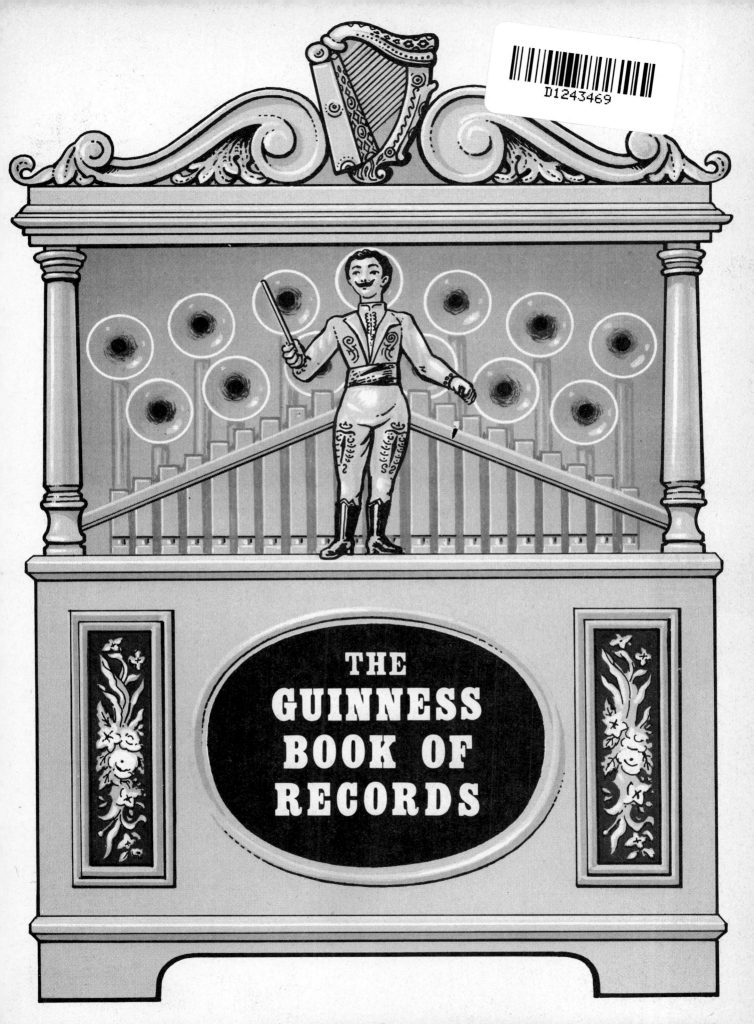

THE GUINNESS BOOK OF RECORDS

Editors and Compilers NORRIS AND ROSS McWHIRTER

Standard Book Number ISBN: 0 900424 13 3
Copyright 1973 by Guinness Superlatives Limited

Standard Book Number ISBN: 0 900424 15 X
Australian Edition
Standard Book Number ISBN: 0 900424 14 1
South African Edition
© 1973 by Guinness Superlatives Limited
World Copyright Reserved
Twentieth Edition

Note.
In keeping with the standardization sought by the Booksellers' Association,
The Library Association and The Publishers' Association,
editions have been designated thus:

Edition	Published		Edition	Published	
First Edition	October	1955	Eleventh Edition	November	1964
Second Edition	October	1955	Twelfth Edition	November	1965
Third Edition	November	1955	Thirteenth Edition	October	1966
Fourth Edition	January	1956	Fourteenth Edition	October	1967
Fifth Edition	October	1956	Fifteenth Edition	October	1968
Sixth Edition	December	1956	Sixteenth Edition	October	1969
Seventh Edition	November	1958	Seventeenth Edition	October	1970
Eighth Edition	November	1960	Eighteenth Edition	October	1971
Ninth Edition	April	1961	Nineteenth Edition	October	1972
Tenth Edition	November	1962	Twentieth Edition	October	1973

Note.
No back numbers are now available. Orders for current editions published overseas
will willingly be passed on to the publishers concerned.

OVERSEAS AND FOREIGN LANGUAGE EDITIONS
Dates refer to the first or earliest year of publication in the country concerned.

Guinness Book of World Records   1956   Casebound   U.S.A.
Guinness Book of World Records   1962   Paperback   U.S.A.
Le Livres des Extrêmes   1962   Casebound   French
Guinness Rekord bog Først og Størst Sidst og Mindst   1967   Casebound   Danish
Guinness Das Buch Der Rekorde   1967   Paperback   German
Guinness Rekord bok Først og Størst Sist og Minst   1967   Casebound   Norwegian
Guinness Korega Sekai Ichi   1968   Paper (2 vols.)   Japanese
Enciclopedia Guinness de Superlativos Mundiales   1968   Paperback   Spanish
Il Guinness dei Primati   1968   Italian
Guinnessin Ennätysten Kirja   1968   Casebound   Finnish
Guinness Rekord bok Först och Störst   1968   Casebound   Swedish
Het Groot Guinness Rekord Boek   1971   Casebound   Dutch
Guinnessova kniha rekordu   1974   Paperback   Czech
Note: Hebrew, Portuguese and Serbo-Croatian editions have been contracted for publication shortly

Artwork by DENZIL REEVES
Layout by SALLY BENNETT

Made and produced in Great Britain by
Redwood Press Limited
Trowbridge, Wiltshire, England

 GUINNESS SUPERLATIVES LIMITED, 2 CECIL COURT, LONDON ROAD, ENFIELD, MIDDX.

Above: The most tenuously established species of the 474 on the British Bird List—the male of the sole pair of Snowy Owls (*Nyctea scandacia*) now nesting on the Shetland Island of Fetlar (see page 44) *Photo: Bobby Tulloch*

Below: The most valuable animal in captivity in Britain, the Killer Whale (*Orcinus orca*) named "Ramu" at the Windsor Safari Park, valued at £30,000 (see page 36) *Courtesy of Windsor Safari Park*

Above: The world's highest waterfall. The 3,212 ft *979 m* high Angel Falls in Venezuela, South America, which remained undiscovered until 1935. The Auyan-Tepui plateau was first climbed in 1971 (see page 72) *Courtesy of the Venezuelan Embassy*

Below: Mauna Kea, the Hawaiian mountain which measured from its submarine base 3,280 fathoms deep to its summit 13,796 ft *4 025 m* high is the tallest in the world totalling 33,476 ft 10 203 *m* (see p. 71)

George III (1760–1820)
Pattern of 1820
Only 25 specimens of this pattern were struck. The reverse bears the famous St. George and the Dragon *motif* which is still used on the gold coinage of George III's great-great-great-great-grand-daughter Elizabeth II.

George IV (1820–1830)
Pattern of 1826
Some 150 specimens of this pattern were struck. The royal arms on the reverse include those of Hanover. The edge lettering reads *Decus et Tutamen Anno Regni Septimo*—An ornament and a safeguard in the seventh year of our reign.

Victoria (1837–1901)
Proof of 1839
Some 180 of these famous Una and the Lion patterns were included in the proof set of 15 coins made up at the Royal Mint. This proof was designed by W. Wyon R.A. The young queen is wearing the robes of the Order of the Garter.

Victoria (1837–1901)
1887
This Golden Jubilee issue is the least rare of the £5 piece series. A total of 53,844 of these were struck for currency. In addition 797 examples were struck for proof sets on polished flans. The initials J. E. B. on the obverse stand for the engraver J. E. Boehm.

A complete set of the ten 22 carat £5 pieces, which are the highest denomination of the Imperial Coinage. Coins of standard weight (616.37 grains 39.94 g) are officially legal tender. A set of the eight collectable coins would today be worth some £10,000. No £5 piece of William IV was ever struck though six crown pieces were struck in gold.

Victoria (1837–1901)
1893
A total of 20,405 examples of this Widow's Head type were struck for currency and 773 for proof sets. The obverse was engraved by Thomas Brock and Pistrucci's St. George and the Dragon design was retained.

Edward VII (1901–1910)
1902
A total of 24,911 examples of this coin were struck for currency and circulated in the Near East, India and S.W. Asia.

George V (1910–1936)
Proof of 1911
Only 2,812 examples were struck—all for issue in the official sets of the proof coins for the new reign.

Edward VIII (Jan-Dec 1936) Pattern 1937
An undisclosed number of patterns were struck. The King of 326 days insisted on breaking the 12 reign long tradition of alternation of head by facing the same way as his predecessor. There are probably fewer than 8 examples extant of which none is in private hands.

George VI (1936–1952)
Proof of 1937
These were the last £5 gold pieces issued. A total of 5,501 were struck for the official Royal Mint proof sets.

Elizabeth II
(acceded 1952)
Proof of 1953
No more than 12 examples of the gold £5 piece of the present reign were struck of which again none is in private hands.

Above: The array of 63 mirrors forming the world's largest solar furnace at Odeillo in the French Pyrenees. The project was begun in 1969. Temperatures of up to 3 725° C or *6,735° F* have been achieved (see page 159)
Photo: Gazuait-Rapho

Below: The reflector base of the world's largest optical telescope — the U.S.S.R. 6 m *236.2 in* diameter telescope sited on Mount Semirodriki (6,830 ft *[2,080 m]*) in the Caucasus Mountains. (see page 90)
Photo: Novosti Press Agency

Below: The launch of the U.S. rocket *Pioneer X* on 2 March 1972 from Cape Kennedy, Florida, which attained the unprecedented speed of 31,700 m.p.h. *51 000 km/h* (see pages 84 and 85)
Photo: N.A.S.A.

Above: An artist's impression of the fully deployed *Skylab I*—the heaviest (89.17 ton [*90 601 kg*]) and largest (118 ft [*35,96 m*] long) object ever put into Earth orbit. (see page 84)
Photo: N.A.S.A.

Below: A 159 m.p.h. *255 km/h* New Tokaido service train passing Japan's highest mountain, Fuji 12,388 ft *3 775 m.* On one stretch it covers 112 miles *180 km* in 60 min (see page 150)
Courtesy of The Japanese Embassy

Right: The twin towers of the World Trade Center on Manhattan, New York City comprise the world's most capacious office building, with 4,370,000 square feet (100.32 acres [*40,6 ha*] of rentable space in each of the 110 storey towers (see page 121)
Courtesy of The Port of New York Authority

Above: Sears Tower Chicago—the world's tallest inhabited building rising to 1,453 ft *443 m,* topped out on 4 May 1973 and due for completion in 1974 (see page 121)
Courtesy of Sears Roebuck and Company

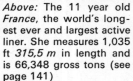

Above: The 11 year old *France,* the world's longest ever and largest active liner. She measures 1,035 ft *315,5 m* in length and is 66,348 gross tons (see page 141)
Courtesy of Compagnie Générale Transatlantique

Left: The British Aircraft Corporation / Aérospatiale supersonic passenger aircraft, *Concorde* during take-off. It first exceeded Mach 2 1,320 m.p.h. *2 124 km/h* on 4 November 1970 (see page 155)
Courtesy of The British Aircraft Corporation

Left: The Blue Flame, the natural gas / hydrogen peroxide rocket powered vehicle which momentarily touched 650 m.p.h. in its world record measured kilometre run of 631.368 m.p.h. *1 016, 088 km/h* (see page 145). The driver is the now injured Gary Gabelich
Courtesy of The Goodyear Tyre and Rubber Company

Left: The largest mobile object ever constructed by man—the Japanese built British owned tanker of 483,664 deadweight tons, *Globtik Tokyo,* completed in February 1973. Her upper deck is so vast it could accommodate 79 tennis courts (see page 142)
Courtesy of Ishikawajima-Halima Heavy Industries Ltd

Above: Italian Motor cycle ace Giacomo Agostini, winner of most F.I.M. World Championships —12 titles in the 7 years 1966–72 (see Chapter 12—Motor Cycling)
Photo: Syndication International

Above: Robert Seagren (U.S.) clearing 18 ft 5¾ in *5,63 m* to set a world Pole Vault record in Eugene, Oregon in 1972 (see Chapter 12—Track & Field Athletics)
Photo: Ed Lacey

Below: Rounding Tattenham Corner in the 1972 Derby won by Roberto ridden by Lester Piggott. This was Piggott's sixth Derby win—an unsurpassed total (see Chapter 12—Horse Racing)
Photo: Fox Photos

Right: Shane Gould (Australia) multi world swimming record holder and triple Olympic gold medallist (see Chapter 12—Swimming)
Photo: Syndication International

Left: John Akii-Bua (Uganda)—world record holder for 400 m hurdles with 47.8 sec (See Chapter 12—Track & Field Athletics) *Photo: Ed Lacey*

Left: Renate Stecher (East Germany), double Olympic gold medallist at Munich. In 1973 she lowered the world record for 100 metres to 10.9 sec (see Chapter 12—Track & Field Athletics)

Right: Iain Macdonald-Smith, M.B.E. and Lt. Rodney Pattisson, M.B.E., R.N., in their yacht *Superdocious* in which they won the Olympic gold medal at Acapulco, Mexico in 1968. Mr. Pattisson went on to win a second gold in the 1972 Olympics at Keil (see Chapter 12—Yachting) *Photo: Ed Lacey*

Left: Holder of most world wrestling championships Aleksandr Medved (U.S.S.R.) seen on his way to winning his eighth world title at the 1972 Olympics at Munich (see Chapter 12—Wrestling) *Photo: Stewart Fraser/Colour Sport*

Right: Twice winner of the Olympic Grand Prix in 1952 and 1964, Pierre d'Oriola of France (see Chapter 12—Equestrian Sports) *Photo: Ed Lacey*

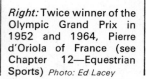

CONTENTS

FOREWORD

By the Rt. Hon. The Earl of Iveagh

When we first brought out this book, some eighteen years ago, we did so in the hope of providing a means for peaceful settling of arguments about record performances in this record-breaking world in which we live. We realise, of course, that much joy lies in the argument, but how exasperating it can be if there is no final means of finding the answer.

In the event, we have found that the interest aroused by this book has exceeded our wildest expectations. We have now produced more than 12,500,000 copies, and twelve editions in the United States. Translations into Czech, Danish, Dutch, French, Finnish, German, Hebrew, Italian, Japanese, Norwegian, Serbo-Croatian, Spanish and Swedish and special editions for Australia and Southern Africa are showing the universality of its appeal.

Whether the discussion concerns the smallest fish ever caught, the most expensive wine, the greatest weight lifted by a man, the furthest reached in space, the world's most successful racehorse, or—an old bone of contention—the longest river in the world, I can but quote the words used in introducing the first edition, "How much heat these innocent questions can raise: Guinness, in producing this book, hopes that it may assist in resolving many such disputes, and may, we hope, turn heat into light".

Iveagh

Chairman
Arthur Guinness, Son & Co., Ltd.
St. James's Gate Brewery, Dublin
Park Royal Brewery, London   October 1973

PREFACE

This twentieth Edition has been completely revised, re-set in Times type and re-illustrated throughout.

For the first time the British edition has been metricated so that readers may have the benefit of whichever system of measurement is the more familiar to them. Imperial weights and distances have been converted to their metric equivalents or *vice versa* to the appropriate same number of *significant* figures. We have endeavoured to avoid conversions being meaninglessly more "accurate" than the basic measurement justified.

There has been in recent months a marked increase in efforts to establish records for sheer endurance in many activities. In the very nature of record-breaking the duration of such 'marathons' will tend to be pushed to greater and greater extremes and it should be stressed that marathon attempts are not without possible dangers. Organizers of such events would be well counselled to seek medical advice before and surveillance during marathons which involve extended periods without sleep.

Norris McWhirter

Ross McWhirter

Editors and compilers

October 1973   Guinness Superlatives Limited, 2 Cecil Court, London Road, Enfield, Middlesex

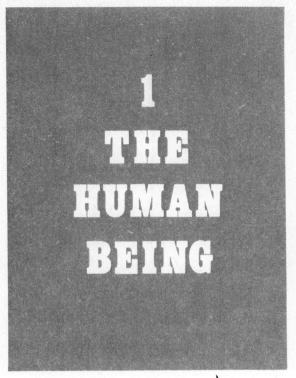

1 THE HUMAN BEING

1. DIMENSIONS

TALLEST GIANTS

The height of human giants is a subject on which accurate information is frequently obscured by exaggeration and commercial dishonesty. The only admissible evidence on the true height of giants is that collected in the last 90 years under impartial medical supervision.

The Biblical claim that Og, the Amorite king of Bashan in *c.* 1450 B.C., stood 9 Hebrew cubits (13 ft 2½ in [*4.02 m*]) is based solely on the length of his basalt sarcophagus or "iron bedstead". The assertion that Goliath of Gath (*c.* 1060 B.C.) stood 6 cubits and a span (9 ft 6½ in [*290 cm*]) suggests a confusion of units or some over-zealous exaggeration by the Hebrew chroniclers. The Jewish historian Flavius Josephus (born in A.D. 37 or 38, died after A.D. 93) and some of the manuscripts of the Septuagint (the earliest Greek translation of the Old Testament) attribute to Goliath the more credible height of 4 Greek cubits and a span (6 ft 10 in [*208 cm*]).

Extreme mediaeval data, taken from bone measurements, invariably refer to specimens of extinct whale, giant cave bear, mastodon, woolly rhinoceros or other prehistoric non-human remains.

Paul Topinard (1830–1911), a French anthropometrist, stated that the tallest man who ever lived was Daniel Mynheer Cajanus (1714–49) of Finland, standing 283 cm *9 ft 3.4 in*. In 1872 his right femur, now in Leyden Museum, in the Netherlands, was measured by Prof. Carl Langer of Germany and indicated a height of 222 cm *7 ft 3.4 in*. Pierre Lemolt reported in 1847 that Ivan Stepanovich Lushkin (1811–44), a drum major in the Russian Imperial Regiment of Guards at Preobrazhenskiy, measured 3 arshin 9¼ vershok (8 ft 3⅜ in [*253 cm*]) and was "the tallest man that has ever lived in modern days". However, his left femur and tibia, which are now in the Museum of the Academy of Sciences in Leningrad, U.S.S.R., indicate a height of 7 ft 10¼ in *239 cm*.

Circus giants and others who are exhibited are normally under contract not to be measured and are, almost traditionally, billed by their promoters at heights up to 18 in *45 cm* in excess of their true heights. There are many notable examples of this, and 23 instances were listed in the *Guinness Book of Records* (14th edition). The acromegalic giant Eddie Carmel (b. Tel Aviv, Israel, 1938), formerly "The Tallest Man on Earth" of Ringling Bros. and Barnum & Bailey's Circus (1961–68) is allegedly 9 ft 0⅝ in *275 cm* tall (weighing 38 st. 3 lb. [*242 kg*]), but photographic evidence suggests that his true height was about 7 ft 6 in *229 cm*. He died in New York City on 14 Aug. 1972.

An extreme case of exaggeration concerned Siah Khān ibn Kashmir Khān (b. 1913) of Bushehr (Bushire), Iran. Prof. D. H. Fuchs showed photographs of him at a meeting of the Society of Physicians in Vienna, Austria, in January 1935, claiming that he was 320 cm *10 ft 6 in* tall. Later, when Siah Khān entered the Imperial Hospital in Teheran for an operation, it was revealed that his actual height was 220 cm *7 ft 2.6 in*.

World Modern opinion is that the tallest recorded man of whom there is irrefutable evidence was Robert Pershing Wadlow, born at 6.30 a.m. on 22 Feb. 1918 in Alton, Illinois, U.S.A. Weighing 8½ lb. *3 kg 860* at birth, his abnormal growth began almost immediately. His height progressed as follows:

Age in Years	Height		Weight in lb.	kg	Age in Years	Height		Weight in lb.	kg
5	5'4"	*163 cm*	105	48	15	7'8"	*234 cm*	355	*161*
8	6'0"	*183 cm*	169	77	16	7'10½"	*240 cm*	374	*170*
9	6'2½"	*189 cm*	180	82	17	8'0½"	*245 cm*	315*	*143*
10	6'5"	*196 cm*	210	95	18	8'3½"	*253 cm*	—	
11	6'7"	*200 cm*	—		19	8'5½"	*258 cm*	480	*218*
12	6'10½"	*210 cm*	—		20	8'6¾"	*261 cm*	—	
13	7'1¾"	*218 cm*	255	*116*	21	8'8½"	*265 cm*	491	*223*
14	7'5"	*226 cm*	301	*137*	22.4†	8'11"	*272 cm*	439	*199*

* Following severe influenza and infection of the foot.
† Wadlow was still growing during his terminal illness.

Dr. C. M. Charles, Associate Professor of Anatomy at Washington University's School of Medicine in St. Louis, Missouri, measured Robert Wadlow at 272 cm *8 ft 11.1 in* in St. Louis on 27 June 1940. Wadlow died 18 days later, at 1.30 a.m. on 15 July 1940, in Manistee, Michigan, as a result of cellulitis of the feet aggravated by a poorly fitted brace.

He was buried in Oakwood Cemetery, Alton, Illinois in a coffin measuring 10 ft 9 in *328 cm* in length, 32 in *81 cm* wide and 30 in *76 cm* deep. His greatest recorded weight was 35 st. 1 lb. *222 kg 70*, on his 21st birthday. He weighed 31 st. 5 lb. *199 kg* at the time of his death. His shoes were size 37AA (18½ in *47 cm* long) and his hands measured 12¾ in *32 cm* from the wrist to the tip of the middle finger.

The only other men for whom heights of 8 ft *244 cm* or more have been reliably reported are the seven listed below. In each case gigantism was followed by acromegaly, a disorder which causes an enlargement of the nose, lips, tongue, lower jaw, hands and feet, due to renewed activity by the already swollen pituitary gland, which is located at the base of the brain.

John F. Carroll (1932–69) of Buffalo, New York State, U.S.A. (a) 8 ft 7¾ in *263,5 cm*.
John William Rogan (1871–1905), a Negro of Gallatin, Tennessee, U.S.A. (b) 8 ft 6 in *259,1 cm*.
Don Koehler (b. 1929-*fl.* 1973) of Denton, Montana, U.S.A. (c) 8 ft 2 in *248,9 cm*, now lives in Chicago.
Väinö Myllyrinne (1909–63) of Helsinki, Finland (d) 8 ft 1.2 in *247 cm*.
Gabriel Estavão Monjane (b. 1944) of Monjacaze, Mozambique (e) 8 ft 1 in *246,3 cm*.
"Constantine" (1872–1902) of Reutlingen, West Germany (f) 8 ft 0.8 in *246 cm*.
Sulaimān 'Alī Nashnush (b. 1943) of Tripoli, Libya (g) 8 ft 0.4 in *245 cm*.

(a) *Severe kypho-scoliosis (two dimensional spinal curvature). The figure represents his height with assumed normal spinal curvature, calculated from a standing height of 8 ft 0 in 244 cm, measured on 14 Oct. 1959. His standing height was 7 ft 8¼ in 234 cm shortly before his death.*
(b) *Measured in a sitting position. Unable to stand owing to ankylosis (stiffening of the joints through the formation of adhesions) of the knees and hips.*
(c) *He has a twin sister who is 5 ft 9 in 175 cm tall.*
(d) *Stood 7 ft 3½ in 222 cm at the age of 21 years. Experienced a second phase of growth in his late thirties and may have stood 8 ft 3 in 251 cm at one time.*
(e) *Abnormal growth started at the age of 10, following a head injury. Some kypho-scoliosis. Present height c. 7 ft 10 in 239 cm. A height of 8 ft 6 in 259 cm is claimed.*
(f) *Height estimated, as both legs were amputated after they turned gangrenous. He claimed a height of 259 cm 8 ft 6 in.*
(g) *Operation to correct abnormal growth in Rome in 1960 was successful.*

A table of the tallest giants of all-time in the 31 countries with men taller than 7 ft 4 in *223,5 cm* was listed in the 15th edition of the *Guinness Book of Records* (1968) at page 9.

The claim that Sa'id Muhammad Ghazi (b. 1909) of Alexandria, Egypt (formerly United Arab Republic) attained a height of 8 ft 10 in *269 cm* in February 1941 is now considered unreliable. Photographic evidence suggests his height was more nearly 7 ft 10½ in *240 cm*, though he may have reached 8 ft *244 cm* at the time of his death.

England The tallest Englishman ever recorded was William Bradley (1788–1820), born in Market Weighton, in the East Riding of Yorkshire. He stood 7 ft 9 in *236 cm*. John Middleton (1578–1623), the famous Childe of Hale, in Lancashire, was claimed to be 9 ft 3 in *282 cm*. Hat pegs were accurately but inconclusively measured in October 1969 to be 12 ft 9 in *389 cm* above the present floor of his cottage. James Toller (1795–1819) of St. Neots, near Huntingdon, was alleged to be 8 ft 6 in *259 cm* but was actually 7 ft 6 in *229 cm*. Albert Brough (1871–1919), a publican of Nottingham, reached a height of 7 ft 7½ in *207 cm*. Frederick Kempster (1889–1918) of Bayswater, London, was reported to have measured 8 ft 4½ in *255 cm* at the time of his death, but photographic evidence suggests that his height was 7 ft 8½ in *235 cm*. He measured 234 cm *7 ft 8.1 in* in 1913. Henry Daglish, who stood 7 ft 7 in *231 cm*, died in Upper Stratton, Wiltshire, on 16 March 1951, aged 25. The much-publicized Edward (Ted) Evans (1924–58) of Englefield Green, Surrey, was reputed to be 9 ft 3 in

William Bradley, the tallest recorded Englishman who stood 7 ft 9 in *236 cm*

282 cm but actually stood 7 ft 8½ in *235 cm*. The tallest fully mobile man now living in Great Britain is Christopher Paul Greener (b. New Brighton, Cheshire, 21 Nov. 1943) of Hayes, Kent, who measures 7 ft 4¾ in *225 cm*. Terence Keenan (b. 1942) of Rock Ferry, Birkenhead, Cheshire measures 7 ft 6 in *229 cm*, but is unable to stand erect owing to a leg condition. His abnormal growth began at the age of 17 when he was only 5 ft 4 in *163 cm* tall.

Scotland The tallest Scotsman, and the tallest recorded "true" (non-pathological) giant, was Angus Macaskill (1825–63), born on the island of Berneray, in the Sound of Harris, in the Outer Hebrides. He stood 7 ft 9 in *236 cm* and died in St. Ann's, on Cape Breton Island, Nova Scotia, Canada. Lambert Quételet (1796–1874), a Belgian anthropometrist, considered that a Scotsman named MacQuail, known as "the Scotch Giant", stood 8 ft 3 in *251 cm*. He served in the famous regiment of giants of Frederick William I (1688–1740), King of Prussia. His skeleton, now in the Staatliche Museum zu Berlin, East Germany, measures 220 cm *7 ft 2.6 in*. Sam McDonald (1762–1802) of Lairg in Sutherland, was reputed to be 8 ft *244 cm* tall but actually stood 6 ft 10 in *208 cm*. The tallest Scotsman now living is George Gracie (b. 1938) of Forth, Lanarkshire. He stands 7 ft 3 in *221 cm* and weighs 28 st. *178 kg*. His brother Hugh (b. 1941) is 7 ft 0½ in *215 cm*.

Wales The tallest Welshman ever recorded was George Auger (1886–1922), born in Cardiff, Glamorgan. He stood 7 ft 5 in *226 cm* and died in New York City, N.Y., U.S.A.

Ireland The tallest Irishman was Patrick Cotter O'Brian (1760–1806), born in Kinsale, County Cork. He died at Hotwells, Clifton, Bristol. He said that he was 8 ft 7¾ in *264 cm* at the age of 26, but his actual living height was 7 ft 10.86 in *241 cm*, calculated from measurements of his long bones made by Dr. Edward Fawcett, Professor of Anatomy at University College, Bristol, on 3 March 1906, after his coffin had been accidentally exposed during excavation work.

The tallest Irishman now living is believed to be Jim Cully (b. 1926) of Tipperary, a former boxer and wrestler. He stands 7 ft 2 in *218 cm*.

Isle of Man The tallest Manxman ever recorded was Arthur Caley (b. 16 Nov. 1829) of Sulby. He was variously credited with heights of 8 ft 2 in *249 cm* and 8 ft 4 in *254 cm*, but actually stood 7 ft 6 in *229 cm*. He died at Clyde, New Jersey, U.S.A., on 12 Feb. 1889 aged 60.

TALLEST GIANTESSES

World
All-time Giantesses are rarer than giants but their heights are still spectacular. The tallest woman in medical history was the acromegalic giantess Jane ("Ginny") Bunford, born on 26 July 1895 at Bartley Green, Northfield, Birmingham. Her abnormal growth started at the age of 11 following a head injury, and on her 13th birthday she measured 6 ft 6 in *198 cm*. Shortly before her death on 1 April 1922 she stood 7 ft 7 in *231 cm* tall, but she had a severe curvature of the spine and would have measured about 7 ft 11 in *241 cm* with assumed normal curvature. Her skeleton, now preserved in the Anatomical Museum in the Medical School at Birmingham University, has a mounted height of 7 ft 4 in *229 cm*. Archaeologists announced on 10 Feb. 1972 the discovery of a mediaeval giantess at a still unsubstantiated 8 ft 3 in *251 cm* in the Laga mountains near Abruzzi, Italy. Anna Hanen Swan (1846–88) of Nova Scotia, Canada, was billed at 8 ft 1 in *246 cm* but actually measured 7 ft 5½ in *227 cm*. In London on 17 June 1871 she married Martin van Buren Bates (1845–1919) of Whitesburg, Letcher County Kentucky, U.S.A., who stood 7 ft 2½ in *220 cm*. Ella Ewing (1875–1913) of Goring, Missouri, U.S.A., was billed at 8 ft 2 in *249 cm* and reputedly measured 6 ft 9 in *206 cm* at the age of 10 (*cf.* 6 ft 5 in [*196 cm*] for Robert Wadlow at this age). She measured 7 ft 4½ in *225 cm* at the age of 23 and may have attained 7 ft 6 in *229 cm* before her death.

Living The tallest living woman is believed to be a eunuchoidal giantess named Tiliya (b. 1947) who lives in the village of Saidpur in Bihar State, north-eastern India. She stands 7 ft 5 in *226 cm* tall. In Nov. 1971 a height of 7 ft 2¾ in *220 cm* was reported for Mildred Tshakayi (b. 1946), a Rhodesian bush dweller. The tallest woman recently living was believed to be Delores Ann Johnson, *née* Pullard (b. 13 August 1946), a negress from De Quincy, Louisiana, U.S.A. She measured 6 ft 10 in *208 cm* in March 1961 and grew to 7 ft 5 in *226 cm* by October 1964. She reportedly wore size 52 dresses and size 23 shoes and weighed 31 st. 1 lb. *197 kg*. At the time of her death in Houston, Texas on 19 May 1971 she was credited with a height of 8 ft 2 in *249 cm*, but her true stature was 7 ft 5½ in *227 cm*.

SHORTEST DWARFS

The strictures which apply to giants apply equally to dwarfs, except that exaggeration gives way to understatement. In the same way as 9 ft *274 cm* may be regarded as the limit towards which the tallest giants tend, so 23 in *58 cm* must be regarded as the limit towards which the shortest mature dwarfs tend (*cf.* the average length of new-born babies is 18–20 in [*46–50 cm*]). In the case of child dwarfs the age is often enhanced by their agents or managers.

The shortest type of dwarf is an ateliotic dwarf, known as a midget. In this form of dwarfism the skeleton tends to remain in its infantile state. Midgets seldom grow to more than 40 in *102 cm* tall. The most famous midget in history was Charles Sherwood Stratton, *alias* "General Tom Thumb", born on 11 Jan. 1832 in Bridgeport, Connecticut, U.S.A. He measured 25 in *64 cm* at the age of 5 months and grew to only 70 cm *27.6 in* by the age of 13½. He was 30½ in *77 cm* tall at the age of 18 and 35 in *89 cm* at 30. He stood 40 in *102 cm* tall at the time of his death from apoplexy on 15 July 1883.

Jane Bunford at 7 ft 11 in *241 cm* compared with Pauline Musters, the world's shortest human at 23.2 in *59 cm*

Another celebrated midget was Józef ('Count') Boruwalaski (b. November 1739) of Poland. He measured only 8 in *20 cm* long at birth, growing to 14 in *36 cm* at the age of one year. He stood 17 in *43 cm* at 6 years, 21 in *53 cm* at 10, 25 in *64 cm* at 15, 35 in *89 cm* at 25 and 39 in *99 cm* at 30. He died near Durham, England, on 5 Sept. 1837, aged 97.

World The shortest mature human of whom there is independent evidence was Pauline Musters ('Princess Pauline'), a Dutch midget. She was born at Ossendrecht, on 26 Feb. 1876 and measured 12 in *30 cm* at birth. At the age of 9 she was 55 cm *21.65 in* tall and weighed only 1 kg 50 *3 lb. 5 oz.* She died, at the age of 19, of pneumonia, with meningitis, her heart weakened from alcoholic excesses, on 1 March 1895 in New York City, N.Y., U.S.A. Although she was billed at 19 in *48 cm*, she was found to be 59 cm *23.2 in* tall. A *post mortem* examination showed her to be exactly 24 in *61 cm* (her body was slightly elongated after death). Her mature weight varied from 7½ lb. to 9 lb. *3 kg 40–4 kg* and her "vital statistics" were 18½-19-17 *47-48-43 cm*.

The Italian girl Caroline Crachami, born in Palermo, Sicily, in 1815, was only 20.2 in *51.3 cm* tall when she died in London in 1824, aged 9. At birth she measured 7 in *18 cm* long and weighed 1 lb. *0 kg 50*. Her skeleton, measuring 19.8 in *50,3 cm*, is now part of the Hunterian collection in the Museum of the Royal College of Surgeons, London.

Male The shortest recorded adult male dwarf was Calvin Phillips, born on 14 Jan. 1791 in Bridgewater, Massachusetts, U.S.A. He weighed 2 lb. *0 kg 910* at birth and stopped growing at the age of 5. When he was 19 he measured 26½ in *67 cm* tall and weighed 12 lb. *5 kg 40* with his clothes on. He died two years later, in April 1812, from progeria, a rare disorder characterised by dwarfism and premature senility.

The world's shortest living man Mihaly Meszaros arriving at Kennedy Airport prior to joining the Ringling Barnum circus

William E. Jackson, *alias* "Major Mite", born on 2 Oct. 1864 in Dunedin, New Zealand, measured 9 in *23 cm* long and weighed 12 oz. *0 kg 34* at birth. In November 1880 he stood 21 in *53 cm* and weighed 9 lb. *4 kg*. He died in New York City, N.Y., U.S.A., on 9 Dec. 1900, when he measured 27 in *70 cm*.

The world's shortest living man is claimed to be Mihaly Meszaros (b. Hungary, 1939), a circus acrobat standing 33 in *83 cm*. However Manoel Souza (b. 1942) of Marenno, Brazil is perhaps 31 in *76,2 cm*.

United Kingdom The shortest mature human ever recorded in Britain is believed to be Miss Joyce Carpenter (b. 21 Dec. 1929), a rachitic dwarf of Charford, Worcestershire, who stands 29 in *74 cm* tall and weighs 30 lb. *13 kg 60*. Her mother is 5 ft 9 in *175 cm* tall. Hopkins Hopkins (1737–54) of Llantrisant, Glamorgan, South Wales was 31 in *79 cm*. Hopkins, who died from progeria (see above) weighed 19 lb. *8 kg 620* at the age of 7 and 13 lb. *6 kg* at the time of his death. There are an estimated 2,000 people of severely restricted growth living in Britain today.

The famous "Sir" Geoffrey Hudson (b. 1619) of Oakham, Rutland, was reputedly 18 in *46 cm* tall at the age of 30, but this extreme measurement is not borne out in portraits which show he was then about 3 ft 6 in *107 cm*. At the time of his death in London in 1682 he measured 3 ft 9 in *114 cm*.

Ireland The shortest recorded Irish adult dwarf was Mrs. Catherine Kelly (b. in August 1756), known as "the Irish fairy", who stood 34 in *86 cm* tall and weighed 22 lb. *10 kg*. She died in Norwich, Norfolk, on 15 Oct. 1785. David Jones (b. 28 April 1903) of Lisburn, County Antrim, Northern Ireland, reputedly measured 26 in *66 cm* at the time of his death on 1 April 1970 aged 66. But as he weighed 4 st. *25 kg*, his height was probably nearer 36 in *91 cm*.

Most variable stature Adam Rainer, born in Graz, Austria, in 1899, measured 1,18 m *3 ft 10.45 in* at the age of 21. But then he suddenly started growing upwards at a rapid rate, and by 1931 he had reached 2,18 m *7 ft 1¾ in*. He became so weak as a result that he was bed-ridden for the rest of his life. He died on 4 March 1950 aged 51.

RACES

Tallest The tallest race in the world is the Tutsi (also called Batutsi, Watutsi, or Watussi), Nilotic herdsmen of Rwanda and Burundi, Central Africa whose males average 6 ft 1 in *185 cm*, with a maximum of 7 ft 6 in *229 cm*. The Tehuelches of Patagonia, long regarded as of gigantic stature (*i.e.* 7 to 8 ft [*213 to 244 cm*]), have in fact an average height (males) of 5 ft 10 in *178 cm* with a maximum of just over 2 m *6 ft 6¾ in*. A tribe with an average height of more than 6 ft was discovered in the inland region of Passis Manua of New Britain in December 1956. In May 1965 it was reported that the Crahiacoro Indians in the border district of the states of Mato Grosso and Pará, in Brazil, are exceptionally tall—certainly with an average of more than 6 ft *183 cm*. A report in May 1966 specifically attributed great stature to the Kranhacacore Indians of the Xingu region of the Mato Grosso. In December 1967 the inhabitants of Barbuda, Leeward Islands were reported to have an average height in excess of 6 ft *183 cm*. The tallest people in Europe are the Montenegrins of Yugoslavia, with a male average of 5 ft 10 in *178 cm* (in the town of Trebinje the average height is 6 ft [*183 cm*]), compared with the men of Sutherland, at 5 ft 9½ in *176,5 cm*. In 1912 the average height of the men living in Balmaclellan, Kirkcudbrightshire was reported to be 179 cm *5 ft 10.4 in*.

Shortest The world's shortest known race is the negrito Onge tribe, of whom only 22 (12 men, 10 women) survived on Little Andaman Island in the Indian Ocean by May 1956. Few were much more than 4 ft *122 cm*. The smallest pygmies are the Mbuti, with an average height of 4 ft 6 in *137 cm* for men and 4 ft 5 in *135 cm* for women, with some groups averaging only 4 ft 4 in *132 cm* for men and 4 ft 1 in *124 cm* for women. They live in the forests near the river Ituri in the Congo (Kinshasa), Africa. In June 1936 there was a report, not subsequently substantiated, that there was a village of dwarfs numbering about 800 in the Hu bei (Hupeh) province of Central China between Wu han and Lishan in which the men were all less than 4 ft *122 cm* tall and the women slightly taller. In October 1970 a tribe of pygmies, reportedly measuring only 1 m *3 ft 3.4 in* tall, was discovered in the border area of Bolivia, Brazil and Peru.

WEIGHT

Heaviest heavyweights World Men The heaviest recorded human of all time was the 6-ft 0½-in *184 cm* tall Robert Earl Hughes (b. 4 June 1926) of Monticello, Illinois, U.S.A. An 11¼ lb. *5 kg* baby, he weighed 14½ st. *92 kg* at six years, 27 st. *171 kg* at ten, 39 st. *248 kg* at 13, 49½ st. *314 kg* at 18, 64 st. *406 kg* at 25 and 67½ st. *428 kg* at 27. His greatest recorded weight was 76 st. 5 lb. *485 kg* in Feb. 1958, and he weighed 74 st. 5 lb. *472 kg* at the time of his death. His claimed waist of 122 in *310 cm*, his chest of 104 in *264 cm* and his upper arm of 40 in *102 cm* were also the greatest on record. He died of uraemia (a condition caused by retention of urinary matter in the blood) in a trailer at Bremen, Indiana, on 10 July 1958, aged 32, and was buried in Binville Cemetery, near Mount Sterling, Illinois, U.S.A. His coffin, measuring 7 ft *213 cm* by 4 ft 4 in *132 cm* and weighing more than half a ton *508 kg*, was the size of a piano case, and had to be lowered by crane. It was once claimed by a commercial interest that Hughes had weighed 107 st. 2 lb. *680 kg*—a 40 per cent exaggeration.

Johnny Alee (1853–87) of Carbon (now known as Carbonton) North Carolina, U.S.A. is reputed to have weighed 80 st. 12 lb. *513 kg* at the time of his death, but the accuracy of this report has not yet been fully substantiated. He died from a heart attack after plunging through the flooring of his log cabin, which had been his "prison" for 19 years.

The only other men for whom weights of 57 st. 2 lb. *363 kg* or more have been reliably reported are the 7 listed below:

	Stone	lb.	kg
Mills Darden (1798–1857)			
U.S.A. (7 ft 6 in [*2,29 m*])	72	12	*463*
John Hanson Craig (1856–94)			
U.S.A. (6 ft 5 in [*1,95 m*]) (a)	64	11	*411*
Arthur Knorr (1914–60)			
U.S.A. (6 ft 1 in [*1,85 m*]) (b)	64	4	*408*
Toubi (b. 1946) Cameroon	61	3½	*389*
T. A. Valenzuela (1895–1937)			
Mexico (5 ft 11 in [*1,80 m*])	60	10	*386*
David Maquire (1904–*fl.* 1935)			
U.S.A. (5 ft 10 in [*1,78 m*])	57	12	*367*
William J. Cobb (b. 1926)			
U.S.A. (6 ft 0 in [*1,83 m*]) (c)	57	4	*364*

(a) *Won $1,000 in a "Bonny Baby" contest in New York City in 1858.*
(b) *Gained 300 lb. 136 kg in the last 6 months of his life.* (c) *Reduced to 16 st. 8 lb. 105 kg by July 1965.*

Michael Walker (b. 1934) was treated for obesity and drug-induced bulimia (morbid desire to overeat) in a caravan outside the Ben Taub Hospital, Houston, Texas in December 1971. A business partner in the company which exhibited him claimed that in the summer of 1971 he had reached a peak of 1,187 lb. (84 st. 11 lb.) *538 kg 414*. Photographic evidence suggests this weight may not be exaggerated for a man of 6 ft 2 in *1,88 m*.

Women The heaviest woman ever recorded was the late Mrs. Percy Pearl Washington, 46 who died in a hospital in Milwaukee, on 9 Oct. 1972. The hospital scales registered only up to 800 lb. (57 st. 2 lb.) *362 kg 80* but she was believed to weigh about 880 lb. (62 st. 12 lb.) *399 kg 10*. The previous feminine weight record had been set 84 years earlier at 850 lb. *386 kg*.

A more reliable and better documented case was that of Mrs. Flora Mae Jackson (*née* King), a 5 ft 9 in *175 cm* negress born in 1930 at Shugualak, Mississippi, U.S.A. She weighed 10 lb. *4 kg 50* at birth, 19 st. 1 lb. *121 kg* at the age of 11, 44 st. 5 lb. *282 kg* at 25 and 60 st. *381 kg* shortly before her death in Meridian, Florida, on 9 Dec. 1965. She was known in show business as "Baby Flo".

Great The heaviest recorded man in Great Britain was
Britain William Campbell, who was born in Glasgow in 1856
Men and died on 16 June 1878, when a publican at High Bridge, Newcastle upon Tyne, Northumberland. He was 6 ft 3 in *191 cm* tall and weighed 53 st. 8 lb. *340 kg* with an 85-in *216 cm* waist and a 96-in *244 cm* chest. His coffin weighed 1,500 lb *680 kg*. He was "a man of considerable intelligence and humour". The only other British man with a recorded weight of more than 50 st. *317 kg 50* was the celebrated Daniel Lambert (1770–1809) of Leicester. He stood 5 ft 11 in *180 cm* tall, weighed 52 st. 11 lb. *335 kg* shortly before his death and had a girth of more than 92 in *234 cm*.

The highest weight attained by any man living in Britain today was that of Arthur Armitage (born a 5 lb. *2 kg 30* baby on 28 June 1929) of Knottingley, Yorkshire, who scaled 40 st. 6 lb. *257 kg* in his clothes on 15 Feb. 1970. He is 5 ft 9 in *175 cm* tall and his vital statistics were 76-80-80 *193-203-203 cm*. By March 1972 he had reduced by dieting (600 calories per day) to 18 st. 2 lb. *115 kg*.

George MacAree (b. 24 Dec. 1923) of Newham, London, who scaled 38½ st. *241 kg 30* in January 1973 is now the heaviest man in Britain. He is 5 ft 10½ in *179 cm* tall and has vital statistics of 72½-71-80 *194-180-203 cm*.

Women The heaviest recorded woman in Great Britain was Miss Nellie Lambert (b. 3 April 1894) of Leicester, who weighed 40 st. 3 lb. *255 kg* at the age of 19 years.

She stood 5 ft 3 in *160 cm* tall, with a waist of 88 in *224 cm* and 26-in *66 cm* upper arm. She claimed to be a great-granddaughter of Daniel Lambert (see above). The heaviest woman living in Britain today is Miss Jean Renwick (b. 1939) of Brixton, London, who weighed 40 st. 2 lb. *255 kg* (height 5 ft 3½ in [*161 cm*]) in January 1972. She was recently reported to be dieting.

Ireland The heaviest Irishman is reputed to have been Roger Byrne, who was buried in Rosenallis, County Laoighis (Leix), on 14 March 1804. He died in his 54th year and his coffin and its contents weighed 52 st. *330 kg*. Another Irish heavyweight was Lovelace Love (1731–66), born in Brook Hill, County Mayo. He weighed "upward of 40 st. *254 kg*" at the time of his death.

Heaviest The heaviest twins in the world are the McCreary
twins twins (b. 1948), farmers of Hendersonville, North Carolina, U.S.A., who in March 1970 weighed 47 st. 2 lb. *299 kg* and 45 st. 10 lb. *290 kg*. Since 1972 they have been billed as Billy and Benny McGuire, tag wrestlers.

Lightest The lightest adult human on record was Lucia Zarate
lightweights (b. San Carlos, Mexico 2 Jan. 1863, d. October 1889),
World an emaciated Mexican ateliotic dwarf of 26½ in *67 cm*, who weighed 2 kg 125 *4.7 lb.* at the age of 17. She "fattened up" to 13 lb. *5 kg 90* by her 20th birthday. At birth she weighed 2½ lb. *1 kg 10*. The lightest adult ever recorded in the United Kingdom was Hopkins Hopkins (Shortest dwarfs, see p. 18).

Eddie Masher *alias* the "Skeleton Dude", who weighed only 48 lb. *22 kg* at the height of his career

The thinnest recorded adults of normal height are those suffering from Simmonds' Disease (Hypophyseal cachexia). Losses up to 65 per cent of the original body-weight have been recorded in females, with a "low" of 3 st. 3 lb. *20 kg*. In cases of anorexia nervosa, weights of under 5 st. *32 kg* have been reported. Edward C. Hagner (1892–1962), *alias* Eddie Masher (U.S.A.) is alleged to have weighed only 3 st. 6 lb. *22 kg* at a height of 5 ft 7 in *170 cm*. He was also known as "the Skeleton Dude". In August 1825 the biceps measurement of Claude-Ambroise Seurat (b. 10 April 1797, d. 6 April 1826) of Troyes, France was 4 in *10 cm* and the distance between his back and his chest was less than 3 in *8 cm*. According to one report he stood 5 ft 7½ in *171 cm* and weighed 5 st. 8 lb.

35 kg, but in another account was described as 5 ft 4 in *163 cm* and only 2 st. 8 lb. *16 kg.* It was recorded that the American exhibitionist Rosa Lee Plemons (b. 1873) weighed 27 lb. *12 kg* at the age of 18.

Slimming The greatest recorded slimming feat was that of William J. Cobb (b. 1926), *alias* "Happy Humphrey", a professional wrestler of Macon, Georgia, U.S.A. It was reported in July 1965 that he had reduced from 57 st. 4 lb. *364 kg* to 16 st. 8 lb. *105 kg,* a loss of 40 st. 10 lb. *259 kg* in 3 years. His waist measurement declined from 101 in to 44 in *257 cm* to *112 cm.*

The U.S. circus fat lady Mrs. Celesta Geyer (b. 1901), *alias* Dolly Dimples, reduced from 553 lb. *251 kg* to 152 lb. *69 kg* in 1950–51, a loss of 401 lb. *182 kg* in 14 months. Her vital statistics diminished *pari passu* from 79-84-84 *200-213-213 cm* to a *svelte* 34-28-36 *86-71-91 cm.* Her book "How I lost 400 lbs." was not a best-seller because of the difficulty of would-be readers identifying themselves with the dressmaking problems of losing more than 28 st. *178 kg* when 4 ft 11 in *150 cm* tall. In December 1967 she was reportedly down to 7 st. 12 lb. *50 kg.* The speed record for slimming was established by Paul M. Kimelman, 21, of Pittsburgh, Pennsylvania, U.S.A., who from 25 Dec. 1966 to August 1967 went on a crash diet of 300 to 600 calories per day to reduce from 30 st. 7 lb. *194 kg* to 9 st. 4 lb. *59 kg.* In his prime he wore size 56 trousers into one leg of which he can now step easily.

Arthur Armitage (see p. 19) reportedly lost 12 st. *76 kg* in 6 weeks in November-December 1970 when reducing from 40 st. *254 kg* towards his target of 16 st. *102 kg.* The feminine Weight Watchers champion in Britain was Mrs. Dolly Wages (b. 1933) of London S.E.7. who, between Sept. 1971 when weighing 31 st. 0½ lb. *197 kg* and 22 May 1973 when weighing 11 st. *69 kg* 853 lost 20 st. 0½ lb. *127 kg.*

Weight gaining A probable record for gaining weight was set by Arthur Knorr (b. 17 May 1914), who died on 7 July 1960, aged 46, in Reseda, California, U.S.A. He gained 21 st. 6 lb. *136 kg* in the last 6 months of his life and weighed 64 st. 4 lb. *408 kg* when he died. Miss Doris James of San Francisco, California, U.S.A. is alleged to have gained 23 st. 3 lb. *147 kg* in the 12 months before her death in August 1965, aged 38, at a weight of 48 st. 3 lb. *306 kg.* She was only 5 ft 2 in *157 cm* tall.

Man *(Homo sapiens)* is a species in the sub-family Homininae of the family Hominidae of the super-family Hominoidea of the sub-order Simiae (or Anthropoidea) of the order Primates of the infra-class Eutheria of the sub-class Theria of the class Mammalia of the sub-phylum Vertebrata (Craniata) of the phylum Chordata of the sub-kingdom Metazoa of the animal kingdom.

2. ORIGINS

EARLIEST MAN

SCALE OF TIME
If the age of the Earth-Moon system (latest estimate at least 4,700 million years) is likened to a single year, Handy Man appeared on the scene at about 8.35 p.m. on 31 December, Britain's earliest known inhabitants arrived at about 11.32 p.m., the Christian era began about 13 sec before midnight and the life span of a 113-year-old man (see page 22) would be about three-quarters of a second. Present calculations indicate that the Sun's increased heat, as it becomes a "red giant", will make life insupportable on Earth in about 10,000 million years. Meanwhile there may well be colder epicycles. The period of 1,000 million years is sometimes referred to as an aeon.

World The earliest known primates appeared in the Palaeocene period of about 70,000,000 years ago. The sub-order of higher primates, called Simiae (or Anthropoidea), evolved from the catarrhine or old-world sect nearly 30,000,000 years later in the Lower Oligocene period. During the Middle and Upper Oligocene the super-family Hominoidea emerged. This contains three accepted families, *viz* Hominidae (bipedal, ground-dwelling man or near man), Pongidae (brachiating forest apes) and Oreopithecidae, which includes *Apidium* of the Oligocene and *Oreopithecus* of the early Pliocene. Opinion is divided on whether to treat gibbons and their ancestors as a fourth full family (Hylobatidae) or as a sub-family (Hylobatinae) within the Pongidae. Some consider that Proconsulidae should also comprise a family, although others regard the genus *Proconsul,* who lived on the open savannah, as part of another sub-family of the Pongidae.

Earliest Hominid There is a conflict of evidence on the time during which true but primitive Hominidae were evolving. Fossil evidence indicates that it was some time during the Upper Miocene (about 10,000,000 to 12,000,000 years ago). The characteristics of the Hominidae, such as a large brain, very fully distinguish them from any of the other Hominoidea. Evidence published in August 1969 indicated that the line of descent of *Ramapithecus,* from the north-eastern Indian sub-continent, was not less than 10,000,000 years old and that of *Australopithecus,* from Eastern Africa 5,500,000 years old.

Earliest Genus Homo The earliest known true member of the genus *Homo* was found to the East of Lake Rudolf in Northern Kenya by Mr. Ngeneo and announced on 9 Nov. 1972 by Richard Leakey, Director of the Kenya National Museum's Centre for Pre-History and Palaeontology. In addition to an almost complete skull, pieced together by Dr. Maeve Leakey, femur, tibula and fibula leg bones were also found. The cranial capacity was about 800 cm³ compared to less than 500 cm³ of *Australopithecus.* The remains have been dated to 2,600,000 years ago. Richard Leakey is the son of the late Louis Leakey (1903–72).

Anthropologist Richard Leakey showing top, the 2½ million year old skull and bottom a one million year old *Austra-lopithecus*

Earliest Homo sapiens The earliest recorded remains of the species *Homo sapiens,* variously dated from 300,000 to 450,000 years ago in the Middle Pleistocene, were discovered on 24 Aug. 1965 by Dr. László Vértes in a limestone quarry at Vértesszöllös, about 30 miles west of Budapest, Hungary. The remains, designated *Homo sapiens palaeo-hungaricus,* comprised an almost complete occipital bone, part of a skull with an estimated cranial capacity of nearly 1 400 cm³ *85 in³.*

Earliest man in the Americas date from at least 50,000 B.C. and "more probably 100,000 B.C." according to Dr. Leakey after the examination of some hearth stones found in the Mojave Desert, California and announced in October 1970. The earliest human relic is a skull found in the area of Los Angeles, California dated in December 1970 to be from 22,000 B.C.

British Isles The earliest known inhabitants of the British Isles who belonged to the genus *Homo* were Clactonian man (probably fewer than 200 of them), one of whose middens was discovered in Aug. 1969 by Dr. John Waechter in the Lower Gravels of the Barnfield Pit at Swanscombe, Kent, together with some of their discarded choppers made of flint cores and blunted flake tools. They probably lived in the Thames valley area during the first third of the Great Interglacial 500,000–475,000 B.C. The oldest human remains ever found in Britain are pieces of a brain case from a specimen of *Homo sapiens fossilis*, believed to be a woman, recovered in June 1935 and March 1936 by Dr. Alvan T. Marston from the Boyn Hill terrace in the Barnfield Pit, near Swanscombe, northern Kent. This find is attributed to Acheulian man, type *III* or *IV*, dating from the warm Hoxnian interglacial period, about 250,000 years ago.

The mandible found in the Red Crag at Foxhall, near Ipswich, in 1863, but subsequently lost in the United States, has been claimed as a Clactonian relic and thus possibly anything up to 100,000 years older than Swanscombe man. There is however very considerable doubt about these details.

No remains from the Mesolithic period (*ante* 3500 B.C.) have yet been found but a site at Portland Bill is expected to yield some.

3. LONGEVITY

No single subject is more obscured by vanity, deceit, falsehood and deliberate fraud than the extremes of human longevity. Extreme claims are generally made on behalf of the very aged rather than by them.

Many hundreds of claims throughout history have been made for persons living well into their second century and some, insulting to the intelligence, for people living even into their third. Centenarians surviving beyond their 110th year are in fact of the extremest rarity and the present absolute proven limit of human longevity does not yet admit of anyone living to celebrate a 114th birthday.

It is highly significant that in Sweden, where alone proper and thorough official investigations follow the death of every allegedly very aged citizen, none has been found to have surpassed 110 years. The most reliably pedigreed large group of people in the world, the British peerage, has, after ten centuries, produced only one peer who reached even his 100th birthday. However, this is possibly not unconnected with the extreme draughtiness of many of their residences.

Scientific research into extreme old age reveals that the correlation between the claimed density of centenarians in a country and its regional illiteracy is 0.83 ± 0.03. In late life, very old people often tend to advance their ages at the rate of about 17 years per decade. This was nicely corroborated by a cross analysis of the 1901 and 1911 censuses of England and Wales. Early claims must necessarily be without the elementary corroboration of birth dates. England was among the earliest of all countries to introduce compulsory local registers (Sept. 1538) and official birth registration (1 July 1837) which was made fully compulsory only in 1874. Even in the United States, where in 1971 there were reputed to be 12,642 centenarians, 45 per cent of births occurring between 1890 and 1920 were unregistered.

Several celebrated super-centenarians are believed to have been double lives (father and son, brothers with the same names or successive bearers of a title). The most famous example is Christian Jakobsen Drackenberg allegedly born in Stavanger, Norway on 18 Nov. 1626 and died in Aarhus, Denmark aged seemingly 145 years 326 days on 9 Oct. 1772. A number of instances have been commercially sponsored, while a fourth category of recent claims are those made for political ends, such as the 100 citizens of the Russian Soviet Federative Socialist Republic (population about 132,000,000 at mid-1967) claimed in March 1960 to be between 120 and 156. From data on documented centenarians, actuaries have shown that only one 115-year life can be expected in 2,100 million lives (*cf.* world population was estimated to be 3,860 million at mid-1973).

The height of credulity was reached on 5 May 1933, when a newsagency solemnly filed a story from China with a Peking date-line that Li Chung-yun, the "oldest man on Earth", born in 1680, had just died aged 256 years (*sic*). Currently the most extreme case of longevity claimed in the U.S.S.R. is 168 years for Shirali "Baba" Muslimov of Barzavu, Azerbaijan, reputedly born on 26 Mar. 1805. No interview of this man has ever been permitted to any Western journalist or scientist. He still rides a horse and says he married his 120 year old wife 102 years ago. It was reported in 1954 that in the Abkhasian Republic of Georgia, U.S.S.R., 2.58 per cent of the population was aged over 90—25 times the proportion in the U.S.A. In 1972 there were an estimated 25,000 centenarians living in the world.

The Andean valley of Vilcabamba in Ecuador became the source of reports of extreme longevity after the 1971 census in which 9 of the 819 inhabitants were returned at ages of more than 100, of whom 3 were listed as over 120. The two oldest were Miguel Carpio Mendreta or Mendieta and José David Toledo, who were reputedly 122 and 140. Publication of transcripts of the local baptismal register since 1830 and of their ages as returned in earlier censuses are awaited.

Charlie Smith of Bartow, Florida, U.S.A. obtained a Social Security card in 1955 when claiming to be born on 4 July 1842 in Liberia. The U.S. Department of Health, Education and Welfare state that they are "unable to disclose the type of evidence used" to determine Mr. Smith's age because such disclosure "would infringe on the confidentiality of the individual's record". The essential data on the ages entered for him in any of the 10 censuses from 1860 to 1950 remains undisclosed.

Mythology often requires immense longevity; for example Larak the god-king lived, according to Sumerian mythology, 28,800 years and Dumuzi even longer. The most extreme biblical claim is that for Methuselah at 969 years (Genesis V, verse 27).

Oldest authentic centenarian *World* The greatest authenticated age to which a human has ever lived is 113 years 124 days in the case of Pierre Joubert, a French-Canadian bootmaker. He was born in Charlesbourg, Québec Province, Canada, on 15 July 1701, son of Pierre Joubert (b. 1670) and Magdeleine Boesmier, and died in Québec on 16 Nov. 1814. His longevity was the subject of an investigation in 1870 by Dr. Tache, Official Statistician to the Canadian Government, and the proofs published are irrefutable. The following national records can be taken as authentic:

AUTHENTICATED NATIONAL LONGEVITY RECORDS

	Years	Days		Born		Died
Canada (a)	113	124	Pierre Joubert	15 July	1701	16 Nov. 1814
United States (b)	113	1	John B. Salling	15 Mar.	1846	16 Mar. 1959
Morocco	>112		El Hadj Mohammed el Mokri (Grand Vizier)		1844	16 Sept. 1957
United Kingdom (c)	>112		Alice Stevenson	10 July	1861	fl. July 1973
Ireland	111	327	The Hon. Katherine Plunket	22 Nov.	1820	14 Oct. 1932
South Africa (d)	111	151	Johanna Booyson	17 Jan.	1857	16 June 1968
Czechoslovakia	111	+	Marie Bernatkova	22 Oct.	1857	fl. Oct. 1968
Channel Islands	110	321	Margaret Ann Neve (née Harvey)	18 May	1792	4 April 1903
Yugoslavia	110	150+	Demitrius Philipovitch	9 Mar.	1818	fl. Aug. 1928
Japan (e)	110	114	Yoshigiku Ito	3 Aug.	1856	26 Nov. 1966
Australia (f)	110	39	Ada Sharp (Mrs.)	6 April	1861	15 May 1971
Northern Ireland	110	+	Elizabeth Watkins (Mrs.)	10 Mar.	1863	fl. July 1973
U.S.S.R. (g)	110	+	Khasako Dzugayev	7 Aug.	1860	fl. Aug. 1970
Netherlands	110	5	Baks Karnebeek (Mrs.)	2 Oct.	1849	7 Oct. 1959
France	109	309	Marie Philoméne Flassayer	13 June	1844	18 April 1954
Italy	109	179	Rosalia Spoto	25 Aug.	1847	20 Feb. 1957
Scotland	109	14	Rachel MacArthur (Mrs.)	26 Nov.	1827	10 Dec. 1936
Norway	109	+	Marie Olsen (Mrs.)	1 May	1850	fl. May 1959
Tasmania	109	+	Mary Ann Crow (Mrs.)	2 Feb.	1836	1945
Germany (h)	108	128	Luise Schwatz	27 Sept.	1849	2 Feb. 1958
Portugal	108	+	Maria Luisa Jorge	7 June	1859	fl. July 1967
Finland	107	+	Marie Anderson	3 Jan.	1829	1936
Belgium	106	267	Marie-Joseph Purnode (Mrs.)	17 April	1843	9 Nov. 1949
Austria	106	231	Anna Migschitz	3 Feb.	1850	1 Nov. 1956
Sweden	106	98	Emma Gustaffsson (Mrs.)	18 June	1858	14 Sept. 1964
Spain (i)	106	14	Jose Palido	15 Mar.	1866	29 Mar. 1972
Malaysia	106	+	Hassan Bin Yusoff	14 Aug.	1865	fl. Jan. 1972
Isle of Man	105	221	John Kneen	12 Nov.	1852	9 June 1958

(a) *Mrs. Ellen Carroll died in North River, Newfoundland, Canada on 8 December 1943, reputedly aged 115 years 49 days.*
(b) *Mrs. Betsy Baker (née Russell) was allegedly born 20 August 1842 in Brington, Northamptonshire, and died in Tecumseh, Nebraska, U.S.A. on 24 October 1955, reputedly aged 113 years 65 days. The 67-year-old son of Mrs. Tatzumbie Dupea, a Piute Indian at the Good Hope Convalescent Center, Los Angeles claimed that her birthday on 26 July 1969 was not her 112th but her 120th. Sarah Collins, d. 3 May 1971 was allegedly born in slavery 116 years before.*
(c) *London-born Miss Isabella Shepheard was allegedly 115 years old when she died at St. Asaph, Flintshire, North Wales, on 20 Nov. 1948, but her actual age was believed to have been 109 years 90 days. Charles Alfred Nunez Arnold died in Liverpool on 15 Sept. 1941 reputedly aged 112 years 66 days based on a baptismal claim (London, 10 Nov. 1829).*

(d) *Mrs. Susan Johanna Deporter of Port Elizabeth, South Africa, was reputedly 114 years old when she died on 4 August 1954. Mrs. Sarah Lawrence, Cape Town, South Africa was reputedly 112 on 3 June 1968.*
(e) *A man named Nakamura of Kamaishi, northern Japan, was reported to have died on 4 May 1969 aged 116 years 329 days.*
(f) *Reginald Beck of Sydney, New South Wales, Australia was allegedly 111 years old when he died on 13 April 1928.*
(g) *There are allegedly 22,000 centenarians in U.S.S.R. (c.f. 7,000 in U.S.A.).*
(h) *Friedrich Sadowski of Heidelberg reputedly celebrated his 111th birthday on 31 October 1936. Franz Joseph Eder d. Spitzburg 3 May 1911 allegedly aged 116.*
(i) *Juana Ortega Villarin, Madrid, Spain, was allegedly 112 in February 1962. Ana Maria Parraga of Murcia was reportedly 107 in Nov. 1969.*

In the face of the above data the claim published in the April 1961 issue of the Soviet Union's *Vestnik Statistiki* ("Statistical Herald") that there were 224 male and 368 female Soviet citizens aged in excess of 120 recorded at the census of 15 Jan. 1959, indicates a reliance on hearsay rather than evidence. Official Soviet insistence on the unrivalled longevity of the country's citizenry is curious in view of the fact that the 592 persons in their unique "over 120" category must have spent at least the first 78 years of their prolonged lives under Tsarism. It has recently been suggested that the extreme ages claimed by some men in Georgia, U.S.S.R., are the result of attempts to avoid military service when they were younger, by assuming the identities of older men.

Great Britain The oldest living Briton among an estimated population of 1,300 (1,130 women and 170 men) centenarians is Miss Alice Stevenson (b. Piccadilly, London 10 July 1861) now living at Brambleacres Old People's Home, Worcester Road, Sutton, Surrey. The oldest living man is Frederick Victor Butterfield of Harrogate, Yorkshire, who was born on 28 Feb. 1864. He retired from pharmacy at the age of 99.

Most reigns The greatest number of reigns during which any English subject could have lived is ten. A person born on the day (11 April) that Henry VI was deposed in 1471 had to live to only the comparatively modest age of 87 years 7 months and 6 days to see the accession of Elizabeth I on 17 Nov. 1558. Such a person could have been Thomas Carn of London, born 1471 and died 28 Jan. 1578 in his 107th year.

Miss Alice Stevenson, who at 112 became the oldest woman of all time with birth certification

4. REPRODUCTIVITY

MOTHERHOOD

Most children
World The greatest number of children produced by a mother in an independently attested case is 69 by the first wife of Fyodor Vassilet, a peasant of the Moscow Jurisdiction, Russia, who, in 27 confinements, gave birth to 16 pairs of twins, 7 sets of triplets and 4 sets of quadruplets. Most of the children attained their majority. Mme. Vassilet (1816–72) became so renowned that she was presented at the court of Tsar Alexander II.

Currently the highest reported figure is a 38th child born to Raimundo Carnauba, 58 and Josimar Carnauba, 54 of Belém, Brazil. She was married at 15 and so far has had 14 sons and 24 daughters at yearly intervals. The mother in May 1972 said "They have given us a lot of work and worry but they are worth it", and the father "I don't know why people make such a fuss".

Great Britain The British record is probably held by Mrs. Elizabeth Greenhille (d. 1681) of Abbot's Langley, Hertfordshire. It is alleged that she gave birth to 39 children (32 daughters and 7 sons), all of whom attained their majority. She was married at 16, had a world record 38 confinements and died reputedly aged 64. Her last son Thomas (d. *c.* 1740) became surgeon to the 10th Duke of Norfolk and was the author of the "Art of Embalming" (1705). According to an inscription on a gravestone in Conway Church cemetery, Caernarvonshire, North Wales, Nicholas Hookes (d. 27 March 1637) was the 41st child of his mother Alice Hookes, but further details are lacking. It was reported in December 1634 that the wife of a Scottish weaver living in Newcastle upon Tyne had borne her husband 62 children. It has not been possible to corroborate or refute this report.

Great Britain's champion mothers of today are believed to be Mrs. Margaret McNaught, 50 of Balsall Heath, Birmingham (12 boys and 10 girls, all single births) and Mrs. Mable Constable, 53 of Long Itchington, Warwickshire who also has had 22 children including a set of triplets and two sets of twins.

Oldest mother
World Medical literature contains extreme but unauthenticated cases of septuagenarian mothers. The oldest recorded mother of whom there is certain evidence is Mrs. Ruth Alice Kistler (*née* Taylor), formerly Mrs. Shepard, of Portland, Oregon, U.S.A. She was born at Wakefield, Massachusetts, on 11 June 1899 and gave birth to a daughter, Suzan, at Glendale, near Los Angeles, California, on 18 Oct. 1956, when her age was 57 years 129 days. The incidence of quinquagenarian births varies widely with the highest known rate in Albania (nearly 5,500 per million).

Great Britain The oldest British mother reliably recorded is Mrs. Winifred Wilson (*née* Stanley) of Eccles, Lancashire. She was born in Wolverhampton on 11 Nov. 1881 or 1882 and had her tenth child, a daughter Shirley, on Nov. 14 1936, when aged 54 or 55 years and 3 days.

At Southampton on 10 Feb. 1916, Mrs. Elizabeth Pearce gave birth to a son when aged 54 years 40 days. It is believed that live births to quinquagenarian mothers occur only twice in each million births in England and Wales.

Ireland The oldest Irish mother recorded was Mrs. Mary Higgins of Cork, County Cork (b. 7 Jan. 1876) who gave birth to a daughter, Patricia, on 17 March 1931 when aged 55 years 69 days.

Raimundo and Josimar Carnauba, currently the world's most prolific parents with their family. Some "extras" were needed to support the younger members of the cast

Descendants In polygamous countries, the number of a person's descendants can become incalculable. The last Sharifian Emperor of Morocco, Moulay Ismail (1672–1727), known as "The Bloodthirsty", was reputed to have fathered a total of 548 sons and 340 daughters.

Capt. Wilson Kettle (b. 1860) of Grand Bay, Port aux Basques, Newfoundland, Canada, died on 25 Jan. 1963, aged 102, leaving 11 children by two wives, 65 grandchildren, 201 great-grandchildren and 305 great-great-grandchildren, a total of 582 living descendants. Mrs. Johanna Booyson (see page 22), of Belfast, Transvaal, was estimated to have 600 living descendants in South Africa in January 1968.

Mrs. Sarah Crawshaw (d. 25 Dec. 1844) left 397 descendants, according to her gravestone in Stones Methodist Church, Ripponden, Halifax, Yorkshire.

Multiple great grand-parents Theoretically a great-great-great-great-grandparent is a possibility, though in practice countries in which young mothers are common generally have a low expectation of life. Mrs. Ella M. Prince of the U.S.A., who died, aged 91, on 29 May 1970, had three great-great-great-grandchildren among her 60 living descendants, while Hon. General Walter Washington Williams (1855–1959) of Houston, Texas, U.S.A., was reportedly several times a great-great-great-grand-father. On 8 Oct. 1971 Mrs. Mary Williams allegedly born 18 Mar. 1856) died at Forest Park, Atlanta, Georgia. She reportedly left, among 192 living descendants, 7 great-great-great-great-great-grand-children. This was most probably a confusion with her leaving five generations, since an age of 115 and seven successive generations producing children at an average interval of 16 years strains all credence.

MULTIPLE BIRTHS

Quinde-caplets It was announced by Dr. Gennaro Montanino of Rome that he had removed the foetuses of 10 girls and 5 boys from the womb of a 35-year-old housewife on 22 July 1971. A fertility drug was responsible for this unique and unsurpassed instance of quindecaplets.

Nonuplets With multiple births, as with giants and centenarians, exaggeration is the rule. Since 1900 two cases of nonuplets, five cases of octuplets, 19 cases of septuplets and at least 23 cases of sextuplets have been reported. Mrs. Geraldine Broderick, 29, gave birth to 5 boys (two still-born) and 4 girls—the only certain nonuplets—at the Royal Hospital, Sydney, Australia on 13 June 1971. The last survivor, Richard (12 oz. [340 g]) died on the sixth day. Archbishop Estsathios of Salonika, Greece (d. 1150) once alluded to a woman in the Peloponese, named Geyfyra, who produced nine surviving nonuplets. Jamaica has the highest incidence of multiple births (i.e. triplet and upward) at 4 per 1,000.

Octuplets The only confirmed case of live-born octuplets was the four boys and four girls born to Señora María Teresa Lopez de Sepulveda, aged 21, in a nursing home in Mexico City, Mexico, between 7 p.m. and 8 p.m. on 10 March 1967. They had an aggregate weight of 9 lb. 10 oz. *4 kg 40* and ranged between 1 lb. 3 oz. *539 g* down to 14 oz. *397 g*. All the boys were named José and all the girls Josefina. They all died within 14 hours.

There have been four unconfirmed reports of octuplets since 1900: to Señora Enriquita Ruibi at Tampico, Mexico, in 1921; seven boys and one girl to Mme. Tam Sing at Kwoom Yam Sha, China, in June 1934; a case near Tientsin, China, on 29 Sept. 1947 (one baby died); and still-born babies to Señora Celia Gonzalez at Bahía Blanca, Argentina, on 2 May 1955.

Septuplets There have been 7 confirmed cases of septuplets since 1900; still-born babies to Britt Louise Ericsson,

aged 34, in Uppsala, Sweden, in August 1964; five girls and two boys to Mme. Brigitte Verhaeghe-Denayer in Brussels, Belgium, on 25 March 1966 (all the babies died soon afterwards); four girls and three boys to Mrs Sandra Cwikielnik in Boston, Massachusetts, U.S.A., on 1 Oct. 1966 (one was born dead and the others died within minutes); a still-born set in Sweden in 1966; a case from Addis Ababa, Ethiopia in March 1969 of seven babies to Mrs. Verema Jusuf of whom two died immediately; and a set of 3 girls and 4 boys (none survived more than 12 hrs) in Santa Clara, Cal. on 17 March 1972 to a 24 year old nullipara. They were delivered by Dr. Anthony J. Damore.

Sextuplets Among sextuplet births, the case of Mrs. Philip Speichinger provided the earliest irrefutable evidence in the person of a surviving daughter, Marjorie Louise of Mendon, Missouri, U.S.A., born on 9 Aug. 1936. The other five children were still-born. Mrs. Alincia Parker (*née* Bushnell) was always cited as last survivor of the sextuplets reputedly born on 18 Sept. 1866 to Mrs. James B. Bushnell in Chicago, Illinois, U.S.A. She died, aged 85, in Warsaw, New York State, U.S.A., on 27 March 1952. The birth was registered by Dr. James Edwards but, for obscure reasons, was unrevealed until about 1912. The other children were identified as Lucy (died at 2 months), Laberto (died at 8 months), Norberto (died in 1934), Alberto (died in Albion, N.Y., in *c.* 1940) and Mrs. Alice Elizabeth Hughes (*née* Bushnell) who died in Flagstaff, Arizona, on 2 July 1941. From the sextuplets born to Maria Garcia wife of an Indian farmer in Michoacán State, Mexico, on 7 Sept. 1953, three (one boy and two girls) are reputedly still living. Mrs. Wahed Ali, living in Coshi, Faridpur district of East Pakistan, allegedly gave birth to six sons on 11 Nov. 1967.

Mrs. Sheila Ann Thorns (*née* Manning) (b. Birmingham 2 Oct. 1938) of Northfield, Birmingham, England, gave birth by Caesarean section to sextuplets at the New Birmingham Maternity Hospital on 2 Oct. 1968. In order of birth they were Lynne (2 lb. 6 oz. [*1 kg 080*], died 22nd), Ian (2 lb. 13 oz. [*1 kg 280*] died 13th), Julie (3 lb. 1 oz. [*1 kg 390*]), Susan (2 lb. 11 oz. [*1 kg 219*]), Roger (2 lb. 10 oz. [*1 kg 190*]) and Jillian (died after one hour). A seventh child did not develop beyond the third month of this pregnancy which had been induced by a fertility drug. A second set of British sextuplets were delivered, after use of a fertility drug, of Mrs. Rosemary Letts (*née* Egerton) (b. Watford, 1946) of Chorleywood, Hertfordshire by Caesarean section at University College Hospital, London on 15 Dec. 1969. One girl was still-born but the others Cara Dawn (2 lb. 13 oz. [*1 kg 280*]), Sharon Marie (2 lb. 9 oz. [*1 kg 160*]), Joanne Nadine (2 lb. 7 oz. [*1 kg 110*]), Gary John (1 lb. 11½ oz. [*0 kg 780*]) and Tanya Odile (2 lb. 1 oz. [*936 g*]) survived.

Quintuplets The earliest quintuplets in which all survived were: Emilie (died 6 Aug. 1954, aged 20), Yvonne (now in a convent), Cécile (now Mrs. Philippe Langlois), Marie (later Mrs. Florian Houle died 28 Feb. 1970) and Annette (now Mrs. Germain Allard), born in her seventh pregnancy to Mrs. Oliva Dionne, aged 25, at Corbeil, near Callander, Ontario, Canada, on 28 May 1934 (aggregate weight 13 lb. 6 oz. [*10 kg 60*] with an average of 2 lb. 11 oz. [*1 kg 220*]).

Quintuplets were recorded in Wells, Somerset on 5 Oct. 1736 where four boys and a girl were all christened. Quins (three boys and two girls) were born to Mrs. Elspet Gordon of Rothes, Morayshire, Scotland in 1858 but all died within 12 hours, and at Over Darwen, Lancashire on 24 April 1786 Mrs. Margaret Waddington produced five girls (three still-born) weighing a total of 2 lb. 12 oz. *1 kg 250*.

Quins were born to Mrs. Irene Mary Hanson (*née* Brown) 33, of Rayleigh, Essex at the Queen Charlotte's Maternity Hospital, Hammersmith, London on

13 Nov. 1969. They are Joanne Lesley (2 lb. 7 oz. [*1 kg 110*]), Nicola Jane (2 lb. 13 oz. [*1 kg 280*]), Julie Anne (2 lb. 15 oz. [*1 kg 330*]), Sarah Louise (3 lb. 7 oz. [*1 kg 560*]) and Jacqueline Mary (2 lb. 6½ oz. [*1 kg 090*]). A fertility drug was used.

Heaviest It was reported that quintuplets weighing 25 lb. *11 kg 340* were born on 7 June 1953 to Mrs. Lui Saulien of Chekiang province, China. A weight of 25 lb. *11 kg 340* was also reported for girl quins born to Mrs. Kamalammal in Pondicherry, India, on 30 Dec. 1956. All died shortly afterwards.

Quadruplets The heaviest quadruplets ever recorded are the three
Heaviest girls and one boy born to Mrs. Penny McPherson on
World 8 July 1972 at Liverpool Maternity Hospital. They aggregated 21 lb. 5 oz. *9 kg 660*—Fiona (5 lb. 1 oz. [*2 kg 30*]), Kirsten (5 lb. 15 oz. [*2 kg 690*]), Rachel (4 lb. 11 oz. [*2 kg 210*]) and Guy (5 lb. 10 oz. *2 kg 550*])

United The earliest recorded quadruplets to have all survived
Kingdom in the United Kingdom were the Miles quads, born at St. Neots, Huntingdon on 28 Nov. 1935—Ann (now Mrs. Robert Browning), Ernest, Paul and Michael (total weight 13 lb. 15½ oz. [*6 kg 340*]). Sarah Coe, one of the quads born to Mrs. Mary Coe of Cambridge on 6–7 Oct. 1766 was reportedly still alive 42 years later in 1808. The other three died at 2, 15 and 20 months respectively. Quadruplets reputedly survived birth near Devil's Bridge, Cardiganshire, Wales in 1856 only to die of cholera later in the same year. The lightest were Yana (3 lb. 8 oz. [*1 kg 590*]), Edward (3 lb. 3½ oz. [*1 kg 460*]), Lucille (3 lb. 8 oz. [*1 kg 590*]) and Christopher (2 lb. 7½ oz. [*1 kg 120*]), totalling 12 lb. 11 oz. *4 kg 730* born to Mrs. Phoebe Meacham (*née* Buckley) (b. 1928) of Leigh-on-Sea in Rochford Hospital, Essex on 3 Jan. 1962.

Ireland The first surviving quadruplets born in Ireland were those born on 23 Jan. 1965 to Mrs. Eileen O'Connell, aged 36, of Pallasgreen, Co. Limerick, in the Limerick Regional Hospital. On 31 Jan. 1965 they were weighed: Catherine Mary (2 lb. 2 oz. [*0 kg 963*]), Gerard Michael (3 lb. 6 oz. [*1 kg 530*]), John Paul (3 lb. 11 oz. [*1 kg 670*]) and Margaret Anne (3 lb. 0 oz. [*1 kg 360*]).

Triplets There is an unconfirmed report of triplets (two boys
Heaviest and a girl) weighing 26 lb. 6 oz. *11 kg 960* born to a 21-year-old Iranian woman reported on 18 March 1968. Three boy triplets weighing 23 lb. 1 oz. *10 kg 430* were born in the Yarrawonga District Hospital, Victoria, Australia on 8 Aug. 1946. They weighed 7 lb. 13 oz. *3 kg 540*, 7 lb. 12 oz. *3 kg 520* and 7 lb. 8 oz. *3 kg 40*. The heaviest recorded triplets born in the United Kingdom, were Timothy Stuart (7 lb. 3 oz. [*3 kg 260*]), Martin James (6 lb. 10 oz. [*3 kg 010*]) and Guy Thomas (8 lb. 11 oz. [*3 kg 940*]) born at 9.0 a.m. to 9.10 a.m. on 21 Feb. 1972 to Mrs. Elizabeth A. Parker aged 31 of Buxton, Derbyshire in the Stepping Hill Hospital, Stockport, Cheshire. They aggregated 22 lb. 8 oz. *7 kg 370*.

Most The greatest reported number of sets of triplets born to one woman is 15 (*cf.* 7 to Mme Vassilet, page 23) to Maddalena Granata (1839–*fl.* 1886) of Nocera Superiore, Italy.

Oldest The oldest known surviving triplets in the world are Richard Henry, John James and Catherine Vivian (now Mrs. Ellis) Lutey born in Carfury, Cornwall on 24 April 1891.

Twins The heaviest recorded live-born twins have been John
Heaviest and Jane weighing 14 lb. *6 kg 350* and 13¾ lb. *6 kg 240* born to Mrs. J. P. Haskin on 20 Feb. 1924 in Fort Smith, Arkansas. The heaviest recorded stillborn twins were two boys, the first weighing 17 lb. 8 oz. *7 kg 940* and the second 18 lb. *8 kg 160*. This was

reported in a letter from Derbyshire in *The Lancet* of 6 Dec. 1884.

Lightest The lightest recorded birthweight for a pair of surviving twins has been 2 lb. 3 oz. *992 g* in the case of Mary 16 oz. *453 g* and Margaret 19 oz. *538 g* born to Mrs. Florence Stimson, Queens Road, Old Fletton, Peterborough, England, delivered by Dr. Macaulay on 16 Aug. 1931. Margaret is now Mrs. M. J. Hurst.

Margaret (left) and Mary Stimson the lightest recorded pair of surviving twins, at the age of two

Oldest The chances of identical twins both reaching 100 are said to be one in 1,000 million. The oldest recorded twins were Gulbrand and Bernt Morterud, born at Nord Odal, Norway, on 20 Dec. 1858. Bernt died on 1 Aug. 1960 in Chicago, Illinois, U.S.A. aged 101, and his brother died at Nord Odal on 12 Jan. 1964, aged 105. Twin sisters, Mrs. Vassilka Dermendjhieva and Mrs. Vassila Yapourdjieva of Sofia, Bulgaria allegedly celebrated their joint 104th birthday on 27 Sept. 1966.

Most The highest recorded number of sets of twins born to one mother is 16 in the case of Mme. Fyodor Vassilet (see page 23). The British record is 15 by Mrs. Mary Jonas who died aged 85 on 4 Dec. 1899 near Chester. All the sets were boy and girl. She also had three single babies.

"Siamese" Conjoined twins derived the name "Siamese" from the celebrated Chang and Eng Bunker, born at Maklong, Thailand (Siam), on 11 May 1811. They were joined by a cartilaginous band at the chest and married in April 1843 the Misses Sarah and Adelaide Yates and fathered ten and twelve children respectively. They died within three hours of each other on 17 Jan. 1874, aged 62. There is no genealogical evidence for the existence of the much-publicized Chalkhurst twins, Mary and Aliza, of Biddenden, Kent, allegedly born in *c.* 1550 (not 1100). Daisy and Violet Hilton, born in Brighton, Sussex on 5 Feb. 1908, were joined at the hip. They died in Charlotte, North Carolina, U.S.A., on 5 Jan. 1969 aged 60. The earliest successful separation of Siamese twins was performed on Prisna and Napit Atkinson (b. May 1953 in Thailand) by Dr. Dragstedt at the University of Chicago on 29 March 1955.

BABIES

Largest The heaviest normal new-born child recorded in
World modern times was a boy weighing 11 kg *24 lb. 4 oz.*, born on 3 June 1961 to Mrs. Saadat Cor of Cegham, Southern Turkey. A report from Dezful, S.W. Iran, that Mrs. Massoumeh Valizadeh or Valli-Ullah 32, had given birth to a 12 kg *26 lb. 6½ oz.* boy on 7 Feb. 1972, was later officially stated to be incorrect. There is

also an unconfirmed report of a woman giving birth to a 27 lb. *12 kg 250* baby in Essonnes, a suburb of Corbeil, central France, in June 1929. A deformed baby weighing 29¼ lb. *13 kg 280* was born in May 1939 in a hospital at Effingham, Illinois, U.S.A., but only lived for 2 hours.

United Kingdom The greatest recorded live birth weight in the United Kingdom is 21 lb. *9 kg 530* for a child born on Christmas Day, 1852. It was reported in a letter to the *British Medical Journal* (1 Feb. 1879) from a doctor in Torpoint, Cornwall. The only other reported birth weight in excess of 20 lb. *9 kg 070* is 20 lb. 2 oz. *9 kg 130* for a boy born to a 33-year-old schoolmistress in Crewe, Cheshire, on 12 Nov. 1884. A baby of 33 lb. *14 kg 970* was reportedly born to a Mrs. Lambert of Wandsworth Road, London *c.* 1930 but its measurements indicate a weight of about 17 lb. *7 kg 70*. The *British Medical Journal* reported in February 1935 the case of a boy aged 2 years 9 months who weighed 7 st. 2½ lb. *45 kg 590*.

Most Bouncing Baby The most bouncing baby on record is Elias Daou (b. Suniani, Ghana on 12 Oct. 1969). At the age of 22 months Elias weighed 4 st. 5½ lb. *27 kg 90*, his circumference was 91 cm *35¾ in*.

Smallest The lowest birth weight for a surviving infant, of which there is definite evidence, is 10 oz. *283 g* in the case of Marion Chapman, born on 5 June 1938 in South Shields, County Durham. She was 12¼ in *31 cm* long. By her first birthday her weight had increased to 13 lb. 14 oz. *6 kg 290*. She was born unattended and was nursed by Dr. D. A. Shearer, who fed her hourly through a fountain pen filler. Her weight on her 21st birthday was 7 st. 8 lb. *48 kg 080*. The smallest viable baby reported from the United States has been Jacqueline Benson born at Palatine, Illinois on 20 Feb. 1936, weighing 12 oz. *340 g*.

A weight of 8 oz. *227 g* was reported on 20 March 1938 for a baby born prematurely to Mrs. John Womack, after she had been knocked down by a lorry in East Louis, Illinois, U.S.A. The baby was taken alive to St. Mary's Hospital, but further information is lacking. On 23 Feb. 1952 it was reported that a 6 oz. *170 g* baby only 6½ in *17 cm* long lived for 12 hours in a hospital in Indianapolis, Indiana, U.S.A. A twin was still-born. English law has accepted pregnancies with extremes of 174 days (*Clark* v. *Clark*, 1939) and 349 days (*Hadlum* v. *Hadlum*, 1949).

Longest pregnancy The longest pregnancy reported is one of 389 days for a woman aged 25 in Woking Maternity Hospital, Surrey, England (*Lancet*, 3 Dec. 1954). The baby, weighing 7 lb. 14 oz. *3 kg 570*, was still-born. The average pregnancy is 273 days. The longest medically accepted pregnancy for a live-born baby was one of 390 days in the case of Mrs. Christine Houghton, 28, of Walberton, Sussex on 22 May 1971. The baby, Tina, weighed 7 lb. 7 oz. *3 kg 370*.

Coincident Birthdates On 21 Jan. 1971 it was reported from Torrente, Spain that a fourth consecutive child had been born to Mrs. Teresa Gomez Olivares on her birthday. The odds against 5 such births would be 1 to 17,748,855,000 if this were random chance.

5. PHYSIOLOGY AND ANATOMY

A French medical publication in 1970 set a value of £1.40 on the raw materials in an average weight human body. It may be a commentary on world inflation that a pre-war figure was 39 U.S. cents, then 1s 7½d. (8p). Hydrogen (63%) and oxygen (25.5%) constitute the commonest of the 24 elements in the human body. In 1972 four more trace elements were added—fluorine, silicon, tin and vanadium. The "essentiality" of nickel is now being studied.

BONES

Longest The thigh bone or *femur* is the longest of the 206 bones in the human body. It constitutes usually 27½ per cent of a person's stature, and may be expected to be 19¾ in *50 cm* long in a 6-ft *183 cm* -tall man. The longest recorded bone was the femur of the German giant Constantine, who died in Mons, Belgium, on 30 March 1902, aged 30 (see page 16). It measured 76 cm *29.9 in*. The femur of Robert Wadlow, the tallest man ever recorded, measured approximately 29½ in *75 cm*.

Smallest The *stapes* or stirrup bone, one of the three auditory ossicles in the middle ear, is the smallest human bone, measuring from 2,6 to 3,4 mm *0.10 to 0.17 in*. in length and weighing from 2,0 to 4,3 mg *0.03 to 0.065 gr*. Sesamoids are not included among human bones.

MUSCLES

Largest Muscles normally account for 40 per cent of the body weight and the bulkiest of the 639 muscles in the human body is the *gluteus maximus* or buttock muscle, which extends the thigh.

Smallest The smallest muscle is the *stapedius*, which controls the *stapes* (see above), an auditory ossicle in the middle ear, and which is less than 1/20th in *0,127 cm* long.

Smallest waists Queen Catherine de Medici (1519–89) decreed a waist measurement of 13 in *33 cm* for ladies of the French court. This was at a time when females were more diminutive. The smallest recorded waist among women of normal stature in the 20th century is a reputed 13 in *33 cm* in the case of the French actress Mlle. Polaire (1881–1939) and Mrs. Ethel Granger (b. 12 April 1905) of Peterborough who reduced from a natural 22 in *56 cm* over the period 1929–1939.

Catherine de Medici, wife of Henry II of France, who decreed a waist measurement of 13 in *33 cm* for ladies of her court

Largest chest measurements The largest chest measurements are among endomorphs (those with a tendency toward globularity). In the extreme case of Hughes (see page 18) this was reportedly 124 in *315 cm* but in the light of his known height and weight a figure of 104 in *264 cm* would be more supportable. George MacAree (see Britain's heaviest man) has a chest measurement of 72½ in *184 cm*. Among muscular subjects (mesomorphs), chest measurements above 56 in *142 cm* are extremely rare. The largest such chest measurement ever recorded was that of Angus Macaskill (1825–63) of Berneray, Scotland (see page 16), who may well have been the strongest man who ever lived. His chest must have measured 65 in *165 cm* at his top weight of 37½ st. *235 kg*.

Ivan Sergeyvich Turgenev left, owner of the heaviest brain ever recorded, and Anatole France whose brain weighed only 2 lb. 4 oz. *1 017 g* at his death

BRAIN

Largest The brain has 1.5×10^{10} cells each containing 10^{10} macromolecules. Each cell has 10^4 interconnections with other cells. After the age of 18 the brain loses some 10^3 cells per day but the macromolecular contingent of each cell is renewed 10^4 times in a normal life span. The brain of an average adult male (*i.e.* 30–59 years) weighs 1 410 g *3 lb. 1.73 oz.* falling to 1 030 g *2 lb. 4.31 oz.* The heaviest brain ever recorded was that of Ivan Sergeyvich Turgenev (1818–83), the Russian author. His brain weighed 2 012 g *4 lb. 6.96 oz.* The brain of Oliver Cromwell (1599–1658) reputedly weighed 2 222 g *4 lb. 14.8 oz.*, but the size of his head in portraits does not support this extreme figure. The brain of Lord Byron, who died in Greece in 1824 aged 36, reportedly weighed 6 Neopolitan pounds (1 924 g or *4 lb. 3.86 oz.*), but this also included a certain amount of blood. In January 1891 the *Edinburgh Medical Journal* reported the case of a 75-year-old man in the Royal Edinburgh Asylum whose brain weighed 1 829 g *4 lb. 0.5 oz.*

Smallest The brain of Anatole France (1844–1924), the French writer, weighed only 1 017 g *2 lb. 4 oz.* without the membrane, but there was some shrinkage due to old age. His brain probably weighed *c.* 1 130 g *2 lb. 7.78 oz.* at its heaviest.

Brains in extreme cases of microcephaly may weigh as little as 300 g *10.6 oz.* (*cf.* 20 oz. [*567 g*] for the adult male gorilla, and 16–20 oz. [*454–567 g*] for other anthropoid apes).

Longest necks The maximum measured extension of the neck by the successive fitting of copper coils, as practised by the Padaung or Mayan people of Burma, is 15¾ in *40 cm.*

From the male viewpoint the practice serves the dual purpose of enhancing the beauty of the female and ensuring fidelity. The neck muscles can become so atrophied that the removal of the support of the coils can produce asphyxiation.

Commonest illness The commonest illness in the world is coryza (acute nasopharyngitis) or the common cold. Only 3,540,000 working days were reportedly lost as a result of this illness in Great Britain between mid 1970 and mid 1971, since absences of less than three days are not reported. The greatest reported loss of working time in Britain is from bronchitis, which accounted for 33,750,000, or 10.74 per cent, of the total of 314,130,000 working days lost in the same period.

DISEASE

Commonest The commonest disease in the world is dental caries or tooth decay. In Great Britain 13 per cent of people have lost all their teeth before they are 21 years old. During their lifetime few completely escape its effects. Infestation with pinworm (*Enterobius vermicularis*) approaches 100 per cent in some areas of the world.

Rarest Medical literature periodically records hitherto undescribed diseases. A disease as yet undescribed but predicted is podocytoma of the kidney—a tumor of the epithelial cells lining the glomerulus of the kidney. Of once common diseases, rabies (hydrophobia) was last contracted in Britain in 1922 and last recorded in 1964. Kuru, or laughing sickness, afflicts only the Fore tribe of eastern New Guinea and is 100 per cent fatal. The rarest fatal diseases in England and Wales have been those from which the last deaths (all males) were all recorded more than 40 years ago—yellow fever (1930), cholera nostras (1928) and bubonic plague (1926).

Most and least infectious The most infectious of all diseases is the pneumonic form of plague, with a mortality rate of about 99.99 per cent. Leprosy transmitted by *Mycobacterium leprae* is the least infectious of communicable diseases.

Highest morbidity Rabies in humans has been regarded as uniformly fatal when associated with the hydrophobia symptom. A 25-year-old woman Candida de Sousa Barbosa of Rio de Janeiro, Brazil, was believed to be the first ever survivor of the disease in November 1968. In 1969 all 515 cases reported were fatal.

Most notorious carrier The most notorious of all typhoid carriers has been Mary Mallon, known as Typhoid Mary, of New York City, N.Y., U.S.A. She was the source of the 1903 outbreak, with 1,300 cases. Because of her refusal to leave employment, often under assumed names, involving the handling of food, she was placed under permanent detention from 1915 until her death in 1938.

Most Bee Stings The greatest number of bee stings sustained by any surviving human subject is 2,443 by Johannes Relleke, at the Gwaii River in the Wankie District of Rhodesia, on 28 Jan. 1962.

Touch sensitivity The extreme sensitivity of the fingers is such that a vibration with a movement of 0.02 of a micron can be detected. On 12 Jan. 1963 the Soviet newspaper

Izvestiya reported the case of a totally blindfolded girl, Rosa Kulgeshova, who was able to identify colours by touch alone. Later reports confirmed in 1970 that under rigorous test conditions this claimed ability totally disappeared.

Most fingers Voigt records a case from Marmont, France of a boy *c.* 1790 with 13 fingers and 12 toes. Polydactylism is common in the Urdes district of Spain.

Longest finger nails The longest recorded finger nails were reported from Shanghai in 1910, in the case of a Chinese priest who took 27 years to achieve nails up to 22¾ in *58 cm* in length. Probably the longest nails now grown are those of Ramesh Sharma of Delhi, whose nails on his left hand now aggregate 52½ in *133 cm* after 10 years, with his best at 15 in *38 cm*. Human nails normally grow from cuticle to cutting length in from 117 to 138 days.

Longest hair The longest recorded hair was that of Swami Pandarasannadhi, the head of the Thiruvadu Thurai monastery in India. His matted hair was reported in 1949 to be 26 ft *7,93 m* in length. The hair of Jane Bunford (see p. 17) which she wore in two plaits, reached down to her ankles, indicating a length in excess of 8 ft *2,43 m*.

Longest beard The longest beard preserved was that of Hans N. Langseth (b. 1846 in Norway) which measured 17½ ft *533 m* at the time of his death in 1927 after 15 years residence in the United States. The beard was presented to the Smithsonian Institution, Washington, D.C. in 1967. Richard Latter (b. Pembury, Kent, 1831) of Tunbridge Wells, Kent, who died in 1914 aged 83, reputedly had a beard 18 ft *5,49 m* long but contemporary independent corroboration is lacking and photographic evidence indicates this figure was exaggerated. The beard of the bearded lady Janice Deveree (b. Bracken Co., Kentucky, U.S.A., 1842) was measured at 14 in *36 cm* in 1884.

Longest moustache The longest moustache on record is that of Masuriya Din (b. 1908), a Brahmin of the Partabgarh district in Uttar Pradesh, India. It grew to an extended span of 8 ft 6 in *2,59 m* between 1949 and 1962, and costs £13 per annum in upkeep. The longest moustache in Great Britain is that of Mr. John Roy (b. 14 Jan. 1910), licensee of the "Cock Inn" at Beazely End, near Braintree, Essex. It attained a span of 44 in *112 cm* between 1939 and 9 Nov. 1971 when measured on the *Magpie* T.V. programme.

Blood groups The preponderance of one blood group varies greatly from one locality to another. On a world basis Group O is the most common (46 per cent), but in some areas, for example London and Norway, Group A predominates.

The full description of the commonest sub-group in Britain is O MsNs, P+, Rr, Lu(a−), K−, Le(a−b+), Fy(a+b+), Jk(a+b+), which occurs in one in every 270 people.

The rarest blood group on the ABO system, one of nine systems, is AB, which occurs in less than three per cent of persons in the British Isles. The rarest type in the world is a type of Bombay blood (sub-type A-h) found so far only in a Czechoslovak nurse in 1961 and in a brother and sister in New Jersey, U.S.A. reported in February 1968. The American male has started a blood bank for himself.

Richest Natural Resources Joe Thomas of Detroit, Michigan, U.S.A. was reported in August 1970 to have the highest known count of Anti-Lewis B, the rare blood antibody. A U.S. biological supply firm pays him $1,500 per quart—an income of $12,000 (£4,615) per annum.

The Internal Revenue regard this income as a taxable liquid asset.

Champion blood donor Joseph Elmaleh (b. 1915) of Marseilles, France, donated on 22 May 1968 his 339th litre of blood making a total of 74 gal 5 pt (597 pints) since 1931. A 50-year-old haemophiliac Warren C. Jyrich required 2,400 pt *1 364 litres* of blood when undergoing open heart surgery at the Michael Reese Hospital, Chicago, U.S.A., in December 1970. The most blood got from a Stone is believed to be that from Norman Stone, a Liverpool bus driver who became a regular donor in 1966. His is the rare AB Rh+.

Largest vein The largest vein in the human body is the cardiac vein known as the vena cava.

Most alcoholic subject It is recorded that a hard drinker named Vanhorn (1750–1811), born in London, averaged more than four bottles of ruby port per day for the 23 years 1788 to his death aged 61 in 1811. The total of his "empties" was put at 35,688.

The United Kingdom's legal limit for motorists is 80 mg of alcohol per 100 ml of blood. The hitherto recorded highest figure in medical literature of 600 mg per 100 ml was submerged when the late Mr. Michael Spring, 41, of Derby was found to have a level of 605 mg by a pathologist after a fatal road accident on 7 Jan. 1972.

Longest coma The longest duration of human unconsciousness was 32 years 99 days endured by Karoline Karlsson (b. Mönsterås, Sweden in 1862) from 25 Dec. 1875 to 3 April 1908. She died on 6 April 1950 aged 88. The longest recorded coma of any person still living is that of Elaine Esposito (b. 3 Dec. 1934) of Tarpon Springs, Florida, U.S.A. She has never stirred since an appendicectomy on 5 Aug. 1941, when she was six, in Chicago, Illinois, U.S.A.

Fastest reflexes The results of experiments carried out in 1943 have shown that the fastest messages transmitted by the nervous system travel at 265 m.p.h. *426 km/h*. With advancing age impulses are carried 15 per cent more slowly.

BODY TEMPERATURE

Highest In Kalow's case (*Lancet*, 31 Oct. 1970) a woman following halothane anaesthesia ran a temperature of 112° F *44,4° C*. She recovered after a procainamide infusion. Marathon runners in hot weather attain 105.8° F *41° C*.

A temperature of 155° F *46,1° C* was recorded in the case of Christopher Legge in the Hospital for Tropical Diseases, London, on 9 Feb. 1934. A subsequent examination of the thermometer disclosed a flaw in the bulb, but it is regarded as certain that the patient sustained a temperature of more than 110° F *43,3° C*.

Lowest The lowest body temperature ever recorded for a living person was 60.8° F *16,0° C* in the case of Vickie Mary Davis (b. 25 Dec. 1953) of Milwaukee, Wisconsin, when she was admitted to the Evangelical Hospital, Marshalltown, Iowa, U.S.A., on 21 Jan. 1956. The house in which she had been found unconscious on the floor was unheated and the air temperature had dropped to −24° F *−31° C*. Her temperature returned to normal (98.4° F or *36,9° C*) after 12 hours and may have been as low as 59° F *15,0° C* when she was first found.

Heart stoppage The longest recorded heart stoppage is 3 hours in the case of a Norwegian boy, Roger Arntzen, in April 1962. He was rescued, apparently drowned, after 22 minutes under the waters of the River Nideelv, near Trondheim.

The longest recorded interval in a *post mortem* birth was one of at least 80 minutes in Magnolia, Mississippi, U.S.A. Dr. Robert E. Drake found Fanella Anderson, aged 25, dead in her home at 11.40 p.m. on 15 Oct. 1966 and he delivered her of a son weighing 6 lb. 4 oz. *2 kg 830* by Caesarean operation in the Beacham Memorial Hospital on 16 Oct. 1966.

Largest stone The largest stone or vesical calculus reported in medical literature was one of 13 lb. 14 oz. *6 294 g* removed from an 80-year-old woman by Dr. Humphrey Arthure at Charing Cross Hospital, London, on 29 Dec. 1952.

Earliest influenza An epidemic bearing symptoms akin to influenza was first recorded in 412 B.C. by Hippocrates (*c.* 460–*c.* 375 B.C.). The earliest description of an epidemic in Great Britain was in the *Chronicle of Melrose* in 1173, although the term influenza was not introduced until 1743 by John Huxham (1692–1768) of Plymouth, Devon.

Earliest duodenal ulcer The earliest description in medical literature of a duodenal ulcer was made in 1746 by Georg Erhard Hamberger (1696–1755).

Earliest slipped disc The earliest description of a prolapsed intervertebral cartilage was by George S. Middleton and John H. Teacher of Glasgow, Scotland, in 1911.

Pill-taking It is recorded that among hypochondriacs Samuel Jessup (b. 1752), a wealthy grazier of Heckington, Lincolnshire, has never had a modern rival. His consumption of pills from 1794 to 1816 was 226,934, with a peak annual total of 51,590 in 1814. He is also recorded as having drunk 40,000 bottles of medicine before death overtook him at the surprisingly advanced age of 65.

Most tattoos Vivian "Sailor Joe" Simmons, a Canadian tattoo artist, had 4,831 tattoos on his body. He died in Toronto on 22 Dec. 1965 aged 77. Britain's most tattooed man is Arthur (Eddy) Noble (b. 8 Feb. 1923) of Newcastle, who filled in his last gaps with 114 more tattoos in 1970 making a total of more than 400. Britain's most tattooed woman is Rusty Field (b. 1944) of Aldershot, Hampshire, who after 12 years under the needle, is nearing totality.

Hiccoughing The longest recorded attack of hiccoughs was that afflicting Jack O'Leary of Los Angeles, California, U.S.A. It was estimated that he "hicked" more than 100,000,000 times in an attack which lasted from 13 June 1948 to 1 June 1956, apart from a week's respite in 1951. His weight fell from 9 st. 12 lb. *62 kg 60* to 5 st. 4 lb. *33 kg 570*. In June 1973 it was reported that Charles Osborne, 79, of Iowa, U.S.A. had been affected for 51 years. The infirmary at Newcastle upon Tyne is recorded to have admitted a young man from Long Witton, Northumberland on 25 March 1769 suffering from hiccoughs which could be heard at a range of more than a mile.

Sneezing The most chronic sneezing fit ever recorded was that of June Clark, aged 17, of Miami, Florida, U.S.A. She started sneezing on 4 Jan. 1966, while recovering from a kidney ailment in the James M. Jackson Memorial Hospital, Miami. The sneezing was stopped by electric "aversion" treatment on 8 June 1966, after 155 days. The highest speed at which expelled particles have been measured to travel is 103.6 m.p.h. *167 km/h.*

Snoring *Loudest* Research at the Ear, Nose and Throat Department of St. Mary's Hospital, London, published in November 1968, shows that a rasping snore can attain a loudness of 69 decibels (*c.f.* 70–90 for a pneumatic drill).

Yawning In Lee's case, reported in 1888, a fifteen-year-old female patient yawned continuously for a period of five weeks.

SWALLOWING

The worst known case of compulsive swallowing was reported in the *Journal of the American Medical Association* in December 1960. The patient, who complained only of swollen ankles, was found to have 258 items in his stomach, including a 3 lb. *1 kg 360* piece of metal, 26 keys, 3 sets of rosary beads, 16 religious medals, a bracelet, a necklace, 3 pairs of tweezers, 4 nail clippers, 39 nail files, 3 metal chains and 88 assorted coins.

Coins The most extreme recorded case of coin swallowing was revealed by Sedgefield General Hospital, County Durham, on 5 Jan. 1958, when it was reported that 366 halfpennies, 26 sixpences, 17 threepences, 11 pennies and four shillings (424 coins valued at £1 17s. 5d.), plus 27 pieces of wire totalling 5 lb. 1 oz. *2 kg 30*, had been extracted from the stomach of a 54-year-old man.

Sword The longest length of sword able to be "swallowed" by a practised exponent, after a heavy meal, is 27 in *69 cm*. Perhaps the greatest exponent is Alex Linton, born on 25 Oct. 1904 in Boyle, County Roscommon, Ireland. He stands 5 ft 3 in *1,6 m* tall and has "swallowed" four 27 in *69 cm* blades at one time. He now lives in Sarasota, Florida, U.S.A.

DENTITION

Earliest The first deciduous or milk teeth normally appear in infants at five to eight months, these being the mandibular and maxillary first incisors. There are many records of children born with teeth, the most famous example being Prince Louis Dieudonné, later Louis XIV of France, who was born with two teeth on 5 Sept. 1638. Molars usually appear at 24 months, but in 1956 Bellevue Hospital in New York City, N.Y., U.S.A., reported a molar in a one-month-old baby, Robert R. Clinton.

Louis XIV of France who was born in 1638 with two teeth

Most Cases of the growth in late life of a third set of teeth have been recorded several times. A reference to an extreme case in France of a fourth dentition, known as Lison's case was published in 1896. A triple row of teeth was noted in 1680 by Albertus Hellwigius.

Most dedicated dentist Brother Giovanni Battista Orsenigo of the Ospedale Fatebenefratelli, Rome, Italy, a religious dentist, conserved all the teeth he extracted in three enormous cases during the time he exercised his profession from 1868 to 1904. In 1903 the number was counted and found to be 2,000,744 teeth.

OPTICS

Smallest visible object The resolving power of the human eye is 0.0003 of a radian or an arc of one minute (1/60th of a degree), which corresponds to 100 microns at 10 in. A micron is a thousandth of a millimetre, hence 100 microns is 0.003937, or less than four thousandths, of an inch. The human eye can, however, detect a bright light source shining through an aperture only 3 to 4 microns across.

Colour sensitivity The unaided human eye, under the best possible viewing conditions, comparing large areas of colour, in good illumination, using both eyes, can distinguish 10,000,000 different colour surfaces. The most accurate photo-electric spectrophotometers possess a precision probably only 40 per cent as good as this.

Colour blindness The most extreme form of colour blindness, monochromatic vision, is very rare. The highest recorded rate of red-green colour blindness is in Czechoslovakia and the lowest rate among Fijians and Brazilian Indians.

VOICE

Highest and lowest The highest and lowest recorded notes attained by the human voice before this century were a C in *alt-altissimo* (C^{iv}) by Lucrezia Agujari (1743–83), noted by the Austrian composer Wolfgang Amadeus Mozart (1756–91) in Parma, northern Italy, in 1770, and an A_1 (55 cycles per sec) by Kaspar Foster (1617–73). Since 1950 singers have achieved high and low notes far beyond the hitherto accepted extremes. However, notes at the bass and treble extremities of the register tend to lack harmonics and are of little musical value. Frl. Marita Günther, trained by Alfred Wolfsohn, has covered the range of the piano from the lowest note, A_{11}, to C^v. Of this range of $7\frac{1}{4}$ octaves, six octaves are considered to be of musical value. Mr. Roy Hart, also trained by Wolfsohn, has reached notes below the range of the piano. The highest note being sung by a tenor is G in *alt-altissimo* by Louis Lavelle, coached by Mr. S. Pleeth, in *Lovely Mary Donelly*. The lowest note put into song is a D_{11} by the singer Tom King, of King's Langley, Hertfordshire. The highest note called for in singing was an $f^{iv}\sharp$, which occurred twice in Zerbinetta's Recitative and Aria in the first (1912) version of the opera *Ariadne auf Naxos* by Richard Georg Strauss (1864–1949). It was transposed down a tone in 1916.

Greatest range The normal intelligible outdoor range of the male human voice in still air is 200 yd *180 m*. The *silbo*, the whistled language of the Spanish-speaking Canary Island of La Gomera, is intelligible across the valleys, under ideal conditions, at five miles *8 km*. There is a recorded case, under freak acoustic conditions, of the human voice being detectable at a distance of $10\frac{1}{2}$ miles *17 km* across still water at night. It was said that Mills Darden (see page 19) could be heard 6 miles *9 km* away when he shouted at the top of his voice.

At the "World" Shouting Competition at Scarborough, Yorkshire on 17 Feb. 1973 the titles were won by Skipper Kenny Leader with 111 decibels and Mrs. Margaret Featherstone with 106.6 decibels.

Lowest detectable sound The intensity of noise or sound is measured in terms of power. The power of the quietest sound that can be detected by a person of normal hearing at the most sensitive frequency of *c.* 2.750 Hz is 1.0×10^{-16} of a watt per cm^2. One tenth of the logarithm (to the base of 10) of the ratio of the power of a noise to this standard provides a unit termed a decibel. Noises above 150 decibels will cause immediate permanent deafness, while a noise of 30 decibels is negligible.

Highest detectable pitch The upper limit of hearing by the human ear has long been regarded as 20,000 Hz (cycles per sec), although children with asthma can often detect a sound of 30,000 cycles per sec. It was announced in February 1964 that experiments in the U.S.S.R. had conclusively proved that oscillations as high as 200,000 cycles per sec can be heard if the oscillator is pressed against the skull.

OPERATIONS

Longest The most protracted operations are those involving brain surgery. Such an operation lasting up to 31 hr was performed on Victor Zazueta, 19, of El Centro at San Diego Hospital, California by Dr. John F. Alksne and his team on 17–18 Jan. 1972.

Oldest subject The greatest recorded age at which a person has been subjected to an operation is 111 years 105 days in the case of James Henry Brett, Jr. (b. 25 July 1849, d. 10 Feb. 1961) of Houston, Texas, U.S.A. He underwent a hip operation on 7 Nov. 1960. The oldest age established in Britain was the case of Miss Mary Wright (b. 28 Feb. 1862) who died during a thigh operation at Boston, Lincolnshire on 22 April 1971 aged 109 years 53 days.

Youngest subject The youngest reported subject in a heart operation has been identified only as "Hamish". He underwent such an operation at the Royal Alexandra Hospital, Sydney, Australia on 15 April 1971 at the age of two days.

Heart The first human heart transplant operation was performed on Louis Washkansky, aged 55, at the Groote Schuur Hospital, Cape Town, South Africa, between 1.00 a.m. and 6 a.m., on 3 Dec. 1967, by a team of 30 headed by Prof. Christiaan Neethling Barnard (b. Beaufort West, South Africa, 8 Oct. 1922). The donor was Miss Denise Ann Darvall, aged 25. Washkansky died on 21 Dec. 1967. The longest surviving heart transplant patient has been the American negro Harry Lewis (b. 1923), who received his replacement heart in August 1968. He entered the 39th month of his second life in November 1971. Britain's longest-surviving heart transplant patient has been Mr. Charles Hendrick who died in Guy's Hospital of a lung infection on 31 Aug. 1969—107 days after his operation.

Earliest appendicectomy The earliest recorded successful appendix operation was performed in 1736 by Claudius Amyand (1680–1740). He was Serjeant Surgeon to King George II (reigned 1727–60).

Longest in iron lung The longest survival in an "iron lung" is 23 years since 5 Oct. 1949 by Mr. Dennis Atkin in Lodge Moor Hospital, Sheffield, England.

Earliest anaesthesia The earliest recorded operation under general anaesthesia was for the removal of a cyst from the neck of James Venable by Dr. Crawford Williamson Long (1815–78), using diethyl ether ($C_2H_5)_2O$), in Jefferson, Georgia, U.S.A., on 30 March 1842. The earliest use of an anaesthetic in Great Britain was by Robert Liston (see also below) at the University College Hospital, London on 21 Dec. 1846 for an amputation on a man.

Surgeon Robert Liston, whose record amputation time of 33 sec through his patient's thigh included three of his assistant's fingers

Fastest amputation The shortest time recorded for the amputation of a limb in the pre-anaesthetic era was 33 sec through a patient's thigh by Robert Liston (1794–1847) of Edinburgh, Scotland. This feat caused his assistant the loss of three fingers from his master's saw.

Surgical instruments The largest surgical instruments are robot retractors used in abdominal surgery introduced by Abbey Surgical Instruments of Chingford, Essex in 1968 and weighing 11 lb. *5 kg*. Some bronchoscopic forceps measure 60 cm *23½ in* in length. The smallest is Elliot's eye trephine, which has a blade 0.078 in *0,20 cm* in diameter.

Highest I.Q. On the Terman index for Intelligence Quotients, 150 represents "genius" level. The indices are sometimes held to be immeasurable above a level of 200 but a figure of 210 has been attributed to Kim Ung-Yong of Seoul, South Korea (b. 7 March 1963). He composed poetry and spoke four languages (Korean, English, German and Japanese), and performed integral calculus at the age of 4 years 8 months on television in Tokyo on "The World Surprise Show" on 2 Nov. 1967. Both his parents are University professors and were both born at 11 a.m. on 23 May 1934. Research into past geniuses at Stanford University, California, U.S.A., has produced a figure of "over 200" for John Stuart Mill (United Kingdom) (1806–73), who began to learn ancient Greek at the age of three. A similar rating has also been attributed to Emanuel Swedenborg (1688–1772) and Johann Wolfgang von Goethe (1749–1832). More than 20 per cent of the 15,000 members of the international Mensa society have an I.Q. of 161 or above on the Cattell index which is equivalent to 142 on the Terman index.

Herbert B. de Grote of Mexico City, Mexico has been attested to have extracted the 19th root of a 133-digit number by an algorithm of his own invention by purely mental application in a test in Mexico City on 15 May 1973. His answer was 9,126,254. No comparable mental feat has been recorded. Baron de Grote (b. 9 July 1892) had previously uniquely extracted 7th and 13th roots and is probably the oldest person to set a world record.

Human memory Mehmed Ali Halici of Ankara, Turkey on 14 Oct. 1967 recited 6,666 verses of the Koran from memory in six hours. The recitation was followed by six Koran scholars. Rare instances of eidetic memory—the ability to re-project and hence "visually" recall material—are known to science.

The greatest number of places of π The greatest number of places to which Pi has been memorised is 930, in May 1973, by Nigel Hodges, 14, of Morwenna, Polzeath, Cornwall, England who attends Bodmin Grammar School. The making of the tape recording was invigilated by The *Cornish Guardian*.

Sleeplessness Researches indicate that on the Circadian cycle for the majority peak efficiency is attained between 8 p.m. and 9 p.m. and the low point comes at 4 a.m. The longest recorded period for which a person has voluntarily gone without sleep, while under medical surveillance, is 282 hr 55 min (11 days 18 hr 55 min) by Mrs. Bertha Van Der Merwe, aged 52, a housewife of Cape Town, South Africa, ending on 13 Dec. 1968.

It was reported that Toimi Artturinpoika Silvo, a 54-year-old port worker of Hamina, Finland, stayed awake for 32 days 12 hr from 1 March to 2 April 1967. He walked 17 miles per day and lost 33 lb. *14 kg 970* in weight. Mr. Eustace Rushworth Burnett (b. 1880) of Hose, Leicestershire, claimed to have lost all desire to sleep in 1907 and that he never again went to bed. He died in January 1965, 58 years later, aged 85.

Motionlessness The longest that a man has voluntarily remained motionless is 4½ hr by Private (1st Class) William A. Fuqua of Fort Worth, Texas, U.S.A. He is a male mannequin or "fashioneer" in civil life earning up to $1,300 (£541) per hr for his ability to "freeze". The job is hazardous for it was reported in November 1967 that he was stabbed in the back by a man "proving" to his wife that he was only a dummy.

Fastest talker Few people are able to speak articulately at a sustained speed above 300 words per min. The fastest broadcaster has been regarded as Jerry Wilmot, the Canadian ice hockey commentator in the post World War II period. Raymond Glendenning (b. Newport, Monmouth, 25 Sept. 1907) of the B.B.C. once spoke 176 words in 30 sec while commentating on a greyhound race. In public life the highest speed recorded is a 327 words per min burst in a speech made in December 1961 by John Fitzgerald Kennedy (1917–63), then President of the United States. In October 1965 it was reported that Peter Spiegel, 62 of Essen, West Germany, achieved 908 syllables in 1 min at a rally of shorthand writers.

Dr. Charles Hunter of Rochdale, Lancashire, England on 31 Dec. 1972 demonstrated an ability to recite audibly the 262 words of the soliloquy *To Be or Not To Be* from Shakespeare's *Hamlet* (Act III, Scene 1) in 36 sec or at a rate of 436.6 words per min in the recording of the B.B.C. T.V. series *Record Breakers*.

Fasting Most humans experience considerable discomfort after an abstinence from food for even 12 hr but this often passes off after 24–28 hr. Records claimed without unremitting medical surveillance are of little value.

The longest period for which anyone has gone without food is 382 days by Angus Barbieri (b. 1940) of Tayport, Fife, who lived on tea, coffee, water, soda water and vitamins in Maryfield Hospital, Dundee, Angus, from June 1965 to July 1966. His weight declined from 33 st. 10 lb. *214 kg 10* to 12 st. 10 lb. *80 kg 740*. Dr. Stephen Taylor, 43, of Mount Roskill, New Zealand, fasted 40 days with only a glass of water per day in a political protest in 1970.

Hunger strike The longest recorded hunger strike was one of 94 days by John and Peter Crowley, Thomas Donovan, Michael Burke, Michael O'Reilly, Christopher Upton, John Power, Joseph Kenny and Seán Hennessy in Cork Prison, Ireland, from 11 Aug. to 12 Nov. 1920. These nine survivors owed their lives to expert medical attention and an appeal by Arthur Griffith. The longest recorded hunger strike with forcible feeding in a British gaol is 375 days by Ronald Barker, 28, in Lincoln Jail and Armley Prison, Leeds from 23 Jan. 1970. He was protesting his innocence of a robbery in Louth, Lincolnshire in which he was found uninvolved in a re-trial at Northamptonshire Assizes on 2 Feb. 1971. The feeding was done with "Complan" by tube orally.

Most voracious fire eater Sheik Michael (Mr. Michael Taylor, 37) blew a flame from his mouth estimated at 12 ft *3,62 m* in length at North Wooton, Norfolk on 26 Jan. 1973. Three years previously he had spent 17 weeks in hospital with a lung injury from a blow back.

The youngest member of the Masi tribe to walk the white hot coals (400° F [*204° C*]) on the island of Bega, Fiji has been Maikeli Masi, aged 11 outside the Korolevu Beach Hotel on 15 Dec. 1972.

Underwater The world record for voluntarily staying underwater is 13 min 42.5 sec by Robert Foster, aged 32, an electronics technician of Richmond, California, who stayed under 10 ft *3,05 m* of water in the swimming pool of the Bermuda Palms Motel at San Rafael, California, U.S.A., on 15 March 1959. He hyperventilated with oxygen for 30 min before his descent. The longest unprepared record is 6 min 29.8 sec by M. Pouliguin in Paris in Nov. 1912. It must be stressed that record-breaking of this kind is *extremely* dangerous.

Human salamanders The highest dry-air temperature endured by naked men in the U.S. Air Force experiments in 1960 was 400° F *204,4° C* and for heavily clothed men 500° F *260° C*. Steaks require only 325° F *162,8° C*. Temperatures of 140° C *284° F* have been found quite bearable in *Sauna* baths.

g forces The acceleration g, due to gravity, is 32 ft 1.05 in per sec per sec *978,02 cm/sec²* at sea-level at the Equator. A *sustained* acceleration of 31 g was withstood for 5 sec by R. Flanagan Gray, aged 39, at the U.S. Naval Air Development Center in Warminster, Pennsylvania, in 1959. This makes the bodyweight of a 13 st. 3 lb. *83 kg 910* man seem like 2.54 tons *2 585 kg*. The highest value endured in a dry capsule is 25 g. The highest g value endured on a water-braked rocket sled is 82.6 g for 0.04 of a sec by Eli L. Beeding Jr. at Holloman Air Force Base, New Mexico, U.S.A., on 16 May 1958. He was put in hospital for 3 days. A man who fell off a 185-ft *56,39 m* cliff (before 1963) has survived a *momentary* g of 209 in decelerating from 68 m.p.h. *109 km/h* to stationary in 0.015 of a sec.

Isolation The longest recorded period for which any volunteer has been able to withstand total deprivation of all sensory stimulation (sight, hearing and touch) is 92 hr, recorded in 1962 at Lancaster Moor Hospital, Lancashire.

Extra-sensory perception The highest consistent performer in tests to detect powers of extra-sensory perception is Pavel Stepánek (Czechoslovakia) known in parapsychological circles as "P.S.". His performance on nominating hidden white or green cards from May 1967 to March 1968 departed from a chance probability yielding a Chi² value corresponding to $P < 10^{-50}$ or odds of more than 100 octillion to one against the achievement being one of chance. One of the two appointed referees recommended that the results should not be published. The highest published scores in any E.S.P. test were those of a 26-year-old female tested by Prof. Bernard F. Reiss of Hunter College, New York in 1936. In 74 runs of 25 guesses each she scored one with 25 all correct, two with 24 and an average of 18.24 instead of the random 5.00. Such a result would depart from chance probability by a factor $> 10^{700}$.

Most durable ghosts Ghosts are not immortal and, according to the *Gazeteer of British Ghosts*, seem to deteriorate after 400 years. The most outstanding exception to their normal "half-life" is the ghost of a Roman centurion that still reportedly haunts Strood, Mersea Island, Essex after 15½ centuries. The book's author, Peter Underwood, states that Britain has more reported ghosts per square mile than any other country with Borley Rectory near Long Melford, Suffolk the site of unrivalled activity between 1863 and its destruction by fire in 1939.

Britain's most haunted rectory, at Borley near near Long Melford, Suffolk

2 ANIMAL AND PLANT KINGDOMS

ANIMAL KINGDOM
GENERAL RECORDS

Note—Guinness Superlatives Ltd. has newly published a specialist volume entitled *The Guinness Book of Animal Facts and Feats*. This work treats the dimensions and performances of all the Classes of the Animal Kingdom in greater detail giving also the sources and authorities for much of the material in this chapter.

Largest and heaviest The largest and heaviest animal in the world, and probably the biggest creature which has *ever* existed, is the Blue or Sulphur-bottom whale (*Balaenoptera musculus*), also called Sibbald's rorqual. The largest accurately measured specimen on record was a female landed at an Argentine Whaling Station, South Georgia *c.* 1912 which measured 33.58 m *110 ft 2½ in* in length. Another female measuring 96¾ ft *29,48 m* brought into the shore station at Prince Olaf, South Georgia in *c.* 1931 was calculated to have weighed 163.7 tons *166 tonnes*, inclusive of blood, judging by the number of cookers that were filled by the animal's blubber, meat and bones. The total weight of this whale was believed to have been 174 tons *177 tonnes*.

In November 1947 a weight of 190 tons *193 tonnes* was reported for a 90¾ ft *27,66 m* Blue whale weighed piecemeal by the Russians during the first cruise of the "Slava" whaling fleet in the Antarctic, but this figure was a misprint and should have read 140 tons *142 tonnes*. On the principle that the weight should vary as the cube of linear dimensions, a 100 ft *30,48 m* Blue whale in good condition should weigh about 160 tons *163 tonnes*, but in the case of pregnant females the weight could be as much as 190–200 tons *193–203 tonnes*—equivalent to 35 African elephants.

Tallest The tallest living animal is the Giraffe (*Giraffa camelopardalis*), which is now found only in the dry savannah and semi-desert areas of Africa south of the Sahara. The tallest ever recorded was a Masai bull (*G. camelopardalis tippelskirchi*) shot in Kenya before 1930 which measured 19 ft 3 in *5,86 m* between pegs (tip of forehoof to tip of "false" horn with neck erect) and must have stood about 19 ft *5,80 m* when alive. It was thus 4½ ft *137 m* taller than a London double-decker bus. Less credible heights of up to 23 ft *7 m* have been claimed.

The first giraffe ever seen in England was a six-month-old cow of the Nubian race (*G.c. camelopardalis*) presented to George IV (1762–1830) by Mohammed Ali, Pasha of Egypt. The 9 ft 2 in *2,79 m* tall animal arrived in London in August 1827. It was kept at Windsor for 26 months, grew another 18 in *45 cm* and died in Oct. 1829.

Longest The longest animal ever recorded is the giant jellyfish *Cyanaea arctica*, which is found in the north-western Atlantic Ocean. One specimen washed up in Massachusetts Bay, Mass., U.S.A., in *c.* 1865 had a bell diameter of 7½ ft *2,29 m* and tentacles measuring 120 ft *36,5 m*, thus giving a theoretical tentacular span of some 245 ft *75 m*.

Smallest The smallest of all free-living organisms are pleuro-pneumonia-like organisms (P.P.L.O.) of the *Mycoplasma*. One of these, *Mycoplasma laidlawii*, first discovered in sewage in 1936, has a diameter during its early existence of only 100 millimicrons, or 0.000004 of an in. Examples of the strain known as H.39 have a maximum diameter of 300 millimicrons and weigh an estimated 1.0×10^{-16} of a gramme. Thus a 174 ton *177 tonnes* Blue whale would weigh 1.77×10^{23} or 177,000 trillion times as much.

Longest lived Few non-bacterial creatures live longer than humans. It would appear that tortoises are the longest lived such animals. The greatest authentic age recorded for a tortoise is 152-plus years for a male Marion's tortoise (*Testudo sumeirii*) brought from the Seychelles to Mauritius in 1766 by the Chevalier de Fresne, who presented it to the Port Louis army garrison. This specimen (it went blind in 1908) was accidentally killed in 1918. When the famous Royal Tongan tortoise "Tu'malilia" (believed to be a specimen of *Testudo radiata*) died on 19 May 1966 it was reputed

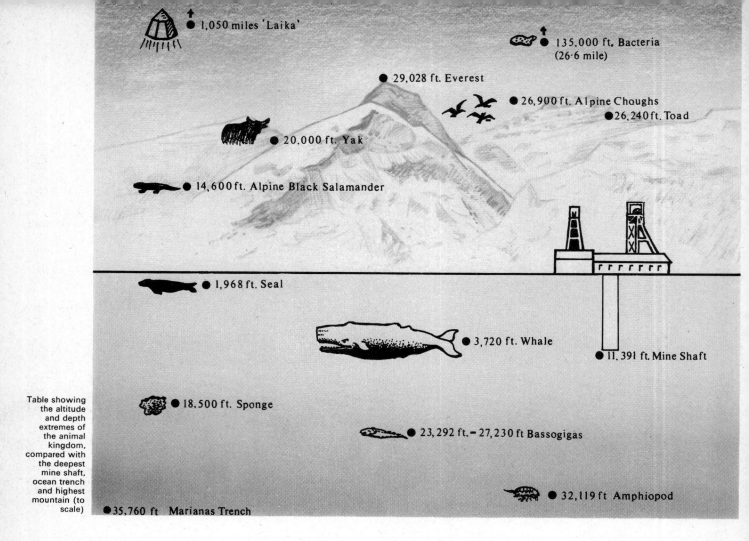

1,050 miles 'Laika'

135,000 ft. Bacteria
(26·6 mile)

29,028 ft. Everest

26,900 ft. Alpine Choughs

26,240 ft. Toad

20,000 ft. Yak

14,600 ft. Alpine Black Salamander

1,968 ft. Seal

3,720 ft. Whale

11,391 ft. Mine Shaft

18,500 ft. Sponge

23,292 ft. – 27,230 ft Bassogigas

32,119 ft Amphiopod

35,760 ft Marianas Trench

Table showing the altitude and depth extremes of the animal kingdom, compared with the deepest mine shaft, ocean trench and highest mountain (to scale)

to be over 200 years old, having been presented to the then King of Tonga by Captain James Cook (1728–79) on 22 Oct. 1773, but this record lacks proper documentation.

The bacteria *Thermoactinomyces vulgaris* has been found alive in cores of mud taken from the bottom of Windermere, Westmorland, England which have been dated to 1,500 yrs before the present.

Fastest The fastest reliably measured speed of any animal is 106.25 m.p.h. *171 km/h* for the Spine-tailed swift (*Chaetura caudacuta*) reported from the U.S.S.R. in 1942. In 1934 ground speeds ranging from 171.8 to 219.5 m.p.h. *276,5–353,3 km/h* were recorded by stop-watch for spine-tailed swifts over a 2-mile *3 km* course in the Cachar Hills of north-eastern India, but scientific tests since have revealed that this species of bird cannot be seen at a distance of 1 mile *1,6 km*, even with standard binoculars. This bird is the fastest moving living creature and has a blood temperature of 112.5° F *44,7° C*. Speeds even higher than a "free fall" maximum of 185 m.p.h. *297 km/h* have been ascribed to the Peregrine falcon (*Falco peregrinus*) in a stoop, but in recent experiments in which miniature air speedometers were fitted, the maximum recorded diving speed was 82 m.p.h. *132 km/h*.

Rarest The best claimant to the title of the world's rarest land animal is probably the tenrec *Dasogale fontoynonti*, which is known only from the type specimen collected in eastern Madagascar and now preserved in the Paris Museum of Natural History.

Commonest It has been estimated that man shares the earth with about 3,000,000,000,000,000,000,000,000,000,000,000 (3,000 quintillion or 3×10^{33}) other living things. Of these, more than 75 per cent are bacteria, namely 2,200 quintillion or 2.2×10^{33}.

Fastest growth The fastest growth in the Animal Kingdom is that of the Blue whale calf (see above). A barely visible ovum weighing a fraction of a milligramme (0.000035 of an oz.) grows to a weight of *c.* 26 tons *26 tonnes* in $22\frac{3}{4}$ months, made up of $10\frac{3}{4}$ months gestation and the first 12 months of life. This is equivalent to an increase of 30,000 million-fold.

Largest egg The largest egg of any living animal is that of the whale-shark (*Rhiniodon typus*). One egg case measuring 12 in by 5.5 in by 3.5 in *30 × 14 × 9 cm* was picked up by the shrimp trawler "Doris" on 29 June 1953 at a depth of 31 fathoms (186 ft *[56,6 m]*) in the Gulf of Mexico 130 miles *209 km* south of Port Isabel, Texas, U.S.A. The egg contained a perfect embryo of a whale-shark 13.78 in *35 cm* long.

Greatest size difference between sexes The largest female deep-sea angler fish of the species *Ceratias holboelki* on record weighed half a million times as much as the smallest known parasitic male. It has been suggested that this fish would make an appropriate emblem for the Women's Lib. Movement.

Heaviest brain The Sperm whale (*Physeter catodon*) has the heaviest brain of any living animal. The brain of a 49 ft *14,93 m* bull processed in the Japanese factory ship *Nissin Maru No. 1* in the Antarctic on 11 Dec. 1949 weighed 9,2 kg *20.24 lb.* compared with 6,9 kg *15.38 lb.* for a 90 ft *27 m* Blue whale. The heaviest brain recorded for an elephant is 16.5 lb. *7 kg 50* in the case of an Asiatic cow. The normal brain weight for an adult African bull is 12 lb. *5 kg 440*.

Largest eye The giant squid *Architeuthis sp.* has the largest eye of any living animal. The ocular diameter may exceed 38 cm *15 in* compared to 10–12 cm *3.93 to 4.71 in* for the largest Blue whales.

34

1. MAMMALS (*Mammalia*)

Largest and heaviest
World For details of the Blue whale (*Balaenoptera musculus*) see page 33. Further information: the tongue and heart of a 27.6 m *90 ft 8 in* long female Blue whale taken by the Salva whaling fleet in the Antarctic on 17 March 1947 weighed 4.22 tons *4,29 tonnes* and 1,540 lb. *698 kg 50* respectively.

British waters The largest Blue whale ever recorded in British waters was probably an 88 ft *26,8 m* specimen killed near the Bunaveneader station in Harris in the Outer Hebrides, Scotland in 1904. In Sept. 1750 a Blue whale allegedly measuring 101 ft *30,75 m* in length ran aground in the River Humber estuary. Another specimen stranded on the west coast of Lewis, Outer Hebrides, Scotland in *c.* 1870 was credited with a length of 105 ft *32 m* but the carcase was cut up by the local people before the length could be verified. In both cases the length was probably exaggerated or taken along the curve of the body instead of in a straight line from the tip of the snout to the notch in the flukes. Four Blue whales have been stranded on British coasts since 1913. The last occurrence (*c.* 60 ft [*18 m*]) was at Wick, Caithness, Scotland on 15 Oct. 1923.

Blue whales inhabit the colder seas and migrate to warmer waters in the winter for breeding. Observations made in the Antarctic in 1947–48 showed that a Blue whale can maintain a speed of 20 knots (23 m.p.h. [*37 km/h*]) for ten minutes when frightened. It has been calculated that a 90 ft *27 m* Blue whale travelling at 20 knots *37 km/h* would develop 520 h.p. *527 c.v.* Newborn calves measure 6,5 to 8,6 m *21 ft 3½ in to 28 ft 6 in* in length and weigh up to 3,000 kg *2.95 tons*.

It has been estimated that there were 100,000 Blue whales living throughout the oceans in 1930, but that only 19,000 to 24,000 survived in January 1973.

Deepest dive The greatest *recorded* depth to which a whale has dived is 620 fathoms (3,720 ft [*1,134 m*]) by a 47 ft *14,32 m* bull Sperm whale (*Physeter catodon*) found with its jaw entangled with a submarine cable running between Santa Elena, Ecuador and Chorillos, Peru, on 14 Oct. 1955. At this depth the whale withstood a pressure of 1,680 lb/in² *118 kg.f/cm²* of body surface. On 25 August 1969 a Sperm whale was killed 100 miles *160 km* south of Durban after it had surfaced from a dive lasting 1 hr 52 min, and inside its stomach were found two small sharks which had been swallowed about an hour earlier. These were later identified as *Scymnodon sp.*, a species found only on the sea floor. At this point from land the depth of water is in excess of 1,646 fathoms (10,476 ft [*3 193 m*]) for a radius of 30–40 miles *48–64 km*, which now suggests that the Sperm whale sometimes may descend to a depth of over 10,000 ft *3 000 m* when seeking food.

Largest on land
World The largest living land animal is the African bush elephant (*Loxodonta africana africana*). The average adult bull stands 10 ft 6 in *3,20 m* at the shoulder and weighs 5.6 tons *5,7 tonnes*. The largest specimen ever recorded was a bull shot 48 miles *77 km* north-west of Macusso, Angola on 13 Nov. 1955. Lying on its side this elephant measured 13 ft 2 in *4,01 m* in a projected line from the highest point of the shoulder to the base of the forefoot, indicating that its standing height must have been about 12 ft 6 in *3,8 m*. Other measurements included an over-all length of 33 ft 2 in *10,10 m* (tip of extended trunk to tip of extended tail) and a maximum bodily girth of 19 ft 8 in *5,99 m*. The weight was estimated at 24,000 lb. (10.7 tons [*10,9 tonnes*]). On 6 March 1959 the mounted specimen was put on display in the rotunda of the U.S. National Museum in Washington, D.C., U.S.A. (see also Shooting, Chapter 12). Another outsized bull elephant known as "Dhulalamithi" (Taller than the Trees),

reputed to stand over 12 ft *3,65 m* at the shoulder, was shot east of the Lundi River, Rhodesia in Aug. 1967 by a South African police officer, after straying outside its reserve.

Britain The largest wild mammal in the British Isles, excluding the wild pony (*Equus caballus*) is the Red deer (*Cervus elephus*). A full-grown stag stands 3 ft 8 in *1,11 m* at the shoulder and weighs 230–250 lb *104–113 kg*. The heaviest ever recorded was probably a stag weighing 462 lb. *209 kg* killed in Glenmore Deer-forest, Inverness, Scotland in 1877. The heaviest park Red deer on record was a stag weiging 476 lb. *215 kg 90* (height at shoulder 4 ft 6 in [*1,37 m*]) killed at Woburn, Bedfordshire in 1836. The wild population in 1968 was estimated at 180,000 to 185,000.

Tallest The tallest mammal is the giraffe (*Giraffa camelopardalis*). For details see page 33.

Smallest
Land The smallest recorded mammal is Savi's white-toothed pygmy shrew (*Suncus etruscus*), also called the Etruscan shrew, which is found along the coast of the northern Mediterranean and southwards to Cape Province, South Africa. Mature specimens have a head and body length of 36–52 mm *1.32–2.04 in*, a tail length of 24–29 mm *0.94–1.14 in* and weigh between 1,5 and 2,5 g *0.052 and 0.09 oz*. The smallest mammal found in the British Isles is the European pygmy shrew (*Sorex minutus*). Mature specimens have a head and body length of 43–64 mm *1.69–2.5 in*, a tail length of 31–46 mm *1.22–1.81 in* and weigh between 2,4 and 6,1 g *0.084 and 0.213 oz*.

Marine The smallest totally marine mammal is the Sea otter (*Enhydra lutris*), which is found in coastal waters off California, western Alaska and the Komandorskie and Kurile Islands in the Bering Sea. Adult specimens measure 120–156 cm *47.24–61.5 in* in total length and weigh 25–38 kg 50 *55–81.4 lb*.

Rarest The rarest placental mammal in the world is now the Javan rhinoceros (*Rhinoceros sondaicus*). In mid-1972 there were an estimated 35–40 in the Udjung-Kulon (also called Oedjoeng Kuelon) Reserve of 117 miles² *300 km²* at the tip of western Java, Indonesia, but there may also be a few left in the Tenasserim area on the Thai-Burmese border. Among sub-species, there are believed to be only a dozen specimens of the Javan tiger (*Leo tigris sondaica*) left in the wild, all of them in east Java. The rarest marine mammal is Hose's Sarawak dolphin (*Lagenodelphis hosei*), which is known only from the type specimen collected at the mouth of the Lutong River, Barama, Borneo in 1895.

The rarest British land mammal is the Pine marten (*Martes martes*), which is found in the highlands of Scotland, particularly in Coille na Glas, Leitire, Ross and Cromarty, and thinly distributed in North Wales and the Scottish border country. The largest specimens measure up to 34 in *863 mm* from nose to tip of tail (tail 6–9 in [*152–228 mm*]) and weigh up to 4 lb. 6 oz. *1 984 g*.

Fastest
World The fastest of all land animals over a short distance (*i.e.* up to 600 yds [*549 m*]) is the Cheetah or Hunting leopard (*Acinonyx jubatus*) of the open plains of East Africa, Iran, Turkmenia and Afghanistan, with a probable maximum speed of 60–63 m.p.h. *96–101 km/h* over suitably level ground. Speeds of 71, 84 and even 90 m.p.h. *114, 135 and 145 km/h* have been claimed for this animal, but these figures must be considered exaggerated. Tests in London in 1937 showed that on an oval greyhound track over 345 yds *316 m* a female cheetah's average speed over three runs was 43.4 m.p.h. *69,8 km/h* (*cf.* 43.26 m.p.h. [*69,6 km/h*] for the fastest racehorse), but this specimen was not running flat out. The fastest land animal over a sustained distance (*i.e.* 1,000 yds [*914 m*] or more) is

the Pronghorn antelope (*Antilocapra americana*) of the western United States. Specimens have been observed to travel at 35 m.p.h. for 4 miles *56 km/h for 6 km*, at 42 m.p.h. for 1 mile *67 km/h for 1,6 km* and 55 m.p.h. for half a mile *88,5 km/h for 0,8 km*. On 14 Aug. 1936 at Spanish Lake, in Lake County, Oregon a hard-pressed buck was timed by a car speedometer at 61 m.p.h. *98 km/h* over 200 yds *183 m*.

Britain The fastest British land mammal over a sustained distance is the Roe deer (*Capreolus capreolus*), which can cruise at 25–30 m.p.h. *40–48 km/h* for more than 20 miles *32 km*, with occasional bursts of up to 40 m.p.h. *64 km/h*. On 19 Oct. 1970 a frightened runaway Red deer (*Cervus elephus*) registered a speed of 42 m.p.h. *67,5 km/h* on a police radar trap as it charged through a street in Stalybridge, Cheshire.

Slowest The slowest moving land mammal is the Ai or Three-toed sloth (*Bradypus tridactylus*) of tropical America. The usual ground speed is 6 to 8 ft *c. 2,10 m* a minute (0.068 to 0.098 m.p.h. *[0,109–0,158 km/h]*), but one mother sloth, speeded up by the calls of her infant, was observed to cover 14 ft *4 m* in one minute (0.155 m.p.h. *[0,249 km/h]*). In the trees this speed may be increased to 2 ft *0,61 m* a sec (1.36 m.p.h. *[2,19 km/h]*) (*cf.* these figures with the 0.03 m.p.h. *[0,05 km/h]* of the common garden snail and the 0.17 m.p.h. *[0,27 km/h]* of the giant tortoise).

Longest lived No mammal can match the extreme proven age of 113 years attained by Man (*Homo sapiens*) (see page 21). It is probable that the closest approach is among Blue and Fin whales (*Balaenoptera physalus*) the annual growth layers in the ear plugs of which indicate an age of 90–100 years. A bull Killer whale (*Orcinus orca*) with distinctive physical characteristics known as "Old Tom" was seen every winter from 1843 to 1930 in Twofold Bay, Eden, New South Wales, Australia.

The longest lived land mammal, excluding Man, is the Asiatic elephant (*Elephas maximus*). The greatest age that has been verified with reasonable certainty is an estimated 69 years in the case of a cow named "Jessie", who arrived at Taronga Park Zoo in Sydney, New South Wales, Australia in 1882. She was destroyed on 26 Sept. 1939. Her age on arrival was believed to have been 12, but may have been as high as 20. An elephant's life span is indicated by the persistence of its teeth, which generally wear out around the 50–55th year.

"Jessie", the oldest recorded elephant, celebrating her 64th birthday at Taronga Park Zoo, Sydney, Australia

Highest living The highest living mammal in the world is probably the Yak (*Bos grunniens*), the wild ox of Tibet and Szechwan, China, which occasionally climbs to an altitude of 20,000 ft *6,100 m* when foraging in the Himalayas.

Largest herds The largest herds on record were those of the Springbok (*Antidorcas marsupialis*) during migration across the plains of the western parts of southern Africa in the 19th century. In 1849 John Fraser (later Sir John Fraser) saw a *trekbokken* that took three days to pass through the settlement of Beaufort West, Cape Province. Another herd seen moving near Nels Poortje, Cape Province in 1888 was estimated to contain 100,000,000 head.

Longest and shortest gestation periods The longest of all mammalian gestation periods is that of the Asiatic elephant (*Elephas maximus*), with an average of 609 days or just over 20 months and a maximum of 760 days—more than two and a half times that of a human. The gestation period of the American opossum (*Didelphis marsupialis*), also called the Virginian opossum, is normally 12 to 13 days but may be as short as eight days.

The gestation periods of the rare Water opossum or Yapok (*Chironectes minimus*) of Central and northern South America (average 12–13 days) and the Eastern native cat (*Dasyurus viverrinus*) of Australia (average 12 days) may also be as short as 8 days.

The viviparous amphibian Alpine Black Salamander (*Salamandra atra*) can have a gestation period of up to 38 months when living above 14,600 ft *4 450 m* in Switzerland.

Largest litter The greatest recorded number of young born to a *wild* mammal at a single birth is 32 (not all of which survived) in the case of the Common tenrec (*Centetes ecaudatus*) found in Madagascar and the Comoro Islands. The average litter size is thirteen to fourteen. In March 1961 a litter of 32 was also reported for a House mouse (*Mus musculus*) at the Roswell Park Memorial Institute in Buffalo, N.Y., U.S.A. (average litter size 13–21) (see also Chapter 9 Agriculture, prolificacy records—pigs).

Fastest breeder The Streaked tenrec (*Hemicentetes semispinosus*) of Madagascar is weaned after only 5 days, and females are capable of breeding 3–4 weeks after birth.

CARNIVORES

Largest Land World The largest living terrestrial carnivore is the Kodiak bear (*Ursus arctos middendorffi*), which is found on Kodiak Island and the adjacent Afognak and Shuyak islands in the Gulf of Alaska, U.S.A. The average adult male has a nose to tail length of 8 ft *2,4 m* (tail about 4 in [*10 cm*]), stands 52 in *132 cm* at the shoulder and weighs between 1,050 and 1,175 lb. *476–533 kg*. In 1894 a weight of 1,656 lb. *751 kg* was recorded for a male shot at English Bay, Kodiak Island, whose *stretched* skin measured 13 ft 6 in *4,11 m* from the tip of the nose to the root of the tail. This weight was exceeded by a male in the Cheyenne Mountain Zoological Park, Colorado Springs, Colorado, U.S.A. which scaled 1,670 lb. *757 kg* at the time of its death on 22 Sept. 1955.

Weights in excess of 1,600 lb. *725 kg* have also been reported for the Polar bear (*Ursus maritimus*), but the average adult male weighs 850–900 lb. *386–408 kg* and measures 7¾ ft *2,4 m* nose to tail. In 1960 a polar bear allegedly weighing 2,210 lb. *1 002 kg* before skinning was shot at the polar entrance to Kotzebue Sound, north-west Alaska. In April 1962 the 11 ft 1½ in *3,39 m* tall mounted specimen was put on display at the Seattle World Fair, Washington. U.S.A

Britain The largest land carnivore found in Britain is the Common badger (*Meles meles*). The average adult boar measures 3 ft *90 cm* including a 4 in *10 cm* tail and weighs 25–30 lb. *11–13 kg*. The heaviest recorded but not authenticated specimen was a boar weighing 68 lb. *31 kg* killed at Ampleforth, Yorkshire on 10 Feb. 1942. Specimens over 40 lb *18 kg 20* are not disputed.

Sea The largest toothed mammal ever recorded is the Sperm whale (*Physeter catodon*), also called the cachalot. The average adult bull measures 47 ft *14,30 m* in length and weighs about 33 tons *33,5 tonnes*. The largest accurately measured specimen on record was a 71 ft *21,64 m* bull taken on the Aleutian coast and towed to the Akutan Whaling Station, Alaska, U.S.A. in 1921. It was not weighed but must have scaled 88 tons *89,5 tonnes*. On 25 June 1903 a measurement of 68 ft *21 m* was reported for a bull killed 60 miles *96 km* west of Shetland and landed at the Norrona whaling station, but the measurement was believed to have been taken over the curve of the body instead of in a straight line. Eleven cachalots have been stranded on British coasts since 1913. The largest, a bull measuring 61 ft 5 in *19 m* was washed ashore at Birchington, Kent on 18 Oct. 1914. Another bull measuring 60 ft *18 m* was stranded at North Roe, Shetland on 30 May 1958.

Smallest The smallest living carnivore is the Least weasel (*Mustela rixosa*), also called the Dwarf weasel, which is circumpolar in distribution. Four races are recognised, the smallest of which is *M.r. pygmaea* of Siberia. Mature specimens have an overall length of 177–207 mm *6.96–8.14 in* and weigh between 35 and 70 g *1¼ and 2½ oz.*

Largest feline The largest member of the cat family (Felidae) is the long-furred Siberian tiger (*Pantheria tigris altaica*), also called the Amur or Manchurian tiger. Adult males average 10 ft 4 in *3,15 m* in length (nose to tip of extended tail), stand 39–42 in *99–107 cm* at the shoulder and weigh about 585 lb. *265 kg*. The heaviest specimen on record was one shot by a German hunter near the Amur river in c. 1933 which weighed 350 kg *770 lb*. In 1970 the total wild population, now strictly protected, was estimated at 160–170 animals in the wild and 296 in captivity.

The average adult African lion (*Pantheria leo*) measures 9 ft *2,7 m* overall, stands 36–38 in *91–97 cm* at the shoulder and weighs 400–410 lb *181–185 kg*. The heaviest wild specimen on record was one weighing 690 lb. *313 kg* shot by Mr. Lennox Anderson just outside Hectorspruit in the eastern Transvaal, South Africa in 1936. In July 1970 a weight of 826 lb. *375 kg* was reported for an 11-year-old black-maned lion named "Simba" (b. Dublin Zoo, 1959) at Colchester Zoo, Essex. He died on 16 Jan. 1973 at Knaresborough Zoo, Yorkshire. In 1953 a weight of 750 lb. *340 kg* was recorded for an 18-year-old male liger (a lion-tigress hybrid) living in Bloemfontein Zoological Gardens, South Africa.

Smallest The smallest member of the cat family is the Rusty-spotted cat (*Felis rubiginosa*) of southern India and Ceylon. The average adult male has an overall length of 25–28 in *64–71 cm* (tail 9–10 in [*23–25 cm*]) and weighs about 3 lb *1 kg 350*.

PINNIPEDS (Seals, Sea-lions and Walruses)

Largest World The largest of the 32 known species of pinniped is the Southern elephant seal (*Mirounga leonina*), which inhabits the sub-Antarctic islands. Adult bulls average 16½ ft *5 m* in length (tip of inflated snout to the extremities of the outstretched tail flippers), 12 ft *3,7 m* in maximum bodily girth and weigh about 5,000 lb. (2.18 tons *2 268 kg*). The largest accurately measured specimen on record was a bull killed in Possession

The 690 lb. *313 kg* lion shot by Mr. Lennox Anderson in the Transvaal in 1936

Bay, South Georgia on 28 February 1913 which measured 21 ft 4 in *6,50 m* after flensing (original length about 22½ ft [*6,85 m*]) and probably weighed at least 4 tons/*tonnes*. There are old records of bulls measuring 25, 30 and even 35 ft *10,66 m* but these figures must be considered exaggerated.

British The largest pinniped among British fauna is the Grey seal (*Halichoerus grypus*), also called the Atlantic seal, which is found mainly on the western coasts of Britain. Adult bulls have been recorded up to 9 ft 6 in *2,90 m* in length and 700 lb. *318 kg* in weight.

Smallest The smallest pinniped is the Baikal seal (*Pusa sibrica*) of Lake Baikal, a large freshwater lake in southern Siberia, U.S.S.R. Adult specimens measure about 4 ft 6 in *1,37 m* from nose to tail and weigh about 140 lb. *63 kg*.

Fastest and deepest The highest speed recorded for a pinniped is 25 m.p.h. *40 km/h* for a Californian sea lion (*Zalophus californianus*). The deepest diving pinniped is the Weddell seal (*Leptonychotes weddelli*), which is found along the Antarctic mainland and neighbouring islands. In March 1966 a large bull with a depth-gauge attached to it recorded a dive of 600 m *1,968 ft* in McMurdo Sound. At this depth the seal withstood a pressure of 875 lb./in² *61 kg f/cm²* of body area.

Longest lived A female Grey seal (*Halichoerus grypus*) shot at Shunni Wick in the Shetland Islands on 23 April 1969 was believed to be "at least 46 years old" based on a count of dental annuli.

Rarest The Caribbean or West Indian monk seal (*Monachus tropicalis*) has not been recorded since 1962 when a single specimen was sighted on the beach of Isla Mujueres off the Yucatan Peninsula, Mexico, and the species is now believed to be on the verge of extinction.

BATS

Largest World The only flying mammals are bats (order Chiroptera), of which there are about 1,000 living species. That with the greatest wing span is the Fruit Bat (*Camvampyrus*) found in Indonesia and New Guinea. It has a wing span of up to 1700 mm *5 ft 7 in* and weighs up to 900 g *31.7 oz.*

Britain The largest bat found in Britain is the very rare Large mouse-eared bat (*Myotis myotis*). Mature specimens have a wing span of 355–450 mm *13.97–17.71 in* and weigh up to 45 g *1.58 oz.*

Smallest The smallest known species of bat is the rare Tiny
World pipistrelle (*Pipistrellus nanulus*) found in West Africa. It has a wing span of about 152 mm *6 in* and weighs about 2,5 g *0.088 oz.*, which means it rivals the Etruscan pygmy shrew (*Suncus etruscus*) for the title of "smallest living mammal".

Britain The smallest native British bat is the Pipistrelle (*Pipistrellus pipistrellus*). Mature specimens have a wing span of 200–230 mm *7.87–9.05 in* and weigh between 5.5 and 7.5 g *0.19–0.26 oz.*

Fastest Because of the great practical difficulties little data on bat speeds have been published. The greatest speed attributed to a bat is 32 m.p.h. *51 km/h* in the case of a Free-tailed or Guano bat (*Tadarida mexicana*) which flew 31 miles *50 km* in 58 min. This speed is closely matched by the Noctule bat (*Nyctalus noctula*) and the Long-winged bat (*Miniopterus schreibersi*), both of which have been timed at 31 m.p.h. *50 km/h.*

Rarest The rarest native British bat is Bechstein's bat (*Myotis*
Britain *bechsteini*), which is confined to a small area in southern England, with the New Forest as the main centre of population. There have been about a dozen records since 1900. In January 1965 fifteen specimens of the Grey long-eared bat (*Plecotus austriacus*) were discovered in the roof of the Nautre Conservancy's Research Station at Furzebrook, Dorset. Up to then this species, which is found all over Europe, had only been recorded once in Britain (Hampshire, 1875).

Longest The greatest age reliably reported for a bat is "at least
lived 24 years" for a female Little brown bat (*Myotis lucifugus*) found on 30 April 1960 in a cave on Mount Aeolis, East Dorset, Vermont, U.S.A. It had been banded at a summer colony in Mashpee, Massachusetts on 22 June 1937.

Highest Because of their ultrasonic echolocation bats have the
detectable most acute hearing in the animal world. Vampire bats
pitch (*Desmodontidae*) and fruit bats (*Pteropodidae*) can hear frequencies as high as 150 k Hz (*cf.* 20 k Hz for the adult human limit but 153 k Hz for the bottle-nosed dolphin (*Tursiopis truncatus*)).

PRIMATES

Largest The largest living primate is the Mountain Gorilla (*Gorilla gorilla beringei*) which is found on the Virunga Mountains, the volcanic range in the eastern Congo and South Western Uganda. The average adult bull stands 5 ft 8 in *1,72 m* tall (including crest) and measures 58 to 60 in *147–152 cm* round the chest and weighs 370 to 420 lb. *168–190 kg.* The average adult female stands at about 4 ft 8 in *1,42 m* and weighs 190 to 230 lb. *86–104 kg.* The greatest height (top of crest to heel) recorded for a Mountain Gorilla is 6 ft 2 in *1,88 m* for a bull shot in the Eastern Congo in *c.* 1921.

The heaviest gorilla ever kept in captivity was a bull of the mountain race named "Mbongo", who died in San Diego Zoological Gardens, California, U.S.A. on 15 March 1942. During an attempt to weigh him shortly before his death the platform scales "fluctuated from 645 pounds to nearly 670 *[293–304 kg]*". This specimen measured 5 ft 7½ in *1,71 m* in height and 69 in *175 cm* around the chest.

Smallest The smallest known primate is the Lesser mouse lemur (*Microcebus murinus*) of Madagascar. Adult specimens have a head and body length of 125–150 mm *4.9–5.9 in* and a tail of about the same length. The weight varies from 45 to 85 g *1.58–2.99 oz.*

Longest The greatest irrefutable age reported for a primate
lived (excluding humans) is 50 years 3 months for a male chimpanzee (*Pan troglodytes*) named "Heine" at Lincoln Park Zoological Gardens, Chicago, Illinois, U.S.A. He arrived there on 10 June 1924 when aged about 3 years and died on 10 September 1971.

Rarest The rarest primate is the Hairy-eared mouse lemur (*Cheirogaleus trichotis*) of Madagascar which, until fairly recently, was known only from the type specimen and two skins. In 1966, however, a live example was found on the east coast near Mananara.

Strength In 1924 "Boma", a 165 lb. *74,80 kg* male chimpanzee at Bronx Zoo, New York, N.Y., U.S.A. recorded a right-handed pull (feet braced) of 847 lb. *384 kg* on a dynamometer (*cf.* 210 lb. *[95 kg]* for a man of the same weight). On another occasion an adult female chimpanzee named "Suzette" (estimated weight 135 lb. *[61 kg]*) at the same zoo registered a right-handed pull of 1,260 lb. *572 kg* while in a rage. A record from the U.S.A. of a 100 lb. *45 kg* chimpanzee achieving a two-handed dead lift of 600 lb. *272 kg* with ease suggests that a male gorilla could with training raise 1,800 lb. *362 kg*!

MONKEYS

Largest The largest member of the monkey family is the Mandrill (*Mandrillus sphinx*) of equatorial West Africa. Adult males have an average head and body length of 24–30 in *61–76 cm* and weigh 55–70 lb. *25–32 kg.* The greatest reliable weight recorded for a mandrill is 54 kg *119 lb.* for a specimen which had a head and body length of 36 in *91 cm*, but unconfirmed weights up to 130 lb. *59 kg* have been reported.

Smallest The smallest known monkey is the Pygmy marmoset (*Cebuella pygmaea*) of Ecuador, northern Peru and western Brazil. Mature specimens have a maximum total length of 304 mm *12 in* half of which is tail, and weigh from 49 to 80 g *1.7 to 2.81 oz.*, which means it rivals the mouse lemur for the title of the smallest living primate (see page 38).

Longest The greatest reliable age reported for a monkey is *c.*
lived 46 years for a male mandrill (*Mandrillus sphinx*) named "George" of London Zoological Gardens, who died on 14 March 1916. He had originally been imported into Europe in 1869.

Most and Of sub-human primates, chimpanzees appear to have
least the most superior intelligence. Lemurs have less
intelligent learning ability than any monkey or ape and, in some tests, are inferior to dogs and even pigeons.

The world's heaviest gorilla in captivity, Samson at Milwaukee Zoological Park, U.S.A.

RODENTS

Largest The world's largest rodent is the Capybara (*Hydrochoerus hydrochaeris*), also called the carpincho or water hog, which is found in tropical South America. Mature specimens have a head and body length of 3¼ to 4½ ft *0,99–1,4 m* and weigh up to 150 lb. *68 kg*. Britain's largest rodent is now the Coypu (*Myocastor coypus*), also known as the Nutria, which was introduced from Argentina by East Anglian fur-breeders in 1927. In 1937 four escaped from a nutria-farm near Ipswich, Suffolk. Adult males measure 30–36 in *76–91 cm* in length (including short tail) and weigh up to 28 lb. *13 kg* in the wild state (40 lb. [*18 kg*] in captivity).

Smallest The smallest rodent is probably the Old World harvest mouse (*Micromys minutus*), of which the British form measures up to 135 mm *5.3 in* in total length and weighs between 4,2 and 10,2 g *0.15 to 0.36 of an oz.* In June 1965 it was announced that an even smaller rodent had been discovered in the Asian part of the U.S.S.R. (probably a more diminutive form of *M. minutus*), but further information is lacking.

Rarest The rarest rodent in the world is believed to be the James Island rice rat (*Oryzomys swarthi*), also called Swarth's rice rat. Four specimens were collected on this island in the Galapagos group in 1906, and it was not heard of again until January 1966 when the skull of a recently dead animal was found.

Longest lived The greatest reliable age reported for a rodent is 22 years for an Indian crested porcupine (*Hystrix indica*) which died in Trivandrum Zoological Gardens, south-western India in 1942.

INSECTIVORES

Largest The largest insectivore is the Moon rat (*Echinosorex gymnurus*), also known as Raffles gymnure, which is found in Burma, Thailand, Malaysia, Sumatra and Borneo. Mature specimens have a head and body length of 265–445 mm *10.43–17.52 in*, a tail measuring 200–210 mm *7.87–8.26 in.* and weigh up to 1,400 g *3.08 lb*. Although Anteaters feed on termites and other soft-bodied insects they are not insectivores, but belong to the order Edentata, which means "without teeth".

Smallest The smallest insectivore is Savi's white-toothed shrew (see Smallest mammal, page 35).

Longest lived The greatest reliable age recorded for an insectivore is 10½ years for a Hedgehog tenrec (*Setifer setosus*), which died in London Zoo in 1971.

ANTELOPES

Largest The largest of all antelopes is the rare Derby eland (*Taurotragus derbianus*), also called the Giant eland, of West and north-central Africa, which may surpass 2,000 lb. *907 kg*. The Common eland (*T. oryx*) of East and South Africa has the same shoulder height of up to 5 ft 10 in *1,78 m* but is not quite so massive, although there is one record of a 5 ft 5 in *1,65 m* bull shot in Nyasaland (now Malawi) in *c.* 1937 which weighed 2,078 lb. *943 kg*.

Smallest The smallest known antelope is the Royal antelope (*Neotragus pygmaeus*) of West Africa. Mature specimens measure 10–12 in *25–31 cm* at the shoulder and weigh only 7–8 lb. *3–3 kg 60* which is the size of a large Brown hare (*Lepus europaeus*). The slender Swayne's dik-dik (*Madoqua swaynei*) of Somalia, East Africa weighs only 5–6 lb. *2 kg 30–2 kg 70* when adult, but this species stands about 13 in *33 cm* at the shoulder.

Rarest The rarest antelope is probably Jentink's duiker (*Cephalophus jentinki*), also known as the Black-headed duiker, which is found only in a restricted area of tropical West Africa. Its total population may be anything from a few dozen to possibly a few hundred.

DEER

Largest The largest deer is the Alaskan moose (*Alces alces gigas*). A bull standing 7 ft 8 in *2,3 m* at the withers and weighing an estimated 1,800 lb. *816 kg* was shot on the Yukon River in the Yukon Territory, Canada in Sept. 1897. Unconfirmed measurements up to 8½ ft *2,59 m* at the withers and estimated weights up to 2,600 lb. *1 180 kg* have been claimed. The record antler span is 78½ in *199 cm*.

Smallest The smallest true deer (family Cervidae) is the pudu (*Pudu mephistophiles*) of Ecuador the male of which stands 13–15 in *33–38 cm* at the shoulder and weighs 18–20 lb. *8–9 kg*. The smallest known ruminant is the Lesser Malayan chevrotain or Mouse deer (*Tragulus javanicus*) of south-eastern Asia. Adult specimens measure 8–10 in *20–25 cm* at the shoulder and weigh 6–7 lb. *2 kg 70–3 kg 20*.

Rarest The rarest deer in the world is Fea's muntjac (*Muntiacus feae*), which is known only from two specimens collected on the borders of Tennasserim, Lower Burma and Thailand.

Oldest The greatest reliable age recorded for a deer is 26 years 6 months 2 days for a Red Deer (*Cervus elephus*) which died in the National Zoological Park, Washington, D.C., U.S.A. on 24 March 1941.

TUSKS

Longest The longest recorded elephant tusks (excluding prehistoric examples) are a pair from the eastern Congo (Zaïre) preserved in the National Collection of Heads and Horns kept by the New York Zoological Society in Bronx Park, New York City, N.Y., U.S.A. The right tusk measures 11 ft 5½ in *3,49 m* along the outside curve and the left 11 ft *3,35 m*. Their combined weight is 293 lb. *133 kg*. A single tusk of 11 ft 6 in *3,50 m* has been reported, but further details are lacking.

Heaviest The heaviest recorded tusks are a pair in the British Museum of Natural History, London which were collected from an aged bull shot at the foot of Mount Kilimanjaro, Kenya in 1897. They were sent to London for auction in 1901. The tusks were measured in 1955, when the first was found to be 10 ft 2½ in *3,11 m* long, weighing 226½ lb. *102 kg 70* and the other 10 ft 5½ in *3,18 m* weighing 214 lb. *97 kg* giving a combined weight of 440½ lb. *199 kg 80*. The tusks, when fresh, were reportedly 236 lb. and 225 lb. *107 and 102 kg* giving a combined weight of 461 lb. *209 kg*. Another pair collected in Dahomey, West Africa exhibited at the Paris Exposition of 1900 allegedly weighed 117 kg *258 lb.* and 97 kg *213 lb.* making a total of 214 kg *471 lb.* All trace of this record pair has now been lost.

HORNS

Longest The longest recorded animal horn was one measuring 81¼ in *206 cm* on the outside curve, with a circumference of 18¼ in *46 cm*, found on a specimen of domestic Ankole cattle (*Bos taurus*) near Lake Ngami, Botswana (formerly Bechuanaland).

Wild animal The longest horns grown by a wild animal are those of the Pamir argali (*Ovis poli*), also called Marco Polo's argali, a wild sheep found in the mountains of Soviet Central Asia. One of these has been measured at 75 in *191 cm* along the front curve, with a maximum circumference of 16 in *41 cm*.

Rhinoceros The longest recorded anterior horn of a rhinoceros is one of 62¼ in *158 cm* found on a female southern race White rhinoceros (*Ceratotherium simum simum*) shot in South Africa in *c.* 1848. The interior horn measured 22¼ in *57 cm*. There is also an unconfirmed record of an anterior horn measuring 81 in *206 cm*.

Blood tempera- tures The highest mammalian blood temperature is that of the Domestic goat (*Capra hircus*) with an average of 103.8° F *39,9° C*, and a normal range of from 101.7° to 105.3° F *38,7° to 40,7° C*. The lowest mammalian blood temperature is that of the Spiny anteater (*Tachyglossus aculeatus*), a monotreme found in Australia and New Guinea, with a normal range of 72° to 87° F *22,2° to 24,4° C*. The blood temperature of the Golden hamster (*Mesocricetus auratus*) sometimes falls as low as 38.3° F *3,5° C* during hibernation, and an extreme figure of 29.6° F *1,4° C* has been reported for a myotis bat (family Vespertilionidae) during a deep sleep.

Most valuable furs The highest-priced animal pelts are those of the Sea otter (*Enhydra lutris*), also known as the Kamchatka beaver, which fetched up to $2,700 (then £675) before their 55-year-long protection started in 1912. The protection ended in 1967, and at the first legal auction of sea otter pelts at Seattle, Washington, U.S.A. on 31 January 1968 Neiman-Marcus, the famous Dallas department store, paid $9,200 (then *£3,832*) for four pelts from Alaska. On 30 Jan. 1969 a New York company paid $1,100 *£457* for an exceptionally fine pelt from Alaska. On 26 Feb. 1969 forty selected pelts of the mink-sable cross-breed "Kojah" from the Piampiano Fur Ranch, Zion, Illinois, U.S.A. realised $2,700 *£1,125* in New York City. In May 1970 a Kojah coat costing $125,000 *£52,083* was sold by Neiman-Marcus to Welsh actor Richard Burton for his wife.

Ambergris The heaviest piece of ambergris (a fatty deposit in the intestine of the Sperm whale) on record was a 1,003 lb. *455 kg* lump recovered from a Sperm whale (*Physeter catodon*) taken in Australian waters on 3 Dec. 1912 by a Norwegian whaling fleet. It was later sold in London for £23,000.

MARSUPIALS

Largest The largest of all marsupials is the Red kangaroo (*Macropus rufus*) of southern and eastern Australia. Adult males or "boomers" stand 6–7 ft *1,83–2,13 m* tall, weigh 150–175 lb. *68–79 kg* and measure up to 8 ft 11 in *2,71 m* in a straight line from the nose to the tip of the extended tail. The Great grey kangaroo (*Macropus giganteus*) of eastern Australia and Tasmania is almost equally as large, and there is an authentic record of a boomer measuring 8 ft 8 in *2,64 m* from nose to tail (9 ft 7 in *[2,92 m]* along the curve of the body) and weighing 200 lb. *90 kg 70*. The skin of this specimen is preserved in the Australian Museum, Sydney, New South Wales.

Smallest The smallest known marsupial is the rare Kimberley planigale or marsupial mouse (*Planigale subtilissima*), which is found only in the Kimberley district of Western Australia. Adult males have a head and body length of 44.5 mm *1.75 in*, a tail length of 51 mm *2 in* and weigh about 4 g *0.141 oz*. Females are smaller than males.

Rarest The rarest marsupial is the sandhill Dunnart, (*Sminthopsis psammophila*) also known as the narrow-footed marsupial mouse, which is known only from the type specimen collected in 1894 near Lake Amadeus, Northern Territory, Australia.

Highest and longest jumps The greatest measured height cleared by a hunted kangaroo is 10 ft 6 in *3,20 m* over a pile of timber. During the course of a chase in January 1951 a female Red kangaroo (*Macropus rufus*) made a series of bounds which included one of 42 ft *12,80 m*. There is also an unconfirmed report of a Great grey kangaroo (*M. canguru*) jumping nearly 13,5 m *44 ft 8½ in* on the flat.

HORSES AND PONIES

Largest The heaviest horse ever recorded was a 19.2-hand (6 ft 6 in *[1,98 m]*) pure-bred Belgian stallion named

"Firpon", the tallest horse ever recorded standing 21.1 hands

"Brooklyn Supreme" (foaled 12 April 1928) owned by Ralph Fogleman of Callender, Iowa, U.S.A. who weighed 1.42 tons *1,44 tonnes* shortly before his death on 6 Sept. 1948 aged 20. The heaviest horse living in Britain today is "Saltmarsh Silver Crest" (foaled 1955), an 18¼-hand (6 ft 1 in *[1,85 m]*) champion Percheron stallion owned by George E. Sneath of Money Bridge near Pinchbeck, Lincolnshire. He weighed 2,772 lb. *1 257 kg* in 1967.

Tallest The tallest horse ever recorded was the Percheron-Shire cross "Firpon" (foaled 1959) which stood 21.1 hands (7 ft 1 in *[2,16 m]*) and weighed 2,976 lb. *1 350 kg*. He died on the Olavarria Ranch, Argentina on 14 Mar. 1972. The tallest horse living in Britain is "Fort d'Or" at 18.2 hands (see Horse Racing, Chapter 12).

Smallest The smallest breed of horse are those bred by Julio Falabella at the El Peludo Ranch, Argentina. Adult specimens range from under 12 in to 42 in *31–107 cm* at the shoulder and weigh up to 150 lb. *68 kg*. The upper accepted limit for the American Miniature Horse Breeders Association is 34 in *86,3 cm*. The smallest breed of pony is the Shetland pony, which usually measures 8–10 hands (32–40 in *[81–102 cm]*) and weighs 275–385 lb. *125–175 kg*. In March 1969 a measurement of 3.2 hands (14 in *[36 cm]*) was reported for a "miniature" Shetland pony named "Midnight", owned by Miss Susan Perry of Worths Circus, Melbourne, Victoria, Australia.

Oldest The greatest reliable age recorded for a horse is 52 years for a 17 hands (5 ft 8 in *[1,73 m]*) light draught-horse named "Monty", owned by Mrs. Marjorie Cooper of Albury, New South Wales, Australia, who died on 25 Jan. 1970. He was foaled in Wodonga, New South Wales in 1917. The jaws of this horse are now preserved in the School of Veterinary Science at Melbourne University. On 1 Nov. 1969 a mare named "Nellie" died of a heart attack on a farm near Danville, Missouri, U.S.A. reputedly foaled in March 1916 and then aged 53½, but this claim has not yet been fully substantiated. The greatest reliable age recorded for a pony is 54 years for a stallion owned by a farmer in Central France which was still alive in 1919. In June 1970 a Welsh pony living on a farm near Pebbles Bay, Gower Peninsula, South Wales was reported to be 66 years old, but this claim lacks proper documentation.

Strongest *draught* The greatest load hauled by a pair of draught horses (probably Shires) was 50 logs comprising 36,055 board-feet of timber (= 53.8 tons [*55 tonnes*] on a sledge litter across snow at the Nester Estate, Ewen, Ontonagon County, Michigan, U.S.A. in 1893. In a test at Liverpool Road, Islington, London on 25 Feb. 1924 an 8-year-old draught-horse "Umber" moved a 2 ton 9½ cwt *2 515 kg* cart carrying 16 tons *16 tonnes* of iron on stone setts.

DOGS

Largest The heaviest breed of domestic dog (*Canis familiaris*) is the St. Bernard. The heaviest recorded example was "Schwarzwald Hof Duke", owned by Dr. A. M. Bruner of Oconomowoc, Wisconsin, U.S.A. He was whelped on 8 Oct. 1964 and weighed 21 st. 1 lb. *133 kg 80* on 2 May 1969, dying three months later aged 4 years 10 months. The largest St. Bernard ever weighed in Britain was one named "Brandy", owned by Miss Gwendoline L. White of Chinnor, Oxfordshire. He weighed 18 st. 7 lb. *117 kg 50* on 11 Feb. 1966, dying 23 days later aged 6½ years. "Montmorency of Hollesley", also known as "Monty", an Old English mastiff owned by Mr. Randolph Simon of Wilmington, Sussex, was also of comparable size. He was whelped on 1 May 1962 and weighed 18 st. 7 lb. *117 kg 50* in July 1969. In April 1970 his weight was estimated to be 19 st. *120 kg*. He was put to sleep in April 1971 aged 8 years 11 months. In January 1973 a 5 year old English mastiff named Jason owned by Mr. C. B. Skinner of Worthing, Sussex reportedly weighed more than 17 st. *107 kg 90*.

Tallest The world's tallest breed of dog is the Irish wolfhound. The extreme recorded example was "Broadbridge Michael" (b. 1926) owned by Mrs. Mary Beynon of Sutton-at-Hone, Kent, He stood 39½ in *100,3 cm* at the shoulder in 1928 when aged two years. The tallest dog now living in Britain is "Fatherwell Alexander", also known as "Kelly", owned by Mrs. Jeanette Coffer of Herne Bay, Kent. He stands 39 in *99,1 cm* and was whelped in 1971.

Smallest The smallest breed of dog is the Chihuahua from Mexico. New-born pups average 3½–4½ oz. *99–127 g* and weigh 2–4 lb. *0 kg 910–1 kg 80* when fully grown, but some "miniature" specimens weigh only 16 oz. *453 g*. The smallest British breed is the Yorkshire terrier, one of which named "Cody Queen of Dudley" was reported in July 1968 to have weighed only 20 oz. *567 g* at 16 months. In January 1971 a full-grown white toy poodle named "Giles", owned by Mrs. Sylvia Wyse of Bucknall, Staffordshire, stood 4½ in *11 cm* at the shoulder and weighed 13 oz. *368 g*. Shortly afterwards he was exported to Canada.

Oldest Authentic records of dogs living over 20 years are extremely rare, but even 34 years has been accepted by one authority. The greatest reliable age recorded for a dog is 27 years 3 months for a black Labrador gun-dog named "Adjutant", who was whelped on 14 August 1936 and died on 20 Nov. 1963 in the care of his lifetime owner, James Hawkes, a gamekeeper at the Reversby Estate, near Boston, Lincolnshire. Less reliable is a claim of 28 years for an Irish terrier which died in 1951.

Rarest The rarest breed of dog is the Löwchen ("Little Lion"), of which only 65–70 were reported in March 1973. The Chinese crested dog (now extinct in China) is also extremely rare. In 1972 the world population was estimated at less than 150.

Fastest The fastest breed of dog (excluding the greyhound or possibly the whippet) is the Saluki, also called the Arabian gazelle hound or Persian greyhound. Speeds up to 43 m.p.h. *69 km/h* have been claimed, but tests

"Monty" the United Kingdom's heaviest recorded dog. He tipped the scales at 19 st. *120 kg*

in the Netherlands have shown that it is not as fast as the present-day greyhound which has attained a measured speed of 41.7 m.p.h. *67,1 km/h* on a track.

Largest litter The largest recorded litter of puppies is one of 23 thrown on 11 February 1945 by "Lena", a foxhound bitch owned by Commander W. N. Ely of Ambler, Pennsylvania, U.S.A. On 9 February 1895 a St. Bernard bitch named "Lady Millard", owned by a Mr. Thorpe of Northwold, Norfolk, produced a litter of 21.

Most prolific The greatest sire of all time was the champion greyhound "Low Pressure", nicknamed "Timmy", whelped in September 1957 and owned by Mrs. Bruna Amhurst of Regent's Park, London. From December 1961 until his death on 27 November 1969 he fathered 2,414 registered puppies, with at least 600 others unregistered. The report from Rushholme, Manchester, England on 4–5 June 1972 of the birth of 24 live pups to an Alsatian bitch remains unsatisfactory.

Most popular The breed with the most Kennel Club registrations in 1972 was the Alsatian with 15,078. In 1973, Cruft's Dog Show (founded in 1886 for terriers only) had an entry of 7,581, compared with the record entry of 10,650 dogs in 1936 before entrants were restricted to prize winners.

Most expensive In June 1972 Mrs. Judith Thurlow of Great Ashfield, Suffolk turned down an offer of £14,000 for her champion greyhound "Super Rory" who was whelped in October 1970. The highest price ever paid for a dog is £2,000 by Mrs. A. H. Hempton in December 1929 for the champion greyhound "Mick the Miller" (whelped in Ireland in June 1926 and died 1939). In 1947 a figure of £2,000 was also quoted for a champion English bulldog sold to an American breeder, but further details are lacking.

"Top dog" The greatest altitude attained by an animal is 1,050 miles *1 690 km* by the Samoyed husky bitch fired as a passenger in Sputnik II on 3 Nov. 1957. The dog was variously named "Kudryavka" (feminine form of "Curly"), "Limonchik" (diminutive of lemon), "Malyshka", "Zhuchka" or by the Russian breed name for husky, "Laika".

Highest and longest jump The canine "high jump" record is held by the British dog "Mikeve", who scaled a wall of 9 ft 6 in *2,89 m* off a springboard in a test in Kensington, London, in 1934. The longest recorded canine long jump was one of 30 ft *9,14 m* by a greyhound named "Bang" made in jumping a gate in coursing a hare at Brecon Lodge, Gloucestershire in 1849.

Strongest The greatest load ever shifted by a dog is 3,260 lb. *1 479 kg* pulled over 15 ft *4,5 m* in under 90 sec in accordance with international rules by a champion Newfoundland dog "Newfield's Nelson" aged 6½ and weighing 164 lb. *74 kg* on 10 Oct. 1970 at Bethell, Washington, U.S.A. owned by Mr. and Mrs. Allen A. Wolman. The record time for the annual 15 mile *24 km* dog sled race at Whitehorse, Yukon Territory, Canada is 59 min 33 sec by the driver "Charlie", 33 in March 1969.

Ratting The greatest ratter of all time was Mr. James Searle's bull terrier bitch "Jenny Lind", who killed 500 rats in 1 hr 30 min at "The Beehive", Old Crosshall Street, Liverpool on 12 July 1853. Another bull terrier named "Jacko", owned by Mr. Jemmy Shaw, was credited with killing 1,000 rats in 1 hr 40 min, but the feat was performed over a period of ten weeks in batches of 100 at a time. The last 100 were accounted for in 5 min 28 sec in London on 1 May 1862.

Tracking The greatest tracking feat on record was performed by a Doberman named "Sauer", trained by Detective-Sergeant Herbert Kruger. In 1925 he tracked a stock-thief 100 miles *160 km* across the Great Karroo, South Africa by scent alone. In Jan. 1969 an Alsatian bitch was reported to have followed her master 745 miles *1 200 km* from Brindisi to Milan, Italy in four months. The dog's owner had left her behind when he went on a visit. An Alsatian's sense of smell is one million times better than man's.

Police Dogs The highest score recorded in the National Police Dog championships is 938½ out of a possible 1,000 points by "Skol of Baswich" near Cheltenham, Gloucestershire on 26–30 May 1963. Obedience, agility, searching, chase and attack tests are included. "Skol" was prepared by Chief Inspector (then Sgt.) J. Howell.

Greatest Dog Funeral The greatest dog funeral on record was for the mongrel dog belonging to the eccentric King Norbert I of the United States, Defender of Mexico, held in San Francisco, California in 1860 which was attended by an estimated 10,000 people.

CATS

Heaviest The heaviest domestic cat (*Felis catus*) on record was probably a female tabby named "Gigi" (1959–72), owned by Miss Ann Clark of Carlisle, Cumberland. The weight of this cat normally fluctuated between 37 and 40 lb. *17 and 18 kg* but in April 1970 she weighed 42 lb. *19 kg* and had a maximum bodily girth of 37 in *94 cm*. The average weight for an adult cat is 11 lb. *5 kg*.

Oldest Cats are longer-lived animals than dogs and there are a number of authentic records over 20 years. Information on this subject is often obscured by two or more cats bearing the same nickname. The oldest cat ever recorded was probably the tabby "Puss", owned by Mrs. T. Holway of Clayhidon, Devon who celebrated his 36th birthday on 28 November 1939 and died the next day. A more recent and better-documented case was that of the female tabby "Ma", owned by Mrs. Alice St. George Moore of Drewsteignton, Devon. She was put to sleep on 5 November 1957 aged 34. According to the American Feline Society a cat living in Hazleton, Pennsylvania celebrated its 37th birthday on 1 November 1958 but it was later discovered by the Society that two or more cats were involved. The oldest cat living in Britain today is believed to be a long

"Chan Lass" the Siamese cat, with her litter of 11 kittens which survived from the 13 born to her

haired tabby named "Jane" owned by Mrs. D. Strotton of Worthing, Sussex. She is at least 30 years old and was acquired in May 1944 when it was an estimated ten months old.

Largest litter The largest live litter ever recorded was one of 13 kittens born on 13 April 1969 to "Boccaccio Blue Danielle", a one-year-old blue-pointed Siamese cat owned by Mrs. Helen J. Coward of Klemzig, South Australia. On 23 April 1972 a one-year-old seal point Siamese cat named "Chan-Lass", owned by Mrs. Harriet Smith of Southsea, Hants., gave birth to a litter of 13 kittens, 11 of which survived. In July 1970 a litter of 19 kittens (four incompletely formed) was reportedly born by Caesarean section to "Tarawood Antigone", a brown Burmese owned by Mrs. Valerie Gane of Church Westcote, Kingham, Oxfordshire, but this claim has never been fully substantiated.

Most prolific A cat named "Dusty", aged 17, living in Bonham, Texas, U.S.A., gave birth to her 420th kitten on 12 June 1952. A 21-year-old cat "Tippy" living in Kingston-upon-Hull, Yorkshire gave birth to her 343rd kitten in June 1933.

Greatest Escape On 15 July 1972 "Fat Olive" a black and white tom cat, survived a fall of 160 ft *48,77 m* from a Toronto penthouse, breaking only two legs.

"Most Lives" "Thumper", a 2½-year-old tabby owned by Mrs. Reg Buckett of Westminster, London was rescued from a lift shaft on 29 March 1964 after being trapped for 52 days.

Richest and most valuable Dr. William Grier of San Diego, California, U.S.A. died in June 1963 leaving his entire estate of $415,000 to his two 15-year-old cats "Hellcat" and "Brownie". When the cats died in 1965 the money went to the George Washington University in Washington, D.C. In 1967 Miss Elspeth Sellar of Grafham, Surrey turned down an offer of 2,000 guineas (£2,100) from an American breeder for her champion copper-eyed white Persian tom "Coylum Marcus" (b. 28 March 1965).

Rarest breed The rarest of the 52 recognised breeds of cat in Britain is the Red self Persian or Long-haired red self.

Ratting and mousing The greatest ratter on record was probably the female tabby named "Minnie" who during the six year period 1927 to 1933 killed 12,480 rats at the White City

Stadium, London. The greatest mouser on record was a tabby named "Mickey", owned by Shepherd & Sons Ltd. of Burscough, Lancashire which killed more than 22,000 mice during 23 years with the firm. He died in November 1968.

Cat population The largest cat population is that of the U.S.A. with 28,000,000. Of Britain's cat population of 6,000,000, an estimated 100,000 are "employed" by the Civil Service.

RABBITS

Largest The largest breed of domestic rabbit (*Oryctolagus cuniculus*) is the Flemish giant, which has an average toe to toe length of 36 in *91 cm* when fully extended and weighs 12–14 lb. *5 kg 40–6 kg 30*. The heaviest recorded specimen was a male named "Floppy" who weighed 25 lb. *11 kg 30* shortly before his death in June 1963 aged eight. In May 1971 a weight of 25 lb. *11 kg* was also reported for a four-year-old Norfolk Star named "Chewer", owned by Mr. Edward Williams of Attleborough, Norfolk.

Oldest The greatest reliable age recorded for a domestic rabbit is 18 years for a doe which was still alive in 1947. A buck rabbit named "Blackie" owned by Mrs. H. H. Chivers of Brixham, Devon died on 13 March 1971 aged 16 years 3 months.

Most prolific The most prolific domestic breed is the Norfolk Star. Females produce 9 to 10 litters a year, each containing about 10 young (*cf.* five litters and three to seven young for the wild rabbit). "Chewer" (see above) fathered 36,772 offspring up to 3 July 1972.

2. BIRDS (*Aves*)

Largest Ratite The largest living bird is the North African ostrich (*Struthio camelus camelus*), which is found in reduced numbers south of the Atlas Mountains from Upper Senegal and Niger across to the Sudan and central Ethiopia. Male examples of this flightless or ratite bird have been recorded up to 9 ft *2,74 m* in height and 345 lb. *156 kg 50* in weight.

Carinate The heaviest flying bird or carinate is the Kori bustard or Paauw (*Otis kori*) of East and South Africa. Cock birds weighing up to 40 lb. *18 kg 10* have been shot in South Africa, and one enormously fat specimen killed in the western Transvaal in *c.* 1892 with a wing span of 8 ft 4 in *2,54 m* was estimated to weigh 54 lb. *24 kg 490*. The Mute swan (*Cygnus olor*), which is resident in Britain, also exceeds 40 lb. *18 kg* on occasion, and there is a record from Poland of a cob weighing 22 kg 50 *49.5 lb*. The heaviest flying bird of prey is the Andean condor (*Vultur gryphus*). Adult males average 20–25 lb. *9–11 kg*, but one specimen shot on San Gallan Island off the coast of Peru in 1919 weighed 26½ lb. *12 kg 020*.

Largest wing span The Wandering albatross (*Diomedea exulans*) of the southern oceans has the largest wing span of any living bird, adult males averaging 10 ft 2 in *3,09 m* with wings tightly stretched. The largest recorded specimen was a male measuring 11 ft 10 in *3,60 m* caught by banders in Western Australia in *c.* 1957, but some unmeasured birds may reach or possibly just exceed 12 ft *3,65 m*. This size is closely matched by the Andean condor (*Vultur gryphus*). Adult males commonly have a wing span of 9 ft 3 in *2,82 m* and some specimens exceed 10 ft *3,04 m*. One bird killed in the Ilo Valley, southern Peru in *c.* 1714 allegedly measured 12 ft 3 in *373 cm*, but this figure must be considered excessive. In extreme cases the wing span of the Marabou stork (*Leptoptilus crumeniferus*) may also exceed 10 ft *305 cm* (average span 9 ft [*274 cm*]), and there is an unconfirmed record of 13 ft 4 in *406 cm* for a specimen shot in Central Africa in the 1930s. In August 1939 a wing span of 12 ft *366 cm* was recorded for a Mute swan (*Cygnus olor*) named "Guardsman" (d. 1945) at the famous swannery at Abbotsbury, near Weymouth, Dorset. The average span is 8½–9 ft *259–274 cm*.

Smallest World The smallest bird in the world is the bee hummingbird *Mellisuga helenae*, also known as Helena's hummingbird or "the fairy hummer", found in Cuba. An average adult male has a wing-span measurement of 28.4 mm *1.11 in.*, a total length of 58 mm *2.28 in.* and weighs about 2 g *0.070 oz.* This means it is lighter than a Sphinx moth which weighs about 0.080 oz *2,3 g*. Adult females are slightly larger than males. The bee hummingbird *Acestruta bombus* of Ecuador is about the same size as *M. helenae*, but is slightly heavier.

United Kingdom The smallest resident British bird is the Goldcrest (*Regulus regulus*), also known as the Golden-crested wren or Kinglet. Adult specimens measure 90 mm *3.5 in* in total length and weigh between 3.8 and 4.5 g *0.108 and 0.127 oz.*

Most abundant The most abundant species of bird is the chicken, the domesticated form of the wild Red jungle fowl (*Gallus gallus*) of south-east Asia. There are believed to be about 3,500,000,000 in the world, or nearly one chicken for every member of the human race. The fowl stock in Britain was estimated at 190,000,000 in 1971, producing 270,000,000 chicks annually. The most abundant species of wild bird is believed to be the Starling (*Sturnus vulgaris*) with an estimated world population of well over 1,000,000,000. The most abundant of all sea birds is Wilson's petrel (*Oceanites oceanicus*).

The most abundant species of bird ever recorded was the Passenger pigeon (*Ectopistes migratoria*) of North America. It has been estimated that there were between 5,000,000,000 and 9,000,000,000 of these birds before 1840. Thereafter the birds were killed in vast numbers, and the last recorded specimen, a female named "Martha", died in Cincinnati Zoological Gardens, Ohio, U.S.A. at 1 p.m. Eastern standard time on 1 Sept. 1914 aged about 12 years. The mounted specimen is now on display in the U.S. National Museum, Washington, D.C.

The Andean condor, which has the longest wing span of any predatory bird

United Kingdom The commonest wild breeding birds in Great Britain are the Blackbird (*Turdus merula*), the Chaffinch (*Fringilla coelebs*), the House Sparrow (*Passer domesticus*) and the Wood Pigeon (*Columba palumbus*) all of which have an estimated population of 10,000,000. It was estimated in 1967 that 250,000 pigeon fanciers owned an average of 40 racing pigeons per loft, making a population of *c.* 10,000,000 in Great Britain.

Rarest World Perhaps the best claimants to this title would be the ten species last seen in the 19th century but still just possibly extant. They are the New Caledonian lorikeet (*Vini diadema*) (New Caledonia *ante* 1860); the Himalayan mountain quail (*Ophrysia superciliosa*) (eastern Punjab, 1868); Forest Spotted Owlet (*Athene blewitti*) (Central India, *c.* 1972); the Samoan wood rail (*Pareudiastes pacificus*) (Savaii, Samoa, 1873); the Fiji bar-winged rail (*Rallina poeciilopterus*) (Ovalau and Viti Levu, 1890); the Kona "finches" (*Psittirostra flaviceps* and *P. palmeri*) (Kona, Hawaii, 1891 and 1896); the Akepa (*Loxops coccinea*) (Oahu, Hawaii, 1893); the Kona "finch" (*Psittirostra kona*) (Kona, Hawaii, 1894) and the Mamo (*Drepanis pacifica*) (Hawaii, 1898). The Puerto Rican nightjar (*Caprimulgus ruficollis*), believed extinct since 1888, was rediscovered in 1962, and the Ivory-billed woodpecker (*Campephilus principalis*) has been confirmed as surviving since 1963.

United Kingdom There are about 30 species of bird (8 of them unconfirmed) which have been recorded only once in the British Isles. That which has not recurred for the longest period is the black-capped petrel (*Pterodroma hasitata*), also known as the Diablotin. A specimen was caught alive on a heath at Southacre, near Swaffham, Norfolk in March or April 1850. The most tenuously established British bird is probably the Snowy owl (*Nyctea scandiaca*), now breeding as a single pair on Fetlar in the Shetland Islands.

Longest lived The greatest irrefutable age reported for any bird is 68 years in the case of a female European eagle-owl (*Bubo bubo*) which was still alive in 1899. Other records which are regarded as *probably* reliable include 73 years (1818–91) for a Greater sulphur-crested cockatoo (*Cacatua galerita*); 72 years (1797–1869) for an African grey parrot (*Psittacus erithacus*); 70 years (1770–1840) for a Mute swan (*Cygnus olor*) and 69 years for a Raven (*Corvus corax*). An Egyptian vulture (*Neophron percnopterus*) which died in the menagerie at Schönbrunn, Vienna, Austria in 1824 was stated to have been 118 years old, but the menagerie was not founded until 1752. In 1972 a Southern Ostrich (*Struthio camelus australis*) aged 62 years and 3 months was killed in the Ostrich Abattoir at Oudtshoorn, Cape Province, South Africa.

Fastest flying The fastest flying bird is the spine-tailed swift (*Chaetura caudacuta*). For details see page 34.

The bird which presents the hunter with the greatest difficulty is the Spur-wing goose (*Plectropterus gambiensis*), with a recorded air speed of 60 m.p.h. *96 km/h* in level flight and 88 m.p.h. *141 km/h* in an escape dive.

The fastest recorded wing beat of any bird is that of the hummingbird (*Heliactin cornuta*) of tropical South America with a rate of 90 beats a sec. Large vultures (family Vulturidae) can soar for hours without beating their wings, but sometimes exhibit a flapping rate as low as one beat per sec.

Fastest swimmer The fastest swimming bird is the Gentoo penguin (*Pygoscelis papua*). In January 1913 a small group were timed at 10 m a sec *22.3 m.p.h.* under water near the Bay of Isles, South Georgia. This is a respectable flying speed for some birds.

Longest flights The greatest distance covered by a ringed bird during migration is 12,000 miles *19 300 km* by an Arctic tern (*Sterna paradisaea*), which was banded as a nestling on 5 July 1955 in the Kandalaksha Sanctuary on the White Sea coast and was captured alive by a fisherman 8 miles *13 km* south of Fremantle, Western Australia on 16 May 1956.

Highest flying The celebrated example of a skein of 17 Egyptian geese (*Alopochen aegptiacus*) photographed by an astronomer at Dehra Dun, northern India on 17 Sept. 1919 as they crossed the sun at an estimated height of between 11 and 12 miles (58,080–63,360 ft [*17 700–19 310 m*]), has been discredited by experts.

The highest acceptable altitude recorded for a bird is 8 200 m *26,902 ft* for a small number of Alpine choughs (*Pyrrhocorax graculus*) which followed the British Everest expedition of 1924, but their take-off point may have been as high as 20,000 ft *6 100 m*. On three separate occasions in 1959 a radar station in Norfolk picked up flocks of small passerine night migrants flying in from Scandinavia at heights up to 21,000 ft *6 400 m*. They were probably Warblers (*Sylviidae*), Chats (*Turnidae*) and Flycatchers (*Muscicapidae*).

Most airborne The most "airborne" of all birds is the common swift (*Apus apus*) which remains aloft for at least nine months of the year.

Most acute vision Tests have shown that under favourable conditions the Long-eared owl (*Asio otus*) and the Barn owl (*Tyto alba*) can swoop on targets from a distance of 6 ft *1,83 m* or more in an illumination of only 0.00000073 of a ft candle (equivalent to the light from a standard candle at a distance of 1,170 ft [*356 m*]). This acuity is 50–100 times as great as that of human night vision. In good light and against a contrasting background a Golden eagle (*Aquila chrysaetos*) can detect an 18 in *46 cm* long hare at a range of 2,150 yds *1 966 m* (possibly even 2 miles [*3,2 km*]).

Eggs Largest The largest egg produced by any living bird is that of the ostrich (*Struthio camelus*). The average example measures 6–8 in *15–20 cm* in length, 4 to 6 in *10–15 cm* in diameter and weighs 3.63 to 3.88 lb. *1 kg 650–1 kg 780* (equal to the volume of two dozen hen's eggs). It requires about 40 min for boiling. The shell is one-sixteenth of an in *15,8 mm* thick and can support the weight of a 20 st. *127 kg* man. The largest egg laid by any bird on the British list is that of the Mute swan (*Cygnus olor*), which measures from 4.3 to 4.9 in *109–124 mm* in length and between 2.8 and 3.1 in *71–78,5 mm* in diameter. The weight is 12–13 oz. *340–368 g*.

Smallest The smallest egg laid by any bird is that of the bee hummingbird *Mellisuga helenae*, the world's smallest bird (see page 43). A specimen collected at Boyate, Santiago de Cuba on 8 May 1906 and later presented to the U.S. National Museum, Washington, D.C., U.S.A. measures 11,4 mm *0.45 in* in length, 8 mm *0.32 in* in diameter and weighs 0,5 of a g *0.176 oz*. The smallest egg laid by a bird on the British list is that of the Goldcrest (*Regulus regulus*), which measures 12,2–14,5 mm *0.48–0.57 in* in length and between 9,4 and 9,9 mm *0,37 and 0,39 in* in diameter.

Incubation Longest and shortest The longest incubation period is that of the Wandering albatross (*Diomedea exulans*), with a normal range of 75 days to 82 days. The shortest incubation period is probably that of the Hawfinch (*Coccothraustes coccothraustes*), which is only 9–10 days. The idlest of cock birds are hummingbirds (family Trochilidae), among whom the hen bird does 100 per cent of the incubation, whereas the female Common kiwi (*Apteryx australis*) leaves this entirely to the male for 75 to 80 days.

Feathers
Longest The longest feathers grown by any bird are those of the cock Long-tailed fowl or Onagadori (a strain of *Gallus gallus*) bred at Kochi in Shikoku, Japan which have tail coverts measuring up to 20 ft *6,10 m* in length.

Most In a series of "feather counts" on various species of bird a Whistling swan (*Cygnus columbianus*) was found to have 25,216 feathers. A Ruby-throated hummingbird (*Archilochus colubris*) had only 940, although hummingbirds have more feathers per area of body surface than any other living bird.

Earliest and latest cuckoo It is unlikely that the Cuckoo (*Cuculus canorus*) has ever been *heard and seen* in Britain earlier than 2 March, on which date one was observed under acceptable conditions by Mr. W. A. Haynes of Trinder Road, Wantage, Berkshire in 1972. The two latest dates are 16 Dec. 1912 at Anstey's Cove, Torquay, Devon and 26 Dec. 1897 or 1898 in Cheshire.

DOMESTICATED BIRDS

Chicken
Heaviest The heaviest chicken on record is "Weirdo", a 4 year old White Sully of 22 lb. *9 kg 980* reported in Calaveras County, California in Jan. 1973. "Weirdo" murdered an 18 lb. *8 kg 160* son, crippled a dog, and has so far injured his owner to the extent of 8 stitches besides killing two cats.

Turkey
Heaviest The greatest *live* weight recorded for a Turkey (*Meleagris gallapavo*) is 70 lb. *31 kg 70*, reported in December 1966 for a White Holland stag named "Tom" owned by a breeder in California, U.S.A. The U.S. record for a dressed bird is 68½ lb. *31 kg 070* in 1953. The British record for a *clean plucked* turkey is 66 lb. 8 oz. *30 kg 150* for a stag reared by Mr. Lawrence Mack of Norfolk in Dec. 1972. It's liveweight was probably 69 lb. 4 oz. *31 kg 440*. Turkeys were introduced into Britain *via* Germany from Mexico in 1549.

Longest lived The longest lived domesticated bird (excluding the Ostrich) is the domestic goose which normally lives about 25 years. In January 1973 a figure of 42 years was reported for a gander named George owned by Mrs. Florence Hull of Thornton, Lancashire. It was reported in June 1972 that Mrs. Kathleen Leck, 32, still has a 31-year-old canary (*Serinus canaria*) bartered by her father, Mr. Ross of Hull, in Calabar, Nigeria when she was 1. A budgerigar named "Pretty Boy" (hatched Nov. 1948), owned by Mrs. Anne Dolan of Loughton, Essex, died on 25 February 1972 aged 23 years 3 months. The largest caged budgerigar (*Melopsittacus undulatus*) population is probably that of the United Kingdom with an estimated 3½–4 million. In 1956 the population was about 7 million. This small parakeet is found wild in Australia.

Most talkative The world's most talkative bird is a male African grey parrot (*Psittacus erythacus*) named "Prudle", owned by Mrs. Lyn Logue of Golders Green, London, which has won the "Best talking parrot-like bird" title at the National Cage and Aviary Bird Show in London for the nine years 1965–1973. Prudle was taken from a nest in a tree about to be felled at Jinja, Uganda in 1958.

3. REPTILES (*Reptilia*)
(Crocodiles, snakes, turtles, tortoises and lizards.)

Largest and heaviest The largest reptile in the world is the Estuarine or Salt-water crocodile (*Crocodylus porosus*) of south-east Asia, northern Australia, New Guinea, the Philippines and the Solomon Islands. Adult bulls average 12–14 ft *3,7–4,3 m* in length and scale about 1,100 lb. *499 kg*. In 1823 a notorious man-eater measuring 27 ft *8,23 m* in length and weighing an estimated 2 tons/*tonnes* was shot at Jala Jala on Luzon Island in the Philippines after terrorising the

neighbourhood for many years. Its skull, the largest on record if we exclude fossil remains, is now preserved in the Museum of Comparative Zoology at Harvard University, Cambridge, Massachusetts, U.S.A. Another outsized example with a reputed length of 33 ft *10,05 m* and a maximum bodily girth of 13 ft 8 in *4,16 m* was shot in the Bay of Bengal in 1840, but the dimensions of its skull (preserved in the British Museum of Natural History, London) suggest that it must have come from a crocodile measuring about 24 ft *7,31 m*. In April 1966 an Estuarine crocodile measuring 20 ft 9 in *6,32 m* in length and weighing more than a ton was shot at Liaga, on the south-east coast of Papua.

Smallest The smallest known species of reptile is believed to be *Sphaerodactylus parthenopiom*, a tiny gecko found only on the island of Virgin Gorda, one of the British Virgin Islands, in the West Indies. It is known only from 15 specimens, including some gravid females found between 10 and 16 Aug. 1964. The three largest females measured 18 mm *0.71 in* from snout to vent, with a tail of approximately the same length. It is possible that another gecko, *Sphaerodactylus elasmorhynchus*, may be even smaller. The only known specimen was an apparently mature female with a snout-vent length of 17 mm *0.67 in* and a tail the same measurement found on 15 March 1966 among the roots of a tree in the western part of the Massif de la Hotte in Haiti. A species of dwarf chameleon, *Evoluticauda tuberculata* found in Madagascar, and known only from a single specimen, has a snout-vent length of 18 mm *0.71 in* and a tail length of 14 mm *0.55 in*. Chameleons, however, are more bulky than geckos, and it is not yet known if this specimen was fully grown.

The smallest reptile found in Britain is the Viviparous or Common lizard (*Lacerta vivipara*). Adult specimens have an overall length of 108–178 mm *4.25–7 in*.

Fastest The highest speed measured for any reptile on land is 18 m.p.h. *29 km/h* for a Six-lined racerunner (*Cnemidophorus sexlineatus*) pursued by a car near McCormick, South Carolina, U.S.A. in 1941. The highest speed claimed for any reptile in water is 22 m.p.h. *35 km/h* by a frightened Pacific leatherback turtle (see below).

The Komodo monitor or Ora the world's largest lizard

Lizards
Largest The largest of all lizards is the Komodo monitor or Ora (*Varanus komodoensis*), a dragonlike reptile found on the Indonesian islands of Komodo, Rintja, Padar and Flores. Adult males average 8 ft *2,43 m* in length and weigh 175–200 lb *79–91 kg*. Lengths up to 23 ft *7,01 m* (sic) have been quoted for this species, but the largest specimen to be accurately measured was a male presented to an American zoologist in 1928 by the Sultan of Bima which taped 3,05 m *10 ft 0.8 in*. In 1937 this animal was put on display in St. Louis Zoological Gardens, Missouri, U.S.A. for a short period. It then measured 10 ft 2 in *3,10 m* in length and weighed 365 lb. *166 kg*.

Oldest The greatest age recorded for a lizard is more than 54 years for a male Slow worm (*Anguis fragilis*) kept in the Zoological Museum in Copenhagen, Denmark from 1892 until 1946.

Chelonians The largest of all chelonians is the Pacific leatherback
Largest turtle (*Dermochelys coriacea schlegelii*). The average adult measures 6–7 ft *1,83–2,13 m* in overall length (length of carapace 4–5 ft [*122–152 cm*]) and weighs between 660 and 800 lb. *299–363 kg*. The greatest weight reliably recorded is 1,908 lb. *865 kg* for a specimen captured off Monterey, California, U.S.A. in 1961 which is now on permanent display at the Wharf Aquarium, Fisherman's Wharf, Monterey. The largest chelonian found in British waters is the Atlantic leatherback turtle (*Dermochelys coriacea coriacea*). One weighing 997 lb. *452 kg* and measuring more than 7 ft *2,13 m* in length was caught by a French fishing trawler in the English Channel on 8 May 1958, and another specimen reportedly weighing 1,345 lb. *610 kg* was caught by a fishing vessel in the North Sea on 6 Oct. 1951.

The largest living tortoise is *Geochelone* (*Testudo*) *gigantea* of the Indian Ocean islands of Aldabra, Mauritius, Réunion and Seychelles (introduced 1874). Adult males sometimes exceed 350 lb. *158 kg* in weight and a specimen weighing 900 lb. *408 kg* was allegedly collected in Aldabra in 1847.

Longest Tortoises are the longest lived of all vertebrates. (See
lived Animal Kingdom Records above.) Other reliable records over 100 years include a Common box tortoise (*Testudo carolina*) of 138 years and a European pond-tortoise (*Emys orbicularis*) of 120+ years. The greatest proven age of a continuously observed tortoise is 116+ years for a Mediterranean spur-thighed tortoise (*Testudo graeca*) which died in Paignton Zoo, Devon in 1957. On 19 May 1966 the death was reported of "Tu'imalilia" or "Tui Malela", the famous but much battered Madagascar radiated tortoise (*Testudo radiata*) reputedly presented to the King of Tonga by Captain James Cook in 1773, but this record lacks proper documentation.

Slowest Tests on a giant tortoise (*Geochelone gigantea*) in
moving Mauritius show that even when hungry and enticed by a cabbage it cannot cover more than 5 yds *4,57 m* in a min (0.17 m.p.h.) [*0,27 km/h*] on land. Over longer distances its speed is greatly reduced.

SNAKES

Longest The longest (and the heaviest) of all snakes is the
World Anaconda (*Eunectes murinus*) of tropical South America. The largest anaconda on record was probably a specimen shot on the upper Orinoco River, eastern Colombia in 1944 which later recovered and escaped. It had been provisionally measured at 37½ ft *11,43 m*. Another anaconda killed on the lower Rio Guaviare, in south-eastern Colombia in November 1956 reportedly measured 10,25 m *33 ft 7½ in*, but nothing of this snake was preserved. In 1912 a Reticulated python (*Python reticulatus*) measuring 10 m *32 ft 9½ in* was killed near a mining camp on the north coast of Celebes in the Malay Archipelago. An African rock python (*Python sebae*) measuring 9,81 m *32 ft 2¼ in* was killed in the grounds of a school at Bingerville, Ivory Coast in 1932.

In Captivity The longest snake ever kept in a zoo was probably "Colossus", a female Reticulated python (*Python reticulatus*), who died of reptilian tuberculosis on 15 April 1963 in the Highland Park Zoological Gardens, Pittsburgh, Pennsylvania, U.S.A. She measured 28 ft 6 in *8,68 m* on 15 Nov. 1956 and was probably at least 29 ft *8,84 m* at the time of her death. Her maximum girth before a feed was measured at 36 in *91 cm* on 2 March 1955 and she weighed 22 st. 12 lb. *145 kg* on 12 June 1957. A long-standing reward

of \$5,000 (now £*1,923*) offered by the New York Zoological Society in Bronx Park, New York City, U.S.A. for the skin or vertebral column of a snake measuring more than 30 ft *9,14 m* has never been collected.

The longest snake living in captivity anywhere in the world today is a female Reticulated python named "Cassius" owned by Mr. Adrian Nyoka at Knaresborough Zoo, Yorkshire. In January 1973 this specimen (collected in Malaysia in 1972) measured 27 ft 4 in *8,33 m* in length and weighed 220 lb. *99 kg*.

British The longest snake found in Britain is the Grass snake (*Natrix natrix*), which is found throughout southern England, parts of Wales and in Dumfries-shire, Scotland. Adult males average 610 mm *24.01 in* in length and adult females 760 mm *29.92 in*. The longest accurately measured specimen on record was probably a female killed in South Wales in 1887 which measured 1 775 mm *5 ft 9.88 in*.

Shortest The shortest known snake is the thread snake (*Leptotyphlops bilineata*), which is found on the islands of Martinique, Barbados and St. Lucia in the West Indies. It has a maximum recorded length of 11,9 cm *4.7 in*.

Heaviest The heaviest snake is the Anaconda (*Eunectes murinus*). The specimen shot in eastern Colombia in 1944 (see above) probably weighed nearly 1,000 lb. *454 kg*. The heaviest venomous snake is the Eastern diamond-back rattlesnake (*Crotalus adamanteus*) of the southeastern United States. One specimen measuring 7 ft 9 in *2,36 m* in length weighed 34 lb. *15 kg*. Less reliable lengths up to 8 ft 9 in *2,66 m* and weights up to 40 lb. *18 kg* have been reported. A 15 ft 7 in *4,75 m* King cobra (*Ophiophagus hannah*) captured alive on Singapore Island and presented to Raffles Museum weighed 26½ lb. *12 kg*.

Venomous The longest venomous snake in the world is the King
Longest and cobra (*Ophiophagus hannah*), also called the Hama-
Shortest dryad, of south-east Asia and the Philippines. A specimen collected near Port Dickson in the state of Negri Sembilan, Malaya in April 1937 grew to 18 ft 9 in *5,71 m* in London Zoo. The shortest venomous snake is probably Peringuey's adder (*Bitis peringueyi*) of south-west Africa which has a maximum recorded length of 12 in *31 cm*.

Oldest The greatest irrefutable age recorded for a snake is 35 years 6 months in the case of a common boa (*Boa constrictor constrictor*) at Philadelphia Zoological Gardens, Philadelphia, Pennsylvania, U.S.A. which was still alive on 10 Aug. 1972.

Fastest The fastest moving land snake is probably the slender
moving Black mamba (*Dendroaspis polylepis*). On 23 April 1906 an angry Black mamba was timed at a speed of 7 m.p.h. *11 km/h* over a measured distance of 47 yds *43 m* near Mbuyuni on the Serengeti Plains, Kenya. Stories that Black mambas can overtake galloping horses (maximum speed 43.26 m.p.h. [*69,62 km/h*]) are wild exaggerations, though a speed of 15 m.p.h. *24 km/h* may be possible for short bursts over level ground. The British grass snake (*Natrix natrix*) has a maximum speed of 4.2 m.p.h. *6,8 km/h*.

Most The world's most venomous snake is now believed to
venomous be the sea snake (*Hydrophis belcheri*) which has a venom one hundred times as effective as that of the Australian taipan. The snake abounds round Ashmore Reef in the Timor Sea, off North West Australia. The most venomous land snake is probably the peninsular tiger snake (*Notechis ater niger*) found on Kangaroo Island and in the Sir Joseph Banks Group in Spencers Gulf, South Australia which grows to a length of 4 to 5 ft *1,22 m–1,52 m*. The average venom yield is sufficient to kill 300 sheep. It is estimated that

between 30,000 and 40,000 people (excluding Chinese and Russians) die from snakebite each year, 75 per cent of them in densely populated India. Burma has the highest mortality rate with 15.4 deaths per 100,000 population per annum.

Britain The only venomous snake in Britain is the Adder (*Vipera berus*). Since 1890 nine people have died after being bitten by this snake, including five children. The most recently recorded death was on 13 May 1957 when a 14-year-old boy was bitten on the right hand at Carey Camp, near Wareham, Dorset and died three hours later. The longest specimen recorded was one of 38 in *9,65 cm* killed on Walberswick Common, Suffolk on 7 July 1971.

Longest The longest fangs of any snake are those of the
fangs Gaboon viper (*Bitus gabonica*) of tropical Africa. In a 6 ft *1,83 m* long specimen they measured 50 mm *1.96 in*. On 12 Feb. 1963 a Gaboon viper bit itself to death in the Philadelphia Zoological Gardens, Philadelphia, Pennsylvania, U.S.A. Keepers found the dead snake with its fangs deeply embedded in its own back.

4. AMPHIBIANS (*Amphibia*)

Largest The largest species of amphibian is the Chinese giant
World salamander (*Megalobatrachus davidianus*), which lives in the cold mountain streams and marshy areas of north-eastern, central and southern China. The average adult measures 1 m *39,37 in* in total length and weighs 11–13 kg *24.2 to 28.6 lb*. One huge individual collected in Kweichow (Guizhou) Province in southern China in the early 1920s measured 5 ft *1,52 m* in total length and weighed nearly 100 lb. *45 kg*. The Japanese giant salamander (*Megalobatrachus japonicus*) is slightly smaller, but one captive specimen weighed 40 kg *88 lb*. when alive and 45 kg *100 lb*. after death, the body having absorbed water from the aquarium.

Britain The largest British amphibian is the Warty or Great crested newt (*Triturus cristatus*). One specimen collected at Hampton, Middlesex measured 16,2 cm *6.37 in* in total length, and another one collected at Dunbar, East Lothian, Scotland weighed 10,6 g *0.37 oz*.

Newt The largest newt in the world is the Pleurodele or Ribbed newt (*Pleurodeles waltl*), which is found in Morocco and on the Iberian Peninsula. Specimens measuring up to 40 cm *15.74 in* in total length and weighing over 1 lb. *450 g* have been reliably reported.

Frog The largest known frog is the rare Goliath frog (*Rana*
World *goliath*) of Cameroun and Spanish Guinea, West Africa. A female weighing 3 306 g *7 lb. 4.5 oz*. was caught in the rapids of the River Mbia, Spanish Guinea on 23 Aug. 1960. It had a snout-vent length of 34 cm *13.38 in* and measured 81,5 cm *32.08 in* overall with legs extended. In December 1960 another giant frog known locally as "agak" or "carn-pnag" and said to measure 12–15 in *30–38 cm* snout to vent and weigh over 6 lb. *2 kg 70* was reportedly discovered in central New Guinea, but further information is lacking. In 1969 a new species of giant frog was discovered in Sumatra.

Britain The largest frog found in Britain is the *introduced* Marsh frog (*Rana r. ridibunda*). Adult males have been measured up to 9,6 cm *3.77 in* snout to vent, and adult females up to 12,6 cm *4.96 in*, the weight ranging from 60 to 95 g *1.7 oz*. to *3 oz*.

Tree frog The largest species of tree frog is *Hyla vasta*, found only on the island of Hispaniola (Haiti and the Dominican Republic) in the West Indies. The average snout-vent length is about 9 cm *3.54 in* but a female collected from the San Juan River, Dominican Republic, in March 1928 measured 14,3 cm *5.63 in*.

Toad The most massive toad in the world is probably the
World Marine toad (*Bufo marinus*) of tropical South America. An enormous female collected on 24 Nov. 1965 at Miraflores Vaupes, Colombia and later exhibited in the Reptile House at Bronx Zoo, New York City, U.S.A. had a snout vent length of 23,8 cm *9.37 in* and weighed 1 302 g *2 lb. 11¼ oz*. at the time of its death in 1967.

Britain The largest toad found in Britain is the Common toad (*Bufo vulgaris*). An adult female of 10,2 cm *3.94 in* in length has been recorded.

Smallest The smallest species of amphibian is believed to be the
World arrow-poison frog *Sminthillus limbatus*, found only in Cuba. Adult specimens have a snout-vent length of 8,5–12,4 mm *0.33–0.48 in*.

Britain The smallest amphibian found in Britain is the Palmate newt (*Triturus helveticus*). Adult specimens measure 7,5–9,2 cm *2.95–3.62 in* in total length and weigh up to 2,39 g *0.083 oz*. The Natterjack or Running toad (*Bufo calamita*) has a maximum snout-vent length of only 8 cm *3.14 in*, but it is a bulkier animal.

Newt The smallest newt in the world is believed to be the Striped newt (*Notophthalmus perstriatus*) of the south-eastern United States. Adult specimens average 51 mm *2.01 in* in total length.

Tree frog The smallest tree frog in the world is the Least tree frog (*Hyla ocularis*), found in the south-eastern United States. It has a maximum snout-vent length of 15,8 mm *0.62 in*.

The world's smallest species of toad, from Mozambique which have a maximum length of 0.94 in *24 mm*

Toad The smallest toad in the world is the sub-species *Bufo taitanus beiranus*, first discovered in *c*. 1906 near Beira, Mozambique, East Africa. Adult specimens have a maximum recorded snout-vent length of 24 mm *0.94 in*.

Salamander The smallest species of salamander is the Pygmy salamander (*Desmognathus wrighti*), which is found only in Tennessee, North Carolina and Virginia, U.S.A. Adult specimens measure from 37 to 50,8 mm *1.45 to 2.0 in*. in total length.

Longest The greatest authentic age recorded for an amphibian
lived is about 55 years for a male Japanese giant salamander (*Megalobatrachus japonicus*) which died in the aquarium at Amsterdam Zoological Gardens on 3 June 1881. It was brought to Holland in 1829, at which time it was estimated to be three years old.

Highest and lowest The greatest altitude at which an amphibian has been found is 8 000 m *26,246 ft* for a Common toad (*Bufo vulgaris*) collected in the Himalayas. This species has also been found at a depth of 340 m *1,115 ft* in a coal mine.

Most poisonous The most active known poison is the batrachotoxin derived from the skin secretions of the Kokoi (*Phyllobates latinasus*), an arrow-poison frog found in north-western Colombia, South America. Only about 1/100,000th of a gramme *0.0000004 oz.* is sufficient to kill a man.

Longest jump Frog The record for three consecutive leaps is 32 ft 3 in *9,83 m* by a 2 in *5 cm* long South African sharp-nosed frog (*Rana oxyrhyncha*) named "Leaping Lena" (later discovered to be a male) on Green Point Common, Cape Town on 16 Jan. 1954. At the annual Calaveras County Jumping Frog Jubilee at Angels Camp, California, U.S.A. in May 1955 another male of this species made an unofficial *single* leap of over 15 ft *4,57 m* when being retrieved for placement in its container.

5. FISHES (*Pisces, Bradyodonti, Selachii, Marsipoli*)

Largest Marine World The largest fish in the world is the rare plankton-feeding Whale shark (*Rhiniodon typus*), which is found in the warmer areas of the Atlantic, Pacific and Indian Oceans. It is not, however, the largest marine animal, since it is smaller than the larger species of whales (mammals). In 1919 a Whale shark measuring 59 ft *18 m* in length and weighing an estimated 42.4 tons *43 tonnes* was trapped in a bamboo stake-trap at Koh Chik, in the Gulf of Siam. The largest carnivorous fish (excluding plankton eaters) is the rare Great white shark (*Carcharodon carcharias*), also called the "Man-eater", which is found mainly in tropical and sub-tropical waters. In June 1930 a specimen measuring 37 ft *11,27 m* in length was found trapped in a herring weir at White Head Island, New Brunswick, Canada. Another Great white shark which ran aground in False Bay, near the Cape of Good Hope, South Africa many years ago reportedly measured 43 ft *13,10 m* but further information is lacking. The longest of the bony or "true" fishes (Pisces) is the Russian sturgeon (*Acipenser huso*), also called the Beluga, which is found in the temperate areas of the Adriatic, Black and Caspian Seas but enters large rivers like the Volga and the Danube for spawning. Lengths up to 8 m *26 ft 3 in* have been reliably reported, and a gravid female taken in the estuary of the Volga in 1827 weighed 1 474 kg 20 *1.44 tons*. The heaviest bony fish in the world is the Ocean sunfish (*Mola mola*), which is found in all tropical, sub-tropical and temperate waters. On 18 Sept. 1908 a huge specimen was accidentally struck by the S.S. *Fiona* off Bird Island about 40 miles *65 km* from Sydney, New South Wales, Australia and towed to Port Jackson. It measured 14 ft *4,26 m* between the anal and dorsal fins and weighed 2.24 tons/*2,28 tonnes*.

Britain The largest fish ever recorded in the waters of the British Isles was a Basking shark (*Cetorhinus maximus*) measuring 40 ft *12 m* in length and 25 ft *7,62 m* in maximum girth killed off Mutton Island, Galway Bay, western Ireland. It weighed an estimated 14 tons /*tonne*. The largest bony fish found in British waters is the Ocean sunfish (*Mola mola*). A specimen measuring 6 ft 6 in *1,98 m* between the anal and dorsal fins and weighing 672 lb. *305 kg* was washed ashore at Kessingland near Lowestoft, Suffolk on 19 Dec. 1948.

Largest Freshwater World The largest fish which spends its whole life in fresh or brackish water is the European catfish or Wels (*Silurus glanis*). In September 1918 a specimen measuring nearly 11 ft *3,35 m* in length and weighing 256 kg 70 *564.74 lb.* was caught in the Desna River, six miles

9 km from Chernigou in the Ukraine, U.S.S.R. Another one caught in the Dnieper River near Kremenchug, U.S.S.R. allegedly weighed 300 kg *660 lb.*, but further details are lacking. The Arapaima (*Arapaima gigas*), also called the Pirarucu, found in the Amazon and other South American rivers and often claimed to be the largest freshwater fish, averages 6½ ft *2 m* and 150 lb. *68 kg*. The largest 'authentically recorded" measured 8 ft 1½ in *2,48 m* in length and weighed 325 lb. *147 kg*. It was caught in the Rio Negro, Brazil in 1836.

Britain The largest fish ever caught in a British river was a Common sturgeon (*Acipenser sturio*) weighing 460 lb. *208 kg* taken in the Esk, Yorkshire in 1810. Another one allegedly weighing "over 500 lb. *[227 kg]*" was caught in the Severn at Lydney, Glos. on 1 June 1937 and sent to Billingsgate, London, but further details are lacking. Larger specimens have been taken at sea—notably one weighing 700 lb. *317 kg* and 10 ft 5 in *3,18 m* long netted by the trawler *Ben Urie* off the Orkneys and landed at Aberdeen on 18 Oct. 1956.

Smallest Marine The smallest recorded marine fishes are the Marshall Islands goby (*Eviota zonura*) measuring 12 to 16 mm *0.47 to 0.63 in* and *Schindleria praematurus* from Samoa, measuring 12 to 19 mm *0.47 to 0 74 in*, both in the Pacific Ocean. Mature specimens of the latter fish, which was not described until 1940, have been known to weigh only 2 mg, equivalent to 17,750 to the oz—the lightest of all vertebrates and the smallest catch possible for any fisherman. The smallest British marine fish is the Diminutive or Scorpion goby (*Gobios scorpoides*) of the English Channel which measures 20 to 25 mm *0.78 to 0.98 in* in length.

Freshwater The shortest known fish, and the shortest of all vertebrates, is the Dwarf pygmy goby (*Pandaka pygmaea*), a colourless and nearly transparent fish found in the streams and lakes of Luzon in the Philippines. Adult males measures only 7,5 to 9,9 mm *0.28 to 0.38 in* in length and weigh 4 to 5 mg *0.00014 to 0.00017 oz.*

Fastest The Sailfish (*Isiophorus platypterus*) is generally considered to be the fastest species of fish, although the practical difficulties of measurement make data extremely difficult to secure. A figure of 68.18 m.p.h. *109,73 km/h* (100 yds [*91 m*] in 3 sec) has been cited for one off Florida, U.S.A. The Swordfish (*Xiphias gladius*) has also been credited with very high speeds, but the evidence is based mainly on bills that have been found deeply embedded in ships' timbers. A speed of 50 knots (57.6 m.p.h. [*92,7 km/h*]) has been calculated from a penetration of 22 in *56 cm* by a bill into a piece of timber, but 30 to 35 knots (35 to 40 m.p.h. [*56-64 km/h*]) is the most conceded by some experts. Speeds in excess of 35 knots (40 m.p.h. [*64 km/h*]) have also been attributed to the Marlin (*Tetrapturus sp.*), the Wahoo (*Acanthocybium solandri*), the Great blue shark (*Prionace glauca*) and the Bonefish (*Albula vulpes*), and the Bluefin tuna (*Thunnus thynnus*) has been scientifically clocked at 43.4 m.p.h. *69,8 km/h* in a 20 sec dash. The Four-winged flying fish (*Cypselurus hetererurs*) may also exceed 40 m.p.h. *64 km/h* during its rapid rush to the surface before take-off (the average speed in the air is about 35 m.p.h. [*56 km/h*]). Record flights of 42 sec, 36 ft *11 m* in altitude and 1,200 ft *366 m* length have been recorded in the tropical Atlantic.

Longest lived Aquaria are of too recent origin to be able to establish with certainty which species of fish can fairly be regarded as the longest lived. Early indications are that it is the Lake sturgeon (*Acipenser fulvescens*). One specimen 6 ft 7 in *2,01 m* long caught in the Lake Winnebago region, Wisconsin, U.S.A. was believed to be 82 years old based on a count of the growth rings (*annuli*) in the marginal ray of the pectoral fin. Another Lake sturgeon 6 ft 9 in *2,05 m* long and weighing

215 lb. *97 kg* caught in the Lake of the Woods, Kenora, Ontario, Canada on 15 July 1953 was believed to be 150 years old based on a growth ring count, but this extreme figure has been questioned by some authorities. A figure of 150 years has also been attributed to the Mirror carp (*Cyprinus carpion*), but the greatest authoritatively accepted age is "more than 50 years". Other long-lived fish include the European sterlet (*Acipenser ruthenus*) with 69 years, the European catfish (*Silurus glanis*) with 60+ years, the European freshwater eel (*Anguilla anguilla*) with 55 years and the American eel (*Anguilla chrisypa*) with 50 years.

Oldest goldfish The exhibition life of a Goldfish (*Carassius auratus*) is normally about 17 years, but much greater ages have been reliably reported. There is a record of a goldfish living in a water-butt for 40 years.

Shortest lived There are several contenders for the title of shortest-lived fish. One of them is the Transparent or White goby (*Latrunculus pellucidus*), which hatches, grows, reproduces and dies in less than a year. Other "annuals" include the Top minnow (*Gambusia holbrookii*), the Sea horse (*Hippocampus hudsonius*), the Dwarf pygmy goby (*Pandaka pygmaea*) and the Ice fishes (family Chaenichthyidae) of the Antarctic.

Deepest The greatest depth from which a fish has been recovered is 8 300 m *27,230 ft* in the Puerto Rico Trench (27,488 ft [*8 366 m*]) in the Atlantic by Dr Gilbert L. Voss of the U.S. research vessel *John Elliott* who took a 6½ in *16,5 cm* long *Bassiogigas profundissimus* in April 1970. It was only the fifth ever caught. Dr. Jacques Piccard and Lieutenant Don Walsh, U.S. Navy, reported they saw a sole-like fish about 1 ft *33 cm* long (tentatively identified as *Chascanopsetta lugubris*) from the bathyscaphe *Trieste* at a depth of 35,802 ft *10 912 m* in the Challenger Deep (Marianas Trench) in the western Pacific on 24 Jan. 1960. This sighting, however, has been questioned by some authorities, who still regard the brotulids of the genus *Bassogigas* as the deepest-living vertebrates.

Most eggs The Ocean sunfish (*Mola mola*) produces up to 300,000,000 eggs, each of them measuring about 0.05 in *0,127 mm* in diameter. The egg yield of the guppy *Poecilia reticulatus* is usually only 40–50, but these are borne to maturity. A female measuring 1¼ in *31 mm* in length had only four in her ovaries.

Most venomous The most venomous fish in the world are the Stonefish (family Synanceidae) of the tropical waters of the Indo-Pacific. Direct contact with the spines of their fins, which contain a strong neurotoxic poison, often proves fatal.

Most electric The most powerful electric fish is the Electric eel (*Electrophorus electricus*), which is found in the rivers of Brazil, Columbia, Venezuela and Peru. An average sized specimen can discharge 400 volts at 1 ampere, but measurements up to 650 volts have been recorded.

6. STARFISHES (*Asteroida*)

Largest The largest of the 1,600 known species of starfish in terms of total diameter is the very fragile *Brisingid midgardia xandaros*. A specimen collected by the Texas A & M University research vessel *Alaminos* in the southern part of the Gulf of Mexico in the late summer of 1968, measured 1 380 mm *54.33 in* on tip to tip but the diameter of its disc was only 26 mm *1.02 in*. Its dry weight was only 70 g *2.46 oz*. The most massive species of starfish is probably the five-armed *Evasterias echinosomo* of the North Pacific. One specimen collected by a Russian expedition in the flooded crater of a volcano in Broughton Bay, Semushir, one of the Kurile Islands in June 1970 measured 96 cm *37.79 in* in total diameter and weighed more

The smallest starfish found in British waters, *Asterrina gibbosa*, known as the Cushion Starfish

than 5 kg *11 lb*. The largest starfish found in British waters is the northern sun star (*Solaster endeca*), which has been measured up to 40 cm *15.74 in* in total diameter.

Smallest The smallest recorded starfish is the North Pacific deep-sea species *Leptychaster propinquus*, which has a maximum total diameter of 18,3 mm *0.72 in*. The smallest starfish found in British waters is the Cushion starfish (*Asterrina gibbosa*), which has a maximum total diameter of 60 mm *2.36 in*.

Deepest The greatest depth from which a Starfish has been recovered is 7 584 m *24,880 ft* for a specimen of *Porcellanaster sp.* collected by the U.S.S.R. research ship *Vityaz* in the Marianas Trench, in the Pacific in 1959. These parasitic crabs are found in the mantle cavities of the bivalve molluscs such as oysters, muscles and scallops.

7. ARACHNIDS (*Arachnida*)

SPIDERS (Order Araneae)

Largest World The world's largest known spider is the bird-eating spider *Theraphosa leblondi* of northern South America. A male specimen with a leg span of 10 in *25 cm* when fully extended and a body length of 3½ in *8,9 cm* was collected at Montagne la Gabrielle, French Guiana in April 1925. It weighed nearly 2 oz *56 g*. The heaviest spider ever recorded was a female "tarantula" of the genus *Lasiodora* collected at Manaos, Brazil in 1945. It measured 9½ in *241 mm* across the legs and weighed almost 3 oz *85 g*.

Britain Of the 617 known British species of spider covering an estimated population of over 500,000,000,000,000, the Cardinal spider (*Tegenaria parietina*) has the greatest leg span, males sometimes exceeding 5 in *125 mm* (length of body up to 19 mm [*or 0.75 in*]). This spider is found only in southern England. The well-known "Daddy Longlegs" spider (*Pholcus phanlangoides*) rarely exceeds 3 in *75 mm* in leg span, but one outsized specimen collected in England measured 6 in *152 mm* across. The heaviest spider found in Britain is probably the orb weaver *Araneus quadratus* (formerly called *Araneus reaumuri*). An averaged-sized specimen collected in October 1943 weighed 1,174 g *0.041 oz.* and measured 15 mm *0.58 in* in body length.

Smallest World The smallest known spider is *Microlinypheus bryophilus* (family Argiopedae), discovered in Lorne, Victoria, Australia in January 1928. Adult males have a body length of 0,6 mm *0.023 in* and adult females 0,8 mm *0.031 in*. The smallest spider found in Britain is the money spider *Glyphesis cottonae*, which is confined to a swamp near Beaulieu Road Station, New Forest, Hants and Thurley Heath, Surrey. Adult specimens of both sexes have a body length of 1 mm *0.039 in.*

Largest webs The largest webs are the aerial ones spun by the tropical orb weavers of the genus *Nephila*, which have been measured up to 18 ft 9¾ in *573 cm* in circumference. The smallest webs are spun by spiders like *Glyphesis cottonae*, etc. which are about the size of a postage stamp.

Most venomous The most venomous spider in the world is probably *Latrodectus mactans* of the Americas, which is better known as the "black widow" in the United States. Females of this species (the much smaller males are harmless) have a bite capable of killing a human being, but deaths are rare. The Funnel web spider (*Atrax robustus*) of Australia, the Jockey spider (*Latrodectus hasseltii*) of Australia and New Zealand, the Button spider (*Latrodectus indistinctus*) of South Africa, the Podadora (*Glyptocranium gasteracanthoides*) of Argentina and the Brown recluse spider (*Loxosceles reclusa*) of the central and southern United States have also been credited with fatalities.

Rarest The most elusive of all spiders are the primitive atypical tarantulas of the genus *Liphistius*, which are found in south-east Asia. The most elusive spider in Britain is the handsome crimson and black Lace web eresus spider (*Eresus niger*), found in Hampshire, Dorset and Cornwall, which is known only from eight specimens (seven males and one female). In the early 1950s a specimen was reportedly seen at Sandown on the Isle of Wight, but it escaped.

Fastest The highest speed recorded for a spider on a level surface is 1.73 ft *53 cm/sec* (1.17 m.p.h. [*1,88 km/h*]) in the case of a specimen of *Tegenaria atrica*.

Longest lived The longest lived of all spiders are the primitive *Mygalomorphae* (tarantulas and allied species). One mature female tarantula collected at Mazatlan, Mexico in 1935 and estimated to be 12 years old at the time, was kept in a laboratory for 16 years, making a total of 28 years. The longest-lived British spider is probably the purse web spider (*Atypus affinis*). One specimen was kept in a greenhouse for nine years.

8. CRUSTACEANS (*Crustacea*)

(Crabs, lobsters, shrimps, prawns, crayfish, barnacles, water fleas, fish lice, woodlice, sandhoppers, kril, etc.)

Largest World The largest of all crustaceans (although not the heaviest) is the giant spider crab (*Macrocheira kaempferi*), also called the stilt crab, which is found in deep waters off the south-eastern coast of Japan. Mature specimens usually have a 12–14 in *30–35 cm* wide body and a claw-span of 8–9 ft *2,43–2,74 m* but unconfirmed measurements up to 19 ft *5,79 m* have been reported. A specimen with a claw span of 12 ft 1½ in *3,69 m* weighed 14 lb. *6 kg.*

The largest species of lobster, and the heaviest of all crustaceans, is the American or North Atlantic lobster (*Homarus americanus*). One weighing 42 lb. 7 oz. *19 kg 050* and measuring 4 ft *121 cm* from the end of the tail-fan to the tip of the claw was caught by the smack *Hustler* in a deep-sea trawl off the Virginia Capes, Virginia, U.S.A. in 1934 and is now on display in the Museum of Science, Boston, Massachusetts. Another specimen allegedly weighing 48 lb. *21 kg 772* was caught off Chatham, New England, U.S.A. in 1949.

Britain The largest crustacean found in British waters is the common or European lobster (*Homarus vulgarus*), which averages 2–3 lb. *900–1 360 g* in weight. On 17 Aug. 1967 a lobster weighing 14½ lb. *6 kg 575* was

Skin diver David Rollinson with an 11 lb. crab—the biggest landed in Britain this century

caught by a skin-diver off St. Ann's Head, Pembrokeshire, Wales. It is now mounted in the "Coracle Restaurant" at the Glan-y-môr Country Club, Laugharne, Carmarthenshire. The largest crab found in British waters is the Edible or great crab (*Cancer pagurus*). In 1895 a crab measuring 11 in *279 mm* across the shell and weighing 14 lb. *6 kg 350* was caught off the coast of Cornwall.

Smallest The smallest known crustaceans are water fleas of the genus *Alonella*, which may measure less than 0,25 mm *0.0098 in* in length. They are found in British waters. The smallest known lobster is the Cape lobster (*Homarus capensis*) of South Africa which measures 10–12 cm *3.93–4.72 in* in total length. The smallest crabs in the world are the aptly named pea crabs (family Pinnotheridae). Some species have a shell diameter of only 0.25 in *63 mm*, including *Pinnotheres pisum* which is found in British waters.

Longest lived The longest lived of all crustaceans is the American lobster (*Homarus americanus*). Very large specimens may be as much as 50 years old.

Deepest The greatest depth from which a crustacean has been recovered is 9 790 m *32.119 ft* for an amphiopod (order Amphiopoda) collected by the Galathea Deep Sea Expedition in the Philippine Trench in 1951. The marine crab *Ethusina abyssicola* has been taken at a depth of 14,000 ft *4 265 m.*

9. INSECTS (*Insecta*)

Heaviest World The heaviest insect in the world is the Goliath beetle *Goliathus giganteus* of equatorial Africa. One specimen measuring 14,85 cm *5.85 in* in length (jaw to tip of abdomen) and 10 cm *3.93 in* across the back weighed 3.52 oz. *99,8 g.* The longhorn beetles *Titanus giganteus* of South America and *Xinuthrus heros* of the Fiji Islands are also massive insects, and both have been measured up to 15 cm *5.9 in* in length. The largest beetle found in Britain is the stag beetle (*Lucanus cervus*) widely distributed over southern England. The largest specimen on record was a male collected at Sheerness, Kent, in 1871 and now preserved in the British Museum (Natural History), London, which measures 77,4 mm *3.04 in* in length (body plus mandibles) and probably weighed over 6,000 mg when alive. The large tortoise shell (*Nymphalis polychloros*), which is now confined mainly to Essex and the Kent–Sussex border, has not been reported to have bred in Britain for several years.

Longest The longest insect in the world is the tropical stick-insect *Pharnacia serratipes*, females of which have been measured up to 33 cm *12.99 in* in body length. The longest known beetle (excluding antenae) is the Hercules beetle (*Dynastes hercules*) of Central and South America, which has been measured up to 18 cm *7.08 in*, but over half of this length is accounted for by the "prong" from the thorax. The longhorn beetle *Batocera wallacei* of New Guinea has been measured up to 26,7 cm *10.5 in*, but 19 cm *7.5 in* of this was antenna.

Smallest The smallest insects recorded so far are the "Hairy-
World winged" beetles of the family Trichopterygidae and the "battledore-wing fairy flies" (parasitic wasps) of the family Mymaridae. They measure only 0,2 mm *0.008 in* in length, and the fairy flies have a wing span of only 1 mm *0.04 in*. This makes them smaller than some of the protozoa (single-celled animals). The male bloodsucking banded louse (*Enderleinellus zonatus*), ungorged, and the parasitic wasp *Caraphractus cinctus* may each weigh as little as 0,005 mg, *or 567,000 to an oz.* The eggs of the latter each weigh 0.0002 mg, *or 14,175,000 to the oz.*

Fastest Experiments have proved that the widely publicised
flying claim by an American entomologist in 1926 that the Deer bot-fly (*Cephenemyia pratti*) could attain a speed of 818 m.p.h. *1 316 km/h* (*sic*) was wildly exaggerated. Acceptable modern experiments have now established that the highest maintainable air-speed of any insect, including the Deer bot-fly, is 24 m.p.h. *39 km/h*, rising to a maximum of 36 m.p.h. *58 km/h* for short bursts. A relay of bees (maximum speed 11 m.p.h. [*18 km/h*]) would use only a gallon of nectar in cruising 4,000,000 miles *6,5 million km* at an average speed of 7 m.p.h. *11 km/h.*

Longest The longest-lived insects are queen termites (*Isoptera*),
lived which have been known to lay eggs for up to 50 years.

Loudest The loudest of all insects is the male cicada (family Cicadidae). At 7,400 pulses/min its tymbal organs produce a noise (officially described by the United States Departments of Agriculture as "Tsh-ee-EEEE-e-ou") detectable more than a quarter of a mile *400 m* distant. The only British species is the very rare Mountain cicada (*Cicadetta montana*), which is confined to the New Forest area in Hampshire.

Southern- The farthest south at which any insect has been found
most is 77° S (900 miles [*1 450 km*] from the South Pole) in the case of a springtail (order Collembola).

Largest The greatest swarm of Desert locusts (*Schistocerea*
locust *gregaria*) ever recorded was one covering an estimated
swarm 2,000 miles² *5 180 km²* observed crossing the Red Sea in 1889. Such a swarm must have contained about 250,000,000,000 insects weighing about 500,000 tons *508 000 tonnes.*

Fastest The fastest wing beat of any insect under natural
wing beat conditions is 62,760 a min by a tiny midge of the genus *Forcipomyia*. In experiments with truncated wings at a temperature of 37° C *98.6° F* the rate increased to 133,080 beats/min. The muscular contraction-expansion cycle in 0.00045 or 1/2,218th of a sec, further represents the fastest muscle movement ever measured.

Slowest The slowest wing beat of any insect is 300 a min by
wing beat the swallowtail butterfly (*Papilo machaon*). Most butterflies beat their wings at a rate of 460 to 636 a min.

Largest ants The largest ant in the world is the Driver ant (*Dinoponera grandis*) of Africa, workers of which measure up to 33 mm *1.31 in* in length. The largest of the 27 species found in Britain is the Wood ant (*Formica rufa*), males reaching 9 mm *0.35 in* and queens 11 mm *0.43 in*. The smallest is the Thief ant (*Solenopsis fugax*), whose workers measure 1,5–3 mm *0.059–0.18 in.*

Hive record The greatest reported amount of wild honey ever extracted from a single hive is 300 lb. *136 kg* recorded by Mr A. I. Root in Medina, Ohio, U.S.A. *c* 1895.

Bush- The bush-cricket with the largest wing span is the New
cricket Guinean grasshopper *Siliquofera grandis* with female
Largest examples measuring more than 10 in *254 mm*. *Pseudophyllanax imperialis*, found on the island of New Caledonia in the south-western Pacific has antennae measuring up to 8 in *203 mm*. The largest bush-cricket found in Britain is *Tettigonia viridissima*, which normally has a body length of 1¼ in *31,8 mm*. In August 1953 a female measuring 77 mm *3.03 in* in body length (including ovipositor) was caught in a sand pit at Grays, Essex and later presented to London Zoological Gardens. The largest of the 14 true grass-hoppers found in Britain is *Mecostethus grossus*, females of which measure up to 39 mm *1.53 in* in body length.

Dragonflies The largest dragonfly in the world is *Tetracanthagyne*
Largest *plagiata* of north-eastern Borneo, which is known only from a single specimen preserved in the British Museum of Natural History, London. This dragonfly has a wing span of 194 mm *7.63 in* and an overall length of 108 mm *4.25 in*. The largest dragonfly found in Britain is the Golden-ringed dragonfly (*Cordulegaster boltoni*), which has been measured up to 84 mm *3.3 in* in overall length and may have a wing span of more than 100 mm *3.93 in*. The smallest British dragonfly is the Scarce ischnura (*Ischnura pumilio*), which has a wing span of 33 mm *1.3 in.*

Flea The largest known flea is *Hystricopsylla schefferi*
Largest discovered in Seattle, Washington, U.S.A. in 1913. Females measure up to 8 mm *0.31 in* in length, which is the diameter of a pencil The largest flea (61 species) found in Britain is the Mole and vole flea (*H talpae*), females of which have been measured up to 6 mm *0.23 in.*

Jump The champion jumper among fleas is the common flea
Longest (*Pulex irritans*). In one American experiment carried out in 1910 a specimen allowed to leap at will performed a long jump of 13 in *330 mm* and a high jump of 7¾ in *197 mm*. In jumping 130 times its own height a flea subjects itself to a force of 200 g. Siphonapterologists recognise 1,830 varieties.

Smallest The smallest known tick is a male *Ixodes soricis* from
and largest a British Columbian shrew, and the largest an en-
tick gorged female, *Amblyomma varium* from a Venezuelan sloth.

BUTTERFLIES AND MOTHS (order Lepidoptera)

Largest The largest known butterfly is the giant birdwing
World *Troides victoriae* of the Solomon Islands in the south-western Pacific. Females may have a wing span exceeding 12 in *30 cm* and weigh over 5 g *0.176 oz*. The largest moth in the world is the Hercules emperor moth (*Coscinoscera hercules*) of tropical Australia and New Guinea. Females measure up to 10½ in *266 mm* across the outspread wings and have a wing area of up to 40.8 in² *263,2 cm²*. The rare Owlet moth (*Thysania agrippina*) of Brazil has been measured up to 30 cm *11.81 in* in wing span, and the Atlas moth (*Attacus atlas*) of south-east Asia up to 28 cm *11.02 in*, but both these species are less bulky than *C. hercules*.

Britain The largest (but not the heaviest) of the 21,000 species of insect found in Britain is the very rare Death's head

CENTIMETRES

INCHES

The world's largest species of moth, a female *Coscinoscera hercules*
found in tropical Australia and New Guinea

hawk moth (*Acherontia atropos*), females of which have
a body length of 60 mm *2.36 in*, a wing span of up to
133 mm *5.25 in* and weigh about 1,6 g *0.065 oz*. The
largest butterfly found in Britain is the Monarch
butterfly (*Danaus plexippus*), also called the Milkweek
or Black-veined brown butterfly, a rare vagrant which
breeds in the southern United States and Central
America. It has a wing span of up to 5 in *127 mm* and
weighs about 1 g *0.04 oz*. The largest *native* butterfly
is the Swallowtail (*Papilo machaon*), females of which
have a wing span of 70–100 mm *2.75–3.93 in*. This
species is now confined to a small area of the Norfolk
Broads.

Smallest The smallest of the 140,000 known species of Lepidop-
World tera is the moth *Nepticula microtheriella*, which has a
wing span of 3–4 mm *0.11–0.15 in* and a body length
of 2 mm *0.078 in*. It is found in Britain. The world's
smallest known butterfly is the dwarf blue (*Brephidium
barberae*) of South Africa. It has a wing span of 14 mm
0.55 in. The smallest butterfly found in Britain is the
Small blue (*Cupido minimus*), which has a wing span of
19–25 mm *0.75–1.0 in*.

Rarest The rarest of all butterflies (and the most valuable) is
the giant birdwing *Troides allottei*, which is found
only on Bougainville in the Solomon Islands. A
specimen was sold for £750 at an auction in Paris on
24 Oct. 1966. The rarest British butterfly is the large
blue (*Maculinea arion*), which is now confined to few
localities in north Cornwall. The total population is
now so small (estimated at only 100–150 in 1972) that
the British Butterfly Conservation Society believe that
it would only need poor weather conditions during the
flight season for this species to become extinct in
Britain. Britain's rarest moth is the Tree-lichen Beauty
(*Briophila algae*), one specimen of which was captured
in Manchester in July 1858.

Most acute The most acute sense of smell exhibited in nature is
sense of that of the male True silkworm moth (*Bombyx mori*)
smell which, according to German experiments in 1961,
can detect the sex signals of the female at the almost
unbelievable range of 11 km *6.8 miles* upwind. This
scent has been identified as one of the higher alcohols
($C_{16}H_{29}OH$), of which the female carries less than
0.0001 mg.

10. CENTIPEDES (*Chilopoda*)

Longest The longest known species of centipede is a large
variant of the widely distributed *Scolopendra morsitans*,
found on the Andaman Islands, Bay of Bengal. Specimens have been measured up to 13 in *330 mm* in
length and 1½ in *38 mm* in breadth. The longest centipede found in Britain is *Haplophilus subterraneus*,
which measures up to 70 mm *2.75 in* in length and
1,4 mm *0.005 in* across the body.

Shortest The shortest recorded centipede is an unidentified
species which measures only 5 mm *0.19 in*. The shortest
centipede found in Britain is *Lithobius dubosequi*, which
measures up to 9,5 mm *0.374 in* in length and 1,1 mm
0.043 in across the body.

Most legs The centipede with the greatest number of legs is
Himantarum gabrielis of southern Europe which has
171–177 pairs when adult.

Fastest The fastest centipede is probably *Scutiger coleoptrata* of
southern Europe which can travel at a rate of 50 cm
19.68 in a sec or 4.47 m.p.h. *7,19 km/h*.

11. MILLIPEDES (*Diplopoda*)

Longest The longest known species of millipede are *Graphi-
dostreptus gigas* of Africa and *Scaphistostreptus
seychellarum* of the Seychelles in the Indian Ocean,
both of which have been measured up to 280 mm
11.02 in in length and 20 mm *0.78 in* in diameter.
The longest millipede found in Britain is *Cylindroiulus
londinensis* which measures up to 50 mm *1.96 in*.

Shortest The shortest millipede in the world is the British species
Polyxenus lagurus, which measures 2,1–4,0 mm *0.082–
0.15 in* in length.

Most legs The greatest number of legs reported for a millipede is
355 pairs (710 legs) for an unidentified South African
species.

12. SEGMENTED WORMS (*Annelida* or *Annulata*)

Longest The longest known species of earthworm is *Megascolides australis*, first discovered in Brandy Creek,
southern Gippsland, Victoria, Australia in 1868. An
average-sized specimen measures 4 ft *121 cm* in length
(2 ft [*61 cm*] when contracted) and nearly 7 ft *213 cm*
when *naturally* extended. The longest accurately
measured *Megascolides* on record was one collected
before 1930 in southern Gippsland which measured
7 ft 2 in *218 cm* in length and over 13 ft *396 cm* when
naturally extended. The eggs of this worm measure
2–3 in *50–75 mm* in length and 0.75 in *19 mm* in
diameter. In November 1967 a specimen of the African
giant earthworm *Microchaetus rappi* (= *M. microchaetus*) measuring 11 ft *335 cm* in length and 21 ft
640 cm when naturally extended was found on the
road between Alice and King William's Town,
Eastern Cape Province, South Africa. The *average*
length of this species, however, is 3 ft 6 in *105 cm* and
6–7 ft *180–210 cm* when naturally extended. The
longest segmented worm found in Britain is *Lumbricus
terrestris*, which has been reliably measured up to
350 mm *13.78 in* when naturally extended.

Shortest The shortest known segmented worm is *Chaetogaster
annandalei*, which measures less than 0,5 mm *0.019 in*
in length.

13. MOLLUSCS (*Mollusca*)
(Squids, octopuses, shellfish, snails, etc.)

Largest squid The heaviest of all invertebrate animals is the Atlantic giant squid (*Architeuthis sp.*). The largest specimen ever recorded was one measuring 55 ft *16,76 m* in total length (head and body 20 ft [*6,09 m*] tentacles 35 ft [*10,66 m*]) captured on 2 Nov. 1878 after it had run aground in Thimble Tickle Bay, Newfoundland, Canada. It weighed an estimated 2 tons/tonnes. In October 1887 a giant squid (*Architeuthis longimanus*) measuring 57 ft *17,37 m* in total length was washed up in Lyall Bay, New Zealand, but 49 ft *14,93 m* of this was tentacle. The largest squid ever recorded in British waters was one found at the head of Whalefirth Voe, Shetland on 2 Oct. 1949 which measured 24 ft *7,31 m* in total length.

Largest octopus The largest known octopus is the Common Pacific octopus (*Octopus apollyon*). One specimen trapped in a fisherman's net in Monterey Bay, California, U.S.A. had a radial spread of over 20 ft *6,09 m* and scaled 110 lb. *49 kg 90*, and a weight of 125 lb. *56 kg 70* has been reported for another individual. In 1874 a radial spread of 32 ft *9,75 m* was reported for an octopus (*Octopus hong-kongensis*) speared in Illiuliuk Harbour, Unalaska Island, Alaska, U.S.A., but the body of this animal only measured 12 in *305 mm* in length and it probably weighed less than 20 lb. *9 kg*. The largest octopus found in British waters is the Common octopus (*Octopus vulgaris*), which has been measured up to 7 ft *2,13 m* in radial spread and may weigh more than 10 lb. *4 kg 50*.

Most ancient mollusc The longest existing living creature is *Neopilina galatheae*, a deep-sea worm-snail which had been believed extinct for about 320,000,000 years. In 1952, however, specimens were found at a depth of 11,400 ft *3 470 m* off Costa Rica by the Danish research vessel *Galathea*. Fossils found in New York State, U.S.A., Newfoundland, Canada, and Sweden show that this mollusc was also living about 500,000,000 years ago.

SHELLS

Largest The largest of all existing bivalve shells is the marine Giant clam (*Tridacna derasa*), which is found on the Indo-Pacific coral reefs. A specimen measuring 43 in *109,2 cm* by 29 in *73,6 cm* and weighing 579½ lb. *262 kg 90* (over a quarter of a ton) was collected from the Great Barrier Reef in 1917, and is now preserved in the American Museum of Natural History, New York City, N.Y., U.S.A. The largest bivalve shell found in British waters is the Fan mussel (*Pinna fragilis*). One specimen found at Tor Bay, Devon measured 37 cm *14.56 in* in length and 20 cm *7.87 in* in breadth at the hind end.

Smallest The smallest bivalve shell found in British waters, and one of the smallest in the world, is *Neolepton skysi*, which measures less than 16 mm *0.629 in* in length. This species is only known from a few specimens collected off Guernsey in the Channel Islands in 1894.

Rarest The most highly prized of all molluscan shells in the hands of conchologists is the 3 in *7,5 cm* long White-tooth cowrie (*Cypraea leucodon*), which is found in the deep waters off the Philippines. Only three examples are known, including one in the British Museum of Natural History, London. The highest price ever paid for a sea shell is £1,350 in a sale at Sotheby's, London, on 4 March 1971 for one of the four known examples of *Conus bengalensis*. The 4-in *10 cm* long shell was trawled by fishermen off north-western Thailand in December 1970.

Longest lived The longest lived mollusc is probably the Freshwater mussel (*Margaritan margaritifera*) which has been credited with a potential maximum longevity of 100 years. The Giant clam (*Tridacna derasa*) lives about 30 years.

SNAILS

Largest The largest known species of snail is the sea hare *Tethys californicus*, which is found in coastal waters off California, U.S.A. The average weight is 7 to 8 lb. *315–360 g* but one specimen scaled 15 lb. 13 oz. *7 kg 172*. The largest known land snail is the African giant snail (*Achatina fulica*), which has been recorded up to 10¾ in *273 mm* in overall length and 1 lb. 2 oz. *510 g* in weight. The largest land snail found in Britain is the Roman or Edible snail (*Helix pomatia*), which measures up to 4 in *10 cm* in overall length and weighs up to 3 oz. *85 g*. The smallest British land snail is *Punctum pygmaeum*, which has a shell measuring 0.023–0.035 of an in *6–9 mm* by 0.047–0.059 of an in *12–15 mm*.

Speed The fastest-moving species of land snail is probably the common garden snail (*Helix aspersa*). According to tests carried out in the United States of America absolute top speed for *Helix aspersa* is 0.0313 m.p.h., (or 55 yds [*50,3 m*] per hr.) while some species are at full stretch at 0.00036 m.p.h., (or 23 in [*58 cm*]] per hr). This snail would thus take over 16 weeks to cover a mile, provided it did not stop for rest or food.

14. RIBBON WORMS (*Nermertina* or *Rhynchopods*)

Longest The longest of the 550 recorded species of ribbon worms, also called nemertines (or nemerteans), is the "Boot-lace worm" (*Lincus longissimus*), which is found in the shallow waters of the North Sea. A specimen washed ashore at St. Andrews, Fifeshire, Scotland in 1864 after a severe storm measured more than 180 ft *55 m* in length, making it easily the longest recorded worm of any variety.

15. JELLYFISHES (*Scyphozoa* or *Scyphomedusia*)

Largest and smallest The largest jellyfish is *Cyanea arctica*. For details see page 33.

The largest coelenterate found in British waters is the rare "Lion's mane" jellyfish (*Cyanea capillata*), which is also known as the Common sea blubber. One specimen measured at St. Andrew's Marine Laboratory, Fifeshire, Scotland had a bell diameter of 91 cm *35.82 in* and tentacles stretching over 45 ft *13,7 m*. Some true jellyfishes have a bell diameter of less than 20 mm *0.78 in*.

Most venomous The most venomous coelenterates are the box jellies of the genera *Chiropsalmus* and *Chironex* of the Indo-Pacific region, which carry a neuro-toxic venom similar in strength to that found in the Asiatic cobra. These jellyfish have caused the deaths of at least 60 people off the coast of Queensland, Australia in the past 25 years. Victims die within 1–3 min. The most effective defence is women's panty hose.

16. SPONGES (*Parazoa, Porifera* or *Spongida*)

Largest The largest known sponge is the barrel-shaped Logger-head sponge (*Spheciospongia vesparium*) of the West Indies and the waters off Florida, U.S.A. Single individuals measure up to 3 ft 6 in *105 cm* in height and 3 ft *91 cm* in diameter. Neptune's cup or goblet (*Poterion patera*) of Indonesia grows to 4 ft *120 cm* in height, but it is a less bulky animal. In 1909 a Wool sponge (*Hippospongia canaliculatta*) measuring

6 ft *183 cm* in circumference was collected off the Bahama Islands. When first taken from the water it weighed between 80 and 90 lb. *36 and 41 kg* but after it had been dried and relieved of all excrescences it scaled 12 lb. *5 kg 440* (this sponge is now preserved in the U.S. National Museum, Washington, D.C., U.S.A.).

Smallest The smallest known sponge is the widely distributed *Leucosolenia blanca*, which measures 3 mm *0.11 in* in height when fully grown.

Deepest Sponges have been recovered from depths of up to 18,500 ft *5 637 m*.

17. EXTINCT ANIMALS

Longest The first dinosaur to be scientifically described was
World *Megalosaurus* ("large lizard"), a 20 ft *6,09 m* long bipedal theropod, in 1824. A lower jaw and other bones of this animal had been found before 1818 in a slate quarry at Stonesfield, near Woodstock, Oxfordshire. It stalked across what is now southern England about 130,000,000 years ago. The word "dinosaur" ("fearfully great lizard") was not used for such reptiles until 1842. The longest recorded dinosaur was *Diplodocus* ("double-beam"), an attenuated sauropod which ranged over western North America about 150,000,000 years ago. A composite skeleton of three individuals excavated near Split Mountain, Utah between 1909 and 1922 and mounted in the Carnegie Museum of the Natural Sciences in Pittsburgh, Pennsylvania measures 87½ ft *26,67 m* in total length (neck 22 ft, body 15 ft, tail 50 ft 6 in [*6,70; 4,57; 15,40 m*])—nearly the length of three London double-decker buses—and 11 ft 9 in *3,6 m* at the pelvis (the highest point on the body). This animal weighed a computed 10,56 metric tons in life.

Britain Britain's longest dinosaur was the sauropod *Cetiosaurus* ("whale lizard"), which lived in what is now England about 165,000,000 years ago. It measured up to 60 ft *18,28 m* in total length and weighed over 15 tons/*tonnes*. The bones of this dinosaur were first discovered in the No. 1 Brickyard at the New Peterborough Brick Co., Peterborough, Northamptonshire in May 1898 and subsequently in Oxfordshire.

Heaviest The heaviest of all prehistoric animals, and the heaviest land vertebrate of all time, was probably *Brachiosaurus* ("arm lizard"), the remains of which have been found in East Africa (Rhodesia and Tanzania), Colorado, Oklahoma and Utah, U.S.A. from 135,000,000 and 165,000,000 years ago. A complete skeleton excavated near Tendaguru Hill, southern Tanganyika (Tanzania) in 1909 and now mounted in the Museum für Naturkunde, East Berlin, Germany, measures 74 ft 6 in *22,68 m* in total length and 21 ft *6,40 m* at the shoulder. This reptile weighed a computed 78,26 metric tons in life, but isolated bones have since been discovered in East Africa which indicate that some specimens may have weighed as much as 100 tons *102 tonnes* and measured over 90 ft *27 m* in total length.

In the summer of 1972 the remains of another enormous sauropod, new to science, was discovered in a flood-plain bonejam in Colorado, U.S.A. by an expedition from Brigham Young University, Provo, Utah. Excavations are still continuing, but a study of the incomplete series of cervical vertebrae indicate that this dinosaur must have. had a neck length of approximately 39 ft *11,88 m* (compare 22 ft [*6,70 m*] for *diplodocus*) and measured over 100 ft *30,48 m* in total length when alive.

Largest It is now known that some carnosaurs were even
predator larger than the 6¾ ton/*tonnes* 47 ft *14,32 m Tyrannosaurus*. In 1930 the British Museum Expedition to East Africa dug up the pelvic bones and part of the vertebrae of another huge carnosaur at Tendaguru Hill which must have measured about 54 ft *16,45 m* in total length when alive. During the summers of 1963–65 a Polish-Mongolian expedition discovered the remains of a carnosaur in the Gobi Desert which had 8 ft 6 in *2,59 m* long forelimbs! It is not yet known, however, whether the rest of this dinosaur was built on the same colossal scale.

Most *Stegosaurus* ("plated reptile"), which measured up to
brainless 30 ft *9 m* in total length and weighed 1¾ ton/*tonnes*, had a walnut-sized brain weighing only 2½ oz. *70 g*, which represented 0.004 of one per cent of its body weight (*cf.* 0.074 of 1 per cent for an elephant and

The longest recorded species of dinosaur, the Diplodocus, which was nearly the length of three London double-decker buses

The 1¾ ton Stegosaurus, which was the most brainless of the extinct animals. His brain was no bigger than a walnut

1.88 per cent for a human). It roamed widely across the Northern Hemisphere about 150,000,000 years ago.

Largest dinosaur eggs The largest known dinosaur eggs are those of *Hypselosaurus priseus*, a 30 ft *9,14 m* long sauropod which lived about 80,000,000 years ago. Some specimens found in the valley of the Durance near Aix-en-Provence, southern France in October 1961 would have had, uncrushed, a length of 12 in *300 mm* and a diameter of 10 in *255 mm*.

Largest flying creature The largest flying creature was probably the winged reptile *Pteranodon ingens*, a dynamic soarer which glided over what is now the State of Kansas, U.S.A. about 80,000,000 years ago. It had a wing-span of up to 27 ft *8,23 m* and weighed an estimated 40 lb. *18 kg*.

Largest marine reptile The largest marine reptile ever recorded was *Kronosaurus queenslandicus*, a short-necked pliosaur which swam in the seas around what is now Australia about 100,000,000 years ago. It measured up to 55 ft *16,76 m* in length and had an 11½ ft *3,60 m* long skull.

Largest crocodile The largest known crocodile was *Phobosuchus* ("horror crocodile"), which lived in the lakes and swamps of what are now the States of Montana and Texas, U.S.A. about 75,000,000 years ago. It measured up to 50 ft *15,24 m* in total length and had a 6 ft *1,83 m* long skull. The gavial *Rhamphosuchus*, which lived in what is now northern India about 7,000,000 years ago, also reached a length of 50 ft *15,24 m* but it was not so bulky.

Largest chelonians The largest prehistoric marine turtle was probably *Archelon ischyros*, which lived in the shallow seas over what are now the states of South Dakota and Kansas, U.S.A. about 80,000,000 years ago. An almost complete skeleton with a carapace (shell) measuring 6 ft 6 in *1,98 m* in length was discovered in August 1895 near the south fork of the Cheyenne River in Custer County, South Dakota. The skeleton, which has an overall length of 11 ft 4 in *3,45 m* (20 ft [*6,09 m*] across the outstretched flippers) is now preserved in the Peabody Museum of Natural History at Yale University, New Haven, Connecticut, U.S.A. This specimen is estimated to have weighed 6,000 lb. (2.7 tons/*tonnes*]) when it was alive. In 1914 the fossil remains of another giant marine turtle (*Cratochelone berneyi*) which must have measured at least 12 ft *3,65 m* in overall length when alive were discovered at Sylvania Station, 20 miles *32 km* west of Hughenden, Queensland, Australia.

The largest prehistoric tortoise was *Colossochelys atlas*, which lived in what is now northern India between 7,000,000 and 12,000,000 years ago. The fossil remains of a specimen with a carapace 5 ft 5 in *165 cm* long (7 ft 4 in [*2,23 m*] over the curve) and 2 ft 11 in *89 cm* high were discovered near Chandigarh in the Siwalik Hills in 1923. This animal had a nose to tail length of 8 ft *2,43 m* and is computed to have weighed 2,100 lb. *952 kg* when it was alive.

Longest snake The longest prehistoric snake was the python-like *Gigantophis garstini*, which inhabited what is now Egypt about 50,000,000 years ago. Parts of a spinal column and a small piece of jaw discovered at El Faiyum indicate a length of about 42 ft *12,80 m*.

Largest amphibian The largest amphibian ever recorded was the alligator-like *Eogyrinus* which lived between 280,000,000 and 345,000,000 years ago. It measured nearly 15 ft *4,57 m* in length.

Largest fish The largest fish ever recorded was the great shark (*Carcharodon megalodon*), which lived between 1,000,000 and 25,000,000 years ago. In 1909 the American Museum of Natural History undertook a restoration of the jaws of this giant shark, basing the size on 4 in *10 cm* long fossil teeth, and found that the jaws measured 9 ft *2,7 m* across and had a gape of 6 ft *1,82 m*. The length of this fish was estimated at 80 ft *24 m*. Other fossil teeth measuring up to 6 in *15 cm* in length and weighing 12 oz. *340 g* have since been discovered near Bakersfield, California, U.S.A.

Largest insect The largest prehistoric insect was the dragonfly *Meganeura monyi*, which lived between 280,000,000 and 325,000,000 years ago. Fossil remains (*i.e.* impressions of wings) discovered at Commentry, central France, indicate that it had a wing span reaching up to 70 cm *27.5 in*.

Most southerly The most southerly creature yet found is a freshwater salamander-like amphibian *Labyrinthodont*, represented by a 2½ in *63,5 mm* piece of jawbone found near Beardmore Glacier, Antarctica, 325 miles *523 km* from the South Pole, dating from the early Jurassic of 200,000,000 years ago. This discovery was made in December 1967.

Largest bird The largest prehistoric bird was the Elephant bird (*Aepyornis maximus*), also known as the "Roc bird", which lived in southern Madagascar. It was a flightless bird standing 9–10 ft *2,74–3,04 m* in height and weighing nearly 1,000 lb. *453 kg*. Aepyornis also had the largest eggs of any known animal. One example preserved in the British Museum of Natural History, London measures 33¾ in *86 cm* round the long axis with a circumference of 28½ in *72 cm* giving a capacity of 2.35 gal *10,68 litres*—seven times that of an ostrich egg. A more cylindrical egg preserved in the Academie des Sciences, Paris, France measures 12⅞ by 15¾ in *32,7–39 cm* and probably weighed about 27 lb. *12 kg* with its contents. This bird may have survived until *c.* 1660. The flightless moa *Dinornis giganteus* of North Island, New Zealand was taller, attaining a height of over 13 ft *3,96 m* but it only weighed about 500 lb. *227 kg*. In May 1962 a single fossilised ankle joint of an enormous flightless bird was found at Gainsville, Florida, U.S.A.

The largest prehistoric bird actually to fly was probably the condor-like *Teratornis incredibilis* which lived in what is now North America about 100,000,000 years ago. Fossil remains discovered in Smith Creek Cave, Nevada in 1952 indicate it had a wing span of 5 m *16 ft 4¼ in* and weighed nearly 50 lb. *22 kg* 50 A wing span measurement of 5 m *16ft 4¼ in* has also been reported for another flying bird named *Ornithodesmus latidens*, which flew over what is now Hampshire and the Isle of Wight about 90,000,000 years ago.

Another gigantic flying bird named *Osteodontornis orri*, which lived in what is now the State of California, U.S.A. about 20,000,000 years ago, had a wing span of 16 ft *4,87 m* and was probably even heavier. It was related to the pelicans and storks. The albatross-like *Gigantornis eaglesomei*, which flew over what is now Nigeria between 34,000,000 and 58,000,000 years ago, has been credited with a wing span of 20 ft *6,09 m* on the evidence of a single fossilised breastbone.

Largest mammal The largest prehistoric mammal, and the largest land mammal ever recorded, was *Baluchitherium* (= *Indricotherium, Paraceratherium, Aceratherium, Thaumastotherium, Aralotherium* and *Benaratherium*), a long-necked hornless rhinoceros which lived in Europe and central western Asia between 20,000,000 and 40,000,000 years ago. It stood up to 17 ft 9 in *5,41 m* to the top of the shoulder hump (27 ft *[8,23 m]* to the crown of the head), measured 27–28 ft *8,23–8,53 m* in length and probably weighed at least 20 tons/*tonnes*. The bones of this gigantic browser were first discovered in 1907–08 in the Bugti Hills in east Baluchistan, Pakistan.

Tusks Longest The longest tusks of any prehistoric animal were those of the straight-tusked elephant *Hesperoloxodon antiquus germanicus*, which lived in what is now northern Germany about 2,000,000 years ago. The average length in adult bulls was 5 m *16 ft 4¾ in*. A single tusk of a woolly mammoth (*Mammonteus primigenius*) preserved in the Franzens Museum at Brno, Czechoslovakia measures 5,02 m *16 ft 5½ in* along the outside curve. In *c*. August 1933, a single tusk of an Imperial mammoth (*Archidiskodon imperator*) measuring 16+ ft *4,87+ m* (anterior end missing) was unearthed near Post, Gorza County, Texas, U.S.A. In 1934 this tusk was presented to the American Museum of Natural History in New York City, N.Y., U.S.A.

The heaviest tusk on record is one weighing 330 lb. *149 kg 70* with a maximum circumference of 35 in *89 cm* now preserved in the Museo Civico di Storia Naturale, Milan, Italy. It measures 11 ft 9 in *3,58 m* in length. The heaviest recorded mammoth tusks are a pair in the University of Nebraska Museum, Lincoln, Nebraska, U.S.A. which have a combined weight of 498 lb. *226 kg* and measure 13 ft 9 in *4,21 m* and 13 ft 7 in *4,16 m* respectively and which were found near Campbell, Nebraska in April 1915.

Horns Longest The prehistoric Giant deer (*Megaceros giganteus*), which lived in northern Europe and northern Asia as recently as 50,000 B.C., had the longest horns of any known animal. One specimen recovered from an Irish bog had greatly palmated antlers measuring 14 ft *4,3 m* across.

18. PROTISTA AND MICROBES

PROTISTA

Protista were first discovered in 1676 by Anton van Leeuwenhoek of Delft (1632–1723), a Dutch microscopist. Among Protista characteristics common to both plants and animals are exhibited. The more plant-like are termed Protophyta (protophytes) and the more animal-like are placed in the phylum Protozoa (protozoans).

Largest The largest protozoans which are known to have existed were the now extinct Nummulities, which each had a diameter of 0.95 of an in *24,1 mm*. The largest existing protozoan is *Pelomyxa palustris*, which may attain a length of up to 0.6 of an in *15,2 mm*.

Smallest The smallest of all free-living organisms are pleuropneumonia-like organisms (P.P.L.O.) of the *Mycoplasma*. For fuller details see page 33. The smallest of

all protophytes is *Micromonas pusilla*, with a diameter of less than 2 microns.

Fastest moving The protozoan *Monas stigmatica* has been measured to move a distance equivalent to 40 times its own length in a second. No human can cover even seven times his own length in a second.

Fastest reproduction The protozoan *Glaucoma*, which reproduces by binary fission, divides as frequently as every three hours. Thus in the course of a day it could become a "six greats grandparent" and the progenitor of 510 descendants.

Densest The most densely existing species in the animal kingdom is the sea water dinoflagellate *Gymnodinium breve*, which exists at a density of 240 million/ga. or *52 million/litre* of sea water in certain conditions of salinity and temperature off the coast of Florida, U.S.A.

BACTERIA

Largest The largest of the bacteria is the sulphur bacterium *Beggiatoa mirabilis*, which is from 16 to 45 microns in width and which may form filaments several millimetres long.

Highest In April 1967 the U.S. National Aeronautics and Space Administration reported that bacteria had been recently discovered at an altitude of 135,000 ft (25.56 miles) *41 100 m*.

Longest lived The oldest deposits from which living bacteria are claimed to have been extracted are salt layers near Irkutsk, U.S.S.R., dating from about 600,000,000 years ago. The discovery, not accepted internationally, of their survival was made on 26 Feb. 1962 by Dr. H. J. Dombrowski of Freiberg University, West Germany.

Toughest The bacterium *Micrococcus radiodurans* can withstand atomic radiation of 6.5 million röntgens or 10,000 times that fatal to the average man.

VIRUSES

Largest The largest true viruses are the brick-shaped pox viruses (*e.g.* smallpox, vaccina, orf etc.) measuring *c*. 250 × 300 millimicrons (mμ) or 0.0003 of a mm.

Smallest Of more than 1,000 identified viruses, the smallest is the potato spindle tuber virus measuring less than 20 mμ in diameter.

Sub viral infective agents Evidence was announced from the Institute of Research on Animal Diseases at Compton, Berkshire, in January 1967 for the existence of a form of life more basic than both the virus and nucleic acid. It was named SF or Scrapie factor, from the sheep disease. If proven this will become the most fundamental replicating particle known. Its diameter is believed to be not more than 7 millionths of a mm. Having now been cultured, it has been allocated back to its former status of an ultra-virus.

19. PLANT KINGDOM (*Plantae*)

Earliest life World If one accepts the definition of life as the ability of an organism to make replicas of itself by taking as building materials the simpler molecules in the medium around it, life probably appeared on Earth about 3,300 million years ago. On 24 April 1972 the Ames Research Laboratory, Mountain View, California, announced this date for the earliest photosynthesing plant from the Onverwacht strata of the South Africa-Swaziland border. The oldest known living life-form was announced in December 1970 by Drs. Sanford and Barbara Siegel of Harvard University, U.S.A., to be a microscopic organism, similar in form

Earliest of their type

Type	Scientific name and year of discovery	Location	Estimated years before present
Ape	*Aegyptopitherus zeuxis* (1966)	Fayum, U.A.R.	28,000,000
Primate	tarsier-like	Indonesia	70,000,000
	lemur	Madagascar	70,000,000
Social insect	*Sphecomyrma freyi* (1967)	New Jersey, U.S.A.	100,000,000
Bird	*Archaeopteryx lithographica* (1861)	Bavaria, W. Germany	140,000,000
Mammal	shrew-like (1966)	Thaba-ea-Litau, Lesotho	190,000,000
Reptiles	*Hylonomus, Archerpeton, Protoclepsybrops, Romericus*	all in Nova Scotia	290,000,000
Amphibian	*Ichthyostega* (first quadruped)	Greenland	350,000,000
Spider	*Palaeostenzia crassipes*	Aberdeenshire, Scotland	370,000,000
Insect	*Rhyniella proecursor*	Aberdeenshire, Scotland	370,000,000
Vertebrates	Agnathans (Jawless fish)	near Leningrad, U.S.S.R.	480,000,000
Mollusc	*Neophilina galatheae* (1952)	off Costa Rica	500,000,000
Crustacean	*Karagassiema* (12 legged)	Sayan Mts., U.S.S.R.	*c.* 650,000,000

to an orange slice, first collected near Harlech, Merionethshire, Wales in 1964. It has been named *Kakabekia barghoorniana* and has existed from 2,000 million years ago.

United Kingdom The oldest micro-fossils found in Great Britain are those suggestive of blue-green algae mucilage identified in pre-Cambrian chert pebbles from north-west Scotland announced in April 1970. The age of the rock antedates the oldest Torridonian rocks of 935 million years and may derive from the fossiliferous Greenland sediments as old as 1,700 million years.

Earliest flower The oldest fossil of a flowering plant with palm-like imprints was found in Colorado, U.S.A., in 1953 and dated about 65,000,000 years old.

Largest forest **World** The largest afforested areas in the world are the vast coniferous forests of the northern U.S.S.R., lying mainly between latitude 55° N. and the Arctic Circle. The total wooded areas amount to 2,700,000,000 acres (25 per cent of the world's forests), of which 38 per cent is Siberian larch. The U.S.S.R. is 34 per cent afforested.

Great Britain The largest forest in England is Kielder Forest (72,336 acres [*29 273 ha*]), in Northumberland. The largest forest in Wales is the Coed Morgannwg (Forest of Glamorgan) (42,555 acres [*17 221 ha*]). Scotland's most extensive forest is the Glen Trool Forest (51,376 acres [*20 791 ha*]) in Kirkcudbrightshire. The United Kingdom is 7 per cent afforested.

PLANT

Rarest Plants thought to be extinct are rediscovered each year and there are thus many plants of which specimens are known in but a single locality. The flecked pink spurred coral-root (*Epipogium aphyllum*) is usually cited as Britain's rarest orchid, having been unrecorded between 1931 and 1953. The rose purple Alpine coltsfoot (*Homogyne alpina*), recorded by Don prior to 1814 in the mountains of Clova, Angus, Scotland, was not again confirmed until 1951. The only known location of the adder's-tongue spearwort (*Ranunculus ophioglossifolius*) in the British Isles is the Badgeworth Nature Reserve, Gloucestershire (see page 62). There were only two or three plants of the Lady's Slipper orchid (*Cyripedium calceolus*) in a single locality in 1971.

Commonest **World** The most widely distributed flowering plant in the world is *Cynodon dactylon*, a toothed grass found as far apart as Canada, Argentina, New Zealand, Japan and South Africa.

British The most widely distributed plant in Great Britain appears to be Ribwort plantain.

Northernmost The yellow poppy (*Papaver radicatum*) and the Arctic willow (*Salix arctica*) survive, the latter in an extremely stunted form, on the northernmost land (83° N.).

Southernmost The most southerly plant life recorded is seven species of lichen found in 1933–34 by the second expedition of Rear-Admiral Richard E. Byrd, U.S. Navy, in latitude 86° 03′ S. in the Queen Maud Mountains, Antarctica. The southernmost recorded flowering plant is the carnation (*Colobanthus crassifolius*), which was found in latitude 67° 15′ S. on Jenny Island, Margaret Bay, Graham Land (Palmer Peninsula), Antarctica.

Highest The greatest altitude at which any flowering plant has been found is 20,130 ft *6 135 m* in the Himalaya for *Stellaria decumbens*.

Deepest roots The greatest reported depth to which roots have penetrated is a calculated 400 ft *120 m* in the case of a wild fig tree at Echo Caves, near Ohrigstad, East Transvaal, South Africa.

TREES

World's largest living thing The most massive living thing on Earth is the biggest known California big tree (*Sequoiadendron giganteum*) named the "General Sherman", standing 272 ft 4 in *83 m* tall, in the Sequoia National Park, California, U.S.A. It has a true girth of 79.1 ft *24,11 m* (at 5 ft [*1,52 m*] above the ground). The "General Sherman"

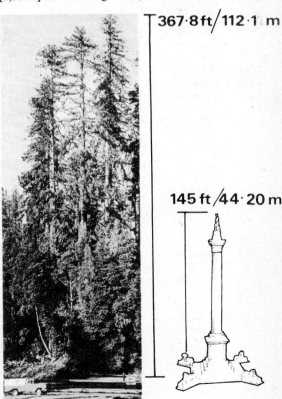

367·8 ft/112·1 m

145 ft/44·20 m

The world's tallest tree, which stands 367.8 ft *112,10 m* tall, in Humboldt County, California, U.S.A.

57

has been estimated to contain the equivalent of 600,120 board feet of timber, sufficient to make 40 five-roomed bungalows, The foliage is blue-green, and the red-brown tan bark may be up to 24 in *61 cm* thick in parts. In 1968 the official published figure for its estimated weight was "2,145 tons" (1,915 long tons [*2 030 tonnes*]).

The seed of a "big tree" weighs only 1/6,000th of an oz. *4,7 mg*. Its growth at maturity may therefore represent an increase in weight of over 250,000 million fold.

Tallest World The world's tallest known species of tree is the coast redwood (*Sequoia sempervirens*), now found only growing indigenously near the coast of California from just across the Oregon border south to Monterey.

The tallest example is now believed to be the Howard Libbey Tree in Redwood Creek Grove, Humboldt County, California announced at 367.8 ft *112,10 m* in 1964 but discovered to have an apparently dead top and re-estimated at 366.2 ft *111,60 m* in 1970. The nearby tree announced to a Senate Committee by Dr. Rudolf W. Becking on 18 June 1966 to be 385 ft *117,34 m*, proved on re-measurement to be no more than 311.3 ft *94,88 m* tall. It has a girth of 44 ft *13,41 m*. The tallest non-sequoia is a Douglas fir at Quinault Lake Park trail, Washington, U.S.A. of *c*. 310 ft *94,5 m*.

All-time The identity of the tallest tree of all-time has never been satisfactorily resolved. In 1872 a mountain ash (*Eucalyptus regnans*) found in Victoria, Australia, measured 435 ft *132,58 m* from its roots to the point where the trunk had been broken off by its fall. At this point the trunk's diameter was 3 ft *91 cm* so the overall height was probably at least 500 ft *152 m*. Its diameter was 18 ft *5,48 m* at 5 ft *1,52 m* above the ground. Another specimen, known as the "Baron Tree", was reported to be 464 ft *141,42 m* in 1868. Modern opinion tends to the view that the highest accurately measured Australian "big gum" tree is one 346 ft *105,46 m* tall felled near Colac, Victoria, in 1890. Claims for a Douglas fir (*Pseudotsuga taxifolia*) of 417 ft *127,10 m* with a 77 ft *23,47 m* circumference felled in British Columbia in 1940 remain unverified. The tallest specimen now known is *c*. 310 ft *94,5 m* (see above). The most probable claimant was thus a coast redwood of 367 ft 8 in *112,06 m* felled in 1873 near Guernville, California, U.S.A., thus being the same height as the Howard Libbey Tree as originally measured.

Great Britain The tallest tree in Great Britain is a Grand fir (*Abies grandis*) at Leighton Park, Montgomeryshire, Wales, now about 185 ft *56,38 m* tall. The tallest in England is a Wellingtonia (*Sequoiadendron giganteum*) measured at 165 ft *50,29 m* in February 1970 at Endsleigh, Devon.

The tallest measured in Scotland is the Grand fir (*Abies grandis*) at Strone' Cairndow, Argyllshire, planted in 1876, and 175 ft *53,34 m* when measured in May 1969 and now estimated to be at least 180 ft *54,86 m* tall.

Ireland The tallest tree in Ireland is a Sitka spruce (*Picea sitchensis*) 162 ft *49,37 m* tall at Shelton Abbey, County Wicklow. The Sitka spruce, planted in 1835, at Curraghmore, 160 ft *48,77 m* tall, in 1968 has ceased upward growth but one 151 ft *46,02 m* tall in 1966 at Powerscourt, Co. Wicklow should now be as tall.

Greatest girth World The Santa Maria del Tule Tree, in the state of Oaxaca, in Mexico is a Montezuma cypress (*Taxodium mucronatum*) with a girth of 112–113 ft *34,1–34,4 m* (1949) at a height of 5 ft *1,52 m* above the ground. A figure of 204 ft *62 m* in circumference was reported for the European chestnut (*Castanea sativa*) known as the "Tree of the 100 Horse" (Castagno di Cento Cavalli) on the edge of Mount Etna, Sicily, Italy in 1770.

The tree of greatest girth in Britain is a Sweet Chestnut at Canford, Dorset, with a bole 43 ft 9 in *13,33 m* in circumference.

Britain's greatest oaks The largest-girthed living British oak is one at Chirk, Denbighshire measuring 40 ft 2 in *12,24 m* (April 1971). It may, however, be a pollard. The largest "maiden" oak is the Majesty Oak at Fredville, Kent, with a girth of 37 ft 5 in *11,40 m*.

OLDEST

World The oldest recorded living tree is a bristlecone pine (*Pinus longaeva*) designated WPN–114, growing at 10,750 ft *3 275 m* above sea-level on the north-east face of Wheeler Peak (13,063 ft [*3 981 m*]) in eastern Nevada, U.S.A. During studies in 1963 and 1964 it was found to be about 4,900 years old. The oldest dated California big tree (*Sequoiadendron giganteum*) is a 3,212-year-old stump felled in 1892, but larger standing specimens are estimated to be between 3,500 and 4,000 years as in the case of the "General Sherman" tree from a ring count from a core drilled in 1931. Dendrochronologists estimate the *potential* life-span of a bristlecone pine at nearly 5,500 years, but that of a "big tree" at perhaps 6,000 years. Ring count dating extends back to 5,150 B.C. by examination of fallen bristlecone pine wood. Such tree-ring datings have led archaeologists to realize that some radiocarbon datings could be 1,000 years or more too young.

Great Britain Of all British trees that with the longest life is the yew (*Taxus baccata*), for which a maximum age well in excess of 1,000 years is usually conceded. The oldest known is the Fortingall Yew near Aberfeldy, Perthshire, part of which still grows. In 1777 this tree was

TALLEST TREES IN GREAT BRITAIN AND IRELAND—BY SPECIES

		ft	m			ft	m
Alder (Italian)	Westonbirt, Gloucester	92	28	Larch (Japanese)	Blair Castle, Perthshire	121	36
Alder (Common)	Sandling Park, Kent	85	25	Lime	Duncombe Park, Yorkshire	150	45
Ash	Duncombe Park, Yorkshire	148	45	Metasequoia	Savill Gardens, Windsor, Berkshire	57	17
Beech	Yester House, East Lothian	142	43	Monkey Puzzle	Endsleigh, Devon	86	26
Cedar	Petworth House, Sussex	132	40	Oak (Common)	Fountains Abbey, Yorkshire	120	36
Chestnut (Horse)	Petworth House, Sussex	125	38	Oak (Sessile)	Whitfield House, Hereford	135	41
Chestnut (Sweet)	Godinton Park, Kent	118	35	Oak (Red)	West Dean, Sussex	115	35
Cypress (Lawson)	Endsleigh, Devon	126	38	Pine (Corsican)	Stanage Park, Radnor	144	43
Cypress (Monterey)	Tregothnan, Cornwall	120	36	Plane	Bryanston, Dorset	145	44
Douglas Fir	Powis Castle, Montgomery	180	54	Poplar (Black Italian)	Fairlawne, Kent	140	42
Elm (Wych)	Rossie Priory, Nr. Dundee	128	39	Poplar (Lombardy)	Marble Hill, Twickenham	118	35
Elm (Jersey)	Wilton, Wiltshire	121	36	Silver Fir	Dupplin Castle, Perthshire	154	46
Eucalyptus (Blue Gum)	Glengarriff, Co. Cork	140	42	Spruce (Sitka)	Murthly, Perth	174	53
Grand Fir	Leighton Park, Montgomeryshire	185	56	Sycamore	Drumlanrig Castle, Dumfries-shire	112	34
Ginkgo	Linton Park (Maidstone), Kent	93	28	Tulip-tree	Taplow House, Buckingham	119	36
Hemlock (Western)	Benmore, Argyllshire	157	47	Walnut	Laverstoke Park, Hampshire	82	24
Holly	Staverton Thicks, Suffolk	74	22	Wellingtonia	Endsleigh, Devon	165	50
Hornbeam	Durdans, Epsom, Surrey	105	32	Yew	Midhurst, Sussex	85	25
Larch (European)	Parkhatch, Surrey	142	43				

The loneliest tree in the world. Standing in the Ténéré Desert, it has survived being rammed by a lorry. There is no other tree for 50 km *31 miles* in any direction

over 50 ft *15,24 m* in girth and it cannot be much less than 1,500 years old today.

Earliest The earliest species of tree still surviving is the maidenhair tree (*Ginkgo biloba*) of Chekiang, China, which first appeared about 160,000,000 years ago, during the Jurassic era. It was "re-discovered" by Kaempfer (Netherlands) in 1690 and reached England c. 1754. It has been grown in Japan since c. 1100 where it was known as *ginkyō* ("silver apricot") and is now known as *icho*.

Fastest growing Discounting bamboo, which is not botanically classified as a tree, but as a woody grass, the fastest growing tree is *Eucalyptus deglupta*, which has been measured to grow 35 ft *10,66 m* in 15 months in New Guinea. The youngest recorded age for a tree to reach 100 ft *30,48 m* is 7 years for *E. regnans* in Rhodesia and for 200 ft *60,96 m* is 40 years for a Monterey pine in New Zealand.

Slowest growing The speed of growth of trees depends largely upon conditions, although some species, such as box and yew, are always slow-growing. The extreme is represented by a specimen of Sitka spruce which required 98 years to grow to 11 in *28 cm* tall with a diameter of less than 1 in *2,5 cm* on the Arctic tree-line. The growing of miniature trees or *bonsai* is an oriental cult mentioned as early as c. 1320.

Most spreading The greatest area covered by a single clonal growth is that of the wild box huckleberry (*Gaylussacia brachyera*), a mat-forming evergreen shrub first reported in 1796. A colony covering 8 acres *3,2 hectares* was discovered in 1845 near New Bloomfield, Pennsylvania. Another colony, covering about 100 acres, was "discovered" on 18 July 1920 near the Juniata River, Pennsylvania. It has been estimated that this colony began 13,000 years ago.

Remotest The tree remotest from any other tree is believed to be one at an oasis in the Ténéré Desert, Niger Republic. In Feb. 1960 it survived being rammed by a lorry driven by a Frenchman. There are no other trees within 50 km *31 miles*.

Most expensive The highest price ever paid for a tree is $51,000 (then £18,214) for a single Starkspur Golden Delicious apple tree from near Yakuma, Washington, U.S.A., bought by a nursery in Missouri in 1959.

WOOD

Heaviest The heaviest of all woods is black ironwood (*Olea laurifolia*), also called South African ironwood, with a specific gravity of up to 1.49, and weighing up to 93

lb./ft³ *1 490 kg/m³*. The heaviest British wood is boxwood (*Buxus sempervivens*) with an extreme of 64 lb./ft³ *1 025 kg/m³*.

Lightest The lightest wood is *Aeschynomene hispida*, found in Cuba, which has a specific gravity of 0.044 and a weight of only 2¾ lb./ft³ *44 kg/m³*. The wood of the balsa tree (*Ochroma pyramidale*) is of very variable density—between 2½ and 24 lb./ft³ *40 and 384 kg/m³* The density of cork is 15 lb./ft³ *240 kg/m³*.

BAMBOO

Tallest The tallest recorded species of bamboo is *Dendrocalamus giganteus*, native to southern Burma. It was reported in 1904 that there were specimens with a culm-length of 30 to 35 m *100 to 115 ft* in the Botanic Gardens at Peradeniya, Ceylon.

Fastest growing Some species of the 45 genera of bamboo have attained growth rates of up to 36 in *91 cm* per day (0.00002 m.p.h. [*0,00003 km/h*]), on their way to reaching a height of 100 ft in less than three months.

BLOOMS

Largest World The mottled orange-brown and white parasitic stinking corpse lily (*Rafflesia arnoldi*) has the largest of all blooms. These attach themselves to the cissus vines of the jungle in south-east Asia and measure up to 3 ft *91 cm* across and ¾ of an in *1,9 cm* thick, and attain a weight of 15 lb. *7 kg*.

The largest known inflorescence is that of *Puya raimondii*, a rare Bolivian plant with an erect panicle (diameter 8 ft [*2,4 m*]) which emerges to a height of 35 ft *10,7 m*. Each of these bears up to 8,000 white blooms (see also Slowest-flowering plant, below).

The world's largest blossoming plant is the giant Chinese wisteria at Sierra Madre, California, U.S.A. It was planted in 1892 and now has branches 500 ft *152 m* long. It covers nearly an acre, weighs 225 tons *228 tonnes* and has an estimated 1,500,000 blossoms during its blossoming period of five weeks, when up to 30,000 people pay admission to visit it.

Great Britain The largest bloom of any indigenous British flowering plant is that of the wild white water lily (*Nymphaea alba*), which measures 6 in *15 cm* across. Other species bear much larger inflorescences.

Smallest flowering plant The smallest of all flowering plants are duckweeds, seen on the surface of ponds. Of these the rootless *Wolffia punctata* has fronds only 1/50th to 1/35th of an in *0,5 to 0,7 mm* long. Another species, *Wolffia arrhiza*, occurs in Great Britain but rarely, if ever, flowers there. The smallest plant regularly flowering in Britain is the chaffweed (*Cetunculus minimus*), a single seed of which weighs 0.00003 of a gramme.

Slowest flowering plant The slowest flowering of all plants is the rare *Puya raimondii*, the largest of all herbs, discovered in Bolivia in 1870. The panicle emerges after about 150 years of the plant's life. It then dies. (See also above under Largest blooms.)

Largest bouquet The largest bouquet on record is one of 243 Baccara red roses made by Jayne Foster of *The Florist* magazine and presented by the Lord Mayor of London to Madame Mayor of Lancaster on the occasion of the opening of the Midland Link joining these two cities, 243 miles *391 km* apart, on 23 May 1972.

Largest wreath The largest wreath ever constructed was a Christmas wreath of 765 lb. *347 kg* and 19½ ft *5,94 m* in diameter by the Oshkosh Warriors of Wisconsin, U.S.A., and hung in the Grand Mall for 25 Dec. 1971.

Longest daisy chain The longest daisy chain on record is one of 1,463 ft *446 m*, made by class 4A of Hessle Junior School, Yorkshire on 25 May 1973.

LEAVES

Largest
World The largest leaves of any plant belong to the raffia palm (*Raphia raffia*) of the Mascarene Islands, in the Indian Ocean, and the Amazonian bamboo palm (*R. toedigera*) of South America, whose leaf blades may measure up to 65 ft *19,81 m* in length with petioles up to 13 ft *3,96 m*.

The largest undivided leaf is that of *Alocasia macrorrhiza*, found in Sabah, East Malaysia. One found in 1966 measured 9 ft 11 in *3,02 m* long and 6 ft 3½ in *1,92 m* wide, and had an area of 34.2 ft² *3,17 m²* on one side.

Great
Britain The largest leaves to be found in outdoor plants in Great Britain are those of *Gunnera manicata* from Brazil with leaves 6 to 10 ft *1,82–3,04 m* across on prickly stems 5 to 8 ft *1,52–2,43 m* long.

FRUIT

Most and
least
nutritive An analysis of the 38 commonly eaten fruits shows that the one with by far the highest calorific value is avocado (*Persea drymifolia*), with 1,200 calories per lb. That with the lowest value is cucumber with 73 calories per lb. The fruit with the highest percentage of invert sugar by weight is plantain or cooking banana (*Musa paradisiaca*) with 25.3 per cent. Apple (*Malus pumila*)

and quince (*Cydonia oblonga*) are the least proteinous, at 0.3 of one per cent.

ORCHID

Largest The largest of all orchids is *Grammatophyllum speciosum*, native to Malaysia. A specimen recorded in Penang, West Malaysia, in the 19th century had 30 spikes up to 8 ft *2,4 m* tall and a diameter of more than 40 ft *12 m*. The largest orchid flower is that of *Selenipedium caudatum*, found in tropical areas of America. Its petals are up to 18 in *46 cm* long, giving it a maximum outstretched diameter of 3 ft *91 cm*. The flower is, however, much less bulky than that of the stinking corpse lily (see Largest blooms, above.)

Tallest The tallest of all orchids is the terrestrial tree-orchid (*Angraecum infundibulare*), which grows in the swamps of Uganda to a height of 12 ft *3,65 m*.

Smallest The smallest orchid plant is believed to be *Notylia norae*, found in Venezuela. The smallest orchid flower is that of *Bulbophyllum minutissium*, found in Australia.

Highest
priced The highest price ever paid for an orchid is 1,150 guineas (£1,207.50), paid by Baron Schröder to Sanders of St. Albans for an *Odontoglossum crispum*

RECORD DIMENSIONS AND WEIGHTS FOR FRUIT, VEGETABLES AND FLOWERS GROWN IN THE UNITED KINGDOM

Most data subsequent to 1958 comes from the annual *Garden News* Giant Vegetable and Fruit Contest.

Apple	3 lb. 1 oz.	*1 kg 40*	V. Loveridge	Ross-on-Wye, Herefordshire	1965
Artichoke	8 lb.	*3 kg 60*	A. R. Lawson	Tollerton, Yorkshire	1964
Beetroot	24 lb.	*11 kg*	R. G. Arthur	Longlevens, Gloucestershire	1971
Broad Bean	23⅜ in	*59,37 cm*	T. Currie	Jedburgh, Roxburghshire	1963
Broccoli	28 lb. 14¾ oz.	*13 kg 10*	J. T. Cooke	Funtington, Sussex	1964
Brussels Sprout[1]	7 lb. 10 oz.	*3 kg 50*	J. Marsh	Whitfield, Kent	1966
Cabbage[2]	69 lb. 8 oz.	*313 kg 250*	P. Hayes	Uttoxeter, Staffordshire	1965
Carrot[3]	7 lb. 5 oz.	*3 kg 30*	R. Clarkson	Freckleton, Lancashire	1970
Cauliflower	52 lb. 11½ oz.	*236 kg 30*	J. T. Cooke	Funtington, Sussex	1966
Celery	27 lb. 8 oz.	*122 kg 70*	E. E. Allen	Heston, Middlesex	1970
Cucumber	10 lb. 2 oz. (indoor)	*4 kg 60*	W. Hodgson	Birkenhead, Cheshire	1967
	4 lb. 14 oz. (outdoor)	*2 kg 20*	M. Housden	Efford Hill, Hampshire	1966
Dwarf Bean	14½ in	*36,8 cm*	E. E. Jenkins	Shipston-on-Stour, Warwickshire	1970
Gourd	196 lb.	*89 kg*	J. Leathes	Herringfleet Hall, Suffolk	1846
Kale	12 ft tall	*3,7 m*	B. T. Newton	Mullion, Cornwall	1950
Leek	9 lb. 4 oz.	*4 kg 20*	E. E. Jenkins	Shipston-on-Stour, Warwickshire	1968
Lemon	1 lb. 12 oz. (girth 15 in [*38 cm*])	*0 kg 790*	T. P. Matthews	Iver Heath, Buckinghamshire	1969
Lettuce	16 lb. 2¼ oz.	*7 kg 30*	J. T. Cooke	Funtington, Sussex	1966
Mangold	46 lb.	*21 kg*	D. Bolland	Spalding, Lincolnshire	1964
Marrow[4]	60 lb.	*27 kg*	A. V. Bishop	Snailwell, Cambridgeshire	1963
Mushroom[5]	54 in circum.	*1,4 m*	—	Hasketon, Suffolk	1957
Onion	5 lb. 13 oz.	*2 kg 60*	W. Taylor	Leicester	1965
Parsnip[6]	9 lb. 4 oz. (31 in [*78 cm*] long)	*4 kg 20*	P. C. Richardson	Heighington, Lincolnshire	1962
Pea Pod	10⅛ in	*25,7 cm*	T. Currie	Jedburgh, Roxburghshire	1964
Pear	1 lb. 12¼ oz.	*794 g*	A. Bratton	Shifnal, Shropshire	1966
Potato[7]	7 lb. 1 oz.	*3 kg 20*	J. H. East	Spalding, Lincolnshire	1963
Pumpkin[8]	204 lb. 8 oz.	*92 kg 80*	F. H. Smith	Coventry, Warwickshire	1970
Radish	16 lb. 8 oz.	*7 kg 50*	E. E. Allen	Heston, Middlesex	1966
Red Cabbage	33 lb. 2 oz.	*14 kg 970*	A. Bratton	Ryton, Shropshire	1963
Rhubarb	5 ft 1 in	*155 cm*	A. C. Setterfield	Englefield, Reading, Berkshire	1968
Runner Bean	33¾ in	*85,7 cm*	A. Bratton	Ryton, Shropshire	1966
Savoy	38 lb. 8 oz.	*17 kg 50*	W. H. Neil	Retford, Nottinghamshire	1966
Shallot	1 lb. 7 oz.	*652 g*	H. H. May	Inkpen, Berkshire	1962
Strawberry	7¼ oz.	*205 g*	E. Oxley	Walton, Essex	1968
Sugar Beet	21 lb.	*9 kg 50*	L. Hawcroft	Holme-on-Spalding Moor, Yorkshire	1971
Sunflower	15 ft 2 in tall	*4,6 m*	Mrs. J. A. Hawkins	Capel, Surrey	1969
Swede[9]	32 lb. 8 oz.	*14 kg 70*	R. T. Leeson	Irchester, Northamptonshire	1963
Tomato	3 lb.	*1 kg 40*	B. Austin	Uttoxeter, Staffordshire	1964
Tomato Plant	20 ft tall, 34 lb. fruit	*6 m, 15 kg 40*	—	Southport, Lancashire	1957
Tomato Truss	10 lb. 4 oz.	*4 kg 60*	A. L. Smith	Hove, Sussex	1971
Turnip[10]	35 lb. 4 oz.	*15 kg 99*	C. W. Butler	Nafferton, Yorkshire	1972

1 A Brussels Sprout plant measuring 9 ft 6½ in *2,90 m* tall was grown by W. Lawrence at Kidderminster, Worcs. in June 1972.
2 A 75 lb. *34 kg* cabbage has been reported (since 1930) from Bolton, Lancashire. The Swalwell, County Durham cabbage of 1865 grown by R. Collingwood reputedly weighed 123 lb. *56 kg*.
3 One of 7 lb. 7 oz. *3 kg 402* (15 in [*38 cm*] long) reported grown by Police Sgt. Alfred Garwood of Blidworth, Nottinghamshire in November 1970.
4 A 96 lb. *43 kg 545* marrow has been reported from Suffolk.
5 Same size reported by J. Coombes at Mark, Somerset on 28 July, 1965. In Sept. 1968 one weighing 18 lb. 10 oz. *8 kg 450* was reported from Whidbey Is., Washington, U.S.A.

6 50 in *1,32 m* long; G. Chesterton near Wyberton, Lincolnshire, April 1959.
7 One weighing 18 lb. 4 oz. *8 kg 278* reported dug up by Thomas Siddal in his garden in Chester on 17 Feb. 1795. A yield of 1,242 lb. 14 oz. 563 kg 750 from 6 plants reported on 28 Sept. 1969 by J. T. Cooke (see Broccoli above).
8 One weighing 353 lb. *160 kg 130* grown by E. Van Wyck of Roland, Manitoba reported in 1971. 5 of 298 lb. *135 kg* (biggest 82 lb. [*37 kg*]) on one plant by George F. Ould, Feniton, Devon in Oct. 1970.
9 One weighing 39 lb. 8 oz. *18 kg* claimed by E. R. Reay of Gaitsgill Hall, Dalston, Cumberland in 1940 (unratified).
10 A 73 lb. *33 kg* turnip was reported in December 1768.

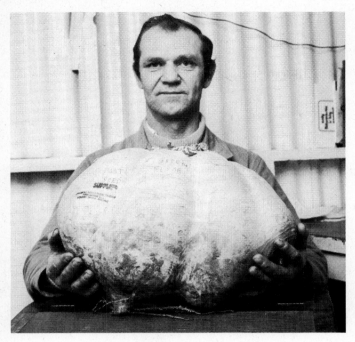

Mr. C. W. Butler proud owner of Britain's heaviest recorded turnip

(variety *pittianum*) at an auction by Protheroe & Morris of Bow Lane, London, on 22 March 1906.

Tallest lupin The largest lupin reported is one of 6 ft 0½ in *1,84 m* grown by Mr. J. Lawlor of New Malden, Surrey in 1971.

Tallest sunflower A sunflower 16 ft 2 in *4,92 m* in height was grown by G. E. Hooking of Kington Langley, Wilts., and was cut down in October 1971.

Longest seaweed Claims made that seaweed off Tierra del Fuego, South America, grows to 600 ft *182,5 m* and even to 1,000 ft *305 m* in length have gained currency. More recent and more reliable records indicate that the longest species of seaweed is the Pacific giant kelp (*Macrocystis pyrifera*), which does not exceed 196 ft *60 m* in length. It can grow 45 cm *17¾ in* in a day. The longest of the 700 species of seaweed recognised around the coasts of Britain is the brown seaweed *Chorda filum* which grows up to a length of 20 ft *6,10 m*. The largest British seaweed is *Saccorhiza polyschides* single plants of which may weigh 2 cwt./*100 kg*.

Mosses The smallest of mosses is the pygmy moss (*Ephemerum*) and the longest is the brook moss (*Fontinalis*), which forms streamers up to 3 ft *91 cm* long in flowing water.

FUNGUS
Largest The largest recorded ground fungus was a specimen of the giant puff ball (*Calvatia gigantea*) which was 5 ft 4 in *1,63 m* in diameter, and 9½ in *24 cm* high. It was discovered in New York State, U.S.A., in 1877.

The largest officially recorded tree fungus was a specimen of *Oxyporus* (*Fomes*) *nobilissimus*, measuring 56 in *142 cm* by 37 in *94 cm* and weighing at least 300 lb. *136 kg* found by J. Hisey in Washington State, U.S.A., in 1946. The largest recorded in the United Kingdom is an ash fungus (*Fomes fraxineus*) measuring 50 in by 15 in *127 cm* by *38 cm* wide, found by the forester A. D. C. LeSueur on a tree at Waddesdon, Buckinghamshire, in 1954.

Largest rose tree A "Lady Banks" rose tree at Tombstone, Arizona, U.S.A., has a trunk 40 in *101 cm* thick, stands 9 ft *2,74 m* high and covers an area of 5,380 ft² *499 m²* supported by 68 posts and several thousand feet of iron

piping. This enables 150 people to be seated under the arbour. The cutting came from Scotland in 1884.

Largest rhododendron The largest species of rhododendron is the scarlet *Rhododendron arboreum*, examples of which reach a height of 60 ft *18,25 m* at Mangalbaré, Nepal. The cross-section of the trunk of a *Rhododendron giganteum*, reputedly 90 ft *27,43 m* high from Yunnan, China is preserved at Inverewe Garden, Ross-shire. The largest in the United Kingdom is one 25 ft *7,60 m* tall and 272 ft *82,90 m* in circumference at Government House, Hillsborough, Co. Down.

Largest aspidistra The aspidistra (*Aspidistra elatior*) was introduced to Britain as a parlour palm from Japan and China in 1822. The biggest aspidistra in the world is one 49¾ in *126 cm* tall and grown by George Munns at Perth University, Western Australia and measured in January 1972.

Largest vines The largest recorded grape vine was one planted in 1842 at Carpinteria, California, U.S.A. By 1900 it was yielding more than 9 tons/*tonnes* of grapes in some years, and averaging 7 tons/*tonnes* per year. It died in 1920. Britain's largest vine (1898–1964) was at Kippen, Stirling with a girth, measured in 1956, of 5 ft *1,52 m*. England's largest vine is the Great Vine, planted in 1768 at Hampton Court, Greater London. Its girth is 38 in *96,5 cm* with branches up to 110 ft *33,5 m* long and an average yield of 1,200 lb. *545 kg*.

Most Northerly Vineyard On 6 April 1972, 300 grape vines from Neustadt, West Germany were planted by the Old Bishop's Palace in Lincoln at Lat 53° 15′ N.

Tallest hedge *World* The world's tallest hedge is the Meikleour beech hedge in Perthshire, Scotland. It was planted in 1746 and has now attained a trimmed height of 85 ft *26 m*. It is 600 yds *550 m* long.

Yew The tallest yew hedge in the world is in Earl Bathurst's Park, Cirencester, Gloucestershire. It was planted in 1720, runs for 135 yds *124 m* reaches 36 ft *11 m*, is 12 ft *3,65 m* thick and takes 20 man-days to trim.

Box The tallest box hedge is 35 ft *10,7 m* in height at Birr Castle, Offaly, Ireland dating from the 18th century.

Largest cactus The largest of all cacti is the saguaro (*Cereus giganteus* or *Carnegieia gigantea*), found in Arizona, New Mexico and California, U.S.A., and Sonora, Mexico. The green fluted column is surmounted by candelabra-like branches rising to a height of 53 ft *16,15 m* in the case of a specimen found in 1950 near Madrona, New Mexico. They have waxy white blooms which are followed by edible crimson fruit. A cardon cactus in Baja California, Mexico was reputed to reach a height of 58 ft *17,67 m* and a weight of 9 tons/*tonnes*.

Most poisonous toadstool The yellowish-olive death cap (*Amanita phalloides*) is regarded as the world's most poisonous fungus. It is found in England. From six to fifteen hours after tasting, the effects are vomiting, delirium, collapse and death. Among its victims was Cardinal Giulio de' Medici, Pope Clement VII (b. 1478) on 25 Sept. 1534.

The Registrar General's Report states that between 1920 and 1950 there were 39 fatalities from fungus poisoning in the United Kingdom. As the poisonous types are mostly *Amanita* varieties, it is reasonable to assume that the deaths were predominantly due to *Amanita phalloides*. The most recent fatality was probably in 1960.

FERNS
Largest The largest of all the more than 6,000 species of fern is the tree fern (*Alsophila excelsa*) of Norfolk Island, in the South Pacific, which attains a height of up to 80 ft *24,38 m*.

The planting of the most northerly vineyard by the Old Bishop's Palace, Lincoln

Smallest The world's smallest ferns are *Hecistopteris pumila*, found in Central America, and *Azolla caroliniana*, which is native to the United States.

SEED

Largest The largest seed in the world is that of the double coconut or Coco de Mer (*Lodoicea seychellarum*), the single-seeded fruit of which may weigh 40 lb. *18 kg.* This grows only in the Seychelles Islands, in the Indian Ocean.

Smallest The smallest seeds are those of *Epiphytic* orchids, at 35,000,000 to the oz. (*cf.* grass pollens at up to 6,000,000,000 grains/oz.). A single plant of the American ragweed can generate 8,000,000,000 pollen grains in five hours.

Most viable The most viable of all known seeds are those of the Arctic Lupin (*Lupinus arcticus*) found in frozen silt at Miller Creek in the Yukon, Canada in July 1954. They were germinated in 1966 and dated by the radio carbon method to at least 8,000 B.C. and more probably to 13,000 B.C.

GRASS

Longest The tallest of the 160 grasses found in Great Britain is the common reed (*Phragmites communis*), which reaches a height of 9 ft 9 in *2,97 m.*

Shortest The shortest grass native to Great Britain is the very rare sand bent (*Mibora minima*) from Anglesey, which has a maximum growing height of under 6 in *15 cm.*

Hay fever The highest recorded grass pollen count in Britain was one of 720 (mean number of grains/m³ of air noon to noon) near London on 15–16 June 1964. A figure of 2,160 for plane tree pollen was recorded on 9 May 1971. The lowest counts are nil.

Worst weeds The most intransigent weed is the mat-forming water weed *Salvinia auriculata*, found in Africa. It was detected on the filling of Kariba Lake in May 1959 and within 11 months had choked an area of 77 miles² *199 km²* rising by 1963 to 387 miles² *1,002 km².* The world's worst land weeds are regarded as purple nut sedge, Bermuda grass, barnyard grass, junglerice,

goose grass, Johnson grass, Guinea grass, cogon grass and lantana. The most damaging and widespread cereal weeds in Britain are the wild oats *Avena fatua* and *A. ludoviciana*. Their weeds can withstand temperatures of 240° F *115,6° C* for 15 minutes and remain viable.

Ten-leafed A certified ten-leafed clover (*Trifolium pratense*) **clover** found by Phillipa Smith in Woodborough, Nottinghamshire in 1966. Another case was reported from Columbus, Ohio, in October 1972.

20. PARKS, ZOOS, AQUARIA AND OCEANARIA

PARKS

Largest The world's largest park is the Wood Buffalo National *World* Park in Alberta, Canada (established 1922), which has an area of 11,172,000 acres (17,560 miles² [*45 480 km²*]).

Britain The largest National Park in Great Britain is the Lake District National Park which has an area of 866 miles² *2 240 km².* The largest private park in the United Kingdom is Woburn Park (3,000 acres [*1 200 ha*]), near Woburn Abbey, the seat of the Dukes of Bedford. The largest common in the United Kingdom is Llansantffraed Cwmdauddwr (28,819 acres [*11 662 ha*]) in Radnorshire, Wales.

Smallest The world's smallest nature reserve is believed to be the Badgeworth Nature Reserve (346 yds² [*289 m²*]), near Cheltenham, Gloucestershire. Owned by the Society for the Promotion of Nature Reserves, it is leased to the Gloucestershire Trust for Nature Conservation to protect the sole site in the British Isles of the adder's-tongue spearwort (*Ranunculus ophioglossifolius*).

ZOOS

Largest It has been estimated that throughout the world there *game* are some 500 zoos with an estimated annual atten-*reserve* dance of 330,000,000. The largest zoological preserve in the world has been the Etosha Reserve, South West Africa established in 1907 with an area which grew to 38,427 miles² *99 525 km².* In 1970 it was announced that the Kaokoveld section of 26,000 miles² *67 350 km²* had been de-proclaimed in the interests of the 10,000 Ovahimba and Ovatjimba living in the area.

Largest collection The largest collection in any zoo is that in the Zoological Gardens of West Berlin, Germany. At 1 Jan. 1973 the zoo had a total of 13,373 specimens from 2,409 species. This total included 1,061 mammals (232 species), 2,808 birds (747 species), 623 reptiles (304 species), 307 amphibians (95 species), 2,351 fishes (775 species) and 6,223 invertebrates (256 species).

Oldest The earliest known collection of animals was that set up by Hatshepsut the Egyptian queen of the 18th dynasty in Egypt, *c.* 1495 B.C. This "Garden of Amon" contained leopards, giraffe, monkeys, an elephant and an aviary. The oldest known zoo is that at Schönbrunn, Vienna, Austria, built in 1752 by the Holy Roman Emperor Franz I for his wife Maria Theresa. The oldest privately owned zoo in the world is that of the Zoological Society of London, founded in 1826. Its collection, housed partly in Regent's Park, London (36 acres [*14.5 ha*]) and partly at Whipsnade Park, Bedfordshire (541 acres [*219 ha*], opened 1931) is the most comprehensive in the United Kingdom. At the stocktaking on 31 Dec. 1972 there were a total of 8,670 specimens including 1,808 mammals (302 species), 2,352 birds (644 species), 486 reptiles (213 species), 454 amphibians (42 species), 2,450 fish (276 species), and 1,120 invertebrates (106 species). The record annual attendances are 3,031,571 in 1950 for Regent's Park and 756,758 in 1961 for Whipsnade.

Largest aquarium The world's largest aquarium is the John G. Shedd Aquarium on 12th Street and Grant Park, Chicago, Illinois, U.S.A., completed in November 1929 at a cost of $3,250,000 (now £1,354,166). The total capacity

of its display tanks is 375,000 gal *1,7 million litres* with reservoir tanks holding 1,665,000 gal *7,5 million litres*. Exhibited are 7,500 specimens from 350 species. Salt water is brought in road and rail tankers from Key West, Florida, and a tanker barge from the Gulf of Mexico. The record attendances are 78,658 in a day on 21 May 1931, and 4,689,730 visitors in the single year of 1931.

The largest marine mammal ever held in captivity was a female pacific grey whale (*Eschrichtius gibbosus*), named "Gigi", who was captured in Scammon's lagoon, Baja California, Mexico, on 13 March 1971 and then transferred to the Sea World Aquarium in Mission Bay, San Diego, California, U.S.A. She measured 18 ft 2 in *5,53 m* in length on arrival, and weighed 4,300 lb. *1 950 kg*. She was released at sea off the San Diego coast on 13 March 1972, after she had grown to an unmanageable 27 ft *8,23 m* and 14,000 lb. *6 350 kg*.

OCEANARIA

Earliest and largest The world's first oceanarium is Marineland of Florida, opened in 1938 at a site 18 miles *29 km* south of St. Augustine, Florida, U.S.A. Up to 5,800,000 gal *26,3 million litres* of sea-water are pumped daily through two major tanks, one rectangular (100 ft [*30,48 m*] long by 40 ft [*12,19 m*] wide by 18 ft [*5,48 m*] deep) containing 375,000 gal *1,7 million litres* and one circular (233 ft [*71 m*] in circumference and 12 ft [*3,65 m*] deep) containing 330,000 gal *1,5 million litres*. The tanks are seascaped, including coral reefs and even a shipwreck. The salt water tank at the Marineland of the Pacific Palos Verdes Peninsula, California, U.S.A. is 251½ ft *76,65 m* in circumference and 22 ft *6,7 m* deep, with a capacity of 530,000 gal *2,4 million litres*. The total capacity of this whole oceanarium is 1,830,000 gal *8,3 million litres*.

An old German fort in the world's largest Game Reserve at Namutoni, South West Africa

3
THE
NATURAL
WORLD

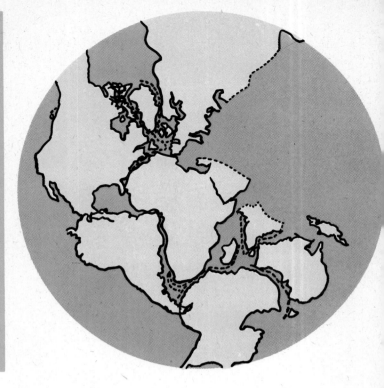

THE EARTH

The Earth is not a true sphere, but flattened at the poles and hence an ellipsoid. The polar diameter of the Earth (7,899.809 miles [*12 713,510 km*]) is 25.576 miles *41,161 km* less than the equatorial diameter (7,926.385 miles [*12 756,280 km*]). The Earth also has a slight ellipticity of the equator since its long axis (about longitude 37° W) is 174 yds *159 m* greater than the short axis. The greatest departures from the reference ellipsoid are a protuberance of 266 ft *81 m* in the area of New Guinea and a depression of 371 ft *113 m* south of Ceylon, in the Indian Ocean.

The greatest circumference of the Earth, at the equator, is 24,901.47 miles *40 075,03 km*, compared with 24,859.75 miles *40 007,89 km* at the meridian. The area of the surface is estimated to be 196,937,600 miles^2 *510 066 000 km^2*. The period of axial rotation, *i.e.* the true sidereal day, is 23 hrs 56 min 4.0996 sec, mean time.

The mass of the Earth is 5,882,000,000,000,000,000,000 tons *5 976 × 10^{18} tonnes* and its density is 5.517 times that of water. The volume is an estimated 259,875,424,000 miles^3 *1 083 208 018 000 km^3*. The Earth picks up cosmic dust but estimates vary widely with 40,000 tons/*tonnes* a day being the upper limit. Modern theory is that the Earth has an outer shell or lithosphere about 25 miles *40 km* thick, then an outer and inner rock layer or mantle extending 1,800 miles *2 900 km* deep, beneath which there is an iron-nickel core at an estimated temperature of 3 700° C *6,700° F*, and at a pressure of 22,000 tons/*tonnes* per in^2 or 3,400 kb. If the iron-nickel core theory is correct, iron must be by far the most abundant element in the Earth.

1. NATURAL PHENOMENA

EARTHQUAKES

Greatest It is estimated that each year there are some 500,000 **World** detectable seismic or micro-seismic disturbances of which 100,000 can be felt and 1,000 cause damage.

Using the comparative scale of Mantle Wave magnitudes (defined in 1968), the world's largest earthquake since 1930 has been the cataclysmic Alaska, U.S.A., or Prince William Sound earthquake (epicentre Latitude 61° 10′ N., Longitude 147° 48′ W.) of 1964 March 28 with a magnitude of 8.9. The Kamchatka, U.S.S.R., earthquake (epicentre Lat. 52° 45′ N., Long. 159° 30′ E.) of 1952 Nov. 4 and the shocks around Lebu, south of Concepción, Chile on 1960 May 22 are both now assessed at a magnitude of 8.8. Formerly the largest earthquake during this period had been regarded as the submarine shock (epicentre Lat. 39° 30′ N., Long. 144° 30′ E.) about 100 miles off the Sanriku coast of north-eastern Honshū, Japan of 1933 March 2 estimated at 8.9 on the Gutenberg-Richter scale (1956). It is possible that the earthquake in Lisbon, Portugal, of 1755 Nov. 1 would have been accorded a magnitude of between 8¾ and 9 if seismographs, invented in 1853, had been available to record traces. The first of the three shocks was at 9.40 a.m. and lasted for between 6 and 7 min. Lakes in Norway were disturbed. The energy of an earthquake of magnitude 8.9 is about $5.6 × 10^{24}$ ergs, which is equivalent to an explosion of 140 megatons (140 million short tons/*127 million tonnes* of trinitrotoluene [$C_7H_5(NO_2)_3$] called T.N.T.).

Scene after the Alaska earthquake 27 March 1964, the car is straddling a fissure

Worst death roll The greatest loss of life occurred in the earthquake in Shensi Province, China, of 1556 Jan. 23, when an estimated 830,000 people were killed. The greatest material damage was in the earthquake on the Kwanto plain, Japan, of 1923 Sept. 1 (magnitude 8.2, epicentre in Lat. 35° 15′ N., Long. 139° 30′ E.). In Sagami Bay the sea-bottom in one area sank 400 m *1,310 ft*. The official total of persons killed and missing in the *Shinsai* or great 'quake and the resultant fires was 142,807. In Tōkyō and Yokohama 575,000 dwellings were destroyed. The cost of the damage was estimated at £1,000 million (now more than £3,000 million).

The East Anglian or Colchester earthquake of 1884 April 22 (9.18 a.m.) (epicentres Lat. 51° 48′ N., Long. 0° 53′ E., and Lat. 51° 51′ N., Long. 0° 55′ E.) caused damage estimated at £10,000 to 1,200 buildings, and the death of a child at Rowhedge. Langenhoe Church was wrecked. Windows and doors were rattled over an area of 53,000 miles² *137 250 km²* and the shock was felt in Exeter and Ostend, Belgium. The most marked since 1844 and the worst since instruments have been in use (*i.e.* since 1927) occurred in the Midlands at 3.43 p.m. on 1957 Feb. 11, showing a strength of between five and six on the Davison scale. The strongest Scottish tremor occurred at Inverness at 10.45 p.m. on 1816 Aug. 13, and was felt over an area of 50,000 miles² *130 000 km²*. The strongest Welsh tremor occurred in Swansea at 9.45 a.m. on 1906 June 27 (epicentre Lat. 51° 38′ N., Long 4° W.). It was felt over an area of 37,800 miles² *97 900 km²*.

Ireland No earthquake with its epicentre in Ireland has ever been instrumentally measured, though the effects of remoter shocks have been felt. However, there was a shock in 1734 August which damaged 100 dwellings and five churches.

VOLCANOES

The total number of known active volcanoes in the world is 455 with an estimated 80 more that are submarine. The greatest active concentration is in Indonesia, where 77 of its 167 volcanoes have erupted within historic times. The name volcano derives from the now dormant Vulcano Island in the Aeolian group in the Mediterranean.

Greatest eruption The total volume of matter discharged in the eruption of Tambora, a volcano on the island of Sumbawa, in Indonesia, 5–7 April 1815, has been estimated at 36.4 miles³ *151,7 km³*. The energy of this eruption was 8.4×10^{26} ergs. The volcano lost about 1 250 m *4,100 ft* in height and a crater seven miles *11 km* in diameter was formed. This compares with a probable 15 miles³ *62,5 km³* ejected by Santoríni and 4.3 miles³ *18 km³* ejected by Krakatoa (see below). The internal pressure causing the Tambora eruption has been estimated at 46,500,000 lb./in² or more than 20,000 tons/in² *315 000 kg/cm²*.

Greatest explosion The greatest volcanic explosion in historic times was the eruption in *c.* 1470 B.C. of Thíra (Santoríni), a volcanic island in the Aegean Sea. It is highly probable that this explosion destroyed the centres of the Minoan civilization in Crete, about 80 miles *130 km* away, with a *tsunami* 50 m *165 ft* high. Evidence was published in December 1967 of an eruption that spewed lava over 100,000 miles² *260 000 km²* of Oregon, Idaho, Nevada and northern California about 3,000,000 years ago.

The greatest explosion since Santoríni occurred at 9.56 a.m. (local time), or 2.56 a.m. G.M.T., on 27 Aug. 1883, with an eruption of Krakatoa, an island (then 18 miles² *47 km²*) in the Sunda Strait, between Sumatra and Java, in Indonesia. A total of 163 villages were wiped out, and 36,380 people killed by the wave it caused. Rocks were thrown 34 miles *55 km* high and dust fell 3,313 miles *5 330 km* away 10 days later. The explosion was recorded four hours later on the island of Rodrigues, 2,968 miles *4 776 km* away, as "the roar of heavy guns" and was heard over 1/13th part of the surface of the globe. This explosion has been estimated to have had about 26 times the power of the greatest H-bomb test detonation but was still only a fifth part of the Santoríni cataclysm.

Highest Extinct The highest extinct volcano in the world is Cerro Aconcagua (22,834 ft *[6 960 m]*) on the Argentine side of the Andes. It was first climbed on 14 Jan. 1897 and was the highest summit climbed anywhere until 12 June 1907.

Dormant The highest dormant volcano is Volcán Llullaillaco (22,058 ft *[6 723 m]*), on the frontier between Chile and Argentina.

Active The highest volcano regarded as active is Volcán Antofalla (20,013 ft *[6 100 m]*), in Argentina, though a more definite claim is made for Volcán Guayatiri or Guallatiri (19,882 ft *[6 060 m]*), in Chile, which erupted in 1959.

Northernmost and southernmost The northernmost volcano is Beeren Berg (7,470 ft *[2 276 m]*) on the island of Jan Mayen (71° 05′ N.) in the Greenland Sea. It erupted on 20 Sept. 1970 and the island's 39 male inhabitants had to be evacuated. It was possibly discovered by Henry Hudson in 1607 or 1608, but definitely visited by Jan Jacobsz May (Netherlands) in 1614. It was annexed by Norway on 8 May 1929. The most southerly known active volcano is Mount Erebus (12,450 ft *[3 795 m]*) on Ross Island (77° 35′ S.), in Antarctica. It was discovered on 28 Jan. 1841 by the expedition of Captain (later Rear-Admiral Sir) James Clark Ross, R.N. (1800–1862), and first climbed at 10 a.m. on 10 March 1908 by a British party of five, led by Professor (later Lieut.-Col. Sir) Tannatt William Edgeworth David (1858–1934).

Sir James Clark Ross, discoverer of the Magnetic Pole in 1831, and ten years later the most southerly known active volcano, Mt. Erebus

Largest crater The world's largest *caldera* or volcano crater is that of Mount Aso (5,223 ft *[1 590 m]*) in Kyūshū, Japan, which measures 17 miles *27 km* north to south, 10 miles *16 km* east to west and 71 miles *114 km* in circumference. The longest lava flows known as *pahoehoe* (twisted cord-like solidifications) are 60 miles *96 km* in length in Iceland.

GEYSERS

World's tallest The Waimangu geyser, in New Zealand, erupted to a height in excess of 1,000 ft *300 m* in 1909, but has not been active since it erupted violently in 1917. Currently the world's tallest active geyser is the "Giant", discovered in 1872 in what is now the Yellowstone National Park, Wyoming, U.S.A., which erupts at intervals of more than 7 days, throwing a spire 200 ft *60 m* high at a rate of 580,000 gal *2 637 000 litres* per hr. The most regularly erupting geyser is the nearby "Old Faithful", whose 140 ft *42,5 m* spire rarely varies more than 21 minutes either side of its 66 min average. The *Geysir* ("gusher") near Mount Hekla in south-central Iceland, from which all others have been named, spurts, on occasions, to 180 ft *55 m*.

2. STRUCTURE AND DIMENSIONS

OCEANS

Largest The area of the Earth covered by the sea is estimated to be 139,670,000 miles^2 *361 743 000 km^2* or 70.92 per cent of the total surface. The mean depth of the hydrosphere was once estimated to be 12,450 ft *3 795 m*, but recent surveys suggest a lower estimate, of 11,660 ft *3 550 m*. The total weight of the water is estimated to be 1.3×10^{18} tons, or 0.022 per cent of the Earth's total weight. The volume of the oceans is estimated to be 308,400,000 miles^3 *1 285 × 10^9 km^3* compared with only 8,400,000 miles^2 *3,5 × 10^7 km^3* of fresh water.

The largest ocean in the world is the Pacific. Excluding adjacent seas, it represents 45.8 per cent of the world's oceans and is about 63,800,000 miles^2 *165 250 000 km^2* in area. The shortest navigable trans-Pacific distance from Guayaquil, Ecuador to Bangkok, Thailand is 10,905 miles *17 550 km*.

Most southerly The most southerly part of the oceans is 85° 34' S., 154° W., at the snout of the Robert Scott Glacier, 305 miles *490 km* from the South Pole.

Deepest World The deepest part of the ocean was first discovered in 1951 by H.M. Survey Ship *Challenger* in the Marianas Trench in the Pacific Ocean. The depth was measured by sounding and by echo-sounder and published as 5,960 fathoms (35,760 ft [*10 900 m*]). Subsequent visits to the Challenger Deep have resulted in claims by echo-sounder only, culminating in one of 6,033 fathoms (36,198 ft [*11 033 m*]) by the U.S.S.R.'s research ship *Vityaz* in March 1959. A metal object, say a pound ball of steel, dropped into water above this trench would take nearly 63 min to fall to the sea-bed 6.85 miles *11,03 km* below. The average depth of the Pacific Ocean is 14,000 ft *4 267 m*.

British waters The deepest point in the territorial waters of the United Kingdom is an area 6 cables (1,200 yds) off the island of Raasay, Inverness-shire, in the Inner Sound at Lat 57° 30′ 33″ N, Long. 5° 57′ 27″ W. A depth of 1,038 ft (173 fathoms) was found in Dec. 1959 by H.M.S. *Yarnton* (Lt.-Cdr. A. C. F. David, R.N.).

Sea temperature The temperature of the water at the surface of the sea varies from $-2°$ C (*28.5° F*) in the White Sea to 35.6° C (*96° F*) in the shallow areas of the Persian Gulf in summer. A freak geo-thermal temperature of 56° C (*132.8° F*) was recorded in February 1965 by the survey ship *Atlantis II* near the bottom of Discovery Deep (7,200 ft [*2 195 m*]) in the Red Sea. The normal sea temperature in the area is 22° C (*71.6° F*).

Remotest spot from land The world's most distant point from land is a spot in the South Pacific, approximately 48° 30′ S., 125° 30′ W., which is about 1,660 miles *2 670 km* from the nearest points of land, namely Pitcairn Island, Ducie Island and Cape Dart, Antarctica. Centred on this spot, therefore, is a circle of water with an area of

"Old Faithful", the world's most active geyser at Yellowstone National Park erupting into action

about 8,657,000 miles^2 *22 421 500 km^2*—about 7,000 miles^2 *18 000 km^2* larger than the U.S.S.R., the world's largest country (see Chapter 11).

Largest sea The largest of the world's seas (as opposed to oceans) is the South China Sea, with an area of 1,148,500 miles^2 *2 974 600 km^2*. The Malayan Sea comprising the waters between the Indian Ocean and the South Pacific, south of the Chinese mainland covering 3,144,000 miles^2 *8 142 900 km^2* is not now an entity accepted by the International Hydrographic Bureau.

Largest gulf The largest gulf in the world is the Gulf of Mexico, with an area of 580,000 miles^2 *1 500 000 km^2* and a shoreline of 3,100 miles *4 990 km* from Cape Sable, Florida, U.S.A., to Cabo Catoche, Mexico.

Largest bay The largest bay in the world is the Bay of Bengal, with a shoreline of 2,250 miles *3 620 km* from south-eastern Ceylon to Pagoda Point, Burma. Its mouth measures 1,075 miles *1 730 km* across. Great Britain's largest bay is Cardigan Bay which has a 140 mile *225 km* long shoreline and measures 72 miles *116 km* across from the Lleyn Peninsula, Caernarvonshire to St. David's Head, Pembrokeshire in Wales.

Highest seamount The highest known submarine mountain, or seamount is one discovered in 1953 near the Tonga Trench, between Samoa and New Zealand. It rises 28,500 ft *8 690 m* from the sea bed, with its summit 1,200 ft *365 m* below the surface.

STRAITS

Longest The longest straits in the world are the Malacca Straits between West Malaysia (formerly called Malaya) and Sumatra, in Indonesia, which extend for 485 miles *780 km*.

Broadest The broadest straits in the world are the Mozambique Straits between Mozambique and Madagascar, which are at one point 245 miles *394 km* across.

Narrowest The narrowest navigable straits are those between the Aegean island of Euboea and the mainland of Greece.

The gap is only 45 yds *40 m* wide at Chalkis. The Seil Sound, Argyllshire, Scotland, narrows to a point only 20 ft *6 m* wide where a bridge joins the island of Seil to the mainland and is thus said to span the Atlantic.

HIGHEST WAVES

The highest officially recorded sea wave was measured by Lt. Frederic Margraff U.S.N. from the U.S.S. *Ramapo* proceeding from Manila, Philippines, to San Diego, California, U.S.A., on the night of 6–7 Feb. 1933, during a 68-knot (78.3 m.p.h. [*126 km/h*]) gale. The wave was computed to be 112 ft *34 m* from trough to crest. A stereo photograph of a wave calculated to be 24,9 m (*81.7 ft*) high was taken from the U.S.S.R.'s diesel-electric vessel *Ob'* in the South Pacific Ocean, about 600 km *370 miles* south of Macquarie Island, on 2 April 1956. The highest instrumentally measured wave was one 77 ft *23,5 m* high, recorded by the British ship *Weather Adviser* on station Juliette, in the North Atlantic at noon on 17 March 1968. Its length was 1,150 ft *350 m* and its period was 15 sec. It has been calculated on the statistics of the Stationary Random Theory that one wave in more than 300,000 may exceed the average by a factor of 4.

On 9 July 1958 a landslip caused a wave to wash 1,740 ft *530 m* high along the fjord-like Lituya Bay, Alaska, U.S.A.

U.S.S. *Ramapo*, from whom the reading of the highest officially recorded wave was taken in 1933

Seismic wave The highest recorded *tsunami* (often wrongly called a tidal wave), was one of 220 ft *67 m* which appeared off Valdez, south-west Alaska, after the great Prince William Sound earthquake of 28 March 1964. *Tsunami* (a Japanese word which is singular and plural) have been observed to travel at 490 m.p.h. *790 km/h*. Between 479 B.C. and 1967 there were 286 instances of devastating *tsunami*.

CURRENTS

Greatest The greatest current in the oceans of the world is the Antarctic Circumpolar Current, which was measured in 1969 in the Drake Passage between South America and Antarctica to be flowing at a rate of 9,500 million ft³ *270 000 000 m³* per sec—nearly treble that of the Gulf Stream. Its width ranges from 185 to 620 miles *300 to 1 000 km* and has a surface flow rate of ¾ of a knot *1,4 km/h*.

Strongest The world's strongest currents are the Saltstraumen in the Saltfjord, near Bodø, Norway, which reach 15.6 knots (18.0 m.p.h. [*29 km/h*]). The flow rate through the 500-ft *150 m* wide channel surpasses 500,000 cu secs *14 250 m³/sec*. The fastest current in British territorial waters is 10.7 knots *19,8 km/h* in the Pentland Firth between the Orkney Islands and Caithness, Scotland's northernmost mainland county.

GREATEST TIDES

World The greatest tides in the world occur in the Bay of Fundy, which separates Nova Scotia, Canada, from the United States' north-easternmost state of Maine and the Canadian province of New Brunswick.

The highest recorded wave, compared with the Bishop Rock Lighthouse, Isles of Scilly

Burncoat Head in the Minas Basin, Nova Scotia, has the greatest mean spring range with 47.5 ft *14,50 m* and an extreme range of 53.5 ft *16,30 m*.

United Kingdom The place with the greatest mean spring range in Great Britain is Beachley, on the Severn, with a range of 40.7 ft *12,40 m*, compared with the British Isles' average of 15 ft *4,57 m*. Prior to 1933 tides as high as 28.9 ft *8,80 m* above and 22.3 ft *6,80 m* below datum (total range 51.2 ft [*15,60 m*]) were recorded at Avonmouth though an extreme range of 52.2 ft *15,90 m* for Beachley was officially accepted. In 1883 a freak tide of greater range was reported from Chepstow, Monmouthshire.

Ireland The greatest mean spring tidal range in Ireland is 17.3 ft *5,27 m* at Mellon, Limerick, on the banks of the River Shannon.

ICEBERGS

Largest The largest iceberg on record was an Antarctic tabular 'berg of over 12,000 miles² *31 000 km²* (208 miles [*335 km*]) long and 60 miles [*97 km*] wide and thus larger than Belgium) sighted 150 miles *240 km* west of Scott Island, in the South Pacific Ocean, by the U.S.S. *Glacier* on 12 Nov. 1956. The 200-ft *61 m* thick Arctic ice island T.1 (140 miles² [*360 km²*]) was discovered in 1946, and was still being plotted in 1963.

Most southerly Arctic The most southerly Arctic iceberg was sighted in the Atlantic in 30° 50′ N., 45° 06′ W., on 2 June 1934. The tallest on record was one calved off north-west Greenland with 550 ft *165 m* above the surface. The southernmost iceberg reported in British home waters was one sighted 60 miles *96 km* from Smith's Knoll, on the Dogger Bank, in the North Sea.

Most northerly Antarctic The most northerly Antarctic iceberg was a remnant sighted in the Atlantic by the ship *Dochra* in Latitude 26° 30′ S., Longitude 25° 40′ W., on 30 April 1894.

LAND

There is satisfactory evidence that at one time the Earth's land surface comprised a single primeval continent of 80 million miles² *2 × 10⁸ km²*, now termed Pangaea, and that this split about 190,000,000 years ago, during the Jurassic period, into two supercontinents, termed Laurasia (Eurasia, Greenland and Northern America) in the north and Gondwanaland (Africa, Arabia, India, South America, Oceania and Antarctica) and named after Gondwana, India. The South Pole was apparently in the area of the Sahara as recently as the Ordovician period of *c.* 450 million years ago.

The most southerly
Arctic iceberg

The most northerly
Antarctic iceberg

THE WORLD

The world,
showing the
latitudes of the
most southerly
Arctic iceberg
and the most
northerly
Antarctic
iceberg

ROCKS

The age of the Earth is generally considered to be within the range of 4600 ± 100 million years, by analogy with directly measured ages of meteorites and of the moon. However, no rocks of this great age have yet been found on the Earth since geological processes have presumably destroyed the earliest record.

Oldest The greatest recorded age for any reliably dated rock
World is 3800 ± 50 million years for the Amitsoq Gneiss from the Godthaab area of West Greenland, as measured by the rubidium-strontium method by workers at Oxford University. A date of 3550 million years has been reported for the Morton Gneiss of Minnesota, U.S.A., measured by the uranium-lead method by American workers, whilst a number of dates in the general range 3200–3400 million years have been reported from Africa, India and the U.S.S.R.

Britain A considerable proportion of the Lewisian Complex of the Northwest Mainland of Scotland and of the Outer Hebrides has been proved to be 2800–2900 million years old by measurements using the rubidium-strontium and uranium-lead methods.

Largest The largest exposed rocky outcrop is the 1,237-ft *377 m* high Mount Augustus (3,627 ft [*1 105 m*] above sea-level), discovered on 3 June 1858, 200 miles *320 km* east of Carnarvon, Western Australia. It is an up-faulted monoclinal gritty conglomerate 5 miles *8 km* long and 2 miles *3 km* across and thus twice the size of the celebrated monolithic arkose Ayer's Rock (1,100 ft [*335 m*]), 250 miles *400 km* south-west of Alice Springs, in Northern Territory, Australia.

CONTINENTS

Largest Only 29.08 per cent, or an estimated 57,270,000 miles² *148 329 000 km²* of the Earth's surface is land, with a mean height of 2,480 ft *756 m* above sea-level. The Eurasian land mass is the largest, with an area (including islands) of 21,053,000 miles² *54 527 000 km²*.

Smallest The smallest is the Australian mainland, with an area of about 2,940,000 miles² *7 614 500 km²*, which, together with Tasmania, New Zealand, New Guinea and the Pacific Islands, is described sometimes as Oceania. The total area of Oceania is about 3,450,000 miles² *8 935 000 km²* including West Irian (formerly West New Guinea), which is politically in Asia.

Land There is an as yet unpinpointed spot in the Dzoosotoyn
remotest Elisen (desert), northern Sinkiang, China, that is
from the sea more than 1,500 miles *2 400 km* from the open sea
World in any direction. The nearest large town to this point is Wulumuchi (Urumchi) to its south.

Great The point furthest from the sea in Great Britain is a
Britain point near Meriden, Warwickshire, England, which is 72½ miles *117 km* equidistant from the Severn Bridge, the Dee and Mersey estuaries and the Welland estuary in the Wash. The equivalent point in Scotland is in the Forest of Atholl, Perthshire, 40½ miles *65 km* equidistant from the head of Loch Leven, Inverness Firth and the Firth of Tay.

Peninsula The world's largest peninsula is Arabia, with an area of about 1,250,000 miles² *3 250 000 km²*.

ISLANDS

Largest Discounting Australia, which is usually regarded as a
World continental land mass, the largest island in the world is Greenland (part of the Kingdom of Denmark), with an area of about 840,000 miles² *2 175 000 km²*. There is some evidence that Greenland is in fact several islands overlayed by an ice-cap.

Great The mainland of Great Britain (Scotland, England
Britain and Wales) is the eighth largest in the world, with an area of 84,186 miles² *218 041 km²*. It stretches 603½

miles *971 km* from Dunnet Head in the north to Lizard Point in the south and 287½ miles *463 km* across from Porthaflod, Pembrokeshire, Wales to Lowestoft, Suffolk. The island of Ireland (32,594 miles² [*84 418 km²*]) is the 20th largest in the world.

Details of the British Islands will appear in the forthcoming **Guinness Book of British Islands.**

Freshwater The largest island surrounded by fresh water is the Ilha de Marajó (1,553 miles² [*4 022 km²*]), in the mouth of the River Amazon, Brazil. The world's largest inland island (*i.e.* land surrounded by rivers) is Ilha do Bananal, Brazil. The largest island in a lake is Manitoulin Island (1,068 miles² [*2 766 km²*]) in the Canadian (Ontario) section of Lake Huron. This island itself has on it a lake of 41.09 miles² *106,42 km²* called Manitou Lake, in which there are several islands. The largest lake island in Great Britain is Inchmurrin in Loch Lomond with an area of 284 acres *115 ha*.

Remotest The remotest island in the world is Bouvet Øya
World (formerly Liverpool Island), discovered in the South
Uninhabited Atlantic by J. B. C. Bouvet de Lozier on 1 Jan. 1739, and first landed on by Capt. George Norris on 16 Dec. 1825. Its position is 54° 26′ S., 3° 24′ E. This uninhabited Norwegian dependency is about 1,050 miles *1 700 km* from the nearest land—the uninhabited Queen Maud Land coast of eastern Antarctica.

Inhabited The remotest inhabited island in the world is Tristan da Cunha, discovered in the South Atlantic by Tristao da Cunha, a Portuguese admiral, in March 1506. It has an area of 38 miles² *98 km²* (habitable area 12 miles² [*31 km²*]) and was annexed by the United Kingdom on 14 Aug. 1816. The island's population was 235 in August 1966. The nearest inhabited land is the island of St. Helena, 1,320 miles *2 120 km* to the north-east. The nearest continent, Africa is 1,700 miles *2 735 km* away.

British The remotest of the British islets is Rockall 191 miles *307 km* west of St. Kilda, allocated to the County of Inverness in 1971. This 70-ft *21 m* high rock measuring 83 ft *25 m* across was not formally annexed until 18 Sept. 1955. The remotest British island which has ever been inhabited is North Rona which is 44 miles *70,8 km* from the next nearest land at Cape Wrath and the Butt of Lewis. It was evacuated *c.* 1844. Muckle Flugga, off Unst, in the Shetlands, is the northernmost inhabited with a population of 3 (1971) and is in a latitude north of southern Greenland. Just to the north of it is Out Stack.

Newest The world's newest island is a volcanic one about 100 ft *30 m* high, which began forming in 1970 south of Gatukai Island in the British Solomon Islands, southwest Pacific.

Greatest The world's greatest archipelago is the 3,500-mile
archipelago *5 600 km* long crescent of more than 3,000 islands which forms Indonesia.

Northern- The most northerly land is Kaffeklubben Øyen (the
most land Coffee Club Island) off the north-east of Greenland, 440 miles *708 km* from the North Pole, discovered by Dr. Lange Koch in 1921, but determined only in June 1969 to be in Latitude 83° 40′ 6″.

Largest atoll The largest atoll in the world is Kwajalein in the Marshall Islands, in the central Pacific Ocean. Its slender 176-mile *283 km* long coral reef encloses a lagoon of 1,100 miles² *2 850 km²*. The atoll with the largest land area is Christmas Island, in the Line Islands, in the central Pacific Ocean. It has an area of 184 miles² *477 km²*. Its two principal settlements, London and Paris, are 4 miles *6 km* apart.

Longest reef The longest reef is the Great Barrier Reef off Queensland, north-eastern Australia, which is 1,260 geographical miles *2 027 km* in length. Between 1959 and 1971 a large section between Cooktown and Townsville was destroyed by the proliferation of the Crown of Thorns starfish (*Acanthaster planci*).

MOUNTAINS

Highest An eastern Himalayan peak of 29,028 ft *8 848 m* above
World sea-level on the Tibet-Nepal border (in an area first designated Chu-mu-lang-ma on a map of 1717) was discovered to be the world's highest mountain in 1852 by the Survey Department of the Government of India, from theodolite readings taken in 1849 and 1850. In 1860 its height was computed to be 29,002 ft *8 840 m*. The 5½ mile *8,85 km* peak was named Mount Everest after Sir George Everest, C.B. (1790–1866), formerly Surveyor-General of India. After a total loss of 11 lives since the first reconnaissance in 1921, Everest was finally conquered at 11.30 a.m. on 29 May 1953. (For details of ascents, see under Mountaineering in Chapter 12.) The mountain whose summit is farthest from the Earth's centre is the Andean peak of Chimborazo (20,561 ft [*6 267 m*]), 98 miles *158 km* south of the equator in Ecuador, South America. The highest mountain on the equator is Volcán Gayambe (19,285 ft [*5 878 m*]), Ecuador, in Long. 83°.

The highest insular island in the world is Mt. Sukarno (Carstensz Pyramide) (17,096 ft [*5 210 m*]) in West Irian (formerly New Guinea), Indonesia.

Highest The highest mountain in the United Kingdom is Ben
U.K. and Nevis (4,406 ft [*1 343 m*] excluding the 12-ft [*3,65 m*]
Ireland cairn), 4¼ miles *6,85 km* south-east of Fort William, Inverness-shire, Scotland. It was climbed before 1720 but was not discovered to be higher than Ben Macdhui (4,300 ft [*1 310 m*]) until 1870. In 1830 Ben Macdhui and Ben Nevis (Gaelic, Beinn Nibheis) were respectively quoted as 4,418 ft *1 346 m* and 4,358 ft *1 328 m*.

The United Kingdom's highest mountain Ben Nevis, at 4,406 ft *1 343 m*. Ireland is visible from the summit on a very clear day

There is some evidence that, before being ground down by the ice-cap, mountains in the Loch Bà area of the Island of Mull were 15,000 ft *4 575 m* above sea-level.

HIGHEST POINTS IN THE GEOGRAPHICAL COUNTIES OF THE UNITED KINGDOM AND THE REPUBLIC OF IRELAND

Numbers in brackets indicate the order of the counties with the highest point. New Administration Areas will become operative in Great Britain as from 1 April 1974.

The first person known to have visited the highest point in every English and Welsh county is Mr. Basil Harris of Gloucester.

ENGLAND

40 Geographical counties	Height in ft	Height in m	Location
Bedfordshire	798	243	Dunstable Downs
Berkshire	974	296	Walbury Hill
Buckinghamshire	857	261	Aston Hill
Cambridgeshire and Isle of Ely	478	145	300 yds 275 m south of the Hall, Great Chishill
Cheshire	1,908	581	Black Hill
Cornwall	1,377	419	Brown Willy
Cumberland (1)	3,210	978	SCAFELL PIKE
Derbyshire (9)	2,088	636	Kinder Scout
Devon (10)	2,038	621	High Willhays
Dorset	908	276	Pilsdon Pen
Durham, County (6)	2,449	746	Near Burnhope Seat
Essex	480	146	In High Wood, nr. Langley
Gloucestershire	1,083	330	Cleeve Cloud
Hampshire (inc. Isle of Wight)	937	285	Pilot Hill, nr. Ashmansworth
Herefordshire (7)	2,306	702	Black Mountains
Hertfordshire	802	244	Hastoe
Huntingdon and Peterborough	c. 267	81	South of Stamford
Kent	824	251	Westerham (old fort trig. point)
Lancashire (4)	2,631	801	Old Man of Coniston
Leicestershire	912	277	Bardon Hill, nr. Coalville
Lincolnshire	550	167	Normanby-le-Wold
London, Greater	809	246	33 yds 30 m S.E. of "Westerham Heights" (a house) on the Kent-G.L.C. boundary
Monmouthshire (8)	2,228	679	Chwarel-y-Fan
Norfolk	329	100	Roman Camp, Sheringham
Northamptonshire	734	223	Arbury Hill
Northumberland (3)	2,676	815	The Cheviot
Nottinghamshire	652	198	S. side of Herrods Hill
Oxfordshire	835	254	Portobello
Rutland	646	196	West of Oakham
Shropshire	1,772	540	Brown Clee Hill
Somerset	1,705	519	Dunkery Beacon
Staffordshire	1,684	513	Oliver Hill
Suffolk	420	128	Rede
Surrey	965	294	Leith Hill
Sussex	919	280	Blackdown Hill
Warwickshire	854	260	Ilmington Downs
Westmorland (2)	3,118	950	Helvellyn
Wiltshire	964	293	Milk Hill and Tan Hill
Worcestershire	1,394	424	Worcestershire Beacon
Yorkshire (5)	2,591	789	Mickle Fell

SCOTLAND   33 Geographical counties

Aberdeenshire (2)	4,296	1 309	Ben Macdhui (shared with Banffshire)
Angus (7)	3,504	1 068	Glas Maol
Argyll (6)	3,766	1 147	Bidean nam Bian
Ayrshire	2,565	781	Kirriereoch Hill
Banffshire (2)	4,296	1 309	Ben Macdhui (shared with Aberdeenshire)
Berwickshire	c. 1,730	527	Meikle Says Law (slopes of)
Bute	2,868	874	Goat Fell, Arran
Caithness	2,313	705	Morven
Clackmannanshire	2,364	720	Ben Cleugh (Clach) (Ochils)
Dumfries-shire	2,696	821	White Coomb
Dunbarton (10)	3,092	942	Ben Vorlich
East Lothian	1,755	534	Meikle Says Law
Fife	1,713	522	West Lomond
Inverness-shire (1)	4,406	1 342	BEN NEVIS
Kincardineshire	2,555	778	Mount Battock (on Angus border)
Kinross-shire	1,630	496	Innerdouny Hill (Ochils)
Kirkcudbrightshire	2,770	844	Merrick
Lanarkshire	2,455	748	Culter Fell
Midlothian	2,137	651	Blackhope Scar
Moray	2,329	709	Càrn A 'Ghille Chearr
Nairnshire	2,162	658	Càrn-Glas-Choire
Orkney	1,570	478	Ward Hill, Hoy
Peebles-shire	2,756	840	Broad Law (shared with Selkirkshire)
Perthshire (4)	3,984	1 214	Ben Lawers
Renfrewshire	1,713	522	Hill of Stake (on Ayrshire border)
Ross and Cromarty (5)	3,880	1 182	Carn Eige (on Inverness-shire border)
Roxburghshire	2,433	741	Nr. Auchope Cairn (on English border)
Selkirkshire	2,756	840	Broad Law (shared with Peebles-shire)
Shetland	1,486	452	Ronas Hill, Northmavine
Stirlingshire (9)	3,192	972	Ben Lomond
Sutherland (8)	3,273	997	Ben More Assynt
West Lothian	1,023	311	The Knock
Wigtownshire	1,051	320	Craigairie Fell

WALES   12 Geographical counties

Anglesey	720	219	Caer y Twr
Breconshire (3)	2,906	885	Pen-y-Fan (Cader Arthur)
Caernarvonshire (1)	3,560	1 085	SNOWDON (YR WYDDFA)
Cardiganshire	2,468	752	Plynlimon
Carmarthenshire (6)	2,500+	762+	Carmarthen Fan Foel
Denbighshire (4)	2,713	826	Moel Sych (shared with Montgomeryshire)
Flintshire	1,820	554	Moel Fammau
Glamorgan	1,969	600	Cefnfford
Merionethshire (2)	2,974	905	Aran Fawddwy, nr. Bala
Montgomeryshire (4)	2,713	826	Moel Sych (shared with Denbighshire)
Pembrokeshire	1,760	536	Foel Cwmcerwyn
Radnorshire	2,166	660	In Radnor Forest

NORTHERN IRELAND   (6 Counties)

Antrim	1,817	553	Trostàn
Armagh	1,894	577	Slieve Gullion
Down (1)	2,796	852	SLIEVE DONARD
Fermanagh	2,188	666	Cuilcagh
Londonderry	2,240	682	Sawel Mountain
Tyrone	2,240	682	Sawel Mountain

†REPUBLIC OF IRELAND   (26 Counties)

Carlow (6)	2,610	795	Mount Leinster
Cavan	2,188	666	Cuilcagh
Clare	1,746	532	Glennagalliagh
Cork	2,321	707	Knockboy
Donegal	2,466	751	Errigal
Dublin	2,475	754	Kippure
Galway	2,395	729	Benbaun
Kerry (1)	3,414	1 040	CARRAUNTOOHILL
Kildare	1,248	380	Cupidstown Hill
Kilkenny	1,694	516	Brandon
Leitrim	2,113	644	Truskmore (slopes)
Leix	1,734	528	Arderin
Limerick (3)	3,018	919	Galtymore
Longford	916	279	Cornhill
Louth	1,935	589	Slieve Foye
Mayo (5)	2,688	819	Mweelrea
Meath	911	277	Carnbune East
Monaghan	1,255	382	Slieve Beagh (slopes)
Offaly	1,734	528	Arderin
Roscommon	c. 1,350	411	Corry Mountain (slopes)
Sligo	2,120	646	Truskmore
Tipperary (3)	3,018	919	Galtymore
Waterford (8)	2,609	795	Knockmealdown
Westmeath	855	260	Mullaghmeen
Wexford (6)	2,610	795	Mount Leinster
Wicklow (2)	3,039	926	Lugnaquillia

† Relative to the Poolbeg (Dublin) datum.

Peaks over 3,000 ft There are 577 peaks and tops over 3,000 ft *915 m* in the whole British Isles and 165 peaks and 136 tops in Scotland higher than England's highest point, Scafell Pike. The highest mountain off the mainland is Sgùrr Alasdair (3,309 ft [*1 008 m*]) on Skye named after Alexander (in Gaelic Alasdair) Nicolson, who made the first ascent in 1873.

Highest unclimbed Excluding subsidiary summits, the highest separate unclimbed mountain in the world is Gasherbrum III (26,090 ft [7 952 m]) in the Karakoram followed by Kangbachen (25,925 ft [7 900 m]) in the Himalaya. These rank, respectively, 15th and 19th in height in the world.

Largest The world's tallest mountain measured from its submarine base (3,280 fathoms [6 000 m]) in the Hawaiian Trough to peak is Mauna Kea (Mountain White) on the Island of Hawaii, with a combined height of 33,476 ft 10 203 m of which 13,796 ft 4 205 m are above sea-level. Another mountain whose dimensions, but not height, exceed those of Mount Everest is the Hawaiian peak of Mauna Loa (Mountain Long) at 13,680 ft 4 170 m. The axes of its elliptical base, 15,000 ft 4 572 m below sea-level, have been estimated at 74 miles 119 km and 53 miles 85 km. It should be noted that Cerro Aconcagua (22,834 ft [6 960 m]) is more than 38,800 ft 11 826 m above the 16,000-ft 4 875 m deep Pacific abyssal plain or 42,834 ft 13 055 m above the Peru-Chile Trench which is 180 miles 290 km distant in the South Pacific.

Greatest ranges The world's greatest land mountain range is the Himalaya-Karakoram, which contains 96 of the world's 109 peaks of over 24 000 ft 7 315 m. The greatest of all mountain ranges is, however, the submarine mid-Atlantic Ridge, which is 10,000 miles 16 100 km long and 500 miles 805 km wide, with its highest peak being Mount Pico in the Azores, which rises 23,615 ft 7 198 m from the ocean floor (7,615 ft [2 320 m] above sea-level).

Greatest plateau The most extensive high plateau in the world is the Tibetan Plateau in Central Asia. The average altitude is 16,000 ft 4 875 m and the area is 77,000 miles² 200 000 km².

Highest halites Along the northern shores of the Gulf of Mexico for 725 miles 1 160 km there exist 330 subterranean "mountains" of salt, some of which rise more than 60,000 ft 18 300 m from bed rock and appear as the low salt domes first discovered in 1862.

Largest swamp The world's largest tract of swamp is in the basin of the Pripet or Pripyat River—a tributary of the Dnieper in the U.S.S.R. These swamps cover an estimated area of 18,125 miles² 46 950 km².

Sand dunes The world's highest measured sand dunes are those in the Saharan sand sea of Isaouane-N-Tiferine of east central Algeria in Lat. 26° 42′ N, Long. 6° 43′ E. They have a wavelength of nearly 3 miles 5 km and attain a height of 430 metres [1,410 ft].

DEPRESSIONS

Deepest World The deepest depression so far discovered is beneath the Hollick-Kenyon Plateau in Marie Byrd Land, Antarctica, where, at a point 5,900 ft 1 800 m above sea-level, the ice depth is 14,000 ft 4 267 m, hence indicating a bed rock depression 8,100 ft 2 468 m below sea-level. The greatest submarine depression is a large area of the floor of the north west Pacific which has an average depth of 15,000 ft 4 570 m.

The deepest exposed depression on land is the shore surrounding the Dead Sea, 1,291 ft 393 m below sea-level. The deepest point on the bed of this lake is 2,600 ft 792 m below the Mediterranean. The deepest part of the bed of Lake Baykal in Siberia, U.S.S.R., is 4,872 ft 1 484 m below sea-level.

Great Britain The lowest lying area in Great Britain is in the Holme Fen area of the Great Ouse, in northern Huntingdon and Peterborough, at 9 ft 2,75 m below sea-level. The deepest depression in England is the bed of part of Windermere, 94 ft 28,65 m below sea-level, and in Scotland the bed of Loch Morar, 987 ft 300,8 m below sea-level.

Largest The largest exposed depression in the world is the Caspian Sea basin in the Azerbaydzhani, Russian, Kazakh and Turkmen Republics of the U.S.S.R. and northern Iran (Persia). It is more than 200,000 miles² 518 000 km² of which 143,550 miles² 371 792 km² is lake area. The preponderant land area of the depression is the Prikaspiyskaya Nizmennost', lying around the northern third of the lake and stretching inland for a distance of up to 280 miles 450 km.

RIVERS

The river systems of the world are estimated to contain 55,000 miles³ 230 000 km³ of fresh water.

Longest World The two longest rivers in the world are the Amazon (Amazonas), flowing into the South Atlantic, and the Nile (Bahr-el-Nil) flowing into the Mediterranean. Which is the longer is more a matter of definition than of simple measurement.

The true source of the Amazon was discovered in 1953 to be a stream named Huarco, rising near the summit of Cerro Huagra (17,188 ft [5 238 m]) in Peru. This stream progressively becomes the Toro then the Santiago then the Apurímac, which in turn is known as the Ene and then the Tambo before its confluence with the Amazon prime tributary the Ucayali. The length of the Amazon from this source to the South Atlantic via the Canal do Norte was measured in 1969 to be 4,007 miles 6 448 km (usually quoted to the rounded off figure of 4,000 miles [6 437 km]).

If, however, a vessel navigating down the river turns to the south of Ilha de Marajó through the straits of Breves and Boiuci into the Pará, the total length of the watercourse becomes 4,195 miles 6 750 km. The Pará is not however a tributary of the Amazon, being hydrologically part of the basin of the Tocantins.

The length of the Nile watercourse, as surveyed by M. Devroey (Belgium) before the loss of a few miles of meanders due to the formation of Lake Nasser, behind the Aswan High Dam, was 4,145 miles 6 670 km. This course is the hydrologically acceptable one from the source in Ruanda of the Luvironza branch of the Kagera feeder of the Victoria Nyanza via the White Nile (Bahr-el-Jebel) to the delta.

Ireland The longest river in Ireland is the Shannon, which is longer than any river in Great Britain. It rises 258 ft 78,6 m above sea-level, in County Cavan, and flows through a series of loughs to Limerick. It is 240 miles 386 km long, including the 56 mile 90 km long estuary to Loop Head. The basin area is 6,060 miles² 15 695 km².

Great Britain The longest river in Great Britain is the Severn, which empties into the Bristol Channel and is 220 miles 354 km long. Its basin extends over 4,409 miles² 11 419 km². It rises in south-western Montgomeryshire, in Wales and flows through Shropshire, Worcestershire and Gloucestershire. The longest river wholly in England is the Thames, which is 215 miles 346 km long to the Nore. Its remotest source is at Seven Springs, Gloucestershire, whence the River Churn joins the other head waters. The source of the Thames proper is Trewsbury Mead, Coate, Cirencester, Gloucestershire. The basin measures 3,841 miles² 9 948km². The longest river wholly in Wales is the Towy, with a length of 64 miles 102 km. It rises in Cardiganshire and flows out into Carmarthen Bay. The longest river in Scotland is the Tay, with Dundee, Angus, on the shore of the estuary. It is 117 miles 188 km long from the source of its remotest head-stream, the River Tummel, Perthshire and has the greatest volume of any river in Great Britain, with a flow of up to 49,000 cusecs 1 387 m³ per sec. Its basin extends over 1,961 miles² 5 078 km².

Shortest river The strongest claimant to the title of the world's shortest river is the D River, Lincoln, Oregon, U.S.A., which connects Devil Lake to the Pacific Ocean and is 440 ft *134 m* long at low tide.

Greatest flow The greatest flow of any river in the world is that of the Amazon, which discharges an average of 4,200,000 cusecs *120 000 m^3/sec* into the Atlantic Ocean, rising to more than 7,000,000 cusecs *200 000 m^3/sec* in full flood. The lowest 900 miles *1 450 km* of the Amazon average 300 ft *90 m* in depth.

Largest basin and longest tributary The largest river basin in the world is that drained by the Amazon (4,007 miles [*6 448 km*]). It covers about 2,720,000 miles^2 *7 045 000 km^2*. It has about 15,000 tributaries and subtributaries, of which four are more than 1,000 miles *1 609 km* long. These include the Madeira, the longest of all tributaries, with a length of 2,100 miles *3 380 km*, which is surpassed by only 14 rivers in the whole world.

Longest sub-tributary The longest sub-tributary is the Pilcomayo (1,000 miles [*1 609 km*] long) in South America. It is a tributary of the Paraguay (1,500 miles [*2 415 km*] long), which is itself a tributary of the Paraná (2,500 miles [*4 025 km*]).

Submarine river In 1952 a submarine river 250 miles *400 km* wide, known as the Cromwell current, was discovered flowing eastward 300 ft *90 m* below the surface of the Pacific for 3,500 miles *5 625 km* along the equator. Its volume is 1,000 times that of the Mississippi.

Sub-terranean river In August 1958 a crypto-river was tracked by radio isotopes flowing under the Nile with a mean annual flow six times greater—560,000 million m^3 *20 million million ft^2*.

Longest estuary The world's longest estuary is that of the Ob', in the northern U.S.S.R., at 450 miles *725 km*.

Largest delta The world's largest delta is that created by the Ganga (Ganges) and Brahmaputra in Bangla Desh (formerly East Pakistan) and West Bengal, India. It covers an area of 30,000 miles^2 *75 000 km^2*.

RIVER BORES

World The bore on the Ch'ient'ang'kian (Hang-chou-fe) in eastern China is the most remarkable in the world. At spring tides the wave attains a height of up to 25 ft *7,5 m* and a speed of 13 knots *24 km/h*. It is heard advancing at a range of 14 miles *22 km*. The bore on the Hooghly branch of the Ganges travels for 70 miles *110 km* at more than 15 knots *27 km/h*. The annual downstream flood wave on the Mekong sometimes reaches a height of 46 ft *14 m*. The greatest volume of any tidal bore is that of the Canal do Norte (10 miles [*16 km*] wide) in the mouth of the Amazon.

The river bore on the Hang-chou-fe, the roar of which can be heard at a distance of 14 miles *22 km*

Great Britain The most notable river bore in the United Kingdom is that on the River Severn, which attained a measured height of 9¼ ft *2,8 m* on 15 Oct. 1966 downstream of Stonebench, and a speed of 13 m.p.h. *20 km/h*. It travels 21 miles *33 km* from Awre to Gloucester.

Fastest rapids The fastest rapids which have ever been navigated are the Lava Falls on the River Colorado, U.S.A. At times of flood these attain a speed of 30 m.p.h. *48 km/h* (26 knots) with waves boiling up to 12 ft *3,65 m*.

WATERFALLS

Highest The highest waterfall in the world is the Angel Falls, in Venezuela, on a branch of the River Carrao, an upper tributary of the Caroní with a total drop of 3,212 ft *979 m*—the longest single drop is 2,648 ft *807 m*. It was discovered in 1935 by a United States pilot named Jimmy Angel (died 8 Dec. 1956), who crashed nearby. The Auyan-Tepui plateau was first climbed on 13 Jan. 1971.

United Kingdom The tallest waterfall in the United Kingdom is Eas-Coul-Aulin, in the parish of Eddrachillis, Sutherland, Scotland, with a drop of 658 ft *200 m*. England's highest fall is Caldron (or Cauldron) Snout, on the Tees, with a fall of 200 ft *60 m* in 450 ft *135 m* of cataracts, but no sheer leap. It is at the junction of Durham, Westmorland and Yorkshire. The highest Welsh waterfall is the Pistyll Rhaiadr (240 ft [*73 m*]), on the River Rhaiadr, in southern Denbighshire.

The highest waterfall in Wales, the 240 ft *73 m* Pistyll Rhaiadr, on the River Rhaiadr, Denbighshire

Ireland The highest falls in Ireland are the Powerscourt Falls (350 ft [*106 m*]), on the River Dargle, County Wicklow.

Greatest On the basis of the average annual flow, the greatest waterfall in the world is the Guairá (374 ft [*114 m*] high), known also as the Salto dos Sete Quedas, on the Alto Paraná River between Brazil and Paraguay. Although attaining an average height of only 110 ft *33,5 m*, its estimated annual average flow over the lip (5,300 yds [*4 850 m*] wide) is 470,000 cusecs *13 300 m^3/sec*. The amount of water this represents can be imagined by supposing that it was pouring into the dome of St. Paul's Cathedral—it would fill it completely in three-fifths of a sec. It has a peak flow of 1,750,000 ft^3/sec *50 000 m^3/sec*. The seven cataracts of the Stanley Falls in the Congo (Kinshasa) have an average annual flow of 600,000 ft^3/sec *17 000 m^3/sec*.

Widest The widest waterfalls in the world are the Khône Falls (50 to 70 ft [*15–21 m*] high) in Laos, with a width of 6.7 miles *10,8 km* and a flood flow of 1,500,000 cusecs *42 500 m^3/sec*.

Longest fjords and sea lochs

World The world's longest fjord is the Nordvest Fjord arm of the Scoresby Sund in eastern Greenland, which extends inland 195 miles *313 km* from the sea. The longest of Norwegian fjords is the Sogne Fjord, which extends 183 km *113.7 miles* inland from Sygnefest to the head of the Lusterfjord arm at Skjolden. It averages barely 3 miles *4,75 km* in width and has a deepest point of 4,085 ft *1 245 m*. If measured from Huglo along the Bømlafjord to the head of the Sørfjord arm at Odda, the Hardangerfjorden can also be said to extend 183 km *113.7 miles*. The longest Danish fjord is the Limfjorden (100 miles [*160 km*] long).

Great Britain Scotland's longest sea loch is Loch Fyne, which extends 42 miles *67,5 km* inland into Argyllshire.

LAKES AND INLAND SEAS

Largest

World The largest inland sea or lake in the world is the Kaspiskoye More (Caspian Sea) in the southern U.S.S.R. and Iran (Persia). It is 760 miles *1 225 km* long and its total area is 143,550 miles² *371 800 km²*. Of the total area some 55,280 miles² *143 200 km²* (38.6%) is in Iran, where it is named the Darya-ye-Khazar. Its maximum depth is 980 m *3,215 ft* and its surface is 92 ft *28 m* below sea-level. Its estimated volume is 21,500 miles³ *89 600 km³* of saline water. Since 1930 it has diminished 15,000 miles² *39 000 km²* in area with a fall of 62 ft *18,90 m* while the shore line has retreated more than 10 miles *16 km* in some places.

Freshwater lake

World The freshwater lake with the greatest surface area is Lake Superior, one of the Great Lakes of North America. The total area is 31,800 miles² *82 350 km²*, of which 20,700 miles² *53 600 km²* are in Minnesota, Wisconsin and Michigan, U.S.A. and 11,100 miles² *27 750 km²* in Ontario, Canda. It is 600 ft *182 m* above sea-level. The freshwater lake with the greatest volume is Baykal (see Deepest lake, below) with an estimated volume of 5,750 miles³ *24 000 km³*.

United Kingdom The largest lake in the United Kingdom is Lough Neagh (48 ft [*14,60 m*] above sea-level) in Northern Ireland. It is 18 miles *28,9 km* long and 11 miles *17,7 km* wide and has an area of 147.39 miles² *381,73 km²*. Its extreme depth is 102 ft *31 m*.

Great Britain The largest lake in Great Britain, and the largest inland loch in Scotland is Loch Lomond (23 ft [*7,0 m*] above sea-level), which is 22.64 miles *36,44 km* long and has a surface area of 27.45 miles² *70,04 km²*. It is situated in the counties of Stirling and Dunbarton and its greatest depth is 623 ft *190 m*. The lake with the greatest volume is however Loch Ness with 263,162,000,000 ft³ *7 451 920 000 m³*. The longest lake is Loch Ness which measures 24.23 miles *38,99 km*. The 3 arms of the Y-shaped Loch Awe aggregate however 25.47 miles *40,99 km*. The largest lake in England is Windermere, in the county of Westmorland. It is 10½ miles *17 km* long and has a surface area of 5.69 miles² *14,74 km²*. Its greatest depth is 219 ft *66,75 m* in the northern half. The largest *natural* lake in Wales is Llyn Tegid, with an area of 1.69 miles² *4,38 km²*, although it should be noted that the largest lake in Wales is that formed by the reservoir at Lake Vyrnwy, where the total surface area is 1,120 acres *453,25 ha*.

Republic of Ireland The largest lough in the Republic of Ireland is Lough Corrib in the counties of Mayo and Galway. It measures 27 miles *43,5 km* in length and is 7 miles *11,25 km* across at its widest point with a total surface area of 41,616 acres (65.0 miles² [*168 km²*]).

Lake in a lake The largest lake in a lake is Manitou Lake (41.09 miles² [*106,42 km²*]) on Manitoulin Island (1,068 miles² [*2 766 km²*]) in the Canadian part of Lake Huron.

Loch Fyne, Great Britain's longest sea loch, seen from Strachur, Argyllshire

DEEPEST LAKES

World The deepest lake in the world is Ozero (Lake) Baykal in central Siberia, U.S.S.R. It is 385 miles *620 km* long and between 20 and 46 miles *32–74 km* wide. In 1957 the Olkhon Crevice was measured to be 1 940 m *6,365 ft* deep and hence 1 485 m *4,872 ft* below sea-level.

Great Britain The deepest lake in Great Britain is the 10.30 mile *16,57 km* long Loch Morar, in Inverness-shire. Its surface is 30 ft *9 m* above sea-level and its extreme depth 1,017 ft *310 m*. England's deepest lake is Wast Water (258 ft [*78 m*]), in Cumberland. That with the greatest mean depth is Loch Ness with 433 ft *132 m*.

HIGHEST LAKES

World The highest steam-navigated lake in the world is Lago Titicaca (maximum depth 1,214 ft [*370 m*]), with an area of about 3,200 miles² *8 285 km²* (1,850 miles² [*4 790 km²*] in Peru, 1,350 miles² [*3 495 km²*] in Bolivia), in South America. It is 130 miles *209 km* long and is situated at 12,506 ft *3 811 m* above sea-level. There is a small unnamed lake north of Mount Everest by the Changtse Glacier, Tibet, at an altitude of 20,230 ft *6 166 m* above sea-level.

United Kingdom The highest lake in the United Kingdom is the 1.9 acre *0,76 ha* Lochan Buidhe at 3,600 ft *1 097 m* above sea-level in the Cairngorm Mountains, Scotland. England's highest is Broad Crag Tarn (2,746 ft [*837 m*] above sea-level) on Scafell, Cumberland, and the highest in Wales is a pool above Llyn y Fign (c. 2,540 ft [*774 m*]), 8 miles *12,8 km* east of Dolgellau, Merionethshire.

Longest glaciers It is estimated that 6,020,000 miles² *15 600 000 km²*, or about 10.4 per cent of the Earth's land surface, is permanently glaciated. The world's longest known glacier is the Lambert Glacier, discovered by an Australian aircraft crew in Australian Antarctic Territory in 1956–57. It is up to 40 miles *64 km* wide and, with its upper section, known as the Mellor Glacier, it measures at least 250 miles *402 km* in length. With the Fisher Glacier limb, the Lambert forms a continuous ice passage about 320 miles *514 km* long. The longest Himalayan glacier is the Siachen (47 miles [*75,6 km*]) in the Karakoram range, though the Hispar and Biafo combine to form an ice passage 76 miles *122 km* long.

Greatest avalanches The greatest avalanches, though rarely observed, occur in the Himalaya but no estimates of their volume have been published. It was estimated that 3,500,000 m³ *120 000 000 ft³* of snow fell in an avalanche in the Italian Alps in 1885. (See also Disasters, end of Chapter 11.)

DESERT

Largest Nearly an eighth of the world's land surface is arid with a rainfall of less than 25 cm (*9.8 in*) per annum. The Sahara Desert in N. Africa is the largest in the world. At its greatest length it is 3,200 miles *5 150 km* from east to west. From north to south it is between 800 and 1,400 miles *1 275 and 2 250 km*. The area covered by the desert is about 3,250,000 miles² *8 400 000 km²*. The land level varies from 436 ft *132 m* below sea-level in the Qattâra Depression, United Arab Republic (formerly Egypt), to the mountain Emi Koussi (11,204 ft [*3 415 m*]) in Chad. The diurnal temperature range in the western Sahara may be more than 80° F. or 45° C.

GORGE

Largest The largest gorge in the world is the Grand Canyon on the Colorado River in north-central Arizona, U.S.A. It extends from Marble Gorge to the Grand Wash Cliffs, over a distance of 217 miles *349 km*. It varies in width from 4 to 13 miles *6 to 20 km* and is up to 7,000 ft *2 133 m* deep.

Deepest The deepest visible canyon in the world is Hell's Canyon, dividing Oregon and Idaho, U.S.A. It plunges 7,900 ft *2 400 m* from the Devil Mountain down to the Snake River. The deepest submarine canyon yet discovered is one 25 miles *40 km* south of Esperance, Western Australia, which is 6,000 ft *1 800 m* deep and 20 miles *32 km* wide.

CAVES

Largest The largest known underground chamber in the *World* world is the Big Room of the Carlsbad Caverns (1,320 ft [*400 m*] deep) in New Mexico, U.S.A. It is 4,270 ft *1 300 m* long and reaches 328 ft *99,99 m* in height and 656 ft *200 m* in width. The largest cavern in Britain is a cavern about 2,500 ft *760 m* long, discovered on 13 April 1966 under Mynydd-dhu, a hill in Carmarthenshire, Wales. It contains stalagmites 12 ft *3,65 m* tall and a waterfall with a drop of 100 ft *30 m*.

Longest The most extensive cave system in the world is that under the Mammoth Cave National Park, Kentucky, U.S.A. first discovered in 1799. On 9 Sept. 1972 an exploration group led by Dr. John P. Wilcox completed a connection, pioneered by Mrs. Patricia Crowther on 30 Aug., between the Flint Ridge Cave System (87 miles [*140 km*] long) and the Mammoth Cave system (58 miles [*93 km*] long) so making a combined system with a total mapped passageway length of 145 miles *233 km*. The longest cave system in Great Britain is Ogof Ffynnon Ddu, Breconshire in South Wales, in which 20.3 miles *32,67 km* of passages have so far been surveyed.

DEEPEST CAVES BY COUNTRIES

These depths are subject to continuous revisions.

Ft below Entrance	m		
4,300	1 310	Gouffre de la Pierre Saint-Martin, Pyrenees	France/Spain
3,750	1 143	Gouffre Berger, Sornin Plateau, Vercors	France
2,906	885	Spulga della Preta, Lessinische Alps	Italy
2,427	739	Hölloch, Mustathal, Schwyz	Switzerland
2,329	709	Gruberhorn Höhle, Hoher Göll, Salzburg	Austria
2,099	639	Sniezna, Tatra	Poland
2,040	621	Gouffre de Faour Dara	Lebanon
2,006	611	Sotano del San Agustin	Mexico
1,969	600	Gouffre Juhue	Spain
1,885	574	Ragge favreraige	Norway
1,770	539	Abisso Vereo, Istria	Yugoslavia
1,690	515	Anou Boussouil, Djurdjura	Algeria
>1,300	396	Provetina, Mount Astraka	Greece
1,184	360	Neff's Cave, Utah	U.S.A.
1,115	340	Izvorul Tausoarelor, Rodna	Romania
850	259	Ogof Ffynnon Ddu, Breconshire	Wales
653	199	Oxlow Cavern, Giant's Hole, Derbyshire	England
527	160	Growling Swallet Cave, Tasmania	Australia
330	100	Pollnagollum-Poulelva, County Clare	Ireland

LONGEST CAVE SYSTEMS BY COUNTRIES

These surveyed lengths are subject to continuous revision.

Miles	Km		
145	233	Flint Ridge Cave System, Kentucky	U.S.A.
72	116	Hölloch, Schwyz	Switzerland
32.74	52,69	Sistema Cavernavio de Cuyaguatega	Cuba
*26.10	42,00	Eisriesenwelt, Werfen, Salzburg	Austria
22.74	36,60	Peschtschera Optimistitshcheskaya, Pololien	U.S.S.R.
22.48	36,18	Complejo Palomera-Dolencias, Burgos	Spain
20.3	32,67	Ogof Ffynnon Ddu, Breconshire	Wales
17.00	27,36	Postojnska Jama, Slovenia	Yugoslavia
15.98	25,72	Réseau de la Dent de Crolles	France
13.67	22,00	Baradla Barlang-Jaskyna Domica, Magyarország	Hungary
12.5	20,1	Lancaster Hole—Easegill Caverns, Westmorland	England
7.39	11,89	Poulnagollum-Poulelva Caves, County Clare	Ireland
>6	9,65	Mullamullang Cave	Australia

* Longest ice caves, discovered in 1879. Now rank as seventh longest known.

Longest The longest known stalactite in the world is a wall-*stalactite* supported column extending 195 ft *59 m* from roof to floor in the Cueva de Nerja, near Málaga, Spain. The rather low tensile strength of calcite (calcium carbonate) precludes very long free-hanging stalactites, but one of 38 ft *11,60 m* exists in the Poll an Ionian cave in County Clare, Ireland.

Tallest The tallest known stalagmite in the world is La *stalagmite* Grande Stalagmite in the Aren Armand cave, Lozère, France, which has attained a height of 98 ft *29 m* from the cave floor. It was found in September 1897.

SEA CLIFFS

Highest The location of the highest sea cliffs in the world has yet to be established. These may be in north-west Greenland. Coastal terrain at Dexterity Fjord, north-east Baffin Island rises to 4,000 ft *1 200 m*. The highest cliffs in the British Isles are those on the north coast of Achill Island, in County Mayo, Ireland, which are 2,192 ft *668 m* sheer above the sea at Croaghan. The highest cliffs in the United Kingdom are the 1,300 ft *396 m* Conachair cliffs on St. Kilda, Scotland (1,397 ft [*425 m*]). The highest sheer sea cliffs on the mainland of Great Britain are at Clo Mor, 3 miles *4,8 km* south east of Cape Wrath, Sutherland, Scotland which drop 921 ft *280,7 m*. England's highest cliffs are at Countisbury, North Devon, where they drop 900 ft *274 m*.

NATURAL BRIDGE

Longest The longest natural bridge in the world is the Landscape Arch in the Arches and Canyonlands National Parks, Natural Bridges National Monument, Moab, Utah, U.S.A. This natural sandstone arch spans 291 ft *88 m* and is set about 100 ft *30 m* above the canyon floor. In one place erosion has narrowed its section to 6 ft *1,82 m*. Larger, however, is the Rainbow Bridge, Utah discovered on 14 Aug. 1909 with a span of 278 ft *84,7 m* and more than 22 ft *7 m* wide.

3. WEATHER

The meteorological records given below necessarily relate largely to the last 125 to 145 years, since data before that time are both sparse and unreliable. Reliable registering thermometers were introduced as recently as c. 1820.

Palaeo-entomological evidence is that there was a southern European climate in England c. 90,000 B.C., while in c. 6,000 B.C. the mean summer temperature reached 67° F *19,4° C*, or 6° F *14,4° C* higher than the present. The earliest authentic British weather records relate to the period 26–30 Aug. 55 B.C. The earliest reliably known hot summer was in A.D. 664 during our driest every century and the earliest known severe winter was that of A.D. 763–4. In 1683–84 there was frost in London from November to April. Frosts were recorded during August in the period 1668–89.

Progressive The world's extremes of temperature have been noted
extremes progressively thus:

127.4° F	53,0° C	Ouargla, Algeria	27 Aug. 1884
130° F	54,4° C	Amos, California, U.S.A.	17 Aug. 1885
130° F	54,4° C	Mammoth Tank, California, U.S.A.	17 Aug. 1885
134° F	56,7° C	Death Valley, California, U.S.A.	10 July 1913
136.4° F	58,0° C	Al'Aziziyah (el-Azizia), Libya*	13 Sept. 1922

* *Obtained by the U.S. National Geographic Society but not officially recognized by the Libyan Ministry of Communications.*

A reading of 140° F 60° C at Delta, Mexico, in August 1953 is not now accepted because of over-exposure to roof radiation. The official Mexican record of 136.4° F 58,0° C at San Luis, Sonora on 11 Aug. 1933 is not internationally accepted.

A freak heat flash reported from Coimbra, Portugal, in September 1933 said to have caused the temperature to rise to 70° C 158° F for 120 seconds is apocryphal.

Lowest Screen Temperatures

—73° F	—58,3° C	Floeberg Bay, Ellesmere Is., Canada	1852
—90.4° F	—68° C	Verkhoyansk, Siberia, U.S.S.R.	3 Jan. 1885
—90.4° F	—68° C	Verkhoyansk, Siberia, U.S.S.R.	5 & 7 Feb. 1892
—90.4° F	—68° C	Oymyakon, Siberia, U.S.S.R.	6 Feb. 1933
—100.4° F	—73,5° C	South Pole, Antarctica	11 May 1957
—102.1° F	—74,5° C	South Pole, Antarctica	17 Sept. 1957
—109.1° F	—78,34° C	Sovietskaya, Antarctica	2 May 1958
—113.3° F	—80,7° C	Vostok, Antarctica	15 June 1958
—114.1° F	—81,2° C	Sovietskaya, Antarctica	19 June 1958
—117.4° F	—83,0° C	Sovietskaya, Antarctica	25 June 1958
—122.4° F	—85,7° C	Vostok, Antarctica	7–8 Aug. 1958
—124.1° F	—86,7° C	Sovietskaya, Antarctica	9 Aug. 1958
—125.3° F	—87,4° C	Vostok, Antarctica	25 Aug. 1958
—126.9° F	—88,3° C	Vostok, Antarctica	24 Aug. 1960

Most The location with the most equable recorded temper-
equable ature over a short period is Garapan, on Saipan, in the
temperature Mariana Islands, Pacific Ocean. During the nine years
from 1927 to 1935, inclusive, the lowest temperature
recorded was 19,6° C 67.3° F on 30 Jan. 1934 and
the highest was 31,4° C 88.5° F on 9 Sept. 1931,
giving an extreme range of 11,8° C 21.2° F. Between
1911 and 1966 the Brazilian off-shore island of
Fernando de Noronha had a minimum temperature
of 18,6° C 65.5° F on 17 Nov. 1913 and a maximum
of 32,0° C 89.6° F on 2 March 1965, an extreme
range of 13,4° C 24.1° F.

Humidity Human comfort or discomfort depends not merely on
and temperature but on the combination of temperature,
discomfort humidity, radiation and wind-speed. The United
States Weather Bureau uses a Temperature-Humidity
Index, which equals two-fifths of the sum of the dry
and wet bulb thermometer readings plus 15. When the
THI reaches 75 in still air, at least half of the people
will be uncomfortable while at 79 few, if any, will be
comfortable. When the index reaches 86 inside a
Federal building in Washington, D.C., everybody may
be sent home. A reading of 92 (shade temperature
119° F [48,3° C], relative humidity 22%) was recorded
at Yuma, Arizona, U.S.A., on 31 July 1957, but even
this must have been surpassed in Death Valley,
California, U.S.A.

Greatest The greatest recorded temperature ranges in the
temperature world are around the Siberian "cold pole" in the
ranges eastern U.S.S.R. Olekminsk has ranged 189 deg F
87,2 deg C from —76° F —60° C to 113°F 45° C and
Verkhoyansk (67° 33′ N., 133° 23′ E.) has ranged
192 deg F 88,9 deg C from —94° F —70° C (unofficial)
to 98° F 36,7° C.

The greatest temperature variation recorded in a day
is 100 deg F 37,8 deg C (a fall from 44° F [—6,7° C] to
—56° F [—48,8° C]) at Browning, Montana, U.S.A.,
on 23–24 Jan. 1916. The most freakish rise was
49 deg F 9,4 deg C in 2 min at Spearfish, South
Dakota, from —4° F —20° C at 7.30 a.m. to 45° F

—7,2° C at 7.32 a.m. on 22 Jan. 1943. The British
record is 50.9 deg F 10,5 deg C (34° F [1,1° C] to
84.9° F [29° C]) in 9 hrs at Rickmansworth, Hertfordshire, on 29 Aug. 1936.

Longest The longest recorded unremitting freeze (maximum
freeze temperature 32° F [0° C] and below) in the British Isles
was one of 34 days at Moor House, Westmorland,
from 23 Dec. 1962 to 25 Jan. 1963. This was almost
certainly exceeded at the neighbouring Great Dun Fell,
where the screen temperature never rose above freezing
during the whole of January 1963. Less rigorous early
data includes a frost from 5 Dec. 1607 to 14 Feb.
1608 and a 91 day frost on Dartmoor, Devon in
1854–55.

Upper The lowest temperature ever recorded in the atmo-
atmosphere sphere is —143° C —225.4° F at an altitude of about
50 to 60 miles 80,5–96,5 km, during noctilucent cloud
research above Kronogård, Sweden, from 27 July to
7 Aug. 1963. A jet stream moving at 408 m.p.h.
656 km/h at 154,200 ft 47 000 m (29.2 miles [46 km])
was recorded by Skua rocket above South Uist,
Outer Hebrides, Scotland on 13 Dec. 1967.

Deepest The greatest recorded depth of permafrost is 1,5
permafrost km 4,920 ft reported in April 1968 in the basin of the
River Lena, Siberia, U.S.S.R.

Most intense Difficulties attend rainfall readings for very short
rainfall periods but the figure of 1.23 in 3,12 cm in 1 min at
Unionville, Maryland, U.S.A., at 3.23 p.m. on 4 July
1956, is regarded as the most intense recorded in
modern times. The cloudburst of "near 2 ft [609 mm]
in less than a quarter of half an hour" at Oxford on
the afternoon of 31 May (Old Style) 1682 is regarded
as unacademically recorded. The most intense rainfall
in Britain recorded to modern standards has been 2.0
in 5,08 cm in 12 min at Wisbech, Cambridgeshire on
28 June 1970.

Falsest The legend that the weather on St. Swithin's Day,
St. Swithin's celebrated on 15 July since A.D. 912, determines the
Days rainfall for the next 40 days is one which has long
persisted. There was a brilliant 13½ hrs sunshine in
London on 15 July 1924, but 30 of the next 40 days
were wet. On 15 July 1913 there was a 15-hr downpour,
yet it rained on only 9 of the subsequent 40 days in
London.

Lightning The visible length of lightning strokes varies greatly.
In mountainous regions, when clouds are very low,
the flash may be less than 300 ft 91 m long. In flat
country with very high clouds, a cloud-to-earth flash
sometimes measures 4 miles 6 km though in extreme
cases such flashes have been measured at 20 miles
32 km. The intensely bright central core of the lightning channel is extremely narrow. Some authorities
suggest that its diameter is as little as half an inch 1,27
cm. This core is surrounded by a "corona envelope"
(glow discharge) which may measure 10 to 20 ft
3–6 m in diameter.

The speed of a lightning discharge varies from 100 to
1,000 miles/sec 160,9 to 1609 km/sec for the downward
leader track, and reaches up to 87,000 miles/sec
140 012 km/sec (nearly half the speed of light) for the
powerful return stroke. In Britain there is an average
of 6 strikes/mile^2 per annum, and an average of 4,200
per annum over Greater London alone. Every few
million strokes there is a giant discharge, in which the
cloud-to-earth and the return lightning strokes flash
from the top of the thunder clouds. In these "positive
giants" energy of up to 3,000 million joules (3×10^{16}
ergs) is sometimes recorded. The temperature reaches
about 30,000° C, which is more than five times
greater than that of the surface of the Sun.

Highest waterspout The highest waterspout of which there is a reliable record was one observed on 16 May 1898 off Eden, New South Wales, Australia. A theodolite reading from the shore gave its height as 5,014 ft *1 528 m*. It was about 10 ft *3 m* in diameter. A waterspout moved around Tor Bay, Devon on 17 Sept. 1969 which was according to press estimates 1,000 ft *300 m* in height.

Cloud extremes The highest standard cloud form is cirrus, averaging 27,000 ft *8 250 m* and above, but the rare nacreous or mother-of-pearl formation sometimes reaches nearly 80,000 ft *24 000 m*. The lowest is stratus, below 3,500 ft *1 066 m*. The cloud form with the greatest vertical range is cumulo-nimbus, which has been observed to reach a height of nearly 68,00 ft *20 000 m* in the tropics. Noctilucent "clouds", e.g. over Hampshire on 30 June 1950, are believed to pass at a height of over 60 miles *1 100 km*.

Best and worst British summers According to Prof. Gordon Manley's survey over the period 1728 to 1970 the best (*i.e.* driest and hottest) British summer was that of 1949 and the worst (*i.e.* wettest and coldest) that of 1879. The mean temperature for June, July and August 1911 at Shanklin, Isle of Wight was, however, 2.5° F *16,3° C* higher than in 1949 at 64.9° F *18,3° C*.

Most recent White Christmas and Frost Fair London has experienced seven "White" Christmas Days since 1900. These have been 1906, 1917 (slight), 1923 (slight), 1927. 1938, 1956 (slight) and 1970. These were more frequent in the 19th century and even more so before the change of calendar in 1752. The last of the nine recorded Frost Fairs held on the Thames was in Dec. 1813 to 26 Jan. 1814.

WEATHER RECORDS

	World Records	United Kingdom & Ireland
Highest Shade Temperature:	136.4° F *57,7° C* Al' Aziziyah, Libya, 13.9.1922	100.5° F *38° C*, Tonbridge, Kent, 22.7.1868[1]
Lowest Screen Temperature:	−126.9° F *88,3° C* Vostok, Antarctica, 24.8.1960[2]	−17°F −27,2° C, Braemar, Aberdeenshire, Scotland, 11.2.1895[3]
Greatest Rainfall (24 hours):	73.62 in *1 870 mm*, Cilaos, La Réunion, Indian Ocean, 15–16.3.1952[4]	11.00 in *279 mm*, Martinstown, Dorset, 18–19.7.1955
(Month)	366.14 in *930 mm*, Cherrapunji, Assam, India, July 1861	56.54 in *1 430 mm*, Llyn Llydau, Snowdon, Caernarvonshire, October 1909
(12 Months):	1,041.78 in *2 646 mm*, Cherrapunji, Assam, 1.8.1860–31.7.1861	257.0 in *6 520 mm*, Sprinkling Tarn, Cumberland, in 1954[5]
Greatest Snowfall[6] (12 Months):	1,104 in *2 804 mm*, Tide Lake, Stewart, British Columbia, Canada, 16.5.1971 to 15.5.1972	60 in *1 520 mm*, Upper Teesdale and Denbighshire Hills, 1947
Maximum Sunshine:[7]	97%+ (over 4,300 hours), eastern Sahara, annual average	78.3% (382 hours), Pendennis Castle, Falmouth, Cornwall, June 1925
Minimum Sunshine:	Nil at North Pole—for winter stretches of 186 days	Nil in a month at Westminster, London, in December 1890[8]
Barometric Pressure (Highest):	1,083.8 mb. (32.00 in), Agata, Siberia, U.S.S.R. (alt. 862 ft [*262 m*]), 31.12.1968	1,054.7 mb. (31.15 in), Aberdeen, 31.1.1902
(Lowest):	877 mb. (25.90 in), about 600 miles *965 km* north-west of Guam, Pacific Ocean, 24.9.1958	925.5 mb. (27.33 in), Ochtertyre, near Crieff, Perthshire, 26.1.1884
Highest Surface Wind-speed:[9]	231 m.p.h. *371 km/h*, Mt. Washington (6,288 ft [*1 916 m*]), New Hampshire, U.S.A., 12.4.1934	144 m.p.h. *231 km/h* (125 knots), Coire Cas ski lift (3,525 ft [*1 074 m*]) Cairn Gorm, Inverness-shire, 6.3.1967[10]
Thunder-Days (Year):[11]	322 days, Bogor (formerly Buitenzorg), Java, Indonesia (average, 1916–19)	38 days, Stonyhurst, Lancashire, 1912 and Huddersfield, Yorkshire, 1967
Hottest Place (Annual mean):[12]	Dallol, Ethiopia, 94° F *34,4° C* (1960–66).	Penzance, Cornwall, and Isles of Scilly, both 52.7° F *11,5° C*, average 1931–60
Coldest Place (Annual mean):	Pole of Cold (78° S., 96° E.), Antarctica, −72° F −57,8° C (16° F [−8,9° C] lower than the Pole)	Braemar, Aberdeenshire, 43.7° F *6,5° C*, average 1931–60
Wettest Place (Annual mean):	Mt. Wai-'ale'ale (5,080 ft [*1 548 m*]), Kauai, Hawaii, 486.1 in. *1 235 mm* (average, 1920–58). About 335 rainy days per year	Styhead Tarn (1,600 ft [*487 m*]), Cumberland, 172.9 in. *4 390 mm*
Driest Place (Annual mean):	Nil—In the Desierto de Atacama, near Calama, Chile	Great Wakering, Essex 19.2 in *487 mm* (1916–50)[13]
Longest Drought:	c. 400 years to 1971, Desierto de Atacama, Chile	73 days, Mile End, London, 4.3 to 15.5.1893[14]
Most Rainy Days (Year):	Bahía Felix, Chile, 348 days in 1916	Ballynahinch, Galway, 309 days in 1923
Heaviest Hailstones:[15]	1.67 lb. *750 g* (7½ in. [*19 cm*] diameter, 17½ in. [*44,45 cm*] circumference), Coffeyville, Kansas, U.S.A., 3.9.1970	5 oz *141 g*, Horsham, Sussex, 5.9.1958
Longest Fogs (Visibility less than 1,000 yards):	Fogs persist for weeks on the Grand Banks, Newfoundland, Canada, and the average is more than 120 days per year	London, 26.11 to 1.12.1948 (4 days 18 hours). London, 5.12 to 9.12.1952 (4 days 18 hours).
Windiest Place:	The Commonwealth Bay, George V Coast, Antarctica, where gales reach 200 m.p.h. *320 km/h*	Tiree, Argyllshire (89 ft [*27 m*]); annual average 17.4 m.p.h. *28 km/h*

1 *The shade temperature in London on 8 July 1808 may have reached this figure.*
2 *Vostok s 11,500 ft 3 505 m above sea-level. The coldest permanently inhabited place is the Siberian village of Oymyakon (63° 16′ N., 143° 15′ E.), in the U.S.S.R., where the temperature reached −96° F −71,1° C in 1964.*
3 *The −23° F −30,5° C at Blackadder, Berwickshire on 4 Dec. 1879, and the −20° F −28,9° C at Grantown-on-Spey on 24 Feb. 1955, were not standard exposures. The −11° F −23,9° C reported from Buxton, Derbyshire on 11 Feb. 1895 was not standard. The lowest official temperature in England is −6° F −21,1° C at Bodiam, Sussex on 20 Jan. 1940, at Ambleside, Westmorland on 21 Jan. 1940 and at Hough-all, Durham on 5 Jan. 1941 and 4 March 1947.*
4 *This is equal to 7,435 tons 7554 tonnes of rain per acre. Elevation 1 200 m 3,937 ft.*
5 *The record for Ireland is 154.4 in 3 921 mm near Derriana Lough, County Kerry, in 1948.*
6 *The record for a single snow storm is 175.4 in 4 450 mm at Thompson Pass, Alaska, on 26–31 Dec. 1955, and, for 24 hr, 76 in 1 870 mm at Silver Lake, Colorado, U.S.A., on 14–15 April 1921. London's earliest recorded snow was on 25 Sept. 1885, and the latest on 27 May 1821. Less reliable reports suggest snow on 12 Sept. 1658 and on 12 June 1791.*
7 *St. Petersburg, Florida, U.S.A. recorded 768 consecutive sunny days from 9 Feb. 1967 to 17 March 1969.*
8 *The south-eastern end of the village of Lochranza, Isle of Arran, Bute is in shadow of mountains from 18 Nov. to 8 Feb. each winter.*
9 *The highest speed yet measured in a tornado is 280 m.p.h. 450 km/h at Wichita Falls, Texas, U.S.A., on 2 April 1958.*
10 *The figure of 177.2 m.p.h. 285,2 km/h at R.A.F. Saxa Vord, Unst, in the Shetlands, Scotland, on 16 Feb. 1962, was not recorded with standard equipment. There were gales of great severity on 15 Jan. 1362 and 26 Nov. 1703.*
11 *Between Lat. 35° N. and 35° S. there are some 3,200 thunderstorms each 12 night-time hrs, some of which can be heard at a range of 18 miles 29 km.*
12 *In Death Valley, California, U.S.A., maximum temperatures of over 120° F 48,9° C were recorded on 43 consecutive days—6 July to 17 Aug. 1917. At Marble Bar, Western Australia (maximum 121° F [49,4° C]) 160 consecutive days with maximum temperatures of over 100° F 37,8° C were recorded—31 Oct. 1923 to 7 April 1924. At Wyndham, Western Australia, the temperature reached 90° F 32,2° C or more on 333 days in 1946.*
13 *The lowest rainfall recorded in a single year was 9.29 in 23,6 cm at one station in Margate, Kent, in 1921.*
14 *The longest drought in Scotland was one of 38 days at Port William, Wigtownshire on 3 Apr. to 10 May 1938.*
15 *Much heavier hailstones are sometimes reported. These are usually not single but coalesced stones. An 8½ oz 240 g stone was reported at Bicester, Oxfordshire, on 11 May 1945.*

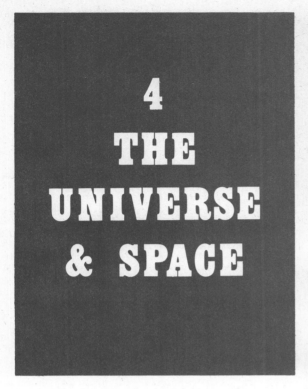

4
THE
UNIVERSE
& SPACE

LIGHT-YEAR—that distance travelled by light (speed 186,282.3960 ± 0.0007 miles/sec or 670,616,625.6 m.p.h. *in vacuo*) in one tropical year (365.24219878 mean solar days at January 0, 12 hrs Ephemeris time in A.D. 1900) and is 5,878,499,772,000 miles. The unit was first used in March 1888. In metric terms the speed of light is *299 792 456,2 m/sec (1079 252 842 km/h)*. The light year is *9 460 528 342 000 km*.

MAGNITUDE—a measure of stellar brightness such that the light of a star of any magnitude bears a ratio of 2.511886 to that of a star of the next magnitude. Thus a fifth magnitude star is 2.511886 times as bright, while one of the first magnitude is exactly 100 (or 2.511886[5]) times as bright, as a sixth magnitude star. In the case of such exceptionally bright bodies as Sirius, Venus, the Moon (magnitude—11.2) or the Sun (magnitude —26.7), the magnitude is expressed as a minus quantity.

PROPER MOTION—that component of a star's motion in space which, at right angles to the line of sight, constitutes an apparent change of position of the star in the celestial sphere.

The universe is the entirety of space, matter and anti-matter. An appreciation of its magnitude is best grasped by working outward from the Earth, through the Solar System and our own Milky Way Galaxy, to the remotest extra-galactic nebulae.

METEOROIDS

Meteor shower Meteoroids are mostly of cometary origin. A meteor is the light phenomenon caused by the entry of a meteoroid into the Earth's atmosphere. The greatest meteor "shower" on record occurred on the night of 16–17 Nov. 1966, when the Leonid meteors (which recur every 33¼ years) were visible between western North America and eastern U.S.S.R. It was calculated that meteors passed over Arizona, U.S.A., at a rate of 2,300 per min for a period of 20 min from 5 a.m. on 17 Nov. 1966.

METEORITES

Largest World When a meteoroid penetrates to the Earth's surface, the remnant is described as a meteorite. This occurs about 150 times per year over the whole land surface of the Earth. Although the chances of being struck are deemed negligible, the most anxious time of day for meteorophobes is 3 p.m. The largest known meteorite is one found in 1920 at Hoba West, near Grootfontein in South West Africa. This is a block about 9 ft *2,75 m* long by 8 ft *2,43 m* broad, weighing 132,000 lb. (59 tons/*tonnes*). The largest meteorite exhibited by any museum is the "Tent" meteorite, weighing 68,085 lb. (30.4 tons [*30 882 kg*]) found in 1897 near Cape York, on the west coast of Greenland, by the expedition of Commander (later Rear-Admiral) Robert Edwin Peary (1856–1920). It was known to the Eskimos as the Abnighito and is now exhibited in the Hayden Planetarium in New York City, N.Y., U.S.A.

The largest piece of stony meteorite recovered is a piece of the Norton County meteorite which fell in Nebraska, U.S.A. on 18 Feb. 1948. The greatest amount of material recovered from any non-metallic meteorite is from the Allende fall of more than 1 ton in Chihuahua, Mexico on 8 Feb. 1969. A piece of this has been dated to 4,610 million years—thus is the oldest dated object on Earth.

There was a mysterious explosion of about 35 megatons in Latitude 60° 55′ N., Longitude 101° 57′ E., in the basin of the Podkamennaya Tunguska river, 40 miles north of Vanavara, in Siberia, U.S.S.R., at 00 hrs 17 min 11 sec U.T. on 30 June 1908. The energy of this explosion was about 10^{24} ergs and the cause has been variously attributed to a meteorite (1927), a comet (1930), a nuclear explosion (1961) and to anti-matter (1965). This devastated an area of about 1,500 miles[2] *3 885 km²* and the shock was felt as far as 1 000 km (more than *600 miles*) away.

United Kingdom and Ireland The heaviest of the 22 meteorites known to have fallen on the British Isles since 1623 was one weighing at least 102 lb. *46 kg 250* (largest piece 17 lb. 6 oz. [*7 kg 880*]), which fell at 4.12 p.m. on 24 Dec. 1965 at Barwell, Leicestershire. Scotland's largest recorded meteorite fell in Strathmore, Perthshire, on 3 Dec. 1917. It weighed 22¼ lb. *10 kg 090* and was the largest of four stones totalling 29 lb. 6 oz. *13 kg 324*. The largest recorded meteorite to fall in Ireland was the Limerick Stone of 65 lb. *29 kg 50* part of a shower weighing more than 106 lb. *48 kg* which fell near Adare, County Limerick, on 10 Sept. 1813. The larger of the two recorded meteorites to land in Wales was one weighing 28 oz. *794 g* of which a piece weighing 25½ oz. *723 g* went through the roof of the Prince Llewellyn Hotel in Beddgelert, Caernarvonshire, shortly before 3.15 a.m. on 21 Sept. 1949.

Largest craters Aerial surveys in Canada in 1956 and 1957 brought to light a gash, or astrobleme, 8½ miles *13,7 km* across near Deep Bay, Saskatchewan, possibly attributable to a very old and very oblique meteorite. U.S.S.R. scientists reported in Dec. 1970 an astrobleme with a 60 mile *95 km* diameter and a maximum depth of 1,300 ft *400 m* in the basin of the River Popigai. There is a possible crater-like formation 275 miles *442,5 km* in diameter on the eastern shore of the Hudson Bay, where the Nastapoka Islands are just off the coast.

The largest proven crater is the Coon Butte or Barringer crater, discovered in 1891 near Canyon Diablo, Winslow, northern Arizona, U.S.A. It is 4,150 ft *1 265 m* in diameter and now about 575 ft *175 m* deep, with a parapet rising 130 to 155 ft *40–48 m* above the surrounding plain. It has been estimated than an iron-nickel mass with a diameter of 200 to 260 ft *61–79 m* and weighing about 2,000,000 tons/ *tonnes* gouged this crater in *c.* 25,000 B.C., with an impact force equivalent to an explosion of 30,000,000 short tons of trinitrotulene or T.N.T. ($C_7H_5O_6N_3$).

Evidence was published in 1963 discounting a meteoric origin for the crypto-volcanic Vredefort Ring (diameter 26 miles [*41,8 km*]), to the south-west of Johannesburg, South Africa, but this has now been re-asserted. The New Quebec (formerly the Chubb) "Crater", first sighted on 20 June 1943 in northern Ungava, Canada, is 1,325 ft *404 m* deep and measures 6.8 miles *10,9 km* round its rim.

Tektites The largest tektite of which details have been published has been of 3 kg 20 *7.04 lb* found *c.* 1932 at Muong Nong, Saravane Province, Laos and now in the Paris Museum.

AURORA

Most frequent Polar lights, known as Aurora Borealis or Northern Lights in the northern hemisphere and Aurora Australis in the southern hemisphere, are caused by electrical solar discharges in the upper atmosphere and occur most frequently in high latitudes. The maximum auroral frequencies, of up to 240 displays per year, have occurred in the Hudson Bay area of northern Canada. The extreme height of auroras has been measured at 1,000 km *620 miles*, while the lowest may descend to 45 miles *72,5 km.*

Southern-most "Northern Lights" Displays occur 90 times a year (on average) in the Shetland Islands, 25 times a year in Edinburgh, seven times a year in London, and once a decade in southern Italy. On 25 Sept. 1909 a display was witnessed as far south as Singapore (1° 25′ N.). The greatest auroral displays over the United Kingdom in recent times occurred on 24–25 Oct. 1870 and 25–26 Jan. 1938.

THE MOON

The Earth's closest neighbour in space and only natural satellite is the Moon, at a mean distance of 238,855 statute miles *384 400 km* centre to centre or 233,812 miles *376 284 km* surface to surface. Its closest approach (perigee) and most extreme distance away (apogee) measured surface to surface are 216,420 and 247,667 miles *348 294 and 398 581 km* respectively or 221,463 and 252,710 miles *356 410/406 697 km* measured centre to centre. It has a diameter of 2,159.9 miles *3 475,92 km* in the plane of the sky and has a mass of 7.23×10^{19} tons *$7,35 \times 10^{19}$ tonnes* with a mean density of 3.34. The average orbital speed is 2,287 m.p.h. *3 680 km/h.*

The first direct hit on the Moon was achieved at 2 min 24 sec after midnight (Moscow time) on 14 Sept. 1959, by the Soviet space probe *Lunik II* near the *Mare Serenitatis.* The first photographic images of the hidden side were collected by the U.S.S.R.'s *Lunik III* from 6.30 a.m. on 7 Oct. 1959, from a range of up to 43,750 miles *70 400 km* and transmitted to the Earth from a distance of 470 000 km *292,000 miles.* The first "soft" landing was made by the U.S.S.R.'s *Luna IX*, launched at about 11 a.m. G.M.T. on 31 Jan. 1966. It landed in the area of the Ocean of Storms (*Oceanus Procellarum*) at 18 hrs 45 min 30 sec G.M.T. on 3 Feb. 1966.

"Blue Moon" Owing to sulphur particles in the upper atmosphere from a forest fire covering 250,000 acres *100 000 ha* between Mile 103 and Mile 119 on the Alaska Highway in northern British Columbia, Canada, the Moon took

on a bluish colour, as seen from Great Britain, on the night of 26 Sept. 1950. The Moon also appeared blue after the Krakatoa eruption of 27 Aug. 1883 (see page 65) and on other occasions.

Crater Largest Only 59 per cent of the Moon's surface is directly visible from the Earth because it is in "captured rotation", *i.e.* the period of revolution is equal to the period of orbit. The largest wholly visible crater is the walled plain Bailly, towards the Moon's South Pole, which is 183 miles *295 km* across, with walls rising to 14,000 ft *4 250 m*. The Orientale Basin, partly on the averted side, measures more than 600 miles *965 km* in diameter.

Deepest The deepest crater is the Newton crater, with a floor estimated to be between 23,000 and 29,000 ft *7 000– 8 850 m* below its rim and 14,000 ft *2 250 m* below the level of the plain outside. The brightest directly visible spot on the Moon is *Aristarchus.*

Highest mountains As there is no water on the Moon, the heights of mountains can be measured only in relation to lower-lying terrain near their bases. The highest lunar mountains were, until 1967, thought to be in the Leibnitz and Doerfel ranges, near the lunar South Pole with a height of some 35,000 ft *10 500 m.* On the discovery from Lunar Orbiter spacecraft of evidence that they were merely crater rims, the names have been withdrawn. It is now established that such an elevation would have been an exaggerated estimate for any feature of the Moon's surface.

Temperature extremes When the Sun is overhead the temperature on the lunar equator reaches 243° F *117,2° C* (31 deg F [*17,2 deg C*] above the boiling point of water). By sunset the temperature is 58° F *14,4° C* but after nightfall it sinks to −261° F *−162,7° C.*

Moon samples The age attributed to the oldest of the moon material brought back to Earth by the *Apollo* programme crews has been soil dated to 4,720 million years. The extreme figures have been modified to less than 4,600 million years due to suspected loss of rubidium.

THE SUN

Distance extremes The Earth's 66,690 m.p.h. *107 325 km/h* orbit of 584,000,000 miles *940 000 000 km* around the Sun is elliptical, hence our distance from the Sun varies. The orbital speed varies between 65,600 m.p.h. *105 570 km/h* (minimum) and 67,800 m.p.h. *109 110 km/h*. The average distance of the Sun is 92,955,840 miles *149 597 900 km.*

The closest approach (perihelion) is 91,395,000 miles *147 082 000 km* and the farthest departure (aphelion) is 94,513,300 miles *152 100 250 km.* The Solar System is revolving around the centre of the Milky Way once in each 225,000 years, at a speed of 481,000 m.p.h. *774 000 km/h* and has a velocity of 42,500 m.p.h. *68 400 km/h* relative to stars in our immediate region such as Vega, towards which it is moving.

Temperature and dimensions The Sun has an internal temperature of about 20,000,000° K., a core pressure of 500,000,000 tons/in² and uses up 4,000,000 tons/*tonnes* of hydrogen per sec, thus providing a luminosity of 3×10^{27} candlepower, with an intensity of 1,500,000 candles/in² *1 530 000 candelas.* The Sun has the stellar classification of a "yellow dwarf" and, although its density is only 1.41 times that of water, its mass is 333,430 times as much as that of the Earth. It has a mean diameter of 865,370 miles *1 392 640 km.* The Sun with a mass of 1.961×10^{27} tons *$1,992 \times 10^{27}$ tonnes* represents more than 99 per cent of the total mass of the Solar System.

Sun-spots Largest To be visible to the *protected* naked eye, a Sun-spot must cover about one two-thousandth part of the Sun's hemisphere and thus have an area of about

500,000,000 miles² *1 300 million km²*. The largest recorded Sun-spot occurred in the Sun's southern hemisphere on 8 April 1947. Its area was about 7,000 million miles² *18 000 million km²* with an extreme longitude of 187,000 miles *300 000 km* and an extreme latitude of 90,000 miles *145 000 km*. Sun-spots appear darker because they are more than 1 500 deg C cooler than the rest of the Sun's surface temperature of 5 660° C. The largest observed solar prominence was one measuring 70,000 miles *112 500 km* across its base and protruding 300,000 miles *480 000 km*, observed on 4 June 1946.

Most frequent In October 1957 a smoothed Sun-spot count showed 263, the highest recorded index since records started in 1755 (*cf.* previous record of 239 in May 1778). In 1943 one Sun-spot lasted for 200 days from June to December.

ECLIPSES

Earliest recorded The earliest extrapolated eclipses that have been identified are 1361 B.C. (lunar) and 2136 B.C. (solar). For the Middle East only, lunar eclipses have been extrapolated to 3450 B.C. and solar ones to 4200 B.C. No centre of the path of totality for a solar eclipse crossed London for the 575 years from 20 March 1140 to 3 May 1715. The most recent occasion when a line of totality of a solar eclipse crossed Great Britain was on 29 June 1927, and the next instance may just clip the Cornish coast on 11 Aug. 1999. On 30 June 1954 a total eclipse was witnessed in Unst, Shetland Islands but the line of totality was to the north of territorial waters.

Longest duration The maximum possible duration of an eclipse of the Sun is 7 min 31 sec. The longest actually occurring since 13 June A.D. 717 was on 20 June 1955 (7 min 8 sec), seen from the Philippines. The longest possible in the British Isles is 5½ min. Those of 15 June 885 and 3 May 1715 were both nearly 5 min, as will be the eclipse of 2381. An annular eclipse may last for 12 min 24 sec. The longest totality of any lunar eclipse is 104 min. This has occurred many times.

Most and least frequent The highest number of eclipses possible in a year is seven, as in 1935, when there were five solar and two lunar eclipses; or four solar and three lunar eclipses, as will occur in 1982. The lowest possible number in a year is two, both of which must be solar, as in 1944 and 1969.

COMETS

Earliest recorded The earliest records of comets date from the 7th century B.C. The speeds of the estimated 2,000,000 comets vary from 700 m.p.h. *1 125 km/h* in outer space to 1,250,000 m.p.h. *2 000 000 km/h* when near the Sun. The successive appearances of Halley's Comet have been traced back to 466 B.C. It was first depicted in in the Nuremburg Chronicle of A.D. 684. The first prediction of its return by Edmund Halley (1656–1742) proved true on Christmas Day 1758, 16 years after his death. Its next appearance should be at 9.9 (*viz.* at 9.30 p.m. on the 9th) February 1986, 75.81 years after the last, which was on 19 April 1910.

Closest approach On 1 July 1770, Lexell's Comet, travelling at a speed of 23.9 miles/sec *38,5 km/sec* (relative to the Sun), came within 1,500,000 miles *2 400 000 km* of the Earth. However, the Earth is believed to have passed through the tail of Halley's Comet, most recently on 19 May 1910.

Largest Comets are so tenuous that it has been estimated that even the head of one rarely contains solid matter much more than *c.* 1 km *0.6 miles* in diameter. In the tail 10,000 miles³ contain less than a cubic inch of solid matter (or *2 500 km³* contains less than *1 cm³*).

Edmund Halley, who correctly predicted the return of Halley's Comet more than sixteen years after his death

These tails, as in the case of the Great Comet of 1843, may trail for 200,000,000 miles *320 million km*.

Comet Bennett which appeared in January 1970 was found to be enveloped in a hydrogen cloud measuring some 8,000,000 miles *12 750 000 km*.

Shortest period Of all the recorded periodic comets (these are members of the Solar System), the one which most frequently returns is Encke's Comet, first identified in 1786. Its period of 1,206 days (3.3 years) is the shortest established. Not one of its 48 returns (up to May 1967) has been missed by astronomers. Now increasingly faint, it is expected to "die" by Feb. 1994. The most frequently observed comets are Schwassmann-Wachmann I, Kopff and Oterma which can be observed every year between Mars and Jupiter.

Longest period At the other extreme is the comet 1910 a, whose path was not accurately determined. It is not expected to return for perhaps 4,000,000 years.

PLANETS

Largest Planets (including the Earth) are bodies within the Solar System and which revolve round the Sun in definite orbits. Jupiter, with an equatorial diameter of 88,070 miles *141 730 km* and a polar diameter of 82,720 miles *133 120 km*, is the largest of the nine major planets, with a mass 317.83 times, and a volume 1,293 times that of the Earth. It also has the shortest period of rotation with a "day" of only 9 hrs 50 min 30.003 sec in the equatorial zone.

Smallest Of the nine major planets, Mercury is the smallest with a diameter of 3,033 miles *4 880 km* and a mass only 0.0555 of that of the Earth or 326 trillion tons *331 × 10¹⁸ tonnes*. Mercury, which orbits the Sun at an average distance of 35,983,100 miles *57 909 200 km* has a period of revolution of 87.9686 days so giving the highest average speed in orbit of 107,030 m.p.h. *172 248 km/h*.

Hottest The U.S.S.R. probe *Venera 7* recorded a temperature of 474° C *885° F* on the surface of Venus on 15 Dec. 1970. The surface temperature of Mercury has now been calculated to be 421° C *790° F* on its daylight side at perihelion (28,566,000 miles [*45 972 500 km*]). The planet with a surface temperature closest to Earth's average figure of 59° F *15° C* is Mars with a value of 55° F *12,8° C* for the sub-solar point at a mean solar distance of 141,636,000 miles *227 940 000 km*.

Coldest The coldest planet is, not unnaturally, that which is the remotest from the Sun, namely Pluto, which has an estimated surface temperature of −420° F *−251° C* (40 deg F [*22 deg C*] above absolute zero). Its mean distance from the Sun is 3,675,300,000 miles *5 914 800 000 km* and its period of revolution is 248.62 years. Its diameter is about 3,400 miles (*c. 5 450 km*) and has a mass about one twentieth of that of the Earth. Pluto was first recorded by Clyde William Tombaugh (b. 4 Feb. 1906) at Lowell Observatory, Flagstaff, Arizona, U.S.A., on 18 Feb. 1930 from photographs taken on 23 and 29 January. Because of its orbital eccentricity Pluto will move closer to the Sun than Neptune between 21 Jan. 1979 and 14 Mar. 1999.

Nearest The fellow planet closest to the Earth is Venus, which is, at times, about 25,700,000 miles *41 360 000 km* inside the Earth's orbit, compared with Mars's closest approach of 34,600,000 miles *55 680 000 km* outside the Earth's orbit. Mars, known since 1965 to be cratered, has temperatures ranging from 85° F *29,4° C* to −190° F *−123° C* but in which infusorians of the *genus* Colpoda *could* survive.

Surface features Mariner 9 photographs have revealed a canyon in the Tithonias Lacus region of Mars which is 62 miles *100 km* wider and 4,000 ft *1 220 m* deeper than the 13 mile *21 km* wide 5,500 ft *1 675 m* deep Grand Canyon on Earth. The volcanic pile Nix Olympica is 305 miles *490 km* across with a 40 mile *64 km* wide crater probably 19,500 ft *5 950 m* high. Mars has elevational differences of 15 km *49,200 ft*.

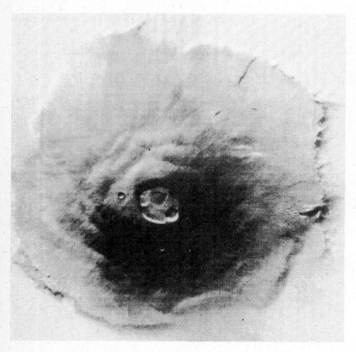

Nix Olympica, seen as a cone instead of a depression, from a mosaic of photographs from *Mariner 9*

Brightest and faintest Viewed from the Earth, by far the brightest of the five planets visible to the naked eye (Uranus at magnitude 5.7 is only marginally visible) is Venus, with a maximum magnitude of −4.4. The faintest is Pluto, with a magnitude of 14. In April 1972 the existence of a

tenth or trans-Plutonian planet more than 6,000 million miles from the Sun with 3 times the mass of Saturn was mooted.

Densest and least Dense Earth is the densest planet with an average figure of 5.517 times that of water, whilst Saturn has an average density only about one eighth of this value or 0.705 times that of water.

Conjunctions The most dramatic recorded conjunction (coming together) of the other seven principal members of the Solar System (Sun, Moon, Mercury, Venus, Mars, Jupiter and Saturn) occurred on 5 Feb. 1962, when 16° covered all seven during an eclipse in the Pacific area. It is possible that the seven-fold conjunction of September 1186 spanned only 12°. The next notable conjunction will take place on 5 May 2000.

SATELLITES

Most Of the nine major planets, all but Mercury, Venus and Pluto have natural satellites. The planet with the most is Jupiter, with four large and eight small moons. The Earth is the only planet with a single satellite. The distance of the Solar System's 32 known satellites from their parent planets varies from the 5,818 miles *9 363 km* of *Phobos* from the centre of Mars to the 14,730,000 miles *23 705 000 km* of Jupiter's ninth satellite (Jupiter IX).

Largest and smallest The largest satellite is *Ganymede* (Jupiter III) with a diameter of 3,450 miles *5 550 km* and a mass 2.11 times that of our Moon. The smallest is Mars's outer "moon" *Deimos* discovered on 18 Aug. 1877 by Asaph Hall (U.S.) with a major axis of 8.4 miles *13,5 km* and a minor one of 7.5 miles *12 km*.

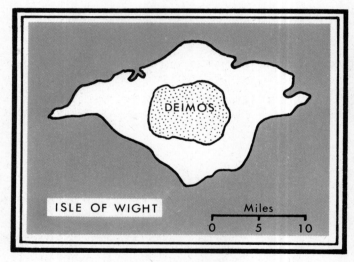

Deimos the smallest of the 32 satellites drawn to scale imposed on the Isle of Wight

Largest asteroids In the belt which lies between Mars and Jupiter, there are some 45,000 (only 3,100 charted) minor planets or asteroids which are, for the most part, too small to yield to diameter measurement. The largest and first discovered (by Piazzi at Palermo, Sicily on 1 Jan. 1801) of these is *Ceres*, with a diameter of 480 miles *772,5 km*. The only one visible to the naked eye is *Vesta* (diameter 260 miles [*418 km*]) discovered on 29 March 1807 by Dr. Heinrich Wilhelm Olbers (1758–1840), a German amateur astronomer. The closest measured approach to the Earth by an asteroid was 485,000 miles *780 000 km* in the case of *Hermes* on 30 Oct. 1937. It was announced in Dec. 1971 that the orbit of *Toro* (disc. 1964), though centered on the Sun, is also in resonance with the Earth-Moon system. Its nearest approach to Earth is 9,600,000 miles *15 450 000 km*. *Amor, Eros*, and *Ivar*, are also in resonance.

STARS

Largest and most massive Of those measured, the star with the greatest diameter is believed to be the cold giant star IRS5 in the Perseus spiral arm of the Milky Way with a diameter larger than that of the entire Solar System of 9,200 million miles *15 000 million km.* This was announced in January 1973. The *Alpha Herculis* aggregation, consisting of a main star and a double star companion, is enveloped in a cold gas. This system, visible to the naked eye, has a diameter of 170,000 million miles *275 000 million km.* The fainter component of Plaskett's star discovered by J. S. Plaskett from the Dominion Astrophysical Observatory, Victoria, British Columbia, Canada *c.* 1920 is the most massive star known with a mass *c.* 55 times that of the Sun.

Smallest The smallest known star is LP 327–186, a "white dwarf" with a diameter only half that of the Moon, 100 light-years distant and detected in May 1962 from Minneapolis, Minnesota, U.S.A. The claim that LP 768–500 is even smaller at <1,000 miles *<1 600 km* is not widely accepted. Some pulsars or neutron stars may however have diameters of only 10–20 miles *16–32 km.*

Oldest The Sun is estimated to be about 7,500 million years old and our galaxy between 10,000 million and 12,000 million years old.

Farthest The Solar System, with its Sun, nine principal planets, 32 satellites, asteroids and comets, was discovered in 1921 to be about 27,000 light-years from the center of the lens-shaped Milky Way galaxy (diameter 100,000 light-years) of about 100,000 million stars. The most distant star in our galaxy is therefore about 75,000 light-years distant.

Nearest Excepting the special case of our own Sun (*q.v.* above) the nearest star is the very faint *Proxima Centauri*, which is 4.3 light-years (25,000,000,000,000 miles $[40 \times 10^{12} km]$) away. The nearest star visible to the naked eye is the southern hemisphere star *Alpha*

Dr. Heinrich Wilhelm Olbers, the amateur astronomer who discovered *Vesta* in 1807—the only asteroid visible to the naked eye

Centauri, or *Rigil Kentaurus* (4.33 light-years), with a magnitude of 0.1.

Brightest Sirius A (*Alpha Canis Majoris*), also known as the Dog Star, is apparently the brightest star of the 5,776 stars visible in the heavens, with an apparent magnitude of −1.58. It is in the constellation *Canis Major* and is visible in the winter months of the northern hemisphere, being due south at midnight on the last day of the year. Sirius A is 8.7 light-years away and has a

PROGRESSIVE RECORDS OF THE MOST DISTANT MEASURED HEAVENLY BODIES

The possible existence of galaxies external to our own Milky Way system was mooted in 1789 by Sir William Herschel (1738–1822). These extra-galactic nebulae were termed "island universes". Sir John Herschel (1792–1871) opined as early as 1835 that some were 48,000 light-years distant. The first direct measurement of any body outside the Solar System was in 1838.

Estimated Distance in Light Years[1]	Object	Method	Astronomer	Observatory	Date
nearly 11 (now 11.08)	61 Cygni	Parallax	F. Bessel	Konigsberg, Germany	1838
>20 (now 26)	Vega	Parallax	F. G. W. Struve	Dorpat (now Tartu), Estonia	1840
c. 200	Limit	Parallax			by 1900
750,000 (now 2.2 m)[2]	Galaxy M31	Cepheid variable	E. P. Hubble	Mt. Wilson, Cal., U.S.A.	1923
900,000 (now 2.2 m)[2]	Galaxy M31	Cepheid variable	E. P. Hubble	Mt. Wilson, Cal., U.S.A.	1924

Millions of Light Years	% of c	Red shift[3]			
250 m	14	Ursa Major Galaxy	E. P. Hubble	Mt. Wilson, Cal., U.S.A.	by 1934[4]
>350 m	>20		M. L. Humason	Palomar, Cal., U.S.A.	by 1952
	37		M. L. Humason	Palomar, Cal., U.S.A.	1954
3,000 m	40	Cluster 1448		Palomar, Cal., U.S.A.	1956
c. 4,500 m	46	3C 295 in Boötes		Palomar, Cal., U.S.A.	June 1960
5,300 m	54.5	QSO 3C 147		Palomar, Cal., U.S.A.	April 1964[5]
8,700 m	80	QSO 3C 9	M. Schmidt	Palomar, Cal., U.S.A.	May 1965
c. 10,000 m	81		Mrs. M. Burbidge	Palomar, Cal., U.S.A.	Dec. 1965
	82.2	QSO 1116+12			Jan. 1966
13,000 m	82.4	QSO PKS 0237−23	J. G. Bolton	Parkes, N.S.W.	March 1967
	83.8	QSO 4C 25.5		Palomar, Cal., U.S.A.	1968
	87.5	QSO 4C 05.34		Kitt Peak, Arizona	May 1970
15,000 m	92	QSO OH 471	Dr. Carswell *et al.*	Steward Observatory, Arizona	March 1973
15,600 m	95	QSO OQ 172	Mrs. M. Burbidge	Lick Observatory, Cal., U.S.A.	Apr. 1973

1 *Term first utilised in 1888.*
2 *Re-estimate by W. Baade in Sept. 1952.*
3 *Discovered by V. M. Slipher from Flagstaff, Arizona, U.S.A., 1920–15.*
4 *In this year Hubble opined that the observable horizon would be 3,000 m light-years.*
5 *Then said that QSO 3C2 and 286 might be more distant—former even 10,000 m light-years.*

Note: *c* is the notation for the speed of light.

luminosity 26 times as much as that of the Sun. It has a diameter of 1,500,000 miles *2,4 million km* and a mass of 4,580,000,000,000,000,000,000,000,000 tons *4,65 × 10²⁷ tonnes*.

Longest Name The longest name for any star is *Shurnarkabtishashutu*, the Arabic for "under the southern horn of the bull".

Most and least luminous If all stars could be viewed at the same distance, the most luminous would be the apparently faint variable *S. Doradûs*, in the Greater Magellanic Cloud (*Nebecula Major*), which can be 300,000 to 500,000 times brighter than the Sun, and has an absolute magnitude of −8.9. The faintest star detected visually is a very red star 30 light-years distant in *Pisces*, with one two-millionth of the Sun's brightness.

Coolest A 16th magnitude star with a surface temperature of only about 425° C *800° F* was detected in *Cygnus* in 1965.

Densest The limit of stellar density is at the neutron state, when the sub-atomic particles exist in a state in which there is no space between them. Theoretical calculations call for a density of 4.7 × 10¹⁵ g/cm³ (*75,000 million tons/in³*) in the innermost core of a pulsar.

Brightest super-nova Super-novae, or temporary "stars" which flare and then fade, occur perhaps five times in 1,000 years. The brightest "star" ever seen by historic man is believed to be the super-nova close to *Zeta Tauri*, visible by day for 23 days from 4 July 1054. The remains, known as the "Crab" Nebula, now appear to have a diameter of about 3 × 10¹³ miles *4,8 × 10¹³ km* and are still expanding at a rate of 800 miles/sec *1 275 km/sec* so indicating a diameter of 1.3 × 10¹⁴ miles *2,1 × 10¹⁴ km* now. It is about 4,100 light-years away, indicating that the explosion actually occurred in about 3000 B.C.

Constellations The largest of the 89 constellations is *Hydra* (the Sea Serpent), which covers 1,302.844 deg² or 6.3 per cent of the hemisphere and contains at least 68 stars visible to the naked eye (to 5.5 mag.). The constellation *Centaurus* (Centaur), ranking ninth in area embraces however at least 94 such stars. The smallest constellation is *Crux Australis* (Southern Cross) with an area of 68.477 deg² compared with the 41,252.96 deg² of the whole sky.

Stellar planets Planetary companions, with a mass of less than 7 per cent of their parent star, have been found to 61 *Cygni* (1942), Lalande 21185 (1960) *Krüger 60, Ci 2354, BD + 20° 2465* and one of the two components of 70 *Ophiuchi*. Barnard's Star (Munich 15040) was discovered to have a planet in April 1963 with 1.1 times the mass of Jupiter and a second planet more recently with 0.8 times this mass. A planet of 6 times the mass of Jupiter 750 million miles *1 200 million km* from *Epsilon Eridani* (see below) was reported by Peter Van de Kemp in January 1973.

Listening operations ("Project Ozma") on the *Tau Ceti* and *Epsilon Eridani* were maintained from 4 April 1960 to March 1961, using an 85-ft *25,90 m* radio telescope at Deer Creek Valley, Green Bank, West Virginia, U.S.A. The apparatus was probably insufficiently sensitive for any signal from a distance of 10.7 light-years to be received. Monitoring has been conducted from Gorkiy, U.S.S.R. since 1969.

Black Holes The first tentative identification of a Black Hole was announced in December 1972 in the binary-star X-ray source Cygnus X-1. After a star suffers gravitational collapse neither matter nor radiation can escape from the resultant Black Hole.

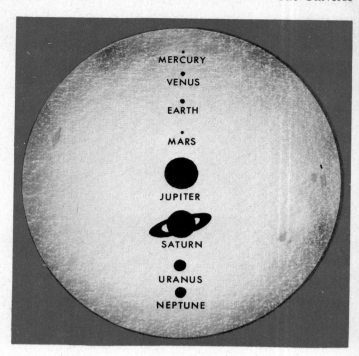

Diagram showing the planets in relation to the earth and the sun

THE UNIVERSE

According to Einstein's Special Theory time dilation effect (published in 1905), time slows down on a moving system as measured by the system at rest, according to the Lorenz transformation

$$T = \frac{T_0}{\sqrt{1-(v/c)^2}}$$

where T_0 = time interval when systems are at rest relatively; c = speed of light constant; v = relative velocity, and T = time measured in one system observing the other moving system.

Outside the Milky Way galaxy, which possibly moves around the centre of the local super-cluster of 2,500 neighbouring galaxies at a speed of 1,350,000 m.p.h. *2 172 500 km/h*, there exist 10,000 million other galaxies. These range in size up to 200,000 light-years in diameter. The nearest heavenly body outside our galaxy is its satellite body the Large Magellanic Cloud near the Southern Cross, at a distance of 160,000 light-years. In 1967 it was suggested by the astronomer G. Idlis (U.S.S.R.) that the Magellanic Clouds were detached from the Milky Way by another colliding galaxy, now in *Sagittarius*, about 3,800,000 years ago.

Farthest visible object The remotest heavenly body clearly visible with the naked eye is the Great Galaxy in *Andromeda* (Mag. 3.47). This is a rotating nebula in spiral form, and its distance from the Earth is about 2,200,000 light-years, or about 13,000,000,000,000,000,000 miles *21 × 10¹⁸ km*. It is just possible however that, under ideal seeing conditions, Messier 33, the Spiral in Triangulum (Mag. 5.79), can be glimpsed by the naked eye of keen-sighted people at a distance of 2,300,000 light-years.

Heaviest Galaxy In April 1971 the heaviest galaxy was found to be 41C 31:04 (a "binary" system) with a mass 45 times that of the Milky Way, thus indicating a figure of 12,000 sextillion tons (1.2 × 10⁴⁰ tons/*tonnes*).

Quasars In November 1962 the existence of quasi-stellar radio sources ("quasars" or QSO's) was established. No satisfactory model has yet been constructed to account for the immensely high luminosity of bodies apparently so distant and of such small diameter. The diameter of 3C 446 is only about 90 light-days, but there are measurable alterations in brightness in less than one day. It is believed to be undergoing the most violent explosion yet detected, since it increased 3.2 magnitudes or 20-fold in less than one year.

"Pulsars" The discovery of the first pulsating radio source or "pulsar" CP 1919 was announced from the Mullard Radio Astronomy Observatory, Cambridge, England, on 29 Feb. 1968. The fastest so far discovered is NP 0532 in the Crab Nebula with a pulse of 33 milli-sec. The now accepted model is that it is a rotating neutron star of immense density.

Remotest object The greatest distance yet ascribed to a radio detected and visibly confirmed body is that ascribed to the quasar QSO OQ172 announced in *Nature* on 7 June 1973. This object was found by Dr. Elennor Margaret Burbidge F.R.S., Director of the Royal Greenwich Observatory, Hertsmonceux Castle, Sussex with the 120 in *304,8 cm* telescope working at the Lick Observatory, Santa Cruz, California, U.S.A., with Drs. E. J. Wampler, L. B. Robinson and J. B. Baldwin. The object has a stellar magnitude of 17.5 and exhibited a red-shift of $Z = 3.53$, which is consistent with a body receding at 95.5 per cent of the speed of light (177,000 miles/sec [*286 000 km/sec*]) and a distance of 15,600 million light years or 9,170,000,000,000,000,000,000 miles *14,75 $\times$ 10^{21} km.*

Quasar OH 471 detected from the Royal Radar Establishment Malvern in March 1973 (see Table p. 81) at a distance of 9,000,000,000,000, 000,000,000 miles

A trace of the analysed light from the Quasar 4C 05.34 (see table p. 81) which took over 14,000 million years to reach the Earth. The shift of the spectral lines towards the red-end of the spectrum indicate that this body is receding from our Galaxy at a speed of 87.5 per cent of the speed of light or 163,000 miles *262 000 km* each second *(Kitt Peak National Observatory)*

Age of the Universe Proponents of the oscillation theory of cosmology believe that the Universe is between 16 and 20,000 million years advanced on the expanding phase of an 80,000 million year expansion-contraction cycle. The number of previous cycles, if any, is not determinable.

ROCKETRY AND MISSILES

Earliest experiments The origin of the rocket dates from war rockets propelled by a charcoal-saltpetre-sulphur gunpowder, made by the Chinese as early as *c.* 1100. These early rockets became known in Europe by 1258. The pioneer of military rocketry in Britain was Col. Sir William Congreve, Bt., M.P. (1772–1828), Comptroller of the Royal Laboratory, Woolwich and Inspector of Military Machines, whose "six-pound [*2,72 kg*] rocket" was developed to a range of 2,000 yds *1 825 m* by 1805 when used by the Royal Navy against Boulogne, France.

The first launching of a liquid-fuelled rocket (patented 14 July 1914) was by Dr. Robert Hutchings Goddard (1882–1945) of the United States, at Auburn, Massachusetts, U.S.A., on 16 March 1926, when his rocket reached an altitude of 41 ft *12,5 m* and travelled a distance of 184 ft *56 m*. The U.S.S.R.'s earliest rocket was the semi-liquid fuelled GIRD-IX tested on 17 Aug. 1933.

Longest ranges On 16 March 1962, Nikita Khrushchyov, then Prime Minister of the U.S.S.R., claimed in Moscow that the U.S.S.R. possessed a "global rocket" with a range of

History's earliest military rockets as used in the English Channel in 1805

30 000 km (about 19,000 miles) i.e. more than the Earth's semi-circumference and therefore capable of hitting any target from either direction.

Most powerful World It has been suggested that the U.S.S.R. manned spacecraft booster which blew up at Tyuratam in the summer (? July) of 1969 had a thrust of 10 to 14 million lb. 4,5 to 6,35 million kg. No further details have been released by the U.S.S.R. nor by ELINT (the U.S. Electronic Intelligence Section).

The most powerful rocket that has been publicized is the Saturn V, used for the Project Apollo and Skylab programmes on which development began in January 1962, at the John F. Kennedy Space Center, Merritt Island, Florida, U.S.A. The rocket is 363 ft 8 in 110,85 m tall, with a payload of 199,500 lb 90 490 kg in the case of Skylab I, and gulps 13.4 tons 13,6 tonnes of propellant per sec for 2½ min (2,005 tons [2 042 tonnes]). Stage I (S-IC) is 138 ft 42,06 m tall and is powered by five Rocketdyne F-1 engines, using liquid oxygen (LOX) and kerosene, each delivering 1,514,000 lb. 686 680 kg thrust. Stage II (S-II) is powered by five LOX and liquid hydrogen Rocketdyne J-2 engines with a total thrust of 1,141,453 lb. 517 759 kg while Stage III (designated S-IVB) is powered by a single 228,290 lb. 103 550 kg thrust J-2 engine. The whole assembly generates 175,600,000 h.p. and weighs up to 7,600,000 lb. (3,393 tons [3 447 tonnes]) fully loaded in the case of Apollo 17. It was first launched on 9 Nov. 1967, from Cape Kennedy, Florida.

Highest velocity The first space vehicle to achieve the Third Cosmic velocity sufficient to break out of the Solar System was Pioneer 10 (see page 85). The Atlas SLV-3C launcher with a modified Centaur D second stage Thiokol Te-364-4 third stage left the Earth at an unprecedented 31,700 m.p.h. 51 000 km/h on 2 March 1972. It flys-by Jupiter in Dec. 1973.

Ion rockets Speeds of up to 100,000 m.p.h. 160 000 km/h are envisaged for rockets powered by an ion discharge. It was announced on 13 Jan. 1960 that caesium vapour discharge had been maintained for 50 hrs at the Lewis Research Center in Cleveland, Ohio, U.S.A. Ion rockets were first used in flight by the U.S.S.R.'s Mars probe Zond 2, launched on 30 Nov. 1964.

ARTIFICIAL SATELLITES

The dynamics of artificial satellites were first propounded by Sir Isaac Newton (1642–1727) in his Philosophiae Naturalis Principia Mathematica ("Mathematical Principles of Natural Philosophy"), begun in March 1686 and first published in the summmer of 1687. The first artificial satellite was successfully put into orbit at an altitude of 142/588 miles 228,5/946 km and a velocity of more than 17,500 m.p.h. 28 160 km/h from Tyuratam, a site located 170 miles 275 km east of the Aral Sea on the night of 4 Oct. 1957. This spherical satellite Sputnik ("Fellow Traveller") 1, officially designated "Satellite 1957 Alpha 2", weighed 83 kg 60 184.3 lb., with a diameter of 58 cm 22.8 in, and its lifetime is believed to have been 9 days, ending on 4 Jan. 1958. It was designed under the direction of Dr. Sergey Pavlovich Korolyov (1906–1966).

Earliest successful manned satellite The first successful manned space flight began at 9.07 a.m. (Moscow time), or 6.07 a.m. G.M.T., on 12 April 1961. Cosmonaut Flight Major (later Colonel) Yuriy Alekseyevich Gagarin (born 9 March 1934) completed a single orbit of the Earth in 89.34 min in the U.S.S.R.'s 4.65 ton 4,72 tonnes space vehicle Vostok. The take-off was from Tyuratam in Kazakhstan, and the landing was 108 min later near the village of Smelovka, near Engels, in the Saratov region of the U.S.S.R. The maximum speed was 17,560 m.p.h.

28 260 km/h and the maximum altitude 327 km 203.2 miles. Major Gagarin, invested a Hero of the Soviet Union and awarded the Order of Lenin and the Gold Star Medal, was killed in a jet plane crash near Moscow on 27 March 1968.

First woman in space The first and only woman to orbit the Earth was Junior Lieutenant (now Lieut.-Col.) Valentina Vladimirovna Tereshkova, now Mme. Nikolayev (b. 6 March 1937), who was launched in Vostok 6 from Tyuratam, U.S.S.R., at 9.30 a.m. G.M.T. on 16 June 1963, and landed at 8.16 a.m. on 19 June, after a flight of 2 days 22 hrs 46 min, during which she completed over 48 orbits (1,225,000 miles [1 971 000 km]) and passed momentarily within 3 miles 4,8 km of Vostok 5.

First in flight fatality Col. Vladimir Mikhailovich Komarov (b. 16 March 1927) was launched in Soyuz ("Union") 1 at 00.35 a.m. G.M.T. on 23 April 1967. The spacecraft was in orbit for about 25½ hrs but he impacted on the final descent due to parachute failure and was thus the first man indisputedly known to have died during space flight.

First "walk" in space The first person to leave an artificial satellite during orbit was Lt.-Col. Aleksey Arkhipovich Leonov (b. 30 May 1934), who left the Soviet satellite Voshkod 2 at about 8.30 a.m. G.M.T. on 18 March 1965. Lt.-Col. Leonov was "in space" for about 20 min, and for 12 min 9 sec he "floated" at the end of a tether 5 m 16 ft long.

Longest manned space flight The longest time spent in space by an astronaut was set on 4 June 1973 when Capt. Charles Conrad U.S.N. on the 11th day of the Skylab I mission surpassed the 715 hrs 5 min 25 sec aggregated by Capt. James A. Lovell U.S.N. Skylab I, which had been launched on 14 May 1973, was joined by its crew consisting of Conrad, Cdr. Dr. Joseph P. Kerwin U.S.N. and Cdr. Paul J. Weitz U.S.N. at 0353 G.M.T. 26 May 1973. They surpassed the previous mission duration record of Soyuz 11, set on 6–29 June 1971, at 0715 hrs G.M.T. on 18 June 1973 on their 25th day in space. Future mannings of Skylab may last for as long as 56 days.

Astronauts Oldest and youngest The oldest of the 61 people in space has been Col. Georgyi T. Beregovoiy who was 47 years and 6 months when launched in Soyuz 3 on 26 Oct. 1968. The youngest was Major Gherman Stepanovich Titov aged 25 years 329 days when launched in Vostok 2 on 6 Aug. 1961.

Longest lunar mission The longest duration of any manned lunar orbit was the Apollo XV's command module Endeavour, which set a record of manned lunar orbit with 6 days 1 hr 13 min during a mission of 12 days 7 hrs 12 min from 26 July to 7 Aug. 1971.

Duration record on the Moon The crew of Apollo XVI's lunar exploration module Orion, manned by Capt. John Watts Young U.S.N., 41, and Lt.-Col. Charles M. Duke, Jnr., 36, was on the lunar surface for 71 hrs 2 min on 22–24 April 1972. The crew of Apollo XVII collected a record 249 lb. 113 kg of rock and soil during their 22 hrs 5 min "extra-vehicular activity". They were Capt. Eugene A. Cernan, U.S.N. and Dr. Harrison H. (Jack) Schmitt, who became the 12th man on the moon on 11 Dec. 1972.

First extra-terrestrial vehicle The first wheeled vehicle landed on the Moon was Lunokhod 1 which began its Earth-controlled travels on 17 Nov. 1970. It moved a total of 10,54 km 6.54 miles on gradients up to 30 deg in the Mare Imbrium and did not become non-functioning until 4 Oct. 1971. The lunar speed and distance record was set by the Apollo XVII Rover with 11.2 m.p.h. 18 km/h and 22.4 miles 35,8 km.

Most expensive project The total cost of the U.S. manned space programme up to and including the lunar mission of *Apollo XVII* has been estimated to be $25,541,400,000 (£9,823,150,000). The estimated cost of the Space Shuttle programme to 1990 will be $42,800 million.	**Accuracy record** The most accurate recovery from space was the splashdown of *Gemini IX* on 6 June 1966 only 769 yds *703 m* from the *U.S.S. Wasp* in the Western Atlantic (27° 52′ N., 75° 0′ 24″ W.).

PROGRESSIVE ROCKET ALTITUDE RECORDS

Height in miles	Height in km	Rocket	Place	Launch Date
0.71	*1.14*	A 3-in rocket	near London, England	April 1750
1.24	*2*	Reinhold Tiling[1] (Germany) solid fuel rocket	Osnabrück, Germany	April 1931
3.1	*5*	GIRD-X liquid fuel (U.S.S.R.)	U.S.S.R.	25 Nov. 1933
8.1	*13*	U.S.S.R. "Stratosphere" rocket	U.S.S.R.	1935
52.46	*84,42*	A.4 rocket (Germany)	Peenemünde, Germany	3 Oct. 1942
c. 85	*c. 136*	A.4 rocket (Germany)	Heidelager, Poland	early 1944
118	*190*	A.4 rocket (Germany)	Heidelager, Poland	mid 1944
244	*392,6*	V-2/W.A.C. Corporal (2-stage) Bumper No. 5 (U.S.A.)	White Sands, N.M., U.S.A.	24 Feb. 1949
250	*400*	M.104 *Raketa* (U.S.S.R.)	? Tyuratam, U.S.S.R.	1954
682	*1 097*	Jupiter C (U.S.A.)	Cape Canaveral (now Cape Kennedy), Florida, U.S.A.	20 Sept. 1956
>2,700	*>74 345*	Farside No. 5 (4-stage) (U.S.A.)	Eniwetok Atoll	20 Oct. 1957
70,700	*113 770*	Pioneer I-B Lunar Probe (U.S.A.)	Cape Canaveral (now Cape Kennedy), Florida, U.S.A.	11 Oct. 1958
215,300,000*	*346 480 000*	Luna 1 or Mechta (U.S.S.R.)	Tyuratam, U.S.S.R.	2 Jan. 1959
242,000,000*	*389 450 000*	Mars 1 (U.S.S.R.)	U.S.S.R.	1 Nov. 1962
1,800,000,000[2]	*2 900 000 000*	Pioneer X (U.S.A.) (see page 84)	Cape Kennedy, Florida U.S.A.	2 Mar. 1972

* *Apogee in solar orbit.*
[1] *There is some evidence that Tiling may shortly after have reached 9,500 m. (5.90 miles) with a solid fuel rocket at Wangerooge, East Friesian Islands, West Germany,*
[2] *This distance will be reached by 1980 on its way to passing out of the Solar System's gravitational field.*

ROCKETRY AND SPACE RECORDS

	Earth Orbits	Moon Orbits	Solar Orbits
Earliest Satellite	Sputnik 1, 4 Oct. 1957	Luna 10, 31 March 1966	Luna 1, 2 Jan. 1959
Earliest Planetary Contact	Sputnik 1 rocket—burnt out 1 Dec. 1957	Luna 2 hit Moon, 13 Sept. 1959	Venus III hit Venus, 1 Mar. 1966
Earliest Planetary Touchdown	Discoverer XIII capsule, landed 11 Aug. 1960	Luna 9 soft landed on Moon 3 Feb. 1966	Venus VII soft landed on Venus 15 Dec. 1970
Earliest Rendezvous and Docking	Gemini VIII and Agena VIII, 16 March 1966	Apollo X and LEM 4 docked 23 May 1969	None
Earliest Crew Exchange	Soyuz 4 and 5, 14-15 Jan. 1969	Apollo X and LEM 4, 18 May 1969	None
Heaviest Satellite	89.06 tons *90 490 kg*, 118 ft *35,96 m* long; Skylab I, 14 May 1973	30.34 tons *30 928 kg* Apollo XV, 26 July 1971	13.60 tons *13 818 kg*, Apollo X rocket, 18 May 1969
Lightest Satellite	1.47 lb. *666 g* each, Tetrahedron Research Satellites (TRS), 2 and 3, 9 May, 1963	150 lb. *68 kg*, Interplanetary Monitoring Probe 6, 19 July 1967	13 lb. *5 kg 896*, Pioneer IV, 3 March 1959
Longest First Orbit	42 days, Apollo XII rocket, 14 Nov. 1969	720 minutes, Lunar Orbiter 4, 4 May 1967	636 days, Mariner 6 (Mars Probe), 25 Feb. 1969
Shortest First Orbit	86 minutes 30.6 sec, Cosmos 169 (rocket), 17 July 1967	114 min LEM 9 ascent stage (Apollo XV), 2 Aug. 1971	195 days, Mariner 5 (Venus Probe), 14 June 1967
Longest Expected Lifetime	>1 million years, Vela 12, 8 April 1970	Unlimited, IMP 6 (see above), 19 July 1967	All unlimited
Nearest First Perigee, Pericynthion or Perihelion	63 miles *101 km* Cosmos 169 rocket, 17 July 1967	10 miles *16 km* LEM 6 ascent stage (Apollo XII), 20 Nov. 1969	50,700 miles *81 590 km* Apollo IX rocket, 3 Mar 1969
Furthest First Apogee, Apcynthion or Aphelion	535,522 miles, *861 815 km*, Apollo XII rocket, 14 Nov. 1969	4,900 miles *7 885 km* IMP 6 (see above), 19 July 1967	162,900,000 miles, *262 150 000 km* Mariner 6 (Mars Probe), 25 Feb. 1969

The highest and lowest speeds in solar orbit are by Apollo IX rocket and Mariner 6 (see above), respectively.
NOTE: *The largest artificial satellite measured by volume has been Echo II (diameter 135 ft 41,14 m), weighing 565 lb. 256 kg, launched into orbit (642/816 miles 1033/1313 km) from Vandenberg Air Force Base, California, U.S.A., on 25 Jan. 1964. It was an inflated sphere, comprising a 535 lb. 242 kg balloon, whose* skin *was made of Mylar plastic 0,00035 of an in 0,009 mm thick, bonded on both sides by aluminium alloy foil 0.00018 of an in 0,0045 mm thick, together with equipment. Echo II was the brightest of artificial satellites (its magnitude was about—1) and it has been claimed that it became the man-made object seen by more people than any other. Its lifetime was 1,960 days until it burned up on 7 June 1969.*

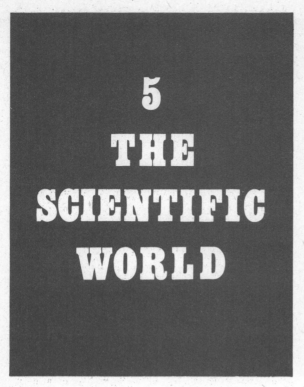

5
THE
SCIENTIFIC
WORLD

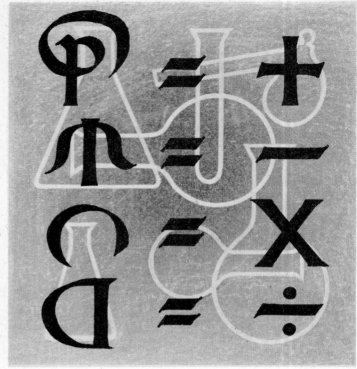

1. ELEMENTS

All known matter in the Solar System is made up of chemical elements. The total of naturally-occurring elements so far detected is 94, comprising, at ordinary temperature, two liquids, 11 gases and 81 solids. The so-called "fourth state" of matter is plasma, when negatively-charged electrons and positively-charged ions are in flux. There are 3.9 million chemical compounds.

Lightest and heaviest sub-nuclear particles The number of fundamental sub-nuclear particles catered for by the 1964 Unitary Symmetry Theory, or SU(3), was 34. The SU(6) system caters for 91 particles, while the later SU(12) system caters for an infinite number, some of which are expected to be produced by higher and higher energies, but with shorter and shorter lifetimes and weaker and weaker interactions. By 1971 some 400 particles and resonances had been recorded. Of SU(3) particles the one with the highest mass is the omega minus, announced on 24 Feb. 1964 from the Brookhaven National Laboratory, near Upton, Long Island, New York State, U.S.A. It has a mass of $1,672.5 \pm 0.5$ Mev and a lifetime of 1.3×10^{-10} of a sec. Of all sub-atomic concepts only the neutrino calls for masslessness. There is experimental proof that the mass, if any, of an electron neutrino, first observed in June 1956, cannot be greater than one ten-thousandth of that of an electron, which itself has a rest mass of 9.10956 $(\pm 0.00005) \times 10^{-28}$ of a g, *i.e.* it has a weight of less than 1.07×10^{-31} of a g.

Least Stable The least stable nuclear particle discovered is the rho prime meson announced on 29 Jan. 1973 from the Stanford Linear Accelerator Center, California. This resonance lasts for 1.0×10^{-24} of a sec. The discovery of the qwark was claimed at Leeds University, England on 23 May 1973.

Fastest particles A search for the existence of super-luminary particles, named tachyons (symbol T^+ and T^-), with a speed *in vacuo* greater than *c.* the speed of light, was instituted in 1968 by Dr. T. Alvager and Dr. M. Kriesler of Princeton University, U.S.A. Such particles would create the conceptual difficulty of disappearing before they exist.

Commonest The commonest element in the Universe is hydrogen, which has been calculated to comprise 90 per cent of all matter and over 99 per cent of matter in interstellar space.

Most and least isotopes The element with the most isotopes is the colourless gas xenon (Xe) with 30 and that with the least is hydrogen with only 3 confirmed isotopes. The metallic element with the most is platinum (Pt) with 29 and that with the least is lithium (Li) with 5. Of stable and naturally-occurring isotopes, tin (Sn) has the most with 10 whilst 20 elements exist in Nature only as single nuclides.

GASES

Lightest Hydrogen, a colourless gas discovered in 1766 by the Hon. Henry Cavendish (1731–1810), a British millionaire, is less than 1/14th the weight of air, weighing only 0.005611 of one lb./ft³ or *89,88 mg/litre*.

Heaviest The heaviest elemental gas is radon, the colourless isotope Em 222 of the gas emanation, which was discovered in 1900 by Friedrich Ernst Dorn (1848–1916) of Germany, and is 111.5 times as heavy as hydrogen. It is also known as niton and emanates from radium salts.

Melting and boiling points Lowest Of all substances, helium has the lowest boiling point $(-268,94°$ C.). This element, which is at normal temperatures a colourless gas, was discovered in 1868 by Sir Joseph Norman Lockyer, K.C.B. (1836–1920) working with Sir Edward Frankland, K.C.B. (1825–1899) and the French astronomer Pierre Jules Cesar Janssen (1824–1907) working independently. Helium was first liquefied in 1908 by Heike Kamerlingh Onnes (1853–1926), a Dutch physicist. Liquid helium, which exists in two forms, can be solidified only under pressure of 26 atmospheres. This was first achieved on 26 July 1926 by Wilhemus H. Keesom (b. Netherlands 1876). At this pressure helium will melt at $-272°$ C.

Highest Of the elements that are gases at normal temperatures, chlorine has the highest melting point $(-101,0°$ C) and the highest boiling point $(-34,1°$ C.). This yellow-green gas was discovered in 1774 by the German-born Karl Wilhelm Scheele (1742–86) of Sweden.

Rarest The Earth's atmosphere weighs an estimated 5,075,000,000,000,000 tons *5,155 × 10¹⁵ tonnes*, of which nitrogen constitutes 78.09 per cent by volume in dry air. The heavy hydrogen isotope tritium exists in the atmosphere to an extent of only 5×10^{-23} of one per cent by volume.

METALS

Lightest The lightest of all metals is lithium (Li), a light golden brown (*in vacuo*) metal, discovered in 1817 by Johan August Afrvedson (1792–1841) of Sweden. It has a density of 0.5333 of a g/cm³ or *33.29 lb./ft³*. The isotope Li 6 (7.56% of naturally-occurring lithium) has a density of only 0.4616 g/cm³ compared with 0.5391 for Li 7. Metallic hydrogen has a density of 1.3.

Densest The densest of all metals and hence the most effective possible paperweight is osmium (Os), a grey-blue metal of the platinum group, discovered in 1804 by Smithson Tennant (1761–1815) of the United Kingdom. It has a density at 20° C of 22,59g/cm³ or *1,410 lb./ft³*. A cubic foot of uranium would weigh 220 lb. *99 kg 70* less than a cubic foot of osmium. During the period 1955–70 iridium was thought by some inorganic chemists to be the densest metal but it has a density of 22.56.

Melting and boiling points Excluding mercury, which is liquid at normal temperatures, caesium (Cs), a silvery-white metal discovered in 1860 by Robert Wilhelm von Bunsen (1811–1899) and Gustav Robert Kirchhoff (1824–87) of Germany, has the lowest metallic melting point at 28,5° C (*83.3° F*).
Lowest

Excluding mercury, which vaporizes at 356,66° C, the metal which vaporizes at the lowest temperature and hence has the lowest boiling point is caesium with a figure of 669° C (*1,236° F*).

Highest The highest melting point of any pure element is that of tungsten or wolfram (W), a grey metal discovered in 1783 by the Spanish brothers, Juan José d'Elhuyar and Fausto d'Elhuyar (1755–1833). It melts at 3 417° C, ±10 deg C.

The most refractory substances known are the tantalum carbide ($TaC_{0.88}$), a black solid, and the hafnium carbide ($HfC_{0.95}$), which melt at 4 010° C ±75 deg C and 3 960° C±20 deg C respectively.

Expansion The highest normal linear thermal expansion of a metal is that of caesium which at 20° C is 9.7×10^{-5} of a cm/cm/1 deg C. The trans-uranic metal plutonium, will, however, expand and contract by as much as 8.9 per cent of its volume when being heated to its melting point of 639.5° C±2 deg C.

The lowest linear expansion is that of the alloy invar, containing 35 per cent nickel, the remainder being iron, with one per cent carbon and manganese. This has a linear thermal expansion of 9×10^{-7} of an in/in/7 deg C at ordinary temperatures. It was first prepared *c.* 1930 by Charles Edouard Guillaume (b. Switzerland 1861, d. 1938).

Highest ductility The most malleable, or ductile, of metals is gold. One oz. (avoirdupois) of gold can be drawn in the form of a continuous wire thread (diameter 2×10^{-4} of an in [*0,005 mm*]) to a length of 43 miles *69 km*. A cubic inch *16,38 cm³* is beaten into a leaf 1/280,000th of an inch *0,000091 mm* thick, so as to cover 1,945 ft² *180 m²* It has been estimated that all the gold mined since A.D. 1500 could be stored in a vault with dimensions of 55 × 55 × 55 ft or *4 711 m³*.

Highest tensile strength The material with the highest known UTS (ultimate tensile strength) is sapphire whisker (Al_2O_3) at 6.2 × 10⁶ lb./in² *4,36 × 10⁵ kgf/cm²*. This is equivalent to a whisker of the thickness of a human hair (an as yet unachieved 70 microns) which could support a weight of 621 lb. *281 kg 70*. Amorphous boron has a maximum cohesive strength of 3.9 × 10⁶ lb./in² *2,74 × 10⁵ kgf/cm²* and thus theoretically a wire 189.4 miles *296,8 km* long could be suspended without parting.

Rarest The fourteen of the fifteen "rare earth" or "lanthanide" elements which have stable isotopes (this includes lutetium) have now been separated into metallic purity exceeding 99.9%. The highly radioactive element promethium (Pm) has been produced artificially with a purity exceeding only 99.8%. The radioactive elements 43 (technetium) and 61 (promethium) were chemically separated from pitch-blende ore in 1961 and 1968 respectively. Because of their relatively short half-lives their existence in Nature is due entirely to the "spontaneous fission" radioactive decay of uranium.

The rarest naturally-occurring element is astatine (element 85) first produced artificially in 1940 and identified in Nature three years later. It has been calculated that only 0,35 g or *1 hundredth of an oz.* exists in the Earth's crust to a depth of 10 miles *16 km*.

The isotope polonium 213 (Po 213) is, however, rarer by a factor of 5×10^{10} which is equivalent to one atom in 3.5×10^{37}.

Several of the trans-uranium elements have been produced on an atom-to-atom basis so that at any one moment only single atoms of these elements may have existed.

Commonest Though ranking behind oxygen (46.60 per cent) and silicon (27.72 per cent) in abundance, aluminium is the commonest of all metals constituting 8.13 per cent by weight of the Earth's crust.

Most magnetic and non-magnetic The most highly magnetic material known, at ordinary temperatures, is a cobalt-copper-samarium compound Co_3Cu_2Sm with a coercive force of 10,500 oersted. The most non-magnetic alloy yet discovered is 963 parts of copper to 37 parts of nickel.

Newest The newest trans-uranium element, number 105, was synthesised in the HILAC heavy-ion linear accelerator in the Lawrence Radiation Laboratory, University of California, Berkeley, California, U.S.A. by an American-Finnish team led by Dr. Albert Ghiorso. The element, for which the name "Hahnium" has been proposed, was first produced on the 5th March 1970 with a mass of 260 and a half-life of 1.6 sec.

Attempts initiated in November 1968 at Berkeley, California, U.S.A. to find traces of elements 110 (eka-platinum) to 114 (eka-lead) have so far proved inconclusive: U.S.S.R. claims to have detected elements 108 and 114 in the Earth's crust have not been substantiated. Element 110 was apparently recorded by the Physics Department of Bristol University, England on emulsion plates sent aloft in a balloon 25 miles *40 km* above Palestine, Texas, U.S.A. in September 1968, but the evidence must be regarded as being very tenuous. The heaviest isotope for which there is definite evidence is that of mass 262 of element 105 (Hahnium 262) synthesised by Ghiorso and others and announced in 1971.

Dr. Glenn Theodore Seaborg (b. 19 April 1912), Chairman of the United States Atomic Energy Commission, estimated in June 1966 that elements up to 126 would be produced by the year 2000.

Most expensive substance In October 1968 the U.S. Atomic Energy Commission announced that minuscule amounts of californium 252 (Element 98) were on sale at $100 for a tenth of a microgramme. A fanciful calculation would indicate that the price of an ingot weighing 1 lb *453,6 g* (if such were available) would at this rate have been

£189,000 million or more than double the then entire national wealth of the United Kingdom. It was announced in August 1970 that by using Am 243 and Cm 244, the price might be reduced to *only* $10 per microgramme.

Longest and shortest half-lives The half-life of a radio-active substance is the period taken for its activity to fall to half of its original value. The highest theoretical figure is $>2 \times 10^{18}$ years for bismuth 209, while the shortest is 2.4×10^{-21} of a second for helium 5.

Purest The purest metal yet achieved is the grey-white metal germanium by the zone refining technique, first mooted in 1939 and published by William G. Pfann of Bell Laboratories, U.S.A. in 1952. By 1967 a purity of 99.99999999 per cent had been achieved, which has been likened to one grain of salt in a freight car-load of sugar.

Hardest substances Prof. Naoto Kawai of Osaka University, Japan announced in June 1967 the production by dint of a pressure of 150 tonnes/cm² *2,133,500 lb.f/in²* of a single crystal of 1 part silica, 1 part magnesium and 4 parts oxygen which was "twice as hard as diamond".

Plastics The plastic with best temperature resistance is modified polymide which can withstand temperatures of up to 500°C *930°F* for short periods. The plastics with the greatest tensile strength are poly-vinyl alcoholic fibres which have been tested to 1.5×10^5 lb.f./in² *1,05 × 10⁴ kgf/cm²*.

SMELLIEST SUBSTANCE

The most pungent of the 17,000 smells so far classified is 4-hydroxy-3-methoxy benzaldehyde or vanillaldehyde. This can be detected in a concentration of 2×10^{-8} of a mg/litre of air. Thus 9.7×10^{-5} (about one ten-thousandth) of an oz. *2,75 × 10⁻³ g* completely volatilized would still be detectable in an enclosed space with a floor the size of a full-sized football pitch (360 ft × 300 ft [*109,73 m × 91,44 m*]) and a roof 45 ft *13,71 m* high. Only 2.94 oz. *83,3 g* would be sufficient to permeate a mile³ *4,16 km³* of the atmosphere. The most evil smelling substance must be a matter of opinion but ethyl mercaptan (C_2H_5SH) and butyl seleno-mercaptan (C_4H_9SeH), are powerful claimants, each with a smell reminiscent of a combination of rotting cabbage, garlic, onions and sewer gas.

Most expensive perfume The costliest perfume in the world is "Adoration", manufactured by Nina Omar of Puerto Real, Cadiz, Spain, and distributed in the United States at a retail price of $185 (£77) per half-oz. Its most expensive ingredient is a very rare aromatic gum from Asia. The most expensive bottle of perfume sold is the outsize bottle of Vivre by Molyneux of Paris sold by Neiman Marcus of Dallas, Texas in 1972 for $4,500 (£1,875).

Sweetest substance The sweetest naturally-occurring substance is exuded from the red serendipity berry (*Dioscoreophyllum cumminsii*) from Nigeria, which was announced in September 1967 to be 1,500 times as sweet as sucrose. The chemical 1-n-propoxy-2-amino-4-nitro-benzene was determined by Verkade in 1946 to be 5,600 times as sweet as 1 per cent sucrose.

Bitterest substance The bitterest known substance is Bitrex, the proprietary name for benzyldiethyl (2:6-xylylcarbamoyl methyl) ammonium benzoate ($C_{28}H_{34}N_2O_3$), first reported from Macfarlan Smith Ltd. of Edinburgh, Scotland. This can be detected in solution at a concentration of one part in 20,000,000 and is thus about 200 times as bitter as quinine sulphate ($[C_{22}H_{24}N_2O_2]_2,H_2SO_42H_2O$).

Strongest acid The strength of acids and alkalis is measured on the pH scale. The pH of a solution is the logarithm to the base 10 of the reciprocal of the hydrogen-ion concentration in g ions/litre. The strongest simple acid is perchloric acid ($HClO_4$). Assessed on its power as a hydrogen-ion donor, the most powerful acid is a solution of antimony pentafluoride in fluosulphonic acid ($SbF_5 + FSO_3H$).

Strongest alkali The strength of alkalis is expressed by pH values rising above the neutral 7.0. The strongest bases are caustic soda or sodium hydroxide (NaOH), caustic potash or potassium hydroxide (KOH) and tetramethylammonium hydroxide ($N[CH_3]_4OH$), with pH values of 14 in normal solutions. True neutrality, pH 7, occurs in pure water at 22° C *71.6° F*.

Most powerful fuel The greatest specific impulse of any rocket propulsion fuel combination is 435 lb.f/sec/lb. or *435 kgf/sec/kg* produced by lithium fluoride and hydrogen. This compares with a figure of 300 for liquid oxygen and kerosene.

POISON

Quickest The barbiturate, thiopentone, if given as a large intracardiac injection, will cause permanent cessation of respiration in one to two seconds.

Most potent The rikettsal disease, Q-fever can be instituted by a *single* organism but is only fatal in 1 in 1,000 cases. Effectually the most poisonous substance yet discovered is the toxin of the bacterium *Pasteurella tularensis*. About 10 organisms can institute tulaeremia variously called alkali disease, Francis disease or deerfly fever, and this is fatal in 50 to 80 cases in 1,000.

Most powerful nerve gas The nerve gas Sarin or GB (isopropylmethylphosphonofluoridate), a lethal colourless and odourless gas, has been developed since 1945 in the United States and is reputedly 30 times as toxic as phosgene ($COCl_2$) used in World War I. In the early 1950s substances known as V-agents, notably VX, 10 times more toxic than GB, were developed at the Chemical Defence Experimental Establishment, Porton Down, Wiltshire, which are lethal at 1 mg per man.

Most powerful drugs The most potent and, to an addict, the most expensive of all naturally-derived drugs is heroin, which is a chemically-processed form of opium from the juice of the unripe seed capsules of the white poppy (*Papaver somniferum*). An oz., which suffices for up to 1,800 hypodermic shots or "fixes", may fetch up to $10,000 (£4,080) in the United States, or a 70,000 per cent profit over the raw material price in Turkey. It has been estimated that an addict who has no income is impelled to steal $44,000's (£17,960) worth of goods per annum to keep him or herself in "fixes". The most potent analgesic drug is Etorphine or M-99, announced in June 1963 by Dr. Kenneth W. Bentley (b. 1925) and D. G. Hardy of Reckitt & Sons Ltd. of Hull, Yorkshire, with almost 10,000 times the potency of morphine.

2. DRINK

The strength of spirituous liquor is gauged by degrees proof. In the United Kingdom proof spirit is that mixture of ethyl alcohol (C_2H_5OH) and water which at 51° F *10,55° C* weighs 12/13ths of an equal measure of distilled water. Such spirit in fact contains 57.06 per cent alcohol by volume, so that pure or absolute alcohol is 75.254° over proof (O.P.). A "hangover" is due to toxic congenerics such as amyl alcohol ($C_5H_{11}OH$).

Most alcoholic Absolute (or 100%) alcohol is 75.254 degrees over proof (U.K.) or 100° O.P. (U.S.). The strongest alcoholic spirits produced are unmarketable raw rums and vodkas at 97.2% alcohol by volume at 60° F *15,6° C* or 70° O.P. (U.K.) or 95.3° O.P. (U.S.). Polish White Spirit vodka produced for the Polish State Spirits Monopoly is 79.8% alcohol and 40°

O.P. (U.K.) or 59.9° O.P. (U.S.). Royal Navy rum, introduced in 1692, was also 40° O.P. (79.8%) before 1948 but was reduced to 4.5° U.P. (under proof) or 54.7% alcohol by volume, before its abolition on 31 July 1970.

BEER

Strongest The world's strongest beer is Thomas Hardy's Ale brewed in July 1968 by Dorchester Brewery, Dorset with 10.15 per cent alcohol by weight and 12.58 per cent by volume. The strongest regularly brewed nationally distributed beer in Britain is Gold Label Barley Wine brewed by Tennant Bros. of Sheffield, a subsidiary of Whitbread & Co. Ltd. It has an alcoholic content of 8.6 per cent by weight and 10.6 per cent by volume.

Weakest The weakest liquid ever marketed as beer was a sweet ersatz beer which was brewed in Germany by Sunner, Colne-Kalk, in 1918. It had an original gravity of 1,000.96° and a strength 1/30th that of the weakest beer now obtainable in the United Kingdom.

WINE

Most The highest price ever paid for a bottle of wine of any *expensive* size is 55,000 francs (*then £4,532*) in Paris for a Jeroboam of *Château Mouton* Rothschild 1870 by Mario Ruspoli in a 'phoned auction bid on 21 Nov. 1972. This bottle 'contained the equivalent of *five* normal bottles and was thus equivalent to about £150 per glass or £37.75 per fluid oz.

A bottle of *Château Lafite* Rothschild 1946 was sold at auction by Mr. Michael Broadbent of Christie's in San Francisco, California on 26 May 1971 and was bought by Laurence H. Bender, 25 on behalf of Hublein's for $5,000 (*then £2,083.33*). This thus worked out at an even higher price of £86.80 per fluid oz. or (*2,84 centilitres*).

Most The most expensive liqueur in France is the orange-*expensive* flavoured *Le Grand Marnier Coronation*. Owing to *liqueurs* excise duties, *Elixir Végétale de la Grande Chartreuse*

which is 24 degrees O.P. is sold only by special order in miniature bottles of 2.8 fl. oz. *7,95 centilitres* at 90p per bottle in the United Kingdom. This liqueur has been produced since 1757, by Carthusian monks from a recipe of 1605, which reputedly contains 130 herbs including *Arnica montana*. Ancient *Chartreuse* (before 1903) has been known to fetch more than £15 per litre bottle *1,76 pints*. An 1878 bottle was sold in 1954 for this price.

Most The most expensive spirit is *Grande Fine Champagne* *expensive* *Arbellot* 1749 brandy, retailed at Fauchon, Paris, at *spirits* 667 francs (*then £48.25*) per bottle. *Hennessy Extra Liqueur* retails in Britain for £22.82 (including V.A.T.) a bottle.

Largest The largest bottle normally used in the wine and spirit *bottles* trade is the Jeroboam (equal to 4 bottles of champagne or, rarely, of brandy) and the Double Magnum (equal, since c. 1934, to 6 bottles of claret or, more rarely, red Burgundy). A complete set of Champagne bottles would consist of a ¼ bottle, through the ½ bottle, bottle, magnum, Jeroboam, Rehoboam, Methuselah, Salmanazer and Balthazar, to the Nebuchadnezzar, which has a capacity of 16 litres (*28.16 pt*), and is equivalent to 20 bottles. In May 1958 a 5 ft *152 cm* tall sherry bottle with a capacity of 20½ Imperial gal *93,19 litres* was blown in Stoke-on-Trent, Staffordshire. This bottle, with the capacity of 131 normal bottles, was named an "Adelaide".

Smallest The smallest and meanest bottles of liquor sold are *bottles* the Thistle bottles of Scotch whisky marketed by The Cumbrae Supply Co. of Glasgow. They contain 24 minims or $\frac{1}{20}$ of a fl. oz. *1,42 millilitres* and retail for 10p.

Champagne The longest distance for a champagne cork to fly from *cork* an untreated and unheated bottle 4 ft *1,22 m* from level *flight* ground is 73 ft 10½ in *22,54 m* popped by the author A. David Beaty D.F.C.* at Hever, Kent on 20 July 1971.

3. GEMS AND OTHER PRECIOUS MATERIALS

Note: The carat was standardised at 205 mg in 1877. The metric carat of 200 mg was introduced in 1913.

PRECIOUS STONE RECORDS

	Largest	Largest Cut Stone	Other records
Diamond (pure crystallised carbon)	3,106 metric carats (over 1¼ lb.) — *The Cullinan,* found by Capt. M. F. Wells 26 Jan. 1905 in the Premier Mine, Pretoria, South Africa. The largest uncut diamond is *The Star of Sierra Leone* found at Kono on 14 Feb. 1972 weighing 969.1 carats. It was sold for an undisclosed amount below its reserve of some $2.6 million in Feb. 1973 to Henry Winston (U.S.).	530.2 metric carats. Cleaved from *The Cullinan* in 1908, in Amsterdam by Jak Asscher and polished by Henri Koe known as *The Star of Africa No. 1* and now in the Royal Sceptre.	Diamond is the *hardest* known naturally-occurring substance, being 90 times as hard as the next hardest mineral, corundum (Al_2O_3). The peak hardness value on the Knoop scale is 8,400 compared with an average diamond of 7,000. The rarest colours for diamond are blue (record—44.4 carat *Hope* diamond) and pink (record—24 carat presented by Dr. John Thoburn Williamson to H.M. The Queen in 1958). Auction record: $1,050,000 (then £437,500) for a 69.42 carat stone bought by Cartier on 13 Oct. 1969 and sold to Richard Burton (at $1,200,000 (then £500,000) for Elizabeth Taylor on 24 Oct. 1969. Tiffany and Co. put a $5 million price on their canary yellow diamond of 1877 for one day on 17 Nov. 1972.
Emerald (green beryl) [$Be_3Al_2 (SiO_3)_6$]	125 lb. *56 kg 70* crystal (up to 15¾ in [*40 cm*] long and 9¾ in [*24,75 cm*] in diameter) from a Ural, U.S.S.R. mine.	2,680 carat unguent jar carved by Dionysio Miseroni in the 17th century owned by the Austrian Government. 1,350 carat of *gem* quality, the *Devonshire* stone from Muso, Columbia.	A necklace of eight major emeralds and one pendant emerald of 75.63 carats with diamonds was sold by Sotheby's in Zurich on 24 Nov. 1971 for £436,550 (then $1,090,000). The Swiss customs at Geneva confirmed on 16th April 1972 the existence of an hexaponal emerald of about 20,000 carats, thus possibly worth more than $100 million.
Sapphire (blue corundum) (Al_2O_3)	2,302 carat stone found at Anakie, Queensland, Australia, in c. 1935, now a 1,318 carat head of President Abraham Lincoln (1809–65).	1,444 carat *Black Star of Queensland* carved in 1953–1955 into a bust of General Dwight David Eisenhower (1890–1969).	*Note:* both the sapphire busts are in the custody of the Kazanjian Foundation of Los Angeles, California, U.S.A.
Ruby (red corundum) (Al_2O_3)	3,421 carat broken stone reported found in July 1961 (largest piece 750 carats).	1,184 carat natural gem stone of Burmese origin.	Since 1955 rubies have been the world's most precious gem attaining a price of up to £4,000 per carat by 1969. The ability to make corundum prisms for laser technology up to over 12 in *30 cm* in length must now have a bearing on the gem market.

RECORDS FOR OTHER PRECIOUS MATERIALS

	Largest	Where Found	Notes On Present Location, etc
Pearl (Molluscan concretion)	14 lb. 1 oz. *6 kg 378* 9½ in *24 cm* long by 5½ in *14 cm* in diameter—*Pearl of Laotze*	At Palawan, Philippines, 7 May 1934 in shell of giant clam.	In a San Francisco bank vault. It is the property since 1936 of Wilburn Dowell Cobb and was valued at $4,080,000 in July 1971.
Opal ($SiO_2.nH_2O$)	Any stone: 220 troy oz. (yellow-orange). Gem stone: 17,700 carats (*Olympic Australis*)	Andamooka, South Australia Jan. 1970. Coober Pedy, South Australia, Aug. 1956.	The Andamooka specimen was unearthed by a bulldozer.
Crystal (SiO_2)	Any stone: 70 tons/*tonnes* (piezo-quartz crystal). Ball: 106¾ lb. *48 kg 420* 12⅞ in *32,7 cm* diameter, the *Warner* sphere	Kazakhstan, U.S.S.R., Sept. 1958. Burma, (originally a 1,000 lb. [*450 kg*] piece).	Note: There is a single rock crystal of 1,728 lb *783 kg 800* placed in the Ural Geological Museum, Sverdlovsk, U.S.S.R., November 1968. U.S. National Museum, in Washington, D.C.
Topaz [$(Al_2SiO_4)_4$ $(F,OH)_2$]	Any stone: 596 lb. *270 kg* Gem stone: 7,725 carats	Minas Gerais, Brazil.	American Museum of Natural History, New York City, since 1951. Also at the American Museum of Natural History.
Amber (Coniferous fossil resin)	33 lb. 10 oz. *15 kg 250.*	Reputedly from Burma acquired in 1860.	Bought by John Charles Bowring (d. 1893) for £300 in Canton, China. Natural History Museum, London, since 1940.
Jade [$NaAl(Si_2O_6)$]	Sub-marine boulder of 5 short tons *4,53 tonnes* valued at $180,000)	Off Monterey, California. Landed 5 June 1971.	Jadeite can be virtually any colour. The less precious nephrite is [Ca_2 $(Mg,Fe)_5(OH)_2(Si_4O_{11})_2$]
Marble (Metamorphosed $CaCO_3$)	90 tons/*tonnes* (single slab)	Quarried at Yule, Colorado, U.S.A.	A piece of over 45 tons/*tonnes* was dressed from this slab for the coping stone of the Tomb of the Unknown Soldier in Arlington National Cemetery, Virginia, U.S.A.
Nuggets— Gold (Au)	7,560 oz. (472½ lb. [*214 kg 318*]) (reef gold) *Holtermann Nugget*	Beyers & Holtermann Star of Hope Gold Mining Co., Hill End, N.S.W., Australia, 19 Oct. 1872	The purest large nugget was the *Welcome Stranger*, found at Tarnagulla, near Moliagul, Victoria, Australia, which yielded 2,248 troy oz. *69 kg 920* of pure gold from 2,280¼ oz. *64 kg 640.*
Silver (Ag)	2,750 lb. troy	Sonora, Mexico	Appropriated by the Spanish Government before 1821.

Other Gems Records:

Largest Stone of Gem Quality:
A 520,000 carat (2 cwt. 5 lb. [*103 kg 800*]) aquamarine (Be_3Al_2 [SiO_3]$_6$) found near Marambaia, Brazil in 1910. Yielded over 200,000 carats of gem quality cut stones.

Rarest:
Taaffeite ($Be_4Mg_4Al_{15}O_{32}$) first discovered in Dublin, Ireland, in November 1945. Only two of these pale mauve stones are known—the larger is of 0.84 of a carat.

Densest Gem Mineral:
Stibotantalite [$(SbO)_2(Ta,Nb)_2O_6$] a rare brownish-yellow mineral found in San Diego County, California, has a density of 7.46. The alloy platiniridium has a density of more than 22.0

The world's largest opals from Andamooka, South Australia

4. TELESCOPES

Earliest Although there is evidence that early Arabian scientists understood something of the magnifying power of lenses, their first use to form a telescope has been attributed to Roger Bacon (*c.* 1214–92) in England. The prototype of modern refracting telescopes was that completed by Johannes Lippershey for the Dutch government on 2 Oct. 1608.

Largest Refractor The largest refracting (*i.e.* magnification by lenses) telescope in the world is the 62 ft *101,6 cm* long 40 in *18,90 m* telescope completed in 1897 at the Yerkes Observatory, Williams Bay, Wisconsin, and belonging to the University of Chicago, Illinois, U.S.A. The largest in the British Isles is the 28 in *71,1cm* at the Royal Greenwich Observatory completed in 1894.

Reflector World The largest telescope in the world is the 6 m *236.2 in* telescope sited on Mount Semirodriki, near Zelenchukskaya in the Caucasus Mountains, U.S.S.R., at an altitude of 6,830 ft *2 080 m*. The mirror, weighing 70 tons/*tonnes* was completed in November 1967 and assembled by October 1970. The overall weight of the 80 ft *24,38 m* long assembly is 850 tons *863 tonnes*. Being the most powerful of all telescopes its range, which includes the location of objects down to the 25th magnitude, represents the limits of the observable

Universe. Its light-gathering power would enable it to detect the light from a candle at a distance of 15,000 miles more than *24 000 km*.

United The largest reflector in the British Isles is the Isaac
Kingdom Newton 98.2 in *249,4 cm* reflector at the Royal Greenwich Observatory, Herstmonceux Castle, Sussex. It was built in Newcastle upon Tyne, Northumberland, weighs 92 tons *93,5 tonnes*, cost £641,000 and was inaugurated on 1 Dec. 1967.

Radio The world's first fully steerable radio telescope is the
Earliest Mark I telescope at the University of Manchester Department of Radio Astronomy, Nuffield Radio Astronomy Laboratories, Jodrell Bank, Macclesfield, Cheshire, on which work began in September 1952. The 750 ton *762 tonnes* 250 ft *76,20 m* diameter bowl of steel plates and 180 ft *54,86 m* high supports weigh 2,000 tons *2 032 tonnes*. Its cost is believed to have been about £750,000 when it was completed in 1957.

Largest The world's largest trainable dish-type radio telescope
steerable is the 100 m *328 ft* diameter, 3,000 ton/*tonnes*
dish assembly at the Max Planck Institute for Radio Astronomy of Bonn in the Effelsberger Valley, West Germany; it became operative in May 1971. The cost of the installation begun in November 1967 was £14,200,000. The University of Manchester Mark V radio telescope at Meiford, Montgomeryshire will have a diameter of 375 ft *120 m* and is due for completion at a cost of some £6 million before 1980.

Largest The world's largest dish radio telescope is the partially-
Dish steerable ionospheric assembly built over a natural bowl at Arecibo, Puerto Rico, completed in November 1963 at a cost of about $9,000,000 (*£3.75 million*). The dish has a diameter of 1,000 ft *304,80 m* and covers 18½ acres *7,28 ha*. Its sensitivity is being raised by a factor of 1,000 and its range to the edge of the observable Universe at some 15,000 million light-years by the fitting of new aluminium plates at a cost of $7.7 million for completion in May 1974. The RATAN-600 radio telescope being built in the Northern Caucasus, U.S.S.R. will have a dish 600 m *1,968.5 ft* in diameter.

Largest The first $3 million instalment for the building of the
World world's largest and most sensitive radio telescope was included by the National Science Foundation in their federal budget for the fiscal year 1973. The instrument termed the VLA (Very Large Array) will be Y-shaped with each arm 13 miles *20,9 km* long with 27 mobile antennae on rails. The site selected will be 50 miles *80 km* west of Socorro in the Plains of San Augustin, New Mexico and the completion date will be 1979 to 1981 at a total cost of $74 million (*now £30.2 million*).

The British Science Research Council 5 Km Radio telescope at Lord's Bridge, Cambridgeshire and Isle of Ely to be operated by the Mullard Radio Astronomy Observatory of Cambridge University will utilize eight mobile 42 ft *12,80 m* rail-borne computer-controlled dish aerials, which will be equivalent to a single steerable dish 5 km *3 miles 188 yds* in diameter. The project, to be operational before the end of 1973, will cost more than £2,100,000.

Solar The world's largest solar telescope is the 480 ft *146,30 m* long McMath telescope at Kitt Peak National Observatory near Tucson, Arizona, U.S.A. It has a focal length of 300 ft *91,44 m* and an 80 in *2,03 m* heliostat mirror. It was completed in 1962 and produces an image measuring 33 in *83,8 cm* in diameter.

Observatory The highest altitude observatory in the world is the
Highest Mauna Kea Observatory, Hawaii at an altitude of 13,824 ft *4 213 m*, opened in 1969. The principal instrument is an 88 in *224 cm* telescope.

The world's oldest astronomical observatory—a 1,341 year old edifice in South Korea

Oldest The earliest astronomical observatory in the world is the Chomsong-dae built in A.D. 632 in Kyongju, South Korea and still extant.

Planetaria The ancestor of the planetarium is the rotatable
World Gottorp Globe, built by Andreas Busch in Denmark between 1654 and 1664 to the orders of the Duke, Frederick III of Holstein's court mathematician Olearius. It is 34.6 ft *10,34 m* in circumference, weighs nearly 3½ tons/*tonnes* and is now preserved in Leningrad, U.S.S.R. The stars were painted on the inside. The earliest optical installation was not until 1923 in the Deutsches Museum, Munich, by Zeiss of Jena, Germany. The world's largest planetarium, with a diameter of 85 ft *25,90 m* is the Washington Planetarium and Space Center in Washington, D.C. The total construction cost was $5 million.

United The United Kingdom's first planetarium was opened
Kingdom at Madame Tussaud's Marylebone Road, London, on 19 March 1958. Accurate images of 8,900 stars are able to be projected on the 70 ft *21,33 m* high copper dome.

5. PHOTOGRAPHY

CAMERAS

Earliest The earliest photograph was taken in the summer of 1826 by Joseph Nicéphore Niépce (1765–1833), a French physician and scientist. It showed the courtyard of his country house at Gras, near St. Loup-de-Varennes. It probably took eight hours to expose and was taken on a bitumen-coated polished pewter plate measuring 7¾ in by 6½ in *20 × 16,5 cm*. The earliest photograph taken in England was one of a diamond-paned window in Laycock (or Lacock) Abbey, Wiltshire, taken in August 1835 by William Henry Fox Talbot, M.P. (1800–77), the inventor of the negative-positive process. This was bought by the Johannesburg City Council for £480 in November 1970. The world's earliest aerial photograph was taken in 1858 by Gaspard Félix Tournachon (1820–1910), *alias* Nadar, from a balloon near Villacoublay, on the outskirts of Paris, France.

Largest The largest camera ever built was the Anderson Mammoth camera, built in Chicago, Illinois, U.S.A., in 1900. When extended, it measured 9 ft high, 6 ft wide and 20 ft long *2,74 × 1,83 × 6,10 m*. Its two lenses were a wide-angle Zeiss with a focal length of 68 in *172,7 cm* and a telescope Rapid Rectilinear of 120 in *304,8 cm* focal length. Exposures averaged 150 seconds and a team of 15 men were required to work it.

Smallest Apart from cameras built for intra-cardiac surgery and espionage, the smallest camera generally marketed is the Japanese Kiku 16 Model II, which measures $6 × 2,5 × 1,5$ cm $2\frac{3}{8} × 1 × \frac{5}{8}$ *of an in.*

Fastest In 1972 Prof. Basor of the U.S.S.R. Academy of Sciences published a paper describing an experimental camera with a time resolution of $5 × 10^{-13}$ of a sec or $\frac{1}{2}$ a picosec. The fastest production camera in the world is the Imacon 600 manufactured by John Hadland (P.I.) Ltd of Bovington, Hertfordshire which is capable of 600 million pictures per sec. Uses include lasar, ballistic, detonic, plasma and corona research.

Most expensive The most expensive range of camera equipment in the world is the F-1 35 mm system of Canon Camera Co. Inc. of Tokyo. The 40 lenses offered range from the Fish Eye 7.5 mm F5.6 to the FL 1200 mm F11, while the accessories available number 180. The total cost of the range would exceed £12,000.

Fastest Lens The world's fastest lens is the Canon × 200 mm. F0.56 mirror lens used for X-Ray work. The fastest lens available in television cameras is the Canon 25 mm TV 16 of maximum aperture f 0.78.

6. NUMEROLOGY

In dealing with large numbers, scientists use the notation of 10 raised to various powers to eliminate a profusion of noughts. For example, 19,160,000,000,000 miles would be written $1.916 × 10^{13}$ miles. Similarly, a very small number, for example 0.0000154324 of a gramme, would be written $1.5432 × 10^{-5}$ g. Of the prefixes used before numbers the smallest is "atto-" from the Danish atten for 18, indicating a trillionth part (10^{-18}) of the unit, and the highest is "tera-" (Greek, teras = monster), indicating a billion (10^{12}) fold.

NUMBERS

Highest The highest generally accepted named number is the centillion, which is 10 raised to the power 600, or one followed by 600 noughts. Higher numbers are named in linguistic literature the most extreme of which is the milli-millimillillion (10 raised to the power 6,000,000,000) devised by Rudolf Ondrejka. The number Megiston written with symbol ⊚ is a number too great to have any physical meaning. The highest named number outside the decimal notation is the Buddhist *asankhyeya*, which is equal to 10^{140} or 100 tertio-vigintillions (British system) or 100 quinto-quadragintillions (U.S. system).

The number 10^{100} (10,000 sexdecillion) is designated a Googol. This was invented by Dr. Edward Kasner (U.S.) (d. 1955). Ten raised to the power of a Googol is described as a Googolplex. Some conception of the magnitude of such numbers can be gained when it is said that the number of atoms in some models of the observable Universe does not exceed 10^{85}. Factorial 10^{85}, approximates to 10 to the power of $43 + 85 × 10^{85}$!

The largest number to have become sufficiently well-known in mathematics to have been named after its begetter is the larger of the two Skewes numbers which is 10 to the power 10 to the power 10 to the power 3, obtained by Prof. Stanley Skewes, M.A.,

Ph.D., now of Cape Town University, South Africa, and published in two papers of 1933 and 1955 concerning the occurrence of prime numbers.

Prime numbers A prime number is any positive integer (excluding 1) having no integral factors other than itself and unity, *e.g.* 2, 3, 5, 7 or 11. The lowest prime number is thus 2. The highest known prime number is $2^{19937}-1$ (a number of 6,002 digits of which the first five are 43,154 and the last three, 471) received by the American Mathematical Society on 18 March 1971 and calculated on an I.B.M. 360/91 computer in 39 mins. 26.4 sec by Dr. Bryant Tuckerman at Yorktown Heights, New York.

Perfect numbers A number is said to be perfect if it is equal to the sum of its divisors other than itself, *e.g.* $1 + 2 + 4 + 7 + 14 = 28$. The lowest perfect number is 6 $(1 + 2 + 3)$. The highest known and the 24th so far discovered, is $(2^{19937} - 1) × 2^{19936}$ which has 12,003 digits of which the first 3 are 931, and the last 3 are 656. It is a consequence of the highest known prime (see above).

Most primitive The lowest limit in enumeration among primitive peoples is among the Yancos, an Amazon tribe who cannot count beyond *poettarrarorincoaroac*, which is their word for "three". The Temiar people of West Malaysia (formerly called Malaya) also stop at three. Investigators have reported that the number "four" is expressed by a look of total stupefaction indistinguishable from that for any other number higher than three. It is said that among survivors of the Aimores, naked nomads of Eastern Brazil, there is no apparent word for "two".

Most accurate and most inaccurate version of "pi" The greatest number of decimal places to which *pi* (π) has been calculated is 500,000 by the French mathematicians Jean Guilloud and Michele Dichampt of the Commissariat à l'Energie Atomique published on 26 Feb. 1967. The published value to 500,000 places, in what has been described as the world's most boring 100 page book, was 3.141592653589793 ... (omitting the next 499,975 places) ... 5138195242. In 1897 the State legislature of Indiana came within a single vote of declaring that pi should be *de jure* 3.2.

Square root of Two The greatest accuracy for $\sqrt{2}$ is an enumeration to 1,000,082 places by Jacques Dutka of Columbia University, N.Y., U.S.A. announced in Oct. 1971 after a $47\frac{1}{2}$ hour run work on a computer.

Earliest measures The earliest known measure of weight is the *beqa* of the Amratian period of Egyptian civilization *c.* 3,800 B.C. found at Naqada, United Arab Republic. The weights are cylindrical with rounded ends from 188.7 to 211.2 g *6.65 to 7.45 oz*. The unit of length used by the megalithic tomb-builders in Britain *c.* 2300 B.C. appears to have been $2.72 ± 0.003$ ft *82,81 ± 82,99* cm.

TIME MEASURE

Longest The longest measure of time is the *kalpa* in Hindu chronology. It is equivalent to 4,320 million years. In astronomy a cosmic year is the period of rotation of the sun around the centre of the Milky Way galaxy, *i.e.* about 225,000,000 years. In the Late Cretaceous Period of *c.* 85 million years ago the Earth rotated faster so resulting in 370.3 days per year while in Cambrian times some 600 million years ago there is evidence that the year contained 425 days.

Shortest Owing to variations in the length of a day, which is estimated to be increasing irregularly at the average rate of about two milliseconds per century due to the Moon's tidal drag, the second has been redefined. Instead of being 1/86,400th part of a mean solar day, it has, since 1960, been reckoned as 1/31,556,925.9747th part of the solar (or tropical) year at A.D. 1900, January 0 to 12 hrs, Ephemeris time. In 1958 the second of Ephemeris time was computed to be equivalent to

9,192,631,770±20 cycles of the radiation corresponding to the transition of a caesium 133 atom when unperturbed by exterior fields. In a nano-second or a milli-micro second (1.0×10^{-9} of a sec) light travels 11.8 in *29,97 cm*.

SMALLEST UNITS

The shortest unit of length is the atto-metre which is 1.0×10^{-16} of a cm. The smallest unit of area is a "shed", used in sub-atomic physics and first mentioned in 1956. It is 1.0×10^{-48} of a cm². A "barn" is equal to 10^{24} "sheds". The reaction of a neutrino occurs over the area of 1×10^{-43} of a cm².

7. PHYSICAL EXTREMES

TEMPERATURES

Highest The highest man-made temperatures yet attained are those produced in the centre of a thermonuclear fusion bomb, which are of the order of 300,000,000 to 400,000,000° C. Of controllable temperatures, the highest effective laboratory figure reported is 50,000,000°C, for 2/100ths of a second by Prof. Lev A. Artsimovich at Tokamuk in the U.S.S.R. in 1969. At very low particle densities even higher figures are obtainable. Prior to 1963 a figure of 3,000 million ° C. was reportedly achieved in the U.S.S.R. with Ogra injection-mirror equipment.

Lowest The lowest temperature reached is 5×10^{-7} degree Kelvin, achieved by Professor A. Abragam (b. 1914) in collaboration with M. Chapellier, M. Goldman, and Vu Hoang Chau at the Centre d'Etudes Nucléaires, Saclay, France, in March 1969. Absolute or thermodynamic temperatures are defined in terms of ratios rather than as differences reckoned from the unattainable absolute zero, which on the Kelvin scale is −273,15° C or −459.67° F. Thus the lowest temperature ever attained is 1 in 5.46×10^8 of the melting point of ice (0° C. or 273.15K or 32° F.).

Highest pressures The highest sustained laboratory pressures yet reported are of 5,000,000 atmospheres (32,800 tons per in² [*51 650 kgf/mm²*]), achieved in the U.S.S.R. and announced in October 1958. Using dynamic methods and impact speeds of up to 18,000 m.p.h. *29 000 km/h*, momentary pressures of 75,000,000 atmospheres (490,000 tons/in² [*771 000 kgf/mm²*]) were reported from the United States in 1958.

Highest vacuum The highest (or 'hardest') vacuums obtained in scientific research are of the order of 1.0×10^{-16} of an atmosphere. This compares with an estimated pressure in inter-stellar space of 1.0×10^{-19} of an atmosphere. At sea-level there are 3×10^{19} molecules/cm³ in the atmosphere, but in inter-stellar space there are probably less than 10/cm³.

Fastest centrifuge The highest man-made rotary speed ever achieved is 1,500,000 revs/sec, or 90,000,000 revs/min, on a steel rotor with a diameter of about 1/100th of an in *0,25 mm* suspended in a vacuum in an ultra-centrifuge installed in March 1961 in the Rouss Physical Laboratory at the University of Virginia in Charlottesville, Virginia, U.S.A. This work is led by Prof. Jesse W. Beams. The edge of the rotor is travelling at 2,500 m.p.h *4 000 km/h* and is subject to a stress of 1,000,000,000 g.

Microscopes *Most powerful* Electron microscopes have now reached the point at which individual atoms are distinguishable. In March 1958 the U.S.S.R. announced an electronic point projector with a magnification approaching × 2,000,000, in which individual atoms of barium and molecules of oxygen can be observed. In 1970 a resolution of 0.88 of an Ångström unit diameter was achieved by Dr. K. Yada (Japan) using a Hitachi Model HU-11B. In February 1969 it was announced

from Pennsylvania State University, U.S.A., that the combination of the field-ion microscope invented by their Prof. Erwing W. Müller in 1956 and a spectrometer enabled single atoms to be identified.

Smallest The smallest high power microscope in the world is the 2,000 × 18 oz. *510 g* McArthur microscope measuring 4 × 2½ × 2 in *10 × 6,3 × 5 cm*. It provides immersion dark ground, phase contrast, polarising and incident illumination and is produced at Landbeach, Cambridge, England.

Electron microscope The most powerful electron microscope in the world is the 3,500 kV installation at the National Scientific Research Centre, Toulouse, France which reached testing stage in October 1969. The high voltage generator and accelerator fill a cylinder 15 ft *4,57 m* in diameter and 30 ft *9,14 m* high. Its six lenses form a column 3 ft by 11 ft *0,91 × 3,35 m* and weigh 20 tons/ *tonnes*.

Highest note The highest note yet attained is one of 60,000 megahertz (60 GHz) (60,000 million vibrations/sec), generated by a "laser" beam striking a sapphire crystal at the Massachusetts Institute of Technology in Cambridge, Massachusetts, U.S.A., in September 1964.

Loudest noise The loudest noise created in a laboratory is 210 decibels or 400,000 acoustic watts reported by N.A.S.A from a 48 ft *14,63 m* steel and concrete horn at Huntsville, Alabama, U.S.A. in October 1965. Holes can be bored in solid material by this means.

Most Powerful Sound System The World's most powerful Sound System is that installed at the Ontario Motor Speedway, California in July 1970. It has an output of 30,800 watts. connectable to 355 horn speaker assemblies and is thus able to communicate the spoken word to 230,000 people above the noise of 50 screaming racing cars.

The control tower of the world's largest and most powerful sound system, at the Ontario Motor Speedway, California

Quietest place The "dead room", measuring 35 ft by 28 ft *10,67 × 3,53 m* in the Bell Telephone System laboratory at Murray Hill, New Jersey, U.S.A., is the most anechoic room in the world, eliminating 99.98 per cent of reflected sound.

Finest balance The most accurate balance in the world is the Q01 quartz fibre decimicro balance made by L. Oertling Ltd. of Orpington, Kent, England which has a readout scale on which one division corresponds to

0.0001 of a mg. It can weigh to an accuracy of 0.0002 of a mg which is equivalent to little more than one third of the weight of the ink on this full stop .

Lowest viscosity The California Institute of Technology, U.S.A. announced on 1 Dec. 1957 that there was no measurable viscosity, *i.e.* perfect flow, in liquid helium II, which exists only at temperatures close to absolute zero (−273.15° C. or −459.67° F.).

Lowest friction The lowest coefficient of static and dynamic friction of any solid is 0.02, in the case of polytetrafluoroethylene ($[C_2F_4]_n$), called P.T.F.E.—equivalent to wet ice on wet ice. It was first manufactured in quantity by E. I. du Pont de Nemours & Co. Inc. in 1943, and is marketed from the U.S.A. as Teflon. In the United Kingdom it is marketed by I.C.I. as Fluon.

At the University of Virginia (see above, Fastest centrifuge) a 30 lb. *13 kg 60* rotor magnetically supported has been spun at 1,000 revs/sec in a vacuum of 10^{-6} mm. of mercury pressure. It loses only one revolution per second per day thus spinning for years.

Most powerful electric current The most powerful electric current generated is that from the Zeus capacitor at the Los Alamos Scientific Laboratory, New Mexico, U.S.A. If fired simultaneously the 4,032 capacitors would produce for a few microseconds twice as much current as that generated elsewhere on Earth.

Most powerful adhesive The most powerful adhesive known is epoxy resin, which, after being supercooled to −450° F. *−267°C* can withstand a shearing pull of 8,000 lb./in² *560 kgf/cm²*.

Most powerful particle accelerator The 1.24 mile *2 km* diameter proton synchrotron at the National Accelerator Laboratory at Weston Illinois, U.S.A. is the largest and most powerful "atom-smasher" in the world. An energy of 400 GeV was attained on 14 Dec. 1972. The plant cost $250 million. The construction of the CERN II 1.37 mile *2,2 km* diameter proton synchrotron on the French-Swiss border at Megrin near Geneva was authorized on 19 Feb. 1971 and should surpass 300 GeV by 1979.

The £32 million CERN intersecting storage rings (ISR) project, started on 27 Jan. 1971, using two 28 GeV proton beams, is designed to yield the equivalent of 1,700 GeV in its centre of mass experiments.

World's largest bubble chamber The largest bubble chamber in the world is at the Argonne National Laboratory, Illinois, U.S.A. It is 12 ft *3,65 m* in diameter and contains 5,330 gal *24 227 litres* of liquid hydrogen at a temperature of −247° C. A 30 000 litre *6,600 gal* chamber is being built at CERN, near Geneva.

Strongest magnet The heaviest magnet in the world is one measuring 60 m *196 ft* in diameter, with a weight of 36,000 tons/*tonnes* for the 10 GeV synchrophasotron in the Joint Institute for Nuclear Research at Dubna, near Moscow, U.S.S.R. The largest super-conducting magnet is a niobium-zirconium magnet, weighing 15,675 lb. *7 kg 110* completed in June 1966 by Avco Everett Research Laboratory, Massachusetts, U.S.A. It produces a magnetic field of 40,000 gauss and the windings are super-cooled with 6 000 litres *1,320 gal* of liquid helium.

Strongest magnetic field The strongest recorded magnetic fields are ones of 10 megagauss, fleetingly produced by explosive flux compression devices reported in Sept. 1968. The first megagauss field was announced also from the United States in March 1967.

The strongest steady magnetic field yet achieved is one of 255,000 gauss in a cylindrical bore of 1.25 in *3,17 cm* using 10 megawatts of power, called the "1J" magnet designed by D. Bruce Montgomery, which was put into operation at the Francis Bitter National Magnet Laboratory at Massachusetts Institute of Technology in 1964.

WIND TUNNELS

World The world's largest wind tunnel is a low-speed tunnel with a 40 × 80 ft *12,19 × 24,38 m* test section built in 1944 at the Ames Research Center, Moffett Field, California, U.S.A. The tunnel encloses 800 tons/*tonnes* of air and cost approximately $7,000,000 (*now £2,916,666*). The maximum volume of air that can be moved is 60,000,000 ft³ *1 700 000 m³* per min. The most powerful is the 216,000 h.p. *219 000 c.v.* installation at the Arnold Engineering Test Center at Tullahoma, Tennessee, U.S.A. opened in September 1956. The highest Mach number attained with air is Mach 27 at the works of the Boeing Company in Seattle, Washington State, U.S.A. For periods of micro-seconds, shock Mach numbers of the order of 30 have been attained in impulse tubes at Cornell University, Ithaca, New York State, U.S.A.

United Kingdom The most powerful wind tunnel in the United Kingdom is the transonic installation at the Aircraft Research Association at Bedford, with a working area 9 ft × 8 ft *2,74 × 2,43 m* and a tunnel power of 25,000 h.p. *18.5 Mw*. This machine is capable of producing Mach 1.4, which is equivalent to 1,065 m.p.h. *1 714 km/h* at sea level.

Finest cut Biological specimens embedded in epoxy resin can be sectioned by a glass knife microtome under ideal conditions to a thickness of 1/875,000th of an inch or 290 Ångström units.

Brightest light The brightest steady artificial light sources are "laser" beams with an intensity exceeding the Sun's 1,500,000 candles/in² *200 000 candelas/cm²* by a factor well in excess of 1,000. In May 1969 the U.S.S.R. Academy of Sciences announced blast waves travelling through a luminous plasma of inert gases heated to 90,000° K. The flare-up for up to 3 microseconds shone at 50,000 times the brightness of the Sun *viz.* 40,000 million candles/in². Of continuously burning sources, the most powerful is a 200 kW high-pressure xenon arc lamp of

The interior of the remodelled heavy ion linear accelerator at the Lawrence Berkeley Laboratory, University of California which at 2 miles *3,2 km* has been described as the world's longest scientific instrument

600,000 candle-power, reported from the U.S.S.R. in 1965. The most powerful searchlight ever developed was one produced during the 1939–45 war by the General Electric Company Ltd. at the Hirst Research Centre in Wembley, Greater London. It had a consumption of 600 kW and gave an arc luminance of 300,000 candles/in² and a maximum beam intensity of 2,700,000,000 candles from its parabolic mirror (diameter 10 ft [*3,04 m*]).

Longest Lived Electric Battery A battery kept in the Clarendon Laboratory, University of Oxford, has been causing a suspended bob to be electrostatically attracted a few times a second alternately by two small bells since 1840 when it was made by the London firm of scientific apparatus makers Watkins and Hill. It produces about 2 kV at 10^{-8} A and is an example of the so-called "dry column" associated with the names of Marechaux, de Luc, Behrens and Zamboni. The only known use of this form of battery in this century was for an infrared viewer in the 1939–45 war.

Most durable light The electric light bulb was invented in New York City, U.S.A. in 1860 by Heinrich (later Henry) Goebel (1818–93) of Springe, Germany. The average bulb lasts for 750 to 1,000 hrs. There is some evidence that a carbide filament bulb burning in the Fire Department, Livermore, South Alameda County, California has been burning since 1901

Most powerful "laser" beams The first illumination of another celestial body was achieved on 9 May 1962, when a beam of light was successfully reflected from the Moon by the use of an optical "maser" (microwave amplification by stimulated emission of radiation) or "laser" (light amplification by stimulated emission of radiation) attached to a 48-in. *121,9 cm* telescope at Massachusetts Institute of Technology, Cambridge, Massachusetts, U.S.A. The spot was estimated to be 4 miles *6,4 km* in diameter on the Moon. A "maser" light flash is focused into liquid nitrogen-cooled ruby crystal. Its chromium atoms are excited into a high energy state in which they emit a red light which is allowed to escape only in the direction desired. The device was propounded in 1958 by Dr. Charles Hard Townes

(born 1915) of the U.S.A. Such a flash for 1/5,000th of a second can bore a hole through a diamond by vaporization at 10,000° C, produced by 2×10^{23} photons.

COMPUTERS

The modern computer was made possible by the invention of the point-contact transistor by John Bardeen and Walter Brattain announced in July 1948, and the junction transistor by R. L. Wallace, Morgan Sparks and Dr. William Shockley in early 1951.

World The world's most powerful computer is the Control Data Corporation CDC 7600 first delivered in January 1969. It can perform 36 million operations in one second and has an access time of 27.5 nano-sec. It has two internal memory cores of 655,360 and 5,242,880 characters (6 bits per character) supplemented by a Model 817 disc file of 800 million characters. Commerical deliveries have been scheduled from 1972 at a cost of $9 to $15 million (*£3¾ to £6¼ million*) depending on peripherals. The most capacious storage device is the Ampex Terabit Memory which can store 2.88×10^{12} bits.

United Kingdom The computer with the largest memory built in the United Kingdom is the International Business Machines' I.B.M. System/370 Model 168 MP which is a multiprocessing computer with 16,777,216 bytes of main storage. A 'byte' is a unit of storage comprising 8 'bits' collectively equivalent to one alphabetic letter or two numerals. This machine is made at Havant, Hampshire.

Oldest Computer The oldest operative computer in Britain and probably the world is Witch built at Harwell in 1949–50 and still in service at the Wolverhampton and Staffordshire College of Technology since 1957. It has 827 "Dekatron" cathode tubes.

Fastest Switch An electronic device that can be switched in less than 10 billionths of a second (10^{-11} sec) was announced on 18 Jan. 1973. It utilizes the prediction of the English physicist Brian Josephson (b. 1940) in 1962 that ultra-thin insulators can be made superconductive.

The IBM System 370/ Model 168 MP computer, which is the most powerful in Britain

6 THE ARTS AND ENTERTAIN- MENTS

1. PAINTING

Earliest Evidence of Palaeolithic art was first found in 1834 at Chaffaud, Vienne, France by Brouillet when he recognised an engraving of two deer on a piece of flat bone from the cave, dating to *c.* 20,000 B.C. The number of stratigraphically-dated examples of cave art is very limited. The oldest known dated examples came from La Ferrassie, near Les Eyzies in the Périgord, where large blocks of stone engraved with animal figures and symbols were found in the Aurignacian II layer (*c.* 25,000 B.C.).

LARGEST

World All time *Panorama of the Mississippi*, completed by John Banvard (1815–91) in 1846, showing the river for 1,200 miles *1 930 km* in a strip probably 5,000 ft *1 525 m* long and 12 ft *3,65 m* wide, was the largest painting in the world, with an area of more than 1.3 acres *0,52 ha*. The painting is believed to have been destroyed when the rolls of canvas, stored in a barn at Cold Spring Harbor, Long Island, New York State, U.S.A., caught fire shortly before Banvard's death on 16 May 1891.

Existing The largest painting now in existence is probably *The Battle of Gettysburg*, completed in 1883, after 2½ yrs of work, by Paul Philippoteaux (France) and 16 assistants. The painting is 410 ft *125 m* long, 70 ft *21,3 m* high and weighs 5.36 tons *5,45 tonnes*. It depicts the climax of the Battle of Gettysburg, in southern Pennsylvania, U.S.A., on 3 July 1863. In 1964 the painting was bought by Joe King of Winston-Salem, North Carolina, U.S.A. after being stored by E. W. McConnell in a Chicago warehouse since 1933.

"Old Master" The largest "Old Master" is *Il Paradiso*, painted between 1587 and 1590 by Jacopo Robusti, *alias* Tintoretto (1518–94), and his son Domenico on Wall "E" of the Sala del Maggior Consiglio in the Palazzo Ducale (Doge's Palace) in Venice, Italy. The work is 22 m *72 ft 2 in* long and 7 m *22 ft 11½ in* high and contains more than 100 human figures.

United Kingdom The largest painting in the United Kingdom is the giant oval *Triumph of Peace and Liberty* by Sir James Thornhill (1676–1734), on the ceiling of the Painted Hall in the Royal Naval College, Greenwich, London. It measures 106 ft *32,3 m* by 51 ft *15,4 m* and took 20 yrs (1707–1727) to complete.

MOST VALUABLE

World The "Mona Lisa" (*La Gioconda*) by Leonardo da Vinci (1452–1519) in the Louvre, Paris, was assessed for insurance purposes at the highest ever figure of $100,000,000 (*then £35.7 million*) for its move for exhibition in Washington, D.C., and New York City, N.Y., U.S.A., from 14 Dec. 1962 to 12 March 1963. However, insurance was not concluded because the cost of the closest security precautions was less than that of the premiums. It was painted in *c.* 1503–07 and measures 77 × 53 cm *30.5 × 20.9 in*. It is believed to portray Mona (short for Madonna) Lisa Gherardini, the wife of Francesco del Giocondo.

The ceiling of the Painted Hall, Royal Hospital, Greenwich, the largest painting in the United Kingdom

of Florence, who disliked it and refused to pay for it. Francis I, King of France, bought the painting for his bathroom for 4,000 gold florins (now equivalent to £225,000) in 1517.

HIGHEST PRICE

Auction price World The highest price ever bid in a public auction for any painting is £2,310,000 for *Portrait of Juan de Pareja*, also known as *The Slave of Velázquez*, painted in Rome in 1649 by Diego Rodríguez de Silva Velázquez (1599–1660) and sold on 27 Nov. 1970 at the salerooms of Christie, Manson & Woods, London to the Wildenstein Gallery, New York. The painting had been sold at Christie's at auction in 1801 for 39 guineas (£40.95) It was in the possession of the Earls of Radnor from May 1811 until 1970.

Art Auction Sale Highest Total The highest total ever achieved for a single auction of works of art is £3,638,825 by a sale of 27 paintings by Old Masters at the salerooms of Christie, Manson and Woods, London on 25 June 1971. The highest price in the sale was paid for *The Death of Acteon* by Titian (£1,680,000).

By British artist The highest auction price for the work of a British artist is the £280,000 paid by Colnaghi's at Sotheby's for Gainsborough's painting of the Gravenor Family, from the estate of Major J. Townshend, on 19 July 1972. Executed in *c.* 1748, it measures 35½ in *90 cm* square.

Miniature portrait The highest price ever paid for a portrait miniature is the £65,100 given by an anonymous buyer at a sale held by Christie, Manson and Woods, London on 8 June 1971 for a miniature of Frances Howard, Countess of Essex and Somerset by Isaac Oliver, painted *c.* 1605. This miniature, sent for auction by Lord Derby, measured 5⅛ in *13 cm* in diameter.

Modern painting The highest price paid for a modern painting is $1,550,000 (*then £645,833*) paid by the Norton Simon Foundation of Los Angeles, California, U.S.A. at the Parke-Bernet Galleries, New York City on 9 Oct. 1968 for *Le Pont des Arts* painted by Pierre Auguste Renoir (1841–1919) of France in 1868. Renoir sold the picture to the Paris dealer Durand-Ruel for about £16.

Living artist World The highest price paid for paintings in the lifetime of the artist is $1,950,000 (*then £812,500*) paid for the two canvases *Two Brothers* (1905) and *Seated Harlequin* (1922) by Pablo Diego José Francisco de Paula Juan Nepomuceno Crispín Crispiano de la Santisima Trinidad Ruiz y Picasso (1881–1973) of Spain. This was paid by the Basle City Government to the Staechelin Foundation to enable the Basle Museum of Arts to retain the painting after an offer of $2,560,000 (*£1,066,666*) had been received from the United States in December 1967.

Picasso was the most prolific of all painters in a career which lasted 78 years. It has been estimated that Picasso produced about 13,500 paintings or designs, 100,000 prints or engravings, 34,000 book illustrations and 300 sculptures or ceramics. His life-time *oeuvre* has been valued at £300 million.

British The highest price for any painting by a living British artist is £26,000 for a painting of a Pope in "convulsive hysteria" by Francis Bacon, completed in 1953, sent in anonymously and bought by Lefevre Gallery at auction at Sotheby's in 1970.

Pop Art The highest price for an item of Pop Art was for "Big Painting No. 6" (1965) by Roy Lichtenstein (U.S.) which was sold for $79,200 (*then £33,000*) at Parke-Bernet, New York City on 18 Nov. 1970.

Drawing The highest price ever attached to any drawing is £804,361 for the cartoon *The Virgin and Child with*

Leonardo da Vinci's cartoon of the Virgin and Child with St. John the Baptist and St. Anne

St. John the Baptist and St. Anne, measuring 54¼ in by 39¼ in *137 by 100 cm*, drawn in Milan, probably in 1499–1500, by Leonardo da Vinci (1452–1519) of Italy, retained by the National Gallery in 1962. Three United States bids of over $4,000,000 (*then £1,428,570*) were reputed to have been made for the cartoon.

Largest gallery The world's largest art gallery is the Winter Palace and the neighbouring Hermitage in Leningrad, U.S.S.R. One has to walk 15 miles *24 km* to visit each of the 322 galleries, which house nearly 3,000,000 works of art and objects of archaeological interest.

Oldest and youngest R.A. The oldest ever Royal Academician has been (Thomas) Sidney Cooper C.V.O., who died on 8 Feb. 1902 aged 98 yrs 136 days, having exhibited 266 paintings over the record span of 67 consecutive years (1833–1902). The youngest ever R.A. has been Mary Moser (later Mrs. Hugh Lloyd), who was elected on the foundation of the Royal Academy in 1768 when aged 24.

Shortest apprenticeship Derek Myer of Henley-on-Thames, Oxfordshire had his landscape "Forty Inches Per Annum", painted two months after he had taken up painting, accepted for the Royal Academy's Summer Exhibition of 1969.

MURALS

Earliest The earliest known murals on man-made walls are those at Catal Hüyük in southern Anatolia, Turkey, dating from *c.* 5850 B.C.

Largest The world's largest mural is *The March of Humanity*, a mural of 54 panels, covering 48,000 ft² *4 460 m²* by David Alfaro Siqueiros, which was unveiled in 1968 in the Olimpico Hotel, Mexico City, Mexico. A rainbow mural stretching nearly 300 ft *90 m* up the sides of the Hilton Rainbow Hotel, Waikiki, Honolulu was completed in 1968.

HIGHEST-PRICED PAINTINGS—PROGRESSIVE RECORDS

Price	Equivalent 1973 Price	Painter, title, sold by and sold to	Date
£6,500	£61,880	Antonio Correggio's *The Magdalen Reading* (in fact spurious) to Elector Freidrich Augustus II of Saxony.	1746
£8,500	£80,920	Raphael's *The Sistine Madonna* to Elector Friedrich Augustus II of Saxony.	1759
£16,000	£87,500	Van Eyck's *Adoration of the Lamb*, 6 outer panels of Ghent altarpiece by Edward Solby to the Government of Prussia.	1821
£24,600*	£193,250	Murillo's *The Immaculate Conception* by estate of Marshall Soult to the Louvre (against Czar Nicholas I) in Paris.	1852
£70,000	£666,000	Raphael's *Ansidei Madonna* by the 8th Duke of Marlborough to the National Gallery.	1885
£100,000	£952,000	Raphael's *The Colonna Altarpiece* by Sedelmeyer to J. Pierpoint Morgan.	1901
£102,880	£980,000	Van Dyck's *Elena Grimaldi-Cattaneo* (portrait) by Knoedler to Peter Widener (1834–1915).	1906
£102,880	£810,000	Rembrandt's *The Mill* by 6th Marquess of Lansdowne to Peter Widener.	1911
£116,500	£916,000	Raphael's smaller *Panshanger Madonna* by Joseph (later Baron) Duveen (1869–1939) to Peter Widener.	1913
£310,400	£2,440,000	Leonardo da Vinci's *Benois Madonna* to Czar Nicholas II in Paris.	1914
£821,429*	£1,445,000	Rembrandt's *Aristotle Contemplating the Bust of Homer* by estate of Mr. and Mrs. Alfred W. Erickson to New York Metropolitan Museum of Art.	1961
£1,785,714	£2,564,000	Leonardo da Vinci's *Ginevra de' Benci* (portrait) by Prince Franz Josef II of Liechtenstein to National Gallery of Art, Washington, D.C., U.S.A.	1967
£2,310,000*	£2,749,000	Velázquez's *Portrait of Juan de Pareja* by the Earl of Radnor to the Wildenstein Gallery, New York.	1970

Indicates price at auction, otherwise prices were by private treaty.

Largest mobile The largest mobile in the world is one measuring 45 ft by 17 ft *14 by 5 m* and weighing 600 lb. *272 kg* suspended in December 1957 in the main terminal building of the John F. Kennedy International Airport (formerly Idlewild), Long Island, New York State, U.S.A. It was created by Alexander Calder (b. 1898), who invented this art form in 1930 as a reaction to sculptures or "stabiles". The heaviest of all mobiles is *Spirale*, weighing 4,000 lb. *1 800 kg* outside the U.N.E.S.C.O. headquarters in Paris, France. The word "mobile" was coined by Marcel Duchamp in 1932.

Largest mosaic The world's largest mosaic is on the walls of the central library of the Universidad Nacional Autónomao de México, Mexico City. There are four walls, the two largest measuring 12,949 ft² *1 203 m²* each representing the pre-Hispanic past.

MUSEUMS
Oldest The oldest museum in the world is the Ashmolean Museum in Oxford built in 1679.

Largest The largest museum in the world is the American Museum of Natural History on 77th to 81st Streets and Central Park West, New York City, N.Y., U.S.A. Founded in 1874, it comprises 19 interconnected buildings with 23 acres *9 ha* of floor space. The largest museum in the United Kingdom is the British Museum (founded in 1753), which was opened to the public in 1759. The main building in Bloomsbury, London, was built in 1823 and has a total floor area of 17.57 acres *7,11 ha*.

2. SCULPTURE

Earliest World The earliest known examples of sculpture are the so-called Venus figurines from Aurignacian sites, dating to *c.* 25,000–22,000 B.C., *e.g.* the famous Venus of Willendorf from Austria and the Venus of Brassempouy (Landes, France).

Britain The earliest British art object is an engraving of a horse's head on a piece of rib-bone from Robin Hood Cave, Creswell Crag, Derbyshire. It dates from the Upper Palaeolithic period (*c.* 15,000 to 10,000 B.C.). The earliest Scottish rock carving from Lagalochan, Argyllshire dates from pre-3,000 B.C.

Most expensive World The highest price ever paid for a sculpture is the $380,000 (£158,333) given at Sotheby's New York salerooms, Parke-Bernet, on 5 May 1971 for Edgar Degas' (1834–1917) bronze *Petite Danseuse de Quatorze Ans*, executed in an edition of about 12 casts in 1880.

The main entrance of The British Museum, the largest museum in the United Kingdom

Language

Living sculptor The highest price paid for the work of a living sculptor is the $260,000 (£104,000) given at Sotheby's Parke-Bernet Galleries, New York on 1 March 1972 for the wooden carving *Reclining Figure* by Henry Moore, O.M., C.H. (b. Castleford, Yorkshire, 30 July 1898).

Largest The world's largest sculptures are the mounted figures of Jefferson Davis (1808–89), Gen. Robert Edward Lee (1807–70) and Gen. Thomas Jonathan ("Stonewall") Jackson (1824–63), covering 1.33 acres *0,5 ha* on the face of Stone Mountain, near Atlanta, Georgia. They are 20 ft *6 m* higher than the more famous Rushmore sculptures. When completed the world's largest sculpture will be that of the Indian chief Tashunca-Uitco, known as Crazy Horse, of the Oglala tribe of the Dakota or Nadowessioux (Sioux) group. He is believed to have been born in about 1849, and he died at Fort Robinson, Nebraska, on 5 Sept. 1877. The sculpture was begun on 3 June 1948 near Mount Rushormore, South Dakota, U.S.A. A projected 561 ft *170 m* high and 641 ft *195 m* long, it will require the removal of 5,800,000 tons *5 890 000 tonnes* of stone and is the life work of one man, Korczak Ziolkowski. The work will take until at least 1978.

Ground figures In the Nazca Desert, south of Lima, Peru there are straight lines (one 5 miles [*8 km*] long), geometric shapes and plants and animals drawn on the ground by still unknown persons *ante* A.D. 100 for an uncertain but seemingly astronomical purpose.

Hill figures The largest human hill carving in Britain is the "Long Man" of Wilmington, Sussex, 226 ft *68 m* in length. The oldest of all White Horses in Britain is the Uffington White Horse in Berkshire, dating from the late Iron Age (*c.* 150 B.C.) and measuring 374 ft *114 m* from nose to tail and 120 ft *36 m* from ear to heel.

3. LANGUAGE

Earliest Anthropologists have evidence that the truncated pharynx of Neanderthal man precluded his speaking anything akin to a modern language any more than an ape or a modern baby. Cro Magnon man of 40,000 B.C. had however developed an efficient vocal tract. Clay tablets of the neolithic Danubian culture discovered in Dec. 1966 at Tartaria, Moros River, Romania have been dated to the fifth or fourth millennium B.C. The tablets bear symbols of bows and arrows, gates and combs. In 1970 it was announced that writing tablets bearing an early form of the Elamite language dating from 3,500 B.C. had been found in south-eastern Iran. The scientist Alexander Marshack (U.S.) maintains that marked Upper Palaeolithic artifacts, such as a Cro Magnon bone from 30,000 B.C. in the Musée des Antiquités Nationales, outside Paris with 69 marks with 24 stroke changes, are not random but of possibly lunar or menstrual cycle significance.

Oldest The written language with the longest continuous history is Chinese, the orthography of which has survived from *c.* 1400 B.C. such that some 2,000 shell-and-bone characters (*jiăgŭwén*) of that date can be read today.

Oldest words in English Recent research indicates that several river names in Britain date from pre-Celtic times (*ante* 550 B.C.). These include Ayr, Hayle and Nairn. This ascendant, Indo-Germanic tongue, which was spoken from *c.* 3000 B.C. on the Great Lowland Plain of Europe, now has only fragments left in Old Lithuanian, from which the modern English word *eland* derives. The word *land* is traceable to the Old Celtic *landa*, a heath and therefore must have been in use on the continent before the Roman Empire grew powerful in the 6th century B.C.

Sculptor Korczak Ziolkowski beside a scale plaster model 1/34th of the size of his semi-completed statue on Mount Rushmore

Commonest language Today's world total of languages and dialects still spoken is about 5,000 of which some 845 come from India. The language spoken by more people than any other is Northern Chinese, or Mandarin, by an estimated 68 per cent of the population hence 465 million people in 1972. The so-called national language (*Guóyŭ*) is a standardized form of Northern Chinese (*Běifānghuà*) as spoken in the Peking area. This was alphabetized into *zhuyin zimu* of 39 letters in 1918. In 1958 the *pinyin* system, using a Latin alphabet, was introduced. The next most commonly spoken language and the most widespread is English, by an estimated 340,000,000 in mid-1972. English is spoken by 10 per cent or more of the population in 29 sovereign countries.

In Great Britain and Ireland there are six indigenous tongues: English, Scots Gaelic, Welsh, Irish Gaelic, Manx and Romany (Gipsy). Of these English is, of course, predominant, while Manx has almost followed Cornish (whose last fluent speaker, John Davey, died in 1891) into extinction. By 1973 there remained only Mr. Edward (Ned) Maddrell (b. 20 Aug. 1877) of Glen Chass, Port St. Mary, Isle of Man, whose mother tongue is Manx. In the Channel Islands, apart from Jersey and Guernsey *patois*, there survive words of Sarkese, in which a prayer book was published in 1812. A movement exists to revive the use of Cornish.

Most complex The following extremes of complexity have been noted: Chippewa, the North American Indian language of Minnesota, U.S.A., has the most verb forms with up to 6,000; Tillamook, the North American Indian language of Oregon, U.S.A., has the most prefixes with 30; Tabassaran, a language in Daghestan, U.S.S.R., uses the most noun cases with 35, while Eskimaux use 63 forms of the present tense and simple nouns have as many as 252 inflections. In Chinese the *Chung-wên TaTz'û-tien* dictionary lists 49,905 characters. The fourth tone of "i" has 84 meanings, varying as widely as "dress", "hiccough" and "licentious". The written language provides 92 different characters for "i⁴". The most complex written character in Chinese is that representing the sound of thunder which has 52 strokes and is somewhat surprisingly pronounced *ping*. The most complex in current use consists of 36 strokes representing a blocked nose and less surprisingly pronounced *nang*.

Rarest and commonest sounds The rarest speech sound is probably the sound written ř in Czech which occurs in very few languages and is the last sound mastered by Czech children. The *l* sound in the Arabic word *Allah* is seemingly unique as it occurs in no other word in the language. The commonest sound is the vowel *a* (as in the English father); no language is known to be without it.

Most and least regular verbs Esperanto was devised in 1887 without irregular verbs and is now estimated (by text book sales) to have a million speakers. Swahili has a strict 6-class pattern of verbs and no verbs which are irregular to this pattern. According to the more daunting grammars published in West Germany, English has 194 irregular verbs though there are arguably 214.

Vocabulary The English language contains about 490,000 words plus another 300,000 technical terms, the most in any language, but it is doubtful if any individual uses more than 60,000. Those in Great Britain who have undergone a full 16 years of education use perhaps 5,000 words in speech and up to 10,000 words in written communications.

Greatest linguist The most acclaimed linguist of all-time has been Cardinal Giuseppe Caspar Mezzofanti (b. 17 Sept. 1774 at Bologna, d. 1849), the former chief keeper of the Vatican library in Rome, Italy. He was reputed to have worked on the translation of 114 languages and 72 dialects, and to have spoken 39 languages and used 11 others in interviews. The claims made on behalf of Prof. Rasmus Christian Rask (1787–1832) of Copenhagen in 1837 have proved highly exaggerated. The greatest living linguist is probably Georges Schmidt (b. Strasbourg, France in 1915) of the United Nations Translation Department in New York City, U.S.A. who can reputedly speak fluently in 30 languages and has been prepared to embark on the translation of 36 others.

ALPHABET

Oldest The development of the use of an alphabet in place of pictograms occurred in the Sinaitic world between 1700 and 1500 B.C. This northern Semitic language developed the consonantal system based on phonetic and syllabic principles.

Longest and shortest The language with most letters is Cambodian with 74, and Rotokas has least with 11 (just a, ɓ, e, g, i, k, ó, p, ř, t and u). Amharic has 231 formations from 33 basic syllabic forms, each of which has seven modifications, so this Ethiopian language cannot be described as alphabetic.

Most and least consonants and vowels The language with most consonants is the Caucasian mountain language Ubyx, with 80 and that with least is Rotokas, spoken in central Bougainville Island with only 6 consonants. The language with the most vowels is Sedang, a central Vietnamese language with 55 distinguishable vowel sounds and those with the least are those with two such as the Caucasian languages Abaza and Kabardian. The Hawaiian word for "certified" has 8 consecutive vowels—hooiaioia—while the English record is 5 in queueing. The Latin genitive for Aeneas's island consists solely of 6 vowels —aeaeae.

Oldest and Youngest Letters The oldest letter is "O", unchanged in shape since its adoption in the Phoenician alphabet *c.* 1300 B.C. The newest letters in the English alphabet, are "j" and "v" which are of post Shakespearean use *c.* 1630. There are 65 alphabets now in use.

Largest letter The largest permanent letters in the world are the giant 600 ft *183 m* letters spelling READYMIX on the ground in the Nullarbor near East Balladonia, Western Australia. This was constructed in Dec. 1971. In sky-writing (normally at *c.* 8,000 ft [*2 400 m*]) a seven letter word may stretch for 6 miles *9 km* in length and can be read from 50 miles *80 km*. The world's earliest example was over Epsom racecourse, Surrey on 30 May 1922 when Cyril Turner "spelt out" "London Daily Mail" from an S.E.5A biplane.

Most frequently used letters In English the most frequently used letters are, according to a survey carried out by Mr. Arthur Hall of St. John's Preparatory School, Northwood, London, e, t, a, o, i, n, s, h, r, d, l, m, u, w, g, c, f, y, p, b, v, k, j, q, x and z. The most frequent initial letters are found by indexers to be TASHWIOBCFMPDLR NGEUYJKVQZX.

WORDS

Longest words World The longest word ever to appear in literature occurs in *The Ecclesiazusae*, a comedy by Aristophanes (448–380 B.C.). In the Greek it is 170 letters long but transliterates into 182 letters in English, thus: lopadotemachoselachogaleokranioleipsanodrimhypotrimmatosilphioparaomelitokatakechymenokichlepikossyphophattoperisteralektryonoptekephallio kigklopeleiolagoiosiraiobaphetraganopterygon. The term describes a fricassee of 17 sweet and sour ingredients including mullet, brains, honey, vinegar, pickles, marrow and ouzo (a Greek drink laced with anisette).

English The longest word in the Oxford English Dictionary is floccipaucinihilipilification (alternatively spelt in hyphenated form with "n" in seventh place), with 29 letters, meaning "the action of estimating as worthless", first used in 1741, and later by Sir Walter Scott (1771–1832). Webster's Third International Dictionary lists among its 450,000 entries pneumonoultramicroscopicsilicovolcanoconiosis (45 letters), the name of a miners' lung disease.

The nonce word used by Dr. Edward Strother (1675–1737) to describe the spa waters at Bristol was aequeosalinocalcalinoceraceoaluminosocupreovitriolic of 52 letters.

The longest regularly formed English word is praetertranssubstantiationalisticaly (37 letters), used by Mark McShane in his novel *Untimely Ripped*, published in 1963. The medical term hepaticocholangiocholecystenterostomies (39 letters) refers to the surgical creations of new communications between gallbladders and hepatic ducts and between intestines and gallbladders. The longest in common use is disproportionableness (21 letters).

Longest palindromic words The longest known palindromic word is *saippuakauppias* (15 letters), the Finnish word for soap-seller. The longest in the English language are *evitative* and *redivider* (each nine letters), while another nine-letter word, *Malayalam*, is a proper noun given to the language of the Malayali people in Kerala, southern India. The contrived chemical term *detartrated* has 11 letters, as does *kinnikinnik* (sometimes written *kinnik-kinnik*, a 12-letter palindrome), the word for the dried leaf and bark mixture which was smoked by the Cree Indians of North America. Some baptismal fonts in Greece and Turkey bear the circular 25 letter inscription NIΨON ANOMHMATA MH MONAN OΨIN meaning "wash (my) sins not only (my) face". This appears at St. Mary's Church, Nottingham, St. Paul's, Woldingham, Surrey and other churches. The longest palindromic composition devised is one of 242 words by Howard Bergeson of Oregon, U.S.A. It begins "Deliver no evil, avid diva . . . and hence predictably ends . . . avid diva, live on reviled".

Most meanings The most over-worked word in English is the word *jack* which has 10 main substantive uses with 40 sub-uses and two verbal uses.

Longest chemical name The longest chemical term is that describing trypto-phan synthetase A protein, which has the formula $C_{1289}H_{2051}N_{343}O_{375}S_8$ and the 1,913 letter name:

Methionylglutaminylarginyltyrosylglutamylserylleu-cylphenylalanylalanylglutaminylleucyllysylglutamyl-arginyllysyglutamylglycylalanylphenylalanylvalylpro-lylphenylalanylvalylthreonylleucylglycylaspartylpro-lylglycylisoleucylglutamylglutaminylserylleucyllysyli-soleucylaspartylthreonylleucylisoleucylglutamylalanyl-glycylalanylaspartylalanylleucylglutamylleucylglycyli-soleucylprolylphenylalanylserylaspartylprolylleucyl-alanylaspartylglycylprolylthreonylisoleucylgluta-minylasparaginylalanylthreonylleucylarginylalanyl-phenylalanylalanylalanylglycylvalylthreonylprolyl-alanylglutaminylcysteinylphenylalanylglutamylmethi-onylleucylalanylleucylisoleucylarginylglutaminyllysyl-histidylprolylthreonylisoleucylprolylisoleucylglycyl-leucylleucylmethionyltyrosylalanylasparaginylleucyl-valylphenylalanylasparaginyllysylglycylisoleucylaspar-tylglutamylphenylalanyltyrosylalanylglutaminylcy-steinylglutamyllysylvalylglycylvalylaspartylserylvalyl-leucylvalylalanylaspartylvalylprolylvalylglutaminyl-glutamylserylalanylprolylphenylalanylarginylgluta-minylalanylalanylleucylarginylhistidylasparaginyl-valylalanylprolylisoleucylphenylalanylisoleucylcy-steinylprolylprolylaspartylalanylaspartylaspartylas-partylleucylleucylarginylglutaminylisoleucylalanyl-seryltyrosylglycylarginylglycyltyrosylthreonyltyrosyl-leucylleucylserylarginylalanylglycylvalylthreonylgly-cylalanylglutamylasparaginylarginylalanylalanyl-leucylprolylleucylasparaginylhistidylleucylvalylalanyl-lysylleucyllysylglutamyltyrosylasparaginylalanyl-alanylprolylprolylleucylglutaminylglycylphenylalanyl-glycylisoleucylserylalanylprolylaspartylglutaminyl-valyllysylalanylalanylisoleucylaspartylalanylglycyl-alanylalanylglycylalanylisoleucylserylglycylseryl-alanylisoleucylvalyllysylisoleucylisoleucylglutamyl-glutaminylhistidylasparaginylisoleucylglutamylprolyl-glutamyllysylmethionylleucylalanylalanylleucyllysyl-valylphenylalanylvalylglutaminylprolylmethionyllysyl-alanylalanylthreonylarginylserine.

Commonest words In written English the most frequently used words are in order: the, of, and, to, a, in, that, is, I, it, for *and* as. The most used in conversation is I.

Most Homophones The most homophonous sound in English is *rōz* which has 9 meanings: roes (deer); roes (fish); rose (flower); rose (watering can); rose (past tense of rise); rose (compass card); rows (boats); rows (of houses) or rhos (plural of the Greek letter).

Most accents Accents were introduced in French in the reign of Louis XIII (1601–43). The word with most accents is *hétérogénéité*, meaning heterogeneity. An atoll in the Pacific Ocean 320 miles *516 km* E.S.E. of Tahiti is named Héréhérétué.

Worst tongue twisters The most difficult tongue twister in the only anthology of its type *Anthology of British Tongue-Twisters* by Ken Parkin of Teesside, is deemed by the author to be "The sixth sick sheik's sixth sheep's sick"—especially when spoken quickly.

Perhaps the most difficult in the world is the Xhosa (from Transkei, South Africa) for "The skunk rolled down and ruptured its larynx" Iqaqa laziqikaqika kwaze kwaqhawaka uqhoqhoqha. The last word contains three "clicks". A European rival is the vowelless *Strch prst skrz krk*, the Czech for "stick a finger in the throat".

Longest abbreviation The longest known abbreviation is S.O.M.K.H.P.-B.K.J.C.S.S.D.P.M.W.D.T.B., the initials of the Sharikat Orang-Orang Melayu Kerajaan Hilir Perak Berkerjasama-Serkerjasama Kerana Jimat Chermat Serta Simpanan Dan Pinjam Meminjam Wang Dengan Tanggongan Berhad. This is the Malay name for the Lower Perak Malay Government Servant's Co-operative Thrift and Loan Society Limited, in Telok Anson, Perak State, West Malaysia (formerly Malaya). The abbreviation for this abbreviation is not recorded.

Longest anagrams The longest non-scientific English words which can form anagrams are the 16-letter transpositions "inter-laminations" *and* "internationalism" *and* "conserva-tionists" *and* "conversationists".

Shortest holo-alphabetic sentence The contrived headline describing the annoyance of an eccentric in finding inscriptions on the side of a fjord in a rounded valley as "Cwm fjord-bank glyphs vext quiz" represents the ultimate in containing all 26 letters in 26 letters.

Longest sentence The longest sentence in classical western literature is one in *Les Misérables* by Victor Marie Hugo (1802–85) which runs to 823 words punctuated by 93 commas, 51 semi-colons and 4 dashes. A sentence of 958 words appears in "Cities of the Plain" by the French author, Marcel Proust (1871–1922), while some authors such as James Joyce (1882–1941) appear to eschew punctua-tion altogether. The Report of the President of Columbia University 1942–43 contained a sentence of 4,284 words. The first 40,000 words of *The Gates of Paradise* by George Andrzeyevski (Panther) appear to lack any punctuation.

Most Prepositions with which to end The sentence claimed to possess most prepositions with which to end describes the protest of a child against an Australian bed-time story-book thus "Mummy what did you bring that book which I didn't want to be read to out of from about Down Under up for?" Arguably, however, "Down Under" is a proper noun and "up" an adverb.

PLACE-NAMES

Longest World The official name for Bangkok, the capital city of Thailand, is Krungtep Mahanakhon. The full name is however: Krungthep Mahanakhon Bovorn Ratana-kosin Mahintharayutthaya Mahadilokpop Nopara-tratchathani Burirom Udomratchanivetmahasathan Amornpiman Avatarnsathit Sakkathattiyavisnukarm-prasit (167 letters) which in its most scholarly trans-literation emerges with 175 letters. The longest place-

---

LONGEST WORDS IN VARIOUS LANGUAGES—Only the first 6 are to be found in dictionaries

French	Anticonstitutionnellement (25 letters) —anticonstitutionally.
Croatian	Prijestolenaslijeduikovice (26 letters) —wife of an heir apparent.
Italian	Precipitevolissimevolmente (26 letters) —as fast as possible
Russian	Pyeryeosvidyetyel'stvovayushchyegosya (27 Cyrillic letters, transliterated to 36) —of being re-examined (medically).
Japanese	Ryăgū-no-otohime-no-motoyui-no-kirihazushi (36 letters) —a seaweed, literally of small pieces of the paper hair streamers of the underwater princess.
Hungarian	Engedelmeskedhetetlenségeskedéseitekert (39 letters) —because of your continued disobedience.
Dutch	Rijksluchtvaartdienstweerschepenpersoneel (41 letters) —Government aviation department weather ship personnel.
German	Donaudampfschifffahrtselectricitaetenhauptbetriebswerkbauunterbeamtengesellschaft (81 letters) —The club for subordinate officials of the head office management of the Danube steamboat electrical services (Name of a pre-war club in Vienna)
Swedish	Spårvagnsaktiebolagsskensmutsskjutarefackföreningspersonalbeklädnadsmagasinsförrådsförvaltaren (94 letters) —Manager of the depot for the supply of uniforms to the personnel of the track cleaners' union of the tramway company.

Reputedly known as the longest name in the world... **AA**

TAUMATAWHAKATANGI HANGAKOAUAUOTAMATEA TURIPUKAKAPIKIMAUNGA HORONUKUPOKAIWHEN UAKITANATAHU

THE PLACE WHERE TAMATEA, THE MAN WITH THE BIG KNEES, WHO SLID, CLIMBED, AND SWALLOWED MOUNTAINS, KNOWN AS LANDEATER, PLAYED HIS FLUTE TO HIS LOVED ONE.

The signpost for the world's longest place-name near Hawke's Bay, New Zealand

name now in use in the world is Taumatawhakatangi-hangakoauauotamatea (turipukakapikimaungahoronuku) pokaiwhenuakitanatahu, the unofficial 85-letter version of the name of a hill (1,002 ft above sea-level) in the Southern Hawke's Bay district of North Island, New Zealand. This Maori name means "the place where Tamatea, the man with the big knee who slid, climbed and swallowed mountains, known as Traveller, played on his flute to his loved one". The official version has 57 letters (1 to 36 and 65 to 85).

United Kingdom The longest place-name in the United Kingdom is the concocted 58-letter name Llanfairpwllgwyngyllgoger-ychwyrndrobwllllantysiliogogogoch, which is translated: "St. Mary's Church in a hollow by the white hazel, close to the rapid whirlpool, by the red cave of St. Tysilio". This is the name used for the reopened (April 1973) village railway station in Anglesey, Wales, but the *official* name consists of only the first 20 letters. The longest genuine Welsh place-name listed in the Ordnance Survey Gazetteer is Lower Llanfihangel-y-Creuddyn (26 letters), a village near Aberystwyth, Cardiganshire.

England The longest single word (unhyphenated) place-name in England is Blakehopeburnhaugh, a hamlet between Burness and Rochester in Northumberland, of 18 letters. The hyphenated Sutton-under-Whitestonecliffe, Yorkshire has 27 letters on the Ordnance Survey but with the insertion of 'the' and the dropping of the final 'e' 29 letters in the Post Office List. The longest multiple name is North Leverton with Habbelsthorpe (30 letters), Nottinghamshire, while the longest parish name is Saint Mary le More and All Hallows with Saint Leonard and Saint Peter, Wallingford (68 letters) in Berkshire formed on 5 April 1971.

Scotland The longest single word place-names in Scotland are Claddochknockline, on the island of North Uist, in the Outer Hebrides and the nearby Claddochbaleshare both with 17 letters. The statutory name for Kirk-cudbrightshire (18 letters) is however County of Kirkcudbright. A 12-acre *5 ha* loch 9 miles *14 km* west of Stornoway on Lewes is named Loch Airidh Mhic Fhionnlaidh Dhuibh (31 letters).

Ireland The longest place-name in Ireland is Muckanagheder-dauhaulia (22 letters), 4 miles *6 km* from Costello in Carris Bay, County Galway. The name means "soft place between two seas".

Shortest The shortest place names in the world are the French village of Y (population 143), so named since 1241; the Norwegian village of Å (pronounced "Aw"), U in the Caroline Islands, Pacific Ocean; and the Japanese town of Sosei which is alternatively called Aioi or O-o or even O. There was once a 6 in West Virginia, U.S.A. The shortest place-names in Great Britain are the two-lettered villages of Ae (population 199 in 1961) in Dumfriesshire and Oa on the island of Islay off western Scotland. In the Shetland Islands there are skerries called Ve and two stacks called Aa. The island of Iona was originally I. The River E flows into the southern end of Loch Mhór, Inverness-shire. The shortest place-name in Ireland is Ta (or Lady's Island) Lough, a sea-inlet off the coast of County Wexford. Tievelough, in County Donegal, is also called Ea.

Earliest The earliest recorded British place-name is Belerion, the Penwith peninsula of Cornwall, referred to as such by Pytheas of Massalia in *c*. 308 B.C. The earliest distinctive name for what is now Great Britain was Albion by Himilco *c*. 500 B.C. The oldest name among England's 41 counties is Kent, first mentioned in its Roman form of Cantium (from the Celtic *canto*, meaning a rim, *i.e.* a coastal district) from the same circumnavigation by Pytheas. The youngest is Lancashire, first recorded in the 12th century. The earliest mention of England is the form *Angelcynn*, which appeared in the Anglo-Saxon Chronicle in A.D. 880.

Commonest The commonest place-name in England and Wales is Newtown or New Town, with 129 entries in the 1961 Census Gazetteer, and Newton with 47. The British place-name most widely used overseas is Richmond, Yorkshire, which has given its name, according to a list compiled by Mr. David Ball, to 43 other villages, towns and cities, including examples in 20 of the 50 states of the U.S.A.

PERSONAL NAMES

Earliest The earliest personal name which has survived is uncertain. Some experts believe that it is En-lil-ti, a word which appears on a Sumerian tablet dating from *c*. 3000 B.C., recovered before 1936 from Jamdat Nasr, 40 miles south-east of Baghdad, Iraq. Other antiquarians regard it purely as the name of a deity, Lord of the air, and claim that the names Lahma and Lahamu, Sumer gods of silt, are older still. N'armer, the father of Men (Menes), the first Egyptian Pharaoh, dates from about 2900 B.C. The earliest known name of any resident of Britain is Divitiacus, King of the Suessones, the Gaulish ruler of the Kent area *c*. 75 B.C. under the name Prydhain. Scotland, unlike England, was never conquered by the Roman occupiers (A.D. 43–410). Calgācus (b. *c*. A.D. 40), who led this last resistance was the earliest native of Scotland whose name has been recorded.

Longest World The longest name used by anyone is Adolph Blaine Charles David Earl Frederick Gerald Hubert Irvin John Kenneth Lloyd Martin Nero Oliver Paul Quincy Randolph Sherman Thomas Uncas Victor William Xerxes Yancy Zeus Wolfeschlegelsteinhausenberger-dorff, Senior, who was born at Bergedorf, near Hamburg, Germany, on 29 Feb. 1904. On printed forms he uses only his eighth and second Christian names and the first 35 letters of his surname. The full version of the name of 590 letters appeared in the 12th edition of *The Guinness Book of Records*. He now lives in Philadelphia, Pennsylvania, U.S.A., and has shortened his surname to Mr. Wolfe+590, Senior.

The longest Christian or given name on record is Napuamahalaonaonekawehiwehionakuahiweanen-awawakehoonkakehoaalekeeaonanainananiakeao'-Hawaiikawao (94 letters) in the case of Miss Dawn N. Lee so named in Honolulu, Hawaii, U.S.A. in February 1967. The name means "The abundant, beautiful blossoms of the mountains and valleys begin to fill the

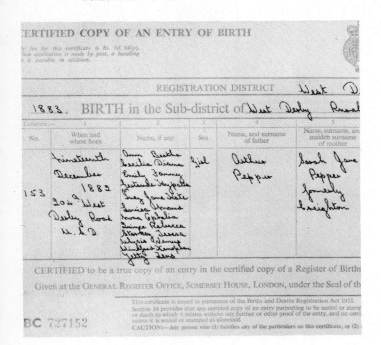

Part of the Birth Certificate of "Alphabet" Pepper, showing her full set of 25 Christian names

air with their fragrance throughout the length and breadth of Hawaii".

Most Christian names The daughter of Arthur Pepper of West Derby, Lancashire, born on 19 Dec. 1882, was christened Ann Bertha Cecilia Diana Emily Fanny Gertrude Hypatia Inez Jane Kate Louisa Maud Nora Orphelia Quince Rebecca Starkey Teresa Ulysis Venus Winifred Xenophen Yetty Zeus Pepper.

United Kingdom The longest surname in the United Kingdom was the six-barrelled one borne by the late Major L.S.D.O.F. (Leone Sextus Denys Oswolf Fraudati filius) Tollemache-Tollemache de Orellana Plantagenet Tollemache Tollemache, who was born in 1884 and died of pneumonia in France on 20 Feb. 1917. Of non-repetitious surnames, the last example of a five-barrelled one was that of the Lady Caroline Jemima Temple-Nugent-Chandos-Brydges-Grenville (1858–1946). The longest single English surname is Featherstonehaugh, correctly pronounced on occasions (but improbably on the correct occasion) Featherstonehaw or Festonhaw or Fessonhay or Freestonhugh or Feerstonhaw or Fanshaw.

Scotland In Scotland the surname nin (feminine of mac) Achinmacdholicachinskerray (29 letters) was recorded in an 18th century parish register.

Shortest The single letter surname O, of which 13 examples appear in the telephone directory in Brussels, besides being the commonest single letter name is the one obviously causing most distress to those concerned with the prevention of cruelty to computers. There exist among the 42,500,000 names on the Ministry of Social Security index four examples of a one-lettered surname. Their identity has not been disclosed, but they are "E", "J", "M" and "X". Two-letter British surnames include By and On.

Commonest World The commonest surname in the world is the Chinese name Chang which is borne according to estimates, by between 9.7% and 12.1% of the Chinese population, so indicating even on the lower estimate that there are at least some 75,000,000 Changs—more than the entire population of all but 7 of the 147 other sovereign countries of the world.

English The commonest surname in the English-speaking world is Smith. There are 671,550 nationally insured Smiths in Great Britain, of whom 7,081 are plain John Smith and another 22,550 are John (plus one or more given names) Smith. Including uninsured persons there are over 800,000 Smiths in England and Wales alone, of whom 90,000 are called A. Smith. There were an estimated 1,678,815 Smiths in the United States in 1964.

"Macs" There are, however, estimated to be 1,600,000 persons in Britain with M', Mc or Mac (Gaelic "son of") as part of their surnames. The commonest of these is Macdonald which accounts for about 55,000 of the Scottish population.

The most common first or single forenames in England and Wales would appear from C. V. Appleton's study of a sample of more than 100,000 from the latest available birth registers at Somerset House, London to be Sarah/Sara for girls and narrowly Paul over David for boys. In the period 1196–1307 William was the commonest boy's name but since 1340 to recent times this had been John.

Most contrived name The palm for the most determined attempt to be last in the local telephone directory must now be awarded to Mr. Zachary Zzzzra of San Francisco, California. He outdid the previous occupant who was a mere Mr. Zeke Zzzypt. In September 1970 Mr. Zero Zzyzx (rhymes with "fizz") was ousted by Mr. Vladimir Zzzyd (rhymes with outdid) in the Miami directory. The alpha and omega of Britain's 62 directories are Mr. M. Aab of Hull and Mr. F. Zzarino of Waltham Cross, Hertfordshire.

TEXTS AND BOOKS

Oldest The oldest known written text is the pictograph expression of Sumerian speech (see Earliest Language, p. 99). The earliest known vellum document dates from the 2nd century A.D.; it contains paragraphs 10 to 32 of Demosthenes' *De Falsa Legatione*. Demosthenes died in the 4th century B.C.

Oldest printed The oldest surviving printed work is a Korean scroll or *sutra* from wooden printed blocks found in the foundations of the Pulguk Sa pagoda, Kyongju, Korea, on 14 Oct. 1966. It has been dated no later than A.D. 704.

Oldest Mechanically printed It is generally accepted that the earliest mechanically printed book was the 42-line Gutenberg Bible, printed at Mainz, Germany, in c. 1455 by Johann Henne zum Gensfleisch zur Laden, called "zu Gutenberg" (c. 1398–c. 1468). Recent work on water marks published in 1967 indicates a copy of a surviving printed Latin grammar was made from paper made in c. 1450. The earliest exactly dated printed work is the Psalter completed on 14 Aug. 1457 by Johann Fust (c. 1400–1466) and Peter Schöffer (1425–1502), who had been Gutenberg's chief assistant The earliest printing in Britain was an Indulgence dated 13 Dec. 1476, issued by Abbot Sant of Abingdon, Berkshire, and printed by William Caxton (c. 1422–1491).

Largest The largest book in the world is *The Little Red Elf*, a story in 64 verses by William P. Wood, who designed, constructed and printed the book. It measures 7 ft 2 in *2.2 m* high and 10 ft *3 m* across when open. The book is at present on show in a case at the Red Elf Cave, Ardentinny near Dunoon. The largest art book ever produced was one 210 cm *82.7 in* high and 80 cm *31.5 in* wide, first shown in Amsterdam, in the Netherlands, in May 1963. It contained five "pages", three the work of Karel Appel (b. 1921), an abstract painter, and two with poems by Hugo Claus. The price was $5,255 (*then £1,876*).

Largest publication The largest publication in the world is the 1,200 volume set of *British Parliamentary Papers* of 1800–1900 by Irish University Press in 1967–1971. A complete set weighs 3¼ tons *3,3 tonnes*, costs £27,000 and would take 6 years to read at 10 hours per day. The production involved the death of 34,000 Indian goats, and the use of £15,000 worth of gold ingots. Further volumes are planned. The total print is 500 sets.

Smallest The smallest book printed in metal type as opposed to any micro-photographic process is one printed for the Gutenberg Museum, Mainz, West Germany. It measures 3.5 mm by 3.5 mm *0.13 of an in square* and consists of the Lord's Prayer in seven languages.

Most valuable The most valuable printed books are the three surviving perfect vellum copies of the Gutenberg Bible, printed in Mainz, Germany, in *c.* 1455 by Gutenberg (see above). The United States Library of Congress copy, bound in three volumes, was obtained in 1930 from Dr. Otto Vollbehr, who paid about $330,000 (*then £68,000*) for it. During 1970 a paper edition in the hands of the New York book dealer, Hans Peter Kraus, was privately bought for $2,500,000 (*£1,041,666*).

Broadsheet The highest price ever paid for a broadsheet has been $404,000 (*£168,333*) for one of the 16 known copies of *The Declaration of Independence*, printed in Philadelphia in 1776 by Samuel T. Freeman & Co., and sold to a Texan in May 1969.

Longest novel The longest important novel ever published is *Les hommes de bonne volonté* by Louis Henri Jean Farigoule (b. 26 Aug. 1885), *alias* Jules Romains, of France, in 27 volumes in 1932–46. The English version *Men of Good Will* was published in 14 volumes in 1933–46 as a "novel-cycle". The novel *Tokuga-Wa Ieyasu* by Sohachi Yamaoka has been serialised in Japanese daily newspapers since 1951. When completed it will run to 40 volumes.

Encyclopaedias **Earliest** The earliest known encyclopaedia was compiled by Speusippas (*post* 408–*c.* 388 B.C.) a nephew of Plato, in Athens *c.* 370 B.C. The earliest encyclopaedia compiled by a Briton was *Liber exerptionum* by the Scottish monk Richard (d. 1173) at St. Victor's Abbey, Paris *c.* 1140.

Most comprehensive The most comprehensive present day encyclopaedia is the *Encyclopaedia Britannica*, first published in Edinburgh, Scotland, in December 1768. A group of booksellers in the United States acquired reprint rights in 1898 and completed ownership in 1899. In 1943 the *Britannica* was given to the University of Chicago, Illinois, U.S.A. The current 24-volume edition contains 28,380 pages, 34,696 articles and 2,247 other entries, 36,674,000 words and 22,670 illustrations. It is now edited in Chicago and in London. There are 10,326 contributors.

Largest The largest encyclopaedia ever compiled was the *Great Standard Encyclopaedia* of Yung-lo ta tien of 22,937 manuscript chapters (370 still survive), written by 2,000 Chinese scholars in 1403–08.

Largest dictionary The largest dictionary now published is the 12-volume Royal quarto *The Oxford English Dictionary* of 15,487 pages published between 1884 and 1928 with a first supplement of 963 pages in 1933 with a further 3-volume supplement, edited by R. W. Burchfield, in which the second and third volumes covering H to Z will appear in 1975 and 1977. The work contains 414,825 words, 1,827,306 illustrative quotations and reputedly 227,779,589 letters and figures.

Manuscripts *Highest price* The highest value ever paid for any manuscript is £100,000 paid in December 1933 by the British Museum, London to the U.S.S.R Government for parts of the manuscript Bible rescued from a shelf in a

1,200 volumes of Parliamentary Papers at the Irish University Press, containing a century of British Parliamentary History

monk's cell in the Monastery of St. Catherine on Mount Sinai, Egypt in 1859. The monks had in May 1844 given 43 leaves from the 129, which had been rescued from a waste paper basket there by Lobegott Friedrich Konstantin von Tischendorf (1815–74). These leaves which were part of the Codex Sinaiticus, are in the University Library at Leipzig and are known as the Codex Friderico-Augustanus. Originally the Mss measured 16 × 28 in *40 × 71 cm* before their edges were sheared off to the present size of 15 × 13½–14 in *38 × 34 cm*. The highest price at auction is 1,100,000 Francs (then *£94,933 incl. tax*) paid by H. P. Krauss, the New York dealer, at the salerooms of Rheims et Laurin, Paris on 24 June 1968 for the late 13th-century North Italian illuminated vellum Manuscript of the Apocrypha.

BIBLE

Oldest The oldest known bible is the *Codex Vaticanus* written in Greek *ante* A.D. 350 and preserved in the Vatican Museum, Rome. The earliest Bible printed in English was one edited by Miles Coverdale, Bishop of Exeter (*c.* 1488–1569), printed in 1535 at Marberg in Hesse, Germany. William Tyndale's New Testament in English had, however, been printed in Cologne and in Worms, Germany in 1525.

Longest and shortest books The longest book in the Authorized version of the Bible is the Book of Psalms, while the longest book including prose is the Book of the Prophet Isaiah, with 66 chapters. The shortest is the Third Epistle of John, with 294 words in 14 verses. The Second Epistle of John has only 13 verses but 298 words.

Longest Psalm, verse sentence and name Of the 150 Psalms, the longest is the 119th, with 176 verses, and the shortest is the 117th, with two verses. The shortest verse in the Authorized Version (King James) of the Bible is verse 35 of Chapter XI of the Gospel according to St. John, consisting of the two words "Jesus wept". The longest is verse 9 of Chapter VIII of the Book of Esther, which extends to a 90-word description of the Persian empire. The total number of letters in the Bible is 3,566,480. The total number of words depends on the method of counting hyphenated words, but is usually given as between 773,692 and 773,746. The word "and" according to Colin McKay Wilson of the Salvation Army appears 46,227 times. The longest personal name in the Bible is Maher-shalal-hash-baz, the symbolic name of the second son of Isaiah (Isaiah, Chapter VIII, verses 1 and 3). The caption of Psalm 22, however, contains a Hebrew title sometimes rendered Al-'Ayyeleth Hash-Shahar (20 letters).

MOST PROLIFIC WRITERS

The most prolific writer for whom a word count has been published was Charles Hamilton, *alias* Frank Richards (1875–1961), the Englishman who created Billy Bunter. At his height in 1908 he wrote the whole of the boys' comics *Gem* (founded 1907) and *Magnet* (1908–1940) and most of two others, totalling 80,000 words a week. His lifetime output was at least 72,000,000 words. He enjoyed the advantages of the use of electric light rather than candlelight and of being unmarried. An even higher though less satisfactory estimate has been made for Charles Andrews, the U.S. short story writer, novelist, journalist, scenario, serial and soap-opera writer who at his height in 1949 reached 100,000 words a week and may well have surpassed 100 million words.

Novels The Belgian writer Georges Simenon (b. Georges Sim in Liège on 13 Feb. 1903), creator of Inspector Maigret, wrote a novel of 200 pages in 8 days actual writing and in April 1973 completed his 214th and last under his own name of which 78 were about Inspector Maigret. He has also written 300 other novels under 19 other pen-names since 1919. These are published in 31 countries in 47 languages and have sold more than 300,000,000 copies. He hates adverbs and has had his children's playroom soundproofed. Since 1931 the British novelist John Creasey (1908–73) has, under his own name and 13 *aliases*, written 564 books totalling more than 40,000,000 words. The authoress with the greatest total of published titles is Miss Ursula Harvey Bloom (Mrs. A. C. G. Robinson), with 468 full-length works to July 1972, starting in 1922 with *The Great Beginning* and including the best sellers *The Ring Tree* (novel) and *The Rose of Norfolk* (non-fiction).

Miss Ursula Bloom, the authoress with the greatest number of published titles

Short stories The highest established count for published short stories is 3,500 in the case of Michael Hervey, B.E.M. (born London, 1914) of Henley, New South Wales, Australia. Aided by his wife Lilyan Brilliant, he has also turned in 60 detective novels and 80 stage and television plays. The most prolific short story writer in Britain is Herbert Harris (born 1911) of Leatherhead, Surrey, with nearly 3,000 published in Britain and in 28 other countries.

Fastest novelist The world's fastest novelist has been Erle Stanley Gardner (1889–1970) of the U.S.A., the mystery writer who created Perry Mason. He dictated up to 10,000 words per day and worked with his staff on as many as seven novels simultaneously. His sales on 140 titles reached 170 million by his death. The British novelist John Creasey (see column 1) has an output of 15 to 20 novels per annum, with a record of 22. He once wrote two books in a week with a half-day off. The most translated British writer has been Enid Blyton with 128 languages.

Writer and playwright Edgar Wallace (1875–1932) began his play *On the Spot* on a Friday and finished it by lunchtime on the following Sunday. This included the stage directions and, unusually, after the production the prompt copy was identical to his original. The shortest time in which he wrote a novel was in the case of *The Three Oaks Mystery* which he started on a Tuesday and delivered typed to his publishers on the following Friday.

Highest paid writer The highest rate ever offered to a writer was $30,000 (*then £10,714*) to Ernest Miller Hemingway (1899–1961) for a 2,000-word article on bullfighting by *Sports Illustrated* in January 1960. This was a rate of $15 (*then £5.35*) per word. In 1958 a Mrs. Deborah Schneider of Minneapolis, Minnesota, U.S.A., wrote 25 words to complete a sentence in a competition for the best blurb for Plymouth cars. She won from about 1,400,000 entrants the prize of $500 (*£178*) every month for life. On normal life expectations she would have collected $12,000 (*£4,285*) per word. No known anthology includes Mrs. Schneider's deathless prose.

Top selling author It was announced on 13 March 1953 that 672,058,000 copies of the works of Marshal Iosif Vissarionovich Dzhugashvili, *alias* Stalin (1879–1953), had been sold or distributed in 101 languages.

Among writers of fiction, sales alone of over 300,000,000 have been claimed for Georges Simenon (see column 1) and for the British authoress Dame Agatha Christie (born Agatha Mary Clarissa Miller), now Lady Mallowan (formerly Mrs. Archibald Christie) (b. Torquay, Devon 15 Sept. 1890). Her paperback sales of 80 novels in the United Kingdom alone are 1½ million per annum.

Text Books Britain's most successful writer of text books is the ex-schoolmaster Ronald Ridout (b. 23 July 1916) who between 1948 and 1972 had 275 titles published with sales of 47,400,000. His *The First English Workbook* has sold 3,365,000 copies.

Oldest authoress The oldest authoress in the world is Mrs. Alice Pollock (*née* Wykeham-Martin, b. 2 July 1868) of Haslemere, Surrey, whose book "Portrait of My Victorian Youth" (Johnson Publications) was published in March 1971 when she was aged 102 years 8 months.

Youngest The youngest recorded commercially-published author is Janet Aitchison of Reigate, Surrey, who wrote *The Pirates' Tale* when aged 5½ years. It was published in a Puffin Book Children's Magazine by Penguin in April 1969 when she was 6½.

POETS LAUREATE

Youngest and oldest The youngest Poet Laureate was Laurence Eusden (1688–1730), who received the bays on 24 Dec. 1718, at the age of 30 years and 3 months. The greatest age at which a poet has succeeded is 73 in the case of William Wordsworth (1770–1850) on 6 April 1843. The longest lived Laureate was John Masefield, O.M., who died on 12 May 1967, aged 88 years 345 days. The longest which any poet has worn the laurel is 41 years 322 days, in the case of Alfred (later the 1st Lord) Tennyson (1809–92), who was appointed on 19 Nov. 1850 and died in office on 6 Oct. 1892.

Longest poem The longest poem ever written was the *Mahabharata* which appeared in India in the period *c.* 400 to 150 B.C. It runs to 220,000 lines and nearly 3,000,000 words.

The longest poem ever written in the English language is one on the life of King Alfred by John Fitchett (1766–1838) of Liverpool which ran to 129,807 lines and took 40 years to write. His editor Robert Riscoe added the concluding 2,585 lines.

Shortest poem The shortest poem in the *Oxford Dictionary of Quotations* is *On the Antiquity of Microbes* and consists of the 3 words "Adam, Had 'em".

Most Successful Sloganeer "Think Mink" invented by Jack Gasnick (b. 1910) in 1929 has sold in metal, celluloid and ribbon 50 million since 1950. His "*Cross at the Green . . . not in Between Enterprises*" of New York City has sold 55 million buttons, badges and tabs and 40 million other pieces.

BEST SELLERS

World The world's best seller is the Bible, portions of which have been translated into 1,315 languages. This compares with 222 languages by Lenin. It has been estimated that between 1800 and 1950 some 1,500,000,000 copies were printed of which 1,100,000,000 were handled by Bible Societies. The total production of Bibles or parts of the Bible in the United States in the year 1963 alone was reputed to be 50,000,000. The distribution of *Good News* (The New Testament in Today's English Version) was 30 million copies from 1967 to Nov. 1971 of which 80 per cent was by its non-profit publisher.

It has been reported that 800,000,000 copies of the red-covered booklet *Quotations from the Works of Mao Tse-tung* were sold or distributed between June 1966, when possession became virtually mandatory in China, and Sept. 1971 when their promoter Marshal Lin Piao was killed. The name of Mao Tse-tung (b. 26 Dec. 1893) means literally "Hair Enrich-East".

Non-fiction The total disposal through non-commercial channels by Jehovah's Witnesses of the 190 page hard bound book *The Truth That Leads to Eternal Life* published by the Watchtower Bible and Tract Society of Brooklyn, New York, published on 8 May 1968, reached 46 million in 67 languages by February 1972.

The commercially best selling non-fiction book is *The Common Sense Book of Baby and Child Care* by Dr. Benjamin McLane Spock (b. 2 May 1903) of New Haven, Connecticut, U.S.A. It was first published in New York in May 1946 and the total sales were 19,076,822 by December 1965 and probably over 23,000,000 by 1970. Dr. Spock's book was written with a ball-point pen and typed by his wife, a silk heiress.

Slowest seller The accolade for the world's slowest selling book (known in U.S. publishing as slooow-sellers) probably belongs to David Wilkins's Translation of the New Testament from Coptic into Latin published by Oxford University Press in 1716 in 500 copies. Selling an average of one each 139 days it was in print for 191 years.

Fiction The novel with the highest sales has been *Valley of the Dolls* (first published 4 July 1967) by Jacqueline Susann with a world wide total of 15,800,000 to June 1973. In the first 6 months Bantam sold 6.8 million. In the United Kingdom the highest print order has been 3,000,000 by Penguin Books Ltd. for their paperback edition of *Lady Chatterley's Lover*, by D. H. (David Herbert) Lawrence (1885–1930). The total sales to May 1973 were 3,750,000 copies.

Post-cards The world's first post-cards were issued in Vienna on 1 Oct. 1869. Pin-up girls came into vogue in 1914 having been pioneered in 1900 by Raphaël Kirchner (1876–1917). The most expensive on record were ones made in ivory for an Indian prince which involved the killing of 60 elephants.

LARGEST PUBLISHERS

World The largest publisher in the world is the United States Government Printing Office in Washington, D.C., U.S.A. The Superintendents of Documents Division dispatches more than 150,000,000 items every year. The annual list of new titles and annuals is about 6,000.

United Kingdom The U.K. published a record 33,489 book titles in 1970 of which a record 9,977 were reprints. The highest figure for new titles was 24,654 in 1972.

LARGEST PRINTERS

World The largest printers in the world are R. R. Donnelly & Co. of Chicago, Illinois, U.S.A. The company, founded in 1864, has plants in seven main centres, turning out $200,000,000 (*£83,300,000*) worth of work per year from 180 presses, 125 composing machines and more than 50 binding lines. Nearly 18,000 tons of inks and 450,000 tons of paper and board are consumed every year.

Print order The print order for the 47th Automobile Association Handbook (1972–73) was 5,200,000 copies. The total print since 1908 has been 58,710,000. It is currently printed by web offset by Petty & Sons of Leeds.

Largest cartoon The largest cartoon ever exhibited was one covering five storeys (50 × 150 ft [*15 × 45 m*]) of a University of Arizona building drawn by Peter C. Kesling for Mom 'n Dad's Day 1954.

Longest lived strip The most durable newspaper comic strip has been the Katzenjammer Kids (Hans and Fritz) created by Rudolph Dirks and first published in the United States in 1897 and currently drawn by Joe Musial. The most read is believed to be "Peanuts" by Charles M. Schulz (b. 1922) which since 1950 has grown to be syndicated to 1,000 U.S. newspapers with a total readership of 90,000,000.

LETTERS

Longest A letter of 325,000 words by Anton van Dam of Arnheim, Netherlands to his pen pal Clementi (now Mrs. H. Randolph Holder) between 24 June 1940 and 15 July 1945 is believed to be the most voluminous.

To an editor *Longest* The longest recorded letter to an editor was one of 13,000 words (a third of a modern novel) written to the editor of the *Fishing Gazette* by A.R.I.E.L. and published in 7-point type spread over two issues in 1884.

Most Britain's, and seemingly the world's, most indefatigable writer of letters to the editors of newspapers is Raymond L. Cantwell, 52, of Oxford, who since 1948 has had more than 12,000 letters published in print or on the air. His peak production has been 425 in 36 hours non-stop in aid of charity.

Shortest The shortest correspondence on record was that between Victor Marie Hugo (1802–85) and his publisher

Hurst and Blackett in 1862. The author was on holiday and anxious to know how his new novel *Les Misérables* was selling. He wrote "?". The reply was "!".

SIGNATURES

Earliest English Regal The earliest English sovereign whose handwriting is known to have survived is Henry III (1207–72). The earliest full signature extant is that of Richard II (dated 26 July 1386). The Magna Carta does not bear even the mark of King John (reigned 1199–1216), but carries only his seal. In 1932 an attested cross of William I (reigned 1066–87) was sold in London.

Most expensive The highest price ever paid on the open market for a single autograph letter signed is $51,000 (*then £10,500*), paid in 1927 for a letter written by the Gloucestershire-born Button Gwinnett (1732–77), one of the three men from Georgia to sign the United States' Declaration of Independence in Philadelphia on 4 July 1776. Such an item would today probably attract bids of $250,000 (*£100,000*). If one of the six known signatures of William Shakespeare (1564–1616) were to come on the market or a new one was discovered the price would doubtless set a record. There is no known surviving signature of Christopher Marlowe (1564–1593).

CROSSWORDS

First The earliest crossword was one with 32 clues invented by Arthur Wynne (b. Liverpool, England, d. 1945) and published in the *New York World* on 21 Dec. 1913. The first crossword published in a British newspaper was one furnished by C. W. Shepherd in the *Sunday Express* of 2 Nov. 1924.

Largest The largest crossword ever published is one with 3,185 clues across and 3,149 clues down, compiled by Robert M. Stilgenbauer of Los Angeles in 7½ years of spare time between 15 May 1938 and publication in 1949. Despite the 125,000 copies distributed not one copy has been returned worked out or even partially worked out. The largest crosswords regularly published are of 1,694 squares compiled by Lennart Fosselins for the Swedish monthly *Chansen*.

Fastest and slowest solution The fastest recorded time for completing *The Times* crossword under test conditions is 3 min 45.0 sec by Roy Dean, 43, of Bromley, Kent in the B.B.C. "Today" radio studio on 19 Dec. 1970. In May 1966 *The Times* of London received an announcement from a Fijian woman that she had just succeeded in completing their crossword No. 673 in the issue of 4 April 1932.

Oldest Map The oldest known map is the Turin Papyrus, showing the layout of the Egyptian gold mines at Wādī Hammāmāt dated c. 1170 B.C.

Christmas cards The greatest number of personal Christmas cards sent out is believed to be 40,000 in 1969 by President and Mrs. Nixon to friends and others, some of whom must have been unilateral acquaintances. In 1972 the average U.S. family sent 68 cards costing with postage $17 (*£6.80*).

LIBRARIES

Largest World The largest library in the world is the United States Library of Congress (founded on 24 April 1800), on Capitol Hill, Washington, D.C. On 30 June 1969 it contained more than 59,000,000 items, including 14,846,000 books and pamphlets. The two buildings cover six acres *2,4 ha* and contain 327 miles *526 km* of book shelves. The tallest library in the world is the University of Massachusetts Library, Amherst, Mass., U.S.A. with 28 storeys and a height of 296 ft 4 in *90,32 m* opened in May 1973.

The Lenin State Library in Moscow, U.S.S.R, claims to house more than 20,000,000 books, but this total is understood to include periodicals.

The world's tallest library, at the University of Massachusetts U.S.A.

The largest non-statutory library in the world is the New York Public Library (founded 1895) on Fifth Avenue with a floor area of 525,276 ft² *48 800 m²*. The main part of its collection is in a private research library which has 4,662,326 volumes on 80 miles *128 km* of shelves, 9,000,000 manuscripts, 120,000 prints, 150,000 gramophone records, and 275,000 maps. There are also 81 tax-supported branch libraries with 3,231,696 books. The central research library used to be open until the civilized hour of 10 p.m. on every day of the year but now closes at 6 p.m. and does not open on Sundays.

United Kingdom The largest library in the United Kingdom is that in the British Museum, London. It contains more than 9,000,000 books, about 115,000 manuscripts and 101,000 charters on 158 miles *254 km* of shelf. There are spaces for 370 readers in the domed Reading Room, built in 1854. The largest public library in the United Kingdom will be the new Birmingham Public Library with a floor area of 230,000 ft² *21 400 m²* or more than 5¼ acres *2 ha*, seating for 1,200 people and an ultimate reference capacity for 1,500,000 volumes on 31 miles *50 km* of shelving. The oldest public library in Scotland is in Kirkwall, Orkney, founded in 1683.

Overdue books It was reported on 7 Dec. 1968 that a book checked out in 1823 from the University of Cincinnati Medical Library on Febrile Diseases (London, 1805 by Dr. J. Currie) was returned by the borrower's great-grandson Richard Dodd. The fine calculated to be $22,646 (*£9,435*) was waived.

NEWSPAPERS

Most It has been estimated that the total circulation of newspapers throughout the world averaged 320,000,000 copies per day in 1966. The country with the greatest number is the U.S.S.R, with 7,967 in 1966. Their average circulation in 1966 was 110,400,000.

The United States had 1,749 English language daily newspapers at 1 Jan. 1968. They had a combined net paid circulation of 61,397,000 copies per day at 30 Sept. 1966. The peak year for U.S. newspapers was 1910, when there were 2,202. The leading newspaper readers in the world are the people of Sweden, where

515 newspapers were sold for each 1,000 of the population in 1967–68. The U.K. figure was 488.

Oldest The oldest existing newspaper in the world is the
World Swedish official journal *Post och Inrikes Tidningar*, founded in 1644. It is published by the Royal Swedish Academy of Letters. The oldest existing commercial newspaper is the *Haarlems Dagblad/Oprechte Haarlemsche Courant*, published in Haarlem, in the Netherlands. The *Courant* was first issued as the *Weeckelycke Courante van Europa* on 8 Jan. 1656 and a copy of issue No. 1 survives.

United The oldest continuously produced newspaper in the
Kingdom United Kingdom is *Berrow's Worcester Journal* (originally the *Worcester Post Man*), published in Worcester. It was traditionally founded in 1690 and has appeared weekly since June 1709. The oldest newspaper title is that of the *Stamford Mercury* dating back to at least 1714 and traditionally to 1695. The oldest daily newspaper in the United Kingdom is *Lloyd's List*, the shipping intelligence bulletin of Lloyd's, London, established as a weekly in 1726 and as a daily in 1734. The *London Gazette* (originally the *Oxford Gazette*) was first published on 16 Nov. 1665. In November 1845 it became the most expensive daily newspaper ever sold in the United Kingdom, priced at 2s. 8d. per copy. The oldest Sunday newspaper in the United Kingdom is *The Observer*, first issued on 4 Dec. 1791.

Largest The most massive single issue of a newspaper was the 7½ lb. *3kg 40 New York Times* of Sunday 10 Oct. 1971. It comprised 15 sections with a total of 972 pages, including about 1,200,000 lines of advertising.

The largest page size ever used has been 51 in by 35 in *130 by 89 cm* for *The Constellation*, printed in 1859 by George Roberts as part of the Fourth of July celebrations in New York City, N.Y., U.S.A. The *Worcestershire Chronicle* was the largest British newspaper. A surviving issue of 16 Feb. 1859 measures 32¼ in by 22½ in *82 by 57 cm*.

The smallest recorded page size has been 3½ in by 4½ in *9 by 11 cm* as used in *Diario di Roma*, an issue of which dated 28 Feb. 1829 survives.

HIGHEST CIRCULATION

The first newspaper to achieve a circulation of 1,000,000 was *Le Petit Journal*, published in Paris, France, which reached this figure in 1886, when selling at 5 centimes (*now about ½p*) per copy.

World The claim exercised for the world's highest circulation is that by the *Asahi Shimbun* (founded 1879) of Japan with a figure which attained more than 10,000,000 copies in October 1970. This, however, has been achieved by totalling the figures for editions published in various centres with a morning figure of 6,100,000 and an evening figure of 3,900,000. The highest circulation of any single newspaper in the world is that of the Sunday newspaper *The News of the World*, printed in Bouverie Street, London. Single issues have attained a sale of 9,000,000 copies with an estimated readership of more than 19,000,000. The paper first appeared on 1 Oct. 1843, averaged 12,971 copies per week in its first year and surpassed the million mark in 1905. To provide sufficient pulp for the 1,500 reels used per week, each measuring 5 miles *8 km* long, more than 780,000 trees have to be felled each year. The latest sales figure is 5,976,657 copies per issue (average for 1 July to 31 Dec. 1972), with a last published estimated readership of 16,635,000.

Daily The highest circulation of any daily newspaper is that
World of the U.S.S.R government organ *Izvestia* (founded in Leningrad on 12 March 1917 as a Menshevik news sheet and meaning "Information") with a figure of 8,670,000 in March 1967. The daily tabloid *Pionerskaya*

A copy of the front page of the earliest known surviving edition of *Lloyd's List*, Britain's oldest daily newspaper

Pravda had an average circulation of 9,181,000 copies per issue in 1966. This is the news organ of the Pioneers, a Communist youth organization founded in 1922.

United The highest daily net sale of any newspaper in the
Kingdom United Kingdom is that of *The Daily Mirror*, founded in London in 1903. A print of 7,161,704 was sold out on 3 June 1953. The latest sales figure is 4,279,490 (for July–December 1972), with an estimated readership of 13,713,000.

Evening The highest circulation of any evening newspaper is that of *The Evening News*, established in London in 1881. The latest figure is 1,683,945 copies per issue (average for 1 July to 31 Dec. 1972), with an average readership of 4,866,000.

"Earliest" The first newspaper to be published in the world each
newspaper day is sometimes said to be the *Fiji Times* because it is closest to the international date-line.

Most read The newspaper which achieves the closest to a saturation circulation is *The Sunday Post*, established in Glasgow in 1914. In 1972 its total estimated readership of 2,947,000 represented more than 79 per cent of the entire population of Scotland aged 15 and over.

PERIODICALS

Largest The largest circulation of any weekly periodical has
circulation been that of *This Week Magazine*, produced in the
World United States to circulate with 43 newspapers which found it uneconomical to run their own coloured Sunday magazine section. The circulation reached 11,889,211 copies at 31 March 1967. In its 30 basic international editions *The Reader's Digest* (established February 1922) circulates more than 30,000,000 copies monthly in 13 languages, including a United States edition of more than 18,000,000 copies (average for July to December 1972) and a United Kingdom edition (established 1939) of 1,600,000 copies.

United The *Botanical Magazine* has been in continuous
Kingdom publication since 1787, as several "parts" a year forming a series of continuously numbered volumes. Britain's oldest weekly periodical is *Lancet* first published in 1823. The monthly *Blackwood's Magazine* has not missed an issue since the first in April 1817. The Editor has always been a Blackwood. Since 1948 it has

been Douglas Blackwood great great-grandson of the founder. The *Scots Magazine* began publication in 1739 and ran till 1826, and with three breaks has been produced continuously since 1924.

The highest circulation of any periodical in the United Kingdom is that of the *Radio Times* (instituted in September 1923). The average weekly sale for July–December 1972 was 3,778,538 copies. The highest sale of any issue was 9,778,062 copies for the Christmas issue of 1955. The materials used include 885 tons *899 tonnes* of paper, 9½ tons *9,6 tonnes* of ink and 355 miles *570 km* of stapling wire per issue. The highest audited readership figure in December 1972 was 10,791,000 for *TV Times* from a lower circulation.

Annual *Old Moore's Almanack* has been published annually since 1697, when it first appeared as a broadsheet, by Dr. Francis Moore (1657–1715) of Southwark, London to advertise his "physiks". The annual sale certified by its publishers W. Foulsham & Co. Ltd. of Slough England is 1,150,000 copies and its aggregate sale must well exceed 100,000,000 copies.

ADVERTISING RATES

The highest ever price for a single page has been $84,100 (*£35,040*) for a four-colour back cover in the now defunct *Life* magazine (circulation 8½ million per week) from Jan. 1969 to Jan. 1971.

The highest expenditure ever incurred on a single advertisement in a periodical is $950,000 (*then, £395,833*) by Uniroyal Inc. for a 40-page insert in the May 1968 issue of the U.S. edition of *The Reader's Digest*. The British record is some £100,000 for a 20-page colour supplement by Woolworths in the *Radio Times* of 16 Nov. 1972. The colour rate for a single page in the *Radio Times* is £5,800.

Longest editorship The longest editorship of any national newspaper has been more than 59 years by C. P. Scott (1846–1932) of the (then *Manchester*) *Guardian*, who was appointed aged 25 in 1872 and died on 1 Jan. 1932. The Irish record for editorship of a national newspaper was set by Hector Legge, editor of the *Sunday Independent* from 13 Oct. 1940 to 31 Oct. 1970—30 years 2 weeks.

Most durable feature The longest lasting feature in the British press from one pen is *Your Stars* by Edward Lyndoe. It has run since 1 Oct. 1933.

4. MUSIC

INSTRUMENTS

Oldest The world's oldest surviving musical notation is a heptonic scale deciphered from a clay tablet by Dr. Duchesne-Guillemin in 1966–67. The tablet has been dated to *c.* 1800 B.C. and was found at a site in Nippur, Sumer, now Iraq. Musical history is, however, able to be traced back to the 3rd millennium B.C., when the yellow bell (*huang chung*) had a recognised standard musical tone in Chinese temple music. Whistles and flutes made from perforated phalange bones have been found at Upper Palaeolithic sites of the Aurignacian period (*c.* 25,000–22,000 B.C.) *e.g.* Istállóskö, Hungary and in Molodova, U.S.S.R.

Earliest piano The earliest pianoforte in existence is one built in Florence, Italy, in 1720 by Bartolommeo Cristofori (1655–1731) of Padua, and now preserved in the Metropolitan Museum of Art, New York City.

Organ Largest World The largest and loudest musical instrument ever constructed is the now only partially functional Auditorium Organ in Atlantic City, New Jersey, U.S.A. Completed in 1930, this heroic instrument has

Vox Stellarum; Being a Loyal **ALMANACK** FOR THE Year of Humane Redemption 1718.

Frontispiece of the annual with the highest circulation, Old Moore's Almanack, for the year 1718

two consoles (one with seven manuals and another movable one with five), 1,477 stop controls and 33,112 pipes ranging from $\frac{3}{16}$ of an in *476 mm* to 64 ft *19 m* in length. It is powered with blower motors of 365 horsepower *370 cv*, cost $500,000 (now *£208,333*) and has the volume of 25 brass bands, with a range of seven octaves. The grand organ at Wannamaker's Store, Philadelphia, installed in 1911, was enlarged until by 1930 it had 6 manuals and 30,067 pipes including a 64 ft *19 m* Gravissima.

The world's largest church organ is that in Passau Cathedral, Germany. It was completed in 1928 by D. F. Steinmeyer & Co. It has 16,000 pipes and five manuals.

United Kingdom The largest organ in the United Kingdom is that completed in Liverpool Anglican Cathedral on 18 Oct. 1926, with two five-manual consoles of which only one is now in use, and 9,704 speaking pipes ranging from 32 ft *9,75 m* to ¾ in *19 mm*.

Loudest stop The loudest organ stop in the world is the Ophicleide stop of the Grand Great in the Solo Organ in the Atlantic City Auditorium (see above). It is operated by a pressure of 100 in *254 cm* of water (3½ lb./in² [*1kg 585f/cm²*]) and has a pure trumpet note of ear-splitting volume, more than six times the volume of the loudest locomotive whistles.

Organ marathon The longest organ recital ever sustained was one of 43¼ hrs at Handsworth College Chapel, Birmingham, England, by the Rev. Ian Yates on 9–11 May 1970. The record for playing an electric organ is 122 hrs by drag artiste Vince Bull at the Oswald Hotel, Scunthorpe, Lincs, on 9–14 Feb. 1973. An entirely non-stop record of 51 hrs was set by David J. Klein, from 7–9 March 1973 at Walker's Garage Showrooms, Mansfield, Notts.

Harmonium marathon The longest recorded non-stop harmonium marathon is 72 hrs by Iain Stinson and John Whiteley, both of the Royal Holloway College at Englefield Green, Surrey on 6–9 Feb. 1970.

Brass instrument Largest The largest recorded brass instrument is a tuba standing 7½ ft *2 m* tall, with 39 ft *12 m* of tubing and a bell 3 ft 4 in *1 m* across. This contrabass tuba was constructed for a world tour by the band of John Philip Sousa (1854–1932), the United States composer, in *c.* 1896–98, and is still in use. This instrument is now owned by a circus promoter in South Africa.

Longest alphorn The longest Swiss alphorn, which is of wooden construction, is 26½ ft *8 m* long and was constructed before June 1968 in Maine, U.S.A. by Dr. Allison.

Stringed instrument Largest The largest stringed instrument ever constructed was a pantaleon with 270 strings stretched over 50 ft² *4,6 m²* used by George Noel in 1767.

Most players The greatest number of musicians required to operate a single instrument was the six required to play the gigantic orchestrion, known as the Apollonican, built in 1816 and played until 1840.

Largest guitar The largest and presumably also the loudest playable guitar in the world is one 8 ft 10 in *2,6 m* tall, weighing 80 lb. *36 kg* and with a volume of 16,000 in³ *262 200 cm³* (*c.f.* the standard 1,024 in³ *16,780 cm³*) built by The Harmony Company of Chicago and completed in April 1970.

Largest double bass The largest bass viol ever constructed was an octo-bass 10 ft *3 m* tall, built in *c.* 1845 by J. B. Vuillaume (1798–1875) of France. Because the stretch was too great for any musician's finger-span, the stopping was effected by foot levers. It was played in London in 1851.

Violin Most valuable The highest recorded auction price for a violin is the £84,000 paid by W. E. Hill & Son, London, at Sothebys on 3 June 1971 for the Lady Anne Blunt Stradivarius, made in 1721. On this valuation the "Messie" Stradivarius in the Ashmolean Museum at Oxford, England, is now worth some £200,0000.

Smallest The smallest fully-functional violin made is one 5½ in *14 cm* overall, constructed by Mr. T. B. Pollard of Rock Ferry, Birkenhead, Cheshire, England.

Largest drum The largest drum in the world is the Disneyland Big Bass Drum with a diameter of 10 ft 6 in *3,2 m* and a weight of 450 lb. *204 kg.* It was built in 1961 by Remo Inc. of North Hollywood, California, U.S.A. and is mounted on wheels and towed by a tractor.

ORCHESTRAS

Most The greatest number of professional orchestras maintained in one country is 94 in West Germany. The total number of symphony orchestras in the United States, including "community" orchestras, was estimated to be 1,436 including 30 major and 66 metropolitan ones (as of August 1970).

Largest The vastest orchestra ever recorded were those assembled on Band Day at the University of Michigan, U.S.A. In some years between 1958 and 1965 the total number of instrumentalists reached 13,500. On 17 June 1872, Johann Strauss the younger (1825–99) conducted an orchestra of 2,000, supported by a choir of 20,000, at the World Peace Jubilee in Boston, Massachusetts, U.S.A. The number of violinists was more than 350.

Most Successful Brass band Most British Open Championship titles (inst. 1853) have been won by the Black Dyke Mills Band which has won 19 times from 1862 to 1972.

Marching Band The largest marching band on record was one of 1,976 musicians and 54 drill majors, flag bearers and directors who marched 2 miles down Pennsylvania Avenue in President Nixon's Inaugural Parade on 20 Jan. 1973.

Greatest attendance The greatest attendance at any classical concert was 90,000 for a presentation by the New York Philharmonic Orchestra, conducted by Leonard Bernstein, at Sheep Meadow in Central Park, New York City, N.Y., U.S.A., on 1 Aug. 1966.

Pop Festival The greatest estimated attendance at a Pop Festival has been 400,000 for the Woodstock Music and Art Fair at Bethel, New York State, U.S.A. on 15–17 Aug. 1969. According to one press estimate "at least 90 per cent" were smoking marijuana. The attendance at the third Pop Festival at East Afton Farm, Freshwater, Isle of Wight, England on 30 Aug. 1970 was claimed by its promoters, Fiery Creations, also to be 400,000.

Highest and lowest notes The extremes of orchestral instruments (excluding the organ) range between the piccolo or octave flute, which can reach e^v or 5,274 cycles per sec, and the sub-contrabass clarinet, which can reach C_{11} or 16.4 cycles/sec. The highest note on a standard pianoforte is c^v (4,186 cycles/sec), which is also the violinist's limit. In 1873 a sub double bassoon able to reach $B_{111}\sharp$ or 14.6 cycles/sec was constructed but no surviving specimen is known. The extremes for the organ are g^{vi} (the sixth G above middle C) (12,544 cycles/sec) and

'Band Day" at the University of Michigan, U.S.A., 27 Sept. 1958, with approximately 13,500 bandsmen from 192 bands

C_{111} (8.12 cycles/sec) obtainable from $\frac{3}{4}$-in and 64 ft pipes respectively.

COMPOSERS

Most prolific The most prolific composer of all time was probably Georg Philipp Telemann (1681–1767) of Germany. He composed 12 complete sets of services (one cantata every Sunday) for a year, 78 services for special occasions, 40 operas, 600 to 700 orchestral suites, 44 Passions, plus concertos and chamber music. The most prolific symphonist was Johann Melchior Molter (c. 1695–1765) of Germany who wrote 169. Joseph Haydn (1732–1809) of Austria wrote 104 numbered symphonies some of which are regularly played today.

Most rapid Among composers of the classical period the most prolific was Wolfgang Amadeus Mozart (1756–91) of Austria, who wrote 600 operas, operettas, symphonies, violin sonatas, divertimenti, serenades, motets, concertos for piano and many other instruments, string quartets, other chamber music, masses and litanies, of which only 70 were published before he died, aged 35. His opera *The Clemency of Titus* (1791) was written in 18 days and three symphonic masterpieces, *Symphony No. 39 in E flat major*, *Symphony in G minor* and the *Jupiter Symphony in C*, were reputedly written in the space of 42 days in 1788. His overture *Don Giovanni* was written in full score at one sitting in Prague in 1787 and finished on the day of its opening performance.

National The oldest national anthem is the *Kimigayo* of Japan, *anthems* in which the words date from the 9th century. The anthem of Greece constitutes the first four verses of the Solomos poem, which has 158 verses. The shortest anthems are those of Japan, Jordan and San Marino, each with only four lines. The anthems of Bahrain and Qatar have no words at all.

Longest "God Save the King" was played non-stop 16 or 17 *rendering* times by a German military band on the platform of Rathenau Railway Station, Brandenburg, on the morning of 9 Feb. 1909. The reason was that King Edward VII was struggling inside the train with the uniform of a German Field-Marshal before he could emerge.

Longest The longest of all single classical symphonies is the *symphony* orchestral symphony No. 3 in D minor by Gustav Mahler (1860–1911) of Austria. This work, composed in 1895, requires a contralto, a women's and a boys' choir and an organ, in addition to a full orchestra. A full performance requires 1 hour 34 min, of which the first movement alone takes 45 min. The Symphony No. 2 (the Gothic, now renumbered as No. 1), composed in 1919–22 by Havergal Brian, has been performed only twice, on 24 June 1961 and 30 Oct. 1966. The total *ensemble* included 55 brass instruments, 31 wood wind, six kettledrummers playing 22 drums, four vocal soloists, four large mixed choruses, a children's chorus and an organ. The symphony is continuous and required, when played as a recording on 27 Nov. 1967, 100 min. Brian has written an even vaster work based on Shelley's "Prometheus Unbound' lasting 4 hrs 11 min but the full score has been missing since 1961. He wrote 27 symphonies, 4 grand operas and 7 large orchestral works between 1948 when he was 72 and 1968.

The symphony *Victory at Sea* written by Richard Rodgers and arranged by Robert Russell Bennett for N.B.C. T.V. in 1952 lasted 13 hours.

Longest The longest continuous non-repetitious piece for *piano* piano ever composed has been the Opus Clavicem*composition* balisticum by Kaikhosru Shapurji Sorabji (b. 1892). The composer himself gave it its only public performance on 1 Dec. 1930 in Glasgow, Scotland. The

work is in 12 movements with a theme and 49 variations and a Passacaglia with 81 and a playing time of $2\frac{3}{4}$ hours.

The longest piano piece of any kind is *Vexations* by Erik Satie (France) which consists of a 180-note composition which on the composer's orders must be repeated 840 times such that the whole lasts 18 hrs 40 min. Its first reported public performance in September 1963 in the Pocket Theater, New York City required a relay of ten pianists. The *New York Times* critic fell asleep at 4 a.m. and the audience dwindled to six masochists. Richard Toop played the first solo rendition in London on 10–11 Oct. 1967 in 25 hrs.

Longest The most protracted silence in a modern composition *silence* is one entitled *4 minutes 33 seconds* in a totally silent *opus* by John Cage (U.S.A.). Commenting on this trend among young composers, Igor Fyodorovich Stravinsky (1882–1971) said that he looked forward to their subsequent compositions being "works of major length".

HIGHEST PAID MUSICIANS

Pianist The highest paid concert pianist was Ignace Jan Paderewski (1860–1941), Prime Minister of Poland from 1919 to 1921, who accumulated a fortune estimated at $5,000,000, of which $500,000 was earned in a single season in 1922–23. He once received $33,000 for a concert in Madison Square Garden, New York City, the highest valued fee ever paid for a single performance.

Singers Of great fortunes earned by singers, the highest on record are those of Enrico Caruso (1873–1921), the Italian tenor, whose estate was about $9,000,000 and the Italian-Spanish coloratura soprano Amelita Galli-Curci (1889–1963), who received about $3,000,000. In 1850, up to $653 was paid for a single seat at the concerts given in the United States by Johanna ("Janny") Maria Lind, later Mrs. Otto Goldschmidt (1820–87), the "Swedish Nightingale". She had a range from g to e^{III} of which the middle register is still regarded as unrivalled.

Violinist The Austrian-born Fritz Kreisler (1875–1962) is reputed to have received more than £1,000,000 in his career.

Drummer The most highly paid drummer, or indeed "side man" of any kind, is Bernard ("Buddy") Rich (b. 1917) in the band of Harry James, at more than $75,000 (*£30,000*) per annum.

OPERA

Longest The longest of commonly performed operas is *Die Meisteringer von Nurnberg* by Wilhelm Richard Wagner (1813–83) of Germany. A normal uncut performance of this opera as performed by the Sadler's Wells company between 24 Aug. and 19 Sept. 1968 entailed 5 hrs 15 min of music. *William Tell* by Rossini, never now performed uncut, would according to the *tempi* require some 7 or more hours if performed in full.

Aria The longest single aria, in the sense of an operatic solo, is Brünnhilde's immolation scene in Wagner's *Götterdammerung*. A well-known recording of this has been precisely timed at 14 minutes 46 seconds.

Cadenza The longest recorded cadenza in operatic history occured in c. 1815, when Crevilli, a tenor, sang the two words *felice ognora* ("always happy") as a cadenza for 25 min in the Milan Opera House, Italy.

Opera The largest opera house in the world is the Metropoli*houses* tan Opera House, Lincoln Center, New York City, *Largest* N.Y., U.S.A., completed in September 1966 at a cost of $45,700,000 (*£16,320,000*). It has a capacity of 3,800 seats in an auditorium 451 ft *137 m* deep. The stage is 234 ft *71 m* in width and 146 ft *44,5 m* deep. The tallest opera house is one housed in a 42-storey building on Wacker Drive in Chicago, Illinois, U.S.A.

Most tiers The Teatro della Scala (La Scala) in Milan, Italy, shares with the Bolshoi Theatre in Moscow, U.S.S.R., the distinction of having the greatest number of tiers. Each has six, with the topmost in Moscow being termed the Galurka.

Opera Singers Youngest and Oldest The youngest opera singer in the world has been Jeanette Gloria La Bianca, born in Buffalo, New York on 12 May 1934, who made her debut as Rosina in *The Barber of Seville* at the Teatro dell'Opera, Rome on 8 May 1950 aged 15 years 361 days, having appeared as Gilda in *Rigoletto* at Velletri 45 days earlier. Ginetta La Bianca was taught by Lucia Carlino and managed by Angelo Carlino. Giacomo Lauri-Volpi (Spain) gave a public performance on 26 Jan. 1972 aged 79.

BELLS

Heaviest World The heaviest bell in the world is the Tsar Kolokol, cast in 1733 in Moscow, U.S.S.R. It weighs 193 tons *196 tonnes* measures 22 ft 8 in *6,9 m* in diameter and over 19 ft *5,8 m* high, and its greatest thickness is 24 in *60 cm*. The bell is cracked, and a fragment, weighing about 11 tons/*tonnes* was broken from it. The bell has stood on a platform in the Kremlin, in Moscow, since 1836.

The heaviest bell in use is the Mingoon bell, weighing 87 tons *88 tonnes* in Mandalay, Burma, which is struck by a teak boom from the outside. The heaviest swinging bell in the world is the Kaiserglock in Cologne Cathedral, Germany, which was recast in 1925 at 25 tons/*tonnes*.

United Kingdom The heaviest bell hung in the United Kingdom is "Great Paul" in St. Paul's Cathedral, London. It was cast in 1881, weighs 16 tons 14 cwt. 2 qrs. 19 lb. *17 tonnes* and has a diameter of 9 ft 6½ in *2,9 m*. "Big Ben", the hour bell in the clock tower of the House of Commons, was cast in 1858 and weighs 13 tons 10 cwt. 3 qrs. 15 lb *13 761 kg*.

The heaviest bell ever cast in England and the heaviest tuned bell in the world is the bourdon bell of the Laura Spelman Rockefeller Memorial carillon in Riverside Church, New York City, N.Y., U.S.A. It weighs 18 tons 5 cwt. 1 qr. 18 lb. *18,5 tonnes* and is 10 ft 2 in *3 m* in diameter.

Oldest World The oldest bell in the world is reputed to be that found in the Babylonian Palace of Nimrod in 1849 by Mr. (later Sir) Austen Henry Layard (1817–94). It dates from *c*. 1000 B.C.

United Kingdom The oldest *dated* bell in England is one hanging in Lissett church, near Bridlington, Yorkshire discovered in Oct. 1972 to bear the date MCCLIIII (1254). The oldest inscribed bell is at Caversfield church, Oxfordshire and may be dated *c*. 1210. The uninscribed bell, discovered in 1968, at Whitfield church, Dover, Kent, has a casting date probably *ante* 1200.

The heaviest change ringing peal in the world is the ring of 13 bells, cast in 1938–39, weighing 16½ tons *16,7 tonnes*, in Liverpool Anglican Cathedral. The tenor bell, Emmanuel, weighs 82 cwt. 11 lb. *4 170 kg 80*.

CARILLON

Largest The largest carillon in the world is the Laura Spelman Rockefeller Memorial carillon in Riverside Church. New York City, N.Y., U.S.A. It consists of 72 bells with a total weight of 102 tons *103 tonnes*.

Heaviest The heaviest carillon in the United Kingdom is in St. Nicholas Church, Aberdeen, Scotland. It consists of

48 bells, the total weight of which is 25 tons 8 cwt. 2 qrs. 13 lb. *25 838 kg*. The bourdon bell weighs 4 tons 9 cwt. 3 qrs. 26 lb. *4 571 kg* and the carillon comprises four octaves, less the bottom semi-tone.

BELL RINGING

Eight bells have been rung to their full "extent" (a "Bob Major" of 40,320 changes) only once without relays. This took place in a bell foundry at Loughborough, Leicestershire, beginning at 6.52 a.m. on 27 July 1963 and ending at 00.50 a.m. on 28 July, after 17 hrs 58 min. The peal was composed by Kenneth Lewis of Altrincham, Cheshire, and the eight ringers were conducted by Robert B. Smith, aged 25, of Marple, Cheshire. Theoretically it would take 37 years 355 days to ring 12 bells (maximus) to their full extent of 479,001,600 changes.

SONG

Oldest The oldest known song is the *chadouf* chant, which has been sung since time immemorial by irrigation workers on the man-powered treadwheel Nile water mills (or *saqiyas*) in Egypt (now the United Arab Republic). The English song *Sumer is icumen in* dates from *c*. 1240.

Top songs of all time The most frequently sung songs in English are *Happy Birthday to You* (based on the original *Good morning to all*), by Mildred and Patty S. Hill of New York (published in 1935 and in copyright until 1996); *For He's a Jolly Good Fellow* (originally the French *Malbrouk*), known at least as early as 1781, and *Auld Lang Syne* (originally the Srathspey *I fee'd a Lad at Michaelmass*), some words of which were written by Robert Burns (1759–96). *Happy Birthday* was sung in space by the Apollo IX astronauts on 8 March 1969.

Top selling sheet music Sales of three non-copyright pieces are known to have exceeded 20,000,000 namely *The Old Folks at Home*, *Listen to the Mocking Bird* (1855) and *The Blue Danube* (1867). Of copyright material the two top-sellers are *Let Me Call You Sweetheart* (1910, by Whitson and Friedman) and *Till We Meet Again* (1918, by Egan and Whiting) each with some 6,000,000 by 1967.

Most successful songwriters In terms of sales of single records, the most successful of all song writers have been John Lennon and Paul McCartney (see also Gramophone, Fastest sales, p. 116) of the Beatles. Between 1962 and 1 Jan. 1970 they together wrote 30 songs which sold more than 1,000,000 records each.

HYMNS

Earliest There are believed to be more than 500,000 Christian hymns in existence. "Te Deum Laudamus" dates from about the 5th century, but the earliest exactly datable hymn is the French one "Jesus soit en ma teste et mon entendement" from 1490, translated into the well-known "God be in my head" in 1512.

Longest and shortest The longest hymn is "Hora novissima tempora pessima sunt; vigilemus" by Bernard of Cluny (12th century), which runs to 2,966 lines. In English the longest is "The Sands of Time are sinking" by Mrs. Anne Ross Cousin, *née* Cundell (1824–1906), which is in full 152 lines, though only 32 lines in the Methodist Hymn Book. The shortest hymn is the single verse in Long Metre "Be Present at our Table Lord", anonymous but attributed to "J. Leland".

Most prolific hymnists Mrs. Frances (Fanny) Jan Van Alstyne, *née* Crosby (1820–1915), of the U.S.A., wrote more than 8,000 hymns although she had been blinded at the age of 6 weeks. She is reputed to have knocked off one hymn in 15 min. Charles Wesley (1707–88) wrote about 6,000 hymns. In the seventh (1950) edition of *Hymns Ancient and Modern* the works of John Mason Neale (1818–66) appear 56 times.

The stage at Radio City Music Hall, New York City, the world's largest theatre, with the world's longest chorus line (see page 114)

Longest hymn-in The Cambridge University Student Methodist Society sang through the 984 hymns in the Methodist Hymn Book in 45 hrs 42 min, and completed 1,000 hymns with 16 more requests in 88 min on 7–9 Feb. 1969 in the Wesley Church, Cambridge.

5. THEATRE

Origins Theatre in Europe has its origins in Greek drama performed in honour of a god, usually Dionysus. The earliest amphitheatres date from the 5th century B.C. The largest of all known *orchestras* is one at Megalopolis in central Greece, where the auditorium reached a height of 75 ft *23 m* and had a capacity of 17,000.

Oldest World The oldest indoor theatre in the world is the Teatro Olimpico in Vicenza, Italy. Designed in the Roman style by Andrea di Pietro, *alias* Palladio (1508–80), it was begun three months before his death and finished in 1582 by his pupil Vicenzo Scamozzi (1552–1616). It is preserved today in its original form.

United Kingdom The earliest London theatre was James Burbage's "The Theatre", built in 1576 near Finsbury Fields, London. The oldest theatre still in use in the United Kingdom is the Theatre Royal, Bristol. The foundation stone was laid on 30 Nov. 1764, and the theatre was opened on 30 May 1766 with a "Concert of Music and a Specimen of Rhetorick". The City Varieties Music Hall, Leeds was a singing room in 1762 and so claims to outdate the Theatre Royal. Actors were legally rogues and vagabonds until the passing of an act (5 Geo. IV C.38) in 1824. The first honour for work on the stage was to Henry Irving (1838–1905), b. John Henry Brodribb, who was knighted in 1895. The earliest Dame was Geneviève Ward made D.B.E. in 1921. The first stage peer has been Sir Laurence Kerr Olivier (b. 22 May 1907), created a life Baron on 13 June 1970.

Largest World The world's largest building used for theatre is the National People's Congress Building (*Ren min da hui tang*) on the west side of Tian an men Square, Peking, China. It was completed in 1959 and covers an area of 12.9 acres *5,2 ha*. The theatre seats 10,000 and is occasionally used as such as in 1964 for the play "The East is Red". The largest regular theatre in the world has been Radio City Music Hall in Rockefeller Center, New York City, N.Y., U.S.A. with a seating capacity of more than 6,200 people and thus 8 million per annum. The stage is 144 ft *44 m* wide and 66 ft 6 in *20,26 m* deep, equipped with a revolving turntable 43 ft *13,10 m* in diameter and three elevator sections, each 70 ft *21 m* long.

The greatest seating capacity of any regular theatre in the world is that of the "Chaplin" (formerly the "Blanquita") in Havana, Cuba. It was opened on 30 Dec. 1949 and has 6,500 seats.

United Kingdom The highest capacity theatre is the Odeon, Hammersmith, West London, with 3,485 seats in 1973. The largest theatre stage in the United Kingdom is the Opera House in Blackpool, Lancashire. It was re-built in July 1939 and has seats for 2,975 people. Behind the 45 ft *14 m* wide proscenium arch the stage is 110 ft *33 m* high, 60 ft *18 m* deep and 100 ft *30 m* wide, and there is dressing room accommodation for 200 artistes.

Smallest The smallest regularly operated professional theatre in the United Kingdom is the Little Theatre, Tobermory, Isle of Mull, Scotland with a capacity of 36 seats.

Largest amphitheatre The largest amphitheatre ever built is the Flavian amphitheatre or Colosseum of Rome, Italy, completed in A.D. 80. Covering 5 acres *2 ha* and with a capacity of 87,000, it has a maximum length of 612 ft *187 m* and maximum width of 515 ft *157 m*.

Longest runs Continuous The longest continuous run of any show at one theatre in the world is by *The Mousetrap* by Dame Agatha Mary Clarissa Christie, D.B.E. (*née* Miller, now Lady Mallowan) (b. Torquay, Devon, 15 Sept. 1890) at the Ambassadors Theatre (capacity 453). This thriller opened on 25 Nov. 1952, and had its 8,525th performance on 1 June 1973. On 19 Aug. 1969 a power failure caused one performance to be missed. So far 145 actors have played its 8 roles, while A. Huntley Gordon has been the stage manager since the start.

113

Composite The 19th century morality play *The Drunkard* was revived at the Theatre Mart, Los Angeles on 6 July 1933 and ran for 7,510 performances until 3 Sept. 1953. It continued to run alternate nights until its 8,494th performance on 17 Oct. 1959 with its own musical adaptation entitled *The Wayward Way*, making a composite total of 9,477 performances.

Revue The greatest number of performances of any theatrical presentation is more than 25,000 in the case of *The Golden Horseshoe Revue*—a show staged at Disneyland Park, Anaheim, California, U.S.A. The show was first put on on 17 July 1955. The three main performers Fulton Berley, Bert Henry and Betty Taylor play as many as five houses a day in a routine lasting 45 minutes. In Britain, the Brighton Corporation's variety show *Tuesday Night at the Dome* reached its 1,317th performance in 27 years on 30 Apr. 1973.

Broadway The Broadway record is 3,242 performances by *Fiddler on the Roof* which closed on 3rd July 1972. It had opened on 22 Sept. 1964. Paul Lipson played from the opening including 1,811 times as Tevye during which time he had ten "wives" and 58 "daughters". The world gross earnings reached $64,300,000 (£25.7 million) on an original investment of $375,000. The off-Broadway show *The Fantasticks* achieved however its 5,060th performance on 25 June 1972.

Musical The longest-running musical show ever performed in **shows** Britain was *The Black and White Minstrel Show*, a musical variety presentation which opened at the Victoria Palace, London, on 25 May 1962, was performed *twice* nightly and continued until 24 May 1969 reaching 4,354 performances. The total attendance had been recorded at 5,614,077. One chorus girl claims a pedometer strapped to a leg registered 6½ miles *10 km* in one night. It reopened as *Magic of the Minstrels* on 24 Nov. 1969 and reached its 2,000th performance on 13 Dec. 1972.

One-man The longest run of any one-man show, without **shows** audience participation, has been 327 performances of· *Comedy To Night* by James Young at the Ulster Group Theatre, Belfast from 7 Apr. 1969 to 22 Mar. 1970. He was on stage for 2 hrs 15 min. The longest run of a one-man show on the London stage has been 213 performances of *Brief Lives* by Roy Dotrice (b. Guernsey, 5 May 1923) at the Criterion from 25 Feb. to 6 Sept. 1969.

The longest theatrical run with audience participation is 351 performances extending 46 weeks from 17 Jan. to 2 Dec. 1972 at the Lyric Theatre, Durban, South Africa, by "Romark" (Ronald Markham), the psychological entertainer, in his 3 hour long *Hypnotrix*. The total attendances with his 41 further performances in other Durban theatres were 220,000 (more than 2 in 5 of Durban's population).

Shortest The shortest run on record was that of *The Intimate* **runs** *Revue* at the Duchess Theatre, London, on 11 March **World** 1930. Anything which could go wrong did. With scene changes taking up to 20 min apiece, the management scrapped seven scenes to get the finale on before midnight. The run was described as "half a performance". Even this fractional first night was surpassed by *As You Like It* by William Shakespeare (1564–1616) at the Shaftesbury Theatre, London, in 1888. On the opening night the fire curtain was let down, jammed, and did not rise again that night or ever again on this production.

Broadway Of the many Broadway shows for which the opening and closing nights coincided, the most costly was *Kelly*, a musical costing $700,000 (*then* £250,000) which underwent the double ceremony on 6 Feb. 1965.

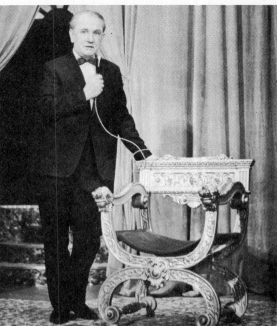
James Young, during one of his record-breaking solo appearances at the Ulster Group Theatre, Belfast

Longest *O'Casey* by Patrick Funge played at the Lantern **play** Theatre, Dublin, lasted 6 hrs 45 min playing time, opening on 24 July 1972 at 3 p.m. and finishing at 11.15 p.m. with a 90 min meal interval. George Begley was never off the stage. The 15th century Cornish Cycle of Mystery Plays was revived in English in July 1969, at the earthwork theatre, St. Piran's Round, Piran, near Perranporth, Cornwall, by the Drama Department of Bristol University. Three parts, *Origo Mundi*, *Passio*, and *Resurrectio*, ran for 12 hrs with two intermissions.

Shakespeare The first all amateur company to have staged all 37 of Shakespeare's plays was The Southsea Shakespeare Actors, Hampshire, England (founded 1947), when in October 1966 they presented *Cymbeline*. The amateur director throughout was Mr. K. Edmonds Gateley, M.B.E. Ten members of Nottingham Theatre Group, Nottingham completed a dramatic reading of all the plays, 154 sonnets and five narrative poems in 44 hrs 46 min on 9–11 March 1973. The longest is *Richard III*.

Longest The world's longest permanent chorus line was that **chorus** formed by the Rockettes in the Radio City Music **line** Hall, which opened in December 1932 in New York City, U.S.A. The 36 girls danced precision routines across its 144 ft *43,9 m* wide stage.

Ice shows The most prolific producer of ice shows has been Gerald Palmer, who, since 1945, has produced 128 Ice Shows including 27 consecutive shows at Empire Pool, Wembley, London with attendances up to 491,000.

6. GRAMOPHONE

Origins The gramophone (phonograph) was first described on 30 April 1877 by Charles Cros (1842–88), a French poet and scientist. The first successful machine was constructed by Thomas Alva Edison (1847–1931) of the U.S.A., who gained his first patent on 19 Feb. 1878. It was on 15 Aug. 1877 that he shouted "Mary had a little Lamb". The first practical hand-cranked foil cylinder phonograph was manufactured in the United States by Chichester Bell and Charles Sumner Tainter in 1886.

The country with the greatest number of record players is the United States, with a total of more than 61,200,000 by Dec. 1971. A total of more than half a

Gramophone
pioneer Thomas
Alva Edison
(b. 1847) in
his laboratory

billion dollars (*now £192 million*) is spent annually on 500,000 juke boxes in the United States.

In the United States retail sales of discs and tapes reached $1,744 million in 1971 of which $1,251 million was for L.P.'s and $96 million for cassettes.

The peak year for value in U.K. sales of records was 1971 with £43,485,000 for 120,524,000 records.

OLDEST RECORD

The oldest record in the British Broadcasting Corporation's gramophone library is a record made by Emile Berliner (b. Berlin, 1851) of himself reciting the Lord's Prayer. It was made in 1884. Berliner invented the flat disc to replace the cylinder in 1888.

The B.B.C. library, the world's largest, contains over 750,000 records, including 5,250 with no known matrix.

Earliest jazz records The earliest jazz record made was *Indiana* and *The Dark Town Strutters Ball*, recorded for the Columbia label in New York City, N.Y., U.S.A., on or about 30 Jan. 1917, by the Original Dixieland Jazz Band, led by Dominick (Nick) James La Rocca (1889–1961). This was released on 31 May 1917. The first jazz record to be released was the O.D.J.B.'s *Livery Stable Blues* (recorded 24 Feb.), backed by *The Dixie Jass Band One-Step* (recorded 26 Feb.), released by Victor on 7 March 1917.

Most successful solo recording artist On 9 June 1960 the Hollywood Chamber of Commerce presented Harry Lillis (*alias* Bing) Crosby, Jr. (b. 2 May 1904 at Tacoma, Washington) with a platinum disc to commemorate a sale of 200,000,000 records from the 2,600 singles and 125 albums he had recorded. On 15 Sept. 1970 he received a second platinum disc for selling 300,650,000 discs with Decca. It was then estimated that his global life-time sales on 88 labels in 28 countries totalled, according to his royalty reports, 362,000,000. His first commercial recording was "*I've Got the Girl*" recorded on 18 Oct. 1926 (master number W142785 (Take 3) issued on the Columbia label). The greatest collection of Crosbiana by Mr. Bob Roberts of Chatham, Kent includes 1,677 records.

Most successful group The singers with the greatest sales of any group have been the Beatles. This group from Liverpool, Lancashire, comprised George Harrison, M.B.E. (b. 25 Feb.

1943), John Ono (formerly John Winston) Lennon, M.B.E. (b. 9 Oct. 1940), James Paul McCartney, M.B.E. (b. 18 June 1942) and Richard Starkey, M.B.E., *alias* Ringo Starr (b. 7 July 1940). Between February 1963 and June 1972 their sales were estimated at 545 million in singles' equivalents. This included 85 million albums. The 40,000 strong Beatles Fan Club had been closed down on 31 Mar. 1972.

GOLDEN DISCS

Earliest The earliest recorded piece eventually to aggregate a total sale of a million copies were performances by Enrico Caruso (b. Naples, Italy, 1873, and d. 2 Aug. 1921) of the aria *Vesti la giubba* (*On with the Motley*) from the opera *I Pagliacci* by Ruggiero Leoncavallo (1858–1919), the earliest version of which was recorded with piano on 12 Nov. 1902. The first single recording to surpass the million mark was Alma Gluck's *Carry me back to old Virginny* on the Red Seal Victor label on the 12-inch *30,48 cm* single faced (later backed) record 74420. The first actual golden disc was one sprayed by R.C.A. Victor for presentation to the U.S. trombonist and band-leader Alton 'Glenn' Miller (1904–44) for his *Chattanooga Choo Choo* on 10 Feb. 1942.

Most The only *audited* measure of million-selling records within the United States, is certification by the Recording Industry Association of America (R.I.A.A.) introduced in 1958. The artist claiming most golden discs is Elvis Aron Presley (b. Tupelo, Mississippi, U.S.A., 8 Jan. 1935) with 116. This total arises from 67 titles which by either each million dollars worth of sales or per million copies sold have produced 103 golden discs. The remaining 13 are for million dollar sales of L.P.s.

Youngest The youngest age at which an artist has achieved sales of 1,000,000 copies of a record is 6 yrs by Osamu Minagawa of Tōkyō, Japan for his single *Kuro Neko No Tango* (*Black Cat Tango*) released on 5 Oct. 1969.

Most recorded song Two songs have each been recorded between 900 and 1,000 times in the United States alone—*St. Louis Blues*, written in 1914 by W. C. (William Christopher) Handy (b. Florence, Alabama 1873 and d. 1958), and *Stardust*, written in 1927 by Hoagland ("Hoagy") Carmichael (b. Bloomington, Indiana, 22 Nov. 1899).

"Glenn" Miller (k. 1944) recipient of the first actual golden disc

Most recordings Miss Lata Mangeshker (b. 1928) between 1948 and 1971 has reportedly recorded not less than 20,000 solo, duet and chorus backed songs in 20 Indian languages. She frequently has 5 sessions in a day.

Biggest sellers The greatest seller of any gramophone record to date is *White Christmas* by Irving Berlin (b. Israel Bailin, at Tyumen, Russia, 11 May 1888). First recorded in 1941, it became the first ever record to reach 9 figures (100,000,000) sales in 1970. The top-selling "pop" record has been *It's Now or Never* by Elvis Presley, issued in 1970 with sales reported in excess of 20,000,000. The top-selling British record of all-time is *I Want to Hold Your Hand* by the Beatles, released in 1963, with world sales of over 12,000,000, including a certified sale of 5,000,000 in the United States.

Best-sellers' charts Radio Luxembourg's "Top Twenty" Sunday night programme, launched in the autumn of 1948, was the first *programme* based on current selling strength though best-selling lists had been appearing in the U.S. periodical *Billboard* since 27 July 1950. The longest stay in the British charts has been by Frank Sinatra's *My Way* released in 1969 which on 23 Oct. 1971 celebrated its 120th consecutive week. The longest stay in the L.P. charts in the U.S.A. has been 490 weeks from late in 1958 to July 1968 by the Columbia album *Johnny's Greatest Hits* (Johnny Mathis). The longest in the U.K. has been *Sound of Music* (sound track) with 356 weeks to 31 Dec. 1972.

Top-selling L.P. The best-selling L.P. is the 20th Century Fox album *Sing We now of Christmas*, issued in 1958 and re-entitled *The Little Drummer Boy* in 1963. Its sales were reported to be more than 14,000,000 by Nov. 1972. The first British L.P. to sell 1,000,000 copies was *With the Beatles* (Parlophone), from November 1963 to January 1964 in the United States and to September 1965 in Britain. The top-selling British L.P. has been the double (4-sided) *Jesus Christ Superstar* by Andrew Lloyd Webber (b. 22 Mar. 1948) and Tim Rice (b. 10 Nov. 1944) released on 10 Oct. 1970. Sales reached 4½ million sets by Jan. 1973.

Top-selling L.P. sound track The all-time best-seller among long-playing records of musical film shows is *The Sound of Music* sound track album, released by Victor in U.S.A. on 2 March and in Britain on 9 April 1965, with more than 19,000,000 to 1 Jan. 1973. In Britain it was No. 1 in the L.P. Charts for 73 weeks.

Top-selling classical L.P. The first classical long-player to sell a million was a performance featuring the pianist Harvey Lavan (Van) Cliburn, Jr. (b. Kilgore, Texas, 12 July 1934) of the *Piano Concerto No. 1* by Pyotr Ilyich Tchaikovsky (1840–93) (more properly rendered Chaykovskiy) of Russia. This recording was made in 1958 and sales reached 1,000,000 by 1961, 2,000,000 by 1965 and about 2,500,000 by January 1970.

Longest L.P. set The longest long-playing record is the 137-disc set of the complete works of William Shakespeare (1564–1616). The recordings, which were made in 1957–1964, cost £260.62½ per set, and are by the Argo Record Co. Ltd., London, S.W.3. The Vienna Philharmonic's playing of Wagner's "The Ring" covers 19 L.P.s, was eight years in the making and requires 14½ hrs playing time.

Fastest selling L.P.s The fastest selling record of all time is *John Fitzgerald Kennedy—A Memorial Album* (Premium Albums), an L.P. recorded on 22 Nov. 1963, the day of Mr. Kennedy's assassination, which sold 4,000,000 copies at 99 cents (*then 35p*) in six days (7–12 Dec. 1963), thus ironically beating the previous speed record set by the satirical L.P. *The First Family* in 1962–63. The fastest selling British record has been the Beatles' double album *The Beatles* (Parlophone) with "nearly 2 million" in its first week in November 1968.

Advance sales The greatest advance sale was 2,100,000 for *Can't Buy Me Love* by the Beatles, released in the United States on 16 March 1964. The Beatles also equalled their British record of 1,000,000 advance sales, set by *I want to Hold Your Hand* (Parlophone transferred to Apple Aug. 1968) on 29 Nov. 1963, with this same record on 20 March 1964. The U.K. record for advance sales of an L.P. is 750,000 for the Parlophone album *Beatles for Sale* released on 4 Dec. 1964.

Highest gross and audience The highest gross taking for an individual pop recording group is $309,000 (*£123,600*) and the highest attendance is 560,800 both for the concert by the British group Led Zeppelin at the Tampa Stadium, Florida, U.S.A., on 5 May 1973.

Longest Silence Silent records (Hush Label) were first placed on juke boxes at the University of Detroit, U.S.A. in January 1959. The longest programme of sponsored silence was one of 6 hrs on Station WS00 of Sault Ste. Marie, Michigan on 1 Jan. 1971.

7. CINEMA

EARLIEST

Origins The greatest impetus in the development of cinematography came from the inventiveness of Etienne Jules Marey (1830–1903) of France

Earliest silent showings The earliest demonstration of a celluloid cinematograph film was given at Lyon (Lyons), France on 22 March 1895 by Auguste Marie Louis Nicolas Lumière (1862–1954) and Louis Jean Lumière (1864–1948), the French brothers. The first public showing was at the Indian Salon of the Hotel Scribe, on the Boulevard des Capucines, in Paris, on 28 Dec. 1895. The 33 patrons were charged 1 franc each and was ten short films, including *Baby's Breakfast*, *Lunch Hour at the Lumière Factory* and *The Arrival of a Train*. The same programme was shown on 20 Feb. 1896 at the Polytechnic Institute in Regent Street, London.

Earliest 'Talkie' The earliest sound-on-film motion picture was achieved by Eugene Augustin Lauste (b. Paris 17 Jan. 1857) who patented his process on 11 Aug. 1906 and produced a workable system using a string galvanometer in 1910 in London. The event is more usually attributed to Dr. Lee de Forest (1873–1961) in New York City, N.Y., U.S.A., on 13 March 1923. The first all-talking picture was *Lights of New York*, shown at The Strand, New York City, on 6 July 1928.

Highest production Japan annually produces most full length films, with 423 films of 1,500 m *4,921 ft* or more completed in 1970, compared with 396 films of 3,400 m *11,155 ft* or more approved by the censor in India in 1970. This compares, however, with Japan's production of 1,000 films in 1928. The average seat price in Japan is 70 yen (7p). In the United Kingdom 90 feature films of 72 or more minutes duration were registered in the year ending 31 Dec. 1971.

Highest cinema-going The people of Taiwan go to the cinema more often than those of any other country in the world with an average of 66 attendances per person per annum according to the latest data. The Soviet Union has the most cinemas in the world, with 147,200 in 1970 including those projecting only 16 mm film. The number of cinemas in the U.K. declined from 4,542 in 1953 to 1,543 at 1 Mar. 1973. The average weekly admissions declined from 24,700,000 in 1953 to 3,150,000 in 1972. Excluding "captive" projectionists, the most persistent voluntary devotee of a film has been Mrs. Myra Franklin (b. 1919) of Cardiff, Wales, who saw *The Sound of Music* more than 900 times.

Most cinema seats The Falkland Islands and the Cook Islands have more cinema seats per total population than any other country in the world, with 250 seats for each 1,000 inhabitants. The Central African Republic has 2 cinemas and hence one seat for 4,100 people.

CINEMAS

Largest The largest open-air cinema in the world is in the
World British Sector of West Berlin, Germany. One end of
the Olympic Stadium, converted into an amphitheatre, seats 22,000 people.

United The United Kingdom's largest cinema is the Odeon
Kingdom Theatre, Hammersmith, London, with 3,485 seats.
The *Playhouse*, Glasgow had 4,235 seats.

Oldest The earliest cinema was the "Electric Theatre", part
of a tented circus in Los Angeles, California, U.S.A. It
opened on 2 April 1902. The oldest building designed
as a cinema is the Biograph Cinema in Wilton Road,
Victoria, London. It was opened in 1905 and originally
had seating accommodation for 500 patrons. Its
present capacity is 700.

Most The most expensive film ever made is the 7 hr 13
expensive min long *War and Peace*, the U.S.S.R. government
film adaptation of the masterpiece of Tolstoy produced
by Sergei Bondarchuk (b. 1921) over the period
1962–67. The total cost has been officially stated to
be more than £40,000,000. More than 165,000
uniforms had to be made. The re-creation of the
Battle of Borodino (7 Sept. 1812) involved 120,000
Red Army "extras" at 3 roubles (£1.38) per month.

Most The highest price ever paid for film rights is
expensive $5,500,000, paid on 6 Feb. 1962 by Warner Brothers
film rights for *My Fair Lady*, which cost $17,000,000 thus
making it the most expensive musical film then made.

Longest The longest film ever shown is *The Human Condition*,
film directed in three parts by Masaki Kobayashi of Japan.
It lasts 8 hrs 50 min, excluding two breaks of 20 min
each. It was shown in Tōkyō in October 1961 at an
admission price of 250 yen (24½p). The longest
film ever released was **** by Andy Warhol (b.
Cleveland, Ohio, 1931) which lasted 24 hrs. It proved,
not surprisingly, except reportedly to its creator, a
commercial failure and was withdrawn and re-released
in 90 min form as *The Loves of Ondine*.

Longest The longest film title is: *Persecution and Assassi-*
title *nation of Jean-Paul Marat as performed by the*
Inmates of the Asylum of Charenton under the direction
of the Marquis de Sade, first distributed by United
Artists in March 1967.

Highest The film which has had the highest world gross
box office earnings (amount paid by cinema owners) is *The*
gross *Godfather* (released in March 1972) which reached
$100,000,000 (£40 million) by March 1973.

Highest The greatest earnings by any film star for one film is
earning by expected to be that of Elizabeth Rosamund Taylor
an actor (b. Hampstead, London, 27 Feb. 1932) in *Cleopatra*
(1963). Her undisputed share of the earnings is
$3,000,000 (*then £1,071,400*) and could eventually
reach $7,000,000 (*now £2,692,300*). Sean Connery
who played James Bond (secret service agent 007)
reputedly earned by way of fees and percentage of
gross takings $13½ million (£5½ *million*) for the first
five Bond films.

Largest The largest complex of film studios in the world are
Studios those at Universal City, South California. The Back
Lot contains 561 buildings and there are 34 sound
stages.

OSCARS

Most Walter (Walt) Elias Disney (1901–1966) won more
"Oscars"—the awards of the United States Academy
of Motion Picture Arts and Sciences, instituted on 16
May 1929 for 1927–28—than any other person. His
total was 35 from 1931 to 1969. The only actress to

Marlon Brando, in the title rôle of *The Godfather*, the top box office earner

win three Oscars in a starring rôle has been Miss
Katharine Hepburn, formerly Mrs. Ludlow Ogden
Smith (b. Hartford, Conn., 9 Nov. 1909) in *Morning
Glory* (1932–3), *Guess Who's Coming to Dinner*
(1967) and *The Lion in Winter* (1968). Oscars are
named after Mr. Oscar Pierce of Texas, U.S.A. The
films with most awards have been *Ben Hur* (1959)
with 11, followed by *West Side Story* (1961) with 10.
The film with the highest number of nominations was
All About Eve (1950) with 14.

Newsreels The world's most durable newsreel commentator has
been Bob Danvers Walker (b. Cheam, Surrey, 11 Oct.
1906), who commentated for Pathé "Gazette" from
June 1940 until its demise in February 1970.

8. RADIO BROADCASTING

Origins The earliest description of a radio transmission
system was written by Dr. Mahlon Loomis (U.S.A.)
(b. Fulton County, N.Y., 21 July 1826) on 21 July
1864 and demonstrated between two kites more than
14 miles *22 km* apart at Bear's Den, Loudoun County,
Virginia in October 1866. He received U.S. patent No.
129,971 entitled Improvement in Telegraphing on 20
or 30 July 1872. He died in 1886.

Earliest The first patent for a system of communication by
patent means of electro-magnetic waves, numbered No.
12039, was granted on 22 June 1896 to the Italian-
Irish Marchese Guglielmo Marconi (1874–1937). A
public demonstration of wireless transmission of
speech was, however, given in the town square of
Murray, Kentucky, U.S.A. in 1892 by Nathan B.
Stubblefield. He died destitute on 28 March 1928.
The first permanent wireless installation was at The
Needles on the Isle of Wight, Hampshire, by Marconi's
Wireless Telegraph Co., Ltd., in November 1896.

Earliest The world's first advertised broadcast was made on 24
broadcast Dec. 1906 by Prof. Reginald Aubrey Fessenden
World (1868–1932) from the 420 ft *128 m* mast of the National
Electric Signalling Company at Brant Rock, Massachusetts, U.S.A. The transmission included the *Largo*
by George Friedrich Händel (1685–1759) of Germany.
Fessenden had achieved the broadcast of highly
distorted speech as early as November 1900.

United Kingdom The first experimental broadcasting transmitter in the United Kingdom was set up at the Marconi Works in Chelmsford, Essex, in December 1919, and broadcast a news service in February 1920. The earliest regular broadcast of entertainment was made from the Marconi transmitter "2 MT" at Writtle, Essex, on 14 Feb. 1922.

Transatlantic transmissions The earliest transatlantic wireless signals (the letter S in Morse Code) were sent by Marconi from a 10 kw station at Poldhu, Cornwall, and received by Percy Wright Paget and G. S. Kemp at Signal Hill, St. John's, Newfoundland, Canada, on 12 Dec. 1901. Human speech was first heard across the Atlantic in November 1915 when a transmission from the U.S. Navy station at Arlington, Virginia was received by U.S. radio-telephone engineers on the Eiffel Tower, Paris.

Most stations The country with the greatest number of radio broadcasting stations is the United States, where there were 6,372 authorized broadcast stations in 1972 of which 4,250 were AM (Amplitude modulation) and 2,122 FM (Frequency modulation).

Radio sets There were an estimated 620,000,000 radio sets in use throughout the world in 1970, equivalent to 92 for each 1,000 people. Of the U.S. total of 354 million for the end of 1971, 92,000,000 were in cars. The equivalent United Kingdom figure is not now available as sound licences were abolished on 1 Feb. 1971. The last figure was 2,074,034 for December 1970.

Highest Listenership The peak recorded listenership on B.B.C. Radio was 30,000,000 adults on 6 June 1950 for the world title boxing fight between Lee Savold (U.S.) and Bruce Woodcock (G.B.).

Longest The longest B.B.C. broadcast was the reporting of the Coronation of Queen Elizabeth II on 2 June 1953. It began at 10.15 a.m. and finished at 5.30 p.m., after 7 hrs 15 min. This was well surpassed by Radio Station ELBC, Monrovia, on 23 Nov. 1961 when a transmission of 14 hrs 20 min was devoted to the coverage of the Queen's visit to Liberia.

Most durable B.B.C. programmes The most durable B.B.C. radio series is *The Week's Good Cause* beginning on 24 Jan. 1926. The longest running record programme is *Desert Island Discs* which began on 29 Jan. 1942 and on which programme the only guests to be thrice stranded have been Arthur Bowden Askey, O.B.E. (b. 6 June 1900) and Robertson Hare (b. 17 Dec. 1891). The *Desert Island* programme has been presented since its inception by Roy Plomley who also devised the idea. The longest running solo radio feature is *Letter from America* by (Alfred) Alistair Cooke, Hon. K.B.E. (b. Manchester 20 Nov. 1908), first commissioned as a series of 13 talks on 6 March 1946. The longest running comedy serial was *The Clitheroe Kid* started in 1958, which entered its 15th successive year in 1972.

9. TELEVISION

Invention The invention of television, the instantaneous viewing of distant objects, was not an act but a process of successive and inter-dependent discoveries. The first commercial cathode ray tube was introduced in 1897 by Karl Ferdinand Braun (1850–1918), but was not linked to "electric vision" until 1907 by Boris Rosing of Russia in St. Petersburg (now Leningrad). The earliest public demonstration of television was given on 26 Jan. 1926 by John Logie Baird (1888–1946) of Scotland, using a development of the mechanical scanning system suggested by Paul Nipkov in 1884. A patent application for the Iconoscope (Number 2,141,059) had been filed on 29 Dec. 1923 by Dr.

Vladimir Kosma Zworykin (born in Russia on 30 July 1889, became a U.S. citizen in 1924), and a short range transmission of a model windmill had been made on 13 June 1925 by C. Francis Jenkins in Washington, D.C., U.S.A. The first experimental transmission in Britain was on 30 Sept. 1929. Public transmissions on 30 lines were made from 22 Aug. 1932 until 11 Sept. 1935.

Earliest service The world's first high definition (*i.e.* 405 lines) television broadcasting service was opened from Alexandra Palace, London, N.22, on 2 Nov. 1936, when there were about 100 sets in the United Kingdom. The Chief Engineer was Mr. Douglas Birkinshaw. A television station in Berlin, Germany, made a low definition (180 line) transmission from 22 March 1935. The transmitter burnt out in Aug. 1935.

Transatlantic transmission The earliest transatlantic transmission by satellite was achieved at 1 a.m. on 11 July 1962, *via* the active satellite *Telstar 1* from Andover, Maine, U.S.A., to Pleumeur Bodou, France. The picture was of Mr. Frederick R. Kappel, chairman of the American Telephone and Telegraph Company, which owned the satellite. The first "live" broadcast was made on 23 July 1962 and the first woman to appear was the *haute couturière*, Genette Spanier, directrice of Balmain, the next day. The earliest satellite transmission was one of 2,700 miles *4 300 km* from California to Massachusetts, U.S.A., *via* the satellite *Echo 1*, on 3 May 1962—the letters M.I.T.

Most sets In 1971 the total estimated number of television transmitters in use or under construction was 6,400 serving 270,500,000 sets (75 for each 1,000 of the world population). Of these, about 92,700,000 were estimated to be in use in the United States where 96 per cent of the population is reached. The number of colour sets in the U.S.A. has grown from 200,000 in 1960 to 31,300,000 by January 1971. The number of licences current in the United Kingdom was 17,124,619 on 31 March 1973 of which 3,331,996 were for colour sets.

Alistair Cooke, author of the longest running solo radio feature *Letter from America*

The cast of television's longest running serial and the longest telecast, *The Forsyte Saga*

Greatest audience The greatest estimated number of viewers for a televised event is 1,000 million for the live and recorded transmissions of the XXth Olympic Games in Munich, West Germany from 26 Aug. to 11 Sept. 1972.

Largest T.V. prizes
World The greatest amount won by an individual in T.V. prizes was $264,000 (*then £94,286*) by Teddy Nadler on quiz programmes in the United States up to September 1958. In March 1960 he failed a test to become a census enumerator because of his inability to distinguish between east and west. His comment was, reportedly, "Those maps threw me".

United Kingdom The largest T.V. prize won in the U.K. is £5,580 by Bernard Davis, aged 33, on Granada T.V.'s "Twenty-one" quiz programme, reached on 24 Sept. 1958.

Most successful appeal The greatest amount raised by any B.B.C. T.V. or Radio Appeal was £1,500,000, raised as a result of an appeal by Richard Samuel Attenborough, C.B.E. (b. Cambridge, 29 Aug. 1923) on behalf of the fund for the East Pakistan Cyclone Disaster of 12–13 Nov. 1970.

LARGEST CONTRACTS

World The largest T.V. contract ever signed was one for $34,000,000 (*£14,166,666*) in a three-year no-option contract between Dino Paul Crocetti (b. 7 June 1917) otherwise Dean Martin, and N.B.C.

Dean Martin was acclaimed in September 1968 as the top-earning show-business personality of all-time with $5,000,000 (*over £2 million*) in a year. Television's highest-paid interviewer has been Garry Moore (b. Thomas Garrison Morfit on 31 Jan. 1915), who was earning $43,000 (*£15,357*) a week in 1963, equivalent to $2,236,000 (*nearly £800,000*) per year.

United Kingdom The largest contract in British television was one of a reported £9,000,000, inclusive of production expenses, signed by Tom Jones (b. Thomas Jones Woodward, 7 June 1950) of Treforest, Glamorgan, Wales in June 1968 with ABC-TV of the United States and ATV in London for 17 one-hour shows per annum from January 1969 to January 1974.

Hourly The world's highest paid television performer based on an hourly rate has been Perry Como (b. Pierino Como, Canonsburg, Pennsylvania, U.S.A., on 18 May 1912) who began as a barber. In May 1969 he signed a contract with N.B.C. to star in four one-hour video specials at $5,000,000 (*£2,083,333*) or at the rate of £8,680.55 per min. The contract required him to provide supporting artistes.

Longest telecast The longest pre-scheduled telecast on record was a continuous transmission for 163 hours 18 mins by GTV 9 of Melbourne, Australia covering the Apollo XI moon mission on 19–26 July 1969.

Most durable performer Bob Barker acted as host for the American T.V. show *Truth or Consequences* from 31 Dec. 1956 to 12 Jan. 1973—3,524 consecutive programmes.

Most durable B.B.C. programme The longest running T.V. programme on B.B.C. is *Panorama* which was first transmitted, first introduced by Patrick Murphy, on 11 Nov. 1953. *Andy Pandy* was first transmitted on 11 July 1950 but consisted of repeats of a cycle of 26 shows until 1970. The News has been featured since 23 March 1938.

Earliest T.V. critic The first man in the world appointed to be a T.V. critic and correspondent was Leonard Marsland Gander (b. 27 June 1902) by the London *Daily Telegraph* in 1935—the year before the B.B.C.'s 405 line transmissions. He retired in July 1970 after spanning 35 yrs with T.V. and 44 yrs with radio.

Biggest sale The greatest number of episodes of any T.V. programme ever sold has been 1,144 episodes of "Coronation Street" by Granada Television to CBKST Saskatoon, Saskatchewan, Canada on 31 May 1971. This constituted 20 days 15 hrs 44 min continuous viewing.

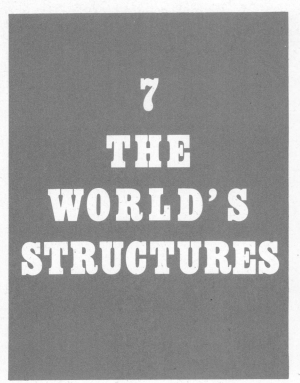

7
THE WORLD'S STRUCTURES

EARLIEST STRUCTURES

World The earliest known human structure is a rough circle of loosely piled lava blocks found in 1960 on the lowest cultural level at the Lower Palaeolithic site at Olduvai Gorge in Tanganyika (now part of Tanzania). The structure was associated with artifacts and bones and may represent a work-floor, dating to *circa* 1,750,000 B.C. (see Chapter 1, Earliest Man). The earliest evidence of *buildings* yet discovered is that of 21 huts with hearths or pebble-lined pits and delimited by stake holes found in October 1965 at the Terra Amata site in Nice, France originally dated to 300,000 B.C. but now thought to be more likely belonging to the Acheulian culture of 120,000 years ago. Excavation carried out between 28 June and 5 July 1966 revealed one hut with palisaded walls with axes of 49 ft *15 m* and 20 ft *6 m*.

United A rudimentary platform of birch branches, stones and
Kingdom wads of clay thrown down on the edge of a swamp at Star Carr, south of Scarborough, Yorkshire, may possibly represent the earliest man-made "dwelling" yet found in Britain (Mesolithic, 7607 B.C. ± 210). Remains of the earliest dated stone shelter and cooking pit were discovered in 1967 on the Isle of Portland, Dorset (Mesolithic, 5200 B.C. ± 135). The rock shelter on Oldbury Hill, ¾ of a mile *1 km* south-west of Ightham, Kent, is believed to have been occupied by the Mousterian people before the onset of the Last Glaciation of the Ice Age, c. 80,000 B.C.

Ireland The carbon dating of the earliest known house in Ireland at Ballynagilly, County Tyrone was announced in 1971 to be 3795 B.C. ± 90. It is made of wood.

1. BUILDINGS FOR WORKING

LARGEST BUILDINGS

Commercial The greatest ground area covered by any building in the world is that by the Autolite-Ford Parts Redistribution Center, Brownstown, Michigan, U.S.A. It encloses a floor area of 3,100,000 ft² or 71.16 acres *28,4 ha*. It was opened on 20 May 1971 and employs 1,400 people. The fire control system comprises 70 miles *112 km* of pipelines with 37,000 sprinklers.

120

The building with the largest cubic capacity in the world is the Boeing Company's main assembly plant at Everett, Washington State, U.S.A. completed in 1968 with a capacity of 200 million ft³ *5,6 million m³*.

Scientific The most capacious scientific building in the world is the Vehicle Assembly Building (VAB) at Complex 39, the selected site for the final assembly and launching of the Apollo moon spacecraft on the Saturn V rocket, at the John F. Kennedy Space Center (KSC) on Merritt Island, near Cape Kennedy (formerly Cape Canaveral), Florida, U.S.A. It is a steel-framed building measuring 716 ft *218 m* in length, 518 ft *158 m* in width and 525 ft *160 m* high. The building contains four bays, each with its own door 460 ft *140 m* high. Construction began in April 1963 by the Ursum Consortium. Its floor area is 343,500 ft² (7.87 acres [*3,18 ha*]) and its capacity is 129,482,000 ft³ *3 666 500 m³*. The building was "topped out" on 14 April 1965 at a cost of $108,700,000 (*then £38,8 million*).

Admini- The largest ground area covered by any office building
strative is that of the Pentagon, in Arlington County, Virginia, U.S.A. Built to house the U.S. Defense Department's offices, it was completed on 15 Jan. 1943 and cost an estimated $83,000,000 (*now £34,583,000*). Each of the outermost sides of the Pentagon is 921 ft *281 m* long and the perimeter of the building is about 1,500 yds *1 370 m*. The five storeys of the building enclose a floor area of 6,500,000 ft² *604 000 m²*. During the day 29,000 people work in the building. The telephone system of the building has over 44,000 telephones connected by 160,000 miles *257 500 km* of cable and its 220 staff handle 280,000 calls a day. Two restaurants, six cafeterias and ten snackbars and a staff of 675 form the catering department of the building. The corridors measure 17 miles *27 km* in length and there are 7,748 windows to be cleaned.

Office The largest office buildings in the world are The World Trade Center in New York City, U.S.A. with a total of 4,370,000 ft² (100.32 acres [*40,6 ha*]) of rentable space in each of the twin towers (see page 9).

Single Office The largest single office in the United Kingdom is that
Largest of the West Midlands Gas Board at Solihull, Warwick-
in U.K. shire, built by Spooners (Hull) Ltd. in 1962. It now measures 753 ft by 160 ft *230 by 49 m* (2.77 acres

[*1,12 ha*]) in one open plan room accommodating 2,170 clerical and managerial workers.

Britain The largest building in Britain is the Ford Parts Centre at Daventry, Northamptonshire, which measures 1,978 × 780 ft *602 × 219 m* and 1.6 million ft² or 36.7 acres *14,86 ha*. It was opened on 6 Sept. 1972 at a cost of nearly £8 million. It employs 1,600 people and is fitted with 14,000 fluorescent lights.

TALLEST BUILDINGS

World The tallest inhabited building in the world is the Sears Tower, the national headquarters of Sears Roebuck & Co. in Wacker Drive, Chicago, Illinois with 109 storeys rising to 1,454 ft *443 m* and due for completion in 1974. Its gross area is 4,400,000 ft² (101.0 acres [*40,8 ha*]). It was "topped out" on 4 May 1973 (see page 9). It surpassed the World Trade Center in New York City in height at 2.35 p.m. on 6 March 1973 with the first steel column reaching to the 104th storey. The addition of two T.V. antennae will bring the total height to 1,800 ft *548,64 m*.

Most storeys The world Trade Center (see above) has 110 storeys—eight more than the Empire State Building. The projects for the 1,300 ft *396 m* Schaumburg Planet Corporation Building with a 250 ft *76 m* antenna and the 1,610 ft *490 m* Barrington Space Needle, Barrington, Illinois, call for 113 and 120 storeys respectively.

United Kingdom The tallest office block in Britain will be The National Westminster tower block in Bishopsgate, City of London due for completion in 1976. It will have 49 storeys and 3 basement levels and will reach a height of 600 ft 4 in *183 m*. The rentable floor area will be 636,373 ft² *59 121 m²*.

HABITATIONS

Greatest altitude The highest inhabited buildings in the world are those in the Chilean sulphur-mining village of Aucanquilca, at an altitude of 17,500 ft *5 334 m* above Amincha (see also Chapter 11). During the 1960–61 Himalayan High Altitude Expedition, the "silver hut", a prefabricated laboratory, was inhabited for four months in the Ming Bo Valley at 18,765 ft *5 720 m*. In April 1961, however, a 3-room dwelling was discovered at 21,650 ft *6 600 m* on Cerro Llullaillaco (22,058 ft [*6 723 m*]), on the Argentine-Chile border, believed to date from the late pre-Columbian period *c.* 1480.

Northernmost The most northerly habitation in the world is the Danish scientific station set up in 1952 in Pearyland, northern Greenland, over 900 miles *1 450 km* north of the Arctic Circle. Eskimo hearths dated to before 1000 B.C. were discovered in Pearyland in 1969. The U.S.S.R. and the United States have maintained research stations on ice floes in the Arctic. The U.S.S.R.'s "North Pole 15" which drifted 1,250 miles *2 000 km* passed within 1¼ miles *2,8 km* of the North Pole in December 1967.

Southernmost The most southerly permanent human habitation is the United States' Scott–Amundsen I.G.Y. (International Geophysical Year) base 800 yds *730 m* from the South Pole.

EMBASSIES

Largest The largest embassy in the world is the U.S.S.R embassy on Bei Xiao Jie, Peking, China, in the northeastern corner of the Northern walled city. The whole 45 acre *18,2 ha* area of the old Orthodox Church mission (established 1728), now known as the *Bei guan*, was handed over to the U.S.S.R. in 1949. The largest in Great Britain is the United States of America Embassy in Grosvenor Square, London. The Chancery Building, completed in 1960, alone has 600 rooms for a staff of 700, on seven floors with a usable floor area of 255,000 ft² (5.85 acres [*2,37 ha*]).

PLANTS

Atomic The largest atomic plant in the world is the Savannah River Project, near Aiken, South Carolina, U.S.A., extending 27 miles *43 km* along the river and over a total area of 315 miles² *816 km²*. The plant, comprising 280 permanent buildings, cost $1,400 million (£583 million). Construction was started in February 1951 and by September 1952 the labour force had reached 38,500. The present operating strength is 8,500.

Underground The world's largest underground factory was the Mittelwerk Factory, near Nordhausen in the Kohnstein Hills, south of the Harz Mountains, Germany. It was built with concentration camp labour during World War II and had a floor area of 1,270,000 ft² *118 000 m²* and an output of 900 V-2 rockets per month.

Tallest chimneys The world's tallest chimney is the $5.5 million International Nickel Company's stack 1,250 ft 9 in *381,23 m* tall at Copper Cliff, Sudbury, Ontario, Canada,

The Ford Autolite Building in Brownstown Township, Detroit, Michigan, which is the world's largest commercial building, covering an area of 71.16 acres *28.4 ha*

completed in 1970. It was built by the M. W. Kellogg Company and the diameter tapers from 116.4 ft *35,5 m* at the base to 51.8 ft *15,8 m* at the top. It weighs 38,390 tons *39 006 tonnes* and became operational in 1971. The tallest chimney in Great Britain is one of 850 ft *259 m* at Drax Power Station, Yorkshire, begun in 1966 and topped out on 16 May 1969. It was built by Holst & Co. Ltd. of Watford, Hertfordshire.

Cooling towers The largest cooling tower in the world is that at the Columbia River Atomic Power Station, near Ranier, Oregon, U.S.A. standing 499 ft *152 m* and completed in 1972 at a cost of $7.8 million. The largest in the United Kingdom are the Ferrybridge "C" power station, Yorkshire, type measuring 375 ft *114 m* tall and 300 ft *91 m* across the base.

LARGEST HANGARS

World The world's largest hangar is the Goodyear Airship hangar at Akron, Ohio, U.S.A. which measures 1,175 ft *358 m* long, 325 ft *99 m* wide and 200 ft *61 m* high. It covers 364,000 ft^2 (8.35 acres *[3,38 ha]*) and has a capacity of 55,000,000 ft^3 *1,6 million m^3*. The world's largest single fixed-wing aircraft hangar is the Lockheed-Georgia engineering test center at Marietta, Georgia measuring 630 ft by 480 ft *192 by 146 m* (6.94 acres *[2,81 ha]*) completed in 1967. The maintenance hangar at Frankfurt/Main Airport, West Germany has a slightly lesser area but a frontage of 902 ft *275 m*.

The Goodyear Airship inside the world's largest hangar at Akron, Ohio

The largest group of hangars in the world is at the U.S. Air Force Base near San Antonio, Texas, U.S.A. These, including covered maintenance bays, cover 23 acres *9,3 ha*.

United Kingdom The largest hangar building in the United Kingdom is the Britannia Assembly Hall at the former Bristol Aeroplane Company's works at Filton, Bristol, now part of the British Aircraft Corporation. The overall width of the Hall is 1,054 ft *321 m* and the overall depth of the centre bay is 420 ft *128 m*. It encloses a floor area of 7½ acres *3,0 ha*. The cubic capacity of the Hall is 33,000,000 ft^3 *934 000 m^3*. The building was begun in April 1946 and completed by September 1949.

Largest Fair Hall The largest fair hall in the world is that in Hanover, West Germany completed on 1 Apr. 1970 at a cost of 55 million DMk (£6½ *million*) with dimensions of 1,180 ft by 885 ft *360 by 270 m* and a floor area of 877,500 ft^2 *81 500 m^2*.

122

GRAIN ELEVATOR

The world's largest single-unit grain elevator is that operated by the C-G-F-Grain Company at Wichita, Kansas, U.S.A. Consisting of a triple row of storage tanks, 123 on each side of the central loading tower or "head house", the unit is 2,717 ft *828 m* long and 100 ft *30 m* wide. Each tank is 120 ft *37 m* high, with an inside diameter of 30 ft *9 m* giving a total storage capacity of 20,000,000 bushels *7,3 million hl* of wheat The largest collection of elevators in the world is at Thunder Bay, Ontario, Canada, on Lake Superior with a total capacity of 100 million bushels *36 million hl*.

GARAGES

Largest The largest garage in Britain is that completed in September 1961 for the Austin Motor Works at Longbridge, near Birmingham. It has nine storeys and cost £500,000. It has a capacity of 3,300 cars. The United Kingdom's largest underground garage is that for the Victoria Centre, Nottingham opened in June 1972 which has a capacity of 1,650 cars. The East corridor to Marble Arch tube station from the Park Lane Garage (Normand's Ltd) opened on 15 Oct. 1962 is 534 yds *488 m*.

Private The largest private garage ever built was one for 100 cars at the Long Island, New York mansion of William Kissam Vanderbilt (1849–1920).

Filling station The largest filling station of 36,000 in the United Kingdom is the Esso service area on the M4 at Leigh Delamere, Wiltshire, opened on 3 Jan. 1972. It has 48 petrol and diesel pumps and extends over 43 acres *17,4 ha*. It cost £650,000, has a staff of 280 and can service 2 million vehicles a year.

SEWAGE WORKS

Largest World The largest single full treatment sewage works in the world is the West-Southwest Treatment Plant, opened in 1940 on a site of 501 acres *203 ha* in Chicago, Illinois, U.S.A. It serves an area containing 2,940,000 people. It treated an average of 685,000,000 gal *3 114 million litres* of wastes per day in 1971. The capacity of its sedimentation and aeration tanks is 1,125,000 m^3 *1.4 million yds^3*.

United Kingdom The largest full treatment works in Britain and probably in Europe are the G.L.C. Crossness Plant with a tank capacity of 338,000 m^3 *12 million ft^3*, a resident population of 1,600,000 and an average daily flow of 103 million Imperial gal *468 million litres*. This will be overtaken in Sept. 1973 by the G.L.C. Beckton Works which when extended will serve a 2,966,000 population and handle a daily flow of 207 million gal *941 million litres* in a tank capacity of 757,000 ft^3 *21 400 m^3*.

Glasshouse The largest glasshouse in the United Kingdom is one 826 ft long and 348 ft *252 by 106 m* wide, covering 6.5 acres *2.6 ha* at Brough, East Yorkshire, completed in 1971. A total of 420 tons/*tonnes* of glass was used in glazing it.

2. BUILDINGS FOR LIVING

WOODEN BUILDINGS

Oldest The oldest wooden building in the world is the Temple of Horyu (Horyu-ji), built at Nara, Japan, in A.D. 708–715. The largest wooden building in the world, the nearby Daibutsuden, built in 1704–11, measures 285.4 ft long, 167.3 ft wide and 153.3 ft tall *87 × 51 × 46,75 m*.

Largest The municipal building occupied by the Department of Education in Wellington, New Zealand built in 1876 has the largest floor area of any wooden building with 101,300 ft^2 *9 400 m^2*.

CASTLES

Earliest
World Castles in the sense of unfortified manor houses existed in all the great early civilizations, including that of ancient Egypt from 3,000 B.C. Fortified castles in the more accepted sense only existed much later. The oldest in the world is that at Gomdan, in the Yemen, which originally had 20 storeys and dates from before A.D. 100.

British Isles The oldest stone castle extant in Great Britain is Richmond Castle, Yorkshire, built in *c.* 1075. Iron Age relics from the first century B.C. or A.D. have been found in the lower levels of the Dover Castle site.

Ireland The oldest Irish castle is Ferrycarrig near Wexford dating from *c.* 1180. The oldest castle in Northern Ireland is Carrickfergus Castle, County Antrim, which dates from before 1210.

Largest
United Kingdom and Ireland The largest castle in the British Isles and the largest inhabited castle in the world is the Royal residence of Windsor Castle at New Windsor, Berkshire. It is primarily of 12th century construction and is in the form of a parallelogram 1,890 ft by 540 ft *576 by 164 m.* The overall dimensions of Carisbrooke Castle (450 ft by 360 ft [*110 by 137 m*]), Isle of Wight, if its earthworks are included, are 1,350 ft by *825 ft 411 by 251 m.* The largest castle in Scotland was the unfinished Doune Castle, Perthshire, built *c.* 1425. The most capacious of all Irish castles is Carrickfergus (see above) in Antrim but that with the most extensive fortifications is Trim Castle, County Meath, built in *c.* 1205 with a curtain wall 485 yds *443 m* long.

Forts The largest ancient citadel in the world is the Qila (Citadel) at Halab (Aleppo) in Syria. It is oval in shape and has a surrounding wall 1,230 ft long and 777 ft wide *375 × 237 m.* It dates, in its present form, from the Humanid dynasty of the 10th century A.D. Fort George, Ardersier, Inverness-shire, built in 1748–1769 measures 2,100 ft *640 m* in length and has an average width of 620 ft *189 m.* The total site covers 42½ acres *17,2 ha.*

Thickest walls The most massive keep in the world was that belonging to the 13-century château at Coucy-le-Château-Auffrique, in the Department of L'Aisne, France. It was 177 ft *54 m* high, 318 ft *97 m* in circumference and had walls over 22½ ft *7 m* in thickness. It was levelled to its foundations by the Germans in 1917. The walls of Babylon north of Al Hillah, Iraq, built in 600 B.C., were up to 85 ft *26 m* in thickness. The walls of part of Dover Castle, Kent, measure 20 ft *6 m* in thickness. The largest Norman keep in Britain is that of Colchester Castle measuring 152½ ft *46 m* by 111½ ft *34 m.*

PALACES

Largest
World The largest palace in the world is the Imperial Palace (*Gu gong*) in the centre of Peking (*Bei jing*, the northern capital), China, which covers a rectangle 1,050 yds by 820 yds *960 by 750 m* an area of 177.9 acres *72 ha.* The outline survives from the construction of the third Ming Emperor Yong le of 1307–20, but due to constant re-arrangements most of the intra-mural buildings are 18th century. These consist of 5 halls and 17 palaces of which the last occupied by the last Empress was the Palace of Accumulated Elegance (*Chu xia gong*) until 1924.

Residential The largest residential palace in the world is the Vatican Palace, in the Vatican City, an enclave in Rome, Italy. Covering an area of 13½ acres *5,5 ha* it has 1,400 rooms, chapels and halls, of which the oldest date from the 15th century.

United Kingdom The largest palace in the United Kingdom in Royal use is Buckingham Palace, London, so named after its site, bought in 1703 by John Sheffield, the 1st Duke

Carrickfergus Castle, County Antrim, Northern Ireland's oldest castle, which is more than 700 years old

of Buckingham and Normanby (1648–1721). Buckingham House was reconstructed in the Palladian style between 1835 and 1836, following the design of John Nash (1752–1835). The 610 ft *186 m*-long East Front was built in 1846 and refaced in 1912. The Palace, which stands in 39 acres *15,8 ha* of garden, has 600 rooms including a ballroom 111 ft *34 m* long.

The largest ever Royal palace has been Hampton Court Palace, Greater London, acquired by Henry VIII from Cardinal Wolsey in 1525 and greatly enlarged by the King and later by William III, Anne and George I, whose son George II was its last resident monarch. It covers 4 acres *1,6 ha* of a 669 acre *270,7 ha* site.

Largest
moat The world's largest moats are those which surround the Imperial Palace in Peking (see above). From plans drawn by French sources it appears to measure 54 yds *49 m* wide and have a total length of 3,600 yds *3 290 m.*

FLATS

Largest The largest block of private flats in Britain is Dolphin Square, London, covering a site of 7½ acres *3 ha.* The building occupies the four sides of a square enclosing gardens of about three acres *1,2 ha.* Dolphin Square contains 1,220 separate and self-contained flats, an underground garage for 300 cars with filling and service station, a swimming pool, eight squash courts, a tennis court and an indoor shopping centre. It cost £1,750,000 to build in 1936 but was sold to Westminster City Council for £4,500,000 in January 1963. Its nine storeys house 3,000 people.

The Hyde Park development in Sheffield, Yorkshire, comprises 1,322 dwellings and an estimated population of 4,675 persons. It was built between 1959 and 1966.

Tallest
World The tallest block of flats in the world are Lake Point Towers of 70 storeys, and 645 ft *197 m* in Chicago, Illinois, U.S.A.

Britain The tallest residential blocks in the United Kingdom are the two tower blocks in the Barbican in the City of London, E.C.2, which have between 39 and 41 levels of flats and rise to a height of 417 ft *127 m* above the street. The first tower was "topped out" in May 1971.

HOTELS

Largest
World The hotel with most rooms in the world is the 12 storey Hotel Rossiya in Moscow, U.S.S.R., with 3,200 rooms providing accommodation for 5,500 guests. It

would thus require more than 8½ years to spend one night in each room. In addition there is a 23 storey "Presidential" tower in the central courtyard. The hotel employs about 3,000 people, and has 93 lifts. The ballroom is reputed to be the world's largest. Muscovites are not permitted as residents while foreigners are charged 16 times more than the very low rate charged to U.S.S.R officials.

The largest commercial hotel building in the world, is the Waldorf Astoria, on Park Avenue, New York City, N.Y., U.S.A. It occupies a complete block of 81,337 ft² (1.87 acres [0,75 ha]) and reaches a maximum height of 625 ft 7 in 191 m. The Waldorf Astoria has 47 storeys and 1,900 guest rooms and maintains the largest hotel radio receiving system in the world. The Waldorf can accommodate 10,000 people at one time and has a staff of 1,700. The restaurants have catered for parties up to 6,000 at a time. The coffee-makers' daily output reaches 1,000 gal 4 546 litres. The electricity bill is about $360,000 (£150,000) each year. The hotel has housed 6 Heads of States simultaneously and has both a resident gynaecologist and mortician.

United The greatest capacity of any hotel in the United
Kingdom Kingdom is that of the Regent Palace Hotel, Piccadilly Circus, London (opened on 20 May 1915). It has 1,140 rooms accommodating 1,670 guests. The total staff numbers 1,200. The largest hotel is the Grosvenor House Hotel, Park Lane, London, which was opened in 1929. It is of 8 storeys covering 2½ acres 1 ha and caters for more than 100,000 visitors per year in 470 rooms. The Great Room is the largest hotel room in Great Britain measuring 181 ft by 131 ft 55 by 40 m with a height of 23 ft 7 m. Banquets for 1,500 are frequently handled.

Tallest The world's tallest hotel is the 34-storey Ukrania in Moscow, U.S.S.R, which, including its tower, is 650 ft 198 m tall. The highest hotel rooms in the world are those on the topmost 50th storey of the 509 ft 155 m tall Americana Hotel, opened on 24 Sept. 1962 on 7th Avenue at 52nd Street, New York City, N.Y., U.S.A. On completion in October 1975 the 1,200 room $50 million Peachtree Plaza Hotel, Atlanta, Georgia, U.S.A. with 70 storeys rising to 700 ft 213 m will be the world's tallest. Britain's tallest hotel is the 33-storey London Hilton (328 ft [100 m]) tall, completed in Park Lane, London, W.1, in 1962. It was opened on 17 April 1963.

Most The world's costliest hotel accommodation is The
expensive Celestial Suite on the ninth floor of the Astroworld Hotel, Houston, Texas which is rented for $2,500 (£1,000) a day. It makes the official New York City Presidential Suite in the Waldorf Astoria at $450 (£180) a day seem positively middle-class.

The most expensive hotel suites in Britain are the luxury suites in the London Hilton, Park Lane, London, W.1. Some suites are 90 guineas (£94.50) per night in 1973.

SPAS
The largest spa in the world measured by number of available hotel rooms is Vichy, Allier, France, with 14,000 rooms. Spas are named after the watering place in the Liège province of Belgium where hydropathy was developed from 1626. The highest French spa is Baréges, Hautes-Pyrénées, at 4,068 ft 1 240 m above sea level.

Barracks The oldest purpose built barracks in the world are believed to be Collins Barracks, formerly the Royal Barracks, Dublin, Ireland completed in 1704 and still in use.

HOUSING
Largest The largest housing estate in the United Kingdom is
estate the 1,670-acre 675 ha Becontree Estate, on a site of

3,000 acres 1 214 ha in Barking and Redbridge, Greater London, built between 1921 and 1929. The total number of homes is 26,822, with an estimated population of nearly 90,000.

New towns Of the 23 new towns being built in Great Britain that with the largest eventual planned population will be Milton Keynes, Buckinghamshire, with 250,000 by 1992.

Largest The largest private house in the world is the 250-room
house Biltmore House in Asheville, North Carolina, U.S.A.
World It is owned by George and William Cecil, grandsons of George Washington Vanderbilt II (1862–1914). The house was built between 1890 and 1895 in an estate of 119,000 acres 48 160 ha, at a cost of $4,100,000 (now (£1,708,333) and now valued at $55,000,000 with 12,000 acres 4 856 ha. The most expensive private house ever built is La Cuesta Encunada at San Simeon, California, U.S.A. It was built in 1922–39 for William Randolph Hearst (1863–1951), at a total cost of more than $30,000,000 (then £6,120,000). It has more than 100 rooms, a 104 ft 32 m long heated swimming pool, an 83 ft 25 m long assembly hall and a garage for 25 limousines. The house required 60 servants to maintain it.

United The largest house in the United Kingdom is Went-
Kingdom worth Woodhouse, near Rotherham, Yorkshire, formerly the seat of the Earls Fitzwilliam. The main part of the house, built over 300 years ago, has more than 240 rooms with over 1,000 windows, and its principal façade is 600 ft 183 m long. The Royal residence, Sandringham House, Norfolk, has been reported to have 365 rooms. The largest house in Ireland is Castletown in County Kildare, formerly owned by Lord Carew. Scotland's largest house is Hopetoun House, West Lothian, built between 1696 and 1756 with a west façade 675 ft 206 m long.

Stately The most visited stately home, for which figures are
home most published in the United Kingdom, is Beaulieu, Hamp-
visited shire, owned by Lord Montagu of Beaulieu with 630,212 visitors in 1972. The figures for Woburn Abbey, Bedfordshire, owned by the Duke of Bedford, have not been published sinec 1963 but reached 470,000 as early as 1961.

Smallest The smallest house in Britain is the 19th century fisherman's cottage on Conway Quay, Caernarvonshire, North Wales. It has a 72 in 182 cm frontage, is 122 in 315 cm high and has two tiny rooms and a staircase.

Most The most expensive private house in Britain is one
expensive overlooking Hampstead Heath in London bought by Mr Ravi Tikkoo (b. 1933) former Sub-Lieutenant in the Indian Navy now owner of a fleet of the largest tankers, on 1 May 1973 for £500,000. On 4 May 1973 the corner house on Belgrave Square and Belgrave Mews South, London was leased for 74 years by the Grosvenor Estates for a reported £500,000.

3. BUILDINGS FOR ENTERTAINMENT

STADIUMS
Largest The world's largest stadium is the Strahov Stadium in
World Praha (Prague), Czechoslovakia. It was completed in 1934 and can accommodate 240,000 spectators for mass displays of up to 40,000 Sokol gymnasts.

Football The largest football stadium in the world is the Maracaña Municipal Stadium in Rio de Janeiro, Brazil, where the football ground has a normal capacity of 205,000, of whom 155,000 may be seated. A crowd of 199,854 was accommodated for the World Cup final between Brazil and Uruguay on 16 July 1950. A dry moat, 7 ft 2,10 m wide and more than 5 ft 1,5 m deep, protects players from spectators and *vice*

Britain's most expensive house, for which Mr. Ravi Tikoo paid £500,000 in May 1973

versa. Britain's most capacious football stadium is Hampden Park, Glasgow opened on 31 Oct. 1903 and once surveyed to accommodate 184,000 compared with the present licensed limit of 135,000 (see also below).

Covered The largest covered stadium in the world is the Empire Stadium, Wembley, London, opened in April 1923. It was the scene of the 1948 Olympic Games and the final of the 1966 World Cup. In 1962–63 the capacity under cover was increased to 100,000, of whom 45,000 may be seated. The original cost was £1,250,000. The Azteca Stadium, Mexico City, Mexico, opened in 1968, has a capacity of 107,000 of whom nearly all are under cover.

Roofed The transparent acryl glass "tent" roof over the Munich Olympic Stadium, West Germany measures 914,940 ft² (21.0 acres [*8,5 ha*]) in area resting on a steel net supported by masts.

Indoor The world's largest completed indoor stadium is the Harris County Sports Stadium, or Astrodome, in Houston, Texas, U.S.A. opened in April 1965. It has a capacity of 45,000 for baseball and 66,000 (maximum) for boxing. The domed stadium covers 9½ acres *3,8 ha* and is so large that an 18-storey building could be built under the roof (208 ft [*63 m*] high). The total cost was $45,350,000. The architects of the $151 million 280 ft *85 m* tall Superdome due to be completed in New Orleans, Louisiana by mid-1974 say that the Astrodome could fit comfortably inside it. Its capacity will be 103,402.

United Kingdom The highest capacity stadium in the United Kingdom is that at Hampden Park, Glasgow, which accommodated a football crowd of 149,547 on 17 April 1937.

Largest ballroom The largest ballroom in the United Kingdom is the Orchid Ballroom, Purley, Surrey. The room is over 200 ft *60 m* long and 117 ft *35,7 m* wide, and has a total floor area of 23,320 ft² *2 170 m²*. When laid out for dance championships, the floor of the Earl's Court Exhibition Hall is 256 ft *78 m* in length. The Empress Ballroom, Blackpool, Lancashire, when used for dances, can accommodate 4,500 couples.

Amusement resort The world's largest amusement resort is Disney World in 27,443 acres *11 105 ha* of Orange and Osceola counties, 20 miles *32 km* south west of Orlando in central Florida. It was opened on 1 Oct. 1971. This $400 million investment attracted 10,700,000 visitors in its first year.

Holiday Camps The largest of the 8 major holiday camps in Britain is that at Filey, Yorkshire opened by Butlins Ltd. It extends over 500 acres *200 ha* and can house 11,000 residents.

RESTAURANTS

Highest The highest restaurant in Great Britain is the Ptarmigan Observation Restaurant at 3,650 ft *1 112 m* above sea-level on Cairngorm (4,084 ft [*1 244 m*]) near Aviemore, Inverness-shire, Scotland.

KITCHEN

Largest The largest kitchen ever set up has been the Indian Government field kitchen set up in April 1973 at Ahmadnagar, Maharashtra in the famine area which daily provides 1.2 million subsistence meals.

NIGHT CLUBS

Oldest The oldest night club (*boîte de nuit*) is "Le Bal des Anglais" at 6 Rue des Anglais, Paris 5*me*, France. It was founded in 1843.

Largest The largest night club in the world is that in the Imperial Room of the Concord Hotel in the Catskill Mountains, New York State, U.S.A., with a capacity of 3,000 patrons. In the more classical sense the largest night club in the world is "The Mikado" in the Akasaka district of Tōkyō, Japan, with a seating capacity of 2,000. It is "manned" by 1,250 hostesses, some of whom earn an estimated £4,800 per annum. A binocular is essential to an appreciation of the floor show.

Loftiest The highest night club will be that on the 52nd storey of the Antigone Building, now under construction, in Montparnasse, Paris, at 187 m *613.5 ft* above street level.

Lowest The lowest night club is the "Minus 206" in Tiberias, Israel, on the shores of the Sea of Galilee. It is 206 m *676 ft* below sea-level. An alternative candidate is "Outer Limits", opposite the Cow Palace, San Francisco, California which was raided for the 151st time on 1 Aug. 1971. It has been called both "The Most Busted Joint" and "The Slowest to Get the Message".

PLEASURE BEACH

Largest The largest pleasure beach in the world is Virginia Beach, Virginia, U.S.A. It has 28 miles *45 km* of beach front on the Atlantic and 10 miles *16 km* of estuary frontage. The area embraces 255 miles² *660 km²* and 134 hotels and motels.

Longest pleasure pier The longest pleasure pier in the world is Southend Pier at Southend-on-Sea in Essex. It is 1.33 miles *2,14 km* in length. It was built in 1889, with final extensions made in 1929. It is decorated with more than 75,000 lamps.

FAIRS

Earliest The earliest major international fair was the Great Exhibition of 1851 in the Crystal Palace, Hyde Park, London which in 141 days attracted 6,039,195 admissions.

Largest The largest fair ever held was the New York World's Fair, covering 1,216½ acres *492 ha* of Flushing Meadow Park, Queens Borough, Long Island, New York, U.S.A. The fair was open at times between 20 April 1939 and 21 Oct. 1940 and there were 25,817,265 admissions and an attendance of 51,607,037 for the 1964–65 Fair there.

Record attendance The record attendance for any fair was 65,000,000 for Expo 70 held on an 815-acre *330 ha* site at Osaka, Japan from March to 13 Sept. 1970. It made a profit of more than £11,000,000.

Big Wheel The original Ferris Wheel, named after its constructor, George W. Ferris (1859–96), was erected in 1893 at the Midway, Chicago, Illinois, U.S.A., at a cost of $300,000 (*now £125,000*). The wheel was 250 ft *76 m* in diameter, 790 ft *240 m* in circumference, weighed 1,070 tons *1 087 tonnes* and carried 36 cars each seating 40 people, making a total of 1,440 passengers. The structure was removed in 1904 to St. Louis, Missouri, and was eventually sold as scrap for $1,800 (*now £750*). In 1897 a Ferris Wheel with a diameter of 300 ft *91 m* was erected for the Earls Court Exhibition, London. It had ten 1st-class and 30 2nd-class cars. The largest wheel now operating is the Riesenrad in the Prater Park, Vienna, Austria with a diameter of 197 ft *60 m*. It was built by the British engineer Walter Basset in 1896 and carried 15 million people in its first 75 years to 13 June 1971.

Fastest switchback The world's fastest gravity switchback has been the "Bobs" in the Belle Vue Amusement Park, Manchester, Lancashire. The cars attained a peak speed of 61 m.p.h. *98 km/h*. The track was 862 yds 2 in *788 m* long with a maximum height of 76 ft *23 m*. It had been imported from the U.S.A. in 1929 and now has reportedly been re-imported.

PUBLIC HOUSES

Largest World The largest beer-selling establishment in the world is the Mathäser, Bayerstrasse 5, München (Munich), West Germany, where the daily sale reaches 84,470 pts *48 000 litres*. It was established in 1829, was demolished in World War II and re-built by 1955 and now seats 5,500 people. The through-put at the Dube beer halls in the Bantu township of Soweto, Johannesburg, South Africa may, however, be higher on some Saturdays when the average consumption of 6,000 gal (48,000 pts [*27 280 litres*]) is far exceeded.

United Kingdom The largest public house in the United Kingdom is The Swan at Yardley, Birmingham. It has eight bars with a total drinking area of 13,852 ft² *1 287 m²* with 58 taps and 2 miles *3,2 km* of piping. The sale of beer is equivalent to 31,000 bottles per week. The pub can hold well over 1,000 customers and 320 for banqueting. The permanent staff totals 60 with seven resident. The Swan is owned by Allied Breweries and administered by Ansells Limited.

Smallest Excluding "lock-ups" the smallest pub in the United Kingdom is "The Nutshell", Bury St. Edmunds,

Suffolk with maximum dimensions of 15 ft 10 in by 7 ft 6 in *4,82 × 2,28 m*. The bar in the Spread Eagle, Crewe, Cheshire measures 5 ft 3 in × 3 ft 4 in *1,60 × 1,01 m*.

Highest The highest public house in the United Kingdom is the Tan Hill Inn in Yorkshire. It is 1,732 ft *528 m* above sea-level, on the moorland road between Reeth in Yorkshire and Brough in Westmorland. The White Lady Restaurant, 2,550 ft *777 m* up on Cairngorm (4,084 ft [*1 244 m*]) near Aviemore, Inverness-shire, Scotland, is the highest licensed restaurant.

Oldest There are various claimants to the title of the United Kingdom's oldest inn. The foremost claimants include "The Angel and Royal" (*c*. 1450) at Grantham, Lincolnshire, which has cellar masonry dated 1213; the "George" (early 15th century) at Norton St. Philip, Somerset; the oldest Welsh inn the Skirrid Mountain Inn, Llanvihangel Crucorney, Monmouthshire recorded in 1110; "The Trip to Jerusalem" in Nottingham, with foundations believed to date back to 1070; "The Fighting Cocks", St. Albans, Hertfordshire (an 11th century structure on an 8th century site) and the "Godbegot", Winchester, Hampshire dating to 1002. An origin as early as A.D. 560 has been claimed for "Ye Olde Ferry Boat Inn" at Holywell, Huntingdonshire. There is some evidence that it antedates the local church, built in 980, but the earliest documents are not dated earlier than 1100. There is evidence that the "Bingley Arms", Bardsey, near Leeds, Yorkshire, restored and extended in 1738, existed as the "Priest's Inn" according to Bardsey Church records dated 905.

The Ferry Boat Inn, St. Ives, one of the claimants to the title of the United Kingdom's oldest inn

Longest name The English pub with the longest name was the 39 letter "The Thirteenth Mounted Cheshire Rifleman Inn" at Stalybridge, Cheshire. The word "Mounted" is now omitted making "The London, Chatham and Dover Railway Tavern" (37 letters), the champion.

Shortest name There are two public houses in the United Kingdom with a name of only two letters: the "C.B." Hotel Arkengarthdale, near Richmond, Yorkshire and The H.H. at Cheriton, Hampshire.

Commonest name The commonest pub name in Britain is "Crown", often coupled with the Rose, of which there are some 1,100 examples—more than the total of "Red Lions." of which there are over 900.

Most visits The man who visited most pubs in Britain is Jimmy Young G.M., B.E.M. of "Better Pubs", Crediton, Devon with more than 15,000. Mr Stanley House of Totterdown, Bristol has visited 2,401 pubs with different names by way of public transport only.

Major Civil Engineering Structures

Longest bars
World The longest permanent bar with beer pumps is that built in 1938 at the Working Men's Club, Mildura, Victoria, Australia. It has a counter 287 ft *87 m* in length, served by 32 pumps. Temporary bars have been erected of greater length. The Falstaff Brewing Corp. put up a temporary bar 336 ft 5 in *102 m* in length on Wharf St., St. Louis, Missouri, U.S.A., on 22 June 1970.

United Kingdom The longest bar in the United Kingdom with beer pumps is the French Bar (198 ft 5½ in [*60,5 m*]) at Butlin's Holiday Camp, Filey, Yorkshire. It has 20 beer pumps, 12 tills and stillage for 30 barrels, and is operated by 30 barmaids, 20 floor waiters and 20 other hands. The longest bar in a pub is the 45 ft *13,72 m* counter in Downham Tavern, Bromley, Kent. The Grand Stand Bar at Galway Racecourse, Ireland completed in 1955, measures 210 ft *64 m*.

Wine cellar The largest wine cellars in the world are at Paarl, those of the Ko-operative Wijnbouwers Vereeniging, known as K.W.V. near Cape Town, in the centre of the wine-growing district of South Africa. They cover an area of 25 acres *10 ha* and have a capacity of 30,000,000 gal *136 million litres*. The largest blending vats have a capacity of 45,700 gal *207 750 litres* and are 17 ft *5 m* high, with a diameter of 26 ft *8 m*.

Some visitors at the world's largest wine cellars, at Paarl, near Cape Town, South Africa

4. MAJOR CIVIL ENGINEERING STRUCTURES

TALLEST STRUCTURES

World
Completed The tallest structure in the world is a stayed television transmitting tower 2,063 ft *628 m* tall, between Fargo and Blanchard, North Dakota, U.S.A. It was built at a cost of about $500,000 (*£208,000*) for Channel 11 of KTHI-TV, owned by the Pembina Broadcasting Company of North Dakota, a subsidiary of the Polaris Corporation from Milwaukee, Wisconsin, U.S.A. The tower was erected in 30 days (2 Oct. to 1 Nov. 1963) by 11 men of the Kline Iron and Steel Company of Columbia, South Carolina, U.S.A., who designed and fabricated the tower. The cage elevator in the centre rises to 1,948 ft *593 m*. The tower is built to allow for a sway of up to 13.9 ft *4,2 m* in a wind gusting to 120 m.p.h. *193 km/h* and is so tall that anyone falling off the top would no longer be accelerating just before hitting the ground.

Uncompleted Work was begun in July 1970 on a tubular steel T.V. tower with 15 steel guy ropes near Plock, north-east Poland, which will rise to 2,100 ft *640 m*. The structure, designed by Jan Polak will weigh 650 tons/*660 tonnes* and is due for completion in December 1973.

TALLEST STRUCTURES IN THE WORLD—PROGRESSIVE RECORDS

Height in ft	m	Structure	Location	Material	Building or Completion Dates
204	62	Djoser step pyramid (earliest Pyramid)	Saqqâra, Egypt	Tura limestone	c.2650 B.C.
294	89	Pyramid of Meidun	Meidun, Egypt	Tura limestone	c.2600 B.C.
c.336	102	Snefru Bent pyramid	Dahshûr, Egypt	Tura limestone	c.2600 B.C.
342	104	Snefru North Stone pyramid	Dahshûr, Egypt	Tura limestone	c.2600 B.C.
480.9[1]	146,5	Great Pyramid of Cheops (Khufu)	El Gizeh, Egypt	Tura limestone	c.2580 B.C.
525[2]	160	Lincoln Cathedral, Central Tower	Lincoln, England	lead sheathed wood	c.1307–1548
489[3]	149	St. Paul's Cathedral	London, England	lead sheathed wood	1315–1561
465	141	Minster of Notre Dame	Strasbourg, France	Vosges sandstone	1420–1439
502[4]	153	St. Pierre de Beauvais	Beauvais, France	lead sheathed wood	–1568
475	144	St. Nicholas Church	Hamburg, Germany	stone and iron	1846–1847
485	147	Rouen Cathedral	Rouen, France	cast iron	1823–1876
513	156	Köln Cathedral	Cologne, West Germany	stone	–1880
555	169	Washington Memorial	Washington, D.C., U.S.A.	stone	1848–1884
985.9[5]	300,5	Eiffel Tower	Paris, France	iron	1887–1889
1,046	318	Chrysler Building	New York City, U.S.A.	steel and concrete	1929–1930
1,250[6]	381	Empire State Building	New York City, U.S.A.	steel and concrete	1929–1930
1,572	479	KWTV Television Mast	Oklahoma City, U.S.A.	steel	Nov. 1954
1,610[7]	490	KSWS Television Mast	Roswell, New Mexico, U.S.A.	steel	Dec. 1956
1,619	493	WGAN Television Mast	Portland Maine, U.S.A.	steel	Sept. 1959
1,676	510	KFVS Television Mast	Cape Girardeau, Missouri, U.S.A.	steel	June 1960
1,749	533	WTVM & WRBL TV Mast	Columbus, Georgia, U.S.A.	steel	May 1962
1,749	533	WBIR-TV Mast	Knoxville, Tennessee, U.S.A.	steel	Sept. 1963
2,063	628	KTHI-TV Mast	Fargo, North Dakota, U.S.A.	steel	Nov. 1963
c.2,100	640	Polish T.V. Service Tower	Plock, Poland	galvanised steel	1970–1973

1 Original height. With loss of pyramidion (topmost stone) height now 449 ft 6 in 137 m.
2 Fell in a storm.
3 Struck by lightning and destroyed 4 June 1561.
4 Fell April 1573, shortly after completion.
5 Original height. With addition of T.V. antenna in 1957, now 1,052 ft 4 in 320,75 m.

6 Original height. With addition of T.V. tower on 1 May 1951 now 1,472 ft 449 m. On 11 Oct. 1972 it was revealed that the top 15 storeys might be replaced by 33 to give the old champion 113 storeys and a height of 1,494 ft 455,37 m.
7 Fell in gale in 1960.

127

United Kingdom The tallest structure in the United Kingdom is the Independent Television Authority's mast at Belmont, north of Horncastle, Lincolnshire, completed in 1965 to a height of 1,265 ft *385 m* with 7 ft *2 m* added by meteorological equipment installed in September 1967. It serves Anglia T.V. and was severely threatened by the icing on 21 March 1969 which two days earlier felled the 1,265 ft *385 m* Emley Moore mast in Yorkshire, which was replaced in 1971 by the 1,080 ft *329 m* self-supporting concrete tower.

TALLEST TOWERS

World The tallest self-supporting tower (as opposed to a guyed mast) in the world is the 1,749 ft *533 m* tall tower at Ostankino, Greater Moscow, U.S.S.R., "topped out" in May 1967. It is of reinforced concrete construction and weighs over 22,000 tons *22 350 tonnes* A three-storey restaurant revolves at the 882 ft *269 m* level and there is a balcony at 1,050 ft *320 m*. In a high wind the T.V. antennae may sway up to 26 ft *8 m* but the restaurant only 3.14 in *7,98 cm*. The tower was designed by N. V. Nikitin. This will be surpassed in 1974 by a $21 million tower 1,805 ft *550,16 m* on the Waterfront, Toronto, Canada on which work was started on 12 Feb. 1973. A 360 seat restaurant will revolve at the 1,100 ft *335 m* level.

The tallest tower built before the era of television masts is the Eiffel Tower, in Paris, France, designed by Alexandre Gustav Eiffel (1832–1923) for the Paris exhibition and completed on 31 March 1889. It was 300,51 m *985 ft 11 in* tall, now extended by a T.V. antenna to 1,052 ft 4 in *320,75 m* and weighs 7,224 tons *7 340 tonnes*. The maximum sway in high winds is 5 in *11 cm*. The whole iron edifice which has 1,792 steps, took 2 years, 2 months and 2 days to build and cost 7,799,401 francs 31 centimes. The 352nd suicide committed from the tower had occurred by 1 Jan. 1970.

The architects André and Jan Polak put forward a design in February 1969 for a tower 2,378.6 ft *725 m* in height to be erected at La Défense in Paris.

United Kingdom The tallest self-supported tower in the United Kingdom is the 1,080 ft *329,18 m* tall Independent Broadcasting Authority transmitter at Emley Moor, near Huddersfield, Yorkshire, completed in September 1971. The structure which cost £900,000 has an enclosed room at the 865 ft *263,65 m* level and weighs with its foundations more than 15,000 tons/*tonnes*.

5. BRIDGES

OLDEST

World Arch construction was understood by the Sumerians as early as 3200 B.C. but the oldest surviving bridge in the world is the slab stone single arch bridge over the River Meles in Smyrna (now Izmir), Turkey, which dates from *c.* 850 B.C. The oldest iron bridge used for vehicular traffic is the Tickford Bridge over the River Lovat, Buckinghamshire built in 1810.

Britain The clapper bridges of Dartmoor and Exmoor (*e.g.* the Tarr Steps over the River Barle, Exmoor, Somerset) are thought to be of prehistoric types although none of the existing examples can be certainly dated. They are made of large slabs of stone placed over boulders. The Romans built stone bridges in England and remains of these have been found at Corbridge (Roman, Corstopitum), Northumberland dating to the 2nd century A.D.; Chester, Northumberland and Willowford, Cumberland. Remains of a very early wooden bridge have been found at Ardwinkle, Northamptonshire.

LONGEST

Cable suspension World The world's longest single span bridge is the Verrazano-Narrows Bridge stretching across the entrance to New York City harbour from Richmond, Staten Island to Brooklyn. Work on the $305,000,000 (*then £109 million*) project began on 13 Aug. 1959 and the bridge was opened to traffic on 21 Nov. 1964. It measures 6,690 ft *2 039 m* between anchorages and carries two decks, each of six lanes of traffic. The centre span is 4,260 ft *1 298 m* and the tops of the main towers (each 690 ft [*210 m*] tall) are 1⅝ in *4 cm* out of parallel, to allow for the curvature of of the Earth. The traffic in the first 12 months is 17,000,000 vehicles, and is rising towards 48,000,000 with the completion of the second deck. The bridge was designed by Othmar H. Ammann (1879–1965), a Swiss-born engineer.

The Mackinac Straits Bridge between Mackinaw City and St. Ignace, Michigan, U.S.A., is the longest suspension bridge in the world measured between anchorages (8,344 ft [*2 543 m*]) and has an overall length, including viaducts of the bridge proper measured between abutment bearings, of 19,205 ft 4 in *5 853,78 m*. It was opened in Nobember 1957 (dedicated 28 June 1958) at a cost of $100 million (*then £35,700,000*) and has a main span of 3,800 ft *1 158 m*.

Even longer main spans are planned for completion in 1977 across the Humber Estuary (4,626 ft [*1 410 m*]) costing £27.6 million, and one of even 9,000 ft *2 740 m* with piers 400 ft *122 m* deep, across the Messina Straits, Italy.

An artist's impression of the Humber Suspension Bridge, which will contain the world's longest bridge span of 4,626 ft *1410 m*

United Kingdom The longest span bridge in the United Kingdom is the Firth of Forth Road Bridge with a main channel span of 3,300 ft *1 005 m* and side spans of 1,340 ft *408 m* each, opened on 4 Sept. 1964. The main towers each stand 512 ft *156 m* high. It is the seventh longest span in the world and cost £11,000,000 including the viaducts but excluding the approach roads which cost £9 million.

Cantilever World The Quebec Bridge (Pont de Québec) over the St. Lawrence River in Canada has the longest cantilever truss span of any in the world—1,800 ft *548 m* between the piers and 3,239 ft *987 m* overall. It carries a railway

LONGEST BRIDGE SPANS IN THE WORLD—BY TYPE

Type	ft	m	Location	Completion Date
Cable Suspension	4,260	1 298,4	Verrazano-Narrows, New York, N.Y., U.S.A.	1964
Cantilever Truss	1,800	548,6	Quebec Railway, Quebec, Canada	1917
Steel Arch	1,652	503,6	Bayonne (Kill Van Kull), New York, N.Y., U.S.A.	1931
Covered Bridge	1,282	390,8	Hartland, New Brunswick, Canada	1899
Continuous Truss	1,232	375,5	Astoria, Columbia River, Oregon, U.S.A.	1966
Cable-Stayed	1,148	350,0	Duisburg-Nuenkamp, West Germany	1970
Chain Suspension	1,114	339,5	Florianópolis, Santa Catarina, Brazil	1926
Concrete Arch	1,000	304,8	Gladesville, Sydney, Australia	1964
Plate and Box Girder	984	300,0	Rio-Niterói, Rio de Janeiro, Brazil	1974
Stone Arch	295	89,9	Plauen, East Germany	1903

track and 2 carriageways. Begun in 1899, it was finally opened to traffic on 3 Dec. 1917 at a cost of 87 lives, and \$Can.22,500,000 (then £4,623,000).

United Kingdom The longest cantilever bridge in the United Kingdom is the Forth Bridge. Its two main spans are 1,710 ft *521 m* long. It carries a double railway track over the Firth of Forth 150 ft *45 m* above the water level. Work commenced in November 1882 and the first test trains crossed on 22 Jan. 1890 after an expenditure of £3 million. It was officially opened on 4 March 1890. Of the 4,500 workers who built it, 57 were killed in various accidents.

Longest steel arch *World* The longest steel arch bridge in the world is the Bayonne Bridge over the Kill Van Kull, which has connected Bayonne, New Jersey, to Staten Island New York, since its completion in November 1931. Its span is 1,652 ft 1 in *503 m*—25 in *63 cm* longer than the Sydney Harbour Bridge, Australia (see below).

United Kingdom The longest steel arch bridge in the United Kingdom is the Runcorn-Widnes bridge from Widnes, Lancashire, to Runcorn, Cheshire, opened on 21 July 1961. It has a span of 1,082 ft *329 m* and a total length including viaducts of 3,489 ft *1 063 m*.

Largest steel arch The largest steel arch bridge in the world is the Sydney Harbour Bridge in Sydney, New South Wales, Australia. Its main arch span is 1,650 ft *503 m* long and it carries two electric overhead railway tracks, eight lanes of roadway, a cycleway and a footway, 172 ft *52 m* above the waters of Sydney Harbour. It took eight years to build and was officially opened on 19 March 1932 at a cost of \$A9,500,000 (then £7,600,000). Its total length is 2¾ miles *4,42 km* including complex viaducts.

Floating bridge *Longest* The longest floating bridge in the world is the Second Lake Washington Bridge, Seattle, Washington State, U.S.A. completed in 1963. Its total length is 12,596 ft *3 839 m* and its floating section measures 7,518 ft *2 291 m* (1.42 miles [2,29 km]). It was built at a total cost of \$15,000,000 (£6,250,000) and completed in August 1963.

Railway bridge *Longest* The longest railway bridge in the world is the Huey P. Long Bridge, Metairie, Louisiana, U.S.A. with a railway section 22,996 ft *7 009 m* (4.35 miles [7 km]) long. It was completed on 16 Dec. 1935 with a longest span of 790 ft *240 m*. The longest railway bridge in Britain is the second Tay Bridge (11,653 ft [*3 552 m*]), joining Fife and Angus, opened on 20 June 1887. Of the 85 spans, 74 (length 10,289 ft [*3 136 m*]) are over the waterway.

HIGHEST

World The highest bridge in the world is the bridge over the Royal Gorge of the Arkansas River in Colorado, U.S.A. It is 1,053 ft *321 m* above the water level. It is a suspension bridge with a main span of 880 ft *268 m* and was constructed in 6 months, ending on 6 Dec. 1929. The highest railway bridge in the world is the single track span at Fades, outside Clermont-Ferrand,

France, It was built in 1901–09 with a span of 472 ft *143 m* and is 430 ft *131 m* above the River Sioule.

United Kingdom The highest railway bridge in the United Kingdom was the Crumlin Viaduct, Monmouthshire, completed in June 1857 to a height of 200 ft *60 m*.

WIDEST

The world's widest long-span bridge is the Sydney Harbour Bridge (160 ft [*48 m*] wide). The Crawford Street Bridge in Providence, Rhode Island, U.S.A., has a width of 1,147 ft *350 m*. The River Roch is bridged for a distance of 1,460 ft *445 m* where the culvert passes through the centre of Rochdale, Lancashire.

Deepest foundations The deepest foundations of any structure are those of the 3,323 ft *1 012 m* span Ponte de Salazar, which was opened on 6 Aug. 1966, at a cost of £30,000,000, across the Rio Tejo (the River Tagus), in Portugal. One of the 625 ft *190 m* tall towers extends 260 ft *79 m* down.

Longest Bridging The world's longest bridging is the second Lake Pontchartrain Causeway, completed on 23 March 1969, joining Lewisburg and Metairie, Louisiana, U.S.A. It has a length of 126,055 ft *38 421 m* (23.87 miles). It cost \$29,900,000 (£12.45 million) and is 228 ft *69 m* longer than the adjoining First Causeway completed in 1956. The longest railway viaduct in the world is the rock-filled Great Salt Lake Railroad Trestle, carrying the Southern Pacific Railroad 11.85 miles *19 km* across the Great Salt Lake, Utah, U.S.A. It was opened as a pile and trestle bridge on 8 March 1904, but converted to rock fill in 1955–60.

The longest stone arch bridging in the world is the 3,810 ft *1 161 m* long Rockville Bridge north of Harresburg, Pennsylvania, U.S.A., with 48 spans containing 196,000 tons/*tonnes* of stone and completed in 1901.

AQUEDUCTS

World *Longest* *Ancient* The greatest of ancient aqueducts was the Aqueduct of Carthage in Tunisia, which ran 141 km *87.6 miles* from the springs of Zaghouan to Djebel Djougar. It was built by the Romans during the reign of Publius Aelius Hadrianus (A.D. 117–138). By 1895, 344 arches still survived. Its original capacity has been calculated at 7,000,000 gal *31,8 million litres* per day. The triple-tiered aqueduct Pont du Gard, built in A.D. 19 near Nîmes, France, is 160 ft *48 m* high. The tallest of the 14 arches of Aguas Livres Aqueduct, built in Lisbon, Portugal, in 1748 is 213 ft 3 in *65 m*.

Modern The world's longest aqueduct, in the modern sense of a water conduit, is the Colorado River Aqueduct in south-eastern California, U.S.A. The whole system, complete with the aqueduct conduit, tunnels and syphons, is 242 miles *389 km* long and was completed in 1939. The California Aqueduct is 444 miles *714 km* long and was in use in 1973.

129

Pontcysyllte Aqueduct, Denbighshire, the United Kingdom's longest aqueduct

United Kingdom The longest aqueduct in the United Kingdom is the Pontcysyllte in Denbighshire, Wales, on the Frankton to Llantisilio branch of the Shropshire Union Canal. It is 1,007 ft *307 m* long, has 19 arches up to 121 ft *36 m* high and crosses the valley of the Dee. It was designed by Thomas Telford (1757–1834) of Scotland, and was opened for use in 1803.

6. CANALS

EARLIEST

World Relics of the oldest canals in the world, dated by archaeologists to 5000 B.C., were discovered near Mandali, Iraq early in 1968.

Britain The first canals in Britain were undoubtedly cut by the Romans. In the Midlands the 11 mile *17 km* long Fossdyke Canal between Lincoln and the River Trent at Torksey was built in about A.D. 65 and was scoured in 1122. Part of it is still in use today. Though Exeter Canal was cut as early as 1564–68, the first wholly artificial major navigation canal in the United Kingdom was the Bridgewater canal dug in 1759–61. It ran from Worsley to Manchester, Lancashire. Parts of the Sankey Canal from St. Helens to Widnes, Lancashire, were however, dug before the Bridgewater Canal.

LONGEST

World The longest canalized system in the world is the Volga-Baltic Canal opened in April 1965. It runs 1,850 miles *2 300 km* from Astrakhan up the Volga, *via* Kuybyshev, Gor'kiy and Lake Ladoga, to Leningrad, U.S.S.R. The longest canal of the ancient world has been the Grand Canal of China from Peking to Hangchou. It was begun in 540 B.C. and not completed until the 13th century by which time it extended for 1,107 miles *1 781 km*. Having been allowed by 1950 to silt up to the point that it was in no place more than 6 ft *1,8 m* deep, it is reported to have been reconstructed.

The Beloye More (White Sea) Baltic Canal from Belomorsk to Povenets, in the U.S.S.R., is 141 miles *227 km* long with 19 locks. It was completed with the use of forced labour in 1933 and cannot accommodate ships of more than 16 ft *5 m* in draught.

The world's longest big ship canal is the still inoperative (since June 1967) Suez Canal in the United Arab Republic, opened on 16 Nov. 1869. The canal was planned by the French diplomatist Count

Ferdinand de Lesseps (1805–94) and work began on 25 April 1859. It is 100.6 miles *161,9 km* in length from Port Said lighthouse to Suez Roads and 60 m *197 ft* wide. The work force was 8,213 men and 368 camels.

United Kingdom The longest inland waterway in the United Kingdom is the Grand Union Canal Main Line from Brentford Lock Junction, Middlesex, to Langley Mull, a total distance of 167⅜ miles *269 km*. The Grand Union System was originally 255 miles *410 km* long when nine canals, including the Grand Junction, were amalgamated in 1929. The voyage along the whole length of the Grand Union Canal, Main Line, would involve the negotiation of 169 locks.

Largest seaway The world's longest artificial seaway is the St. Lawrence Seaway (189 miles [*304 km*] long) along the New York State-Ontario border from Montreal to Lake Ontario, which enables 80 per cent of all ocean-going ships, and bulk carriers with a capacity of 26,000 tons *26 400 tonnes* to sail 2,342 miles *3 769 km* from the North Atlantic, up the St. Lawrence estuary and across the Great Lakes to Duluth, Minnesota, U.S.A., on Lake Superior (602 ft [*183 m*] above sea-level). The project cost $470,000,000 (*then £168 million*) and was opened on 25 April 1959.

Irrigation canal The longest irrigation canal in the world is the Karakumskiy Kanal, stretching 528 miles *850 km* from Haun-Khan to Ashkhabad, Turkmenistan, U.S.S.R. In Sept. 1971 the "navigable" length reached 280 miles *450 km*. The length of the £370 million project will reach 870 miles *1 400 km* by 1975.

LOCKS

Largest World The world's largest locking system is the Miraflores lock system in the Panama Canal, opened on 15 Aug 1914. The two lower locks are 1,050 ft *320 m* long, 110 ft *33 m* wide and have gates 82 ft *25 m* high, 65 ft *19 m* long and 7 ft *2 m* thick, with doors weighing 652 to 696 tons *662–707 tonnes* each. The largest liner ever to transit was S.S. *Bremen* (51,730 gross tons with a length of 899 ft *274 m*, a beam of 101.9 ft *31 m* and a draught of 48.2 ft *14,7 m*, on 15 Feb. 1939. The swimmer Albert H. Oshiver was charged a toll of 45 cents in Dec. 1962.

The world's largest single lock is that connecting the Schelde with the Kanaaldok system at Zandvliet, west of Antwerp, Belgium. It is 500 m *1,640 ft* long and 57 m *187 ft* wide and is an entrance to an impounded sheet of water 18 km *11.2 miles* long.

United Kingdom The largest lock on any canal system in the United Kingdom is the Eastham Large Lock, Eastham, Cheshire, on the Manchester Ship Canal. It can handle craft up to 600 ft *182 m* long and 80 ft *24 m* beam.

Deepest The world's deepest lock is the Wilson dam lock at Muscle Shoals, Alabama, U.S.A. on the Tennessee River completed in Nov. 1959. It can raise or lower barges 100 ft *30 m* and has twin-leaf gates weighing 1,400 tons/*tonnes*.

Longest flight The world's highest lock elevator is at Arzwiller-Saint Louis in France. The lift was completed in 1969 to replace 17 locks on the Marne-Rhine canal system. It drops 146 ft *44,5 m* over a ramp 383.8 ft *116,9 m* long on a 41 degree gradient.

The longest flight of locks in the United Kingdom is on the Worcester and Birmingham Canal at Tardebigge, Worcestershire, where a 2½ mile *4 km* long flight of 30 consecutive locks raises the canal level 217 ft *66 m*.

Largest cut The Gaillard Cut (known as "the Ditch") on the Panama Canal is 270 ft *82 m* deep between Gold Hill and Contractor's Hill with a bottom width of 300 ft *91 m*. In one day in 1911 as many as 333 dirt trains each carrying 357 tons *363 tonnes* left this site. The total amount of earth excavated for the whole Panama Canal was 8,910,000 tons *9 053 000 tonnes* which total will be raised by the widening of the Gaillard Cut to 500 ft *152 m*. In 1968 there were a record 14,807 transits.

7. DAMS

Earliest The earliest dam ever built was the Sadd al-Kafara, seven miles south-east of Helwan, United Arab Republic. It was built in the period 2950 to 2750 B.C. and had a length of 348 ft *106 m* and a height of 37 ft *11 m*.

Most massive Measured by volume, the largest dam in the world is the Fort Peck Dam, completed in 1940 across the Missouri River in Montana, U.S.A. It contains 125,628,000 yds^3 *96 050 000 m^3* of earth and rock fill, and is 21,026 ft (3.98 miles [*6 408 m*]) long and up to 251 ft *76,5 m* high. It maintains a reservoir with a capacity of 19.1 million acre/ft *2,35 million ha/m*. Work began in Dec. 1967 on the Tarbela Dam across the River Indus, in the Hazara District, West Pakistan. The total expenditure on the 485 ft *147 m* tall, 9,000 ft *2 743 m* long construction is expected to reach $815 million (£339.6 million) by completion in 1975 including the $623 million contract awarded to the Impregilo Consortium. The total volume of the dam will be 186,000,000 yds^3 *142 million m^3*.

Largest concrete The world's largest concrete dam, and the largest concrete structure in the world, is the Grand Coulee Dam on the Columbia River, Washington State, U.S.A. Work on the dam was begun in 1933, it began working on 22 March 1941 and was completed in 1942 at a cost of $56 million. It has a crest length of 4,173 ft *1 272 m* and is 550 ft *167 m* high. It contains 10,585,000 yds^3 *8 092 000 m^3* of concrete and weighs about 19,285,000 tons *19 595 000 tonnes*. The hydro-electric power plant (now being extended) will have a capacity of 9,771,000 kw.

Highest The highest dam in the world is the Grande Dixence in Switzerland, completed in September 1961 at a cost of 1,600 million Swiss francs (£151,000,000). It is 932 ft *284 m* from base to rim, 2,296 ft *700 m* long and the total volume of concrete in the dam is 7,792,000 yds^3 *5 957 000 m^3*. The earth fill Nurek dam on the Vakhsh-Amu Darya river, U.S.S.R. will be 1,017 ft *310 m* high, have a crest length of 2,390 ft *730 m* and a volume of 70,806,000 yds^3 *54 million m^3*. The concrete Ingurskaya dam in western Georgia, U.S.S.R., was planned to have a final height of 988 ft *301 m*, a crest length of 2,390 ft *728 m* but may be completed only to 892 ft *271 m*.

Longest The longest river dam in the world is the Hirakud Dam on the Mahanadi River, near Sambalpur, Orissa, India completed in 1956. It consists of a main concrete and masonry dam (3,768 ft [*1 148 m*]), an Earth Dam (11,980 ft [*3 652 m*]), the Left Dyke (five sections of 32,275 ft [*9 837 m*]) and the Right Dyke (35,500 ft [*10 820 m*]), totalling 15.8 miles *25,4 km* altogether.

The longest sea dam in the world is the Afsluitdijk stretching 20.195 miles *32,5 km* across the mouth of the Zuider Zee in two sections of 1.553 miles *2,499 km* (mainland of North Holland to the Isle of Wieringen) and 18.641 miles *30 km* from Wieringen to Friesland. It has a sea-level width of 293 ft *89 m* and a height of 24 ft 7 in *7,5 m*.

United Kingdom The most massive (5,630,000 yds^3 [*4 304 000 m^3*]), the highest (240 ft [*73 m*]) and longest high dam (2,050 ft [*625 m*] crest length) in the United Kingdom is the Scammonden Dam, West Riding of Yorkshire, begun in November 1966 and completed in the summer of 1970. This rock fill dam carries the M62 on its crest and was built by Sir Alfred McAlpine's. The cost of

Power plant on the Fort Peck Dam, on the Missouri River, the world's largest rock fill dam

the project together with the 6½ miles *10 km* motorway was £8,400,000. There are longer low dams or barrages of the valley cut-off type notably the Hanningfield Dam, Essex, built from July 1952 to August 1956 to a length of 6,850 ft *2 088 m* and a height of 64.5 ft *19,7 m*. The rock fill Llyn Brianne Dam in Carmarthenshire, is Britain's highest dam reaching 298½ ft *91 m* in Nov. 1971 and becoming operational on 20 July 1972.

LARGEST RESERVOIR

World The largest man-made is Bratsk reservoir (River Angara) U.S.S.R., with a volume of 137,214,000 acre/ft *16 925 000 ha/m*. The dam was completed in 1964. A volume of 149,000,000 acre/ft *18 379 000 ha/m* was quoted for Kariba Lake, Zambia-Rhodesia in 1959 but is now more reliably estimated at 130,000,000 acre/ft *16 035 000 ha/m*. The Volta Lake, Ghana, which filled behind the Akosombo dam from May 1964 to late 1968, also often referred to as the world's largest man-made lake, has a capacity of 120,000,000 acre/ft *14 802 000 ha/m*.

The completion in 1954 of the Owen Falls Dam near Jinja, Uganda, across the northern exit of the White Nile from the Victoria Nyanza marginally raised the level of that lake by adding 166,000,000 acre/ft *20 476 000 ha/m*, and technically turned it into a reservoir with a surface area of 17,169,920 acres *6,9 million ha* (26,828 miles^2 [*69 484 km^2*]).

The most grandiose reservoir project mooted is the Xingu-Araguaia river plan in central Brazil for a reservoir behind a dam at Ilha da Paz with a volume of 780,000 million yds^3 *596 000 million m^3* extending over 22,800 miles^2 *59 000 km^2*. A dam at Obidos on the Amazon would produce a 744 mile *1 197 km* long back-up and a 68,400 mile^2 *177 100 km^2* reservoir at an estimated cost of $3,000 million (£1,200 million).

United Kingdom The largest wholly artificial reservoir in the United Kingdom is the Queen Mary Reservoir, built from August 1914 to June 1925, at Littleton, near Staines, with an available storage capacity of 8,130 million gal *2 956 million litres* and a water area of 707 acres *286 ha*. The length of the perimeter embankment is 20,766 ft *6 329 m* (3.93 miles [*6,32 km*]). Of valley cut-off type reservoirs the most capacious is Llyn Celyn, North Wales with a capacity of 17,800 million gals *809 million hectolitres*. The capacity of Haweswater, Westmorland, was increased by 18,660 million gal *6 786 million litres* by the building in 1929–41 of a 1,540 ft *470 m* long concrete buttress dam 120 ft *36 m* high. The natural surface area was trebled to 1,050 acres *425 ha*. The deepest reservoir in Europe is Loch Morar, in Inverness-shire, Scotland, with a maximum depth of 1,017 ft *310 m* (see also Chapter 3).

Largest polder The largest of the five great polders in the old Zuider Zee, Netherlands, will be the 149,000 acre *60 300 ha* (232.8 miles² [*602,9 km²*]) Markerwaard. Work on the 66 mile *106 km* long surrounding dyke was begun in 1957. The water area remaining after the erection of the 1927–32 dam is called IJssel Meer, which will have a final area of 487.5 miles² *1 262,6 km²*.

Largest levees The most massive earthworks ever carried out are the Mississippi levees begun in 1717 but vastly augmented by the U.S. Federal Government after the disastrous floods of 1927. These extend for 1,732 miles *2 787 km* along the main river from Cape Girardeau, Missouri, to the Gulf of Mexico and comprise more than 1,000 million yds³ *765 000 m³* of earthworks. Levees on the tributaries comprise an additional 2,000 miles *3 200 km*.

8. TUNNELS

LONGEST

Water supply World The world's longest tunnel of any kind is the New York City West Delaware water supply tunnel begun in 1937 and completed in 1945. It has a diameter of 13 ft 6 in *4,1 m* and runs for 85.0 miles *136 km* from the Rondout Reservoir into the Hillview Reservoir, in the northern part of Manhattan Island, New York City, N.Y., U.S.A.

United Kingdom The longest water supply tunnel in the United Kingdom is the Thames water tunnel from Hampton-on-Thames to Walthamstow, Greater London, completed in 1960 with a circumference of 26 ft 8 in *8,1 m* and a length of 18.8 miles *30,3 km*.

RAILWAY

World The world's longest main-line tunnel is the Simplon II Tunnel, completed after 4 year's work on 16 Oct. 1922. Linking Switzerland and Italy under the Alps, it is 12 miles 559 yds *19,5 km* long. Over 60 were killed boring this and the Simplon I (1898–1906), which is 22 yds *20 m* shorter. Its greatest depth below the surface is 7,005 ft *2 135 m*.

Subway tunnel The world's longest continuous vehicular tunnel is the London Transport Executive underground railway line from Morden to East Finchley, *via* Bank. In use since 1939, it is 17 miles 528 yds *27,8 km* long and the diameter of the tunnel is 12 ft *3,7 m* and the station tunnels 22.2 ft *6,8 m*.

United Kingdom The United Kingdom's longest main-line railway tunnel is the Severn Tunnel (4 miles 628 yds *[6 km]*), linking Gloucestershire and Monmouthshire, completed with 76,400,000 bricks between 1873 and 1886.

ROAD

World The longest road tunnel is the tunnel 7.2 miles *11,6 km* long under Mont Blanc (15,771 ft *[4 807 m]*) from Pèlerins, near Chamonix, France, to Entrèves, near Courmayeur in Valle d'Aosta, Italy, on which work began on 6 Jan. 1959. The holing through was achieved on 14 Aug. 1962 and it was opened on 16 July 1965, after an expenditure of £22,800,000. The 29½ ft *9 m* high tunnel with its carriage-way of two 12 ft *3,7 m* lanes is expected to carry 600,000 vehicles a year. There were 23 deaths during tunnelling.

Sub-aqueous The world's longest sub-aqueous road tunnel is the Kanmon Tunnel, completed in 1958, which runs 6.15 miles *9,90 km* from Shimonseki, Honshū, to Kyūshū, Japan. The 33.6 mile *54 km* long Seikan Tunnel, 460 ft *140 m* beneath the sea-bed of the Tsugaru Strait between Tappi Saki, Honshū, and Fukushima, Hokkaidō, Japan, is due to be completed by 1980 at a cost of £240 million. Tests started on the sub-aqueous section (14.5 miles *[23,3 km]*) in 1963 and construction in April 1971.

Channel tunnel On 8 July 1966 the United Kingdom and French governments reached agreement on a Channel Tunnel for electric trains. It would run in two passages, each of 35.6 miles *57,3 km*, 21 miles *34 km* being sub-aqueous, between Westenhanger, near Dover, Kent, and Sangatte, near Calais. The project, now known as the "Chunnel", was first mooted in 1802. It will cost more than £900,000,000, if proceeded with.

United Kingdom The longest road tunnel in the United Kingdom is the Mersey Tunnel, joining Liverpool, Lancashire, and Birkenhead, Cheshire. It is 2.13 miles *3,43 km* long, or 2.87 miles *4,62 km* including branch tunnels. Work was begun in December 1925 and it was opened by H.M. King George V on 18 July 1934. The total cost was £7¾ million. The 36 ft *11 m* wide 4-lane roadway carries nearly 7½ million vehicles a year. The first tube of the second Mersey Tunnel was opened on 24 June 1971.

Largest The largest diameter road tunnel in the world is that blasted through Yerba Buena Island, San Francisco, California, U.S.A. It is 76 ft *23 m* wide, 58 ft *17 m* high and 540 ft *165 m* long. More than 35,000,000 vehicles pass through on its two decks every year.

HYDRO-ELECTRIC OR IRRIGATION

World The longest irrigation tunnel in the world is the 51.5 mile *82,9 km* long Orange-Fish Rivers Tunnel, South Africa, begun in 1967 at an estimated cost of £60 million. The boring was completed in April 1973. The lining to a minimum thickness of 9 inches *23 cm* will give a completed diameter of 17 ft 6 ins *5,33 m*. The total work force was at times more than 5,000. Some of the access shafts in the eight sections descend more than 1,000 feet *305 m*.

United Kingdom The longest in the United Kingdom is that at Ben Nevis, Inverness-shire, which has a mean diameter of 15 ft 2 in *4,6 m* and a length of 15 miles *24 km*. It was begun in June 1926 and was holed through into Loch Treig on 3 Jan. 1930 for hydro-electric use.

BRIDGE-TUNNEL

The world's longest bridge-tunnel system is the Chesapeake Bay Bridge-Tunnel, extending 17.65 miles *28,40 km* from the Delmarva Peninsula to Norfolk, Virginia, U.S.A. It cost $200,000,000 (then £71.4 million) and was completed after 42 months and opened to traffic on 15 April 1964. The longest bridged section is Trestle C (4.56 miles [*7,34 km*] long) and the longer tunnel is the Thimble Shoal Channel Tunnel (1.09 miles [*1,75 km*]).

CANAL TUNNELS

Longest World The world's longest canal tunnel is that on the Rove canal between the port of Marseilles, France and the river Rhône, built in 1912–27. It is 4.53 miles *7,29 km* long, 72 ft *22 m* wide and 50 ft *15 m* high, involving 2¼ million yds³ *1,7 million m³* of excavation.

United Kingdom The longest of the 49 canal tunnels in the United Kingdom is the Standedge Tunnel in the West Riding of Yorkshire on the Huddersfield Narrow Canal built from 1794 to 4 April 1811. It measures 3 miles 135 yds *3,5 km* in length and was closed on 21 Dec. 1944. The Huddersfield Narrow Canal is also the highest in the United Kingdom, reaching a height at one point of 638 ft *194 m* above sea-level.

Tunnelling record The world's records for rapid tunnelling were set on 18 March 1967 in the 8.6 mile *13,8 km* long Blanco Tunnel, in Southern Colorado when the "mole" (giant boring machine) crew advanced the 10 ft *3 m* diameter heading 375 ft *114 m* in one day and on 26 June 1972 in the 20½ ft *6,95 m* diameter Navajo Tunnel 3 project, New Mexico with an advance of 247 lineal ft *75,28 m*.

9. SPECIALISED STRUCTURES

SEVEN WONDERS OF THE WORLD

The Seven Wonders of the World were first designated by Antipater of Sidon in the 2nd century B.C. They included the Pyramids of Gîza, built by three Fourth Dynasty Egyptian Pharaohs, Hwfw (Khufu or Cheops), Kha-f-Ra (Khafre, Khefren or Chephren) and Menkaure (Mycerinus) near El Gîza (El Gizeh), south-west of El Qâhira (Cairo) in Egypt (now the United Arab Republic). The Great Pyramid ("Horizon of Khufu") was finished *c.* 2580 B.C. Its original height was 480 ft 11 in *146 m* (now, since the loss of its topmost stone or pyramidion, reduced to 449 ft 6 in [*137 m*]) with a base line of 756 ft *230 m* and thus originally covering slightly more than 13 acres *5 ha*. It has been estimated that a work force of 4,000 required 30 years to manoeuvre into position the 2,300,000 limestone blocks averaging 2½ tons/*tonnes* each, totalling about 5,750,000 tons *5 840 000 tonnes* and a volume of 90,700,000 ft³ *2 568 000 m³*.

Of the other six wonders only fragments remain of the Temple of Artemis (Diana) of the Ephesians, built in *c.* 350 B.C. at Ephesus, Turkey (destroyed by the Goths in A.D. 262), and of the Tomb of King Mausolus of Caria, built at Halicarnassus, now Bodrum, Turkey, in *c.* 325 B.C. No trace remains of the Hanging Gardens of Semiramis, at Babylon, Iraq (*c.* 600 B.C.); the 40 ft *12 m* tall marble, gold and ivory statue of Zeus (Jupiter), by Phidias (5th century B.C.) at Olympia, Greece (lost in a fire at Istanbul); the 117 ft *35 m* tall statue by Charles of Lindos of the figure of the god Helios (Apollo) called the Colossus of Rhodes (sculptured 292–280 B.C., destroyed by an earthquake in 224 B.C.); or the 400 ft *122 m* tall lighthouse built by Soscratus of Cnidus during the 3rd century B.C. (destroyed by earthquake in A.D. 1375) on the island of Pharos (Greek, *pharos* = lighthouse), off the coast of El Iskandarîya (Alexandria), Egypt (now the United Arab Republic).

PYRAMIDS

Largest The largest pyramid, and the largest monument ever constructed, is the Quetzalcóatl at Cholula de Rivadahia, 63 miles *101 km* south-east of Mexico City, Mexico. It is 177 ft *54 m* tall and its base covers an area of nearly 45 acres *18,2 ha*. Its total volume has been estimated at 4,300,000 yds³ *3 300 000 m³* compared with 3,360,000 yds³ *2,5 million m³* for the Pyramid of Cheops (see above). The pyramid-building era here was between the 6th and 12th centuries A.D.

Oldest The oldest known pyramid is the Djoser step pyramid at Saqqâra, Egypt constructed to a height of 204 ft *62 m* of Tura limestone in *c.* 2650 B.C. The oldest New World pyramid is that on the island of La Venta in south-eastern Mexico built by the Olmec people *c.* 800 B.C. It stands 100 ft *30 m* tall with a base diameter of 420 ft *128 m*.

TALLEST FLAGSTAFF

World The tallest flagstaff ever erected was that outside the Oregon Building at the 1915 Panama-Pacific International Exposition in San Francisco, California, U.S.A. Trimmed from a Douglas fir, it stood 299 ft 7 in *91 m* in height and weighed 45 tons *47 tonnes*. The tallest unsupported flag pole in the world is a 220 ft *67 m* tall metal pole weighing 28,000 lb. *12 700 kg* erected in 1955 at the U.S. Merchant Marine Academy in King's Point, New York, U.S.A. The pole, built by Kearney-National Inc., tapers from 24 in to 5½ in *61 cm to 14 cm* at the jack.

United Kingdom The tallest flagstaff in the United Kingdom is a 225 ft *68 m* tall Douglas fir staff at Kew, London. Cut in Canada, it was shipped across the Atlantic and towed up the River Thames on 7 May 1958, to replace the old 214 ft *65 m* tall staff of 1919.

The 105 ft *32 m* Maypole erected at Lanreath, Cornwall on 1 May 1973

Tallest totem pole The tallest totem pole in the world is one 160 ft tall in McKinleyville, California, U.S.A. It weighs 57,000 lb. (25.4 tons [*25,8 tonnes*]), was carved from a 500 year old tree and was erected in May 1962.

Maypole The tallest reported Maypole erected in England was one of 105 ft *32 m* including the brush put up in Lanreath, Cornwall on 1 May 1973.

MONUMENTS

Tallest The world's tallest monument is the stainless steel Gateway to the West Arch in St. Louis, Missouri, U.S.A., completed on 28 Oct. 1965 to commemorate the westward expansion after the Louisiana Purchase of 1803. It is a sweeping arch spanning 630 ft *192 m* and rising to the same height of 630 ft *192 m* and costing $29,000,000 (*£12,083,000*). It was designed in 1947 by Eero Saarinen (died 1961).

The tallest monumental column in the world is that commemorating the battle of San Jacinto (21 April 1836), on the bank of the San Jacinto river near Houston, Texas, U.S.A. General Sam Houston (1793–1863) and his force of 743 Texan troops killed 630 Mexicans (out of a total force of 1,600) and captured 700 others, for the loss of nine men killed and 30 wounded. Constructed in 1936–39, at a cost of $1,500,000 (*now £625,000*), the tapering column is 570 ft *173 m* tall, 47 ft *14 m* square at the base, and 30 ft *9 m* square at the observation tower, which is surmounted by a star weighing 196.4 tons *199,6 tonnes*. It is built of concrete, faced with buff limestone, and weighs 31,384 tons *31 888 tonnes*.

Prehistoric Largest Britain's largest megalithic prehistoric monuments are the 28½ acre *11,5 ha* earthworks and stone circles of Avebury, Wiltshire, rediscovered in 1646. This is believed to be the work of the Beaker people of the later Neolithic period of *c.* 1700 to 1500 B.C. The whole work is 1,200 ft *365 m* in diameter with a 40 ft *12 m* ditch around the perimeter and required an estimated 15 million man-hours of work. The largest trilithons exist at Stonehenge, to the south of Salisbury Plain, Wiltshire, with single sarsen blocks weighing over 45 tons/*tonnes* and requiring over 550 men to drag them up a 9° gradient. The dating of the ditch was in 1969 revised to 2180 B.C.±105. Whether Stonehenge was a lunar calendar or an eclipse-predictor remains debatable.

Largest earthwork The greatest prehistoric earthwork in Britain is Wansdyke, originally Woden's Dyke, which ran 86

133

miles *138 km* from Portishead, Somerset to Inkpen Beacon and Ludgershall, south of Hungerford, Berkshire. It is believed to have been built by the pre-Roman Wessex culture. The most extensive single site earthwork is the Dorset Cursus near Gussage St. Michael, dating from *c.* 1900 B.C. The workings are 6 miles *9,7 km* in length, involving an estimated 250,000 yds³ *191 000 m³* of excavations. The largest of the Celtic hill-forts is that known as Mew Dun, or Maiden Castle, 2 miles *3 km* south-west of Dorchester, Dorset. It covers 115 acres *46,5 ha* and was abandoned shortly after A.D. 43.

Largest The largest artificial mound in Europe is Silbury Hill,
mound 6 miles *9,7 km* west of Marlborough, Wiltshire, which involved the moving of an estimated 670,000 tons *681 000 tonnes* of chalk to make a cone 130 ft *39 m* high with a base of 5½ acres *2 ha*. Prof. Richard Atkinson in charge of the 1968 excavations showed that it is based on an innermost central mound, similar to contemporary round barrows, and may be dated to *c.* 2200 B.C. The largest long barrow in England is that inside the hill-fort at Maiden Castle (see above). It originally had a length of 1,800 ft *548 m* and had several enigmatic features such as a ritual pit with pottery, limpet shells, and animal bones. In 1934–37 the remains of a man of 25–35 was discovered, who had been hacked to pieces after death. The longest long barrow containing a megalithic chamber is that at West Kennet (*c.* 2200 B.C.), near Silbury, measuring 385 ft *117 m* in length.

Henges There are in Britain some 80 henges built *c.* 2100–1500 B.C. of which the largest is Darrington, Yorks with an average diameter of 1,550 ft *472 m*.

Youngest Of all the ancient monuments scheduled in Great
ancient Britain, the youngest is Fort Wallington, near Ports-
monument mouth, Hampshire. It was begun in 1860, when a French invasion was thought possible, and was not completed until 1870.

The main entrance to Fort Wallington, Britain's Youngest Ancient Monument

OBELISKS (Monolithic)

Oldest The longest an obelisk has remained *in situ* is that at Heliopolis (now Masr-el-Gedîda) United Arab Republic (Egypt), erected by Senusret I *c.* 1750 B.C.

The world's largest standing obelisk in the Piazza of St. John in Lateran, Rome, which measures 110 ft *33 m* high

Largest The largest standing obelisk in the world is that in the Piazza of St. John in Lateran, Rome, erected in 1588. It came originally from the Circus Maximus (erected A.D. 357) and before that from Heliopolis, Egypt (erected *c.* 1450 B.C.). It is 110 ft *33 m* in length and weighs 450 tons *457 tonnes*. The largest obelisk in the United Kingdom is Cleopatra's Needle on the Embankment, London, which is 68 ft 5½ in *20 m* tall and weighs 186.36 tons *189,35 tonnes*. It was towed up the Thames from Egypt on 20 Jan. 1878.

Largest The largest tomb in the world is that of Emperor
tomb Nintoku (died *c.* A.D. 428) south of Osaka, Japan. It measures 1,594 ft *485 m* long by 1,000 ft *305 m* wide by 150 ft *45 m* high.

Largest The largest surviving ziqqurat (from the verb *zaqaru*
ziqqurat to build high) or stage-tower is the Ziqqurat of Ur (now Muqqayr, Iraq) with a base 200 ft by 150 ft *60 by 45 m* built to at least three storeys of which the first and part of the second now survive to a height of 60 ft *18 m*. It was built by the Akkadian King Ur-Nammu (*c.* 2113–2006 B.C.) to the moon god Nanna covering 30,000 ft² *2 800 m²*.

STATUES

Tallest The tallest free-standing statue in the world is that of "Motherland", an enormous pre-stressed concrete female figure on Mamayev Hill, outside Volgograd, U.S.S.R., designed in 1967 by Yevgenyi Vuchetich, to commemorate victory in the Battle of Stalingrad (1942–43). The statue from its base to the tip of the sword clenched in her right had measures 270 ft *82,30 m*.

The U.S. sculptor Felix de Welton has announced a plan to replicate the Colossus of Rhodes to a height of 308 ft *93,87 m*.

Longest Near Bamiyan, Afghanistan there are the remains of the recumbent Sakya Buddha, built of plastered rubble, which was "about 1,000 ft *305 m*" long and is believed to date from the 3rd or 4th century A.D.

LARGEST DOME

World The world's largest dome is the Louisiana Superdome, New Orleans, U.S.A. It has a diameter of 680 ft *207,26 m*. (See page 125 for futher details.) The largest dome of ancient architecture is that of the Pantheon, built in Rome in A.D. 112, with a diameter of 142½ ft *43 m*.

Britain The largest dome in Britain is that of the Bell Sports Centre, Perth, Scotland with a diameter of 222 ft *67 m* designed by D. B. Cockburn and constructed in Baltic whitewood by Muirhead & Sons Ltd. of Grangemouth, Stirlingshire.

Tallest columns The tallest columns (as opposed to obelisks) in the world are the sixteen 82 ft *25 m* tall pillars in the Palace of Labour in Torino (Turin), Italy, for which the architect was Pier Luigi Nervi (born 21 June 1891). They were built of concrete and steel in only 8 days. The tallest load-bearing stone columns in the world are those measuring 69 ft *21 m* in the Hall of Columns of the Temple of Amun at Al Karnak, the northern part of the ruins of Thebes, the Greek name for the ancient capital of Upper Egypt (now the United Arab Republic). They were built in the 19th dynasty in the reign of Rameses II in *c.* 1270 B.C.

HARBOUR WORKS

Longest jetty The longest deep water jetty in the world is the Quai Hermann du Pasquier at Le Havre, France, with a length of 5,000 ft *1 524 m*. Part of an enclosed basin, it has a constant depth of water of 32 ft *9,8 m* on both sides.

Longest pier
World The world's longest pier is the Damman Pier at El Hasa, Saudi Arabia, on the Persian Gulf. A rock-filled causeway 4.84 miles *7,79 km* long joins the steel trestle pier 1.80 miles *2,90 km* long, which joins the Main Pier (744 ft [*226 m*] long), giving an overall length of 6.79 miles *10,93 km*. The work was begun in July 1948 and completed on 15 March 1950.

United Kingdom The longest pier in Great Britain is the Bee Ness Jetty, completed in 1930, which stretches 8,200 ft *2 500 m* along the west bank of the River Medway, 5 to 6 miles *8 to 9,6 km* below Rochester, at Kingsnorth, Kent.

Longest breakwater
World The world's longest breakwater system is that which protects the Ports of Long Beach and Los Angeles, California, U.S.A. The combined length of the four breakwaters is 43,602 ft (8.26 miles [*13,29 km*]) of which the Long Beach section, built between 1941 and February 1949, is the longest at 13,350 ft (2.53 miles [*4,07 km*]). The North breakwater at Tuticorin, Madras Province, Southern India on which construction began in 1968 extends to 13,589 ft *4,14 km*.

United Kingdom The longest breakwater in the United Kingdom is the North Breakwater at Holyhead, Anglesey, which is 9,860 ft (1.86 miles [*3 005 m*]) in length and was completed in 1873.

LARGEST DRY DOCK

World The world's largest dry dock is the Lisnave dock, Lisbon, Portugal begun in 1969 and completed at a cost of £10,000,000 in 20 months. It measures 1,700 × 318 × 53 ft *518 × 97 × 16,15 m*.

United Kingdom The largest dry dock in the United Kingdom is the Belfast Harbour Commission and Harland and Wolff building dock at Belfast, Northern Ireland. It has been excavated by Wimpey's to a length of 1,825 ft *556 m* and a width of 305 ft *93 m* and can accommodate tankers of 1,000,000 d.w.t. Work was begun on 26 Jan. 1968 and completed on 30 Nov. 1969 and involved the excavation of 400,000 yds³ *306 000 m³*. (See also Largest crane.)

Work started at Nagasaki, Japan on 16 Sept. 1970 on a building dock capable of taking a tanker of 1,200,000 d.w.t. for Mitsubishi Heavy Industries Co. at a cost of £32,000,000.

LARGEST FLOATING DOCKS

Sectional The highest capacity floating docks ever constructed are the United States Navy's advanced base sectional docks (A.B.S.D.). These consist of 10 sectional units

Aerial view of Lisnave dock, Lisbon, Portugal, which is the world's largest dry dock

giving together an effective keel block length of 827 ft *252 m* and clear width of 140 ft *42 m* with a lifting capacity of up to 80,000 tons *81 000 tonnes*. Floating Dock No. 2 at Palermo, Sicily, Italy, measures 285 m *936 ft* long and 46 m *151 ft* in the beam.

Single unit The largest single unit floating dock is Admiralty Floating Dock (AFD) 35, which was towed from the Royal Navy's dockyard in Malta to the Cantieri Navali Santa Maria of Genoa, Italy, in May 1965. It has a lifting capacity of 65,000 tons *66 000 tonnes* and an overall length of 857 ft 8 in *261 m*. It had been towed to Malta from Bombay, India, where it was built in 1947.

LIGHTHOUSES

Brightest
World The lighthouse with the most powerful light in the world is Créac'h d'Ouessant lighthouse, established in 1638 and last altered in 1939 on l'Ile d'Ouessant, Finistère, Brittany, France. It is 163 ft *50 m* tall and, in times of fog, has a luminous intensity of up to 500 million candelas *490.5 million candles*.

The lights with the greatest visible range are those 1,092 ft *332 m* above the ground on the Empire State Building, New York City, N.Y., U.S.A. Each of the four-arc mercury bulbs has a rated candlepower of 450,000,000, visible 80 miles *130 km* away on the ground and 300 miles *490 km* away from aircraft. They were switched on on 31 March 1956.

United Kingdom The lighthouse in the United Kingdom with the most powerful light is the shorelight Orfordness, Suffolk. It has an intensity of 7,500,000 candelas. The Irish light with the greatest intensity is Aranmore on Rinrawros Point, County Donegal.

Tallest The world's tallest lighthouse is the steel tower 348 ft *106 m* tall near Yamashita Park in Yokohama, Japan. It has a power of 600,000 candles and a visibility range of 20 miles *32 km*.

Remotest The most remote Trinity House lighthouse is The Smalls, about 16 sea miles (18.4 statute miles [*29,6 km*]) off the Pembrokeshire coast. The most remote Scottish lighthouse is Sule Skerry, 35 miles *56 km* off shore and 45 miles *72 km* north-west of Dunnet Head, Caithness. The most remote Irish light is Blackrock, about 9 miles *14 km* off the Mayo coast.

WINDMILLS

Earliest The earliest recorded windmills are those used for grinding corn in Iran (Persia) in the 7th century A.D.

The earliest known in England was the post-mill at Bury St. Edmunds, Suffolk, recorded in 1191. The oldest Dutch mill is the towermill at Zedden, Gelderland built in c. 1450. The oldest working mill in England is the post-mill at Outwood, Surrey, built in 1665, though the Ivinghoe Mill in Pitstone Green Farm, Buckinghamshire, dating from 1627, has been restored.

Largest The largest Dutch windmill is the Dijkpolder in Maasland built in 1718. The sails measure 95¾ ft *29 m* from tip to tip. The tallest windmill in the Netherlands is De Walvisch in Schiedam built to a height of 108 ft *33 m* in 1794. The largest conventional windmill in England is a disused one at Sutton, Norfolk.

WATERWHEEL

Largest The largest waterwheel in the world is the Moham-
World madieh Noria wheel at Hama, Syria with a diameter of 131 ft *40 m* dating from Roman times. The Lady Isabella wheel at Laxey, Isle of Man is the largest in the British Isles and was built in Lancashire for draining a lead mine and completed on 27 Sept. 1854, has a circumference of 228 ft *69 m*, a diameter of 72½ ft *22 m* and an axle weighing 9 tons/*tonnes*. The largest waterwheel in Great Britain is claimed to be the Pitchback indoor wheel of 45 ft *13,70 m* diameter which provided power from 1862–1932 for the mill of James Wilson & Son Ltd. of Keighley, Yorkshire.

Barns The largest barn in Britain is one at Manor Farm, Cholsey, near Wallingford, Berkshire. It is 303 ft *92 m* in length and 54 ft *16 m* in breadth (16,362 ft² [*1 520 m²*]). The Ipsden Barn, Oxfordshire, is 385½ ft *117 m* long but 30 ft *9 m* wide (11,565 ft² [*1 074 m²*]).

The longest tithe barn in Britain is one measuring 268 ft *81 m* long at Wyke Farm, near Sherborne, Dorset.

NUDIST CAMP

Largest The first nudist camps were established in Germany in 1912. The largest such camp in the world was that at l'Ile du Levant, southern France, which had up to 15,000 *adeptes* before most of it was taken over for defence purposes by the French Navy in 1965.

LONGEST WALL

World The Great Wall of China, completed during the reign of Shih Huang-ti (246–210 B.C.), is 1,684 miles *2 710 km* in length, with a height of from 15 to 39 ft *4,5 to 12 m* and up to 32 ft *9,8 m* thick. Its erection is the most massive construction job ever undertaken by the human race. It runs from Shanhaikuan, on the Gulf of Pohai, to Chiayukuan in Kansu and was kept in repair up to the 16th century.

Britain The longest of the Roman Walls built in Britain was the 15–20 ft *4,5–6 m* tall Hadrian's Wall, built in the period A.D. 122–126. It ran across the Tyne-Solway isthmus of 74½ miles *120 km* from Bowness-on-Solway, Cumberland, to Wallsend-on-Tyne, Northumberland, and was abandoned in A.D. 383.

LONGEST FENCE

The longest fence in the world is the dingo-proof fence enclosing the main sheep areas of Queensland, Australia. The wire fence is 6 ft *1,8 m* high, one foot *30 cm* underground and stretches for 3,437 miles.

DOORS

Largest The largest doors in the world are the four in the
World Vertical Assembly Building near Cape Kennedy, Florida, with a height of 460 ft *140 m* (see page 120).

The largest doors in the United Kingdom are those to the Britannia Assembly Hall, at Filton, Bristol. The doors are 1,035 ft *315 m* in length and 67 ft *20 m* high, divided into three bays each 345 ft *105 m* across. The largest simple hinged door in Britain is that of Ye Old

A section of Hadrian's Wall, the great Roman wall built in Britain in A.D. 122–126

Bull's Head, Beaumaris, Anglesey, Wales, which is 12 ft *3,7 m* wide and 30 ft *9 m* high.

Oldest The oldest doors in Britain are those of Hadstock Church, Essex, which date from c. 1040 and exhibit evidence of Danish workmanship.

LARGEST WINDOWS

The largest sheet of glass ever manufactured was one of 50 m² *538.2 ft²*, or 20 m *65 ft 7 in* by 2,5 m *8 ft 2½ in*, exhibited by the Saint Gobian Company in France at the *Journées Internationales de Miroiterie* in March 1958. The largest windows in the world are the three in the Palace of Industry and Technology at Rond-point de la Défense, Paris, with an extreme width of 218 m *715.2 ft* and a maximum height of 50 m *164 ft*.

LONGEST STAIRS

World The world's longest stairs are reputedly at the Mår power station, Øverland, western Norway. Built of wood, these are 4,101 ft *1 250 m* in length, rising in 3,875 steps at an angle of 41 degrees inside the pressure shaft. The length of a very long, now discontinuous, stone stairway in the Rohtang Pass, Manali, Kulu, Northern India, is still under investigation.

Britain The longest stairs in Britain are those from the transformer gallery to the surface 1,065 ft *324 m* (1,420 steps) in the Cruachan Power Station, Argyll, Scotland.

TALLEST FIRE ESCAPE

The world's tallest mobile fire escape is a 250 ft *76 m* tall turntable ladder built in 1962 by Magirus, a West German firm.

LARGEST MARQUEE

World The largest tent ever erected was one covering an area of 188,368 ft² (4.32 acres [*17 500 m²*]) put up by the firm of Deuter from Augsburg, West Germany, for the 1958 "Welcome Expo" in Brussels, Belgium.

Britain The largest marquee in Britain is one made by Piggot Brothers in 1951 and used by the Royal Horticultural Society at their annual show (first held in 1913) in the grounds of the Royal Hospital, Chelsea, London. The marquee is 310 ft *94 m* long by 480 ft *146 m* wide and consists of 18¾ miles *30 km* of 36 in *91 cm* wide canvas covering a ground area of 148,800 ft² *13 820 m²*. A tent 390 ft *119 m* long was erected in one lift by the Army for the Colchester Tattoo in Kings Head Meadow with 135 men in July 1970.

LARGEST VATS

The largest vats in the United Kingdom are those used in cider brewing by H. P. Bulmer & Company. Their standard oak vats hold 60,000 gal *272 760 litres* and reinforced concrete vats hold up to 100,000 gal *454 600 litres*. Largest of all is Apollo XI, a lined steel vat with a capacity of 1,100,000 gal *5 million litres* and a diameter of 60 ft *18 m* at Hereford.

The world's largest fermentation vessel is the giant stainless steel container, No. 26M, built by the A.P.V. Co. Ltd. of Crawley, Sussex, for the Guinness Brewery, St. James's Gate, Dublin, Ireland. This has a nominal capacity of 8,000 standard barrels, or 2,304,000 Imperial pints *1 309 200 litres*, and dimensions of 63 ft *19 m* long by 28 ft 9 in *8,8 m* wide by 29 ft 7 in *8,9 m* high.

ADVERTISING SIGNS

Largest The greatest advertising sign ever erected was the electric Citroën sign on the Eiffel Tower, Paris. It was switched on on 4 July 1925, and could be seen 24 miles *38 km* away. It was in six colours with 250,000 lamps and 56 miles *90 km* of electric cables. The letter "N" which terminated the name "Citroën" between the second and third levels measured 68 ft 5 in *20,8 m* in height. The whole apparatus was taken down after 11 years in 1936. For the largest ground sign see Chapter 6, page 100—Letters, largest.

The world's largest neon sign was that owned by the Atlantic Coast Line Railroad Company at Port Tampa, Florida, U.S.A. It measured 387 ft 6 in *118 m* long and 76 ft *23 m* high, weighed 175 tons *178 tonnes* and contained about 4,200 ft *1 280 m* of red neon tubing. It was demolished on 19 Feb. 1970. Broadway's largest billboard in New York City is 11,426 ft² *1 062 m²* in area—equivalent to 107 ft *32,6 m* square. Britain's largest illuminated sign is the word PLAY-HOUSE extending 90 ft *27 m* across the frontage of the new theatre in Leeds, Yorkshire opened in 1970.

The world's largest working sign was that in Times Square at 44 & 45th Streets, New York City, U.S.A., in 1966. It showed two 42½ ft *13 m* tall "bottles" of Haig Scotch Whisky and an 80 ft *24 m* long "bottle" of Gordon's Gin being "poured" into a frosted glass. The world's tallest free-standing advertising sign is the 188 ft *57 m* tall, 93 ft *28 m* wide Stardust Hotel sign at Las Vegas, Nevada, U.S.A. completed in February 1968. It uses 25,000 light bulbs and 2,500 ft *762 m* of neon tubing and has letters up to 22 ft *6,7 m* tall.

Highest World The highest advertising sign in the world is the "R.C.A." on the Radio Corporation of America Building in Rockefeller Plaza, New York City, U.S.A. The top of the 25 ft *7,6 m* tall illuminated letters is 825 ft *251 m* above street level.

United Kingdom The highest advertising sign in the United Kingdom was the revolving name board of the contractors "Peter Lind" on the Post Office Tower, London. The illuminated letters were 12 ft *3,7 m* tall and 563 to 575 ft *171 to 175 m* above the street.

LARGEST GASHOLDER

World The world's largest gasholder is that at Fontaine l'Evêque, Belgium, where disused mines have been adapted to store up to 500 million m³ *17,650 million ft³* of gas at ordinary pressure. Probably the largest conventional gasholder is that at Wein-Simmering, Vienna, Austria, completed in 1968, with a height of 274 ft 8 in *84 m* and a capacity of 10.59 million ft³ *300 000 m³*.

United Kingdom The largest gasholder ever constructed in the United Kingdom is the East Greenwich Gas Works No. 2 Holder built in 1891 with an original capacity for 12,200,000 ft³ *346 000 m³*. As reconstructed its capacity is 8.9 million ft³ *252 000 m³* with a water tank 303 ft *92 m* in diameter and a full inflated height of 148 ft *45 m*. The No. 1 holder (capacity 8.6 million ft³ [*243 500 m³*]) has a height of 200 ft *61 m*. The River Tees Northern Gas Board's 1,186 ft *361 m* deep underground storage in use since January 1959 has a capacity of 330,000 ft³ *9 300 m³*.

TALLEST FOUNTAIN

World The world's tallest fountain is the Fountain at Fountain Hills, Arizona built at a cost of $1,500,000 for McCulloch Properties Inc. At full pressure of 375 lb./in² *26,3 kg/cm²* and at a rate of 5,828 Imp. gal *26 500 litres/min* the 560 ft *170 m* tall column of water weighs more than 8 tons/*tonnes*. The nozzle speed achieved by the three 600 h.p. pumps is 46.7 m.p.h. *75 km/h.*

The 560 ft *170 m* fountain at Fountain Hills Arizona, which supports a column of 8 tons of water in the air

United Kingdom The tallest fountain in the United Kingdom is the Emperor Fountain at Chatsworth, Bakewell, Derbyshire. When first tested on 1 June 1844, it attained the then unprecedented height of 260 ft *79 m*. Since the war it has not been played to more than 250 ft *76 m* and rarely beyond 180 ft *55 m*.

Bonfire Largest The largest Guy Fawkes bonfire constructed was one using 150 tons *152 tonnes* of timber and 1,500 tyres built to a height of 75 ft *23 m* by The First Company of Torrington Cavaliers in Torrington, Devon for 5 Nov. 1971. At College Station, Texas on Thanksgiving Eve 1969 a bonfire of 107 ft 10 in *32,85 m* was built.

CEMETERIES

The world's largest cemetery is that in Leningrad, U.S.S.R., which contains over 500,000 of the 1,300,000 victims of the German army's siege of 1941–42. The largest cemetery in the United Kingdom is Brookwood Cemetery, Brookwood, Surrey. It is owned by the London Necropolis Co. and is 500 acres *200 ha* in extent with 225,436 interments to April 1973.

CREMATORIA

Earliest The oldest crematorium in Britain is one built in 1879 at Woking, Surrey. The first legal cremation took place there on 20 March 1885.

Largest The largest crematorium in the world is at the Nikolo-Arkhangelskoye Cemetery, East Moscow completed to a British design in March 1972. It has seven twin furnaces and several Halls of Farewell for atheists. Britain's largest is the Enfield Crematorium, Middlesex which extends over 40 acres *16 ha* and also carries out most cremations.

10. BORINGS

DEEPEST

World Man's deepest penetration into the Earth's crust is the Baden No. 1 gas wildcat well, Beckham County, Oklahoma, U.S.A. After 546 days drilling the Loffland Brothers Drilling Co. reached 30,050 ft *9 159 m* (5.69 miles [*9,16 km*]) on 29 Feb. 1972. The hole temperature at the bottom was 420° F. *215° C*. A conception of the depth of this hole can be gained by the realization that it was sufficient in depth to lower the Sears Tower down it more than 20 times.

The most recent in a succession of announcements of intentions to drill down 15 km *49,213 ft* from the U.S.S.R was in February 1972 from the Baku Scientific Research Institute. A depth of 21,620 ft *6 590 m* has been reached at the Kura River valley site in Southern Azerbaijan. The target here remains 48,000 ft (9.09 miles [*14,6 km*]).

PROGRESSIVE RECORDS IN DEEP DRILLING

Depth in ft	m	Location	Date
475	*144*	Duck Creek, Ohio (brine)	1841
550	*167*	Perpignan, France (artesian)	1849
5,735	*1 748*	Schladebach, Germany	1886
6,570	*2 002*	Schladebach, Germany	1893
7,230	*2 203*	Schladebach, Germany	1909
8,046	*2 452*	Olinda, Calif.	1927
8,523	*2 597*	Big Lake, W. Texas	1928
9,280	*2 828*	Long Beach, Calif.	1929
9,753	*2 972*	Midway, Calif.	1930
10,030	*3 057*	Rinconfield, Calif.	1931
10,585	*3 226*	Vera Cruz, Mexico	1931
10,944	*3 335*	Kettleman Hills, Calif.	1933
11,377	*3 467*	Belridge, Calif.	1934
12,786	*3 897*	Gulf McElroy, W. Texas	1935
15,004	*4 573*	Wasco, Calif.	1938
15,279	*4 657*	Pecos County, W. Texas	1944
16,246	*4 951*	S. Coles Levee, Calif.	1944
16,655	*5 076*	Brazos County, Texas	1945
16,668	*5 080*	Miramonte, Calif.	1946
17,823	*5 432*	Caddo County, Oklahoma	1947
18,734	*5 710*	Ventura County, Calif.	1949
20,521	*6 254*	Sublette County, Wyoming	1949
21,482	*6 547*	Bakersfield, Calif.	1953
22,570	*6 879*	Plaquemines, Louisiana	1956
25,340	*7 723*	Pecos County, W. Texas	1958
25,600	*7 802*	St. Bernard Parish, Louisiana	1970
28,500	*8 686*	Pecos County, W. Texas	1972
30,050	*9 159*	Beckham County, Oklahoma	1972

United Kingdom The deepest oil well in the United Kingdom is the British Petroleum well drilled to a depth of 9,355 ft *2 851 m* at Tetney Lock, near Cleethorpes, Lincolnshire, in 1963. A depth of 19,171 ft *5 843 m* was attained at an undisclosed site in the U.K. North Sea fields in 1970.

OIL FIELDS

The world's total proved reserves have been estimated to be 666,000 million U.S. barrels *105 800 hectolitres* or 36 more year's worth at 1972 production levels. The largest oil field in the world is the Ghawar field, Saudi Arabia operated by ARAMCO which measures 150 miles by 22 miles (*240 km by 35 km*). It has been asserted that the Groningen gas field in the Netherlands is the largest discovered. It was estimated in 1968 that the United Kingdom's segment of the North Sea gas field contains 2.5×10^{13} ft³ *7,0 × 10¹¹ m³* of almost pure methane of which the Leman Field (discovered April

The head gear above Baden No. 1 well in Oklahoma—man's deepest penetration into the earth of 30,050 ft *9 159 m* or 5.69 miles

1966), operated by the Shell-Esso-Gas Council-Amoco group, accounts for about half.

Greatest gusher The most prolific wildcat recorded is the 1,160 ft *353 m* deep Lucas No. 1, at Spindletop, about 3 miles *4,8 km* south of Beaumont, Texas, U.S.A., on 10 Jan. 1901. The gusher was heard more than a mile away and yielded 800,000 barrels during the 9 days it was uncapped. The surrounding ground subsequently yielded 142,000,000 barrels.

Greatest flare The greatest gas fire was that which burnt at Gassi Touil in the Algerian Sahara from noon on 13 Nov. 1961 to 9.30 a.m. on 28 April 1962. The pillar of flame rose 450 ft *13,7 m* and the smoke 600 ft *182 m*. It was eventually extinguished by Paul Neal ("Red") Adair, aged 47, of Austin, Texas, U.S.A., using 550 lb. *245 kg* of dynamite. His fee was understood to be about $1,000,000 (*then £357,000*).

WATER WELLS

Deepest world The world's deepest water bore is the Stensvad Water Well 11-W1 of 7,320 ft *2 231 m* drilled by the Great Northern Drilling Co. Inc. in Rosebud County, Montana, U.S.A. in October-November 1961. The Thermal Power Co. geothermal steam well begun in Sonora County, California in 1955 is now down to 9,029 ft *2 752 m*.

United Kingdom The deepest well in the United Kingdom is a water table well 2,842 ft *866 m* deep in the Staffordshire coal measures at Smestow. The deepest artesian well in Britain is that at the White Heather Laundry, Stonebridge Park, Willesden, London, N.W.10, bored in 1911 to a depth of 2,225 ft *678 m*.

Largest Hand-dug The largest hand-dug well was one 100 ft *30 m* in circumference and 109 ft *33 m* deep dug in 1877-8 at Greensburg, Kansas, U.S.A.

MINES

Earliest The earliest known mining operations were in the Ngwenya Hills of the Hhohho District of northwestern Swaziland where haematite (iron ore) was mined for body paint *c.* 41,000 B.C. The earliest known mines in England are the Neolithic flint mines at Church Hill, Findon, Sussex dated to 3390 B.C. ±150.

Deepest The world's deepest mine is the Western Deep Levels
World Mine at Carltonville, South Africa. A depth of 11,391 ft *3 471 m* (2.15 miles) was attained in March 1973. At such extreme depths where the rock temperature attains temperatures of 126° F *52,2° C* refrigerated ventilation is necessary. The other great hazard is rock bursts due to the pressures. The deepest terminal below any vertical mine shaft in the world is No. 3 sub-vertical main shaft on the Western Deep Levels Mine reaching 9,783 ft *2 981 m* below the surface. The longest vertical shaft is No. 3 Ventilation Shaft at the mine which measures 9,673 ft *2 948 m* in one continuous hole. The longest sub-incline shaft is the Angelo Tertiary at E.R.P.M. with a length of 6,656 ft *2 028 m* (1.26 miles [*2.03 km*]).

United The all-time record depth is 4,132 ft *1 259 m* in the
Kingdom Arley Seam of the Parsonage Colliery, Leigh, Lancashire in Feb. 1949. The record in Scottish coalmines was 3,093 ft *942 m* in the Michael Colliery, Barncraig, Fife, reached in August 1939. The deepest present mine workings are the Hem Heath Colliery (Moss Seam), Trentham, Staffordshire, England at 3,300 ft *1 005 m*. The deepest in Scotland is the Great Seam at Monkton Hall Colliery, Millerhill, Midlothian, at 2,930 ft *893 m*. The deepest ever shaft in England, is that of the Cleveland Potash Ltd. at Boulby, North Riding, Yorkshire at 3,754 ft *1 144 m* completed in February 1973 and the deepest in Scotland was Monkton Hall No. 1, Midlothian at 3,054 ft *930 m*. The deepest Cornish tin mine was Dolcoath mine, near Camborne. The Williams shaft was completed in 1910 to 550 fathoms (3,300 ft [*1 005 m*]) from adit or approximately 3,600 ft *1 097 m* from the surface.

GOLDMINES

Largest The largest goldmining area in the world is the
area Witwatersrand gold field extending 30 miles *48 km* east and west of Johannesburg, South Africa. Gold was discovered there in 1886 and by 1944 more than 45 per cent of the world's gold was mined there by 320,000 Bantu and 44,000 Europeans. Currently 78% of the free world's supply comes from this area whose production reached a peak *999 857 kg 984 tons* in 1970.

Largest The largest goldmine in area is the East Rand Pro-
World prietary Mines Ltd., whose 8,785 claims cover 12,100 acres *4 900 ha*. The largest, measured by volume extracted, is Randfontein Estates Gold Mine Co. Ltd. with 170 million yds³ *129 million m³*—enough to cover Manhattan Island to a depth of 8 ft *2,4 m*. The main tunnels if placed end to end would stretch a distance of 2,600 miles *4 184 km*.

United The most productive goldmine in Britain was Clogan
Kingdom St. David's, Merionethshire, Wales, in which county
and Ireland gold was discovered in 1836. This mine yielded 120,000 fine oz. in 1854–1914. Alluvial gold deposits are believed to have been worked in the Wicklow Mountains, Ireland, as early as 1800 B.C.

Richest The richest goldmine has been Crown Mines with nearly 45 million ounces *1 275 million g* and still productive. The richest in yield per year was West Driefontein which averaged more than 2½ million oz *71 million g* per year until disrupted in November 1968 by flooding. The only large mine in South Africa yielding more than one ounce per ton *28,8 g/tonne* milled is Free State Geduld.

Iron The world's largest iron-mine is at Lebedinsky, U.S.S.R., in the Kursk Magnetic Anomaly which has altogether an estimated 20,000 millions tons *20 320 million tonnes* of rich (45–65 per cent) ore and 10,000,000 million tons *10,16 × 10¹² tonnes* of poorer ore in seams up to 2,000 ft *610 m* thick. The world's greatest reserves

are, however, those of Brazil, estimated to total 58,000 million tons *58 930 million tonnes* or 35 per cent of the world's total surface stock.

Copper Historically the world's most productive copper mine has been the Bingham Canyon Mine (see below) belonging to the Kennecott Copper Corporation with over 9,000,000 short tons *8 million tonnes* in the 65 years 1904–68. Currently the most productive is the Chuquicamata mine of the Anaconda Company 150 miles *240 km* north of Antofagasta, Chile with 334,578 short tons *303 524 tonnes* in 1966.

The world's largest underground copper mine is at El Teniente, 50 miles *80 km* south-east of Santiago, Chile with more than 200 miles *320 km* of underground workings and an annual output of nearly 11,000,000 tons *11 176 000 tonnes* of ore.

Silver, The world's largest lead, zinc and silver mine is the
lead and Sullivan Mine at Kimberley, British Columbia,
zinc Canada, with 248 miles *399 km* of tunnels. Since 1970 the world's leading lead mine has been the Viburnum Trend, S.E. Missouri, U.S.A. with 495,090 short tons/ *449 140 tonnes* in 1972, from which is extracted some 10 per cent of the world's output of lead. The world's largest zinc smelter is the Cominco Ltd. plant at Trail, British Columbia, Canada which has an annual capacity of 263,000 tons *267 000 tonnes* of zinc and 800 tons *813 tonnes* of cadmium.

Spoil heap The world's largest artificial heap is the sand dump on the Randfontein Estates Gold Mines, South Africa, which comprises 42 million tons *42,6 million tonnes* of crushed ore and rock waste and has a volume six times that of the Great Pyramid. The largest colliery tip in Great Britain covers 114 acres *46 ha* (maximum height 130 ft *40 m*) with 18 million tons *18,3 million tonnes* of slag at Cutacre Clough, Lancashire.

QUARRIES

Largest The world's largest excavation is the Bingham Canyon
World Copper Mine, 30 miles *48 km* south of Salt Lake City, Utah, U.S.A. From 1906 to mid-1969 the total excavation has been 2,445 million long tons *2 484 million tonnes* over an area of 2.08 miles² *5,39 km²* to a depth of 2,280 ft *695 m*. This is five times the amount of material moved to build the Panama Canal. Three shifts of 900 men work round the clock with 38 electric shovels, 62 locomotives hauling 1,268 wagons and 18 drilling machines for the 28 tons/*tonnes* of explosive used daily. The average daily extraction is 96,000 tons *97 500 tonnes* of one per cent ore and 225,000 tons *229 000 tonnes* of overburden.

The world's deepest open pit is the Kimberley Open Mine in South Africa, dug over a period of 43 years (1871 to 1914) to a depth of nearly 1,200 ft *365 m* and with a diameter of about 1,500 ft *457 m* and a circumference of nearly a mile, covering an area of 36 acres *14,5 ha*. Three tons/*tonnes* (14,504,566 carats) of diamonds were extracted from the 21,000,000 tons *21 337 000 tonnes* of earth dug out. The inflow of water has now made the depth 845 ft *257 m* to the water surface. The "Big Hole" was dug by pick and shovel.

United The largest quarry in Britain is Imperial Chemical
Kingdom Industries Ltd.'s Tunstead Quarry, near Buxton, Derbyshire. The working face is 1½ miles *2,4 km* long and 120 ft *36,5 m* high.

Largest The largest mined slab of quarried stone is one
stone measuring 68 ft by 14 ft by 14 ft *20 by 4 by 4 m* weighing about 1,590 tons *1 615 tonnes* at Ba'labakk (Baalbeck), in the Lebanon. The largest able to be moved from this mine were slabs of 805 tons *818 tonnes* for the trilithon of the nearby Temple of Jupiter.

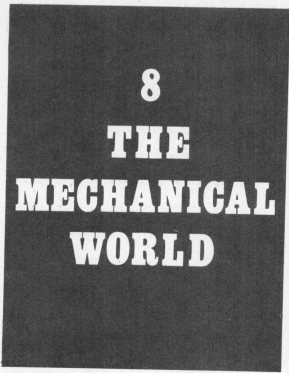

8 THE MECHANICAL WORLD

1. SHIPS

EARLIEST BOATS

The earliest known vessel which is still sea-worthy is a 102 ft *31,1 m* long sailing vessel dated to the Egyptian sixth dynasty from *c.* 2420 B.C. Oars found in bogs at Magle Mose, Sjaelland, Denmark and Star Carr Yorkshire, England, have been dated to the eighth millenium B.C. Evidence for sea faring between the Greek mainland at Melos to trade obsidian *c.* 7250 B.C. was published in 1971.

Earliest power The earliest experiments with marine steam engines date from those on the river Seine, France, in 1775. Propulsion was first achieved when in 1783 the Marquis Jouffroy d'Abbans ascended a reach of the river Saône near Lyons, France, in the 180 ton *182 tonnes* paddle steamer *Pyroscaphe*.

The tug *Charlotte Dundas* was the first successful power-driven vessel. She was a paddle-wheel steamer built in Scotland in 1801–02 by William Symington (1763–1831), using a double-acting condensing engine constructed by James Watt (1736–1819). The earliest regular steam run was by the *Clermont*, built by Robert Fulton (1765–1815), a U.S. engineer, which maintained a service from New York to Albany from 17 Aug. 1807.

Oldest Steam vessel The oldest steamer is believed to be the *Skibladner* (206 gross tons), which was built in Motala, Sweden, in 1856 and sank on Lake Mjøsa, Norway, in February 1967 but was raised and refitted for re-commission. Mr. G. H. Pattinson's 40 ft *12,20 m* steam launch, raised from Ullswater in 1962 and now on Lake Windermere, may date from a year or two earlier. The oldest motor vessel afloat in British waters is the *Prøven* on a run from the Clyde to the Inner Hebrides. She was built in Norway in 1866.

Earliest turbine The first turbine ship was the *Turbinia*, built in 1894 at Wallsend-on-Tyne, Northumberland, to the design of the Hon. Sir Charles Algernon Parsons, O.M., K.C.B. (1854–1931). The *Turbinia* was 100 ft *30,48 m* long and of 44½ tons *45,2 tonnes* displacement with machinery consisting of three steam turbines totalling about 2,000 shaft horsepower. At her first public demonstration in 1897 she reached a speed of 34.5 knots (39.7 m.p.h. [*63,9 km/h*]).

Atlantic crossings Earliest The earliest crossing of the Atlantic by a power vessel, as opposed to an auxiliary engined sailing ship, was a 22-day voyage begun in April 1827, from Rotterdam, Netherlands, to the West Indies by the *Curaçao*. She was a wooden paddle boat of 438 registered tons, built in Dundee, Angus, in 1826 and purchased by the Dutch Government for the West Indian mail service. The earliest Atlantic crossing entirely under steam (with intervals for desalting the boilers) was by H.M.S. *Rhadamanthus* from Plymouth to Barbados in 1832. The earliest crossing of the Atlantic under continuous steam power was by the condenser-fitted packet ship *Sirius* (703 tons [*714 tonnes*]) from Queenstown (now Cóbh), Ireland, to Sandy Hook, N.Y., U.S.A., in 18 days 10 hours on 4–22 April 1838.

Fastest World The fastest Atlantic crossing was made by the *United States* (then 51,988, now 38,216 gross tons), flagship of the United States Lines Company. On her maiden voyage between 3 and 7 July 1952 from New York City, N.Y., U.S.A., to Le Havre, France, and Southampton, England, she averaged 35.59 knots, or 40.98 m.p.h. *65,95 km/h* for 3 days 10 hrs 40 min (6.36 p.m. G.M.T. 3 July to 5.16 a.m. 7 July) on a route of 2,949 nautical miles *5 465 km* from the Ambrose Light Vessel to the Bishop Rock Light, Isles of Scilly, Cornwall. During this run, on 6–7 July 1952, she steamed the greatest distance ever covered by any ship in a day's run (24 hrs)—868 nautical miles *1 609 km*, hence averaging 36.17 knots (41.65 m.p.h. [*67,02 km/h*]). Her maximum speed is 41.75 knots (48 m.h.p. [*77,24 km/h*]) on a full power of 240,000 shaft horse-power. The s.h.p. figure was only revealed by the U.S. Defense Department in 1968.

British The fastest crossing of the Atlantic by a British ship is 3 days 15 hrs 48 min by the Cunard liner *Queen Mary* in September 1946 on a 2,710 mile *4 361 km* voyage from Halifax, Nova Scotia, Canada, to Southampton at an average of 30.86 knots (35.54 m.p.h. [*57,19 km/h*]). On her 2,938-mile *4 728 km* crossing from the Ambrose Light to Bishop Rock on 10–14 Aug. 1938, she averaged 31.69 knots (36.49 m.p.h. [*58,72 km/h*]) for 3 days 20 hrs 42 min.

Submerged The fastest disclosed submerged Atlantic crossing is 6 days 11 hrs 55 min by the U.S. nuclear-powered

PROGRESSIVE LIST OF WORLD'S LARGEST AND LONGEST LINERS

Gross Tonnage	Name	Propulsion	Overall Length ft	m	Dates
1,340	Great Western (U.K.)	Paddle wheels	236	72	1838–1856
1,862	British Queen (U.K.)	Paddle wheels	275	83	1839–1844
2,360	President (U.K.)	Paddle wheels	268	81	1840–1841
3,270	Great Britain (U.K.)	Single screw	322	98	1845–1937
4,690	Himalaya (U.K.)	Single screw	340	103	1853–1927
18,914[1]	Great Eastern (U.K.)	Paddles and screw	692	210	1858–1888
10,650	City of New York (later Harvard, Pittsburgh) (U.S.)	Twin screw	528	160	1888–1923
17,274	Oceanic (U.K.)	Twin screw	705	214	1899–1914
20,904	Celtic (U.K.)	Twin screw	700	213	1901–1928
21,227	Cedric (U.K.)	Twin screw	700	213	1903–1932
23,884	Baltic (U.K.)	Twin screw	726	221	1904–1933
31,550	Lusitania (U.K.)	4 screws	790	240	1907–1915
31,938	Mauretania (U.K.)	4 screws	787	239	1907–1935
45,300	Olympic (U.K.)	Triple screw	882	271	1911–1935
46,328	Titanic (U.K.)	Triple screw	882	268	1912–1912
52,022	Imperator (Germany) (later Berengaria [U.K.])	4 screws	919	280	1913–1938
54,282[2]	Vaterland (Germany) (later Leviathan [U.S.])	4 screws	950	289	1914–1938
56,621	Bismarck (Germany) (later Majestic [U.K.] and H.M. Training Ship Caledonia)	4 screws	954	290	1922–1939
79,280[3]	Normandie (France) (later U.S.S. Lafayette)	4 screws	1,029	313	1935–1946
80,774[4]	Queen Mary (U.K.) (later sold to U.S. interests)	4 screws	1,019	310	1936–
83,673[5]	Queen Elizabeth (U.K.) (later sold to U.S., then Hong Kong interests)	4 screws	1,031	314	1940–
66,348	France (France)	4 screws	1,035	315	1961–

[1] Originally 22,500 tons.
[2] Listed as 59,957 gross tons under U.S. registration, 1922–31, but not internationally accepted as such.
[3] Gross tonnage later raised by enclosure of open deck space to 83,423 gross tons.
[4] Later 81,237 gross tons.
[5] Later 82,998 gross tons.

submarine *Nautilus*, which travelled 3,150 miles *5 069 km* from Portland, Dorset, to New York City, N.Y., U.S.A., arriving on 25 Aug. 1958.

Most crossings Between 1856 and June 1894 Captain Samuel Brooks (1832–1904) crossed the North Atlantic 690 times— equal to 2,437,712 statute miles *3 923 117 km*. In 1850–51 he had sailed in the brig *Bessie* as an Able Bodied seaman round The Horn to Panama coming home to Liverpool as her master. His life-time sailing distance was at least 2,513,000 miles *4 044 000 km.*

Pacific crossing The fastest crossing of the Pacific Ocean (Yokohama, Japan to San Francisco, U.S.A.) is 8 days 35 min achieved by the 14,114 ton *14 340 tonnes* diesel cargo liner *Italy Maru* in August 1967.

EXTREMITIES REACHED

Northern-most The farthest north ever attained by a surface vessel is 86° 39′ N. in 47° 55′ E. by the drifting U.S.S.R. icebreaker *Sedov* on 29 Aug. 1939. She was locked in the Arctic ice floes from 23 Oct. 1937 until freed on 13 Jan. 1940.

Southern-most The farthest south ever reached by a ship was achieved on 3 Jan. 1955, by the Argentine icebreaker *General San Martin* in establishing the General Belgrano Base, Antarctica, on the shores of the Weddell Sea at 78° S., 39° W., 830 miles *1 335 km* from the South Pole.

PASSENGER LINERS

Largest The world's longest and largest active liner (66,348 gross tons) is the *France*, built at St. Nazaire, owned by the Compagnie Générale Transatlantique. She measures 1,035 ft 2 in *315,52 m* overall and made her official maiden voyage from Le Havre, France, to New York City, N.Y., U.S.A., on 3 Feb. 1962 and cost £29,000,000. She has a service sea speed of 31 knots. Britain's largest liner is R.M.S. *Queen Elizabeth 2* of 65,863 gross tons and an overall length of 963 ft *293 m*, completed for the Cunard Line Ltd. in 1969. She set a "turn round" record of 8 hrs 3 min at New York on 17 May 1972.

Largest ever The R.M.S. *Queen Elizabeth* (finally 82,998 but formerly 83,673 gross tons), of the Cunard fleet, was the largest passenger vessel ever built and had the largest displacement of any liner in the world. She had an overall length of 1,031 ft *314 m* and was 118 ft 7 in *36 m* in breadth and was powered by steam turbines which developed 168,000 h.p. Her last passenger voyage ended on 15 Nov. 1968. In 1970 she was removed to Hong Kong to serve as a floating marine university and renamed *Seawise University*. On 9 Jan. 1972 she was fired by 3 simultaneous fires and was gutted.

WARSHIPS

Battleships Largest World The largest battleships in the world are now the U.S.S. *Iowa* (completed 22 Feb. 1943) and U.S.S. *Missouri* (completed 11 June 1944) each of which has a full load displacement of 57,950 tons *58 880 tonnes* and mounts nine 16 in *40,6 cm* and 20 × 5 in *126 mm* guns. The U.S.S. *New Jersey* (57,216 tons [*58 134 tonnes*] full load displacement) is, however, longer than either by 9 in *22,8 cm* with an overall length of 888 ft *270 m*. She was the last fire support ship on active service in the world and was de-commissioned on 17 Dec. 1969.

Largest all-time The Japanese battleships *Yamato* (completed on 16 Dec. 1941 and sunk south west of Kyūshū, Japan, by U.S. planes on 7 April 1945) and *Musashi* (sunk in the Philippine Sea by 11 bombs and 16 torpedoes on 24 Oct. 1944) were the largest battleships ever constructed, each with a full load displacement of 72,809 tons *73 977 tonnes*. With an overall length of 863 ft *263 m*, a beam of 127 ft *38,7 m* and a full load draught of 35½ ft *10,8 m* they mounted nine 460 mm *18.1 in* guns and three triple turrets. Each gun weighed 162 tons *164,6 tonnes* and was 75 ft *22,8 m* in length, firing a 3,200 lb. *1 451 kg* projectile.

Britain Britain's largest ever and last battleship was H.M.S. *Vanguard* with a full load displacement of 51,420 tons *52 245 tonnes*, overall length 814 ft *248,1 m*, beam 108½ ft *33,07 m*, with a maximum draught of 36 ft *10,9 m*. She mounted eight 15 in *38 cm* and 16 × 5.25 in *13,33 cm* guns. A shaft horse-power of 130,000 gave her a sea speed of 29½ knots (34 m.p.h. [*54 km/h*]). The *Vanguard* was laid down in John Brown & Co. Ltd's yard at Clydebank, Dunbartonshire, on 20 Oct. 1941, launched on 30 Nov. 1944 and completed on 25 April 1946. She was sold for scrap in August 1960 for £500,000 having cost a total of £14,000,000.

Guns The largest guns ever mounted in any of H.M. ships were the 18 in *45 cm* pieces in the light battle cruiser (later aircraft carrier) H.M.S. *Furious* in 1917. In 1918 they were transferred to the monitors H.M.S. *Lord Clive* and *General Wolfe*. The thickest armour ever carried was in H.M.S. *Inflexible* (completed 1881), measuring 24 in *60 cm*.

AIRCRAFT CARRIERS

Largest The warship with the largest full load displacement in
World the world is the aircraft carrier U.S.S. *Nimitz* at 95,100 tons *96 626 tonnes*. She was launched on 13 May 1972 and will be commissioned in Sept. 1973. U.S.S. *Enterprise* is, however, 1,101½ ft *335,7 m* long and thus 65½ ft *19,9 m* longer. U.S.S. *Nimitz*, which will have a speed well in excess of 30 knots *56 km/h* will cost $536,000,000 (£223.3 million). She will be followed by a sister ship U.S.S. *Eisenhower*, which will be only 9½ ft *2,8 m* shorter than the *Enterprise*.

Britain Britain's largest ever aircraft carrier is H.M.S. *Ark Royal*, completed on 25 Feb. 1955, with a full load displacement of 50,786 tons *51 601 tonnes* (previously 53,340 tons *54 196 tonnes*), 845 ft *257,5 m* overall, 166 ft *50,5 m* wide, maximum draught 36 ft *10,9 m*, with a full complement of 2,640 and a capacity of 30 naval jet aircraft and 6 helicopters. Her 152,000 shaft horse-power give her a maximum speed of 31.5 knots (36.27 m.p.h. [*58,37 km/h*]).

Most deck The pilot who has made the greatest number of deck
landings landings is Capt. Eric M. Brown, C.B.E., D.S.C., A.F.C., R.N. with 2,407. Capt. Brown (b. Edinburgh, 1919), who retired in 1970, flew a record 325 types of aircraft during his career and also set a world record with 2,721 catapult launchings.

Most The Fleet Escort Ships (formerly cruisers) with the
powerful greatest fire power are the three Albany class ships
cruiser U.S.S.'s *Albany*, *Chicago* and *Columbus* of 13,700 tons *13 920 tonnes* and 673 ft *205,1 m* overall. They carry 2 twin Talos and 2 twin Tartar suface-to-air missiles and an 8-tube Asroc launcher. The world's largest ever cruiser was the U.S.S. *Newport News* of 21,500 tons, full load commissioned on 29 Jan. 1949 and since extensively modified as a flagship. The Royal Navy's largest ever cruiser, H.M.S. *Belfast* displacing 10,000 tons, is now moored on exhibition above the Tower Bridge, London.

Fastest The highest speed attained by a destroyer was 45.02
destroyer knots (51.84 m.p.h. [*83,42 km/h*]) by the 3,750 ton *3 810 tonnes* French destroyer *Le Terrible* in 1935. She was powered by four Yarrow small tube boilers and two geared turbines giving 100,000 shaft horse-power. She was removed from the active list at the end of 1957.

Fastest The world's fastest warship is H.M.C.S. *Bras d'Or*, the
warship 180 ton *182 tonnes*, 150.8 ft *45,96 m* long Canadian Navy Hydrofoil commissioned in 1967 and laid up in 1971. On 17 July 1969 outside Halifax harbour, Nova Scotia she attained 61 knots (70.2 m.p.h. [*112,9 km/h*]). The 100 ton/*tonne* U.S. Navy test vehicle SES-100B has a design speed of 80 plus knots *148 km/h* and attained more than 70 knots *129 km/h* during a trial on 1 March 1973.

SUBMARINES

Largest The world's largest submarines are believed to be the 25 nuclear-powered U.S.S.R. "Y" Class submarines with a submerged displacement of 9,000 tons and an overall length of 426.5 ft *130 m*. The largest submarines built for the Royal Navy are the four atomic-powered nuclear missile R class boats with a surface displacement of 7,500 tons *7 620 tonnes* and 8,400 tons *8 534 tonnes* submerged, a length of 425 ft *129,5 m*, a beam of 33 ft *10 m* and a draught of 30 ft *9,1 m*.

Fastest The world's fastest submarines are the 35-knot U.S. Navy's tear-drop hulled nuclear vessels of the *Skipjack* class. They have been listed semi-officially as

A United States *Skipjack* submarine, the world's fastest

capable of a speed of 45 knots (51.8 m.p.h. *83,3 km/h*) submerged. In November 1968 the building of attack submarines with submerged speeds in the region of 50 knots *92 km/h* was approved for the U.S. Navy.

Deepest The greatest depth recorded by a true submarine was 8,310 ft *2 533 m* by the Lockheed *Sea Quest* off California, U.S.A., on 29 Feb. 1968. The 51 ft *15,4 m* long *Aluminaut* launched by the Reynolds Metals Co. on 2 Sept. 1964 is designed for depths of up to 15,000 ft *4 572 m* but is prevented from descending below 6,250 ft *1 905 m* by prohibitive insurance costs. The U.S. Navy's nuclear-powered NR-1 being built by General Dynamics Inc. will be able to operate at a "very great" but classified depth which is assumed to be lower than the published figure of 20,000 ft *6 096 m* for the first 7-man Deep Submergence Search Vehicle DSSV due in service in 1973.

Largest The largest submarine fleet in the world is that of the
fleet U.S.S.R. Navy or *Krasni Flot*, which numbers 408 boats, of which 95 (73 ballistic missile armed) are nuclear-powered and 331 conventional. The U.S. Navy has 41 nuclear submarines with ballistic missiles, 60 nuclear attack submarines and 35 others.

TANKERS

Largest The world's largest tanker is the *Globtik Tokyo* of 483,664 tons deadweight and 1,243 ft 5 in *379 m* length overall. She is 203 ft 5 in *62 m* in the beam, draws 92 ft *28 m* and is powered by an I.H.I. turbine set rated at 44,385 s.h.p. She was built by Ishikawajima-Harima Heavy Industries Co. Ltd. at Kure, Japan and was launched on 14 Oct. 1972 and completed in Feb. 1973 costing £22,878,000. She has a crew of 38 and flies the Red Ensign. She is equipped with a helicopter, which can take off or land on her deck which is as large as 79 tennis courts or 20 688 m². A sister ship, *Globtik London*, will be completed in March 1974 and another in Sept. 1975. Shell has two 540,000 tonners due for delivery in 1976 from French shipyards and a preliminary agreement for a 707,000 tonner has been made by Globtik Tankers for delivery in late 1977.

Longest The largest ships ever launched in Britain are two Esso class tankers, which have a length of 1,143 ft 3 in *348,46 m*—108 ft *32,94 m* longer than the world's longest ever liner, *France*. They have a deadweight tonnage of 253,000 tons *257 060 tonnes*, a gross registered tonnage of 127,150 and a beam of 170 ft 2 in *51,86 m*. Some idea of this length can be conveyed by the thought that it would take a golfer, standing on the stem, a full-blooded drive and a chip shot to reach the stern. The largest vessels of this class are the *Esso Hibernia* and the *Esso Caledonia* launched in 1970 and 1971 respectively. They are also the longest ships ever launched in the United Kingdom.

CARGO VESSELS

Largest The largest vessel in the world capable of carrying dry cargo is the Japanese *Usa Maru* of 264,523 d.wt. tons *142 246 g.r.t.* with a length of 1,108 ft *337,71 m* and a beam of 178 ft *54,25 m*. The largest British ore/bulk oil carrier is the P & O's *Lauderdale*, built in Japan in 1972, of 260,424 d.wt. tons, which has the highest gross tonnage figure of 143,957 g.r.t.

Fastest built During the Second World War "Liberty ships" of prefabricated welded steel construction were built at seven shipyards on the Pacific coast of the United States, under the management of Henry J. Kaiser (1882–1967). The record time for assembly of one ship of 7,200 gross tons (10,500 tons deadweight) was 4 days 15½ hrs. In January 1968, 900 Liberty ships were still in service.

Largest cable ship The world's largest cable-laying ship is the American Telephone & Telegraph Co.'s German-built *Long Lines* (11,200 gross tons), completed by Deutsche Werft of Hamburg in April 1963, at a cost of £6,800,000. She has a fully-laden displacement of 17,000 tons, measures 511 ft 6 in *156 m* overall and is powered by twin turbine electric engines.

Largest whale factory The largest whale factory ship is the U.S.S.R.'s *Sovietskaya Ukraina* (32,034 gross tons), with a summer deadweight of 46,000 tons *46 738 tonnes* completed in October 1959. She is 714.6 ft *217,8 m* in length and 94 ft 3 in *28,7 m* in the beam.

Most powerful tug World The world's largest and most powerful tugs are the two 17,500 i.h.p. *Oceanic* class boats of 2,046 gross tons, 284 ft 5 in *86 m* overall, a beam of 46 ft 11 in *14,3 m*, a speed of 22 knots *40 km/h* and a range of

m.t. *Lloydsman*, the most powerful British tug at 16,000 s.h.p. *16 221 c.v.*, owned by United Towing Ltd. and built in Scotland

20,000 miles *32 186 km*. The largest ship ever to take another in tow is S.S. *Ardlui*, the 214,180 deadweight ton tanker which towed S.S. *British Architect* (22,729 gross tons) 73 miles *117 km* in the China Sea on 16 June 1970.

British The most powerful tug ever built for a British owner is m.t. *Lloydsman* completed in June 1971 for United Towing Limited of Hull by Robb Caledon Shipbuilders Ltd. She is rated at 16,000 h.p. *16 221 c.v.* with a bollard pull of 135 tons *137 tonnes*. A 5,000 ton tug of 20,000 tons b.h.p. is being built by Robbs for early 1975.

Fastest tow H.M.S. *Scylla* (Cdr., now Comdre., A. F. C. Wemyss, O.B.E., R.N.) towed her sister ship, H.M.S. *Penelope* (Cdr. S. Idiens R.N.) in the Western Mediterranean on 25 Sept. 1970 with an 11 in *28 cm* mile *1,6 km* long nylon rope (breaking strain 165 tons [*167 tonnes*]) at a speed of 24 knots *44 km/h*. The £10,000 Viking Nylon Braidline hawser, made by British Ropes, stretched 38% to 7,325 ft *2 232,6 m*.

Largest car ferry The world's largest car and passenger ferry is the 502 ft *153 m* long *Finlandia* (8,100 gross tons), delivered by Wärtsilä Ab. of Helsinki in May 1967, for service between Helsinki and Copenhagen with Finska Angfartygs Ab. She can carry 321 cars and up to 1,200 passengers and achieved a speed of 22 knots (25 m.p.h. [*40 km/h*]) during trials.

Largest hydrofoil The world's largest naval hydrofoil is the 212 ft *65 m* long *Plainview* (310 tons [*314 tonnes*] full load), launched by the Lockheed Shipbuilding and Construction Co. at Seattle, Washington, U.S.A., on 28 June 1965. She has a service speed of 50 knots (57 m.p.h. [*92 km/h*]). A larger hydrofoil, carrying 150 passengers and 8 cars at 40 knots *74 km/h* to ply the Göteborg-Ålborg crossing, came into service in June 1968. It was built by Westermoen Hydrofoil Ltd. of Mandal, Norway.

Most powerful icebreaker The world's most powerful icebreaker and the first atomic-powered ship has been the U.S.S.R.'s 18 knot *33 km/h* 44,000 s.h.p. *Lenin* (16,000 gross tons), which was launched at Leningrad on 2 Dec. 1957 and began her maiden voyage on 18 Sept. 1959. In 1971-2 mystery surrounded her continued existence. She is or was 439¾ ft *134 m* long and 90½ ft *27,5 m* in the beam. In March 1970 the U.S.S.R. announced the building of

Esso Northumbria, the longest vessel to be launched in the United Kingdom, on the slipway prior to her launch by H.R.H. The Princess Anne on 2 May 1969

The world's first atomic icebreaker, the U.S.S.R.'s 18 knot *Lenin* whose whereabouts are now unknown

a more powerful atomic-powered icebreaker to be named *Arctika*, able to go through ice 7 ft *2,1 m* thick at 4 knots *7 km/h*.

The largest *converted* icebreaker has been the 1,007 ft *306,9 m* long S.S. *Manhattan* (43,000 s.h.p.), which was converted by the Humble Oil Co. into a 150,000 ton *152 407 tonnes* icebreaker with an armoured prow 69 ft 2 in *21,08 m* long. She made a double voyage through the North-West Passage in arctic Canada from 24 Aug. to 12 Nov. 1969. The North-West Passage was first navigated in 1906.

Largest dredger The world's largest dredger is one reported to be operating in the lower Lena basin in May 1967, with a rig more than 100 ft *30 m* tall and a cutting depth of 165 ft *50 m*. The pontoon is 750 ft *228,6 m* long. The largest dredging grabs in the world are those of 635 ft³ *17,98 m³* capacity built in 1965 by Priestman Bros. Ltd. of Hull, Yorkshire for the dredging pontoon *Biarritz*.

Most successful trawler The greatest tonnage of fish ever landed from any British trawler in a year is 4,169 tons *4 235 tonnes* in 1969 from the freezer stern trawler *Lady Parkes* owned by Boston Deep Sea Fisheries Ltd. (est. 1894).

Wooden ship The heaviest wooden ship ever built was the *Richelieu*, 333 ft 8 in *101,70 m* long and of 8,534 tons launched in Toulon, France on 3 Dec. 1873. H.M. Battleship *Lord Warden*, completed 1869, displaced 7,940 tons. The longest sea-going wooden ship ever built was the New York built *Rochambeau* (1867–1872) formerly *Dunderberg*. She measured 377 ft 4 in *115 m* overall.

SAILING SHIPS

Largest The largest sailing vessel ever built was the *France II* (5,806 gross tons), launched at Bordeaux in 1911. The *France II* was a steel-hulled, five-masted barque (square-rigged on four masts and fore and aft rigged on the aftermost mast). Her hull measured 418 ft *127,4 m* overall. Although principally designed as a sailing vessel with a stump topgallant rig, she was also fitted with two steam engines. She was wrecked in 1922. The only 5 masted full-rigged ship ever built was the *Preussen*, built in 1902, of 5,548 gross tons and 410 ft *125 m* overall. Her total sail area was 59,000 ft² *5 480 m²*.

Largest junks The largest junk on record was the sea-going *Cheng Ho* of *c.* 1420, with a displacement of 3,100 tons *3 150 tonnes* and a length variously estimated at from 300 ft to 440 ft *91 to 134 m*.

A river junk 361 ft *110 m* long, with treadmill-operated paddle-wheels, was recorded in A.D. 1161. In *c.* A.D. 280 a floating fortress 600 ft *182,8 m* square, built by Wang Chün on the Yangtze, took part in the Chin-Wu river war. Modern junks do not, even in the case of the Chiangsu traders, exceed 170 ft *51,8 m* in length.

Longest day's run under sail The longest day's run by any sailing ship was one of 465 nautical miles (535.45 statute miles [*861,72 km*]) by the clipper *Champion of the Seas* (2,722 registered tons) of the Liverpool Black Ball Line running before a north-westerly gale in the south Indian Ocean under the command of Capt. Alex. Newlands. The elapsed time between the fixes was 23 hrs 17 min giving an average of 19,97 knots *37,00 km/h*.

Greatest speed The highest speed by a sailing merchantman is 22 knots (25.3 m.p.h. [*40,7 km/h*]) in 4 consecutive watches, by *Lancing* (ex *La Péreire*) when "running her easting down" on a passage to Melbourne in 1890/91. She was the last 4 masted full-rigged ship (36 sails) and at 405 ft *123,4 m* the longest. Her main and mizzen masts were 203 ft *61,8 m* from keelson to truck with yards 98 ft 9 in *30,09 m* across.

Slowest voyage Perhaps the slowest passage on record was that of the *Red Rock* (1,600 tons [*1 625 tonnes*]), which was posted missing at Lloyd's of London after taking 112 days for 950 miles *1 529 km* across the Coral Sea from 20 Feb. to 12 June 1899, at an average speed of less than 0.4 of a knot *0,7 km/h*.

Largest sails The largest spars ever carried were those in H.M. Battleship *Temeraire*, completed at Chatham, Kent, on 31 Aug. 1877. The fore and main yards measured 115 ft *35 m* in length. The mainsail contained 5,100 ft *1 555 m* of canvas, weighing 2 tons *2,03 tonnes* and the total sail area was 25,000 ft² *2 322 m²*. At 8,540 tons *8 677 tonnes* the *Temeraire* was the largest brig ever built but was primarily steam-powered. The main masts of H.M.S. *Achilles*, *Black Prince* and *Warrior* all measured 175 ft *53 m* from truck to deck.

Largest propeller The largest ship's propellers are of 30 ft 2 in *9,19 m* diameter from blade tip to blade tip and weighing 58 tons *59 tonnes* built for the 483,664 ton tankers *Globtik Tokyo* and *Globtik London*.

Deepest anchorage The deepest anchorage ever achieved is one of 24,600 ft *7 498 m* in the mid-Atlantic Romanche Trench by Capt. Jacques-Yves Cousteau's research vessel *Calypso*, with a 5½ mile *8,9 km* long nylon cable, on 29 July 1956.

Largest Oil Platforms The largest fixed leg drilling platforms are two due for completion in spring 1974 for British Petroleum with 464 ft *141,4 m* legs weighing 57,000 tons for the Forties Field 115 miles *185 km* out in the North Sea.

Largest wreck The largest ship ever wrecked has been the Japanese-built, Royal Dutch/Shell owned, 206,600 ton (deadweight) tanker *Marpessa* after a tank explosion when sailing in ballast from Rotterdam, 50 miles northwest of Dakar, Senegal on 15 Dec. 1969. She was 1,067 ft 5 in *325 m* long. The largest vessel ever to be wrecked in British waters has been the 965 ft *294 m* long tanker, *Torrey Canyon*, of 61,275 tons gross and 118,285 tons deadweight, which struck the Pollard Rock of the Seven Stones Reef between the Isles of Scilly and Land's End, Cornwall, England, at 08.50 on 18 March 1967. The resultant oil pollution from some 30,000 tons *30 481 tonnes* of Kuwait crude was "on a scale which had no precedent anywhere in the world". In an attempt to fire the remaining oil, the ship was bombed to virtual destruction on 28–30 March 1967.

Oldest wreck The oldest vessel regarded as salvageable in British waters is the carrack *Mary Rose* of 1509, which sank off Ryde, Isle of Wight in 1545. On 18 Sept. 1970 a 4 cwt *203 kg* 8 ft *2,4 m* long breech-loader was recovered from her hull, which appears to have been preserved in a blue clay layer of the sea bed.

Greatest Roll The ultimate in rolling was recorded in heavy seas off Coos Bay, Oregon, U.S.A. on 13 Nov. 1971, when the U.S. Coast Guard motor lifeboat *Intrepid* made a 360 degree roll.

2. ROAD VEHICLES

Guinness Superlatives has now published automotive records in much greater detail in the more specialist publication "Car Facts and Feats" (price £2.00) and obtainable from any good bookshop or, if in difficulties, from the address in the front of this volume.

COACHING

Before the advent of the McAdam road surfaces in *c.* 1815 coaching was slow and hazardous. The zenith was reached on 13 July 1888 when J. Selby, Esq., drove the "Old Times" coach 108 miles *173 km* from London to Brighton and back with 8 teams and 14 changes in 7 hrs 50 min to average 13.79 m.p.h. *22,19 km/h*. Four-horse carriages could maintain a speed of 21¼ m.p.h. *34 km/h* for nearly an hour.

MOTOR CARS

Earliest automobiles The earliest automobile of which there is record is a two-foot-long steam-powered model constructed by *Model* Ferdinand Verbiest (d. 1687) a Belgian Jesuit priest, and described in his *Astronomia Europaea*. His model of 1668 was possibly inspired either by Giovanni Branca's description of a steam turbine, published in his *La Macchina* in 1629, or by writings on "fire carts" during the Chu dynasty (*c.* 800 B.C.) in the library of the Emperor Khang-hi of China, to whom he was an astronomer during the period *c.* 1665–80. A 3-wheeled model steam locomotive was built at Redruth, Cornwall by William Murdoch (1754–1839) in 1785–6.

Passenger-carrying The earliest mechanically-propelled passenger vehicle was the first of two military steam tractors, completed at the Paris Arsenal in 1770 by Nicolas-Joseph Cugnot (1725–1804). This reached 2¼ m.p.h. *3,6 km/h* Cugnot's second, larger tractor, completed in May 1771, today survives in the *Conservatoire Nationale des Arts et Métiers* in Paris. Britain's first steam carriage carried eight passengers on 24 Dec. 1801 and was built by Richard Trevithick (1771–1833) at Cambourne, Cornwall.

Internal combustion The first true internal-combustion engined vehicle was that built by the Londoner Samuel Brown whose 4 h.p. *4,05 c.v.* two cylinder engined carriage climbed Shooters Hill, Blackheath, Kent in May 1826.

Earliest petrol-driven cars The first successful petrol-driven car, the Motorwagen, built by Karl-Friedrich Benz (1844–1929) of Karlsruhe, ran at Mannheim, Germany, in late 1885. It was a 5 cwt. *250 kg* 3-wheeler reaching 8–10 m.p.h. *13–16 km/h*. Its single cylinder chain-drive engine (bore 91.4 mm., stroke 160 mm.) delivered 0.85 h.p. *0,86 c.v.* at 200 r.p.m. It was patented on 29 Jan. 1886. Its first 1 kilometre road test was reported in the local newspaper, the *Neue Badische Landeszeitung*, of 4 June 1886, under the heading "Miscellaneous". Two were built in 1885 of which one has been preserved in "running order" at the Deutsche Museum, Munich since 1959.

Earliest British cars In Britain Edward Butler (1863–1940) built a 1,042 c.c. twin cylinder petrol-engined tricycle automobile in 1888 but the earliest successful British built car with an internal combustion engine was the Bremer car built at Walthamstow, Greater London, by the engineer Frederick William Bremer (1872–1941) which first took the road in December 1894 though the body was not completed until the following month. The car has a single cylinder horizontal, water cooled 600 c.c. engine with a two speed chain drive and tiller steering. The maximum speed is about 15 m.p.h. and the car in 1965 completed the London–to–Brighton run. It is now housed in the Vestry House Museum, London E.17.

Oldest The oldest internal-combustion engine car seen on British roads has been the Danish "Hammel". Designed by Albert Hammel, who took out the original

The renovated car designed by Frederick Bremer in 1894, the first successful car on British roads, now housed at the Vestry House Museum, Walthamstow

patents in 1886, it was completed in 1887. In 1954 it completed the London-to-Brighton run in 12½ hrs, averaging 4¼ m.p.h. *7,24 km/h*. The engine is a twin-cylinder, horizontal water-cooled four-stroke with a capacity of 2,720 c.c., bore and stroke 104.5 mm × 160 mm, and a compression ratio of 3.5:1.

Most durable The automotive writer Boyd Eugene Taylor of Atlanta, Georgia, U.S.A. in 1956 surpassed the 1,000,000 mile mark in his 1936 Ford two-door car. The "clock" on its 11th trip round showed (1 million and) 37,000 miles.

Earliest registrations The world's first plates were probably introduced by the Parisian police in France in 1893. Registration plates were introduced in Britain in 1903. The original A1 plate was secured by the 2nd Earl Russell (1865–1931) for his 12 h.p. *12,1 c.v.* Napier. This plate, willed in September 1950 to Mr. Trevor T. Laker of Leicester, was sold in August 1959 for £2,500 in aid of charity. It was reported in April 1973 that a number plate changed hands for £14,000 in a private deal.

FASTEST CARS

Rocket engined The highest speed attained by any wheeled land vehicle is 631.368 m.p.h. *1 016,088 km/h* over the first measured kilometre of *The Blue Flame*, a liquid natural gas-powered 4-wheeled vehicle driven by Gary Gabelich on the Bonneville Salt Flats, Utah, on 23 Oct. 1970. Momentarily Gabelich exceeded 650 m.p.h. *1 046 km/h*. The tyres were made by Goodyear. The car was powered by a liquid natural gas/hydrogen peroxide rocket engine delivering 22,000 lb.s.t. maximum and thus theoretically capable of 900 m.p.h. *1 448 km/h*. The building of a 1200 km/h (*745 m.p.h.*) racing car, the Nikitin *Khadi-9*, by the Institute of Automotive Transport, Khomkov, Ukraine was announced in May 1973.

Jet The highest speed attained by any jet-engined car is 613.995 m.p.h. *988,129 km/h* over a flying 666.386 yds *609 342 m* by the 34 ft 7 in *10,5 m* long 9,000 lb. *4 080 kg* Spirit of America–Sonic I, driven by Norman Craig Breedlove (b. 23 March 1938, Los Angeles) on Bonneville Salt Flats, Tooele County, Utah, U.S.A., on 15 Nov. 1965. The car was powered by a General Electric J79 GE-3 jet engine, developing 15,000 lb.s.t. *6 080 kg* at sea-level.

Wheel-driven The highest speed attained by a wheel-driven car is 429.311 m.p.h. *690,909 km/h* over a flying 666.386 yds *609,342 m* by Donald Malcolm Campbell, C.B.E.

(1921–67), a British engineer, in the 30 ft *9,10 m* long *Bluebird*, weighing 9,600 lb. *4 354 kg* on the salt flats at Lake Eyre, South Australia, on 17 July 1964. The car was powered by a Bristol-Siddeley 705 gas-turbine engine developing 4,500 s.h.p. Its *peak* speed was c. 440 m.p.h. *708 km/h*. It was rebuilt in 1962, after a crash at about 360 m.p.h. *579 km/h* on 16 Sept. 1960.

Piston engine The highest speed attained by a piston-engined car is 418.504 m.p.h. *673,516 km/h* over a flying 666.386 yds *609,342 m* by Robert Sherman Summers (born 4 April 1937, Omaha, Nebraska) in *Goldenrod* at Bonneville Salt Flats on 12 Nov. 1965. The car, measuring 32 ft *9,75 m* long and weighing 5,500 lb. *2 494 kg* was powered by four fuel-injected Chrysler Hemi engines (total capacity 27,924 c.c.) developing 2,400 b.h.p.

Production The world's fastest and most powerful production car (more than 25 examples produced within 12 months) ever produced was the German Porsche 4.9 litre Type 917 built in 1970 and 1971. It had a flat 12-cylinder air-cooled 4.99 litre engine developing 600 b.h.p. at 8,600 r.p.m. A Type 917L reached a speed calculated to be 238 m.p.h. *383 km/h* during practice on the Le Mans Mulsanne straight on 18 April 1971.

LARGEST

World Of cars produced for private road use, the largest has been the Bugatti "Royale" type 41, known in Britain as the "Golden Bugatti", of which only six (not seven) were made at Molsheim, France by the Italian Ettore Bugatti, and some survive. First built in 1927, this machine has an 8-cylinder engine of 12.7 litres capacity, and measures over 22 ft *6,7 m* in length. The bonnet is over 7 ft *2 m* long. The blood red 1933 Model J Victoria Duesenberg custom-built for Greta Garbo measures 24 ft *7,30 m* overall. The longest present-day limousine is the Stageway Coaches Inc. 10 door Travelall 18 seat model measuring 25 ft 4¼ in *7,7 m* overall. (For cars not intended for private use, see Largest engines.)

Heaviest The heaviest standard production car is the U.S.S.R.'s Zil 114, which weighs 7,000 lb. 3.12 ton *3 175 kg*.

MOST EXPENSIVE

Special The most expensive car to build has been the U.S. Presidential 1969 Lincoln Continental Executive delivered to the U.S. Secret Service on 14 Oct. 1968. It has an overall length of 21 ft 6.3 in *6,56 m* with a 13 ft 4 in *4 m* wheel-base and with the addition of two tons *2,03 tonnes* of armour plate weighs 5.35 tons *5,43 tonnes* (12,000 lb. [*5 443 kg*]). The estimated research, development and manufacture cost was $500,000 (*then £208,000*) but it is rented at $5,000 (*now £1,923*) per annum. Even if all four tyres were shot out it can travel at 50 m.p.h. *80 km/h* on inner rubber-edged steel discs.

Production The most expensive standard car now available is the 19 ft 10 in *6 m* long 7-seat Rolls-Royce Phantom VI (V8, 6,230 c.c. engine) with coachwork by Park Ward at £15,559. The cost of a 4.9 litre Series 2 Porsche Type 917 *ex* works with import duty and purchase tax would have been more than £37,000 but none were imported. The Ferrari Boxer is expected to be priced at some $48,000 in 1974. The all-time dollar record was a Bugatti Royale in 1931 for $55,000 (*then £14,850*).

Used The greatest price paid for any used car has been $153,000 (*then £62,448*) for the armour plated 8 seat 230 h.p. Mercedes straight 8 used in parades by Hitler. The purchaser at Scottsdale, Arizona on 6 Jan. 1973 was Earl Clark of Lancaster, Pennsylvania. The greatest collection of vintage cars is the William F. Harrah Collection of 1,440, estimated to be worth more than $3 million (*£1¼ million*), at Reno, Nevada, U.S.A. Mr. Harrah is still looking for a Chalmer's Detroit 1909 Tourabout, an Owen car of 1910–12 and a Nevada Truck of 1915.

A Porsche 917 L the world's fastest production car (238 m.p.h. [*383 km/h*])

Most inexpensive The cheapest car of all-time was the U.S. 1908 Brownicker for children, but designed for road use, which sold for $150 (*then £30 17s. 3d.*). The Kavan of 1905, also of U.S. manufacture, was listed at $200 (*then £41 3s.*). The early models of the King Midget cars were sold in kit form for self-assembly for as little as $100 (*then £24 16s.*) as late as 1948.

Longest production The longest any car has been in production is 42 years (1910–52), including wartime interruptions, in the case of the "Flat Twin" engined Jowett produced in Britain. The Ford Model T production record of 15,007,033 cars (1908–1927) was surpassed by the Volkswagen "Beetle" series when their 15,007,034th car came off the production line on 17 Feb. 1972.

LARGEST ENGINES

Cars are compared on the basis of engine capacity. Distinction is made between those designed for normal road use and machines specially built for track racing and outright speed records.

All-time record The world's most powerful piston engine car is "Quad Al." It was designed and built in 1964 by Jim Lytle and was first shown in May 1965 at the Los Angeles Sports Arena. The car featured four Allison V12 aircraft engines with a total of 6840 in³ (112,087 c.c.) displacement and 12,000 h.p. The car has 4-wheel drive, 8 wheels and tyres, and dual six-disc clutch assemblies. The wheelbase is 160 in, and weighs 5,860 lb. *2 658 kg*. It has 96 spark plugs and 96 exhaust pipes.

The largest car ever used was the "White Triplex", sponsored by J. H. White of Philadelphia, Pennsylvania, U.S.A. Completed early in 1928, after two year's work, the car weighed about 4 tons *4,06 tonnes* and was powered by three Liberty V12 aircraft engines with a total capacity of 81,188 c.c., developing 1,500 b.h.p. at 2,000 r.p.m. It was used to break the world speed record but crashed at Daytona, Florida on 13 March 1929.

The largest racing car was the "Higham Special", which first raced in 1923 at Brooklands driven by its owner Count Louis Vorow Zborowski, the younger (k. 1924). John Godfrey Parry Thomas renamed the car "Babs" and used it to break the land speed record. Powered by a V12 Liberty aircraft engine with a capacity of 27,059 c.c., developing 400 to 500 b.h.p. at 2,000 r.p.m. The car was wrecked, and Thomas killed, during an attempt on this record at Pendine Sands, Carmarthenshire, Wales, on 3 March 1927.

Production car The highest engine capacity of a production car was 13½ litres (*824 in³*), in the case of the U.S. Pierce-Arrow 6-66 Raceabout of 1912–18, the U.S. Peerless 6-60 of 1912–14 and the Fageol of 1918. The largest currently available is the V8 engine of 500.1 in³ (*8,195 c.c.*), developing 235 b.h.p. net, used in the 1972 Cadillac Fleetwood Eldorado.

Petrol The world record for fuel economy on a closed circuit **consump-** course (one of 14.08 miles [*22,65 km*]) was set by R. J. **tion** 'Bob' Greenshields, C. A. 'Skeeter' Hargrave, Jan Evans and Earl Elmqvist in a highly modified 1956 Austin Healey in the annual Shell Research Laboratory contest at Wood River, Illinois on 19 Sept. 1970 with 302.7 ton miles per U.S. gal. and 145.5 miles *234,1 km* on one U.S. gal. of *3,78 litres*. These figures are equivalent to 324.57 ton miles and 174.7 miles *281,1 km* on an Imperial gallon of *4,54 litres*.

On 24 Aug. 1969 a 4-seat 600 c.c. Reliant Regal 3-wheeler driven by Brian Lodwick plus an R.A.C. observer, described as 'large', achieved 103.6 miles *166,7 km* on one gal *4,5 litres* at Mallory Park, Leicestershire.

The best recorded figure in an unmodified 4-wheeled car using pump petrol is 96.59 m.p.g. *34,19 km/litres* by a Fiat 500 driven on an out and home course from Cheltenham to Evesham, Worcestershire, England, by W. (Featherfoot Joe) Dembowski on 1 July 1965.

BUSES

Earliest The first municipal motor omnibus service in the world was inaugurated on 12 April 1903 between Eastbourne railway station and Meads, Sussex, England.

Longest The longest buses in the world are the 65 ft *20 m* long articulated buses for 160 passengers built by Bus Bodies (S.A.) Ltd. of Port Elizabeth, South Africa for use in Johannesburg.

Longest The longest regularly scheduled bus route is the **route** Greyhound "Supercruiser" Miami, Florida to San Francisco, California route over 3,240 miles *5 214 km* in 81 hrs 50 min (average speed of travel 39.59 m.p.h. [*63,71 km/h*]). The total Greyhound fleet numbers 5,500 buses.

A Greyhound "Supercruiser", one of the fleet which travel the longest regularly scheduled bus route, Miami, Florida to San Francisco, California

Largest The largest trolleybuses in the world are the articu- **trolleybuses** lated vehicles put into service in Moscow, U.S.S.R., in May 1959, with a length of 57 ft *17 m* and a capacity of 200.

A Euclid R-210 Hauler, the world's largest Dumper Truck, and the most expensive at £200,000

Most The most massive vehicle ever constructed is the **massive** Marion eight-caterpillar crawler used for conveying **vehicle** *Saturn V* rockets to their launching pads at the John F. Kennedy Space Center, Florida (see Chapter 4, Most powerful rocket). It measures 131 ft 4 in *40 m* by 114 ft *34,7 m* and cost $12,300,000 (*then £5,125,000*) for two. The loaded train weight is 8,036 tons *8 165 tonnes*. Its windscreen wipers with 42 in *106 cm* blades are the world's largest. Two were built.

Largest The world's largest lorry is the M-200 Lectra Haul **lorry** built by Unit Rig and Equipment Co. of Fort Worth, Texas with a capacity of 200 tons *203 tonnes*. It is powered by a 1,650 h.p. diesel and twin 750 h.p. electric motors. It is 43 ft *13 m* long and 20 ft *6 m* high.

The most powerful British-engined prime mover is the Rotinoff Tractor Super Atlantic with a 400 b.h.p. Rolls-Royce engine. In May 1958, one of these hauled the first of 12 atomic power station heat-exchangers at Bradwell, Essex. The gross train weight was 370 tons *375 tonnes*. The Aveling Barford Sn 35 Dump Truck is fitted with a 450 b.h.p. engine.

Longest The longest vehicle in the world was the 572 ft *174,3 m* **vehicle** long, 54-wheeled U.S. Army Overland Train Mk. II, built by R.G. Le Tourneau Inc. of Longview, Texas, U.S.A. Its gross weight was 400 tons *406 tonnes* and it had a top speed of 20 m.p.h. *32 km/h* from four engines with a combined s.h.p. of 4,680, which required a capacity of 6,522 Imperial gallons *29 648 litres* of fuel. Despite a cost of $3,755,000, it was sold for scrap for $47,900 (*then £18,425*) in 1971.

Largest The world's largest bulldozer is the Caterpillar SXS **bulldozers** D9G with a 24 ft *7,3 m* dozer blade weighing 84.8 tons *86,1 tonnes*. The largest road grader in the world is the 25.0 ton *25,4 tonnes* 31 ft 5 in *9,5 m* long CMI Corporation Autograde 55 with a 325 h.p. engine.

Largest The world's largest dumper truck is the Euclid Inc. **Dumper** R-210 Hauler announced on 31 Aug. 1971. This **Truck** 111.6 ton *113,3 tonnes* 8 wheeled vehicle measuring 42 ft 6 in *12,95 m* overall, 23 ft 3 in *7,08 m* wide and 16 ft 11 in *5,15 m* high costs $500,000 (*now £200,000*).

The world's most powerful tractor in action, the 142.8 ton *145,1 tonne* K-205 Pacemaker

Largest tractor The most powerful tractor in the world is the 142.8 ton *145,09 tonnes* K-205 Pacemaker with a 1,260 horse-power rating. It is built by R. G. Le Tourneau, Inc., of Longview, Texas, U.S.A.

Driving in Reverse The largest recorded drive backwards was one of 136 km *84½ miles* from near Injebara to Bahar Dar, Ethiopia in a Volkswagen 1200 with a jammed gear box by Patrick Gilkes at Easter 1967.

Largest taxi fleet The largest taxi fleet was that of New York City, which amounted to 29,000 cabs in October 1929, compared with the 1969 figure of 11,500.

Fastest caravan The world record for towing a caravan in 24 hours is 1,689 miles *2 718 km* (average speed 70.395 m.p.h. [*113,289 km/h*]) by a Ford Zodiac Mk. IV towing a Sprite Major 5-berth caravan, 16 ft *4,8 m* long and weighing 14½ cwt. *736 kg* at Monza Autodrome near Milan, Italy, on 15–16 Oct. 1966. The drivers were Ian Mantle, John Risborough and Michael Bowler, all of Great Britain.

Longest motor caravan journey The longest motor caravan tour on record is one of 68,000 miles *109 435 km* carried out in a 1966 Commer Highwayman through 69 sovereign countries between 27 Dec. 1966 and 20 Oct. 1971 by Sy Feldman, his wife Christine, and two sons, Greg and Tim.

Round Britain motoring *The Guinness Book of Records does not publish place to place or rally records made on public roads due to public policy unless these are under the aegis of H.M. Armed Forces, the R.A.C. or the Police.*

On 7–11 May 1971 an R.A.F. team of Corporals, Peter Mitchell and Ken Jones, and Junior Technician John Housley from Leuchars, Fife, completed 3,542 miles *5 700 km* in 97¾ hours in a rally round the coast of Great Britain in a 1961 Mark 2, 2.4 Jaguar.

LOADS

The world's record road load is one of 400 short tons *363 tonnes*. This reactor was moved from Avila Beach for 10 miles *16 km* to Diablo Canyon, California in November 1970. The conveyance called "Atlas", built by the Bigge Drayage Co. itself weighs 211 short tons *191 tonnes* has 192 wheels in 16 groups of twelve.

Heaviest and largest The heaviest road loads moved in the United Kingdom have been 305.5 ton *310,4 tonne* generator inner cores moved both by Pickfords Heavy Haulage Ltd. and Robert Wynn & Sons Ltd. for the C.E.G.B. to various power stations since 25 June 1971 when Pickfords hauled the first to Dungeness "B" Station, Kent. The longest load moved on British roads has been a 171 ft *52,1 m* long Carbon dioxide absorber column, by Pickfords from Linhouse Works to Glasgow Docks in May 1971. The bulkiest load moved was a 212 ton *215 tonnes* cracking tower 111½ ft *33,9 m* long with a diameter of 28½ ft *8,68 m* for a distance of 17 miles *27 km* by Wynn's from Birkenhead to the Shell Refinery, Stanlow, Cheshire. By 1976 it is anticipated that loads of up to 600 tons *609 tonnes* will be being moved on British roads.

Tallest The tallest load ever conveyed by road comprised two 98 ft *30 m* tall cableway towers, each weighing 70 tons *71 tonnes* which were taken 25 miles *40 km* from Ohakuri to Aratiatia, New Zealand, in June 1961. The loads were carried on a 68-wheel trailer, towed by a 230 h.p. Leyland Buffalo tractor, for George Dale and Son Ltd.

Amphibious vehicle The only trans-Atlantic crossing by an amphibious vehicle was achieved by Ben Carlin (U.S.A.) in an amphibious jeep called "Half-Safe". He completed the cross channel leg on 24 Aug. 1951.

Longest skid marks The longest recorded skid marks on a public road have been those 950 ft *290 m* long left by a Jaguar car involved in an accident on the M1 near Luton, Bedfordshire, on 30 June 1960. Evidence given in the High Court case *Hurlock* v. *Inglis and others* indicated a speed "in excess of 100 m.p.h. *160 km/h*" before the application of the brakes. The skid marks made by the jet-powered *Spirit of America*, driven by Craig Breedlove, after the car went out of control at Bonneville Salt Flats, Utah, U.S.A., on 15 Oct. 1964, were nearly 6 miles *9,6 km* long.

The "Atlas" conveyance, built by the Bigge Drayage Co. for moving the heaviest load of 400 short tons *363 tonnes*, it moves on 192 wheels

Largest tyres The world's largest tyres are the 4000-57 OR tyre built in 1971 by Bridgestone Tyre Co. of Japan which have a diameter of 11 ft 10 in *3,6 m* and weigh 7,275 lb. (3.24 tons [*3,29 tonnes*]).

Petrol Station The largest gallonage sold claimed through a single pump is 2,597 gal *11 085 litres* in 24 hours on 15–16 July 1972 at Pitcher's Garage, St. Helier, Jersey.

"L" test *Most failures* The record for persistence in taking the Ministry of Transport's Learners' Test is held by Mrs. Miriam Hargrave, 62, of Wakefield, Yorkshire, who failed her 39th driving test in eight years on 29 April 1970. She triumphed at her 40th attempt on 3 Aug. 1970. The examiner was alleged not to have known about her previous 39 tests.

Most Durable Examiner The most durable examiner has been Mr. Charles James Sugrue, M.B.E. of Lewes, Sussex who in 37 years (March 1935 to 1972) survived at least 42,500 tests.

Oldest driver In a survey by the U.S. Social Security Administration of 300 centenarians in 1968 it was discovered that one, identified as a Mr. Dring, drove his car to work every day. Britain's oldest recorded driver was the Rev. Wilfred Lionel de Buckenhold Thorold of Petersfield, Hampshire, who was banned in June 1971 from further driving without a test when aged 98. The oldest age at which anyone has passed the then Ministry of Transport driving test was on 20 September 1969 at Sutton-in-Derwent, Yorkshire, when Mr. Arthur Daniel passed at his second attempt aged 85. The highest year number ever displayed on a Veteran Motorist's badge was "75" by Walter Herbert Weake, who started his accident free career in 1894 and drove daily until his death in 1969, aged 91.

Garage Work Record The fastest time recorded for taking out a car engine and replacing it is 5 mins 20 sec in the case of a Volkswagen by Bobby Ervin and Larry Allen at Tustin, California in Nov. 1972.

MOTORCYCLES

Earliest The earliest internal combustion-engined motorized bicycle was a wooden-framed machine built at Bad Canstatt in Nov. 1886 by Gottlieb Daimler (1834–1900) of Germany and first ridden by Wilhelm Maybach (1846–1929). It had a top speed of 12 m.p.h. and developed one-half of one horse-power from its single cylinder 264 c.c. four-stroke engine at 700 r.p.m. The first entirely British motorcycle was the 3 h.p. Holden flat-four produced in 1898. The earliest factory which made motorcycles in quantity was opened in 1894 by Henry and William Hildebrand and Alois Wolfmüller at München (Munich), Bavaria, Germany. In its first two years this factory produced over 1,000 machines, each having a water-cooled 1,488 c.c. twin-cylinder four-stroke engine developing about 2.5 b.h.p. at 600 r.p.m.

Fastest road machine The fastest standard motorcycle ever produced is the Dunstall Norton Commando powered by a twin cylinder 850 c.c. engine developing 72 b.h.p. at 7,000 r.p.m. and capable of 140 m.p.h. *225 km/h.*

Fastest racing machine The fastest racing motorcycle ever has been the 748 c.c. 105 b.h.p. Kawasaki 3-cylinder two-stroke produced in Dec. 1971 and capable of 185 m.p.h. *297 km/h* (see also Motorcycle racing, Chapter 12). Of British machines the fastest ever were the 741 c.c. 3-cylinder B.S.A. Rocket 3 and Triumph Trident racers used in the "Daytona 200" on 14 March 1971. They developed 84 b.h.p. and were capable of 170 m.p.h. *273 km/h.*

Largest The largest motorcycle ever put into production was the 1,488 c.c. Hildebrand Wolfmüller (see above).

Most expensive The most expensive road motorcycle in current production is the Italian M.V.-Agusta 750 Sport which retails in the United Kingdom for £2,175 (Oct. 1972).

The most expensive British-made motorcycle in current production is the 850 c.c. Dunstall Norton Commando which retail for up to £1,071 in June 1973.

BICYCLES

Earliest Though there were many velocipedes before that time, the term bicycle was first used in 1868. The earliest portrayal of such a vehicle is in a stained glass window, dated 1642, in Stoke Poges Church, Buckinghamshire, depicting a man riding a hobby horse or celeripede.

The first machine propelled by cranks and pedals, with connecting rods, was that invented in 1839 by Kirkpatrick Macmillan (1810–78) of Dumfries. It is now in the Science Museum, South Kensington, London.

Penny-Farthing record The record for riding from Land's End to John o'Groats on Ordinary Bicycles, more commonly known in the 1870's as Penny-Farthings, is 13 days (123½ hours riding) by Brian Thompson, 34 in 1970.

Longest The longest tandem 'bicycle' ever built is the 31-man 50 ft *15 m* long trigintapede built in Queanbeyan, Australia in November, 1971.

Smallest The world's smallest rideable bicycle is a 5 in *12 cm* high model with front and rear wheels of 2⅛ and 4 in *5,4 and 10 cm* made and ridden by Midshipman Arthur L. Nalls of Annapolis, Maryland, U.S.A.

The world's smallest bicycle, compared with a Dollar Note, the bicycle is 5 in *12,7 cm* high

Largest tricycle The largest tricycle ever made was one manufactured in 1897 for the Woven-Hose and Rubber Company of Boston, Massachusetts, U.S.A. Its side wheels were 11 ft *3,4 m* in diameter and it weighed nearly a ton *1,01 tonnes*. It could carry eight riders.

Tallest unicycle The tallest unicycle ever mastered is one 32 ft *9,7 m* tall ridden by Steve McPeak of Seattle Pacific College, U.S.A., in 1969. McPeak set a duration record when on 26 Nov. 1968 he completed a 2,000 miles *3 218 km* journey from Chicago, Illinois to Las Vegas, Nevada, U.S.A. in 6 weeks on a 13 ft *4 m* unicycle. He covered 80 miles *128 km* on some days.

LAWN MOWER

Largest The widest gang mower on record is one of 15 overlapping sections manufactured by Lloyds & Co. of Letchworth Ltd., Hertfordshire, England used by The Jockey Club to mow 2,500 acres *1 011 ha* on Newmarket Heath. Its cutting width is 41 ft 6 in *12,6 m* and has a capacity, with a 15 m.p.h. *24 km/h* tractor, of up to 70 acres *28 ha* per hour.

The three lawn mowers which took part in the endurance trials between Washington and New York City in September 1971

Longest lawnmower journey In an endurance trial over 306.6 miles *493,4 km* from Washington, D.C. to New York City on 9–21 Sept. 1971 three Gravely machines (a 12 h.p. walking model, an 8 h.p. lawn tractor and a 16.5 h.p. riding tractor) each covered 144.1 miles *231,9 km* mowing 47 per cent of the time.

3. RAILWAYS

Guinness Superlatives has now published railway records in much greater detail in the more specialist publication "Guinness Book of Rail Facts and Feats" (price £2.75) and obtainable from any good bookshop or, if in difficulties, from the address in the front of this volume.

EARLIEST

Railed trucks were used for mining as early as 1550 at Leberthal, Alsace and by Ralph Allen from Combe Down to the River Avon in 1731, but the first self-propelled locomotive ever to run on rails was that built by Richard Trevithick (1771–1833) and demonstrated over 9 miles *14 km* with a 10 ton *10,2 tonnes* load and 70 passengers in Penydaren, Glamorgan, on 21 Feb. 1804. The earliest established railway to have a steam powered locomotive was the Middleton Colliery Railway, set up by an Act of 1758 running between Middleton Colliery and Leeds Bridge, Yorkshire. This line went over to the use of steam locomotives, built by Matthew Murray, in 1812. The Stockton and Darlington colliery line, County Durham, which ran from Shildon through Darlington to Stockton, opened on 27 Sept. 1825. The 7 ton *7,1 tonnes Locomotion I* (formerly *Active*) could pull 48 tons *48,7 tonnes* at a speed of 15 m.p.h. *24 km/h*. It was designed and driven by George Stephenson (1781–1848). The first regular steam passenger run was inaugurated over a one mile section (between Bogshole Farm and South Street) on the 6¼ mile *10,05 km* track between Canterbury and Whitstable, Kent, on 3 May 1830 hauled by the engine *Invicta*. The first electric railway was Werner von Siemen's 300 yds *274 m* long Berlin electric tramway opened for the Berlin Trades' Exhibition on 31 May 1879.

FASTEST

Electric The world rail speed record is held jointly by two French Railway electric locomotives, the CC7107 and the BB9004. On 28 and 29 March 1955, hauling three carriages of a total weight of 100 tons *101,6 tonnes*, they each achieved a speed of 205.6 m.p.h. *330,8 km/h*. The runs took place on the 1,500 volt D.C. Bordeaux–Dax line, from Facture to Morcenx, and the top speed was maintained by the drivers, H. Braghet and J. Brocca, for 2 km *1.24 miles*. The CC7107 weighs 106 tons *108 tonnes* and has a continuous rating of 4,300 h.p. at 1,500 volts, but developed 12,000 h.p. over the timing stretch. The BB9004 weighs 81 tons *82 tonnes* and has a continuous rating of 4,000 h.p.

Steam The highest speed ever recorded by a steam locomotive was 126 m.p.h. *202 km/h* over 440 yds *402 m* by the 167.1 ton *169,7 tonnes* L.N.E.R. 4-6-2 No. 4468 *Mallard* (later numbered 60022), which hauled seven coaches weighing 240 tons *243 tonnes* gross, near Essendine, down Stoke Bank, between Grantham, Lincolnshire, and Peterborough on 3 July 1938. Driver Duddington was at the controls with Fireman T. Bray.

Fastest regular run The fastest point-to-point schedule in the world is that of the "New Tokaido" service of the Japanese National Railways from Osaka to Okayama, inaugurated on 15 March 1972. The train covers 112.03 miles *180,29 km* in exactly 1 hour. The maximum speed is being raised from 130.5 to 159 m.p.h. *210,0–255 km/h*. The 60 ton *60,9 tonnes* 12-car unit has motors generating 8,880 kW on a single-phase 25,000 volt A.C. system.

The fastest regular run on British Rail is the 203 mile *326 km* stretch from Darlington, Durham, to Stevenage, Herts. in 2 hours 26 min giving an average of 83.5 m.p.h. *134,3 km/h*. The prototype British Rail 2 unit diesel HST (High Speed Train) attained 141 m.p.h. *226,9 km/h* between Northallerton and Thirsk, Yorkshire on 11 June 1973.

LONGEST NON-STOP

The world's longest non-stop run is that of the Auto-Train Corporation daily passenger and automobile service between Lorton, Virginia and Sanford, Florida —a distance of 863 miles *1 388 km*. The longest run on British Rail without any advertised stop is the Night Motorail Service from Kensington Olympia, London to Inverness inaugurated in May 1973. The distance is 565 miles *909 km* and the time taken is 13 hours 20 min.

MOST POWERFUL

World The world's most powerful compound type steam locomotive was No. 700, a triple articulated or triplex 2-8-8-4, the Baldwin Locomotive Co. 6-cylinder engine built in 1916 for the Virginian Railway. It had a tractive force of 166,300 lb. *75 432 kg* working compound and 199,560 lb. *90 518 kg* working simple. In 1918 this railway operated a 4-cylinder compound 2-10-10-2 engine, built by the American Locomotive Co., with a starting (*i.e.* working simple) tractive effort of 176,000 lb. *79 832 kg*. Probably the heaviest train ever hauled by a single engine was one of 15,300 tons *15 545 tonnes* made up of 250 freight cars stretching 1.6 miles *2,5 km* by the *Matt H. Shay* (No. 5014), a 2-8-8-8-2 engine which ran on the Erie Railroad from May 1914 until 1929.

PERMANENT WAY

The longest stretch of continuous four track main line in the United Kingdom is between St. Pancras, London, and Glendon North Junction, Northamptonshire, and is 75 miles *120 km* in length.

Longest straight The longest straight in the world is on the Commonwealth Railways Trans Australian line over the Nullarbor Plain from Mile 496 between Nuringa and Loongana, Western Australia, to Mile 793 between Ooldea and Watson, South Australia, 297 miles *478 km* dead straight although not level. The longest straight on British Rail is the 18 miles *29 km* between Selby and Kingston-upon-Hill, Yorkshire.

Longest line The world's longest run is one of 9 334 km *5,799 miles* on the Trans Siberian line from Moscow to Nakhodka, U.S.S.R. in the Soviet Far East. There are 97 stops.

Widest The widest gauge in standard use is 5 ft 6 in *1,67 m*. This width is used in India, Pakistan, Ceylon, Spain, Portugal, Argentina and Chile. In 1885 there was a lumber railway in Oregon, U.S.A., with a gauge of 8 ft *2,4 m*.

HIGHEST

World The highest standard gauge (4 ft 8½ in [*1,43 m*]) track in the world is on the Central Railway of Peru (owned by the Peruvian Corporation Ltd.) at La Cima, where a branch siding rises to 15,844 ft *4 829 m* above sea-level. The highest point on the main line is 15,688 ft *4 781 m* in the Galera tunnel.

Great Britain The highest point of the British Rail system is at the pass of Druimnachdar on the Perth-Inverness border, where the track reaches an altitude of 1,484 ft *452 m* above sea-level. The highest railway in Britain is the Snowdon Mountain Railway, which rises from Llanberis to 3,493 ft *1 064 m* above sea-level, just below the summit of Snowdon (Yr Wyddfa). It has a gauge of 2 ft 7½ in *0,81 m*.

Lowest The lowest point on British Rail is in the Severn Tunnel—144 ft *43,8 m* below sea-level.

STEEPEST GRADIENTS

World The world's steepest standard gauge gradient by adhesion is 1:11. This figure is achieved by the Guatemalan State Electric Railway between the River Samala Bridge and Zunil.

Great Britain The steepest sustained adhesion-worked gradient on main line in the United Kingdom is the two-mile Lickey incline of 1:37.7 in Worcestershire. From the tunnel bottom to James Street, Liverpool, on the former Mersey Railway, there is a stretch of 1:27; just south of Ilfracombe, Devon, two miles *3,2 km* of 1:36; and between Folkestone Junction and Harbour a mile *1,6 km* of 1:30.

Shallowest The shallowest gradient posted on the British Rail system is one indicated as 1 in 13,707 between Pirbright Junction and Farnborough, Hampshire. This could, perhaps, also be described as England's most obtuse summit.

BUSIEST

Rail system The world's most crowded rail system is the Japanese National Railways, which in 1971 carried 16,495,000 passengers daily. Professional pushers are employed on the Tōkyō Service to squeeze in passengers before the doors can be closed. Among articles lost in 1970 were 419,929 umbrellas, 172,106 shoes, 250,630 spectacles and hats and also assorted false teeth and artificial eyeballs.

Station The world's busiest station is reputedly the main Moscow Station, U.S.S.R. which in 1971 handled some 2,700,000 passengers daily. The busiest railway junction in Great Britain is Clapham Junction on the Southern Region of British Rail, with over 2,070 trains passing through each 24 hours.

STATIONS

Largest World The world's largest railway station is Grand Central Terminal, Park Avenue and 43rd Street, New York City, N.Y., U.S.A., built 1903–13. It covers 48 acres *19 ha* on two levels with 41 tracks on the upper level and 26 on the lower. On average more than 550 trains and 180,000 people per day use it, with a peak of 252,288 on 3 July 1947.

United Kingdom The largest railway station in extent on the British Rail system is the 17-platform Clapham Junction, London, covering 27¾ acres *11,22 ha* and with a total face of 11,185 ft *3 409 m*. The station with the largest number of platforms is Waterloo, London (24½ acres [*9,9 ha*]), with 21 main line and two Waterloo and City Line platforms, with a total face of 15,352 ft *4 679 m*. Victoria Station (21¾ acres [*8,80 ha*]) with 17 platforms has, however, a total face length of 18,412 ft *5 611 m*. The oldest station in Britain is Liverpool Road Station, Manchester, first used on 15 Sept. 1830.

Highest The highest station in the world on standard gauge railways is Ticlio, at 15,685 ft *4 680 m* above sea-level, on the Central Railway of Peru, in South America. The highest passenger station on British Rail is Corrour, Inverness-shire, at an altitude of 1,347 ft *410,5 m* above sea-level.

Waiting rooms The world's largest waiting rooms are those in Peking Station, Chang'an Boulevard, Peking, China, opened in September 1959, with a capacity of 14,000.

Longest platform The longest railway platform in the world is the Kharagpur platform, West Bengal, India, which measures 2,733 ft *833 m* in length. The State Street Center subway platform staging on "The Loop" in Chicago, Illinois, U.S.A., measures 3,500 ft *1 066 m* in length.

The longest platform in the British Rail system is the 1,981 ft *603,8 m* long platform at Colchester, Essex.

PROGRESSIVE RAILWAY SPEED RECORDS

Speed m.p.h.	km/h	Engine	Place	Date
29.1	46,8	The *Rocket* (Stephenson's and Booth's 0-2-2)	Liverpool—Manchester	8 Oct. 1829
36	58	The *Northumbrian*	from Parkside, Newton-le-Willows	15 Sept. 1830
56¾	91,3	Grand Junction Rly., 2-2-2 *Lucifer*	Madeley Bank, Staffordshire	13 Nov. 1839
c.85[1]	137	Atmospheric railway (Frank Elrington)	Dun Laoghaire-Dalkey, Co. Dublin	19 Aug. 1843
74½	119,5	Great Western Rly., 8 ft *2,4 m* single 4-2-2 *Great Britain*	Wootton Bassett, Wiltshire	11 May 1845
74½	119,5	Great Western Rly., 8 ft *2,4 m* single 4-2-2 *Great Western*	Wootton Bassett, Wiltshire	1 June 1846
78	125,5	Great Western Rly., 8 ft *2,4 m* single 4-2-2 *Great Britain*	Wootton Bassett, Wiltshire	11 May 1848
81.8	131,6	Bristol & Exeter Rly., 9 ft *2,7 m* single 4-2-4 tank No. 41	Wellington Bank, Somerset	June 1854
89.48	144	Crompton No. 604 engine	Champigny Pont sur Yvonne, France	20 June 1890
98.4[2]	158,4	Philadelphia & Reading Rly., Engine 206	Skillmans to Belle Mead, New Jersey	July 1890
102.8[2]	165,4	N.Y. Central & Hudson River Rly. Empire State Express No. 999	Grimesville, N.Y., U.S.A.	9 May 1893
112.5[2 3]	181,1	N.Y. Central & Hudson River Rly. Empire State Express No. 999	Crittenden West, N.Y., U.S.A.	11 May 1893
102	164	Pennsylvania Railroad	Landover to Anacosta, U.S.A.	Aug. 1895
90.0	144,8	Midland Rly., 7 ft 9 in *2,4 m* single 4-2-2	Melton Mowbray—Nottingham	Mar. 1897
130[2]	209	*Burlington Route*	Siding to Arion, Iowa, U.S.A.	Jan. 1899
101.0	162,5	Siemens und Halske Electric	near Berlin	1901
120.0[2 4]	193,1	*Savannah, Florida and Western Rly.* mail train	Screven, Florida, U.S.A.	1 Mar. 1901
124.89	200,99	Siemens und Halske Electric	Marienfeld-Zossen, nr. Berlin	6 Oct. 1903
128.43	206,69	Siemens und Halske Electric	Marienfeld-Zossen, nr. Berlin	23 Oct. 1903
130.61	210,19	Siemens und Halske Electric	Marienfeld-Zossen, nr. Berlin	27 Oct. 1903
99–100[5]	159–161	Great Western Rly., 4-4-0 *City of Truro* (Steam Record only)	Wellington Bank, Somerset	9 May 1904
143.0	230,1	Kruckenberg (propeller-driven)	Karstädt-Dergenthin, Germany	21 June 1931
150.9	242,9	Co-Co S.N.C.F. No. 7121	Dijon-Beaune, France	21 Feb. 1953
205.6	330,9	Co-Co S.N.C.F. No. 7107	Facture-Morcenx, France	28 Mar. 1955
205.6	330,9	Bo-Bo S.N.C.F. No. 9004	Facture-Morcenx, France	29 Mar. 1955
235	378	*L'Aérotrain* (jet aero engines)	Gometz le Chatel-Limours, France	4 Dec. 1967

[1] *Speed attributed to runaway compressed air train. No independent timings.*
[2] *Not internationally regarded as authentic.*

[3] *Later alleged to be unable to attain 82 m.p.h. 132 km/h on this track but then hauling 4 coaches.*
[4] *5 miles 8 km in 2½ min to a stop, hence fictitious.*
[5] *Previously unauthenticated at 102.3 m.p.h. 164,6 km/h.*

Longest freight train The longest and heaviest freight train on record was one about 4 miles *6 km* in length consisting of 500 coal cars with three 3,600 h.p. diesels pulling and three more pushing on the Iaeger, West Virginia to Portsmouth, Ohio stretch of 157 miles *252 km* on the Norfolk and Western Railway on 15 Nov. 1967. The total weight was nearly 42,000 tons *42 674 tonnes*.

Greatest load The heaviest single piece of freight ever conveyed by rail was a 1,230,000 lb. *557 918 kg* (549.2 ton [*558 tonnes*]) 106 ft *32,3 m* tall hydrocracker reactor which was carried from Birmingham, Alabama, to Toledo, Ohio, U.S.A., on 12 Nov. 1965.

The heaviest load carried by British Rail was a 122 ft *37,1 m* long boiler drum, weighing 275 tons *279 tonnes* which was carried from Immingham Docks to Killinghome, Lincolnshire in September 1968.

Greatest mileage The greatest mileage covered with a weekly roving ticket on British Rail is 9,082 miles *14 616 km* between 3–9 Feb. 1973 by Michael Parker of Leicester.

Dearest season ticket The most expensive annual season ticket issued by British Rail is a 1st class weekly return between London (Euston) and Inverness for £1,250 issued to Mr. Henry E. Williamson.

UNDERGROUND RAILWAYS

Most extensive The most extensive and oldest (opened 10 Jan. 1863) underground railway system of the 23 in the world is that of the London Transport Executive, with 257 miles *413 km* of route, of which 80 miles *128 km* is bored tunnel and 24 miles *38 km* is "cut and cover". This whole Tube system is operated by a staff of 20,000 serving 278 stations. The 500 trains comprising 4,350 cars carried 654,000,000 passengers in 1971. The greatest depth is 192 ft *58,5 m* at Hampstead. The record for touring all 277 stations was 15 hours precisely by Leslie R. V. Burwood on 3 Sept. 1968. The record for the Paris Metro's 270 stations (7 closed) is 11 hours 13 min by Alan Paul Jenkins of Bushey, Hertfordshire on 30 Aug. 1967.

Busiest The busiest subway in the world is the New York City Transit Authority (opened on 27 Oct. 1904) with a total of 237.22 miles *381,76 km* of track and 2,081,810,464 passengers in 1970. The stations are closer set and total 475. The previous peak number carried was 2,051,400,973 in 1947. The record for travelling the whole system is 22 hours 11½ min by Morgan Chu and 6 others on 3 Aug. 1967.

Model railway The record run for a miniature steam-powered locomotive on a 3½ in *8,89 cm* gauge track is 70 miles *112 km*. This is equivalent to 1,130 miles *1 818 km* to scale.

TRAMS

Longest tram journey The longest tramway journeys now possible are in the Rhein-Ruhr area of West Germany from Dinslaken to Krefold, a distance of 64 km *40 miles*. The record journeys in the United Kingdom have been by the famous illuminated car from Edgehill Works, Liverpool *via* Knotty Ash, St. Helens, Atherton, Leigh, Salford and then branching off to Ashton-under-Lyne on 13 December 1925 and alternatively to Stockport on 14 November 1926. Both journeys were of some 40 miles *64 km* in length.

MONORAIL

Highest Speed The highest speed ever attained on rails is 3,090 m.p.h. *4 972 km/h* (Mach 4.1) by an unmanned rocket-powered sled on the 6.62 mile *10,65 km* long captive track at the U.S. Air Force Missile Development Center at Holloman, New Mexico, U.S.A., on 19 Feb. 1959. The highest speed reached carrying a chimpanzee is 1,295 m.p.h. *2 084 km/h*.

The highest speed attained by a tracked hovercraft is 235 m.p.h. *378 km/h* by the jet-powered *L'Aérotrain*, invented by Jean Bertin (see Progressive speed table page 151).

Speeds as high as Mach 0.8 (608 mp.h. [*978 km/h*]) are planned in 1973 from The Onsoku Kasotai (sonic speed sliding vehicle), a wheelless rocket-powered train running on rollers designed by Prof. H. Ozawa (Japan) and announced in March 1968.

4. AIRCRAFT

Note—The use of the Mach scale for aircraft speeds was introduced by Prof. Acherer of Zürich, Switzerland. The Mach number is the ratio of the velocity of a moving body to the local velocity of sound. This ratio was first employed by Dr. Ernst Mach (1838–1916) of Vienna. Austria in 1887. Thus Mach 1.0 equals 760.98 m.p.h. *1 224,67 km/h* at sea-level at 15° C, and is assumed, for convenience, to fall to a constant 659.78 m.p.h. *1 061,81 km/h* in the stratosphere, *i.e.* above 11,000 m *36,089 ft*.

EARLIEST FLIGHTS

World The first controlled and sustained power-driven flight occurred near the Kill Devil Hill, Kitty Hawk, North Carolina, U.S.A., at 10.35 a.m. on 17 December 1903, when Orville Wright (1871–1948) flew the 12 h.p. chain-driven *Flyer I* at an airspeed of 30 m.p.h. *48 km/h*, a ground speed of 6.8 m.p.h. *10,9 km/h* and an altitude of 8–12 ft *2,4–3,6 m* for 12 sec, watched by his brother Wilbur (1867–1912) and three coastguards and two others. Both the brothers, from Dayton, Ohio, were bachelors because, as Orville put it, they had not the means to "support a wife as well as an aeroplane". The plane is now in the Smithsonian Institution, Washington D.C.

The first man-carrying powered aeroplane to fly, but not entirely under its own power was the monoplane with a hot-air engine built by Félix Du Temple de la Croix (1823–90), a French naval officer, and piloted by a young sailor who made a short hop after taking off, probably down an incline, at Brest, France, in *c.* 1874. The first hop by a man-carrying aeroplane entirely under its own power was made when Clément Ader (1841–1925) of France flew in his *Eole* for about 50 m *164 ft* at Armainvilliers, France, on 9 Oct. 1890.

British Isles The first officially recognised flight in the British Isles was made by "Colonel" Samuel Franklin Cody (1861–1913) of the U.S.A., who flew 1,390 ft *423 m* in his own biplane at Farnborough, Hampshire, on 16 Oct. 1908. Horatio Frederick Phillips (1845–1926) almost certainly covered 500 ft *152 m* in his Philips II *"Venetian blind"* aeroplane at Streatham, in 1907. The first British citizen to fly was Griffith Brewer (1867–1948), as a passenger of Wilbur Wright, on 8 Oct. 1908 at Auvours, France.

The famous illuminated tram which made the longest journeys in Britain, from Liverpool to either Ashton-under-Lyne or Stockport

Cross-Channel The earliest cross-Channel flight by an aeroplane was made on Sunday, 25 July 1909 when Louis Blériot (1872–1936) of France flew his *Blériot XI* monoplane, powered by a 23 h.p. Anzani engine, 26 miles *41,8 km* from Les Baraques, France, to Northfall Meadow near Dover Castle, England, in 36½ minutes, after taking off at 4.41 a.m.

Jet-engined Proposals for jet propulsion date back to Captain Marconnet (1909) of France, and Henri Coanda (1886–1972) of Romania and to the turbojet proposals of Maxime Guillaume in 1921. The earliest test bed run was that of the British Power Jets Ltd.'s experimental W.U. (Whittle Unit) on 12 April 1937, invented by Flying Officer (now Air Commodore Sir) Frank Whittle (b. Coventry, 1 June 1907), who had applied for a patent on jet propulsion in 1930. The first flight by an aeroplane powered by a turbojet engine was made by the Heinkel He 178, piloted by Flug Kapitan Erich Warsitz, at Marienehe, Germany, on 27 Aug. 1939. It was powered by a Heinkel S3B engine (834 lb. s.t. as installed with long tail-pipe) designed by Dr. Hans 'Pabst' von Ohain and first tested in August 1937.

The first British jet flight occurred when Fl. Lt. P. E. G. "Jerry" Sayer, O.B.E., flew the Gloster-Whittle E.28/39 (wing span 29 ft [*8,83 m*] length 25 ft 3 in [*7,69 m*]) fitted with a 860 lb. *390 kg* s.t. Whittle W-1 engine for 17 min at Cranwell, Lincolnshire, on 15 May 1941. The second prototype attained 466 m.p.h. *750 km/h.*

Supersonic flight The first supersonic flight was achieved on 14 Oct. 1947 by Capt. (now Brig.-Gen) Charles ("Chick") E. Yeager, U.S.A.F. (b. 13 Feb. 1923), over Edwards Air Force Base, Muroc, California, U.S.A., in a U.S. Bell XS-1 rocket plane ("Glamorous Glennis"), with Mach 1,015 (670 m.p.h. [*1 078 km/h*]) at an altitude of 42,000 ft *12 800 m.*

TRANS-ATLANTIC

The first crossing of the North Atlantic by air was made by Lt-Cdr. (later Rear Admiral) Albert Cushing Read (1887-1967) and his crew (Stone, Hinton, Rodd, Rhoads and Breese) in the 84 knot *155 km/h* Curtiss flying-boat NC-4 of the U.S. Navy from Trepassey Harbour, Newfoundland, *via* the Azores, to Lisbon, Portugal, on 16 to 27 May 1919. The whole flight of 4,717 miles *7 591 km* originating from Rockaway Air Station, Long Island, N.Y. on 8 May, required 53 hours 58 min terminating at Plymouth, England, on 31 May.

First non-stop The first non-stop trans-Atlantic flight was achieved from 4.13 p.m. G.M.T. on 14 June 1919, from Lester's Field, St. John's Newfoundland, 1,960 miles *3 154 km* to Derrygimla bog near Clifden, County Galway, Ireland, at 8.40 a.m. G.M.T., 15 June, when the pilot Capt. John William Alcock, D.S.C. (1892–1919), and the navigator Lt. Arthur Whitten-Brown (1886–1948) flew across in a Vickers *Vimy*, powered by two 360 h.p. Rolls-Royce *Eagle VIII* engines. Both men were created K.B.E. on 21 June 1919 when Alcock was aged 26 years 286 days and won the *Daily Mail* prize of £10,000.

First solo The 79th man to achieve a trans-Atlantic flight but the first to do so solo was Capt. (later Col.) Charles Augustus Lindbergh (b. 4 Feb. 1902, Detroit) who took off in his 220 h.p. Ryan monoplane "Spirit of St. Louis" at 12.52 pm. G.M.T. on 20 May 1927 from Roosevelt Field, Long Island, New York State, U.S.A. He landed at 10.21 p.m. G.M.T. on 21 May 1927 at Le Bourget airfield, Paris, France. His flight of 3,610 miles *5 810 km* lasted 33 hours 29½ min and he won a prize of $25,000 (*then £5,300*).

Fastest The present New York–Paris trans-Atlantic record is 3 hours 19 min 44.5 sec by a General Dynamics/

The Curtiss flying-boat NC-4 in which Lt. Cdr. Albert Read and his crew made the first crossing of the North Atlantic in May 1919

Convair B-58A *Hustler* "Firefly", piloted by Major William R. Payne, U.S.A.F., on 26 May 1961. The 3,626 miles *5 835 km* were covered at an average of 1,089 m.p.h. *1 752 km/h.* The B-58 was withdrawn from operational service in January 1970.

The fastest time between New York and London is 4 hours 36 min 30.4 sec by Lt.-Cdr. Brian Davies, 35, and Lt.-Cdr. Peter M. Goddard, R.N. 32, of No. 892 Squadron, Royal Navy, on 11 May 1969, flying a McDonnell Douglas F-4K *Phantom II F.G.1* with Rolls-Royce *Spey* engines. Lt.-Cdr. Goddard was participating in the *Daily Mail* trans-Atlantic air race, which he won (prize £5,000) with an overall time of 5 hours 11 min 22 sec from the top of the Empire State Building, New York, to the top of the Post Office Tower, London.

CIRCUMNAVIGATION

Earliest The earliest flight around the world was completed by two U.S. Army Air Service Douglas aircraft "Chicago" (Lt. Lowell H. Smith and Lt. Leslie P. Arnold) and "New Orleans" (Lt. Erik H. Nelson and Lt. John Harding) on 28 Sept. 1924 at Seattle, Washington, U.S.A. The 175-day flight of 26,345 miles *42,398 km* began on 26 April 1924 and involved 57 "hops" and a flying time of 351 hours 11 min. These aircraft had inter-changeable wheels and floats. The earliest solo flight round the world was made from 15 to 22 July 1933 by Wiley Hardeman Post (1898–1935) (U.S.A.) in the Lockheed *Vega* "Winnie Mae" starting and finishing at Floyd Bennett Field, New York City, U.S.A. He flew the 15,596 miles *25 099 km* east-about in 7 days 18 hours 49 min—in 10 hops with a flying time of 115 hours 36 min.

Fastest The fastest circumnavigation of the globe was achieved by three U.S.A.F. B-52 *Stratofortresses*, led by Maj.-Gen. Archie J. Old, Jr., chief of the U.S. 15th Air force. They took off from Castle Air Force Base, Merced, California, at 1 p.m. on 16 Jan. and flew eastwards, arriving 45 hours 19 min later at March Air Force Base, Riverside, California, on 18 Jan. 1957, after a flight of 24,325 miles *39 147 km.* The planes averaged 525 m.p.h. *844 km/h* and were refuelled four times in flight by KC-97 aerial tankers.

Earliest Solo Circum-polar flight Capt. Elgen M. Long, 44, completed at San Francisco International Airport the first ever solo polar circumnavigation in his Piper Navajo in 215 hours and 38,896 miles *62 597 km,* flying from 5 Nov. to 3 Dec. 1971. The cabin temperature sank to −40° F. *−40° C.* over Antarctica.

LARGEST AIRCRAFT

Heaviest and Most Powerful The greatest weight at which an aeroplane has taken off is 820,700 lb. *372 263 kg* (366.38 tons/tonnes), achieved by the prototype Boeing Model 747-200 (747B) commercial transport at Edwards Air Force Base, California, in November 1970. The basic aeroplane weighed 320,000 lb. (142.9 tons [*145,1 tonnes*]), the remaining weight representing fuel, flight test equipment and an artificial payload of sand and water. The 747B has a wing span of 195 ft 8 in *59,63 m*, is 231 ft 4 in *70,51 m* long. It is structurally capable of accepting 4 Pratt & Whitney JT9D-7W turbofans, giving a total thrust of 188,000 lb. *85 275 kg*.

Largest wing span The aircraft with the largest wing span ever constructed was the $40 million Hughes H.2 *Hercules* flying-boat, which was raised 70 ft *21,3 m* into the air in a test run of 1,000 yds *914 m*, piloted by Howard Hughes, off Long Beach Harbor, California, U.S.A., on 2 Nov. 1947. The eight-engined 190 ton *193 tonnes* aircraft had a wing span of 320 ft *97,53 m* and a length of 219 ft *66,75 m* and never flew again.

Most Powerful From Oct. 1971 the 4 Pratt & Whitney JT 9D-7W turbofans gave a total thrust of 188,000 lb. *85 275 kg* s.t., so surpassing the 186,000 lb. s.t. of the 6 engined North American XB-70A *Valkyrie*.

Lightest The lightest aeroplane ever flown is the Whing Ding II, a single seat biplane designed and built by R. W. Hovey of Saugus, California and first flown in Feb. 1971. It has a wing span of 17 ft *5,18 m*, an empty weight of 123 lb. *55,8 kg* (incl. fuel) and 310 lb. *140 kg* fully loaded. It is powered by a 14 h.p. McCulloch Go-Kart engine, driving a pusher propeller and has a maximum speed of 50 m.p.h. *80 km/h* and a range of 20 miles *32 km* on half a gal *2,2 litres* of fuel. The pilot sits on an open seat. At least 100 more Whing Ding IIs were under construction by 1973.

Smallest The smallest aeroplane ever flown is the Stits *Skybaby* biplane, designed, built and flown by Ray Stits at Riverside, California, U.S.A., in 1952. It was 9 ft 10 in *3 m* long, with a wing span of 7 ft 2 in *2,18 m* and weighed 452 lb. *205 kg* empty. It was powered by an 85 h.p. Continental C85 engine, giving a top speed of 185 m.p.h. *297 km/h*.

BOMBERS

Heaviest The world's heaviest bomber is the eight-jet swept-wing Boeing B-52H *Stratofortress*, which has a maximum take-off weight of 488,000 lb. (217.86 tons [*221,35 tonnes*]). It has a wing span of 185 ft *56,38 m* and is 157 ft 6¾ in *48,02 m* in length, with a speed of over 650 m.p.h. *1 046 km/h*. The B-52 can carry 12 750 lb. *5 340 kg* bombs under each wing and 84

A United States Air Force B-52 "Stratofortress" bomber, the world's heaviest, crossing the South Vietnam coastline

A Dassault *Mirage IV* bomber during take-off, this plane is capable of flying at 1,450 m.p.h. *2 333 km/h*

500 lb. *226 kg* bombs in the fuselage, giving the total bomb load of 60,000 lb. *27 215 kg* or 26.78 tons/tonnes. The ten-engined Convair B-36J, weighing 183 tons *185 tonnes* had a greater wing span, at 230 ft *70,10 m* but it is no longer in service. It had a top speed of 435 m.p.h. *700 km/h*.

Fastest The world's fastest operational bombers are the French Dassault *Mirage IV*, which can fly at Mach 2.2 (1,450 m.p.h. [*2 333 km/h*]) at 36,000 ft *10 972 m* and the American General Dynamics FB-111A, which also flies above Mach 2. Under development is a swing-wing Tupolev bomber known to N.A.T.O. as "Backfire", which has an estimated over-target speed of Mach 2.25–2.5 and a range of 4,600 miles *7 400 km*. The fastest Soviet bomber in service is the Tupolev Tu-22 "Blinder", with a speed of Mach 1.4 (925 m.p.h. [*1 488 km/h*]) at 36,000 ft *10 972,8 m*.

AIRLINERS

Largest World The highest capacity jet airliner is the Boeing 747, "Jumbo Jet", first flown on 9 Feb. 1969, which by November 1970 had set a record for gross take-off weight with 820,700 lb. *372 263 kg* (366.38 tons/tonnes) (see Heaviest aircraft) and has a capacity of from 362 to 537 passengers with a maximum speed of 608 m.p.h. *978 km/h*. Its wing span is 195.7 ft *59,64 m* and its length 231.3 ft *70,50 m*. It entered service on 21 Jan. 1970.

United Kingdom The heaviest United Kingdom airliner in service is the B.A.C. Super VC10, which first flew on 7 May 1964. It weighs 335,000 lb. (149.5 tons) *151,8 tonnes* and is 171.7 ft *52,33 m* long, with a wing span of 146.2 ft *44,56 m*. The largest ever British aircraft was the experimental Bristol Type 167 *Brabazon*, which had a maximum take-off weight of 129.4 tons *131,4 tonnes*, a wing span of 230 ft *70,10 m* and a length of 177 ft *53,94 m*. This eight-engined aircraft first flew on 4 Sept. 1949. The *Concorde* (see below) has a maximum take-off weight of 389,000 lb. *176 447 kg* (173.66 tons).

Largest Cargo Compartment The largest cargo compartment of any aircraft is the 39,000 ft³ *11 040 m³* of the American Aero Spacelines. Guppy-201 which was put into service in Sept. 1971. The compartment is more than 25 ft *7,6 m* in diameter.

Fastest World The world's fastest airliner in service is the Convair CV-990 *Coronado*, one of which flew at 675 m.p.h. *1 086 km/h* at 22,500 ft *6 858 m* (Mach 0.97) on 8 May 1961. Its maximum cruising speed is 625 m.p.h. *1 005 km/h*. A Douglas DC-8 Series 40, with Rolls-Royce Conway engines, exceeded the speed of sound in a shallow diver on 21 Aug. 1961. Its true air speed was 667 mp.h. *1 073 km/h* or Mach 1.012 at a height of 40,350 ft *12 298 m*. The U.S.S.R.'s Tu-144 supersonic airliner, with a capacity of 140 passengers, first flew on 31 Dec. 1968, with a design ceiling of 65,000 ft *19 812 m*, and it "went" supersonic on 5 June 1969. It first exceeded Mach 2 on 26 May 1970, and attained 1,565.8 m.p.h. *2 519,9 km/h* (Mach 2.37) at 59,000 ft *17 983 m* in late December 1971. During later flight trials it attained Mach 2.4 (1,585 m.p.h. [*2 550 km/h*]) and was expected to enter the Paris-New York service in 1975 at an average speed of 1,245 m.p.h. *2 000 km/h*.

Britain The fastest British airliner in service is the three-engined Hawker Siddeley *Trident 1C* which has reached 627 m.p.h. *1 009 km/h* (Mach 0.9) in level flight and 667 m.p.h. *1 073 km/h* (Mach 0.96) in a shallow dive at 24,000 ft *7 315 m*. The supersonic BAC/Aérospatiale *Concorde*, first flown on 2 March 1969, with a capacity of 128 passengers, is expected to cruise at up to Mach 2.05 (1,355 m.p.h. [*2 180 km/h*]). It flew at Mach 1.05 on 10 Oct. 1969 and exceeded Mach 2 for the first time on 4 Nov. 1970.

Scheduled flights The longest scheduled non-stop flight is the Buenos Aires, Argentina to Madrid, Spain stage of 6,462 *Longest* statute miles *10 400 km* by Aerolíneas Argentinas inaugurated on 7 Aug. 1967. The Boeing 707-320B requires 11½ hours.

Shortest The shortest scheduled flight in the world is that by Loganair between the Orkney Islands of Westray and Papa Westray which has been flown since September 1967. Though scheduled for 2 min in favourable wind conditions it is accomplished in 70 sec.

HIGHEST SPEED

Official record The official air speed record is 2,070.102 m.p.h. *3 331,506 km/h* by Col. Robert L. Stephens and Lt.-Col. Daniel André (both U.S.A.F.) in a Lockheed YF-12A near Edwards Air Force Base, California, U.S.A. over a 15/25 km course on 1 May 1965.

Air-launched record The fastest fixed-wing aircraft in the world is the U.S. North American Aviation X-15A-2, which flew for the first time (after conversion) on 28 June 1964 powered by a liquid oxygen and ammonia rocket propulsion system. Ablative materials on the airframe have once enabled a temperature of 3,000° F. to be withstood. The landing speed was 210 knots (241.8 m.p.h. [*389,1 km/h*]) momentarily. The highest speed attained was 4,520 m.p.h. *7 274 km/h* (Mach 6.70) when piloted by Major William J. Knight, U.S.A.F. (b. 1930), on 3 Oct. 1967. An earlier version piloted by Joseph A. Walker (1920-66), reached 354,200 ft *107 960 m* (67.08 miles) also over Edwards Air Force Base, California, U.S.A., on 22 Aug. 1963. The programme was suspended after the final flight of 24 Oct. 1968.

The Convair *Coronado*, the fastest airliner in service, one of which flew at a speed of 675 m.p.h. *1 086 km/h*, they have a maximum cruising speed of 625 m.p.h. *1 005 km/h*

An artist's impression of the Mikoyan MiG-25 jet, code name "Foxbat", with a speed of 2,110 m.p.h. *3 395 km/h*

Fastest jet The world's fastest jet aircraft is the U.S.A.F Lockheed SR-71 reconnaissance aircraft (a variant of the YF-12A) which was first flown on 22 Dec. 1964 and is reportedly capable of attaining a speed of 2,200 m.p.h. *3 540 km/h* and an altitude ceiling of close to 100,000 ft *30 480 m*. The SR-71 has a span of 55.6 ft *16,94 m* and a length of 107.4 ft *32,73 m* and weighs 170,000 lb. (75.9 tons [*77,1 tonnes*]) at take-off. Its reported range is 2,982 miles *4 800 km* at Mach 3 at 78,750 ft *24 000 m*. Only 23 are believed to have been built and 9 had been lost by April 1969. The fastest Soviet jet aircraft in service is the Mikoyan MiG-25 fighter (code name "Foxbat") with a speed of Mach 3.2 (2,110 m.p.h. [*3 395 km/h*]). It is armed with air-to-air missiles.

Fastest biplane The fastest recorded biplane was the Italian Fiat C.R.42B, with a 1,010 h.p. Daimler-Benz DB601A engine, which attained 323 m.p.h. *520 km/h* in 1941. Only one was built.

Fastest piston-engined aircraft The fastest speed at which a piston-engined aeroplane has ever been measured was for a cut-down privately owned Hawker *Sea Fury* which attained 520 m.p.h. *836 km/h* in level flight over Texas, U.S.A., in August 1966 piloted by Mike Carroll (k. 1969) of Los Angeles. The official record for a piston-engined aircraft is 482.462 m.p.h. *776,447 km/h* over Edwards AFB California by Darryl C. Greenamyer, 33, (U.S.) in a modified Grumman F8F-2 *Bearcat* on 16 Aug. 1969. The Republic XF-84H prototype U.S. Navy fighter which flew on 22 July 1955 had a top *design* speed of 670 m.p.h. *1 078 km/h* but was abandoned.

Fastest propeller-driven aircraft The Soviet Tu-114 turboprop transport is the world's fastest propeller-driven aeroplane. It has achieved average speeds of more than 545 m.p.h. *877 km/h* carrying heavy payloads over measured circuits. It is developed from the Tupolev Tu-95 bomber, known in the West as the "Bear", and has 14,795 h.p. engines.

Largest propeller The largest aircraft propeller ever used was the 22 ft 7½ in *6,89 m* diameter Garuda propeller, fitted to the Linke-Hofmann R II built in Breslau, Germany, which flew in 1919. It was driven by four 260 h.p. Mercédès engines and turned at only 545 r.p.m.

ALTITUDE

Official record The official world altitude record by an aircraft which took off from the ground under its own power is 113,892 ft (21.57 miles [*34,71 km*]) by Lt.-Col. Georgiy Mosolov (U.S.S.R.) in a Mikoyan E-66A aircraft, powered by one turbojet and one rocket engine at Podmoskovnoe on 28 April 1961. Major R. W. Smith of the U.S. Air Force reached an unofficial record height of 118,860 ft (22.15 miles [*35,64 km*]) in a Lockheed NF-104A over Edwards Air Force Base, California, U.S.A., early in November 1963.

DURATION

The flight duration record is 64 days, 22 hours, 19 min and 5 sec, set up by Robert Timm and John Cook in a Cessna 172 "Hacienda". They took off from McCarran Airfield, Las Vegas, Nevada, U.S.A., just before 3.53 p.m. local time on 4 Dec. 1958, and landed at the same airfield just before 2.12 p.m. on 7 Feb. 1959. They covered a distance equivalent to six times around the world.

AIRPORTS

Largest World The world's largest airport is the Dallas/Fort Worth Airport, Texas, U.S.A., which extends over 17,400 acres *7,040 ha* in the Grapevine area opened in 1973 at a cost of $700 million for the opening phase. It will eventually have 11 runways and 13 terminals with 234 gates and be able to accommodate 200 of the largest cargo aircraft envisaged for AD 2001 with a capacity of more than any seaport. The jet port will have a capacity for 336,960 movements per year handling 60 million passengers.

United Kingdom Sixty-eight airline companies from 57 countries operate scheduled services into London (Heathrow) Airport (2,721 acres [*1 101 ha*]), and during 1972 there were a total number of 279,227 air transport movements handled by a staff of 51,052 employed by the various companies and the British Airports Authority. The total number of passengers, both incoming and outgoing, was 18,621,822 in 1972. The most flights in a day was 972 on 21 July 1972 and the largest number of passengers yet handled in a day was 82,274 on 3 Sept. 1972. Aircraft fly to over 90 countries.

Busiest The world's busiest airport is the Chicago International Airport, O'Hare Field, Illinois, U.S.A., with a total of 641,429 movements (565,826 air carrier movements) in 1971. This represents a take-off or landing every 49 seconds.

The busiest landing area ever has been Bien Hoa Air Base, South Vietnam, which handled more than 1,000,000 take-offs and landings in 1970. The world's largest "helipad" was An Khe, South Vietnam, which serviced U.S. Army and Air Force helicopters.

Highest and lowest The highest airport in the world is El Alto, near La Paz, Bolivia, at 13,599 ft *4 144,9 m* above sea-level. Ladakh airstrip in Kashmir has, however, an altitude of 14,270 ft *4 349 m*. The highest landing ever made by a fixed-wing 'plane is 6,080 m *19,947 ft* on Dhaulagri, Himalaya by a Pilatus Porter, named *Yeti*, supplying the 1960 Swiss Expedition. The lowest landing field is El Lisan on the east shore of the Dead Sea, 1,180 ft *359,6 m* below sea-level, but the lowest international airport is Schiphol, Amsterdam, at 13 ft *3,9 m* below sea-level.

LONGEST RUNWAY

World The longest runway in the world is one of 7 miles *11 km* in length (of which 15,000 ft [*4 572 m*] is concreted) at Edwards Air Force Base on the bed of Rogers Dry Lake at Muroc, California, U.S.A. The whole test centre airfield extends over 65 miles² *168 km²*. In an emergency an auxiliary 12 mile *19 km* strip is available along the bed of the Dry Lake. The world's longest civil airport runway is one of 15,510 ft (2.95 miles [*4,74 km*]) at Salisbury, Rhodesia, completed in 1969.

United Kingdom The longest runway available normally to civil aircraft in the United Kingdom is No. 1 at London (Heathrow) Airport, measuring 12,799 ft (2.42 miles [*3,89 km*]).

HELICOPTERS

Fastest A Bell YUH-1B Model 533 compound research helicopter, boosted by two auxiliary turbojet engines,

attained an unofficial speed record of 316.1 m.p.h. *508,7 km/h* over Arlington, Texas, U.S.A., in April 1969. The official world speed record for a pure helicopter is 220.885 m.p.h. *355,479 km/h* by a Sikorsky S-67 Blackhawk, flown by test pilot Kurt Cannon, between Milford and Branford, Conneticut, U.S.A. on 19 Dec. 1970.

Largest The world's largest helicopter is the Soviet Mil *Mi-12* ("Homer"), also known as the V-12, which set up an international record by lifting a payload of 88,636 lb. (39.5 tons [*40,1 tonnes*]) to a height of 7,398 ft *2 254,9 m* on 6 Aug. 1969. It is powered by four 6,500 h.p. turboshaft engines and has a span of 219 ft 10 in *67 m* over its rotor tips with a fuselage length of 121 ft 4½ in *37,00 m* and weighs 103.3 tons *104,9 tonnes*.

Highest The altitude record for helicopters, still subject to confirmation, is 40,815 ft *12 440 m* by an Aérospatiale SA 315B Lama, over France on 21 June 1972. The highest landing has been at 23,000 ft *7 010 m* below the South-East face of Everest in a rescue sortie in May 1971.

FLYING-BOAT

The fastest flying-boat ever built has been the Martin XP6M-1, the U.S. Navy 4 jet engined minelayer flown in 1955–59 with a top speed of 646 m.p.h. *1 040 km/h*. In Sept. 1946 the Martin Caroline *Mars* flying-boat set a payload record of 68,327 lb. *30 992 kg*. Two Mars flying-boats are still working as forest fire protection water bombers in British Columbia.

AIRSHIPS

Earliest The earliest flight in an airship was by Henri Giffard from Paris in his coal-gas 88,300 ft³ *2 500 m³* 144 ft *43,8 m* long rigid airship on 24 Sept. 1852. The earliest British airship was a 20,000 ft³ *566 m³* 75 ft *22,8 m* long craft built by Stanley Spencer whose maiden flight was from Crystal Palace, London on 22 September 1902. The last airship to be assembled in Britain is the 202,700 ft³ *5 739 m³* 192½ ft *56,67 m* long *Europa* built at Cardington, Bedfordshire by the Goodyear Tyre & Rubber Co. which first flew on 8 March 1972.

Largest Rigid The largest rigid airship ever built was the German *Graf Zeppelin II* (LZ 130), with a length of 245 m *803,8 ft* and a capacity of 7,062,100 ft³ *199 977 m³*. She made her maiden flight on 14 Sept. 1938 and in May and August 1939 made radar spying missions in British air space. She was dismantled in April 1940.

British The largest British airship was the R101 built by the Royal Airship Works, Cardington, Bedfordshire, which

A prototype Sikorsky S-67 Blackhawk helicopter, which holds the world's speed record for a pure helicopter at 220.885 m.p.h. *355,479 km/h*

The Goodyear *Europa* airship, at Cardington, Bedfordshire, the only existing airship built in Britain

first flew on 14 Oct. 1929. She was 777 ft *236,8 m* in length and had a capacity of 5,508,800 ft³ *155 992 m³*. She crashed near Beauvais, France, killing 48 aboard on 5 Oct. 1930.

Non-Rigid The largest non-rigid airship ever constructed was the U.S. Navy ZPG 3-W. It had a capacity of 1,516,300 ft³ *42 937 m³*, was 403.4 ft *122,9 m* long and 85.1 ft *25,93 m* in diameter, with a crew of 21. She first flew on 21 July 1958, but crashed into the sea in June 1960.

Greatest Passenger Load The most people ever carried in an airship was 207 in the U.S. Navy *Akron* in 1931. The trans-atlantic record is 117 by the German *Hindenburg* in 1937.

Earliest The earliest recorded balloon was a hot air model invented by Father Bartolomeu de Gusmão (*né* Lourenço) (b. Santos, Brazil, 1685), which was flown indoors at the Casa da India, Terreiro do Paço, Portugal on 8 Aug. 1709.

Distance record The record distance travelled is 3 052,7 km *1,896.9 miles* by H. Berliner (Germany) from Bitterfeld, Germany, to Kirgishan in the Ural Mountains, Russia, on 8–10 Feb. 1914. The official duration record is 87 hours by H. Kaulen (Germany) set on 13–17 Dec. 1913.

Largest The largest balloon ever to fly is the 800 ft tall balloon built by G. T. Schjeldahl for the U.S.A.F., first tested on 18 July 1966. It was used for a Martian re-entry experiment by N.A.S.A. 130,000 ft *39 624 m* above Walker AFB, New Mexico, U.S.A., on 30 Aug. 1966. Its capacity is 260 million ft³ *7 362 420 m³*. The largest hot air balloon in the world is one of 40,000 ft³ *11 326 m³* known as *Cumulo Nimbus* built by Mr. Don Cameron in 1972.

Human-powered flight The greatest distance achieved in human-powered flight is 1,171 yds *1 070 m* in *Jupiter* by Flt. Lt. John Potter R.A.F. in 1 min 47.4 sec at R.A.F. Benson, Oxfordshire on 29 June 1972. He achieved 1,350 yds *1 234 m* unofficially.

Oldest and Youngest Pilots Thomas Williams, 86, of Sweaberg, Ontario, Canada who first flew in Scotland in 1917 had his license renewed to May 1973. The youngest age at which anyone has ever qualified as a military pilot is 15 years 5 months in the case of Sgt. Thomas Dobney (b. 6 May 1926) of the R.A.F. He had understated his age (14 years) on entry. Miss Betty Bennett took off, flew and landed solo at the age of 10 on 4 Jan. 1952 in Cuba.

HOVERCRAFT

Earliest The inventor of the ACV (air-cushion vehicle) is Sir Christopher Sydney Cockerell, C.B.E., F.R.S. (b. 4 June 1910), a British engineer who had the idea in 1954, published his Ripplecraft Report 1/55 on 25 Oct. 1955 and patented it on 12 Dec. 1955. The earliest patent relating to an air-cushion craft was applied for in 1877 by John I. Thornycroft (1843–1928) of Chiswick, London. The first flight by a hovercraft was made by the 4 ton/*tonnes* Saunders Roe SR-N1 at Cowes on 30 May 1959. With a 1,500 lb. *680 kg* thrust Viper turbojet engine, this craft reached 68 knots *126 km/h* in June 1961. The first hovercraft public service was run across the Dee Estuary by the 60-knot *111 km/h* 24-passenger Vickers-Armstrong VA-3 between July and September 1962.

Largest The largest is the £1,500,000 Westland SR-N4, *Mountbatten*, weighing 168 tons *170 tonnes*, first run on 4 Feb. 1968. It has a top speed of 77 knots *142 km/h* powered by 4 Bristol Siddeley Marine Proteus engines with 19 ft *5,7 m* propellers. It carries 34 cars and 174 passengers and is 130 ft 2 in *39,67 m* long with a 76 ft 10 in *23,41 m* beam.

Longest flight The longest hovercraft journey was one of 5,000 miles *8 047 km* through eight West African countries between 15 Oct. 1969 and 3 Jan. 1970 by the British Trans-African Hovercraft Expedition. The longest non-stop journey on record is one of 550 miles *885,2 km* lasting 33 hours by a Denny Mark II piloted by Sir John Onslow from Poole, Dorset to Fleetwood, Lancashire on 4–5 July 1968.

Greatest Load The heaviest object moved by "hover floatation" is 500 short tons *453,5 tonnes* in the case of a 471 ft *143,5 m* circumference tank by Brocklesby Transport at Quebec City in late Sept. 1971.

MODEL AIRCRAFT

The world record for altitude is 26,929 ft *8 207,9 m* by Maynard L. Hill (U.S.A.) on 6 Sept. 1970 using a radio-controlled model. The speed record is 213.71 m.p.h. *343,93 km/h* by V. Goukoune and V. Myakinin (both U.S.S.R.) with a radio-controlled model at Klementyeva, U.S.S.R., on 21 Sept. 1971. The best

Betty Bennett, who at the age of 10 years flew a plane solo, at the controls of her plane

British performance is 101.5 m.p.h. *163,3 km/h* by an unsponsored home-built 7.9 c.c. engined model of 32 in *0,81 m* wing span by John Crampton at Dunsfold, Surrey on 20 Oct. 1968.

5. POWER PRODUCERS

LARGEST POWER PLANT

World The world's largest power station is the U.S.S.R.'s hydro-electric station at Krasnoyarsk on the river Yenisey, Siberia, U.S.S.R. with a power of 6,096,000 kW. Its third generator turned in March 1968 and the twelfth became operative in December 1970. The turbine hall, completed in June 1968, is 1,378 ft *420 m* long. The reservoir backed up by the dam was reported in Nov. 1972 to be 240 miles *386 km* in length.

The largest non-hydro-electric generating plant in the world is the 2,500,000 kW Tennessee Valley Authority installation at Paradise, Kentucky, U.S.A. with an annual consumption of 8,150,000 tons *8 280 807 tonnes* of coal. It cost $189,000,000 (*then £78,750,000*).

United Kingdom The power station with the greatest installed capacity in the United Kingdom is Longannet, Fife, Scotland which attained 2,400 MW by Dec. 1972. Ferrybridge "C" near Pontefract, Yorkshire, reached full power of 2,000 MW in December 1967, and with the Ferrybridge "A" and "B" forms a 2,430 MW complex. At Drax, Yorkshire, the first stage of 3 × 660 MW sets will be completed in 1973 and there is provision, pending Government decision, to double this figure to 3,960 MW.

The largest hydro-electric plant in the United Kingdom is the North of Scotland Hydro-electricity Board's Power Station at Loch Sloy, Dunbartonshire. The installed capacity of this station is 130,450 kW or 175,000 h.p. The Ben Cruachan Pumped Storage Scheme was opened on 15 Oct. 1965 at Loch Awe, Argyll, Scotland. It has a capacity of 400,000 kW and cost £24,000,000.

Biggest black-out The greatest power failure in history struck seven north-eastern U.S. States and Ontario, Canada, on 9–10 Nov. 1965. About 30,000,000 people in 80,000 miles² *207 200 km²* were plunged into darkness. Only two were killed. In New York City the power failed at 5.27 p.m. Supplies were eventually restored by 2 a.m. in Brooklyn, 4.20 a.m. in Queens, 6.58 a.m. in Manhattan and 7 a.m. in the Bronx.

ATOMIC POWER

Earliest The world's first atomic pile was built in a disused squash court at the University of Chicago, Illinois, U.S.A. It went "critical" at 3.25 p.m. on 2 Dec. 1942.

The world's largest power plant, at Krasnoyarsk, Siberia, U.S.S.R., which has a power output of 6,096,000 kW

Largest The world's largest atomic power station is the Ontario Hydro's Pickering station which in 1973 attained full output of 2,160 Mw.

LARGEST REACTOR

The largest single atomic reactor in the world is the 873 MW Westinghouse Electric Corporation presurized water type reactor installed at Indian Point No. 2 Station, New York, U.S.A., which became operative in 1969.

TIDAL POWER STATION

The world's first major tidal power station is the *Usine marèmotrice de la Rance*, officially opened on 26 Nov. 1966 at the Rance estuary in the Golfe de St. Malo, Brittany, France. It was built in five years at a cost of 420,000,000 francs (*£34,685,000*), and has a net annual output of 544,000,000 kWh. The 880 yd *804 m* barrage contains 24 turbo alternators. This harnessing of the tides has imperceptibly slowed the Earth's rate of revolution. The $1,000 million (*£416 million*) Passamaquoddy project for the Bay of Fundy in Maine, U.S.A., and New Brunswick, Canada, is not expected to be operative before 1978.

LARGEST BOILER

The largest boilers ever designed are those ordered in the United States from The Babcock & Wilcox Company (U.S.A.) with a capacity of 1,330 MW so

THE WORLD'S LARGEST HYDRO-ELECTRIC GENERATING PLANTS

(Progressive List)

Kilowattage	First Operational	Location	River
38,400	1898	De Cew Falls No. 1 (old plant)	Welland Canal
132,500	1905	Ontario Power Station	Niagara
403,900	1922	Sir Adam Beck No. 1 (formerly Queenston-Chippawa)	Niagara
524,000[1]	1967	Guri, Venezuela	Caroní
1,641,000	1942	Beauharnois, Quebec, Canada	St. Lawrence
2,025,000[2]	1941	Grand Coulee, Washington State, U.S.A.	Columbia
2,100,000	1955	Volga-V.I. Lenin Station, Kuybyshev, U.S.S.R.	Volga
2,543,000	1958	Volga-22nd Congress Station, Volgograd, U.S.S.R.	Volga
4,500,000	1961	Bratsk, U.S.S.R.	Angara
6,096,000	1967	Krasnoyarsk, U.S.S.R.	Yenisey
6,400,000	—	Sayano-Shushensk, U.S.S.R.	Yenisey

[1] *Ultimate Kilowattage will be 6,500,000 kW.*
[2] *Ultimate long-term planned kilowattage will be 9,771,000 kW with the completion of the "Third Powerplant" (capacity 7,200,000 kW).*

involving the evaporation of 9,330,000 lb. of steam per hour. The largest boilers now being installed in the United Kingdom are the three 660 MW units for the Drax Power Station (see page 158) designed and constructed by Babcock & Wilcox Ltd.

LARGEST GENERATOR

Generators in the 2,000,000 kW (or 2,000 Mw) range are now in the planning stages both in the U.K. and the U.S.A. The largest under construction is one of 1,300 Mw by the Brown Boveri Co. of Switzerland for the Tennessee Valley Authority.

LARGEST TURBINES

The largest turbines under construction are those rated at 820,000 h.p. with an overload capacity of 1,000,000 h.p., 32 ft *9,7 m* in diameter with a 401-ton *407 tonnes* runner and a 312½ ton *317,5 tonnes* shaft for the Grand Coulee "Third Powerplant" (see page 158).

GAS TURBINE

The largest gas turbine in the world is that installed at the Krasnodar thermal power station in August 1969 with a capacity of 100,000 kW. It was built in Leningrad, U.S.S.R.

LARGEST PUMP TURBINE

The world's largest integral reversible pump-turbine is that made by Allis-Chalmers for the $50,000,000 Taum Sauk installation of the Union Electric Co. in St. Louis, Missouri, U.S.A. It has a rating of 240,000 h.p. as a turbine and a capacity of 1,100,000 gallons *5 000 559 litres*/min as a pump. The Tehachapi Pumping Plant, California (1972) pumps 18,300,000 gal/min *83,2 million litres/min* over 1,700 ft *518 m* up.

SOLAR POWER PLANT

The largest solar furnace in the world is the Laboratoire de l'Energie Solaire, at Odeillo, Pyrénées-Orientales, France. It consists of an array of 63 steerable mirrors with a total area of 2 835 m² *30,515 ft²* or seven tenths of an acre which can generate a heat of 3 725° C *6 735° F*. (see page 8).

LARGEST GAS WORKS

The flow of natural gas from the North Sea is diminishing the manufacture of gas by the carbonisation of coal and the re-forming process using petroleum derivatives. Britain's largest ever gasworks 300 acres *120 ha* were at Beckton, Essex. Currently the most productive gasworks are at the oil re-forming plant at East Greenwich, London, with an output of 420.5 million ft³ *11 907 298 m³* per day.

MOST POWERFUL JET ENGINE

The world's most powerful jet engine was the General Electric GE4/J5 turbojet which attained a thrust of 69,900 lb. *31 706 kg*, with after-burning, on 13 Nov. 1969. The Pratt & Whitney JT 9D-X turbofan first run on 15 Jan. 1972 has a thrust of 62,000 lb. *28 122 kg* at 23° F *−5° C*. The Rolls-Royce RB 211-24 is being developed to power the Lockheed L-1011-2 'Tristar', and will develop 48,000 lb. *21 722 kg* to become the most powerful British made turbofan. The thrust of the Thiokol XLR99-RM-2 rocket motor in each of the three U.S. North American X-15 aircraft was 56,880 lb. *25 800 kg* at sea-level, reaching 70,000 lb. *31 kg 750* at peak altitudes.

Smallest Steam Engine The smallest double acting reciprocating engine ever built was constructed in 1971 by Jon Van de Geer, B.Sc of Salisbury, Wilts, England. It has a bore and a stroke of 0.025 in *0,635 mm* and a spoked fly wheel 0.125 in *3,175 mm* diameter which runs at between 30,000 and 60,000 r.p.m. The engine is run on vacuum to avoid water globules in pressurized air or steam.

6. ENGINEERING

OLDEST MACHINERY

World The earliest machinery still in use is the *dâlu*—a water raising instrument known to have been in use in the Sumerian civilization which originated *c.* 3500 B.C. in Lower Iraq.

Britain The oldest piece of machinery (excluding clocks) operating in the United Kingdom is the snuff mill driven by a water wheel at Messrs. Wilson & Co.'s Sharrow Mill in Sheffield, Yorkshire. It is known to have been operating in 1797 and more probably since 1730.

LARGEST PRESS

The world's two most powerful production machines are forging presses in the U.S.A. The Loewy closed-die forging press, in a plant leased from the U.S. Air Force by the Wyman-Gordon Company at North Grafton, Massachusetts, U.S.A. weighs 9,469 tons *9 620 tonnes* and stands 114 ft 2 in *34,79 m* high, of which 66 ft *20,1 m* is sunk below the operating floor. It has a rated capacity of 44,600 tons *45 315 tonnes*, and went into operation in October 1955. The other similar press is at the plant of the Aluminium Company of America at Cleveland, Ohio. There has been a report of a press in the U.S.S.R. with a capacity of 75 000 tonnes *73,800 tons* at Novo Kramatorsk. The most powerful press in Great Britain is the closed-die forging and extruding press installed in 1967 at the Camelon Iron Works, near Edinburgh, Scotland. The press is 92 ft *28 m* tall (27 ft *[8,2m]* below ground) and exerts a force of 30,000 tons *30 481 tonnes*.

LATHE

The world's largest lathe is the 72 ft *21,9 m* long 385 ton *391 tonnes* giant lathe built by the Dortmunder Rheinstahl firm of Wagner in 1962. The face plate is 15 ft *4,5 m* in diameter and can exert a torque of 289,000 ft/lb. *39 955 m/kg f* when handling objects weighing up to 200 tons *203 tonnes*.

EXCAVATOR

The world's largest excavator is the 33,400 h.p. *33 863 c.v.* Marion 6360 excavator, weighing 12,500 tons *12 700 tonnes*. This vast machine can grab 241 tons *244 tonnes* in a single bite in a bucket of 85 yds³ *65 m³* capacity.

The oldest piece of machinery still working in Britain, the snuff mill at Messrs. Wilson & Co.'s works in Sheffield, Yorkshire

DRAGLINE

World The Ural Engineering Works at Ordzhonikdze, U.S.S.R., completed in March 1962, has a dragline known as the ES-25(100) with a boom of 100 m *328 ft* and a bucket with a capacity of 31.5 yds³ *24 m³*. The world's largest walking dragline is the Bucyrus-Erie 4250W with an all-up weight of 12,000 tons *12 192 tonnes* and a bucket capacity of 220 yds³ *168 m³* on a 310 ft *94,4 m* boom. This machine, the world's largest mobile land machine is now operating on the Central Ohio Coal Company's Muskingum site in Ohio, U.S.A.

United Kingdom The largest dragline excavator in Britain is "Big Geordie", the Bucyrus-Erie 1550W 6250 gross h.p., weighing 3,000 tons *3 048 tonnes* with a forward mast 160 ft *48,7 m* high. On open-cast coal workings at Widdrington, Northumberland in February 1970, it proved able to strip 100 tons *101 tonnes* of overburden in 65 secs with its 65 yard³ *49,7 m³* bucket on a 265 ft *80,7 m* boom. It is operated by Derek Crouch (Contractors) Ltd. of Peterborough.

BLAST FURNACE

The world's largest blast furnace is the No. 3 Blast Furnace at the Nippon Steel Corporation's Kimitsu Steel Works completed in April 1971. It has a daily pig iron production capacity of 10,000 tons *10 160 tonnes*. The No. 1 Blast Furnace at Nippon Steel's Oita Works, Japan has an inner volume of 4 158 m³ *146,838 ft³* and capacity of 10,000 tons/*tonnes* also.

Largest forging The largest forging on record is one 53 ft *16,1 m* long weighing 396,000 lb. (176.79 tons [*179,62 tonnes*]) forged by Bethlehem Steel for the Tennessee Valley Authority nuclear power plant at Brown Ferry Alabama, U.S.A. in Nov. 1969.

LONGEST PIPELINES

Oil The longest crude oil pipeline in the world is the Interprovincial Pipe Line Company's installation from Edmonton, Alberta, to Buffalo, New York State, U.S.A., a distance of 1,775 miles *2 856 km*. Along the length of the pipe 13 pumping stations maintain a flow of 6,900,000 gal *31 367 145 litres* of oil per day. In Britain the longest commercial oil pipeline, 242 miles *389 km* from the Thames to the Mersey, is owned by Chevron, Mobil, Petrofina, Shell-Mex and B.P., and Texaco. It was opened on 19 March 1969 at a cost of £8½ million.

The eventual length of the Trans-Siberian Pipeline will be 2,319 miles *3 732 km*, running from Tuimazy through Omsk and Novosibirsk to Irkutsk. The first 30 mile *48 km* section was opened in July 1957.

Natural gas The longest natural gas pipeline in the world is the TransCanada Pipeline which by mid-1971 had 3,769 miles *6 065 km* of pipe up to 36 in *91,4 cm* in diameter. The mileage will be increased to 4,464 miles *7 184 km*, some of it in 42 in *106,6 cm* pipe, by mid-1973. A system 5,625 miles *9 052 km* in length, with a 3,500 mile *5 632 km* trunk from northern Russia to Leningrad, is under construction in the U.S.S.R., for completion by 1976.

Oil Tank Largest The largest oil tank ever constructed is the Million Barrell Ekofisk Oil Tank completed in 1973 for implanting in the North Sea measuring 92 × 92 82 m high (*301.8 ft square and 269 ft high*) and containing 8 000 metric tons *7,873 tons* of steel and 202,000 metric tons *198 809 tons* of concrete. The capacity of 160 000 m³ *209,272 yds³* is equivalent to 1.42 times the amount of oil which escaped from the *Torrey Canyon*.

Largest Cat Cracker The world's largest catalyst cracker is the American Oil Company's installation at the Texas City Refinery,

The North Sea oil tank named "Ekofisk", which holds 160 000 m³ or one million barrels of oil

Texas, U.S.A., with a capacity of 3,322,000 gal *15 101 689 litres* per day.

Largest nut The largest nuts ever made weigh 29.5 cwt. (1.48 tons [*1,50 tonnes*]) each and have an outside diameter of 43½ in *110,5 cm* and a 26 in *66 cm* thread. known as the Pilgrim Nuts, they are manufactured by Doncaster Moorside Ltd. Of Oldham, Lancashire, for securing propellers.

Smallest spanner The smallest standard ratchet spanner made in the world is the No. 0 model made by the precision engineers Leytool Ltd. of London, E10, with a head outside diameter of ½ in *12,7 mm* and a width of ¼ in *6,35 mm*.

TRANSFORMER

The world's largest single phase transformers are rated at 1,500,000 kVa of which 8 are in service with the American Electric Power Service Corporation. Of these five stepdown from 765 to 345 kV. Britain's largest trasnformers are those rated at 1,000,000 kVa 400/275 kV built by Hackbridge & Hewittic Co. Ltd., Walton-on-Thames, Surrey first commissioned for the CEGB in Oct 1968.

HIGHEST ROPEWAY OR TELEPHERIQUE

World The highest and longest aerial ropeway in the world is the Teleférico Mérida (Mérida téléphérique) in Venezuela, from Mérida City (5,379 ft [*1 639,5 m*]) to the summit of Pico Espejo (15,629 ft [*4 763,7 m*]), a rise of 10,250 ft *3 124 m*. The ropeway is in four sections, involving 3 car changes in the 8 mile ascent in one hour. The fourth span is 10,070 ft *3 069 m* in length. The two cars work on the pendulum system—the carrier rope is locked and the cars are hauled by means of three pull ropes powered by a 230 h.p. *233 c.v.* motor. They have a maximum capacity of 45 persons and travel at 32 ft *9,7 m* per sec (21.8 m.p.h. [*35,08 km/h*]). The longest single span ropeway is the 13,500 ft *4 114 m* long span from The Coachella Valley to Mt. San Jacinto (10,821 ft [*3 298 m*]), California U.S.A., inaugurated on 12 Sept. 1963. The largest cable cars in the world are those at Squaw Valley, California, U.S.A., with a capacity of 121 persons built by Carrosseriewerke A.G. of Aarburg, Switzerland, and first run on 19 Dec. 1968. The breaking strain on the 7,000 ft *2 133 m* cable is 279 tons *283 tonnes*.

Great Britain Britain's longest cabin lift is that at Llandudno, Caernarvonshire, Wales opened in June 1969. It has 42 cabins with a capacity of 1,000 people per hour and is 5,320 ft *1 621 m* in length.

The B.B.C. Radio Mast at Bilsdale North Yorkshire, which holds the United Kingdom's longest lift shaft at 930 ft *283 m*

PASSENGER LIFTS

Fastest The fastest domestic passenger lifts in the world are
World the express lifts to the 103rd floor in the 109 storey, 1,452 ft *442,56 m* tall Sears Tower in Chicago, Illinois, U.S.A. They operate at a speed of 1,800 ft per min. 20.45 m.p.h. *32,91 km/h*. Much higher speeds are achieved in the winding cages of mine shafts. A hoisting shaft 6,800 ft *2 072 m* deep, owned by Western Deep Levels Ltd. in South Africa, winds at speeds of up to 40.9 m.p.h. *65,8 km/h* (3,595 ft *[1 095 m]* per min).

United The longest lift in the United Kingdom is one 930 ft
Kingdom long inside the B.B.C. T.V. tower at Bilsdale, West Moor, North Riding, Yorkshire built by J. L. Eve Construction Co. Ltd. It runs at 130 ft *39,6m/*min. The longest fast lifts are the two 15-passenger cars in the Post Office Tower, Maple Street, London W1 which travel 540 ft *164 m* up at up to 1,000 ft *304 m/*min.

LONGEST ESCALATORS

The longest escalators of the 235 on the London Underground system are those at Leicester Square which measure 175½ ft *53,49 m* comb to comb. Escalators were introduced on the system at Earl's Court station, London, on 3 Oct. 1911. The term was registered in the U.S. on 28 May 1900 and an escalator was installed at the Paris Exhibition in 1900 and on the Liverpool Overhead Railway at Seaforth Sands *c.* 1904–5.

The world's longest "moving sidewalks" are those installed in the air terminal at Montreal International Airport, Canada, comprising two conveyors measuring 475 ft *144,78 m* each.

The longest "travolators" in Great Britain are the pair of 360 ft *109,7 m* and 375 ft *114,3 m* in tandem at

Terminal No. 3, London Airport, installed by Fletcher, Sutcliffe and Wild of Horbury, Leeds, Yorkshire in March-May 1970.

FASTEST PRINTER

The world's fastest printer is the Radiation Inc. electro-sensitive system at the Lawrence Radiation Laboratory, Livermore, California. High speed recording of up to 30,000 lines each containing 120 alphanumeric characters per minute is attained by controlling electronic pulses through chemically impregnated recording paper which is rapidly moving under closely spaced fixed styli. It can thus print the wordage of the whole Bible (773,692 words) in 65 sec—3,333 times as fast as the world's fastest typist.

TRANSMISSION LINES

Longest The longest span between pylons of any power line in the world is that across the Sogne Fjord, Norway, between Rabnaberg and Flatlberg. Erected in 1955, by the Whitecross Co. Ltd. of Warrington, England, as part of the high-tension power cable from Refsdal power station at Vik, it has a span of 16,040 ft *4 888 m* and a weight of 12 tons/*tonnes*. In 1967 two further high tensile steel/aluminium lines 16,006 ft *4 878 m* long, and weighing 33 tons *33,5 tonnes*, manufactured by Whitecross and B.I.C.C. (see below), were erected here. The longest in Britain are the 5,310 ft *1 618 m* lines built by J. L. Eve Co. across the Severn with main towers each 488 ft *148 m* high.

Highest The world's highest are those across the Straits of Messina, with towers of 675 ft *205 m* (Sicily side) and 735 ft *224 m* (Calabria) and 11,900 ft *3 627 m* apart. The highest lines in Britain are those made by British Insulated Callender's Cables Ltd. at West Thurrock, Essex, which cross the Thames estuary suspended from 630 ft *192 m* tall towers at a minimum height of 250 ft *76 m*, with a 130 ton *132 tonnes* breaking load. They are 4,500 ft *1 371 m* in length.

Highest The highest voltages now carried are 800,000 volts
voltages from Volgograd to the Donbas basin, U.S.S.R. The Swedish A.S.E.A. Company has been experimenting with possible 1,500,000 volt A.C./D.C. transmission lines.

LONGEST CONVEYOR BELT

The world's longest single flight conveyor belt is one of 9 miles *14 km* installed near Uniontown, Kentucky, U.S.A. by Cable Belt Ltd. of Camberley, Surrey. It has a weekly capacity of 140,000 short tons *142 247 tonnes* of coal on a 42 in *1,06 m* wide 800 ft *243 m/*min belt and forms part of a 12½ mile *20 km* long system. The longest installation in Great Britain is also by

Longannet Power Station Fife, Scotland which is supplied by a 5⅛ mile *8,24 km* conveyor belt running underground

Cable Belt Ltd. and of 5½ miles *8,9 km* underground at Longannet Power Station, Fife, Scotland. The world's longest multi-flight conveyor is one of 100 km *62 miles* between the phosphate mine near Bucraa and the port of El Aaiun, Spanish Sahara built by Krupps and completed in 1972. It has 11 flights of between 9 and 11 km *5.6–6.8 miles* and is driven at 4,5 m/sec *10.06* m.p.h.

LONGEST WIRE ROPE

The longest wire rope ever spun in one piece was one measuring 46,653 ft *14 219 m* (8.83 miles) long and 3⅛ in *7,93 cm* in circumference, with a weight of 28½ tons *28,9 tonnes*, manufactured by British Ropes Ltd. of Doncaster, Yorkshire.

CLOCKS

Oldest The earliest mechanical clock, that is one with an escapement, was completed in China in A.D. 725 by I Hsing and Liang Ling-tsan.

The oldest surviving working clock in the world is the faceless clock dating from 1386, or possibly earlier, at Salisbury Cathedral, Wiltshire, which was restored in 1956 having struck the hours for 498 years and ticked more than 500 million times. Earlier dates, ranging back to *c.* 1335, have been attributed to the weight-driven clock in Wells Cathedral, Somerset, but only the iron frame is original. A model of Giovanni de Dondi's heptagonal astronomical clock of 1348–64 was completed in 1962.

Largest The world's most massive clock is the Astronomical
World Clock in Beauvais Cathedral, France, constructed between 1865 and 1868. It contains 90,000 parts and measures 40 ft *12,1 m* high, 20 ft *6,09 m* wide and 9 ft *2,7 m* deep. The Su Sung clock, built in China at K'aifeng in 1088–92, had a 20-ton *20,3 tonnes* bronze armillary sphere for 1½ tons *1,52 tonnes* of water. It was removed to Peking in 1126 and was last known to be working in its 40 ft *12,1 m* high tower in 1136.

United The largest clock in the United Kingdom was on the
Kingdom Singer Sewing Machine factory at Clydebank, Dunbartonshire, Scotland. It had four faces, each 26 ft *7,9 m* in diameter, the minute hand was 12 ft 9 in *3,88 m* long and the hour hand 8 ft 9 in *2,66 m*. It was built in 1882, re-modelled in 1926 and operated until 5 p.m. on 5 March 1963. The largest clock face constructed in Britain is the Synchronome turret clock (diameter 60 ft [*18,2 m*]) exhibited at Earl's Court, London, in March 1959.

Public The largest four-faced clock in the world is that on the
clocks building of the Allen-Bradley Company of Milwaukee, Wisconsin, U.S.A. Each face has a diameter of 40 ft 3½ in *12,28 m* with a minute hand 20 ft *6,09 m* in overall length. The tallest four-faced clock in the world is that of the Williamsburgh Savings Bank in Brooklyn, New York City, N.Y., U.S.A. It is 430 ft *131 m* above street level.

Longest The longest stoppage of Big Ben, Palace of West-
stoppage minster, London since the first tick on 31 May 1859 has been 8 hours in 1900 due to a snow-storm. In 1945 a host of starlings slowed the minute hand by 5 min.

Most The most accurate and complicated clockwork in the
accurate world is the Olsen clock, installed in the Copenhagen Town Hall, Denmark. The clock, which has more than 14,000 units, took 10 years to make and the mechanism of the clock functions in 570,000 different ways. The celestial pole motion of the clock will take 25,753 years to complete a full circle and is the slowest moving designed mechanism in the world. The clock is accurate to 0.5 of a second in 300 years.

Most The highest auction price for any portable English
expensive clock is £26,000 for the silver-mounted Barnard ebony

A scale model of the face of the Olsen clock in Copenhagen Town Hall, Denmark, which is accurate to 0.5 of a second in 300 years

bracket clock made by Thomas Tompion (*c.* 1639–1713) in 1702–08 sold at the salerooms of Sotheby & Co., London on 16 Nov. 1970.

WATCHES

Oldest The oldest watch (portable clock-work time-keeper) is one made of iron by Peter Henlein (or Hele) in Nürnberg (Nuremberg), Bavaria, Germany, in *c.* 1504 and now in the Memorial Hall, Philadelphia, Pennsylvania, U.S.A. The earliest wrist watches were those of Jacquet-Droz and Leschot of Geneva, Switzerland, dating from 1790.

Most Excluding watches with jewelled cases, the most
expensive expensive standard men's pocket watch is the Swiss *Grande Complication* by Audemars-Piguet which retails for $25,000 (£9,615). The Vacheron et Constantin Minute repeater has a retail selling price of about £10,000. The "perpetual" calendar however requires resetting at the end of some centuries. On 1 June 1964, a record £27,500 was paid for the Duke of Wellington's watch made in Paris in 1807 by Abraham Louis Bréguet, at the salerooms of Sotheby & Co., London, by the dealers Messrs. Ronald Lee for a Portuguese client.

Smallest The smallest watches in the world are produced by Jaeger Le Coultre of Switzerland. Equipped with a 15-jewelled movement they measure just over half-an-inch *1,2 cm* long and three-sixteenths of an in *0,476 cm* in width. The movement, with its case, weighs under a quarter of an oz. *7 gr.*

TIME MEASURER

Most The most accurate time-keeping devices are the twin
accurate atomic hydrogen masers installed in 1964 in the U.S.
World Naval Research Laboratory, Washington, D.C. They are based on the frequency of the hydrogen atom's transition period of 1,420,450,751,694 cycles/sec. This enables an accuracy to within one sec/1,700,000 years.

United The most accurate measurer in the United Kingdom is
Kingdom the 14 ft *4,2 m* long rubidium resonance Standard Atomic Clock at the National Physical Laboratory, Teddington, Greater London, devised by Dr. Louis Essen, O.B.E. and Mr. J. V. L. Parry and completed in 1962. It is accurate to within one second in 1,000 years.

RADAR INSTALLATIONS

Largest The largest of the three installations in the U.S. Ballistic Missile Early Warning System (B.M.E.W.S.) is

An aerial view of Harland and Wolff's shipbuilding dock at Belfast, Northern Ireland, showing the *Goliath* crane which has test lifted 1,050 tons *1 067 tonnes*

that near Thule, in Greenland, 931 miles *1 498 km* from the North Pole, completed in 1960 at a cost of $500,000,000 (*now £208.3 million*). Its sister stations are one at Cape Clear, Alaska, U.S.A., completed in 1961, and a $115,000,000 (*now £47.9 million*) installation at Fylingdales Moor, Yorkshire, completed in June 1963. A fourth station is being built on an Indian Ocean island site. The 187-mast installation erected at Orfordness, Suffolk for the U.S.A.F. and R.A.F. was closed down on 30 June 1973.

Smallest tubing The smallest tubing in the world is made by Accles and Pollock, Ltd. of Oldbury, Worcestershire. It is of pure nickel with an outside diameter of 0.0005 of an in and was announced on 9 Sept. 1963. The average human hair measures from 0.002 to 0.003 of an inch *0,05–0,075 mm* diameter. The tubing, which is stainless, can be used for the artificial insemination of bees and for the medical process of "feeding" nerves, and weighs only 5 oz. *141 gr* per 100 miles *160 km.*

MOST POWERFUL CRANE

World The crane with the world's greatest lifting capacity is that mounted on the craneship *Thor* (ex-super tanker *Veedol*) which is designed to lift 2,000 tons *2 032 tonnes* over its stern and up to 1,600 tons *1 626 tonnes* while the 250 ft *76,2 m* boom is rotating. This craneship, due for completion in October 1973, which is designed to lift off-shore oil production platforms in the North Sea, is owned by the Heerema Group, the Netherlands off-shore lifting contractors and was built by Boele Bolnef, Netherlands.

British The Goliath crane installed at Harland and Wolff's shipbuilding dock, Belfast, Northern Ireland in 1969 has test lifted 1,050 tons *1 067 tonnes.*

Tallest Mobile The tallest mobile crane in the world is the 810 tonnes Rosenkranz K10001 with a lifting capacity of 1 000 tonnes *948 tons*, a combined boom and jib height of 202 m *663 ft.* It is carried on 10 trucks each limited to 75 ft 8 in *23,06 m* and an axle weight of 118 tonnes *116 tons.* It can lift 30 tonnes *29.5 tons* to a height of 160 m *525 ft.*

Greatest Lift The heaviest lifting operation in engineering history was of the 902 ft *274,9 m* long centre span of the Fremont Bridge over the Willamette River, Portland Oregon on 13–15 Mar. 1973. The $1 million hydraulic jacking system raised the 6,000 short tons *5 443 tonne* section at 4 ft *1,21 m* per hour in 42 hours.

An artist's impression of the crane with the greatest lifting capacity mounted on the crane-ship *Thor*

9
THE BUSINESS WORLD

1. COMMERCE

The $(US) has in this chapter been converted at a fixed mean rate of 2.50 to the £ Sterling, which mainly pertained during those financial years ending 31 Dec. 1972.

OLDEST INDUSTRY

Agriculture is often described as "the oldest industry in the world", whereas in fact there is no evidence that it was practised before *c.* 11,000 B.C. The oldest known industry is flint knapping, involving the production of chopping tools and hand axes, dating from about 1,750,000 years ago.

OLDEST COMPANY

World The oldest company in the world is the Faversham Oyster Fishery Co., referred to in the Faversham Oyster Fishing Act 1930, as existing "from time immemorial", *i.e.* from before 1189.

Britain The Royal Mint has origins going back to A.D. 287. The Whitechapel Bell Foundry of Whitechapel Road, London, E.1, has been in business since 1570. The retail business in Britain with the oldest history is the Cambridge bookshop, which, though under various ownership, has traded from the site of 1 Trinity Street since 1581 and since 1907 under its present title Bowes & Bowes. R. Durtnell & Sons, builders, of Brasted, Kent, has been run by the same family since 1591. The first bill of adventure signed by the English East India Co., was dated 21 March 1601.

GREATEST ASSETS

World The business with the greatest amount in physical assets is the Bell System, which comprises the American Telephone and Telegraph Company, with headquarters at 195 Broadway, New York City, N.Y., U.S.A., and its subsidiaries. The group's total assets on the consolidated balance sheet at 31 Dec. 1972 were valued at $60,625,045,000 (*£24,250 million*). The plant involved included 105.3 million telephones. The number of employees was 1,000,772. The shareholders at 1 Jan. 1973 numbered more than those of any other company, namely more than 3,000,000. A total of 20,109 attended the Annual Meeting in April 1961, thereby setting a world record.

The first company to have assets in excess of $1 billion was the United States Steel Corporation with $1,400 million (*then £287.73 million*) at the time of its creation by merger in 1900.

United Kingdom The enterprise in the United Kingdom, excluding banks, with the greatest capital employed is the Electricity Council and the Electricity Boards in England and Wales with £5,185,000,000 in 1972. This ranks third in the western world to Exxon and General Motors.

The manufacturing company with the greatest net assets employed is Imperial Chemical Industries, Ltd., with £1,869.4 million, as at 31 Dec. 1972. Its staff and payroll averaged 199,000 during the year. The company, which has 426 U.K. and overseas subsidiaries, was formed on 7 Dec. 1926 by the merger of four concerns—British Dyestuffs Corporation Ltd.; Brunner, Mond & Co. Ltd.; Nobel Industries Ltd. and United Alkali Co. Ltd. The first chairman was Sir Alfred Moritz Mond (1868–1930), later the 1st Lord Melchett.

The net assets of The "Shell" Transport and Trading Company, Ltd., at 31 Dec. 1972, were valued at £1,593,636,534. Of this, £1,591,828,400 represented a 40 per cent holding of the net assets of the Royal Dutch/Shell Group, which stands at £3,979,571,000. Group companies have 174,000 employees. "Shell" Transport was formed in 1897 by Marcus Samuel (1853–1927), later the 1st Viscount Bearsted.

Greatest sales The first company to surpass the $1 billion (U.S.) mark in annual sales was the United States Steel Corporation in 1917. Now there are 58 corporations with sales exceeding £1,000 million (36 U.S., 17 European and 5 Japanese). The list is headed by General Motors (see Motor car manufacturer) with sales in 1972 of $30,435,231,414 (*£12,174 million*).

The world's largest retail merchandiser is The Defense Logistics Service Center, Battle Creek, Michigan which sells off surplus U.S. Federal material.

Greatest profit and loss The greatest net profit ever made by one company in a year is $2,162,806,765 (*now £865.1 million*) by General Motors Corporation of Detroit in 1972. The greatest loss ever sustained by a commercial concern in a year is $431.2 million (*£179.6 million*) by Penn

Central Transportation Co. in 1970—a rate of $13.67 (*then £5.69*) per second. The top gross profits in the United Kingdom in 1972 were British Petroleum with £776.4 million and the biggest loss maker was Ford Motor Co. which lost £19,200,000.

Most efficient The major United Kingdom company with highest return on capital in 1972 was Tampimex Oil Products, a London-based company trading in mineral oils and petro-chemicals which showed a net profit of £1,166,000 or 149.7 per cent on a capital employed of £779,000.

Biggest work force The greatest payroll of any civilian organisation in the world is that of the United States Post Office with 696,840 on 1 July 1972. The biggest employer in the United Kingdom is the Post Office with 418,654 employees on 1 Jan. 1973.

Largest Take-Over The largest take-over in commercial history has been the bid of £438,000,000 by Grand Metropolitan Hotels Ltd., for the brewers Watney Mann on 17 June 1972.

Largest Merger The largest merger ever mooted in British business was that of the Hill Samuel Group (£768 million assets) and Slater, Walker Securities (£469 million) in April 1973 with combined assets of £1,237 million. This plan was called off on 19 June 1973.

ADVERTISING AGENTS

The largest advertising agency in the world is J. Walter Thompson Co. Ltd., which in 1972 had total billings of $772,400,000 (*£309 million*).

Biggest advertiser The world's biggest advertiser is Unilever, the Anglo-Dutch group formed on 2 Sept. 1929 whose origins go back to 21 June 1884. The group has more than 500 companies in more than 70 countries and employs 324,000 people, mainly in the production of foods, detergents and toiletries. The advertising bill for over 1,000 branded products is in the region of £110,000,000 per annum.

Aircraft manu-facturer The world's largest aircraft manufacturer is the Boeing Company of Seattle, Washington, U.S.A. The corporation's sales totalled $2,370,000,000 (*£948 million*) in 1972, and it had 58,600 employees and assets valued at $2,127,396,000 (*£850.9 million*) at 31 Dec. 1972. Cessna Aircraft Company of Wichita, Kansas, U.S.A., produced 4,643 civil aircraft (41 models) in the year 1972, with total sales of $248 million (*£99.2 million*). The Company has produced more than 105,000 aircraft since Clyde's Cessna's first was built in 1911. Their record year was 1965–66 with 7,922 aircraft completed.

AIRLINES

Largest The largest airline in the world is the U.S.S.R. State airline "Aeroflot", so named since 1932. This was instituted on 9 Feb. 1923, with the title of Civil Air Fleet of the Council of Ministers of the U.S.S.R., abbreviated to "Dobrolet". It operates 1,300 aircraft over about 435,000 miles *700 000 km* of routes, employs 400,000 people and carried 80 million passengers in 1972 to 57 countries. The commercial airline carrying the greatest number of passengers in 1972 was United Air Lines of Chicago, Illinois, U.S.A. (formed 1931) with 29,591,000 passengers. The company had 48,230 employees and a fleet of 359 jet planes. The commercial airline serving the greatest mileage of routes is Air France, with 293,135 miles *471 755 km* of undupli-cated routes in 1972. In 1972 the company carried 7,327,246 passengers. In March 1973 the British Airways Group were operating a fleet of 222 aircraft, with 11 on order. Staff employed on airline activities totalled 54,000 and some 14,500,000 passengers were carried in the year ended 31 March 1973.

Oldest The oldest commercial airline is Koninklijke-Lucht-vaart-Maatschappij N.V. (KLM) of the Netherlands, which opened its first scheduled service (Amsterdam-London) on 17 May 1920, having been established in 1919. One of the original constituents of B.O.A.C., Aircraft Transport and Travel Ltd., was founded in 1918 and merged into Imperial Airways in 1924, and one of the holding companies of S.A.S., Det Danske Luftfartselskab, was established on 29 Oct. 1918 but operated a scheduled service only between August 1920 and 1946.

Aluminium producer The world's largest producer of aluminium is Alcan Aluminium Limited, of Montreal, Quebec, Canada. With its affiliated companies, the company had an output of 1,853,000 short tons *1 681 000 tonnes* and record consolidated revenues of U.S. $1,529,384,000 (*£611 million*) in 1972. The company's principal subsidiary, the Aluminium Company of Canada, Ltd., owns the world's largest aluminium smelter, at Arvida, Québec, with a capacity of 458,500 short tons *415 900 tonnes* per annum.

Art auctioneer-ring The largest and oldest firm of art auctioneers in the world is Sotheby Parke-Bernet of London and New York, founded in 1744. The turnover in 1971–72 was £43,296,900. The highest total of any single art sale has been $5,852,250 (*£2,438,437*) paid at Parke-Bernet Gallery on 25 Feb. 1970 for 73 impressionist and modern paintings.

Largest Barbers The largest barbering establishment in the world is Norris of Houston, 3200 Audley, Houston, Texas, U.S.A. which employs 60 barbers.

Bicycle factory The 64-acre *25,9 ha* plant of Raleigh Industries Ltd. at Nottingham is the largest factory in the world produc-ing complete bicycles, components, wheeled toys and prams. The company employs 10,000 and in 1973 has targets to make 850,000 wheeled toys and more than 2 million bicycles.

Book shop The world's largest book shop is that of W. & G. Foyle Ltd., of London W.C.2. First established in 1904 in a small shop in Islington, the company is now at 119–125 Charing Cross Road. The area on one site is 75,825 ft² *7 044 m²*. The largest single display of books in one room in the world is in the Norrington Room at Blackwell's Bookshop, Broad Street, Oxford. This subterranean adjunct was opened on 16 June 1966 and contains 160,000 volumes on 2½ miles *4 km* of shelving in 10,000 ft² *929 m²* of selling space.

The Norrington Room in Blackwell's Bookshop, Oxford, which has the largest single display of books in the world

BREWER

Oldest The oldest brewery in the world is the Weihenstephan Brewery, Freising, near Munich, West Germany, founded in A.D. 1040.

Largest World The largest single brewer in the world is Anheuser-Busch, Inc. in St. Louis, Missouri, U.S.A. In 1972 the company sold 26,521,872 U.S. barrels, equivalent to 5,476 million Imperial pints, the greatest annual volume ever produced by a brewing company. The company's St. Louis plant covers 95 acres *38,4 ha* and has a capacity of 9,300,000 U.S. barrels *1,920 million Imperial pints*. The largest brewery on a single site is Adolph Coors Co. of Golden, Colorado, U.S.A. which produced 9,700,000 U.S. barrels *2,002 million Imperial pints* in 1972.

Europe The largest brewery in Europe is the Guinness Brewery at St. James's Gate, Dublin, Ireland, which extends over 58.03 acres *23,48 ha*. The business was founded in 1759.

United Kingdom The largest brewing company in the United Kingdom based on its 9,053 public houses, 1,068 off-licences and 92 hotels, is Bass Charrington Ltd. The company has net assets of £372,500,000, 58,341 employees (including bar-staff) and controls 20 breweries. Their sales figure of £440,500,000 for the year ending 30 Sept. 1972 (53 week end) was however, surpassed by Allied Breweries Ltd. with £484,464,000 for the same period. Allied Breweries lead on assets also with £421.3 million.

Greatest exports The largest exporter of beer, ale and stout in the world is Arthur Guinness, Son & Co. Ltd., of Dublin, Ireland. Exports of Guinness from the Republic of Ireland in the 53 weeks ending 14 April 1973 were 1,141,778 bulk barrels (bulk barrel = 36 Imperial gallons), which is equivalent to 1,772,680 half pint glasses *1 678 862 thirty centilitre glasses* per day.

Brickworks The largest brickworks in the world is the London Brick Company plant at Stewartby, Bedford. The works, established in 1898, now cover 221 acres *90 ha* and produce 17,000,000 bricks and brick equivalent every week.

Building contractors The largest construction company in the United Kingdom is George Wimpey & Co. Ltd. (founded 1880), of London, who undertake building, civil, mechanical, electrical and chemical engineering work. With assets of £156,816,473 and over 25,000 employees, the turnover of work was £242,000,000 in 29 countries in 1972.

Building societies The largest building society in the world is the Halifax Building Society of Halifax, Yorkshire. It was established in 1853 and has total assets exceeding £2,791,000,000. It has 5,245 employees and 245 branches and over 950 agencies. The oldest building society in the world is the Chelmsford and Essex Society, established in July 1845.

Chemist shop chain The largest chain of chemist shops in the world is Boots The Chemists, which has 1,350 retail branches. The firm was founded by Jesse Boot (b. Nottingham, 1850), later the 1st Baron Trent, who died in 1931.

Chemical company The world's largest chemical company is Imperial Chemical Industries Ltd. (see Greatest Assets, U.K. company above.)

Chocolate factory The world's largest chocolate factory is that built by Hershey Foods Corp. of Hershey, Pennsylvania, U.S.A., in 1905. In 1972 sales were $416,191,154 (*£166.4 million*) and the payroll was over 8,000 employees.

DEPARTMENT STORES

World The largest department store chain, in terms of number of stores, is J. C. Penney, Company Inc., founded in Wyoming, U.S.A., in 1902. The company operates almost 2,000 retail units in the U.S.A., Belgium and Italy, with net selling space of 45.4 million ft² *4,21 million m²*. Its turnover was $4,812,238,548 (*£1,723 million*) in the year ending

The Marble Arch, London branch of Marks & Spencer Ltd., the department store with the fastest moving stock

29 Jan. 1972, the sixteenth consecutive year of record sales.

United Kingdom The largest department store in the United Kingdom is Harrods Ltd. of Knightsbridge, London, S.W.1 named after Henry Charles Harrod, who opened a grocery in Knightsbridge Village in 1849. It has a total selling floor space of 23 acres *9,3 ha*, employs 5,000 people and had a total of 12,260,000 transactions in 1972.

Most profitable The department store with the fastest-moving stock in the world is the Marks & Spencer premier branch, known as "Marble Arch" at 458 Oxford Street, London, W. 1. The figure of £250 worth of goods per square foot of selling space per year is believed to have become an understatement when the selling area was raised to 72,000 ft² *6 690 m²* in October 1970. The Company has 250 branches in the U.K. and operates on over 5 million ft² *460 000 m²* of selling space.

Games manufacturer The largest company manufacturing games is Parker Bros. Inc. of Salem, Massachusetts, U.S.A. The company's top-selling line is the real estate game "Monopoly", acquired in 1935. More than 65,000,000 sets were sold by January 1972. The daily print of "money" is equivalent to 215,000,000 "dollars", thus exceeding the dollar output of the U.S. Treasury. In the U.S. version the streets are named after those in Atlantic City, New Jersey whence came its then unemployed inventor Charles Darrow. The longest two-man game of "Monopoly" on record is one of 86 hours by Eric Foxall and Gary Davis at the Power House Youth Club, Birmingham in May 1972. John Raddon also completed the same time against a series of opponents.

Distillery The world's largest distilling company is Distillers Corporation-Seagrams Limited of Canada. Its sales in the year ending 31 July 1972 totalled U.S. $1,585,162,000 (*£634 million*), of which $1,358,167,000 (*£543 million*) were from sales by Joseph E. Seagram & Sons, Inc. in the United States. The group employs about 15,000 people, including about 8,000 in the United States.

The largest of all Scotch whisky distilleries is Carsebridge at Alloa, Clackmannanshire, Scotland, owned by Scottish Grain Distillers Limited. This distillery is capable of producing more than 20,000,000 proof gallons per annum. The largest establishment for blending and bottling Scotch whisky is owned by John Walker & Sons Limited at Kilmarnock, Ayrshire, with a potential annual output of 120,000,000 bottles. "Johnnie Walker" is the world's largest-selling brand of Scotch whisky. The largest malt Scotch whisky distillery is the Tomatin Distillery, Inverness-shire, established at 1,028 ft *313 m* above sea level in 1897, with an annual capacity well in excess of 2 million proof gallons. The world's largest-selling brand of gin is Gordon's.

General merchandise The largest general merchandising firm in the world is Sears, Roebuck and Co. (founded by Richard W. Sears in North Redwood railway station, Minnesota in 1886) of Chicago, Illinois, U.S.A. The net sales were $10,991,001,000 (*£4,396 million*) in the year ending 31 Jan. 1973 when the corporation had 837 retail stores and 2,648 catalogue, retail and telephone sales offices and independent catalogue merchants, and total assets valued at $9,326,162,000 (*£3,730 million*).

Grocery stores The largest grocery chain in the world is Safeway Stores Incorporated of Oakland, California, U.S.A. with sales in the calendar year 1972 amounting to $6,057,633,445 *£2,423 million* and total current assets valued at $605,435,021 as at 30 Dec. 1972. The company has 2,331 stores totalling 44,844,000 ft² *4 826 000 m²*. The total payroll is 105,613.

Largest Hotelier The top revenue-earning hotel business is Holiday Inns Inc., with a 1972 revenue of $775,210,000 (*£310 million*), from 1,480 inns at 31 Dec. 1972 in 24 countries. The business was founded by Charles Kemmons Wilson with his first inn in Summer Avenue, Memphis, Tennessee in 1952. Services include spiritual counselling for potential suicides.

INSURANCE COMPANIES

World The company with the highest volume of insurance in force in the world is the Metropolitan Life Insurance Company of 1 Madison Avenue, New York City with $186 billion (*£74,400 million*) which is more than double the U.K. National Debt figure. The assets of the Prudential Insurance Co. of America of Newark, New Jersey are however greater than those of the Met with a figure of $33.9 billion (*£13,560 million*).

United Kingdom The largest insurance company in the United Kingdom is the Prudential Assurance Co. Ltd. At 1 Jan. 1973 the total funds were £2,935,930,000 and the total amount assured was £11,145,567,637.

Life policies Largest The largest life assurance policy ever written was one of £10,000,000 $25,000,000 for James D. Slater (b. 1929), Chairman of Slater, Walker Securities, the City

The liner *Queen Elizabeth 2*, which was insured for £25.5 million for her trials in 1969

of London Investment bankers. The existence of the policy was made known on 3 June 1971.

Smallest The smallest Whole Life Policy written in the United Kingdom in recent times was one for the Sum Assured of £1.95 on the life of George Parfitt, Chairman of Time Assurance Society, Oldham, Lancashire. His premium is 1p per four weeks. The policy was written on 23 February 1973.

Highest pay-out The highest pay-out on a single life has been some $14 million (*£5.6 million*) to Mrs. Linda Mullendore, wife of an Oklahoma rancher, reported on 14 Nov. 1970. Her murdered husband had paid $300,000 in premiums in 1969.

Marine insurance The greatest insured value of any ship lost has been the $16.5 million (*then £5.89 million*) on the *Torrey Canyon* in 1967. The greatest loss withstood on the London market was $10.8 million (*£4.5 million*) on the *Marpessa* though the loss on the *Andrea Doria* in 1956 was £3.93 million (*then $11.0 million*). The cost of the repairs to the U.S.S. *Guittaro*, the nuclear submarine flooded on 15 May 1969 while fitting out at Mare Island, San Francisco, cost $25 million (*£10.42 million*). The Cunard liner QE2 was insured (builder's value only) on its sea trials in 1969 for £25.5 million (*then $61.2 million*).

Mineral water The world's largest mineral firm is Source Perrier, near Nîmes, France with an annual production of more than 1,600,000,000 bottles, of which more than 330,000,000 come from the single spring near Nîmes, and 550,000,000 from Contrexeville. The net profits for the year 1972 were 36,392,521 francs (*£2,730,000*). The French drink about 50 litres *88 pts* of mineral water per person per year.

MOTOR CAR MANUFACTURER

The largest manufacturing company in the world is General Motors Corporation of Detroit, Michigan, U.S.A. During its peak year of 1972 world wide sales totalled $30,435,231,414 (*£12,174 million*). Its assets at 31 Dec. 1972 were valued at $18,273,382,035 (*£7,309 million*). Its total 1972 payroll was $8,668,224,000 (*£3,467 million*) to an average of 760,000 employees. The greatest total of dividends ever paid for one year was $1,509,740,939 (*£629 million*) by General Motors for 1965.

The largest manufacturer was the British Leyland Motor Corporation, with 1,127,000 vehicles produced. The company is the United Kingdom's largest exporter with record direct exports valued at £355 million in 1971/72 and total overseas sales valued at £560 million.

A bottling line at the Hill Street complex, Kilmarnock, the largest Scotch whisky blending and bottling plant

167

Largest plant The largest single automobile plant in the world is the Volkswagenwerk, Wolfsburg, West Germany, with 54,000 employees turning out 5,000 vehicles daily. The surface area of the factory buildings is 353½ acres *143 ha* and that of the whole plant 1,730 acres *700 ha* with 45 miles *72 km* of rail sidings.

Oil Company Largest The world's largest oil company is the Exxon Corporation (formerly Standard Oil Company [New Jersey]), with 143,000 employees and assets valued at $21,558,257,000 (*£8,623 million*) on 1 Jan. 1973.

Oil refineries Largest The world's largest refinery is the Pernis refinery in the Netherlands, operated by the Royal Dutch/Shell Group of companies with a capacity of 25,000,000 tons *25,4 million tonnes*. The largest oil refinery in the United Kingdom is the Esso Refinery at Fawley, Hampshire. Opened in 1921 and much expanded in 1951, it has a capacity of 19,000,000 tons *19,3 million tonnes* per year. The total investment on the 1,300-acre *3 200 ha* site is more than £140,000,000.

Paper mills The world's largest paper mill is that established in 1936 by the Union Camp Corporation at Savannah, Georgia, U.S.A., with an output of 903,124 short tons *819 296 tonnes*. The largest paper mill in the United Kingdom is the Bowater Paper Corporation Ltd.'s Kemsley Mill near Sittingbourne, Kent with a complex covering an area of 2,500 acres *1 012 ha* and a capacity in excess of 300,000 tons/*tonnes* a year.

Pop-corn plant The largest pop-corn plant in the world is The House of Clarks Ltd. (instituted 1933) of Dagenham, Essex, which in 1972–73 produced an unrivalled 25,000,000 packets of "Butter Kist".

Public relations The world's largest public relations firm is Hill and Knowlton, Inc. of 633 Third Avenue, New York City, N.Y., U.S.A. and seven other U.S. cities. The firm employs a full-time staff of more than 329 and also maintains offices in Brussels, Frankfurt, The Hague, Geneva, London, Paris, Milan, Rome, Singapore and Tōkyō.

Publishing The publishing company generating most revenue is Time Inc. of New York City with $606.8 million (*£233.3 million*) in 1972 of which $142.5 million is from *Time* magazine advertising. Britain's largest publisher is the International Publishing Corporation (part of Reed International Group) with a turnover of £210 million in 1972–73. The largest book publishing concern in the world is the Book Division of McGraw-Hill Inc. of New York with sales of $204 million (*£81.6 million*) in 1971–72.

Restaurateurs The largest restaurant chain in the world is that operated by F. W. Woolworth and Co. with 2,074 throughout six countries. The largest restauratuers in the United Kingdom are Trust House-Forte who have a total staff of 42,000 in the U.K. and turned over £180,107,000 in 1971–72.

BANQUETS

Greatest World Outdoors The greatest banquet ever staged was that by President Loubet, President of France, in the gardens of the Tuileries, Paris, on 22 Sept. 1900. He invited every one of the 22,000 mayors in France and their deputies. With the Gallic *penchant* for round numbers, the event has always been referred to as "le banquet des 100,000 maires".

Indoors The largest banquet ever held has been one for 10,158 at a $15 a plate dinner in support of Mayor Richard J. Daley of Chicago at McCormick Place Convention Hall on the Lake, Chicago on 3 March 1971.

Most Expensive The menu for the main 5½ hr banquet at the Imperial Iranian 2500th Anniversary gathering at Persepolis in October 1971 (see Party, greatest) was probably the most expensive ever compiled. It comprised quail eggs stuffed with Iranian caviar, a mousse of crayfish tails in Nantua sauce, stuffed rack of roast lamb, with a main course of roast peacock stuffed with *foie gras*, fig rings and raspberry sweet champagne sherbet, with wines including *Château Lafite-Rothschild* 1945 at £40 per bottle from the cellars of Maxime, Paris.

Great Britain Britain's largest banquet was one catered for by J. Lyons & Co. Ltd., at Olympia, London, on 8 Aug. 1925. The 8,000 guests were seated at 5 miles *8 km* of tables, served by 1,360 waitresses, supported by 700 cooks and porters. The occasion was a War Memorial fund-raising effort by Freemasons. Of the 86,000 glasses and plates used, 3,500 were broken. The world's largest tea party was one for 25,000 on the Gaslight Coke Company's annual sports day at East Ham, Greater London, in 1939, with Lyons again catering.

Shipbuilding In 1972 there were 26,714,386 gross tons of ships, excluding sailing ships, barges and vessels of less than 100 tons, launched throughout the world, excluding the U.S.S.R., Romania and China (mainland). Japan launched 12,865,851 gross tons (48.16 per cent of the world total), the greatest tonnage launched in peacetime by any single country. The United Kingdom ranked fourth behind also Sweden and West Germany, with 1,233,412 gross tons.

The world's leading shipbuilding firm in 1972 was the Ishikawajima-Harima Co. of Japan, which launched 42 merchant ships of 2,058,740 gross tons from five shipyards.

Physically the largest shipyard in the United Kingdom is Harland and Wolff Ltd. of Queen's Island, Belfast, which covers some 300 acres *120 ha*.

Shipping line The largest shipping owner and operator in the world is the Royal Dutch/Shell Group (see page 164). The Group on 31 March 1973 owned and managed 181 ships of 10,360,277 deadweight tons and had on charter on the same date a total of 235 ships of 18,535,242 deadweight tons. Many of the vessels of this combined fleet of 416 ships of 28,895,519 d.w.t. were mammoth tankers.

Shoe shop The largest shoe shop in the world is that of Lilley & Skinner, Ltd. at 360–366 Oxford Street, London, W.1. The shop has a floor area of 76,000 ft² *7 060 m²* spread over four floors. With a total staff of more than 180 people it offers, in ten departments, a choice of 250,000 pairs of shoes. Every week, on average, over 45,000 people visit this store.

LARGEST SHOPPING CENTRE

The world's largest shopping centre is the Woodfield Shopping Center, Schaumburg, Illinois with a selling space of 2,203,454ft² *204 707 m²* as at September 1973 on the current 191 acre *77,3 ha* site. Britain's largest shopping center is The Victoria Centre, Nottingham opened in 1972 which extends over 17 acres *6,9 ha*.

Largest store The world's largest store is R. H. Macy & Co. Inc. at Broadway and 34th Street, New York City, N.Y., U.S.A. It covers 46.2 acres *18,6 ha* and employs 11,000 who handle 400,000 items. The sales of the company and its subsidaries exceeded $1,000,000,000 (*£400 million*) in 1972–73. Mr. Rowland Hussey Macy's sales on his first day at his fancy goods store on 6th Avenue, on 27 Oct. 1858, were recorded as $11.06 (*now £4.42*).

Largest supermarket U.K. The largest supermarket building in the United Kingdom is the Woolco One-Stop Shopping Centre opened in Bournemouth, Hampshire on 29 Oct. 1968. Currently it has an area of 114,000 ft² *10 590 m²* and parking space for 1,250 cars.

The Woolco store in Bournemouth, Hampshire, the United Kingdom's largest supermarket

Soft drinks The world's top-selling soft drink is Coca-Cola with over 150,000,000 bottles per day at the end of 1972 in more than 130 countries. Coke was invented by Dr. John S. Pemberton of Atlanta, Georgia in 1886 and The Coca-Cola Company was formed in 1892.

STEEL COMPANY

The world's largest producer of steel is Nippon Steel of Tōkyō, Japan which produced 77 774 000 tonnes of steel, steel products and pig iron in 1971–72. The Kimitzu Works has a capacity of more than 10 000 000 tonnes per annum.

United Kingdom Currently the largest single British plant is the Port Talbot works of the British Steel Corporation, Glamorganshire, which extend for 4½ miles *7,2 km*, with an area of 2,600 acres *1 050 ha*. The total number employed at this plant is 13,500 and its capacity is 3 000 000 tonnes. The Anchor Complex, Scunthorpe, Lincolnshire, which went into production in 1973 is planned to have a capacity of 4.4 million tonnes and eventually more than 5 million tonnes.

Tobacco company The world's largest tobacco company is the British American Tobacco Company Ltd. (founded 1902), of London. The group's net assets were £913,320,000 at 30 Sept. 1972. The sales for 1971/72 were £2,037,450,000. The group has 140 factories and over 200,000 employees.

Toy manufacturer The world's largest toy manufacturer is Mattel Toys of Hawthorne, Los Angeles, U.S.A. founded in 1945. Its sales in 1972 were $331,912,000 (*£132.7 million*).

Toy shop *World* The world's biggest toy store is F.A.O. Schwarz, 745 Fifth Avenue at 58th Street, New York City, N.Y., U.S.A. with 50,000 ft² *4 645 m²* on three floors. Schwarz have 16 branch stores with a further 150,000 ft² *13 935 m²*.

United Kingdom Britain's biggest toy shop is that of Hamley of Regent Street Ltd., founded in 1760 in Holborn and removed to Regent Street, London, W.1. in 1901. It has selling space of 24,000 ft² *2 230 m²* on 10 floors and up to 250 employees during the Christmas season.

Vintners The oldest champagne firm is Ruinart Père et Fils founded in 1729. The oldest cognac firm is Augier Freres & Co., established in 1643.

Fisheries The world's highest recorded catch of fish was 55 790 000 tonnes in 1970. Peru had the largest ever national haul with 12 160 000 tonnes in 1970 comprising mostly anchoveta. The United Kingdom's highest figure was 1 206 000 tonnes in 1948. The world's largest fishmongers are MacFisheries, a subsidiary of Unilever Ltd., with 296 retail outlets as at May 1973.

Landowners The world's largest landowner is the United States Government, with a holding of 760,731,000 acres *308 million ha*, including 528,000 acres *213 770 ha* outside the U.S. The total value was $80,738 million (*£32,295 million*). The United Kingdom's greatest ever private landowner was the 3rd Duke of Sutherland, George Granville Sutherland-Leveson-Gower, K.G. (1828–92), who owned 1,358,000 acres *549 560 ha* in 1883. Currently the largest landowner in Great Britain is the Forestry Commission (instituted 1919) with 2,900,000 acres *1 173 000 ha*. The longest tenure is that by St. Paul's Cathedral of land at Tillingham, Essex, given by King Ethelbert before A.D. 616. Currently the landowner with the largest known acreage is the 8th Duke of Buccleuch (b. 1894) with 336,000 acres *136 035 ha*.

LAND VALUES

Highest Currently the most expensive land in the world is that in the City of London. The freehold price on small prime sites reached £1,950/ft² (*£21,230/m²*) in mid 1973. The 600 ft *182,88 m* National Westminster Bank on a 2¼ acre *0,91 ha* site off Bishopsgate has become *pro rata* the world's highest valued building. At rents of £10/ft² on 500,000 net ft² *46 452 m²* and on 18 years purchase, it is worth £90 million. The value of the whole site of 6½ acres *1,6 ha* is £225,000,000. On 1 Feb. 1926 a parcel of land of 1,275 ft² *118,45 m²* was bought by the One Wall Street Realty Corporation for $1,000 (*then £206*) per square foot. In February 1964 a woman paid $510 (*£212.50*) for a triangular piece of land measuring 3 by 6½ by 5¾ in *7,6 × 16,5 × 14,6 cm* at a tax lien auction in North Hollywood, California, U.S.A.—equivalent to $365,182,470 (*£152.1 million*) per acre. The real estate value per square metre of the four topmost French vineyards has not been recently estimated. Recent reports of astronomical prices in Hong Kong were due to a journalist's confusion between U.S. dollars and Hong Kong dollars.

Lowest The historic example of low land values is the Alaska Purchase of 30 March 1867, when William Henry Seward (1801–72), the United States Secretary of State, agreed that the U.S. should buy the whole territory from the Russian Government of Czar Alexander II for $7,200,000 (*now £2,880,000*), equivalent to 1.9 cents per acre *or 4.7 cents per hectare*. When Willem Verhulst bought Manhattan Island, New York, *ante* June in 1626, by paying the Brooklyn Indians (Canarsees) with trinkets and cloth valued at 60 guilders (equivalent to $42 or £16.80), he was buying land now worth up to $425 (*£170*) per square foot for 0.2 of a cent per acre—a capital appreciation of 9,000 million-fold.

Greatest auction The greatest auction was that at Anchorage, Alaska, on 11 Sept. 1969 for 179 tracts 450,858 acres *182 455 ha* of the oil-bearing North Slope, Alaska. An all-time record bid of $72,277,133 for a 2,560 acre *1 036 ha* lease was made by the Amerada Hess Corporation—Getty Oil consortium. This £30,115,472 bid indicated a price of $28,233 (*then £11,763*) per acre.

Highest rent The highest recorded rentals in the world are for modern office accommodation in the prime areas of the City of London. In mid-1973 figures of £21/ft² *£226/m²* were reached exclusive of rates and services. For main thoroughfare ground floor banking halls figures up to £45/ft² *£484/m²* were under negotiation.

Companies The number of companies on the register in Great Britain at 1 Jan. 1973 was 603,935 of which 16,770 were public and the balance private companies.

Most directorships The world record for directorships was set in September 1959 by Harry O. Jasper, a London real estate financier, with 451. If he had attended all their Annual General Meetings this would have involved him, in normal office hours, in an A.G.M. every 4 hrs 33 min.

STOCK EXCHANGES

The oldest Stock Exchange in the world is that at Amsterdam, in the Netherlands, founded in 1602. There were 126 throughout the world as of 13 June 1972.

Most markings The highest number of markings received in one day on the London Stock Exchange is 32,665 after the 1959 General Election on 14 Oct. 1959. The record for a year is 4,396,175 "marks" in the year ending 31 March 1960. There were 9,037 securities (gilt-edged 1,446, company 7,591) quoted at Dec. 1972. Their total nominal value was £57,812 million (gilt-edged £31,080 million, company £26,731 million) and their market value was £184,796 million (gilt-edged £23,922 million, company £160,814 million).

The greatest overall daily movement occurred on 22 Jan. 1972, when the market value of United Kingdom Ordinary shares fell by about £2,000,000,000 or nearly 2 per cent.

The highest figure of *The Financial Times* Industrial Ordinary share index (1 July 1935 = 100) was 543.6 on 19 May 1972. The lowest figure was 49.4 on 28 May 1940. The greatest rise in a day has been 20.5 points to 352.2 on Budget Day on 30 March 1971.

Highest and lowest par values The highest denomination of any share quoted in the world is a single share in F. Hoffmann—La Roche of Basel worth £17,250. The record for the London Stock Exchange is £100 for preference shares in Baring Brothers & Co. Ltd., the bankers.

U.S. records The highest index figure on the Dow Jones average (instituted 8 Oct. 1896) of selected industrial stocks at the close of a day's trading was 1,051.70 on 11 Jan. 1973, when the average of the daily "highs" of the 30 component stocks was 1,067.20. The old record trading volume in a day on the New York Stock Exchange of 16,410,030 shares on 29 Oct. 1929, the "Black Tuesday" of the famous "crash" was unsurpassed until April 1968. The Dow Jones industrial average, which had reached 381.17 on 3 Sept. 1929, plunged 48.31 points in the day, on its way to the Depression's lowest point of 41.22 on 8 July 1932. The total lost in security values was $125,000 million (*now £48,076 million*). World trade slumped 57 per cent from 1929 to 1936. The greatest paper loss in a year was $62,884 million (*£24,186 million*) in 1969. The record daily increase of 28.40 on 30 Oct. 1929 was beaten on 16 Aug. 1971, when the index increased 32.93 points to 888.95. That day's trading was also a record 31,730,960 shares. The largest transaction on record "share-wise" was on 14 Mar. 1972 for 5,245,000 shares of American Motors at $7.25 each. The dollar value for one block was $76,135,026 for 730,312 shares of American Standard Class A Preferred shares at $104.25 a share. The largest deal "value-wise" was for two 2,000,000 blocks of Greyhound shares at $20 each sold to Goldman Sachs and Salomon Brothers. The highest prices paid for seats on the N.Y. Stock Exchange have been $515,000 (*£206,000*) in 1968–69.

Largest Equity The greatest aggregate market value of any Corporation is $50.3 billion (*£20,120 million*) assuming a closing price of $431½ multiplied by the 116,613,551 shares of I.B.M. extant on 30 March 1973.

Largest new issue The American Telegraph & Telephone Co. offered $1,375 million's worth of shares in a rights offer on 27,500,000 shares of convertible preferred stock on the New York market on 2 June 1971. The largest offering on the London Stock Exchange by a United Kingdom company was the £40 million of loan stock by I.C.I. in December 1970.

Greatest appreciation It is not possible to state categorically which shares have enjoyed the greatest appreciation in value. Spectacular "growth stocks" include the International Business Machines Corporation (IBM) in which 100 shares, costing $5,250 in July 1932, grew to 13,472 shares with a market value of $5,813,200 *£2,325,000* on 30 March 1973. In addition $497,300 were paid in dividends. Winnebago Co, makers of "mobile homes" went public in 1965 when shares were $12.50. By Apr. 1972 $5,250 worth of shares was worth $5,241,600. In the United Kingdom an investment of £100 in Drage's Ltd. in 1951 would have been realizable at £108,000 in 1962. The same amount invested in 1947 in the late Mr. Jack Cotton's Mansion House Chambers Co. would have been worth £200,000 in City Centre Properties stock by 1964.

Largest investment house The largest investment company in the world, and also once the world's largest partnership (124 partners, 61,200 stockholders at 31 Dec. 1971) is Merrill, Lynch, Pierce, Fenner & Smith Inc. (founded 6 Jan. 1914, went public in 1971) of New York City, U.S.A. It has 20,662 employees, 279 offices and 1,400,000 separate accounts. The firm is referred to in the United States stock exchange circles as "We" or "We, the people" or "The Thundering Herd". The company's assets totalled $3,991,764,000 at 31 Dec. 1972.

Largest bank The International Bank for Reconstruction and Development (founded 27 Dec. 1945), the United Nations "World Bank" at 1818 H Street N.W., Washington, D.C., U.S.A., has an authorized share capital of $27,000 million (*£10,800 million*). There were 117 members with a subscribed capital of $24,506,200,000 (*£9,802 million*) at 30 June 1972. The International Monetary Fund in Washington, D.C., U.S.A. has 125 members with total quotas of $29,168,600,000 (*£11,667 million*) at 31 Mar. 1973.

The San Francisco headquarters of the world's private bank with the greatest private deposits, the Bank of America

The private bank with the greatest deposits is the Bank of America National Trust and Savings Association, of San Francisco, California, U.S.A., with $35,085,132,000 at 31 Dec. 1972. Its total resources as at 31 Dec. 1972 were $40,888,450,000 (£16,355 million). Barclays Bank (with Barclays Bank International and other subsidiary companies) had nearly 5,000 branches in 50 countries (3,100 in the United Kingdom) in December 1972. Deposits totalled £8,411,964,000 and assets £10,109,304,000 as at 31 Dec. 1972. The largest bank in the United Kingdom is the National Westminster with total assets of £8,760,753,000 and 3,400 branches as at 1 Jan. 1973.

Largest bank building
World
The largest bank building is the 813 ft *247,80m* tall Chase Manhattan Building, completed in May 1961 in New York City, N.Y., U.S.A. It has 64 storeys and contains the largest bank vault in the world, measuring 350 × 100 × 8 ft *106,7 × 30,4 × 2,4 m* and weighing 879 tons *893 tonnes*. Its six doors weigh up to 40 tons *40,6 tonnes* apiece but each can be closed by the pressure of a forefinger. The 60-storey First National Bank of Chicago, completed in 1969, is 850 ft *259 m* tall.

2. MANUFACTURED ARTICLES

Guinness Superlatives Ltd. publishes fine art books in colour on English and Irish Glass; Pottery and Porcelain; English Furniture (2 Volumes); Edged Weapons, Militaria and British Gallantry Decorations, obtainable on order from the publishers or from any good book shop.

Antique
Largest
The largest antique ever sold has been London Bridge in March 1968. The sale was made by Mr. Ivan F. Luckin of the Court of Common Council of the Corporation of London to the McCulloch Corporation of Los Angeles, California, U.S.A. for $2,460,000 (*then £1,029,000*). The 10,000 tons of elevational stonework were re-assembled at Lake Havasu City, Arizona and "re-dedicated" on 10 Oct. 1971.

Armour
The highest price paid for a suit of armour is £25,000, paid in 1924 for the Pembroke suit of armour, made at Greenwich in the 16th century, for the Earl of Pembroke.

Beds
Largest
In Bruges, Belgium, Philip, Duke of Burgundy had a bed 12½ ft wide and 19 ft long *3,81 × 5,79 m* erected for the perfunctory *coucher officiel* ceremony with Princess Isabella of Portugal in 1430. The largest bed in Great Britain is the Great Bed of Ware, dating from *c.* 1580, from the Crown Inn, Ware, Hertfordshire, now preserved in the Victoria and Albert Museum, London. It is 10 ft 8½ in wide, 11 ft 1 in long and 8 ft 9 in tall *3,26 × 3,37 × 2,66 m*. The largest standard bed currently marketed in the United Kingdom is the Super Size bed, 8 ft wide by 8 ft long, *2,43 × 2,43 m*, which sell for £600.

Heaviest
The world's most massive beds are waterbeds which first became a vogue in California, U.S.A. in 1970 when merchandised by Michael V. Zamoro, 53. When filled, king-sized versions measuring 8 ft *2,43 m* square will weigh more than 14 cwt. *711 kg* and are more advisably used on a ground floor.

Beer Mats
The world's largest collection of beer mats is owned by Leo Pisker of Vienna, who has more than 40,000 different mats. The largest collection of purely British mats is 8,142 by Charles Schofield of Glasgow.

Largest candle
The world's biggest candle is Western Candle Ltd.'s 50 ft *15,24 m* high, 18 ft *5,48 m* diameter by U.S. Highway 30, near Scappose, Oregon, completed on 9 May 1971.

CARPETS AND RUGS

Earliest
The earliest carpet known is a white bordered black hair pelt from Pazyryk, U.S.S.R. dated to the 5th century B.C. now preserved in Leningrad. The earliest known in Britain were some depicted at the court of Edward IV *c.* 1480.

Largest
Of ancient carpets the largest on record was the gold-enriched silk carpet of Hashim (dated A.D. 743) of the Abbasid caliphate in Baghdad, Iraq. It is reputed to have measured 180 by 300 ft *54,86 × 91,44 m*.

The world's largest carpet now consists of 88,000 ft² (over two acres *or 0,81 ha*) of maroon carpeting in the Coliseum exhibition hall, Columbus Circle, New York City, N.Y., U.S.A. This was first used for the International Automobile Show on 28 April 1956.

Most expensive
The most magnificent carpet ever made was the Spring carpet of Khusraw made for the audience hall of the Sassanian palace at Ctesiphon, Iraq. It was about 7,000 ft² *650 m²* of silk, gold thread and encrusted with emeralds. It was cut up as booty by a Persian army in A.D. 635 and from the known realisation value of the pieces must have had an original value of some £80,000,000.

It was reported in March 1968 that a 16th century Persian silk hunting carpet was sold "recently" to an undisclosed U.S. museum by one of the Rothschild family for "about $600,000" (*then £205,000*).

The highest price ever paid at auction for a carpet is the $150,000 (£60,000) given at Sotheby Parke Bernet, New York City on 9 Dec. 1972 for an early Louis XIV French Savonnerie carpet measuring 18 ft 6 in by 12 ft 7 in *5,63 × 3,83 m* and dating from the third quarter of the 17th century and woven under the administration of Simon Lourdet.

Most finely woven
The most finely woven carpet known is one with more than 2,490 knots per in² *386 per cm²* from a fragment of an Imperial Mughal prayer carpet of the 17th century now in the Altman collections in the Metropolitan Museum of Art, New York City.

Chair
Largest
The world's largest chair is claimed to be an American ladderback outside Hayes and Kane furniture store, Bennington, Vermont, U.S.A. 19 ft 1 in *5,81 m* tall and weighing 2,200 lb. *998 kg*.

Most Expensive
The highest price ever paid for a single chair is $85,000 (£34,000) for the John Brown Chippendale mahogany corner chair attributed to John Goddard of Newport, Rhode Island, U.S.A. and made in *c.* 1760. This piece was included in the collection of Mr. Lansdell K. Christie dispersed by Sotheby Parke Bernet, New York on 21 Oct. 1972.

Christmas present
Most expensive
The most expensive Christmas present listed in any store's catalogue has been in the 1971 Neiman-Marcus, Dallas, Texas, offering of a "Fortress of the Freeway" for $845,300 (*then £325,115*). This Total Transportational Security Environment features anti-theft device hood ornament, closed-circuit dual-lens infra-red scanning camera, infra-red periscope, 360° vision indestructable cockpit bubble, telephoto periscope, radar, dual-exhaust anti-pollution device, highway signal markers, signals "Stop"—"Too Close", marine prop, retractable tyres, tank-tracks, loudspeakers to warn off passing motorists, multi-level terrain stabilizer, safety air bumpers and padded safety bumpers—absolutely one of a kind.

CIGARS

Largest
The largest cigar in existence is one 5 ft 4½ in *1,63 m* long and 10½ in *26,6 cm* in diameter made by Abraham & Gluckstein, London and now housed at the Northumbrian University Air Squadron. The largest standard cigar in the world is the 9¾ in *24,1 cm* long "Partagas Visible Immensas". The Partagas factory

in Havana, Cuba, manufactures special gift cigars 50 cm *19.7 in* long, which retail in Europe for more than £5 each.

Most expensive The world's most expensive regular cigar has been the "Partagas Visible Immensas". This used to be retailed in the United States for $7.50 (*£3*). The most expensive cigars imported into Britain, where the duty is £4.75 per lb. *£10,47 per kg*, are the Montecristo 'A', which retail at a suggested £1.67½ incl. V.A.T.

Most voracious cigar smoker The only man to master the esoteric art of smoking 13 full-sized cigars simultaneously whilst whistling, talking or giving bird imitations is Mr. Simon Argevitch of Oakland, California, U.S.A. Mr. Bob Fordham of Romford, Essex, England in July 1972 demonstrated the ability to smoke 14 cigars simultaneously.

CIGARETTES

Consumption The heaviest smokers in the world are the people of the United States, where 529,000 million cigarettes (an average of 3,473 per adult) were consumed at a cost of about $11,500 million (*£4,600 million*) in 1972. The peak consumption in the United Kingdom was 3,090 cigarettes per adult in 1972. The peak volume was 243,100,000 lb. *110,2 million kg* in 1961, compared with 216,200,000 lb. *98,0 million kg* in 1972, when 130,500 million cigarettes were sold.

In the United Kingdom 65 per cent of adult men and 42 per cent of adult women smoke. Nicotine releases acetylcholine in the brain, so reducing tension and increasing resolve. It has thus been described as an anodyne to civilization.

Tar/ Nicotine Content Of the 101 brands so far analysed by the Health Education Council the one with highest tar/nicotine content is *Capstan Full Strength* with 38/3.2 mg per cigarette. The lowest is *Silk Cut Extra Mild* with 4/0.3.

Most expensive The most expensive cigarettes in the world are the "Sobranie Imperial Russian" hand made paperholdered cigarettes which retail for U.S. $1.40 (*56 p*) per 10.

Most popular The world's most popular cigarette has been the "Winston", a filter cigarette made by the R. J. Reynolds Tobacco Co., which sold 82,000 million of them in 1969. The largest selling British cigarette in 1972 was John Player and Sons of Nottingham's "Players No. 6." The Wills brand "Passing Cloud" was introduced in 1874.

Longest and shortest The longest cigarettes ever marketed were "Head Plays", each 11 in *27,9 cm* long and sold in packets of 5 in the United States in about 1930, to save tax. The shortest were "Lilliput" cigarettes, each 1¼ in *31,7 mm* long, made in Great Britain in 1956.

Earliest abstention The earliest recorded case of a man giving up smoking was on 5 April 1679 when Johan Kastu, Sheriff of Turku, Finland wrote in his diary "I quit smoking tobacco". He died one month later.

Largest collection The world's largest collection of cigarettes is that of Robert E. Kaufman, M.D., of 950 Park Avenue, New York City 28, N.Y., U.S.A. In May 1973 he had 6,507 different kinds of cigarettes from 161 countries. The oldest brand represented is "Lone Jack", made in the U.S.A. in *c.* 1885. Both the longest and shortest (see above) are represented.

Cigarette lighter *Most Expensive* The most expensive cigarette lighter in the world is made by Alfred Dunhill Ltd. of St. James's, London S.W.1. and costing £2,750. It is made of two-tone bark textured 18 ct. gold, scattered with a fringe of 200 brilliant-cut diamonds.

Player's No. 6 cigarettes, the most popular brand in the United Kingdom

Cigarette packets The world's largest collection of cigarette packets is that of Niels Ventegodt of Frederiksberg Allé 13A, Copenhagen, Denmark. He had 48,524 different packets from 206 countries by May 1973. The countries supplying the largest numbers were the United Kingdom (6,588) and the United States (3,821). The earliest is the Finnish "Petit Canon" packet for 25, made by Tollander & Klärich in 1860. The rarest is the Latvian 700-year anniversary (1201–1901) Riga packet, believed to be unique.

Cigarette cards The earliest known and most valuable cigarette card is that bearing the portrait of the Marquess of Lorne published in the United States *c.* 1879. The only known specimen is in the Metropolitan Museum of Art, New York City. The earliest British example appeared in 1883 in the form of a calendar issued by Allen & Ginter, of Richmond, Virginia, trading from Holborn Viaduct, London. The largest known collection is that of Mr. Edward Wharton-Tigar (b. 1913) of London with a collection of more than 500,000 cigarette and trade cards in about 25,000 sets.

Largest Christmas Cracker The largest cracker ever constructed was one 42 ft *12,80 m* in length and 7 ft *2,13 m* in diameter built in December 1972 for the Christmas showroom display of Cleales Ltd. Garage, Station Road, Saffron Walden, Essex. The cracker concealed a Ford Escort car and took two weeks to build with a metal frame covered with polythene and coloured paper sheets.

Credit Card Collection The largest collection of credit cards is one of 273 (all different) by Walter Cavanagh (b. 1943) of Mount View, California, U.S.A. The cost of acquisition was nil.

Largest curtain The largest curtain ever built has been the bright orange-red 4-ton 185 ft *56 m* high curtain suspended 1,350 ft *411 m* across the Rifle Gap, Grand Hogback, Colorado, U.S.A. by the Bulgarian-born sculptor Christo, 36 (*né* Javacheff) on 10 Aug. 1972. It blew apart in a 50 m.p.h. *80 km/h* gust 27 hrs later. The total cost involved in displaying this work of art was $750,000 (*£300,000*).

Dinner service The highest price ever paid for a silver dinner service is £207,000 for the Berkeley Louis XV Service of 168 pieces, made by Jacques Roettiers between 1736 and 1738, sold at the salerooms of Sotheby & Co., London, in June 1960.

Dress *Most expensive* The most expensive dress ever sold by a Paris fashion house was one by Pierre Balmain (Directrice, Ginette Spanier), to a non-European Royal Personage for £4,500 in 1971.

FABRICS

Most expensive The most expensive fabric obtainable is an evening-wear fabric 40 in *101,6 cm* wide, hand embroidered and sequinned on a pure silk ground in a classical flower pattern. It has 194,400 tiny sequins per yard, and is designed by Alan Hershman of Duke St., London; it cost £135 per yd.

Finest cloth The finest of all cloths is Shahtoosh (or Shatusa), a brown-grey wool from the throats of Indian goats. It is sold by Neiman-Marcus of Dallas, Texas, U.S.A., at $18.50 (£7.71p) per ft² and is both more expensive and finer than Vicuña. A simple hostess gown in Shahtoosh costs up to $5,000 (£2,000). Qiviut, the underwool of a musk ox is about $6.66 per ft².

LARGEST FIREWORK

The most powerful firework obtainable is the Bouquet of Chrysanthemums *hanabi*, marketed by the Marutamaya Ogatsu Fireworks Co. Ltd., of Tōkyō, Japan. It is fired to a height of over 3,000 ft *915 m* from a 36 in *914 mm* calibre mortar. Their chrysanthemum and peony flower shells produce a spherical flower with "twice-thrice changing colours", 2,000 ft *610 m* in diameter. The largest firework produced in Britain is one fired from Brock's 25 in *635 mm*, 22 cwt. *1 117 kg* mortar. The shell weighs 200 lb. *90 kg 70* and is 6½ ft *1,98 m* in circumference and was first used in Lisbon in 1886. The last firing was in London on 8 June 1946 for the World War II Victory Celebration which was the most elaborate show of aerial pyrotechny ever fired. Brock's Fireworks Ltd. of Hemel Hempstead, Hertfordshire was established before 1720.

FLAGS

Oldest The oldest national flag in the world is that of Denmark (a large white cross on a red field), known as the Dannebrog ("Danish Cloth"), dating from 1219, adopted after the Battle of Lindanissa in Estonia, now part of the U.S.S.R. The crest in the centre of the Austrian flag has its origins in the 11th century. The origins of the Iranian flag, with its sword-carrying lion and sun, are obscure but "go beyond the 12th century".

Largest The largest flag in the world is the "Stars and Stripes" displayed annually on the Woodward Avenue side of J. L. Hudson Company store in Detroit, Michigan, U.S.A. The flag 104 by 235 ft *31,69 × 71,62 m* and weighing 1,500 lb. *680 kg* was unfurled on 14 June 1949. The 50 stars are each 5½ ft *1,67 m* high and each stripe is 8 ft *2,43 m* deep. The largest Union Flag (or Union Jack) was one 11,520 ft² (144 by 80 ft [*43,89 × 23,38 m*]) used at a military tattoo in the Olympic Stadium, West Berlin in September 1967. The largest flag *flown* from a public building in Britain is a Union Flag measuring 36 ft *10,97 m* by 18 ft *5,48 m*, flown on occasions from the Victoria Tower of the Palace of Westminster, London.

Largest float The largest float used in any street carnival is the 200 ft *60 m* long dragon *Sun Loon* used in Bendigo, Victoria, Australia. It has 65,000 mirror scales. Six men are needed to carry its head alone.

FURNITURE

Most expensive The highest price ever paid for a single piece of furniture is 165,000 guineas (£173,250) at auction at Christies, London on 24 June 1971, for a Louis XVI *bureau plat* by Martin Carlin in 1778 and once belonging to the Empress Marie-Feodorovna in 1784, sold by the estate of Mrs. Anna Thompson Dodge and bought by Mr. Henri Sabet of Teheran, Iran. It is 51½ in *1,30 m* wide, 30 in *76,2 cm* deep and 30 in *76,2 cm* high in veneered pale tulipwood with a tooled and gilded black leather top and 14 Sèvres porcelain plaques in ormolu frames.

One of the most powerful fireworks exploding, called the *Bouquet of Chrysanthemums*, manufactured in Japan

Oldest British The oldest surviving piece of British furniture is a three-footed tub with metal bands found at Glastonbury, Somerset, and dating from between 300 and 150 B.C.

Largest The largest item of furniture in the world is the Long Sofa—a wooden bench for old seafarers—measuring 72 m *236 ft* in length at Oscarshamn, Sweden.

Gun The highest price ever paid for a single gun is £125,000 given by the London dealers F. Partridge for a French flintlock fowling piece made for Louis XIII, King of France in *c.* 1615 and attributed to Pierre le Bourgeoys of Lisieux, France (d. 1627). This piece was included in the collection of the late William Goodwin Renwick of the United States sold by Sotheby and Co. of London on 21 Nov. 1972.

Gold plate The world's highest auction price for a single piece of gold plate is £40,000 for a 20 oz. 4 dwt. *628,3 g* George II teapot made by James Ker for the King's Plate horse race for 100 guineas at Leith, Scotland in 1736. The sale was by Christie's of London on 13 Dec. 1967 to a dealer from Boston, Massachusetts, U.S.A.

Hat Most expensive The highest price ever paid for a hat is 165,570 francs (*£14,032*) (inc. tax) by Moët et Chandon at an auction by Maîtres Liery, Rheims et Laurin on 23 April 1970 for one last worn by Emperor Napoleon I (1769–1821) on 1 Jan. 1815.

Jade The highest price ever paid for an item in jade is 1,250,000 Swiss Francs (*£156,250*) for a necklace set with 31 graduated beads of Imperial green jade. This was sold by Christie's at the Hotel Richmond, Geneva, Switzerland, on 9 May 1973. The highest price paid for a single piece of jade sculpture is £71,000 for a massive Ming jade buffalo sold by Sotheby's on 15 March 1973.

Largest jig-saw The largest jig-saw ever made is believed to be one of 31,000 pieces, measuring 20 ft 6 in × 10 ft 8 in.

6,24 × 3,25 m exhibited in Jan. 1973 by Condor Toys Ltd. of London Colney, Hertfordshire. The *Festival of Britain* jigsaw by Efroc Ltd., now in Montserrat though of slightly less area contains an estimated 40,000 pieces.

Matchbox labels The oldest match label is that of John Walker, Stockton-on-Tees, County Durham, England in 1827. Collectors of labels are phillumenists, of bookmatch covers philliberumenists and of matchboxes cumyxaphists. The world's longest and perhaps dullest set is one of the U.S.S.R. comprising 600 variations on interior views of the Moscow Metro.

Sheerest nylon The lowest denier nylon yarn ever produced is the 6-denier used for stockings exhibited at the Nylon Fair in London in February 1956. The sheerest stockings normally available are 9-denier. An indication of the thinness is that a hair from the average human head is about 50 denier.

Paperweight The highest price ever paid for a paperweight is £8,500 at Sotheby & Co., London on 16 March 1970 for a Clichy lily-of-the-valley weight.

Penknife
Most blades The penknife with the greatest number of blades is the Year Knife made by the world's oldest firm of cutlers, Joseph Rodgers & Sons Ltd., of Sheffield, England, whose trade mark was granted in 1682. The knife was built in 1822 with 1,822 blades but now has 1,973 to match the year of the Christian era until A.D. 2000, beyond which there will be no further space. It was acquired by Britain's largest hand tool manufacturers, Stanley Works (Great Britain) Ltd. of Sheffield, in 1970.

Pipe
Most expensive The most expensive smoker's pipe is the Charatan *Summa cum Laude* straight-grain briar root pipe available in limited numbers in New York City at $2,500 (*£100*).

Longest In the Braunschweig Museum, Germany, there is exhibited an outsize late 19th century pipe, 15 ft *4,57 m* in length, the bowl of which can accommodate 3 lb. *1 kg 360* of tobacco.

Porcelain and pottery The highest price ever paid for a single piece of porcelain is £220,500 at auction at the salerooms of Christie's, London, on 5 June 1972, for a 14th century Chinese porcelain wine jar in blue and white with a red underglaze decoration, 13¼ in *33,6 cm* high, previously used as an umbrella stand. The most priceless example of the occidental ceramic art is usually regarded as the Portland Vase which dates from late in the first century B.C. or 1st century A.D. It was made in Italy and was in the possession of the Barberini family in Rome from at least 1642. It was eventually bought by the Duchess of Portland in 1792 but smashed while in the British Museum in 1847.

English Porcelain The highest price ever paid for a single piece of English porcelain is £9,450. This was given for a turquoise ground Worcester bowl 6½ in *16,5 cm* in diameter of the 18th century, dating from the 'Dr Wall' period and decorated in the atelier of James Giles, at Christie's, London on 29 Jan. 1973.

Pistols
Most expensive The highest price paid for a pair of pistols is the £60,000 given by an anonymous European collector for a pair of flintlock, breech-loading, repeating pistols by the early 18th century Florentine gunsmith Michele Lorenzoni. These were included in the collection of the late William Goodwin Renwick of Tucson, Arizona, U.S.A., sold at the Bond Street salerooms of Messrs Sotheby and Co. on 17 July 1972.

Largest and Longest ropes The largest rope ever made was a coir fibre launching rope with a circumference of 47 in *119 cm* made in 1858 for the British liner *Great Eastern* by John and Edwin Wright of Birmingham. It consisted of four

The 14th century Chinese porcelain wine jar which was sold for £220,500 in 1972. The vendor had previously used it as an umbrella stand

strands, each of 3,780 yarns. The longest fibre rope ever made without a splice was one of 10,000 fathoms or 11.36 miles *18 288 m* of 6½ in *16,5 cm* circumference manila by Frost Brothers (now British Ropes Ltd.) in London in 1874.

SHOES

Most expensive The most expensive standard shoes obtainable are mink-lined golf shoes with 18 carat gold embellishments and ruby-tipped gold spikes made by Stylo Matchmakers International Ltd., of Nottingham, England which retail for £2,500 per pair.

Largest Excluding cases of elephantiasis, the largest shoes ever sold are a pair size 42 built for the giant Harley Davidson of Avon Park, Florida, U.S.A.

Silver The highest price ever paid for a single piece of silver is £78,000 at Christie's of London on 1 July 1970 for a unique Charles I silver inkstand, hallmarked for 1639, weighing 172 oz. *5 kg 349*. It had been sold also at Christie's on 5 June 1893 for £446.

The highest price for English Silver is £56,000 paid by the London dealer Wartski for the Brownlow James II Tankards at Christie's, London, on 20 Nov. 1968. This pair made in 1686 was in mint condition and weighed nearly 7½ lb. *3 kg 400*. It has been calculated that they appreciated at the rate of 75p per hour since they were sold by Lord Astor for £17,000 in 1963.

Most expensive snuff The most expensive snuff obtainable in Britain is "Café Royale" sold by G. Smith and Sons (Est. 1869) of 74, Charing Cross Road, London. It sells at 92p per oz.

Snuff box The highest price ever paid for a snuff box is the 825,570 francs inc. tax (*£61,609*) given in a sale held by Maîtres Ader and Picard at the Palais Galliera in Paris for a gold and lapis lazuli example by J. A. Meissonnier (d. 1750), dated Paris 1728. This is the only signed example of a snuff box by Meissonnier to have survived although he is known to have been one of the most patronised of French 18th-century goldsmiths. It was made for Marie-Anne de Vaviere-Neubourg, wife of Charles II of Spain. It measures 84 × 29 mm. It was sent for sale by the executors of the estate of the late D. David Weill, and was purchased by Messrs. Wartski of Regent Street, London.

Apostle spoons The highest price ever paid for a set of 13 apostle spoons is $30,000 (*£10,700*), paid by the Clark Institute of Williamstown, Massachusetts, U.S.A. There are only six other complete sets known.

The stuffed Great Auk, which fetched the highest price for a stuffed bird, £9,000

Stuffed bird The highest price ever paid for a stuffed bird is £9,000. This was given in the salerooms of Messrs. Sotheby & Co., London by the Iceland Natural History Museum for a specimen of the Great Auk (*Alca impennis*) in summer plumage, which was taken in Iceland *c.* 1821; this particular specimen stood 22½ in *57 cm* high. The Great Auk was a flightless North Atlantic seabird, which was finally exterminated on Eldey, Iceland in 1844, becoming extinct through hunting. The last British sightings were at Co. Waterford in 1834 and St. Kilda *c.* 1840.

Sword The highest price recorded for a European sword is £21,000 paid at Sotheby's on 23 March 1970 for a swept hilt rapier 48½ in *123 cm* long made by Israel Schuech in 1606 probably for Elector Christian II or Duke Johann Georg of Saxony. The hilt is inset with pearls and semi-precious stones. It should be noted that prices as high as £60,000 have been reported in Japan for important swords by master Japanese swordsmiths such as the incomparable 13th century master Masamune.

TAPESTRY

Earliest The earliest known examples of tapestry weaved linen are three pieces from the tomb of Thutmose IV, the Egyptian Pharaoh and dated to 1483–1411 B.C.

Largest The largest single piece of tapestry ever woven is "Christ in Glory", measuring 74 ft 8 in by 38 ft *22,75 × 11,58 m* designed by Graham Vivian Sutherland, O.M. (b. 24 Aug. 1903) for an altar hanging in Coventry Cathedral, Warwickshire. It cost £10,500 and was delivered from Pinton Frères of Felletin, France, on 1 March 1962.

Longest The longest of all embroideries is the famous Bayeux
Embroidery *Telle du Conquest, dite tapisserie de la reine Mathilde*, a hanging 19½ in *49,5 cm* wide by 231 ft *70,40 m* in length. It depicts events of the period 1064–1066 in 72 scenes and was probably worked in Canterbury, Kent, in *c.* 1086. It was "lost" from 1476 until 1724.

Most The highest price paid for a set of tapestries is
expensive £200,000 for four Louis XV pieces at Sotheby & Co., London on 8 Dec. 1967.

Table cloth The world's largest table cloth is one 60 yds *54,8 m* long by 2½ yds *2,28 m* wide woven in linen in Belfast in January 1972 for King Bhumibol of Thailand whose titles include Brother of the Moon and Half-Brother of the Sun.

Earliest The earliest evidence of tartan is the so-called Falkirk
tartan tartan, found stuffed in a jar of coins in Bells Meadow, north of Callendar Park, Scotland. It is of a dark and light brown pattern and dates from *c.* A.D. 245. The earliest reference to a specific named tartan has been to a Murray tartan in 1618.

Most The Greek Urn painted by Ueuphromios and potted
expensive by the potter Euxitheos in *c.* 530 B.C. was bought by
urn the Metropolitan Museum of Art, New York for $1 million (£400,000) in the summer of 1972.

Largest wig The largest wig yet made is that by Jean Leonard, owner of a salon in Copenhagen, Denmark. It is intended for bridal occasions, made from 24 tresses, measures nearly 8 ft *2,43 m* in length and costs £416.

Most The most expensive wreath on record was that sent to
expensive the funeral of President Kennedy in Washington, D.C.
wreath on 25 Nov. 1963 by the civic authority of Paris. It was handled by Interflora Inc. and cost $1,200 (now £460). The only rival was a floral tribute sent to the Mayor of Moscow in 1970 by Umberto Farmichello, general manager of Interflora which is never slow to scent an opportunity. The largest wreath on record is a Christmas wreath 61 ft 4 in *18,69 m* in diameter weighing 750 lb. *340 kg* built for the Park Plaza, Oshkosh, Wisconsin, U.S.A. in November 1971.

Writing The most expensive writing paper in the world is that
paper sold by Cartier Inc. on Fifth Avenue, New York City at $1,904 (£793) per 100 sheets with envelopes. It is of hand made paper from Finland with deckle edges and a "personalized" portrait watermark. Second thoughts and mis-spellings are costly.

The largest wreath recorded, constructed by the Oshkosh Warriors Drum & Bugle Corps., Wisconsin, U.S.A.

3. AGRICULTURE

ORIGINS

It has been estimated that only 21 per cent of the world's land surface is cultivable and that of this only two-fifths is cultivated. Evidence adduced in 1971 from Nok Nok Tha and Spirit Cave, Thailand tends to confirm plant cultivation and animal domestication was part of the Hoabinhian culture *c.* 11,000 B.C.

Reindeer may have been domesticated as early as *c.* 18,000 B.C. but definite evidence is still lacking.

FARMS

Earliest The earliest dated British farming site is a neolithic one, enclosed within the Iron Age hill-fort at Hembury, Devon, excavated during 1934–5 and now dated to 3330 B.C. ± 150. Pollen analysis from two sites Oakhanger, Hampshire, and Winfrith Heath, Dorset (Mesolithic *c.* 4300 B.C.) indicates that Mesolithic man may have had herds which were fed on ivy during the winter months.

Largest The largest farms in the world are collective farms in
World the U.S.S.R. These have been reduced in number from 235,500 in 1940 to only 36,000 in 1969 and have been increased in size so that units of over 60,000 acres *25 000 ha* are not uncommon.

Britain The largest farms in the British Isles are Scottish hill farms in the Grampians. The largest arable farm is that of Elveden, Suffolk, farmed by the Earl of Iveagh. Here 11,251½ acres *4 553 ha* are farmed on an estate of 22,918 acres *9 274 ha*, the greater part of which was formerly derelict land. The 1972 production included 1,150,045 gal *5 228 062 litres* of milk, 3,762 tons/*tonnes* of grain and 7,938 tons *7 915 tonnes* of sugar beet. The livestock includes 1,457 cattle, 961 ewes and 4,344 pigs.

Largest The world's largest single wheat field was probably
wheat field one of more than 35,000 acres *14 160 ha* first sown in 1951 near Lethbridge, Alberta, Canada.

Largest The largest hop field in the world is one of 710 acres
hop field *287 ha* at Toppenish, Washington State, U.S.A. It is owned by John I. Haas, Inc., the world's largest hop growers, with hop farms in British Columbia (Canada), California, Idaho, Oregon and Washington, with a total net area of 3,065 acres *1 240 ha*.

Cattle The world's largest cattle station was Alexandria
station Station, Northern Territory, Australia, selected in 1873 by Robert Collins, who rode 1,600 miles *2 575 km* to reach it. It has 66 wells, a staff of 90 and originally extended over 7,207,608 acres *2 916 818 ha*—more than the area of the English counties of Yorkshire, Devon, Norfolk and Cambridgeshire put together. The present area is 6,500 miles² *16 835 km²* which is stocked with 58,000 shorthorn cattle. Until 1915 the Victoria River Downs Station, Northern Territory, was over three times larger, with an area of 22,400,000 acres (35,000 miles² [*90 650 km²*]).

Sheep The largest sheep station in the world is Common-
station wealth Hill, in the north-west of South Australia. It grazes between 70,000 and 90,000 sheep in an area of 3,640 miles² *9 425 km²* *i.e.* larger than the combined area of Norfolk and Suffolk.

The largest sheep move on record occurred when 27 horsemen moved a mob of 43,000 sheep 40 miles *64 km* from Barealdine to Beaconsfield Station, Queensland, Australia, in 1886.

Mushroom The largest mushroom farm in the world is the Butler
farm County Mushroom Farm, Inc., founded in 1937 in a disused limestone mine near West Winfield, Pennsylvania, U.S.A. It now has 900 employees working underground, in a maze of galleries 110 miles *177 km* long, producing about 32,000,000 lb. *14 518 tonnes* of mushrooms per year.

Turkey farm Europe's largest turkey farm is that of Bernard Matthews Ltd., at Weston Longville, Norfolk, with up to 300 workers tending 160,000 turkeys.

CROP YIELDS

Wheat Crop yields for highly tended small areas are of little significance. The greatest recorded wheat yield is

Lord and Lady Iveagh at Elveden, Suffolk, Britain's largest arable farm

255.03 U.S. bushels (136.62 cwt./acre [*221,9 hectolitres/ha*]) from 25½ acres *10,3 ha* in 1972 by David Case of Minden, Nebraska, U.S.A. The British record is 71.4 cwt./acre *128,3 hectolitres/ha* (variety Viking) on a field of 9.453 acres *3,825 ha* by J. F. Oliver, near Doncaster, Yorkshire in 1962.

Barley A yield of 82.61 cwt./acre *10 371 kg/ha* of Clermont Spring Barley was achieved in 1972 by John Graham of Kirkland Hall, Wigton, Cumberland from a 13.52 acre *5,47 ha* field.

DIMENSIONS AND PROLIFICACY

Cattle Of heavyweight cattle the heaviest on record was a Hereford-Shorthorn named "Old Ben", owned by Mike and John Murphy of Miami, Indiana, U.S.A. When he died at the age of 8, in February 1910, he had attained a length of 16 ft 2 in *4,92 m* from nose to tail, a girth of 13 ft 8 in *4,16 m*, a height of 6 ft 4 in *1,93 m* at the forequarters and a weight of 4,720 lb. *2 140 kg*. The stuffed and mounted steer is displayed in Highland Park, Kokomo, Indiana, as proof to all who would otherwise have said "there ain't no such animal". The British record is the 4,480 lb. *2 032 kg* of "The Bradwell Ox" owned by William Spurgin of Bradwell, Essex. He was 15 ft *4,57 m* from nose to tail and had a girth of 11 ft *3,35 m*. Weights of 4,000 lb. *1 815 kg* are commonplace among Italian Chianina bulls standing 6½ ft *1,98 m* at the shoulder.

The highest recorded birthweight for a calf is 225 lb. *102 kg* from a British Friesian cow at Rockhouse Farm, Bishopston, Swansea, Glamorganshire, in 1961.

On 25 April 1964 it was reported that a cow named "Lyubik" had given birth to seven calves at Mogilev, U.S.S.R. A case of five live calves at one birth was reported in 1928 by T. G. Yarwood of Manchester, Lancashire. The life-time prolificacy record is 30 in the case of a cross-bred cow owned by G. Page of Warren Farm, Wilmington, Sussex, which died in November 1957, aged 32. A cross-Hereford calved in 1916 and owned by A. J. Thomas of West Hook Farm, Marloes, Pembrokeshire, Wales, produced her 30th calf in May 1955 and died in May 1956, aged 40.

Pigs The heaviest pig ever recorded in Britain was one of 12 cwt. 66 lb. *639 kg 50* bred by Joseph Lawton of Astbury, Cheshire. In 1774 it stood 4 ft 8½ in *1,43 m* in height and was 9 ft 8 in *2,94 m* long. The highest recorded weight for a piglet at weaning (8 weeks) is 81 lb. *36 kg 70* for a boar, one of nine piglets farrowed on 6 July 1962 by the Landrace gilt "Manorport Ballerina 53rd", *alias* "Mary", and sired by a Large White named "Johnny" at Kettle Lane Farm, West Ashton, Trowbridge, Wiltshire.

The highest recorded number of piglets in one litter is 34, thrown on 25–26 June 1961 by a sow owned by Aksel Egedee of Denmark. In February 1955 a Wessex sow owned by Mrs. E. C. Goodwin of Paul's Farm, Leigh, near Tonbridge, Kent, had a litter of 34, of which 30 were born dead. A litter of 32 piglets (26 live born) was thrown in February 1971 by a British saddleback owned by Mr. R. Spencer of Tdingtonod, Gloucestershire. In September 1934 a Large White sow, owned by Mr. H. S. Pedlingham, died after having farrowed 385 piglets in 22 litters in 10 yrs 10 months.

Sheep The highest recorded birthweight for a lamb in Britain is 26 lb. *11 kg 80* in the case of a lamb delivered on 9 Feb. 1967 by Alan F. Baldry from a ewe belonging to J. L. H. Arkwright of Winkleigh, Devonshire. A case of eight lambs at a birth was reported by D. T. Jones of Priory Farm, Monmouthshire, in June 1956, but none lived. A case of a sheep living to 26 years was recorded in flock book records by H. Poole, Wexford, Ireland.

Egg-laying The highest authenticated rate of egg-laying by a hen is 361 eggs in 364 days by a Black Orpington in an official test at Taranaki, New Zealand, in 1930. The U.K. record is 353 eggs in 365 days in a National Laying Test at Milford, Surrey in 1957 by a Rhode Island Red owned by W. Lawson of Welham Grange, Retford, Nottinghamshire. In Aug. 1971 a Rhode Island Red "Penny", owned by Mrs. Treena White of Aston Clinton, Buckinghamshire laid 20 eggs in 7 days and 7 in one day on 11 Sept. 1971.

The largest egg reported is one of 16 oz. *454 g*, with double yolk and double shell, laid by a white Leghorn at Vineland, New Jersey, U.S.A., on 25 Feb. 1956. The largest in the United Kingdom was one of 8¼ oz., *226 g* laid by "Daisy", owned by Peter Quarton, aged 8, at Lodge Farm, Kexby Bridge, near York, in March 1964.

MILK YIELDS

Cows The world lifetime record yield of milk is 334,292 lb. (149.2 tons [*151 632 kg*]) at 3.4 per cent butter fat by the U.S. Holstein cow "College Ormsby Burke" which died at Fort Collins, Colorado in August 1966. The greatest yield of any British cow was that given by the British Friesian "Manningford Faith Jan Graceful", owned by R. and H. Jenkinson of Oxfordshire. This cow yielded 326,451 lb. *148 075 kg* before she died in November 1955, aged 17½ years. The greatest recorded yield for one lactation (365 days) is 45,081 lb. *20 448 kg.* by Mr. R. A. Pierson's British Friesian "Bridge Birch" in England in 1947–48. The British record for milk yield in a day is 198¼ lb. *89 kg 924* by R. A. Pierson's British Friesian "Garsdon Minnie" in 1948.

Milking The hand milking record for cows is 17 lb. 11 oz. *8 kg 022* in two minutes from two cows by Manuel Dutra of Stockton, California at the Cow Palace, San Francisco, California, U.S.A., on 27 Oct. 1970. Dutra known as a fierce competitor, proclaimed "I credit my cows with the victory".

Goats The highest recorded milk yield for any goat is 6,661 pints *9 091 litres* in 365 days by "Malpas Melba", owned by Mr. J. R. Egerton of Bramford, East Anglia, in 1931.

SHEEP SHEARING

The highest recorded speed for lamb shearing in a working day was that of Steve Morrell who machine-sheared 585 lambs (average 65 per hour) in 9 hrs at Ashburton, New Zealand on 29 Dec. 1971. The blade (*i.e.* hand-shearing) record in a 9 hr working day is 350, set in 1899. The female record is held by Mrs. Pamela Warren, aged 21, who machine-sheared 337 Romney Marsh ewes and lambs at Puketutu, near Piopio, North Island, New Zealand on 25 Nov. 1964.

Mr. LaVor Taylor, the sheep-shearer with the highest lifetime total, adding another sheep to his score

Britain British records for 9 hrs have been set at 555 by Roger Poyntz-Roberts (300) and John Savery (255) on 9 June 1971 (sheep caught *by* shearers), and 610 by the same pair (sheep caught *for* shearers) in July 1970. In a shearing marathon by the Kingsbridge Young Farmer's Club, four men machine-shore 776 sheep in 24 hrs on 4–5 June 1971.

Lifetime Total The Sheep Shearer with the largest life-time total is believed to be LaVor Taylor (b. 27 Feb. 1896) of Ephraim, Utah, U.S.A., who with annual totals varying between 8,000 and 22,000 sheep accumulated 225,000 head in 58 years.

LIVESTOCK PRICES

The highest nominal value ever placed on a bull is $1,050,000 (*then £375,000*), implicit in the $350,000 paid on 22 Jan. 1967 for a one-third share in the Aberdeen-Angus bull "Newhouse Jewror Eric", aged 7, by the Embassy Angus Farm of Mississippi, U.S.A.

The highest price ever paid for a bull in Britain is 60,000 guineas (£63,000), paid on 5 Feb. 1963 at Perth, Scotland, by Jock Dick, co-manager of Black Watch Farms, for "Lindertis Evulse", an Aberdeen-Angus owned by Sir Torquil and Lady Munro of Lindertis, Kirriemuir, Angus, Scotland. This bull failed a fertility test in August 1963 when 20 months old thus becoming the world's most expensive piece of beef.

Cow The highest price ever paid for a cow is Can. $62,000 (*£23,890*) for the Holstein-Friesian "Oak Ridges Royal Linda" by Mr. E. L. Vesley of Lapeer, Michigan, U.S.A. at the Oak Ridges, Canada dispersal sale on 12 Nov. 1968.

Sheep The highest price ever paid for a sheep is $A27,200 (*£12,920*) for a Merino ram from John Collins &

Sons, Mount Bryan, South Australia by L. W. Gare & Sons of Burra, South Australia at Adelaide in Sept. 1970.

The British auction record is £6,300 paid by William Hyslop and Son for a Scottish Blackface ram lamb owned by James McWhirter of Dalmellington, Ayrshire at Newton-Stewart, Wigtownshire in Oct. 1972.

The highest price ever paid for wool is $A46 per kg (*£11.09 per lb.*) for a bale of superfine Merino fleece from the Launceston, Tasmania sales in Dec. 1972 set by Mr. C. Stephen of Mount Morrison estate.

Pig The highest price ever paid for a pig is $10,200 (*now £3,920*), paid in 1953 for a Hampshire boar "Great Western" by a farm at Byron, Illinois, U.S.A. The U.K. record is 3,300 guineas (*£3,465*), paid by Malvern Farms for the Swedish Landrace gilt "Blue-gate Ally 33rd" owned by Davidson Trust in a draft sale at Reading on 2 March 1955.

Horse The highest price ever given for a farm horse is £9,500, paid for the Clydesdale stallion "Baron of Buchlyvie" by William Dunlop at Ayr, Scotland, in December 1911.

Donkey Perhaps the lowest ever price for livestock was at a sale at Kuruman, Cape Province, South Africa in 1934 where donkeys were sold for less than 2p each.

Turkey The highest price ever paid for a turkey is $990 (*then £353*) for a 33 lb. *15 kg* stag bird bought at the Arkansas State Turkey Show at Springdale, Arkansas, U.S.A. on 3 Dec. 1955.

BUTTER FAT

The world record lifetime yield is 13,607 lb. *6 172 kg* from 308,569 lb. *139 964 kg* by the U.S. Brown Swiss cow "Ivetta" (1954–71) in the herd of W. E. Naffziger at Pekin, Illinois, U.S.A. in 4,515 days. The British record butter fat yield in a lifetime is 12,144 lb. *5 508 kg* by the Friesian "Lavenham Wallen 87th" (b. 30 Nov. 1946, d. 17 Oct. 1967), owned by Mr. John Lindley of Nowers Farm, Wellington, Somerset. The world's lactation (365 days) record is 1,866 lb. *846 kg* by the U.S. Holstein-Friesian "Princess Breezewood R. A. Patsy" while the British record is 1,799 lb. *816 kg* (33,184 lb. *[15 052 kg]* milk at 5.42 per cent) by A. Drexler's British Friesian "Zenda Bountiful" at Manor Farm, Kidlington, Oxfordshire, in the year ending 3 March 1953. This is sufficient to produce 2,116 lb. *959 kg* of butter. The United Kingdom record for butter fat in one day is 9.30 lb. *4 kg 218* (79 lb. *[35 kg 80]* milk at 11.8 per cent) by Queens Letch Farms' Guernsey Cow "Thisbe's Bronwen of Trewollack".

CHEESE

The most active cheese-eaters are the people of France, with an annual average in 1969 of 29.98 lb. *13 kg 600* per person. The world's biggest producer is the United States with a factory production of 998,800 tons *1 014 827 tonnes* in 1970. The U.K. cheese consumption in 1970 was 11.4 lb. *5 kg 170* per head.

Oldest The oldest and most primitive cheeses are the Arabian *kishk*, made of dried curd of goats' milk. There are today 450 named cheeses of 18 major varieties, but many are merely named after different towns and differ only in shape or the method of packing. France has 240 varieties.

Most expensive The most expensive of all cheeses is the ewe's milk mountain cheese Laruns from the Béarn area of the Pyrenees, France, which is marketed in Paris, at times, for 35 francs per kg (£1.31 per lb.). Britain's most costly cheeses are Blue Cheshire and Windsor Red both at 45p per lb. *99p per kg*. In the U.S. Imported

The world's largest cheese, a 34,591 lb. *15 190 kg* specimen, made in the U.S.A. in 1964

Brie from France may cost $5.80 (*£2.32*) per lb. or *£5.11 kg* retail.

Largest The largest cheese ever made was a cheddar of 34,591 lb. *15 190 kg* made in 43 hrs on 20–22 Jan. 1964 by the Wisconsin Cheese Foundation for exhibition at the New York World's Fair, U.S.A. It was transported in a specially designed refrigerated tractor trailer "Cheese Mobile" 45 ft *13,71 m* long.

Longest sausage The longest sausage ever recorded was one 3,124 ft *952 m* long, made on 29 June 1966 by 30 butchers in Scunthorpe, Lincolnshire. It was made from 6½ cwt. *330 kg* of pork and 1½ cwt. *76 kg 20* of cereal and seasoning.

Piggery The world's largest piggery is the Sljeme pig unit in Yugoslavia which is able to process 300,000 pigs in a year. Even larger units may exist in Romania but details are at present lacking.

Cow shed The longest cow shed in Britain is that of the Yorkshire Agricultural Society at Harrogate. It is 456 ft *139 m* in length with a capacity of 686 cows. The National Agricultural Centre, Kenilworth, Warwickshire, completed in 1967, has, however, capacity for 782 animals.

Chicken Ranch The world's largest chicken ranch is the 600 acre *242 ha* "Egg City" Moor Park, California established by Jules Goldman in 1954. Some 2 million eggs are laid daily by 4.5 million chickens. The manure sale totals $72,000 (*£28,800*) per annum.

Foot-and-mouth disease The worst outbreak of foot-and-mouth disease in Great Britain was that from Shropshire on 25 Oct. 1967 to 25 June 1968 in which there were 2,364 outbreaks and 429,632 animals slaughtered at a direct and consequential loss of £150,000,000. The outbreak of 1871, when farms were much smaller, affected 42,531 farms. The disease first appeared in Great Britain at Stratford near London in August 1839.

Ploughing The world championship (instituted 1953) has been staged in 17 countries and won by ploughmen of ten nationalities of which the United Kingdom has been most successful with 6 champions. The only man to take the title three times has been Hugh Barr of Northern Ireland in 1954–55–56.

The fastest recorded time for ploughing an acre *0,404 ha* (minimum 32 right-hand turns and depth 9 in *[22 cm]*) is 17 min 52.5 sec by Mervyn Ford using a six-furrow 14 inch Ransomes plough towed by a Roadless 114 four-wheel drive tractor at Bowhay Farm, Ide, Exeter, Devon on 25 Sept. 1970.

The greatest recorded acreage ploughed in 24 hrs is 115 acres *46,53 ha* at North Barn Farm, Dorchester, Dorset on 22–23 Nov. 1971 with a County Eleven Twenty Four tractor with a Bamford Kverneland 7 furrow plough to a depth of 6 in *15 cm*.

Honey Record The greatest recorded yield of honey from a single hive has been 100 qrs 300 lb. *136 kg* by the apiarist A. I. Root of Medina, Ohio, U.S.A. in *c.* 1895.

178

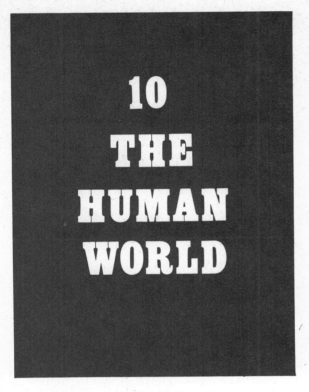

10 THE HUMAN WORLD

1. POLITICAL AND SOCIAL

The land area of the Earth is estimated at 57,270,000 miles² *148 325 000 km²* (including inland waters), or 29.08 per cent of the world's surface area.

Largest political division The British Commonwealth of Nations, a free association of 33 independent sovereign states together with their dependencies, covers an area of 13,095,000 miles² *33 915 000 km²* and had a population estimated to be 875 million in 1972.

COUNTRIES

Total The total number of separately administered territories in the world is 225, of which 150 are independent countries. Of these 26 sovereign and 62 non-sovereign are insular countries. Only 29 sovereign and 3 non-sovereign countries are entirely without a seaboard. Territorial waters vary between extremes of 3 miles *4,82 km* (*e.g.* United Kingdom, Australia, France, Ireland and the U.S.A.) up to 200 miles *321,8 km* (*e.g.* Argentina, Ecuador, El Salvador and Panama).

Largest The country with the greatest area is the Union of Soviet Socialist Republics (the Soviet Union), comprising 15 Union (constituent) Republics with a total area of 22 402 000 km *8,649,500 miles²*, or 15.0 per cent of the world's total land area, and a total coastline (including islands) of 106 360 km *66,090 miles*. The country measures 8 980 km *5,580 miles* from east to west and 4 490 km *2,790 miles* from north to south.

The United Kingdom covers 94,221 miles² *244 030 km²* (including 1,197 miles² [*3 100 km²*] of inland water), or 0.16 per cent of the total land area of the world. Great Britain is the world's eighth largest island, with an area of 84,186 miles² *218 040 km²* and a coastline 5,126 miles *8 249 km* long, of which Scotland accounts for 2,573 miles *4 141 km*, Wales 624 miles *1 004 km* and England 1,929 miles *3 104 km*.

Smallest The smallest independent country in the world is the State of the Vatican City or Holy See (Stato della Città del Vaticano), which was made an enclave within the city of Rome, Italy on 11 Feb. 1929. It has an area of 44 hectares *108.7 acres*.

The world's smallest republic is Nauru, less than 1 degree south of the equator in the Western Pacific, which became independent on 31 Jan. 1968, has an area of 5,263 acres *2 129 ha* and a population of 7,000 (estimate mid-1969).

The smallest colony in the world is Pitcairn Island with an area of 960 acres *388 ha* and a population of 82 (mid-1972).

The official residence, since 1834, of the Grand Master of the Order of the Knights of Malta totalling 3 acres *1,2 ha* and comprising the Villa del Priorato di Malta on the lowest of Rome's seven hills, the 151 ft *46 m* Aventine, retains certain diplomatic privileges and has accredited representatives to foreign governments and is hence sometimes cited as the smallest state in the world.

On 19 Jan. 1972 the two South Pacific atolls of North and South Minerva (400 miles [*640 km*] south of Fiji) were declared to be a sovereign independent Republic under international law by Mr. Michael Oliver formerly of Lithuania.

FRONTIERS

Most The country with the most frontiers is the U.S.S.R., with 13—Norway, Finland, Poland, Czechoslovakia, Hungary, Romania, Turkey, Iran (Persia), Afghanistan Mongolia, People's Republic of China, North Korea and Japan (territorial waters).

Longest The longest continuous frontier in the world is that between Canada and the United States, which (including the Great Lakes boundaries) extends for 3,987 miles *6 416 km* (excluding 1,538 miles [*2 547 km*] with Alaska). The frontier which is crossed most frequently is that between the United States and Mexico. It extends for 1,933 miles *3 110 km* and there are more than 120,000,000 crossings every year. The Sino-Soviet frontier extends for 4,500 miles *7 240 km* with no reported figure of crossings.

Most impenetrable boundary The "Iron Curtain" (858 miles [*1 380 km*]) dividing the Federal Republican (West) and the Democratic Republican (East) parts of Germany, utilises 2,230,000 land mines and 50,000 miles *80 500 km* of barbed wire, much of it of British manufacture, in addition to many watch-towers containing detection devices. The whole strip of 270 yds *246 m* wide occupies 133 miles² *344 km²* of East German territory.

POPULATIONS

World Estimates of the human population of the world depend largely on the component figure for the population of the People's Republic of China (see also below). Her seating in the United Nations on 25 Oct. 1971 may result in the publication of the first census figures since 1953. The world total at mid-1973 can be estimated to be 3,860 million, giving an average density of 28,6 people per km² *74.2 per mile²* of land (including inland waters). This excludes Antarctica and uninhabited island groups. The daily increase in the world's population was running at 208,000 in 1972–73. It is estimated that about 245 are born and about 101 die every minute in 1972–73. The world's population has doubled in the last 50 years and is expected to double again in the next 35 years. It is now estimated that the world's population in the year 2000 will be more than 6,000 million, and probably closer to 7,000 million. The present population "explosion" is of such a magnitude that it has been fancifully calculated that, if it were to continue unabated, there would be one person to each square yard by A.D. 2600, and humanity would weigh more than Earth itself by A.D. 3700. It is estimated that 75,000,000,000 humans have been born and died in the last 600,000 years.

WORLD POPULATION —
Progressive mid-year estimates

Date	Millions	Date	Millions
4000 B.C.	85		
A.D. 1	c. 200–300	1960	2,982
1650	c. 500–550	1965	3,289
1750	750	1970	3,632
1800	960	1971	3,706
1850	1,240	1972	3,782
1900	1,650	1973	3,860
1920	1,862	2000	6,493*
1930	2,070	2007	7,600
1940	2,295	2070	25,000
1950	2,486	2100	48,000

* U.N. Forecasts made on medium variants.

Most populous country The largest population of any country is that of the People's Republic of China. The two most recent quasi-official figures published are 732 million as of 31 Dec. 1967 for the Chinese Revolutionary Committee and 697,260,000 relating to mid-1970, by the Chinese Cartographic Institute when the figure, allowing for a natural increase of 1.8 per cent (U.N. estimate) should have been 765.4 million—a discrepancy of more than 68 million. If the lower figure is accepted, the population of The People's Republic of China would be 720,000,000 in mid 1973.

Colonial The most populous colony in the world is Mozambique, South East Africa with an estimated Dec. 1970 figure of 8,234,000. The capital city of this Portuguese overseas province is Lourenço Marques.

Least populous The independent state with the smallest population is the Vatican City of the Holy See (see Smallest country, page 179), with 880 inhabitants at 1 Jan. 1966.

Most densely populated The most densely populated territory in the world is the Portuguese province of Macau (or Macao), on the southern coast of China. It has an estimated population of 321,000 (30 June 1971) in an area of 6.2 miles² giving a density of 51,775 per mile² *19 990 per km²*.

The Principality of Monaco, on the south coast of France, has a population of 24,000 (estimated 30 June 1971) in an area of 369.9 acres *149,6 ha* giving a density of 41,500/mile² *16 023/km²*. This is being relieved by marine infilling which will increase her area to 447 acres *180 ha*. Singapore has 2,147,000 (mid-1972 estimate) people in an inhabited area of 73 miles² *189 km²*.

Of territories with an area of more than 200 miles² *518 km²*, Hong Kong (398¼ miles² [*1 031,4 km²*]) contains 4,045,000 (estimated mid-1971), giving the territory a density of 10,155/mile² *3 920/km²*. The name Hong Kong is the transcription of the local pronunciation of the Peking dialect version of Xiang gang (a port for incense). About 80 per cent of the population lives in the urban areas of Hong Kong island and Kowloon, on the mainland, and the density there is greater than 200,000/mile² *518 000/km²*. At North Point there are 12,400 people living in 6½ acres *2,6 ha* giving an unsurpassed spot density of more than 1,200,000/mile² *463 000/km²*. In 1959 it was reported that in one house designed for 12 people the number of occupants was 459, including 104 in one room and 4 living on the roof.

Of countries over 1,000 miles² *2 589 km²* the most densely populated is the Netherlands, with a population of 13,330,000 (estimated 1 July 1972) on 12,978 miles² *33 612/km²* of land, giving a density of 1,026 people/mile² *396/km²*. The Indonesian islands of Java and Madura (combined area 51,033 miles² [*132 174 km²*]) had a population of 73,400,000 (estimated for mid-1969), giving a density of 1,438/mile² *555 km²*. The United Kingdom (94,221 miles² [*244 030 km²*]) had an estimated home population of 55,789,000 at 30 June 1972, giving a density of 592.1 people/mile². The projected population figures for 1980 and 2000 are 59,548,000 and 66,100,000. The population density for England alone (50,869 miles²) is 959.8/mile², while that of south-eastern England is more than 1,640/mile².

Most sparsely populated Antarctica became permanently occupied by relays of scientists from October 1956. The population varies seasonally and reaches 1,500 at times.

The least populated territory, apart from Antarctica, is Greenland, with a population of 50,000 (estimated 1 July 1971) in an area of 840,000 miles² *2 175 000 km²*, giving a density of one person to every 16.7 miles² *43,3 km²*. The ice-free area of the island is only 132,000 miles² *340 000 km²*.

BRITISH AND IRISH LARGEST AND SMALLEST COUNTIES / DISTRICTS BY AREA AND IN POPULATION

	By Area (in acres/hectares)						By Home Population (estimate 30 June 1972)			
	Largest			Smallest			Most Populous		Least Populous	
England	North Yorkshire	2,055,109	*831 661*	Isle of Wight	94,141	*38 096*	Greater London	7,353,810	Isle of Wight[1]	109,000
Wales	Dyfed	1,424,668	*576 534*	West Glamorgan	201,476	*81 533*	Mid Glamorgan	530,639[2]	Powys	98,765
Scotland[3]	County of Inverness[4]	2,695,094	*1 090 650*	County of Clackmannan	34,937	*14 138*	County of Lanark	1,494,250[5]	County of Kinross	6,542
Northern Ireland[6]	Fermanagh District	463,515	*187 575*	North Down District	18,174	*7 354*	Belfast District	403,900[1]	Moyle District	14,500[1]
Republic of Ireland	Cork	1,843,408	*745 990*	Louth	202,806	*82 071*	Dublin County	799,048	Longford	28,250

1 Figures based on 1971 Census.
2 Includes the largest town in Wales—the City of Cardiff (pop. 274,920).
3 Scotland's 33 Counties are to be replaced in May 1975 by nine Regions and three Island Areas.
4 The inclusion by Act of Parliament on 10 February 1972 of Rockall in the District of Harris in the County of Inverness put the extremities of the County at the record distance of 365 miles 587 km.
5 Includes the largest town in Scotland—the City of Glasgow (pop. 861,898).
6 There are now no counties in Northern Ireland, which is divided into 26 Districts.

An aerial view
of part of
Hong Kong,
the world's
most densely
populated small
territory

CITIES

Most The most populous city in the world is Shanghai,
populous China with a population in 1970 of 10,820,000 thus
World surpassing the figure for the 23 wards of Tōkyō, Japan.
At the census of 1 Oct. 1970, the "Keihin Metropolitan
Area" (Tōkyō-Yokohama Metropolitan Area) of
1,081 miles² *2 800 km²* however contained an
estimated 14,034,074 people.

The world's largest city not built by the sea or on a
river is Greater Mexico City (Ciudad de Mexico), the
capital of Mexico, with an estimated population of
7,314,900 at Jan. 1970.

United The largest conurbation in Britain is Greater London
Kingdom (established on 1 April 1965), with a provisional for
mid-1972 of 7,353,810 in an area of 396,516 acres
(619.5 miles² [*1 604,4 km²*]). The residential population
of the City of London (677 acres [*273 ha*]) is 4,235
compared with 128,000 in 1801. The peak figure for
Greater London was 8,596,539 in 1939.

Largest The world's largest town, in area, is Mount Isa
in area Queensland, Australia. The area administered by the
City Council is 15,822 miles² *40 978 km²*. The largest
city in the United Kingdom is Greater London with
an area of 619.5 miles² *1 604,4 km²*.

Smallest The only hamlet in Great Britain with an official
hamlet population of one is Gallowhill in the parish of Inver-
avon, Banffshire, Scotland.

Highest The highest capital in the world, before the domina-
World tion of Tibet by China, was Lhasa, at an elevation of
12,087 ft *3 684 m* above sea-level. La Paz, the administrative and *de facto* capital of Bolivia, stands at an
altitude of 11,916 ft *3 631 m* above sea-level. The city
was founded in 1548 by Capt. Alonso de Mendoza on
the site of an Indian village named Chuquiapu. It was
originally called Ciudad de Nuestra Señora de La
Paz (City of Our Lady of Peace), but in 1825 was
renamed La Paz de Ayacucho, its present official name.
Sucre, the legal capital of Bolivia, stands at 9,301 ft
2 834 m above sea-level. The new town of Wenchuan,
founded in 1955 on the Chinghai-Tibet road, north of

the Tangla range is the highest in the world at 5 100 m
16,732 ft above sea-level. The highest village in the
world is the Andean mining village of Aucanquilca, in
Chile, at 17,500 ft *5 300 m* above sea-level.

Great The highest village in England is Flash, in northern
Britain Staffordshire, at 1,518 ft *462 m* above sea-level. The
highest in Scotland is Wanlockhead, in Dumfries-shire
at 1,380 ft *420 m* above sea-level.

Oldest The oldest known walled town in the world is Arīhā
World (Jericho), in Jordan. Radio-carbon dating on specimens from the lowest levels reached by archaeologists
indicate habitation there by perhaps 3,000 people as
early as 7800 B.C. The village of Zawi Chemi Shanidar,
discovered in 1957 in northern Iraq, has been dated
to 8910 B.C. The oldest capital city in the world is
Dimashq (Damascus), the capital of Syria. It has been
continuously inhabited since *c.* 2500 B.C.

Great The oldest town in Great Britain is often cited as
Britain Colchester, the old British Camulodunon, headquarters of Belgic chiefs in the 1st century B.C. However, the place called Ictis, referred to by Pytheas in
c. 308 B.C., has been identified with Marazion, close
to St. Michael's Mount, Cornwall.

Northern- The world's northernmost town with a population of
most more than 10,000 is the Arctic port of Dikson,
U.S.S.R. in 73° 32′ N. The northernmost village is Ny
Ålesund (78° 55′ N.), a coalmining settlement on
King's Bay, Vest Spitsbergen, in the Norwegian
territory of Svalbard, inhabited only during the
winter season. The northernmost capital is Reykjavik,
the capital of Iceland, in 64° 06′ N. Its population was
estimated to be 81,288 at 1 July 1969. The northernmost permanent human occupation is the base at
Alert (82° 31′ N.), on Dumb Bell Bay, on the north-
east coast of Ellesmere Island, northern Canada.

Southern- The world's southernmost village is Puerto Williams
most (population about 350), on the north coast of Isla
Navarino, in Tierra del Fuego, Chile, about 680 miles
1 090 km north of Antarctica. Wellington, North
Island, New Zealand is the southernmost capital city

181

on 41° 17′ S. The world's southernmost administrative centre is Port Stanley (51° 43′ S.), in the Falkland Islands, off South America.

Most remote from sea The largest town most remote from the sea is Wulu-much'i (Urumchi) formerly Tihwa, Sinkiang, capital of the Uighur Autonomous Region of China, at a distance of about 1,400 miles *2 250 km* from the nearest coastline. Its population was estimated to be 275,000 at 31 Dec. 1957.

EMIGRATION

More people emigrate from the United Kingdom than from any other country. A total of 242,200 emigrated from the U.K. for the year ended Sept. 1972. The largest number of emigrants in any one year was 360,000 in 1852, mainly from Ireland in the post-famine period.

IMMIGRATION

The country which regularly receives the most immigrants is the United States, with 370,478 in 1971. It has been estimated that, in the period 1820–1971, the U.S.A. has received 45,533,116 immigrants. The peak year for immigration into the United Kingdom was the 12 months from 1 July 1961 to 30 June 1962, when about 430,000 Commonwealth citizens arrived. The number of immigrants for the year ending Sept. 1972 was 207,200.

MOST TOURISTS

In 1971 Italy received 33,230,000 foreign visitors—more than any other country except Canada, which in 1970 received 37,735,000, of whom more than 62 per cent entered and left the same day. In 1972 the United Kingdom received 7,400,000 visitors who spent an estimated £538,000,000.

BIRTH RATE

Highest and lowest The highest 1965–70 figure is 52.3 for Swaziland. The rate for the whole world was 34 per 1,000 in 1965–71.

Excluding Vatican City where the rate is negligible, the lowest recorded rate is 9.2 for Monaco (1970).

The 1972 rate in the United Kingdom was 13.9/1,000 (13.6 in England and Wales, 14.7 in Scotland and 19.6 in Northern Ireland), while the 1972 rate for the Republic of Ireland was 22.0 registered births per 1,000.

DEATH RATE

Highest and lowest The highest of the latest available recorded death rates is 29.9 deaths per each 1,000 of the population in Portuguese Guinea. The rate for the whole world was 14 per 1,000 in 1965–71.

The lowest of the latest available recorded rates is 1.5 deaths/1,000 in Tonga in 1970.

The 1972 rate in the United Kingdom was 12.4/1,000 (12.5 in England and Wales, 11.8 in Scotland and 10.9 in Northern Ireland), while the 1972 rate for the Republic of Ireland was 11.3 registered deaths per 1,000. The highest S.M.I. (Standard Mortality Index where the national average is 100) is in Salford, Lancashire with a figure of 133.

NATURAL INCREASE

The highest of the latest available recorded rates of natural increase is 41.6/1,000 in the U.S. Virgin Island. The rate for the whole world was 34 − 14 = 20 per 1,000 in 1965–71.

The 1972 rate for the United Kingdom was 1.5/1,000 (1.1 in England and Wales, 2.9 in Scotland and 8.7 in Northern Ireland). The figure for the Republic of Ireland was 10.7/1,000 in 1972.

The lowest rate of natural increase in any major independent country is in East Germany (birth rate 13.9 death rate 14.1) with a negative figure thus of −0.2/1,000 for 1970. The figure for 1970 in Monaco is however −2.2.

Marriage ages The country with the lowest average ages for marriage is India, with 20.0 years for males and 14.5 years for females. At the other extreme is Ireland, with 31.4 for males and 26.5 years for females. In the People's Republic of China the recommended age for marriage for men is 28 and for women 25.

SEX RATIO

The country with the largest recorded shortage of males is the U.S.S.R., with 1,169 females to every 1,000 males at 15 Jan. 1970. The country with the largest recorded woman shortage is Pakistan, with 900.5 to every 1,000 males at 1 Feb. 1961. The ratio in the United Kingdom was 1,058.1 females to every 1,000 males at 30 June 1972, and is expected to be 1,014.2/1,000 by A.D. 2000.

INFANT MORTALITY

Based on deaths before one year of age, the lowest of the latest available recorded rates is 8.6 deaths per 1,000 live births in Gibraltar in 1970, compared with 11.1 per 1,000 in the Netherlands in 1971.

The highest recorded infant mortality rate recently reported has been 137/1,000 for Liberia in 1970. Many countries with rates more than twice as high have apparently ceased to make returns. Among these is Ethiopia, where the infant mortality rate was unofficially estimated to be nearly 550/1,000 live births in 1969.

The United Kingdom figure for 1972 was 17.0/1,000 live births (England and Wales 17.0, Scotland 20.0, Northern Ireland 23.0). The Republic of Ireland figure for 1972 was 18.0.

LIFE EXPECTATION

There is evidence that life expectation in Britain in the 5th century A.D. was 33 years for males and 27 years for females. In the decade 1890–1900 the expectation of life among the population of India was 23.7 years.

Based on the latest available data, the highest recorded expectation of life at birth is 71.85 years (males) and 76.54 years (females) both in Sweden in 1967.

The lowest recorded expectation of life at birth is 27 years for both sexes in the Vallée du Niger area of Mali in 1957 (sample survey, 1957–58). The figure for males in Gabon was 25 years in 1960–61 but 45 for females.

The latest available figures for England and Wales (1969–71) are 68.8 years for males and 75.1 years for females; for Scotland (1968–70) 66.9 years for males and 73.08 years for females; for Northern Ireland (1969–71) 67.9 years for males and 73.7 years for females and for the Republic of Ireland (1960–62) 68.13 years for males and 71.86 years for females. The British figure for 1901–1910 was 48.53 years for males and 52.83 years for females.

STANDARDS OF LIVING

National incomes The country with the highest income per person in 1972 was Nauru, with some £3,400 *$8,500* per head. In 1970 the U.S. reached $4,825 *£1,930* compared with $2,372 *£949* for the U.K. (1972).

COST OF LIVING

The greatest increase since 1963 (=100) has been in Djakarta, the capital of Indonesia, where the index figure reached 68,807 (food 70,809) by 1970.

In the United Kingdom the official index of retail prices (16 Jan. 1962 = 100) was 178.0 in May 1973 —a rise of 15.4 points or 9.47 per cent in 12 months.

HOUSING

For comparison, dwelling units are defined as a structurally separated room or rooms occupied by private households of one or more people and having separate access or a common passageway to the street.

The country with the greatest recorded number of private housing units is India, with 79,193,602 occupied in 1960. These contain 83,523,895 private households.

Great Britain comes fourth among reporting countries, with 18,839,000 dwellings (England 16,076,000, Wales 961,000, Scotland 1,802,000) at June 1971. The 1968 figure for Northern Ireland was 435,000. The Republic of Ireland had 687,304 private households in 1966. The record number of permanent houses built has been 425,800 in 1968.

PHYSICIANS

The country with the most physicians is the U.S.S.R., with 555,400 in 1969, or one to every 433 persons. In England and Wales there were 24,775 doctors employed by the National Health Service on 30 Sept. 1970.

The country with the highest proportion of physicians is Israel, where there were 7,281 (one to every 400 inhabitants) in 1970. The country with the lowest recorded proportion is Upper Volta, with 58 physicians (one for every 92,759 people) in 1970.

Dentists The country with the most dentists is the United States, where 115,000 were registered members of the American Dental Association in 1971.

Psychia- The country with the most psychiatrists is the United
trists States. The registered membership of the American Psychiatric Association was 18,225 in 1971. The membership of the American Psychological Association was 31,000 in 1971.

HOSPITALS

Largest The largest medical centre in the world is the District
World Medical Center in Chicago, Illinois, U.S.A. It covers 478 acres *193 ha* and includes five hospitals, with a total of 5,600 beds, and eight professional schools with more than 3,000 students.

The largest mental hospital in the world is the Pilgrim State Hospital, on Long Island, New York State, U.S.A., with 12,800 beds. It formerly contained 14,200 beds.

The largest maternity hospital in the world is the Kandang Kerbau Government Maternity Hospital in Singapore. It has 239 midwives, 151 beds for gynaecological cases, 388 maternity beds and an output of 31,255 babies in 1969 compared with the record "birthquake" of 39,856 babies (more than 109 per day) in 1966.

United The largest hospitals of any kind in the United
Kingdom Kingdom are the Rainhill Hospital near Liverpool, with 2,250 staffed beds, and St. Bernard's Hospital, Southall, Middlesex, which has 2,267 staffed beds for mental patients.

The largest general hospital in the United Kingdom is the St. James Hospital, Leeds, Yorkshire, with 1,438 available staffed beds.

The largest maternity hospital in the United Kingdom is the Mill Road Maternity Hospital, Liverpool with 206 staffed beds.

The Kadang Kerbau Maternity Hospital, Singapore, the busiest in the world

The largest children's hospital in the United Kingdom is Queen Mary's Hospital for Children, at Carshalton, Surrey, with 668 staffed beds.

2. ROYALTY AND HEADS OF STATE

Oldest The Emperor of Japan, Hirohito (born 29 April
ruling 1901), is the 124th in line from the first Emperor,
house Jimmu Tenno or Zinmu, whose reign was traditionally from 660 to 581 B.C., but probably from *c.* 40 to *c.* 10 B.C. His Imperial Majesty Muhammad Rizā Shāh Pahlavi of Iran (b. 26 Oct. 1919) claims descent from Cyrus the Great (reigned *c.* 559–529 B.C.).

Her Majesty Queen Elizabeth II (b. 21 April 1926) represents dynasties historically traceable at least back until the 5th century A.D.; notably that of Elesa of whom Alfred The Great was a 13 greats grandson and the Queen is therefore a 49 greats granddaughter.

REIGNS

Longest The longest recorded reign of any monarch is that of Pepi II, a Sixth Dynasty Pharaoh of ancient Egypt. His reign began in *c.* 2272 B.C., when he was aged 6, and lasted 91 years. Musoma Kanijo, chief of the Nzega district of western Tanganyika (now part of Tanzania), reputedly reigned for more than 98 years from 1864, when aged 8, until his death on 2 Feb. 1963. The 6th Japanese Emperor Koo-an traditionally reigned for 102 years (from 392 to 290 B.C.), but probably his actual reign was from about A.D. 110 to about A.D. 140. The reign of the 11th Emperor Suinin was traditionally from 29 B.C. to A.D. 71 (99 years), but probably from A.D. 259 to 291. The longest reign in European history was that of King Louis XIV of France, who ascended the throne on 14 May 1643, aged 4 years 8 months, and reigned for 72 years 110 days until his death on 1 Sept. 1715, four days before his 77th birthday.

Currently the longest reigning monarch in the world is King Sobhuza II, K.B.E. (b. July 1899), the *Ngwenyama* (Paramount Chief) of Swaziland, under United Kingdom protection since December 1899, and independent since 6 Sept. 1968. Hirohito (see above) has been Emperor in Japan since 25 Dec. 1926 while Emperor Haile Sellassie I of Ethiopia (b. 23 July 1892) has been in effectual control of his independent country since 1916 as regent Ras Tafari Makonnen since 1928 as Negus (King) and 1930 as Emperor.

Shortest The shortest recorded reign was that of the Dauphin Louis Antoine, who was technically King Louis XIX of France for the fifteen minutes between the signature of Charles X (1757–1836) and his own signature to the act of abdication, in favour of Henri V, which was executed at the Château de Rambouillet on 2 Aug. 1830.

Highest regnal numbers The highest post-nominal number ever used to designate a member of a Royal House was 74 enjoyed by H.S.H. Prince Henry LXXIV Reuss (1798–1886). All male members of this branch of this family are called Henry and are successively numbered from I upwards each century.

The highest British regnal number is 8, used by Henry VIII (1509–1547), who was the first British user of regnal numbers, and by Edward VIII (1936) who died as H.R.H. the Duke of Windsor, K.G., K.T., K.P., G.C.B., G.C.S.I., G.C.M.G., G.C.I.E., G.C.V.O., G.B.E., I.S.O., M.C. on 28 May 1972. Jacobites liked to style Henry Benedict, Cardinal York (born 1725), the grandson of James II, as Henry IX in respect of his "reign' from 1777 to 1807 when he died the last survivor in the male line of the House of Stuart.

Longest lived 'Royals' The longest life among the Blood Royal of Europe is the 96 years 8 months of H.R.H. Princess Anna of Battenberg, daughter of Nicholas I of Montenegro, who was born 18 Aug. 1874 and died in Switzerland 22 April 1971. The greatest age among European Royal Consorts is the 99 years 3 months of H.S.H. Princess Marie Felixovna Romanovsky-Krassinsky, who was born 19 Aug. 1872 and died in Paris 7 Dec. 1971.

Roman Occupation During the 369 year long Roman occupation of England, Wales and parts of Scotland there were 40 sole and 27 co-Emperors of Rome. Of these the longest reigning was Constantinus I (The Great) from 31 March 307 to 22 May 337—30 years 2 months.

Head of State oldest and youngest The oldest head of state in the world is King Gustav VI of the Goths and Wends (b. 11 Nov 1882), the King of Sweden since 29 Oct. 1950. The youngest head of state is Jean-Claude du Valier, b. (3 July 1951) President of Haiti.

Youngest King and Queen Of the world's 19 monarchies that with the youngest King is Bhutan where King Jigme Singye Wangchuk was born 11 Nov. 1955. Queen Alia, third wife of King Hussein I of Jordan became Queen on the eve of her 24th birthday (b. 25 Dec. 1948).

3. LEGISLATURES

PARLIAMENTS

Oldest The oldest legislative body is the *Alpingi* (Althing) of Iceland founded in A.D. 930. This body, which originally comprised 39 local chieftains, was abolished in 1800, but restored by Denmark to a consultative status in 1843 and a legislative status in 1874. The legislative assembly with the oldest continuous history is the Tynwald Court in the Isle of Man, which is believed to have originated more than 1,000 years ago.

Largest The largest legislative assembly in the world is the National People's Congress of the People's Republic of China. The fourth Congress, which met in March 1969, had 3,500 members.

Smallest quorum The House of Lords has the smallest quorum, expressed as a percentage of eligible voters, of any legislative body in the world, namely less than one-third of one per cent. To transact business there must be three peers present, including the Lord Chancellor or his deputy. The House of Commons quorum of 40 M.P.'s, including the Speaker or his deputy, is 20 times as exacting.

Highest paid legislators The most highly paid of all the world's legislators are Senators of the United States who receive a basic annual salary of $42,500 (*£17,000*). Of this, up to $3,000 (*£1,153*) is exempt from taxation. In addition up to $157,092 (*£62,836*) per annum is allowed for office help, with a salary limit of $30,600 (*£12,240*) for any one staff member (limited to 16 in number). Senators also enjoy free travel, telephones, postage, medical care, telegrams, stationery (limited to 480,000 envelopes per year), flowers and haircuts. They also command very low rates for filming, speech and radio transcriptions and, in the case of women senators, beauty treatment. When abroad they have access to "counterpart funds" and on retirement to non-contributory benefits.

Longest membership The longest span as a legislator was 83 years by József Madarász (1814–1915). He first attended the Hungarian Parliament in 1832–36 as *ablegatus absentium* (*i.e.* on behalf of an absent deputy). He was a full

BRITISH MONARCHY RECORDS

	KINGS	QUEENS REGNANT	QUEENS CONSORT
Longest Reign or tenure	59 years 96 days[1] George III 1760–1820	63 years 216 days Victoria 1837–1901	57 years 70 days Charlotte 1761–1818 (Consort of George III)
Shortest Reign or tenure	77 days[2] Edward V 1483	13 days Jane, July 1553	184 days Anne of Cleves 1540 (4th Consort of Henry VIII)
Longest lived	81 years 239 days George III (b. 1738–d. 1820)	81 years 243 days Victoria (b. 1819–d. 1901)	85 years 303 days Mary of Teck (b. 1867–d. 1953) (Consort of George V)
Most children (legitimate)[3]	16 Edward I 1272–1307	18[4] Anne (b. 1665–d. 1714)	15 Charlotte (b. 1744–d. 1818) (Consort of George III)
Oldest to start reign or consortship	64 years 10 months William IV 1830–1837	37 years 5 months Mary I 1553–1558	56 years 53 days Alexandra (b. 1844–d. 1925) (Consort of Edward VII)
Youngest to start reign or consortship	269 days Henry VI in 1422	6 or 7 days Mary, Queen of Scots in 1542	6 years 11 months Isabella (second consort of Richard II in 1396)
Most married	6 times Henry VIII 1509–1547	3 times Mary, Queen of Scots 1542–1567 (executed 1587)	4 times Catharine Parr (b. c. 1512–d. 1548) (sixth consort of Henry VIII)

Notes (Dates are dates of reigns or tenures unless otherwise indicated).

1 James Francis Edward, the Old Pretender, known to his supporters as James III styled his reign from 16 Sept. 1701 until his death 1 Jan. 1766 (i.e. 64 years 109 days)
2 There is the probability that in pre-Conquest times Sweyn 'Forkbeard', the Danish King of England, reigned for only 40 days in 1013–1014.
3 Henry I (1068–1135) in addition to one (possibly two) legitimate sons and a daughter had at least 20 bastard children (9 sons, 11 daughters), and possibly 22, by six mistresses.
4 None survived infancy. Victoria had nine children all of which survived their infancy.

member in 1848–50 and from 1861 until his death on 31 Jan. 1915.

Filibusters The longest continuous speech in the history of the United States Senate was that of Senator Wayne Morse of Oregon on 24–25 April 1953, when he spoke on the Tidelands Oil Bill for 22 hrs 26 min without resuming his seat. Interrupted only briefly by the swearing-in of a new senator, Senator Strom Thurmond (South Carolina, Democrat) spoke against the Civil Rights Bill for 24 hrs 19 min on 28–29 Aug. 1957. The United States national record duration for a filibuster is 38 hrs 20 min by South Carolina senator J. Ralph Gasque, 55 who began at 12.40 p.m. on 3 April and yielded the floor at 3 a.m. on 5 April 1968. He was opposing a bill regulating the sale of eye-glasses.

ELECTIONS

Largest The largest election ever held was that for the Indian *Lok Sabha* (House of the People) on 1–10 March 1971. About 152,720,000 of the electorate of 272,630,000 chose from 2,785 candidates for 518 seats.

Closest The ultimate in close general elections occurred in Zanzibar (now part of Tanzania) on 18 Jan. 1961, when the Afro-Shirazi Party won by a single seat, after the seat of Chake-Chake on Pemba Island had been gained by a single vote.

Most one-sided North Korea recorded a 100 per cent. turn-out of electors and a 100 per cent vote for the Worker's Party of Korea in the general election of 8 Oct. 1962. The previous record had been set in the Albanian election of 4 June 1962, when all but seven of the electorate of 889,875 went to the polls—a 99.9992 per cent turn-out. Of the 889,868 voters, 889,828 voted for the candidates of the Albanian Party of Labour, *i.e.* 99.9955 per cent of the total poll.

Highest personal majority The highest personal majority was 157,692 from 192,909 votes cast, by H. H. Maharani of Jaipur (born 23 May 1919) in the Indian general election of Feb. 1962.

Communist parties The largest national Communist party outside the Soviet Union (14,254,000 members in 1971) and Communist states has been the Partito Communista Italiano (Italian Communist Party), with a membership of 2,300,000 in 1946. The total was 1,500,000 in 1973. The membership in mainland China was estimated to be 17,000,000 in 1970. The Communist Party of Great Britain, formed on 31 July 1920 in Cannon Street Station Hotel, London, attained its peak membership of 56,000 in December 1942, compared with 28,803 in November 1971. (Latest available figure).

Most parties The country with the greatest number of political parties is Italy with 73 registered for the elections of 19 May 1968. These included "Friends of the Moon" with one candidate.

PRIME MINISTERS

Oldest The longest lived Prime Minister of any country is believed to have been Christopher Hornsrud, Prime Minister of Norway from 28 Jan. to 15 Feb. 1928. He was born on 15 Nov. 1859 and died on 13 Dec. 1960, aged 101 years 28 days.

El Hadji Muhammad el Mokri, Grand Vizier of Morocco, died on 16 Sept. 1957, at a reputed age of 116 Muslim (*Hijri*) years, equivalent to 112.5 Gregorian years.

Longest term of office Prof. Dr. António de Oliveirar Salazar, G.C.M.G. (Hon.) (1889–1970) was the President of the Council of Ministers (*i.e.* Prime Minister) of Portugal from 5 July 1932 until 27 Sept. 1968—36 years 84 days. He was superseded 11 days after going into a coma.

UNITED KINGDOM

Parliament Earliest The earliest known use of the term "parliament" in an official English royal document, in the meaning of a summons to the King's council, dates from 19 Dec. 1241.

The Houses of Parliament of the United Kingdom in the Palace of Westminster, London, had 1,708 members (House of Lords 1,078, House of Commons 630) in June 1972.

Longest The longest English Parliament was the "Pensioners" Parliament of Charles II, which lasted from 8 May 1661 to 24 Jan. 1679, a period of 17 years 8 months and 16 days. The longest United Kingdom Parliament was that of George V, Edward VIII and George VI, lasting from 26 Nov. 1935 to 15 June 1945, a span of 9 years 6 months and 20 days.

Shortest The parliament of Edward I, summoned to Westminster for 30 May 1306, lasted only one day. The parliament of Charles II at Oxford from 21–28 March 1681 lasted 7 days. The shortest United Kingdom Parliament was that of George III, lasting from 15 Dec. 1806 to 29 April 1807, a period of only 4 months and 14 days.

Longest sittings The longest sitting in the House of Commons was one of 41½ hrs from 4 p.m. on 31 Jan. 1881 to 9.30 a.m. on 2 Feb. 1881, on the question of better Protection of Person and Property in Ireland. The longest sitting of the Lords has been 19 hrs 16 min from 2.30 p.m. on 29 Feb. to 9.46 a.m. on 1 March 1968 on the Commonwealth Immigrants Bill (Committee stage).

Most Time Consuming Legislation The most profligate use of parliamentary time was on the Government of Ireland Bill of 1893–4, which required 82 days in the House of Commons of which 46 days was in Committee. The record for a standing committee is 57 sittings (248 hrs and 4,734 Hansard columns) on the Housing Finance Bill between 25 Nov. 1971 and 27 March 1972.

Divisions The record number of divisions in the House of Commons is 43 in the single session of 20–21 March 1907. The largest division was one of 350–310 on a vote of confidence in 1892.

ELECTORATES

Largest and smallest The largest electorate of all time was the estimated 217,900 for Hendon, Middlesex, now part of Greater London, prior to the redistribution in 1941. The largest electorate for a seat in Great Britain is 96,966 for Meriden (1973–74 Register). In Antrim South, Northern Ireland the figure is 115,152. The smallest electorate of all-time was in Old Sarum (number of houses nil, population nil since *c.* 1540) in Wiltshire, with eight electors who returned two members in 1821, thus being 54,475 times as well represented as the Hendon electorate of 120 years later. There were no contested elections in Old Sarum for the 536 years from 1295 to 1831. The smallest electorate for any seat is Western Isles with 23,328 electors.

MAJORITIES

Party The largest party majorities were those of the Liberals, with 307 seats in 1832 and 356 seats in 1906. In 1931 the Coalition of Conservatives, Liberals and National Labour candidates had a majority of 425. The narrowest party majority was that of the Whigs in 1847, with a single seat.

The largest majority on a division was one of 463 (464 votes to 1), on a motion of "no confidence" in the conduct of World War II, on 29 Jan. 1942. Since the war the largest majority has been one of 461 (487 votes to 26) on 10 May 1967, during the debate on the government's application for Britain to join the

European Economic Community (the "Common Market").

Largest personal All-time The largest individual majority of any Member of Parliament was the 62,253 of Sir A. Cooper Rawson, M.P. (Conservative) at Brighton in 1931. He polled 75,205 votes against 12,952 votes for his closer opponent the Labour Candidate, Lewis Coleman Cohen, later Lord Cohen of Brighton (1897–1966), from an electorate of 128,779. The largest majority of any woman M.P. was 38,823 in the same General Election by the Countess of Iveagh (*née* Lady Gwendolen Florence Mary Onslow), C.B.E. (1881–1966), the Conservative member for Southend-on-Sea, Essex, from November 1927 to October 1935.

Current The largest majority in the 1970 Parliament is 41,433 held by James Kilfedder (Ulster Unionist) in Down North where he received 55,679 votes.

Narrowest personal All-time The closest result occurred in the General Election of 1886 at Ashton-under-Lyne, Lancashire when the Conservative and Liberal candidates both received 3,049 votes, The Returning Officer, Mr. James Walker, gave his casting vote for John E. W. Addison (Con.), who was duly returned while Alexander B. Rowley (Gladstone-Liberal) was declared unelected. On 13 Oct. 1892 there was a by-election at Cirencester, Gloucestershire, which resulted in an election petition after which the number of votes cast for the Conservative and Liberal were found to have been equal. A new election was ordered.

Two examples of majorities of one have occurred. At Durham in the 1895 General Election, Matthew Fowler (Lib.) with 1,111 votes defeated the Hon. Arthur R. D. Elliott (Liberal-Unionist) (1,110 votes) after a recount. At Exeter in the General Election of December 1910 a Liberal victory over the Conservatives by 4 votes was reversed on an election petition to a Conservative win by H.E. Duke K.C. (later the 1st Lord Merrivale) (Unionist) with 4,777 votes to R. H. St. Maur's (Lib.) 4,776 votes.

The smallest majority since "universal" franchise was one of two votes by Abraham John Flint (b. 1903), the National Labour candidate at Ilkeston, Derbyshire, on 27 Oct. 1931. He received 17,587 votes, compared with 17,585 for G. H. Oliver, D.C.M. (Labour).

Current The finest economy of effort in getting elected by any member of the 1970 Parliament was a majority of 13 votes by Ernle Money (Conservative) in Ipswich, Suffolk with 27,704 votes over Sir Dingle Foot, Q.C. (Labour) with 27,691.

Most recounts The greatest recorded number of recounts has been 7 in the case of Brighton, Kemptown on 16 Oct. 1964 when Dennis H. Hobden (Labour) won by 7 votes and at Peterborough on 1 April 1966 when Sir Harmer Nicholls Bt. (Conservative) won by 3 votes. The counts from the point of view of the loser Michael J. Ward (Labour) went +163, +163; +2, −2, −6, +1, −2, −3.

Fewest votes The smallest number of votes received by any candidate in a parliamentary election since "universal" franchise is 23 in the case of Richard Wort (Independent Conservative) in the Kinross and West Perthshire by-election of 7 Nov. 1963.

Most rapid change of fortune In 1874 Hardinge Stanley Giffard (Con.), later the 1st Earl of Halsbury (1823–1921), received one vote at Launceston, Cornwall. On 3 July 1877 he was returned unopposed for the same seat.

Greatest swing The greatest swing, at least since 1832, was that at Dartford, Kent when on 27 March 1920 Labour turned a Coalition majority of 9,370 to a win of 9,048.

The scene during one of the seven recounts at the election in 1964, at the Brighton Kemptown constituency

This represented a swing of 38.7 per cent. compared with the swing of 32.94 per cent at Sutton and Cheam, Surrey on 7 Dec. 1972 to elect the Liberal Graham Tope, 29. In the 1970 General Election an Ulster Unionist majority of 22,986 was turned into a Protestant Unionist majority of 2,679 over the sitting Member by Ian Richard Kyle Paisley. Since there was no Protestant Unionist candidate in 1966 no swing figure is therefore calculable. He gained 41.3% of the poll.

Highest poll The highest poll in any constituency since "universal" franchise was 93.42 per cent in Fermanagh and South Tyrone, Northern Ireland, at the General Election of 25 Oct. 1951, when there were 62,799 voters from an electorate of 67,219. The Anti-Partition candidate, Mr. Cahir Healy (b. 1877), was elected with a majority of 2,635 votes. The highest poll in any constituency in the 1970 General Election was 92.18 per cent in Fermanagh and South Tyrone. The highest figure in Great Britain was, as in 1966, North Cornwall with 85.11 per cent.

M.P.s Youngest Edmund Waller (1606–1687) was the Member of Parliament for Amersham, Buckinghamshire, in the Parliament of 1621, in which year he was 15. The official returns, however, do not show him as actually having taken his seat until two years later when, in the Parliament of 1623–24, he sat as Member for Ilchester. In 1435 Henry Long (1420–1490) was returned for an Old Sarum seat also at the age of 15. His precise date of birth is unknown. Minors were debarred in law in 1695 and in fact in 1832. Since that time the youngest Member of Parliament has been the Hon. Esmond Cecil Harmsworth (now the 2nd Viscount Rothermere) who was elected for the Isle of Thanet, Kent, on 28 Nov. 1919, when one day short of being 21 years 6 months. The youngest M.P. in 1970 was Mrs. Michael McAliskey (b. 23 April 1947) who was elected for Mid Ulster on 17 April 1969 and who made her maiden speech the day before her twenty-second birthday.

Oldest The oldest of all members was Samuel Young (b. 14 Feb. 1822), Nationalist M.P. for East Cavan (1892–1918), who died on 18 April 1918, aged 96 years 63 days. The oldest "Father of the House" in Parliamentary history was the Rt. Hon. Charles Pelham Villiers (b. 3 Jan. 1802), who was the Member for Wolverhampton when he died on 16 Jan. 1898, aged 96. He was a Member of Parliament for 63 years 6 days, having been returned at 16 elections. The longest sitting member in the present Parliament is the Rt. Hon. Sir Robin Turton M.C. (b. 8 Aug. 1903), who has been the Member for Thirsk and Malton since 1929. He attributes his original adoption to the sense of economy of his committee, who, on the death of his uncle, did not wish to waste their "Vote for Turton" posters.

Longest span The longest span of service of any M.P., is 63 years 10 months (October 1900 to September 1964) by the Rt. Hon. Sir Winston Leonard Spencer Churchill, K.G., O.M., C.H., T.D. (1874–1965), with a break only from November 1922 to October 1924. The longest unbroken span was that of C. P. Villiers (see below). The longest span in the Palace of Westminster (both Houses of Parliament) has been 73 years by the 10th Earl of Wemyss, G.C.V.O., who, as Sir Francis Wemyss-Charteris-Douglas, served as M.P. for East Gloucestershire (1841–46) and Haddingtonshire (1847–83) and then took his seat in the House of Lords, dying on 30 June 1914, aged 95 years 330 days.

Earliest women M.P.s The first woman to be elected to the House of Commons was Mme. Constance Georgine Markievicz (*née* Gore Booth). She was elected as member (Sinn Fein) for St. Patrick's Dublin, in December 1918. The first woman to take her seat was the Viscountess Astor, C. H. (1879–1964) (b. Nancy Witcher Langhorne at Danville, Virginia, U.S.A.; formerly Mrs. Robert Gould Shaw), who was elected Unionist member for the Sutton Division of Plymouth, Devon, on 28 Nov. 1919, and took her seat three days later.

HOUSE OF LORDS

Oldest Member The oldest member ever was the Rt. Hon. the 5th Baron Penrhyn, who was born on 21 Nov. 1865 and died on 3 Feb. 1967, aged 101 years 74 days. The oldest now is the Rt. Hon. Ethel Sydney Keith, the Countess of Kintore (b. 20 Sept. 1874).

Youngest Member The youngest member of the House of Lords is H.R.H. the Prince Charles Philip Arthur George, K.G., the Prince of Wales (b. 14 Nov. 1948). All Dukes of Cornwall, of whom Prince Charles is the 24th, are technically eligible to sit, regardless of age—in his case from his succession on 6 Feb. 1952, aged 3. The 20th and 21st holders, later King George IV (b. 1762) and King Edward VII (b. 1841), were technically entitled to sit from birth. The youngest creation of a life peer under the Peerage Act 1958 has been that of Lord Tanlaw, formerly the Hon. Simon MacKay (b. 30 March 1934) at the age of 37 years and 8 days. However Lady Masham (b. 14 April 1935) was created Baroness Masham of Ilton at the age of 34 years 262 days.

Longest speech The longest recorded continuous speech in the House of Commons was that of Henry Peter Brougham (1778–1868) on 7 Feb. 1828, when he spoke for 6 hrs on Law Reform. He ended at 10.40 p.m. and the report of this speech occupied 12 columns of the next day's edition of *The Times*. Brougham, created the 1st Lord Brougham and Vaux on 22 Nov. 1830, also holds the House of Lords record, also with six hrs, on 7 Oct. 1831, speaking on the second reading of the Reform Bill.

The longest post-war speech has been one of 2 hrs 37 min by Malcolm K. Macmillan (b. 1913), the Labour member for the Western Isles, on 15–16 March 1961.

Greatest parliamentary petition The greatest petition was supposed to be the Great Chartist Petition of 1848 but of the 5,706,000 "signatures" only 1,975,496 were valid. The all time largest was for the abolition of Entertainment Duty with 3,107,080 signatures presented on 5 June 1951.

PREMIERSHIP

Longest term No United Kingdom Prime Minister has yet matched in duration the continuous term of office of Great Britain's first Prime Minister the Rt. Hon. Sir Robert Walpole, K.G., later the 1st Earl of Orford (1676–1745), First Lord of the Treasury and Chancellor, of the Exchequer from 3 April 1721 to 12 Feb. 1742. The office was not, however, officially recognised until 1905, since when the longest tenure has been that of Herbert Henry Asquith, later the 1st Earl of Oxford and Asquith (1852–1928), with 8 years 243 days from

8 April 1908 to 7 Dec. 1916. This was 7 days longer than the three terms of Sir Winston Churchill, between 1940 and 1955. The Hon. Sir Thomas Playford, G.C.M.G. (b. 5 July 1896) was State Premier of South Australia from 5 Nov. 1938 to 10 March 1965.

Shortest term The Rt. Hon. Sir James Waldegrave, K.G., 2nd Earl of Waldegrave (1715–63) held office for 5 days from 8–12 June 1757 but was unable to form a ministry. The shortest term of any ministry was that of the 1st Duke of Wellington, K.G., G.C.B., G.C.H. (1769–1852), whose third ministry survived only 22 days from 17 Nov. to 9 Dec. 1834.

Most times The only Prime Minister to have accepted office five times was the Rt. Hon. Stanley Baldwin, later the 1st Earl Baldwin of Bewdley (1867–1947). His ministries were those of 22 May 1923 to 22 Jan. 1924, 4 Nov. 1924 to 5 June 1929, 7 June 1935 to 21 Jan. 1936, from then until 12 Dec. 1936 and from then until 28 May 1937.

Longest lived The oldest Prime Minister of the United Kingdom has been the Rt. Hon. Sir Winston Leonard Spencer Churchill, K.G., O.M., C.H., T.D. (b. 30 Nov. 1874), who surpassed the age of the Rt. Hon. William Ewart Gladstone (1809–98) on 21 April 1963 and died on 24 Jan. 1965, aged 90 years 55 days.

Youngest The youngest of Great Britain's 47 Prime Ministers has been the Rt. Hon. the Hon. William Pitt (b. 28 May 1759), who accepted the King's invitation to be First Lord of the Treasury on 19 Dec. 1783, aged 24 years 205 days, He had previously declined on 27 Feb. 1783, when aged 23 years 275 days.

CHANCELLORSHIP

Longest and shortest tenures The Rt. Hon. Sir Robert Walpole, K.G., later the 1st Earl of Orford (1676–1745), served 22 years 5 months as Chancellor of the Exchequer, holding office continuously from 12 Oct. 1715 to 12 Feb. 1742, except for the period from 16 April 1717 to 2 April 1721. The briefest tenure of this office was 26 days in the case of the Baron (later the 1st Earl of) Mansfield (1705–93), from 11 Sept. to 6 Oct. 1767.

Most appointments The only man with four terms in this office was the Rt. Hon. William Ewart Gladstone (1809–98) in 1852–55, 1859–66, 1873–74 and 1880–82.

SPEAKERSHIP

Longest Arthur Onslow (1691–1768) was elected Mr. Speaker on 23 Jan. 1728, at the age of 36. He held the position for 33 years 54 days, until 18 March 1761.

4. MILITARY AND DEFENCE

WAR

In the Autumn of 1973, Guinness Superlatives Ltd. are publishing a specialist volume entitled The Guinness History of Land Warfare *(£2.95) by Kenneth Macksey. It deals with the subject in greater detail, and is available from all good bookshops, or if in difficulties, direct from the publishers at the address at the front of this volume.*

Longest The longest of history's countless wars was the "Hundred Years War" between England and France, which lasted from 1338 to 1453 (115 years), although it may be said that the Holy War, comprising the nine Crusades from the First (1096–1104) to the Ninth (1270–91), extended over 195 years. It has been calculated that in the 3,467 years since 1496 B.C. there have been only 230 years of peace throughout the civilised world.

Last battle on British soil The last pitched land battle in Britain was at Culloden Field, Drummossie Moor, Inverness-shire, on 16 April 1746. The last Clan battle in Scotland was between Clan Mackintosh and Clan MacDonald at Mulroy,

Inverness-shire, in 1689. The last battle on English soil was the Battle of Sedgemoor, Somerset, on 6 July 1685, when the forces of James II defeated the supporters of Charles II's illegitimate son, James Scott (formerly called Fitzroy or Crofts), the Duke of Monmouth (1649–85). During the Jacobite rising of 1745–46, there was a skirmish at Clifton Moor, Westmorland, on 18 Dec. 1745, when the British forces under Prince William, the Duke of Cumberland (1721–65), brushed with the rebels of Prince Charles Edward Stuart (1720–88) with about 12 killed on the King's side and 5 Highlanders. This was a tactical victory for the Scots under Lord George Murray.

Shortest war The shortest war on record was that between the United Kingdom and Zanzibar (now part of Tanzania) from 9.02 to 9.40 a.m. on 27 Aug. 1896. The U.K. battle fleet under Rear-Admiral (later Admiral Sir) Harry Holdsworth Rawson (1843–1910) delivered an ultimatum to the self-appointed Sultan Sa'id Khalid to evacuate his palace and surrender. This was not forthcoming until after 38 minutes of bombardment. Admiral Rawson received the Brilliant Star of Zanzibar (first class) from the new Sultan Hamud ibn Muhammad. It was proposed at one time that elements of the local populace should be compelled to defray the cost of the ammunition used.

Bloodiest war By far the most costly war in terms of human life was World War II (1939–45), in which the total number of fatalities, including battle deaths and civilians of all countries, is estimated to have been 54,800,000 assuming 25 million U.S.S.R. fatalities and 7,800,000 Chinese civilians killed. The country which suffered most was Poland with 6,028,000 or 22.2 per cent of her population of 27,007,000 killed.

In the case of the United Kingdom, however, the heaviest casualties occurred in World War I (1914–18), with 765,399 killed out of 5,500,000 engaged (13.9 per cent), compared with 265,000 out of 5,896,000 engaged (4.49 per cent) in World War II. The heaviest total for one day was 21,392 fatalities and 35,493 wounded in the First Battle of the Somme on 1 July 1916. The total casualties in the Third Battle of Ypres (Passchendaele), from 31 July to 6 Nov. 1917, were about 575,000 (238,313 British and 337,000 German). The total death roll from World War I was only 17.7 per cent of that of World War II, viz 9,700,000.

Most costly Although no satisfactory computation has been published, it is certain that the material cost of World War II far transcended that of the rest of history's wars put together. In the case of the United Kingdom the cost of £34,423 million was over five times as great as that of World War I (£6,700 million) and 158.6 times that of the Boer War of 1899–1902 (£217 million). The total cost of World War II to the Soviet Union was estimated semi-officially in May 1959 at 2,500,000,000,000 roubles (£100,000 million).

Bloodiest civil war The bloodiest civil war in history was the T'ai-p'ing ("Peace") rebellion, in which peasant sympathizers of the Southern Ming dynasty fought the Manchu Government troops in China from 1853 to 1864. The rebellion was led by the deranged Hung Hsiu-ch'üan (poisoned himself in June 1864), who imagined himself to be a younger brother of Jesus Christ. His force was named T'ai-p'ing T'ien Kuo (Heavenly Kingdom of Great Peace). According to the best estimates, the loss of life was between 20,000,000 and 30,000,000, including more than 100,000 killed by Government forces in the sack of Nanking on 19–21 July 1864.

Bloodiest battle
Modern The battle with the greatest recorded number of fatalities was the First Battle of the Somme from 1 July to 19 November 1916, with more than 1,030,000 —614,105 British and French and c. 420,000 (not 650,000) German. The gunfire was heard on Hampstead

Heath, London. The greatest battle of World War II and the greatest ever conflict of armour was the Battle of Kursk of 5–22 July 1943 on the Eastern front, which involved 1,300,000 Red Army troops with 3,600 tanks, 20,000 guns and 3,130 aircraft in repelling a German Army Group which had 2,500 tanks. The final investment of Berlin by the Red Army in 1945 is however, said to have involved 3,500,000 men; 52,000 guns and mortars; 7,750 tanks and 11,000 aircraft on both sides.

Ancient Modern historians give no credence to the casualty figures attached to ancient battles, such as the 250,000 reputedly killed at Plataea (Greeks v. Persians) in 479 B.C. or the 200,000 allegedly killed in a single day at Châlons-sur-Marne, France, in A.D. 451. This view is on the grounds that it must have been logistically quite impossible to maintain forces of such a size in the field at that time.

British soil The bloodiest battle fought on British soil was the Battle of Towton, in Yorkshire, on 29 March 1461, when 36,000 Yorkists defeated 40,000 Lancastrians. The total loss has been estimated at between 28,000 and 38,000 killed. A figure of 80,000 British dead was attributed by Tacitus to the battle of A.D. 61 between Queen Boudicca (Boadicea) of the Iceni and the Roman Governor of Britain Suetonius Paulinus, for the loss of 400 Romans in an Army of 10,000. The site of the battle is unknown but may have been near Borough Hill, Daventry, Northamptonshire, or more probably near Hampstead Heath, London. It is improbable that, for such a small loss, the Romans could have killed more than 20,000 Britons.

GREATEST INVASION

Seaborne The greatest invasion in military history was the Allied land, air and sea operation gainst the Normandy coasts of France on D-day, 6 June 1944. Thirty-eight convoys of 745 ships moved in on the first three days, supported by 4,066 landing craft, carrying 185,000 men and 20,000 vehicles, and 347 minesweepers. The air assault comprised 18,000 paratroopers from 1,087 aircraft. The 42 available divisions possessed an air support from 13,175 aircraft. Within a month 1,100,000 troops, 200,000 vehicles and 750,000 tons of stores were landed.

Airborne The largest airborne invasion was the Anglo-American assault of three divisions (34,000 men), with 2,800 aircraft and 1,600 gliders, near Arnhem, in the Netherlands, on 17 Sept. 1944.

Last on the soil of Great Britain The last invasion of Great Britain occurred on 12 Feb. 1797, when the Irish-American adventurer General Tate landed at Carreg Gwastad with 1,400 French troops. They surrendered near Fishguard, Pembrokeshire, to Lord Cawdor's force of the Castlemartin Yeomanry and some local inhabitants armed with pitchforks. The U.K. Crown Dependency of the Channel Islands were occupied by German armed forces from 30 June 1940 to 8 May 1945.

Worst sieges The worst siege in history was the 880-day siege of Leningrad, U.S.S.R. by the German Army from 30 Aug. 1941 until 27 Jan. 1944. The best estimate is that between 1.3 and 1.5 million defenders and citizens died. The longest siege in military history was that of Centa which was besieged by the Moors under Mulai Ismail for the 26 years 1674 to 1700.

LARGEST ARMED FORCES
Numerically, the country with the largest regular armed force is the U.S.S.R., with 3,375,000 at mid-1972, compared with the U.S.A.'s 2,434,000 at the same date. The Chinese People's Liberation Army, which includes naval and air services, has 2,880,000 regulars, but there is also a civilian home guard militia once claimed to be 200 million strong but regarded by the Institute for Strategic Studies to have an effective element of not more than 5,000,000.

Red Army gunners in the front line during the 880 day siege of Leningrad, 1941-44

DEFENCE

The estimated level of spending on armaments throughout the world in 1972 was $234,000 million (*then £93,600 million*). This represents £24.75 per person per annum, or more than 6 per cent of the world's total production of goods and services. It was estimated in 1970 that there were 14,950,000 full-time military and naval personnel and some 30,000,000 armament workers.

The expenditure on "defence" by the government of the United States in the year ending 30 June 1972 was $76,495 million (*£30,600 million*), or 6.9 per cent of the country's Gross National Product.

The U.S.S.R.'s defence expenditure in 1972 has been estimated to be equivalent to $91,000 million and thus markedly higher than the U.S. level. This represents some 15 per cent of Gross National Product.

At the other extreme is Andorra, whose defence budget, voted in 1972, was reduced to £2.00.

NAVIES

Largest The largest navy in the world is the United States Navy, with a manpower of 602,000 and 198,000 Marines at 30 June 1972. The active strength in 1972 included 14 attack and 2 anti-submarine carriers, 101 nuclear submarines in commission of which 41 are ballistic-missile armed, 73 guided missile ships including 8 cruisers, 29 destroyers and 30 frigates, and 72 amphibious warfare ships.

The strength of the Royal Navy in mid-1972 was an aircraft carrier, 3 commando ships, 2 assault ships, 2 missile armed cruisers, 12 destroyers (9 with guided missiles), 62 frigates, 9 nuclear (including 4 with *Polaris* missiles) and 24 other submarines and 44 minesweepers. The uniformed strength was 82,000 including Fleet Air Arm and Royal Marines in mid-1972. In 1914 the Royal Navy had 542 warships including 31 battleships with 5 building.

Greatest naval battle The greatest number of ships and aircraft ever involved in a sea-air action was 231 ships and 1,996 aircraft in the Battle of Leyte Gulf, in the Philippines. It raged from 22 to 27 Oct. 1944, with 166 United States and 65 Japanese warships engaged, of which 26 Japanese and 6 U.S. ships were sunk. In addition 1,280 U.S. and 716 Japanese aircraft were engaged. The greatest naval battle of modern times was the Battle of Jutland on 31 May 1916, in which 151 Royal Navy warships were involved against 101 German warships. The Royal Navy lost 14 ships and 6,097 men and the German fleet 11 ships and 2,545 men. The greatest of ancient naval battles was the Battle of Lepanto on 7 Oct. 1571, when an estimated 25,000 Turks were lost in 250 galleys, sunk by the Spanish, Venetian and Papal forces of more than 300 ships in the Gulf of Lepanto, now called Korinthiakós, Kólpos, or the Gulf of Kórinthos (Corinth), Greece.

Greatest evacuation The greatest evacuation in military history was that carried out by 1,200 Allied naval and civil craft from the beachhead at Dunkerque (Dunkirk), France, between 27 May and 4 June 1940. A total of 338,226 British and French troops were taken off.

ARMIES

Largest Numerically, the world's largest army is that of the People's Republic of China, with a total strength of about 2,500,000 in mid-1972. The total size of the U.S.S.R.'s army (including the ground elements of the Air Defence Command) in mid-1972 was estimated at 2,000,000 men, believed to be organised into about 164 divisions with a maximum strength of 10,000 each. The strength of the British Army was 180,500 in mid-1972.

Oldest The oldest army in the world is the 83-strong Swiss Guard in the Vatican City, with a regular foundation dating back to 21 Jan. 1506. Its origins, however, extend back before 1400.

Oldest old soldiers The oldest old soldier of all time was probably John B. Salling of the army of the Confederate States of America and the last accepted survivor of the U.S. Civil War (1861–65). He died in Kingsport, Tennessee, U.S.A., on 16 March 1959, aged 113 years 1 day. The oldest Chelsea pensioner, based only on the evidence of his tombstone, was the 111-yeard-old William Hiseland (b. 6 Aug. 1620, d. 7 Feb. 1732). The last survivor of the Afghan war of 1878–79 was Alfred Hawker, who died on 10 Dec. 1962, aged 104 years 41 days.

Tallest soldiers The tallest soldier of all time was Väinö Myllyrinne (1909–63) who was inducted into the Finnish Army when he was 7 ft 3 in *2,20 m* and later grew to 8 ft 1¼ in *2,47 m*. The British Army's tallest soldier was Benjamin Crow who was signed on at Litchfield in November 1947 when he was 7 ft 1 in *2,15 m* tall. Edward Evans (1924–58), who later grew to 7 ft 8½ in *2,34 m* was in the Army when he was 6 ft 10 in *2,08 m*.

British regimental records The oldest regular regiment in the British Army is the Royal Scots, raised in French service in 1633, though the Buffs (Royal East Kent Regiment) can trace back their origin to independent companies in Dutch pay as early as 1572. The Coldstream Guards, raised in 1650, were, however, placed on the establishment of the British Army before the Royal Scots and the Buffs. The oldest armed body in the United Kingdom is the Honourable Artillery Company. Formed from the Finsbury Archers, it received its charter from Henry VIII in 1537, and is now the senior regiment of the Territorial and Army Volunteer Reserve. The infantry regiment with most battle honours is The Royal Hampshire Regt. with 153.

TANKS

Note—Guinness Superlatives Ltd. has newly published a specialist volume entitled The Guinness Book of Tank Facts and Feats *by Kenneth Macksey (£2.75). This work deals with all the aspects of the development and history of the tank and other armoured fighting vehicles in greater detail, and is available from all good bookshops or if in difficulties, direct from the publishers at the address at the front of this volume.*

Earliest The first fighting tank was "Mother" *alias* "Big Willie" built by William Foster & Co. Ltd. of Lincoln,

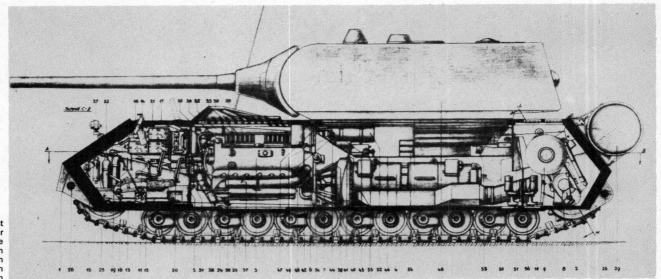

The heaviest tank ever constructed, the German 189 ton Maus II, which was never in action

and first tested on 12 Jan. 1916. Tanks were first taken into action by the Machine Gun Corps (Heavy Section), which later became the Royal Tank Corps, at the battle of Flers, in France, on 15 Sept. 1916. The Mark I male tank was armed with a pair of 6-lb. guns and two machine-guns. The Mark I Male weighed 28 tons *28,4 tonnes* and was driven by a motor developing 105 horse-power which gave it a maximum road speed of 4 to 5 m.p.h. *6–8 km/h.*

Heaviest The heaviest tank ever constructed was the German Panzer Kampfwagen Maus II, which weighed 189 tons *192 tonnes*. By 1945 it had reached only the experimental stage and was not proceeded with.

The heaviest operational tank used by any army was the 81.5 ton *82,8 tonnes* 13-man French Char de Rupture 3C of 1923. It carried a 155 mm. howitzer and had two 250 h.p. engines giving a maximum speed of 8 m.p.h. *12 km/h.* On 7 Nov. 1957, in the annual military parade in Moscow, U.S.S.R., a Soviet tank possibly heavier than the German Jagd Tiger II (71.7 tons [*72,8 tonnes*]), built by Henschel, and certainly heavier than the Stalin III, was displayed.

The heaviest British tank ever built is the 76-ton *77 tonnes* prototype "Tortoise". With a crew of seven and a designed speed of 12 m.p.h. *19 km/h*, this tank had a width two inches *5 cm* less than that of the operational 65-ton *66 tonnes* "Conqueror". The most heavily armed is the 52-ton *52,8 tonnes* "Chieftain", put into service in November 1966, with a 120 mm gun.

GUNS

Earliest Although it cannot be accepted as proved, the best opinion is that the earliest guns were constructed in North Africa, possibly by Arabs, in *c.* 1250. The earliest representation of an English gun is contained in an illustrated manuscript dated 1326 at Oxford. The earliest anti-aircraft gun was an artillery piece on a high angle mounting used in the Franco-Prussian War of 1870 by the Prussians against French balloons.

Largest The remains of the most massive gun ever constructed were found near Frankfurt am Main, Germany, in 1945. It was the "Schwerer Gustav" or "Dora", which had a barrel 94.7 ft *28,87 m* long, with a calibre of 800 mm (31.5 in), and a breech weighing 108 tons *109 tonnes*. The maximum charge was 2,000 kg *4,409 lb.* of cordite to fire a shell weighing 4,800 kg *4.7 tons* a distance of 55 km *34 miles*. The maximum projectile was one of 7 tons *7,1 tonnes* with a range of 22 miles *35 km*. Each gun with its carriage weighed 1,323 tons *1 344 tonnes* and required a crew of 1,500 men.

During the 1914–18 war the British army used a gun of 18 in *457 mm* calibre. The barrel alone weighed 125 tons *127 tonnes*. In World War II the "Bochebuster", a train-mounted howitzer with a calibre of 18 in *457 mm* firing a 2,500 lb. *1 133 kg* shell to a maximum range of 22,800 yds *20 850 m*, was used from 1940 onwards as part of the Kent coast defences.

Greatest range The greatest range ever attained by a gun is by the H.A.R.P. (High Altitude Research Project) gun consisting of two 16.5 in *419 mm* calibre barrels in tandem in Barbados. In 1968 a 200 lb. *90 kg* projectile had been fired to a height of 400,000 ft (75¾ miles [*121,9 km*]). The static V.3 underground firing tubes built in 50 degree shafts near Mimoyecques, near Calais, France to bombard London were never operative due to R.A.F. bombing.

The famous long range guns, which shelled Paris in World War I, were the "Lange Berta" of which seven were built with a calibre of 210 mm (*8.26 in*), a designed range of 79.5 miles *127,9 km* and an achieved range of more than 75 miles *120 km*.

Mortars The largest mortars ever constructed were Mallets mortar (Woolwich Arsenal, London, 1857), and the "Little David" of World War II, made in the U.S.A. Each had a calibre of 36¼ in *920 mm*, but neither was ever used in action.

Largest cannon The highest calibre cannon ever constructed is the *Tsar Puchka* (King of Cannons), now housed in the Kremlin, Moscow, U.S.S.R. It was built in the 16th century with a bore of 36 in *915 mm* and a barrel 17 ft *5,18 m* long. It was designed to fire cannon balls weighing 2 tons but was never used. The Turks fired up to seven shots per day from a bombard 26-ft *7,92 m* long, with an internal calibre of 42 in *1 066 mm* against the walls of Constantinople (now Istanbul) from 12 April to 29 May 1453. It was dragged by 60 oxen and 200 men and fired a stone cannon ball weighing 1,200 lb. *544 kg*.

Military engines The largest military catapults, or onagers, were capable of throwing a missile weighing 60 lb. *27 kg* a distance of 500 yds *457 m*.

Longest march The longest march in military history was the famous Long March by the Chinese Communists in 1934–35. In 368 days, of which 268 days were of movement, from October to October, their force of 90,000 covered 6,000 miles *9 650 km* northward from Kiangis to Yünnan. They crossed 18 mountain ranges and six major rivers and lost all but 22,000 of their force in continual rear-guard actions against Nationalist Kuo-min-tang (K.M.T.) forces.

Most rapid march The most rapid recorded march by foot-soldiers was one of 12 Spanish leagues (42 miles [*67 km*]) in 26 hours on 28–29 July 1809, by the Light Brigade under Brigadier-(later Major-) General Robert Craufurd (1764–1812), coming to the relief of Lieut.-Gen. Sir Arthur Wellesley, later Field Marshall the 1st Duke of Wellington (1769–1852), after the Battle of Talavera (Talavera de la Reina, Toledo, Spain) in the Peninsular War.

The longest recorded march by a body of 60 without any fall-outs was one of 14 hours 23 minutes (13 hours on the march) by the London Rifle Brigade on 18–19 April 1914 from Duke of York Steps, London, to Brighton Aquarium. On 8 April 1922, two officers and 27 other ranks of the London Scottish Regiment covered the 53 miles *85 km* from London to Brighton in 13 hours 59 minutes, each carrying 46 lb. *20,8 kg* of equipment, but two men failed to finish.

AIR FORCES
The earliest autonomous air force is the Royal Air Force whose origin began with the Royal Flying Corps (created 13 May 1912); the Air Battalion of the Royal Engineers (1 April 1911) and the Corps of Royal Engineers Balloon Section (1878) which was first operational in Bechuanaland (now Botswana) in 1884.

Largest The greatest Air Force of all time was the United States Army Air Force (now called the U.S. Air Force), which had 79,908 aircraft in July 1944 and 2,411,294 personnel in March 1944. The U.S. Air Force including strategic air forces had 730,000 personnel and 6,000 combat aircraft in mid-1972. The U.S.S.R. Air Force, with about 550,000 men in mid-1972, had 9,000 combat aircraft. In addition, the U.S.S.R.'s Offensive Strategic Rocket Forces had about 350,000 operational personnel in mid-1972. The strenth of the Royal Air Force was 110,000 with some 500 combat aircraft in mid 1972.

BOMBS
The heaviest conventional bomb ever used operationally was the Royal Air Force's "Grand Slam", weighing 22,000 lb. *9 975 kg* and measuring 25 ft 5 in *7,74 m* long, dropped on Bielefeld railway viaduct, Germany, on 14 March 1945. In 1949 the United States Air Force tested a bomb weighing 42,000 lb. *19 050 kg* at Muroc Dry Lake, California, U.S.A.

Atomic The two atom bombs dropped on Japan by the United States in 1945 each had an explosive power equivalent to that of 20,000 short tons *20 kilotons* of trinitrotoluene ($C_7H_5O_6N_3$), called T.N.T. The one dropped on Hiroshima, known as "Little Boy", was 10 ft *3,04 m* long and weighed 9,000 lb. *4 080 kg*. The most powerful thermo-nuclear device so far tested is one with a power equivalent to 57,000,000 short tons of T.N.T., or 57 megatons, detonated by the U.S.S.R. in the Novaya Zemlya area at 8.33 a.m. G.M.T. on 30 Oct. 1961. The shock wave was detected to have circled the world three times, taking 36 hours 27 min for the first circuit. Some estimates put the power of this device at between 62 and 90 megatons. On 9 Aug. 1961, Nikita Khrushchyov, then the Chairman of the Council of Ministers of the U.S.S.R., declared that the Soviet Union was capable of constructing a 100-megaton bomb, and announced the possession of one in East Berlin, Germany, on 16 Jan. 1963. It has been estimated that such a bomb would make a crater 19 miles *30 km* in diameter and would cause serious fires at a range of from 36 to 40 miles *58–64 km*. The atom bomb became inevitable with the meso-thorium experiments of Otto Hahn, Fritz Strassman and Lise Meitner on 17 Dec. 1938. Work started in the U.S.S.R. on atomic bombs in June 1942 although their first chain

reaction was not achieved until December 1945 by Dr. Igor Kurchatov. The patent for the fusion or H bomb was filed in the United States on 26 May 1946 by Dr. Janos (John) von Neumann (1903–57), a Hungarian-born mathematician, and Dr. Klaus Emil Julius Fuchs (born in Germany, 1911), the defected physicist.

Largest nuclear arsenal It has been estimated that in 1970 the United States total of 1,054 I.C.B.M.s (Inter-Continental Ballistic Missiles) was surpassed by the U.S.S.R. whose 1972 total has been put at 1,530. The greatest S.L.B.M. (Submarine launched Ballistic Missile) armoury was in 1972 that of the United States with 656 compared with 494 in service in the U.S.S.R. Navy. The U.S.S.R.'s arsenal was estimated at 2,100 including 1,530 I.C.B.M.s.

No official estimate has been published of the potential power of the device known as Doomsday, but this far surpasses any tested weapon. A 50,000 megaton cobalt-salted device has been mooted which could kill an entire human race except those who were deep underground and who stayed there for more than five years.

Largest "conventional" explosion The largest use of conventional explosive was for the demolition of German U-Boat pens at Heligoland on 18 Apr. 1947. A charge of 3,997 tons *4 061 tonnes* was detonated by E. C. Jellis aboard H.M.S. Lasso lying 9 miles *14,4 km* out to sea.

5. JUDICIAL

LEGISLATION AND LITIGATION

STATUTES
Oldest The earliest known judicial code was that of King Urnammu during the third dynasty of Ur, Iraq, in *c*. 2145 B.C. The oldest English statute is a section of the Statute of Marlborough of 1267, retitled in 1948 "The Distress Act, 1267". Some statutes enacted by Henry II (d. 1189) and earlier kings are even more durable as they have been assimilated into the Common Law. An extreme example is Alfred, Dooms, c. 43 of *c*. A.D. 890 which contains the passage "judge thou not one doom to the rich, another to the poor".

Longest in the United Kingdom Measured in bulk the longest statute of the United Kingdom, is the Income Tax and Corporation Tax Act, 1970, which runs to 540 sections, 15 schedules and 670 pages. It is 1½ in *37 mm* thick and costs £2.80. However, its 540 sections are surpassed in number by the 748 of the Merchant Shipping Act, 1894.

Of old statutes, 31 George III xiv, the Land Tax Act of 1791, written on parchment, consists of 780 skins forming a roll 1,170 ft *360 m* long.

Shortest The shortest statute is the Parliament (Qualification of Women) Act, 1918, which runs to 27 operative words—"A woman shall not be disqualified by sex or marriage from being elected to or sitting or voting as a Member of the Common House of Parliament". Section 2 contains a further 14 words giving the short title.

Most It was computed in March 1959 that the total number of laws on Federal and State statute books in the United States was 1,156,644. The Illinois State Legislature only discovered in April 1967 that it had made the sale of cigarettes illegal and punishable by a $100 fine for a second offence in 1907.

Earliest English patent The earliest of all known English patents was that granted by Henry VI in 1449 to Flemish-born John of Utynam for making the coloured glass required for the windows of Eton College. The peak number of applications for patents filed in the United Kingdom in any one year was 63,614 in 1969.

Most protracted litigation The longest contested law suit ever recorded ended in Poona, India on 28 April 1966, when Balasaheb Patloji Thorat received a favourable judgment on a suit filed by his ancestor Maloji Thorat 761 years earlier in 1205. The points at issue were rights of presiding over public functions and precedences at religious festivals.

The dispute over the claim of the Prior and Convent of Durham Cathedral to administer the spiritualities of the diocese during a vacancy in the See grew fierce in 1283. It smouldered until 1939, having flared up in 1672, 1890 and 1920. In 1939 the Archbishop of Canterbury exercised his metropolitan rights and appointed the Dean as guardian of spiritualities of Durham "without prejudice to the general issue", then 656 years old.

Most inexplicable Statute Certain passages in several Acts have always defied interpretation and the most inexplicable must be a matter of opinion. A Judge of the Court of Session of Scotland has sent the Editors his candidate which reads, "In the Nuts (unground), (other than ground nuts) Order, the expression nuts shall have reference to such nuts, other than ground nuts, as would but for this amending Order not qualify as nuts (unground) (other than ground nuts) by reason of their being nuts (unground)."

Longest British trial The longest trial in the annals of British justice was the Tichborne personation case. The civil trial began on 11 May 1871, lasted 103 days and collapsed on 6 March 1872. The criminal trial went on for 188 days, resulting in a sentence on 28 Feb. 1874 for two counts of perjury (14 years imprisonment and hard labour) on the London-born Arthur Orton, *alias* Thomas Castro (1834–98), who claimed to be Roger Charles Tichborne (1829–54), the elder brother of Sir Alfred Joseph Doughty-Tichborne, 11th Bt. (1839–66). The whole case, during which, miraculously, no juryman fell ill, thus spanned 827 days and cost £55,315. The jury were out for only 30 minutes.

The impeachment of Warren Hastings (1732–1818), which began in 1788, dragged on for seven years until 23 April 1795, but the trial lasted only 149 days. He was appointed a member of the Privy Council in 1814.

The longest recent criminal trial was that of "The Angry Brigade" concerning 25 explosions and two shootings between Jan. 1968 and July 1971. It began at the Old Bailey on 30 May 1972 and concluded on the 109th day on 4 Dec. 1972. The cost was estimated at £750,000.

Murder The longest murder trial in Britain was that in which Ronald and Reginald Kray (twins), 35, were found guilty of the murder by shooting of George Cornell, 38, at the Blind Beggar public house on 9 Mar. 1966, and by stabbing of Jack "The Hat" McVitie, 38, in Evering Road, Stoke Newington in October 1967. They were sentenced by Mr. Justice Melford Stevenson to imprisonment for not less than 30 years on 5 March 1969 after a 39-day trial at the Old Bailey, London. The costs of the trial were estimated at more than £200,000.

The shortest recorded British murder hearings were *R. v. Murray* on 28 Feb. 1957 and *R. v. Cawley* at Winchester Assizes on 14 Dec. 1959. The proceedings occupied only 30 sec on each occasion.

Divorce The longest trial of a divorce case in Britain was *Gibbons* v. *Gibbons and Roman and Halperin*. On 19 March 1962, after 28 days, Mr. Alfred George

The Kray brothers, left to right, Reginald, Charles and Ronald. The twins Reg and Ron were the central figures in Britain's largest ever murder trial

Boyd Gibbons was granted a decree *nisi* against his wife Dorothy for adultery with Mr. John Halperin of New York City, N.Y., U.S.A.

Longest address The longest address in a British court was in *Globe and Phoenix Gold Mining Co. Ltd. v. Amalgamated Properties of Rhodesia*. Mr. William Henry Upjohn K.C. (1853–1941) concluded his speech on 22 Sept 1916, having addressed the court for 45 days.

Highest bail The highest amount ever demanded as bail was $46,500,000 (*then £16,608,333*) against Antonio De Angelis in a civil damages suit by the Harbor Tank Storage Co. filed in the Superior Court, Jersey City, New Jersey, U.S.A. on 16 Jan. 1964. (See also Greatest swindle, page 199).

The highest bail figure in a British court is £140,000, granted to Manick Banthia at Uxbridge Court, Middlesex on 14 Oct. 1966. The amount involved £30,000 on his own recognizances, a surety of £50,000 and three of £20,000 each. He was charged with an attempt illegally to export £30,000 from London Airport in 60 Bank envelopes. Two other men, Joe Cohen and Amarendra Goswami also charged, had a combined bail of £170,000.

On 2 June 1959 the original bail fixed at Dublin, Ireland, for Dr. Paul Singer, aged 48, managing director of Shanahan's Stamp Auctions Ltd., was £100,000. This was later reduced to £15,000.

Best attended trial The greatest attendance at any trial was that of Major Jesús Sosa Blanco, aged 51, for an alleged 108 murders. At one point in the 12½ hr trial (5.30 p.m. to 6 a.m., 22–23 Jan. 1959), 17,000 people were present in the Havana Sports Palace, Cuba.

Greatest compensation The greatest Crown compensation for wrongful imprisonment was £10,000, paid on 23 Sept. 1931 to T. Boevey Barrett, who had been wrongfully convicted of alleged frauds in 1921. After serving three years' imprisonment in Accra, Ghana, he was granted a free pardon in 1930.

The greatest compensation paid for wrongful imprisonment in the United Kingdom was £6,000 paid in 1929 to Oscar Slater (*né* Leschziner), who had been arraigned for the murder of Miss Marion Gilchrist, aged 83, in Glasgow on 6 May 1909.

GREATEST DAMAGES
The highest damages ever awarded in any court of law were $14,387,674, following upon the crash of a private aircraft at South Lake, Tahoe, California,

U.S.A. on 21 February 1967, to the sole survivor Ray Rosendin, 45, by the Santa Clara Superior Court on 8 March 1972. Rosendin received $1,069,374 for the loss of both legs and disabling arm injuries; $1,213,129 for the loss of his wife and $10,500,000 punitive damages against Avco-Lyconing Corporation which allegedly violated Federal regulations when it rebuilt the aircraft engine owned by Rosendin Corporation.

Breach of contract The greatest damages ever awarded for a breach of contract were £610,392, awarded on 16 July 1930 to the Bank of Portugal against the printers Waterlow & Sons Ltd., of London, arising from their unauthorized printing of 580,000 five-hundred escudo notes in 1925. This award was upheld in the House of Lords on 28 April 1932. One of the perpetrators, Arthur Virgilio Alves Reis, served 16 years (1930–46) in gaol.

Personal injury The greatest damages ever awarded for personal injury are $4,025,000 (*£1,610,000*) to Kelley Niles, 13, of San Francisco, California on 5 Feb. 1973 for paralyzing brain damage sustained in a baseball "whose turn to bat" fight. The damages were awarded against Mount Zion Hospital, a doctor and the school.

The greatest damages ever awarded for personal injury in a British court were £82,500, awarded to David John Butterworth, 22, of Knutsford, Cheshire, for the "catastrophic injuries" received by him in a road accident involving the collision of two cars in 1969. The award, made in the High Court at Manchester on 13 July 1972 by Mr. Justice Wrangham was jointly against the two drivers, Mr. Alfred Sutton of Sandiway, Cheshire, and Peter Frank Dutton. Mr. Butterworth, a passenger, suffered severe brain damage.

On 5 Feb. 1960, the Dublin High Court awarded £87,402 damages for motor injuries to Mr. Kevin P. McMorrow, aged 38, of County Leitrim, against his driver Mr. Edward Knott. It is understood that, after an appeal, a settlement was made out of court for £50,000.

Breach of promise The largest sum involved in a breach of promise suit in the United Kingdom was £50,000, accepted in 1913 by Miss Daisy Markham, *alias* Mrs. Annie Moss (d. 20 Aug. 1962, aged 76), in settlement against the 6th Marquess of Northampton (b. 6 Aug. 1885).

Defamation A sum of $16,800,000 (*£6,720,000*) was awarded to Dr John J. Wild, 58, at the Hennepin District Court, Minnesota, U.S.A., on 30 Nov. 1972 against The Minnesota Foundation and others for defamation, bad-faith termination of a contract, interference with professional business relationship and $10.8 million in punitive damages. These amounts are unappealed.

The greatest damages for defamation ever awarded in the United Kingdom were £117,000, awarded on 21 July 1961 in *The Rubber Improvement Co. Ltd. v. Associated Newspapers Ltd.* for 51 words which appeared in the *Daily Mail* of 23 Dec. 1958. The company was represented by Colin Duncan, M.C. (now a Q.C.) and Mr. (now Sir) Helenus Patrick Joseph Milmo, Q.C. (b. 24 Aug. 1908), who has since become a judge. After appeal proceedings by both sides this action was settled out of court for a substantially smaller amount.

Divorce The highest award made to the dispossessed party in a divorce suit was $70,000 (*then £25,000*), awarded to Mr. Demetrus Sophocles Constandinidi against Dr. Henry William Lance for bigamous adultery with his wife Mrs. Julia Constandinidi. She married Dr. Lance after going through a form of divorce in Sioux Falls, South Dakota, U.S.A., on 27 Feb. 1902.

Greatest Alimony The highest alimony awarded in a British court is £5,000 per annum, but in 1919 the 2nd Duke of Westminster, G.C.V.O., D.S.O. (1879–1953) settled £13,000 per annum upon his first wife, Constance Edwina (*née* Cornwallis-West), C.B.E., later Mrs. Lewis.

HIGHEST SETTLEMENT

Divorce The greatest amount ever paid in a divorce settlement is $9,500,000 (*£3,393,000*) paid by Edward J. Hudson to Mrs. Cecil Amelia Blaffer Hudson, aged 43. This award was made on 28 Feb. 1963 at the Domestic Relations Court, Houston, Texas, U.S.A. Mrs. Hudson was, reputedly, already worth $14,000,000 (*£5,000,000*).

Patent case The greatest settlement ever made in a patent infringement suit is $9,250,000 (*£3,303,000*), paid in April 1952 by the Ford Motor Company to the Ferguson Tractor Co. for a claim filed in January 1948.

Largest Suit The highest amount of damages ever sought is $675,000,000,000,000 (equivalent to the U.S. Government revenue for 3,000 years) in a suit by Mr. I. Walton Bader brought in the U.S. District Court, New York City on 14 April 1971 against General Motors and others for polluting all 50 states.

HIGHEST COSTS

The highest costs in English legal history arose from the case of the *Société Rateau v. Rolls-Royce*, an action concerning the alleged infringement of a French patent of 4 Dec. 1939 for an axial flow jet engine. Mr. Justice Lloyd-Jacob held in April 1967 that the patent had not been infringed. Costs were estimated at £325,000.

Income tax The greatest amount paid for information concerning
Highest a case of income tax delinquency was $79,999.93
reward (*£28,571*) paid by the United States Internal Revenue Service to a group of informers. Payments are limited to 10 per cent of the amount recovered as a direct result of information laid. Informants are often low-income accountants or women scorned. The total of payments in 1965 was $597,731 (*then £213,475*).

Greatest lien The greatest lien ever imposed by the U.S. Internal Revenue Service was one of $21,261,818 (*£7,593,500*), filed against the California property of John A. T. Galvin in March 1963, in respect of alleged tax arrears for 1954–57.

WILLS

Shortest The shortest valid will in the world is "Vše zene", the Czech for "All to wife", written and dated 19 Jan. 1967 by Herr Karl Tausch of Langen, Hesse, Germany. The shortest will contested but subsequently admitted to probate in English law was the case of *Thorn v. Dickens* in 1906. It consisted of the three words "All for Mother".

Longest The longest will on record was that of Mrs. Frederica Cook (U.S.A.), in the early part of the century. It consisted of four bound volumes containing 95,940 words.

JUDGE

Oldest The oldest recorded active judge was Judge Albert R.
World Alexander (1859–1966) of Plattsburg, Missouri, U.S.A. He was the magistrate and probate judge of Clinton County until his retirement aged 105 years 8 months on 9 July 1965.

Britain The greatest recorded age at which any British judge has sat on a bench was 93 years 9 months in the case of Sir William Francis Kyffin Taylor, G.B.E., K.C. (later Lord Maenan), who was born on 9 July 1854 and retired as presiding judge of the Liverpool Court of Passage in April 1948, having held that position since 1903. The greatest age at which a House of Lords judgment has been given is 92 in the case of the 1st Earl of Halsbury (b. 3 Sept. 1823) in 1916.

Youngest The youngest certain age at which any English judge has been appointed is 31, in the case of Sir Francis Buller (b. 17 March 1746), who was appointed Second Judge of the County Palatine of Chester on 27 Nov. 1777, and Puisne Judge of the King's Bench on 6 May 1778, aged 32 years 1 month. The Hon. Daines Barrington (c. 1727–1800) was appointed Justice of the Counties of Merioneth and Anglesey sometime in 1757 and may have been even younger.

Youngest Q.C. The earliest age at which a barrister has taken silk since 1900 is 33 years 8 months in the case of Mr. (later the Rt. Hon. Sir) Francis Raymond Evershed (1899–1966) in April 1933. He was later Lord Evershed, a Lord of Appeal in Ordinary.

Highest paid lawyer It was estimated that Jerry Giesler (1886–1962), an attorney in Los Angeles, California, U.S.A., averaged $50,000 (then £17,850) in fees for each case which he handled during the latter part of his career. Currently, the most highly paid lawyer is generally believed to be Louis Nizer of New York City, N.Y., U.S.A.

Most successful Advocate Sir Lionel Luckhoo K.C.M.G., C.B.E. senior partner of Luckhoo and Luckhoo of Georgetown, Guyana succeeded in getting his 152nd murder acquittal in April 1973.

CRIME AND PUNISHMENT

GREATEST MASS KILLINGS

China The greatest massacre in human history ever imputed is that of 26,300,000 Chinese during the regime of Mao Tse-tung between 1949 and May 1965. This accusation was made by an agency of the U.S.S.R. Government in a radio broadcast on 7 April 1969. This broadcast broke down the figure into four periods:—2.8 million (1949–52); 3.5 million (1953–57); 6.7 million (1958–60); and 13.3 million (1961–May 1965). The highest reported death figures in single monthly announcements on Peking radio were 1,176,000 in the provinces of Anhwei, Cheki-ang, Kiangsu, and Shantung, and 1,150,000 in the Central South Provinces. Po I-po, Minister of Finance, is alleged to have stated in the organ *For a lasting peace, for a people's democracy* "in the past three years (1950–52) we have liquidated more than 2 million bandits". General Jacques Guillermaz, a French diplomat estimated the total executions between February 1951 and May 1952 at between 1 million and 3 million. In April 1971 the Executive *Yuan* or cabinet of the implacably hostile government of The Republic of China in Taipei, Taiwan announced its official estimate of the mainland death roll in the period 1949–69 as "at least 39,940,000". This figure, however, excluded "tens of thousands" killed in the Great Proletarian Cultural Revolution, which began in late 1966. The Walker Report published by the U.S. Senate Committee of the Judiciary in July 1971 placed the parameters of the total death roll since 1949 between 32.25 and 61.7 million.

U.S.S.R. The total death roll in the Great Purge, or *Yezhovs-hchina*, in the U.S.S.R., in 1936–38 has never been published, though evidence of its magnitude may be found in population statistics which show a defici-ency of males from before the outbreak of the 1941–45 war. The reign of terror was administered by the *Narodny Kommissariat Vnutrennykh Del* (N.K.V.D.), or People's Commissariat of Internal Affairs, the Soviet security service headed by Nikolay Ivanovich Yezhov (1895–?1939), described by Nikita

Khrushchyov in 1956 as "a degenerate". S. V. Utechin, an expert on Soviet affairs, regards estimates of 8,000,000 or 10,000,000 victims as "probably not exaggerations".

Nazi Germany At the S.S (*Schutzstaffel*) extermination camp (*Vernichtungslager*) known as Auschwitz-Birkenau (Oswiecim-Brzezinka), near Oswiecim (Auschwitz), in southern Poland, where a minimum of 900,000 people (Soviet estimate is 4,000,000) were extermin-ated from 14 June 1940 to 29 Jan. 1945, the greatest number killed in a day was 6,000. The man who operated the release of the "Zyklon B" cyanide pellets into the gas chambers there during this time was Sergeant Mold. The Nazi (*Nationalsozialistiche Deutsche Arbeiter Partei*) Commandant during the period 1940–43 was Rudolf Franz Ferdinand Höss, who was tried in Warsaw from 11 March to 2 April 1947 and hanged, aged 47, at Oswiecim on 15 April 1947. Erich Koch, the war-time *Gauleiter* of East Prussia and *Reichskommissar* for German-occupied Ukraine, was arrested near Hamburg on 24 May 1949, tried in Warsaw from 20 Oct. 1958 to 9 March 1959 and sentenced to death for his responsibility for, or complicity in, the deaths of 4,232,000 people. The death sentence was later commuted to imprisonment.

Obersturmbannführer (Lt.-Col.) Karl Adolf Eich-mann (b. Solingen, West Germany 19 March 1906) of the S.S. was hanged in a small room inside Ramleh Prison, near Tel Aviv, Israel, at just before midnight (local time) on 31 May 1962, for his complicity in the deaths of 5,700,000 Jews during World War II, under the instruction given in April 1941 by Adolf Hitler (1889–1945) for the "Final Solution" (*Endlösung*), *i.e.* the extermination of European Jewry.

Forced Labour No official figures have been published of the death roll in Corrective Labour Camps in the U.S.S.R., first established in 1918. The total number of such camps was known to be more than 200 in 1946 but in 1956 many were converted to less severe Corrective Labour Colonies. An estimate published in the Netherlands puts the death roll between 1921 and 1960 at 19,000,000. The camps were administered by the *Cheka* until 1922, the O.G.P.U. (1922–34), the N.K.V.D. (1934–46), the M.V.D. (1946–53) and the K.B.G. since 1953. Daily intake has been limited to only 2,400 calories since 1961.

Largest criminal organization The largest syndicate of organized crime is the Mafia or La Cosa Nostra, which has infiltrated the execu-tive, judiciary and legislature of the United States. It consists of some 3,000 to 5,000 individuals in 24 "families" federated under "The Commission", which has a Sicilian-Jewish axis and an estimated annual turnover in vice, gambling, protection rackets and rigged trading of $30,000 million per annum of which some 25 per cent is profit. The biggest Mafia (means *swank* from a Sicilian word for beauty or pride) killing was on 10 Sept. 1931 when the topmost man Salvatore Maranzano, *Il Capo di Tutti Capi*, and 40 allies were liquidated.

Murder rate Highest The country with the highest recorded murder rate is Mexico, with 46.3 registered homicides per each 100,000 of the population in 1970. It has been esti-mated that the number of murders in Colombia during *La Violencia* (1945–62) was about 300,000, giving a rate over a 17-year period of more than 48 a day. A total of 592 deaths was attributed to one bandit leader, Teófilo ("Sparks") Rojas, aged 27, between 1948 and his death in an ambush near Armenia on 22 Jan. 1963. Some sources attribute 3,500 slayings to him.

The highest homicide rates recorded in New York City have been 58 in a week in July 1972 and 13 in a day in August 1972.

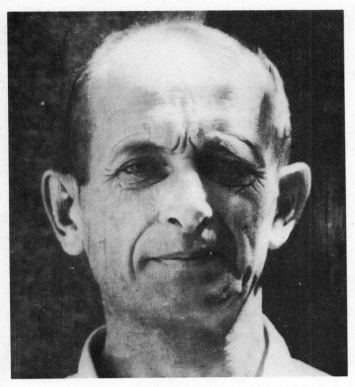

Adolf Eichmann, former Nazi, who was hanged in Israel in May 1962 for his part in the deaths of over 5 million Jews during World War II

Britain In Great Britain the highest annual total of murders since 1900 has been 242 in 1945 ,and the lowest 124 in 1937 and 125 in 1958. The murder rate in Britain is running at less than 3.0 per million.

Lowest The country with the lowest officially recorded rate in the world is Spain, with 39 murders (a rate of 1.23 per each million of the population) in 1967, or one murder every 9 days. In the Indian protectorate of Sikkim, in the Himalayas, murder is, however, practically unknown, while in the Hunza area of Kashmir, in the Karakoram, only one definite case has been recorded since 1900.

MOST PROLIFIC MURDERER

World The greatest number of victims ascribed to an individual has been 610 in the case of Countess Erszebet Báthory (1560–1614) of Hungary. At her trial which began on 2 Jan. 1611 a witness testified to seeing a list of her victims in her own handwriting totalling this number. All were alleged to be young girls from the neighbourhood of her castle at Csejthe where she died on 21 Aug. 1614. She had been walled up in her room for the 3½ years after being found guilty.

Gille de Rays (Raies or Retz) (1404–40) was reputed to have murdered ritually between 140 and 200 kidnapped children. The best estimate put the total of his victims at about 60. He was hanged and burnt at Nantes, France, on 25 Oct. 1440.

The total number of victims of the cannibalistic cave-dwelling Beane family in Galloway, Scotland in the early 17th century is not known but may have run as high as 50 per year. Sawney Beane, head of the family, his wife, 8 sons, 6 daughters and 32 grand-children were taken by an Army detachment to Edinburgh and executed without trial.

The murderer alleged to have most victims was Herman Webster Mudgett (b. 16 May 1860), better known as Harry Howard Holmes who was said to have disposed of between 27 and 150 young women

"paying guests" in his "castle" on 63rd Street, Chicago, Illinois, U.S.A. Holmes was hanged on 7 May 1896, on a charge of murdering his associate, Benjamin F. Pitezel.

A more likely candidate is the German Bruno Lüdke (b. 1909), who confessed to 85 murders of women between 1928 and 29 Jan. 1943. He was executed by injection without trial in a hospital in Vienna on 8 April 1944.

Murderess The greatest total of victims ascribed to a recent murderess is 16, together with a further 12 possible victims, making a total of 28. This was in the case of Bella Poulsdatter Sorensen Gunness *née* Grunt (1859–1908) of La Porte, Indiana, U.S.A. Evidence came to light when her farm was set on fire on 28 April 1908, when she herself was found by a jury to have committed suicide by strychnine poisoning. Her victims, remains of many of whom were dug from her hog-lot, are believed to comprise two husbands, at least eight and possibly 20 would-be suitors lured by "Lonely Hearts" advertisements, three women and three children. A claim that Vera Renzci murdered 35 persons in Romania this century lacks authority.

Britain The only man to be arraigned on a charge of nine murders was Peter Thomas Anthony Manuel, aged 32, a New York born Lanarkshire woodworker. He was found guilty on 29 May 1958 after a 16-day trial at Glasgow High Court, of the capital murders of five females and two males. Two other charges were not proceeded with and three other murders were later admitted by him, making a total of twelve. He was hanged at Barlinnie Prison, near Glasgow, at 8 a.m. on 11 July 1958. The total number of murders committed by "Doctor" William Palmer (b. 1824) of Rugeley, Staffordshire, is not definitely known but was at least 13 and most probably 16, the victims having been poisoned by strychnine or antimony. He was hanged at Stafford on 14 June 1856. Scotland's most prolific known murderer was the Irish-born William Burke (1792–1829) who, in partnership with William Hare, murdered at least 13 derelicts in Edinburgh within 12 months, to sell their corpses. Hare turned King's evidence and Burke was hanged on 28 Jan. 1829.

Gang murders During the period of open gang warfare in Chicago, Illinois, U.S.A., the peak year was 1926, when there were 76 unsolved killings. The 1,000th gang murder in Chicago since 1919 occurred on 1 Feb. 1967. Only 13 cases have ended in convictions.

Thuggee It has been estimated that at least 2,000,000 Indians were strangled by Thugs (*burtotes*) during the period of the Thuggee cult, from 1550 until finally suppressed in 1852. It was established at the trial of Buhram that he had strangled at least 931 victims with his yellow and white cloth strip or *ruhmal* in the Oudh district between 1790 and 1830.

"Smelling out" The greatest "smelling out" recorded in African history occurred before Shaka (1787–1828) and 30,000 Nguni subjects near the River Umhlatuzana, Zululand (now Natal, South Africa) in March 1824. After 9 hrs, over 300 were "smelt out" as guilty of smearing the Royal *Kraal* with blood, by 150 witch-finders led by the hideous female *isangoma* Nobela. The victims were declared innocent when Shaka admitted to having done the smearing himself to expose the falsity of the power of his diviners. Nobela poisoned herself with atropine ($C_{17}H_{23}NO_3$), but the other 149 witch-finders were thereupon skewered or clubbed to death.

Suicide The estimated daily total of suicides throughout the world surpassed 1,000 in 1965. The country with the highest suicide rate is Hungary, with 34.9 per each 100,000 of the population in 1970. The country with the lowest recorded rate is Jordan with a single case in 1970 and hence a rate of 0.04 per 100,000.

In England and Wales there were 3,940 suicides in 1970, or an average of nearly 11 per day. In the northern hemisphere April and May tend to be peak months.

CAPITAL PUNISHMENT

Capital punishment was first abolished *de facto* in Liechtenstein in 1798. The death penalty for murder was abolished on a free vote in the House of Commons by a majority of 158 (343–185) on 16 Dec. and a majority of 46 in the House of Lords on 18 Dec. 1969.

Capital punishment in the British Isles dates from A.D. 450, but fell into disuse in the 11th century, only to be revived in the Middle Ages, reaching a peak in the reign of Edward VI (1547–1553), when an average of 560 persons were executed annually at Tyburn alone. The most people executed at one hanging was 24 at Tyburn (Marble Arch, London) in 1571. Even into the 19th century, there were 223 capital crimes, though people were, in practice, hanged for only 25 of these.

Between 1830 and 1955 the largest number hanged in a year was 27 (24 men, 3 women) in 1903. The least was 5 in 1854, 1921 and 1930. In 1956 there were no hangings in England, Wales or Scotland, since when the highest number in any year has been 5.

Last hangings The last public execution in England took place outside Newgate Prison, London at 8 a.m. on 26 May 1868, when Michael Barrett was hanged for his part in the Fenian bomb outrage on 13 Dec. 1867, when 12 were killed outside the Clerkenwell House of Detention, London. The earliest non-public execution was of the murderer Thomas Wells on 13 Aug. 1868. The last public hanging in Scotland was that of the murderer Joe Bell in Perth in 1866. The last in the United States occurred at Owensboro, Kentucky in 1936. The last hangings were those of Peter Anthony Allen (b. 4 Apr. 1943) at Walton Prison, Liverpool, and John Robson Walby (b. 1 April 1940), *alias* Gwynne Owen Evans, at Strangeways Gaol, Manchester both on 13 Aug. 1964. They had been found guilty of the capital murder of John Alan West, on 7 April 1964. The 14th and last woman executed this century was Mrs. Ruth Ellis, 28, for the murder of David Blakeley, 25, outside The Magdala, Hampstead, on 10 Apr. 1955. She was executed on 13 July at Holloway.

Last from yard-arm The last naval execution at the yard-arm was the hanging of Marine John Dalliger aboard H.M.S. *Leven* in the River Yangtze, China, on 13 July 1860. Dalliger had been found guilty of two attempted murders.

Last public guillotining The last person to be publicly guillotined in France was the murderer Eugen Weidmann before a large crowd at Versailles, near Paris, at 4.50 a.m. on 17 June 1939. The last person guillotined in a French prison was a 34 year old Tunisian child murderer at Marseilles on 12 May 1973. It was the 74 year old executioner's 364th successful execution. Dr. Joseph Ignace Guillotin (1738–1812) died a natural death. He had advocated the use of the machine designed by Dr. Antoine Louis in 1789 in the French constituent assembly.

Youngest Although the hanging of persons under 18 was expressly excluded only in the Children's and Young Person's Act, 1933 (Sec. 33), no person under that age had, in fact, been executed since 1887. Though it has been published widely that a girl of seven was hanged in 1808 and a boy of nine in 1831, the name of

neither can be produced. In 1801 Andrew Benning, aged 13, was executed for housebreaking. The youngest persons hanged since 1900 have been 18 years old:—J. H. Clarkson at Leeds on 29 March 1904; Henry Jacoby on 7 Jan. 1922; Bishop in 1925; another case in 1932; James Farrell on 29 March 1949; and Francis Robert George ("Flossie") Forsyth on 10 Nov. 1960.

Oldest The oldest person hanged in the United Kingdom since 1900 was a man of 71 named Charles Frembd (*sic*) at Chelmsford Gaol on 4 Nov. 1914, for the murder of his wife at Leytonstone, Essex. In 1822 John Smith, said to be 80, of Greenwich, London, was hanged for the murder of a woman.

Most attempts In 1803 it was reported that Joseph Samuels was reprieved in Sydney, Australia after three unsuccessful attempts to hang him in which the rope twice broke.

Slowest The longest delay in carrying out a death sentence in recent history is in the case of Sadamichi Hirasawa (b. 1906) of Tōkyō, Japan, who was sentenced to death in January 1950, after a trial lasting 16 months, on charges of poisoning twelve people with potassium cyanide in a Tōkyō bank. In November 1962 he was transferred to a prison at Sendai, in northern Honshū where he was still awaiting execution in May 1972.

The longest stay on "death row" in the United States has been one of more than 14 years by Edgar Labat, aged 44, and Clifton A. Paret, aged 38, in Angola Penitentiary, Louisiana, U.S.A. In March 1953 they were sentenced to death, after being found guilty of rape in 1950. They were released on 5 May 1967, only to be immediately re-arrested on a local jury indictment arising from the original charge.

Caryl Whittier Chessman, aged 38 and convicted of 17 felonies, was executed on 2 May 1960 in the gas chamber at the California State Prison, San Quentin, California, U.S.A. In 11 years 10 months and one week on "death row", Chessman had won eight stays.

EXECUTIONER

The longest period of office of a Public Executioner was that of William Calcraft (1800–1879), who was in office from 1828 to 1871 and officiated at nearly every hanging outside and later inside Newgate Prison, London. The most "suitably qualified" executioner on the Home Office list for the last remaining gallows at Wandsworth Prison, London against possible use for traitors or violent pirates is believed to be Mr. Harry Allen (b. 1918).

Caryl Chessman, whose stay on "Death Row" totalled 11 years 10 months 1 week, during which he won eight stays of execution

BLOODIEST ASSIZES

In the West Country Assizes of 1685 (Winchester to Wells), George Jeffreys, the 1st Baron Jeffreys of Wem (1645–1689), sentenced 330 persons to be hanged, 841 to be transported for periods of ten or more years and larger numbers to be imprisoned and flogged. These sentences followed the Duke of Monmouth's insurrections.

LONGEST SENTENCES

World The longest recorded prison sentence is one of 7,109 years awarded to a pair of confidence tricksters by an Iranian court on 15 June 1969. The duration of sentences are proportional to the amount of the defalcations involved. A sentence of 384,912 years was demanded at the prosecution of Gabriel March Grandos, 22, at the Palma de Mallorca, Spain on 11 Mar. 1972 for failing to deliver 42,768 letters.

Richard Honeck was sentenced to life imprisonment in the United States in 1899, after having murdered his former schoolteacher. It was reported in November 1963 that Honeck, then aged 84, who was in Menard Penitentiary, Chester, Illinois, was due to be paroled after 64 years in prison, during which time he had received one letter (a four-line note from his brother in 1904) and two visitors, a friend in 1904 and a newspaper reporter in 1963. He was released on 20 Dec. 1963.

Juan Corona, a Mexican-American was sentenced to 25 consecutive life terms, for murdering 25 farm workers in 1970–71 around Feather River, Yuba City, California, at Fairfield on 5 Feb. 1973.

United Kingdom On 17 May 1939, William Burkitt, three times acquitted of murder by a jury (1915, 1925 and 1939), was sentenced by Mr. Justice Cassels "to be kept in prison for the rest of your natural life". Burkitt, whose appeal against the sentence failed in 1948, had served 34 years for manslaughter up to 1954, when he was released. He died on 24 Dec. 1956. Mr. Justice Chapman at Oxford Assizes in October 1971 jailed the police murderer Arthur William Skingle, 25 for life with the first recommendation that "life should mean for life".

The longest single period served by a reprieved murderer in Great Britain this century was 40 years 11 months by John Watson Laurie, the Goat Fell or Arran murderer, who was reprieved on the grounds of insanity in November 1889 and who died in Perth Penitentiary on 4 Oct. 1930.

The longest prison sentence ever passed under United Kingdom law was one of three consecutive and two concurrent terms of 14 years, thus totalling 42 years, imposed on 3 May 1961 on George Blake (b. Rotterdam, 11 Nov. 1922 of an Egyptian-born Jewish-British father and a Dutch mother as George Behar), for treachery. Blake, formerly U.K. vice-consul in Seoul, South Korea, had been converted to Communism during 34 months' internment there from 2 July 1950 to April 1953. It had been alleged that his betrayals may have cost the lives of up to 42 United Kingdom agents. He was "sprung" from Wormwood Scrubs Prison, London, W.12. on 22 Oct. 1966.

Miss Myra Hindley was sentenced at Chester Assizes on 6 May 1966 to life imprisonment with a recommendation she should serve at least 30 years for her part with Ian Brady in the "Moors" murders of Edward Evans, 17 and Lesley Ann Downey, 10.

Broadmoor The longest period for which any person has been detained in the Broadmoor hospital for the criminally insane, near Crowthorne, Berkshire, is 76 years in the case of William Giles. He was admitted as an insane arsonist at the age of 11 and died there on 10 March 1962, at the age of 87.

Oldest prisoner The oldest known prisoner in the United States is John Weber, 95, at the Chillicothe Correctional Institute, Ohio who began his 44th year in prison on 29 Oct. 1970.

Most appearances On 29 May 1971 a statistically-minded magistrate at Leeds, Yorkshire remarked that George Linstrum, 76, was making his 500th appearance on a drink charge since 1922.

Greatest mass arrest The greatest mass arrest in the United Kingdom occurred on 17 Sept. 1961, when 1,314 demonstrators supporting the unilateral nuclear disarmament of the United Kingdom were arrested for wilfully disregarding the directions of the police and thereby obstructing highways leading to Parliament Square, London, by sitting down.

Lynching The worst year in the 20th century for lynchings in the United States has been 1901, with 130 lynchings 105 Negroes, 25 Whites), while the first year with no reported cases was 1952. The last lynching recorded in Britain was that of Panglam Godolan, a Pakistani and a suspected murderer, in London on 27 Oct. 1958. The last case previous to this was of a kidnapping suspect in Glasgow in 1922.

LONGEST PRISON ESCAPES

The longest recorded escape by a recaptured prisoner was that of Leonard T. Fristoe, 77, who escaped from Nevada State Prison, U.S.A., on 15 Dec. 1923 and was turned in by his son on 15 Nov. 1969 at Compton, California. He had had 46 years of freedom under the name Claude R. Willis. He had killed two sheriff's deputies in 1920. The longest period of freedom achieved by a British gaol breaker is more than $15\frac{1}{2}$ years by Irish-born John Patrick Hannan, who escaped from Verne Open Prison at Portland, Dorset, on 22 Dec. 1955 and was still at large in May 1973. He had served only 1 month of a 21-month term for car-stealing and assaulting two policemen.

Broadmoor The longest escape from Broadmoor was one of 39 years by the Liverpool wife murderer James Kelly, who got away on 28 Jan. 1888, using a pass key made from a corset spring. After an adventurous life in Paris, in New York and at sea he returned in April 1927, to ask for re-admission. After some difficulties this was arranged. He died in 1930.

Greatest gaol break The greatest gaol break in Britain was that from Brixton Prison, South London on 30 May 1973 when 20 men got out using a rubbish tipping lorry as a battering ram. Eighteen were captured immediately and one other 5 weeks later, 9 staff were injured.

ROBBERY

Greatest The greatest robbery on record was that of the Reichbank's reserves by a combine of U.S. military personnel and Germans. Gold bars, 728 in number, valued at £3,518,334 were removed from a caché on Klausenkopf mountainside, near Einsiedel, Bavaria on 7 June 1945 together with six sacks of bank notes of 404,840 U.S. dollars and £405 (possibly forged) from a garden in Oberaer. The book *Gold Is Where You Hide It* by W. Stanley Moss (André Deutsch, 1956) named the Town Major of Garmisch-Partenkirken Capt. Robert Mackenzie, *alias* Ben F. Harpman of the Third U.S. Army and the local military governor Captain (later Major) Martin Borg as the instigators. Mackenzie was reputedly sentenced to 10 years after an F.B.I. investigation but Borg vanished from Vitznau, Switzerland on 30 March 1946. In the same area, in which 6 apparently associated murders occurred, 630 cubes of uranium and six boxes of platinum bars and precious stones and 34 forging plates also disappeared. (See, however, Industrial Espionage, page 198.)

Bank On 23 March 1962, 150 *plastiqueurs* of the *Organisation de l'Armée Secrète* (O.A.S.) removed by force

23,500,000 francs (£1,703,000) from the Banque d'Algérie in Oran, Algeria, after the collapse of civil order. The biggest "inside job" was that at the National City Bank of New York, from which the Assistant Manager, Richard Crowe, removed $883,660 (£315,593). He was arrested on 11 April 1949. On 23 Oct. 1969 it was disclosed that $13,193,000 (£5,497,000) of U.S. Treasury bills were inexplicably missing from the Morgan Trust, Wall Street, New York City, U.S.A.

Train The greatest recorded train robbery occurred between about 3.10 a.m. and 3.45 a.m. on 8 Aug. 1963, when a General Post Office mail train from Glasgow, Scotland, was ambushed between Sears Crossing and Bridego Bridge at Mentmore, near Cheddington, Buckinghamshire. The gang escaped with about 120 mailbags conaining £2,595,998 worth of bank notes being taken to London for pulping. Only £343,448 had been recovered by 9 Dec. 1966.

Art The greatest recorded art robbery was the theft of eight paintings, valued at £1,500,000, taken during the night of 30–31 Dec. 1966 from the Dulwich College Picture Gallery in London. The haul included three paintings by Peter Paul Rubens (1577–1640), one was by Adam Ehlsheimer (1578–1610), three by Rembrandt van Rijn (1606–69) and one by Gerard Dou (1613–75). Three of the paintings were recovered on 2 Jan. 1967 and the remaining five on 4 Jan. 1967. It is arguable that the value of the *Mona Lisa* at the time of its theft from The Louvre, Paris on 21 Aug. 1911 was greater than this figure. It was recovered in Italy in 1913 and Vicenzo Perruggia was charged with its theft.

Jewels The greatest recorded theft of gem stones occurred on 13 Nov. 1969 in Freetown, Sierra Leone, when an armed gang stole diamonds belonging to the Sierra Leone Selection Trust worth £1,500,000. The haul from Carrington & Co. Ltd. of Regent Street, London, on 21 Nov. 1965 was estimated to be £500,000. Jewels are believed to have constituted a major part of the Hotel Pierre "heist" on Fifth Avenue, New York City, U.S.A. on 31 Dec. 1971. An unofficial estimate ran as high as $5,000,000 (£2,000,000).

Industrial espionage It has been alleged that about 1966 a division of the American Cyanamid Company lost some papers and vials of micro-organisms through industrial espionage, allegedly organized from Italy, which data had cost them $24,000,000 (*then £8.57 million*) in research and development. It is arguable that this represents the greatest robbery of all-time.

Greatest kidnapping ransom Historically the greatest ransom paid was that for Atahualpa by the Incas to Francisco Pizarro in 1532–33 at Cajamarca, Peru which constituted a hall full of gold and silver worth in modern money some $170 million (£65 million).

The greatest ransom ever extracted in a kidnapping case in modern times has been 7½ million D.Mk (£900,000) for the return after 19 days of Thomas Albrecht, 49 a West German supermarket owner, on 16–17 Dec. 1971.

Greatest Hijack ransom The highest amount ever paid to hijackers has been £2,000,000 in small denomination notes by the West German government to Popular Front for the Liberation of Palestine representatives 30 miles outside Beirut, Lebanon on 23 Feb. 1972. In return a Lufthansa Boeing 747, hijacked an hour out of New Delhi and bound for Athens which had been forced down at Aden, and its 14 crew members were released.

Largest narcotics haul The heaviest recorded haul of narcotics was made off St. Louis at Rhône, France, where 700 cwt. *35,5 tonnes* of floating bales containing unprocessed morphine,

The scene at Dulwich College, after the biggest Art Robbery in Great Britain, showing the door panel through which the thieves removed to gain acceess

opium, heroin and hashish, worth £30 million on the retail U.S. market were found being loaded into canoes by 3 men on 25 Feb. 1971. The most valuable ever haul was of 937 lb. *425 kg* of pure heroin worth $106¼ million (£40.8 million) retail seized aboard the 60 ton shrimp boat *Caprice des Temps* at Marseilles, France on 28 Feb. 1972. The captain, Louis Boucan, 57, who tried to commit suicide was sentenced to 15 years on 5 Jan. 1973.

It was revealed on 31 Jan. 1973 that 398 lb. *180 kg 50* of heroin and cocaine with a street value of $73 million (£29.2 million) had been stolen from the New York Police Department—a record for any law enforcement agency.

Penal camps The largest penal camp systems in the world were those near Karaganda and Kolyma, in the U.S.S.R., each with a population estimated in 1958 at between 1,200,000 and 1,500,000. The official N.A.T.O. estimate for all Soviet camps was "more than one million" in March 1960. It was estimated in 1966 that the total population of penal camps in China was about 10,000,000.

Devil's Island The largest French penal settlement was that of St. Laurent du Maroni, which comprised the notorious Îles du Diable, Royale and St. Joseph (for incorrigibles) off the coast of French Guiana, in South America. It remained in operation for 99 years from 1854 until the last group of repatriated prisoners, including Théodore Rouselle, who had served 50 years, was returned to Bordeaux on 22 Aug. 1953. It has been estimated that barely 2,000 *bagnard* (ex-convicts) of the 70,000 deportees ever returned. These, however, include the executioner Ladurelle (imprisoned 1921–37), who was murdered in Paris in 1938.

PRISONS

Largest World The largest prison in the world is Kharkov Prison, in the U.S.S.R., which has at times accommodated 40,000 prisoners.

British Isles The largest prison in the United Kingdom is Wormwood Scrubs, West London, with 1,134 cells. The highest prison walls in Great Britain are those of Lancaster Prison measuring 36 to 52 ft *11–15,85 m*.

The largest prison in Scotland is Barlinnie, near Glasgow, with 753 single cells. Ireland's largest prison is Mountjoy Prison, Dublin, with 808 cells.

Smallest The smallest prison in the world is usually cited as that on the island of Sark, in the Channel Islands, which has a capacity of two. In fact the prison on Herm, a neighbouring island, is smaller, with a diameter of 13 ft 6 in *4 m*, and must rank with the single person lock-ups such as that at Shenley, Hertfordshire. The smallest prison in England is Kingston Prison, Portsmouth with 93 cells. The smallest in Scotland is Penninghame Open Prison, Wigtownshire with accommodation for 63. Ireland's smallest prison is that at Sligo, with 100 cells.

Highest population The peak prison population, including Borstals and detention centres, for England and Wales was the figure for 15 June 1971 of 40,470. In Scotland the average prison population was 5,338 and in Northern Ireland 1,829 (monthly average for Jan–May 1973).

Most secure prison After it became a maximum security Federal prison in 1934, no convict was known to have lived to tell of a successful escape from the prison of Alcatraz ("Pelican") Island in San Francisco Bay, California, U.S.A. A total of 23 men attempted it but 12 were recaptured, 5 shot dead, one drowned and 5 presumed drowned. On 16 Dec. 1962, three months before the prison was closed, one man reached the mainland alive, only to be recaptured on the spot.

Largest bribe An alleged bribe of £30,000,000 offered to Shaikh Zaid ibn Sultan of Abu Dhabi, Trucial Oman, by a Saudi Arabian official in August 1955, is the highest on record. The affair concerned oil concessions in the disputed territory of Buraimi on the Persian Gulf.

Greatest forgery The greatest recorded forgery was the German Third Reich government's forging operation, code name "Bernhard", engineered by Herr Naujocks in 1940–41. It involved £150,000,000 worth of £5 notes.

Greatest swindle The greatest swindle ever perpetrated in commercial history was that of Antonio (Tino) De Angelis (born 1915), a 5 ft 5 in *1,65 m* 290 lb. *131 kg* ex-hog-cutter of New York City, U.S.A. His Allied Crude Vegetable Oil Refining Corporation (formed 19 Nov. 1955) operated from an uncarpeted office adjoining a converted tank farm in Bayonne, New Jersey. The tanks were rigged with false dipping compartments and were inter-connected such that sea water could be pumped to substitute for phantom salad oil which served as collateral for warehouse receipts. A deficiency of 927,000 short tons of oil valued at $175,000,000 (*then £62.5 million*) was discovered. He was paroled in May 1973.

Biggest fraud The largest amount of money named in a fraud case has been £12,707,726 in the Old Bailey, London trial of Ellis Eser Seillon, 60 and Elias Fahimian, 40. A record total of 3,725 documents were involved. They were sentenced on 14 Jan. 1972 by Judge Stanley Price Q.C. to 5 and 4 years respectively.

Passing bad cheques The record for passing bad cheques was set by Frederick Emerson Peters (1886–1959), who, by dint of some 200 impersonations, netted $250,000 (*£89,300*) with 28,000 bad cheques. Among his many philanthropies was a silver chalice presented to a cathedral in Washington, D.C., U.S.A., also paid for with a bad cheque.

Welfare swindle The greatest welfare swindle yet worked was that of the gypsy Anthony Moreno on the French Social Security in Marseilles. By forging birth certificates and school registration forms, he invented 197 fictitious families and 3,000 children on which he claimed benefits from 1960 to mid-1968. Moreno, nicknamed "El Chorro" (the fountain), was last reported free of extradition worries and living in luxury in his native Spain having absquatulated with an estimated £2,300,000.

FINES

A fine equivalent to £9.83 million was imposed on Juan Vila Reyes, president of the Barcelona textile machinery manufacturer Matesa, by the Currency Crime Court, Madrid, Spain on 19 May 1970 for converting export development funds to his own use. The highest reported individual fine is one of £595,000 made in May 1973 on Pandelis Malachias, a Greek sea captain, for trying to smuggle 8 tons of cigarettes in Italy.

Heaviest The heaviest fine ever imposed in the United Kingdom was one of £277,500, plus £3,717 costs, on I. Hennig & Co. Ltd., the London diamond merchants, at Clerkenwell Magistrates' Court, London, on 14 Dec. 1949. The amount was later reduced on appeal.

Rarest prosecution There are a number of crimes in English law for which there have never been prosecutions. Among unique prosecutions are *Rex v. Crook* in 1662 for praemunire and *Rex v. Gregory* for selling honours under the Honours (Prevention of Abuses) Act, 1924, in 1933. Maundy Gregory (d. 1941) was the honours broker of Lloyd George's 1919–20 Coalition Government.

It is a specific offence on Pitcairn Island in the Pacific to shout "Sail Ho!" when no vessel is in sight. The fine is 25p, which can be commuted to one day's labour on the public roads (there are no cars) or making an oar for the public boat.

6. ECONOMIC

MONETARY AND FINANCE

Largest budget **World** The greatest annual expenditure budgeted by any country has been $230,760 million (*£92,304 million*) by the United States government for the fiscal year ending 30 June 1973. The highest revenue in the United States has been $208,650 million (*£83,460 million*) in 1972–3. The estimated revenue receipts of the U.S.S.R. Government in 1971 were 166,300 million roubles (*officially equivalent to $200,360 million or £83,150 million*).

In the United States, the greatest surplus was $8,419,469,844 in 1947–48, and the greatest deficit was $57,420,430,365 in 1942–43.

United Kingdom The greatest annual budgeted current expenditure of the United Kingdom has been £32,140 million for the fiscal year 1973–74. The highest budgeted current revenue has been the same figure for a balanced budget.

Foreign aid The total net foreign aid given by the United States government between 1 July 1945 and 31 Dec. 1971 was $140,901 million (*£56,360 million*). The country which received most U.S. aid in 1971 was India, with $467 million (*£186.8 million*). U.S. foreign aid began with $50,000 to Venezuela for earthquake relief in 1812 and was the subject of a 4 month long battle in the Senate ending in favour of continuation on 2 March 1972.

TAXATION

Most taxed The major national economy with the highest rate of taxation (central and local taxes, plus social security contribution) is that of France with 53.0 per cent of her National Income in 1970 (latest data). The lowest proportion for any advanced national economy in

1973 was 19.5 per cent in Japan, which also enjoyed the highest economic growth rate. In the United Kingdom in 1971 current taxation receipts were 48.7 per cent of G.N.P.

Least taxed There is no income tax paid by residents on Lundy Island off North Devon, England. This 1,062.4 acre *429,9 ha* island issued its own unofficial currency of Puffins and Half Puffins between the Wars for which offence the owner was prosecuted.

Highest surtax The country with the most confiscatory marginal rate of income tax is Burma, where the rate is 99 per cent for annual incomes exceeding 300,000 kyats (pronounced chuts) (*£23,255*). In November 1969 Premier Ne Win proclaimed "the way of true Socialism—the Burmese way". The second highest marginal rate was in the United Kingdom, where the topmost surtax level was 97.5 per cent in 1950–51 and 96.25 per cent in 1965–66. In 1967–68 a "special charge" of up to 9s. (45p) in the £ additional to surtax brought the top rate to 27s. 3d. (136p) in the £. In 1973–74 the rate for taxable incomes over £20,000 is 75 per cent with a surcharge of a further 15 per cent on any investment income in excess of £2,000 making a rate of 90 per cent. A married man with two children earning £5,000 per year in 1938 would, in March 1973, have to have earned £59,000 to have enjoyed the same standard of living.

Highest and lowest rates in United Kingdom Income tax was introduced in Great Britain in 1799 at the standard rate of 2s. (10p) in the £. It was discontinued in 1815, only to be re-introduced in 1842 at the rate of 7d. (3p) in the £. It was at its lowest as 2d. (0.83p) in the £ in 1875, gradually climbing to 1s. 3d. (6p) by 1913. From April 1941 until 1946 the record peak of 10s. (50p) in the £ was maintained to assist in the finances of World War II. Death Duties (introduced in 1894) on millionaire estates began at 8 per cent (1894–1907) and were raised to a peak of 80 per cent by 1949.

V.A.T. Highest and Lowest The highest *standard* rate of V.A.T. in the E.E.C. is 23% in France and the lowest 10% in the U.K. The lowest "lower" rate is 4% in The Netherlands and the highest luxury Rate is 33⅓% in France.

NATIONAL DEBT

The largest national debt of any country in the world is that of the United States, where the gross federal public debt of the Federal Government with an authorised limit of $465 billion (*£186,000 million*) to 30 June 1973 or $2,225 (*£889*) per citizen. This amount in dollar bills would make a pile 27,528 miles *44,302 km* high, weighing 385,675 tons *391 865 tonnes*.

The United Kingdom National Debt, which became a permanent feature of Britain's economy as early as 1692, was £36,910 million, or £659 per person, at 31 March 1973. This amount placed in a pile of brand new £1 notes would be 2,268.9 miles *3 651,4 km* in height.

Gross National Product The estimated world aggregate of Gross National Products in 1971 was about $3,500 billion *£1,400,000* million. The country with the largest Gross National Product is the United States, with $1,151.8 billion, that is, more than a trillion dollars for 1972. The estimated G.N.P. of the United Kingdom was £53,012 million in 1972.

National wealth The richest large nation, measured by real Gross National Product per head, has been the U.S.A. since about 1910. The average share of G.N.P. in the U.S.A. was $4,138 (*£1,655*) in 1971. It has been estimated that the value of all physical assets in the U.S.A. in 1966 was $2,460,000,000,000 or $12,443 (*£5,184*) per head. The comparative figure for the United Kingdom was £85,423 million at 31 Dec. 1961 (latest available data). External wealth was assessed at £5,905 million in 1972.

Poorest Country According to The World Bank calculations, revised in 1972, the three countries with the lowest annual income per capita are Rwanda, Upper Volta and Burundi each with $60 (*£24*). The U.N. General Assembly using a "category" system places Rwanda as the least "Least Advanced" nation.

National Savings The highest total of National Savings recorded in a year was £573,549,000 (net receipts) in 1945–46. The highest net monthly receipts were £114.1 million in January 1972. The total amount invested was £10,297,300,000 as at 31 March 1973. The greatest monthly withdrawals in a week were £40.0 million in Nov. 1969. Mr Arthur Ellis of Saltergate, Chesterfield between 1958 and his death in June 1971 won one £250, two £100 and 39 £25 premium bond draw prizes. All his winnings were donated to the local parish church.

GOLD RESERVES

The country with the greatest monetary gold reserve is the United States, whose Treasury had $13,151 million (*£5,260 million*) on hand on 1 March 1973. The United States Bullion Depository at Fort Knox, 30 miles south-west of Louisville, Kentucky, U.S.A. is the principal Federal depository of U.S. gold. Gold is stored in standard mint bars of 400 troy ounces *12kg 441* measuring 7 by 3⅝ by 1⅛ in, *17,7×9,2×2,8* and each worth $14,000 (*£5,833*).

The greatest accumulation of gold in the world is now in the Federal Reserve Bank at 33 Liberty Street, New York City, N.Y., U.S.A. The bank has had gold valued at $15,500 million (*£6,200 million*) owned by foreign central banks in Sept. 1972 and stored 85 ft *25,90 m* below street level, in a vault 50 ft *15,24m* by 100 ft *30,48m* behind a steel door weighing 89 tons.

United Kingdom The lowest published figure for the sterling area's gold and convertible currency reserves was $298,000,000 (*then £74 million*) on 31 Dec. 1940. The highest ever figure was the June 1973 figure of £2,716 million (valued at $2.58.20 to the £).

BANK RATE

On 1 Jan. 1972 the highest bank rate in the world was that of Brazil at 20 per cent and the lowest that of Morocco at 3½ per cent. The lowest that the Bank of England bank rate has ever been is 2 per cent, first from 22 April 1852 to 6 Jan. 1853. The highest ever figure was 10 per cent, first on 9 Nov. 1857, and most recently on 6 Aug. 1914. The highest yearly average was 7.35 per cent in 1864 (6 per cent to 9 per cent). The longest period without a change was the 12 years 13 days from 26 Oct. 1939 to 7 Nov. 1951, during which time the rate stayed at 2 per cent.

BALANCE OF PAYMENTS

The highest monthly (seasonally adjusted) visible trade figures have been Exports: £952 million in April 1973 and Imports: £1,119 million in May 1973. The greatest surplus was £181 million for the third quarter of 1971 and the greatest deficit £284 million for the third quarter of 1972.

PAPER MONEY

Paper money is an invention of the Chinese and, although the date of 119 B.C. has been suggested, the innovation is believed to date from the T'ang dynasty of the 7th century A.D. The world's earliest bank notes were issued by the Stockholms Banco, Sweden, in July 1661. The oldest surviving banknote is one for 5 dalers dated 6 Dec. 1662. The oldest surviving printed Bank of England note is one for £555 to bearer, dated 19 Dec. 1699 (4½ × 7¾ in [*11,4 × 19,6 cm*]).

Largest and smallest The largest paper money ever issued was the one kwan note of the Chinese Ming dynasty issue of 1368–99, which measured 9 by 13 in *22,8 × 33,0 cm*. The smallest bank note ever issued was the 5 cent. note of the Chekiang Provincial Bank (established 1908) in China. It measured 55 mm *2.16 in* by 30 mm *1.18 in.*

Highest The highest denomination of paper currency ever
denomina- authorised in the world are United States gold
tions certificates for $100,000 (*£40,000*), bearing the head
World of former President Thomas Woodrow Wilson (1856–1924), issued by the U.S. Treasury in 1934. There also exists in the U.S. Bureau of Engraving and Printing an example of a U.S. Treasury note for $500,000,000 bearing interest coupons for $15,625,000 each 6 months for 14 years at 6¼ per cent.

The highest denomination notes in circulation are U.S. Federal Reserve Bank notes for $10,000 (*£4,000*). They bear the head of Salmon Portland Chase (1808–73). None has been printed since July 1944 and the U.S. Treasury announced in 1969 that no further notes higher than $100 would be issued. By June 1971 only 400 $10,000 bills were in circulation—reputedly mostly around Christmas time in Texas.

United Two Bank of England notes for £1,000,000 still exist,
Kingdom dated before 1812, but these were used only for
Highest internal accounting. The highest issued denominations
value were £1,000 notes, first printed in 1725, discontinued in 1943 and withdrawn on 30 April 1945. A total of 62 of these notes were still unaccounted for up to May 1973 of which only 3 are known to be in the hands of collectors.

Lowest The lowest ever denomination Bank of England note
Value was for penny, dated 10 Jan. 1828, which was adapted from a £5 note and doubtless used to adjust an overnight difference. In 1868 it was purchased by the Bank for £1 from the landlord of the "Blue Last", Bell Alley, in the City of London.

Highest The highest ever Bank of England note circulation in
circulation the United Kingdom was £4,484,577,098 on 20 Dec. 1972—equivalent to a pile of £1 notes 258.69 miles *4 163 km* high.

DEVALUATION
Devaluation was practised by Emperor Nero of Rome (A.D. 54–68), who debased his coinage. Since 1945, 112 of the world's 120 currencies have devalued including the pound twice, the rouble 3 times and the Chilean currency 46 times (since 1 Jan. 1949). The U.S. dollar was never devalued *vis-à-vis* gold from 1934 until 1971.

WORST INFLATION
The world's worst inflation occurred in Hungary in June 1946, when the 1931 gold pengö was valued at 130 trillion ($1.3 × 10^{20}$) paper pengös. Notes were issued for szazmillio billion (100 trillion or 10^{20}) pengös. Currently the worst inflation has been in Indonesia where in the 7 years from 1963 to 1970 the currency depreciated 688 fold.

CHEQUES
Largest The greatest amount paid by a single cheque in the
World history of banking was $960,242,000.00 (*£342,943,571*), paid on 31 Jan. 1961 by the Continental Illinois National Bank of Chicago, Illinois, U.S.A. This bank headed a group which bought the accounts receivable of Sears, Roebuck & Co., to whom the cheque was paid.

United The largest cheque drawn in Britain was one for
Kingdom £119,595,645, drawn on 24 Jan. 1961 by Lazard Brothers & Co. Ltd. and payable to the National Provincial Bank, in connection with the takeover of the British Ford Motor Company. The rate of cheque clearing was, by May 1971, 1,100,000,000 per annum.

The famous 1933 penny of George V of which only one has been found in circulation. The official total striking was 8

COINS
Oldest The earliest certainly dated coins are the electrum
World (alloy of gold and silver) staters of Lydia, in Asia Minor (now Turkey), which were coined in the reign of King Gyges (*c.* 685–652 B.C.). Primitive uninscribed "spade" money of the Chou dynasty of China is now *believed* to date from *c.* 770 B.C. A discovery at Tappeh Nush-i-jan, Iran of silver ingot currency in 1972 has been dated to as early as 760 B.C. Paraguay is probably the only country today without coins.

British The earliest coins to circulate in Britain were Gallo-Belgic gold imitations of the Macedonian staters of Philip II (359–336 B.C.). The Bellovaci type has been tentatively dated *c.* 130 B.C. The earliest date attributed to coins minted in Britain is *c.* 95 B.C. for the Westerham type gold stater.

Heaviest The Swedish copper 10 daler coins of 1659 attained a weight of up to 43½ lb. *19,kg 70*. Of primitive exchange tokens, the most massive are the holed stone discs, or *Fé*, from the Yap Islands, in the western Pacific Ocean, with diameters of up to 12 ft. *3,65 m* A medium-sized one was worth one Yapese wife or an 18 ft *5,18m* canoe.

Smallest The smallest coins in the world have been the Nepalese ¼ dam or Jawa struck *c.* 1740 in silver in the reign of Jeya Prakash Malla. The Jawa of between 0.008 and 0.014 g measuring about 2 × 2 mm were sometimes cut into ½ and even ¼ Jawa of 0.002 g or 14,000 to the oz.

Highest The 1654 Indian gold 200 Mohur (£500) coin of the
denomina- Mughal Emperor Khurram Shihāb-ud-dīn Muham-
tion mad, Shāh Jahān (reigned 1628–57), is both the
World highest denomination coin and that of the greatest intrinsic worth ever struck. It weighed 2 177 g *70 troy oz.* and hence has an intrinsic worth of £2,800. It had a diameter of 5⅜ in *136 mm*. The only known example disappeared in Patna, Bihar, India, in *c.* 1820, but a plaster-cast of this coin exists in the British Museum, London.

British Gold five-guinea pieces were minted from the reign of Charles II (1660–1685) until 1753 in the reign of George II. A pattern 5 guinea piece of George III dated 1777 also exists.

Lowest The 1 aurar piece of Iceland, had a face value of
denomina- 0.0114 of a penny in 1971. Quarter farthings (sixteen
tion to the penny) were struck in copper at the Royal
World Mint, London, in the Imperial coinage for use in Ceylon, in 1839 and 1851–53.

201

Rarest
World More than 100 coins are unique. An example of a unique coin of threefold rarity is one of the rare admixture of bronze with inlaid gold of Kaleb I of Axum (c. A.D. 500) owned by Richard A. Thorud of Bloomington, Minnesota, U.S.A. Only 700 Axumite coins of any sort are known.

The obverse (left) and reverse of an Axumite coin, c. A.D. 500

British There are known to be examples extant of the un-issued Edward VIII 1937 coins from ¼d to £5 excluding the gold £2 piece. Only a single example of a 1933 and a 1954 penny is known to be in private hands.

Most
expensive
World The highest price paid in auction for a single coin is $110,000 (£44,000) for a U.S. Quarter Eagle or $5 gold piece of 1841 by Mr. Lester Merkin of New York City on 12 Feb. 1972. Only 9 others are known. Among the many unique coins that which would attract logically the greatest price on the market would be the unique 1873 dime (U.S. 10 cent piece) with the CC mint mark, since dimes are the most avidly collected series of any coins in the world.

British The highest auction price paid for an English coin is £10,500 paid by the London dealer Spink at the salerooms of Messrs. Glendining and Co. on 17 Oct. 1968 for a gold Edward IV London Noble of the Heavy Coinage period (1461–1464), from the Fishpool Hoard discovered on 22 March 1966. An Irish gold pistole minted in England in 1646 fetched £13,500 at auction at Sotheby's on 16 June 1972. On 24 Nov. 1972 one of the 8 1933 pennies was auctioned at Sotheby's for £7,000.

Legal tender
coins
Oldest The oldest legal tender Imperial coins in circulation are the now rare silver shillings (now 5p) and sixpences (now 2½p) of the reign of George III, dated 1816. All gold coinage of or above the least current weight dated onward from 1838 is still legal tender.

Heaviest
and
highest
denomina-
tion The gold five-pound (£5) piece or quintuple sovereign is both the highest current denomination coin in the United Kingdom and also, at 616.37 grains 1.4066 oz. the heaviest. The most recent specimens available to the public are dated 1937, of which only 5,501 were minted. (See Colour photographs pp. 6–7)

Lightest and
smallest The silver Maundy (new) penny piece is the smallest of the British legal tender coins and, at 7.27 grains (just under 1/60th of an ounce), the lightest. These coins exist for every date since 1822 and are 0.453 in 11,5 mm in diameter.

Greatest
collection It was estimated in November 1967 that the Lilly coin collection of 1,227 U.S. gold pieces now at the Smithsonian Institution, Washington, D.C. U.S.A., had a market value of $5½ million (£2,290,000). The greatest single coin collection ever amassed in Britain was that of Richard Cyril Lockett (1873–1950) of Liverpool, Lancashire. The collection realized a record of £387,457.

The greatest hoard of gold of unknown ownership ever recovered is one valued at about $3,000,000 (£1,070,000) from the lost £8,000,000 (£2,860,000) carried in 10 ships of a Spanish bullion fleet which was sunk by a hurricane off Florida, U.S.A., on 31 July 1715. The biggest single haul was by the diver Kip Wagner on 30 May 1965.

Largest
Treasure
Trove The largest hoard of coins ever found in the United Kingdom was the Tutbury hoard, discovered on the bed of the River Dove in Staffordshire in June 1831. It consisted of about 20,000 silver coins of Edward I and Edward II and some of Henry III. The chest is believed to have been deposited in c. 1324–25. The most valuable hoard ever found was one of more than 1,200 gold coins from the reigns of King Richard II to Edward IV, worth more than £500,000, found on 22 March 1966 by John Craughwell, aged 47, at Fishpool, near Mansfield, Nottinghamshire.

Largest
mint The largest mint in the world is the U.S. Treasury's mint built in 1965–69 on Independence Mall, Philadelphia, covering 11½ acres 4,65 ha with an annual capacity on a 3 shift seven day week production of 8,000 million coins. A single stamping machine can produce coins at a rate of 10,000 per minute.

Greatest
hoarders It was estimated in November 1968 that about $22,500 million (£9,000 million) worth of gold is being retained in personal possession throughout the world and that $4,800 million (£1,920 million) of this total is held by the population of France.

Largest pile The most valuable column of coins amassed for charity was a 6 ft 1,83 m high column of 2 pence pieces worth £1,051.08 (52,554 coins) at the Coundon Hotel, Coventry, on 26 Feb. 1973. The first achievement of a kilometre of New Pence was on 19 May 1973 by 112 children from Tattershall C.E. Primary School, Lincolnshire. They used 50,500 coins on a slip road at R.A.F. Coningsby, Lincolnshire.

TRADE UNIONS

Largest
World The world's largest union is the Industrie-Gewerkschaft Metall (Metal Workers' Union) of West Germany, with a membership of 2,354,975 at 1 Jan. 1973. The union with the longest name is probably the F.N.O.M.M.C.F.E.T.M.F., the National Federation of Officers, Machinists, Motormen, Drivers, Firemen and Electricians in Sea and River Transportation of Brazil.

Britain The largest union in the United Kingdom is the Transport and General Workers' Union, with 1,746,234 members at 1 Jan. 1973.

Oldest The oldest of the 150 trade unions affiliated to the Trade Union Congress (founded 1868) is the National Society of Brushmakers (current membership 2,700) founded in 1747.

Smallest The smallest affiliated union is the Sheffield Wool Shear Workers' Trade Union with a membership of 19. The unaffiliated London Handforged Spoon and Fork Makers' Society instituted in July 1874, has a membership of 6.

LABOUR DISPUTES

Earliest The earliest recorded strike was one by an orchestra leader from Greece named Aristos in Rome c. 309 B.C. The cause was meal breaks.

Largest The most serious single labour dispute in the United Kingdom was the General Strike of 4–12 May 1926, called by the Trades Union Congress in support of the Miners' Federation. During the nine days of the strike 1,580,000 people were involved and 14,500,000 working days were lost.

The smallest Trade Union—the London Handforged Spoon and Fork Makers' Society

During the year 1926 a total of 2,750,000 people were involved in 323 different labour disputes and the working days lost during the year amounted to 162,300,000, the highest figure ever recorded. The figure for 1972 was 23,904,000 working days.

Longest The world's longest recorded strike ended on 4 Jan. 1961, after 33 years. It concerned the employment of barbers' assistants in Copenhagen, Denmark. The longest recorded major strike was that at the plumbing fixtures factory of the Kohler Co. in Sheboygan, Wisconsin, U.S.A., between April 1954 and October 1962. The strike is alleged to have cost the United Automobile Workers' Union about $12,000,000 (£4.8 million) to sustain.

UNEMPLOYMENT

Highest The highest recorded unemployment in Great Britain was on 23 Jan. 1933, when the total of unemployed persons on the Employment Exchange registers was 2,903,065, representing 22.8 per cent of the insured working population. The highest figure for Wales was 244,579 (39.1 per cent) on 22 Aug. 1932.

Lowest The lowest recorded peace-time level of unemployment was 0.9 per cent on 11 July 1955, when 184,929 persons were registered. The peak figure for the total working population in the United Kingdom has been 26,290,000 in September 1966. The figure for June 1972 was 25,377,000.

Largest association The largest single association in the world is the Blue Cross, the U.S.-based medical insurance organization with a membership at 1 Jan. 1971 of 78,715,111. Benefits paid out exceeded $5.30 billion (£2,120 million). The largest association in the United Kingdom is the Automobile Association, with a membership which reached 5,000,000 on 19 June 1973.

FOOD CONSUMPTION

Calories Of all countries in the world, based on the latest available data, Ireland has the largest available total of calories per person. The net supply averaged 3,450 per day in 1968. The United Kingdom average was 3,180 per day in 1968–69. The highest calorific value of any foodstuff is that of pure animal fat, with 930 calories per 100 g *3.5 oz.* Pure alcohol provides 710 calories per 100 g.

Protein Australia and New Zealand have the highest recorded consumption of protein per person, an average of 106 g *3.79 oz.* per day in 1969. The United Kingdom average was 88 g *3.10 oz.* per day in 1968–69.

The lowest *reported* figures are 1,730 calories per day in the Libyan Arab Republic in 1960–62 and 33 g *1.47 oz.* of protein per day in Zaire in 1964–66.

Cereals The greatest consumers of cereal products—flour, milled rice, etc.—are the people of Egypt, with an average of 501 lb. per person *600 g/day* in 1966–67. The United Kingdom average was 160.9 lb. *199 g/day* in 1968–69 and the figure for the Republic of Ireland was 210 lb. *260 g/day* in 1968.

Starch The greatest eaters of starchy food (e.g. bananas, potatoes, etc.) are the people of Gabon, who consumed 4.02 lb. *1 823 g* per head per day in 1964–66. The United Kingdom average was 9.77 oz. *276 g* per day in 1970. The average for Ireland was 12.30 oz. *348 g* in 1968.

Sugar The greatest consumers of sugars are the people of Iceland, with an average of 5.29 oz. *149 g* per person per day in 1964–66. The lowest consumption is 0.70 oz. *19 g* per day in Burundi and Dahomey (both 1964-66). The United Kingdom average was 5.08 oz. *144 g* in 1970 and the average in Ireland was 5.04 oz. *142 g* in 1968.

Meat The greatest meat eaters in the world—figures include offal and poultry—are the people of Uruguay, with an average consumption of 10.93 oz. *309 g* per person per day in 1964–66. The lowest consumption is 0.16 oz. *0,45 g* in Sri Lanka (formerly Ceylon) in 1968. The United Kingdom average was 5.74 oz. *162 g* in 1970 and the Irish average was 7.34 oz. *208 g* in 1967.

BEER

Of reporting countries, the nation with the highest beer consumption per person is Belgium, with 140 l *30.8 gal* per person in 1970. The equivalent figure for the United Kingdom is 100,9 l 22.2 gal per person. In the Northern Territory of Australia, however, the annual intake has been estimated to be as high as 52 gal *236 l* per person. A society for the prevention of alcoholism in Darwin had to disband in June 1966 for lack of support. The January 1970 edition of the U.S.S.R. periodical *Sotsialisticheskaya Industria* claimed that the Russians invented beer.

SPIRITS

The freest spirit drinkers are the white population of South Africa, with 1.71 gal *7,77 l* of proof spirit/person/year, and the most abstemious are the people of Belgium, with 2 pints *1,13 l* per person. It was estimated in 1969 that 13 per cent of all males between 20 and 55 years in France were suffering from alcoholism.

Prohibition The longest lasting imposition of prohibition has been 26 years in Iceland (1908–34). Other prohibitions have been U.S.S.R. (1914–24) and U.S.A. (1920–33).

Largest dish The largest menu item in the world is roasted camel, prepared occasionally for Bedouin wedding feasts. Cooked eggs are stuffed in fish, the fish stuffed in cooked chickens, the chickens stuffed into a roasted sheep carcass and the sheep stuffed into a whole camel.

Most expensive food The most expensive food is white truffle of Alba which fetch, according to seasonal rarity, up to £80 per lb. *£176 per kg* in the market. Truffles in the Périgord district of France require drought between mid-July and mid-August.

Longest Banana Split The longest Banana split ever made was one a mile *1 609 m* in length embracing 10,580 bananas; 33,000 scoops of ice cream; 255 gal of topping, 155 lb *70,33 kg* of chopped nuts and 95 gal of whipped cream at the annual St. Paul Winter Carnival, Minnesota, U.S.A. on 29 Jan. 1973. The calorific value was estimated at 32,670,000.

Largest cake The largest cakes ever baked were a six-sided "birthday" cake weighing 25,000 lb. *11 338 kg*, made in August 1962 by Van de Kemp's Holland Dutch Bakers of Seattle, Washington State, U.S.A., for the Seattle World's Fair (the "Century 21 Exposition"), and a 26 ft *7,92 m* tall creation of the same weight made for the British Columbia Centennial cut on 20 July 1971.

Wedding Cake Most Tiers The most tiers reported for any wedding cake has been 25 for Teresa Doherty at Athlunkard Boat Club Limerick, Ireland in April 1973.

Longest Loaf The longest loaf ever baked was one of 100 ft *30,48 m* by Findlay's Gold Krust Bakeries, Auckland, New Zealand in Nov. 1969.

Largest Easter egg The largest Easter egg ever made was one of 550 lb. *249 kg* and £200 worth of chocolate made at the Liverpool College of Crafts and Catering in March 1971.

Largest meat pie The largest meat pie ever baked weighed 5 tons, measuring 18 × 6 ft and 18 in deep *5,48 × 1,83 × 0,45 m*, the seventh in the series of Denby Dale (West Riding, Yorkshire) pies, to mark four royal births on 5 Sept. 1964. The first was in 1788 to celebrate King George III's return to sanity but the fourth (Queen Victoria's Jubilee, 1887) went a bit "off" and had to be buried in quick-lime.

Largest Mince Pie The largest mince pie recorded was one of 2,260 lb. *1 025 kg*, 20 × 5 ft *6,09 × 1,52 m*, baked at Ashby-de-la-Zouch, Leicestershire in 1932.

Largest Omelette The largest omelette made was one of 1,234 lb. *559,5 kg* made from 5,600 eggs cooked in a 7 × 6 ft *2,13 × 1,83 m* frying tank at the Surrey Agricultural Show, Guildford, Surrey on 28 May 1973. The chief chefs were Tony Stoppani and Barbara Logan with sponsorship from *Poultry World*, SEGAS and the British Egg Information Service.

Largest pizza pie The largest pizza ever baked was one measuring 21 ft *6,40 m* in diameter, hence 346 ft² *32 m²* in area and 1,000 lb *453 kg* in weight at Pizza Pete, South Pulaski Road, Chicago, Illinois, U.S.A. on 3 May 1970.

The ice cream sundae, weighing ¾ ton, made in 1972 by Bob Bercaw of Wooster, Ohio which was surpassed by his 1973 monster

The giant half ton pizza constructed in Chicago in May 1970

Largest sundae The most monstrous ice cream sundae ever concocted is one of 2,011 lb. *912 kg* by Bob Bercaw of Wooster, Ohio, U.S.A. built on 4 July 1973. It contained 133 lb. *60 kg* of pineapple topping, 144 lb. *63 kg* of chocolate syrup and 16 lb. *7 kg* of murichino cherries.

Largest hamburger The largest hamburger on record is one with buns 14 ft *4,26 m* in circumference and 230 lb. *104 kg* of prime beef, 4 gal *15 l* of tomato sauce and a gallon of mustard made by Mister K's Restaurant, Hattiesburg, Mississippi, U.S.A.

SPICES

Most expensive The most expensive of all spices is Mediterranean saffron (*Crocus sativus*). It takes 96,000 stigmas and therefore 32,000 flowers to make a pound. Packets of 1.9 grains are retailed in the United Kingdom for 8½p—equivalent to £19.50 per oz. *68p per gramme*.

"Hottest" The hottest of all spices is the capsicum hot pepper known as Tabasco, first reported in 1868 by Mr. Edmund McIlhenny on Avery Island, Louisiana, U.S.A.

Rarest condiment The world's most prized condiment is Cà Cuong, a secretion recovered in minute amounts from beetles in North Vietnam. Owing to war conditions, the price rose to $100 (*now £40*) per ounce *1,41 g* before supplies virtually ceased.

Sweets The biggest sweet eaters in the world are the people of Britain, with 7.8 oz. *221 g* of confectionery per person per week in 1971. The figure for Scotland was more than 9 oz. *255 g* in 1968.

Tea The most expensive tea marketed in the United Kingdom is "Oolong Leaf Bud", specially imported for Fortnum and Mason of Piccadilly, London, W.1, where, in 1973, it retailed for £4.40 per lb. or 97p/*100 g*. It is blended from very young Formosan leaves. In Britain the *per caput* consumption of tea in 1970 was 139.2 oz. *3 946 g* now overtaken by Libya and Ireland.

The world's largest tea company is Brooke Bond Liebig Limited (a merger of Brooke Bond Tea Ltd. of London founded 1869 and Liebig's Extract of Meat Co. Ltd. made in May 1968), with a turnover of £262,871,000 in the year ended 30 June 1972. The company has 38,887 acres *15 737 ha* of mature plantations in India, Sri Lanka (formerly Ceylon), and East Africa, and ranches in Argentina, Paraguay and Rhodesia extending over 2,663,000 acres *1 077 600 ha* and employs more than 80,000 people.

Coffee The world's greatest coffee drinkers are the people of Finland, who consumed 16,92 kg *37.30 lb.* of coffee per person in 1970. This compares with 1,63 kg *3.59 lb.* for the United Kingdom in 1970. The most expensive coffee is Jamaica Blue Mountain retailed in the U.S. at $5.27 (£2.10) per lb. *£4.62 per kg* in April 1973.

Fresh water The world's greatest consumers of fresh water are the people of the United States, whose average daily consumption reached 308,000 million gal *14 000 million hectolitres* in 1970 or 1,800 U.S. gal *6 813 litres* per head per day.

Oldest tinned food The oldest tinned food known was roast beef canned by Donkin, Hall and Gamble in 1823 and salvaged from H.M.S. *Fury* in the Northwest Passage, Canada. It was opened on 11 Dec. 1958.

Recipe The oldest known surviving recipe is one dated 1657 handed down from Bernice Bardolf of the Black Horse Tavern, Barnsley, Yorkshire found buried in September 1969 in the yard of the Alhambra Hotel Barnsley. Barnsley Bardolf, a variant, is now on the menu.

ENERGY

To express the various forms of available energy (coal, liquid fuels and water power, etc., but omitting vegetable fuels and peat), it is the practice to convert them all into terms of coal. On this basis the world average consumption was the equivalent of 1 889 kg *(37.1 cwt)* of coal, or its energy equivalents, per person in 1970.

The highest consumption in the world is in the United States, with an average of 11 144 kg *219.3 cwt* per person in 1970. The United Kingdom average was 5 362 kg *105.5 cwt* per person in 1970. The lowest recorded average for 1970 was 9 kg *19.8 lb.* per person in Burundi.

MASS COMMUNICATIONS

AIRLINES

The country with the busiest airlines system is the United States, where 135,651 million revenue passenger miles were flown on scheduled domestic and local services in 1971. This was equivalent to an annual trip of 655.3 miles *1 054 km* for every one of the inhabitants of the U.S.A. The United Kingdom airlines flew 192,537,000 miles *309 858 000 km* and carried 15,766,900 passengers in 1972.

MERCHANT SHIPPING

The world total of merchant shipping excluding vessels of less than 100 tons gross, sailing vessels and barges was 57,391 vessels of 268,340,145 tons gross on 1 July 1972. The largest merchant fleet in the world as at mid-1972 was that under the flag of Liberia with 2,234 ships of 44,443,652 tons gross. Liberian registration overtook the United Kingdom Merchant fleet of 21,716,148 tons gross in 1967. The U.K. figure for mid-1972 was 3,700 ships of 28,624,875 tons gross.

Largest and busiest ports Physically, the largest port in the world is New York Harbor, N.Y., U.S.A. The port has a navigable waterfront of 755 miles *121,5 km* (295 miles *4 74km* in New Jersey) stretching over 92 miles² *238 km²*. A total of 261 general cargo berths and 130 other piers give a total berthing capacity of 391 ships at one time. The total warehousing floor space is 422.4 acres *170,9 ha.* The world's busiest port and largest artificial harbour is the Rotterdam-Europoort in the Netherlands which covers 38 miles² *100 km²*. It handled 32,980 sea-going vessels and about 300,000 barges in 1971. It is able to handle 310 sea-going vessels simultaneously up to 251,000 tons and 65 ft *19,80 m* draught. In 1971 232,781,000 tons of seaborne cargo was handled.

RAILWAYS

The country with the greatest length of railway is the United States, with 205,782 miles *331 173 km* of track at 1 Jan. 1971.

The farthest anyone can get from a railway on the mainland island of Great Britain is 54 miles *87 km* in the case of Cape Wrath, Sutherland, Scotland.

The number of journeys made on British Rail in 1972 was 753,608,000, with an average journey of 23.73 miles, compared with the peak year of 1957, when 1,101 million journeys (average 20.51 miles) were made.

ROADS

Oldest The oldest wooden trackway in the world was discovered in 1966 near Abbot's Way, Somerset and known as "Bell B". It is dated to *c* 2900 B.C. The first sod on Britain's first motorway, the M.1 was cut by the Rt. Hon. Harold Watkinson on 31 March 1958.

The country with the greatest length of road is the United States (all 50 States), with 3,730,082 miles *6 003 334 km* of graded roads at 1 Jan. 1970. Regular driving licences are issuable at 15, without a driver education course only in Hawaii and Mississippi. Thirteen U.S. States issue restricted juvenile licences at 14.

The United Kingdom has 223,467 miles of road including 843 miles of motorway at 1 April 1971 and 15,837,128 vehicles in 1971. A total of 23,000,000 vehicles by 1980 has been forecast.

Busiest The highest traffic volume of any point in the world is at the Harbor and Santa Monica Freeways interchange in Los Angeles, California, U.S.A. with a 24-hour average on Fridays of 420,000 vehicles in 1970.

The territory with the highest traffic density in the world is Hong Kong. On 31 May 1970 there were 122,274 motor vehicles on 600 miles *965 km* of serviceable roads giving a density of 8.64 yds *7,90 m* per vehicle. The comparative figure for the United Kingdom in 1971 was 24.82 yds *22,69 m*.

The greatest traffic density at any one point in the United Kingdom is at Hyde Park Corner, London. The average daytime 8 a.m.–8 p.m. flow in 1970 was 164,338 vehicles every 12 hours. The busiest Thames bridge in 1968 was Putney Bridge, with a 12-hour average of 36,249 vehicles. The greatest reported aggregation of London buses was 38, bumper to bumper, along the Vauxhall Bridge Road on 18 Nov. 1965. Censuses are biennial.

Widest The widest street in the world is the Monumental Axis running for 1½ miles *2,4 km* from the Municipal Plaza to the Plaza of the Three Powers in Brasilia, the capital of Brazil. The six-lane Boulevard was opened in April 1960 and is 250 m *273.4 yds* wide. The B Bridge Toll Plaza has 34 lanes (17 in each direction) serving the Bay Bridge, San Francisco, California.

Narrowest The world's narrowest street is St. John's Lane in Rome, with a width of 19 in *48 cm*. The narrowest street in the United Kingdom is Parliament Street, Exeter, Devon, which at one point measures 26 in *66 cm* across.

Longest straight road The longest straight road in the United Kingdom was a stretch of 22¾ miles *33,6 km* between Bailgate in the City of Lincoln and Broughton Village, Lincolnshire. Part of the Roman road Ermine Street, it now comprises sections of Class I (A. 15), Class III and unclassified road, with only two slight deviations of less than 50 ft *15 m* from the true straight line. Part of the road was closed for an airfield, reducing the straight section to 16½ miles *26,5 km*.

205

Longest World The longest motorable road in the world is the Pan-American Highway, which will stretch 17,018 miles *27 387 km* from North West Alaska, to southernmost Chile. There remains a gap known as the Tapon del Darien, in Panama and the Atrato Swamp, Colombia. This was first traversed by the 1972 British Trans-Americas Expedition, led by Major John Blashford-Snell M.B.E., R.E., which emerged from the Atrato swamp after 99 days. On 9 June 1972 the highly modified Range Rover VXC 868K which had made the traverse arrived in Tierra del Fuego, having left Alaska on 3 Dec. 1971.

Most complex interchange The most complex interchange on the British road system is that at Gravelly Hill, north of Birmingham on the Midland Link Motorway section of the M6 opened on 24 May 1972. There are 18 routes on 6 levels together with a diverted canal and river, which consumed 26,000 tons/*tonnes* of steel, 250,000 tons/*tonnes* of concrete, 300,000 tons/*tonnes* of earth and cost £8,200,000.

Longest street This title has been accorded to Figueroa Street which stretches 30 miles *48,2 km* from Pasadena at Colorado Blvd. to the Pacific Coast Highway, Los Angeles, U.S.A.

Britain The longest designated road in Great Britain is the A1 from London to Edinburgh of 404 miles *650 km*. The longest Roman roads were Watling Street, from Dubrae (Dover) 215 miles *346 km* through Londinium (London) to Viroconium (Wroxeter), and Fosse Way, which ran 218 miles *350 km* from Lindum (Lincoln) through Aquae Sulus (Bath) to Isca Dumnoniorum (Exeter). However, a 10-mile *16 km* section of Fosse Way between Ilchester and Seaton remains indistinct. The commonest street name in Greater London is Park Road, of which there are 43.

Shortest The shortest High Street in Britain is that at Ashley Heath, Hampshire which is 40 yds *36,5 m* long.

Longest hill The longest steep hill on any road in the United Kingdom is on the road westwards from Lochcarron toward Applecross in Ross and Cromarty, Scotland. In 6 miles *9,6 km* this road rises from sea-level to 2,054 ft *626 m* with an average gradient of 1 in 15.4, the steepest part being 1 in 4.

Highest World The highest pass ever used by traffic is the Bódpo La (19,412 ft *[5 916 m]* above sea-level), in western Tibet. It was used in 1929 by a caravan from the Shipki Pass on the trade route to Rudok. The highest carriageable road in the world is one 1,180 km *733.2 miles* long between Tibet and south-western Sinkiang, completed in October 1957, which takes in passes of an altitude up to 18,480 ft *5 632 m* above sea-level. Europe's highest pass (excluding the Caucasian passes) is the Col de Restefond (9,193 ft *[2 802 m]*) completed in 1962 with 21 hairpins between Jausiers and Saint-Etienne-de-Tinée, France. It is usually closed between early October and early June. The highest motor road in Europe is the Pico de Veleta in the Sierra Nevada, southern Spain. The shadeless climb of *36 km 22.4 miles* brings the motorist to 11,384 ft *3 469 m* above sea-level and will on the completion of a road on its southern side become also Europe's highest pass.

United Kingdom The highest road in the United Kingdom is the A6293 tarmac extension at Great Dun Fell, Westmorland (2,780 ft *[847 m]*) leading to a Ministry of Defence radar installation. A permit is required to use it. The highest classified road in England is the B6293 at Killhope Cross (2,056 ft *[626 m]*) on the Cumberland-Durham border near Nenthead. The highest classified road in Scotland is the A93 road over the Grampians through Cairnwell, a pass between Blairgowrie, Perthshire, and Braemar, Aberdeenshire, which reaches a height of 2,199 ft *670 m*. The highest classified road in Wales is the Rhondda-Afan Inter-Valley road (A4107), which

The highly modified Range Rover, making the first ever crossing of the Darien Gap, during the 17,000 mile *27 350 km* Trans-America expedition

reaches 1,750 ft *533 m* 2½ miles *4 km* east of Abergwynfi, Glamorganshire.

Lowest The lowest road in the world is that along the Israeli shores of the Dead Sea, 1,290 ft *393 m* below sea-level. The lowest surface roads in Great Britain are just below sea-level in the Holme Fen area of Huntingdon and Peterborough.

Highest motorway The highest motorway in Great Britain is the trans-Pennine M62, which, at the Windy Hill interchange, reaches an altitude of 1,220 ft *371 m*. Its Dean Head cutting is the deepest roadway cutting in Europe at 183 ft *55,7 m*.

Longest viaduct The longest elevated road viaduct on the British road system is the 2.97 mile *5 730 m* Gravelly Hill to Castle Bromwich section of the M6. It was completed in May 1972.

Biggest square The Tian an men (Gate of Heavenly Peace) Square in Peking, described as the navel of China, extends over 98 acres *39,6 ha*. The Maiden e Shah in Isfahan, Iran extends over 20.1 acres *8,1 ha*. The oldest London square is Bloomsbury Square planned in 1754.

Traffic jams The worst traffic jams in the world are in Tōkyō, Japan. Only 9 per cent of the city area is roadway, compared with London (23 per cent), Paris (25 per cent), New York (35 per cent) and Washington, D.C. (43 per cent). In April 1973 it was stated that there were only 247,000 registered cars in Moscow. The longest traffic jam reported in Britain was one of 35 miles *56 km* out of 42.5 miles *75,6 km* road length between Torquay and Yarcombe, Devon, on 25 July 1964 and 35 miles *56 km* on the A30 between Egham, Surrey and Micheldever, Hampshire on 23 May 1970.

Traffic lights Manual 3 colour electric traffic lights were introduced into New York City in 1918. Traffic lights were introduced in Great Britain with a one day trial in Wolverhampton on 11 Feb. 1928. They were first permanently operated in Leeds, Yorkshire on 16 March and in Edinburgh, Scotland on 19 March 1928. The first vehicle-actuated lights were installed at the Cornhill-Gracechurch Junction, City of London in 1932. Semaphore-type traffic signals had been set up in Westminster Square, London in 1868 with red and green gas lamps for night use. It was not an offence to disobey traffic signals until assent was given to the 1930 Road Traffic bill.

Parking meters The earliest parking meters ever installed were those put in the business district of Oklahoma City, Oklahoma, U.S.A., on 19 July 1935. They were the invention of Carl C. Magee (U.S.A.) and reached London in 1958.

Worst driver It was reported that a 75-year-old *male* driver received 10 traffic tickets, drove on the wrong side of the road four times, committed four hit-and-run offences and caused six accidents, all within 20 minutes, in McKinney, Texas, U.S.A., on 15 Oct. 1966.

Milestone Britain's oldest milestone *in situ* is a Roman stone dating from A.D. 150 on the Stanegate, at Chesterholm, near Badron Mill, Northumberland.

TELEPHONES

There were 291,329,000 telephones in the world at 1 Jan. 1972 as estimated by The American Telephone & Telegraph Co. The country with the greatest number was the United States, with 124,665,000 instruments, equivalent to 601.3 for every 1,000 people, compared with the United Kingdom figure of 16,143,102 (third largest in the world to the U.S.A. and Japan), or 288.8 per 1,000 people, at 31 March 1972. The territory with fewest reported telephones is Pitcairn Island with 31.

The country with the most telephones per head of population is Monaco, with 664.8 per 1,000 of the population at 1 Jan. 1972. The country with the least was Upper Volta with 0.3 of a telephone per 1,000 people at 1 Jan. 1970 (latest figure) and Laos and Nepal with 0.6 at 1 Jan. 1972.

The greatest total of calls made in any country is in the United States, with 171,797 million (830.0 calls per person) in 1971. The lowest recorded figure was the Philippines with 0.2 of a call per person in 1971. The United Kingdom telephone service connected 12,117,283,000 calls in the year 1971-72, an average of 217.6 per person.

The city with most telephones is New York City, N.Y., U.S.A., with 5,825,460 (739 per 1,000 people) at 1 Jan. 1972. In 1972 Washington D.C. reached the level of 1,230 telephones per 1,000 people though in some small areas there are still higher densities such as Beverly Hills, north of Los Angeles with a return of about 1,600 per 1,000.

Longest call The longest telephone connection on record was one of 691 hours 6 min from 23 Oct. to 21 Nov. 1969 between co-eds of Zimmermann (Girls) and Ellsworth Hall (male students) at Western Michigan University, Kalamazoo, U.S.A.

Longest cable The world's longest submarine telephone cable is the Commonwealth Pacific Cable (COMPAC), which runs for more than 9,000 miles *14 480 km* from Australia, *via* Auckland, New Zealand and the Hawaiian Islands to Port Alberni, Canada. It cost about £35,000,000 and was inaugurated on 2 Dec. 1963.

POSTAL SERVICES

The country with the largest mail in the world is the United States, whose population posted 85,187 million letters and packages in 1970 when the U.S

Postal Service employed 715,970 people. The United Kingdom total was 13,050 million letters in the year ending 31 March 1971.

The United States also takes first place in the average number of letters which each person posts during one year. The figure was 413 in 1970. The United Kingdom figure was 235 per head in 1970-71. Of all countries the greatest discrepancy between incoming and outgoing mail is for the U.S.A. whence in 1970 only 887 million items were mailed in response to 1,477 million items received from foreign sources.

POSTAGE STAMPS

Earliest The earliest adhesive postage stamps in the world were the "Penny Blacks" of the United Kingdom, bearing the head of Queen Victoria, placed on sale on 1 May for use on 6 May 1840. A total of 64,000,000 were printed. The National Postal Museum possesses a unique full proof sheet of 240 stamps, printed in April 1840, before the corner letters, plate numbers or marginal inscriptions were added.

Largest The largest stamps ever issued were the 1913 Express Delivery stamps of China, which measured 9¾ by 2¼ in *247,5 × 69,8 mm*. The largest postage labels ever printed were the 8RLS (riyal) (70p) air mail stamps issued by the former Trucial State of Fujeira (Fujairah) measuring 2⅝ × 4⅛ in *66,6 × 104,7 mm* on 5 Apr. 1972 for the 1972 Olympic Games. The Universal Postal Union do not regard this as a *bona fide* postal stamp.

Smallest The smallest stamps ever issued were the 10 cents and 1 peso of the Colombian State of Bolívar in 1863-66. They measured 8 mm *0.31 in* by 9,5 mm *0.37 in*. The imperforate 4/4 schilling red of Mecklenburg-Schwerin issued on 1 July 1856 printed in Berlin was divisible into four quarters. Thus a ¼ schilling section measured fractionally over 10 mm² *0.394 in²*.

Highest and lowest denomination The highest denomination stamp ever issued was a red and black stamp for £100, issued in Kenya in 1925-27. Although valid for postage its function was essentially for collection of revenue. The highest denomination stamp ever issued in the United Kingdom was the £5 orange Victoria stamp issued on 21 March 1882. Owing to inflations it is difficult to determine the lowest denomination stamp but it was probably the 1946 3,000 pengö Hungarian stamp, worth at one time only 6.6×10^{-15}p.

Highest price World The highest price ever paid for a single philatelic item is the $380,000 (*then £158,333*) for two 1d. orange "Post Office" Mauritius stamps of 1847 on a cover bought at H. R. Harmer's Inc., New York City, U.S.A. by Raymond H. Weill Co. of New Orleans, Louisiana for their own account from the Liechtenstein-Dale collection on 21 Oct. 1968. The item was discovered in 1897 in an Indian bazaar by a Mr. Charles Williams who paid less than £1 for it.

Most valuable World There are a number of stamps of which but a single specimen is known. Of these the most celebrated is the one cent black on magenta issued in British Guiana (now Guyana) in February 1856. It was originally bought for six shillings from L. Vernon Vaughan, a schoolboy, in 1873. This is the world's most renowned stamp, for which £A16,000 (*then £12,774 sterling*) was paid in 1940, when it was sold by Mrs. Arthur Hind. It was insured for £200,000 when it was displayed in 1965 at the Royal Festival Hall, London. It was sold on 24 March 1970 by Frederick T. Small by auction at the Siegal Galleries, New York City, U.S.A. for $280,000 (*then £116,666*) by Irwin Weinberg. It is now "catalogued" at £120,000. It was alleged in October 1938 that Hind had, in 1928, purchased and burned his stamp's twin.

Great Britain The rarest British stamp which is not an error is the King Edward VII 6d. dull purple Inland Revenue Official stamp issued and withdrawn on 14 May 1904. Only 11 or 12 are known and the only unusued example in private hands was auctioned at Stanley Gibbons, London on 27 Oct. 1972 for £10,000.

Commonest British stamp The most frequently reproduced United Kingdom stamp has been the definitive Elizabeth II 3d. violet, issued from 1 Oct. 1953 to 17 May 1965, of which 19,920 million were issued.

Largest collection The greatest private stamp collection ever auctioned has been that of Maurice Burrus (d. 1959) of Alsace, France, which realised an estimated £1,500,000.

The largest national collection in the world is that at the British Museum, London, which has had the General Post Office collection on permanent loan since March 1963. The British Royal collection, housed in 400 volumes, is also believed to be worth well in excess of £1,000,000. The collection of the U.P.U. (founded 9 Oct. 1874) in Berne, Switzerland receives 400 copies of each new issue of each member nation while the largest international collection open to the public is in the Swiss Postal Museum in Berne.

POSTAL ADDRESSES

Highest numbering The practice of numbering houses began in 1463 on the Pont Notre Dame, Paris, France. The highest numbered house in Britain is No. 2,679 Stratford Road, Solihull, Warwickshire, occupied since 1966 by Mr. & Mrs. H. Hughes. The highest numbered house in Scotland is No. 2,629 London Road, Mount Vernon, Glasgow, which is part of the local police station.

Pillar-boxes Pillar-boxes were introduced into Great Britain at the suggestion of the novelist Anthony Trollope (1815–82). The oldest site on which one is still in service is one dating from 8 Feb. 1853 in Union Street, St. Peter Port, Guernsey though the present box is not the original. The oldest original box in Great Britain is another Victorian example at Barnes Cross, Holwell, near Bishop's Caundle, Dorset, also dating from probably later in 1853.

Post Offices The Post Office's northernmost post office is at Haroldswick, Unst, Shetland Islands. The most southerly in the British Isles is at Samarès, Jersey. The oldest is at Sanquhar, Dumfriesshire which was first referred to in 1763. In England the Post Office at Shipton-Under-Wychwood, Oxfordshire dates back to April 1845.

TELEGRAMS

The country where most telegrams are sent is the U.S.S.R., whose population sent 365,900,000 telegrams in 1970. The United Kingdom total was 10,450,000 including 2,550,000 sent overseas, in the year ending 31 March 1971.

The world's largest telegraph company is the Western Union Telegraph Company of New York City, N.Y., U.S.A. It had 26,269 employees on 1 Jan. 1969, a total of 11,000 telegraphic offices and agencies and 5,734,792 miles of telegraph channels.

The largest British telegraphic undertaking is Cable and Wireless Ltd., which operates 56,234 nautical miles *104 211 km* of ocean cables (including 20,091 miles [*37 232 km*] of telephone cable). It has a fleet of six cable ships, more than 80 overseas stations and 10,152 employees.

INLAND WATERWAYS

The country with the greatest length of inland waterways is Finland. The total length of navigable lakes

Mr. H. Hughes outside his house—the highest numbered in Great Britain, 2679, Stratford Road, Solihull

and rivers is about 50,000 km *31,000 miles*. In the United Kingdom the total length of navigable rivers and canals is 3,940 miles *6 340 km*.

Longest navigable river The longest navigable natural waterway in the world is the River Amazon, which sea-going vessels can ascend as far as Iquitos, in Peru, 2,236 miles *3 598 km* from the Atlantic seaboard. On a National Geographic Society expedition ending on 10 March 1969, Helen and Frank Schreider navigated downstream from San Francisco, Peru, 3,845 miles *6 187 km* up the Amazon, by a balsa raft named *Mamuri* 249 miles *400 km* to Atalaya, thence 356 miles *572 km* to Pucallpa by outboard motor dug-out canoe and thence the last 3,240 miles *5 214 km* towards Belem in the 30 ft *9,14 m* petrol-engined cabin cruiser *Amazon Queen*.

7. EDUCATION

ILLITERACY

Literacy is variously defined as "ability to read simple subjects" and "ability to read and write a simple letter". The looseness of definition and the scarcity of data for many countries preclude anything more than approximations, but the extent of illiteracy among adults (15 years old and over) is estimated to have been 39.3 per cent throughout the world at the opening of the last decade in 1961. In 1969 a United Nations' estimate put the level at 810 million out of 2,335 million adults or 34.7 per cent. The continent with the greatest proportion of illiterates is Africa, where 81.5 per cent of adults are illiterate. The last published figure for the Niger Republic is 99.1 per cent. A U.S.S.R. report published in June 1968, affirmed that more than 300 million people in China are still "completely illiterate".

UNIVERSITIES

World Probably the oldest educational institution in the world is the University of Karueein, founded in A.D. 859 in Fez, Morocco.

United Kingdom The oldest university in the United Kingdom is the University of Oxford, which came into being in *c.* 1167. The oldest of the existing colleges is probably

University College (1249), though its foundation is less well documented than that of Merton College in 1264. The earliest college at Cambridge University is Peterhouse, founded in 1284. The largest college at either university is Trinity College, Cambridge. It was founded in 1546. The oldest university in Scotland is the University of St. Andrews, Fife. It was established in 1411.

The largest College within any British University is London's University College with 4,639 full time students in October 1972.

Greatest enrolment The university with the greatest enrolment in the world is the University of Calcutta (founded 1857) in India, with 178,176 students (internal and external) and 31 professors in 1970–71. Owing to the inadequacy of the buildings and number of lecturers, the students are handled in three shifts per day. The enrolment at all branches of the State University of New York, U.S.A., was 166,363 in January 1971 with 8,461 teachers. The University of London had 33,599 (of which 7,789 were medical or dental) full-time students in 1971–72.

Largest building The largest university building in the world is the M. V. Lomonosov State University on the Lenin Hills, south of Moscow, U.S.S.R. It stands 240 m *787,4 ft* tall, has 32 storeys and contains 40,000 rooms. It was constructed in 1949–53.

PROFESSORS

Youngest The youngest at which anybody has been elected to a chair in a university is 19 years in the case of Colin MacLaurin (1698–1746), who was admitted to Marischal College, Aberdeen as Professor of Mathematics on 30 Sept. 1717. In 1725 he was made Professor of Mathematics at Edinburgh University on the recommendation of Sir Isaac Newton. In July 1967 Dr. Harvey Friedman, Ph.D., was appointed Assistant Professor of Mathematics at Stanford University, California, U.S.A. aged just 19 years.

Most durable The longest period for which any professorship has been held is 63 years in the case of Thomas Martyn (1735–1825), Professor of Botany at Cambridge University from 1762 until his death. His father, John Martyn (1699–1768), had occupied the chair from 1733 to 1762.

Senior Wranglers Since 1910 the Wranglers (first class honours students in the Cambridge University mathematical Tripos, part 2) have been placed in alphabetical order only. In 1890 Miss P. G. Fawcett of Newnham was placed "above the Senior Wrangler".

Oldest Graduation Miss Mabel Purefoy Fitz-Gerald (b. Aug. 1872) received an honorary M.A. from Oxford on 14 Dec. 1972 aged 100 as recognition of her work there and subsequently as a physiologist.

Youngest undergraduate The most extreme recorded case of undergraduate juvenility was that of William Thomson (1824–1907), later Lord Kelvin, O.M., G.C.V.O., who entered Glasgow University aged 10 years 4 months in October 1834 and matriculated on 14 Nov. 1834.

Longest studentship No central records are kept but the closest approach in Britain to an eternal student appears to be that of George A. Goulty of Guildford, Surrey who entered the Southern College of Art, Winchester in 1942 and who, in 1973, after 17 years further education, is at Reading University reading for his seventh qualification, a Ph.D.

Oldest student The oldest student enrolled by the Open University is Miss Mary Carr of Gosforth, Northumberland, aged 79.

SCHOOLS

Largest World The largest school in the world was the De Witt Clinton High School in the Bronx, New York City, N.Y., U.S.A., where the enrolment attained a peak of 12,000 in 1934. It was founded in 1897 and now has an enrolment of 6,000.

United Kingdom The school with the most pupils in the United Kingdom is Thomas Bennett School, Crawley, Sussex with 2,145 in January 1972. The highest figure in Scotland is 2,045 at the Portobello Senior Secondary School, Edinburgh as at April 1972.

Oldest in Britain The title of the oldest existing school in Britain is contested. It is claimed that King's School in Canterbury, Kent, was a foundation of Saint Augustine, some time between his arrival in Kent in A.D. 597 and his death in c. 604. Cor Tewdws (College of Theodosius) at Llantwit Major, Glamorganshire, reputedly burnt down in A.D. 446 was refounded by St. Illtyd in 508 and flourished into the 13th century.

Oldest old school tie The practice of wearing distinctive neckties bearing the colours of registered designs of schools, universities, sports clubs, regiments, etc., appears to date from c. 1880. The practice originated in Oxford University, where boater bands were converted into use as "ribbon ties". The earliest definitive evidence stems from an order from Exeter College for college ties, dated 25 June, 1880.

Most expensive World The most expensive school in the world is the Oxford Academy (established 1906) in Pleasantville, New Jersey, U.S.A. It is a private college-preparatory boarding school for boys with "academic deficiencies". The school has 15 masters and each of the 47 boys is taught individually in each course. The tuition fee for the school year is $8,400 (£3,500).

United Kingdom The most expensive school in the United Kingdom is Millfield at Street, Somerset, founded by R. J. O. Meyer in 1937. The standard annual fee for boarding entries under 15 including standard extras in Sept. 1973 was £1,710. The most expensive girls' school in 1971–72 was Benenden, Kent (founded 1924) with annual fees of £870.

Most Schools The greatest documented number of schools attended by a pupil is 265 by Wilma Williams, now Mrs. R. J. Horton, from 1933–43 when her parents were in show business.

Most "O" and "A" levels Edward Short at St. Kevins Comprehensive School, Kirkby, Lancashire between June 1967 and June 1970 accumulated 11 "O", 12 "A" and 3 "S" levels. His brother Leslie in 1968–71 secured 11 "O", 9 "A" and an "S" level making 47 between them. An anonymous pupil of Marst College, Kingston upon Hull with an IQ of 161 passed 14 "O", 11 "A" and 1 "S" level in 1962–66. Francis L. Thomason of Cleobury Mortimer, in Shropshire had by August 1971 accumulated 22 "O", 7 "A" and 1 "S" levels making a total of 30.

Youngest headmaster The youngest headmaster of a major public school was Henry Montagh Butler (b. 2 July 1835), appointed Headmaster of Harrow School on 16 Nov. 1859, when aged 24 years 137 days. His first term in office began in January 1860.

8. RELIGIONS

LARGEST

Religious statistics are necessarily highly approximate. The test of adherence to a religion varies widely in rigour, while many individuals, particularly in the East, belong to two or more religions.

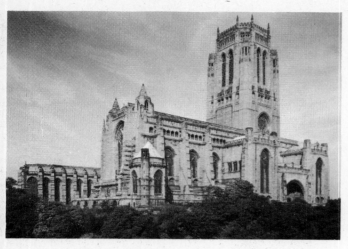

The Anglican Cathedral of Liverpool, the largest in the British Isles

Christianity is the world's prevailing religion, with over 1,020,000,000 adherents in 1972 of whom 575,000,000 have received baptism into the Roman Catholic Church. The largest non-Christian religion is Islam with about 525,000,000 adherents in 1972.

In the United Kingdom the Anglicans comprise members of the Established Church of England, the Dis-established Church in Wales, the Episcopal Church in Scotland and the Church of Ireland. In mid 1970 there were 27,736,000 living persons who had been baptized in Anglican churches in the provinces of Canterbury and York. In the same area it is estimated that there were 9,154,000 persons confirmed, of whom nearly 1,813,892 were Easter communicants in 1970. There were 14,258 parish churches and 17,087 full-time clergymen on 1 Jan. 1972. In Scotland the most numerous group is the Church of Scotland (the Presbyterians), which had 1,133,506 members, apart from adherents.

SMALLEST
In New Zealand the 1966 Census revealed 94 religious sects with a single follower each. These included a Millenarian Heretic and an Aesthetic Hedonist. Such followers might alternatively be described as leaders.

Largest clergy The world's largest religious organization is the Roman Catholic Church, with 584,493,080 members, 425,000 priests and 900,000 nuns. The total number of cardinals, patriarchs, metropolitans, archbishops, bishops, abbots and superiors is 3,967. There are about 420,000 churches.

Jews The total of world Jewry was estimated to be 14.3 million in 1971. The highest concentration was in the United States, with 5,870,000, of whom 2,480,000 were in Greater New York. The total in Israel was 2,530,000. The total of British Jewry is 450,000, of whom 280,000 are in Greater London, 31,500 in Manchester and Salford, and 13,500 in Glasgow. The total in Tōkyō, Japan, is only 250.

Largest Temple The largest religious structure ever built is Angkor Wat (City Temple), enclosing 402 acres *162,6 ha* in Khmer Republic, south-east Asia. It was built to the God Vishnu by the Khmer King Suryavarman II in the period 1113–50. Its curtain wall measures 1,400 by 1,400 yds *1 280 × 1 280 m* and its population before it was abandoned in 1432, was 80,000. The largest Buddhist temple in the world is Borobudur, near Joyjakarta, Indonesia built in the 8th century.

CATHEDRALS
Largest World The world's largest cathedral is the cathedral church of the Diocese of New York, St. John the Divine, with

a floor area of 121,000 ft^2 *11 240 m^2* and a volume of 16,822,000 ft^3 *476 350 m^3*. The corner stone was laid on 27 Dec. 1892, and the Gothic building was still uncompleted in 1967. In New York it is referred to as "Saint John the Unfinished". The nave is the longest in the world, 601 ft *183,18 m* in length, with a vaulting 124 ft *37,79 m* in height.

The cathedral covering the largest area is that of Santa Mariá de la Sede in Sevilla (Seville), Spain. It was built in Spanish Gothic style between 1402 and 1519 and is 414 ft *126,18 m* long, 271 ft *82,60 m* wide and 100 ft *30,48 m* high to the vault of the nave.

United Kingdom The largest cathedral in the British Isles is the Anglican Cathedral of Liverpool. Built in modernized Gothic style, work was begun on 19 July 1904, and when completed will have cost over £3,000,000. The building encloses 100,000 ft^2 *9 300 m^2* and has an overall length of 671 ft *204,52 m*. The Vestey Tower is 331 ft *100,88 m* high.

Smallest United Kingdom The smallest cathedral in use in the United Kingdom (excluding converted parish churches) is St. Asaph in Flintshire, Wales. It is 182 ft *55,47 m* long, 68 ft *20,72 m* wide and has a tower 100 ft *30,48 m* high. Oxford Cathedral in Christ Church (College) is 155 ft *47,24 m* long. The nave of the Cathedral of the Isles on the Isle of Cumbrae, Buteshire measures only 40 × 20 ft *12,19 × 6,09 m*. The total floor area is 2,124 ft^2 *197,3 m^2*.

Longest nave The longest nave in the United Kingdom is that of St. Albans Cathedral, Hertfordshire, which is 285 ft *86,86 m* long.

Largest World The largest church in the world is the basilica of St. Peter, built between 1492 and 1612 in the Vatican City, Rome.

The length of the church, measured from the apse, is 611 ft 4 in *186,33 m*. The area is 18,110 yd^2 *15 142 m^2*. The inner diameter of the famous dome is 137 ft 9 in *41,98 m* and its centre is 119 m *390 ft 5 in* high. The external height is 457 ft 9 in *139,52 m*.

The elliptical Basilique of St. Pie X at Lourdes, France, completed in 1957 at a cost of £2,000,000 has a capacity of 20,000 under its giant span arches and a length of 200 m *656 ft*.

The crypt of the underground Civil War Memorial Church in the Guadarrama Mountains, 45 km *28 miles* from Madrid, Spain, is 260 m *853 ft* in length.

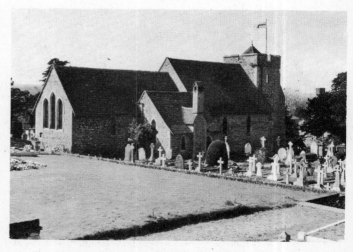

The oldest church in the United Kingdom, St. Martin's, Canterbury, Kent, which dates from A.D. 560

The smallest English parish church in regular use at Culbone, Somerset

It took 21 years (1937–58) to build, at a reported cost of £140,000,000 and is surmounted by a cross 150 m *492 ft* tall.

United Kingdom The largest parish church in the United Kingdom is Holy Trinity Parish Church, Kingston-upon-Hull, Yorkshire. The church exterior is 295 ft *89,91 m* long and 104 ft *31,69 m* wide, and parts of the transept date from 1285. The internal area is 26,384 ft² *2 451 m²*. The parish church of St. Nicholas at Great Yarmouth, Norfolk, after the addition of the Vestries in 1901 reached 25,023 ft² *2 324 m²*, but was destroyed by bombing in 1942. It was rededicated in May 1961.

Smallest World The world's smallest church is the Union Church at Wiscasset, Maine, U.S.A., with a floor area of 31½ ft² *2,92 m²* (7 × 4½ ft [*2,13 × 1,37 m*]). Les Vaubelets Church in Guernsey has an area of 16 × 12 ft *4,87 × 3,65 m*, room for one priest and a congregation of two.

Britain The smallest church in use in England is Bremilham Church, Cowage Farm, Foxley near Malmesbury, Wiltshire which measures 12 × 12 ft *3,65 × 3,65 m* and is used for service twice a year. The smallest completed English church in regular use is that at Culbone, Somerset, which measures 35 × 12 ft *10,66 × 3,65 m*. The smallest Welsh chapel is St. Trillo's Chapel, Rhôs-on-Sea (Llandrillo-yn-Rhos), Denbighshire, measuring only 12 × 6 ft *3,65 × 1,83 m*. The smallest chapel in Scotland is St. Margaret's, Edinburgh, measuring 16½ × 10½ ft *5,02 × 3,20 m*, giving an area of 173¼ ft² *16,09 m²*.

OLDEST

World The earliest known shrine dates from the proto-neolithic Natufian culture in Jericho, where a site on virgin soil has been dated to the ninth millennium B.C. A simple rectilinear red-plastered room with a niche housing a stone pillar believed to be the shrine of a Pre-Pottery fertility cult dating from *c.* 6500 B.C. was also uncovered in Jericho (now Arihā) in Jordan. The oldest surviving Christian church in the world is Qal'at es Salihige in eastern Syria, dating from A.D. 232. A list of the oldest religious buildings in 43 countries was included in the 11th edition of *The Guinness Book of Records*, at page 117. The oldest wooden church in Great Britain, and probably in the world is St. Andrew's, Greensted, near Ongar, Essex dating to A.D. 835 though some of the timbers date to the original building of *c.* A.D. 650.

United Kingdom The oldest church in the United Kingdom is St. Martin's Church in Canterbury, Kent. It was built in A.D. 560 on the foundations of a 1st century Roman church. The oldest church in Ireland is the Gallerus Oratory, built in *c.* 750 at Ballyferriter, near Kilmalkedar, County Kerry. Britain's oldest nunnery is St. Peter and Paul Minster, on the Isle of Thanet, Kent. It was founded in *c.* 748 by the Abbess Eadburga of Bugga.

TALLEST SPIRES

World The tallest cathedral spire in the world is that of the Protestant Cathedral of Ulm in Germany. The building is early Gothic and was begun in 1377. The tower, in the centre of the west façade, was not finally completed until 1890 and is 160,90 m *528 ft* high. The world's tallest church spire is that of the Chicago Temple of the First Methodist Church on Clark Street, Chicago, Illinois, U.S.A. The building consists of a 22-storey skyscraper (erected in 1924) surmounted by a parsonage at 330 ft *100,5 m*, a "Sky Chapel" at 400 ft *121,92 m* and a steeple cross at 568 ft *173,12 m* above street level.

United Kingdom The highest spire in the United Kingdom is that of the church of St. Mary, called Salisbury Cathedral, Wiltshire. The Lady Chapel was built in the years 1220–25 and the main fabric of the cathedral was finished and consecrated in 1258. The spire was

The tallest spire in the world, that of Ulm Cathedral, West Germany which soars 160,90 m *528 ft* in the air

Salisbury Cathedral, which has the tallest spire in the United Kingdom. It was completed to a height of 404 ft *123,12 m* in the 14th century

added later, 1334–65, and reaches a height of 404 ft *123,13 m*. The Central Spire of Lincoln Cathedral completed in *c.* 1307 and which fell in 1548 was 525 ft *160,02 m* tall.

Largest Churchyard The Churchyard beside Walker Parish Church, Newcastle upon Tyne, consecrated in 1848, extends over 11 acres *4,45 ha*.

LARGEST SYNAGOGUES

World The largest synagogue in the world is the Temple Emanu-El on Fifth Avenue at 65th Street, New York City, N.Y., U.S.A. The temple, completed in September 1929, has a frontage of 150 ft *45,72 m* on Fifth Avenue and 253 ft *77,11 m* on 65th Street. The Sanctuary proper can accommodate 2,500 people, and the adjoining Beth-El Chapel seats 350. When all the facilities are in use, more than 6,000 people can be accommodated.

Great Britain The largest synagogue in Great Britain is the Edgware Synagogue, Greater London, completed in 1959, with a capacity of 1,630 seats.

Largest mosque The largest mosque ever built was the now ruinous al-Malawiya mosque of al-Mutawakil in Samarra, Iraq built in A.D. 842–852 and measuring 9.21 acres *3,72 ha* with dimensions of 784 × 512 ft *238,9 × 156,0 m*. The world's largest mosque in use is the Jama Masjid (1644–58) in Delhi, India, with an area of more than 10,000 ft² *929 m²* and two minarets 108 ft *32,91 m* tall. The largest mosque will be the Merdeka Mosque in Djakarta, Indonesia, which was begun in 1962. The cupola will be 45 m *147.6 ft* in diameter and the capacity in excess of 50,000 people.

Tallest minaret The world's tallest minaret is the Qutb Minar, south of New Delhi, India, built in 1194 to a height of 238 ft *72,54 m*.

Tallest pagoda The world's tallest pagoda is the Shwemawdaw in Pegu, Burma of 288 ft *87,78 m*. It was restored by April 1954 having been damaged by an earthquake in 1930. The tallest Chinese temple is the 13-storey Pagoda of the Six Harmonies (*Liu he t'a*) outside Hang-chow. It is "nearly 200 ft [*61 m*] high".

SAINT

Most and least rapidly Canonized The shortest interval that has elapsed between the death of a Saint and his canonization was in the case of St. Anthony of Padua, Italy, who died on 13 June

1251 and was canonized 352 days later on 30 May 1252.

The other extreme is represented by St. Bernard of Thiron for 20 years Prior of St. Sabinus, who died in 1117 and was made a Saint in 1861—744 years later. The Italian monk and painter, Fra Giovanni da Fiesole (*né* Guido di Pietro), called *Il Beato* ("The Blessed") Fra Angelico (*c.* 1400–1455), is still in the first stage of canonization.

POPES

Reign Longest The longest reign of any of the 262 Popes has been that of Pius IX (Giovanni Maria Mastai-Ferretti), who reigned for 31 years 236 days from 16 June 1846 until his death aged 85, on 7 Feb. 1878.

Shortest Pope Stephen II was elected on 24 March 752 and died two days later, but he is not included in the *Liber pontificalis* or the Catalogue of the Popes. The shortest reign of any genuine Pope is that of Giambattista Castagna (1521–90), who was elected Pope Urban VII on 15 Sept. 1590 and died twelve days later on 27 Sept. 1590

Oldest It is recorded that Pope St. Agatho (reigned 678–681) was elected at the age of 103 and lived to 106, but recent scholars have expressed doubts. The oldest of recent Pontiffs has been Pope Leo XIII (Vincenzo Gioacchino Pecci), who was born on 2 March 1810, elected Pope at the third ballot on 20 Feb. 1878 and died on 20 July 1903, aged 93 years 140 days.

Youngest The youngest of all Popes was Pope Benedict IX (Theophylact), who had three terms as Pope: in 1032–44; April to May 1045; and 8 Nov. 1047 to 17 July 1048. It would appear that he was aged only 11 or 12 in 1032, though the Catalogue of the Popes admits only to his "extreme youth".

Last non-Italian ex-Cardinalate and English Popes The last non-Italian Pope was the Utrecht-born Cardinal Priest Adrian Dedel (1459–1523) of the Netherlands. He was elected on 9 Jan. 1522, crowned Pope Adrian VI on 31 Aug. 1522 and died on 14 Sept. 1523. The last Pope elected from outside the College of Cardinals was Bartolomeo Prignano (1318–89), Archbishop of Bari, who was elected Pope Urban VI on 8 April 1378. The only Englishman to be elected Pope was Nicholas Breakspear (born at

Part of the interior of the world's largest synagogue, Temple Emanu-El, New York, U.S.A.

Abbots Langley, near Watford, Hertfordshire, in *c.* 1100), who, as Cardinal Bishop of Albano, was elected Pope Adrian IV on 4 Dec. 1154, and died on 1 Sept. 1159.

Last married The first 37 Popes had no specific obligation to celibacy. The last married Pope was Adrian II (867–872). Rodrigo Borgia was the father of at least four children before being elected Pope Alexander VI in 1492.

Slowest election After 31 months without declaring *Habemus Papam* ("We have a Pope"), the cardinals were subjected to a bread and water diet and the removal of the roof of their conclave by the Mayor before electing Teobaldo Visconti (*c.* 1210–76), the Archbishop of Liège, as Pope Gregory X at Viterbo on 1 Sept. 1271. Cardinal Eugenio Maria Guiseppe Giovanni Pacelli (1876–1958), who took the title of Pius XII, was reputedly elected by 61 votes out of 62 at only the third ballot on 2 March 1939, his 63rd birthday.

CARDINALS

Oldest By 2 February 1973 the Sacred College of Cardinals contained a record 145 declared members compared with 116 in 1972. The oldest is Cardinal José da Costa Nuñes (born Cardelaria, Portugal, 15 March 1880).

Youngest The youngest Cardinal of all time was Giovanni de' Medici (b. 11 Dec. 1475), later Pope Leo X, who was made a Cardinal Deacon in March 1489, when aged 13 years 3 months. The youngest Cardinal is Antonio Ribeiro, Patriarch of Lisbon, Portugal, who was named on 2 Feb. 1973 aged 45.

BISHOPS

Oldest The oldest serving bishop (excluding Suffragans and Assistants) in the Church of England at 1 July 1973 was the Rt. Rev. Robert Cecil Mortimer (b. 6 Dec. 1902), the 67th Bishop of Exeter.

The oldest Roman Catholic bishop in recent years was Mgr. Alfonso Carinci (b. 9 Nov. 1862), who was titular Archbishop of Seleucia, in Isauria, from 1945 until his death on 6 Dec. 1963, at the age of 101 years 27 days. He had celebrated Mass about 24,800 times.

Bishop Herbert Welch of the United Methodist Church who was elected a bishop for Japan and Korea in 1916 died on 4 April 1969 aged 106.

Youngest The youngest bishop of all time was H.R.H. The Duke of York and Albany K.G., G.C.B., G.C.H., the second son of George III, who was elected Bishop of Osnabrück, through his father's influence as Elector of Hanover, at the age of 196 days on 27 Feb. 1764. He resigned after 39 years' enjoyment.

The youngest serving bishop (excluding Suffragans and Assistants) in the Church of England at 1 Jan. 1973 was the Rt. Rev. Ronald Oliver Bowlby (b. 16 Aug. 1926), the 9th Bishop of Newcastle.

BISHOPRIC

Longest tenure The longest tenure of any Church of England bishopric is 57 years in the case of the Rt. Rev. Thomas Wilson, who was consecrated Bishop of Sodor and Man on 16 Jan. 1698 and died in office on 7 March 1755. Of English bishoprics the longest tenure, if one excludes the unsubstantiated case of Aethelwulf, reputedly bishop of Hereford from 937 to 1012, are those of 47 years by Jocelin de Bohun (Salisbury) 1142–1189 and Nathaniel Crew or Crewe (Durham) 1674–1721.

STAINED GLASS

Oldest The oldest stained glass in the world represents the Prophets in a window of the cathedral of Augsburg, Bavaria, Germany, dating from *c.* 1050. The oldest datable stained glass in the United Kingdom is represented by 12th century fragments in the Tree of Jesse in the north aisle of the nave of York Minster, dated *c.* 1150, and medallions in Rivenhall Church, Essex which appear to date from the first half of that century. Dates late in the previous century have been attributed to glass in a window of the church at Compton, Surrey and a complete window in St. Mary the Virgin, Brabourne, Kent.

Largest The largest stained glass window is one measuring 300 × 23 ft *91,44 × 7,01 m* high at the John F. Kennedy International Airport, Long Island, New York, U.S.A. The largest single stained glass window in Great Britain is the East window in Gloucester Cathedral measuring 72 × 38 ft *21,94 × 11,58 m*, set up to commemorate the Battle of Crécy (1346), while the largest area of stained glass is 125 windows, totalling 25,000 ft² *2 322 m²* in York Minster.

BRASSES

The world's oldest monumental brass is that commemorating Bishop Ysowilpe in St. Andrew's Church, Verden, near Hanover, West Germany, dating from 1231. The oldest in Great Britain is of Sir John D'Abernon at Stoke D'Abernon, near Leatherhead, Surrey, dating from 1277.

Longest incumbency The longest incumbency on record is one of 76 years by the Rev. Bartholomew Edwards, Rector of St. Nicholas, Ashill, Norfolk from 1813 to 1889. There appears to be some doubt as to whether the Rev. Richard Sherinton was installed at Folkestone from 1524 or 1529 to 1601. If the former is correct it would surpass the Norfolk record. The parish of Iden, East Sussex had only two incumbents in the 117-year period from 1807 to 1924.

Longest serving chorister Mr. Leonard Thompson (b. 19 Feb. 1883) of Kidderminster, Worcestershire has been in St. Mary's Church choir continuously since 1891 except when his voice was breaking *c.* 1896.

Oldest parish register The oldest parish registers in England are those of St. James Garlickhythe and St. Mary Bothaw, two old City of London parishes, dating from 1536. Scotland's oldest surviving register is that for Anstruther-Wester, Fife, with burial entries from 1549.

Largest crowd The greatest recorded number of human beings assembled with a common purpose was more than 5,000,000 at the 21-day Hindu festival of Kumbh-Mela, which is held every 12 years at the confluence of the Yamuna (formerly called the Jumna), the Ganges and the invisible "Sarasviti" at Allahabad, Uttar Pradesh, India, on 21 Jan. 1966. According to the Jacob Formula for estimating the size of crowds, the allowance of area per person varies from 4 ft² *0,37 m²* (tight) to 9½ ft² *0,88 m²* (loose). Thus such a crowd must have occupied an area of more than 700 acres *283 ha.*

Largest funeral The greatest attendance at any funeral is the estimated 4 million who thronged Cairo, Egypt, for the funeral of President Gamal Abdel Nasser (b. 15 Jan. 1918) on 1 Oct. 1970.

Biggest demonstrations A figure of 2.7 million was published from China for the demonstration against the U.S.S.R. in Shanghai on 3–4 April 1969 following the border clashes, and one of 10 million for the May Day celebrations of 1963 in Peking.

ACCIDENTS AND DISASTERS

Type	WORST IN THE WORLD			WORST IN THE UNITED KINGDOM		
	Number	Location / Description	Date	Number	Location / Description	Date
Pandemic	75,000,000	The Black Death (bubonic, pneumonic and septicaemic plague)	1347–1351	800,000	The Black Death (bubonic, pneumonic and septicaemic plague)	1347–1350
	21,640,000	Influenza	April–Nov. 1918	225,000	Influenza	Sept.–Nov. 1918
Famine	9,500,000[1]	Northern China	Feb.–Nov. 1878	1,500,000[13]	Ireland (famine and typhus)	1846–1851
Flood	3,700,000	Hwang-ho River, China	Aug. 1931	c. 2,000[14]	Severn Estuary	20 Jan. 1606
Circular Storm[2]	1,000,000	Ganges Delta Islands, Bangladesh	12–13 Nov. 1970	c. 8,000	"The Channel Storm"	26 Nov. 1703
Earthquake	830,000	Shensi Province, China	23 Jan. 1556	1	City of London	6 April 1580
Marine (single ship)	c. 7,700	Wilhelm Gustloff (24,484 tons) torpedoed off Danzig by U.S.S.R. submarine S-13	30 Jan. 1945	c. 4,000	H.M. Troopship Lancastria (16,243 tons) off St. Nazaire	17 June 1940
Atomic Bomb	91,223[4]	Hiroshima, Japan	6 Aug. 1945			
Conventional Bombing[3]	135,000	Dresden, Germany	13–15 Feb. 1945	1,436	London	10–11 May 1941
Landslide	200,000	Kansu Province, China	16 Dec. 1920	144	Paniglas coal tip No. 7, Aberfan, Glamorganshire	21 Oct. 1966
Panic	c. 4,000	Chungking (Zhong qing) China air raid shelter	c. 8 June 1941	183[15]	Victoria Hall, Sunderland	16 June 1883
Dam Burst	2,209	South Fork Dam, Johnstown, Pennsylvania	31 May 1889	270	Bradfield Reservoir, Dale Dyke, near Sheffield (embankment burst)	11 Mar. 1864
Snow Avalanche	c. 5,000[5]	Huarás, Peru	13 Dec. 1941	8	Lewes, Sussex (snowdrifts)	27 Dec. 1836
Explosion	1,963[6]	Halifax, Nova Scotia, Canada	6 Dec. 1917	134	Chilwell, Notts. (explosives factory)	1 July 1918
Fire[7] (single building)	1,670	The Theatre, Canton, China	May 1845	173	Bethnal Green Tube Station (air raid siren)	3 Mar. 1943
Mining[8]	1,572	Honkeiko Colliery, China (coal dust explosion)	26 April 1942	439	Universal Colliery, Senghenydd, Glam., Wales	14 Oct. 1913
Riot	c. 1,200	New York City anti-conscription riots	13–16 July 1863	565 (min.)	London anti-Catholic Gordon riots	2–13 June 1780
Crocodiles	c. 900	Japanese soldiers, Ramree Is., Burma	19–20 Feb. 1945			
Fireworks	>800	Dauphine's Wedding, Seine, Paris	16 May 1770	1	Rowhedge, Essex	22 April 1884
Tornado	689	South Central States, U.S.A.	18 Mar. 1925			
Railway	543	Modane, France	12 Dec. 1917	227[17]	Triple collision at Quintins Hill, Dumfries-shire	22 May 1915
Man-eating Tigress[9]	436	Champawat district, India, shot by Col. Jim Corbett	1907			
Hail	246	Moradabad, Uttar Pradesh, India	30 April 1888	60[16]	Widecombe, Devon	21 Oct. 1638
Aircraft (Civil)	176[10]	Krasnaya Polyana, U.S.S.R. Ilyushin 62	1 Oct. 1972	118[18]	B.E.A. Trident 1-C, Staines, Middlesex	18 June 1972
Submarine	129	U.S.S. Thresher off Cape Cod, Massachusetts, U.S.A.	10 April 1963	99	H.M.S. Thetis, during trials, Liverpool Bay	1 June 1939
Road[11]	>125	Two trucks crashed into a crowd of dancers. Sotouboua, Togo	6 Dec. 1965	24	R.M. Cadets, run down by bus, Gillingham, Kent	4 Dec. 1951
Mountaineering	40[12]	U.S.S.R. Expedition on Mount Everest	Dec. 1952	6	On Cairngorm, Scotland (4,084 ft)	21 Nov. 1971
Space Exploration	3	Apollo oxygen fire, Cape Kennedy, Fla., U.S.A.	27 Jan. 1967			
	3	Soyuz 11 re-entry over U.S.S.R.	29 June 1971			

[1] In 1770 the great Indian famine carried away a proportion of the population estimated as high as a third, hence a figure of tens of millions. The figure for Bengal alone was also probably about 10 million. It has been estimated that more than 5,000,000 died in the post-World War I famine of 1920–21 in the U.S.S.R. The U.S.S.R. government in July 1923 informed Mr. (later President) Herbert Hoover that the A.R.A. (American Relief Administration) had since August 1921 saved 20,000,000 lives from famine and famine diseases.

[2] This figure published in 1972 for the East Pakistan disaster was from Dr. Afzal, Principle Scientific Officer of the Atomic Energy Authority Centre, Dacca. One report asserted that less than half of the population of the 4 islands of Bhola, Charjabbar, Hatia and Ramagati (1961 Census 1.4 million) survived. The most damaging hurricane recorded was the billion dollar Betsy (name now retired) in 1965 with an estimated insurance pay-out of $750 million.

[3] The number of civilians killed by the bombing of Germany has been put variously as 593,000 and "over 635,000". A figure of c.140,000 deaths in the U.S.A.F. fire raids on Tokyo of 10 Mar. 1945 has been attributed. The Hiroshima Peace Memorial Museum gives a figure of 240,000, excluding later deaths.

[5] A total of 10,000 Austrian and Italian troops is reputed to have been lost in the Dolomite valley of Northern Italy on 13 Dec. 1916 in more than 100 avalanches. The total is probably exaggerated though bodies were still being found in 1952.

[6] Some sources maintain that the final death roll was over 3,000.

[7] Worst ever hotel fire 162 killed, Hotel Taeyonkak, Seoul, South Korea 25 Dec. 1971.

[8] The worst gold mining disaster in South Africa was 152 killed due to flooding in the Witwatersrand Gold Mining Co. Gold Mine in 1909.

[9] In the period 1941–42 c. 1,500 Kenyans were killed by a pride of 22 man-eating lions. Eighteen of these were shot by a hunter named Rushby.

[10] A figure of 176 was first issued for the Nigerian Airways charter crash at Kano on 29 Jan. 1973.

[11] The worst ever years for road deaths in the U.S.A. and the U.K. have been respectively 1969 (56,400) and 1941 (9,169). The U.S.'s 2 millionth victim since 1899 died in Jan. 1973. The world's highest death rate is said to be in Queensland, Australia but global statistics are not available. The greatest pile-up on British roads was on the M6 near Lymm Interchange involving 200 vehicles on 13 Sept. 1971 with 11 dead and 60 injured.

[12] According to Polish sources, not confirmed by the U.S.S.R. 23 died on Mount Fuji, Japan after blizzard and avalanche on 20 Mar. 1972.

[13] Based on the net rate of natural increase between 1841 and 1851, a support-able case for a loss of population of 3 million can be made out if rates of under-enumeration of 25 per cent (1841) and 10 per cent (1851) are accepted.

[14] Death rolls of 100,000 were reputed in England and Holland in the floods of 1099, 1421 and 1446.

[15] In July 1212 c. 3,000 were killed in the crash, burned or drowned when London Bridge caught fire at both ends. The death roll in the Great Fire of London of 1666 was only 8. History's first "fire storm" occurred in the Blitz on 7–8 Sept. 1940. Dockland casualties were 306 killed and injured.

[16] Killed and injured.

[17] The 213 yd long troop train was telescoped to 67 yds. Signalmen Meakin and Tinsley were sentenced for manslaughter.

[18] The worst crash by a U.K. registered aircraft was that of the B.O.A.C. Boeing 707 which broke up in mid-air near Mount Fuji, Japan, on 5 March 1966. The crew of 11 and all 113 passengers (total 124) were killed. The cause was violent CAT (Clean Air Turbulence).

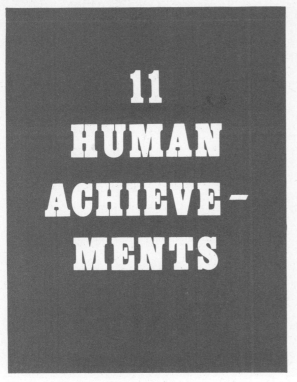

11 HUMAN ACHIEVE-MENTS

1. ENDURANCE AND ENDEAVOUR

LUNAR CONQUEST

Neil Alden Armstrong (b. Wapakoneta, Ohio, U.S.A. of Scoto-Irish and German ancestry, on 5 Aug. 1930), command pilot of the Apollo XI mission, became the first man to set foot on the Moon on the Sea of Tranquillity at 02.56 and 20 sec G.M.T. on 21 July 1969. He was followed out of the Lunar Module *Eagle* by Col. Edwin Eugene Aldrin, Jr. U.S.A.F. (b. Montclair, New Jersey, U.S.A. of Swedish, Dutch and British ancestry, on 20 Jan. 1930), while the Command Module *Columbia* piloted by Lt.-Col. Michael Collins, U.S.A.F. (b. Rome, Italy, of Irish and pre-Revolutionary American ancestry, on 31 Oct. 1930) orbited above.

Eagle landed at 20.17 hours 42 sec G.M.T. on 20 July and lifted off at 17.54 G.M.T. on 21 July, after a stay of 21 hours 36 min. The Apollo XI had blasted off from Cape Kennedy, Florida at 13.32 G.M.T. on 16 July and was a culmination of the U.S. space programme, which, at its peak, employed 376,600 people and attained in the year 1966–67 a peak budget of $5,900,000,000 (*then £2,460 million*).

ALTITUDE

Man The greatest altitude attained by man was when the crew of the ill-fated Apollo XIII were at apocynthion (*i.e.* their furthest point) 158 miles *254 km* above the lunar surface and 248,655 miles *400 187 km* above the Earth's surface at 1.21 a.m. B.S.T. on 15 April 1970. The crew were Capt. James Arthur Lovel, U.S.N. (b. Denver, Colorado, 30 Aug. 1931), Frederick Wallace Haise Jr. (b. Cleveland, Ohio, 25 March 1928) and John L. Swigert Jr. (b. Biloxi, Miss. 14 Nov. 1933).

Woman The greatest altitude attained by a woman is 231 km *143.5 miles* by Jnr. Lt. (now Lt. Col.) Valentina Vladimirovna Tereshkova-Nikolayev (b. 6 Mar. 1937) of the U.S.S.R., during her 48-orbit flight in *Vostok 6* on 16 June 1963. (See also Chapter 4.) The record for an aircraft is 24 336 m *79,842 ft* by Natalia Prokhanova (U.S.S.R.) (b. 1940) in an E-33 jet, on 22 May 1965.

SPEED

Man The fastest speed at which any human has travelled is 24,791 m.p.h. *39 897 km/h* when the Command Module of Apollo X carrying Col. Thomas P. Stafford, U.S.A.F. (b. Weatherford, Okla. 17 Sept. 1930), and Cdrs. Eugene Andrew Cernan (b. Chicago, 14 Mar. 1934) and John Watts Young, U.S.N. (b. San Francisco, 24 Sept. 1930), reached this maximum value at the 400,000 ft *121 192 km* altitude interface on its trans-Earth return flight on 26 May 1969.

Woman The highest speed ever attained by a woman is 28 115 km/h *17,470 m.p.h.* by Jnr. Lt. (now Lt. Col.) Valentina Vladimirovna Tereshkova-Nikolayev (b. 6 March 1937) of the U.S.S.R. in *Vostok 6* on 16 June 1963. The highest speed ever achieved in an aeroplane is 2 300 km/h *1,429.2 m.p.h.* by Jacqueline Cochran (Mrs. Floyd Bostwick-Odlum) (U.S.A.), in an F-104G1 *Starfighter* jet over Edwards Air Force Base, California, U.S.A., on 11 May 1964. The first woman in Britain to fly at over 1,000 m.p.h. *1 609 km/h* was Flt. Off. Jean Oakes, who flew at 1,125 m.p.h. *1 810,5 km/h* in an R.A.F. Lightning Mark 4 on 6 Sept. 1962.

LAND SPEED

Man The highest speed ever achieved on land is 650 m.p.h. *1 046 km/h* momentarily during the 627.287 m.p.h. *1 009,520 km/h* run of *The Blue Flame* driven by Gary Gabelich (b. San Pedro, California, 29 Aug. 1940) on Bonneville Salt Flats, Utah, U.S.A., on 23 Oct. 1970 (see Mechanical World, page 145). The car built by Reaction Dynamics Inc. of Milwaukee, Wisconsin, is designed to withstand stresses up to 1,000 m.p.h. *1 600 km/h* while the tyres have been tested to speeds of 850 m.p.h. *1 365 km/h.*

Woman The highest land speed recorded by a woman is 539,243 km/h *335.070 m.p.h.* by Mrs Lee Ann Breedlove (*née* Roberts) (born 1937) of Los Angeles, California, U.S.A., driving her husband's *Spirit of America—Sonic I* (see page 145) over the timing kilometre on the Bonneville Salt Flats, Utah, U.S.A., on 4 Nov. 1965.

WATER SPEED

Unofficial The highest speed ever achieved on water is 328 m.p.h. *527,8 km/h* by Donald Malcolm Campbell, C.B.E. (1921–67) of the U.K., on his last and fatal run in the

HUMAN ACHIEVEMENTS

turbo-jet engined 2¼ ton *2 285 kg* *Bluebird* K7, on Coniston Water, Lancashire, England, on 4 Jan. 1967.

Official The official record is 285.213 m.p.h. *459,005 km/h* (average of two 1 mile runs) by Lee Taylor, Jr. (b. 1934) of Downey, California, U.S.A., in the hydroplane *Hustler* on Lake Guntersville, Alabama, U.S.A., on 30 June 1967.

Propeller The world record for propeller-driven craft is 200.42 *driven* m.p.h. *322,54 km/h* held by Roy Duby (U.S.A.) in his Rollys-Royce-engined hydroplane on Lake Guntersville, Alabama, U.S.A., on 17 April 1962.

TRAVELLING

Most The man who has visited more countries than anyone **travelled** is J. Hart Rosdail (b. 1915) of Elmhurst, Illinois, **man** U.S.A. Since 1934 of the 150 sovereign countries and 75 non-sovereign territories of the world making a total of 225 he has visited all but 6. He estimates his mileage as 1,231,560 miles *1 982 003 km* by Sept. 1972. The only sovereign countries which he has not visited are the People's Republic of China, Cuba, North Korea and North Vietnam.

The most countries visited by a disabled person is 119 by Lester Nixon of Sarasota, Florida, U.S.A. who is confined to a wheelchair.

An artist's impression of the first untethered ascent by a Hot Air Balloon, at Fauxbourg, Paris in November 1783

PROGRESSIVE HUMAN ALTITUDE RECORDS

Ft	m	Pilot	Vehicle	Place	Date
84*	25	Jean François Pilâtre de Rozier (France)	Hot Air Balloon (tethered)	Fauxbourg, Paris	15 & 17 Oct. 1783
210	64	J. F. Pilâtre de Rozier (France)	Hot Air Balloon (tethered)	Fauxbourg, Paris	19 Oct. 1783
262	80	J. F. Pilâtre de Rozier (France)	Hot Air Balloon (tethered)	Fauxbourg, Paris	19 Oct. 1783
325	99	de Rozier and Girand de Villette (France)	Hot Air Balloon (tethered)	Fauxbourg, Paris	19 Oct. 1783
c. 330	c. 100	de Rozier and the Marquis François-Laurent d'Arlandes (1742–1809) (France)	Hot Air Balloon (free flight)	La Muette, Paris	21 Nov. 1783
c. 2,000	c. 600	Dr. Jacques-Alexandre-César Charles (1746–1823) and Ainé Robert (France)	Charlière Hydrogen Balloon	Tuileries, Paris	1 Dec. 1783
c. 9,000	c. 2 750	J.-A.-C. Charles (France)	Hydrogen Balloon	Nesles, France	1 Dec. 1783
c. 13,000	c. 4 000	James Sadler (G.B.)	Hydrogen Balloon	Manchester	May 1785
c. 20,000	c. 6 100	E. G. R. Robertson (U.K.) and Loest (Germany)	Hydrogen Balloon	Hamburg, Germany	18 July 1803
22,965	7 000	Joseph Louis Gay-Lussac (France)	Hydrogen Balloon	Paris	15 Sept. 1804
c. 25,000	c. 7 620	Charles Green, Edward Spencer (G.B.)	Coal Gas Balloon *Nassau*	Vauxhall, London	24 July 1837
25,400[1]	7 740	James Glaisher (U.K.)	Hydrogen Balloon	Wolverhampton	17 July 1862
27,950	8 520	H. T. Sivel, J. E. Crocé-Spinelli, Gaston Tissandier (only survivor)	Coal Gas Balloon *Zenith*	La Villette, Paris	15 April 1875
31,500	9 615	Prof. A. Berson (Germany)	Hydrogen Balloon *Phoenix*	Strasbourg, France	4 Dec. 1894
35,433	10 800	Prof. Berson and Dr. R. J. Süring (Germany)	Hydrogen Balloon *Preussen*	Berlin, Germany	30 June 1901
36,565	11 145	Sadi Lecointe (France)	Nieuport Aircraft	Issy-les-Moulineaux, France	30 Oct. 1923
42,470[2]	12 945	Capt. Hawthorne C. Gray (U.S.A.)	Hydrogen Balloon	Scott Field, Illinois	4 May 1927
42,470	12 945	Capt. Hawthorne C. Gray (U.S.A.)	Hydrogen Balloon	Scott Field, Illinois	4 Nov. 1927
43,166	13 157	Lt. Apollo Soucek (U.S.A.)	U.S. Navy Wright *Apache*	Washington, D.C.	4 June 1930
51,961	15 837	Prof. Auguste Piccard and Paul Kipfer (Switzerland)	F.N.R.S. I Balloon	Augsburg	27 May 1931
53,139	16 196	Piccard & Dr. Max Cosyns (Belgium)	F.N.R.S. I Balloon	Dübendorf, nr. Zürich	18 Aug. 1932
60,695[3]	18 500	G. Profkoviev, F. N. Birnbaum and K. D. Godunov (U.S.S.R.)	Army Balloon *U.S.S.R.*	Moscow, U.S.S.R.	30 Sept. 1933
61,237	18 665	Lt.-Col. T. G. W. Settle, U.S.N. and Major Chester L. Fordney, U.S.M.C.	Hydrogen Balloon *Century of Progress*	Akron, Ohio	20 & 21 Nov. 1933
72,178[4]	22 000	Raul F. Fedoseyenko, A. B. Vasienko and E. D. Ususkin (U.S.S.R.)	*Osaviakhim* Balloon	Moscow, U.S.S.R.	30 Jan. 1934
72,395	22 066	Capts. Orvill A. Anderson and Albert W. Stevens (U.S. Army—Air Corps)	U.S. *Explorer II* Helium Balloon	Rapid City, South Dakota, U.S.A.	11 Nov. 1935
79,600	24 262	William Barton Bridgeman (U.S.A.)	U.S. Douglas D558-II *Skyrocket*	California, U.S.A.	15 Aug. 1951
83,235	25 370	Lt.-Col. Marion E. Carl, U.S.M.C.	U.S. Douglas D558-II *Skyrocket*	California, U.S.A.	21 Aug. 1953
c. 93,000	c. 28 350	Major Arthur Murray (U.S.A.F)	U.S. Bell *X-1A* Rocket 'plane	California, U.S.A.	4 June 1954
126,200	38 465	Capt. Iven C. Kincheloe, Jnr. (U.S.A.F.)	U.S. Bell *X-2* Rocket 'plane	California, U.S.A.	7 Sept. 1956
136,500	41 605	Major Robert M. White (U.S.A.F)	U.S. *X-15* Rocket 'plane	California, U.S.A.	12 Aug. 1960
169,600	51 694	Joseph A. Walker (U.S.A.)	U.S. *X-15* Rocket 'plane	California, U.S.A.	30 Mar. 1961

Statute miles	Km	Pilot	Vehicle	Place	Date
203.2	327	Flt.-Major Yuriy A. Gagarin (U.S.S.R.)	U.S.S.R. *Vostok I* Capsule	Orbital flight	12 April 1961
253.5	408	Col. Vladimir M. Komarov, Lt. Boris B. Yegorov and Konstantin P. Feoktistov	U.S.S.R. *Voskhod I* Capsule	Orbital flight	12 Oct. 1964
309.2	497,6	Col. Pavel I. Belyayev and Lt.-Col. Aleksey A. Leonov (U.S.S.R.)	U.S.S.R. *Voskhod II* Capsule	Orbital flight	18 Mar. 1965
474.4	763,4	Cdr. John Watts Young, U.S.N. and Major Michael Collins, U.S.A.F.	U.S. *Gemini X* Capsule	Orbital flight	19 July 1966
850.7	1 369,0	Cdr. Charles Conrad, Jr. U.S.N. and Lt.-Cdr. Richard F. Gordon, Jr., U.S.N.	U.S. *Gemini XI* Capsule	Orbital flight	14 Sept. 1966
234,473	377 347	Col. Frank Borman, U.S.A.F., Capt. James Arthur Lovell Jr. U.S.N. and Major William A. Anders, U.S.A.F.	U.S. *Apollo VIII* Command Module	Circum-lunar flight	25 Dec. 1968
248,433	399 814	Cdr. Eugene Andrew Cernan U.S.N. and Col. Thomas P. Stafford U.S.A.F.	U.S. *Apollo X* Lunar Module	Circum-lunar flight	22 May 1969
242,285[5]	389 920	Neil Alden Armstrong, Col. Edwin Eugene Aldrin, Jnr. and Lt.-Col. Michael Collins U.S.A.F.	U.S. *Apollo XI*	Circum-lunar flight and first Moon landing	21 & 22 July 1969
248,655	400 187	Capt. James Arthur Lovell Jr. U.S.N., Frederick Wallace Haise Jr. and John L. Swigert Jr.	U.S. *Apollo XIII*	Abortive lunar landing mission	15 April 1970

* *There is some evidence that Father Bartolomu de Gusmão flew in his hot-air balloon in his 4th experiment ante Aug. 1709 in Portugal.*
1 *Glaisher, with Henry Coxwell, claimed 37,000 ft 11 275 m from Wolverhampton on 5 Sept. 1862. Some writers accept 30,000 ft 9 145 m.*
2 *Neither of Gray's altitudes were official records because he had to parachute on his first descent and he landed dead from his second ascent to an identical height.*

3 *None survived the ascent.*
4 *All died on descent.*
5 *Note. This historic space flight did not establish an altitude record but has been included for reference only.*

PROGRESSIVE ABSOLUTE HUMAN SPEED RECORDS

The progression of the voluntary human speed record is listed below. It is perhaps noteworthy that the petrol-engined car at no time featured in this compilation.

Speed m.p.h.	Km/h	Person and Vehicle	Place	Date
<25	<40	Running	—	*ante* 6500 B.C.
>25	>40	Sledging	Southern Finland	*c.* 6500 B.C.
>35	>55	Ski-ing	Fenno-Scandia	*c.* 3000 B.C.
>35	>55	Horse-riding	Anatolia, Turkey	*c.* 1400 B.C.
<50	<80	Ice Yachts (earliest patent)	Netherlands	A.D. 1600
56¾	95	Grand Junction Railway 2-2-2 *Lucifer*	Madeley Banks, Staffs., England	13 Nov. 1839
74.5[1]	119	Great Western Railway 4-2-2 *Great Britain*	Wootton Bassett, Wiltshire, England	11 May 1845
74.5	119,8	Great Western Railway 2-2-2 8 ft single *Great Western*	Wootton Bassett, Wiltshire, England	1 June 1846
78	125,5	Great Western Railway 4-2-2 8 ft single *Great Britain*	Wootton Bassett, Wiltshire, England	11 May 1848
81.8	131,6	Bristol & Exeter Railway 4-2-4 tank 9 ft single No. 41	Wellington Bank, Somerset, England	June 1854
87.8	141,3	Tommy Todd, downhill skier	La Porte, California, U.S.A.	Mar. 1873
89.48	144	Crompton No. 604 engine	Champigny-Pont sur Yonne, France	20 June 1890
90.0	144,8	Midland Railway 4-2-2 7 ft 9 in single	Ampthill, Bedford, England	Mar. 1897
101.0	162,5	Siemens und Halske electric engine	near Berlin, Germany	1901
124.89	201	Siemens und Halske electric engine	Marienfeld-Zossen, near Berlin	6 Oct. 1903
128.43	206,7	Siemens und Halske electric engine	Marienfeld-Zossen, near Berlin	23 Oct. 1903
130.61	210,2	Siemens und Halske electric engine	Marienfeld-Zossen, near Berlin	27 Oct. 1903
c. 150	*c.* 257,5	Frederick H. Marriott, Stanley Steamer *Rocket* (*fl.* 1957)	Ormond Beach, Florida, U.S.A.	26 Jan. 1907
>210	>338	World War I fighters in dives including Martinsyde F.4's and Nieuport *Nighthawks*	over England and Flanders	1918–19
210.64	339	Sadi Lecointe (France) Nieuport-Delage 29	Villesauvage, France	25 Sept. 1921
211.91	341	Sadi Lecointe (France) Nieuport-Delage 29	Villesauvage, France	21 Sept. 1922
243.94	392,64	Brig.-Gen. William Mitchell (U.S. Army (1879–1936)) Curtiss R-6	Detroit, Michigan	18 Oct. 1922
270.5	435,3	Lt. Alford Joseph Williams (U.S.N.), Curtiss R.2 C-1	Mitchell Field, Long Is., N.Y.	4 Nov. 1923
274.2	441,3	Lt. A. Brown (U.S.N.), Curtiss H.S. D-12	Mitchell Field, Long Is., N.Y.	4 Nov. 1923
278.47[2]	448,15	Adj. Chef Florentin Bonnet (France) Bernard-Ferbois V-2	Istres, France	11 Dec. 1924
284	457	Fg. Off. Sidney Norman Webster A.F.C. Supermarine S.5	Calshot, Hampshire	14 July 1927
>300	>482	Flt. Lt. Sidney Norman Webster, A.F.C. Supermarine S.5	Venice, Italy	26 Sept. 1927
313.59	504,67	Major Mario de Bernardi (Italy) Macchi M-52	Venice, Italy	4 Nov. 1927
322.6[3]	519,1	Lt. Alford J. Williams (U.S.N.) Kirkham-Williams	Mitchell Field, Long Is., N.Y.	7 Nov. 1927
348.6	561	Col. Mario de Bernardi (Italy) Macchi M-52 R	Venice, Italy	30 Mar. 1928
362	582	Capt. Guiseppe Motta Macchi 67	Lago di Garda, Italy	22 Aug. 1929
>370	>595,4	Fg. Off. Henry Richard D. Waghorn, A.F.C. and Fg. Off. Richard Llewellyn Roger Atcherley (1904–70) (later Air Marshall Sir, K.B.E., C.B., A.F.C*) Supermarine S.6's	Solent, Hampshire, England	7 Sept. 1929
375	603	Lt. Ariosti Nevi Macchi 72	Desenzaro, Italy	July 1931
394	634	Lt. Ariosti Nevi Macchi 72	Desenzaro, Italy	Aug. 1931
415.2	668,2	Flt. Lt. (later Wing Cdr.) George Hedley Stainforth, A.F.C. Supermarine S.6 B	Lee-on-Solent, England	29 Sept 1931
430.32[4]	692,529	W.O. Francesco Agello (Italy) Macchi-Castoldi 72	Lago di Garda, Italy	10 April 1933
>434.96[5]	>700	Col. Mario Bernasconi (Italy) Macchi-Castoldi 72	Desenzaro, Italy	18 April 1934
441.22	710,07	Sec. Lt. Francesco Agello (Italy) Macchi-Castoldi 72	Lago di Garda, Italy	23 Oct. 1934
463.94[2]	746,64	Flugkapitan Hans Dieterle (Germany) Heinkel He. 100V-8	Oranienburg, E. Germany	30 Mar. 1939
486	782	Flugkapitan Fritz Wendel (Germany) Messerschmitt 209 V-1	Augsburg, E. Germany	26 April 1939
c. 525	*c.* 845	Heinkel 176 test flight	Peenemünde, Germany	3 July 1939
571.78	920,2	Flugkapitan Heinz Dittmar Me. 163V-1	Peenemünde, Germany	July–August 1941
623.85	1 004	Flugkapitan Heinz Dittmar Me. 163V-1	Peenemünde, Germany	2 Oct. 1941
624.62	1 005	Unnamed test pilot—possibly Gerd Linter Me. 262V-12	Insterburg, Germany	July 1944
c. 652	*c.* 1 050	Franz Rösle Me. 163B	Brandis, Germany	March–April 1945
c. 640–660	*c.* 1 030–1 060	Geoffrey Raoul de Havilland, O.B.E., (1910–46) D.H. 108 *Swallow*	Egypt Bay, Kent, England	27 Sept. 1946
652.6	1 050,3	Cdr. Turner F. Caldwell, U.S.N., Douglas *Skystreak* D-558-I	Muroc Dry Lake, California	20 Aug. 1947
653.4	1 051,5	Major (later Lt.-Col.) Marion E. Carl, U.S.M.C., Douglas *Skystreak* D-558-I	Muroc Dry Lake, California	25 Aug. 1947
670	1 078	Capt. Charles E. Yeager, U.S.A.F., Bell XS-1 *Glamorous Glennis* (Mach 1.015)	Muroc Dry Lake, California	14 Oct. 1947
967	1 556	Capt. Charles E. Yeager, U.S.A.F., Bell XS-1	Muroc Dry Lake, California	1948
1,135	1 826,6	William Barton Bridgeman, Douglas *Skyrocket* D-558-II	Muroc Dry Lake, California	18 May 1951
1,181	1 900,6	William Barton Bridgeman, Douglas *Skyrocket* D-558-II	Muroc Dry Lake, California	11 June 1951
1,221	1 965,0	William Barton Bridgeman, Douglas *Skyrocket* D-558-II	Muroc Dry Lake, California	23 June 1951
1,238	1 992,3	William Barton Bridgeman, Douglas *Skyrocket* D-558-II	Muroc Dry Lake, California	7 Aug. 1951
1,241	2 013,2	William Barton Bridgeman, Douglas *Skyrocket* D-558-II	Muroc Dry Lake, California	Dec. 1951
1,272	2 047,0	Albert Scott Crossfield, Douglas *Skyrocket* D-558-II	Muroc Dry Lake, California	14 Oct. 1953
1,328	2 137,2	Albert Scott Crossfield, Douglas *Skyrocket* D-558-II	Muroc Dry Lake, California	20 Nov. 1953
1,612	2 594,2	Major Charles E. Yeager, *Bell X-1A*	Muroc Dry Lake, California	12 Dec. 1953
1,934	3 112,4	Lt.-Col. Frank K. Everest, Jr. *Bell X-2*	Muroc Dry Lake, California	23 July 1956
2,094	3 369,9	Capt. Milburn G. Apt, *Bell X-2*	Muroc Dry Lake, California	27 Sept. 1956
2,111	3 397,3	Joseph A. Walker, North American *X-15*	Muroc Dry Lake, California	12 May 1960
2,196	3 534,1	Joseph A. Walker, North American *X-15*	Muroc Dry Lake, California	4 Aug. 1960
2,275	3 661,1	Major Robert M. White, North American *X-15*	Muroc Dry Lake, California	7 Feb. 1961
2,905	4 675,1	Major Robert M. White, North American *X-15*	Muroc Dry Lake, California	7 Mar. 1961
c. 17,560	*c.* 28 260	Flt. Maj. Yuriy Alekseyevich Gagarin, *Vostok 1*	Earth orbit	12 April 1961
17,558	28 257	Cdr. Walter Marty Schirra, Jr. U.S.N., *Sigma 7*	Earth orbit	3 Oct. 1962
c. 17,600	*c.* 28 325	Air Eng. Col. Vladimir Mikhaylovich Komarov, Lt. Boris Borisovich Yegorov and Konstantin Petrovich Feoktistov, *Voskhod 1*	Earth orbit	12 Oct. 1964
c. 17,750	*c.* 28 565	Col. Pavel Ivanovich Belyayev and Lt. Col. Aleksey Arkhipovich Leonov, *Voskhod 2*	Earth orbit	18 Mar. 1965
17,943	28 876	Cdr. Charles Conrad, Jr., Lt-Cdr. Richard F. Gordon, Jr., U.S.N. *Gemini XI*	Earth orbit	14 Sept. 1966
24,226	38 988	Col. Frank Borman, U.S.A.F., Capt. James Arthur Lovell, Jr., U.S.N., Major William A. Anders, U.S.A.F. *Apollo VIII*	Trans-lunar injection	21 Dec. 1968
24,752	39 834	Col. Frank Borman, U.S.A.F., Capt. James Arthur Lovell, Jr., U.S.N., Major William A. Anders, U.S.A.F. *Apollo VIII*	Re-entry after lunar orbit	27 Dec. 1968
24,791	39 897	Cdrs. Eugene Andrew Cernan and John Watts Young, U.S.N. and Col. Thomas P. Stafford, U.S.A.F. *Apollo X*	Re-entry after lunar orbit	26 May 1969

1 *A speed of 85 m.p.h. 137 km/h was claimed by Frank Elrington in a run-away compressed air railway from Kingstown (now Dún Laoghaire) to Dalkey, County Dublin on 19 Aug. 1843. It was, however, self-timed.*
2 *Average of 4 runs, individual runs not officially published.*
3 *Self-timed unofficial run.*
4 *Earlier runs at 421.58 m.p.h,, 678,477 km/h and 424.17 m.p.h. 682.637 km/h.*
5 *Unofficial single run.*

Flying The greatest number of flying hours claimed is more than 40,000 by the light aircraft pilot Max A. Conrad (b. 1903) of the U.S.A., who began his flying career on 13 March 1928. Capt. Charles Blair (Pan American World Airways) logged 35,000 flying hours and more than 10,000,000 miles *16 095 000 km* including 1,450 Atlantic crossings up to July 1969. Capt. Gordon R. Buxton surpassed 8,000,000 miles *12 875 000 km* in 22,750 flying hours in 38 years to 22 May 1966. He retired as Senior B.O.A.C. captain, aged 60, having passed all medicals.

Space The most travelled man in history is Capt. Charles "Pete" Conrad, Jr. U.S.N. (b. Philadelphia 2 June 1930) between 21 Aug. 1965 and 22 June 1973. He made four space flights totalling 1,183 hours 38 min. He was commander of the Skylab 2 crew which alone covered an estimated 11.7 milion miles *18,83 million*

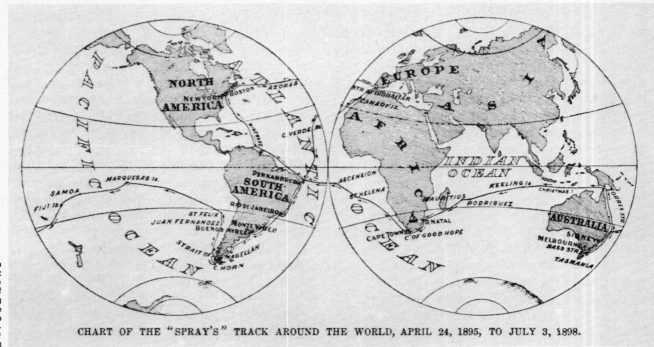

A reproduction of the chart showing the progress of 'Spray" during her voyage, the first solo circum-navigation of 1895-98

CHART OF THE "SPRAY'S" TRACK AROUND THE WORLD, APRIL 24, 1895, TO JULY 3, 1898.

MARINE CIRCUMNAVIGATION RECORDS

A true circumnavigation entails passing through two antipodal points (which are at least 12,429 statute miles apart).

CATEGORY	VESSEL	NAME	START PLACE AND DATE	FINISH DATE AND DURATION
Earliest	*Vittoria* Expedition of Fernão de Magalhães, *c.* 1480–1521	Juan Sebastion de Eleano (d. 1526) and 17 crew including Andrews of Bristol (first Briton)	Guadalquivir, Spain 20 Sept. 1519	6 Sept. 1521 30,700 miles *49 400 km*
Earliest British	*Golden Hind* (ex *Pelican*) 100 tons/*tonnes*	Francis Drake (*c.* 1540–1596) (Knighted 4 April 1581).	Plymouth, 13 Dec. 1577	26 Sept. 1580
Earliest Woman	*La Bordeuse*	Crypto-female valet of M. de Commerson		1764
Earliest Solo	*Spray* 36¾ ft *11,20 m* gaff yawl	Capt. Joshua Slocum, 51, (U.S.) (a non-swimmer)	Newport, Rhode Island, U.S.A. *via* Magellan Straits, 24 Apr. 1895	3 July 1898 46,000 miles *74 000 km*
Earliest Solo Eastabout *via* Cape Horn	*Lehg II* 31¼ ft *9,52 m* Bermuda Ketch	Vito Dumas (Argentina)	Buenos Aires, 27 June 1942	7 Sept. 1943 (272 days)
Smallest Boat	*Trekka* 20½ ft *6,25 m* Bermuda Ketch	John Guzzwell (G.B.)	Victoria B.C., 10 Sept. 1955 Westabout *via* Panama	12 Sept. 1959 (4 years 2 days)
Earliest Submarine	*U.S.S. Triton*	Capt. Edward L. Beach U.S.N. plus 182 crew	New London, Connecticut 16 Feb. 1960	10 May 1960 30,708 miles *49 422 km*
Earliest Solo with One Stop Over	*Gipsy Moth IV* 53 ft *16,15 m* Bermuda Yawl	Sir Francis Chichester K.B.E. (1901–72)	Plymouth to Sydney 27 Aug. 1966	Sydney to Plymouth 28 May 1967 29,626 miles *47 678 km*
Earliest non-stop Solo	*Suhaili* 32.4 ft *9,87 m* Bermuda Ketch	Robin Knox-Johnston C.B.E. (b. 1939)	Falmouth, 14 June 1968	22 Apr. 1969 (313 days)
Fastest Solo	*Victress* 40 ft *12,19 m* Trimaran	Lt-Cdr. Nigel C. W. Tetley R.N. (S. Africa) (1924–72)	Plymouth, 16 Sept. 1968	Tied the Knot in 179 days
Earliest non-stop Solo Westabout	*British Steel* 59 ft *17,98 m* ketch (largest solo)	Charles 'Chay' Blyth C.B.E., B.E.M. (b. 1940)	The Hamble 18 Oct. 1970	6 Aug. 1971 292 days

km. His total previous distance in space was 9 118 948,8 km *5,666,252.1 miles.*

Round the World The fastest time for a round the world trip on commercial flights is 36 hours 19 min 33 sec by Harry J. Cooper, 55 of Greenwich, Connecticut, U.S.A. from Chicago *via* London, Moscow, Tokyo and Anchorage, Alaska to Chicago at a cost of $1,440 (*£576*) on 12–13 April 1973.

Cross-Channel record The record for travelling the 214 miles *344,4 km* between Paris (Arc de Triomphe) and London (Marble Arch) is 40 min 44 sec by Sqn. Ldr. Charles G. Maughan, R.A.F. (b. 1924), by motorcycle, helicopter and Hunter jet aircraft on 22 July 1959, so winning the *Daily Mail* award.

POLAR CONQUESTS

North Pole The claims of neither of the two U.S. Arctic explorers, Dr. Frederick Albert Cook (1865–1940) nor Civil Engineer Robert Edwin Peary, U.S.N. (1856–1920) in reaching the North Pole is subject to positive proof. Cook, accompanied by the Eskimos, Ah-pellah and Etukishook, two sledges and 26 dogs, struck north from a point 60 miles *96,5 km* north of

Svartevoeg, on Axel Heibert Is., Canada, 460 miles *740 km* from the Pole on 21 March 1908, allegedly reaching Lat. 89° 31′N. on 19 April and the Pole on 21 April. Peary, accompanied by his negro assistant, Matthew Alexander Henson (1866–1955) and the four Eskimos, Ooqueah, Egingwah, Seegloo, and Ootah (1875–1955), struck north from his Camp Bartlett (Lat. 87° 44′ N.) at 5 a.m. on 2 April 1909. After travelling another 134 miles *215 km*, he allegedly established his final camp, Camp Jessup, in the proximity of the Pole at 10 a.m. on 6 April and marched a further 42 miles *67,5 km* quartering the sea-ice before turning south at 4 p.m. on 7 April. On excellent pack ice Herbert's 1968–9 Expedition attained a best day's route mileage of 23 miles *37 km* in 15 hours. Cook claimed 26 miles *41,8 km* twice while Peary claimed a surely unsustainable average of 38 miles *61 km* for 8 consecutive days.

The earliest indisputable attainment of the North Pole over the sea-ice was at 3 p.m. (Central Standard Time) on 19 April 1968 by Ralph Plaisted (U.S.) and three companions after a 42-day trek in four Skidoos (snow-mobiles). Their arrival was indpendently verified 18 hours later by a U.S. Air Force weather aircraft.

TRANS-ATLANTIC MARINE RECORDS (compiled by Sq. Ldr. D. H. Clarke, D.F.C., A.F.C.)

Earliest Trimaran	John Mikes +2 crew (U.S.)	*Non Pareil*, 25 ft *7,62 m*	New York (4 June)	Southampton	43 days	1868
Earliest Solo Sailing	Alfred Johnson (Denmark)	*Centennial* 20 ft *6,09 m*	Nova Scotia	Wales	46 days	1876
Earliest Woman Sailing	Mrs. Joanna Crapo (Scotland)	*New Bedford* 20 ft *6,09 m*	Chatham, Mass.	Newlyn, Cornwall	51 days	1877
Earliest Single-handed race	J. W. Lawlor (U.S.)	*Sea Serpent* 15 ft *4,57 m*	Boston (17 June)	Coverack, Cornwall	47 days	1891
Earliest Rowing	George Harbo and Frank Samuelson (U.S.)	*Richard K. Fox* 18½ ft *5,58 m*	New York City (6 June)	Isles of Scilly (1 Aug.)	55 days	1896
Fasting Sailing Ship	Captain and crew	*Lancing* 4 masts	New York	Cape Wrath	6 days 18 hours	1916
Fastest Solo Sailing West-East	J. V. T. McDonald (G.B.)	*Inverarity* 38 ft *11,58 m*	Nova Scotia	Ireland	16 days	1922
Earliest Canoe (with sail)	E. Romer (Germany)	*Deutches Sport* 19½ ft *5,94 m*	Cape St. Vincent (17 Apr.)	St. Thomas, West Indies	58 days	´1928
Fastest Solo Sailing East West (Northern)	Cdr. R. D. Graham R.N. (G.B.)	*Emanuel* 30 ft *9,14 m*	Bantry, Ireland	St. John's, Newfoundland	24.35 days	1934
Earliest Woman Solo-Sailing	Mrs. Ann Davison (G.B.)	*Felicity Ann* 23 ft *7,01 m*	Plymouth (18 May 1952)	Miami, Florida (13 Aug. 1953)	454 days	1952 /1953
Smallest East-West (Northern)	John Riding (G.B.)	*Sjø Ag* 12 ft *3,65 m*	Plymouth, July 1964	Newport, Rhode Is. (17 Aug. 1965)	403 days	1964 /1965
Smallest West-East	William Verity (U.S.)	*Nonoalca* 12 ft *3,65 m*	Ft. Lauderdale, Florida	Tralee, Kerry (12 July)	68 days	1966
Earliest Rowing (G.B.)	Capt. John Ridgway M.B.E. Sgt. Charles Blyth B.E.M. (G.B.)	*English Rose III* 22 ft *6,70 m*	Cape Cod (4 June)	Inishmore (3 Sept.)	91 days	1966
Fastest Crossing Sailing (Trimaran)	Eric Tabarly (France) +2 crew	*Pen Duick IV* 63 ft *19,20 m*	Tenerife	Martinique	251.4 miles *404,5 km*/day (10 days 12 hours)	1968
Smallest East-West (Southern)	Hugo S. Vihlen (U.S.)	*The April Fool* 5 ft 11½ in *1,81 m*	Casablanca (29 Mar.)	Ft. Lauderdale, Florida (21 June)	85 days	1968
Fastest Solo East-West (Northern)	Geoffrey Williams (G.B.)	*Sir Thomas Lipton* 57 ft *17,37 m*	Plymouth (1 June)	Brenton Reef (27 June)	25.85 days	1968
Fastest Solo Rowing East-West	Sidney Genders, 51 (G.B.)	*Khaggavisana* 19¾ ft *6,02 m*	Sennen Cove, Cornwall	Miami, Florida *via* Antigua (27 June)	37.3 miles *60 km*/day	1970
Earliest Solo Rowing East-West	John Fairfax (G.B.)	*Britannia* 22 ft *6,70 m*	Las Palmas (20 Jan.)	Ft. Lauderdale, Florida (19 July)	180 days	1969
Fastest Solo East-West (Southern)	Sir Francis Chichester K.B.E. (G.B.)	*Gipsy Moth V* 57 ft *17,37 m*	Portuguese Guinea	Nicaragua	179.1 miles *288,2 km*/day (22.4 days)	1970
Earliest Solo Rowing West-East	Tom McClean (Ireland)	*Super Silver* 20 ft *6,90 m*	St. John's, Newfoundland (17 May)	Black Sod Bay, Ireland (27 July)	70.7 days	1969
Fastest Solo East-West (Multi-hull)	Prof. Alain Colas (France)	*Pen Duick IV* 70 ft *21,33 m* trimaran	Plymouth (17 June)	Newport, Rhode Is. (7 July)	20½ days	1972

TRANS-PACIFIC MARINE RECORDS

Fastest	Eric Tabarly (France)	*Pen Duick IV* 70 ft *21,33 m* trimaran	Los Angeles, Cal.	Honolulu, Hawaii	8.54 days 260.5 miles *419,2 km*/day	1969
First Solo (Woman)	Sharon Sites Adam	*Sea Harp* 31 ft *9,45 m*	Yokohama, Japan	San Diego, Cal.	75 days	1969
Earliest Rowing	John Fairfax (G.B.) Sylvia Cook (G.B.)	*Britannia II* 35 ft *10,66 m*	San Francisco, Cal. 26 Apr 1971	Hayman Is. Australia 22 Apr. 1972	362 days	1971 /1972

N.B.—The earliest single-handed Pacific crossings were achieved East-West by Bernard Gilboy (U.S.) in 1882 in the 18 ft *5,48 m* double-ender *Pacific* and West-East by Fred Rebel (Latvia) in 1932 in the 18 ft *5,48 m Elaine*.

Arctic crossing The first crossing of the Arctic sea-ice was achieved by the British Trans-Arctic Expedition which left Point Barrow, Alaska on 21 Feb. 1968 and arrived at the Seven Island Archipelago north-east of Spitzbergen 464 days later on 29 May 1969 after a haul of 2,920 statute miles *4 699 km* and a drift of 700 miles *1 126 km* compared with the straight line distance of 1,662 miles *2 674 km*. The team was Wally Herbert (leader), 34, Major Ken Hedges, 34, R.A.M.C., Allan Gill, 38, and Dr. Roy Koerner, 36 (glaciologist), and 40 huskies. This was the longest sustained journey ever made on polar pack ice. Temperatures were down to −47° F *−43,8° C*.

South Pole The first ship to cross the Antarctic circle (Lat. 66° 30′ S.) was the *Resolution* (462 tons/*tonnes*), under Capt. James Cook (1728–79), on 17 Jan. 1773. The first person to sight the Antarctic *mainland*—on the best available evidence and against claims made for British and Russian explorers—was Nathaniel Brown Palmer (U.S.) (1799–1877). On 17 Nov. 1820 he sighted the Orleans Channel coast of the Palmer Peninsular from his 45 ton/*tonnes* sloop *Hero*.

The South Pole was first reached on 14 Dec. 1911 by a Norwegian party led by Capt. Roald Amundsen (1872–1928), after a 53-day march with dog sledges from the Bay of Whales, to which he had penetrated in the *Fram*. Olav Olavson Bjaaland, the first to arrive, was the last survivor, dying in June 1961, aged 88. The others were the late Helmer Hanssen, Sverre H. Hassell and Oskar Wisting.

Antarctic crossing The first crossing of the Antarctic continent was completed at 1.47 p.m. on 2 March 1958, after a trek of 2,158 miles *3 473 km* lasting 99 days from 24 Nov. 1957, from Shackleton Base to Scott Base *via* the Pole. The crossing party of twelve was led by Dr. (now Sir) Vivian Ernest Fuchs (born 11 Feb. 1908).

Longest sledge journey The longest polar sledge journey was one of 3,720 statute route miles *5 986 km* in 476 days by the British Trans-Arctic Expedition from 21 Feb. 1968 to 10 June 1969 (see above). The longest totally self-supporting Polar sledge journey ever made was one of 1,080 miles *1 738 km* from West to East across Greenland on 18 June to 5 Sept. 1934 by Capt. M. Lindsay (now Sir Martin Lindsay, Bt., C.B.E., D.S.O.); Lt. Arthur S. T. Godfrey, R.E., (later Lt. Col., D.S.O., k. 1942), Andrew N. C. Croft and 49 dogs.

MOUNTAINEERING

Highest by man The conquest of the highest point on Earth, Mount Everest (29,028 ft [*8 847 m*]) was first achieved at

Hugo Vihlen in his *April Fool* (overall length 5 ft 11½ in [*1,81 m*]) the smallest boat ever to cross the Atlantic

OCEAN DESCENTS—PROGRESSIVE RECORDS

Ft	m	Vehicle	Divers	Location	Date	
c.245	75	Steel Sphere	Ernest Bazin (France)	Belle Île		1865
c.830	253	Diving Bell	Balsamello Bella Nautica (Italy)			1889
c.1,650	500	Hydrostat	Hartman			1911
2,200	670	Bathysphere	Dr. Charles William Beebe (1887–1962) and Dr. Otis Barton (b. 1901) (U.S.A.)	S.E. Bermuda	22 Sept.	1932
2,510	765	Bathysphere	Dr. C. W. Beebe and Dr. O. Barton (U.S.A.)	S.E. Bermuda	11 Aug.	1934
3,028	923	Bathysphere	Dr. C. W. Beebe and Dr. O. Barton (U.S.A.)	S.E. Bermuda	15 Aug.	1934
7,850	2 390	Converted U-boat	Heinz Sellner (Germany) (unwitnessed)	Murmansk	Aug.	1947
4,500	1 370	Benthoscope	Dr. Otis Barton (U.S.A.)	off Santa Cruz, California	16 Aug.	1949
5,085	1 550	Bathyscaphe F.N.R.S. 3	Lt-Cdr. Georges S. Houet and Lt. Pierre-Henri Willm (France)	off Toulon	12 Aug.	1953
6,890	2 100	Bathyscaphe F.N.R.S. 3	Lt-Cdr G. S. Houet and Lt. P.-H. Willm (France)	off Cap Ferrat	14 Aug.	1953
10,335	3 150	Bathyscaphe Trieste	Prof. Auguste and Dr. Jaques Piccard (Switzerland)	Ponza Is.	30 Sept.	1953
13,287	4 050	Bathyscaphe F.N.R.S. 3	Lt.-Cdr. G. S. Houet and Eng. Off. P.-H. Willm (France)	off Dakar, Senegal	15 Feb.	1954
18,600	5 670	Bathyscaphe Trieste	Dr. J. Piccard (Swiss) and Andreas B. Rechnitzer (U.S.A.)	Marianas Trench	14 Nov.	1959
24,000	7 315	Bathyscaphe Trieste	Dr. J. Piccard (Swiss) and Lt. D. Walsh, U.S.N.	Marianas Trench	7 Jan.	1960
35,802	10 912	Bathyscaphe Trieste	Dr. J. Piccard (Swiss) and Lt. D. Walsh, U.S.N.	Marianas Trench	23 Jan.	1969

11.30 a.m. on 29 May 1953, by Edmund Percival Hillary (New Zealand) and the Sherpa Tenzing Norkhay (see Mountaineering, Chapter 12).

Highest by woman The greatest altitude attained by a woman mountaineer is 26,223 ft *7 992 m* by Miss Setsuko Watanabe, 31 (Japan) on Everest in May 1970. The highest mountain summit reached by women is Qungar I (Kongur Tiube Tagh) (*c.* 25,146 ft), climbed in 1961 by Shierab and another (unnamed) Tibetan woman.

GREATEST OCEAN DESCENT

The record ocean descent was achieved in the Challenger Deep of the Marianas Trench, 250 miles *400 km* south-west of Guam, in the Pacific Ocean, when the Swiss-built U.S. Navy bathyscaphe *Trieste*, manned by Dr. Jacques Piccard (b. 1914) (Switzerland) and Lt. Donald Walsh, U.S.N., reached the ocean bed 35,082 ft (6.78 miles [*10 912 m*]) down, at 1.10 p.m. on 23 Jan. 1960 (but see also Chapter 3). The pressure of the water was 16,883 lb./in^2 *1 183 kg f/cm^2* and the temperature 37.4° F *3° C*. The descent required 4 hours 48 min and the ascent 3 hours 17 min.

Deep diving records The record depth for the extremely dangerous activity of breath-held diving is 250 ft *76 m* by Enzio Maiorca (Italy) at Syracuse, Sicily on 11 Aug. 1971. The record dive with Scuba (self-contained under-water breathing apparatus) is 437 ft *133 m* by John J. Gruener and R. Neal Watson (U.S.A.) off Freeport, Grand Bahama on 14 Oct. 1968. The record dive utilizing gas mixtures is a simulated dive of 2,001 ft *609 m* in a chamber by Patrice Chemin and Robert Gauret (France) at the Comex Chamber, Marseille, France reported in June 1972.

SALVAGING

Deep sea diving The world's record depth for a salvage observation chamber is that established by the Admiralty salvage ship *Reclaim* on 28 June 1956, In an observation chamber measuring 7 ft *2,13 m* long and 3 ft *0,91 m* internal diameter, Senior Com. Boatswain (now Lt.-Cdr.) George A. M. Wookey, M.B.E., R.N., descended to a depth of 1,060 ft *323 m* in Oslo Fjord, Norway.

Deepest The greatest depth at which salvage has been achieved is 16,500 ft *5 029 m* by the bathyscaphe *Trieste II* (Lt.-Cdr. Mel Bartels U.S.N.) to attach cables to an "electronic package" on the sea bed 400 miles *645 km* north of Hawaii on 20 May 1972.

Flexible dress divers The deepest salvaging operation ever carried out was on the wreck of the S.S. *Niagara*, sunk by a mine in 1940, 438 ft *133,5 m* down off Bream Head, Whangarei North Island, New Zealand. All but 6 per cent of the £2,250,000 of gold in her holds was recovered in 7 weeks. The record recovery was that from the White Star Liner *Laurentic*, which was torpedoed in 114 ft *34,7 m* of water off Malin Head, Donegal, Ireland, in 1917, with £5,000,000 of gold ingots in her Second Class baggage room. By 1924, 3,186 of the 3,211 gold bricks had been recovered with immense difficulty.

Largest vessel The largest vessel ever salvaged was the U.S.S. *Lafayette*, formerly the French liner *Normandie* (83,423 tons), which keeled over during fire-fighting operations at the West 49th Street Pier, New York Harbour, U.S.A., on 9 Feb. 1942. She was righted in October 1943, at a cost of $4,500,000 (*then £1,250,000*) and was broken up at Newark, New Jersey, beginning September 1946.

Most Expensive Operation The most expensive salvage operation ever conducted was that by the U.S. Navy off Palomares, southern Spain, for the recovery of a 2,800 lb. *1 270 kg* 20 megaton H-bomb, dropped from a crashing B-52 bomber, at a cost of $30,000,000 (*then £12.5 million*). A fleet of 18 ships and 2,200 men took part between 17 Jan. and 7 Apr. 1966. A CURV (Cable-controlled Underwater Research Vehicle) was flown from California and, directed by the 2 man submarine *Alvin*, retrieved the bomb from a depth of 2,850 ft *368 m*.

MINING DEPTHS

Greatest penetration Man's deepest penetration made into the ground is in the Western Deep Levels Mine at Carltonville, Transvaal, South Africa. On 13 April 1973 a record depth of 3 481 m *11,387 ft* was attained on the way to a target of 3 608 m *11,837 ft* by June 1974. The rock temperature at this depth is 52,2° C *126° F*.

Shaft sinking record The one month (31 days) world record is 1 251 ft *381,3 m* for a standard shaft 26 ft *7,92 m* in diameter at Buffelsfontein Mine, Transvaal, South Africa, in March 1962. The British record is 336 ft *102,4 m* in 31 days in January 1961 at the No. 2 shaft of Kellingley Colliery, Knottingley, Yorkshire.

RUNNING

Mensen Ehrnst (1799–1846) of Norway is reputed to have run from Istanbul, Turkey, to Calcutta, in West Bengal, India, and back in 59 days in 1836, so averaging an improbable 92.4 miles *151,6 km* per day. The greatest non-stop run recorded is 121 miles 440 yds *195,132 km* in 22 hours 27 min by Jared R. Beads, 41, of Westport, Maryland in October 1969. The 24-hour running record is 159 miles 562 yds *256,399 km* (6 marathons plus 3,532 yds [*3 229 m*]) by Wally H. Hayward, 45 (South Africa) at Motspur Park, Surrey on 20–21 Nov. 1954. The best distance by a 19th century "wobbler" was 150 miles 395 yds *245,013 km* by Charles Rowell in New York City in February 1882.

Six-day races The greatest distance covered by a man in six days (*i.e.* the 144 permissible hours between Sundays in Victorian times) was 623¾ miles *1 003,828 km* by George Littlewood (England), who required only 139 hours 1 min for this feat in December 1888 at the old Madison Square Gardens, New York City, U.S.A.

Greatest mileage The greatest life-time mileage recorded by any runner is 153,445 miles *246 945 km* by Ken Baily of Bournemouth, England up to 12 June 1973. This is more than 6 times round the Equator. When running at night in a luminous track suit he has been attacked by owls.

Longest race The longest race ever staged was the 1929 Transcontinental Race (3,665 miles [*5 898 km*]) from New York City, N.Y., to Los Angeles, California, U.S.A. The Finnish-born Johnny Salo (killed 6 Oct. 1931) was the winner in 79 days, from 31 March to 17 June. His elapsed time of 525 hours 57 min 20 sec gave a running average of 6.97 m.p.h. *11,21 km/h.*

Hottest Travel The traverse of the 120 mile *193 km* long Death Valley, California in both directions was accomplished by Paul Pfau with ground temperatures reaching 140° F *60° C* on 22–24 Jan. (30½ elapsed hours) for the southbound and on 3–5 March 1971 (26 hours 10 min) for the northbound traverse. Bill Emerton, 52 (Australia) made the 115 mile *185 km* traverse in July walking in 2 days 15 hours on 22–24 July 1972.

"Go As You Please" Chief Warrant Officer Philippe Latulippe (b. March 1919) of Canada walked 300.14 miles *483 km* at Petawawa Base, Ontario, Canada on 1–4 Oct. 1972.

WALKING

Longest Lt-Col. Richard Crawshaw O.B.E., T.D. (b. 1917), M.P. for Toxteth, Liverpool walked 255.84 miles *411,73 km* in 76 hours 10 min round the 1.64 mile *2,63 km* long Aintree Motorcycle track near Liverpool, Lancashire, on 21–24 April 1972 in support of N.S.P.C.C. fund raising. He had six brief stops.

Non-Stop The greatest distance ever walked literally non-stop is 230.8 miles *371,4 km* in 68½ hours near Napier, New Zealand on 11–14 Sept. 1971, by John Sinclair, 54, of Great Britain.

North America coast to coast John Lees, (b. 23 Feb. 1945) of Brighton, England between 11 Apr. and 3 June 1972, walked 2,876 miles *4 628 km* across the U.S.A. from City Hall, Los Angeles to City Hall, New York City in 53 days 12 hours 15 min (average 53.746 miles [*86,495 km*] a day). This bettered the 53 days 23 hours 12½ min (average 53.291 miles [*85,764 km*] a day) for *running* the distance completed by John Ball, 45 of East London, South Africa between 5 March and 28 April 1972.

Walking Backwards The greatest ever exponent of reverse pedestrianism has been Plennie L. Wingo (b. 1895) of Abilene, Texas, who started on his 8,000 mile *12 874 km* transcontinental walks from Fort Worth, Texas to Istanbul, Turkey, from 15 Apr. 1931 to 24 Oct. 1932. The record distance for walking backwards in 24 hours is 50 miles 90 yds *80,549 km* by Geoff Laycock at Horsham, Australia on 10–11 Mar. 1973.

SWIMMING

The greatest recorded distance ever swum is 1,826 miles *2 938 km* down the Mississippi, U.S.A. by Fred P. Newton, 27, from 6 July to 29 Dec. 1933. He was 742 hours in the water between Ford Dam near Minneapolis and Carrollte Ave., New Orelans, Louisiana. The water temperature fell to 47° F *8,3° C* and Newton used olive oil and axle grease.

Duration The longest duration swim ever achieved was one of 168 continuous hours, ending on 24 Feb. 1941, by the legless Charles Zibbelman, *alias* Zimmy (b. 1894) of the U.S.A., in a pool in Honolulu, Hawaii, U.S.A. The longest duration swim by a woman was 87 hours 27 min in a pool by Mrs. Myrtle Huddleston of New York City, N.Y., U.S.A., in 1931.

The greatest distance covered in a continuous swim is 288 miles *463,5 km* by Clarence Giles from Glendive to Billings, Montana in the Yellowstone River in 71 hours 3 min on 30 June to 3 July 1939.

Longest on a raft The longest recorded survival alone on a raft is 133 days (4½ months) by Second Steward Poon Lim (born Hong Kong) of the U.K. Merchant Navy, whose ship, the S.S. *Ben Lomond*, was torpedoed in the Atlantic 565 miles *910 km* west of St. Paul's Rocks in

Lt.-Col. Richard Crawshaw M.P. (centre) at the start of his marathon walk

Lat. 00 30′ N Long. 38° 45′ W at 11.45 a.m. on 23 Nov. 1942. He was picked up by a Brazilian fishing boat off Salinópolis, Brazil, on 5 April 1943 and was able to walk ashore. In July 1943, he was awarded the B.E.M.

The longest international single-handed voyage on a raft was one of 7,450 miles *11 990 km* by William Willis (born in Germany, 1893) of the U.S.A., who arrived at Upolu, Western Samoa, on 12 Nov. 1963, accompanied by two cats, on his steel-hulled trimaran raft *Age Unlimited* (32 × 20 ft [*9,75 × 6,10 m*]), after a 130-day voyage across the Pacific Ocean. He had been cast off 50 miles *85 km* off Callao, Peru, on 5 July 1963.

CYCLING

The duration record for cycling on a track is 168 hours (7 days) by Syed Muhammed Nawab, aged 22, of Lucknow, India, in Addis Ababa, Ethiopia, in 1964. The monocylce duration record is 11 hours 21 min (83.4 miles [*134,2 km*]) by Raymond Le Grand at Maubeuge, France, on 12 Sept. 1955. The longest cycle tour on record is one of 135,000 miles *217 250 km* by Mishreelal Jaiswal (b. 1924) of India, through 107 countries from 1950 to 5 April 1964, ending in San Francisco, California, U.S.A. He wore out five machines.

Ray Reece, 41, of Alverstoke, Hants., circumnavigated the world by bicycle (13,000 road miles [*20 900 km*]) between 14 June and 5 Nov. (143 days) in 1971. Peter Duker of Worthing, Sussex in circumnavigating the world (15,000 miles [*24 140 km*]) in 236 days set a coast-to-coast Trans-America record (Santa Monica, California to New York City) in 18 days 2½ hours in 1972.

MARRIAGE AND DIVORCE

Most The greatest number of marriages accumulated in the monogamous world is 19 by Glynn de Moss Wolfe (U.S.) (b. 1908) who married for the 19th time since 1930 his 17th wife Gloria, aged 23, on 22 Feb. 1969. His total number of children is, he says, 31. In 1955 he was reputedly worth $500,000 but recently testified to be living on welfare. The most often marrying millionaire was Thomas F. Manville (1894–1967) who contracted his 13th marriage to his 11th wife Christine Erdlen Popa (1940–71) aged 20, in New York City, U.S.A., on 11 Jan. 1960 when aged 65. His shortest marriage (to his seventh wife) effectively lasted only 7½ hours. His fortune of $20 million came from asbestos, none of which he could take with him.

Mrs. Beverly Nina Avery, then aged 48, a barmaid from Los Angeles, California, U.S.A., set a monogamous world record in October 1957 by obtaining her sixteenth divorce from her fourteenth husband, Gabriel Avery. She alleged outside the court that five of the 14 had broken her nose.

Britain Seven times married individuals in Britain include Sir Francis Ferdinand Maurice Cook Bt. (b. 21 Dec. 1907) and Mr. Lionel Birch.

Oldest Bride and Bridegroom The oldest bridegroom on record was Ralph Cambridge, 105, who married Mrs. Adriana Kapp, 70, at Knysna, South Africa on 30 Sept. 1971. The British record was set by Edward Simpson, (1873–1973), who married Mrs. Eva Midwinter, 82, at Swindon, Wilts. on 8 Dec. 1971 when aged 98 years 10 months.

The British record for collective age is 187 years by Alfred Caple, 91, and Kate Benson, Britain's oldest bride at 96 married in Stoke Newington, London, on 3 Aug. 1971.

Longest Engagements The longest engagement on record is one of 67 years between Octavio Guillen, 82 and Adriana Martinez, 82. They finally took the plunge in June 1969 in Mexico City, Mexico.

Most arduous Courtship It is recorded that in the reign of George III (1760–1820) a Kentish labourer named Stephen Hogben walked from Acryse to Faversham, Kent and back to see his betrothed in the period 1771–1778 for a total mileage of 16,000 miles *25 750 km*. The girl, whose name is not recorded, died of consumption and Mr. Hogben became the epitome of the proverb "it is better to travel hopefully than to arrive".

Longest Marriage *World* The longest recorded marriage is one of 86 years between Sir Temulji Bhicaji Nariman and Lady Nariman from 1853 to 1940 resulting from a cousin marriage when both were five. Sir Temulji (b. 3 Sept. 1848) died, aged 91 years 11 months, in August 1940 at Bombay. The only reliable instance of an 83rd anniversary celebrated by a couple marrying at normal ages is that between the late Edd (105) and Margaret (99) Hollen. who celebrated their 83rd anniversary on 7 May 1972. They were married in Kentucky on 7 May 1889.

Britain James Frederick Burgess (born 3 March 1861, died 27 Nov. 1966) and his wife Sarah Ann, *née* Gregory (born 11 July 1865, died 22 June 1965) were married on 21 June 1883 at St. James's, Bermondsey, London, and celebrated their 82nd anniversary in 1965.

Most married James and Mary Grady of Illinois, U.S.A. have married each other 27 times as a protest against the existence of divorce in the period 1964–69. They have married in 25 different States, 3 times in a day (16 Dec. 1968), twice in an hour and twice on television.

Mass ceremony The largest mass wedding ceremony was one of 791 couples officiated over by Sun Myung Moon of the Holy Spirit Association for the Unification of World Christianity in Seoul, South Korea in October 1970. The response to the question "Will you swear to love your spouse for ever?" is "Ye".

Eating out The world champion for eating out is Fred E. Magel of Chicago, Illinois, U.S.A. who since 1928 has dined in 36,000 restaurants in 60 nations as a restaurant grader (to March 1973). He asserts the one serving the largest helpings is Zehnder's Hotel, Frankenmuth, Michigan, U.S.A. Mr. Magel's favourite dishes are South African rock lobster and mousse of fresh English strawberries.

Party giving The most expensive private party ever thrown was that of Mr. and Mrs. Bradley Martin of Troy, N.Y., U.S.A. staged at the Waldorf Hotel, Manhattan in February 1897. The cost to the host and hostess was estimated to be $369,200 in the days when dollars were made of gold.

Toast-masters The Guild of Professional Toastmasters (founded 1962) has only 12 members. Its founder and President, Ivor Spencer, has listened to more than 25,000 speeches in the period 1956–72, including one in excess of 2 hours by the maudlin victim of a retirement luncheon. The Guild also elects the most boring speaker of the year, but for professional reasons, will not publicize the winner's name until A.D. 2000. Red coats were introduced by the earliest professional, William Knight-Smith (d.1932) *c.* 1900.

Lecture Agency The world's largest lecture agency is the American Program Bureau of Boston, Mass., U.S.A., with 400 Personalities on 40 Topics and a turnover of some $5 million. The top rate is $4,000 (*£1,600*) per hour commanded by Ralph Nader. This is $66.66 (*£26.66*) per min.

Working week The longest working week (maximum possible 168 hours) is up to 139 hours at times by some housemen and registrars in some hospitals. This peak value was alleged by Dr. Adrian Cox at the Norfolk and Norwich Hospital in November 1971.

Working career The longest recorded working career in one job in Britain was that of Miss Polly Gadsby who started work with Archibald Turner & Co. of Leicester at the age of 9. In 1932, after 86 years service, she was still at her bench wrapping elastic, aged 95. Mr. Theodore C. Taylor (1850–1952) served 86 years with J. T. & T. Taylor of Batley, Yorkshire including 56 years as chairman. Mr. Ernest Turner of Ramsgate, Kent has been working since 1886 (minding sheep at 2s. 6d. a week) and in July 1973 was a canteen cleaner for Volkswagen, aged 94. His son, a old age pensioner working part-time, has to get up at 6.30 a.m. every morning to drive 'my dad' to work.

Longest pension Miss Millicent Barclay, daughter of Col. William Barclay was born posthumously on 10 July 1872 and became eligible for a Madras Military Fund pension to continue until her marriage. She died unmarried on 26 Oct. 1969 having drawn the pension for every day of her life of 97 years 3 months.

Teaching career The longest teaching career on record is a span of 61 years from 1 Oct. 1911 by John Grant (b. 1888) of Corstorphine, Edinburgh.

Most Jobs The greatest number of different paid jobs recorded in a working life is the 110 accumulated by D. H. "Nobby" Clarke, the yachting author, of Ipswich, Suffolk.

MISCELLANEOUS ENDEAVOURS

Apple peeling The longest single unbroken apple peel on record is one of 130 ft 8½ in *39,86 m* peeled by Frank Freer (U.S.) in 8 hours at Wolcott, N.Y., on 17 Oct. 1971. The apple was 15 in *38 cm* in circumference.

Apple picking The greatest recorded performance is 270 U.S. bushels (261.6 Imperial bushels [*95,14 hectolitres*]) picked in 8 hours by Harold Oaks, 22, at his father's ranch, Hood River, Oregon, U.S.A. on 30 Sept. 1972.

Bag carrying The record time for the annual "World Coal Carrying Championship" over the uphill 1,080 yd *987 m* course at Ossett cum Gawthorpe, Yorkshire, England with a 112 lb. *50 kg 80* sack is 4 min 36 sec by Tony Nicholson, 26, of Penrith, Cumberland on 3 Apr. 1972. The non-stop distance record carrying 1 cwt. *50 kg 80* is 12.6 miles *20,2 km* from Spetchley to Evesham, Worcestershire by Norman Staite, 26, on 29 Oct. 1972.

Bag-pipes The longest duration pipe has been one of 50 hours by William Donaldson, Donald Grant, John Lovie and William Wotherspoon of Aberdeen University on 21–23 April 1969. The comment of some local inhabitants after the "lang blaw" was "Thank God there's nae smell".

Balancing on one foot The longest recorded duration for continuous balancing on one foot is 6½ hours by Garry Plotecki, 13 at West Perth, Western Australia in 1972. The disengaged foot may not be rested on the standing foot nor may any sticks be used for support or balance.

Balloon racing The largest balloon release on record has been one of 100,000 helium balloons at the opening of "Transpo 72" at Dallas Airport, Washington, D.C. on 27 May 1972. The longest reported toy balloon flight is one of 9,000 miles *14 500 km* from Atherton, California (released by Jane Dorst on 21 May 1972) and found on 10 June at Pietermaritzburg, South Africa.

Ballooning (Hot Air) The world's distance record for hot-air ballooning is 255 miles *410 km* by Matt. Wiedertehr, 42, in an AX-5 from St. Paul, Minnesota to Bankston, Iowa on 29 March 1972. The altitude record is 35,971 ft *10 963 m* by Julian Richard Prothro Not, b. 22 June 1944 (G.B.) over Hereford on 14 July 1972. The endurance record is 11 hr 14 min by Bob Sparks (U.S.A.) in a flight from Lafayette, U.S.A. on 12 Dec. 1972. The record-holder for hot-air ballooning records is Ray Munro with 34 F.A.I. ratified records. On 1 Feb. 1970 he flew 158.34 miles across the Irish Sea in 4 hours 52 min. He also has 50 honorary citizenships.

Ball punching Ron Renaulf (Australia) equalled his own world duration ball punching record of 125 hours 20 min at 10.20 p.m. on 31 Dec. 1955, at the Esplanade, Southport, Queensland, Australia.

Band marathons The longest recorded "blow-in" is 12 hours 10 min by the Hammond Sauce Works Junior Band at Dockfield, Shipley, Yorks. on 19 May 1973. Each bandsman was allowed 5 min per hour to regain his wind. The record for a one-man band is 7 hours (no breaks) by Johnny Magoo on drums, harmonica and stylaphone at Strood, Kent on 22 May 1971.

One Man Band The greatest number of musical instruments played in a single tune is 41 by Roy Castle, who performed "Whistle While you Work" in 3 min 51 sec on BBC T.V. *Record Breakers* on 6 Nov. 1972.

Barrow pushing The heaviest loaded barrow pushed for a minimum 20 ft *6,09 m* is one loaded with 202 bricks weighing 606 kg *11.92 cwt.* by Jerry Ward in Birmingham on 3 May 1972.

Barrel jumping The greatest number of barrels jumped by a skater is 17 (total length 28 ft 8 in [*8,73 m*]) by Kenneth LeBel at the Grossinger Country Club, New York State, U.S.A., on 9 Jan. 1965.

Bed of nails The duration record for lying on a bed of nails (needle-sharp 6-inch [*15,2 cm*] 2 in [*5 cm*] apart) is 25 hours 20 min by Vernon C. Craig (Komar, the Hindu *fakir*) at Wooster, Ohio, U.S.A. 22–23 July 1971. Much longer durations are claimed by uninvigilated *fakirs*—the most extreme case being *Silki* who claimed 111 days in Sao Paulo, Brazil ending on 24 Aug. 1969. The greatest weight borne on a bed of nails is also by Komar with 4 persons aggregating 1,082½ lb. (77 st. 4½ lb. [*491 kg 00*]) standing on him in Boulder, Colorado on 30 July 1972.

Bed-pushing The longest recorded push of a normally sessile object is of 604 miles *972 km* in the case of a wheeled hospital bed by a team of 12 from Box Hill High School, Victoria, Australia on 19–24 Aug. 1972.

Bed race The record time for the annual Knaresborough Bed Race (established 1966) in Yorkshire is 15 min 54 sec for the 2½ mile *4 km* course across the River Nidd by the Leeds Regional Hospital Board team, from a field of 34, on 5 June 1971.

Roy Castle playing one of the record 43 instruments during his rendition of a single tune during the B.B.C. television programme "Record-Breakers"

Best man The world's champion "best man" is Mr. Wally Gant, a bachelor fishmonger from Wakefield, Yorkshire, who officiated for the 50th time since 1931 in December 1964.

Big Wheel riding The endurance record for riding a Big Wheel is 14 days 21 hours by David Trumayne, 22, at Ramsgate, Kent ending on 8 June 1969. He completed 62,207 revolutions. Richard Ford, 30, sat for 20 days 16½ hours in a 40 ft *12,19 m* Ferris Wheel in San Francisco, California in January 1971. It did not, however, revolve at night.

Billiard Table jumping Joe Darby (1861–1937) cleared a full-sized billiard table lengthwise, taking off from a 4 in *10 cm* high solid wooden block, at Wolverhampton on 5 Feb. 1892.

Body jump The greatest number of "bodies" cleared in a motorcycle ramp jump is 41 by Sgt.-Maj. Thomas Gledhill, B.E.M., 41, of the Royal Artillery Motorcycle Display Team on a 441 c.c. B.S.A. Victor G.P. at Woolwich, Greater London on 4 June 1971. The 41st man was Capt. Tony Scarisbrick. Tony Yeates cleared 84 ft *25,60 m* (*equivalent* to 55 men) at Swindon in 1970.

Bomb defusing The highest reported number of unexploded bombs defused by any individual is 8,000 by Werner Stephan in West Berlin, Germany, in the 12 years from 1945 to 1957. He was killed by a small grenade on the Grunewald blasting site on 17 Aug. 1957.

Bond signing The greatest feat of bond signing was that performed by L. E. Chittenden (d. 1902), the Registrar of the United States Treasury. In 48 hours (20–22 March 1863) he signed 12,500 bonds worth $10,000,000 (*now £4 million*), which had to catch a steam packet to England. He suffered years of pain and the bonds were never used.

Boomerang throwing The earliest mention of a word similar to *boomerang* is *wo-mur-rang* in Collins *Acct. N.S. Wales Vocab.* published in 1798. The earliest certain account of a returning boomerang (term established, 1827) was in 1831 by Major (later Sir Thomas) Mitchell.

223

The longest measured throw for a return type is one of 108.4 yds *99,1 m* with an orbital perimeter of 250 yds *230 m* with an 8½ oz. *242 g* wooden boomerang by Herb A. Smith on 17 June 1972 at Littlehampton, Sussex.

Brewing Mr. E. Cogans of the Durden Park Beer Circle of Hayes, Middlesex won 5 of the 8 classes in the 1972 B.E.A. Beer Festival and "Master Brewer of the Year" title.

Brick carrying The record for the annual Narrogin Brick Carrying contest in Western Australia (instituted in 1960) is 40.0 miles *64,37 km* by Ronald D. Hamilton on 10 Oct. 1970. The 8 lb. 12 oz. *3 kg 968* wire-cut semi-pressed brick has to be carried in a downward position with a nominated ungloved hand. The feminine record for a 7¾ lb. *3 kg 515* brick is 1.6 miles *2,57 km* by Pat McDougall, aged 16, but Jeanette Bartlett of Swindon, Wiltshire carried an 8 lb. 13¾ oz. *4 kg 018* brick more than 1.49 miles *2,39 km* on 4 July 1969.

Bricklaying The world record for bricklaying was established in 1937 by Joseph Raglon of East St. Louis, Illinois, U.S.A., who, supported by assistants, placed 3,472 bricks in 60 min of foundation-work—at a rate of nearly 58 a minute.

The record for constructional bricklaying was set when J. E. Bloxham, of Stratford-upon-Avon, England laid a 13½ ft *4,11 m* wall of 5,188 bricks in 7 hours 35 min with two assistants on 28 May 1960. It was also reported that Mr. C. Hull of Sheffield, Yorkshire laid 860 bricks in 60 min on 24 Nov. 1924.

Brick throwing The greatest reported distance for throwing a standard 5 lb. *2 kg 268* building brick is 135 ft 8 in *41,35 m* by Robert Gardner at Stroud, Gloucestershire, England, in the annual contest on 18 July 1970.

Burial alive The longest recorded burial alive is one of 100 days ending on 17 Sept. 1968 in Skegness by Mrs. Emma Smith of Ravenshead, Nottinghamshire, England. The male record is 78 days by Bill Kearns, 36, of South Hiendley, Yorkshire, from 21 June to 7 Sept. 1969.

The record in a "regulation" size coffin is 242 hours 58 min by Tim Hayes of Cóbh, Ireland from 23 May to 2 June 1971 14 ft *4,26 m* down in Naas, Co. Kildare. His coffin was 6 ft 3 in long, 14 in deep and 21 in wide *1,90 × 0,35 × 0,53 m* at the shoulder tapering to 12 in *30,4 cm* at the ankle.

Cat's Cradle Leslie Fitzpatrick, 12 and Cindy Gibson, 12 achieved 9,020 "cradles" in 20½ hours in Chamblee, Georgia, U.S.A. on 27 Dec. 1972.

Champagne Fountain The tallest successfully filled column of champagne glasses is one 10 high filled from the top by Giuseppi Massari, 34 at Sutton Coldfield Hotel, Warwickshire in April 1973.

Clapping The duration record for continuous clapping is 14 hours 31 min by Thomas C. Andrews (b. 30 Apr. 1961) at Charleston, West Virginia, U.S.A. on 15 Nov. 1972. He sustained an average of 120 claps per minute and an audibility range of at least 100 yds *91,44 m*.

Club swinging Bill Franks set a world record of 17,280 revolutions (4.8 per sec) in 60 min at Webb's Gymnasium, Newcastle, N.S.W., Australia on 2 Aug. 1934. M. Dobrilla swung continuously for 144 hours at Cobar, N.S.W. finishing on 15 Sept. 1913.

Coal shovelling The record for filling a half-ton *508 kg* hopper with coal is 56.6 sec by D. Coghlan of Reefton, New Zealand on 3 Jan. 1969.

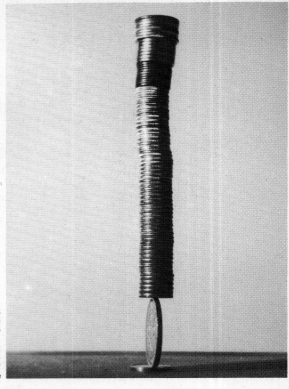

126 coins balanced on a silver dollar, the result of Mr. Alex Chervinsky's 23 years of practice

Coin balancing The greatest recorded feat of coin-balancing is the stacking of 126 coins on top of a silver U.S. dollar on edge by Alex Chervinsky, 65 of Lock Haven, Pennsylvania on 16 Sept. 1971 after 23 years practice.

Commuter Most durable Bruno Leuthardt commuted 370 miles *59,5 km* each day for the 11 years 1957—67 from Hamburg to teach in the Bodelschwingh School, Dortmund, West Germany. He was late only once due to the 1962 Hamburg floods.

Competition winnings The largest individual competition prize win on record is $307,500 (*then £109,821*) by Herbert J. Idle, 55, of Chicago in an encyclopaedia contest run by Unicorn Press Inc. on 20 Aug. 1953.

The highest value first prize offered in Britain has been a £21,000 cash alternative to a $50,000 New York spending spree offered by Soft Blue Band Luxury Margarine in a contest which closed on 30 Nov. 1971. It was won by Mrs. Susan B. Jenkins of Kirkby, Lancashire, who took the cash.

Cow Chip tossing The record distance for throwing a dried cow chip is 166 ft 1 in *50,62 m* for men by Harold 'Hurler' Smith and 101 ft 1 in *30,81 m* for women by the aptly named Patti Bruce at the world championships at Beaver, Oklahoma on 21 April 1973. These distances are anxiously studied by party political campaign managers.

Crawling The longest crawl (on hands and knees) on record is one of 8,9 km *5.53 miles* in 9 hours 16 min by Morgan Remil, 38 of Denmark from Fuengirola to Mijas, Spain in Sept. 1972.

Custard Pie throwing The most times champion in the annual World Custard Pie Championships at Coxheath, Kent (instituted 1967) have been the "The Birds" and the Coxheath Man each with 3 wins. The target (face) must be 8 ft 3⅞ in *2,53 m* from the thrower who must throw a pie no more than 10¾ in *27,3 cm* in diameter. Six points are scored for a square hit full in the face.

DANCING

The largest dance ever staged was that put on by the Houston Livestock Show at the Astro Hall, Houston,

Texas, U.S.A. on 8 Feb. 1969. The attendance was more than 16,500 with 4,000 turned away.

Marathon dancing must be distinguished from dancing mania, which is a pathological condition. The worst outbreak of dancing mania was at Aachen, Germany, in July 1374, when hordes of men and women broke into a frenzied dance in the streets which lasted for hours till injury or complete exhaustion ensued.

The most severe marathon dance staged as a public spectacle in the U.S.A. was one lasting 3,780 hours (22 weeks 3½ days) completed by Callum L. deVillier, 24 and Vonny Kuchinski, 20 at Sommerville, Massachusetts, U.S.A. from 28 Dec. 1932 to 3 June 1933. In the last two weeks the rest allowance was cut from 15 min per hour to only 3 min while the last 52½ hours were continuous. The prize of $1,000 was equivalent to less than 26½ cents per hour.

Ballet In the *entrechat* (a vertical spring from the fifth position with the legs extended criss-crossing at the lower calf), the starting and finishing position each count as one such that in an *entrechat douze* there are *five* crossings and uncrossings. This was performed by Wayne Sleep for the B.B.C. *Record Breakers* programme on 7 Jan. 1973. He was in the air for 0.71 of a second.

Most turns The greatest number of spins called for in classical ballet choreography is the 32 *fouettés rond de jambe en tournant* in "Swan Lake" by Pyotr Ilych Chaykovskiy (Tschaikovsky) (1840–1893). Miss Rowena Jackson, M.B.E. (b. 1926) of New Zealand, achieved 121 such turns at her class in Melbourne, Victoria, Australia, in 1940.

Most curtain calls The greatest recorded number of curtain calls ever received by ballet dancers is 89 by Dame Peggy Arias, D.B.E. *née* Hookham (born Reigate, Surrey, 18 May 1919), *alias* Margot Fonteyn, and Rudolf Hametovich Nureyev (born in a train near Ufa, U.S.S.R., 17 Mar. 1939) after a performance of "Swan Lake" at the Vienna Staatsoper, Austria, in October 1964.

Largest Cast The largest number of ballet dancers used in a production in Britain has been 2,000 in the London Coster Ballet of 1962, directed by Lillian Rowley, at the Royal Albert Hall, London.

Mr. and Mrs. Fox of Palmerston North, New Zealand, winners of the most consecutive national amateur dancing titles

Ballroom Marathon The individual continuous world record for ballroom dancing is 106 hours 5 min 10 sec by Carlos Sandrini in Buenos Aires, Argentina, in September 1955. Three girls worked shifts as his partner.

Champions The world's most successful professional ballroom dancing champions have been Bill Irvine, M.B.E. and Bobby Irvine, M.B.E., who won 10 world titles between 1960 and 1968.

The most consecutive national titles won is 10 in the New Zealand Old Time Championship by Mr. Fox and his wife Royce of Palmerston North in 1963–72.

Charleston The Charleston duration record is 25 hours by Tom Garrett, 23, at Pensacola, Florida, U.S.A. on 8–9 Oct. 1971.

Flamenco The fastest flamenco dancer ever measured is Solero de Jerez aged 17 who in Brisbane, Australia in Sept. 1967 in an electrifying routine attained 16 heel taps per second or a rate of 1,000 a minute.

Go-go The duration record for go-go dancing (Boogoloo or Reggae) is 108 hours (with 5 min breaks each hour) by Jane Berins, 16, of Glinton, Peterborough on 24–28 March 1970.

High Kicking The world record for high kicks is 8,005 in 4 hrs 40 min by Veronica Evans (*née* Steen), (b. Liverpool, 20 Feb. 1910) at the Pathétone Studios, Wardour Street, London in summer 1939.

Jiving The duration record for non-stop jiving is 40 hours by Gordon Lightfoot and Kathleen Fowler at Penrith, on 22–24 April 1960. Breaks of 3½ min per hour were permitted for massage. This time was equalled by Terry Ratcliffe, aged 16, and Christina Woodcroft, aged 17, at Traralgon, Victoria, Australia, from 10.15 p.m. on 28 May to 2.13 p.m. on 30 May 1965.

Limbo The lowest height for a bar under which a limbo dancer has passed is 6½ in *16,5 cm* by Teresa Marquis of St. Lucia, West Indies, at the Guinness Distribution Depot, Grosvenor Road, Belfast, Northern Ireland

Morgan Remil, in action during his most protracted recorded crawl

225

on 15 April 1970. Her vital statistics are 34-24-36 in *86–61–91 cm*. The record for going under a flaming bar is 8½ in *21,5 cm* by "Safari" on the B.B.C. T.V. programme *Record Breakers* on 18 Dec. 1972.

Tap The fastest *rate* ever measured for any tap dancer has been 1,440 taps per min (24 per sec) by Roy Castle on the B.B.C. T.V. *Record Breakers* programme on 14 Jan. 1973.

Twist The duration record for the twist is 102 hours by Mrs. Cathie Harvey (then Mrs. Cathy Connelly) at the Theatre Royal, Tyldesley, Lancashire ending on 29 Nov. 1964. She had 5 min time out per hour and 20 min every 4 hours.

Modern The longest recorded dancing marathon (50 min per hour) in modern style is one of 74½ hours by Julia Reece and Vic Jones at the Starlight Ballroom, Crawley, Sussex on 9–12 July 1970.

Dance band The most protracted session for a dance band is one of 321 hours (13 days 9 hours) by the Black Brothers of West Germany at Bonn ending on 2 Feb. 1968. Never less than a quartet were in action during the marathon.

Demolition work Fifteen members of the International Budo Association led by Phil Milner (3rd Dan Karate) demolished a 6-roomed early Victorian house at Idle, Bradford, Yorkshire by head, foot and empty hand in 6 hours on 4 June 1972. On completion they bowed to the rubble.

The fifteen members of the International Budo Association, and the remains of the house which they demolished with their bare hands

Disc-jockey The longest continuous period of acting as a disc-jockey is 506 hours by Robert Airbright, 20, at the Sighthill Community Centre, Edinburgh, Scotland on 4 to 25 June 1971. L.P.'s are limited to 50% of total playing time. Tony Santos of Kingston-upon-Thames, Surrey played singles only without rest periods for 208 hours at Gullivers Club, Mayfair, London on 13–21 March 1973.

Drumming The world's duration drumming record is 215 hours by Trevor Mitchell, at Oswald Hotel, Scunthorpe,

Lincolnshire on 15–24 Jan. 1973. He had a 5 min rest allowance per hour.

Ducks and Drakes The best accepted ducks and drakes (stone-skipping) or Gerplunking record is 17 skips by Cdr. E. F. Tellefson U.S.N. of Mackinac Island, Michigan, U.S.A. in 1932. The modern video-tape verified record is a 13 skipper (7 plinkers and 6 pitty-pats) by Rolf Anselm in the Open Championship at Mackinac on 2 July 1971.

Egg and spoon racing Len Dean and Mike O'Kane of Bournemouth College completed a 27 mile *43,45 km* fresh egg and dessert spoon marathon in 5 hours 38 min on 25 Oct. 1972.

Egg-shelling Two kitchen hands, Harold Witcomb and Gerald Harding shelled 1,050 dozen eggs in a 7¼ hour shift at Bowyers, Trowbridge, Wiltshire on 23 Apr. 1971. Both are blind.

Egg throwing The longest recorded distance for throwing a fresh hen's egg without breaking is 303 ft 6 in *92,50 m* at their 119th exchange by Rauli Rapo and Markku Kuikka at Rilhimäki, Finland on 9 Oct. 1971.

Escapology The most renowned of all escape artists has been Ehrich Weiss *alias* Harry Houdini (1874–1926), who pioneered underwater escapes from locked, roped and weighted containers while handcuffed and shackled with irons. Jack Gently performed an escape from a straight jacket when suspended from a crane 300 ft *91,4 m* from the ground for A.T.V.'s *Today* in Nov. 1972.

Reynir Oern Leossen (born 1938) succeeded in breaking out of a prison in Iceland in 1972 from a cell in which he had been locked with three handcuffs behind his back and his hands tied by 5 mm chains each able to withstand a force of 1 270 kg *2,800 lb*. His feet were fastened with footcuffs and he was further loaded with 5 mm and 10 mm (tensile strength 6 050 kg) chains weighing in all 20 kg *44 lb*. Leossen broke out in five hours and 50 min and emerged through a 28 mm *1.1 in* thick 15 cm *5.9 in* wide glass window which he had "extended" by breaking some of the adjoining brickwork. In a laboratory on 24 May 1974 he demonstrated the ability of parting 10 mm *0.4 in* chain which had a tensile strength of 6 100 kg *13,448 lb. or 6.00 tons*.

Face-slapping The face-slapping contest duration record was set in Kiev, U.S.S.R., in 1931, when a draw was declared between Vasilly Bezbordny and Goniusch after 30 hours.

Faux Pas Greatest If measuring by financial consequence, the greatest *faux pas* on record was that of the young multi-millionaire, James Gordon Bennett, committed on 1 Jan. 1877 at the family mansion of his demure fiancée one Caroline May, in Fifth Avenue, New York City. Bennett arrived in a two-horse cutter late and obviously in wine. By dint of intricate footwork, he gained the portals to enter the withdrawing room where he was the cynosure of all eyes. He mistook the fireplace for a plumbing fixture more usually reserved for another purpose. The May family broke the engagement and Bennett was obliged to spend the rest of his foot-loose and fancy-free life based in Paris with the resultant loss of millions of dollars to the U.S. Treasury.

Ferret legging Record durations for keeping a ferret down a pair of trousers with ankle ties are unsatisfactory owing to reports of the ferrets being tranquilized. The competitors are abusing the National Health Services in applications for free anti-tetanus injections.

Fire Pump pulling The longest unaided tow of a fire appliance was one of 102.2 miles *164,7 km* for an iron-tyred pump on 29–30 Sept. 1972 from Kennett Square, Pennsylvania to Laurel, Delaware, U.S.A. by a Kennett Fire Co. team of 40 men. The tow took 34 hours 8 min.

Frisbee throwing Competitive Frisbee throwing began in 1958. The longest throw over level ground on record is one of 285 ft *86,86 m* by Robert F. May in San Francisco on 2 July 1971.

Gold panning The fastest time recorded for "panning" eight planted gold nuggets is 18.5 sec by Mrs. Marie Bertles of Palmdale, California, in the 1970 World Gold Panning Championships held at Tropico, California, U.S.A.

Grave digging It is recorded that Johann Heinrich Karl Thieme, sexton of Aldenburg, Germany, dug 23,311 graves during a 50-year career. In 1826 his understudy dug *his* grave.

Guitar playing The longest recorded solo guitar playing marathon is one of 93 hours by Peter Baco, 21, in Winnipeg, Canada in July 1970.

Gun running The record for the Royal Tournament naval gun run competition (instituted 1900, with present rules since 1919) is 2 min 48.0 sec by the Fleet Air Arm Gun Crew at Earl's Court, London in 1971. The barrel alone weighs 8 cwt. *406 kg*. The wall is 5 ft *1,52 m* high and the chasm 28 ft *8,53 m* across. This F.A.A. team trained by CPO R. Wilson, achieved an unofficial 2 min 42.4 sec in a practice run at Lee-on-the-Solent, Hampshire in 1971.

Hairdressing The world's most expensive men's hairdresser is Tristan of Hollywood, California, U.S.A. who charges any "client" $100 (£40) on their first visit. This consists of a "consultation" followed by "remedial grooming". Derek Applegate-Rees cut, set and styled hair for 81 hrs 1 min at "She" Hair Fashions, Penrhyndeudraeth, Merionethshire, on 23–26 June 1972.

Handbell ringing The longest recorded handbell ringing recital was one of 10 hours 10 min by 10 ringers of the Chalk Handbell Ringers, Kent playing in unison with 1 min breaks between pieces and 5 min breaks each hour on 13 May 1972.

Handshaking The world record for handshaking was set up by Theodore Roosevelt (1858–1919), President of the U.S.A., who shook hands with 8,513 people at a New Year's Day, White House Presentation in Washington, D.C., U.S.A. on 1 Jan. 1907. Outside public life the record has become meaningless because aspirants merely arrange circular queues and shake the same hands repetitively.

Hand writing The longest recorded hand writing marathon was one of 78 hours 40 min by Raymond L. Cantwell of Oxford for a charitable fund-raising effort on 24–27 Oct. 1972.

HIGH DIVING

The highest regularly performed dive is that of professional divers from La Quebrada ("the break in the rocks") at Acapulco, Mexico, a height of 118 ft *36 m*. The leader of the 27 divers in the exclusive Club de Clavadistas is Raul Garcia (b. 1928) with more than 35,000 dives. The base rocks, 21 ft *6,40 m* out from the take-off, necessitate a leap of 27 ft *8,22 m* out. The water is 12 ft *3,65 m* deep.

On 18 May 1885, Sarah Ann Henley, aged 24, jumped from the Clifton Suspension Bridge, which crosses the Avon, England. Her 250 ft *76 m* fall was slightly cushioned by her voluminous dress and petticoat acting as a parachute. She landed, bruised and

Members of the Fleet Air Arm gun crew, holders of the gun running record, at a demonstration

bedraggled, in the mud on the Gloucestershire bank and was carried to hospital by four policemen. On 11 Feb. 1968 Jeffrey Kramer, 24, leapt off the George Washington Bridge 250 ft *76 m* above the Hudson River, New York City, N.Y. and survived. Of the 436 (to 13 Dec. 1971) people who have made suicide dives from the Golden Gate Bridge, San Francisco, California, U.S.A. since 1937, four survived. On 10 July 1921 a stuntman named Terry leapt from a seaplane into the Ohio River at Louisville, Kentucky. The alleged altitude was 310 ft *94,5 m*.

Samuel Scott (U.S.A.) is reputed to have made a dive of 497 ft *151,48 m* at Pattison Fall (now Manitou Falls) in Wisconsin, U.S.A., in 1840, but this would have entailed an entry speed of 86 m.p.h. *138 km/h*. The actual height was probably 165 ft *50,30 m*.

Hitch-hiking The title of world champion hitch-hiker is claimed by Devon Smith who from 1947 to 1971 thumbed lifts totalling 291,000 miles *468 300 km*. In 1957 he covered all the then 48 U.S. States in 33 days. It was not till his 6,013th 'hitch' that he got a ride in a Rolls Royce.

The hitch-hiking record for the 873 miles *1 405 km* from Land's End, Cornwall, to John o' Groats, Caithness, Scotland, is 29 hours by J. F. Hornsey on 12–13 Aug. 1971. The time before the first "hitch" on the first day is excluded. This time was equalled in the reverse direction by Bernard Atkins, aged 18, of Donnington, Lincolnshire in 11 lifts on 28 July 1966. The fastest time recorded for the round trip is 77 hours 20 min by Christine Elvery, 20 and Gwendolen Sherwin, 20, of which 61 hours 20 min was travelling on 24–27 March 1969.

Hiking The longest recorded hike is one of 18,500 miles *29 775 km* through 14 countries from Singapore to London by David Kwan, aged 22, which occupied 81 weeks from 4 May 1957, or an average of 32 miles *52 km* a day.

Hoop rolling In 1968 it was reported that Zolilio Diaz (Spain) had rolled a hoop 600 miles *965 km* from Mieres to Madrid and back in 18 days.

House of cards The greatest number of storeys achieved in building houses of cards is 34 in the case of a tower using 7 packs by R. F. Gompers of the University of Kent, Canterbury on 3 May 1971. The highest claim authenticated by affidavit for a 7 or 8 card per storey "house" is 27 storeys by Joe Whitlam of Barnsley, Yorkshire on 28 Feb. 1972.

Human cannon-ball The record distance for firing a human from a cannon is 175 ft *53,3 m* in the case of Emanuel Zacchini in the Ringling Bros. and Barnum & Bailey Circus, Madison Square Gardens, New York City, U.S.A., in 1940. His muzzle velocity was 145 m.p.h. *233 km/h*. On his retirement the management were fortunate in finding that his daughter Florinda was of the same calibre.

Ironing The longest recorded ironing marathon was one won by Mrs. J. Maassen, 37 after 89 hours 32 min in Melbourne, Australia on 9 March 1973.

Juggling The only juggler in history able to juggle—as opposed to "shower"—10 balls or eight plates was the Italian Enrico Rastelli, who was born in Samara, Russia, on 19 Dec. 1896 and died in Bergamo, Italy, on 13 Dec. 1931.

Kissing The most prolonged osculatory marathon in cinematic history is one of 185 sec by Regis Toomey and Jane Wyman in *You're In the Army Now* released in 1940.

Kite-flying The largest kite on record was built in Naruto City, Japan in 1936 of 3,100 panes of paper weighing 8½ tons/*tonnes*. The greatest reported height attained by kites is 35,530 ft *10 829 m* by a train of 19 flown near Portage by 10 Gary, Indiana high school boys on 13 June 1969. The flight took 7 hours and was assessed by telescopic triangulation using 56,457 ft *17 208 m* of line. The longest officially recorded flight is one of 61 hours 25 min by Vincent Tuzo of Bermuda on 6–9 May 1973.

Kite flights (Manned) Bill Moyes of Sydney, Australia descended to earth from a plane-towed kite from an altitude of 8,610 ft *2 624 m* over Amery, Wisconsin, U.S.A. on 14 Oct. 1971.

The greatest free-flight descent from a land take-off is 5,757 ft *1 754 m* by Bill Bennett, 40, of Sydney, Australia from Dante's Peak to the floor of Death Valley, California on 24 Feb. 1972.

Knitting The longest recorded knitting marathon is one of 90 hours by Mrs. Janice Marwick (with 5 min time out allowances per hour), at Pukekohe, New Zealand on 30 Aug.–3 Sept. 1971. The world's most prolific hand-knitter of all time has been Mrs. Gwen Matthewman (b. 1927) of Featherstone, Yorkshire, who retired on 31 Dec. 1970. In her last year she knitted 615 garments involving 7,022 oz. *199 066 g* of wool (equivalent to the fleece of 57 sheep). She had been timed to average 108 stitches per min in a 30-min test. Her technique has been filmed by the world's only Professor of Knitting—a Japanese. The finest recorded knitting is a piece of 2,464 stitches per in² by Douglas Milne of Mount Florida, Glasgow, Scotland in May 1969.

Knot-tying The non-stop knot-tying marathon record is 534,158 links of a drummer's chain knot in ¾ in *1,9 cm* tarred sisal rope in 170 hours by 12 members of the 2nd Noble Park Venture Unit, Victoria, Australia on 26 Aug. to 2 Sept. 1972.

Leap frogging Twelve members of Lisle Senior High School, Lisle, Illinois, U.S.A. covered 50 miles *80,46 km* on a 440 yds track on 6 May 1973. An average of more than 40 leaps per lap was maintained.

Lightning most times struck The only living man in the world to be struck by lightning 4 times is Park Ranger Roy "Dooms" C. Sullivan (U.S.), the human lightning conductor of Virginia. Dooms' attraction for lightning began in 1942 (lost big toe nail), and was resumed in July 1969 (lost eyebrows), in July 1970 (left shoulder seared) and, he hopes, finally on 16 April 1972 (hair set on fire).

Human cannonballs, of the Zacchini family, rocketing from an X-15 Human Missile Rocket

Lion-taming The greatest number of lions mastered and fed in a cage by an unaided lion-tamer was 40, by "Captain" Alfred Schneider in 1925. Clyde Raymond Beatty (1903–65) handled more than 40 "cats" (mixed lions and tigers) simultaneously. Twenty-one lion-tamers have died of injuries since 1900. The youngest legally licensed animal trainer is Carl Ralph Scott Norman (Captain Carl) of Garforth, Yorkshire (b. 23 Mar. 1968) who was licensed under the Performing Animals (Regulation) Act, 1925 on 13 Mar. 1970 aged 1 year 11 months.

Log rolling The most protracted log rolling contest on record was one in Chequamegon Bay, Ashland, Wisconsin, U.S.A., in 1900, when Allan Stewart dislodged Joe Oliver from a 24 in *60 cm* diameter log after 3 hours 15 min birling.

Message in a bottle The longest voyage recorded for a message in a bottle was one estimated to be about 25,000 miles *40 000 km* in the drifts, from the Pacific to the shore of the island of Sylt in the North Sea on 3 Dec. 1968. The bottle had been dropped on 27 May 1947.

Morse The highest recorded speed at which anyone has received morse code is 75.2 words per minute—over 17 symbols per second. This was achieved by Ted R. McElroy of the United States in a tournament at Asheville, North Carolina, U.S.A. on 2 July 1939.

Needle threading The record number of strands of cotton threaded through a number 13 needle (eye ½ in by 1/16 of an in *12,7 mm × 1,6 mm*) in 2 hours is 3,795 by Miss Brenda Robinson of the College of Further Education, Chippenham, Wiltshire on 20 March 1971.

Omelette making The greatest number of two-egg omelettes made in 30 min is 105 (26 min 25 sec) by Clement Raphael Freud (b. 1924) at The Victoria, Nottingham on 15 July 1971. (see also page 204).

Pancake tossing Roy Woodward of the Preston Venture Scouts Unit, Wembley, London succeeded in tossing a pancake 2,105 times at Ealing on 15 Feb. 1972.

Paper Aircraft A paper aircraft was reported to have been flown 1 030 m *1,126 yds* by Greg Raddue, 11 at San Geronimo Valley Elementary School, California on 31 May 1973.

Paper Chains The longest recorded paper link chain made by first or second grade school-children was one of 6,077 ft *1 852 m* in 17 hours by 23 seven and eight year olds at Rome City Elementary School, Indiana, U.S.A. on 20 Dec. 1972 to 13 Feb. 1973.

PARACHUTING

Longest fall without a parachute The greatest altitude from which anyone has bailed out with a parachute and survived is 6 700 m *21,980 ft.* This occurred in January 1942, when Lt. (now Lt.-Col.) I. M. Chisov (U.S.S.R.) fell from an Ilyushin 4 which had been severely damaged. He struck the ground a glancing blow on the edge of a snow-covered ravine and slid to the bottom. He suffered a fractured pelvis and severe spinal damage. It is estimated that the human body reaches 99 per cent of its low level terminal velocity after falling 1,880 ft *573 m* which takes 13 to 14 sec. This is 117–125 m.p.h. *188–201 km/h* at normal atmospheric pressure in a random posture, but up to 185 m.p.h. *298 km/h* in a head down position.

PARACHUTING RECORDS

First from Tower	Sébastian Lenormand	quasi-parachute	Lyons, France	1783
First from Balloon	André-Jacques Garnerin (1769–1823)	2,230 ft *680 m*	Monceau Park, Paris	22 Oct. 1797
First from Aircraft (man)	Capt. Albert Berry	U.S. Army	St. Louis, Missouri	1 Mar. 1912
(woman)	Miss 'Tiny' Broadwick (b. 1896)		Griffiths Park, Los Angeles	1913
First Free Fall	Leslie LeRoy Irvin (1895–1966)	over McCook Field	Dayton, Ohio	19 April 1919
Lowest Escape	S/Ldr. J. Spencer, R.A.F.	30–40 ft *9–12 m*	Wismar Bay, Baltic	19 April 1945
Longest Fall	Lt. Col. Wm. H. Rankin U.S.M.C.	40 min due to thermals	North Carolina	26 July 1956
Highest Escape	Flt. Lt. J. de Salis and Fg. Off. P. Lowe, R.A.F.	56,000 ft *17 068 m*	Monyash, Derby	9 April 1958
Longest Delayed Drop (man)	Capt. Joseph W. Kittinger*	84,700 ft 16.04 miles *25 816 m* from balloon at 102,200 ft *31 150 m*	Tularosa, North Mexico	16 Aug. 1960
(woman)	O. Kommissarova (U.S.S.R.)	14 100 m *46,250 ft*	over U.S.S.R.	21 Sept. 1965
Most Southerly	T/Sgt. Richard J. Patton	Operation Deep Freeze	South Pole	1967
Most Northerly	Ray Munro (Canada)	−39° F (−39,4° C)	In 89° 39' N	31 Mar. 1969
Career Total	Lt.-Col. Ivan Savkin (U.S.S.R.)	More than 5,000	over U.S.S.R.	12 Aug. 1969
Highest Landing	Ten U.S.S.R. parachutists†	23,405 ft *7 133 m*	Lenina Peak	May 1969
Heaviest Load	U.S.A.F. C-130 Hercules	22.52 tons *22,88 tonnes* steel plates 6 parachutes	El Centro, California	28 Jan. 1970
Highest from Bridge	Donald R. Boyle	1,053 ft *320 m*	Royal Gorge, Colorado	7 Sept. 1970
Highest Tower Jump	Herb Schmidt (U.S.A.)	KTUL-TV Mast 1,984 ft *604 m*	Tulsa, Oklahoma	4 Oct. 1970
Biggest Star	24 Skydivers	from 14,500 ft *4 420 m*	Perris Valley, California	16 Jan. 1972
Most Travelled	Kevin Seaman from a Cessna Skylane (pilot Charles Meritt)	12,186 miles *19 611 km*	Jumps in all 50 U.S. States	26 July–15 Oct. 1972
24 Hour Total	Woody Binnacker	201 in 17 hours 351	Barnwell, S. Carolina	12 Jan. 1973

* Maximum speed in rarefied air was 614 m.p.h. *988 km/h*

† Four were killed.

Vesna Vulović, 23 a Jugoslavenski Aerotransport hostess, survived when her DC9 blew up at 33,330 ft *10 160 m* over the Czechoslovak village of Česká Kamenice on 26 Jan. 1972. She was found inside a section of tail unit.

The British record is 18,000 ft *5 485 m* by Flt.-Sgt. Nicholas Stephen Alkemade, aged 21, who jumped from a blazing R.A.F. *Lancaster* bomber over Germany on 23 March 1944. His headlong fall was broken by a fir tree and he landed without a broken bone in a snow bank 18 in *45 cm* deep.

Piano-playing The longest piano-playing marathon has been one of 1,091 hours (45 days 11 hours) playing 22 hours every day from 11 Oct. to 24 Nov. 1970 by James Crowley, Jr., 30 at Scranton, Pennsylvania, U.S.A. The British record is 198 hours 30 min (with 5 min breaks each hour) set by Reg Goode at Wilmcote Working Men's Club, Stratford-upon-Avon on 20–29 Nov. 1972.

The women's world record is 133 hours (5 days 13 hours) by the late Mrs. Marie Ashton, aged 40, in a theatre in Blyth, Northumberland, on 18–23 Aug. 1958.

Piano smashing The record time for demolishing an upright piano and passing the entire wreckage through a circle 9 in *22,8 cm* in diameter is 2 min 26 sec by six men representing Ireland led by Johnny Leydon of Sligo, at Merton, Surrey, England on 7 Sept. 1968. The Robin Hood Karate Club of Sherwood, Nottinghamshire smashed a piano with bare hands in 41 min 29 sec on 10 March 1973.

Pillar box standing The record number of people to pile on top of a pillar box (oval top of 6 ft² *[0,55 m²]*) is 29, all students of the City of London College, Moorgate, in Finsbury Circus, London, E.C.2 on 21 Oct. 1971.

Pilot *Youngest* The youngest age at which anyone has ever qualified as a military pilot is 15 years 5 months in the case of Sgt. Thomas Dobney (b. 6 May 1926) of the R.A.F. He had overstated his age (14 years) on entry.

Pipe smoking The duration record for keeping a pipe (3.3 g *[0.1 oz]* of tobacco) continuously alight with only an initial match is 253 min 28 sec by Yrjö Pentikäinen of Kuopio, Finland on 15–16 March 1968.

Plate spinning The greatest number of plates spun simultaneously is 44 by Holley Gray, on the *Blue Peter* T.V. show at the B.B.C. T.V. Centre, London on 31 Jan. 1972.

Pogo Stick Jumping The greatest number of jumps achieved in 2 hours is 14,325 (at a rate of 2.1 per sec) by Scott Hemeon, 11 at South Yarmouth, Maine, U.S.A., on 26 May 1973.

Pole-squatting Modern records do not, in fact, compare with that of St. Daniel (A.D. 409–493), called Stylites (Greek, *stylos*=pillar), a monk who spent 33 years 3 months on a stone pillar in Syria. This is probably the oldest of all human records.

There being no international rules, the "standards of living" atop poles vary widely. The record squat is 8 months 4 days by Jim Dean, 34 of Dallas, Texas, atop a 60 ft *18,28 m* pole from May 1972–Jan. 1973. His perch was fully glazed.

The British record is 32 days 14 hours by John Stokes, aged 32, of Moseley, in a barrel on a 45 ft *13,70 m* pole in Birmingham, ending on 27 June 1966. This is claimed as a world record for a barrel.

"Pond" baling Elaborate rules exist for baling a "village pond" with a No. 1 size sewing thimble. The record is 94 gal 2 pts *428,4 litres* in 12 hours by 14 members of Soham Church Youth Club, Soham, nr. Ely, Cambs., on 12 May 1973.

Pop group The duration record for a 4-man pop-playing group is 132 hours 2 min by the Phlint at Freewheelers Club, Leicester on 21–26 May 1973. The group at no time sank below a trio.

Pram pushing The greatest distance covered in pushing a pram in 24 hours is 319 miles *513 km* on a track by a 60 strong team from the White Horse Sports and Social Club, Stony Stratford, Bucks. on 19–20 May 1973. A team of 10 with an adult "baby" from Flore Moderns at Flore, Northants. covered 200.4 miles *322,5 km* on 10–11 June 1972.

Fastest "psychiatrist" The world's fastest "psychiatrist" was the osteopath Dr. Albert L. Weiner of Erlton, New Jersey, U.S.A., who dealt with up to 50 patients a day in four treatment rooms. He relied heavily on narcoanalysis, muscle relaxants and electro-shock treatments. In December 1961 he was found guilty on 12 counts of manslaughter from using unsterilized needles.

Quiz league The largest and oldest (established 1959) quiz league in the world is the Merseyside Quiz League, England with 120 teams and 20 major trophies.

Quoit throwing The world's record for rope quoit throwing is an unbroken sequence of 4,002 pegs by Bill Irby, Snr. of Australia in 1968.

Riding in armour The longest recorded ride in full armour is one of 146 miles *234,9 km* from Glasgow to Dumphrief *via* Lanark and Peebles, Scotland in 3 days 3 hrs 40 min by Dick Brown, 42 on 12–15 June 1973.

Riveting The world's record for riveting is 11,209 in 9 hours by J. Moir at the Workman Clark Ltd. shipyard, Belfast, Northern Ireland, in June 1918. His peak hour was his seventh with 1,409, an average of nearly 23½ per min.

Rocking-chair The longest recorded duration of a "Rockathon" is 307 hrs 30 min by Michael Smith of Aubrey, California, U.S.A., at the Fresno Fashion Fair on 24 Aug. –6 Sept. 1972.

Rolling pin The record distance for a woman to throw a 2 lb. *907 g* rolling pin is 140 ft 4 in *42,77 m* by Sheri Salyer at Stroud, Oklahoma on 18 July 1970. The British record is 135 ft 2 in *41,19 m* by Marilyn Roberts at Eastbourne, Sussex on 16 June 1971.

Rope tricks Will Rogers (1879–1935) of the United States demonstrated an ability to rope three separate objects with 3 lariats at a single throw.

Scooter riding The greatest distance covered by a team of 25 in 24 hours is 304.8 miles *490,5 km* by the Peakhurst-Lugarno Catholic Youth Organisation, Lugarno, Australia on 27–28 Jan. 1973.

See-saw The most protracted session for see-sawing is one of 384 hours (16 days) by Ed. Garcia, 18 and Steve Pontes, 17 of San Leandro, California, U.S.A. on 29 Nov. to 8 Dec. 1971. Total time out was only 6 hours 39 min or 1.73 per cent. The "constant motion" record is 200 hours by Tom Adamo and Bob Rowell at Manassa, Va., U.S.A. from 16 Aug. 1971.

Sermon The longest sermon on record was delivered by Clinton Locy of West Richland, Washington, U.S.A., in February 1955. It lasted 48 hours 18 min and ranged through texts from every book in the Bible. A congregation of eight was on hand at the close. From 31 May to 10 June 1969 the 14th Dalai Lama (b. 6 July 1934) the exiled ruler of Tibet, completed a sermon on Tantric Buddhism for five to seven hours per day to total 60 hours in India.

Shaving The fastest barber on record is Gerry Harley, who shaved 130 men in 60 min at The Plough, Gillingham, Kent on 1 April 1971. In an attempt to set a marathon he ran out of volunteer subjects.

Sheaf tossing The world's best performance for tossing an 8 lb. *3 kg 620* sheaf is 56 ft *17,06 m* by C. R. Wiltshire of Geelong, Victoria, Australia in 1956. Contests date from 1914.

Shoeshine Boys In this category (limited to Boy Scouts (aged 11 to 13) and Cubs) 4 scouts shined 707 pairs of shoes in 18 hours in Lincoln on 8 Apr. 1972. They were S. Quincy, P. Gadd, A. Doyle and A. Taylor.

Fastest shorthand The highest recorded speeds ever attained under championship conditions are: 300 words per min (99.64 per cent accuracy) for five minutes and 350 w.p.m. (99.72 per cent accuracy, that is, two insignificant errors) for two minutes by Nathan Behrin (U.S.A.) in New York in December 1922. Behrin (b. 1887) used the Pitman system invented in 1837. Morris I. Kligman of New York currently claims to be the world's fastest shorthand writer at 300 w.p.m.

He has taken 50,000 words in five hours and transcribed them in under five hours. Mr. G. W. Bunbury of Dublin, Ireland held the unique distinction of writing at 250 w.p.m. for 10 min on 23 Jan 1894. The record for the Gregg system was held by Mr. Leslie Bear at 220 w.p.m. He retired as editor of Hansard in Feb. 1972.

Currently the fastest shorthand writer in Britain is Mrs. June Meader (*née* Swan) of North Finchley with a Pitman's Certificate for 230 w.p.m. She demonstrated the ability to write at the *rate of* 260 w.p.m. with a syllabic density of 1.5, on the B.B.C. T.V. Show *Record Breakers* on 31 Dec. 1972.

In Great Britain only four shorthand writers have passed the official Pitman test at 250 w.p.m. for five min:

Miss Edith Ulrica Pearson of London, on 30 June 1927.
Miss Emily Doris Smith of London, on 22 March 1934.
Miss Beatrice W. Solomon of London, in March 1942.
Mrs. Audrey Boyes (*née* Bell) of Finchley, London, in 1956.

Miss Emily Smith, one of the only four shorthand writers to gain a Pitman certificate for 250 w.p.m.

Shouting The greatest number of wins in the national town criers' contest is eight by Herbert T. Waldron of Great Torrington, Devon. He won every year from 1957 to 1965, except for 1959. (See also Longest-ranged voice, Chapter I.) He retired in Sept. 1971.

Showering The most prolonged continuous shower bath on record is one of 174 hours by David Hoffman at the University, Gary, Indiana from 21–27 Jan. 1972. The feminine record is 98 hours 1 min by Paula Glenn, 18 and Margaret Nelson, 20 in Britain on 24 Nov. 1971.

Singing The longest recorded solo singing marathon is one of 72 hours 31 min by Eamonn McGirr in Eccles, Lancashire on 18–21 June 1973. He sang *Now is the Hour* as his wife Mary brushed his teeth, and 88 other songs. In support of the Oakland Community Chest Drive, California, Joan Shepherd Morse sang 8 hours literally non-stop on 7 Oct. 1949.

Skipping The greatest number of turns ever performed without a break is variously reported as 32,089 and 32,809 by J. P. Hughes of Melbourne, Victoria, Australia, in 3 hours 10 min on 26 Oct. 1953.

Other records made without a break:

Most turns in one jump	5 by Katsumi Suzuki, Tokyo, early 1968.
Most turns in 1 min	286 by J. Rogers, Melbourne, 10 Nov. 1937. and T. Lewis, Melbourne, 16 Sept. 1938.
Most turns in 2 hours	22,806 by Tom Morris, Sydney, 21 Nov. 1937.
Double turns	2,001 by K. Brooks, Brisbane, Jan. 1955.
Treble turns	70 by J. Rogers, Melbourne, 17 Sept. 1951.
Duration	1,264 miles *2 034 km* by Tom Morris, Brisbane-Cairns, Queensland, 1963.

Slinging The greatest distance recorded for a sling-shot is 1,147 ft 4 in *349,70 m* using a 34 in *86 cm* long sling and a 7½ oz. *212 g* stone by Melvyn Gaylor on Newport Golf Course, Shide, Isle of Wight on 25 Sept. 1970.

Smoke ring blowing The highest recorded number of smoke rings formed from a single pull of a cigarette is 86 by Robert Reynard, 46 of George and Pilgrim's Inn, Glastonbury, Somerset, on 31 Dec. 1971.

Snakes and Ladders The longest recorded game of Snakes and Ladders has been one of 100 hours by a team of 6 (4 always in play) pupils of Bay House School, Gosport, Hampshire on 12–16 April 1973.

Snow Shoeing The fastest time recorded for covering a mile *1 609,34 m* is 5 min 18.6 sec by Clifton Cody (U.S.) at Somersworth, New Haven, on 19 Feb. 1939.

"Space Hopping" A longest marathon claimed is one of 144 miles 452 yds *232,158 km* in 41 hours by a team of 12 in a S.C.A.S. team at R.A.F. St. Athan, Barry, Glamorgan, Wales on 10–12 Dec. 1971.

Spinning The duration record for spinning a clock balance wheel by hand is 5 min 26.8 sec by Philip Ashley, aged 16, of Leigh, Lancashire, on 20 May 1968.

Spitting The greatest distance achieved at the annual tobacco spitting classic (instituted 1955) at Raleigh, Mississippi is 25 ft 10 in *7,87 m* by Don Snyder, 22, set in August 1970. He achieved 31 ft 6 in *9,60 m* at the Mississippi State University on 21 Apr. 1971. Distance is dependent on the quality of salivation, absence of cross wind, two finger pressure and the co-ordination of the quick hip and neck snap. Sprays smaller than a dime do not count. The record for projecting a melon seed is 44 ft 1¾ in *13,45 m* by Dale Blaylock of Oklahoma achieved at Neosho, Missouri, U.S.A. in 1972. Spitters who care about their image wear 12 in *30,4 cm* boots so practice spits can be measured without a tape.

Stilt-walking The highest stilts ever successfully mastered were more than 21 ft *6,40 m* from the ankle to the ground by the late Albert Yelding ("Harry Sloan") 1901–1971 of Great Yarmouth, Norfolk. Hop stringers use stilts up to 15 ft *4,57 m*. In 1892 M. Garisoain of Bayonne stilt-walked the last 8 km *4.97 miles* into Biarritz in 42 min to average 11,42 km/h *7.10 m.p.h.* In 1891 Sylvain Dornon stilt-walked from Paris to Moscow *via* Vilno in 50 stages for the 1,830 miles *2 945 km*. Another source gives his time as 58 days.

Stretcher bearing The longest recorded carry of a stretcher case with a 10 st. *63 kg 50* "body" is 52 miles *83,6 km* in 14½ hours by a team of 8 from the International Budo Association tion, Dinnington, Yorks., on 12 May 1973.

String Ball Largest The largest ball of string on record is one 11 ft *3,35 m* in diameter, weighing 4½ tons/*tonnes* amassed by Francis A. Johnson of Darwin, Minnesota, U.S.A., since 1950.

Sub-mergence The longest submergence in a frogman's suit is 100 hours 3 min by Mrs. Jane Lisle Baldasare, aged 24, at Pensacola, Florida, U.S.A., ending on 24 Jan. 1960. Mrs. Baldasare also holds the feminine underwater distance record at 14 miles *22,5 km*. Her ex-husband, Fred Baldasare, aged 38, set the underwater distance record of 42 miles *67,6 km* in his France-England Channel crossing of 18 hours 1 min ending 10–11 July 1962.

Suggestion boxes The most prolific example on record of the use of any suggestion box scheme is that of Mr. John Drayton of Pontypool, Monmouthshire, who plied British Rail with a total of 25,000 suggestions.

Swinging Jim Anderson and Lyle Hendrickson completed a 100 hour marathon on a swing at the Seattle Sea Fair, Washington, U.S.A. on 1 Aug. 1971.

Switchback riding The world endurance record for rides on a roller coaster is 465 circuits of the John Collins Pleasure Park switchback at Barry Island, Glamorgan by a group of four men and two women. The test lasted 31 hours, with two brief breaks, on 15–16 Aug. 1968.

Tailoring The highest speed in which the making of a 2 piece suit has been made from sheep to finished article is 1 hour 52 min 18.5 sec to the order of Bud Macken of Mascot, N.S.W., Australia on 23 Dec. 1931. The shearing took 35 sec, the carding and teasing 19 min and the weaving 20 min.

Talking The world record for non-stop talking is 138 hours (5 days 18 hours) by Victor Villimas of Cleveland, Ohio, U.S.A. in Leeds, Yorkshire, England, from 25–31 Oct. 1967. The longest continuous political speech on record was one of 29 hours 5 min by Gerard O'Donnell in Kingston-upon-Hull, Yorkshire, on 23–24 June 1959. The longest recorded lecture was one of 45 hours on "The Christian Faith and its Response" by the Rev. Roger North, 26, at Hartley Victoria Methodist College, Manchester on 15–17 May 1971.

A feminine non-stop talking record was set by Mrs. Alton Clapp of Greenville, North Carolina, U.S.A., in August 1958, with 96 hours 54 min 11 sec. In the U.S.A. such contests have been referred to as "gab fests".

T-bone dive The so-called T-bone dives by cars off ramps over and onto parked cars are often measured by the number of cars, but owing to their variable size, distance is more significant. The record is 116 ft *35,35 m* by Dusty Russell in a 1939 Dodge in a film sequence at Lodi, California, U.S.A., in March 1973.

For the different event of motor cycle long jumping over cars, Gary Davis and Rex Blackwell both cleared 21 Datsun cars taking off at 85 m.p.h. *136 km/h* in record 138 ft *42,06 m* jumps at Ontario, California, U.S.A. in March 1972. Evel Knievel, who jumped over 19 regular-size and compact cars 129 ft *39,31 m* disputes this on the grounds that 4 of these 21 cars were parked *under* the ramps. Knievel (b. 1938) had suffered 431 bone fractures by his 1972 season.

Teeth-pulling The man with "the strongest teeth in the world" is John Massis of Gand, Belgium, who in 1969 demonstrated the ability to pull two railway trucks weighing 36 tons/*tonnes* along rails with a bit in his teeth.

TIGHTROPE WALKING

The greatest 19th century tightrope walker was Jean François Gravelet, *alias* Charles Blondin (1824–1897), of France, who made the earliest crossing of the Niagara Falls on a 3 in *76 mm* rope, 1,100 ft *335 m* long, 160 ft *48,75 m* above the Falls on 30 July 1855. He also made a crossing with Harry Colcord, pick-a-back on 15 Sept. 1860. Though other artists find it difficult to believe, Colcord was his agent.

Endurance The world tightrope endurance record is 384 hours by Henri Rochetain (b. 1926) of France on a wire 394 ft *120 m* long, 82 ft *25 m* above a supermarket in Saint Etienne, France on 28 Mar.–13 Apr. 1973. The feminine record is 34 hours 15 min by Francine Pary, aged 17, on a wire 50 ft *15,24 m* high at Toulouse, France, in February 1957.

Longest The longest walk by any funambulist was achieved by Henri Rochetain (b. 1926) of France on a wire 3,790 yds *3 465 m* long slung across a gorge at Clermont Ferrand, France on 13 July 1969. He required 3 hours 20 min to negotiate the crossing.

The first crossing of the River Thames was achieved by Franz Burbach, 31 on an 800 ft *243 m* wire 55 ft *16,75 m* above the water in 13 min on 25 Aug. 1972.

High-wire act The greatest drop beneath any high wire act was over the Tallulah Gorge, Georgia, U.S.A., where, on 18 July 1970, Karl Wallenda (b. 21 Jan. 1905) walked 821 ft *250 m* in 616 steps with a 35 lb. *15 kg 870* pole in 17 min including pauses for two headstands. The gorge was 750 ft *228 m* deep. The highest altitude high-wire act was that of the Germans Alfred and Henry Traber on a 520 ft *158,5 m* rope stretched from the Zugspitze (9,738 ft [*2 968 m*]) to the Western Peak, Bavaria, Germany, during July and August 1953.

Tree-climbing The fastest tree-climbing record is one of 36 sec for a 90 ft *27,32 m* pine by Kelly Stanley (Canada) at the Toowoomba Show, Queensland, Australia in 1968.

Tree-sitting The duration record for sitting in a tree is 56 days 2 hrs 40 min from 22 July–16 Sept. 1930 by Norman L. Zellers, 13, 12 ft *3,65 m* aloft in a cottonwood tree in the front garden of 921 Marshall Ave., Matoon, Illinois, U.S.A.

Tunnel of fire Dick Sheppard of the "Disaster Squad" negotiated a 65 ft 7½ in *20 m* roofed tunnel of fire with a cross-section measuring 8 ft × 8 ft *2,43 × 2,43 m* at Shanklin, Isle of Wight on 20 Aug. 1972.

The longest tunnel of fire (petrol-soaked hoops of straw) negotiated by a trick motorcyclist is of 164 ft *50 m* by the late Stephen Ladd, 25 of Tottenham, London on a 500 c.c. B.S.A. Scrambler at Wintry Park Farm, Epping, Essex on 21 Nov. 1972. He died attempting a repeat run.

TYPEWRITING

Fastest The highest recorded speeds attained with a ten-word penalty per error on a manual machine are:

One Min: 170 words, Margaret Owen (U.S.A.) (Underwood Standard), New York, 21 Oct. 1918.
One Hour: 147 words (net rate per min) Albert Tangora (U.S.A.) (Underwood Standard), 22 Oct. 1923.

The official hour record on an electric machine is 9,316 words (40 errors) on an I.B.M. machine, giving a net rate of 149 words per min, by Margaret Hamma, now Mrs. Dilmore (U.S.A.), in Brooklyn, New York City, N.Y., U.S.A. on 20 June 1941.

In an official test in 1946 Stella Pajunas now Mrs. Garnand attained a speed of 216 words per min on an I.B.M. machine.

Slowest Chinese typewriters were so complex that even the most skilled operator could not select characters from the 1,500 offered at a rate of more than 11 words a minute. The Hoang typewriter first produced in 1962 now has 5,850 Chinese characters. The keyboard is 2 ft *60 cm* wide and 17 in *43 cm* high.

Longest The world duration record for typewriting on an electric machine is 150 hours by David J. Carnochan,

22, of the University College London Union from noon on 24 Feb. to 6 p.m. 2 March 1970. His breaks were 70 min less than the permitted 5 min per hour.

The longest duration typing marathon on a manual machine is 120 hours 15 min by Mike Howell, a 23 year-old blind office worker from Greenfield, Oldham, Lancashire on 25–30 Nov. 1969 on an Olympia manual typewriter in Liverpool. In aggregating 561,006 strokes he performed a weight movement of 2,482 tons *2 521 tonnes* plus a further 155 tons *157 tonnes* on moving the carriage for line spacing. On an electric machine the total figure would have been 565 tons *574 tonnes*.

Unsupported Circle The highest recorded number of people who have demonstrated the physical paradox of all being seated without a chair is an unsupported circle of 80 staff and students of the Department of Foundation Studies, West Surrey College of Art and Design, Farnham, Surrey on 22 May 1973.

Walking on hands The duration record for walking on hands is 1 400 km *871 miles* by Johann Hurlinger, of Austria, who in 55 daily 10-hour stints, averaged 1.58 m.p.h. *2,54 km/h* from Vienna to Paris in 1900.

Wall of death The greatest endurance feat on a wall of death was 3 hours 4 min by the motorcyclist Louis W. "Speedy" Babbs on a silo, 32 ft *9,75 m* in diameter refuelling in motion, at the Venice Amusement Pier, California on 11 Oct. 1929. In 1934 Babbs performed 1,003 consecutive loop the loops sitting side-saddle in a globe 18 ft *5,48 m* at Ocean Park Pier, California, U.S.A. In a life of stunting, Babbs, who proclaims "Stuntmen are not fools", has broken 56 bones.

Whip cracking The longest stock whip ever "cracked" (*i.e.* the end made to travel above the speed of sound—760 m.p.h. *1 223 km/h* is one of 55 ft *16,76 m* by "Saltbush" Bill Mills of Australia.

Wood-cutting The earliest competitions date from Tasmania in 1874. The best times ever recorded on Australian hardwoods in competition on 12 in *30,4 cm* logs are thus:

Underhand	20.0 sec	Gus De Blanc	1921
Standing Block	13.7 sec	C. Stewart	1965
Hard Hitting	17 hits	G. Parker and Tom Kirk	1958
Tree Felling	1 min 20.0 sec	Bill Youd	1970

The fastest times ever recorded for sawing Australian hardwoods are: single (18 in [*45,7 cm*] logs) 34.2 sec D. M. Rattray in 1967 and Double-handed (24 in [*60,9 cm*] logs) 21.8 sec R. Chalker and C. Johnson in 1967.

The world's most complicated typewriter, the Chinese Hoang typewriter, with a keyboard of 1,500 characters

Eighty members of the West Surrey College of Art and Design, achieving the paradox of all being seated without a chair

Writing Backwards The only recorded instance of a man able to write decipherably backwards, upside down, laterally inverted (mirror-style) while blindfold is Frank H. Keith of Naperville, Illinois, U.S.A.

Yo-yo The yo-yo originates from a Filipino jungle fighting weapon recorded in the 16th century weighing 4 lb. with a 20 ft *6 m* cord. The word means "come-come". The craze was started by Louis Marx (U.S.A.) in 1929. The most difficult modern yo-yo trick is the double-handed cross-over loop the loop. Art Pickles of Shere, Surrey, the 1933–53 world champion once achieved 1,269 consecutive loop the loops. The individual continuous endurance record is 50 hours by Damian Doherty, 21 at the University of Leicester on 22–24 Feb. 1973.

Largest circus The world's largest permanent circus is Circus Circus Las Vegas, Nevada, U.S.A. opened on 18 Oct. 1968 at a cost of $15,000,000 (*then £6,250,000*). It covers an area of 129,000 ft² *11 984 m²* capped by a tent-shaped flexiglass roof 90 ft *27,43 m* high. The new Moscow Circus, completed in 1968, has a seating capacity of 3,200.

WEALTH AND POVERTY

The measurement of extreme personal wealth is beset with immense difficulty. Quite apart from reticence and the element of guessing in approximating the valuation of assets, as Mr. Getty (see below) once said "if you can count your millions you are not a billionaire". The term millionaire was invented *c.* 1740 and billionaire in 1861. The earliest dollar billionaires were John Davison Rockefeller (1863–1937); Henry Ford (1863–1947) and Andrew William Mellon (1855–1937). In 1937, the last year all 3 were alive, a billion U.S. dollars were worth £205 million but that amount of sterling would today have a purchasing power of £1,138 million.

Living Billionaires There are currently five proclaimed U.S. dollar billionaires (a billion dollars is now £400,000,000): Jean Paul Getty (b. Minneapolis, Minnesota, 15 Dec. 1892); Howard Robard Hughes (b. Houston, Texas 24 Dec. 1905) now in London; John Donald Mac-Arthur (b. Pittston, Pennsylvania, 1897); Haroldson Lafayette Hunt (b. 1889) of Dallas, Texas and Daniel K. Ludwig (b. South Haven, Mich., June 1897). H. Ross Perot of Texas (b. Texarkana, Texas, 1930) was in December 1969 worth in excess of a billion dollars on paper.

Fortune Magazine, which in May 1968 assessed Mr. Getty at $1.338 billions and Mr. Hughes at $1.373 billion, stated in January 1972 that Mr. Ludwig was richer than either. On proved oil reserve revaluations, however, Mr. Getty would appear to be unsurpassable.

Europeans with family assets in excess of the equivalent of a billion dollars, include the Wallenburg family in Sweden. The wealthiest United Kingdom citizen, at the time of his death, was Sir John Reeves Ellerman 2nd Bt. (1909–73), whose fortune was estimated at £600 million (*$1.5 billion*).

Highest Incomes The greatest incomes derive from the collection of royalties per barrel by rulers of oil-rich sheikhdoms, who have not abrogated personal entitlement. Before his death in 1965, H. H. Sheikh Sir Abdullah as-Salim as-Sabah G.C.M.G., C.I.E. (b. 1895), the 11th Amir of Kuwait was accumulating royalties payable at a rate of £2.6 million per week or £145 million a year.

The highest gross income ever achieved in a single year by a private citizen is an estimated $105,000,000 (*then £21½ million*) in 1927 by the Sicilian born Chicago gangster Alphonse ("Scarface Al") Capone (1899–1947). This was derived from illegal liquor trading and alky-cookers (illicit stills), gambling establishments, dog tracks, dance halls, "protection" rackets and vice. On his business card Capone described himself as a "Second Hand Furniture Dealer".

Proved Wills and Death Duties Sir John Reeves Ellerman, Bt., C.H. (1862–1933), left £36,684,994, the largest will ever proved in the United Kingdom. The highest death duties ever paid have been £18,000,000 on the estate of Hugh Richard Arthur Grosvenor, G.C.V.O., D.S.O., the 2nd Duke of Westminster (1879–1953), paid between July 1953 and August 1964. The greatest will proved in Ireland was that of the 1st Earl of Iveagh (1847–1927), who left £13,486,146.

Million-airesses The world's wealthiest woman was probably Princess Wilhelmina Helena Pauline Maria of Orange-Nassau (1880–1962), formerly Queen of the Netherlands (from 1890 to her abdication, 4 Sept. 1948), with a fortune which was estimated at over £200 million. The largest amount proved in the will of a woman in the United Kingdom has been the £4,075,550 (duty paid £3,233,454) of Miss Gladys Meryl Yule, daughter of Sir David Yule, Bt. (1858–1928), in August 1957. Mrs. Anna Dodge (later Mrs. Hugh Dillman) who was born in Dundee, Scotland, died on 3 June 1970 in the United States, aged 103, and left an estate of £40,000,000.

The world's largest permanent circus, known as Circus Circus, in Las Vegas, Nevada, U.S.A.

Youngest The youngest person ever to accumulate a millionaire estate was the child film actress Shirley Temple (b. Santa Monica, California 23 April 1928), formerly Mrs. John Agar, Jr., now Mrs. Charles Black, of the U.S.A. Her accumulated wealth exceeded $1,000,000 (*then £209,000*) before she was 10 years old. Her child actress career spanned 1934–39.

Earliest The earliest recorded self-made millionairess was Mrs. Annie M. Pope-Turnbo Malone (d. 1957), a laundress from St. Louis, Missouri, U.S.A. who in 1905 perfected the permanent straight treatment for those with crinkly hair.

Richest families In May 1968 it was estimated that three members of the Irish-American Mellon family of the U.S.A., from Omagh, County Tyrone: Mrs. Alisa Mellon Bruce (1902–1969), Paul Mellon (b. 11 June 1907) and Richard King Mellon (b. 1900) were each worth between $500 million and $1,000 million (*then £416.6 million*). Another 1968 estimate put the family fortune at more than $3,000 million (*then £1,255 million*). It has also been tentatively estimated that the combined wealth of the much larger du Pont family of some 2,100 members may be in excess of this figure. The newest billionaire family are the Vihlein family of Milwaukee, U.S.A. whose stock in Schlitz beer was estimated at $1.3 billion (*£520 million*) in January 1973 having risen $595,600,000 in 1972.

The largest number of millionaires estates in one family in the British Isles is that of the Wills family of the Imperial Tobacco Company, of whom 14 members have left estates in excess of £1,000,000 since 1910. These totalled £55 million, of which death duties (introduced in 1894) have taken over £27,000,000.

Largest dowry The largest recorded dowry was that of Elena Patiño, daughter of Don Simón Iturbi Patino (1861–1947), the Bolivian tin millionaire, who in 1929 bestowed £8,000,000 from a fortune at one time estimated to be worth £125,000,000.

Greatest miser Henrietta (Hetty) Howland Green (*née* Robinson) (1835–1916) who kept a balance of over $31,400,000 (*then £6.2 million*) in one bank alone, was so mean that her son had to have his leg amputated because of the delays in finding a *free* medical clinic. She herself lived off cold porridge because she was too mean to heat it and died of apoplexy in an argument over the virtues of skimmed milk. Her estate proved to be of $95 million (*then £19 million*).

SALARIES AND EARNINGS

Highest World In Japan the National Tax Administration Agency publishes all identities and earnings of the preceding year. The 1971 "Number One Man" was Mr. Heima Seki, President of Sekihei Seibaku Co. of Sendai-shi with a gross income of Yen 3,890,940,000 (*£4,851,546 at Y802.56 per £*). Though his company is ostensibly in business for cleaning barley the income was generated by selling forest land to his own real estate company. The highest salary currently paid in the United States is to the Chairman of the Ford Motor Co., Mr. Henry Ford II who in 1972 earned in salary and bonus $874,567 (*£349,800*) which compared with $812,494 (*£325,000*) to Harold S. Geneen, Chairman of I.T.T. in 1971.

United Kingdom Britain's highest paid business executive is Mr. Richard Tompkins, Chairman of Green Shield Trading Stamp Company which he founded in 1958. His service agreement entitled him to 15 per cent of profits which for the year ending 31 Oct. 1971 would have earned him £395,000. He waived £135,000. On 1972/73 full standard taxation rates it has been calculated that £185,600 of the £260,000 would be payable in income tax and surtax.

The highest straight salary paid in British business is the £75,948 payable to the managing director of Shell Trading and Transport, Mr. F. S. McFadzean.

Highest wage The highest recorded wages in Britain are those paid to long haulage lorry drivers and tower crane drivers on bonuses. A specific case of £350 a week has been cited.

Biggest Loss The biggest recorded paper loss in one day was $24,768,630 (*£9,907,000*) by Arthur Decio, President of Skyline Corporation of Elkhart, Indiana on 26 Dec. 1972 due to share depreciation.

Lowest incomes The poorest people in the world are the surviving Pintibu (or Bindibu) of whom 42 were found in the Northern Territory of Australia in July 1957. They subsist with water from soak holes and by eating rats, lizards and yams. In September 1971 some 20 to 25 were still living. In September 1957 Chinese Government sources admitted that in some areas of the mainland the average annual income of peasants was 42 yuans (*£6.90*) per head. In 1964 China's average income per head was estimated at £25 per annum and the daily calorie intake at 2,200.

Return of cash The largest amount of cash ever found and returned to its owners was $500,000 (U.S.) found by Lowell Elliott, 61 on his farm at Peru, Indiana, U.S.A. It had been dropped in June 1972 by a parachuting hi-jacker.

Greatest bequests The greatest bequest in a life-time of a millionaire were those of the late John Davison Rockefeller (1839–1937), who gave away sums totalling $750,000,000 (*now £312.5 million*). The greatest benefactions of a British millionaire were those of William Richard Morris, later the Viscount Nuffield, G.B.E., C.H. (1877–1963), which totalled more than £30,000,000 between 1926 and his death on 22 Aug. 1963. The Scottish-born U.S. citizen Andrew Carnegie (1835–1919) is estimated to have made benefactions totalling £70 million during the last 18 years of his life. These included 7,689 church organs and 2,811 libraries. He had started life in a bobbin factory at $1.20 per week.

The largest bequest made in the history of philanthropy was the $500,000,000 (*£178,570,000*) gift, announced on 12 Dec. 1955, to 4,157 educational and other institutions by the Ford Foundation (established 1936) of New York City, N.Y., U.S.A. The assets of the Foundation had a book value of $3,370,521,943 (*now £1,348 million*) in 1971.

Best dressed women The longest reign as the "Best Dressed Woman" was 15 years from 1938 to 1953 by the Duchess of Windsor (b. Bessie Wallis Warfield at Blue Ridge Summit, Pennsylvania, 19 June 1896, formerly Mrs. Spencer, formerly Mrs. Simpson). In January 1959 the New York Dress Institute put the Duchess and Mrs. William S. "Babe" Paley beyond annual comparison by elevating them to an ageless "Hall of Fame". Also later elevated was Mrs. Jacqueline Lee Kennedy-Onassis *née* Bouvier (born at Southampton, Long Island, New York, 28 July 1929). Including furs and jewellery, some perennials, such as Mrs. Winston F. C. "Cezee" Guest, Mrs. Paley and Mrs. Gloria Guinness, known as "The Ultimate", are reputed to spend up to $100,000 (*now £40,000*) a year on their wardrobes. Mrs. Henry M. Flagler, the chatelaine of Whitehall, her husband's $300,000 establishment in Palm Beach, Florida, U.S.A. in the era 1902–1914, never wore any dress a second time. Her closets were nonetheless moth proof.

In January 1960 the Institute decided it was politic to list a Top Twelve, not in order of merit, but alphabetically. The youngest winner was Mrs. Amanda Carter Burden, aged 22, a step-daughter of the twice blessed Mr. William Paley (see above), on 13 Jan. 1966. After 1966 rankings were re-established.

GASTRONOMIC RECORDS

Records for eating and drinking by trenchermen do not match those suffering from the rare disease of bulimia (morbid desire to eat) and polydipsia (pathological thirst). Some bulimia patients have to spend 15 hours a day eating, with an extreme consumption of 384 lb. 2 oz. *174 kg 236* of food in six days by Matthew Daking, aged 12, in 1743 (known as Mortimer's case). Some polydipsomaniacs have been said to be unsatisfied by less than 96 pints *54,55 litres* of liquid a day. Miss Helge Andersson (b. 1908) of Lindesberg, Sweden was reported in January 1971 to have been drinking 40 pints *22,73 litres* of water a day since 1922—a total of 87,600 gal *3 982 hectolitres*.

The world's greatest trencherman is Edward Abraham ("Bozo") Miller (b. 1909) of Oakland, California, U.S.A. He consumed up to 25,000 calories per day or more than 11 times that recommended. He stands 5 ft 7½ in *1,71 m* tall but weighs from 20 to 21½ st. *127–139 kg* with a 57 in *144 cm* waist. He has been undefeated in eating contests since 1931 (see below). The bargees on the Rhine are reputed to be the world's heaviest eaters with 5,200 calories a day. However the New Zealand Sports Federation of Medicine reported in Dec. 1972 that a long-distance road runner consumed 14,321 calories in 24 hours.

While no healthy person has been reported to have succumbed in any contest for eating or drinking non-alcoholic or non-toxic drinks, such attempts, from a medical point of view, must be regarded as *extremely* inadvisable, particularly among young people. Guinness Superlatives will not list any records involving the consumption of more than 2 litres *3.52 Imperial pints* of beer nor any at all involving spirits.

Specific records have been claimed as follows:

Baked Beans 1,510 cold beans one by one with a cocktail stick in 30 min by Martin Mead, 23 at Gerrard's Cross, Buckinghamshire on 18 Feb. 1973.

Bananas 63 in 10 min by Michael Gallen, 23 in Cairns, Australia on 11 Oct. 1972.

Beer Lawrence Hill (b. 1942) of Bolton, Lancashire, drained a 2½ pt *1,42 litres* Yard of Ale in 6½ sec on 17 Dec. 1964. A 3 pt *1,70 litre* yard was downed in 10.15 sec by Jack Boyle, 52, at The Bay Horse, Ormsgill, Barrow-in-Furness, Lancashire on 14 May 1971.
The Oxford University "sconce" record is 8.8 sec for 2 pt *113,6 centilitres* of beer set by David Clark (Brasenose College) on 12 Mar. 1973. The record for a single pt *56,8 centilitres* is 1.18 sec (from lips to drained glass) by Bob Farrow, 20 of Diss, Norfolk on 13 June 1973. The record for 2 litres *3.52 Imperial pints* is 11 sec by J. H. Cochran (Class of 1925, Princeton University, New Jersey, U.S.A.) in Harry's New York Bar, Paris, on 26 June 1932.

Beer Upsidedown 2 pt *113,6 centilitres* in 44.2 sec by Ernie Driver at Corby, Northampton on 23 Jan. 1972.

Champagne 1,000 bottles per annum by Bobby Acland of the "Black Raven", Bishopsgate, London.

Cheese 16 oz. *453 g* of Cheddar in 4 min 30 sec by John Lombino of Alhambra High School, California, U.S.A., on 25 May 1971.

Chicken 27 (2 lb. [*907 g*] pullets) by "Bozo" Miller (see above) at a sitting at Trader Vic's, San Francisco, California, U.S.A., in 1963.

Clams 437 in 10 min by Joe Gagnon (U.S.) at Everett, Washington, U.S.A. in January 1971.

Doughnuts 20 in 15 min by a student at Durham, England in Dec. 1971.

Eels 1 lb. *453 g* of elvers in 43 sec by Leslie Cole, 37 at Frampton-on-Severn, Gloucestershire on 13 Apr. 1971.

Eggs (Hard Boiled) 44 in 30 min by Georges Grogniet of Belgium on 31 May 1956. (Soft Boiled) 25 in 3 min 1.8 sec by Bill (Dink) Hewit, Bethlehem, Pennsylvania on 2 Oct. 1971.

Frankfurters 18 (2 oz. [*56,6 g*]) in 5 min by Mike Wright, 28 at Dewdrop Inn, Littlehampton, Sussex in Dec. 1971.

Gherkins 1 lb. *453 g* in 1 min 47.5 sec by Peter L. Citron in Omaha, Nebraska, U.S.A. on 20 May 1971.

Goldfish (live) 225 by Roger Martinez at St. Mary's University, San Antonio, Texas, U.S.A. on 6 Feb. 1970.

Grapes 1 lb. *453 g* (unpipped) in 65.0 sec by Leslie Carter, 24 at Bhisworth Fête, Northamptonshire, on 20 May 1972.

Haggis 24 oz. *680 g* in 2 min 42 sec by W. McVeigh at Corby, Northamptonshire on 23 Jan. 1972.

Hamburgers 83 at a 2½ hour sitting by Robert Matern, 21 at Univeristy of Rhode Island on 3 May 1973.

Ice Cream 7 lb. 13 oz. (50 2½ oz. [*70 g*] scoops) in 16 min by Archie Leggatt, 22 in Hamilton, Lanarkshire, Scotland on 9 Feb. 1972.

Lemons 12 quarters (3 lemons) whole (including skin and pips) in 137 sec by Christopher J. Novack of Silver Springs, Md., U.S.A. on 19 Jan. 1973.

Meat One whole roast ox in 42 days by Johann Ketzlar of Munich, Germany in 1880.

Meat Pies 19 5 oz. *141 g* by Geoffrey Heenan in Arbroath, Fife, Scotland on 25 Oct. 1972.

Milk 2 pt (1 Imperial quart or [*113,5 centilitres*]) in 5.2 sec by M. Barsby at Corby, Northampton on 22 Aug. 1971.

Oysters 500 in 60 min by Councillor Peter Jaconelli, Mayor of Scarborough, Yorkshire at The Castle Hotel (only 48 min 7 sec required) on 27 Apr. 1972. The official record for opening oysters is 100 in 3 min 37 sec in Paris in 1954 by *le Champion du Monde des Ecaillers* M. Williams Bley.

Pancakes (6 in [*15,2 cm*] diameter buttered with syrup) 23 in 7 min by Jim Parker of Decatur, Illinois on 3 Mar. 1973.

Peanuts 100 (whole) singly in 59.2 sec by Chris Ambrose in Clerkenwell, London on 3 Apr. 1973.

Pickled Onions 66 in 2 min by James Wilson at Ilmington, Warwickshire on 5 May 1973.

Potatoes 3 lb. *1,360 g* in 8 min by Arthur L. Warner at Newcastle, N.S.W. on 1 Apr. 1971.

Potato Crisps 30 2 oz. *56,6 g* bags in 24 min 33.6 sec, without a drink, by Paul G. Tully of Brisbane University in May 1969. The largest single crisp on record is one measured to be 5 in × 3 in *12,7 × 7,6 cm* found at Reeds School, Cobham, Surrey by John Nicol, 16, on 2 Feb. 1971.

Prunes 130 in 105 sec by Dave Man at Eastbourne on 16 June 1971.

Ravioli 324 (first 250 in 70 min) by "Bozo" Miller (see above) at Rendezvous Room, Oakland, California, U.S.A., in 1963.

Raw Eggs 26 in 9.0 sec by Leslie Jones on Harlech T.V., Cardiff on 10 Nov. 1970. David Taylor at St. Leonards-on-Sea, Sussex ate 16 raw eggs with their shells in 3 min 20 sec on 8 Jan. 1970.

Sandwiches 39 (jam "butties" 5 × 3 × ½ in [*12,7 × 7,6 × 1,3 cm*]) in 60 min by Paul Hughes, 13 at Ruftwood School, Kirkby, Liverpool on 16 July 1971.

Sausage Meat 89½ Danish 1 oz. *28,3 g* sausages in 6 min by Lee Hang in Hong Kong on 3 May 1972.

Shrimps (Boiled) 5 lb. 10 oz. *2 kg 550* in 2 hours by Mrs Jo-Ann Hoss at Freeport, Texas on 4 July 1971.

Spaghetti 262.6 yds *240 m* (2.1 lb. [*952 g*]) by Tom L. Cresci at Dino's Restaurant San Diego, California, U.S.A. on 20 May 1970. 100 yds *91,44 m* in 42.0 sec by Tony Danico, Danny Signor, John Burse and Frank Busato in Sydney, N.S.W., Australia on 11 June 1972.

Whelks 81 (unshelled) in 15 min by William Corfield, 35 at the Helyar Arms, East Coker, Somerset on 6 Sept. 1969.

2. HONOURS, DECORATIONS AND AWARDS

Eponymous record The largest object to which a human name is attached is the super cluster of galaxies known as Abell 7, after the astronomer Dr. George O. Abell of the University of California, U.S.A. The group of clusters has an estimated linear dimension of 300,000,000 light years and was announced in 1961.

ORDERS AND DECORATIONS

Oldest The earliest of the orders of chivalry is the Venetian order of St. Marc, reputedly founded in A.D. 831. The Castilian order of Calatrava has an established date of foundation in 1158. The prototype of the princely Orders of Chivalry is the Most Noble Order of the Garter founded by King Edward III in *c.* 1348.

Most titles The most titled person in the world is the 18th Duchess of Alba (Albade Termes), Doña María del Rosario Cayetana Fitz-James Stuart y Silva. She is 8 times a duchess, 15 times a marchioness, 21 times a countess and is 19 times a Spanish grandee.

British Rarest The rarest British medal is the Union of South Africa King's Medal for Bravery in Gold. The unique recipient was Francis C. Drake, aged 14, who rescued a child from a deep well at Parys, in the Orange Free State, on 6 Jan. 1943. However, the Queen's Fire Services Medal for Gallantry (instituted in 1954), which can only be won posthumously, has yet to be awarded.

Of War Medals, only three Naval General Service Medals (1793–1840) were issued with seven bars: (Admiral of the Fleet Sir James Gordon G.C.B.; Admiral Sir John Hindmarsh K.H.; and Gunner Thomas Haines) and only two Military General Service Medals (1793–1814) with 15 bars (James Talbot of the 45th Foot and Daniel Loochstadt of the 60th Foot).

Commonest Of gallantry decorations, the most unsparingly given was the Military Medal, which was awarded to 115,589 recipients between 1916 and 1919. The most frequently awarded decoration in the 1939–45 war was the Distinguished Flying Cross, which was awarded (including bars) 21,281 times.

Most expensive The highest price paid for any United Kingdom decoration is £4,400 for the diamond studded 'Royal Star' of a Dame Grand Cross of the Order of the British Empire (G.B.E.) made in 1927 for H.R.H. The Princess Mary, The Princess Royal, The Dowager Countess of Harewood C.I., G.C.V.O., G.B.E., R.R.C., T.D., C.D. (1897–1965). It was sold at Sotheby's to the Leeds Coin Centre in June 1973.

HUMAN ACHIEVEMENTS

VICTORIA CROSS

Most bars The only three men ever to have been awarded a bar to the Victoria Cross (instituted 1856) are:

Surg.-Capt. (later Lt.-Col.) Arthur Martin-Leake, V.C.*, V.D., R.A.M.C. (1874–1953) (1902 and bar 1915).
Capt. Noel Godfrey Chavasse, V.C.*, M.C., R.A.M.C. (1884–1917) (1916 and bar posthumously 14 Sept. 1917).
Second Lieut. (later Capt.) Charles Hazlett Upham, V.C.*, N.Z.M.F. (born 1911) (1941 and bar 1942).

Oldest The greatest reported age at which a man has won the V.C. is 69 in the case of Lieut. (later Capt.) William Raynor of the Bengal Veteran Establishment, in defence of the magazine at Delhi, India, on 11 May 1857. Recent evidence indicates that he was not older than 66.

Youngest The lowest established age for a V.C. is 15 years 100 days for Hospital Apprentice Arthur Fitzgibbon (born at Peteragurh, northern India, 13 May 1845) of the Indian Medical Services for bravery at the Taku Forts in northern China on 21 Aug. 1860. Later, as an assistant surgeon, he was dismissed for insubordination and died in 1879. The youngest living V.C. is Lance-Corporal Rambahadur Limbu (b. Nepal, 1939) of the 10th Princess Mary's Own Gurkha Rifles. The award, announced on 22 April 1966, was for his courage while fighting in the Bau district of Sarawak, East Malaysia, on 21 Nov. 1965.

Longest lived The longest lived of all the 1,349 winners of the Victoria Cross was Captain (later General Sir) Lewis Stratford Tollemache Halliday, V.C., K.C.B., of the Royal Marine Light Infantry. He was born on 14 May 1870, won his V.C. in China in 1900, and died on 9 March 1966, aged 95 years 299 days. The oldest living V.C. is Maj. Gen. Dudley Graham Johnson, V.C., C.B., D.S.O. and bar, M.C. (b. 13 Feb. 1884), who won his decoration as an Acting Lt.-Col. attached to the 2nd Batt. Royal Sussex Regt. at the Sumbre Canal, France on 4 Nov. 1918. He also received the Queen's South Africa Medal in 1900 aged 16.

Most awards The two organizations whose members have won most V.C.s are Eton College (35) and The Church Lads' Brigade with 22. The Eton College Combined Cadet Force (formerly Junior Training Corps and formerly Officers' Training Corps) has more V.C.s to its credit than any other British Military Unit with 32; Eton's first 3 V.C.s left before the unit was founded in 1863.

Most mentions in despatches The record number of "mentions" is 24 by Field Marshal the Rt. Hon. Sir Frederick Sleigh Roberts Bt., the Earl Roberts, V.C., K.G., K.P., G.C.B., O.M., G.C.S.I., G.C.I.E., V.D. (1832–1914).

Most post-nominal letters Lord Roberts was the only subject with 8 sets of official post-nominal letters. Currently the record number is seven by Admiral of the Fleet the Earl Mountbatten of Burma (born 25 June 1900) K.G., G.C.B., O.M., G.C.S.I., G.C.I.E., G.C.V.O., D.S.O.

U.S.S.R. The U.S.S.R.'s highest award for valour is the Gold Star of a Hero of the Soviet Union. Over 10,000 were awarded in World War II. Among the 109 awards of a second star were those to Marshall Iosif Vissarionovich Dzhugashvili, *alias* Stalin (1879–1953) and Lt.-General Nikita Sergeyevich Khrushchyov (1894–1971). The only war-time triple awards were to Marshal Georgiy Konstantinovich Zhukov, Hon. G.C.B. (b. 1896) (subsequently awarded a fourth Gold Star, unique until Mr. Khrushchyov's fourth award) and the leading air aces Guards' Colonel (now Aviation Maj.-Gen.) Aleksandr Ivanovich Polkyrshkin and Aviation Maj.-Gen. Ivan Nikitaevich Kozhedub.

U.S.A. The highest U.S. decoration is the Congressional Medal of Honor. Five marines received both the Army and Navy Medals of Honor for the same acts in 1918 and 14 officers and men from 1863 to 1915 have received the medal on two occasions.

C.P.O. Arthur Blore, M.M., winner of the unique award of the Conspicuous Gallantry Medal and bar

RECORD NUMBER OF BARS (repeat awards) EVER GAZETTED TO BRITISH GALLANTRY DECORATIONS
* = a bar or repeat award

V.C.* A first bar has been three times awarded to the Victoria Cross (see above).

D.S.O.*** A third bar has been 16 times awarded to the Distinguished Service Order.

R.R.C.* Over 100 first bars have been awarded to the R.R.C., but of these Dame Sarah Elizabeth Oram, D.B.E., R.R.C.* (1860–1946) uniquely was gazetted *twice* (1896 and 1901) before receiving a bar in 1918, thus indicating 3 awards.

D.S.C.*** A third bar has been uniquely awarded to the Distinguished Service Cross won by Cdr. Norman Eyre Morley, R.N.V.R.

M.C.*** A third bar has been four times awarded to the Military Cross.

D.F.C.** A second bar has been 54 times awarded to the Distinguished Flying Cross.

A.F.C.** A second bar has been 12 times awarded to the Air Force Cross.

D.C.M.** A second bar has been 11 times awarded to the Distinguished Conduct Medal.

C.G.M.* A first bar has been uniquely awarded to the Conspicuous Gallantry Medal won by C.P.O. Arthur Robert Blore, M.M. (1890–1947) and a second medal to Able Seaman D. Barry.

G.M.* A first bar has been 25 times awarded to the George Medal.

K.P.M.** A second bar has been uniquely awarded to the King's/Queen's Police Medal for Gallantry won by Supt. Frederick William O'Gorman, C.I.E., O.B.E. (d. 1949).

E.M.* A first bar has twice been awarded to the Edward Medal (1st Class or in Silver).

D.S.M.*** A third bar has been uniquely awarded to the Distinguished Service Medal won by Petty Officer William Henry Kelly.

M.M.*** A third bar has been uniquely awarded to the Military Medal won by Cpl. Ernest Albert Correy (1888–1972).

D.F.M.** A second bar has been uniquely awarded to the Distinguished Flying Medal won by Flt.-Sgt. (now Group Capt.) Donald Ernest Kingaby, D.S.O., A.F.C.

A.F.M.* A first bar has been 8 times awarded to the Air Force Medal.

S.G.M.* A first bar has been uniquely awarded to the Sea Gallantry Medal won by Chief Officer James Whiteley.

B.E.M.* A first bar has been 4 times awarded to the British Empire Medal for Gallantry (as instituted in 1957).

No bars have yet been awarded to the George Cross (G.C.) or the Conspicuous Gallantry Medal (Flying) (C.G.M.). No bars were ever awarded to the now obsolete Albert Medal in Gold (A.M.), the Albert Medal (A.M.), the Edward Medal (in bronze) (E.M.) or the Empire Gallantry Medal (E.G.M.), which have all been superceded by the G.C.

Most bemedalled The most bemedalled chest is that of H.I.M. Field-Marshal Hailé Selassié, K.G., G.C.B. (Hon.), G.C.M.G. (Hon.) (born, as Ras Tafari Makonnen, on 23 July 1892), Emperor of Ethiopia, who has over 50 medal ribbons worn in up to 14 rows.

TOP SCORING AIR ACES (World Wars I and II)

World 80 Rittmeister Manfred, Freiherr (Baron) von Richthofen (Germany). 352[1] Major Erich Hartman (Germany).

United Kingdom 73[2] Capt. (acting Major) Edward Mannock, V.C.‘ D.S.O.**, M.C.*. 38[3] Wg.-Cdr. (now Air Vice Marshal) James Edgar Johnson, C.B., C.B.E., D.S.O.**, D.F.C.*.

A compilation of the top air aces of 13 combatant nations in World War I and of 22 nations in World War II was included in the 13th edition of *The Guinness Book of Records.*

1 *All except one of the aircraft in this unrivalled total were Soviet combat aircraft on the Eastern Front in 1942–45. The German air ace with most victories against the R.A.F. was Oberleutnant Hans-Joachim Marseille (killed 30 Sept. 1942), who, in 388 actions, shot down 158 Allied aircraft, 151 of them over North Africa.*

2 *Recent research suggests that Mannock's total may have been lower than that of Major James Thomas Byford McCudden, V.C., D.S.O.*, M.C.*, M.M. (57 victories).*

3 *The greatest number of successes against flying bombs (V.I's) was by Sqn. Ldr. Joseph Berry, D.F.C.** (b. Nottingham, 1920, killed 2 Oct. 1944), who brought down 60 in 4 months. The most successful R.A.F. fighter pilot was Sqn. Ldr. Marmaduke Thomas St. John Pattle, D.F.C.*, of South Africa, with a known total of at least 40.*

Top jet ace The greatest number of kills in jet to jet battles is 16 by Capt. Joseph Christopher McConnell, Jr., U.S.A.F. (b. Dover, New Hampshire, 30 Jan. 1922) in the Korean war (1950–53). He was killed on 25 Aug. 1954. It is possible that an Israeli ace may have surpassed this total in the period 1967–70 but the identity of pilots is subject to strict security.

Top woman ace The record score for any woman fighter pilot is 12 by Jnr. Lt. Lydia Litvak (U.S.S.R.) (b. 1921) on the Eastern Front between 1941 and 1943. She was killed in action on 1 Aug. 1943.

Anti-submarine successes The highest number of U-boat kills attributed to one ship in the 1939–45 war was 13 to H.M.S. *Starling* (Capt. Frederick J. Walker, C.B., D.S.O.***, R.N.). Captain Walker was in overall command at the sinking of a total of 25 U-boats between 1941 and the time of his death on 9 July 1944. The U.S. Destroyer Escort *England* sank six Japanese submarines in the Pacific between 18 and 30 May 1944.

Most successful U-boat captain The most successful of all World War II submarine commanders was Korvetten-Kapitän (now Kapitän zur See) Otto Kretschmer (b. 1911), captain of the U.23 and later the U.99. He sank one Allied destroyer and 43 merchantmen totalling 263,682 gross registered tons in 16 patrols before his capture on 17 March 1941. He is a Knight's Cross of the Iron Cross with Oakleaves and Swords. In World War I Kapitän-Leutnant Lothar von Arnauld de la Perière, in the U.35 and U.139, sank 194 allied ships totalling 453, 716 gross tons. The most successful boats were U.48, which in World War I sank 54 ships of 90,350 g.r.t. in

Alfred Bernhard Nobel, the Swedish chemist, who instigated the Nobel Prize Foundation under the terms of his will

a single voyage and 535,900 g.r.t. all told, and U.53 which sank 53 ships of 318,111 g.r.t. in World War II.

NOBEL PRIZES

The Nobel Foundation of £3,200,000 was set up under the will of Alfred Bernhard Nobel (1833–96), the unmarried Swedish chemist and chemical engineer, who invented dynamite, in 1866. The Nobel Prizes are presented annually on 10 Dec., the anniversary of Nobel's death and the festival day of the Foundation. Since the first Prizes were awarded in 1901, the highest cash value of the award, in each of the six fields of Physics, Chemistry, Medicine and Physiology, Literature, Peace and Economics was £42,000 in 1972.

MOST AWARDS

By countries The United States has shared in the greatest number of awards (including those made in 1972) with a total of 83, made up of 21 for Physics, 14 for Chemistry, 25 for Medicine-Physiology, 6 for Literature, 14 for Peace and 3 for Economics.

The United Kingdom has shared in 56 awards, comprising 14 for Physics, 15 for Chemistry, 12 for Medicine-Physiology, 6 for Literature, 8 for Peace and 1 for Economics.

By classes, the United States holds the record for Medicine-Physiology with 25, for Physics with 21 and for Peace with 14; Germany for Chemistry with 21; and France for Literature with 12.

Individuals Individually the only person to have won two Prizes outright is Dr. Linus Carl Pauling (b. 28 Feb. 1901), Professor of Chemistry at the California Institute of Technology, Pasadena, California, U.S.A. since 1931. He was awarded the Chemistry Prize for 1954 and the Peace Prize for 1962. The only other persons to have won two prizes are Madame Marie Curie (1867–1934), who was born in Poland as Marja Sklodowska. She shared the 1903 Physics Prize with her husband Pierre Curie (1859–1906) and Antoine Henri Becquerel (1852–1908), and won the 1911 Chemistry Prize outright. Professor John Bardeen (b. 23 May 1908) shared the physics prize in 1956 and 1972. The Peace Prize has been awarded three times to the International Committee of the Red Cross (founded 29 Oct. 1863), of Geneva, Switzerland,

The King's Police Medal and two bars, uniquely awarded to Supt. F. W. O'Gorman

The Rev. Dr. Martin Luther King, the youngest winner of a Nobel Prize for Peace

namely in 1917, 1944 and in 1963, when it was shared with the International League of Red Cross Societies.

Oldest The oldest prizeman has been Professor Francis Peyton Rous (1879–1970) of the United States. He shared the Medicine Prize in 1966, at the age of 87.

Youngest The youngest laureate has been Professor Sir William Lawrence Bragg, C.H., O.B.E., M.C. (1890–1971), of the U.K., who, at the age of 25, shared the 1915 Physics Prize with his father, Sir William Henry Bragg, O.M., K.B.E. (1862–1942), for work on X-rays and crystal structures. Bragg and also Theodore William Richards (1868–1928) of the U.S.A., who won the 1914 Chemistry prize, carried out their prize work when aged 23. The youngest Literature prizeman has been Joseph Rudyard Kipling (1865–1936) at the age of 41 in 1907. The youngest Peace prize-winner has

been the Rev. Dr. Martin Luther King, Jr. (1929–68) of the U.S.A., in 1964.

Greatest reception The greatest ticker-tape reception ever given on Broadway, New York City, N.Y., U.S.A., was that for Lt.-Col. (now Col.) John Herschel Glenn, Jr. (b. 18 July 1921) on 1 March 1962, after his return from his tri-orbital flight. The New York Street Cleaning Department estimated that 3,474 tons/*tonnes* of paper descended. This total compared with 3,249 tons/*tonnes* for General of the Army Douglas MacArthur (1880–1964) in 1951 and 1,800 tons/*tonnes* for Col. Charles Augustus Lindbergh (b. 4 Feb. 1902) in June 1927.

Most statues The world record for raising statues to oneself was set by Generalissimo Dr. Rafael Leónidas Trujillo y Molina (1891–1961), former President of the Dominican Republic. In March 1960 a count showed that there were "over 2,000". The country's highest mountain was named Pico Trujillo (now Pico Duarte). One Province was called Trujillo and another Trujillo Valdez. The capital was named Ciudad Trujillo (Trujillo City) in 1936, but reverted to its old name of Santo Domingo de Guzmán on 23 Nov. 1961. Trujillo was assassinated in a car ambush on 30 May 1961, and 30 May is now celebrated annually as a public holiday. The man to whom most statues have been raised is undoubtedly Vladimir Ilyich Ulyanov, *alias* Lenin (1870–1924), busts of whom have been mass-produced as also in the case of Mao Tse-tung. (b. 26 Dec. 1893) and Hô Chi Minh (1890–1969).

PEERAGE

Most ancient creation The year 1223 has been ascribed to the premier Irish barony of Kingsale (formerly de Courcy), though on the Order of Precedence the date is listed as 1397. The premier English barony, de Ros, was held until her death on 8 Oct. 1956, by a Baroness in her own right and 26th in her line, dating from 14 Dec. 1264. It was called out of abeyance on 29 Aug. 1958 in favour of a grand-daughter, Mrs. Georgiana Angela Maxwell (born 1933). The earldom of Arundel, a subsidiary title of the Duke of Norfolk, dates from 1139.

Astronaut John Glenn during his ride down Broadway in 1962, when New York gave him the greatest ticker tape reception ever

Lord Salter, the oldest living peer

Oldest creation The greatest age at which any person has been raised to the peerage is 93 years 337 days in the case of Sir William Francis Kyffin Taylor, G.B.E., K.C. (b. 9 July 1854), who was created Baron Maenan of Ellesmere, County Salop (Shropshire), on 10 June 1948, and died, aged 97, on 22 Sept. 1951, when the title became extinct.

Longest lived peer The longest lived peer ever recorded was the Rt. Hon. Frank Douglas-Pennant, the 5th Baron Penrhyn (b. 21 Nov. 1865), who died on 3 Feb. 1967, aged 101 years 74 days. The oldest peeress recorded was the Countess Desmond, who was alleged to be 140 when she died in 1604. This claim is patently exaggerated but it is accepted that she may have been 104. Currently the oldest holder of a peerage, and the oldest Parliamentarian, is the Rt. Hon. (Ethel) Sydney Keith, formerly Baird (*née* Keith-Falconer), the Countess of Kintore and the Dowager Viscountess Stonehaven, born on 20 Sept. 1874. The oldest peer is the Rt. Hon. Sir (James) Arthur Salter, G.B.E., K.C.B., the Baron Salter, who was born on 15 Mar. 1881.

Youngest peers Twelve Dukes of Cornwall automatically became peers at birth as the eldest son of a Sovereign; and the 9th Earl of Chichester posthumously inherited his father's (killed 54 days previously) earldom at his birth on 14 April 1944.

The youngest age at which a person has had a peerage conferred on them is 7 days old in the case of the Earldom of Chester on H.R.H. the Prince George (later George IV) on 19 Aug. 1762.

Longest and shortest peerages The peer who has sat longest in the House of Lords was Lt.-Col. Charles Henry FitzRoy, O.B.E., the 4th Baron Southampton (b. 11 May 1867), who succeeded to his father's title on 16 July 1872, took his seat on 23 Jan. 1891, 18 months before Mr. W. E. Gladstone's fourth administration began, and died, aged 91, on 7 Dec. 1958, having held the title for 86 years 144 days.

The shortest enjoyment of a peerage was the "split second" by which the law assumes that the Hon. Wilfrid Carlyle Stamp (b. 28 Oct. 1904), the 2nd Baron Stamp, survived his father, Sir Josiah Charles Stamp, G.C.B., G.B.E., the 1st Baron Stamp, when both were killed as a result of German bombing of London on 16 April 1941. Apart from this legal

fiction, the shortest recorded peerage was one of 30 minutes in the case of Sir Charles Brandon, K.B., the 3rd Duke of Suffolk, who died, aged 13 or 14, just after succeeding his brother, Sir Henry, the 2nd Duke, when both were suffering a fatal illness, at Buckden, Huntingdonshire, on 14 July 1551.

Highest numbering The highest succession number borne by any peer is that of the present 35th Baron Kingsale (John de Courcy, b. 27 Jan. 1941), who succeeded to the 746-year-old Barony on 7 Nov. 1969.

Most creations The largest number of new hereditary peerages created in any year was the 54 in 1296. The record for all peerages (including 40 life peerages) is 55 in 1964. The greatest number of extinctions in a year was 16 in 1923 and the greatest number of deaths was 44 in 1935.

Longest abeyance The longest abeyance of any peerage was that of the barony of Strabolgi, which was called out on 9 May 1916, more than 546 years in abeyance since 10 Oct. 1369.

Most prolific The most prolific peers of all time are believed to be the 1st Earl Ferrers (1650–1717) and the 3rd Earl of Winchelsea (*c.* 1620–1689) each with 27 legitimate children. In addition, the former reputedly fathered 30 illegitimate children. Currently the peer with the largest family is the Rt. Hon. Bryan Walter Guinness, 2nd Baron Moyne (b. 27 Oct. 1905) with 6 sons and 5 daughters.

The most prolific peeress is believed to be Elizabeth (*née* Barnard), who bore 22 children to her husband Lord Chandos of Sudeley (1642–1714).

BARONETS

Oldest The greatest age to which a baronet has lived is 101 years 188 days, in the case of Sir Fitzroy Donald Maclean, 10th Bt., K.C.B., (1835–1936). He was the last survivor of the Charge of the Light Brigade at Balaclava in the Crimea, Russia, on 25 Oct. 1854.

Most and least creations The largest number of creations this century was 51 in 1919. There were none in 1940 and none have been created since 1965.

Philosopher the Earl Russell, the longest lived holder of the Order of Merit

KNIGHTS

Youngest and oldest The youngest age for the conferment of a knighthood is 29 days for H.R.H. the Prince Albert Edward (b. 9 Nov. 1841) (later Edward VII) by virtue of his *ex officio* membership of the Order of the Garter (K.G.) consequent upon his creation as Prince of Wales on 8 Dec. 1841. The greatest age for the conferment of a knighthood is 91 years 128 days in the case of Charles Shaw-Lefevre, 1st Viscount Eversley (1794–1888) created G.C.B. (civil) on 30 June 1885.

ORDER OF MERIT

The Order of Merit (instituted on 23 June 1902) is limited to 24 members. Up to April 1973 there were 124 awards including only 3 women, plus 9 honorary awards to non-British citizens. The longest lived holder has been the Rt. Hon. Bertrand Arthur William Russell, 3rd Earl Russell, who died on 2 Feb. 1970 aged 97 years 260 days. The oldest recipient was Admiral of the Fleet the Hon. Sir Henry Keppel, G.C.B., O.M. (1809–1904), who received the Order aged 93 years 56 days on 9 Aug. 1902. The youngest recipient has been H.R.H. the Duke of Edinburgh, K.G., K.T., O.M., G.B.E. who was appointed on his 47th birthday on 10 June 1968.

Most freedoms Probably the greatest number of freedoms ever conferred on any man was 57 in the case of Andrew Carnegie (1835–1919), who was born in Dunfermline, Fife but emigrated to the United States in 1848. The most freedoms conferred upon any citizen of the United Kingdom is 42, in the case of the Rt. Hon. Sir Winston Leonard Spencer Churchill, K.G., O.M., C.H., T.D. (1874–1965).

Herbert C. Hoover, who received a total of 89 honorary degrees, a record number

A characteristic photograph of Sir Winston Churchill, who had a total of 42 freedoms bestowed on him, and also set the record for the longest ever entry in *Who's Who*

Who's Who The longest entry in *Who's Who* (founded 1849) was that of the Rt. Hon. Sir Winston Leonard Spencer Churchill, K.G., O.M., C.H., T.D. (1874–1965), who had 211 lines in the 1965 edition. Apart from those who qualify for inclusion by hereditary title, the youngest entry has been Yehudi Menuhin, Hon. K.B.E. (b. New York City, U.S.A. 22 April 1916), the concert violinist, who first appeared in the 1932 edition. The longest entry of the 66,000 entries in *Who's Who in America* is that of Prof. Richard Buckminster Fuller, Jr. (b. 12 July 1895) whose all-time record of 139 lines compares with the 23 line sketch on President Nixon.

Most honorary degrees The greatest number of honorary degrees awarded to any individual is 89, given to Herbert Clark Hoover (1874–1964), former President of the United States (1929–33).

Greatest vote The largest monetary vote made by Parliament to a subject was the £400,000 given to the 1st Duke of Wellington (1769–1852) on 12 April 1814. He received in all £864,000. The total received by the 1st, 2nd and 3rd Dukes to January 1900 was £1,052,000.

Professor Richard Buckminster Fuller Jr., the holder of the record for the lengthiest entry in *Who's Who in America* with 139 lines

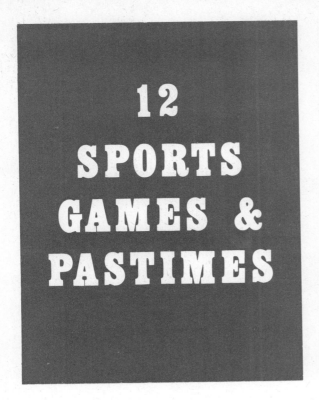

12 SPORTS GAMES & PASTIMES

CITIUS ALTIUS FORTIUS

ALL SPORT

Earliest The origins of sport stem from the time when self-preservation ceased to be the all-consuming human preoccupation. Archery was a hunting skill in mesolithic times (by *c.* 8000 B.C.), but did not become an organized sport until *c.* A.D. 300, among the Genoese. The earliest dated evidence for sport is *c.* 2450 B.C. for fowling with throwing sticks, and hunting. Ball games by girls depicted on Middle Kingdom murals at Ben Hasan, Egypt have been dated to *c.* 2050 B.C.

Fastest The governing body for aviation, *La Fédération Aéronautique Internationale*, records maximum speeds in lunar flight of up to 24,791 m.p.h. *39 897 km/h.* However, these achievements, like all air speed records since 1923, have been para-military rather than sporting. In shooting, muzzle velocities of up to 7,100 ft/sec (4,840 m.p.h. [*7 790 km/h*]) are reached in the case of a U.S. Army Ordnance Department standard 0.30 calibre M1903 rifle. The highest speed reached in a non-mechanical sport is in sky-diving, in which a speed of 185 m.p.h. *295 km/h* is attained in a head-down free falling position, even in the lower atmosphere. In delayed drops a speed of 614 m.p.h. *988 km/h* has been recorded at high rarefied altitudes. The highest projectile speed in any moving ball game is *c.* 160 m.p.h. *260 km/h* in pelota. This compares with 170 m.p.h. *273 km/h* (electronically-timed) for a golf ball driven off a tee.

Slowest In wrestling, before the rules were modified towards "brighter wrestling", contestants could be locked in holds for so long that single bouts could last for 11 hours 40 min. In the extreme case of the 2 hours 41 min pull in the regimental tug o' war in Jubbulpore, India, on 12 Aug. 1889, the winning team moved a net distance of 12 ft *3,6 m* at an average speed of 0.00084 m.p.h. *0,000135 km/h.*

Longest The most protracted sporting test was an automobile duration test of 222,618 miles *358 268 km* by Appaurchaux and others in a Ford Taunus. This was contested over 142 days in 1963. The distance was equivalent to 8.93 times around the equator.

The most protracted non-mechanical sporting event is the *Tour de France* cycling race. In 1926 this was over 3,569 miles *5 743 km* lasting 29 days. The total damage to the French national economy of this annual event, now reduced to 23 days, is immense. If it is assumed that one-third of the total working population works for only two-thirds of the time during the currency of *Le Tour* this would account for a loss of more than three-quarters of one per cent of the nation's annual Gross National Product. In 1972 this was more than £50,000 million, so the loss would have been about £375,000,000.

Shortest Of sports with timed events the briefest recognized for official record purposes is the quick draw in shooting in which electronic times down to 0.02 of a second have been returned in self-draw events.

Most expensive The most expensive of all sports is the racing of large yachts—"J" type boats, last built in 1937, and International 12-metre boats. The owning and racing of these is beyond the means of individual millionaires and is confined to multi-millionaires or syndicates.

Largest crowd The greatest number of live spectators for any sporting spectacle is the estimated 1,000,000 (more than 20 per cent of the population) who line the route of the annual San Sylvestre road race of 8,600 m *5 miles 605 yds* through the streets of São Paulo, Brazil, on New Year's night. However, spread over 23 days, it is estimated that more than 10,000,000 see the annual *Tour de France* along the route (see also above).

The largest crowd travelling to any sporting venue is "more than 400,000" for the annual *Grand Prix d'Endurance* motor race on the Sarthe circuit near Le Mans, France. The record stadium crowd was one of 199,854 for the Brazil *v.* Uruguay match in the Maracaña Municipal Stadium, Rio de Janeiro, Brazil, on 16 July 1950.

Largest field The largest pitch of any ball game is that of polo, with 12.4 acres *5,0 ha*, or a maximum length of 300 yd *274 m* and a width, without side boards, of 200 yd *182 m.*

Most participants The annual Nijmegen Vierdaagse march in the Netherlands over distances up to 50 km *31 miles 120 yds* attracted 16,667 participants in 1968. The Vasa ski race attracted 8,755 starters in 1973 of whom 7,565 finished.

The world's heaviest sportsman, William J. Cobb, *alias* Happy Humphrey, with his house on wheels, which he uses to promote his wrestling matches

Heaviest sportsmen The heaviest sportsman of all-time was the wrestler William J. Cobb of Macon, Georgia, U.S.A., who in 1962 was billed as the 802 lb. (57 st. 4 lb. [*363 kg*]) "Happy Humphrey". The heaviest player of a ball-game has been Bob Pointer, the U.S. Football tackle formerly on the 1967 Santa Barbara High School Team California, U.S.A. and still playing in 1972 at 480 lb. (34 st. 4 lb. [*217 kg*]).

Worst disasters The worst sports disaster in recent history was when an estimated 604 were killed after some stands at the Hong Kong Jockey Club racecourse collapsed and caught fire on 26 Feb. 1918. During the reign of Antoninus Pius (A.D. 138–161) the upper wooden tiers in the Circus Maximus, Rome collapsed during a gladiatorial combat killing some 1,112 spectators. Britain's worst sports disaster was when 66 were killed and 145 injured at the Rangers *v.* Celtic football match at Exit 13 of Ibrox Park stadium, Glasgow on 2 Jan. 1971.

Youngest world record breakers The youngest age at which any person has broken a world record is 12 years 328 days in the case of Karen Yvette Muir (born 16 Sept. 1952) of Kimberley, South Africa, who broke the women's 110 yds backstroke world record with 1 min 08.7 sec at Blackpool on 10 Aug. 1965.

Youngest and oldest inter-nationals The youngest age at which any person has won international honours is 8 years in the case of Miss Joy Foster, the Jamaican singles and mixed doubles table tennis champion in 1958. It would appear that the greatest age at which anyone has actively competed for his country is 73 years in the case of Oscar G. Swahn (Sweden), who won a silver medal for shooting in the Olympic Games at Antwerp in 1920.

Youngest and oldest champions The youngest age at which anyone has successfully participated in a world title event is 12 years in the case of Bernard Malvoire (France), cox of the winning coxed fours in the Olympic regatta at Helsinki in 1952. The youngest individual Olympic winner was Miss Marjorie Gestring (U.S.A.), who took the spring-board diving title at the age of 13 years 9 months at the Olympic Games in Berlin in 1936. The greatest age at which anyone has held a world title is 60 years in the case of Pierre Etchbaster, who retired, in 1955 after 27 years as undefeated world tennis champion from May 1928.

Longest reign The longest reign as a world champion is 27 years by Pierre Etchbaster (France) (see above).

The longest reign as a British champion is 41 years by the archer Miss Alice Blanche Legh (1855–1948) who first won the Championship in 1881 and for the 23rd and final time in 1922.

Greatest earnings The greatest fortune amassed by an individual in sport is an estimated £17,000,000 by the late Sonja Henie of Norway (1912–1969), the triple Olympic figure skating champion (1928–32–36), when later (1936–56) a professional ice skating promoter starring in her own ice shows and 11 films. The most earned for a single event is the reported $2,500,000 (*£1,000,000*) each by the boxers Joe Frazier and Muhammad Ali (*née* Cassius Clay) in their heavyweight world title fight over 15 rounds in Madison Square Gardens, New York City on 8 March 1971. This works out at £23,148.14 per min of actual fighting. The highest contract paid to any sportswoman is $2.5 million (*£1 million*) for 3 years to Janet Lynn, the 1972 Olympic bronze medal figure skater on 20 June 1973.

Largest following The sport with most participants in Britain is swimming with 6¾ million. The highest number of paid admissions is 7¾ million for Association Football, which also attracts more than 21 million T.V. viewers.

Most sportsmen According to a report issued in April 1971, 28,400,000 men and 15,200,000 women are actively involved in 209,000 physical culture and sports groups in the U.S.S.R. where there are 6.1 million track athletes, 5.6 million volleyball players, 3.9 million footballers and 891,000 weightlifters. The report lists 2,918 stadiums, 430 indoor and 475 outdoor swimming pools for 791,000 swimmers.

242

ANGLING

LARGEST SINGLE CATCH

The largest fish ever caught on a rod is an officially ratified man-eating great white shark (*Carcharodon carcharias*) weighing 2,664 lb. *1 208 kg* and measuring 16 ft 10 in *5,13 m* long, caught on a 130 lb. *58 kg* test line by Alf Dean at Denial Bay, near Ceduna, South Australia, on 21 April 1959. Capt. Frank Mundus (U.S.A.) harpooned a 17 ft *5,18 m* long 4,500 lb. *2 040 kg* white shark after a 5-hour battle, off Montauk Point, New York, U.S.A., in 1964.

The largest marine animal ever killed by *hand* harpoon was a blue whale 97 ft *29,56 m* in length, killed by Archer Davidson in Twofold Bay, New South Wales, Australia, in 1910. Its tail flukes measured 20 ft *6,09 m* across and its jaw bone 23 ft 4 in *7,11 m*. To date this has provided the ultimate in "fishing stories".

SMALLEST CATCH

The smallest full-grown fish ever caught is the *Schindleria praematurus*, weighing 1/14,000 of an oz. *0,002 g* (see page 48) found in Samoa, in the Pacific.

Spear fishing The largest fish ever taken underwater was an 804 lb. *364 kg* Giant Black Grouper or Jewfish by Don Pinder of the Miami Triton Club, Florida, U.S.A., in 1955. The British spearfishing record is 89 lb. 0 oz. *40 kg 30* for an angler fish by J. Brown (Weymouth Association Divers) in 1969.

Casting record The longest freshwater cast ratified under I.C.F. (International Casting Federation) rules is 175,01 m *574 ft 2 in* by Walter Kummerow (West Germany), for the Bait Distance Double-Handed 30 g event held at Lenzerheide, Switzerland in the 1968 Championships. The British National record is 148,78 m *488 ft 1 in* by A. Dickison on the same occasion.

Longest fight The longest recorded individual fight with a fish is 32 hrs 5 min by Donal Heatley (b. 1938) (New Zealand) with a broadbill (estimated length 20 ft *6,09 m* and weight 1,500 lb. *680 kg*) off Mayor Island off Tauranga, North Island on 21–22 Jan. 1968. It towed the 12 ton/*tonnes* launch 50 miles *80 km* before breaking the line.

Elliot J. Fishman with his world record Blue Marlin of 845 lb. *383 kg 285* caught off St. Thomas, Virgin Islands

Rarest fish The burbot or eel-pout, the rarest British freshwater fish, is "almost extinct", so it has been agreed that no record for this species should be published, at least until Nov. 1974, in the interests of conservation.

Angling marathon Miss Lynda Hamilton of Kelvedon and District Angling Club fished for 137 hours at Rivenhall Sand Pit, near Silver End, Essex between 4 and 10 Aug. 1972. Approximately five minutes per hour were used as rest breaks.

WORLD RECORDS (All tackle)

(Sea fish as ratified by the International Game Fish Association to 1 Jan. 1973. Freshwater fish, ratified by "*Field & Stream*", are marked*)

Species	Weight lb. oz.	kg/g	Name of Angler	Location	Date
Amberjack	149 0	67,585	Peter Simons	Bermuda	21 June 1964
Barracuda	83 0	37,648	K. J. W. Hackett	Lagos, Nigeria	13 Jan. 1952
Bass (Giant Sea)	563 8	255,599	James D. McAdam	Anacapa Is., California, U.S.A.	20 Aug. 1968
*Carp†	55 5	25,089	Frank J. Ledwein	Clearwater Lake, Minnesota, U.S.A.	10 July 1952
Cod	98 12	44,792	Alphonse J. Bielevich	Isle of Shoals, Massachusetts, U.S.A.	8 June 1969
Marlin (Black)	1,560 0	707,604	Alfred C. Glassell, Jr.	Cabo Blanco, Peru	4 Aug. 1563
Marlin (Blue)	845 0	383,285	Elliot J. Fishman	St. Thomas, Virgin Is.	4 July 1998
Marlin (Pacific Blue)	1,153 0	522,992	Greg D. Perez	Ritidian Point, Guam	21 Aug. 1969
Marlin (Striped)	415 0	188,240	B. C. Bain	Cape Brett, New Zealand	31 Mar. 1964
Marlin (White)	159 8	72,347	W. E. Johnson	Pompano Beach, Florida, U.S.A.	25 April 1953
*Pike (Northern)	46 2	20,921	Peter Dubuc	Sacandaga Reservoir, N.Y., U.S.A.	15 Sept. 1940
Sailfish (Atlantic)	141 1	63,984	Tony Burnand	Ivory Coast, Africa	26 Jan. 1961
Sailfish (Pacific)	221 0	100,243	C. W. Stewart	Santa Cruz Is., Galapagos Is.	12 Feb. 1947
*Salmon (Chinook)††	92 0	41,730	Heinz Wichmann	Skeena River, British Columbia, Canada	19 July 1959
Shark (Blue)	410 0	185,972	Richard C. Webster	Rockport, Massachusetts, U.S.A.	1 Sept. 1960
	410 0	185,972	Martha C. Webster	Rockport, Massachusetts, U.S.A.	17 Aug. 1967
**Shark (Shortfin Mako)	1,061 0	481,261	James B. Penwarden	Mayor Island, New Zealand	17 Feb. 1970
Shark (White or Man-eating)	2,664 0	1 208,370	Alfred Dean	Denial Bay, Ceduna, South Australia	21 April 1959
Shark (Porbeagle)	430 0	195,044	Desmond Bougourd	South of Jersey, C.I.	29 June 1969
Shark (Thresher)	729 0	330,668	Mrs. V. Brown	Mayor Island, New Zealand	3 June 1959
Shark (Tiger)	1,780 0	807,394	Walter Maxwell	Cherry Grove, South Carolina, U.S.A.	14 June 1964
*Sturgeon (White)	360 0	163,293	Willard Cravens	Snake River, Idaho, U.S.A.	24 April 1956
Swordfish	1,182 0	536,146	L. E. Marron	Iquique, Chile	7 May 1953
Tarpon	283 0	128,366	M. Salazar	Lago de Maracaibo, Venezuela	19 Mar. 1956
*Trout (Lake)‡	Record being reviewed.				
Tuna (Allison or Yellowfin)	296 0	134,263	Edward C. Malnar	San Benedicto Is, Mexico	7 Mar. 1971
Tuna (Atlantic Big-eyed)	321 12	145,943	Vito Locaputo	Hudson Canyon, New York, U.S.A.	19 Aug. 1972
Tuna (Pacific Big-eyed)	435 0	197,312	Dr. Russel V. A. Lee	Cabo Blanco, Peru	17 April 1957
Tuna (Bluefin)	1,065 0	483,075	Robert Glen Gibson	Cape Breton, Nova Scotia, Canada	19 Nov. 1970
Wahoo	149 0	67,585	John Pirovano	Cat Cay, Bahamas	15 June 1962

† *A carp weighing 83 lb. 8 oz. 37 kg 874 was taken (not by rod) near Pretoria, South Africa.*

†† *A salmon weighing 126 lb. 8 oz. 57 kg 379 was taken (not by rod) near Petersburg, Alaska, U.S.A.*

** *A 1,295 lb. 587 kg specimen was taken by two anglers off Natal, South*

Africa on 17 March 1939 and a 1,500 lb. 680 kg specimen harpooned inside Durban Harbour, South Africa in 1933.

‡ *A 102 lb. 46 kg 266 trout was taken from Lake Athabasca, northern Saskatchewan, Canada, on 8 Aug. 1961.*

Championship Records

World The *Confederation Internationale de la Pêche Sportive* Championships were inaugurated in 1954. France has won 6 times and Robert Tesse (France) the individual title in 1959–60–65.

British The National Angling Championship (instituted 1906) has been won seven times by Leeds (1909–10–14–28–48–49–52). Only James H. R. Bazley (Leeds) has ever won the individual title twice (1909–1927). The record catch is 76 lb. 9 oz. *34 kg 720* by David Burr (Rugby) in the Huntspill, Somerset in 1965. The team record is 136 lb. 15¼ oz. *62 kg 120* by Sheffield Amalgamated also in the Huntspill in 1955.

BRITISH ROD-CAUGHT RECORDS

(as ratified by the British Record [rod-caught] Fish Committee of the National Angler's Council)

(Selected from the complete list of about 100 species)

Species	Weight lb.	oz.	kg/g	Name of Angler	Location	Year
Angler Fish	74	8	*33,792*	J. J. McVicar	S.W. Eddystone	1972
Bass	18	2	*8,221*	F. C. Borley	Felixstowe Beach, Suffolk	1943
Black Bream	6	1	*2,749*	F. W. Richards	The Skerries, Dartmouth	1969
Red Bream	7	8	*3,401*	A. F. Bell	Fowey, Cornwall	1925
Brill	16	0	*7,257*	A. H. Fisher	Derby Haven, Isle of Man	1950
Bull Huss (Greater Spotted Dogfish)	21	3	*9,610*	J. Holmes	Hat Rock, Cornwall	1955
Coalfish	30	12	*13,947*	A. F. Harris	S. of Eddystone	1973
Cod	53	0	*24,040*	G. Martin	Off Start Point, Devon	1972
Conger	92	13	*42,098*	P. H. Ascott	Torquay, Devon	1970
Dab	2	10¾	*1,211*	A. B. Hare	The Skerries, Dartmouth	1968
Dogfish (Lesser Spotted)	4	8	*2,041*	J. Beattie	off Ayr Pier, Ayrshire	1969
Dogfish (Spur)	20	3	*9,156*	J. Newman	Off Needles Lighthouse	1972
Flounder	5	11½	*2,593*	A. G. L. Cobbledick	Fowey, Cornwall	1956
Garfish	2	9⅛	*1,165*	A. W. Bodfield	Dartmouth, Devonshire	1963
Grey Mullet	10	1	*4,564*	P/O. P.C. Libby	Portland, Dorset	1952
Gurnard	11	7¼	*5,195*	C. W. King	Wallasey, Cheshire	1952
Gurnard (Red)	3	2	*1,417*	W. S. Blunn	Stoke, nr. Plymouth, Devon	1970
Haddock	10	12	*4,876*	A. H. Hill	Looe, Cornwall	1972
Hake	25	5½	*11,495*	Herbert W. Steele	Belfast Lough	1962
Halibut	161	12	*73,368*	W. E. Knight	Orkney	1968
John Dory	10	12	*4,876*	B. Perry	Porthallow, Cornwall	1963
Ling	45	0	*20,411*	H. C. Nicholl	Penzance, Cornwall	1912
Lumpsucker	14	3	*6,435*	W. J. Burgess	Felixstowe Beach, Suffolk	1970
Mackerel	5	6½	*2,452*	S. Beasley	N. of Eddystone Lighthouse	1969
Megrim	3	10	*1,644*	D. DiCicco	Ullapool, Ross-shire	1966
Monkfish	66	0	*29,937*	G. C. Chalk	Shoreham, Sussex	1965
Mullet (Red)	3	10	*1,644*	John E. Martel	St. Martin's, Guernsey	1967
Plaice	7	15	*3,600*	Ian B. Brodie	Salcombe, Devon	1964
Pollack	23	8	*10,569*	G. Bartholomew	Newquay, Cornwall	1957
Pouting	5	8	*2,494*	R. S. Armstrong	off Berry Head, Devon	1969
Ray (Spotted)	16	3	*7,342*	E. Lockwood	Lerwick Harbour, Shetland	1970
Ray (Thornback)	38	0	*17,236*	J. Patterson	Rustington, Sussex	1935
Scad	3	4½	*1,488*	D. O. Cooke	Mewstone, Plymouth	1971
Allis Shad	3	4½	*1,488*	Bernard H. Sloane	Torquay, Devon	1964
Twaite Shad	3	2	*1,417*	T. Hayward	Deal, Kent	1949
	3	2	*1,417*	S. Jenkins	Tor Bay, Devon	1954
Shark (Blue)	218	0	*98,883*	N. Sutcliffe	Looe, Cornwall	1959
Shark (Mako)	500	0	*226,796*	Mrs. J. Yallop	Eddystone Lighthouse	1971
Shark (Porbeagle)	430	0	*195,044*	see world record list		
Shark (Thresher)	280	0	*127,005*	H. A. Kelly	Dungeness, Kent	1933
Skate (Common)	226	8	*102,738*	R. S. Macpherson	Dury Voe, Shetland	1970
Sole	4	1⅞	*1,867*	R. A. Austin	Bordeaux Vale, Guernsey	1967
Sting Ray	59	0	*26,761*	J. M. Buckley	Clacton-on-Sea, Essex	1952
Three-bearded Rockling	2	14¼	*1,311*	S. F. Bealing	Poole Bay, Dorset	1972
Tope	74	11	*33,877*	A. B. Harries	Caldy Island, Pembrokeshire	1964
Tunny	851	0	*386,007*	L. Mitchell-Henry	Whitby, Yorkshire	1933
Turbot	31	4	*14,174*	Paul Hutchings	off Eddystone Lighthouse	1972
Greater Weever	2	4	*1,020*	P. Ainslie	Brighton, Sussex	1927
Whiting	6	3	*2,806*	Mrs. R. Barrett	Rame Head, Cornwall	1971
Wrasse (Ballan)	7	10	*3,458*	B. K. Lawrence	Trevose Head, Cornwall	1970

FRESHWATER FISH

It will be noted that seven former "records" achieved between 1923 and 1955 have been discarded because they cannot be substantiated under the existing rules. These are noted as being "open to claim" if a specimen comes up to or over the "minimum qualifying standard".

Species	Weight lb.	oz.	kg/g	Name of Angler	Location	Year
Barbel	13	12	*6,236*	J. Day	Royalty Fishery, Christchurch, Hampshire	1962
Bleak	0	3⅞	*0,109*	D. Pollard	Staythorpe, Notts.	1971
Bream (Common)	12	14	*5,840*	G. J. Harper	Stour, Great Cornard, Suffolk	1971
Bream (Silver)	record open to claim (over 1 lb. 8 oz. *680 g*)					
Carp	44	0	*19,958*	Richard Walker	Redmire Pool, Herefordshire	1952
Chub	record open to claim (over 7 lb. *3 kg 175*)					
Crucian Carp	4	15½	*2,253*	J. Johnstone	Johnsons Lake, New Hythe, Kent	1972
Dace	1	4¼	*0,574*	J. L. Gasson	Little Ouse, Thetford, Norfolk	1960
Eel	8	10	*3,912*	A. Dart	Hunstrete Lake, Somerset	1969
Grayling	record open to claim (over 3 lb. *1 kg 360*)					
Gudgeon	0	4	*0,113*	M. Morris	Susworth Roach Ponds, Lincs.	1971
Gwyniad (Whitefish)	1	4	*0,566*	J. R.Williams	Llyn Tegid, Merionethshire	1965
Loch Lomond Powan	1	7	*0,651*	J. M. Ryder	Loch Lomond, Scotland	1972
Perch	4	12	*2,154*	S. F. Baker	Oulton Broad, Suffolk	1962
Pike[1]	record open to claim					
Roach	3	14	*1,757*	W. Penney	Lambeth Reservoir, Molesey, Surrey	1938
	3	14	*1,757*	A. Brown	Pit, near Stamford, Lincolnshire	1964
Rudd	4	8	*2,041*	Rev. E. C. Alston	Mere, near Thetford, Norfolk	1933
"Ruffe"	0	4	*0,113*	B. B. Poyner	River Stour, Warwickshire	1969
Salmon[2]	64	0	*29,029*	Miss G. W. Ballantyne	River Tay, Scotland	1922
Tench	9	1	*4,110*	John Salisbury	Hemingford Grey, Huntingdonshire	1963
Trout (Brown)[3]	18	2	*8,221*	K. J. Grant	Loch Garry, Inverness-shire	1965
Trout (Rainbow)	10	0¼	*4,543*	M. Parker	From a private lake, King's Lynn	1970
Trout (Sea)	record open to claim					

1 *A Pike of allegedly 52 lb.* 23 kg *was recovered when Whittlesea Mere, Cambridgeshire and Isle of Ely, was drained in 1851. A pike of reputedly 72 lb.* 32,65 kg *was landed from Loch Ken, Kirkcudbrightshire in 1796.*
2 *The 8th Earl of Home is recorded as having caught a 69¾ lb.* 31 kg 638 *specimen in the R. Tweed in 1730. J. Wallace claimed a 67-pounder* 30 kg *at Barjarg, Dumfries-shire in 1812.*
3 *In 1866 W. C. Muir is reputed to have caught a 39½ lb.* 17 kg 916 *specimen in Loch Awe and in 1816 a 36 lb.* 16 kg *specimen was reported from the R. Colne, near Watford, Hertfordshire.*

IRISH ANGLING RECORDS (as ratified by the Irish Specimen Fish Committee)

Species	Weight lb. oz.	kg/g	Name of Angler	Location	Date
SEA FISH					
Angler Fish	71 8	*32,431*	Michael Fitzgerald	Cork (Cóbh) Harbour	5 July 1964
Bass	16 6	*7,427*	James McClelland	Causeway Coast	13 Nov. 1972
Sea Bream (Red)	9 6	*4,252*	P. Maguire	Valentia, Kerry	24 Aug. 1963
Coalfish	24 7	*11,084*	J. E. Hornibrook	Kinsale, Cork	26 Aug. 1967
Cod	42 0	*19,050*	I. L. Stewart	Ballycotton, Cork	1921
Conger	72 0	*32,658*	J. Greene	Valentia, Kerry	June 1914
Dab	1 12½	*0,807*	Ian V. Kerr	Kinsale, Cork	10 Sept. 1963
Dogfish (Greater Spotted)	19 12	*8,958*	Michael Courage	Bray, Co. Wicklow	6 July 1969
Dogfish (Spur)	16 4	*7,370*	Crawford McIvor	Strangford Lough, Co. Down	20 June 1969
Flounder	4 3	*1,899*	J. L. McMonagle	Killala Bay, Co. Mayo	5 Aug. 1963
Garfish	3 10¼	*1,651*	Evan G. Bazzard	Kinsale, Cork	16 Sept. 1967
Gurnard (Grey)	3 1	*1,389*	Brendan Walsh	Rosslare Bay	21 Sept. 1967
Gurnard (Red)	3 9½	*1,630*	James Prescott	Belmullet, Co. Mayo	17 July 1968
Gurnard (Tub)	10 8	*4,762*	Clive Gammon	Belmullet, Co. Mayo	18 June 1970
Haddock	10 13½	*4,918*	F. A. E. Bull	Kinsale, Cork	15 July 1964
Hake	25 5½	*11,495*	Herbert W. Steele	Belfast Lough	28 April 1962
Halibut	156 0	*70,760*	Frank Brogan	Belmullet, Co. Mayo	23 July 1972
John Dory	7 1	*3,203*	Stanley Morrow	Tory Island, Co. Donegal	6 Sept. 1970
Ling	46 8	*21,092*	Andrew J. C. Bull	Kinsale, Cork	26 July 1965
Mackerel	3 8	*1,587*	Roger Ryan	Clogherhead Pier, Co. Louth	1 July 1972
Monkfish	69 0	*31,297*	Mons. Michael Fuchs	Westport, Co. Mayo	1 July 1958
Mullet (Grey)	7 10	*3,458*	Kevin Boyle	Killybegs Pier, Donegal	8 June 1972
Plaice	7 0	*3,175*	Ernest Yemen	Portrush, Antrim	28 Sept. 1964
Pollack	19 3	*8,703*	J. N. Hearne	Ballycotton, Cork	1904
Pouting	4 10	*2,097*	W. G. Pales	Ballycotton, Cork	1937
Ray (Blonde)	36 8	*16,556*	D. Minchin	Cork (Cóbh) Harbour	9 Sept. 1964
Ray (Thornback)	37 0	*16,782*	M. J. Fitzgerald	Kinsale, Cork	28 May 1961
Shark (Blue)	206 0	*93,440*	J. L. McMonagle	Achill, Co. Mayo	7 Oct. 1959
Shark (Porbeagle)	365 0	*165,561*	Dr. M. O'Donel Browne	Keem Bay, Achill, Co. Mayo	28 Sept. 1932
Skate (Common)	221 0	*100,243*	T. Tucker	Ballycotton, Cork	1913
Skate (White)	165 0	*74,842*	Jack Stack	Clew Bay, Westport, Co. Mayo	7 Aug. 1966
Sting Ray	51 0	*23,133*	John K. White	Kilfenora Strand, Fenet	8 Aug. 1970
Tope	60 12	*27,555*	Crawford McIvor	Strangford Lough, Co. Down	12 Sept. 1968
Turbot	26 8	*12,020*	J. F. Eldridge	Valentia, Kerry	1915
Whiting	4 8½	*2,055*	Eddie Boyle	Kinsale, Cork	4 Aug. 1969
Wrasse (Ballan)	7 6	*3,345*	Anthony J. King	Killybegs, Donegal	26 July 1964
FRESHWATER FISH					
Bream	11 12	*5,329*	A. Pike	River Blackwater, Co. Monaghan	July 1882
Carp	18 12	*8,504*	John Roberts	Abbey Lake	6 June 1958
Dace	1 2	*0,510*	John T. Henry	River Blackwater, Cappoquin	8 Aug. 1966
Eel (River)	5 15	*2,693*	Edmund Hawksworth	River Shannon, Clondra	25 Sept. 1968
Perch	5 8	*2,494*	S. Drum	Lough Erne	1946
Pike	42 0*	*19,050*	M. Watkins	River Barrow	22 Mar. 1964
Roach	2 13½	*1,289*	Lawrie Robinson	River Blackwater, Cappoquin	11 Aug. 1970
	2 13½	*1,289*	Ronald Frost	River Blackwater, Cappoquin	29 Aug. 1972
Rudd	3 1	*1,389*	A. E. Biddlecombe	Kilglass Lake	27 June 1959
Rudd-Bream hybrid	5 5	*2,409*	W. Walker	Coosan Lough, Garnafailagh, Athlone	5 June 1963
Salmon	57 0†	*25,854*	M. Maher	River Suir	1874
Tench	7 13¼	*3,550*	R. Webb	River Shannon, Lanesboro	25 May 1971
Brown Trout (Lake)	26 2††	*11,850*	William Meares	Lough Ennell	15 July 1894
Brown Trout (River)	20 0	*9,071*	Major Hugh H. Place	River Shannon, Corbally	22 Feb. 1957
Sea Trout	12 0	*5,443*	Thomas Regan	River Dargle, Co. Wicklow	3 Oct. 1958

* *A Pike in excess of 92 lb.* 41 kg *is reputed to have been landed from the Shannon at Portumna, County Galway, in c. 1796.*

† *A 58 lb.* 26 kg *Salmon was reported from the River Shannon in 1872 while one of 62 lb.* 28 kg *was taken in a net on the lower Shannon on 27 March 1925.*

†† *A 35½ lb.* 16 kg 102 *Brown Trout is repu ed to have been caught at Turlaghvan, near Tuam, in August 1738. "Pepper's Ghost", the 30 lb. 8 oz.* 13 kg 834 *fish caught by J. W. Pepper in Lough Derg in 1860 has now been shown to have been a salmon.*

ARCHERY

Earliest references Late Palaeolithic drawings of archers indicate that bows and arrows are an invention of *c.* 15,000 B.C. Archery developed as an organized sport at least as early as the 4th century A.D. The oldest archery body in the British Isles is the Royal Company of Archers, the Sovereign's bodyguard for Scotland, dating from 1676, though the Ancient Scorton Arrow meeting in Yorkshire was first staged in 1673. The world governing body is the *Fédération Internationale de Tir à l'Arc* (FITA), founded in 1931.

Flight shooting The longest recorded distance ever shot is 1 mile 101 yds 1 ft 9 in *1 701,89 m* in the unlimited footbow class by the professional Harry Drake of Lakeside, California, U.S.A. at Ivanpah Dry Lake, California on 3 Oct. 1970. Drake also holds the flight records for the handbow at 856 yds 1 ft 8 in *783,23 m* and the crossbow at 1,359 yds 2 ft 5 in *1 243,4 m* both at Ivanpah Dry Lake on 14–15 Oct. 1967.

The British record is 647 yds 1 ft 11 in *592,19 m* by Alan Webster at York on 20 April 1969.

HIGHEST SCORES

World The world records for a single FITA Round are: men 1,268 points (possible 1,440) by John C. Williams (U.S.A.) at Munich, West Germany on 7–8 Sept. 1972, and women 1,236 points (possible 1,440) by Emma Gapchenko (U.S.S.R.) at Novaya Kakhovka, U.S.S.R. on 22 April 1973.

The record for a FITA Double Round is 2,528 points (possible 2,880) by Williams in securing his Olympic title (see above). The feminine record is 2,426 points by Anna Keunova (U.S.S.R.) at Tallin, U.S.S.R. on 5 June 1972.

British York Round (6 dozen at 100 yds, 4 dozen at 80 yds and 2 dozen at 60 yds).
Single Round, 1,097 J. Ian Dixon at Oxford, on 4 July 1968.
Double Round, 2,138 Roy D. Matthews at Oxford, on 3–4 July 1968.
Hereford (Women) (6 dozen at 80 yds, 4 dozen at 60 yds and 2 dozen at 50 yds).
Single Round, 1,102 Miss Pauline Edwards at Oxford, 27 June 1973.
Double Round, 2,200 Miss Pauline Edwards at Oxford, 27–28 June 1973.
FITA Round (Men) (3 dozen each at 90, 70, 50 and 30 m).
Single Round, 1,218 Roy D. Matthews at Windermere, Westmorland, 9 June 1973.
Double Round, 2,386 Roy D. Matthews at Windermere, Westmorland, 9–10 June 1973.
FITA Round (Women's) (3 dozen each at 70,60,50 and 30 m).
Single Round, 1,211 Miss Lynne A. Thomas at Warsaw, Poland, on 19–20 Sept. 1970.
Double Round, 2,313 Mrs. Lynne A. Evans (*née* Thomas) at Munich, West Germany, 7–10 Sept. 1972.

Most titles The greatest number of world titles (instituted 1931) ever won by a man is four by H. Deutgen (Sweden) in

1947–48–49–50. The greatest number won by a woman is seven by Mrs. Janina Spychajowa-Kurkowska (Poland) in 1931–32–33–34, 1936, 1939 and 1947.

The greatest number of British Championships is 12 by Horace A. Ford (b. 1822) between 1849 and 1867, and 23 by Miss Alice Blanche Legh (1855–1948) in 1881, 1886–87–88–89–90–91–92, 1895, 1898–99–1900, 1902–03–04–05–06–07–08–09, 1913 and 1921–22. Miss Legh was inhibited from winning from 1882 to 1885—because her mother Mrs. Piers Legh was Champion and also for four further years 1915 to 1918 because there were no Championships held owing to the first World War.

Marathon The highest recorded score over 24 hours by a pair of archers is 30,709 during 31 Portsmouth Rounds (60 arrows at 20 yds with a 2 in *5 cm* diameter 10 ring) shot by Barry Davison and Cpl. Bob Pritchard at the Odeon Cinema, Colchester, Essex, on 26–27 Feb. 1972.

For Athletics see Track and Field Athletics.

BADMINTON

Origins The game was devised *c.* 1863 at Badminton Hall in Gloucestershire, the seat of the Dukes of Beaufort.

Thomas Cup The International Championship or Thomas Cup (instituted 1948) has been won 5 times by Indonesia in 1957–58, 1960–61, 1963–64 ,1970–71 and 1972–73.

Miss Alice Blanche Legh (right), whose British Archery Championships spanned 41 years, with her mother and sister

Most titles Most wins in the All-England Championships (instituted 1899):

Event	Times	Holder	Dates
Men's Singles	7	Erland Kops (Denmark)	1958, 1960–63, 1965, 1967
Women's Singles	10	Mrs. G. C. K. Hashman (*née* Judy Devlin) (U.S.A.)	1954, 1957–58, 1960–64, 1966–67
Most titles (*i.e.* including doubles):			
Men	21	G. A. Thomas (later Sir George Thomas, Bt. d. 1972)	from 1903 to 1928
Women	17	Miss M. Lucas (U.K.)	from 1899 to 1910
	17	Mrs. G. C. K. Hashman (*née* Judy Devlin) (U.S.A.)	from 1954 to 1967

Most internationals Most international appearances:

	Times	Men	Times	Women
England	100	A. D. Jordan, M.B.E., 1951 to 1970	52	Mrs. W. C. E. Rogers (*née* Cooley), 1955 to 1969
Ireland	50	K. Carlisle, 1954 to 1972	53	Miss Y. Kelly, 1955 to 1973
Scotland	53	R. S. McCoig, 1956 to 1973	28	Miss C. E. Dunglison, 1956 to 1967
Wales	20	D. Colmer, 1964 to 1970	22	Mrs. L. W. Myers, 1928 to 1939

The Ladies International Championship or Uber Cup (instituted 1956) has been most often won by Japan with a fourth win in 1972.

Inter County Championships The most successful county has been Surrey with 17 wins between 1955 and 1973. The championships were instituted on 30 Oct. 1930.

Longest hit Frank Rugani drove a shuttlecock 79 ft 8½ in *24,29 m* in tests at San Jose, California, U.S.A., on 29 Feb. 1964.

Longest games The longest recorded game has been one of 291 hrs by 5 boys from Kirkham Grammar School, Lancs. from 7 July to 19 July 1972, who maintained continuous singles. The longest doubles marathon has been one of 205 hrs 6 min maintained by 8 players (4 men and 4 girls) from Carlisle Y.M.C.A., Cumberland between 18 and 26 Aug. 1972 playing in two teams with 6 hr shifts.

Shortest Game In the 1969 Uber Cup in Jakarta, Indonesia, Miss N. Takagi (Japan) beat Miss P. Tumengkol in 9 min.

BASEBALL

Earliest game "Baste-Ball" was a pursuit banned at Princeton, New Jersey, U.S.A., as early as 1786. On 4 Feb. 1962, it was claimed in *Nedelya*, the weekly supplement to the Soviet newspaper *Izvestiya*, that "Beizbol" was an old Russian game. The earliest baseball game under the Cartwright rules was at Hoboken, New Jersey, U.S.A., on 19 June 1846, with the New York Nine beating the Knickerbockers 23–1 in 4 innings.

Highest batting average The highest average in a career is .367 by Tyrus Raymond Cobb (1886–1961), the "Georgia Peach" of Augusta, Anniston, Detroit (1905–26) and Philadelphia

(1927–28). During his career Ty Cobb made a record 2,244 runs from a record 4,191 hits made during a record 11,429 times at bat in a record 3,033 major league games.

HOME RUNS

Most The highest number of home runs hit in a major league career is the 714 by George Herman ("Babe") Ruth (1895–1948) of Baltimore-Providence, Boston Red Sox (American League), New York Yankees and Boston (National League), between 1914 and 1935. His major league record for home runs in one year is 60 in 154 games between 15 April and 30 Sept. 1927. Roger Maris (b. 1935) (New York Yankees) hit 61 homers in a 162-game schedule in 1961. Josh Gibson (1912–1947) of Homestead Grays, a Negro League club, achieved a career total of 800 homers and 84 in one season, and in 1972 was elected to the Hall of Fame.

Longest The longest home run ever measured was one of 188,4 m *618 ft* by Roy Edward Carlyle in a minor league game at Emeryville Ball Park, California, U.S.A., on 4 July 1929. In 1919 "Babe" Ruth hit a 178,9 m *587 ft* homer in a Boston Red Sox *v.* New York Giants match at Tampa, Florida, U.S.A. The longest throw (ball weighs between 141 and 148 g *5 and 5¼ oz.* is 135,88 m *445 ft* 10 in by Glen Gorbaus on 1 Aug. 1957. The longest throw by a woman is 90,2 m *296 ft* by Miss Mildred "Babe" Didrikson (later Mrs. George Zaharis) (U.S.) (1914–56) at Jersey City, New Jersey, U.S.A. on 25 July 1931. The fastest time for circling bases is 13.3 sec by Evar Swanson at Columbus, Ohio, in 1932.

Pitching The first "perfect game" (no hits, no runs) pitched in a World Series was by Don Larsen (New York Yankees) with 97 pitches (71 in the strike zone) against Brooklyn Dodgers on 8 Oct. 1956.

Highest earnings The greatest earnings of a baseball player is $1,091,477 amassed by "Babe" Ruth between 1914 and 1938.

Record attendances and receipts The World Series record attendance is 420,784 (6 games with total receipts of $2,626,973.44) when the Los Angeles (ex-Brooklyn) Dodgers beat the Chicago White Sox 4–2 on 1–8 Oct. 1959. The single game record is 92,706 for the fifth game (receipts $552,774.77) at the Memorial Coliseum, Los Angeles, California, on 6 Oct. 1959. The record net receipts for a series has been $3,954,542 from a paid attendance of 363,149 who saw the Oakland A's beat the Cincinnati Reds 4–3 on 14–22 Oct. 1972. The highest seating capacity in a baseball stadium is 76,977 in the Cleveland Municipal Stadium, Ohio, U.S.A.

The all-time season record for attendances for both leagues has been 29,193,417 in 1971.

"Babe" Ruth, the most famous baseball player ever, hitter of the longest major league home run at 587 ft *178,9 m*

Highest catch Joe Spring (San Francisco Seals) caught a baseball at the fifth attempt dropped from an airship at about 1,000 ft *304 m* over Treasure Island, San Francisco, U.S.A. in 1939. The force of the ball broke his jaw.

BASKETBALL

Origins The game of "Pok-ta-Pok" was played in the 7th century B.C., by the Mayas in Mexico, and closely resembled basketball in its concept. "Ollamalitzli" was a variation of this game, played by the Aztecs in Mexico as late as the 16th century. If the solid rubber ball was put through a fixed stone ring the player was entitled to the clothing of all the spectators. Modern basketball was devised by the Canadian-born Dr. James A. Naismith (1861–1939) at the Training School of the International Y.M.C.A. College at Springfield, Massachusetts, U.S.A., in December 1891 and first played on 20 Jan. 1892. The game is now a global activity. The International Amateur Basketball Federation (F.I.B.A.) was founded in 1932, and the Amateur Basket Ball Association, the governing body for the game in England, was founded in 1936.

Olympic Champions The U.S.A. won all seven Olympic titles from the time the sport was introduced to the Games in 1936 until 1968, without losing a single match. In 1972 in Munich their run of 64 consecutive victories in matches in the Olympic Games was broken when they lost 50–51 to the U.S.S.R. in the Final match.

World Champions Brazil are the only country to win the World Championship (instituted 1950) on more than one occasion. They won the title in 1959 and again in 1963.

British International Championship The most British International Championships have been won by England with five victories, out of the eleven competitions since the tournament was introduced in 1960.

American Professional titles The most National Basketball Association titles (instituted 1947), played for between the leading professional teams in the United States, have been won by the Boston Celtics with 11 victories.

English National Champions The most English National Championship Cup wins (instituted 1936) have been by London Central Y.M.C.A., with eight wins in 1957, 58, 60, 62, 63, 64, 1967 and 69.

English Women's titles Most English Women's titles (instituted 1965) have been won by the Malory Club of South London, with 4 wins.

Highest score The highest score recorded in any match is 242 by Bestwood against Meadow Jets (222–20) at Nottingham, England on 20 Jan. 1972.

Highest aggregate The highest aggregate score in a match is 316 in a match between the Philadelphia Warriors (169 points) and the New York Knickerbockers (147 points) at Hershey, Pennsylvania on 2 March 1962.

International matches The highest score recorded in an international match is 153 by U.S.S.R. against Switzerland (25) on 4 June 1956 in the European Women's Championship. The highest score in a men's international is 148 by Sweden against Norway (44) on 13 April 1968 in Reykjavik, Iceland.

Highest Individual score Clarence (Bevo) Francis of Rio Grande College, Rio Grande, Ohio, U.S.A., scored 150 points in a single match in 1954.

The highest individual score in Britain is 142 points by Peter Beresford, playing for Cavendish School, Hemel Hempstead against Sir Frederic Osborne School in the Hertfordshire schools' under-19 cup in May 1973.

Most points in career Wilton Norman Chamberlain (b. 21 Aug. 1936), reached a total of 30,003 points in N.B.A. matches on 16 Feb. 1972, in his 941st match. The record for the most points scored in a season, is 4,065 by Travis Grant for Kentucky State in 1971–72.

Tallest players The tallest player of all time has been Emili Rached of Brazil, who competed in the 1971 Pan American Games when measuring 233 cm *7 ft 7⅝ in.* The tallest woman player is Gwendalin Bachman of Englewood, California at 7 ft 0¼ in *213 cm.* The tallest British player has been the 7 ft 4¾ in *225 cm* tall Christopher Greener (see p. 16) of London Latvians whose International debut for England was *v.* France on 17 Dec. 1969.

Most expensive In 1972 Peter Press Maravich of Louisiana State University signed a 5 year contract with Atlanta Hawks for a reputed $1.5 to $2.0 million *£600,000 to £800,000.*

Most accurate The greatest goal shooting demonstration has been by the professional trick specialist Bunny Levitt 5 ft 4 in *162 cm* who in 1935 in Chicago scored 499 consecutive free throws. In 1936 he did 561 in practice. Ted St. Martin of Riverdale, California, scored 10,944 out of 12,099 free throws for a 90.4 per cent average on 30–31 July 1971.

Longest recorded goal The longest recorded field goal in a match is 84 ft 11 in *25,88 m* by George Line, aged 20, of the University of Alabama against University of North Carolina at Tuscaloosa, Alabama, in January 1955. In practice in 1953, Larry Slinkard at Arlington Heights High School, Illinois, scored with a shot from 88 ft *26,82 m.*

Marathon records The longest recorded basketball marathon with 24 players (substitutes permitted) is 144 hours by school teams at William Tennent High School, Warminster, Pennsylvania ending on 6 June 1973. The longest recorded marathon between two teams of five without substitutes (or rest breaks) is 44 hours by Galt High School, Galt, California ending 18 April 1973. The best time with rest breaks (now not allowed) is 46 hrs

"Curly" Neal of the *Harlem Globetrotters*, the most spectacular of all basketball teams

38 min achieved at H.M. Training Prison, Beechworth, Victoria, Australia.

Most travelled team The Harlem Globetrotters have travelled over 5,000,000 miles *8 000 000 km,* visited 87 countries on six continents, and have been watched by an estimated 53,000,000. The team was founded by the London-born Abraham M. Saperstein (1903–66) of Chicago, Illinois, U.S.A., and their first game was played at Hinckley, Illinois on 7 Jan. 1927. The team have recorded over 9,000 victories, with fewer than 400 defeats, but they have been entertainers rather than competitive players for much of their existence.

Largest ever gate The Harlem Globetrotters (U.S.A.) played an exhibition in front of 75,000 in the Olympic Stadium, West Berlin, Germany, in 1951. The largest indoor basketball attendance was at the Astrodome, Houston, Texas, U.S.A., where 52,693 watched the match between University of Houston and University of California at Los Angeles (U.C.L.A.), on 20 Jan. 1968.

BILLIARDS

Earliest mention The earliest recorded mention of billiards was in France in 1429, and it was mentioned in England in 1588 in inventories of the Duke of Norfolk's Howard House and the Earl of Leicester's property at Wanstead House, Essex. The first recorded public billiards room in England was the Piazza, Covent Garden, London, in the early part of the 19th century. Rubber cushions were introduced in 1835 and slate beds in 1836.

Highest breaks Tom Reece (1873–1953) made an unfinished break of 499,135, including 249,152 cradle cannons (2 points each), in 85 hrs 49 min against Joe Chapman at Burroughes' Hall, Soho Square, London, between 3 June and 6 July 1907. This was not recognized because press and public were not continuously present. The highest certified break made by the anchor cannon is 42,746 by W. Cook (England) from 29 May to 7 June 1907. The official world record under the then baulk-line rule is 1,784 by Joe Davis, O.B.E. (b. 15 April 1901) in the United Kingdom Championship on 29 May 1936. Walter Lindrum (Australia) made an official break of 4,137 in 2 hrs 55 min against Joe Davis at Thurston's on 19–20 Jan. 1932, before the baulk-line rule was in force. The amateur record is 702 by Robert Marshall *v.* Tom Cleary, both of Australia, in the Australian Amateur Championship at Brisbane on 17 Sept.

1953. Davis has an unofficial personal best of 2,502 (mostly pendulum cannons) in a match against Tom Newman (1894–1943) (England) in Manchester in 1930.

Fastest Walter Lindrum, M.B.E. (1898–1960) of Australia
century made an unofficial 100 break in 27.5 sec in Australia on 10 Oct. 1952. His official record is 100 in 46.0 sec set in Sydney in 1941.

Most The greatest number of world championship titles
world (instituted 1870) won by one player is eight by John
titles Roberts, Jnr. (England) in 1870 (twice), 1871, 1875 (twice), 1877 and 1885 (twice). The greatest number of United Kingdom titles (instituted 1934) won by any player is seven (1934–39 and 1947) by Joe Davis (England), who also won four world titles (1928–30 and 1932) before the series was discontinued in 1934. Willie Hoppe (U.S.A.) won 51 "world" titles in the United States variants of the game between 1906 and 1952.

Most The record for world amateur titles is four by Robert
amateur Marshall (Australia) in 1936–38–51–62. The greatest
titles number of British Amateur Championships (instituted 1888) ever won is eight by Sidney H. Fry (1893 to 1925) and A. Leslie Driffield (1952–54, 1957–59, 1962 and 1967).

Bar billiards The duration record for bar billiards is 120 hr 15 min
marathon by R. D. Winsborough, P. Duncliffe, M. Corby, P. Schooley, and J. Southon, at the Royal Hussar, Brighton, Sussex, England ending on 30 May 1973. The score was 1,448,350.

Walter Lindrum of Australia, the billiard player with the fastest recorded 100 break in 27.5 sec

BOBSLEIGH

Origins The oldest known sledge is dated *c.* 6500 B.C. and came from Heinola, southern Finland. The word toboggan comes from the Micmac American Indian word *tobaakan*. The oldest bobsleigh club in the world is St. Moritz Tobogganing Club, home of the Cresta Run, founded in 1887. Modern world championships were inaugurated in 1924. Four-man bobs were included in the first Winter Olympic Games at Chamonix in 1924 and two-man boblets from the third Games at Lake Placid, U.S.A., in 1932.

Olympic The Olympic four-man bob title has been won four
and world times by Switzerland (1924–36–56–72). The U.S.A.
titles (1932, 1936), Italy (1956, 1968) and Germany (1952 and (West) 1972) have won the Olympic boblet event twice.

The world four-man bob title has been won eleven times by Switzerland (1924–36–39–47–54–55–56–57–1971–72–73). Italy won the two-man title 13 times (1954–56–57–58–59–60–61–62–63–66–68–69–71). Eugenio Monti (Italy) (b. 23 Jan. 1928) has been a member of eleven world championship crews.

TOBOGGANING

Cresta Run The skeleton one-man toboggan dates, in its present form, from 1892. On the 1,325 yds *1 210 m* long Cresta Run at St. Moritz, Switzerland, dating from 1884 the record from the Junction (2,868 ft [*875 m*]) is 43.45 sec by Bruno Bischofberger of Switzerland in Feb. 1973. The record from Top (3,981 ft [*945 m*]) is 54.21 sec by Paul Marou of Italy in 1971, reaching 85 m.p.h. *136 km/h* near the finish.

The greatest number of wins in the Cresta Run Grand National (inst. 1885) is eight by the 1948 Olympic champion Nino Bibbia (Italy) (b. 9 Sept 1924) in 1960–61–62–63–64–66–68–73. The greatest number of wins in the Cresta Run Curzon Cup (inst. in 1910) is eight by Bibbia in 1950–57–58–60–62–63–64–69 who hence won the Double in 1960–62–63–64.

Eugenio Monti holder of 11 world boblet championships in action at Garmisch-Partenkirchen in 1958

LUGEING

In lugeing the rider adopts a sitting, as opposed to a prone position. It was largely developed by British tourists at Klosters, Switzerland, from 1883. The first European championships were at Reichenberg, East Germany, in 1914 and the first world championships at Oslo, Norway, in 1953. The International Luge Federation was formed in 1957. Lugeing attracts more than 15,000 competitors in Austria.

Most world titles The most successful rider in the world championships is Thomas Köhler (East Germany) (b. 25 June 1940), who won the single-seater title in 1962, 1964 (Olympic), and 1967 and shared the two-seater title in 1967 and 1968 (Olympic). In the women's championship Otrun Enderlein (East Germany) (b. 12 Jan. 1943) has won thrice 1964 (Olympic), 1965 and 1967.

Highest speed The fastest luge run is at Krynica, Poland, where speeds of more than 80 m.p.h. *128 km/h* have been recorded.

BOWLING (TEN PIN)

Origins The ancient German game of nine-pins was exported to the United States in the early 17th century. In about 1845 the Connecticut and New Haven State Legislatures prohibited the game so a tenth pin was added to evade the ban; but there is some evidence of 10 pins being used in Suffolk about 300 years ago.

In the United States there were 8,922 bowling establishments with 139,483 bowling lanes and 29,500,000 bowlers in 1970–71. The world's largest bowling centre is the Tōkyō World Lanes Centre, Japan with 252 lanes. The largest in Europe is the Excel Bowl at Nottingham, England, where the game was introduced in 1960, with 48 lanes on two floors (24 on each floor).

Highest scores World The highest individual score for three sanctioned games (possible 900) is 886 by Albert (Allie) Brandt of Lockport, New York, U.S.A., on 25 Oct. 1939. The record for consecutive strikes in sanctioned match play is 29 by Frank Caruana at Buffalo, New York, on 5 Mar. 1924, and 29 by Max Stein at Los Angeles, California, on 8 Oct. 1939. The highest number of sanctioned 300 games is 24 (till July 1973) by Elvin Mesger of Sullivan, Missouri, U.S.A. The maximum 900 for a three-game series has been recorded three times in unsanctioned games—by Leo Bentley at Lorain, Ohio, U.S.A., on 26 March 1931; by Joe Sargent at Rochester, New York State, U.S.A., in 1934, and by Jim Margie in Philadelphia, Pennsylvania, U.S.A., on 4 Feb. 1937. Such series must have consisted of 36 consecutive strikes (*i.e.* all pins down with one ball).

United Kingdom The United Kingdom record for a three-game series is 775 by Geoffrey Liddiard at Harrow, Greater London on 3 Oct. 1971. The record score for a single game is 300, first achieved by Albert Kirkham, aged 34, of Burslem, Staffordshire, on 5 Dec. 1965, which has since been equalled on several occasions. The highest score for a woman player is 299 by Mrs. Carole Cuthbert, 38, at the Airport Bowl, West London on 16 Mar. 1972.

World championships The world championships were instituted in 1954. The highest pinfall in the individual men's event is 5,963 (in 28 games) by Ed. Luther (U.S.) at Milwaukee, Wisconsin, in 1971.

Marathon Bob W. Petersen (U.S.A.) bowled 1,252 games (knocked down 104,553 pins) scoring 1,228 strikes, walked 192 miles *308 km*, and lifted 12½ tons/*tonnes* in 82 hrs 20 min at Sacramento, California on 7–10 June 1973.

SKITTLES

The duration record for knocking down skittles (9-pins) is 70 hrs (40,102 pins down) by seven skittlers from Westbury-on-Severn at the White Hart Inn, Aston Crews, Herefordshire ending on 26 Feb. 1973. The highest score in 24 hrs is 97,643 pins by 12 players from The Plough Inn, Everden, Northamptonshire, on 7–8 July 1972.

BOWLS (LAWN)

Origins Bowls can be traced back to at least the 13th century in England. The Southampton Town Bowling was formed in 1299. After falling into disrepute, the game was rescued by the bowlers of Scotland who, headed by W. W. Mitchell, framed the modern rules in 1848–49.

World title In the inaugural World Championship held in Sydney, Australia in October 1966 the Singles Title was won by David John Bryant (b. 1931) (England) and the team title (Leonard Cup) by Australia. In the second Championships at Worthing in 1972 the singles was won by Malwyn Evans (Wales) and Scotland won the Leonard Cup.

Most title wins In the annual International Championships (instituted 1903) Scotland have won 26 times to England's 20. The most consecutive wins are eight by Scotland from 1965 to 1972.

English titles The record number of English Bowls Association championships is 11 won or shared by David Bryant, M.B.E., of Clevedon, Somerset. His record of four Singles wins (1960, 1966, 1971 and 1972) is equalled by E. Percy C. Baker (Poole Park, Dorset) (1932, 1946, 1952 and 1955). Bryant has also shared in two Pairs wins (1965 and 1969), a Triples win (1966) and uniquely is involved in all four titles with four Rinks or Fours championships (1957, 1968, 1969 and 1971).

Most internationals The greatest number of international appearances by any bowler is 78 reached by Syd Thompson for Ireland in 1973.

Syd Thompson of Ireland, who has made 78 international appearances in lawn bowls

BOXING

Earliest references Boxing with gloves was depicted on a fresco from the Isle of Thera, Greece which has been dated 1520 B.C. The earliest prize-ring code of rules was formulated in England on 16 Aug. 1743 by the champion pugilist Jack Broughton (1704–89), who reigned from 1729 to 1750. Boxing, which had, in 1867, come under the Queensberry Rules formulated for John Sholto Douglas, 8th Marquess of Queensberry, was not established as a legal sport in Britain until after the ruling R. v. Roberts and others of Mr. Justice Grantham on 24 April 1901, following the death of Billy Smith (Murray Livingstone).

Longest fight The longest recorded fight with gloves was between Andy Bowen of New Orleans (k. 1894) and Jack Burke in New Orleans, Louisiana, U.S.A., on 6–7 April 1893.

The fight lasted 110 rounds and 7 hr 19 min from 9.15 p.m. to 4.34 a.m., but was declared a no contest when both men were unable to continue. The longest recorded bare knuckle fight was one of 6 hr 15 min between James Kelly and Jack Smith at Melbourne Australia, on 19 Oct. 1856. The greatest recorded number of rounds is 278 in 4 hr 30 min when Jack Jones beat Patsy Tunney in Cheshire in 1825.

Shortest fight There is a distinction between the quickest knock-out and the shortest fight. A knock out in $10\frac{1}{2}$ sec (including a 10 sec count) occurred on 26 Sept. 1946, when Al Couture struck Ralph Walton while the latter was adjusting a gum shield in his corner at Lewiston, Maine, U.S.A. If the time was accurately taken it is clear that Couture must have been more than half-way across the ring from his own corner at the opening bell. The shortest fight on record appears to be one at Palmerston, New Zealand on 8 July 1952 when Ross Cleverly (R.N.Z.A.F.) floored D. Emerson (Pahiatua) with the first punch and the referee stopped the contest with a count 7 sec from the bell. Teddie Barker (Swindon) scored a technical knock-out over Bob Roberts (Nigeria) at the first blow in a welterweight fight at Maesteg, Glamorganshire, Wales, on 2 Sept. 1957. The referee, Joe Brimell, stopped the fight without a count 10 sec from the bell.

The shortest world heavyweight title fight occurred when Tommy Burns (b. 17 June 1881 d. 10 May 1955) (née Noah Brusso) of Canada knocked out Jem Roche in 1 min 28 sec in Dublin, Ireland, on 17 March 1908. The duration of the Clay v. Liston fight at Lewiston, Maine, U.S.A., on 25 May 1965 was 1 min 52 sec (including the count) as timed from the video tape recordings, despite a ringside announcement giving a time of 1 min. Charles "Sonny" Liston (b. 8 May 1932) died 30 Dec. 1970. The shortest world title fight was when Al McCoy knocked out George Chip in 45 sec for the middleweight crown in New York on 7 April 1914. The shortest ever British title fight was one of 40 sec (including the count), when Dave Charnley knocked out David "Darkie" Hughes in a lightweight championship defence in Nottingham on 20 Nov. 1961.

Tallest The tallest boxer to fight professionally was Gogea Mitu (b. 1914) of Romania in 1935. He was 7 ft 4 in 223 cm and weighed 23 st. 5 lb. 148 kg (327 lb.). John Rankin, who won a fight in New Orleans, Louisiana, U.S.A., in November 1967, was reputedly also 7 ft 4 in 223 cm.

WORLD HEAVYWEIGHT CHAMPIONS

Longest and shortest reigns The longest reign of any world heavyweight champion is 11 years 8 months and 7 days by Joe Louis (born Joseph Louis Barrow, Lafayette, Alabama, 13 May 1914), from 22 June 1937, when he knocked out

Ross Cleverly (N.Z.) winner of the shortest boxing match on record

James J. Braddock in the eighth round at Chicago, Illinois, U.S.A., until announcing his retirement on 1 March 1949. During his reign Louis made a record 25 defences of his title. The shortest reign was by Primo Carnera (Italy) for 350 days from 29 June 1933 to 14 June 1934. However, if the disputed title claim of Marvin Hart is allowed, his reign from 3 July 1905 to 23 Feb. 1906 was only 235 days.

Heaviest and lightest The heaviest world champion was Primo Carnera (1906–67) of Italy, the "Ambling Alp", who won the title from Jack Sharkey in 6 rounds in New York City, N.Y., U.S.A., on 29 June 1933. He scaled 267 lb. (19 st. 1 lb. [121 kg]) for this fight but his peak weight was 270 lb. 122 kg. He had an expanded chest measurement of 53 in 134 cm, the longest reach at $85\frac{1}{2}$ in 217 cm (finger tip to finger tip) and also the largest fists with a $14\frac{3}{4}$ in. 37 cm circumference. The lightest champion was Robert Prometheus Fitzsimmons (1862–1917), who was born at Helston, Cornwall, and at a weight of 167 lb. (11 st. 13 lb. [75 kg]), won the title by knocking out James J. Corbett in 14 rounds at Carson City, Nevada, U.S.A., on 17 March 1897.

The greatest differential in a world title fight was 86 lb. 39 kg between Carnera (270 lb. or 19 st. 4 lb. [122 kg]) and Tommy Loughran (184 lb. or 13 st. 2 lb. [83 kg]) of the U.S.A., when the former won on points at Miami, Florida, U.S.A., on 1 March 1934.

Tallest and shortest The tallest world champion according to measurements by the Physical Education Director of the Hemingway Gymnasium, Harvard University, was Carnera at 6 ft 5.4 in 196,59 cm although he was widely reported and believed to be up to 6 ft $8\frac{1}{2}$ in 204 cm. Jess Willard (1881–1968), who won the title in 1915, often stated to be 6 ft $6\frac{1}{4}$ in 199 cm was in fact 6 ft 5.25 in 196,21 cm. The shortest was Tommy Burns (1881–1955) of Canada, world champion from

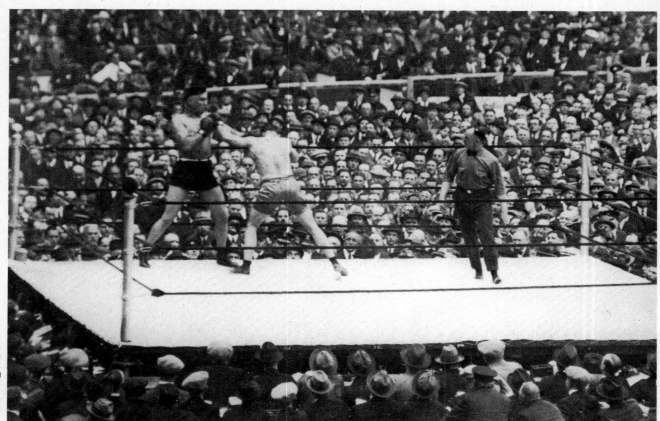

Jess Willard (left) the longest lived heavyweight boxing champion, seen in his 40th year beating Floyd Johnson in 1923

23 Feb. 1906 to 26 Dec. 1908, who stood 5 ft 7 in *170 cm* and weighed 12 st 11 lb. *81 kg.*

Oldest and youngest The oldest man to win the heavyweight crown was Jersey Joe Walcott (b. Arnold Raymond Cream, 31 Jan. 1914 at Merchantville, New Jersey, U.S.A.) who knocked out Ezzard Charles on 18 July 1951 in Pittsburgh, Pennsylvania, when aged 37 years 168 days. Walcott was the oldest holder at 38 years 7 months 23 days losing his title to Marciano on 23 Sept. 1952 and in 1953 the oldest challenger. The youngest age at which the world title has been won is 21 years 331 days by Floyd Patterson (b. Waco, North Carolina, 4 Jan. 1935) of the U.S.A. After the retirement of Marciano, Patterson won the vacant title by beating Archie Moore in 5 rounds in Chicago, Illinois, U.S.A., on 30 Nov. 1956. He is also the only man ever to regain the heavyweight championship. He lost to Ingemar Johansson (Sweden) on 26 June 1959 but defeated him on 20 June 1960 at the New York Polo Grounds Stadium.

Longest lived The longest lived of any heavyweight champion of the world has been Jess Willard (U.S.A.), who was born 29 Dec. 1881 at St. Clere, Kansas, and died 15 Dec. 1968 at Pacoima, California aged 86 years 351 days.

Earliest title fight The first world heavyweight title fight, with gloves and 3 min rounds, was that between John Lawrence Sullivan (b. 15 Oct. 1858 d. 2 Feb. 1918) and "Gentleman" James J. Corbett (b. 1 Sept. 1866 d. 18 Feb. 1933) in New Orleans, Louisiana, U.S.A., on 7 Sept. 1892. Corbett won in 21 rounds.

Undefeated Only James Joseph (Gene) Tunney (b. Greenwich Village, New York City, 25 May 1898) (1926–1928) and Rocky Marciano (1952–56) *finally* retired as champions, undefeated in the heavyweight division.

WORLD CHAMPIONS (any weight)

Longest and shortest reign Joe Louis's heavyweight duration record of 11 years 252 days stands for all divisions. The shortest reign has been 54 days by the French featherweight Eugène

Criqui from 2 June to 26 July 1923. The disputed flyweight champion Emile Pladner (France) reigned only 47 days from 2 March to 18 April 1929, as did also the disputed featherweight champion Dave Sullivan, from 26 Sept. to 11 Nov. 1898.

Youngest and oldest The youngest age at which any world championship has been claimed is 19 years 6 days by Pedlar Palmer (b. 19 Nov. 1876), who won the disputed bantamweight title in London on 25 Nov. 1895. Willie Pep (b. William Papaleo, 20 Nov. 1922), of the U.S.A., won the featherweight crown in New York on his 20th birthday, 22 Nov. 1942. After Young Corbett knocked out Terry McGovern (b. 9 Mar. 1880 d. 26 Feb. 1918) in two rounds at Hartford, Connecticut, U.S.A., on 28 Nov. 1901, neither was able to get his weight down to nine stone, and the featherweight title was claimed by Abe Attell, when aged only 17 years 251 days. The oldest world champion was Archie Moore (b. Archibald Lee Wright, Collinsville, Illinois on either 13 Dec. 1913 or 1916) (U.S.A.) who was recognized as a light heavyweight champion up to early 1962 when his title was removed. He was then believed to be between 45 and 48. Bob Fitzsimmons (1862–1917) had the longest career of any official world titleholder with over 32 years from 1882 to 1914. He won his last world title aged 41 years 174 days in San Francisco, California on 25 Nov. 1903. He was an amateur from 1880 to 1882.

Longest fight The longest world title fight (under Queensberry Rules) was that between the lightweights Joe Gans (b. 25 Nov. 1874 d. 10 Aug. 1910), of the U.S.A., and Oscar Matthew "Battling" Nelson (b. 5 June 1882, d. 7 Feb. 1954), the "Durable Dane", at Goldfield, Nevada, U.S.A., on 3 Sept. 1906. It was terminated in the 42nd round when Gans was declared the winner on a foul.

Most recaptures The only boxer to win a world title five times at one weight is "Sugar" Ray Robinson (b. Walker Smith, Jr., in Detroit, 3 May 1920) of the U.S.A., who beat Carmen Basilio (U.S.A.) in the Chicago

Stadium on 25 March 1958, to regain the world middleweight title for the fourth time. The other title wins were over Jake LaMotta (U.S.A.) in Chicago on 14 Feb. 1951, Randolph Turpin (United Kingdom) in New York on 12 Sept. 1951, Carl "Bobo" Olson (U.S.A.) in Chicago on 9 Dec. 1955, and Gene Fullmer (U.S.A.) in Chicago on 1 May 1957. The record number of title bouts in a career is 33 or 34 (at bantam and featherweight) by George Dixon (b. 29 July 1870, d. 6 Jan. 1909), *alias* Little Chocolate, of the U.S.A., between 1890 and 1901.

Greatest weight span The only man to hold world titles at three weights *simultaneously* was Henry ("Homicide Hank") Armstrong (b. 22 Dec. 1912), now the Rev. Harry Jackson, of the U.S.A., at featherweight, lightweight and welterweight from August to December 1938.

Greatest "tonnage" The greatest "tonnage" recorded in any fight is 700 lb. *317 kg* when Claude "Humphrey" McBride (Oklahoma) 340 lb. (24 st. 4 lb. [*154 kg*]) knocked out Jimmy Black (Houston, Texas), who weighed 360 lb. (25 st. 10 lb. [*163 kg*]) in the third round at Oklahoma City on 4 May 1971. The greatest "tonnage" in a world title fight was 488¾ lb. (34 st. 12¾ lb. [*221 kg 69*]) when Carnera (then 259¼ lb. [*117 kg 59*]) fought Paolino Uzcuden (229½ lb. [*104 kg 09*]) of Spain in Rome on 22 Oct. 1933.

Smallest champion The smallest man to win any world title has been Pascual Perez (b. Mendoza, Argentina, on 4 March 1926) who won the flyweight title in Tōkyō on 26 Nov. 1954 at 7 st. 9 lb. (107 lb. [*48 kg 5*]) and 4 ft 11½ in *1,51 m*. Jimmy Wilde (b. Merthyr Tydfil, 1892–1969) who held the flyweight title from 1916–23 was reputed never to have fought above 7 st. 10 lb. (108 lb. [*48 kg 9*]).

Most knock-downs in title fights Vic Toweel (South Africa) knocked down Danny O'Sullivan of London 14 times in 10 rounds in their world bantamweight fight at Johannesburg on 2 Dec. 1950, before the latter retired.

ALL FIGHTS

Largest purse The greatest purse has been $2,500,000, (*then £1,041,667*) guaranteed to both Joseph Frazier (b. Beaumont, South Carolina, U.S.A., 17 Jan. 1944) and Muhammad Ali Haj (formerly Cassius Marcellus Clay 7th) (b. Louisville, Kentucky, U.S.A., 17 Jan 1942) for their 15-round fight at Madison Square Garden, New York City, on 8 March 1971.

Bare knuckle stake The largest stake ever fought for in this era was $22,500 (*then £4,633*) in the 27-round fight between

Jack Cooper and Wolf Bendoff at Port Elizabeth, South Africa on 29 July 1889.

Attendances Highest The greatest paid attendance at any boxing fight has been 120,757 (with a ringside price of $27.50) for the Tunney *v.* Dempsey world heavyweight title fight at the Sesqui-centennial Stadium, Philadelphia, Pennsylvania, U.S.A., on 23 Sept. 1926. The indoor record is 37,321 at the Clay *v.* Ernie Terrell fight in the Astrodome, Houston, Texas, on 6 Feb. 1967.

The highest non-paying attendance is 135,132 at the Tony Zale *v.* Billy Prior fight at Juneau Park, Milwaukee, Wisconsin, U.S.A., on 18 Aug. 1941.

Lowest The smallest attendance at a world heavyweight title fight was 2,434 at the Clay *v.* Liston fight at Lewiston, Maine, U.S.A., on 25 May 1965.

Highest earnings in career The largest known fortune ever made in a fighting career is an estimated $8,000,000 amassed by Muhammad Ali. Including earnings for refereeing and promoting, Jack Dempsey had grossed over $10,000,000 to 1967.

Most knock-outs The greatest number of finishes classed by the rules prevailing as "knock-outs" in a career (1936 to 1963) is 141 by Archie Moore of the U.S.A. The record for consecutive K.O.'s is 44, set by Lamar Clark of Utah at Las Vegas, Nevada, U.S.A., on 11 Jan. 1960. He knocked out 6 in one night (5 in the first round) at Bingham, Utah, on 1 Dec. 1958.

Most fights The greatest recorded number of fights in a career is 1,309 by Abraham Hollandersky, *alias* Abe the Newsboy (U.S.A.), in the fourteen years from 1905 to 1918. He filled in the time with 387 wrestling bouts (1905–1916).

Hal Bagwell, who was undefeated in 183 consecutive fights, with only five draws

Most fights without loss Hal Bagwell, a lightweight, of Gloucester, England, was reputedly undefeated in 183 consecutive fights, of which only 5 were draws, between 10 Aug. 1938 and 29 Nov. 1948. His record of fights in the war-time period (1939–46), is however very sketchy. He never contested a British title.

Greatest weight difference The greatest weight difference recorded in a major bout is 10 st. (140 lb. [*63 kg*]) between Bob Fitzsimmons (12 st. 4 lb. [*78 kg*]) and Ed Dunkhorst (22 st. 4 lb. [*141 kg*]) at Brooklyn, New York City, N.Y., U.S.A., on 30 April 1900. Fitzsimmons won in two rounds.

Longest career The heavyweight Jem Mace, known as "the gypsy" (b. Norwich, 8 April 1831), had a career lasting 35

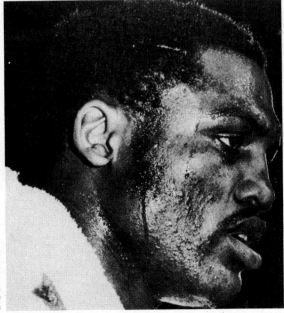

Joe Frazier whose fight with Muhammad Ali in 1971 earned him £385.80 per sec

253

years from 1855 to 1890, but there were several years in which he had only one fight. He died, aged 79, in Jarrow-on-Tyne on 30 Nov., and was buried in Liverpool on 6 Dec. 1910. Walter Edgerton, the "Kentucky Rosebud", knocked out John Henry Johnson aged 45, in 4 rounds at the Broadway A.C., New York City, N.Y., U.S.A., on 4 Feb. 1916, when aged 63.

British titles The most defences of a British heavyweight title is 13 by "Bombardier" Billy Wells (b. 31 Aug. 1889–1967) from 1911 to 1919. The only British boxer to win three Lonsdale Belts outright has been Henry William Cooper, O.B.E. (b. Camberwell, London, 3 May 1934), heavyweight champion (1959–69, 1970–71). He retired on 16 Mar. 1971.

Most Olympic gold medals The only amateur boxer to win three Olympic gold medals is the southpaw László Papp (b. 1926) (Hungary), who took the middleweight (1948) and the light-middleweight titles (1952 and 1956). The only man to win two titles in one celebration was O. L. Kirk (U.S.A.), who took both the bantam and featherweight titles in St. Louis, Missouri, U.S.A., in 1904, when the U.S. won all the titles. In 1908 Great Britain won all the titles.

A.B.A. TITLES

Most The greatest number of A.B.A. titles won by any boxer is 6 by Joseph Steers at middleweight and heavyweight between 1890 and 1893.

Longest span The greatest span of A.B.A. title-winning performances is that of the heavyweight H. Pat Floyd, who won in 1929 and gained his fourth title 17 years later in 1946.

László Papp of Hungary, the only boxer to have won three Olympic gold medals

Class	Instituted	Wins	Name	Years
Flyweight (8 st. [50 kg 80] or under)	1920	5	T. Pardoe	1929–33
Bantamweight (8 st. 7 lb. [54 kg] or under)	1884	4	W. W. Allen	1911–12, 1914, 1919
Featherweight (9 st. [57 kg] or under)	1888	5	G. R. Baker	1912–14, 1919, 1921
Lightweight (9 st. 7 lb. [60 kg] or under)	1881	4	M. Wells	1904–7
		4	F. Grace	1909, 1913, 1919–20
Light-Welterweight (10 st. [63 kg 50] or under)	1951	2	D. Stone	1956–57
		2	R. Kane	1958–59
		2	L./Cpl. B. Brazier	1961–62
		3	R. McTaggart	1963, 1965
Welterweight (10 st. 8 lb. [67 kg] or under)	1920	3	N. Gargano	1954–55–56
Light-Middleweight (11 st. 2 lb. [70 kg] or under)	1951	2	B. Wells	1953–54
		2	B. Foster	1952, 1955
		2	S. Pearson	1958–59
Middleweight (11 st. 11 lb. [74 kg] or under)	1881	2	T. Imrie	1966, 1969
		5	R. C. Warnes	1899, 1901, 1903, 1907, 1910
		5	H. W. Mallin	1919–23
Light-Heavyweight (12 st. 10 lb. [80 kg] or under)	1920	5	F. Malil	1928–32
Heavyweight (any weight)	1881	4	H. J. Mitchell	1922–25
		5	F. Parks	1899, 1901–02, 1905–06

BRITISH COMMONWEALTH GAMES

These quadrennial Games, second only to the Olympic Games for international participation, have been allocated as follows:

I	Hamilton, Ontario, Canada	16–23 Aug. 1930
II	London, England	4–11 Aug. 1934
III	Sydney, Australia	5–12 Feb. 1938
IV	Auckland, New Zealand	4–11 Feb. 1950
V	Vancouver, British Columbia, Canada	30 July–7 Aug. 1954
VI	Cardiff, Wales	18–26 July 1958
VII	Perth, Western Australia	22 Nov.–1 Dec. 1962
VIII	Kingston, Jamaica	4–13 Aug. 1966
IX	Edinburgh, Scotland	16–25 July 1970
X	Christchurch, New Zealand	24 Jan.–2 Feb. 1974
XI	Edmonton, Alberta, Canada	Aug. 1978

MOST GOLD MEDALS

The most gold medals won is nine by Henry William Furse Hoskyns, M.B.E. (England) (b. 19 March 1931) for fencing: 1958 Epée and Sabre individual and team; 1966 Foil team and Epée individual and team; 1972 Epée individual and team.

Individual The most individual gold medals won is five by Mrs. Valerie I. Young (née Sloper) (N.Z.): Shot putt 1958, 1962 and 1966 and Discus 1962 and 1966.

At one Games Decima J. Norman (Australia) won five gold medals (100 yards, 220 yards, 440 yards relay, 660 yards relay and long jump) at the 1938 Games in Sydney.

National Out of the 799 gold medals awarded from 1930–1970, England has won most with 225 compared with 210 by Australia and 104 by Canada.

Youngest Gold Medallist Ved Prakash (India) of Delhi, who won the light fly-weight wrestling title at Edinburgh in 1970, was 14 years old according to his passport but only 12 according to his other team members.

MOST MEDALS

Ivan G. Lund (Australia) won a record for any sport of 3 gold, 6 silver and 4 bronze medals (13) for fencing in 1950, 54, 58, 62.

The record for a woman is 6 golds and 2 silver (8) for swimming in 1958 and 1962 by Miss Dawn Fraser (now Mrs. Gary Ware, O.B.E.) (Australia).

MOST GOLD MEDALS BY SPORTS

Badminton (introduced 1966)	2	Tan Aik Huang (Malaysia) 1966 Angela M. Bairstow (England) 1966 Margaret B. Boxall (England) 1970
Bowls (lawn) (introduced 1930 but once omitted in 1966)	3	David Bryant, M.B.E. (England) 1966, 70
Boxing (since 1930)	2	Anthony Madigan (Australia) 1958, 62 Eddie Blay (Ghana) 1962, 66 Sulley Shitter (Ghana) 1966, 70 Philip Waruingi (Kenya) 1966, 70
Cycling (introduced 1934)	2	Edgar L. Gray (Australia) 1934, 38 Russell Mockridge (Australia) 1950 Richard Ploog (Australia) 1954, 58 Norman H. Sheil (England) 1954, 58 Roger Gibbon (Trinidad & Tobago) 1966
Fencing (introduced 1950)	9	H. W. F. Hoskyns (England) 1958, 66, 70
Rowing (1930, 38, 50, 54, 1958, 62)	4	Mervyn T. Wood (Australia) 1950, 54
Shooting (1966 only)		No marksman has yet won a second gold medal
Swimming & Diving (since 1930)	7	Michael Wenden (Australia) 1966, 70
Track & Field Athletics (since 1930)	7	Marjory Nelson (née Jackson) (Australia) 1950, 54
Weightlifting (introduced 1950)	3	Louis George Martin, M.B.E. (England) 1962, 66, 70
Wrestling (since 1930)	3	Richard E. Gerrard (Australia) 1934, 38, 1950 Muhammad Bashir (Pakistan) 1958, 62, 66 Muhammad Faiz (Pakistan) 1962, 66, 70

Dawn Fraser of Australia, the holder of the record number of 8 (6 gold, 2 silver) medals for a woman in the British Commonwealth Games

BRITISH COMMONWEALTH GAMES RECORDS

Of the eleven sports which have been on the programme of the Games, five (Cycling, Shooting, Swimming, Track and Field Athletics and Weightlifting) have official records as follows:

CYCLING

	Time min sec	Name and Nationality	Place	Year
1,000 metres Time Trial	1:08.69	H. Kent (New Zealand)	Edinburgh	1970
4,000 metres Individual Pursuit	4:56.6	Hugh Porter (England)	Kingston	1966
10 miles Track	20:46.72	Jocelyn B. Lowell (Canada)	Edinburgh	1970

SHOOTING

	Score			
Centre Fire Pistol	576	James Lee (Canada)	Kingston	1966
.22 Rapid Fire Pistol	585	Anthony James Clark (England)	Kingston	1966
.22 Free Pistol	544	Charles Henry Sexton (England)	Kingston	1966
Small-bore Rifle—prone	587	Gil Boa (Canada)	Kingston	1966
.303 Rifle	394	The Rt. Hon. Sir John Hussey Hamilton Vivian Bt., 4th Baron Swansea (Wales)	Kingston	1966

SWIMMING

MEN

Event	Time min sec	Name and Nationality	Place	Year
100 metres freestyle	53.06	Michael Wenden (Australia)	Edinburgh	1970
200 metres freestyle	1:56.69	Michael Wenden (Australia)	Edinburgh	1970
400 metres freestyle	4:08.48	Graham White (Australia)	Edinburgh	1970
1,500 metres freestyle	16:23.82	Graham Windeatt (Australia)	Edinburgh	1970
100 metres backstroke	1:01.65	William R. Kennedy (Canada)	Edinburgh	1970
200 metres backstroke	2:12.0[1]	Peter Reynolds (Australia)	Kingston	1966
100 metres breaststroke	1:08.2[2]	Ian O'Brien (Australia)	Kingston	1966
200 metres breaststroke	2:28.0[3]	Ian O'Brien (Australia)	Kingston	1966
100 metres butterfly	58.44	A. Byron Macdonald (Canada)	Edinburgh	1970
200 metres butterfly	2:08.97	Toomas Arusoo (Canada)	Edinburgh	1970
200 metres individual medley	2:13.72	George W. Smith (Canada)	Edinburgh	1970
400 metres individual medley	4:48.87	George W. Smith (Canada)	Edinburgh	1970
4 × 100 metres freestyle relay	3:35.6[4]	Australia (Michael Wendon, John Ryan, David Dickson, Robert Windle)	Kingston	1966
4 × 200 metres freestyle relay	7:50.77	Australia (Greg Rogers, William Devenish, Graham White, Michael Wendon)	Edinburgh	1970
4 × 100 metres medley relay	4:01.10	Canada (William R. Kennedy, William V. Mahony, A. Byron Macdonald, Robert A. Krasting)	Edinburgh	1970

WOMEN

100 metres freestyle	59.5[2]	Dawn Fraser (Australia)	Perth	1962
200 metres freestyle	2:09.78	Karen Moras (Australia)	Edinburgh	1970
400 metres freestyle	4:27.38	Karen Moras (Australia)	Edinburgh	1970
800 metres freestyle	9:02.45	Karen Moras (Australia)	Edinburgh	1970
100 metres backstroke	1:07.10	Lynn Watson (Australia)	Edinburgh	1970
200 metres backstroke	2:22.86	Lynn Watson (Australia)	Edinburgh	1970
100 metres breaststroke	1:17.40	Beverley Whitfield (Australia)	Edinburgh	1970
200 metres breaststroke	2:44.12	Beverley Whitfield (Australia)	Edinburgh	1970
100 metres butterfly	1:06.3[2]	Elaine B. Tanner (Canada)	Kingston	1966
200 metres butterfly	2:24.67	Maree Robinson (Australia)	Edinburgh	1970
200 metres individual medley	2:28.89	Denise Langford (Australia)	Edinburgh	1970
400 metres individual medley	5:10.74	Denise Langford (Australia)	Edinburgh	1970
4 × 100 metres freestyle relay	4:06.41	Australia (Debbie Cain, Lynn Watson, Jenny Watts, Denise Langford)	Edinburgh	1970
4 × 100 metres medley relay	4:30.66	Australia (Lynn Watson, Beverly Whitfield, Allyson Mabb, Denise Langford)	Edinburgh	1970

[1] *Time over the longer distance of 220 yds.*
[2] *Time over the longer distance of 110 yds.*
[3] *Time in a preliminary and over the longer distance of 220 yds.*
[4] *Time over the longer distance of 4 × 110 yds.*

TRACK AND FIELD ATHLETICS

MEN

Event	ft	in	Time	Name and Nationality	Place	Date
100 metres			10.3[1]	Keith A. St. H. Gardner (Jamaica)	Cardiff	19 July 1958
			10.3[1]	Harry Winston Jerome (Canada)	Kingston (twice)	6 Aug. 1966
			10.3[1]	Tom Robinson (Bahamas)	Kingston	6 Aug. 1966
200 metres			20.5[2]	Stanley Allotey (Ghana)	Kingston	8 Aug. 1966
			20.5	Donald O'Riley Quarrie (Jamaica)	Edinburgh	22 July 1970
400 metres			44.9[3]	Wendell A. Mottley (Trinidad & Tobago)	Kingston	11 Aug. 1966
800 metres			1:46.2[4]	Noel S. Clough (Australia)	Kingston	8 Aug. 1966
1,500 metres			3:36.6	Hezekieh Kipchoge Keino (Kenya)	Edinburgh	22 July 1970
5,000 metres			13:22.8	Ian Stewart (Scotland)	Edinburgh	25 July 1970
10,000 metres			28:11.8	J. Lachie Stewart (Scotland)	Edinburgh	18 July 1970
Marathon (best performance)			2H09:28.0	Ronald Hill (England)	Edinburgh	23 July 1970
110 metres hurdles			14.0[5]	Keith A. St. H. Gardner (Jamaica)	Cardiff	24 July 1958
400 metres hurdles			49.4[6]	Gerhardus Cornelius Potgeiter (South Africa)	Cardiff	23 July 1958
3,000 metres steeplechase			8:26.2	Antony P. Manning (Australia)	Edinburgh	23 July 1970
	ft	**in**	**metres**			
High Jump	7	$0\frac{1}{4}$	*2,14*	Lawrence William Peckham (Australia)	Edinburgh	18 July 1970
Pole Vault	16	$8\frac{3}{4}$	*5,10*	Michael Anthony Bull (Northern Ireland)	Edinburgh	23 July 1970
Long Jump	26	2	*7,99*[7]	Lynn Davies, M.B.E. (Wales)	Kingston	8 Aug. 1966
Triple Jump	54	$10\frac{1}{4}$	*16,72*	Phil J. May (Australia)	Edinburgh	25 July 1970
Shot Putt	63	$0\frac{1}{4}$	*19,21*	David L. Steen (Canada)	Edinburgh	25 July 1970
Discus Throw	193	$7\frac{1}{2}$	*59,02*	George Puce (Canada)	Edinburgh	22 July 1970
Hammer Throw	222	5	*67,80*	Andrew Howard Payne (England)	Edinburgh	18 July 1970
Javelin Throw	261	9	*79,78*	John Henry Peter FitzSimons (England)	Kingston	6 Aug. 1966
Decathlon			7,492 points	Geoff J. Smith (Australia)	Edinburgh	21–22 July 1970
4 × 100 metres Relay			39.4	Jamaica (Errol Stewart, Lennox Miller, Carl Lawson, Donald O'Riley Quarrie)	Edinburgh	25 July 1970
4 × 400 metres Relay			3:01.8[8]	Trinidad & Tobago (Lennox Yearwood, Kent Bernard, Edwin Roberts, Wendell A. Mottley)	Kingston	13 Aug. 1966
20 miles Walk (best performance)			2H33:33.0	Noel F. Freeman (Australia)	Edinburgh	18 July 1970

[1] *Converted from an actual 9.4 sec 100 yds. Faster 1970 times were wind assisted.*
[2] *Converted from an actual 20.6 sec 220 yds. Faster 1970 times were wind assisted.*
[3] *Converted from an actual 45.2 sec 440 yds.*
[4] *Converted from an actual 1:46.9 sec 880 yds.*
[5] *Actually run over 120 yds* (109,72 m.) *Faster 1970 times were wind assisted.*
[6] *Converted from an actual 49.7 sec 440 yds hurdles.*
[7] *Superior 1970 distance was wind assisted.*
[8] *Converted from an actual 3:02.8 sec 4 × 440 yds relay.*

WOMEN

Event	ft	in	Time	Name and Nationality	Place	Date
100 metres			11.5[1]	Diane Burge (Australia)	Kingston	6 Aug. 1966
200 metres			23.5[2]	Marlene Mathews-Willard (Australia)	Cardiff	24 July 1958
400 metres			51.0	Marilyn Fay Neufville (Jamaica)	Edinburgh	23 July 1970
800 metres			2:02.9[3]	Dixie Isobel Willis (Australia)	Perth	1 Dec. 1962
1,500 metres			4:18.8	Rita Ridley (England)	Edinburgh	23 July 1970
100 metres hurdles			13.2	Pamela Kilborn, M.B.E. (Australia)	Edinburgh	23 July 1970
	ft	**in**	**metres**			
High Jump	5	10	*1,78*	Robyn Woodhouse (Australia)	Perth	26 Nov. 1962
	5	10	*1,78*	Debbie A. Brill (Canada)	Edinburgh	25 July 1970
Long Jump	22	$0\frac{3}{4}$	*6,73*	Sheila Sherwood (England)	Edinburgh	23 July 1970
Shot Putt	54	$1\frac{3}{4}$	*16,50*	Valerie I. Young (New Zealand)	Kingston	6 Aug. 1966
Discus Throw	178	8	*54,46*	Christine Rosemary Payne (Scotland)	Edinburgh	18 July 1970
Javelin Throw	188	4	*57,40*	Anna Pazera (Australia)	Cardiff	24 July 1958
Pentathlon			4,524 points (1971 Tables)	Mary Elizabeth Peters, M.B.E. (Northern Ireland)	Edinburgh	21–22 July 1970
4 × 100 metres Relay			44.1	Australia (Maureen Caird, Jennifer Lamy, Marion Hoffman, Raelene Ann Boyle)	Edinburgh	25 July 1970

[1] *Converted from an actual 10.5 sec 100 yds. Faster 1970 times were wind assisted.*
[2] *Converted from an actual 23.6 sec 220 yds. Faster 1970 times were wind assisted.*
[3] *Converted from an actual 2:03.7 sec 880 yds.*

WEIGHTLIFTING

Bodyweight Class	Lift	Lifted lb.	Lifted kg	Name and Nationality	Place	Year
Flyweight	Snatch	$198\frac{1}{4}$	*90*	A. Ghafoor (Pakistan)	Edinburgh	1970
	Jerk	259	*117,5*	A. Ghafoor (Pakistan)	Edinburgh	1970
	Total	$457\frac{1}{4}$	*207,5*	A. Ghafoor (Pakistan)	Edinburgh	1970
Bantamweight	Snatch	225	*102,5*	Chua Phung Kim (Singapore)	Perth	1962
	Jerk	$286\frac{1}{2}$	*130*	Precious McKenzie (England)	Edinburgh	1970
	Total	*496	*225*	Precious McKenzie (England)	Edinburgh	1970
Featherweight	Snatch	$231\frac{1}{4}$	*105*	Chua Phung Kim (Singapore)	Edinburgh	1970
	Jerk	$308\frac{1}{2}$	*140*	M. L. Ghosh (India)	Kingston	1966
	Total	*518	*235*	P. K. Chua (Singapore)	Edinburgh	1970
Lightweight	Snatch	248	*112,5*	George Newton (England)	Edinburgh	1970
	Jerk	330	*150*	Tan Howe Liang (Singapore)	Cardiff	1958
	Total	*$556\frac{1}{2}$	*252,5*	George Newton (England)	Edinburgh	1970
Middleweight	Snatch	281	*127,5*	Pierre St. Jean (Canada)	Kingston	1966
	Jerk	350	*159*	Tan Howe Liang (Singapore)	Perth	1962
	Total	*$622\frac{1}{2}$	*282*	Pierre St. Jean (Canada)	Kingston	1966
Light Heavyweight	Snatch	$297\frac{1}{2}$	*135*	Nicolo Ciancio (Australia)	Edinburgh	1970
	Jerk	$369\frac{1}{4}$	*167,5*	Nicolo Ciancio (Australia)	Edinburgh	1970
	Total	$666\frac{3}{4}$	*302,5*	Nicolo Ciancio (Australia)	Edinburgh	1970
Middle Heavyweight	Snatch	315	*142,5*	Louis George Martin (England)	Perth	1962
	Jerk	$385\frac{3}{4}$	*175*	Louis George Martin (England)	Kingston	1966
	Total	*$694\frac{1}{4}$	*315*	Louis George Martin (England)	Kingston	1966
Heavyweight	Snatch	$319\frac{1}{2}$	*145*	Russell Prior (Canada)	Edinburgh	1970
	Jerk	$402\frac{1}{4}$	*182,5*	E. Price Morris (Canada)	Edinburgh	1970
	Total	*722	*327,5*	Russell Prior (Canada)	Edinburgh	1970
Super Heavyweight	Snatch	$319\frac{1}{2}$	*145*	Terrence R. J. Purdue (Wales)	Edinburgh	1970
	Jerk	$440\frac{3}{4}$	*200*	Donald Oliver (New Zealand)	Kingston	1966
	Total	$743\frac{3}{4}$	*337,5*	Donald Oliver (New Zealand)	Kingston	1966

* This total record is a calculation based on official records but is *not* yet ratified.

In 1973 there were 46 countries affiliated to the British Commonwealth Games Federation. The record entry of countries was 42 and the record number of competitors was 1,383, both at the 1970 Games at Edinburgh. The most gold medals by countries for each of the 11 sports are:

Badminton	6	England	Shooting	2	Canada
Bowls (Lawn)	10	England		2	England
Boxing	22	England	Swimming & Diving	81	England
Cycling	17	Australia	Track & Field Athletics	71	Australia
Fencing	37	England	Weightlifting	13	England
Rowing	12	Australia	Wrestling	18	Pakistan

England has gained most titles five times: 1930 (25), 1934 (29), 1954 (23), 1958 (29), 1966 (33).
Australia has gained most titles in the four remaining celebrations: 1938 (24), 1950 (33), 1962 (38), 1970 (36).

BULLFIGHTING

The first renowned professional *espada* was Francisco Romero of Ronda, in Andalusia, Spain, who introduced the *estoque* and the red muleta *c.* 1700. Spain now has some 190 active matadors. Since 1700, 42 major matadors have died in the ring.

Largest stadiums The world's largest bullfighting ring is the Plaza, Mexico City, with a capacity of 48,000. The largest of Spain's 312 bullrings is Las Ventas, Madrid with a capacity of 28,000.

Most successful matadors The most successful matador measured by bulls killed was Lagartijo (1841–1900), born Rafael Molina, whose lifetime total was 4,867. The longest career of any 20th century *espada* was that of Juan Belmonte (1892–1962) of Spain who survived 29 seasons from 1909–1937, killing 3,000 bulls and being gored 50 times. In 1919 he took part in 109 *corridas*. Recent Spanish law requires compulsory retirement at 55 years of age. Currently Antonio Bienvenida is the doyen at 51.

Most kills in a day In 1884 Romano set a record by killing 18 bulls in a day in Seville and in 1949 El Litri (Miguel Báes) set a Spanish record with 114 *novilladas* in a season.

Highest paid The highest paid bullfighter in history is El Cordobés (b. Manuel Benítez Pérez, probably on 4 May 1936, Palma del Rio, Spain), who became a sterling millionaire in 1966, when he fought 111 *corridas* up to 4 October of that year. On 19 May 1968 he received £9,000 for a *corrida* in Madrid. In 1970 he received an estimated £750,000 for 121 fights.

The most highly paid bullfighter in history, El Cordobes leaves the ring after a *corrida*

CANOEING

Origins The acknowledged pioneer of canoeing as a sport was John Macgregor, a British barrister, in 1865. The Canoe Club was formed on 26 July 1866.

Most Olympic gold medals Gert Fredriksson (b. 21 Nov. 1919) of Sweden has won most Olympic gold medals with 6: the 1,000 m Kayak singles in 1948, 1952 and 1956, the 10,000 m Kayak singles in 1948 and 1956 and the 1,000 m Kayak doubles in 1960.

Most World championships In addition to his 6 Olympic championships Gert Fredriksson has 3 other world titles in non-Olympic years: 1,000 m K.1 in 1950 and 1954 and 500 m K1 in 1954, for a record total of 9. The olympic 1,000 m best performance of 3 min 14.02 sec by the U.S.S.R. K4 represents an average speed of 11.53 m.p.h. *18,55 km/h* and a striking rate of about 125 strokes per min.

Most British titles The most British Open titles (instituted 1936) ever won is 24 by Alistair Wilson (Ayrshire Kayak Club) from 1962 to 1971 including 12 individual events and by John Laurence Oliver (Lincoln Canoe Club) (b. 12 Jan. 1943) from 1966 to 1972 including 10 individual events. David Mitchell (Chester S. & C.C.) won his sixth consecutive British slalom title in 1968.

The only United Kingdom canoeists to win world titles have been Paul Farrant (died 18 April 1960) of Chalfont Park Canoe Club, who won the canoe slalom at Geneva, Switzerland, in August 1959, and Alan Emus, who won the canoe sailing at Hayling Island, Hampshire, in August 1961 and on the Boden See (Lake of Constance) in August 1965.

Longest journey The longest journey ever made by canoe is one of 7,165 miles *11 530 km* from New York City to Nome, Alaska on the North American river system by paddle and portage by Geoffrey Westbrook Pope aged 24 and Sheldon Penfield Taylor aged 25, from 24 Apr. 1936 to 11 Aug. 1937.

Circumnavigation The first man to circumnavigate Great Britain by canoe is Geoffrey Hunter, 26, who started from and returned to Maidstone Bridge, Kent in 188 days (3 May–7 Nov. 1970). He lost one canoe and had to cling to a buoy for 14 hr in the Solway Firth.

Cross-Channel The singles record for canoeing across the English Channel is 3 hr 36 min by David Shankland, aged 29, of Cardiff, in a home-made N.C.K.I. named "Jelly Roll" from Shakespeare Bay, Dover, to Cap Gris-Nez, France, on 21 June 1965. The doubles record is 3 hr 20 min 30 sec by Capt. William Stanley Crook and the late Ronald Ernest Rhodes in their glass-fibre K.2 "Accord", from St. Margaret's Bay, Dover, to Cap Blanc Nez, France on 20 Sept. 1961.

The record for a double crossing is 14 hr 14 min in K.1 canoes by J. McCann, B. Cowburn, Mrs. J. Ledger and Mrs. G. Crow on 18–19 July 1971.

Devizes-Westminster The Senior Class record for the annual Devizes-Westminster Challenge Cup race (instituted 1948) over 125 miles *201 km* with 77 locks is 18 hrs 37 min 48 sec by A. Alan-Williams and T. Cardale (Royal Marine Canoe Federation) to win the 1973 race.

Eskimo rolls The record for Eskimo rolls is 400 in 27 min 29 sec by Terence Russell, 15, of Swanley, Kent at Eltham Baths, Greater London on 18 Dec. 1971. A "hand-rolling" record of 100 rolls in 5 min 52 sec was set in Portsmouth by Peter Mooney on 26 Nov. 1972.

DOWN STREAM CANOEING

River	Miles	Km			Date	
Rhine	708	*1 139*	Sgt. Charles Kavanagh	Chur, Switzerland to Willemstad, Neths.	13 Feb. 1961	17½ days
Rhine	726	*1 168*	L.Cpl. Peter Salisbury Spr. Simon Chivers	Chur, to Hook of Holland with greater portages	17 Apr.–9 May 1972	21½ days
Murray	1,300	*2 100*	Phillip Davis, 16, and Robert S. Lodge (15½ ft [*4,7 m*] canoe)	Albury, N.S.W. to Murray Bridge	27 Dec. 1970– 1 Feb. 1971	36 days
Murray	287	*461*	A. Powell (K.1)	Yarrawonga to Swan Hill	28 Dec. 1971– 1 Jan. 1972	33 hrs 49 min 37.8 sec
Nile	4,000	*6 500*	John Goddard (U.S.), Jean Laporte and André Davy (France)	Kagera to the Delta	Nov. 1953–July 1954	9 months
Amazon	4,000	*6 500*	Stephen Z. Bezuk (U.S.) (Kayak)	Atalaya to Belem	21 June–Nov. 1970	4½ months

CAVING

Duration (trogging) The endurance record for staying in a cave is 463 days by Milutin Veljkovič (b. 1935) (Yugoslavia) in the Samar Cavern, Svrljig Mountains, northern Yugoslavia from 24 June 1969 to 30 Sept. 1970. The British record is 130 days by David Lafferty, aged 27, of Hampstead, who stayed in Boulder Chamber, Goughs' Cave, Cheddar Gorge, Somerset, from 27 March to 4 Aug. 1966. He was alone until 1 Aug. when he thought it was 7 July.

PROGRESSIVE WORLD DEPTH RECORDS

ft	m	Cave	Cavers	Date
210	*64*	Lamb Lair, near West Harptree, Somerset	John Beaumont (explored)	*c.* 1676
454	*138*	Macocha, Moravia	Joseph Nagel	May 1748
742	*226*	Grotta di Padriciano, Trieste	Antonio Lindner, Svetina	1839
1,079	*328*	Grotta di Trebiciano, Trieste	Antonio Lindner	6 April 1841
1,293	*394*	Nidlenloch, Switzerland	—	1909
1,433	*436*	Geldloch, Austria		1923
1,476	*449*	Abisso Bertarelli, Yugoslavia	R. Battelini, G. Cesca	24 Aug. 1925
1,491	*454*	Spluga della Preta, Venezia, Italy	*L. de Battisti	18 Sept. 1927
1,775	*541*	Antro di Corchia, Tuscany, Italy	E. Fiorentino Club	1934
1,980	*603*	Trou de Glaz, Isère, France	F. Petzl, C. Petit-Didier	4 May 1947
2,389	*728*	Gouffre de la Pierre Saint Martin, Basses-Pyrénées, France	*Georges Lépineux	15 Aug. 1953
2,428	*740*	Gouffre Berger, Sornin Plateau, Vercors, France	J. Cadoux, G. Garby	11 Sept. 1954
2,963	*903*	Gouffre Berger, Sornin Plateau, Vercors, France	*F. Petzl and 6 men	25 Sept. 1954
3,230	*984*	Gouffre Berger, Sornin Plateau, Vercors, France	L. Potié, G. Garby *et al.*	29 July 1955
>3,600	*>1 100*	Gouffre Berger, Sornin Plateau, Vercors, France	Jean Cadoux and 2 others	11 Aug. 1956
>3,600	*>1 100*	Gouffre Berger, Sornin Plateau, Vercors, France	*Frank Salt and 7 others	23 Aug. 1962
3,743	*1 141*	Gouffre Berger, Sornin Plateau, Vercors, France	Kenneth Pearce	4 Aug. 1963
<3,850	*<1 174*	Gouffre de la Pierre Saint Martin, Basses-Pyrénées, France	C. Queffélec and 3 others	Aug. 1966
<3,850	*<1 174*	Gouffre de la Pierre Saint Martin, Basses-Pyrénées, France	C. Queffélec and 10 others	Aug. 1968
3,850	*1 174*	Gouffre de la Pierre Saint Martin, Basses-Pyrénées, France	Ass. de Rech. Spéléo Internant.	8–11 Nov. 1969

*Leader

WORLD'S DEEPEST CAVES

The depth of caves are under continuous reassessment. According to the latest available (June 1973) revised measurements, the deepest caves in the world are:

ft	m	Cave	Location
3,851	*1 174*	Resea de la Pierre St. Martin	Western Pyrénées, France
3,743	*1 141*	Gouffre Berger	Dauphin Alps, France
3,149	*960*	Choroum des Aguilles	Dauphin Alps, France
3,018	*920*	Abisso Michele Gortani	Julian Alps, Italy
2,979	*908*	Gouffre de Cambou de Liard	Central Pyrénées, France
2,952	*900*	Reseau Felix Trombe	Eastern Pyrénées, France

NOTE: *El Sotano Cave, Mexico has the world's longest vertical pitch of 1,345 ft 410 m*
The highest known cave entrance in the world is that of the Rakhiot Cave, Nanga Parbat, Kashmir at 21,860 ft 6 660 m

CHESS

Origins The name chess is derived from the Persian word *shah* (a king or ruler). It is a descendant of the game *Chaturanga*. The earliest reference is from the Middle Persian Karnamak (*c.* A.D. 590–628), though there are grounds for believing its origins are from the 2nd century owing to the discovery, announced in March 1973, of two ivory chessmen in the Uzbek Soviet Republic dateable to that century. It reached Britain in *c.* 1255. The *Fédération Internationale des Eschecs* was established in 1924. There were an estimated 7,000,000 competitive players in the U.S.S.R. in 1973.

It has been calculated that the four opening moves can be made in 197,299 ways leading to some 72,000 different positions. The approximate number of different games possible is 2.5×10^{116}—a number astronomically higher than the number of atoms in the observable universe.

World champions World champions have been generally recognized since 1886. The longest tenure was 27 years by Dr. Emanuel Lasker (1868–1941) of Germany, from 1894 to 1921. The women's world championship has been most often won by Nona Gaprindashvili (U.S.S.R.) in 1963–66–69–72. Robert J. Fischer (b. Chicago, U.S.A. 9 Mar. 1943) is reckoned on the officially adopted Elo System to be the greatest Grandmaster of all-time. He has an I.Q. of 187 (Terman index) and became at 15 the youngest ever International Grand Master.

British titles Most British titles have been won by Dr. Jonathan Penrose, O.B.E. (b. 1934) of East Finchley, London with 10 titles in 1958–63, 1966–69. Mrs. Rowena M. Bruce (b. 1919) of Plymouth won 11 titles in 1937 as Miss Dew and in 1950–51–54–55 (shared)–59–60–62–63–67 (shared) and 1969 (shared).

Longest games The most protracted chess match on record was one drawn on the 191st move between H. Pilnik (Argentina) and Moshe Czerniak (Israel) at Mar del Plata, Argentina, in April 1950. The total playing time was 20 hrs. A game of 21½ hrs, but drawn on the 171st move (average over 7½ min per move), was played between Makagonov and Chekover at Baku, U.S.S.R., in 1945. A game of 221 moves between Arthur Williams (G.B.) and Kenneth Rogoff (U.S.A.) occurred at Stockholm, Sweden in August 1969 but required only 4 hrs 25 min.

Marathon The longest recorded session is one of 101 hours between John P. Cameron and Jon Stevens at Ipswich Civic College, Suffolk, England, on 21–25 March 1970. The longest game at "lightning chess" (*i.e.* all moves completed by a player in five minutes) is 81 hrs 32 min by Nigel Williams, 16 and Michael Ashton, 15 at the Hurstbourne Tarrant Church Hall, Hants on 28–31 May 1973 with no breaks longer than 3 min.

Slowest The slowest recorded move (before modern rules) was one of 11 hours between Paul Murphy, the U.S. Champion of 1852–62, and a chess master named Paulsen.

Most opponents Records by chess masters for numbers of opponents tackled simultaneously depend very much on whether or not the opponents are replaced as defeated, are in relays, or whether they are taken on in a simultaneous start. The greatest number tackled on a replacement basis is 400 (379 defeated) by the Swedish master Gideon Ståhlberg (died 26 May 1967) in 36 hrs of play in Buenos Aires, Argentina, in 1940. The greatest number of opponents reported in a simultaneous start is 117, of whom 93 lost and 11 only drew, taken on by Jude F. Acers at the Lloyd Shipping Center, Portland, Oregon, U.S.A. on 21 Apr. 1973. The trial took 13 hrs 41 min. Georges Koltanowski (Belgium, now of U.S.A.) tackled 56 opponents "blindfold" and won 50, drew 6, lost 0 in 9¾ hrs at Fairmont Hotel, San Francisco, California, U.S.A., on 13 Dec. 1960.

COURSING

Origins The sport of dogs chasing hares was probably of Egyptian origin in *c.* 3000 B.C. and brought to England by the Normans in 1067. The classic event is the annual Waterloo Cup, instituted at Altcar, near Liverpool, in 1836. A government bill to declare the sport illegal was "lost" owing to the dissolution of Parliament on 29 May 1970. The number of clubs in Britain has dwindled from 169 in 1873 to 25 in 1973.

Most successful dog The most successful Waterloo Cup dog recorded was Colonel North's *Fullerton*, sired by *Greentich*, who tied for first in 1889 and then won outright in 1890–91–92.

The only dogs to win the Victorian Waterloo Cup (instituted 1873) three times have been *Bulwark* in 1906–07–09, at which time it was known as the Australian Waterloo Cup, and *Byamee* in 1953–54–55.

Longest course The longest authenticated course is one of 4 min 10 sec, when Major C. Blundell's *Blackmore* beat *Boldon* in a Barbican Cup decider on 2 March 1934.

CRICKET

Earliest match The earliest evidence of the game of cricket is from a drawing depicting two men playing with a bat and ball dated *c.* 1250. The game was played in Guildford, Surrey, at least as early as 1550. The earliest major match of which the score survives was one in which a team representing England (40 and 70) was beaten by Kent (53 and 58 for 9) by one wicket at the Artillery Ground in Finsbury, London, on 18 June 1744. Cricket was played in Australia as early as 1803.

BATTING

Highest innings The highest recorded innings by any team was one of 1,107 runs by Victoria against New South Wales in an Australian inter-State match at Melbourne, Victoria, on 27–28 Dec. 1926.

England The highest innings made in England is 903 runs for 7 wickets declared, by England in the 5th Test against Australia at the Oval, London, on 20, 22 and 23 Aug. 1938. The highest innings in a county championship match is 887 by Yorkshire *versus* Warwickshire at Edgbaston on 7–8 May 1896.

Lowest The lowest recorded innings is 12 made by Oxford University *v.* the Marylebone Cricket Club (M.C.C.) at Oxford on 24 May 1877, and 12 by Northamptonshire *v.* Gloucestershire at Gloucester on 11 June 1907. On the occasion of the Oxford match, however, the University batted a man short. The lowest score in a Test match is 26 by New Zealand *v.* England in the 2nd Test at Auckland on 28 March 1955.

The lowest aggregate for two innings is 34 (16 in first and 18 in second) by Border *v.* Natal in the South African Currie Cup at East London on 19 and 21 Dec. 1959.

Greatest victory The greatest recorded margin of victory is an innings and 851 runs, when Pakistan Railways (910 for 6 wickets declared) beat Dera Ismail Khan (32 and 27) at Lahore on 2–4 Dec. 1964. The largest margin in England is one of an innings and 579 runs by England over Australia in the 5th Test at the Oval on 20–24 Aug. 1938 when Australia scored 201 and 123 with two men short in both innings. The most one-sided county match was when Surrey (698) defeated Sussex (114 and 99) by an innings and 485 runs at the Oval on 9–11 Aug. 1888.

FASTEST SCORING

The greatest number of runs scored in a day is 721 all out (10 wickets) in 6 hrs by the Australians *v.* Essex at Southchurch Park, Southend-on-Sea on the first day on 15 May 1948.

The Test record for runs in a day is 588 at Old Trafford on 27 July 1936 when England put on 398 and India were 190 for 0 in their second innings by the close.

Innings of 200 or more The fastest recorded exhibition of hitting occurred in a Kent *v.* Gloucestershire match at Dover on 20 Aug. 1937, when Kent scored 219 runs for 2 wickets in 71 min, at the rate of 156 runs for each 100 balls bowled.

Fastest 50 The fastest 50 ever hit was completed in 8 min (1.22 to 1.30 p.m.) and in 11 scoring strokes by Clive C. Inman (b. Colombo, Ceylon, 29 Jan. 1936) in an innings of 57 not out for Leicestershire *v.* Nottinghamshire at Trent Bridge, Nottingham on 20 Aug. 1965.

Century The fastest century ever hit was completed in 35 min by Percy George Herbert Fender (b. 22 Aug. 1892), when scoring 113 not out for Surrey *v.* Northamptonshire at Northampton on 26 Aug. 1920. The most prolific scorer of centuries in an hour or less was Gilbert Laird Jessop (1874–1955), with 11 between 1897 and 1913. The fastest Test century was one of 70 min by Jack Morrison Gregory (b. 14 Aug. 1895) of New South Wales, for Australia *v.* South Africa in the 2nd Test at Johannesburg on

12 Nov. 1921. Edwin Boaler Alletson (1884–1963) scored 189 runs in 90 min for Nottinghamshire *v.* Sussex at Hove on 20 May 1911.

Double century The fastest double century was completed in 120 min by Gilbert Jessop (1874–1955) (286) for Gloucestershire *v.* Sussex at Hove on 1 June 1903.

Treble century The fastest treble century was completed in 181 min by Denis Charles Scott Compton, C.B.E. (b. Hendon, 23 May 1918) of Middlesex, who scored 300 for the M.C.C. *v.* North-Eastern Transvaal at Benoni on 3–4 Dec. 1948.

1,000 in May The most recent example of scoring 1,000 runs *in May* was by Charles Hallows (Lancashire) (b. 4 April 1895), who made precisely 1,000 between 5–31 May 1928. Dr. W. G. Grace (9–30 May 1895) and W. R. Hammond (7–31 May 1927) surpassed this feat with 1,016 and 1,042 runs. The greatest number of runs made *before the end of May* was by T. W. Hayward with 1,074 from 16 April to 31 May in 1900.

Slowest scoring The longest time a batsman has ever taken to open his scoring is 1 hr 37 min by Thomas Godfrey Evans (b. Finchley, 18 Aug. 1920) of Kent, who scored 10 not out for England *v.* Australia in the 4th Test at Adelaide on 5–6 Feb. 1947. Richard Gorton Barlow (1850–1919) utilized 2½ hrs to score 5 not out for Lancashire *v.* Nottinghamshire at Nottingham on 8 July 1882. During his innings his score remained unchanged for 80 min.

The slowest century on record was by Derrick John (Jackie) McGlew (b. 11 March 1929) of South Africa in the Third Test *v.* Australia at Durban on 25 and 27 Jan. 1958. He required 9 hrs 35 min for 105, reaching the 100 in 9 hrs 5 min. The slowest double century recorded is one of 10 hrs 8 min by Robert Baddeley Simpson (b. 3 Feb. 1936) of New South Wales, during an innings of 311, lasting 12 hrs 42 min, for Australia *v.* England in the Fourth Test at Old Trafford on 23, 24 and 25 July 1964.

Highest individual innings The highest individual innings recorded is 499 in 10 hrs 40 min by Hanif Muhammad (b. Junagadh, Pakistan, 21 Dec. 1934) for Karachi *v.* Bahawalpur at Karachi, Pakistan, on 8, 9 and 11 Jan. 1959. The record for a Test match is 365 not out in 10 hrs 8 min by Garfield St. Aubrun Sobers (b. Barbados, 28 July 1936) playing for the West Indies in the Third Test against Pakistan at Sabina Park, Kingston, Jamaica, on 27 Feb.–1 March 1958. The England Test record is 364 by Sir Leonard Hutton (b. Fulneck, Pudsey, Yorkshire, 23 June 1916) *v.* Australia in the 5th Test at the Oval on 20, 22 and 23 Aug. 1938. The highest score in England is 424 in 7 hrs 50 min by Archibald Campbell MacLaren (1871–1944) for Lancashire *v.* Somerset at Taunton on 15–16 July 1895.

Longest innings The longest innings on record is one of 16 hrs 39 min for 337 runs by Hanif Muhammad (Pakistan) *v.* the West Indies in the 1st Test at Bridgetown, Barbados, on 20–23 Jan. 1958. The English record is 13 hrs 17 min by Hutton (see above).

Least runs in a career S. Clarke the Somerset wicket-keeper, played five matches for his county in 1930, scoring no runs in each of his nine innings of which 7 were ducks.

Most runs off an over The first batsman to score the possible of 36 runs off a six-ball over was Garfield Sobers (Nottingham) off Malcolm Andrew Nash (Glamorgan) at Swansea on 31 Aug. 1968. The ball (recovered from the last hit from the road by a small boy) resides in Nottingham's Museum.

BIGGEST SCORERS

Season The greatest number of runs ever scored in a season is

260

Glen Turner, the most recent scorer of 1,000 runs before the end of May, in the innings in which he scored his 1,000th run, on 30 May 1973

3,816 in 50 innings (8 not out) by Denis Compton (Middlesex) in 1947. His batting average was 90.85.

Most runs in a career The greatest aggregate of runs in a career is 61,237 in 1,315 innings (106 not out) between 1905 and 1934 by Sir John (Jack) Berry Hobbs (1882–1963) of Surrey and England. His career average was 50.65.

Test matches The greatest number of runs scored in Test matches is 7,626 in 150 innings (20 not out) by Garfield St. Aubrun Sobers (b. Bridgetown, Barbados, 28 July 1936) of Barbados and Nottingham playing for the West Indies since 1952–53 and 1972. His average is 58.66.

CENTURIES

Season The record for the greatest number of centuries in a season is also held by Compton with eighteen in 1947. With their restricted fixture list the Australian record is eight by Sir Donald George Bradman (b. 27 Aug. 1908) in only 12 innings in the 1947–48 season.

Career The most centuries in a career is 197 by Sir John Hobbs between 1905 and 1934. The Australian record is Sir Donald Bradman's 117 centuries between 1927 and 1949.

Test matches The greatest number of centuries scored in Test matches is 29 by Sir Donald Bradman (Australia) between 1928 and 1948. The English record is 22 by Walter Hammond (1903–65) of Gloucestershire, between 1927 and 1947, and 22 by Colin Cowdrey (Kent) between 1954–55 and 1971.

Highest averages The highest recorded seasonal batting average in England is 115.66 for 26 innings (2,429 runs) by Don

Bradman (Australia) in England in 1938. The English record is 100.12 by Geoffrey Boycott (b. 21 Oct. 1940) of Yorkshire and England for 30 innings (2,503 runs) including 13 centuries and 5 times not out in 1971. The world record for a complete career is 95.14 for 338 innings (28,067 runs) by Bradman between 1927 and 1949. The record for Test matches is 99.94 in 80 innings (6,996 runs) by Bradman in 1928–48. The English career record is 56.37 for 500 innings (62 not out) by Kumar Shri Ranjitsinhji (1872–1933) later H. H. the Jam Saheb of Nawanagar, with 24,692 runs between 1893 and 1920.

Double centuries The only batsman to score double centuries in both innings is Arthur Edward Fagg (b. 18 June 1915), who made 244 and 202 not out for Kent v. Essex at Colchester on 13–15 July 1938.

Longest hit The longest measured drive is one of 175 yds *160 m* by Walter (later the Rev.) Fellows (1834–1901) of Christ Church, Oxford University, in a practice on their ground off Charles Rogers in 1856. J. E. C. Moore made a measured hit of 170 yds 1 ft 5 in *155,59 m* at Griffith, New South Wales, Australia, in February 1930. Peter Samuel Heine (b. 28 June 1929) of the Orange Free State is said to have driven a ball bowled by Hugh Joseph Tayfield (b. 30 Jan. 1929) of Natal for approximately 180 yds *164,5 m* at Bloemfontein on 3 Jan. 1955.

Most sixes in an innings The highest number of sixes hit in an innings is 15 by John Richard Reid, O.B.E. (b. 3 June 1928), in an innings of 296, lasting 3 hrs 47 min, for Wellington v. Northern Districts in the Plunket Shield Tournament at Wellington, New Zealand, on 14–15 Jan. 1963. The Test record is 10 by Walter Hammond in an innings of 336 not out for England v. New Zealand at Auckland on 31 March and 1 April 1933.

Most sixes in a match The highest number of sixes in a match is 17 (10 in the first and 7 in the second innings) by William James

Geoffrey Boycott, holder of the English record for the highest seasonal batting average

Stewart (b. 31 Aug. 1934) for Warwickshire v. Lancashire at Blackpool on 29–31 July 1959. His two innings were of 155 and 125.

Most boundaries in an innings The highest number of boundaries in an innings was 68 (all in fours) by Percival Albert Perrin (1876–1945) in an innings of 343 not out for Essex v. Derbyshire at Chesterfield on 18–19 July 1904.

Most runs off a ball The most runs scored off a single hit is 10 by Samuel Hill Hill-Wood (1872–1949) off Cuthbert James Burnup (1875–1960) in the Derbyshire v. M.C.C. match at Lord's, London, on 26 May 1900.

GREATEST PARTNERSHIP

World The record stand for any partnership is the fourth wicket stand of 577 by Gul Muhammad (b. 15 Oct. 1921), who scored 319, and Vijay Samuel Hazare (b. 11 March 1915) (288) in the Baroda v. Holkar match at Baroda, India, on 8–10 March 1947.

England The highest stand in English cricket, and the world record for a first wicket partnership, is 555 by Percy Holmes (1886–1971) (224 not out) and Herbert Sutcliffe (313) for Yorkshire v. Essex at Leyton on 15–16 June 1932.

Highest score by a No. 11 The highest score by a No. 11 batsman is 163 by Thomas Peter Bromly Smith (1908–67) for Essex v. Derbyshire at Chesterfield in August 1947.

BOWLING

Most wickets The largest number of wickets ever taken in a season is 304 by Alfred Percy ("Tich") Freeman (1888–1965) of Kent, in 1928. Freeman bowled 1,976.1 overs, of which 423 were maidens, with an average of 18.05 runs per wicket. The greatest wicket-taker in history is Wilfred Rhodes (1877–1973) who took 4,187 wickets for 69,993 runs (average 16.71 runs per wicket) between 1898 and 1930. The highest percentage of wickets gained unassisted is 73.50 % (1,479 from 2,012) by Schofield Haigh, who played for Yorkshire from 1895 to 1913.

Jack Hobbs, whose lifetime total of 61,237 runs remains the greatest recorded

Three record-holding cricketers, Leslie Ames, "Tich" Freeman, and Jack Hobbs

Tests The greatest number of wickets taken in Test matches is 307 for 6,625 runs (average 21.57) by Frederick Sewards Trueman (b. Scotch Springs, Yorkshire, 6 Feb. 1931), in 67 Tests between June 1952 and June 1965. The lowest bowling average in a Test career (minimum 15 wickets) is 61 wickets for 775 runs (12.70 runs per wicket) by John James Ferris (1867–1900) in 9 Tests (8 for Australia and 1 for England) between 1886 and 1892.

Fastest The highest measured speed for a ball bowled by any bowler is 93 m.p.h. *149 km/h* by Harold Larwood (b. Nuncargate, Notts., 14 Nov. 1904) in 1933. The fastest bowler of all time is regarded by many as Charles Jesse Kortright (1871–1952) who played for Essex from 1889 to 1907. Albert Cotter (1883–1917) of New South Wales, Australia, is reputed to have broken a stump more than 20 times. Wesley Winfield Hall (b. 12 Sept. 1937) of Barbados was timed to bowl at 91 m.p.h. *146 km/h* in practice in 1962–63, when playing for Queensland, Australia.

Most consecutive wickets No bowler in first class cricket has yet achieved five wickets with five consecutive balls. The nearest approach was that of Charles Warrington Leonard Parker (1884–1959) (Gloucestershire) in his own benefit match against Yorkshire at Bristol on 10 Aug. 1922, when he struck the stumps with five successive balls but the second was called as a no-ball. The only man to have taken 4 wickets with consecutive balls more than once is Robert James Crisp (b. 28 May 1911) for Western Province v. Griqualand West at Johannesburg on 23–24 Dec. 1931 and against Natal at Durban on 3 March 1934.

Most "hat tricks" The greatest number of "hat tricks" is seven by Douglas Vivian Parson Wright (b. 21 Sept. 1914) of Kent, on 3 and 29 July 1937, 18 May 1938, 13 Jan. and 1 July 1939, 11 Aug. 1947 and 1 Aug. 1949. In his own benefit match at Lord's on 22 May 1907, Albert Edwin Trott (Middlesex) took four Somerset wickets with four consecutive balls and then later in the same innings achieved a "hat trick".

Most wickets in an innings The taking of all ten wickets by a single bowler has been recorded many times but only one bowler has achieved this feat on three occasions—Alfred Percy Freeman of Kent, against Lancashire at Maidstone on 24 July 1929, against Essex at Southend on 13–14 Aug. 1930 and against Lancashire at Old Trafford on 27 May 1931. The fewest runs scored off a bowler taking all 10 wickets is 10, when Hedley Verity

1905–43) of Yorkshire dismissed (8 caught, 1 l.b.w., 1 stumped) every Nottinghamshire batsman in 118 balls at Leeds on 12 July 1932. The only bowler to have "clean bowled" a whole side out was John Wisden (1826–84) of Sussex, playing for the North v. the South at Lord's in 1850.

Most wickets in a match James Charles Laker (b. Frizinghall, Yorkshire, 9 Feb. 1922) of Surrey took 19 wickets for 90 runs (9–37 and 10–53) for England v. Australia in the 4th Test at Old Trafford on 26–31 July 1956. No other bowler has taken more than 17 wickets in a first class match. Henry Arkwright (1837–66) took 18 wickets for 96 runs in a 12-a-side match, M.C.C. v. Gentlemen of Kent, at Canterbury on 14–17 Aug. 1861. Alfred Percy Freeman (Kent) took ten or more wickets in a match on 140 occasions between 1914 and 1936.

Most wickets in a day The greatest number of wickets taken in a day's play is 17 by Colin Blythe (1879–1917) for 48 runs, for Kent against Northamptonshire at Northampton on 1 June 1907; by Hedley Verity for 91 runs, for Yorkshire v. Essex at Leyton on 14 July 1933; and by Thomas William John Goddard (1900–66) for 106 runs, for Gloucestershire v. Kent at Bristol on 3 July 1939.

Most expensive bowling The greatest number of runs hit off one bowler in one innings is 362, scored off Arthur Alfred Mailey (b. 3 Jan. 1888) in the New South Wales v. Victoria inter-State match at Melbourne on 24–28 Dec. 1926. The greatest number of runs ever conceded by a bowler in one match is 428 by C. S. Nayudu in the Holkar v. Bombay match at Bombay on 4–9 March 1945, when he also made the record number of 917 deliveries.

Most maidens Hugh Joseph Tayfield bowled 16 consecutive 8-ball maiden overs (137 balls without conceding a run) for

Jim Laker, holder of the Test record for the most wickets in a match with 19 wickets for 90 runs

Hugh Tayfield, who bowled 16 consecutive 8 ball overs without conceding a run in 1957

South Africa v. England at Durban on 25–27 Jan. 1957. The greatest number of consecutive 6-ball maiden overs bowled is 21 (130 balls) by Ragunath G. ("Bapu") Nadkarni (b. 4 April 1932) for India v. England at Madras on 12 Jan. 1964. The English record is 17 overs (105 balls) by Horace L. Hazell (b. 30 Sept. 1909) for Somerset v. Gloucestershire at Taunton on 4 June 1949, and 17 (104 balls) by Graham Anthony (Tony) Richard Lock (b. 5 July 1929) of Surrey, playing for the M.C.C. v. the Governor-General's XI at Karachi, Pakistan, on 31 Dec. 1955. Alfred Shaw (1842–1907) of Nottinghamshire bowled 23 consecutive 4-ball maiden overs (92 balls) for North v. the South at Nottingham in 1876.

Most balls The greatest number of balls sent down by any bowler in one season is 12,234 (651 maidens: 298 wickets) by Alfred Percy Freeman (Kent) in 1933. The most balls bowled in an innings is 588 (98 overs) by Sonny Ramadhin (b. 1 May 1930) of Trinidad, playing for the West Indies in the First Test v. England at Birmingham on 30 May and 1, 3 and 4 June 1957. He took 2 for 179.

Best average The lowest recorded bowling average for a season is one of 8.61 runs per wicket (177 wickets for 1,525 runs) by Alfred Shaw of Nottinghamshire in 1880.

FIELDING

Most catches in an innings The greatest number of catches in an innings is seven, by Michael James Stewart (b. 16 Sept. 1932) for Surrey v. Northamptonshire at Northampton on 7 June 1957, and by Anthony Stephen Brown (b. 24 June 1936) for Gloucestershire v. Nottinghamshire at Trent Bridge on 26 July 1966.

In a match Walter Reginald Hammond (1903–65) held a record total of 10 catches (4 in the first innings, 6 in the second) for Gloucestershire v. Surrey at Cheltenham on 16–17 Aug. 1928. The record for a wicket-keeper is 11.

In a season and in a career The greatest number of catches in a season is 78 by Walter Hammond (Gloucestershire) in 1928, and 77 by Michael James Stewart (Surrey) in 1957. The most catches in a career is 1,011 by Frank Edward Woolley (b. 27 May 1887) of Kent in 1906–1938. The Test record is 117 by Michael Colin Cowdrey between 1954–55 and 1971.

Longest throw The longest recorded throw of a cricket ball (5½ oz. [155 g]) is 140 yds 2 ft (422 ft [128,6 m]) by R. Percival on Durham Sands Racecourse on Easter Monday, 14 April 1884.

WICKET KEEPING

In an innings The most dismissals by a wicket-keeper in an innings is eight (all caught) by Arthur Theodore Wallace Grout (1927–68) for Queensland against Western Australia at Brisbane on 15 Feb. 1960. The Test record is six (all caught) by A. T. W. Grout (see below) for the First Australia v. South Africa Test at Johannesburg on 27–28 Dec. 1957; six (all caught) by Denis Lindsay (b. 4 Sept. 1939) of North-Eastern Transvaal, for South Africa v. Australia in the First Test at Johannesburg on 24 Dec. 1966; six (all caught) by John Thomas Murray (b. 1 April 1935) of Middlesex, for England v. India in the second Test at Lord's, London on 22 June 1967.

In a match The greatest number of dismissals by a wicket-keeper in a match is 12 by Edward Pooley (1838–1907) (eight caught, four stumped) for Surrey v. Sussex at the Oval on 6–7 July 1868; nine caught, three stumped by Don Tallon (b. 17 Feb. 1916) of Australia for Queensland v. New South Wales at Sydney on 2–4 Jan. 1939; and also nine caught, three stumped by Hedley Brian Taber (b. 29 April 1940) of New South Wales against South Australia at Adelaide 17–19 Dec. 1968. The record for catches is 11 (seven in the first innings and four in the second) by Arnold Long (b. 18 Dec. 1940), for Surrey v. Sussex at Hove on 18 and 21 July 1964. The Test record for dismissals is 9 (eight caught, one stumped) by Gilbert Roche Andrews Langley of South Australia, playing for

"Wally" Grout, who dismissed eight players in an innings in Australia in 1960

Australia *v.* England in the 2nd Test at Lord's, London, on 22–26 June 1956.

In a season The record number of dismissals for any wicket-keeper in a season is 127 (79 caught, 48 stumped) by Leslie Ethelbert George Ames, C.B.E. (b. 3 Dec. 1905) of Kent in 1929. The record for the number stumped is 64 by Ames in 1932. The record for catches is 96 by James Graham Binks (b. 5 Oct. 1935) of Yorkshire in 1960.

In a career The highest total of dismissals in a wicket-keeping career is 1,468 (a record 1,215 catches, plus 253 stumpings) by Herbert Strudwick (1880–1970) of Surrey between 1902 and 1927. The most stumpings in a career is 415 by Ames (1926–1951). The Test record is 219 in 91 innings by Godfrey Evans.

Least byes The best wicket keeping record for preventing byes is that of Archdale Palmer Wickham (1855–1935) when, keeping for Somerset *v.* Hampshire at Taunton on 20–22 July 1899, he did not concede a single bye in a total of 672 runs. The record for Test matches is no byes in 659 runs by Godfrey Evans for England in the 2nd Test *v.* Australia at Sydney, New South Wales, on 14, 16, 17 and 18 Dec. 1946.

Most byes The records at the other extreme are those of Philip Harman Stewart-Brown (b. 30 April 1904) of Harlequins, who let through 46 byes in an Oxford University innings of only 188 on 21–23 May 1927 and 48 byes let through by Anthony William Catt of Kent in a Northamptonshire total of 374 at Northampton on 20–22 Aug. 1955.

TEST RECORDS

Most Test appearances The record number of Test appearances is 109 by Michael Colin Cowdrey (England) between 1954–55 and 1971. The highest number of Test captaincies is 41, including 35 consecutive games, by Peter Barker Howard May (b. 31 Dec. 1929) of Cambridge University and Surrey, who captained England from 1955 to 1961 and played in a total of 66 Tests. The most innings batted in Test matches is 179 in 109 Tests by Cowdrey of Kent, playing for England between 1954–55 and 1971. Garfield Sobers (West Indies) holds the record for consecutive Tests, with 85 from April 1955 to April 1972.

Longest match The lengthiest recorded cricket match was the "timeless" Test between England and South Africa at Durban on 3–14 March 1939. It was abandoned after 10 days (8th day rained off) because the boat taking the England team home was due to leave. The lengthiest in England was the 6-day 5th England *v.* Australia Test on 6–12 Aug. 1930, when rain prevented play on the fifth day.

Largest crowds The greatest recorded attendance at a cricket match is 350,534 (receipts £30,124) for the Third Test between Australia and England at Melbourne on 1–7 Jan. 1937. For the whole series the figure was a record 933,513 (receipts £87,963). The greatest recorded attendance at a cricket match on one day was 90,800 on the second day of the Fifth Test between Australia and the West Indies at Melbourne on 11 Feb. 1961, when the receipts were £A13,132 (£10,484 sterling). The English record is 159,000 for the Fourth Test between England and Australia at Headingley, Leeds, on 22–27 July 1948, and the record for one day probably a capacity of 46,000 for a match between Lancashire and Yorkshire at Old Trafford on 2 Aug. 1926. The English record for a Test series is 549,650 (receipts £200,428) for the series against Australia in 1953.

Greatest receipts The world record for receipts from a match is £82,914, from the attendance paid by 82,538 at the Second Test between England and Australia at

Leslie Ames C.B.E., see also page 262, in action at the wicket, three years after the season in which he made the record number of dismissals

Lord's, London on 22–26 June 1972. The Test series record is £261,283 paid by 294,845 for the five England *v.* Australia Tests of June–August 1972.

ENGLISH COUNTY CHAMPIONSHIP

The greatest number of victories has been secured by Yorkshire with 29 outright wins up to 1968, and one shared with Middlesex in 1949. They have never been lower than 13th (1969 and 1971) on the table. The most "wooden spoons" have been won by Northamptonshire, with ten since 1923. They did not win a single match between May 1935 and May 1939. The record number of consecutive title wins is 7 by Surrey from 1952 to 1958. The greatest number of consecutive appearances for one county is 423 by Kenneth G. Suttle (b. 25 Aug. 1928) of Sussex in 1954–69.

Oldest and youngest county cricketers The youngest player to represent his county was William Wade Fitzherbert Pullen (1866–1937), for Gloucestershire against Middlesex at Lord's on 5 June 1882, when aged 15 years 346 days. The oldest regular County players have been William George Quaife (1872–1951) of Sussex and Warwickshire, who played his last match for Warwickshire against Hampshire at Portsmouth on 27–30 Aug. 1927, when aged 55, and John Herbert King (1871–1946) of Leicestershire, who played his last match for his county against Yorkshire at Leicester on 5–7 Aug. 1925, when aged 54.

Highest benefit The highest "benefit" ever accorded a player is £14,000 for Cyril Washbrook (b. 6 Dec. 1914) in the Lancashire *v.* Australians match at Old Trafford on 7–10 Aug. 1948. The total received in benefits by Jim Parks (b. 21 Oct. 1931) of Sussex since 1964 reached £14,900 on 10 Nov. 1972.

MINOR CRICKET RECORDS
(where excelling those in First Class Cricket)

Bowling Stephen Fleming bowling for Marlborough College "A" XI, New Zealand *v.* Bohally Intermediate at Blenheim, New Zealand in Dec. 1967 took 9 wickets in 9 consecutive balls. In February 1931 in a schools match in South Africa Paul Hugo also took 9 wickets with 9 consecutive balls for Smithfield School *v.* Aliwal North.

Highest individual innings In a Junior House match between Clarke's House and North Town, at Clifton College, Bristol, 22–23–26–7–8 June 1899, A. E. J. Collins (b. India, 1886—k. Flanders, Nov. 1914) scored an unprecedented 628 not out in 6 hrs 50 min, over five afternoons' batting, carrying his bat through the innings of 836. The scorer, E. W. Pegler, gave the score as "628—plus or minus 20, shall we say".

Fastest individual scoring S. K. Coen (South Africa) scored 50 runs (11 fours and 1 six) in 7 min for Gezira v. the R.A.F. in 1942, compared with the First Class record of 8 min. Cecil George Pepper hit a century in 24 min in a Services match in Palestine in 1943. Cedric Ivan James Smith hit 9 successive sixes for a Middlesex XI v. Harrow and District at Rayners' Lane, Harrow, in 1935. This feat was repeated by Arthur Dudley Nourse, Jr. in a South African XI v. Military Police match at Cairo in 1942–43. Nourse's feat included six sixes in one over.

Highest scoring rate In the match Royal Naval College, Dartmouth v. Seale Hayne Agricultural College in 1923, K. A. Sellar (now Cdr. "Monkey" Sellar, D.S.O., D.S.C., R.N.) and L. K. A. Block (now Judge Block, D.S.C.) were set to

score 174 runs in 105 min but achieved this total in 33 min, so averaging 5.27 runs per min.

Lowest score There are at least 60 recorded instances of sides being dismissed for 0. A recent instance was in July 1970 when, in a 2nd XI House match at Brentwood School, West dismissed North for 0 with 13 balls.

Greatest stand T. Patten and N. Rippon made a third wicket stand of 641 for Buffalo v. Whorouly at Gapsted, Victoria, Australia, on 19 March 1914.

Wicket-keeping In a Repton School match for Priory v. Mitre, the late H. W. P. Middleton caught one and stumped eight batsmen in one innings on 10 July 1930.

Longest Game A match under M.C.C. rules was played by 22 members of the Cambridge University Cricket Society on Parker's Piece for 24 hours on 14–15 June 1973. A total of 1,395 runs was scored from 367 overs in 10 innings.

CROQUET

Earliest references Croquet, in its present-day form, originated as a country-house lawn game in Ireland in 1852.

Most championships The greatest number of victories in the Open Croquet Championships (instituted at Evesham, Worcestershire, 1867) is ten by John William Solomon (b. 1932) (1953, 1956, 1959, 1961, 1963 to 68). He has also won the Men's Championship on 10 occasions (1951, 1953, 1958 to 60, 1962, 1964–65, 1971 and 1972), the Open Doubles (with E. Patrick C. Cotter) on 10 occasions (1954–55, 1958–59, 1961 to 65 and 1969) and the Mixed Doubles once (with Mrs. N. Oddie) in 1954, making a total of 31 titles. Solomon has also won the President's Silver Cup (inst. 1934) on 9 occasions (1955, 1957 to 59, 1962 to 64, 1968 and 1971). He has also been Champion of Champions on all four occasions that this competition was run (1967–70).

International Trophy The MacRobertson International Shield (instituted 1925) has been played for 9 times. It has been won most often by England with 5 wins (in 1925, 1937, 1956, 1963 and 1969). The only player to make 5 international appearances is J. C. Windsor (Australia) in 1925, 1928, 1930, 1935 and 1937. The English record is 4 appearances by John W. Solomon in 1951, 1956, 1963 and 1969.

H. O. Hicks, whose handicap at croquet was the lowest ever at minus 5½

Miss Dorothy D. Steel who won a record 31 titles in Croquet Championships between 1919 and 1939

Miss Dorothy D. Steel, fifteen times winner of the Women's Championship (1919 to 39), won the Open Croquet Championship four times (1925, 1933, 1935–36). She had also five Doubles and seven Mixed Doubles titles making a total of 31 titles.

Lowest handicap The lowest playing handicap has been that of Humphrey O. Hicks (Devon) with minus 5½. In 1964 the limit was fixed at minus 5, which handicap is held by J. W. Solomon, E. Patrick C. Cotter, H. O. Hicks, G. Nigel Aspinall, Keith F. Wylie, Dr. William P. Ormerod, Dr. Roger W. Bray and William de B. Prichard.

Largest club The largest number of courts at any one club is eleven, at the Sussex County (Brighton) Croquet and Lawn Tennis Club.

Most Protracted Game The longest croquet match on record is one of 50 hrs 32 min by 4 students of Leeds University on 12–14 June 1972.

CROSS-COUNTRY RUNNING

International championships The earliest recorded international cross-country race took place over 14,5 km *9 miles 18 yds* from Ville d'Avray, outside Paris, on 20 March 1898, between England and France (England won by 21 points to 69). The inaugural International Cross-Country Championships took place at the Hamilton Park Racecourse, Glasgow, on 28 March 1903. The greatest margin of victory is 56 sec or 390 yds *356 m* by Jack T. Holden (England) at Ayr Racecourse, Scotland, on 24 March 1934. The narrowest win was that of Jean-Claude Fayolle (France) at Ostend, Belgium, on 20 March 1965, when the timekeepers were unable to separate his time from that of Melvyn Richard Batty (England), who was placed second.

The greatest team wins have been those of England, with a minimum of 21 points (the first six runners to finish) on two occasions, at Gosforth Park, Newcastle upon Tyne, Northumberland, on 22 March 1924, and at the Hippodrome de Stockel, Brussels, Belgium, on 20 March 1932.

Most wins The greatest number of victories in the International Cross-Country Race is four by Jack Holden (England) in 1933–34–35 and 1939, and four by Alain Mimoun-o-Kacha (France) in 1949, 1952, 1954 and 1956. England have won 43 times to 1973.

Most appearances The runners of participating countries with the largest number of international championship appearances are:

Belgium	20	M. Van de Wattyne, 1946–65
Wales	14	D. Phillips, 1922, 1924, 1926–37
England	12	J. T. Holden, 1929–39, 1946
Spain	12	A. L. Amoros, 1951–62
Scotland	12	A. H. Brown, 1955–56, 1958, 1960–68
France	11	A. Mimoun-o-Kacha, 1949–50, 1952, 1954, 1956, 1958–62, 1964

English championship The English Cross-Country Championship was inaugurated at Roehampton, South London, in 1877. The greatest number of individual titles achieved is four by P. H. Stenning (Thames Hare and Hounds) in 1877–80 and Alfred E. Shrubb (1878–1964) (South London Harriers) in 1901–04. The most successful club in the team race has been Birchfield Harriers from Birmingham with 27 wins and one tie between 1880 and 1953.

Largest field The largest recorded field was one of 1,815 starters (1,020 completed the course) at Gosforth Park, Newcastle upon Tyne in the summer of 1916. It was staged by the Northern Command of the Army and was won by Sapper G. Barber in 35 min 7.2 sec, by a margin of over 40 yds *36 m*.

CURLING

Origins An early form of the sport is believed to have originated in the Netherlands about 450 years ago. The first club was formed at Kilsyth, Stirlingshire, in 1510. Organized administration began in 1838 with the formation of the Royal Caledonian Curling Club, the international legislative body based in Edinburgh. The first indoor ice rink to introduce curling was at Southport in 1879.

The U.S.A. won the first Gordon International Medal series of matches, between Canada and the U.S.A., at Montreal in 1884. The first Strathcona Cup match between Canada and Scotland was won by Canada in 1903. Although demonstrated at the Winter Olympics of 1924, 1932 and 1964, curling has never been included in the official Olympic programme.

Most titles The record for international team matches for the Scotch Cup and Air Canada Silver Broom (instituted 1959) is 12 wins by Canada, in 1959–60–61–62–63–64–1966–68–69–70–71–72. The most Strathcona Cup wins is seven by Canada (1903–09–12–23–38–57–65) against Scotland.

Marathon The longest recorded curling match is one of 37 hrs

A curling match taking place in Scotland

9 min by the Schwarzwald Curling Club at Baden Baden, West Germany on 22–23 Feb. 1973.

Most Durable Player In 1972 Howard "Pappy" Wood competed in his 65th consecutive annual bonspiel of the Manitoba Curling Association since 1908.

Largest rink The world's largest curling rink is the Big Four Curling Rink, Calgary, Alberta, Canada opened in 1959 at a cost of $Can. 2,250,000 *£867,050,* Each of the two floors has 12 rinks, accommodating 48 teams and 192 players.

CYCLING

Earliest race The earliest recorded bicycle race was a velocipede race over 2 km *1.24 miles* at the Parc de St. Cloud, Paris, on 31 May 1868, won by James Moore (G.B.).

Slow cycling Slow bicycling records came to a virtual end in 1965 when Tsugunobu Mitsuishi, aged 39, of Tōkyō, Japan stayed stationary for 5 hrs 25 min.

Highest speed The highest speed ever achieved on a bicycle is 127.243 m.p.h. *204,777 km/h* by Jose Meiffret (b. April 1913) of France, using a 275 in *698 cm* gear behind a windshield on a racing car at Freiburg, West Germany, on 19 July 1962. The first Mile a Minute was achieved by Charles Minthorne Murphy (b. 1872) behind a pacing locomotive on the Long Island Railroad on 30 June 1899 in 57⅘ sec for an average of 62.28 m.p.h. *100,23 km/h.* Antonio Maspes (Italy) recorded an unofficial unpaced 10.8 sec for 200 m (42.21 m.p.h. [*67,93 km/h*]) at Milan on 28 Aug. 1962.

The greatest distance ever covered in one hour is 122,862 km *76 miles 604 yds* by Leon Vanderstuyft (Belgium) on the Montlhery Motor Circuit, France, on 30 Sept. 1928. This was achieved from a standing start paced by a motorcycle. The 24 hr record behind pace is 860 miles 367 yds *1 384,367 km* by Hubert Opperman in Australia in 1932.

Jose Meiffret, holder of the speed record on a bicycle, seen being paced by a motorcycle. Note the gearing

Most world titles The greatest number of world titles for a particular event won since the institution of the amateur championships in 1893 and the professional championships in 1895 are:

Amateur Sprint	4	William J. Bailey (U.K.)	1909–10–11, 1913
	4	Daniel Morelon (France)	1966–67, 1969–70
Amateur 100 km Paced	7	Leon Meredith (U.K.)	1904–05, 1907–09, 1911, 1913
Amateur Road Race	2	Giuseppe Martano (Italy)	1930, 1932
	2	Gustave Schur (East Germany)	1958–59
Professional Sprint	7	Jeff Scherens (Belgium)	1932–37, 1947
	7	Antonio Maspes (Italy)	1955–56, 1959–62, 1964
Professional 100 km Paced	6	Guillermo Timoner (Spain)	1955, 1959–60, 1962, 1964–65
Professional Road Race	3	Alfredo Binda (Italy)	1927, 1930, 1932
	3	Henri (Rik) Van Steenbergen (Belgium)	1949, 1956–57
Women's titles	7	Beryl Burton (G.B.)	1959–60–62–63–66 (pursuits) 1960–67 (Road)
	7	Yvonne Reynders (Belgium)	1961–64–65 (pursuits) 1959–61–63–66 (Road)

WORLD RECORDS   OPEN AIR TRACKS

MEN

Distance	hr	min	sec	Name and nationality	Place	Date	
Professional unpaced standing start:							
1 km.		1	08.6	Reginald Hargreaves Harris, O.B.E. (U.K.)	Milan	20 Oct.	1952
5 kms.		5	51.6	Ole Ritter (Denmark)	Mexico City	4 Oct.	1968
10 kms.		11	53.2	Eddy Merckx (Belgium)	Mexico City	25 Oct.	1972
20 kms.		24	6.8	Eddy Merckx (Belgium)	Mexico City	25 Oct.	1972
100 kms.	2	14	2.5	Ole Ritter (Denmark)	Mexico City	15 Nov.	1971
1 hour	30 miles 700 yd *49 km 408*			Eddy Merckx (Belgium)	Mexico City	25 Oct.	1972
Professional unpaced flying start:							
200 metres			10.8	Antonio Maspes (Italy)	Rome	21 July	1960
500 metres			28.8	Marino Morettini (Italy)	Milan	29 Aug.	1955
1,000 metres		1	02.6	Marino Morettini (Italy)	Milan	26 July	1961
Professional motor-paced:							
100 kms.	1	03	40.0	Walter Lohmann (W. Germany)	Wuppertal	24 Oct.	1955
1 hour	58 miles 737 yd *94 km 015*			Walter Lohmann (W. Germany)	Wuppertal	24 Oct.	1955

Distance	hr	min	sec	Name and nationality	Place	Date

Amateur unpaced standing start:

	hr	min	sec	Name and nationality	Place	Date
1 km.		1	02.4[4]	Pierre Trentin (France)	Zürich	15 Nov. 1970
4 kms.		4	37.5[4]	Mogens Frey (Denmark)	Mexico City	17 Oct. 1968
5 kms.		6	01.6	Mogens Frey (Denmark)	Mexico City	5 Oct. 1969
10 kms.		12	23.8	Mogens Frey (Denmark)	Mexico City	5 Oct. 1969
20 kms.		25	00.5	Mogens Frey (Denmark)	Mexico City	5 Oct. 1969
100 kms.	2	18	43.6	Jorn Lund (Denmark)	Rome	19 Sept. 1971
1 hour	29 miles 921 yd *47 km 513*			Mogens Frey (Denmark)	Mexico City	5 Oct. 1969

Amateur unpaced flying start:

	sec	Name and nationality	Place	Date
200 metres	10.61	Omari Phakadze (U.S.S.R.)	Mexico City	22 Oct. 1967
500 metres	27.85	Pierre Trentin (France)	Mexico City	21 Oct. 1967
1,000 metres	1 01.14	Luigi Borghetti (Italy)	Mexico City	21 Oct. 1967

WOMEN

Amateur unpaced standing start:

	hr	min	sec	Name and nationality	Place	Date
1 km		1	15.1	Irena Kirichenko (U.S.S.R.)	Yerevan	8 Oct. 1966
3 kms.		4	01.7	Raisa Obdovskaya (U.S.S.R.)	Brno	20 Aug. 1969
5 kms.		7	03.3	Nina Sadovaya (U.S.S.R.)	Irkutsk	2 July 1955
10 kms.		14	27.0	Elsy Jacobs (Luxembourg)	Milan	9 Nov. 1958
20 kms.		28	58.4	Mrs. Beryl Burton, O.B.E. (U.K.)	Milan	11 Oct. 1960
100 kms.	2	44	54.8	R. Mykkanen (Finland)	Helsinki	23 Sept. 1971
1 hour	25 miles 1,354 yd *41 km 471*			Maria Cressari (Italy)	Mexico City	25 Nov. 1972

Amateur unpaced flying start:

	sec	Name and nationality	Place	Date
200 metres	12.3	Lyubov Razuvayeva (U.S.S.R.)	Irkutsk	17 July 1955
500 metres	32.5	Irena Kirichenko (U.S.S.R.)	Irkutsk	1967
1,000 metres	1 10.6	Irena Kirichenko (U.S.S.R.)	Irkutsk	1967

COVERED TRACKS

MEN

Professional unpaced standing start:

	hr	min	sec	Name and nationality	Place	Date
1 km.		1	08.0	Reginald Hargreaves Harris, O.B.E. (U.K.)	Zürich	19 July 1957
5 kms.		6	05.6	Ferdinand Bracke (Belgium)	Brussels	5 Dec. 1964
10 kms.		12	26.8	Roger Rivière (France)	Paris	19 Oct. 1958
20 kms.		25	18.0	Siegfried Adler (W. Germany)	Zürich	2 Aug. 1968
1 hour	29 miles 162 yd *46 km 819*			Siegfried Adler (W. Germany)	Zürich	2 Aug. 1968

Professional unpaced flying start:

	sec	Name and nationality	Place	Date
200 metres	10.99	Oscar Plattner (Switzerland)	Zürich	1 Dec. 1961
500 metres	28.6	Oscar Plattner (Switzerland)	Zürich	17 Aug. 1956
1,000 metres	1 01.23	Patrick Sercu (Belgium)	Antwerp	3 Feb. 1967

Professional motor-paced:

	hr	min	sec	Name and nationality	Place	Date
100 kms.	1	23	59.8	Guillermo Timoner (Spain)	San Sebastian	12 Sept. 1965
1 hour	46 miles 669 yd *74 km 641*			Guy Solente (France)	Paris	13 Feb. 1955

Amateur unpaced standing start:

	hr	min	sec	Name and nationality	Place	Date
1 km.		1	06.76	Patrick Sercu (Belgium)	Brussels	12 Dec. 1964
5 kms.		6	06.0	Xavier Kurmann (Switzerland)	Zürich	28 Nov. 1968
10 kms.		12	26.2	Xavier Kurmann (Switzerland)	Zürich	1 Dec. 1968
20 kms.		25	14.6	Ole Ritter (Denmark)	Zürich	30 Oct. 1966
1 hour	28 miles 575 yd *45 km 587*			Alfred Ruegg (Switzerland)	Zürich	16 Nov. 1958

Amateur unpaced flying start:

	sec	Name and nationality	Place	Date
200 metres	10.72	Daniel Morelon (France)	Zürich	4 Nov. 1967
500 metres	28.89	Pierre Trentin (France)	Zürich	4 Nov. 1967
1,000 metres	1 02.44	Pierre Trentin (France)	Zürich	15 Nov. 1970

WOMEN

Amateur unpaced standing start:

	sec	Name and nationality	Place	Date
1,000 metres	1 15.5	Elizabeth Eichholz (Germany)	Berlin	4 Mar. 1964

Amateur unpaced flying start:

	sec	Name and nationality	Place	Date
200 metres	13.2	Karla Günther (Germany)	Berlin	7 Mar. 1964
500 metres	35.0	Karla Günther (Germany)	Berlin	7 Mar. 1964

Most British Titles Beryl Burton, O.B.E. (b. 12 May 1937), 14 times British all-round time trial champion (1959–72) also holds 10 B.C.F. road race titles, 11 track pursuit titles and 40 R.T.T.C. titles. Albert White won 12 individual National track championships from the ¼ mile to 25 miles in 1920–25.

Beryl Burton, 13 times British all-round champion (1959–71) won her 21st track title on 12 Aug. 1972.

Most Olympic titles Cycling has been on the Olympic programme since the revival of the Games in 1896. The greatest number of gold medals ever won is four by Marcus Hurley (U.S.A.) over the ¼, ⅓, ½ and 1 mile in 1904.

ROAD CYCLING RECORDS
(British) as recognized by the Road Time Trials Council (out-and-home records).

Distance	hr	min	sec	Name	Course area	Date
MEN						
25 miles		51	00	Alf Engers	Catterick, Yorkshire	30 Aug. 1969
30 miles	1	04	56	Dave Dungworth	Derby	10 June 1967
50 miles	1	43	46	John Watson	Boroughbridge, Yorkshire	23 Aug. 1970
100 miles	3	46	37	Anthony Taylor	Boroughbridge, Yorkshire	31 Aug. 1969
12 hours	281.87 miles *453,62 km*			John Watson	Blyth, Nottinghamshire	7 Sept. 1969
24 hours	507.00 miles *815,93 km*			Roy Cromack	Cheshire	26–27 July 1969
WOMEN						
10 miles		21	25	Beryl Burton, O.B.E.	Blyth, Nottinghamshire	29 Apr. 1973
25 miles		54	44	Beryl Burton, O.B.E.	Boroughbridge, Yorkshire	22 July 1972
30 miles	1	12	20	Beryl Burton, O.B.E.	St. Neots, Huntingdonshire	3 May 1969
50 miles	1	55	4	Beryl Burton, O.B.E.	Catterick, Yorkshire	21 Sept. 1969
100 miles	3	55	5	Beryl Burton, O.B.E.	Essex	4 Aug. 1968
12 hours	277.25 miles *446,19 km*			Beryl Burton, O.B.E.	Wetherby, Yorkshire	17 Sept. 1967
24 hours	427.86 miles *688,57 km*			Christine Minto (*née* Moody)	Cheshire	26–27 July 1969

ROAD RECORDS ASSOCIATION'S STRAIGHT-OUT DISTANCE RECORDS

Distance	days	hr	min	sec	Name	Date
25 miles			47	0	Peter Crofts	10 Oct. 1971
50 miles		1	39	23	Derek Cottington	2 May 1970
100 miles		3	28	40	Ray Booty	28 Sept. 1956
1,000 miles	2	10	40	0	Reg Randall	19–21 Aug. 1960
12 hours	276½ miles *444,9 km*				Harry Earnshaw	4 July 1939
24 hours	475¾ miles *765,64 km*				Ken Joy	26–27 July 1954

PLACE TO PLACE RECORDS
(British) as recognized by the Road Records Association

	days	hr	min	sec	Name	Date
London to Edinburgh (380 miles [*610 km*])		18	49	42	Cliff Smith	2 Nov. 1965
London to Bath and back (212 miles [*341 km*])		9	31	19	Bob Addy	14 Sept. 1972
London to York (197 miles [*317 km*])		7	41	13	Bob Addy	6 Aug. 1972
London to Brighton and back (107 miles [*172 km*])		4	18	18	Les West	3 Oct. 1970
Land's End to London (287 miles [*461 km*])		12	34	0	Robert Maitland	17 Sept. 1954
Land's End to John O'Groats (879 miles [*1 414 km*])	1	23	46	35	Richard W. E. Poole	18 June 1965

Tour de France The greatest number of wins in the Tour de France (inaugurated 1903) is five by Jacques Anquetil (b. 8 Jan. 1934) of France, who won in 1957, 1961, 1962, 1963 and 1964. The closest race ever was that of 1968 when after 2,898.7 miles *4 665 km* over the 25 days (27 June–21 July) Jan Janssen (Netherlands) (b. 1940) beat Herman van Springel (Belgium) in Paris by 38 sec. Eddie Merckx (b. Belgium, 1945) equalled Anquetil's record of 4 consecutive wins in 1969–70–71–72.

The Land's End to John O'Groats (879 miles [*1 414 km*]) feminine record is 2 days 11 hrs 7 min (average speed 14.75 m.p.h. [*23,73 km/h*]) by Mrs. Eileen Sheridan (b. 1925) on 9–11 June 1954. She continued to complete 1,000 miles *1 610 km* in 3 days 1 hr.

Roller cycling The greatest recorded distance registered in a 12 hr roller team cycling test is 511 miles 605 yds *822,927 km* by Ross Mullenger, John Dupen, Melvyn Phillips and Phillip Brown of the Godric C.C. at Bungay, Suffolk on 2 June 1973.

The eight-man 24 hr record is 1,008 miles 1,320 yds *1 623,423 km* by the Barnwell C.R.S. at Cambridge on 9–10 Jan. 1970. The team was Jim Bowyer, Ian Cannell, Colin Chapman, John Day, Bob Sampson, Peter Scarth, Chris Stevens and Richard Voss.

Endurance The greatest endurance feat in cycling was by Tommy Godwin (G.B.) who in the 365 days of 1939 covered 75,065 miles *120 805 km* or an average of 205.65 miles *330,96 km* per day. He then completed 100,000 miles *160 934 km* in 500 days on 14 May 1940.

Ken Webb of Crawley Wheelers, Sussex claimed to have bettered the 365 day mileage record on 10 Aug. 1972 with an unconfirmed 75,347 miles *121 259 km*.

Trans-Continental Record The North American trans-continental record from San Francisco to New York City Hall is 13 days by Paul Cornish, 25, on 4–17 Mar. 1973.

Jacques Anquetil of France, who has won the Tour de France five times. during the race in 1957, the year he first won the title

Tandem Marathon David Martin (b. 3 Jan. 1957) and Scott Parcel (b. 16 Aug. 1957) set out from San Francisco, California on 4 Feb. 1973 and pedalled 4,837 miles *7 784 km* around the United States finishing in Washington, D.C. on 5 June 1973.

CYCLO-CROSS
The greatest number of world championships (inst. 1950) have been won by E. de Vlaeminck (Belgium) who took the Open title in 1967 and the professional world titles in 1968–69–70–71–72–73. British titles (inst. 1955) have been won most often by John Atkins (Coventry R.C.) with 5 Amateur (1961–62–66–67–68) and 5 professional (1968–69, 1969–70, 1970–71, 1971–72 and 1972–73).

DARTS

Origins The origins of darts date from the use by archers of heavily weighted ten-inch throwing arrows for self-defence in close quarters fighting. The "dartes" were used in Ireland in the 16th century and darts was played on the *Mayflower* by the Plymouth pilgrims in 1620. Today there are an estimated 6,000,000 dart players in the British Isles—a higher participation than in any other sporting pastime. The National Darts Association of Great Britain (inst. 1953) is seeking to standardize the throwing distances and treble boards.

Lowest possible scores The lowest number of darts to achieve standard scores are: 201 four darts, 301 six darts, 501 nine darts, 1,001 seventeen darts. The four and six darts "possibles" have been many times achieved, the nine darts 501 occasionally but never the seventeen darts 1,001 which would require 15 treble 20's, a treble 17 and a 50. The lowest even number which cannot be scored with three darts (ending on a double) is 162. The lowest odd number which cannot be scored with three darts (ending on a double) is 159.

Fastest match The fastest time taken for a match of three games of 301 is 2½ min by Jim Pike (1903–1960) at Broadcasting House, Broad Street, Birmingham, in 1952.

Fastest "round the board" The record time for going round the board in "doubles" at arm's length is 14.5 sec by Jim Pike at the Craven Club, Newmarket, in March 1944. The record for this feat at the nine-feet *2,7 m* throwing distance, retrieving own darts, is 2 min 13 sec by Bill Duddy at The Plough, Hornsey Road, Holloway North London on 29 Oct. 1972.

Million and one up The shortest recorded time to score 1,000,001 up *on one board*, under the rules of darts, is 9 hrs 31 min 32 sec (scoring rate of 29.16 per sec) by eight players from the Associated Book Publishers Sports and Social Club, Andover, Hampshire on 17 March 1973.

Most doubles The record number of doubles scored in 10 hrs is 2,030 (in 8,699 darts) for a percentage of 23.33 by Ray Smith, 27 at the Crosville Bus Depot, Heswell, Cheshire on 25 June 1972.

Marathon record John Reynolds, Albert Wills, Andrew Earl and Robert Harris played non-stop for 358 hr 8 min at the Rose and Crown, Selling, Kent. They played on a shift system, finishing on 30 June 1973.

Most titles Re-instituted in 1947, the annual *News of the World* England and Wales individual Championships consist of the best of 3 legs 501 up, "straight" start and finish on a double with an 8 ft *2,4 m* throwing distance. The only men to win twice are Tommy Gibbons (Ivanhoe Working Men's Club) of Conisbrough, Yorkshire, in 1952 and 1958; Tom Reddington of New Inn, Stonebroom, Derbyshire in 1955 and of George Hotel, Alfreton, Derbyshire 1960; and Tom M. Barrett (Odco Sports Club, London) in 1964 and 1965.

The National Darts Association of Great Britain Individual title was won by Tom O'Regan of the Northern Star, New Southgate, North London in 1970–71–72.

EQUESTRIAN SPORTS

SHOW JUMPING

Origins Evidence of horse-riding dates from an Anatolian statuette dated *c.* 1400 B.C. Pignatelli's academy of horsemanship at Naples dates from the 16th century. The earliest show jumping was in Paris in 1886. Equestrian events have been included in the Olympic Games since 1912.

Most Olympic medals The greatest number of Olympic gold medals is 5 by Hans-Günter Winkler (West Germany) who won 4 team gold medals as captain in 1956, 1960, 1964 and 1972 and won the individual Grand Prix in 1956. The most team wins in the Prix des Nations is five by Germany in 1936, 1956, 1960, 1964 and 1972. The lowest score obtained by a winner was no faults by František Ventura on *Eliot* (Czechoslovakia) in 1928. Pierre Jonqueres d'Oriola (France) is the only two time winner of the individual gold medal in 1952 and 1964. Richard John Hannay Meade, M.B.E. (b. 4 Dec. 1938) (Great Britain) is the only 3 day event rider to win 3 gold medals—the individual in 1972 and the team in 1968 and 1972.

Jumping records The official *Fédération Equestre Internationale* high jump record is 8 ft 1¼ in *2,47 m* by *Huasó*, ridden by Capt. Alberto Larraguibel Morales (Chile) at Vina del Mar, Santiago, Chile, on 5 Feb. 1949, and 27 ft 2¾ in *8,30 m* for long jump over water by *Amado Mio* ridden by Lt.-Col. Lopez del Hierro (Spain), at Barcelona, Spain on 12 Nov. 1951. *Heatherbloom*, ridden by Dick Donnelly was reputed to have covered 37 ft *11,28 m* in clearing an 8 ft 3 in *2,51 m* puissance jump at Richmond, Virginia, U.S.A. in 1903. *Solid Gold* cleared 36 ft 3 in *11,05 m* over water at the Wagga Show, New South Wales, Australia in August 1936 for an Australian record. *Jerry M.* allegedly cleared 40 ft *12,19 m* over the water at Aintree in 1912.

"Heatherbloom" the first horse to clear the eight-foot barrier, making a demonstration jump of 8 ft 2 in *2,49 m* in 1905

Richard Meade, the only Three Day Event rider to win three Olympic Gold Medals

At Cairns, Queensland, *Golden Meade* ridden by Jack Martin cleared an unofficially measured 8 ft 6 in *2,59 m* on 25 July 1946. *Ben Bolt* was credited with clearing 9 ft 6 in *2,89 m* at the 1938 Royal Horse Show, Sydney, Australia. The Australian record is 8 ft 4 in *2,54 m* by *Flyaway* (Colin Russell) in 1939 and *Golden Meade* (A. L. Payne) in 1946. The world's unofficial best for a woman is 7 ft 5½ in *2,27 m* by Miss B. Perry (Australia) on *Plain Bill* at Cairns, Queensland, Australia in 1940. The greatest recorded height reached bareback is 6 ft 7 in *2,00 m* by *Silver Wood* at Heidelberg, Victoria, Australia, on 10 Dec. 1938.

The highest British performance is 7 ft 6¼ in *2,29 m* by the 16.2 hands *167 cm* bay gelding *Swank*, ridden by Donald Beard, at Olympia, London, on 25 June 1937. On the same day, the Lady Wright (*née* Margery Avis Bullows) set the best recorded height for a British equestrienne on her liver chestnut *Jimmy Brown* at 7 ft 4 in *2,23 m*. These records were over the now unused sloping poles. Harvey Smith on *O'Malley* cleared 7 ft 3 in *2,21 m* in Toronto, Canada in 1967.

Most titles The most B.S.J.A. championships won is four by Alan Oliver (1951–54–59–69). The only horses to have won twice are *Maguire* (Lt.-Col. Nathaniel Kindersley) in 1945 and 1947, *Sheila* (Hayes) in 1949–50 and *Red Admiral* (Oliver) in 1951 and 1954. The record for the Ladies' Championship is 8 by Miss Patricia Smythe (b. 22 Nov. 1928), now Mrs. Samuel Koechlin, O.B.E. (1952–53–55–57–58–59–61–62). She was on *Flanagan*, owned by Robert Hanson, C.B.E., in 1955, 1958 and 1962—the only three time winner.

George V Gold Cup Four men have thrice won this premier award (first held in 1911): the late Lt.-Col. J. A. Talbot-Ponsonby (1930–32–34), Lt.-Col. Harry M. Llewellyn, C.B.E. (1948–50–53 on *Foxhunter*), Piero d'Inzeo (Italy) (1957–61–62) and David Broome (b. 1 Mar. 1940) in 1960 on *Sunsalve*, 1966 on *Mister Softee* and 1972 on *Sportsman*.

Marathon The longest continuous period spent in the saddle is 42 hrs 20 min by Joseph Roberts of Newport Pagnell, Buckinghamshire, from Brighton, Sussex to Bletchley, Buckinghamshire on 6–8 July 1972.

End to End Jack Bailey and Graham Miles of High Wycombe, Buckinghamshire rode on *Jason* and *Minstrel* 900 miles *1 450 km* from John O'Groats to Land's End from 26 Aug. to 5 Oct. 1972.

Lady Wright, who achieved the highest recorded jump for a British equestrienne at 7 ft 4 in *2,23 m*

FENCING

Origins "Fencing" (fighting with single sticks) was practised as a sport in Egypt as early as c. 1360 B.C. The first governing body for fencing in Britain was the Corporation of Masters of Defence founded by Henry VIII before 1540 and fencing has been practised as sport, notably in prize fights, since that time. The foil was the practice weapon for the short court sword from the 17th century. The épée was established in the mid-19th century and the light sabre was introduced by the Italians in the late 19th century.

Most Olympic titles The greatest number of individual Olympic Gold Medals won is three by Ramón Fonst (Cuba) (b. 1883) in 1900 and 1904 (2) and by Nedo Nadi (Italy) (b. 9 June 1894) in 1912 and 1920 (2). Nadi also won three team gold medals in 1920 making a then unprecedented total of five gold medals at one celebration. Aladár Gerevich (Hungary) (b. 16 Mar. 1910) was in the winning sabre team in 1932, 36, 48, 52, 56 and 60. He also holds the record of 10 Olympic medals (7 gold, 1 silver, 2 bronze). The women's record is 6 medals (2 gold, 3 silver, 1 bronze) by Ildikó Sagine-Rejtö (formerly Ujlaki-Rejtö) (Hungary) (b. 11 May 1937) from 1960 to 1972.

Most World titles The greatest number of individual world titles won is 4; this record is shared by d'Oriola and Pawlowski (see details in table), but note that d'Oriola also won 2 Individual Olympic titles. Likewise of the three

Christian D'Oriola holder of the greatest number of world fencing titles, during a match against R. R. C. Paul (G.B.) in Rome, 1955

women foilists with 3 world titles, only Elek also won 2 individual Olympic titles.

British Olympic records The only British fencer to win 3 Olympic medals has been Edgar Seligman with silver medals in the épée team event in 1906, 08 and 12. Allan Louis Neville Jay, M.B.E. (b. 30 June 1931) has competed most often for Great Britain with 5 Olympic appearances (1952 to 1968).

MOST OLYMPIC AND MOST WORLD TITLES

Event	Olympic Gold Medals		World Championships (not held in Olympic years)	
Men's Foil, Individual	2	Christian d'Oriola (France) b. 3 Oct. 1928 (1952, 56)	4	Christian d'Oriola (France) b. 3 Oct. 1928 (1947, 49, 53, 54)
Men's Foil, Team	5	France (1924, 32, 48, 52, 68)	12	Italy (1929–31, 33–35, 37, 38, 49, 50, 54, 55)
Men's Epée, Individual	2	Ramón Fonst (Cuba) b. 1883 ((1900, 04)	3	Georges Buchard (France) b. 21 Dec. 1893 (1927, 31, 33)
Men's Epée Team	6	Italy (1920, 28, 36, 52, 56, 60)	3	Aleksey Nikanchikov (U.S.S.R.) b. 30 July 1940 (1966, 67, 70)
Men's Sabre, Individual	2	Dr. Jenö Fuchs (Hungary) b. 29 Oct. 1882 (1908, 12)	10	Italy (1931, 33, 37, 49, 50, 53–55, 57, 58)
	2	Rudolf Kárpáti (Hungary) b. 17 July 1920 (1956, 60)	4	Jerzy Pawlowski (Poland) b. 25 Oct. 1932 (1957, 65, 66, 68)
Men's Sabre, Team	9	Hungary (1908, 12, 28, 32, 36, 48, 52, 56, 60)	13	Hungary (1930, 31, 33–35, 37, 51, 53–55, 57, 58, 66)
Women's Foil, Individual	2	Ilona Schacherer-Elek (Hungary) b. 1907 (1936, 48)	3	Helene Mayer (Germany) 1910–53 (1929, 31, 37)
			3	Ilona Schacherer-Elek (Hungary) b. 1907 (1934, 35, 51)
			3	Ellen Muller-Preiss (Austria) (1947, 49, 50 (shared))
Women's Foil, Team	3	U.S.S.R. (1960, 68, 72)	11	Hungary (1933–35, 37, 53–55, 59, 62, 65, 67)

MOST AMATEUR FENCING ASSOCIATION TITLES

Foil	(Instituted 1898)	7	John Emrys Lloyd	1928, 1930–33, 1937–38
Epée	(Instituted 1904)	5	Robert Montgomerie	1905, 1907, 1909, 1912, 1914
Sabre	(Instituted 1898)	6	Dr. R. F. Tredgold	1937, 1939, 1947–49, 1955
Foil (Ladies)	(Instituted 1907)	10	Miss Gillian M. Sheen (now Mrs. R. G. Donaldson)	1949, 1951–58, 1960

FIVES

ETON FIVES

A handball game against the buttress of Eton College Chapel was recorded in 1825, but a court existed at Lord Weymouth's School, Warminster, as early as 1773 and a handball game against the church wall at Babcary, Somerset, was recorded in June 1765. New courts were built at Eton in 1840, the rules were codified in 1877, rewritten laws were introduced in 1931 and the laws were last drawn up in 1950.

Most titles Only one pair have won the Amateur Championship (Kinnaird Cup) six times—Anthony Hughes and Arthur James Gordon Campbell (1958, 1965–68 and 1971). Hughes was also in the winning pair in 1963 making seven titles in all.

RUGBY FIVES

As now known, this game dates from c. 1850 with the first inter-public school matches recorded in the early 1870s. The Oxford v. Cambridge contest was inaugurated in 1925 and the Rugby Fives Association was founded in the home of Dr. Cyriax, in Welbeck Street, London, on 29 Oct. 1927. The dimensions of the Standard Rugby Fives court were approved by the Association in 1931.

David E. Gardiner, the first person to hold all ten National and Provincial fives titles during his playing career

Most titles The greatest number of Amateur Singles Championships (instituted 1932) ever won is four by John Frederick Pretlove in 1953, 1955–56 and 1958, and by Eric Marsh in 1960–61–62–63. Pretlove also holds the record for the Amateur Doubles Championship (instituted 1925), being co-champion in 1952, 1954, 1956–57–58–59 and 1961. The first person to have held all ten National and Provincial titles during his playing career is David E. Gardner. To 1973 he had won 12 Scottish titles (5 singles and 7 doubles), 14 North of England titles (4 singles and 10 doubles), 7 West of England titles (2 singles and 5 doubles), Lancashire Open (1 singles, 2 doubles), the Amateur Singles in 1964 and the Amateur Doubles in 1960, 1965, 1966, 1970, 1971, and 1972.

FOOTBALL (ASSOCIATION)

Origins A game with some similarities termed *Tsu-chin* was played in China in the 3rd and 4th centuries B.C. The earliest clear representation of the game is an Edinburgh print dated 1672–73. It became standardized with the formation of the Football Association in England on 26 Oct. 1863. A 26-a-side game, however, existed in Florence, Italy, as early as 1530, for which rules were codified in *Discorsa Calcio* in 1580. The oldest club is Sheffield F.C., formed on 24 Oct. 1857. Eleven per side was standardized in 1870.

HIGHEST SCORES

Teams The highest score recorded in a British first-class match is 36. This occurred in the Scottish Cup match between Arbroath and Bon Accord on 5 Sept. 1885, when Arbroath won 36–0 on their home ground. But for the lack of nets and the consequent waste of retrieval time the score would have been even higher. The same day Dundee Harp beat Aberdeen Rovers 35–0.

The highest margin recorded in an international match is 17. This occurred in the England v. Australia match at Sydney on 30 June 1951, when England won 17–0. This match is not listed by England as a *full* international. The highest in the British Isles was when England beat Ireland 13–0 at Belfast on 18 Feb. 1882. The highest score in an F.A. Cup match is 26, when Preston North End beat Hyde 26–0 at Deepdale, Preston on 15 Oct. 1887. This is also the highest score between English clubs. The biggest victory in a final tie is 6 when Bury beat Derby County 6–0 at Crystal Palace on 18 April 1903, in which year Bury did not concede a single goal in the five Cup matches.

The highest score by one side in Football League (Division I) match is 12 goals when West Bromwich Albion beat Darwen 12–0 at West Bromwich on 4 March 1892; when Nottingham Forest beat Leicester Fosse by the same score at Nottingham on 21 April 1909; and when Aston Villa beat Accrington 12–2 at Villa Park on 12 March 1892.

The highest aggregate in League Football was 17 goals when Tranmere Rovers beat Oldham Athletic 13–4 in a 3rd Division (North) match at Prenton Park, Birkenhead, on Boxing Day, 1935. The record margin in a League match has been 13 in the Newcastle United 13, Newport County 0 Division II match on 5 Oct. 1946 and in the Stockport County 13, Halifax 0 Division III (North) match on 6 Jan. 1934.

Individuals The most scored by one player in a first-class match is 16 by Stains for Racing Club de Lens v. Aubry-Asturies, in Lens, France, on 13 Dec. 1942. The record for any British first-class match is 13 by John Petrie in the Arbroath v. Bon Accord Scottish Cup match in 1885 (see above). The record in League Football is 10 by Joe Payne (b. Bolsover, Derbyshire) for Luton Town v. Bristol Rovers in a 3rd Division (South) match at Luton on 13 April 1936. The English 1st Division record is 7 goals by Ted Drake (b. Southampton, Hampshire) for Arsenal v. Aston Villa at Birmingham on 14 Dec. 1935, and James Ross for Preston North End v. Stoke at Preston on 6 Oct. 1888. The Scottish 1st Division record is 8 goals by James McGrory for Celtic v. Dunfermline Athletic at Celtic Park, Glasgow, on 14 Jan. 1928.

The record for individual goal-scoring in a British home international is 6 by Joe Bambrick for Ireland v. Wales at Belfast on 1 Feb. 1930.

Career Artur Friedenreich (b. 1892) is believed to have scored an undocumented 1,329 goals in Brazilian football, but the greatest total of goals scored in a specified period is 1,026 by Edson Arantes do Nascimento (b. Baurú, Brazil, 28 June 1940), known as Pelé, the Brazilian inside left from 1957 to the World Cup final on 21 June 1970. His best year was 1958 with 139 and the *milesimo* (1,000th) came in a penalty for his club Santos in the Maracaña Stadium, Rio de Janerio on 19 Nov. 1969 when playing his 909th first-class match. He passed 1,000 goals in club matches during 1972. Franz ("Bimbo") Binder (b. 1911) scored 1,006 goals in 756 games in Austria and Germany between 1930 and 1950.

The best season League records are 60 goals in 39 League games by William Ralph ("Dixie") Dean (b. Birkenhead, Cheshire, 1906) for Everton (Division I) in 1927–28 and 66 goals in 38 games by Jim Smith for Ayr United (Scottish Division II) in the same season. With 3 more in Cup ties and 19 in representative matches Dean's total was 82.

Ted Drake (Arsenal) holder of the First Division record of seven goals in one match

Bobby Charlton, in his characteristic goal scoring position, which has gained him some of his 49 goals for England

The international career record for England is 49 goals by Robert ("Bobby") Charlton, O.B.E. (b. Ashington, Northumberland, 11 Oct. 1937). His first was *v.* Scotland in 1958 and his last on 20 May 1970 *v.* Colombia.

The greatest number of goals scored in British first-class football is 550 (410 in League matches) by James McGrory of Glasgow Celtic (1922–38). The most scored in League matches is 434, for West Bromwich Albion, Fulham, Leicester City and Shrewsbury Town, by George Arthur Rowley (b. Wolverhampton, Staffordshire, 1926) between 1946 and April 1965. Rowley also scored 32 goals in the F.A. Cup and 1 for England "B".

Fastest Goals The fastest goal on record is 6 sec jointly held by Albert Mundy of Aldershot in a Fourth Division match against Hartlepools United at Victoria Ground, Hartlepool on 25 Oct. 1958 and Keith Smith of Crystal Palace in a Second Division match against Derby County at Baseball Ground, Derby on 12 Dec. 1964. A goal 4 sec after the kick-off is claimed by Jim Fryatt of Bradford in a Fourth Division match against Tranmere Rovers at Park Avenue, Bradford on 25 April 1964. Jimmy Scarth (Gillingham) scored 3 goals in 2 min against Leyton Orient at Priestfield Stadium, Gillingham on 1 Nov. 1952. John McIntyre (Blackburn Rovers) scored 4 goals in 5 min *v.* Everton at Ewood Park, Blackburn, on 16 Sept. 1922. W. G. ("Billy") Richardson (West Bromwich Albion) scored 4 goals in 5 min against West Ham United at Upton Park on 7 Nov. 1931. Frank Keetley scored 6 goals in 21 min in the 2nd half of the Lincoln City *v.* Halifax Town league match on 16 Jan. 1932.

The international record is 3 goals in $3\frac{1}{2}$ min by Willie Hall (Tottenham Hotspur) for England against Ireland on 16 Nov. 1938 at Old Trafford, Manchester.

Goal-less streak In Oct.–Dec. 1919 Coventry played 11 successive games without scoring.

MOST APPEARANCES

Robert Frederick ("Bobby") Moore, O.B.E. (b. Barking, Essex, 12 April 1941) of West Ham United set up a new record of full international appearances by a British footballer by playing in his 107th game for England *v.* Italy on 14 June 1973 in Turin. His first appearance was *v.* Peru on 20 May 1962.

England The greatest number of appearances for England secured in the International Championship is 38 by William (Billy) Ambrose Wright C.B.E. (b. Ironbridge Shropshire, 6 Feb. 1924) in 1946–1959.

Wales The record number of appearances for Wales in the International Championship is 48 by William (Billy) Meredith (Manchester City and United) in the longest international span of 26 years (1895–1920). This is a record for any of the four home countries. Ivor Allchurch, M.B.E. (born 29 Dec. 1929) of Swansea, Newcastle, Cardiff City and Worcester City played 68 times for Wales, including 37 times against the home countries, between 15 Nov. 1950 and Feb. 1968.

Scotland The Scottish record for International Championship matches is 30 by Alan Morton (Queen's Park and Glasgow Rangers) from 1920 to 1932. Morton also had a single foreign international making a total of 31 caps. George Young (Glasgow Rangers) has a record total of 53 appearances for Scotland, of which 29 were for International Championship matches, between 1946 and 1957.

Ireland The greatest number of appearances for Ireland is 59 by Terry Neill (b. Belfast) (Arsenal and Hull City) (1961 to 1973).

Oldest cap The oldest cap has been William Henry (Billy) Meredith (1874–1958), who played outside right for Wales *v.* England at Highbury, London, on 15 March 1920 when aged 45 years 229 days.

Youngest caps The youngest cap in the four home countries internationals has been Norman Kernoghan (Belfast Celtic) who played for Ireland *v.* Wales in 1936 aged 17 years 80 days. It is possible, however, that W. K. Gibson (Cliftonville) who played for Ireland *v.* Wales in 1894 at 17 was slightly younger. England's youngest home international was Duncan Edwards (b. Dudley, Staffordshire, 1 Oct. 1936, d. 21 Feb. 1958, 15 days after the Munich air crash) the Manchester United left half, against Scotland at Wembley on 2 April 1955, aged 18 years 6 months. The youngest Welsh cap was John Charles (b. Swansea, 27 Dec. 1931) the Leeds United centre half, against Ireland at Wrexham on 8 March 1950, aged 18 years 71 days. Scotland's youngest international has been Denis Law (b. Aberdeen, 24 Feb. 1940) of Huddersfield Town, who played against Wales on 18 Oct. 1958, aged 18 years 236 days. Jackie Robinson played for England *v.* Finland in 1937 aged 17 years 9 months. Research remains to be completed on the date of birth of David Black of Hurlford, Ayrshire, who may have been 17 when he played for Scotland *v.* Ireland in 1889.

Longest match The duration record for first class fixtures was set in the Copa Libertadores in Santos, Brazil, on 2–3 Aug. 1962, when Santos drew 3–3 with Penarol F.C. of Montevideo, Uruguay. The game lasted $3\frac{1}{2}$ hours (with interruptions), from 9.30 p.m. to 1 a.m.

The longest British match on record was one of 3 hours 23 min between Stockport County and Doncaster Rovers in the second leg of the 3rd Division (North) Cup at Edgeley Park, Stockport, on 30 March 1946.

Heaviest goalkeeper The biggest goalkeeper in representative football was the England international Willie J. "Fatty" Foulke (1874–1916), who stood 6 ft 3 in *1,90 m* and weighed 22 st. 3 lb. *141 kg*. His last games were for Bradford, by which time he was 26 st. *165 kg*. He once stopped a game by snapping the cross bar.

TRANSFER FEES

The world's highest reported transfer fee is £414,667 paid by the Italian club Roma for Pierino Prati in the week of 8–14 July 1973. The British cash record is *c.* £225,000 for the Leicester City full-back David Nish (b. Measham, Leicestershire, 1947) paid by Derby County on 25 Aug. 1972.

The British aggregate record is held by the centre forward Tony Hateley (b. Derby, 1942) who in six moves from July 1963 to 28 Oct. 1970 was reportedly valued at £393,500.

Signing fee On 26 May 1961, Luis Suarez, the Barcelona inside forward, was transferred to Internazionale (Milan) for £144,000, of which Suarez himself received a record £59,000. The British record is £10,000 for John Charles (Leeds United to Juventus, Turin on 19 April 1957), and Denis Law (Manchester City to Torino, Italy on 13 June 1961).

CROWD AND GATES

The greatest recorded crowd at any football match was 205,000 (199,854 paid) for the Brazil *v.* Uruguay World Cup match in the Maracaña Municipal Stadium, Rio de Janeiro, Brazil on 16 July 1950.

The record attendance for a European Cup match is 127,621 at the European Champions Cup Final between Real Madrid and Eintracht Frankfurt at Hampden Park, Glasgow on 18 May 1950.

The British record paid attendance is 149,547 at the Scotland *v.* England international at Hampden Park, Glasgow, on 17 April 1937. It is, however, probable that this total was exceeded (estimated 160,000) on

Bobby Moore who has made 107 full international appearances for England

the occasion of the F.A. Cup Final between Bolton Wanderers and West Ham United at Wembley Stadium on 28 April 1923, when the crowd broke in on the pitch and the start was delayed 40 min until the pitch was cleared. The counted admissions were 126,047.

The Scottish Cup record attendance is an estimated 170,000 when Celtic played Aberdeen at Hampden Park on 24 April 1937. The record for a British inter-club fixture is 143,570 at the Rangers *v.* Hibernian match at Hampden Park, Glasgow, on 27 March 1948.

Smallest The smallest crowd at a full home international was 4,946 for the Northern Ireland *v.* Wales match of 19 May 1973 at Goodison Park, Everton. The smallest crowd at a Football League fixture was for the Stockport County *v.* Leicester City match at Old Trafford, Manchester, on 7 May 1921. Stockport's own ground was under suspension and the "crowd" numbered 13.

RECEIPTS

The record gross F.A. Cup receipts at Wembley, Greater London, is £233,800 (excluding radio and television fees) for the final on 5 May 1973.

The greatest receipts at any World Cup final were £204,805, from an attendance of 96,924 for England *v.* West Germany at the Empire Stadium, Wembley, on 30 July 1966.

The record for a British international match is £193,000 for the England *v.* Scotland match at Wembley on 19 May 1973 (attendance 100,000). The receipts for the Manchester United *v.* Benfica match at Wembley on 29 May 1968 were £118,000 (attendance 100,000).

Most successful national coach The most successful national coach has been George Raynor (b. 1907) for Sweden. His teams won the 1948 Olympic competition and were 2nd in the 1958 World Cup and 3rd in both the 1950 World Cup and in the 1952 Olympic competition.

F.A. CHALLENGE CUP

Wins The greatest number F.A. Cup wins is 7 by Aston Villa in 1887, 1895, 1897, 1905, 1913, 1920 and 1957 (nine final appearances). Of the 6-time winners Newcastle United have been in the final 10 times, as have 5-time winners West Bromwich Albion. The highest aggregate scores have been 6–1 in 1890, 6–0 in 1903 and 4–3 in 1953.

The greatest number of Scottish F.A. Cup wins is 22 by Celtic in 1892, 1899, 1900, 1904, 1907–08, 1911–12, 1914, 1923, 1925, 1927, 1931, 1933, 1937, 1951, 1954, 1965, 1967, 1969, 1971 and 1972.

Youngest player The youngest player in the F.A. Cup Final was Howard Kendall (b. 22 May 1946) of Preston North End, who played against West Ham United on 2 May 1964, 20 days before his 18th birthday. Note however, that Derek Johnstone (Rangers) (b. 4 Nov. 1953) was 16 years 11 months old when he played in the Scottish League Cup Final against Celtic on 24 Oct. 1970.

Most medals Three players have won 5 F.A. Cup Winner's Medals: James Forrest (Blackburn Rovers) (1884–85–86–90–91); the Hon. Sir Arthur Fitzgerald Kinnaird K.T. (Wanderers) (1873–77–78) and Old Etonians (1879–82) and C. H. R. Wollaston (Wanderers) (1872–73–76–1877–78).

Longest tie The most protracted F.A. Cup tie in the competition proper was that between Stoke City and Bury in the 3rd round with Stoke winning 3–2 in the fifth meeting after 9 hours 22 min of play in January 1955. The matches were at Bury (1–1) on 8 January; Stoke on Trent 12 January (abandoned after 22 min of extra time with the score 1–1); Goodison Park (3–3) on 17 January; Anfield (2–2) on 19 January; and finally at Old Trafford on 24 January. In the 1972 final qualifying round Alvechurch beat Oxford City after five previous drawn games.

MOST LEAGUE CHAMPIONSHIPS

The greatest number of League Championships (Division I) is 8 jointly held by Arsenal in 1931, 1933, 1934, 1935, 1938, 1948, 1953 and 1971 and Liverpool in 1901, 1906, 1922, 1923, 1947, 1964, 1966, and 1973. The record number of points is in Division I 67 by Leeds United in 1969 while the lowest has been 8 by Doncaster Rovers (Division II) in 1904–5. Doncaster Rovers scored 72 points from 42 games in Division III (North) in 1947.

The only F.A. Cup and League Championship "doubles" are those of Preston North End in 1889, Aston Villa in 1897, Tottenham Hotspur in 1961 and Arsenal in 1971. Preston won the League without losing a match and the Cup without having a goal scored against them throughout the whole competition. Glasgow Rangers have won the Scottish League Championship 33 times between 1899 and 1964 and were joint champions on another occasion. Their 76 points in the Scottish 1st Division in 1921 represents a record in any division.

Closest win In 1923–24 Huddersfield won the Division I championship over Cardiff by 0.02 of a goal with a goal average of 1.81.

Most durable player The most durable player in League history has been Jimmy Dickinson (b. Alton, Hampshire, 1925) who made 764 appearances for Portsmouth F.C. between 1946 and 1965.

Jimmy Dickinson who made a total of 764 appearances for Portsmouth F.C. in 19 years

WORLD CUP

The *Fédération Internationale de Football* (F.I.F.A.) was founded in Paris on 21 May 1904 and instituted the World Cup Competition on 13 July 1930, in Montevideo, Uruguay.

The only country to win three times has been Brazil in 1958, 1962 and 1970. Brazil was also third in 1938 and second in 1950, and is the only one of the 40 participating countries to have played in all 9 competitions. Antonio Carbajal (b. 1923) played for Mexico in goal in the competitions of 1950–54–58–62 and 1966. The record goal scorer has been Just Fontaine (France) with 13 goals in 6 games in the final stages of the 1958 competition in Sweden. The most goals scored in a final is 3 by Geoffrey Hurst (b. Ashton-under-Lyne, 1941) (West Ham United) for England v. West Germany on 30 July 1966.

EUROPEAN CHAMPIONSHIP

The European equivalent of the World Cup started in 1958 and is staged every 4 years. Each tournament takes 2 years to run with the semi-finals and final in the same country. The U.S.S.R. won the first when they beat Yugoslavia 2–1 in Paris on 10 July 1960 followed by Spain (1964), Italy (1968) and West Germany (1972).

EUROPEAN CHAMPIONS CUP

The European Cup for the League champions of the respective nations was approved by F.I.F.A. on 8 May 1955 and was run by the European governing body U.E.F.A. (Union of European Football Associations) which came into being in the previous year. Real Madrid defeated Rheims 4–3 in the first final in 1956 and went on to win the Cup in the next 4 seasons and in 1966. They took part in all competitions, either as holders or Spanish champions up to and including 1969–70. Ajax, Amsterdam won the cup for three successive years 1971, 1972 and 1973.

Glasgow Celtic became the first British club to win the Cup when they beat Inter-Milan 2–1 in the National Stadium, Lisbon, Portugal, on 25 May 1967. At the same time they established the record of being the only club to win the European Cup and the two senior domestic tournaments (League and Cup) in the same season.

EUROPEAN CUP WINNERS CUP

A tournament for the national Cup winners started in 1960–1 with 10 entries. Fiorentina beat Glasgow Rangers on 4–1 aggregate in a two-leg final in May 1961. Tottenham Hotspur were the first British club to win the trophy, beating Atletico Madrid 5–1 in Rotterdam in 1963 and were followed by West Ham United in 1965, Manchester City in 1970, Chelsea in 1971 and Glasgow Rangers in 1972.

U.E.F.A. CUP

Originally known as the International Inter-City Industrial Fairs Cup, this club tournament began in 1955. The first competition lasted 3 years, the second 2 years. In 1960–61 it became an annual tournament and since 1971–72 has been replaced by the U.E.F.A. Cup. The first British club to win the trophy were Leeds United in 1968 and were followed by Newcastle United in 1969, Arsenal in 1970, Leeds again in 1971, Tottenham Hotspur in 1972 and Liverpool in 1973.

WORLD CLUB CHAMPIONSHIP

This club tournament was started in 1960 between the winners of the European Cup and the Copa Libertadores, the South American equivalent. Three clubs have won it twice: Penarol, Uruguay in 1961, 1966; Santos, Brazil in 1962, 1963; and Inter-Milan in 1964, 1965.

FOOTBALL (Amateur)

Most Olympic wins The only country to have won the Olympic football title 3 times is Hungary in 1952, 1964 and 1968. The United Kingdom won the unofficial tournament in 1900 and the official tournaments of 1908 and 1912. The highest Olympic score is Denmark 17 *v.* France "A" 1 in 1908.

Highest scores The highest aggregate score in a home Amateur International is 11 goals in the England *v.* Scotland match (8–3) at Dulwich on 11 March 1939. The foreign record was when England beat France 15–0 in Paris on 1 Nov. 1906.

The highest score in an F.A. Amateur Cup Final is 8, when Northern Nomads beat Stockton 7–1 at Sunderland in 1926, and when Dulwich Hamlet beat Marine (Liverpool) by the same score at Upton Park in 1932.

In the match between Sandygate Youth Club *v.* 1st Burnley Boys' Brigade at Burnley, Lancashire on 10 Sept. 1955, the half time score was 27–0 and after 80 min play 53–0. Sandygate's top scorer was Roy Swift with 14 goals.

Individual The highest individual scores in amateur internationals are 6 by William Charles Jordan for England *v.* France (12–0) at Park Royal, London, on 23 March 1908; 6 by Vivian J. Woodward for England *v.* Holland (9–1) at Stamford Bridge, London, on 11 Dec. 1909; and 6 also by Harold A. Walden for Great Britain *v.* Hungary in Stockholm, Sweden, on 1 July 1912.

Most caps The record number of England amateur caps is held by Rod Haider, the Hendon captain and half-back, who made his 57th amateur international appearance for England *v.* Yugoslavia on 20 June 1973.

F.A. Amateur Cup wins The greatest number of F.A. Amateur Cup (instituted 1893) wins is 10 by Bishop Auckland who won in 1896, 1900, 1914, 1921–22, 1935, 1939, 1955, 1956 and 1957.

Largest crowd The highest attendances at amateur matches has been 100,000, first reached at the Cup Final between Pegasus and Bishop Auckland at Wembley on 21 April 1951. The amateur gate record is £29,305 at the final between Bishop Auckland and Hendon on 16 April 1955.

Heading The highest recorded number of repetitions for heading a ball is 3,412 in 34 min 8 sec by Colin Jones, aged 15, at Queensferry, near Chester, on 8 March 1961.

Most and Least Successful Teams Laughton Boys F.C., Yorkshire, in 1972–73 in league and cup competitions won 37 out of 37 matches with a score of 413–18 so averaging 11.16 goals per match. The Nomads F.C. who participate in the Norwich Lads and Minor League lost 20 out of 20 matches in 1972–73 with a score of 11–431 (a goal average of minus 21.55) despite buying a new goalkeeper for 25p. The club was awarded the League's Best Sportsmen Cup.

Most Goals The greatest number of goals in a season reported for an individual player in junior league football is 96 by Tom Duffy, who played centre-forward professionally for Ardeer Thistle F.C., Ayrshire in the 1960–61 season. The highest season figure reported in any class of competitive football for an individual is 294 goals in 67 matches by centre forward Michael Jones of Afan Lido F.C., St. Joseph's School and Port Talbot Boys XI in 1972–73. His total (65 headers, 120 right boot and 109 left boot) included an 11, a 10 and 6 triple hat-tricks.

Fastest Own Goal The fastest own goal on record was one in 7 sec "scored" by Ascot Sports F.C. in the South Derbyshire Premier League in Sept. 1972. The feat was achieved by dint of two deft back passes. Hilton Athletic F.C. went on to cement this early bonus with a further 9 goals.

Longest ties The aggregate duration of ties in amateur soccer have not been collated but it is recorded that in the London F.A. Intermediate Cup first qualifying round Highfield F.C. Reserves had to meet Mansfield House F.C. on 19 and 26 Sept. and 3, 10 and 14 Oct. 1970 to get a decision after 9 hours 50 min play with scores of 0–0, 1–1, 1–1, 3–3, and 0–2.

In the Hertfordshire Intermediate Cup, London Colney beat Leavesden Hospital after 12 hours 41 min play and 7 ties on 6 Nov. to 17 Dec. 1971.

Most disciplined Coleridge F.C. of the Cambridgeshire F.A. completed 19 years without a single member having been cautioned, sent off or otherwise disciplined since its formation in 1954.

Most indisciplined In the local Cup match between Tongham Youth Club, Surrey and Hawley, Hampshire, England on 3 Nov. 1969 the referee booked all 22 players including one who went to hospital, and one of the linesmen. The match, won by Tongham 2–0, was described by a player as "A good, hard game". In a Dorset Junior Shield match at Chideock on 19 Dec. 1970 referee Douglas Chainey sent the entire R.A.O.C. team off.

Oldest Player A contest by the magazine *Goal* to find Britain's oldest footballer resulted in the finding in May 1970 of left-back Guiseppi "Pimple" Brusaferro (b. Nov. 1908) of Strollers XI, Chiswick and Regent Street Polytechnic F.C. playing out his 51st season watched by his father.

Referee Most Durable The longest recorded service of any referee is 56 years (1904–60) in the case of William B. McCallum of Hillhead, Glasgow for 10 years convener of the Scottish Football Referees Association.

Longest marathons The longest recorded 11-a-side football match played under F.A. rules without substitutes has been one of 28 hours (184–140) by Brentwood S.C. and Village Lantern Tavern S.C. in the Long Island Soccer Football League, New York on 21–22 June 1973.

The longest recorded authenticated 5-a-side games have been: outdoors: 41 hours 40 min by two teams (no substitutes) from Duke of York's Royal Military School, Dover, Kent from 25–27 June 1973 and indoors: 63 hours by two teams (no substitutes) from Belle Vue Boys School, Bradford, Yorks. from 12–14 April 1973. Arthur Clement completed the last 15 hours with a broken nose.

FOOTBALL (GAELIC)

Earliest references The game developed from inter-parish "free for all" with no time-limit, no defined playing area nor specific rules. The formation of the Gaelic Athletic Association was in Thurles, Ireland, on 1 Nov. 1884.

Most titles The greatest number of All Ireland Championships ever won by one team is 22 by Ciarraidhe (Kerry) between 1903 and 1970. The greatest number of successive wins is four by Wexford (1915–18) and four by Kerry (1929–32).

Highest scores The highest score in an All-Ireland final was when Cork (6 goals, 6 points) beat Antrim (1 goal, 2 points) in 1911. The highest combined score was when Kerry (2 goals, 19 points) beat Meath (no goals, 18 points) in 1970. A goal equals 3 points.

Lowest scores In four All-Ireland finals the combined totals have been 7 points; 1893 Wexford (1 goal [till 1894 worth 5 points], 1 point) v. Cork (1 point); 1895 Tipperary (4 points) v. Meath (3 points); 1904 Kerry (5 points) v. Dublin (2 points); 1924 Kerry (4 points) v. Dublin (3 points).

Most appearances The most appearances in All-Ireland finals is ten by Dan O'Keeffe (Kerry) of which seven (a record) were on the winning side.

Individual score The highest recorded individual score in an All-Ireland final has been 2 goals, 5 points by Frank Stockwell (Galway) in the match against Cork in 1956.

Largest crowd The record crowd is 90,556 for the Down v. Offaly final at Croke Park, Dublin, in 1961.

The 1972 All-Ireland Gaelic Football final between Kerry, holders of the title 22 times, and Offaly

Inter-provincials The province of Leinster has won most championships (Railway Cup) with 17 between 1928 and 1962. Sean O'Neill (Down) holds the record of 8 medals with Ulster (1960–71).

FOOTBALL (RUGBY LEAGUE)

Origins The Rugby League was formed originally in 1895 as "The Northern Rugby Football Union" by the secession of 22 clubs in Lancashire and Yorkshire from the parent Rugby Union. Though payment for loss of working time was a major cause of the breakaway the "Northern Union" did not itself embrace full professionalism until 1898. A reduction in the number of players per team from 15 to 13 took place in 1906 and the present title of "Rugby League" was adopted in 1922.

Most wins Under the one-league Championship system (1907–62 and 1965–71) the club with the most wins was Wigan with nine (1909, 1922, 1926, 1934, 1946, 1947, 1950, 1952 and 1960).

In the Rugby League Challenge Cup (inaugurated 1896–97) the club with the most wins is Leeds with 8 in 1910–23–32–36, 1941–42 (wartime), 1957 and 1968. Oldham is the only club to appear in four consecutive Cup Finals (1924–27) and Bradford Northern is the only football club (Rugby League or Association) to have appeared at Wembley in three consecutive years (1947–48–49).

Only three clubs have won all four major Rugby League trophies (Challenge Cup, League Championship, County Cup and County League) in one season: Hunslet in 1907–08, Huddersfield in 1914–15 and Swinton in 1927–28.

In addition to the three "All Four Cup clubs", on only five other occasions has a club taken the Cup and League honours in one season: Broughton Rangers (1902); Halifax (1903); Huddersfield (1913); Warrington (1954); and St. Helens (1966).

World Cup The record aggregate score in a World Cup match is 72 points when Great Britain beat New Zealand at Hameau Stadium, Pau, France by 53 points to 19 on 4 Nov. 1972.

There have been six World Cup Competitions. Australia were winners in 1957, 1968 and 1970. Great Britain won in 1954, 1960 and 1972.

Senior match The highest aggregate score in Cup or League football in a game where a senior club has been concerned, was 121 points, when Huddersfield beat Swinton Park

Rangers by 119 points (19 goals, 27 tries) to 2 points (one goal) in the first round of the Northern Union Cup on 28 Feb. 1914.

Cup Final The record aggregate in a Cup Final is 47 points when Featherstone Rovers beat Bradford Northern 33–14 at Wembley on 12 May 1973.

The greatest winning margin was 34 points when Huddersfield beat St. Helens 37–3 at Oldham on 1 May 1915.

Touring teams The record score for a British team touring the Commonwealth is 101 points by England v. South Australia (nil) at Adelaide in May 1914.

The record for a Commonwealth touring team in Britain is 92 points (10 goals, 24 tries) by Australia against Bramley's 7 points (2 goals, one try) at the Barley Mow Ground, Bramley, near Leeds, on 9 Nov. 1921.

Record crowds and receipts The greatest attendance at any Rugby League match is 102,569 for the Warrington v. Halifax Cup Final replay at Odsal Stadium, Bradford, on 5 May 1954.

The highest receipts for a match in the United Kingdom have been £125,826 40p for the Featherstone Rovers v. Bradford Northern Cup Final at Wembley Stadium on 12 May 1973.

Most international caps Test Matches between Great Britain (formerly England) and Australia are regarded as the highest distinction for an R.L. player in either hemisphere and Jim Sullivan (b. 2 Dec. 1903), the Wigan full-back and captain, holds a Test record for a British player with 15 appearances in these games between 1924 and 1933, though Mick Sullivan (no kin) of Huddersfield, Wigan, St. Helens and York, played in 16 G.B. v. Australia games in 1954–64, of which 13 were Tests and 3 World Cup matches.

In all Tests, including those against New Zealand and France, Mick Sullivan made the record number of 47 appearances and scored 43 tries.

Most Cup Finals Two players have appeared in seven Cup Finals: Alan Edwards (Salford, Dewsbury, and Bradford Northern) between 1938 and 1949, and Eric Batten (Leeds, Bradford Northern and Featherstone Rovers) between 1941 and 1952.

Eric Ashton, M.B.E. (b. 24 Jan. 1935), Wigan and Great Britain centre has the distinction of captaining Wigan at Wembley in six R.L. Cup Finals in nine years 1958–66, taking the trophy three times (1958, 1959 and 1965).

The youngest player in a Cup Final was Reg Lloyd (Keighley) who was 17 years 8 months when he played at Wembley on 8 May 1937.

Most goals The record number of goals in a season is 228 by David Watkins (Salford) (b. 5 Mar. 1942) in the 1972–

David Watkins (Salford), who on 1 Dec. 1972 scored 13 points v. Barrow in under 5 min

1973 season. His total was made up of 221 in League, Cup, other competitions, and a Salford v. New Zealand match, plus 7 in two pre-season friendly fixtures.

MOST TRIES

Season Albert Aaron Rosenfeld (Huddersfield), an Australian-born wing-threequarter, scored 80 tries in the 1913–14 season.

Career Brian Bevan, an Australian-born wing-threequarter, scored 834 tries in League, Cup, representative or charity games in the 18 seasons (16 with Warrington, 2 with Blackpool Borough) from 1946 to 1964.

MOST POINTS

Cup C. H. ("Tich") West of Hull Kingston Rovers scored 53 points (10 goals and 11 tries) in a 1st Round Challenge Cup-tie v. Brookland Rovers on 4 March 1905.

League Lionel Cooper of Huddersfield scored 10 tries and kicked two goals against Keighley on 17 Nov. 1951.

Season The record number of points in a season was scored by B. Lewis Jones (Leeds) with 496 in season 1956–57 (he also scored 9 points in a friendly game). David

HIGHEST SCORES

The highest aggregate scores in international Rugby League football are:

Match	Points	Score
Great Britain v. Australia (*Test Matches*)	62	Australia won 50–12 (Swinton, 9 Nov. 1963)
Great Britain v. New Zealand (*Test Matches*)	72	Great Britain won 52–20 (Wellington, 30 July 1910)
Great Britain v. France (*Test Matches*)	65	Great Britain won 50–15 (Leeds, 14 March 1959)
England v. Wales	63	England won 40–23 (Leeds, 18 Oct. 1969)
England v. France	55	France won 42–13 (Marseilles, 25 Nov. 1951)
England v. Other Nationalities	61	England won 34–27 (Workington, 30 March 1933)
Wales v. France	50	France won 29–21 (Bordeaux, 23 Nov. 1947)
Wales v. Other Nationalities	48	Other Nationalities won 27–21 (Swansea, 31 March 1951)
Australia v. Great Britain	76	Australia won 63–13 (Paris, 31 Dec. 1933)
Australia v. Wales	70	Australia won 51–19 (Wembley, 30 Dec. 1933)
Australia v. France (*Test Matches*)	62	Australia won 56–6 (Brisbane, 2 July 1960)
Australia v. New Zealand (*Test Matches*)	74	New Zealand won 49–25 (Brisbane, 28 June 1952)
New Zealand v. France (*Test Matches*)	53	France won 31–22 (Lyon, 15 Jan. 1956)

279

Watkins (Salford) scored 493 points in season 1972–73 (he also scored 14 points in two friendly games).

Career Jim Sullivan (Wigan) scored 6,192 points (2,955 goals and 94 tries) in a senior Rugby League career extending from 1921 to 1946.

Record transfer fees The highest R.L. transfer fee is the reputed £15,000 deal which took Colin Dixon (b. 3 Dec. 1943), the Halifax forward, to Salford on 19 Dec. 1968. David

Watkins (Welsh R.U.) received an £11,000 signing fee at a guaranteed £1,000 p.a. for 5 years from Salford in Oct. 1967.

Longest kick The longest claimed place kick was one of 80 yds *73 m* by H. H. (Dally) Messenger for Australia *v.* Hull in Hull, Yorkshire in 1908 but this was apparently only estimated. In April 1940 Martin Hodgson (Swinton) kicked a goal on the Rochdale ground later measured to be 77¾ yds *71 m*.

FOOTBALL (RUGBY UNION)

Origins The game is traditionally said to have originated from a breach of the rules of the football played in November 1823 at Rugby School by William Webb Ellis (later the Rev.) (*c.* 1807–72). This handling code of football evolved gradually and was known to have been played at Cambridge University by 1839. The Rugby Football Union was not founded until 1871.

MOST CAPPED PLAYERS

The totals below are limited to matches between the seven member countries of the "International Rugby Football Board" and France. Benoit Dauga of France has appeared in 63 internationals of all kinds since 1964.

Ireland	54	Thomas J. Kiernan	1960–73
New Zealand	53	Colin E. Meads	1957–71
France	50	Benoit Dauga	1964–72
Wales	44	Kenneth J. Jones, M.B.E.	1947–57
Australia	42	Peter G. Johnson	1958–72
Scotland	40	Hugh F. McLeod, O.B.E.	1954–62
	40	David M. D. Rollo	1959–68
South Africa	38	Frik C. H. Du Preez	1960–71
England	34	Derek Prior Rogers, O.B.E.	1961–69

Most Olympic Gold Medals Rugby Football was included four times in the Olympic Games: 1900, 1908, 1920 and 1924. Four United States players, in the 1920 winning team won second gold medals in 1924: Charles W. Doe, John T. O'Neil, John C. Patrick and Rudolph J. Scholz. Daniel B. Carroll, who was in the winning Australian team in 1908, won a second gold medal in the 1920 U.S. team.

HIGHEST TEAM SCORES

Internationals The highest score in any full International was when France beat Romania by 72 points (7 goals, six tries and 2 penalty goals) to 3 (1 penalty goal) in the Olympic Games at Colombes, Paris in May 1924.

The above aggregate score also equalled the International Championship record of 75 points when Wales beat France at Swansea in 1910 by 59 points (8 goals, 1 penalty goal, 2 tries) to 16 (1 goal, 2 penalty goals and 1 try).

The highest aggregate score for any International match between the Four Home Unions is 69 when England beat Wales by 69 points (7 goals, 1 drop goal and six tries) to 0 at Blackheath, Kent in 1881.

The highest score by any Overseas side in an International in the British Isles is 53 points (7 goals, 1 drop goal and 2 tries) to 0 when South Africa beat Scotland at Murrayfield, Edinburgh on 24 Nov. 1951.

Tour match The record score for any international tour match is 125–0 (17 goals, 5 tries and 1 penalty goal) when New Zealand beat Northern New South Wales at Quirindi, Australia, on 30 May 1962.

Inter-Club Roundhay Rams defeated R.A.F. Catterick on 28 Feb. 1973 by 154 points to nil (30 tries and 17 conversions).

Schools Scores of over 200 points have been recorded in club matches, for example Radford School beat Hills Court by 31 goals and 7 tries (in current values 214 points) to nil on 20 Nov. 1886.

HIGHEST INDIVIDUAL SCORES

Internationals The highest individual points score in any match between members of the International Board is 24 by W. Fergie McCormick—1 drop goal, 3 conversions and 5 penalty goals for New Zealand against Wales at Auckland on 14 June 1969.

Ian S. Smith (Scotland) has scored most consecutive tries in international matches with 6; 3 in the second half of Scotland *v.* France in 1925 and 3 in the first half against Wales two weeks later.

Senior Inter-Club Malcolm Young (Gosforth) contributed 37 points (4 tries, 3 penalties and 6 conversions) in a 53–3 win over Waterloo on 10 Feb. 1973.

Schools In a match in November 1963 between Stucley's and Darracott's in a junior house match at Bideford G.S., Devon the scrum-half, Alan McKenzie, 14, contributed 86 points (13 tries and 17 conversions) to Stucley's winning score.

Season Record The English first class rugby scoring record for a season is 581 points (incl. 47 points for England) by Samuel Arthur Doble (b. 9 Mar. 1944) of Moseley (in 44 matches) in the 1971–72 season.

Longest kicks The longest recorded successful drop-goal is 90 yds *82 m* by G. Brand for South Africa *v.* England at Twickenham, London, in 1932. This was taken 7 yds *6 m* inside the England "half" 55 yds *50 m* from the posts and dropped over the dead ball line.

The place kick record is reputed to be 100 yds *914 m* at Richmond Athletic Ground, Surrey, by D. F. T. Morkell in an unsuccessful penalty for South Africa *v.* Surrey on 19 Dec. 1906. This was not measured until 1932.

At the Greenyards, Melrose, Roxburghshire on 14 April 1973, George Fairbairn (Kelso) converted the ball which soared out of the ground into a passing lorry. The driver found it when unloading at Yetholm 19 miles *30,5 km* distant.

In the match Bridlington School 1st XV *v.* an Army XV at Bridlington, Yorkshire in 1944, Ernie Cooper, captaining the school, landed a penalty from a measured 81 yds *74 m* from the post with a kick which carried over the dead ball line.

Longest try The longest "try" ever executed was that over 166.5 miles *267,9 km* from Wolverhampton Polytechnic to Cardiff Arms Park, by fifteen players from the Wolverhampton Polytechnic, R.F.C., in 23 hrs 29 min on 9–10 March 1973. There were no forward passes or knock-ons, and the ball was touched down between the posts in the prescribed manner (Law 12).

Fox Hunting

Greatest crowd A crowd of 95,000 has twice been reported: when the British Lions beat South Africa by 1 point at Ellis Park, Johannesburg, on 6 Aug. 1955, and when France met Romania at Bucharest on 19 May 1957, as a curtain raiser for an Association match. The British record is 78,300 for the Calcutta Cup match (England v. Scotland) at Murrayfield, Edinburgh, on 17 March 1962.

County Championships *Most Titles* The County Championships (instituted in 1889) have been won most often by Yorkshire (1889, 1890, 1892–96, 1926, 1928, 1953) and Gloucestershire (1910, 1913, 1920–22, 1930–32, 1937, 1972) each with 10 wins.

The greatest winning margin in a final and highest winning score has been 31–4 in 1921 when Gloucestershire beat Leicestershire.

The highest aggregate score in the final was in 1938 when Lancashire beat Surrey 24–12.

First Seven-a-Sides Seven-a-Side rugby dates from 1883 when Melrose R.F.C., Roxburghshire finding themselves in reduced circumstances due to the formation of a splinter club at Galashiels, Selkirkshire, staged a Seven-a-Side tournament. This idea was that of Ned Haig, the town's butcher. Melrose and Galashiels tied in the final. In extra time, Melrose scored and decamped with the trophy declaring themselves to be the winners. Hence the present day tradition of "sudden death" extra-time.

Middlesex Seven-a-Sides The Middlesex Seven-a-Sides were inaugurated in 1926. The most successful side has been Harlequins with 7 wins (1926–27–28–29–33–35–67).

The only players to be in five winning "sevens" have been N. M. Hall (d. 1972) (St. Mary's Hospital 1944–1946 and Richmond 1951–53–55), and J. A. P. Shackleton and I. H. P. Laughland both of London Scottish (1960–61–62–63–65).

Highest posts The world's highest Rugby Union goal posts measure 93 ft 10½ in *28,61 m* and are made of metal. They are at the Municipal Grounds, Barberton, Transvaal, South Africa.

NED HAIG
The Founder of Seven-a-sides.

Ned Haig, from an original photograph

ALL TIME SCORING RECORDS — AGGREGATE and MARGIN of VICTORY in the ten annual matches in the "International Championship".

Records are determined in terms of current scoring values, i.e. a try at 4 points, a dropped goal, penalty or goal from a mark at 3 points, and a conversion at 2 points, which are given in italics. The actual score in accordance with which ever of the 9 systems was in force at the time is also given in brackets.

		Aggregate Record Current pts. value		Record Margin Current pts. value
England v. Scotland	Scotland (28) beat England (19) in 1931	*57*	England (19) beat Scotland (0) in 1924	*21*
			England (24) beat Scotland (5) in 1947	*21*
England v. Ireland	England (36) beat Ireland (14) in 1938	*61*	Ireland (22) beat England (0) in 1947	*27*
England v. Wales	England beat Wales by 7 goals, 1 drop goal and 6 tries to nil in 1881	*69**	England beat Wales by 7 goals, 1 drop goal and 6 tries to nil in 1881	*69*
England v. France	England (49) beat France (15) in 1907	*64*	England (37) beat France (0) in 1911	*44*
Scotland v. Ireland	Scotland (29) beat Ireland (14) in 1913	*51*	Scotland beat Ireland by 6 goals and 2 tries to nil in 1877	*44*
Scotland v. Wales	Scotland (20) beat Wales (0) in 1887	*56*	Scotland (20) beat Wales (0) in 1887	*56*
Scotland v. France	Scotland (31) beat France (3) in 1912	*41*	Scotland (31) beat France (3) in 1912	*33*
Ireland v. Wales	Wales (28) beat Ireland (4) in 1920 and	*36*	Wales (29) beat Ireland (0) in 1907	*34*
	Wales (23) beat Ireland (9) in 1971	*36*		
Ireland v. France	France (27) beat Ireland (6) in 1964	*40*	Ireland (24) beat France (0) in 1913	*30*
Wales v. France	Wales (49) beat France (14) in 1910	*75*	Wales (47) beat France (5) in 1909	*52*

FOX HUNTING

EARLIEST REFERENCES

Hunting the fox in Britain became prevalent only from the middle of the 17th century though there is a reference to a hunt staged as early as 28 Feb. 1557. Prior to that time hunting was confined principally to the deer or the hare with the fox being hunted only by mistake. It is now estimated that huntsmen account for 10,000 of the 50,000 foxes killed each year.

Pack Oldest The oldest pack of foxhounds in existence in England is the Sinnington (1680), but the old Charlton Hunt in Sussex, now extinct, the Mid-Devon and the Duke of Buckingham in the Bilsdale country, Yorkshire, hunted foxes prior to that time.

Largest The pack with the greatest number of hounds has been the Duke of Beaufort's hounds maintained at Badminton, Gloucestershire, since c. 1780. At times hunting eight times a week, this pack had 120 couples.

HUNT

Longest The longest recorded hunt was one led by Squire Sandys which ran from Holmbank, northern Lancashire, to Ulpha, Cumberland, a total of nearly 80 miles *128 km* in reputedly only six hours, in January or February 1743. The longest hunt in Ireland is probably a run of 24 miles *38 km* made by the Scarteen Hunt, County Limerick, from Pallas to Knockoura in 1914. The longest duration hunt was one of 10 hours 5 min by the Charlton Hunt of Sussex, which ran from East Dean Wood at 7.45 a.m. to kill over 24½ miles *39 km* away at 5.50 p.m. on 26 Jan. 1736.

Largest fox The largest fox ever killed by a hunt in England was a

23¾ lb. *10 kg 770* dog on Cross Fell, Cumberland, by an Ullswater Hunt in 1936. A fox weighing 28 lb. 2 oz. *12 kg 750* measuring 54 in *137 cm* from nose to tail was shot on the Staffordshire-Worcestershire border on 11 March 1956.

BEAGLING

The oldest beagle hunt is the Royal Rock Beagle Hunt, Wirral, Cheshire, whose first outing was on 28 March 1845. The Newcastle and District Beagles claim their origin from the municipally-supported Newcastle Harriers existing in 1787. The Royal Agricultural College beagle pack killed 75½ brace of hares in the 1966–67 season.

GAMBLING

World's biggest win The world's biggest gambling win was £770,000 for a bet of 14p in the Brazilian football pools Loteria Esportiva by Eduardo Teixeira, 23 on 30 Apr. 1972.

Largest Casino The largest casino in the world is the Casino, Mar del Plata, Argentina with average daily attendances of 14,500 rising to 25,000 during carnivals. The Casino has more than 150 roulette tables running simultaneously. The gambling capital of the world is the State of Nevada whose casinos in 1971 removed $662,000,000 from its clients.

BINGO

Origins Bingo is a lottery game which, as keno, was developed in the 1880s from lotto, whose origin is thought to be the 17th century Italian game *tumbule*. It has long been known in the British Army (called Housey-Housey) and the Royal Navy (called Tombola). The winner was the first to complete a random selection of numbers from 1–90. The U.S.A. version called Bingo differs in that the selection is from 1–75.

Largest house The largest 'house' in Bingo sessions was staged at the Empire Pool, Wembley, Greater London, on 25 April 1965 when 10,000 attended. "Full House" calls have occurred when as few as 41 or as many as 67 of the 90 numbers have been called.

Eduardo Teixeira, 23, a factory worker of Rio de Janeiro whose win of £770,000 for a bet of 14p is the world record gambling win

Largest prize Prizes have been controlled since 1 July 1970 by the Betting and Gaming Act 1968. Prior to limitation, prizes in linked games between more than 50 clubs reached £16,000. The largest in a single game was £5,000 won in the Mecca National Rally at the Empire Pool, Wembley on 29 March 1970.

Longest session A session of 60 hrs (two callers) was held at St. Mark's Church Hall, London W.1 on 1–3 April 1970 and at the Royal Bingo, Haverfordwest, Pembrokeshire by Ron Taylor and Ron McKenzie (1,255 games and 72,790 calls) later in April 1970.

FOOTBALL POOLS

The winning dividend paid out by Littlewoods Pools Ltd. in their first week in February 1923 was £2.12s.0d. In April 1937 a record £30,780 was paid to R. Levy of London on 4 away wins, and in April 1947 a record £64,450 for a 1d. points pool.

Progressive list of individual record winnings

Amount	Recipient	Date
£75,000	P.C. Frank H. Chivers, 54, Aldershot, Hampshire	6 April 1948
£91,832	George A. Borrett, Huyton Lancashire	26 Sept. 1950
£94,335	Thomas A. Wood, 42, Carlisle	10 Oct. 1950
£104,990	Mrs. Evelyn Knowlson, 43, Manchester	7 Nov. 1950
£75,000 (limit)	(45 limit winners)	from 20 Nov. 1951 to 10 Sept. 1957
£205,235	Mrs. Nellie McGrail (now Mrs. Albert Cooper), 37, of Reddish, Cheshire	5 Nov. 1957
£206,028	W. John Brockwell, 29, Epsom, Surrey	18 Feb. 1958
£209,079	Tom Riley, 58, of Horden, Co. Durham	1 April 1958
£209,837	Ronald Smith of Liverpool	23 Dec. 1958
£260,104	John Dunn, 45, of Chelsea, London	27 Oct. 1959
£265,352	Arthur Webb, 70, of Scarborough, Yorkshire	24 Nov. 1959
£301,739.45	Lawrence Freedman, 54, of Willesden, London	8 Dec. 1964
£338,356.80	Percy Harrison, 52 of East Stockwith, Lincolnshire	30 Aug. 1966
£401,792	Albert Crocker, 54, of Dobwalls, Cornwall	17 April 1971
£512,683	Cyril Grimes, 62 of Hampshire	4 Mar. 1972
£536,313	A man from Kent	11 Mar. 1972
£542,252	James Wood, 56, of Bradford, Yorkshire	28 Feb. 1973
£547,172	A London woman	3 Mar. 1973
£629,801	Colin Carruthers, 24, of Kirkintilloch, Dunbartonshire	17 Mar. 1973

In order to earn £629,801 net of tax, a single man would have to have a salary of £2,499,819.

The odds for selecting 8 draws (if there are 8 draws) from 54 matches for an all-correct line are 1,040,465,789 to 1 against.

HORSE RACING

Highest ever odds The highest recorded odds ever secured by a backer were 560,000 to 1 by A. Stone in the Penny Jackpot Accumulator run by A. Williams Ltd. betting shop branch at Kingston, Surrey, England on 18 April 1970. On the Newbury card he won 6 races and was paid out £2,337.30 for 1 (old) penny. The world record odds on a 'double' are 24,741 to 1 secured by

Mr. Montague Harry Parker of Windsor, England, for a £1 each-way 'double' on *Ivernia* and *Golden Sparkle* with William Hill.

Biggest tote win The best recorded tote win was one of £341 2s 6d. to 2s. (£341.12½ to 10p) by Mrs. Catharine Unsworth of Blundellsands, Liverpool at Haydock Park on a race won by *Coole* on 30 Nov. 1929. The highest odds in Irish tote history were £184 7s. 6d. on a 2s. 6d. (£184.37½ on a 12½p) stake, *viz.* 1,475 to 1 on *Hillhead VI* at Baldoyle on 31 Jan. 1970.

Most complicated bet The most complicated bet is the Harlequin, a compound wager on 4 horses with 2,028 possible ways of winning. It was invented by Monty H. Preston of London who has been reputed to be the fastest settler of bets in the world. He once completed 3,000 bets in a 4½-hour test.

Largest bookmaker The world's largest bookmaker is Ladbroke's of London with a turnover which from mid 1972 to mid 1973 was estimated at £160 million. The largest chain of Betting Shops is Ladbroke's with 1,130 shops plus 12 credit offices in the United Kingdom.

Topmost tipster The only recorded instance of a racing correspondent forecasting 8 out of 8 winners on a race card was at Taunton, Somerset, on 15 April 1969 by Tom Cosgrove of the London *Evening News*.

Greatest pay out The greatest published pay out on a single bet is £69,375 by Ladbroke's to Bernard Sunley on the Derby victory of *Santa Claus* in 1964. In 1944 it was said that a backer won £200,000 in an ante post bet on *Garden Path*, which won the 2,000 Guineas.

ROULETTE

The longest run on an ungaffed (*i.e.* true) wheel reliably recorded is 6 successive coups (in No. 10) at El San Juan Hotel, Puerto Rico on 9 July 1959. The odds were 1 in 133,448,704.

Longest Marathon The longest 'marathon' on record is one of 31 days from 10 April to 11 May 1970 at The Casino de Macao organised by Paddy O'Neil-Dunne, author of 'Roulette for the Millions,' to test the validity or invalidity of certain contentions in 20,000 spins.

ELECTIONS

Ladbroke's biggest turnover on any topic is on General Elections. The highest ever individual bet was £50,000 on Labour to win the 1964 Election by Sir Maxwell Joseph. He made £37,272 on the odds offered.

GLIDING

Emanuel Swedenborg (1688–1772) of Sweden made sketches of gliders in *c.* 1714. (see under I.Q. levels, Chapter 1).

The earliest man-carrying glider was designed by Sir George Cayley (1773–1857) and carried his coachman (possibly John Appleby) about 500 yds *460 m* across a valley near Brompton Hall, Yorkshire in the summer of 1853. Gliders now attain speeds of 145 m.p.h. *233 km/h* and the Jastrzab aerobatic sailplane is designed to withstand vertical dives at up to 280 m.p.h. *450 km/h*.

Highest standard A Gold C with three diamonds (for goal flight, distance and height) is the highest standard in gliding. This has been gained by 30 British pilots up to July 1973.

Most Titles World World individual championships (inst. 1948) have been 4 times won by West Germans, including two Standard titles by Heinz Huth (1960, 1963). The only two British wins have been by Philip A. Wills (1952) and H. C. N. Goodhart and F. Foster (2 seater, 1956).

British The British national championship (instituted 1939) has been won most often by Philip A. Wills (b. 26 May 1907), in 1948-49-50 and 1955. The first woman to win this title was Mrs. Anne Burns of Farnham, Surrey on 30 May 1966.

Walter Neubert and his Kestrel 604 glider, in which he broke the world speed record over a triangular course

Kite Descents The greatest altitude from which a manned kite descent has been made is 10,500 ft *3 200 m* by Bill Moyes near Sydney, Australia on 7 Apr. 1973. He launched himself from a balloon and glided 12 miles *19 km*. The longest reported flight duration for hang-gliding is 3 hrs 3 min by Robert L. Wills (U.S.) at Torrey Pines, California, U.S.A. on 7 Dec. 1972.

SELECTED WORLD RECORDS (Single-seaters)

Distance	907.7 miles *1 460,8 km*	Hans-Werner Grosse (W. Germany) in an ASW-12 on 25 Apr. 1972 from Lübeck to Biarritz
Declared Goal Flight	653.1 miles *1 051,2 km*	Klaus Tesch (W. Germany) in an LS-1, on 25 Apr. 1972 from Hamburg to Nantes.
Absolute Altitude	46,266 ft *14 102 m*	Paul F. Bikle, Jr. (U.S.A.) in a Schweizer SGS 1-23E, over Mojave, California (released at 3,963 ft [*1 207 m*] on 25 Feb. 1961 (also record altitude gain—42,303 ft [*12 894 m*])
Goal and Return	782 miles *1 260 km*	W. C. Holbrook (U.S.A.) in a Libelle 301 on 5 May 1973
Speed over Triangular Course 100 km	96.34 m.p.h. *155,06 km/h*	Walter Neubert (W. Germany) in a Kestrel 604 over the U.S.A. on 5 July 1970
300 km	94.16 m.p.h. *151,53 km/h*	Walter Neubert (W. Germany) in a Kestrel 604 over Kenya on 3 Mar. 1972
500 km	85.25 m.p.h. *137,19 km/h*	M. Jackson (South Africa) in a BJ-3 in South Africa on 28 Dec. 1967

BRITISH NATIONAL RECORDS[1] (Single-seaters)

460.5 miles *741,1 km*	P. D. Lane in a Skylark 3F, Geilenkirchen to Hiersac, Germany on 1 June 1962
360 miles *579 km*	Rear-Ad. H. C. N. Goodhart in a Skylark 3, Lasham, Hants to Portmoak, Scotland on 10 May 1959
42,814 ft *13 050 m*	Michael Field in a Skylark IV over Oxford—Swindon on 9 May 1972
408 miles *658 km**	Fl. Lt. John S. Williamson in a Standard Libelle over Australia on 20 Jan. 1973
78.5 m.p.h. *126,04 km/h*	Edward P. Hodge in a Diamant 16.5 over Rhodesia on 1 Nov. 1970
81.33 m.p.h. *130,88 km/h*	Edward Pearson in a Standard Cirrus over South Africa on 1 Jan. 1972
75 m.p.h. *121 km/h**[2]	J. Delafield in a Kestrel 19 over South Africa on 21 Dec. 1972

[1] *British National records may be set up by British pilots in any part of the world.*
[2] *Mrs. Anne Burns (G.B.) holds the women's world record for this event with 64.20 m.p.h. 103,31 km/h in a Standard Austria at Kimberley, South Africa on 25 Dec. 1963.*
* *Subject to ratification.*

GOLF

Origins The earliest mention of golf occurs in a prohibiting law passed by the Scottish Parliament in March 1457 under which "golfe be utterly cryed downe". The Romans had a cognate game called *paganica* which may have been carried to Britain before A.D. 400. In February 1962 the Soviet newspaper *Izvestiya* claimed that the game was of 15th century Danish origin while the Chinese Nationalist Golf Association claim the game is of Chinese origin ("the ball hitting game") in the 3rd or 2nd century B.C. Gutta percha balls succeeded feather balls in 1848 and were in turn succeeded in 1902 by rubber-cored balls, invented in 1899 by Haskell (U.S.A). Steel shafts were authorized in 1929.

CLUBS

The oldest club of which there is written evidence is the Gentlemen Golfers (now the Honourable Company of Edinburgh Golfers) formed in March 1744—10 years prior to the institution of the Royal and Ancient Club at St. Andrews, Fife. The oldest existing club in North America is the Royal Montreal Club (1873).

Largest The only club in the world with 15 courses is the Eldorado Golf Club, California, U.S.A. The club with the highest membership in the world is the Wanderer's Club, Johannesburg, South Africa, with 9,120 members, of whom 850 are golfers. The club with the highest membership in the British Isles is the Royal and Ancient Golf Club at St. Andrews, Fife (1,750). The largest in England is Wentworth Club, Virginia Water, Surrey, with 1,702 members, and the largest in Ireland is Royal Portrush, Co. Antrim with 1,224 members.

COURSES

Highest The highest golf course in the world is the Tuctu Golf Club in Morococha, Peru, which is 4 369 m *14,335 ft* above sea-level at its lowest point. Golf has, however, been played in Tibet at an altitude of over 4 875 m *16,000 ft*.

The highest golf course in Great Britain is one of 9 holes at Leadhills, Lanarkshire, 1,500 ft *457 m* above sea-level.

Lowest The lowest golf course in the world was that of the Sodom and Gomorrah Golfing Society at Kallia, on the north-eastern shores of the Dead Sea, 380 m *1,250 ft* below sea-level. The clubhouse was burnt down in 1948 but the game is now played on Kallia Hotel course.

Longest The longest hole in the world is the 17th hole (par 6) of 681 m *745 yds* at the Black Mountain Golf Club, North Carolina, U.S.A. It was opened in 1964. In August 1927 the 6th hole at Prescott Country Club in Arkansas, U.S.A., measured 766 m *838 yds*. The longest hole on a championship course in Great Britain is the sixth at Troon, Ayrshire, which stretches 580 yds *530 m*. The 9th at Hillsborough Golf Course, Wadsley, Sheffield, Yorkshire is 654 yds *598 m*.

Largest green Probably the largest green in the world is the 5th green at Runaway Brook G.C., Bolton, Massachusetts, U.S.A. with an area greater than 2 600 m² *28,000 ft²*.

Biggest bunker The world's biggest bunker (called a trap in the U.S.A.) is Hell's Half Acre on the seventh hole of the Pine Valley course, New Jersey, U.S.A., built in 1912 and generally regarded as the world's most trying course.

Longest "Course" Floyd Satterlee Rood used the United States as a course, when he played from the Pacific surf to the Atlantic surf from 14 Sept. 1963 to 3 Oct. 1964 in

114,737 strokes. He lost 3,511 balls on the 3,397.7 mile *5 468 km* trail.

LOWEST SCORES

9 holes and 18 holes Men The lowest recorded score on any 18-hole course with a par score of 70 or more is 55 (15 under bogey) first achieved by A. E. Smith, the Woolacombe professional, on his home course on 1 Jan. 1936. The course measured 4,248 yds *3 884 m*. The detail was 4, 2, 3, 4, 2, 4, 3, 4, 3 = 29 out, and 2, 3, 3, 3, 3, 2, 5, 4, 1 = 26 in. Homero Blancas (b. 7 Mar. 1938, of Houston, Texas) also scored 55 (27 + 28) on a course of 4 592 m *5 022 yds* (par 70) in a tournament at the Premier Golf Course, Longview, Texas, U.S.A., on 19 Aug. 1962. The lowest recorded score on a long course (over 6,000 yds [*5 486 m*]) in Britain is 58 by Harry Weetman (1920–72) the British Ryder Cup golfer, for the 6,171 yds *5 642 m* Croham Hurst Course, Croydon, on 30 Jan. 1956.

Nine holes in 25 (4, 3, 3, 2, 3, 3, 1, 4, 2) was recorded by A. J. "Bill" Burke in a round in 57 (32 + 25) on the 5 842 m *6,389 yds* par 71 Normandie course St. Louis, Missouri, U.S.A. on 20 May 1970.

The United States P.G.A. tournament record for 18 holes is 60 by Al Brosch (30 + 30) in the Texas Open on 10 Feb. 1951; William Nary in the El Paso Open, Texas on 9 Feb. 1952; Ted Kroll (b. August 1919) in the Texas Open on 20 Feb. 1954; Wally Ulrich in the Virginia Beach Open on 11 June 1954; Tommy Bolt (b. 31 March 1918) in the Insurance City Open on 25 June 1954; Mike Souchak (b. May 1927) in the Texas Open on 17 Feb. 1955 and Samuel Jackson Snead (b. 27 May 1912) in the Dallas Open, Texas on 14 Sept. 1957. Snead went round in 59 in the 3rd round of the Sam Snead Festival, a non-P.G.A. tournament, at White Sulphur Springs, West Virginia, U.S.A., on 16 May 1959.

Women The lowest recorded score on an 18-hole course for a woman is 62 (30 + 32) by Mary (Mickey) Kathryn Wright (b. 14 Feb. 1935) of Dallas, Texas, on the Hogan Park Course (5 747 m [*6,286 yds*]) at Midland, Texas, U.S.A., in November 1964.

United Kingdom The British Tournament 9-hole record is 28 by John Panton (b. 1917) in the Swallow-Penfold Tournament at Harrogate, Yorkshire, in 1952; by Bernard John Hunt (b. 2 Feb. 1930) of Hartsbourne in the Spalding Tournament at Worthing, Sussex, in August 1953; and by Lionel Platts (b. 10 Oct. 1934, Yorkshire), of Wanstead in the Ulster Open at Shandon Park, Belfast, on 11 Sept. 1965. The lowest score recorded in a first class professional tournament on a course of more than 6,000 yds *5 486 m* in Great Britain was set at 61 (29 + 32), by Thomas Bruce Haliburton (b. Scotland, on 5 June 1915) of Wentworth G.C. in the Spalding Tournament at Worthing, Sussex, in June 1952. Peter J. Butler (b. 25 Mar. 1932) equalled the 18-hole record with 61 (32 + 29) in the Bowmaker Tournament on the Old Course at Sunningdale, Berkshire, on 4 July 1967.

36 holes The record for 36 holes is 122 (59 + 63) by Snead in the 1959 Sam Snead Festival on 16–17 May 1959. Horton Smith (see below) scored 63 + 58 = 121 on a short course on 21 Dec. 1928. The lowest score by a British golfer has been 61 + 65 = 126 by Tom Haliburton (b. 5 June 1915).

72 holes The lowest recorded score on a first-class course is 257 (27 under par) by Mike Souchak (born May 1927) in the Texas Open at San Antonio in February 1955, made up of 60 (33 + 27), 68, 64, 65 (average 64.25 per round) exhibiting, as one critic said: "up and down" form.

Horton Smith (1908–1963), a U.S. Masters Champion, scored 245 (63, 58, 61 and 63) for 72

Tom Haliburton, holder of the British record of 126 for 36 holes and also the lowest score recorded in a first class professional tournament

holes on the 4,700 yd *1 432 m* course (par 64) at Catalina Country Club, California, U.S.A., to win the Catalina Open on 21–23 Dec. 1928.

The lowest 72 holes in a national championship is 262 by Percy Alliss (G.B.) (b. 8 Jan. 1897) in the 1932 Italian Open at San Remo, and by Liang Huan Lu (Formosa) (b. 1936) in the 1971 French Open at Biarritz. The lowest for four rounds in a British first class tournament is 262 (66, 63, 66 and 67) by Bernard Hunt in the Piccadilly Stroke Play tournament on Wentworth East Course, Virginia Water, Surrey on 4–5 Oct. 1966. Kelvin D. G. Nagle (b. 21 Dec. 1920) of Australia shot 260 (64, 65, 66 and 65) in the Irish Hospitals Golf Tournament at Woodbrook Golf Club, near Bray, Ireland, on 21–23 July 1961.

Eclectic record The lowest recorded eclectic (from the Greek *eklektikos* = choosing) score, i.e. the sum of a player's all-time personal low scores for each hole, for a course of more than 6,000 yds *5 486 m* is 33 by the club professional Jack McKinnon on the 6,538 yd *1 992 m* Capilano Golf and Country Club course, Vancouver, British Columbia, Canada. This was compiled over the period 1937–1964 and reads 2-2-2-1-2-2-2-2-1 (= 16 out) and 2-1-2-2-1-2-2-2-3 (= 17 in) = 33. The British record is 39 by John W. Ellmore at Elsham Golf Club, Lincolnshire (6,070 yds [*5 550 m*]). This is made up of 2, 3, 2, 2, 2, 2, 2, 3, 2 = 20 (out) and 3, 1, 2, 1, 2, 2, 3, 3, 2 = 19 (in).

Highest scores The highest score for a single hole in the British Open is 21 by a player in the inaugural meeting at Prestwick in 1860. Double figures have been recorded on the card of the winner only once, when Willie Fernie (1851–1924) scored a 10 at Musselburgh, Midlothian, in 1883. Ray Ainsley of Ojai, California, took 19 strokes for the par-4 16th hole during the second round of the U.S. Open at Cherry Hills Country Club, Denver, Colorado, on 10 June 1938. Most of the strokes were used in trying to extricate the ball from a brook. Hans Merell of Mogadore, Ohio, took 19

strokes on the par-3 16th (222 yds [*202 m*]) during the third round of the Bing Crosby National Tournament at Cypress Point Club, Del Monte, California, U.S.A., on 17 Jan. 1959. It is recorded that Chevalier von Cittern went round 18 holes in 316 at Biarritz, France, in 1888.

Most shots for one hole A woman player in the qualifying round of the Shawnee Invitational for Ladies at Shawnee-on-Delaware, Pennsylvania, U.S.A., in *c.* 1912, took 166 strokes for the short 130 yds *118 m* 16th hole. Her tee shot went into the Binniekill River and the ball floated. She put out in a boat with her exemplary, but statistically minded husband at the oars. She eventually beached the ball 1½ miles *2,4 km* downstream but was not yet out of the wood. She had to play through one on the home run.

Fastest and slowest rounds With such variations in lengths of courses, speed records, even for rounds under par, are of little comparative value. Bob Williams at Eugene, Oregon, U.S.A., completed 18 holes (6,010 yds [*5 495 m*]) in 27 min 48.2 sec in 1971 but this test permitted the striking of the ball whilst still moving. The record for a still ball is 31 min 22 sec by Len Richardson, the South African Olympic athlete at Mowbray, Cape Town (6,248 yds [*5 713 m*]) in Nov. 1931.

Fastest round Members of Doon Valley Golf Club, Kitchener, Ontario, Canada completed the 18 hole 6,358 yds *5 813 m* course there in 10 min 58.4 sec on 16 July 1972.

The slowest stroke play tournament round was one of 5 hours 15 min by Sam Snead and Ben W. Hogan (b. 13 Aug. 1912) of the U.S.A. *v.* Stan Leonard and Al Balding (b. 29 Apr. 1924) of Canada in the Canada Cup contest on the West Course, at Wentworth, Surrey, in 1956. This was a 4-ball medal round, everything holed out.

Most rounds in a day The greatest number of rounds played in 24 hours is 22 rounds 5 holes (401 holes) by Ian Colston 35 at Bendigo G.C. Victoria (6,061 yds [*5 542 m*]) on 27–28 Nov. 1971. He covered more than 100 miles *160 km* in 23¾ hrs play. Edward A. Ferguson of Detroit, Michigan, U.S.A., played 828 holes (46 rounds) in 158 hrs from 6.00 p.m. 25 Aug. to 8.00 a.m. 1 Sept. 1930. He walked 327½ miles *527 km*.

Youngest and oldest champions The youngest winner of the British Open was Tom Morris, Jr. (born St. Andrew's 1850, died 25 Dec. 1875) at Prestwick, Ayrshire, in 1868 aged 18. The youngest winner of the British Amateur title was John Charles Beharrel (born 2 May 1938) at Troon, Ayrshire, on 2 June 1956, aged 18 years 1 month. The oldest winner of the British Amateur was the Hon. Michael Scott at Hoylake, Cheshire in 1933, when 54. The oldest British Open Champion was "Old Tom" Morris (b. St Andrew's 16 June 1821), who was aged 46 in 1867. In recent times the 1967 champion, Robert de Vicenzo (Argentina) (b. 14 April 1923) was aged 44 years 93 days. The oldest United States Amateur Champion was Jack Westland (b. 1905) at Seattle, Washington, in 1952 aged 47.

Longest drives In long-driving contests 330 yds *300 m* is rarely surpassed at sea level. The United States P.G.A. record is 311 m *341 yds* by Jack William Nicklaus (born, Columbus, Ohio, 21 Jan. 1940), in July 1963. Bill Calise, 32 won the McGregor contest at Wayne Country Club, New Jersey on 20 June 1954 with 333 m *365 yds*. The Irish Professional Golfers Association record is however 392 yds *358 m* by their amateur member William Thomas (Tommie) Campbell (Foxrock Golf Club) made at Dun Laoghaire, Co. Dublin, in July 1964. Under freak conditions of wind, slope, parched or frozen surfaces, or ricochet from a stone or flint, even greater distances are achieved. The greatest recorded drive is one of 445 yds *406 m* by

285

Tommie Campbell, the Irish golfer whose drive of 392 yards *358 m* in 1964 is the longest in any long-driving contest

Edward C. Bliss (1863–1917), a 12 handicap player, at the 9th hole of the Old Course, Herne Bay, Kent, in August 1913. Bliss, 6 ft *1,82 m* tall and over 13 st. *82 kg 500*, drove to the back of the green on the left-handed dog-leg. The drive was measured by a government surveyor, Capt. L. H. Lloyd, who also measured the drop from the tee to resting place as 57 ft *17 m*.

Other freak drives include the driving of the 483 yds *441 m* 13th at Westward Ho! by F. Lemarchand, backed by a gale; and to the edge of the 465 yd *425 m* downhill 9th on the East Devon Course, Budleigh Salterton, by T. H. V. Haydon in September 1934. Neither drive was accurately measured.

Perhaps the longest recorded drive on level ground was one of an estimated 430 yds *393 m* by Craig Ralph Wood (born 18 Nov. 1901) of the U.S.A. on the 530 yd *484 m* fifth hole at the Old Course, St. Andrews Fife, in the Open Championship in June 1933. The ground was parched and there was a strong following wind.

Tony Jacklin, O.B.E. (b. 7 July 1944) hit a ball from the roof of the Savoy Hotel (125 ft [*38 m*] above the pavement) 353 yds *322 m* to splash into the River Thames on 26 Nov. 1969. A drive of 2,640 yds *2 414 m* (1½ miles) across ice was achieved by an Australian meteorologist named Nils Lied at Mawson Base, Antarctica, in 1962. Arthur Lynskey claimed a drive of 200 yds *182 m* horizontal and 2 miles *3 200 m* vertical off Pikes Peak, Colorado (14,110 ft [*4 300 m*]) on 28 June 1968. On the Moon the energy expended on a mundane 300 yd *274 m* drive would achieve, craters permitting, a distance of a mile *1,6 km*.

Longest hitter The golfer regarded as the longest consistent hitter the game has ever known is the 6 ft 5 in *195 cm* tall, 17 st. 2 lb. *108 kg 86* George Bayer (U.S.A.), the 1957 Canadian Open Champion. His longest measured drive was one of 420 yds *384 m* at the fourth in the Las Vegas Invitational, Nevada, in 1953. It was measured as a precaution against litigation since the ball struck a spectator. Bayer also drove a ball pin high on a 426 yd *389 m* hole in Tucson, Arizona, U.S.A. Radar measurements show that an 87 m.p.h. *140 km/h* impact velocity for a golf ball falls to 46 m.p.h. *74 km/h* in 3.0 seconds.

Longest Putt The longest recorded putt in a major tournament was one of 86 ft *26 m* on the vast 13th green at the Augusta

National, Georgia by Cary Middlecoff (b. Jan. 1921) in the 1955 Master's Tournament.

The Open The Open Championship was inaugurated in 1860 at Prestwick, Ayrshire, Scotland. The lowest score for 9 holes is 29 by Tom Haliburton (Wentworth) and Peter W. Thompson, M.B.E. (Australia) (b. 23 Aug. 1929) in the first round of the Open on the Royal Lytham and St. Anne's course at Lytham St. Anne's, Lancashire on 10 July 1963.

The lowest scoring round is 63 (all in qualifying rounds) by Frank Jowle (b. 14 May 1912) at the New Course, St. Andrews (6,526 yds [*5 967 m*]), on 4 July 1955; by P. W. Thomson of Melbourne, Australia (see above) at Royal Lytham and St. Anne's (6,635 yds [*6 067 m*]) on 30 June 1958; and Maurice Bembridge (Little Aston) (b. 21 Feb. 1945) at Delamare Forest, Cheshire, on 7 July 1967. The best by an amateur is 65 by Ronnie David Bell Mitchell Shade, M.B.E. (b. 15 Oct. 1938) in a qualifying round on the Eden Course (6,250 yds [*5 714 m*]), St. Andrews, on 4 July 1964. The lowest rounds in The Open itself have been 65 by (Thomas) Henry Cotton, M.B.E. (b. Holmes Chapel, Cheshire, 26 Jan. 1907) at Royal St. George's, Sandwich, Kent in the 2nd round on 27 June 1934 to complete a 36-hole record of 132 (67 + 65); by Eric Chalmers Brown (b. 15 Feb. 1925) at Royal Lytham and St. Anne's, Lancashire in the third round on 3 July 1958: by Christy O'Connor (b. County Donegal, Ireland, 1925) (Royal Dublin) at Lytham in the 2nd round on 10 July 1969; by Neil C. Coles (b. 26 Sept. 1934) (Coombe Hill) on the Old Course, St. Andrews in the 1st round on 8 July 1970 and by Nicklaus at Troon in the 4th round on 14 July 1973. The lowest 72-hole aggregate is 276 (71, 69, 67, 69) by Arnold Daniel Palmer (b. 10 Sept. 1929) of Latrobe, Pennsylvania, U.S.A., at Troon, Ayrshire, ending on 13 July 1962 and Tom Weiskopf (b. 9 Nov. 1942) also at Troon on 11–14 July 1973 (68, 67, 71, 70).

British Amateur The lowest score for nine holes in the British Amateur Championship (inaugurated in 1885) is 29 by Richard

Cary Middlecoff who sank a putt of 86 ft *26 m*—the longest recorded in a major tournament

Jack Nicklaus, the highest earner in professional golf, coming out of a bunker at the 18th green during the 1970 Piccadilly World Match-play tournament

Davol Chapman (born 23 March 1911) of the U.S.A. at Sandwich in 1948.

Michael Francis Bonallack, O.B.E. (b. 31 Dec. 1924) shot a 61 (32 + 29) on the par-71 6,905 yd *6 313 m* course at Ganton, Yorkshire, on 27 July 1968 in the first 18 of the 36 holes in the final round of the English Amateur championship.

U.S. Open The United States Open Championship was inaugurated in 1894. The lowest 72-hole aggregate is 275 (71, 67, 72 and 65) by Jack Nicklaus on the Lower Course (6 414 m [*7,015 yds*]) at Baltusrol Country Club, Springfield, New Jersey, on 15–18 June 1967 and 275 (69, 68, 69 and 69) by Lee Trevino (born near Horizon City, Texas, 1 Dec. 1939) at Oak Hill Country Club, Rochester, N.Y., on 13–16 June 1968. The lowest score for 18 holes is 63 by John Miller (b. 29 Apr. 1947) on the 6,921 yd *6 328 m* par-71 Oakmont Club course, Pennsylvania on 17 June 1973.

U.S. Masters The lowest score in the U.S. Masters (instituted on the par-72 6 382 m *6,980 yds* Augusta National Golf Course, Georgia, in 1934) has been 271 by Jack Nicklaus in 1965. The lowest rounds have been 64 by Lloyd Mangrum (b. Aug. 1914) (1st round, 1940) and Jack Nicklaus (3rd round, 1965).

Richest prizes The greatest first place prize money was $60,000 (total purse $300,000 [*£125,000*]) in the Dow Jones Open Invitational played at Upper Montclair Country Club, Clifton, New Jersey on 27–30 Aug. 1970 won by Bobby Nichols (U.S.) and £25,000 ($60,000) in the John Player Golf Classic at Hollinwell, Nottinghamshire, England on 3–6 Sept. 1970.

Highest earnings The all time professional money-winner is Jack Nicklaus who surpassed Arnold Palmer's record with $1,477,200.86 (*then £615,500*) on 6 March 1972. His record for official tournaments in a year is $320,542 (*£128,216*) in 1972. The earnings for a woman have

MOST TITLES

The most titles won in the world's major championships are as follows:

The Open	Harry Vardon (1870–1937)	6	1896–98–99, 1903–11–14
British Amateur	John Ball (1861–1940)	8	1888–90–92–94–99, 1907–10–12
U.S. Open	W. Anderson	4	1901–03–04–05
	Robert Tyre Jones, Jr. (1902–71)	4	1923–26–29–30
	Ben William Hogan (b. 13 Aug. 1912)	4	1948–50–51–53
U.S. Amateur	R. T. Jones, Jr. (1902–71)	5	1924–25–27–28–30
P.G.A. Championship (U.S.A.)	Walter Charles Hagen	5	1921–24–25–26–27
Masters Championship (U.S.A.)	Arnold D. Palmer	4	1958–60–62–64
U.S. Women's Open	Miss Elizabeth (Betsy) Earle-Rawls	4	1951–53–57–60
	Miss "Mickey" Wright	4	1958–59–61–64
U.S. Women's Amateur	Mrs. Glenna C. Vare (*née* Collett)	6	1922–25–28–29–30–35
British Women's	Miss Charlotte Cecilia Pitcairn Leitch	4	1914–20–21–26
	Miss Joyce Wethered (born 1901) (now Lady Heathcoat-Amory)	4	1922–24–25–29

NOTE: *Jones won 13 major titles in 1923–30 while Nicklaus is the only golfer to have won 5 different such titles and the Open, U.S. Open, Masters and P.G.A. titles twice.*

been $332,117 (£127,737) by Kathy Whitworth (U.S.A.) (b. 27 Sept. 1938) up to 15 Jan. 1972.

Most tournament wins The record for winning tournaments in a single season is 19 (out of 31) by Byron Nelson (b. 4 Feb. 1912) of Fort Worth, Texas, in 1945. Of these 11 were consecutive, including the P.G.A., Canadian P.G.A. and Canadian Open, from 16 March to 15 August. He was a money prize winner in 113 consecutive tournaments. Miss Whitworth (see above) won 54 Ladies P.G.A. tournaments to the end of 1971.

Most club championships The British record for amateur club championships is 20 consecutive wins (1937–39 and 1946–62) by R. W. H. Taylor at the Dyke Golf Club, Brighton, Sussex, who retired unbeaten in July 1963, and by Edward Christopher Chapman (b. 9 April 1909), who won the Tunbridge Wells G.C. Scratch Championship 20 consecutive years from 1951 to 1971.

HOLES IN ONE

Longest The longest hole ever holed in one shot is the 10th hole (406 m [444 yds]) at Miracle Hills Golf Club, Omaha, Nebraska, U.S.A. Robert Mitera achieved a hole-in-one there on 7 Oct. 1965. Mitera, aged 21, stands 167 cm 5 ft 6 in tall and weighs 165 lb. 74 kg 842 (11 st. 11 lb.). He is a two handicap player who can normally drive 245 yds 224 m. A 50 m.p.h. 80 km/h gust carried his shot over a 290 yd 265 m drop-off. The ground in front testified to the remaining 154 yds 140 m. The feminine record is 393 yds 359 m by Marie Robie of Wollaston, Massachusetts, U.S.A., on the first hole of the Furnace Brook Golf Club, western Massachusetts, on 4 Sept. 1949.

The longest hole in one performed in the British Isles is the 5th (380 yds [347 m]) on Tankersley Park Course, near Sheffield, Yorkshire, by David Hulley in 1961.

Most The record total number of "aces" recorded in the United States in a year has been 18,319 (indicating more than 100 on some days) in 1969. The greatest number of holes-in-one in a career is 37 by Art Wall, Jr. (b. 23 Nov. 1923) between 1936 and 1967. The British record is 30 by Charles T. Chevalier (b. 22 July 1902) of Heaton Moor Golf Club, Stockport, Cheshire between 20 June 1918 and 17 July 1965. The late Dr. Joseph O. Boydstone was reputed to have scored holes-in-one at the 3rd, 4th and 9th holes on the Bakersfield Public Golf Course, California, U.S.A., on 10 Oct. 1962. The holes measured 192 m, 120 m and 123 m 210, 132 and 135 yds. Further investigation by the *Bakersfield Californian* did not however impress its editor with the validity of the claim.

Double albatross There is no recorded instance of a golfer performing three consecutive holes-in-one but there are at least 15 cases of "aces" being achieved in two consecutive holes of which the greatest was Norman L. Manley's unique "double albatross" on the par-4 301 m 330 yd 7th and par-4 265 m 290 yd 8th holes on the Del Valle Country Club Course, Saugus, California, on 2 Sept. 1964. Three examples by Britons have been by Roger Game at Walmer and Kingsdown, Kent in 1964; Charles Fairlie at Gourock in June 1968, and by the professional John Hudson, 25, of Hendon at Royal Norwich (11th eagle and 12th albatross) in the Martini International on 11 June 1971.

Youngest and oldest The youngest golfer recorded to have shot a hole-in-one was Tommy Moore (6 years 36 days) of Hagerstown, Maryland on the 132 m 145 yd 4th at the Woodbrier Golf Course, Martinsville, West Virginia, on 8 March 1968. The oldest golfer to have performed the feat is Walter Fast, aged 92 years 199 days, at Madison G.C., Peoria, Illinois on the 128 m 140 yd 13th hole on 25 June 1971. The Canadian Charles Youngman of the Tam O'Shantar Club, Toronto is reputed to have holed-in-one aged 93.

Byron Nelson, whose total of 19 wins out of 31 tournaments in one season is a world record

Shooting your age The record for scoring one's age in years over an 18-hole round is held by Weller Noble who between 1955 (scoring 64 aged 64) on 13 Dec. 1971 has amassed 644 "age scores" on the Claremont Country Club, Oakland, California par-68 course of 5 244 m 5,375 yds. The course is provenly harder than many of 5 500 m 6,000 yds or more on which to produce low scores.

The oldest player to score under his age is C. Arthur Thompson (b. 1869) of Victoria, British Columbia, Canada, who scored 96 on the Uplands course of 5 682 m 6,215 yds on 3 Oct. 1966. He was reported to be still in action aged 101 in April 1971.

Largest Tournament The *Daily Mirror* North of England Amateur (Match Play) Tournament in 1973 attracted a record 4,843 amateur competitors.

World Cup (formerly Canada Cup) The World Cup (instituted as the Canada Cup in 1953) has been won most often by the U.S.A., with eleven victories in 1955–1956–1960–1961–1962–1963–1964–1966–1967–1969–1971. The only man to have been on six winning teams has been Arnold Palmer (1960, 62–64, 66–67). Only Nicklaus has taken the individual title 3 times (1963–64–71). The lowest aggregate score for 144 holes is 545 by Australia (Bruce Devlin [b. 10 Oct. 1937] and David Graham) at San Isidro, Buenos Aires, Argentina on 12–15 Nov. 1970. The lowest individual score has been 269 by Roberto de Vicenzo then 47 (Argentina) also in 1970.

Ryder Trophy The biennial Ryder Cup professional match between U.S.A. and the British Isles or Great Britain was instituted in 1927. The U.S.A. have won 14½ to 4½ to date. William (Billy) Casper (U.S.A) has the record of winning most singles with 11 wins in 1961–1969. Dai Rees (G.B.) played in 9 matches (1937–61).

Walker Cup The biennial Walker Cup amateur match between U.S.A. and G.B. and Ireland was instituted in 1921. The U.S.A. have won 21½–2½ to date. Joe Carr (G.B. & I) played in 10 contests (1947–67).

Throwing the golf ball The lowest recorded score for throwing a golf ball round 18 holes (over 5 500 m [6,000 yds]) is 84 by Douglas V. Shipe at the 5 687 m 6,220 yds A. L. Gustin Course, University of Missouri, Columbia, Missouri, U.S.A. on 16 Nov. 1971.

288

GREYHOUND RACING

Earliest meeting In Sept. 1876 a greyhound meeting was staged at Hendon, North London with a railed hare operated by a windlass. Modern greyhound racing originated with the perfecting of the mechanical hare by Oliver P. Smith at Emeryville, California, U.S.A., in 1919. The earliest greyhound race behind a mechanical hare in the British Isles was at Belle Vue, Manchester, opened on 24 July 1926.

Derby The only two dogs to have won the English Greyhound Derby twice (held since 1928 over 525 yd [*480 m*] at the White City Stadium, London) are *Mick the Miller* (whelped in Ireland, June 1926 and died 1939) on 25 July 1929, when owned by Albert H. Williams, and on 28 June 1930 (owned by Mrs. Arundel H. Kempton) and *Patricias Hope* on 24 June 1972 (when owned by Gordon and Basil Marks and Brian Stanley) and 23 June 1973 (when owned by G. & B. Marks and J. O'Connor). *Mick the Miller* won a record 19 consecutive races from 19 March to 20 Aug. 1930. The highest prize was £12,500 to *Patricias Hope* for the Derby on 23 June 1973. The only dogs to win the English, Scottish and Welsh Derby "triple" are *Trev's Perfection*, owned by Fred Trevillion in 1947, *Mile Bush Pride*, owned by Noel W. Purvis, in 1959, and *Patricias Hope* (see above) in 1972.

Grand National The only dog to have thrice won the Greyhound Grand National (instituted 1927) over 525 yd *480 m* and 4 flights is *Sherry's Prince*, a 75 lb. *32 kg* dog whelped in April 1967, owned by Mrs. Joyce Mathews of Sanderstead, Surrey. He won in 1970, 1971 (record 29.22 sec) and 1972 when he won by 6¼ lengths.

Mick the Miller, the first dog to win the English Derby twice, in 1929 and 1930

Fastest 525 yds timings The fastest *photo*-timing is 28.17 sec or 38.12 m.p.h. *61,34 km/h* by *Easy Investment* on 30 June 1973. The fastest *photo*-timing over 525 yds *480 m* hurdles is 29.10 sec (36.90 m.p.h. [*59,38 km/h*]) by *Sherry's Prince* on 8 May 1971.

Fastest dog The highest speed at which any greyhound has been timed is 41.72 m.p.h. *67,14 km/h* (410 yd [*374 m*] in 20.1 sec) by *The Shoe* on the then straightaway track at Richmond, N.S.W., Australia on 25 Apr. 1968. It is estimated that he covered the last 100 yds *91,44 m* in 4.5 sec or at 45.45 m.p.h. *73,14 km/h*. The highest speed recorded for a greyhound in Great Britain is 39.13 m.p.h. *62,97 km/h* by *Beef Cutlet*, when covering a straight course of 500 yds *457 m* in 26.13 sec at Blackpool, Lancashire, on 13 May 1933.

GYMNASTICS

Earliest references Gymnastics were widely practised in Greece during the period of the ancient Olympic Games (776 B.C. to A.D. 393) but they were not revived until *c.* 1780.

World Championships The greatest number of individual titles won by a man in the World Championships is 10 by Boris Shakhlin (U.S.S.R.) between 1954 and 1964. He also won 3 team titles. The female record is 10 individual wins and 5 team titles by Larissa Semyonovna Latynina (born 1935, retired 1966) of the U.S.S.R., between 1956 and 1964.

Olympic Games Italy has won most Olympic team titles with four victories in 1912, 1920, 1924 and 1932.

The only man to win six individual gold medals is Boris Shakhlin (U.S.S.R.), with one in 1956, four (two shared) in 1960 and one in 1964. He was also a member of the winning Combined Exercises team in 1956.

Vera Caslavska-Odlozil (Czechoslovakia), has won most individual Gold Medals with 7, three in 1964 and four (one shared) in 1968. Latynina won six individual Gold Medals and was in three winning teams in 1956–64 making 9 gold medals. She also won 5 silver and 4 bronze medals making 18 in all—an Olympic record for either sex in any sport.

British Championship The most times that the British Gymnastic Championship has been won is 10 by Arthur Whitford in 1928–36 and 39. He was also in four winning Championship teams. The women's record is 5 wins by Miss Margaret Bell, 1965–69.

Rope climbing The United States Amateur Athletic Union records are tantamount to world records: 6 m *20 ft* hands alone—2.8 sec, Don Perry (U.S.A.) at Champaign, Illinois, U.S.A., on 3 April 1954; 7,6 m *25 ft* (hands alone). 4.7 sec, Garvin S. Smith at Los Angeles, California, U.S.A., on 19 April 1947.

Chinning the bar The greatest number of chin-ups (from a dead hang position) recorded is 106 by William D. Reed at the Weightman Hall, University of Pennsylvania, U.S.A. on 23 June 1969. The feminine record for one-handed chin-ups is 27 in Hermann's Gym, Philadelphia, Pennsylvania, U.S.A. in 1918 by Lillian Leitzel (Mrs. Alfredo Codona) (U.S.A), who was killed in Copenhagen, Denmark on 12 Feb. 1931. Her total would be unmatched by any male but it is doubtful if they were achieved from a 'dead hang' position. It is believed that only one person in 100,000 can chin a bar one-handed. Francis Lewis (b. 1896) of Beatrice, Nebraska, U.S.A. in May 1914 achieved 7 consecutive chins using only the middle finger of his left hand. His bodyweight was 158 lb. *71 kg 667*.

Press-ups The greatest recorded number of consecutive press-ups is 6,006 in 3 hr 54 min by Chick Linster, aged 16, of Wilmette, Illinois, U.S.A. on 5 Oct. 1965. Masura Noma of Mihara, Japan did 1,227 press-ups in 37 min in January 1968. James Ullrich at the Yutan High School, Nebraska on 10 Mar. 1973 achieved 115 press-ups on his right arm only in 70 sec followed by 80 on his left arm in 51 sec. Noel Barry Mason performed 101 press-ups on the finger tips at Abbots Bromley, Staffordshire on 2 Feb. 1973.

Sit-ups The greatest recorded number of consecutive sit-ups on a hard surface without feet pinned down is 25,222 in 11 hr 14 min by Richard John Knecht, aged 8 at the Idaho Fall High School Gymnasium, Idaho, on 23 Dec. 1972.

Jumping Jacks The greatest recorded numbers of side-straddle hops is 14,053 performed in 3 hr 53 min (better than 1 per sec) by Dale H. Cummings Jr. of Atlanta, Georgia, U.S.A. on 6 Dec. 1966.

Greatest tumbler The greatest tumbler of all time is Dick Browning (U.S.A.) who made a backward somersault over a 7 ft 3 in *220 cm* bar at Santa Barbara, California, in April 1954. In his unique repertoire was a 'round-off', backward handspring, backward somersault with half twist, walk-out, tinsica tigna round-off, backward handspring, double backward somersault.

Hand-to-hand balancing The longest horizontal dive achieved in any hand-to-hand balancing act is 22 ft *6,7 m* by Harry Berry (top mounter) and the late Nelson Soule (understander) of the Bell-Thazer Brothers from Kentucky, U.S.A., who played at State fairs and vaudevilles from 1912 to 1918. Berry used a 10 ft *3 m* tower and trampoline for impetus.

Largest gymnasium The world's largest gymnasium is Yale University's Payne Whitney Gymnasium at New Haven, Connecticut, U.S.A., completed in 1932 and valued at $18,000,000 (£7,500,000). The building, known as the 'Cathedral of Muscle' has nine storeys with wings of five storeys each. It is equipped with four basketball courts, three rowing tanks, 28 squash courts, 12 handball courts, a roof jogging track and a 25 yds

The *gamine* U.S.S.R. gymnast Olga Korbut, who appeared with the U.S.S.R. team at Earl's Court on 8–10 May 1973 which attracted a record crowd for the sport of 13,922

22,8 m by 42 ft *12,8 m* swimming pool on the first floor and a 55 yd *50,2 m* long pool on the third floor.

HANDBALL (COURT)

Origins Handball played against walls or in a court is a game of ancient Celtic origin. In the early 19th century only a front wall was used but gradually side and back walls were added. The earliest international contest was in New York City, U.S.A., in 1887 between the champions of the U.S.A. and Ireland. The court is now a standardized 60 ft *18 m* by 30 ft *9 m* in Ireland, Ghana and Australia, and 40 ft *12 m* by 20 ft *6 m* in Canada, Mexico and the U.S.A. The game is played with both a hard and soft ball in Ireland and soft ball only in Australia, Canada, Ghana, Mexico and the U.S.A.

Championships World championships were inaugurated in New York in October 1964 with competitors from Australia, Canada, Ireland, Mexico and the U.S.A. The U.S.A. won in 1964; Canada and U.S.A. shared the title in 1967 and Ireland won in 1970.

Most titles In Ireland the most titles (instituted 1925) have been won as follows:

Hardball

Singles	John J. Gilmartin (Kilkenny)	
	10	1936–42, 1945–47
Doubles	John Ryan and John Doyle (Wexford)	
	6	1952, 1954–58

Softball

Singles	Paddy Perry (Roscommon)	
	8	1930–37
Doubles	James O'Brien and Patrick Downey (Kerry)	
	7	1955–56, 1960–64

The U.S. Championship 4 wall singles has been won 6 times by Jimmy Jacobs in 1955–56–57–60–64–65.

HANDBALL (FIELD)

Origins Handball, similar to association football with a substitution of the hands for the feet, was first played *c.* 1895. It was introduced into the Olympic Games at Berlin in 1936 as an 11-a-side outdoor game with Germany winning, but in 1972 it was an indoor game with 7-a-side, which has been the standard size of team since 1952.

By 1972 there were 41 countries affiliated to the International Handball Federation, a World Cup competition and an estimated 5 million participants. The earliest international match was when Sweden beat Denmark on 8 March 1935.

HOCKEY

Origins A representation of two hoop players with curved snagging sticks apparently in an orthodox "bully" position was found in Tomb No. 17 at Beni Hasan, Egypt and has been dated to *c.* 2050 B.C. There is a British reference to the game in Lincolnshire in 1277. The first country to form a national association was England with the first Hockey Association founded at Canon Street Hotel, London on 16 April 1875.

The oldest club with a continuous history is Teddington H.C. formed in the autumn of 1871. They played Richmond on 24 Oct. 1874 and used the first recorded circle *versus* Surbiton at Bushey Park on 9 Dec. 1876.

MEN

Earliest International The first international match was the Wales v. Ireland match at Rhyl on 26 Jan. 1895. Ireland won 3–0.

Highest International score The highest score in international hockey was when India defeated the United States 24–1 at Los Angeles, California, U.S.A., in the 1932 Olympic Games. The Indians were Olympic Champions from the re-inception of Olympic hockey in 1928 until 1960, when Pakistan beat them 1–0 at Rome. They had their seventh win in 1964. Four Indians have won 3 Olympic gold medals—Dhyan Chand and Richard J. Allen (1928, 1932, 1936) and Leslie Claudius and Randhir Gentle (1948, 1952, 1956). The greatest number of goals in a home international match was when England defeated France 16–0 at Beckenham on 25 March 1922. The 1971 World Cup was won by Pakistan at Barcelona.

Longest game The longest international game on record was one of 145 min (into the sixth period of extra time), when Netherlands beat Spain 1–0 in the Olympic tournament at Mexico City on 25 Oct. 1968. The longest club match on record was one of 175 min between Perth H.C. and Aberdeen G.S.F.P. at the North Inch, Perth in the Scottish Cup quarter-final on 24 Feb. 1973.

Most appearances The most by a home countries player is 106 by Harold A. Cahill (b. 9 June 1930) with 71 for Ireland and 35 for Great Britain won from 1953 to 1973.

England 55, Michael W. Corby (b. 18 Feb. 1940) (1961–72)
Wales 69, David J. Prosser (1961–72)
Scotland 64, Frederick H. Scott (b. 29 Nov. 1932) (up to 1971)
Ireland 79, H. D. Judge (b. 19 Jan. 1936) (1957–73)
Great Britain 56, John W. Neill (England) (1959–68)

Five brothers In the England v. Ireland match of 1904, the Irish team included five brothers, Jack, Cecil, Willie, Walter and Nick Peterson of the Palmerston Club. A sixth brother, Bertie, had played for Ireland v. Wales in 1900 and 1902.

Greatest scoring feat M. C. Marckx (Bowdon 2nd XI) scored 19 goals against Brooklands 2nd XI (score 23–0) on 31 Dec. 1910. He was selected for England in March 1912 but declined due to business priorities.

WOMEN

Origins The earliest women's club was East Molesey in Surrey, England formed in c. 1887. The first national

The six Peterson brothers, all of whom played for Ireland, five of them in the same match v. England in 1904

association was the Irish Ladies' Hockey Union founded in 1894. The All England Womens' Hockey Association held its first formal meeting in Westminster Town Hall, London, on 23 Nov. 1895. The first international match was an England v. Ireland game in Dublin in 1896. Ireland won 2–0. In the 1971 World Tournament of 15 nations at Auckland, N.Z. the Netherlands were the only unbeaten team.

Highest international score The highest score in a women's international match occurred when England defeated France 23–0 at Merton, Surrey, on 3 Feb. 1923.

Most appearances The England records are 53 caps by Miss Mildred Mary Knott (1923–39) and 17 seasons by Miss Mabel Bryant (1907–1929), who won 39 caps. The Irish record is 58 (46 full caps and 12 touring) by Mrs. Sean Kyle (born Maeve Esther Enid Shankey, 6 Oct. 1928) between November 1947 and 1966.

Highest attendance The highest attendance at a women's hockey match was 65,000 for the match between England and Wales at the Empire Stadium, Wembley, Greater London, on 8 March 1969.

HORSE RACING

Origins Horsemanship was an important part of the Hittite culture of Anatolia, Turkey in the 2nd millenium B.C. The 23rd ancient Olympic Games of 624 B.C. in Greece featured horse racing. The earliest horse race recorded in England was one held in about A.D. 210 at Netherby, Yorkshire, among Arabians brought to Britain by Lucius Septimius Severus (A.D. 146–211), Emperor of Rome. The oldest race still being run annually is the Lanark Silver Bell, instituted in Scotland by William Lion (1165–1214).

The Jockey Club was formed in 1750–51 and the General Stud Book started in 1791. Racing colours (silks) became compulsory in 1889.

RACECOURSES

Largest The world's largest racecourse is the Newmarket course (founded 1636) on which the Beacon Course, the longest of the 19 courses, is 4 miles 397 yds *6,80 km*

long and the Rowley Mile is 167 ft *50 m* wide. The border between Suffolk and Cambridgeshire runs through the Newmarket course. The world's largest grandstand is that opened in 1968 at Belmont Park, Nassau County, Long Island, N.Y., U.S.A. at a cost of $30,700,000 (*£12.8 million*). It is 110 ft *33 m* tall, 440 yd *402 m* long and contains 908 mutuel windows. The highest seating capacity at any racetrack is 40,000 at Atlantic City Audit, New Jersey, U.S.A.

Smallest The world's smallest racecourse is the Lebong racecourse, Darjeeling, West Bengal, India (altitude 7,000 ft [*2 125 m*]), where the complete lap is 481 yd *439 m*. It was laid out c. 1885 and used as a parade ground.

HORSES

Greatest record The horse with the best recorded win-loss record and the only one on which it was safe to bet was *Kincsem*,

291

a Hungarian mare foaled in 1874, who was unbeaten in 54 races (1877–1880), including the Goodwood Cup of 1878. *Camarero* owned by Don José Coll Vidal of Puerto Rico, foaled in 1951, had a winning streak of 56 races from 19 April 1953 to 17 Aug. 1955. He died 'from a colic' on 26 Aug. 1956 the day after his 73rd win in 77 starts.

Tallest The tallest horse ever to race is *Fort d'Or*, owned by Lady Elizabeth (Eliza) Nugent (*née* Guinness) of Berkshire, England. He stands 18.2 hands *187 cm*.

Highest price The highest price ever paid for a horse is $6,080,000 (*£2,432,000*) paid by Mrs. Penny Tweedy and 28 other members of a $197,000 per unit syndicate in February 1973 for the 16.0½ hand chestnut *Secretariat*. This price was equivalent to $345 (*£138*) per oz. or $12,166 *per kg* which was then quadruple the price per unit of 22 carat gold. *Secretariat* duly became the U.S.'s ninth Triple Crown winner in taking the Belmont Stakes by an unprecedented 31 lengths in a world record dirt track time of 2 min 24.0 sec.

Greatest winning The greatest amount ever won by a horse is $1,977,896 (*then £706,391*) by *Kelso* (foaled in 1957) in the U.S.A., between 1959 and his retirement on 10 March 1966. He is now the supreme status symbol of the hunt under Mrs. Richard C. du Pont. In 63 races he won 39, came second in 12 and third in 2. The most successful horse of all time has been *Buckpasser*, whose career winnings were $1,462,014 (*£609,172*) in 1965–66–67. He won 25 races out of 31. The most won by a mare is $783,674 (*£279,883*) by *Cicada*. In 42 races she won 23, came second in 8 and third in 6. The most won in a year is $817,941 (*£340,808*) by *Damascus* in 1967. His total reached $1,176,781.

Largest prizes The richest race ever held is the All-American Futurity, a race for quarter-horses over 400 yds *365 m* at Ruidoso Downs, New Mexico, U.S.A. The prizes in 1971 totalled $753,910 (*then £314,129*). *Laico Bird*, the winner in 1967 in 20.11 sec received $228,300 (*£81,535*). The largest single prize ever paid was 1,094,126 francs, plus 78 per cent. of the entry fees,

making 1,480,000 francs (*then*) *£107,000* to the owner of *Prince Royal II*, winner of the 43rd Prix de l'Arc de Triomphe at Longchamp, Paris, on 4 Oct. 1964.

JOCKEYS

The most successful jockey of all time has been Willie Shoemaker (b. weighing 2½ lb. [*1 kg 133*] on 19 Aug. 1931) now weighing 98 lb. *44 kg* after 23 years in the saddle, beating Johnny Longden's life-time record of 6,032 winners at Del Mar, California, U.S.A. on 7 Sept. 1970. Shoemaker, stands 4 ft 11½ in *151 cm* and rode his 6,223rd winner on his 40th birthday. From 19 March 1949 his winnings have been $46,000,000. His 485 wins from 1,683 mounts in 1953 constitute a record for any one year.

The greatest amount ever won by any jockey in a year is $3,088,888 by Braulio Baeza (b. Panama) in the U.S.A. in 1967. The oldest jockey was Levi Barlingame (U.S.A.), who rode his last race at Stafford, Kansas, U.S.A., in 1932 aged 80. The youngest jockey was Frank Wootton (English Champion jockey 1909–12), who rode his first winner in South Africa aged 9 years 10 months. The lightest recorded jockey was Kitchener (died 1872), who won the Chester Cup on *Red Deer* in 1844 at 3 st. 7 lb. *22 kg 226*. He was said to have weighed only 2 st. 12 lb. *18 kg 143* in 1840.

The greatest number of winners ridden on one card is 8 by Hubert S. Jones at Caliente, California, U.S.A. on 11 June 1944 of which 5 were photo-finishes. The longest winning streak is 12 by Sir Gordon Richards with 12 (last race at Nottingham on 3 Oct, 6 out of 6 at Chepstow on 4 Oct. and the first 5 races next day at Chepstow) in 1933.

Trainers The greatest amount ever won by a trainer in one year is $2,456,250 (*then £881,519*) by Eddie A. Neloy (U.S.A.) in 1966 when his horses won 93 races.

Dead heats There is no recorded case in turf history of a quintuple dead heat. The nearest approach was in the

292

Astley Stakes, at Lewes, England, in August 1880 when *Mazurka*, *Wandering Nun* and *Scobell* triple dead-heated for first place, just ahead of *Cumberland* and *Thora*, who dead-heated for fourth place. Each of the five jockeys thought he had won. The only two known examples of a quadruple dead heat were between *The Defaulter*, *Squire of Malton*, *Reindeer* and *Pulcherrima* in the Omnibus Stakes at The Hoo, England, on 26 April 1851, and between *Overreach*, *Lady Go-Lightly*, *Gamester* and *The Unexpected* at the Houghton Meeting at Newmarket on 22 Oct. 1855. The earliest recorded photo-finish dead heat in Britain was between *Phantom Bridge* and *Resistance* in the 5-furlong *1 005 m* Beechfield Handicap at Doncaster on 22 Oct. 1947.

Longest race The longest recorded horse race was one of 1,200 miles *1 925 km* in Portugal, won by a horse *Emir* bred from Egyptian-bred Blunt Arab stock. The holder of the world's record for long distance racing and speed is *Champion Crabbet*, who covered 300 miles *482 km* in 52 hrs 33 min carrying 17½ st. *111 kg 130*, in 1920. In 1831 Squire George Osbaldeston (1787–1866), M.P. of East Retford covered 200 miles *321 km* in 8 hrs 42 min at Newmarket, using 50 mounts, so averaging 22.99 m.p.h. *36,99 km/h*. In 1967 G. Steecher covered 100 miles *160 km* on a single horse in 11 hrs 4 min in Victoria, Australia.

Shortest price The shortest odds ever quoted for any racehorse are 10,000 to 1 on for *Dragon Blood*, ridden by Lester Piggott (G.B.) in the Premio Naviglio in Milan, Italy on 1 June 1967. Odds of 100 to 1 on were quoted for the United States horse *Man o' War* (foaled 29 March 1917, died 1 Nov. 1947) on three separate occasions in 1920, and for the two British horses, *Ormonde* in the Champion Stakes on 14 Oct. 1886 (three runners), and *Sceptre* in the Limekiln Stakes on 27 Oct. 1903 (two runners).

BRITISH TURF RECORDS

Most expensive horses The highest price ever paid for a horse in the British Isles is £250,000, paid in February 1953 for *Tulyar* by the Irish National Stud to the Rt. Hon. Aga Sultan Sir Mohammed Shah, H.H. Aga Khan III, G.C.S.I., G.C.M.G., G.C.I.E., G.C.V.O. (1877–1957) of Iran (Persia). A sum of £250,000 was also paid to Mr J. McShain for *Ballymoss* by a syndicate in September 1958. The French horse *Charlottesville* was bought by a syndicate for £336,000 from H.H. Shah Karim, Aga Khan IV (b. 13 Dec. 1936), in November 1960. The record payment for a horse in training is 136,000 guineas (£142,800) to Mr. L. B. Holliday for *Vaguely Noble* at Park Paddocks, Newmarket auction sale by Dr. Robert A. Franklyn (U.S.) on 7 Dec. 1967. *Sir Ivor* commands a covering fee of £8,000.

Most successful horses Only fillies are eligible to win all five classics. *Sceptre* came closest in 1902 when she won the 1,000 Guineas, 2,000 Guineas, Oaks and St. Leger. In 1868 *Formosa* won the same four but dead-heated in the 2,000 Guineas. The most races won in a season is 23 by *Fisherman* in 1856. *Catherina* won 79 out of 174 races between 1833 and 1841. The only horse to win the same race in seven successive years was *Dr. Syntax*, who won the Preston Gold Cup (1815–21). The most successful sire was *Stockwell*, whose progeny won 1,153 races (1858–76) and in 1866 set a record of 132 races won. The first English horse to win more than £200,000 in prize money on English racecourses is *Brigadier Gerard* who won £243,924 10p during the 1970–1–2 seasons.

Most successful owners The greatest amount of stake money won is £1,025,592 from 784 races by H.H. Aga Khan III (1877–1957) from 1922 until his death. These included 35 classics, of which 17 were English classics. The record for a season was set by Mr. C. W. Engelhard, who surpassed the previous record of £120,924 by winning £182,056

in 1970. The most wins in a season is 109 by Mr. David Robinson. The most English classics won is 20 by the 4th Duke of Grafton, K.G. (1760–1844), from 1813 to 1831.

Most successful trainers Captain Sir Cecil Charles Boyd-Rochfort, K.C.V.O. (b. 16 April 1887) earned more than £1,500,000 for his patrons. The record for a season is £256,899 by Charles Francis Noel Murless (born 1910) in 1967. Noel Murless has also earned more than £1,500,000 for his patrons. The most classics won by a trainer is 40 or 41 by John Scott, including 16 St. Leger winners between 1827 and 1862.

Most successful jockeys Sir Gordon Richards (b. 5 March 1904) retired in 1954, having won 4,870 races from 21,834 mounts since his first win at Leicester on 31 March 1921. In 1953, after 27 attempts, he won the Derby, six days after being knighted. In 1947 he won a record 269 races. The most classic races won by a jockey is 27 by Frank Buckle (1766–1832), between 1792 and 1827.

Most runners The most horses in a race is 66 (a world record) in the Grand National of 22 March 1929. The record for the flat is 58 in the Lincolnshire Handicap on 13 March 1948. The most runners at a meeting were 214 (flat) in seven races at Newmarket on 15 June 1915 and 229 (National Hunt) in eight races at Worcester on 13 Jan. 1965.

THE DERBY

The greatest of England's five classic races, the Epsom Derby, was inaugurated on 4 May 1780 by the 12th Earl of Derby (1752–1834). It has been run over 1 mile 885 yds *2,418 km* since 1784 (1½ miles [*2,414 km*] since World War I) on Epsom Downs, Surrey, except for the two war periods, when it was run at Newmarket. Since 1884 the race has been for three-year-old colts carrying 9 st. *57 kg* and fillies carrying 8 st. 9 lb. *54 kg 884*.

Highest prize The highest prize for winning any English race was £74,489.50 for *Charlottown* in the Derby on 25 May 1966.

Most winning owners The only owner with five outright winners was the 3rd Earl of Egremont (1751–1837) with *Assassin* (1782), *Hannibal* (1804), *Cardinal Beaufort* (1805), *Election* (1807) and *Lapdog* (1826). H.H. Aga Khan III (1877–1957) had four winners in *Blenheim* (1930), *Bahram* (1935), *Mahmoud* (1936) and *Tulyar* (1952) and a half-share in *My Love* (1948).

Mahmoud, led by the most successful owner H. H. Aga Khan (black top hat), after winning the 1936 Derby in a record time of 2 min 33.8 sec

Steve Donoghue, who rode six Derby winners between 1915 and 1925

Trainer The only two trainers with seven winners were John Porter with *Blue Gown* (1868), *Shotover* (1882), *St. Blaise* (1883), *Ormonde* (1886), *Sainfoin* (1890), *Common* (1891) and *Flying Fox* (1899), and Robert Robson with *Waxy* (1793), *Tyrant* (1802), *Pope* (1809), *Whalebone* (1810), *Whisker* (1815), *Azor* (1817), and *Emilius* (1823). Fred Darling had seven winners, including two in the war-time meetings at Newmarket (1940–41)—*Captain Cuttle* (1922), *Manna* (1925), *Coronace* (1926), *Cameronian* (1931), *Bois Roussel* (1938), *Pont l'Evique* (1940), and *Owen Tudor* (1941).

Jockey The most successful jockeys have been Jem Robinson, won won six times in 1817, 1824–25, 1827–28 and 1836 and Lester Piggott (1954–57–60–68–70–72). Steve Donogue (1884–1945) rode six winners (1915–1925) but the first two were war-time races not on the Epsom Course.

Record time The record time for the Derby is 2 min 33.8 sec (average speed 35.06 m.p.h. [*56,42 km/h*]) by *Mahmoud* ridden by Charlie Smirke, owned by H.H. Aga Khan III, trained by Frank Butters (1878–1957), winning at 100 to 8 by three lengths from a field of 22 in 1936. The fastest time recorded over the Derby course is, however, the hand-timed 2 min 33.0 sec by the four-year-old *Apelle* in winning the 1928 Coronation Cup. The fastest mechanically timed run was 2 min 33.49 sec by *Knockroe* in the 3.10 p.m. on 8 June 1973.

Dead heats The two instances of dead heats were in 1828, when *Cadland* beat *The Colonel* in the run off, and in 1884 between *Harvester* and *St. Gatien* (stakes divided).

Disqualifications The two disqualifications were of *Running Rein* (race awarded to *Orlando*) in 1844 and of *Craganour* (race awarded to *Aboyeur*) in the 'Suffragette Derby' on 4 June 1913, when Miss Emily Davison killed herself by impeding King George V's horse *Anmer*.

Other records The only greys to have won were *Gustavus* (1821), *Tagalie* (1912), *Mahmoud* (1936) and *Airborne* (1946). Only two black horses have ever won—*Smolensko* (1813) and *Grand Parade* (1919). The longest odds quoted on a placed Derby horse were 200–1 against for *Black Tommy*, second to *Blink Bonny* in 1857. The shortest priced winner was *Ladas* (1894) at 9–2 on and the highest priced winners were *Jeddah* (1898), *Signorinetta* (1908) and *Aboyeur* (1913), all at 100 to 1 against. The smallest field was four in 1794 and the largest 34 in 1862. The smallest winner was *Little Wonder* (14 hands 3½ in [*151,12 cm*]) in 1840.

Starter of most classics The only man to start more than 100 classics has been Alec Marsh, Senior Jockey Club starter who retired after his 101st classic start in 1972. His first was the 2,000 Guineas in 1952.

GRAND NATIONAL

Most wins *Horse* The first official Grand National Steeplechase may be regarded as the Grand Liverpool Steeplechase of 26 Feb. 1839 though the race was not so named until some years later. The first winner of the Grand Liverpool Steeplechase was Mr. Pott's *The Duke* in 1837. The race is for six-year-olds and over (since 1930) and is run over a course of 4 miles 856 yds *7,220 km*, with 30 jumps, at Aintree, near Liverpool. No horse has won three times but six share the record of two wins:

Peter Simple	1849 and 1853	*The Colonel*	1869 and 1870
Abd-el-Kader	1850 and 1851	*Manifesto*	1897 and 1899
The Lamb	1868 and 1871	*Reynoldstown*	1935 and 1936

Manifesto was entered eight times (1895–1904) and won twice, came third three times and fourth once. *Poethlyn* won in 1919 having won the war-time Gatwick race in 1918.

Jockey The only jockey to ride five winners was George Stevens on *Free Trader* (1856), *Emblem* (1863), *Emblematic* (1864) and *The Colonel* (1869–70).

Owner The only owners with three winners, since the race became a handicap in 1843, are Captain Machell with *Disturbance* (1873), *Reughy* (1874) and *Regal* (1876); and Sir Charles Assheton-Smith with *Cloister* (1893), *Jerry M* (1912) and *Covertcoat* (1913).

Trainer The only trainer with four winners was the Hon. Aubrey Hastings with *Ascetic's Silver* (1906), *Ally Sloper* (1915), *Ballymacad* (1917, Gatwick) and *Master Robert* (1924).

Highest prize The highest prize was £25,765.50 won by *Well to Do* on 8 April 1972.

SPEED RECORDS

Distance	Time min sec	m.p.h.	km/h	Name	Course	Date
¼ mile	20.8	43.26	*69,62*	*Big Racket* (U.S.A.)	Lomas de Sotelo, Mexico	5 Feb. 1945
½ mile (straight)	45.0	40.00	*64,37*	*Gloaming* (N.Z.)	Wellington, New Zealand	12 Jan. 1921
½ mile	45.0	40.00	*64,37*	*Beau Madison* (U.S.A.)	Phoenix, Arizona, U.S.A.	30 Mar. 1957
	45.0	40.00	*64,37*	*Another Nell* (U.S.A.)	Cicero, Ill., U.S.A.	8 May 1967
⅝ mile	53.6	41.98	*67,56*	*Indigenous* (G.B.)	Epsom, Surrey	2 June 1960
¾ mile	1:07.4	40.06	*64,47*	*Zip Pocket* (U.S.A.)	Phoenix, Arizona, U.S.A.	6 Dec. 1966
	1:07.4	40.06	*64,47*	*Vale of Tears* (U.S.A.)	Ab Sar Ben, Omaha, Neb., U.S.A.	7 June 1969
	1:06.2	40.78	*65,62*	*Broken Tindril* (G.B.)	*Brighton, Sussex	6 Aug. 1929
Mile	1:31.8	39.21	*63,10*	*Soueida* (G.B.)	*Brighton, Sussex	19 Sept. 1963
	1:31.8	39.21	*63,10*	*Loose Cover* (G.B.)	*Brighton, Sussex	9 June 1966
	1:32.2	39.04	*62,82*	*Dr. Fager* (U.S.A.)	Arlington, Ill., U.S.A.	24 Aug. 1968
1½ miles	2:23.0	37.76	*60,76*	*Fiddle Isle* (U.S.A.)	Arcadia, Cal., U.S.A.	21 Mar. 1970
2 miles**	3:15.0	36.93	*59,43*	*Polazel* (G.B.)	Salisbury, Wiltshire	8 July 1924
3 miles	5:15.0	34.29	*55,18*	*Farragut* (Mexico)	Agua Caliente	9 Mar. 1941

* *Course downhill for two thirds of a mile.*
** *A more reliable modern record is 3 min 16.75 sec by Il Tempo (N.Z.) at Trentham, Wellington, New Zealand on 17 Jan. 1970.*

Alec Marsh, Senior Jockey Club starter, who has started 101 classics

Fastest time The record time is 9 min 1.9 sec set by *Red Rum* ridden by Brian Fletcher, owned by Noel Le Maire, 84 and trained by Donald McCain, 42 of Southport in 1973. He won by ¾ length from the joint favourite *Crisp*, which was earlier 20 lengths clear.

Highest jump The 15th jump, known as the 'Chair', is 5 ft 2 in *1,57 m* high and 3 ft 9 in *1,14 m* thick. The ditch on the take-off side is 6 ft *1,82 m* wide and the guard rail in front of the ditch is 1 ft 6 in *45 cm* in height.

STEEPLECHASING

Golden Miller won the Cheltenham Gold Cup on 14 March 1935 in very heavy conditions carrying 12 st. *76 kg* over 3 miles 3 furlongs *5,43 km* in 6 min 30 sec so averaging an unsurpassed 31.15 m.p.h. *50,13 km/h.*

Jockey The first National Hunt jockey to reach 1,000 wins is Stan Mellor (b. 1938). This he achieved on *Ouzo* at Nottingham on 18 Dec. 1971.

HURLING

Earliest reference A game of very ancient origin, hurling only became standardized with the formation of the Gaelic Athletic Association in Thurles, Ireland, on 1 Nov. 1884.

Most titles The greatest number of All-Ireland Championships won by one team is 22 by Tipperary in 1887, 1895–96, 1898–99–1900, 1906, 1908, 1916, 1925, 1930, 1937, 1945, 1949–50–51, 1958, 1961–62, 1964–65 and 1971. The greatest number of successive wins is the four by Cork (1941–44).

Highest score The highest score in an All-Ireland final was in 1896 when Tipperary (8 goals, 14 points) beat Dublin (no goals, 4 points). The record aggregate score was when Cork (6 goals, 21 points) defeated Wexford (5 goals, 10 points) in 1970. A goal equals 3 points.

Lowest score The lowest score in an All-Ireland final was when Tipperary (1 goal, 1 point) beat Galway (nil) in the first championship at Birr in 1887.

Most The most appearances in All-Ireland finals is ten shared by Christy Ring (Cork) and John Doyle Tipperary). They also share the record of All-Ireland medals won with 8 each. Ring's appearances on the winning side were in 1941–42–43–44, 1946 and 1952–53–54, while Doyle's were in 1949–50–51, 1958, 1961–62 and 1964–65.

Individual score The highest recorded individual score was by Nick Rackard (Wexford), who scored 7 goals and 7 points against Antrim in the 1954 All-Ireland semi-finals.

Largest crowd The largest crowd was 84,856 for the final between Cork and Wexford at Croke Park, Dublin, in 1954.

Inter-provincials Munster holds the greatest number of inter-provincial (Railway Cup) championships with 32 (1928–1970). Christy Ring (Cork and Munster) played in a record 22 finals (1942–63) and was on the winning side 18 times.

Longest stroke The greatest distance for a "lift and stroke" is one of 129 yds *117 m* credited to Tom Murphy of Three Castles, Kilkenny, in a "long puck" contest in 1906. The record for the annual *An Poc Fada* (Long Puck) contest (instituted 1961) in the ravines of the Cooley Hills, north of Dundalk, County Louth, is 65 pucks (drives) plus 87 yds *79 m* over the course of 3 miles 320 yds *5,120 km* by Fionnbar O'Neill (Cork) in 1966. This represents an average of 84.8 yds *77,5 m* per drive.

Tipperary, winners of 22 All Ireland Championships, on the way to winning their 22nd title in 1971

ICE HOCKEY

Origins There is pictorial evidence that hockey was played on ice in the 17th century in The Netherlands. The game was probably first played in North America in 1860 at Kingston, Ontario, Canada, but Montreal and Halifax also lay claim to priority.

Olympic Games Canada has won the Olympic Championship six times (1920–24–28–32–48–52) and the world title 19 times, the last being at Geneva in 1961. The longest Olympic career is that of Richard Torriani (Switzerland) from 1928 to 1948. The most gold medals won by any player is three achieved by Vitaliy Davidov, Anatoliy Firssov, Viktor Kuzkin and Aleksandr Ragulin of the U.S.S.R. teams that won the Olympic titles in 1964–68 and 1972. Davidov and Ragulin had played in 9 World championship teams prior to the 1972 Games.

Stanley Cup The Stanley Cup, presented by the Governor-General Lord Stanley (original cost $48.67), became emblematic of world professional team supremacy several years after the first contest at Montreal in 1893. It has been won most often by the Montreal Canadiens [*sic*], with 18 wins in 1916, 1924, 1930, 1931, 1944, 1946, 1953, 1956 (winning a record 45 games), 1957, 1958, 1959, 1960, 1965, 1966, 1968, 1969, 1971 and 1973. Henri Richard and Jean Beliveau played in their tenth finals in 1971.

Longest match The longest match was 2 hrs 56 min 30 sec when Detroit Red Wings eventually beat Montreal Maroons 1–0 in the sixth period of overtime at the Forum, Montreal, at 2.25 a.m. on 25 March 1936.

Most goals The greatest number of goals recorded in a World Championship match has been 31–1 when Hungary beat Belgium in 1971. The N.H.L. record is 21 goals when Montreal Canadiens beat Toronto St. Patrick's at Montreal, 14–7 on 10 Jan 1920.

Most National Hockey League goals in a season: 76 goals by Phil Esposito of the Boston Bruins in 1970–71. The most points in a season is 152 (76 goals and 76 assists) by Phil Esposito (Boston Bruins) also in 1970–71. The North American career record for goals is 786 by Gordie Howe (b. 31 Mar. 1928) (Detroit Red Wings) in 25 seasons ending in 1970–71. He has also collected 500 stitches in his face. Two players have scored 1,000 goals in Great Britain—Chick Zamick (Nottingham Panthers and Wembley Lions) and George Beach (Wembley Monarchs and later Wembley Lions).

Fastest scoring Toronto scored 8 goals against the New York Americans in 4 min 52 sec on 19 March 1938. Bill Mosienko (Chicago) scored three goals in 21 sec against New York Rangers on 23 March 1952.

The Canadian Ice Hockey ace, Bobby Hull who has been timed skating at 29.7 m.p.h. *47,7 km/h*

Most points one game The most points scored in one game is 10 (3 goals, 7 assists) by Jim Harrison (Toronto) on 30 Jan. 1973.

Fastest player The highest speed measured for any player is 29.7 m.p.h. *47,7 km/h* for Bobby Hull (Chicago Black Hawks) (born 3 Jan. 1939). The highest puck speed is also attributed to Hull, whose left-handed slap shot has been measured at 118.3 m.p.h. *190,3 km/h*.

BRITISH LEAGUE

The highest score in a League match has been 23–0 when Durham Wasps beat Paisley Vikings on 31 Jan. 1967. The highest aggregate score has been 29 when Ayr Bruins beat Whitley Warriors 17–12 at Ayr on 24 Jan. 1971.

Most wins The British League championship (instituted 1934 but ended in 1960) has been won most often by the Wembley Lions with four victories in 1936–37, 1952 and 1957.

Fastest scoring Kenny Westman (Nottingham Panthers) scored a hat trick in 30 sec *v.* Brighton Tigers on 3 March 1955.

ICE SKATING

Origins The earliest reference to ice skating is that of a Danish writer dated 1134. The earliest English account of 1180 refers to skates made of bone. Metal blades date from probably *c.* 1600. The earliest skating club was the Edinburgh Skating Club formed in 1742. The earliest artificial ice rink in the world was the "Glaciarium" in Chelsea, London, in 1876.

Olympic The most Olympic gold medals won in speed skating is six by Lidia Skoblikova (b. 8 March 1939) of Chelyaminsk, U.S.S.R., in 1960 (2) and 1964 (4). The male record is by Ivor Ballangrad (b. 7 March 1904) who won 4 gold, 2 silver and 1 bronze medal.

FIGURE SKATING

World The greatest number of world men's figure skating titles (instituted 1896) is ten by Ulrich Salchow (b. 7 Aug. 1877) of Sweden, in 1901–05 and 1907–11. The only British figure skater to win has been Henry Graham Sharp (b. 19 Dec. 1917) in Budapest on 18–19 Feb. 1939. The women's record (instituted 1906) is ten titles by Frk. Sonja Henie (b. 8 April 1912) of Norway, between 1927 and 1936. She died on 12 Oct. 1969.

Olympic The most Olympic gold medals won by a figure skater is three by Gillis Graftström (b. 7 June 1893) of

Sweden in 1920, 1924 and 1928 (also silver medal in 1932); and by Sonja Henie (see above) in 1928, 1932 and 1936.

British The record number of British titles is 11 by Jack Page (Manchester S.C.) in 1922–31 and 1933, and six by Miss Cecilia Colledge (b. 28 Nov. 1920) (Park Lane F.S.C., London) in 1935–36–37(2)–38 and 1946.

Most Difficult Jump The triple Lutz has been performed by only 3 skaters—by Donald Jackson (U.S.) (b. 2 April 1940) in Prague, 1962; by Haïg B. Oundjian (G.B.) (b. 16 May 1949) in the Grand Prix de Saint Gervais in Aug. 1969 and by John Mischa Petkevich, (b. 3 Mar. 1949) the 1971 U.S. champion.

Longest race The longest race regularly held is the "Elfstedentocht" ("Tour of the Eleven Towns") in the Netherlands. It covers 200 km *124 miles 483 yds* and the fastest time is 7 hrs 35 min by Jeen van den Berg (b. 8 Jan. 1928) on 3 Feb. 1954.

Skating marathon The longest recorded skating marathon is one of 82 hrs 30 min by Tony Hocking, 19 at the Toombul Ice Rink, Brisbane, Australia in April 1973. The fastest time to complete 100 miles *160 km* is 5 hrs 35 min by Robert B. Kerns on 20 Feb. 1972 at Glacier Falls Ice Rink, Anaheim, California, U.S.A.

Largest rink The world's largest indoor ice rink is the quadruple rink at Burnaby, British Columbia, Canada, completed in Dec. 1972, which has an ice area of 68,000 ft² *6 317 m²*. The largest artificial outdoor rink is the Fujikyu Highland Promenade Rink, Japan opened at a cost of £335,000 in 1967 and with an area of 165,750 ft² *15 400 m²* (3.8 acres *1,5 ha*). The largest in the U.K. has been the Crossmyloof Ice Rink, Glasgow, with an ice area of 225 ft *68 m* by 97 ft *29 m*.

SPEED SKATING

Most titles World The greatest number of world speed skating titles (instituted 1893) won by any skater is five by Oscar Mathisen (Norway) in 1908–09 and 1912–14, and Clas

Holder of four world records and winner of three Olympic gold medals in 1972, Ard Schenk of the Netherlands on the way to his third gold in Sapporo, Japan

Thunberg (b. 5 April 1893) of Finland, in 1923, 1925, 1928–29 and 1931. The most titles won by a woman is four by Mrs. Inga Voronina, *née* Artomonova (1936–66) of Moscow, U.S.S.R., in 1957, 1958, 1962 and 1965.

WORLD SPEED SKATING RECORDS

	Distance	min sec	Name and Nationality	Place	Date
MEN	500 metres	38.00*	Leo Linkovesi (Finland)	Davos, Switzerland	8 Jan. 1972
		38.00*	Hasse Borjes (Sweden)	Inzell, West Germany	4 Mar. 1972
		38.00*	Erhard Keller (West Germany)	Inzell, West Germany	4 Mar. 1972
		38.00*	Lasse Efskind (Norway)	Davos, Switzerland	13 Jan. 1973
	1,000 metres	1:17.60	Lasse Efskind (Norway)	Davos, Switzerland	13 Jan. 1973
	1,500 metres	1:58.70	Ard Schenk (Netherlands)	Davos, Switzerland	15 Feb. 1971
	3,000 metres	4:08.30	Ard Schenk (Netherlands)	Inzell, West Germany	2 Mar. 1972
	5,000 metres	7:09.80	Ard Schenk (Netherlands)	Inzell, West Germany	4 Mar. 1972
	10,000 metres	14:55.96	Ard Schenk (Netherlands)	Inzell, West Germany	14 Mar. 1971
WOMEN	500 metres	41.8†	Sheila Young (U.S.A.)	Davos, Switzerland	20 Jan. 1973
	1,000 metres	1:26.1†	Tatiana Averina (U.S.S.R.)	Medeo, U.S.S.R.	20 Mar. 1973
	1,500 metres	2:13.4†	Galina Stepanskaya (U.S.S.R.)	Medeo, U.S.S.R.	19 Mar. 1973
	3,000 metres	4:46.5†	Stien Kaiser (Netherlands)	Davos, Switzerland	16 Jan. 1971
	5,000 metres	9:01.60	Rimma Zhukova (U.S.S.R.)	Medeo, U.S.S.R.	24 Jan. 1953

BRITISH OUTDOOR RECORDS

	Distance	min sec	Name	Place	Date
MEN	500 metres	40.90	A. John Tipper	Cortina d'Ampezzo, Italy	28 Jan. 1970
	1,000 metres	1:23.1	A. John Tipper	Davos, Switzerland	8 Jan. 1972
	1,500 metres	2:08.40	A. John Tipper	Cortina d'Ampezzo, Italy	28 Jan. 1970
	3,000 metres	4:34.70	John B. Blewitt	Cortina d'Ampezzo, Italy	16 Jan. 1968
	5,000 metres	7:51.2	John B. Blewitt	Davos, Switzerland	22 Jan. 1972
	10,000 metres	16:30.10	Terence A. Malkin	Oslo, Norway	19 Jan. 1964
WOMEN	500 metres	51.90	Patricia K. Tipper	Cortina d'Ampezzo, Italy	16 Jan. 1968
	1,000 metres	1:44.20	Patricia K. Tipper	Inzell, West Germany	7 Jan. 1968
	1,500 metres	2:42.80	Patricia K. Tipper	Cortina d'Ampezzo, Italy	17 Dec. 1967
	3,000 metres	5:39.40	Patricia K. Tipper	Cortina d'Ampezzo, Italy	16 Dec. 1967

* This represents a speed of 29.43 m.p.h. 47,36 km/h.
† Awaiting ratification.

ICE AND SAND YACHTING

Origin The sport originated in The Netherlands from the year 1600 (earliest patent granted) and along the Baltic coast. The earliest authentic record is Dutch, dating from 1768. Land or Sand yachts of Dutch construction were first reported on beaches (now in Belgium) in 1595. The earliest International championship was staged in 1914.

Record Speeds The largest known ice yacht was *Icicle*, built for Commodore John E. Roosevelt for racing on the

Ice Hudson River, New York, in *c.* 1870. It was 68 ft 11 in *21 m* long and carried 1,070 ft² *99 m²* of canvas. The highest speed officially recorded is 143 m.p.h. *230 km/h* by John D. Buckstaff in a Class A stern-steerer on Lake Winnebago, Wisconsin, U.S.A., in 1938. Such a speed is possible in a wind of 72 m.p.h. *115 km/h.*

Sand The fastest recorded speed for a sand yacht is 57.69 m.p.h. *92,84 km/h* (measured mile in 62.4 sec) by *Coronation Year Mk. II* owned by R. Millett Denning and crewed by J. Halliday, Bob Harding, J. Glassbrook and Cliff Martindale at Lytham St. Anne's, Lancashire, England in 1956.

INDOOR GAMES

CONTRACT BRIDGE

Earliest references Bridge (a corruption of Biritch) is of Levantine origin, having been played in Greece in the early 1880s. The game was known in London in 1886 under the title of "Biritch" or Russian Whist.

Auction Bridge (highest bidder names trump) was introduced in 1904 but was swamped by the Contract game, which was devised by Harold S. Vanderbilt (U.S.A.) on a Caribbean voyage in November 1925. The new version became a world-wide craze after the U.S.A. *v.* Great Britain challenge match between Ely Culbertson (b. Romania, 1891) and Lt.-Col. Walter Thomas More Buller (1886–1938) at Almack's Club, London, on 15 Sept. 1930. The U.S.A. won the 54-hand match by 4,845 points.

World titles The World Championship (Bermuda Bowl) has been won most often by Italy's Blue Team (*Squadra Azzura*) (1957–58–59, 1961–62–63, 1965–66–67, 1969, 1973), whose team also won the Olympiad in 1964, 1968 and 1972. Two of the Italian players, Giorgio Belladonna (b. 1923) and Pietro Forquet, were in 13 of these winning teams. The team retired in 1969 but came back to defeat the Dallas Aces (1970–71 World Champions) 338–254 in Las Vegas, Nevada in December 1971, and take the Olympiad in Miami, Florida in June 1972.

Perfect deals The mathematical odds against dealing 13 cards of one suit are 158,753,389,899 to 1, while the odds against receiving a "perfect hand" consisting of all 13 spades are 635,013,559,599 to 1. The odds against each of the 4 players receiving a complete suit (a "perfect deal") are 2,235,197,406,895,366,368,301,559,999 to 1. Instances of this are reported frequently but the chances of it happening genuinely are extraordinarily remote—in fact if all the people in the world were grouped in bridge fours, and each four were dealt 120 hands a day, it would require 62×10^{12} years before one "perfect deal" should recur.

A "perfect" perfect deal with the dealer (South) with 13 clubs, round to East with 13 spades was the subject of affidavits by Mrs. E. F. Gyde (dealer), Mrs. Hennion, David Rex-Taylor and Mrs. P. Dawson at Richmond Community Centre, Surrey, on 25 Aug. 1964. This deal, 24 times more remote than a "perfect

The world's leading woman bridge player Mrs. Rixi Markus (G.B.)

deal", the second of the rubber, was with a pack not used for the first deal. In view of the fact that there should be 31,201,794 deals with two perfect hands for each deal with four perfect hands and that reports of the latter far outnumber the former, it can be safely assumed that reported occurrences of perfect deals are almost without exception bogus.

Longest session The longest recorded session is one of 180 hr by 4 students at Edinburgh University on 21–28 April 1972.

Most master points In 1971 a new world ranking list based on Master Points was instituted. The leading male player in the world was Giorgio Belladonna (Italy) a member of the Blue team with 1,333 points as at Feb. 1973, followed by five more Italians. The leading Briton is Boris Schapiro (b. 1911) in 16th place with 353 points. The world's leading woman player was Mrs. Rixi Markus (G.B.) with 195 points. Britain had 4 more in the Top Ten.

HIGHEST POSSIBLE SCORES (excluding penalties)

Opponents bid 7 of any suit or No Trumps doubled and redoubled and vulnerable

	Opponents make no trick	
Above Line	1st undertrick	400
	12 subsequent undertricks at 600 each	7,200
	All Honours	150
		7,750

Bid 1 No Trump, double and redouble, vulnerable

Below Line	1st trick (40 × 4)	160
Above Line	6 over tricks (400 × 6)	2,400
	2nd game of 2-Game Rubber	*350
	All Honours	150
	Bonus for making redoubled contract	50
	(Highest Possible Positive Score)	3,110

* *In Practice, the full bonus of 700 points is awarded after the completion of the second winning game rather than 350 after each game.*

DRAUGHTS

Origins Draughts, known as checkers in North America, has origins earlier than chess. It was played in Egypt in the first millenium B.C. The earliest book on the game was by Antonio Torquemada of Valencia, Spain in 1547. The earliest U.S. *v.* Great Britain international was

in 1905 and was won by the Scottish Masters, 73–34 with 284 draws. The U.S. won in 1927 in New York 96–20 with 364 draws.

The British Championship (biannual) was inaugurated in 1926. The only man to win 5 titles has been Mr. J.

Marshall (Fife) in 1948–50–52–54–66. The longest tenure of invincibility in freestyle play was that of Melvin Pomeroy (U.S.), who was internationally undefeated from 1914 until his death in 1933.

Longest game In competition the prescribed rate of play is not less than 30 moves per hour with the average game lasting about 90 min. In 1958 a match between Dr. Marian Tinsley (U.S.) and Derek Oldbury (G.B.) lasted 7½ hours.

Most opponents Newell W. Banks (b. Detroit 10 Oct. 1887) played 140 games simultaneously winning 133 and drawing 7 in Chicago, Illinois in 1933. His playing time was 145 min so averaging about one move per sec.

SCRABBLE

Origins This word game was invented in 1949 by Jim Brunot (U.S.). It was introduced into the United Kingdom in 1953. The National Scrabble Championships were instituted in 1971.

Record The single move record score is 1,751 points by Mrs. Margaret Eddleston of Hitchin, Hertfordshire published in July 1973. The rules were codified by the periodical *Games and Puzzles* in their November 1972 issue.

Marathon The longest Scrabble game on record is one of 100

hours set by Mike Borrello, Pat Edmond, Rick Varyas and Mike Wilson at Lakewood, California on 14–18 April 1973.

TABLE FOOTBALL

Bar The most protracted 2-a-side table football on record was one of 300 hours maintained by six members of the sixth form of Bournemouth School, Hants., England on 25 June–7–July 1973.

Subbuteo The longest recorded Subbuteo table soccer marathon was one of 122 hours by 6 boys (aged under 17) who played continuously at Redditch Youth Centre, Worcestershire on 9–14 March 1973.

WHIST

Whist, first referred to in 1529, was the world's premier card game until 1930. The rules were standardized in 1742.

Highest Score No collated records exist but the highest scores notified to the editors have been—for 24 hands—209 by Mrs. E. Heslop in the Shaldon Over 60 Club, Teignmouth, Devon on 5 Jan. 1973.

Collection of Jokers The largest reported collection of jokers (terms first used in 1885) is one of 1,200 different examples from 8 countries amassed by Derek Haddon of Willenhall, Warwickshire.

JUDO (JIU-JITSU)

Origins Judo is a modern combat sport which developed out of an amalgam of several old Japanese fighting arts, the most popular of which was ju-jitsu (jiu-jitsu), which is thought to be of pre-Christian Chinese origin. Judo has been greatly developed by the Japanese since 1882, when it was first devised by *Shihan* Dr. Jigoro Kano.

World championships were inaugurated in Tōkyō on 5 May 1956. The only two men to have won 3 world titles have been Antonius (Anton) J. Geesink (b. 6 Apr. 1934) of the Netherlands, who won the 1963 (Open), 1964 (Olympic Open) and 1965 Heavyweight title at 120 kg *19 st.*, 6 ft 6 in *1,98 cm* and Wilhem Ruska (Netherlands), who won the 1971 Heavyweight and the 1972 Olympic Heavyweight and Open titles.

Great Britain has won most consecutive European championships (instituted in 1951) with 3 victories (1957–58–59). France won in 1951–52, 1954–55, and 1962. Britain won again in 1971.

Highest grade The efficiency grades in Judo are divided into pupil (*kyu*) and master (*dan*) grades. The highest awarded is the extremely rare red belt *Judan* (10th dan), given only to seven men. The Judo protocol provides for an *11th dan* (*Juichidan*) who also would wear a red belt and even a *12th dan* who would wear a white belt twice as wide as an ordinary belt, but these have never been bestowed. The highest British native Judo grade is *7th dan* by Trevor P. Leggett (b. 22 Aug. 1914).

Marathon The longest recorded Judo marathon with continuous action by two of 8 Judoka in 5 min stints is 24 hrs from St. Andrews Judo Club, London N.19, on 20–21 July 1973.

KARATE

Origins Based on techniques devised from the 6th century Chinese art of *Chuan-fa* (Kempo), karate (empty hand) was developed by an unarmed populace in Okinawa as a weapon against armed oppressors. Transmitted to Japan in the 1920's by Funakoshi Gichin, the founder of modern karate, this method of combat was further refined and organised into a sport with competitive rules. The five major styles of karate in Japan are: *Shotokan*, *Wado-ryu*, *Goju-ryu*, *Shito-ryu* and *Kyokushinkai*, each of which place different emphasis on speed and power etc. *Tae kwan-do* is a lethal Korean variation on Karate, which has been used for military purposes.

The Governing Body for the sport in Britain is the British Karate Control Commission on which the major karate styles in this country are represented. Great Britain became the first country ever to defeat the Japanese in competition when they won in the World championships in Paris in 1972.

Most Titles The only winner of three All-Japanese titles has been Takeshi Oishi who won in 1969–70–71.

Billy Corbett who broke a pile of 5,000 bricks in half in 17 hours with his Karate Chop

Greatest force Considerably less emphasis is placed on *Tamashiwara* (wood breaking etc.) than is generally supposed. Most styles use it only for demonstration purposes. However, the force needed to break a brick with the abductor *digiti quinti* muscle of the hand is 130–140 lb. *59–63 kg* up to a maximum of 196 lb. *88 kg*. The greatest brick breaking feat was 294 per hour for 17 hours (total 5,000) by Billy Corbett in Bellvue, Washington, U.S.A. on 29 April–1 May 1972. The bricks used were $2 \times 3\frac{1}{2} \times 12$ in $5 \times 8,9 \times 30$ cm Roman bricks, of which he once broke 8 at a blow.

Top exponents The highest dan among karatekas is Yamaguchi Gogen (b. 1907) a 10th dan of the *Goju-ryu* Karate Do.

The leading exponents in the United Kingdom are Tatsuo Suzuki (7th dan, *Wado-ryu*), chief instructor to the United Kingdom Karate Federation; Keinosuke Enoeda (7th dan, *Shotokan*), resident instructor to the Karate Union of Great Britain and Steve Arneil (5th dan, *Kyokushinkai*) British national born in South Africa.

LACROSSE

Origin The game is of American Indian origin, derived from the inter-tribal game *baggataway*, and was played before 1492 by Iroquois Indians in lower Ontario, Canada and upper New York State, U.S.A. It was introduced into Great Britain in 1867. The English Lacrosse Union was formed in 1892. The Oxford *v.* Cambridge match was instituted in 1903 and the game was included in the Olympic Games of 1908 and featured as an exhibition sport in the 1928 and 1948 Games.

World championship The first World Tournament was held at Toronto, Canada in 1967 and the U.S.A. won.

Longest throw The longest recorded throw is 162.86 yds *148,91 m* by Barney Quinn of Ottawa on 10 Sept. 1892.

Most titles The English Club Championship (Iroquois Cup), instituted in 1890, has been won most often by Stockport with 15 wins between 1897 and 1934.

Highest scores The highest score in any international match was Australia's 19–3 win over England at Manchester in May 1972. The highest score in the annual North of England *v.* South of England match has been 26–2 in 1927.

The record number of international representations for England is 14 by John Hall of Mellor, Cheshire to 1972. G. H. Metcalfe played for the South of England 30 times (1949–69).

The record for women is 52 for Scotland by Caro Macintosh (1952–1969).

LAWN TENNIS

Origins The modern game is generally agreed to have evolved as an outdoor form of the indoor game of Tennis (see separate entry). "Field Tennis" is mentioned in an English magazine—*Sporting Magazine*—of 29 Sept. 1793. The earliest club for such a game, variously called Pelota or Lawn Rackets, was the Leamington Club founded in 1872 by Major Harry Gem. The earliest attempt to commercialise the game was by Major Walter Clopton Wingfield, M.V.O. (1833–1912) who patented a form called "sphairistike" in February 1874. It soon became called Lawn Tennis. Amateur players were permitted to play with and against professionals in 'Open' tournaments in 1968.

ALL TIME RECORDS

Greatest Domination The grand slam is to win all four of the world's major championship singles: Wimbledon, the United States, Australian and French (on hard courts) championships. The first man to have won all four was Frederick John Perry (G.B.) (born 1909) with the French title in 1935. The first man to hold all four championships simultaneously was J. Donald Budge (U.S.A.) (born 1915) with the French title in 1938. The first man to achieve the grand slam twice was Rodney George Laver (Australia) (born 9 Aug. 1938) having won in 1962 as an amateur and again in 1969 when the titles were 'open' to professionals.

Only two women have achieved the grand slam: Maureen Catherine Connolly (U.S.A.) (1934–1969), later Mrs. Norman Brinker with the French title in 1953; and Mrs. Barry M. Court, M.B.E., (*née* Margaret Smith) (Australia) (born 1942) in 1970.

Fastest service The fastest service ever *measured* was one of 154 m.p.h. *247 km/h* by Michael J. Sangster (U.K.) (b. 1940) in June 1963. Crossing the net the ball was travelling at 108 m.p.h. *173 km/h*. Some players consider the service of Robert Falkenberg (U.S.A.) (b. 1926) the 1948 Wimbledon Champion as the fastest ever used.

Greatest crowd The greatest crowd at a tennis match was 25,578 at the first day of the Davis Cup Challenge Round between Australia and the United States at the White City, Sydney, New South Wales, Australia, on 27 Dec. 1954.

Highest Prize Money The highest prize money won in a year is $292,717 (£121,965) by Rodney George Laver (Australia) (b. 9 Aug. 1938) in 1971. His career total in nine professional seasons was thus brought to a record $1,006,947

The tennis court designed in 1874 by Major Walter Clopton Wingfield, an account of which was first published in *The Field* on 21 March 1874

(*£419,561*). The highest prize money won by a woman in a season is $117,000 (*£48,750*) by Mrs. Billie-Jean King (*née* Moffitt) (U.S.A.) also in 1971, which was more than any American male player. The biggest single prize, $50,000 (*£20,833*) was first won by Kenneth R. Rosewall (Australia) (b. 2 Nov. 1934) in the World Championship Tennis final play-offs at Dallas, Texas in 1971.

Lawn tennis marathons The longest recorded non-stop lawn tennis doubles game is one of 41 hr 35 min by four players of Stobsmuir Lawn Tennis Club in Dundee, Scotland ending on 1 July 1973. The duration record for singles by 2 players is 73 hr 25 min by Mel Baleson and Glen Grisillo (S.A.), at Reno, Nevada, U.S.A. on 6–9 May 1971.

WIMBLEDON RECORDS

Youngest champions The youngest ever champion at Wimbledon was Miss Charlotte Dod (1871–1960), who was 15 years 8 months when she won in 1887. The youngest male singles champion was Wilfred Baddeley (b. 11 Jan. 1872 d. 1929) who won the Wimbledon title in 1891 at the age of 19.

Richard Dennis Ralston (b. 27 July 1942) of Bakersfield, California, U.S.A., was 25 days short of his 18th birthday when he won the men's doubles with Rafael H. Osuna (1938–69) of Mexico in 1960.

Most appearances Arthur W. Gore (1868–1928) of the U.K. made 36 appearances at Wimbledon between 1888 and 1927, and was in 1909 at 41 years the oldest ever singles winner. In 1964, Jean Borotra (b. 13 Aug. 1898) of France made his 35th appearance since 1922. In 1972 he appeared in the Veterans' Doubles aged 73.

Most wins Miss Elizabeth Ryan (U.S.A.) (b. 1894) won her first title in 1914 and her 19th in 1934 (12 women's doubles with 5 different partners and 7 mixed doubles with 5 different partners). The post-war record is 17 Championships by Mrs. Billie-Jean King (*née* Moffitt) (U.S.A.), with five singles, nine women's doubles and three mixed doubles during the period 1961 to 1973.

Arthur Gore, who made a total of 36 appearances at the Wimbledon championships between 1888 and 1927

Men The greatest number of wins by a man at Wimbledon has been William Charles Renshaw (1861–1904) (G.B.) who won 7 singles titles (1881–2–3–4–5–6–9) and 7 doubles (1880–1–4–5–6–8–9), partnered by his twin brother (James) Ernest. Hugh Lawrence Doherty (1875–1919) won 5 singles (1902–3–4–5–6), 8 men's doubles (1897–8–9–1900–01 and 1903–4–5), partnered by his brother Reginald Frank Doherty (1872–1910), and two mixed doubles (then unofficial) in 1901–02, partnered by Mrs. Charlotte Sterry (*née* Cooper).

MOST GAMES AND LONGEST MATCHES

Note: The increasing option since 1970 by tournament organisers to use various "tie break" systems, which are precisely designed to stop long sets, is reducing the likelihood of these records, which may shortly become of mere historic interest, being broken.

	No. of Games	Players and score	Place	Date
Any match	147	Dick Leach/Dick Dell (Michigan Univ.) bt. Tommy Mozur/ Lenny Schloss 3–6, 49–47, 22–20	Newport, Rhode Island, U.S.A.	18–19 Aug. 1967
Any singles	126	Roger Taylor (G.B.) bt. Wieslaw Gasiorek (Poland) 27–29, 31–29, 6–4 (4 hr 35 min)	King's Cup, Warsaw, Poland	5 Nov. 1966
Any women's singles	62	Kathy Blake (U.S.A.) bt. Elena Subirats (Mexico) 12–10, 6–8, 14–12	Riping Rock, Locust Valley, N.Y., U.S.A.	1966
Any women's match	81	Nancy Richey/Carole Graebner (*née* Caldwell) bt. Justina Bricka/Carol Hanks (all U.S.A.) 31–33, 6–1, 6–4	South Orange, New Jersey, U.S.A.	1964
Any mixed doubles	71	William F. Talbot/Margaret du Pont (*née* Osborne) bt. Robert Falkenburg/Gertrude Moran (all U.S.A.) 27–25, 5–7, 6–1	Forest Hills, N.Y., U.S.A.	1948
Any set	96	see middle set of Any match above		
Longest time for Any Match	6 hr 23 min	Mark Cox/Robert K. Wilson (U.K.) bt. Charles M. Pasarell/ Ron E. Holmburg (U.S.A.) 26–24, 17–19, 30–28	U.S. Indoor Championships, Salisbury, Maryland, U.S.A.	18–19 Aug. 1967
Any Wimbledon match	112	Ricardo Alonzo Gonzalez (U.S.A.) bt. Charles M. Pasarell (U.S.A.) 22–24, 1–6, 16–14, 6–3, 11–9	First round	24–25 June 1969
Any Wimbledon doubles	98	Eugene L. Scott (U.S.A.)/Nicola Pilic (Yugoslavia) bt. G. Cliff Richey (U.S.A.)/Torben Ulrich (Denmark) 19–21, 12–10, 6–4, 4–6, 9–7	First round	22 June 1966
Any Wimbledon set	62	Pancho Segura (Ecuador)/Alex Olmedo (Peru) bt. Abe A. Segal/Gordon L. Forbes (S. Africa) 32–30	Second round	June 1968
Longest time for any Wimbledon match	5 hr 12 min	see Any Wimbledon match above		
Wimbledon men's final	58	Jaroslav Drobny (then Egypt) bt. Kenneth R. Rosewall (Australia) 13–11, 4–6, 6–2, 9–7	Final	July 1954
Wimbledon men's doubles Final	70	John D. Newcombe/Anthony D. Roche (Australia) bt. Kenneth R. Rosewall/Frederick S. Stolle (Australia) 3–6, 8–6, 5–7, 14–12, 6–3	Final	July 1968
Wimbledon women's Final	46	Mrs. Barry M. Court, M.B.E. (*née* Margaret Smith) (Australia) bt. Mrs. L. W. King (*née* Billie-Jean Moffitt) (U.S.A.) 14–12, 11–9. (2 hr 25 min)	Final	July 1970
Wimbledon women's Doubles final	38	Mme. Simone Mathieu (France)/Miss Elizabeth Ryan (U.S.A.) bt. Freda James (now Hammersley)/Adeline Maud Yorke (now Eyres) (both G.B.) 6–2, 9–11, 6–4	Final	July 1933
		Rosemary Casals/Mrs. L. W. King (*née* Moffitt) (both U.S.A.) bt. Maria E. Bueno (Brazil)/Nancy Richey (U.S.A.) 9–11, 6–4, 6–2	Final	July 1963
Wimbledon mixed Doubles final	48	Eric W. Sturgess/Mrs. Sheila Summers (S. Africa) bt. John E. Bromwich (Australia)/Alice Louise Brough (now Clapp) (U.S.A.) 9–7, 9–11, 7–5	Final	July 1949
Any Davis Cup rubber	122	Stanley Smith/Erik van Dillan (U.S.A.) bt. Jaime Filliol/ Patricio Cornejo (Chile) 7–9, 37–39, 8–6, 6–1, 6–3	American Zone Final, North Little Rock, Arkansas, U.S.A.	1973
Any Davis Cup singles	86	Arthur Ashe (U.S.A.) bt. Christian Kuhnke (Germany) 6–8, 10–12, 9–7, 13–11, 6–4	Challenge Round, Cleveland, Ohio, U.S.A.	1970
Any Davis Cup tie i.e. 5 rubbers	281	Italy bt. U.S.A. 3 rubbers to 2	Inter Zone Final, Perth, Western Australia	1960

Singles The greatest number of singles wins was eight by Mrs. F. S. Moody (*née* Helen N. Wills) (b. 6 Oct. 1905), now Mrs. Aiden Roark, of the U.S.A., who won in 1927, 1928, 1929, 1930, 1932, 1933, 1935 and 1938.

The greatest number of singles wins by a man was seven by William C. Renshaw (G.B.) as quoted above.

Doubles The greatest number of doubles wins by men was 8 by the brothers R. F. and H. L. Doherty (G.B.). They won each year from 1897 to 1905 except for 1902 (see above)

The most wins in women's doubles were 12 by Miss Elizabeth Ryan (U.S.A.) between 1914 and 1934 (see above).

The most wins in mixed doubles was 7 by Miss Elizabeth Ryan (U.S.A.) between 1919 and 1932. The male record is four wins shared by Elias Victor Seixias (U.S.A.) (b. 30 Aug. 1923) in 1953–54–55–56 and Kenneth N. Fletcher (Australia) (b. 15 June 1940) in 1963–65–66–68.

DAVIS CUP

Most victories The greatest number of wins in the Davis Cup (instituted 1900) has been (inclusive of 1972) the U.S.A., with 24 wins and Australasia/Australia with 22. The British Isles/Great Britain have won 9 times, in 1903–04–05–06, 1912, 1933–34–35–36.

Individual Performance Nicola Pietrangeli (Italy) played 164 rubbers, 1954 to 1972, winning 120. He played 110 singles (winning 78) and 54 doubles (winning 42). He took part in 66 ties.

OLYMPIC GAMES

Most Medals Lawn Tennis was part of the Olympic programme at the first eight celebrations of the Games (including the 1906 Games). The winner of most medals was Max Decugis (b. 24 Sept. 1882) (France) with six (four gold [a record], one silver and one bronze) in the 1900, 1906 and 1920 tournaments. The British male winners of most medals was Reginald F. Doherty (1872–1910) with four (three gold [a record] and one bronze) and Charles Percy Dixon (one gold, one silver and two bronze).

"Little Mo" (Maureen Connolly), who was the first woman tennis player to achieve the grand slam, pictured here during a match on Court 1 during the Wimbledon championships of 1952

Women The most medals won by a woman player is five by Miss Kitty McKane (later Mrs. L. A. Godfree) (G.B.), with two gold, one silver and one bronze in the 1920 and 1924 tournaments. Her two gold medals is a record shared by Miss Charlotte Cooper (later Mrs. Alfred Sterry) (G.B.); Mrs. Edith M. Hannam (G.B.); Mlle. Suzanne Lenglen (France); Mrs. Hazel Hotchkiss Wightman (U.S.A.) and Miss Helen N. Wills (later Mrs. F. S. Moody and Mrs. A. Roark) (U.S.A.).

MARBLES

Origins Marbles was played by the Romans who are believed to have introduced it into Britain in the 1st Century A.D. It was organised as a competitive sport with the setting up of the British Marbles Board of Control at the Greyhound Hotel, Tinsley Green, Crawley, Sussex in 1926.

The game is also played in Australia, Brazil (as *Gude*), Canada, China, France, Germany, India, Iran, New Zealand, Spain, Syria, Turkey and the United States.

Most championships The British Championship (established 1926) has been won most often by the Toucan Terribles with 18 consecutive titles (1956–1973). Len Smith (b. 13 Oct. 1917) has won the individual title 15 times (1957–64, 1966, 1968–73).

The record for clearing the ring (between $5\frac{3}{4}$ and $6\frac{1}{4}$ ft [*1,75–1,90 m*] in diameter) of 49 marbles is 2 min 57 sec by the Toucan Terribles at Worthing, Sussex in 1971.

MODERN PENTATHLON

Points scores in riding, fencing, cross country and hence overall scores have no comparative value between one competition and another. In shooting and swimming (300 m) the scores are of record significance.

The Modern Pentathlon (Riding, Fencing, Shooting, Swimming and Running) was inaugurated into the Olympic Games at Stockholm in 1912. The Modern Pentathlon Association of Great Britain was formed in 1922.

World			
Shooting	1,066	P. Macken (Australia) and R. Phelps (U.K.), Leipzig	21 Sept. 1965
	1,066	I. Mona (Hungary), Jönköping	11 Sept. 1967
Swimming	1,260	Robert Vonk (Netherlands) San Antonio, Texas	13 Oct. 1971

British		
1,066	R. Phelps, Leipzig	21 Sept. 1965
1,064	L/Cpl. B. Lillywhite, San Antonio, Texas	13 Oct. 1971

MOST TITLES

World The record number of world titles won is 5 by András Balczó (Hungary) in 1963, 1965, 1966, 1967 and 1969.

Olympic The greatest number of Olympic gold medals won is three by András Balczó (Hungary) a member of the winning team in 1960 and 1968 and the 1972 individual champion. Lars Hall (Sweden) has uniquely won two

individual Championships (1952 and 1956). Balczó has won a record number of five medals (three gold and two silver). The best British performance is the fourth place gained by Sgt. Jeremy Robert Fox (b. 1941) at Munich in 1972.

British The pentathlete with most British titles is Sergeant Jeremy Robert Fox, R.E.M.E., with eight (1963–65–66–67–68–70–71–72).

MOTORCYCLING

EARLIEST RACES

The first motorcycle race was one from Paris to Dieppe, France, in 1897. The first closed-circuit race was held at the Parc des Princes, Paris cycle track in 1903. The oldest motorcycle races in the world are the Auto-Cycle Union Tourist Trophy (T.T.) series, first held on the 15.81 mile *25,44 km* "Peel" ("St. John's") course in the Isle of Man on 28 May 1907, and still run in the island on the "Mountain" circuit (37.73 miles [*60,72 km*]) and, until 1959, on the Clypse circuit of 10.79 miles *17,36 km*.

FASTEST CIRCUITS

World The highest average lap speed attained on any closed circuit is 182 m.p.h. *293 km/h* by a Kawasaki racer powered by a 748 c.c. three-cylinder two-stroke engine on a banked circuit in Tōkyō, Japan in December 1971.

The fastest road circuit is the Francorchamps circuit near Spa, Belgium. It is 14,100 km *8 miles 1,340 yd* in length and was lapped in 4 min 0.9 sec (average speed 130.929 m.p.h. [*210,709 km/h*]) by Giacomo Agostini (b. Lovere, Italy, 16 June 1942) on a 500 c.c. three-cylinder M.V.-Agusta during the 500 c.c. Belgian Grand Prix on 1 July 1973.

United Kingdom The fastest circuit in the United Kingdom is the 9.714 mile *15,633 km* Portstewart-Coleraine-Portrush circuit in Londonderry, Northern Ireland. The lap record is 5 min 11.0 sec (average speed 112.445 m.p.h. [*180,962 km/h*]) by Tony Rutter (b. Wordsley, Worcs., 24 Sept. 1941) on a 350 c.c. twin-cylinder Yamaha, on lap 3 of the 350 c.c. event of the North-West 200, on 19 May 1973.

The lap record for the outer circuit (2.767 miles [*4,453 km*]) at the Brooklands Motor Course near Weybridge, Surrey (open between 1907 and 1939) was 80.0 sec (average speed 124.51 m.p.h. [*200,37 km/h*]) by Noel Baddow "Bill" Pope (later Major) (1909–1971) of the United Kingdom on a Brough Superior powered by a supercharged 996 c.c. V-twin "8-80" J.A.P. engine developing 110 b.h.p., on 4 July 1939. The race lap record for the outer circuit at Brooklands was 80.6 sec (average speed 123.588 m.p.h. [*198,895 km/h*]) by Eric Crudgington Fernihough (1905–1938) of the United Kingdom on a Brough Superior powered by an unsupercharged 996 c.c. V-twin J.A.P. engine, on 28 July 1935.

FASTEST RACES

World The fastest race in the world was held at Grenzland-ring, near Wegberg, W. Germany in 1939. It was won by Georg Meier (b. Germany, 1910) at an average speed of 134 m.p.h. *215 km/h* on a supercharged 495 c.c. flat-twin B.M.W.

The fastest road race is the 500 c.c. Belgian Grand Prix held on the Francorchamps circuit (8 miles 1,340 yd [*140,100 km*]) near Spa, Belgium. The record time for this 12-lap (105.136 mile [*169,200 km*]) race is 49 min 5.3 sec (average speed 128.506 m.p.h. [*206,810 km/h*]) by Giacomo Agostini, on a 500 c.c. three-cylinder M.V.-Agusta, on 1 July 1973.

Tony Rutter, Great Britain's fastest road racer, holder of the record time for the North-West "200" road race

United Kingdom The fastest race in the United Kingdom is the 350 c.c. event of the North-West 200 held on the Londonderry circuit (see above). The record time for this 7-lap (67.998 mile [*109,432 km*]) race is 36 min 54.4 sec (average speed 110.546 m.p.h. [*177,906 km/h*]) by Tony Rutter on a 350 c.c. twin-cylinder Yamaha on 19 May 1973.

MOST SUCCESSFUL RIDERS

Tourist Trophy The record number of victories in the Isle of Man T.T. races is 12 by Stanley Michael Bailey Hailwood, M.B.E. (b. Oxford, 2 April 1940), now of Durban, South Africa, between 1961 and 1967. The first man to win three consecutive T.T. titles in two events was James A. Redman, M.B.E. (Rhodesia) (b. Hampstead, London, 8 Nov. 1931). He won the 250 c.c. and 350 c.c. events in 1963–64–65. Mike Hailwood is the only man to win three events in one year, in 1961 and 1967.

World championships The most world championship titles (instituted by the *Fédération Internationale Motorcycliste* in 1949) won are:

13 Giacomo Agostini (Italy)
350 c.c. 1968, 69, 70, 71, 72, 73.
500 c.c. 1966, 67, 68, 69, 70, 71, 72.

Giacomo Agostini is the only man to win two world championships in five consecutive years (350 and 500 c.c titles in 1968–69–70–71–72).

Mike Hailwood is the youngest person to win a world championship. He was 21 when he won the 250 c.c. title in 1961. The oldest was Eric S. Oliver (U.K.) who won the sidecar title in 1953 aged 42.

Giacomo Agostini won 108 races in the world championship series between 1965 and 30 July 1973, including a record 19 in 1970, also achieved by Mike Hailwood in 1966.

Trials Samuel Hamilton Miller (b. Belfast, Northern Ireland, 11 Nov. 1935), won eleven A.-C.U. Solo Trials Drivers' Stars in 1959–69.

Scrambles Jeffrey Vincent Smith, M.B.E. (b. Colne, Lancashire, 14 Oct. 1934) won nine A.-C.U. 500 c.c. Scrambles Stars in 1955–56, 1960–61–62–63–64–65 and 1967.

Joel Robert (b. Chatelet, Belgium, Nov. 1943) has won six 250 c.c. moto-cross world championships (1964, 1968–69–70–71–72). Between 25 April 1964 and 18 June 1972 he won a record fifty 250 c.c. Grand Prix. He became the youngest moto-cross world champion on 12 July 1964 when he won the 250 c.c. championship aged 20 years 8 months.

MOST SUCCESSFUL MACHINES
Italian M.V.-Agusta machines won 36 world championships between 1952 and 1972 and 256 world championship races between 1952 and 1972. Japanese Honda machines won 29 world championship races and five world championships in 1966.

SPEED RECORDS
The official world speed record (average speed for two runs over a 1 km [*1,093.6 yd*] course) is 224.569 m.p.h. *361,408 km/h* (average time 9.961 sec) by William A. "Bill" Johnson, aged 38, of Garden Grove, Los Angeles, California, U.S.A., riding a Triumph Bonneville T120 streamliner, with a 667.25 c.c. parallel twin-cylinder engine running on methanol and nitromethane and developing 75 to 80 b.h.p., at Bonneville Salt Flats, Tooele County, Utah, U.S.A., on 5 Sept. 1962. His machine was 17 ft *5 m* long and weighed 400 lb. *181 kg*. His first run was made in 9.847 sec (227.169 m.p.h. [*365,593 km/h*]).

Calvin G. Rayborn (b. San Diego, California, U.S.A., 20 Feb. 1940) recorded higher speeds over the measured mile *1,6 km*, without F.I.M. observers, at Bonneville on 16 Oct. 1970 riding his 10 ft 3 in *3,12 m* long, 1,480 c.c. V-twin Harley-Davidson streamliner running on methanol and nitromethane. On the first run Rayborn covered the mile *1,6 km* in 13.494 sec (266.785 m.p.h. [*429,348 km/h*]). On the second run his time was 13.626 sec (264.201 m.p.h. [*420,190 km/h*]). The average time for the two runs was 13.560 sec (average speed 265.487 m.p.h. [*427,259 km/h*]).

Jon S. McKibben, 33, of Costa Mesa, California, U.S.A. covered a measured mile *1,6 km* one-way at Bonneville in 12.5625 sec (286.567 m.p.h. [*461,184 km/h*]) in November 1971 riding his 21 ft 6 in *6,5 m* long Reaction Dynamics *Honda Hawk* streamliner powered by two turbocharged 736 c.c. in-line four-cylinder Honda engines developing 140 b.h.p. each running on methanol.

David Lecoq, holder of the world record for two runs over a quarter mile, standing start

Giacomo Agostini (Italy), supreme motor cycling champion, with a total of twelve world championship titles

The world record for two runs over 1 km *1,093.6 yd* from a standing start is 122.77 m.p.h. *197,57 km/h* (18.22 sec) by David John Hobbs (b. Woodford, Essex, 3 June 1947) on his supercharged Triumph *Olympus II* powered by two twin-cylinder 500 c.c. engines each developing 100 b.h.p. using methanol and nitromethane, at Elvington Airfield, Yorkshire on 30 Sept. 1972.

The world record for two runs over 440 yds *402 m* from a standing start is 92.879 m.p.h. *149,474 km/h* (9.69 sec) by David Pierre Lecoq (b. Tunbridge Wells, Kent, 24 April 1940) on the supercharged 1,287 c.c. *Drag-Waye* powered by a flat-four Volkswagen engine developing 150 b.h.p. using methanol, at Elvington Airfield, Yorkshire on 27 Sept. 1970. The faster run was made in 9.60 sec. He equalled this record on the same machine at R.A.F. Fairford, Gloucestershire on 23 Sept. 1972.

The fastest time for a single run over 440 yds *402 m* from a standing start is 8.528 sec (terminal velocity 165.13 m.p.h. [*265,75 km/h*]) by Tom C. Christenson of Kenosha, Wisconsin, U.S.A., riding his 1,490 c.c. *Hogslayer*, powered by two Norton Commando engines developing 150 b.h.p. each using nitromethane, during the National Hot Rod Association's 1st All Pro Supernationals at Ontario Motor Speedway, Ontario, California, U.S.A., on 19 Nov. 1972.

The highest terminal velocity recorded at the end of a 440 yd *402 m* run from a standing start is 180.13 m.p.h. *289,89 km/h* (elapsed time 9.35 sec) by Christenson at U.S. 30 Drag Strip, Gary, Indiana, U.S.A., in Aug. 1972.

MISCELLANEOUS

Longest race The longest race is the 24 hour Bol d'Or. The greatest distance ever covered is 1,835.95 miles *2 954,67 km* (average speed 76.498 m.p.h. *[123,111 km/h]*) by Thomas Dickie (b. Aberdare, Glamorganshire, 22 December 1941) and Paul Anthony Smart (b. Eynsford Kent, 23 April 1943) on a 741 c.c. three-cylinder Triumph Trident at Montlhéry, Paris, France (3 miles 1,610 yd *[6,300 km]* lap) on 12–13 Sept. 1970.

Longest circuit The 37.73 mile *60,72 km* "Mountain" circuit, over which the two main T.T. races have been run since 1911, has 264 curves and corners and is the longest used for any motorcycle race.

MOTOR RACING

EARLIEST RACES

The first automobile trial was one of 20 miles *32 km* from Paris to Versailles and back on 20 April 1887, won by Georges Bouton (1847–1938) of France in his steam quadricycle in 74 min, at an average speed of 16.22 m.p.h. *26,10 km/h*. The first "real" race was from Paris to Bordeaux and back (732 miles *[1 178 km]*) on 11–13 June 1895. The winner was Emile Levassor (d. 1897) (France) driving a Panhard-Levassor two-seater, with a 1.2 litre Daimler engine developing 3½ h.p. His time was 48 hours 47 min (average speed 15.01 m.p.h. *[24,15 km/h]*). The first closed circuit race was held at the Circuit du Sud-Ouest, Pau, France in 1900.

The oldest motor race in the world, still being regularly run, is the R.A.C. Tourist Trophy (36th race held in 1972), first staged on 14 Sept. 1905 in the Isle of Man. The oldest continental races are the Targa Florio (57th in 1973) in Sicily, first held on 9 May 1906, and the French Grand Prix (51st in 1973), first held on 26–27 June 1906.

FASTEST CIRCUITS

World The highest average lap speed attained on any closed circuit is 212.766 m.p.h. *342,413 km/h* by Bobby Unser (b. Colorado Springs, Colorado, U.S.A., 1934) who lapped the 2 mile *3,2 km*, 22-degree banked oval at Texas World Speedway, College Station, Texas, U.S.A. in 33.84 sec, driving a 2 611 c.c. 900 b.h.p. turbocharged Olsonite Eagle Model VI-Offenhauser, on 5 April 1973.

The highest average race lap speed for a closed circuit is over 195 m.p.h. *313 km/h* by Richard Brickhouse (U.S.A.) driving a 1969 Dodge Daytona Charger, powered by a 6 980 c.c. 600 b.h.p. V8 engine, during a 500 mile *804 km* race on the 2.66 mile *4,28 km*, 33-degree banked tri-oval at Alabama International Motor Speedway, Talladega, Alabama, U.S.A. on 14 Sept. 1969.

The fastest road circuit is the Francorchamps circuit near Spa, Belgium. It is 14,10 km *8 miles 1,340 yds* in length and was lapped in 3 min 13.4 sec (average speed 163.086 m.p.h. *[262,461 km/h]*) on lap 7 of the Francorchamps 1000 km sports car race on 6 May 1973, by Henri Pescarolo (b. Paris, France, 25 Sept. 1942) driving a 2 993 c.c. V12 Matra-Simca MS670 Group 5 sports car. The practice lap record is 3 min 12.7 sec (average speed 163.678 m.p.h. *[263,414 km/h]*) by Jacques-Bernard "Jacky" Ickx (b. Brussels, Belgium, 1 Jan. 1945) driving a 2 998.5 c.c. flat-12 Ferrari 312P Group 5 sports car, on 4 May 1973.

United Kingdom The fastest circuit in the United Kingdom is the ex-aerodrome course of 2.927 miles *4,710 km* at Silverstone, Northamptonshire (opened 1948). The race lap record is 1 min 17.5 sec (average speed 135.964 m.p.h. *[218,812 km/h]*) by Bengt Ronald "Ronnie" Peterson (b. Orebro, Sweden, 14 Feb. 1944) driving a Formula One 2 993 c.c. Lotus 72 John Player Special-Cosworth V8 during the 25th *GKN/Daily Express* International Trophy race on 8 April 1973. The practice lap record is 1 min 15.9 sec (138.830 m.p.h. *[223,425 km/h]*) by Albert François Cevert (b. Paris 25 Feb. 1944) and Jackie Stewart, both driving a Tyrrell-Cosworth V8, and by Peterson in May 1973.

The lap record for the outer circuit (2.767 miles *[4,453 km]*) at the Brooklands Motor Course near Weybridge, Surrey (open between 1907 and 1939) was 1 min 9.44 sec (average speed 143.44 m.p.h. *[230,84 km/h]*) by John Rhodes Cobb (1899–1952) in his 3 ton *3,3 tonnes* 23 856 c.c. Napier-Railton, with a Napier *Lion* 12-cylinder aero-engine developing 450 b.h.p., on 7 Oct. 1935. His average speed over a km *0.6 mile* was 151.97 m.p.h. *244,57 km/h* (14.72 sec). The race lap record for the outer circuit at Brooklands was 1 min 9.6 sec (average speed 143.11 m.p.h. *[230,31 km/h]*) by Oliver Henry Julius Bertram (b. Kensington, London, 26 Feb. 1910) driving a 7 963 c.c. Barnato-Hassan Special (Bentley engine), during the 7-lap "Dunlop Jubilee Cup" handicap race on 24 Sept. 1938.

The Motor Industry Research Association (MIRA) High Speed Circuit (2.82 mile *[4,53 km]* lap with 33-degree banking on the bends) at Lindley, Warwickshire, was lapped in 1 min 2.8 sec (average speed 161.655 m.p.h. *[260,158 km/h]*) by David Wishart Hobbs (b. Leamington, Warwickshire, 1939 (driving a 4 994 c.c. V12 Jaguar XJ 13 Group 6 prototype sports car in April 1967.

FASTEST RACES

World The fastest race in the world was the 50 mile *80 km* event at the NASCAR Grand National meeting on the 2.50 mile *4,02 km*, 31-degree banked tri-oval at Daytona International Speedway, Daytona Beach, Florida, U.S.A. on 8 Feb. 1964. It was won by Richard Petty (b. 2 July 1937) of Randleman, North Carolina in 17 min 27 sec (average speed 171.920 m.p.h. *[276,678 km/h]*), driving a 405 b.h.p. 1964 Plymouth V8.

The fastest road race is the Francorchamps 1000 km sports car race held on the Francorchamps circuit (14,100 km *[8 miles 1,340 yd]*) near Spa, Belgium. The record time for this 71-lap (622.055 miles *[1 001,100 km]*) race is 4 hours 1 min 9.7 sec (average speed 154.765 m.p.h. *[249,070 km/h]*) by Pedro Rodriguez (1940–1971) of Mexico and Keith Jack "Jackie" Oliver (b. Chadwell Heath, Essex, 14 Aug. 1942) driving a 4 998 c.c. flat-12 Porsche 917K Group 5 sports car, on 9 May 1971.

United Kingdom The fastest currently held race in the United Kingdom is the *Martini* International Super Sports race. The record was set in the second heat of this race by Wilhelm Kauhsen (W.G.) driving a turbocharged 4 998 c.c. flat-12 Porsche 917/10T Group 7 sports car, at Silverstone, on 20 May 1973. He covered 35 laps (102.445 miles *[164,869 km]*) in 46 min 6.3 sec (average speed 133.320 m.p.h. *[214,557 km/h]*).

The fastest race ever held in the United Kingdom was the Broadcast Trophy Handicap held on the Brooklands outer circuit on 29 March 1937. The 29 mile *46 km* race was won by John Cobb driving his 23 970 c.c. 12-cylinder Napier-Railton at an average speed of 136.03 m.p.h. *218,91 km/h*.

TOUGHEST CIRCUITS

The Targa Florio (first run 9 May 1906) is widely acknowledged to be the most arduous race. Held on

Jackie Stewart, holder of the record time for the most difficult of *Grand Prix* circuits, Monaco, relaxing before a race

the Piccolo Madonie Circuit in Sicily, it now covers eleven laps (492.126 miles [*792,000 km*]) and involves the negotiation of 9,350 corners, over severe mountain gradients, and narrow rough roads. The record time is 6 hours 27 min 48.0 sec (average speed 76.141 m.p.h. [*122,537 km/h*]) by Arturo Merzario (b. Civenna, Italy, 11 March 1943) and Sandro Munari (Italy) driving a 2 995 c.c. flat-12 Ferrari 312P Group 5 sports car in the 56th race on 21 May 1972. The lap record is 33 min 36.0 sec (average speed 79.890 m.p.h. [*128,570 km/h*]) by Leo Juhani Kinnunen (b. Tampere, Finland, 5 Aug. 1943) on lap 11 of the 54th race on 3 May 1970 driving a 2 997 c.c. flat-8 Porsche 908/3 Spyder Group 6 prototype sports car.

The most difficult Grand Prix circuit is generally regarded to be that for the Monaco Grand Prix (first run on 14 April 1929), run round the streets and the harbour of Monte Carlo. It is 3 278 m *2 mile 65 yd* in length and has eleven pronounced corners and several sharp changes of gradient. The race is run over 78 laps (158.875 miles [*255,67 km*]) and involves on average more than 2,000 gear changes. The record time for the race is 1 hour 57 min 44.3 sec (average speed 80.963 m.p.h. [*130,297 km/h*]) by John Young "Jackie" Stewart, O.B.E. (b. Milton, Dunbartonshire, 11 June 1939) driving a 2 993 c.c. Tyrrell-Cosworth V8, on 3 June 1973. The race lap record is 1 min 28.1 sec (average speed 83.231 m.p.h. [*133,947 km/h*]) by Emerson Fittipaldi (b. São Paulo, Brazil, 12 Dec. 1946) driving a 2 993 c.c. Lotus 72 John Player Special-Cosworth V8 on lap 78 of the above race. The practice lap record is 1 min 27.5 sec (average speed 83.802 m.p.h. [*134,866 km/h*]) by Stewart on 1 June 1973.

LE MANS

The world's most important race for sports cars is the 24-hour *Grand Prix d'Endurance* (first held on 26–27 May 1923) on the Sarthe circuit at Le Mans, France.

The greatest distance ever covered is 3,315.210 miles *5 335,313 km* (average speed 138.134 m.p.h. [*222,305 km/h*]) by Dr. Helmut Marko (b. Graz, Austria, 27 April 1943) and Jonkheer Gijs van Lennep (b. Bloemendaal, Netherlands, 16 March 1942) driving a 4 907 c.c. flat-12 Porsche 917K Group 5 sports car, on 12–13 June 1971. The race lap record (8 miles 650 yd [*13,469 km*]) is 3 min 18.7 sec (average speed 151.632 m.p.h. [*244,028 km/h*]) by Pedro Rodriguez (1940–1971) driving a 4 907 c.c. flat-12 Porsche 917L on 12 June 1971. The practice lap record is 3 min 13.6 sec (average speed 155.627 m.p.h. [*250,457 km/h*]) by Jackie Oliver driving a similar car on 18 April 1971. The pre-war record average speed was 86.85 m.p.h. *139,77 km/h* by a 3.3 litre Bugatti in 1939.

Most wins The race has been won by Ferrari cars nine times, in 1949, 1954, 1958 and 1960–61–62–63–64–65. The most wins by one man is four by Olivier Gendebien (b. 1924) (Belgium), who won in 1958 and 1960–61–62.

British wins The race has been won 12 times by British cars, thus: Bentley in 1924 and 1927–28–29–30, once by Lagonda in 1935, five times by Jaguar in 1951, 1953 and 1955–56–57 and once by Aston Martin in 1959.

INDIANAPOLIS 500

The Indianapolis 500-mile *804 km* race (200 laps) was inaugurated in the U.S.A. on 30 May 1911. The most successful drivers have been Warren Wilbur Shaw (1902–1954), who won in 1937, 1939 and 1940; Louis Meyer, who won in 1928, 1933 and 1936, and Anthony Joseph "A.J." Foyt, Jr. (b. Houston, Texas, U.S.A., 1935), who won in 1961, 1964 and 1967. Mauri Rose won in 1947 and 1948 and was the co-driver of Floyd Davis in 1941. The record time is 3 hours 4 min 5.54 sec (average speed 162.962 m.p.h. [*262,261 km/h*]) by Mark Donohue (b. Summit, New Jersey, U.S.A., 18 March 1937) driving a 2 595 c.c. 900 b.h.p. turbocharged Sunoco McLaren M16B-Offenhauser on 27 May 1972. Donohue received $218,767.90 from a record prize fund of $1,011,845.94 for winning this, the 56th, race. The individual prize record is $271,697.72 by Al Unser (b. Albuquerque, New Mexico, U.S.A., 29 May 1939) on 30 May 1970. The race lap record is 47.99 sec (average speed 187.539 m.p.h. [*301,814 km/h*]) by Mark Donohue on lap 150 of the above race. The practice lap record is 45.21 sec (average speed 199.071 m.p.h. [*320,373 km/h*])

An aerial view of the Le Mans circuit, scene of the 24 hour *Grand Prix d'Endurance*

Mark Donohue (No. 66) on his way to winning the Indianapolis 500 race in 1972

by Johnny Rutherford (b. 1938) of Fort Worth, Texas, U.S.A. driving a 2 595 c.c. 900 b.h.p. turbo-charged Gulf McLaren-Offenhauser on lap 3 of his 4-lap qualification run on 12 May 1973.

DRIVERS

Most successful Based on the World Drivers' Championship, inaugurated in 1950, the most successful driver is Juan-Manuel Fangio y Cia (b. Balcarce, Argentina, 24 June 1911) who won five times in 1951–54–55–56–57. He retired in 1958, after having won 24 Grand Prix races (2 shared). The most successful driver in terms of race wins is Stirling Craufurd Moss, O.B.E. (b. Paddington, London, 17 Sept. 1929), with 167 (11 shared) races won, including 16 Grand Prix victories (1 shared), from 18 Sept. 1948 to 11 Feb. 1962. Moss was awarded the annual Gold Star of the British Racing Drivers' Club in 1950–51–52, 1954–55–56–57–58–59 and 1961, a record total of ten awards.

The most Grand Prix victories is 27 by Jackie Stewart between 12 Sept. 1965 and 5 Aug. 1973. Jim Clark, O.B.E. (1936–1968) of Scotland holds the record for Grand Prix victories in one year with 7 in 1963. He won a record 61 Formula One and Formula Libre races between 1959 and 1968. The most Grand Prix starts is 155 (out of a possible 163) between 18 May 1958 and 5 Aug. 1973 by Norman Graham Hill, O.B.E. (b. Hampstead, London) 15 Feb. 1929). Between 20 Nov. 1960 and 5 Oct. 1969 he took part in 90 consecutive Grand Prix.

Oldest and youngest world champions The youngest world champion was Emerson Fittipaldi who won his first world championship on 10 Sept. 1972 aged 25 years 273 days. The oldest world champion was Juan-Manuel Fangio who won his last world championship on 18 Aug. 1957 aged 46 years 55 days.

Oldest and youngest G.P. winners and drivers The youngest Grand Prix winner was Bruce Leslie McLaren (1937–1970) of New Zealand, who won the United States Grand Prix at Sebring, Florida, U.S.A., on 12 Dec. 1959 aged 22 years 104 days. The oldest Grand Prix winner was Tazio Giorgio Nuvolari (1892–1953) of Italy, who won the Albi Grand Prix at Albi, France on 14 July 1946 aged 53 years 240 days. The oldest Grand Prix driver was Louis Alexandre Chiron, O. St-C., L.d'H., C.d'I (b. Monaco, 3 Aug. 1899), who finished 6th in the Monaco Grand Prix on 22 May 1955 aged 55 years 292 days. The youngest

Grand Prix driver was Christopher Arthur Amon (b. Bulls, New Zealand, 20 July 1943), who took part in the Belgian Grand Prix at Spa on 9 June 1963 aged 19 years 324 days.

HILL CLIMBING

Pike's Peak race The Pike's Peak Auto Hill Climb, Colorado, U.S.A. (instituted 1916) has been won by Bobby Unser 11 times between 1956 and 1969 (9 championship, 1 stock and 1 sports car title). On 30 June 1968 in the 46th race, he set a record time of 11 min 54.9 sec in his 5 506 c.c. Chevrolet championship car for the 12.42 mile *19,98 km* course rising from 9,402 ft to 14,110 ft *2 865–4 300 m* through 157 curves.

Most successful drivers The British National Hill Climb Championship (inaugurated in 1947) has been won six times by Anthony Ernest Marsh (b. Stourbridge, Worcestershire, 20 July 1913), 1955–56–57, 1965–66–67. Raymond Mays (b. Bourne, Lincolnshire, 1 Aug. 1899) won the Shelsley Walsh hill climb, near Worcester, 19 times between 1923 and 1950.

RALLIES

Earliest The earliest long rally was promoted by the Parisian daily *Le Matin* in 1907 from Peking, China to Paris over a route of about 7,500 miles *12 000 km*. Five cars left Peking on 10 June. The winner, Prince Scipione Borghesi, arrived in Paris on 10 Aug. 1907 in his 40 h.p. Itala.

Longest The world's longest ever rally was the £10,000 *Daily Mirror* World Cup Rally run over 16,243 miles *26 140 km* starting from Wembley, London on 19 April 1970 to Mexico City *via* Sofia, Bulgaria and Buenos Aires, Argentina passing through 25 countries. It was won on 27 May 1970 by Hannu Mikkola (b. Joensuu, Finland, 24 May 1942) and Gunnar Palm (b. Kristinehamn, Sweden, 25 Feb. 1937) in a 1 834 c.c. Ford Escort. The longest held annually is the East African Safari (first run 1953), run through Kenya, Tanzania and Uganda, which is up to 3,874 miles *6 234 km* long, as in the 17th Safari held between 8–12 April 1971. The smallest car to win the Monte Carlo Rally (founded 1911) was an 841 c.c. Saab driven by Erik Carlsson (b. Sweden, 1929) and Gunnar Häggbom of Sweden on 25 Jan. 1962, and by Carlsson and Gunnar Palm on 24 Jan. 1963.

DRAGGING

Piston engined The highest terminal velocity recorded by a piston-engined dragster is 243.90 m.p.h. *392,51 km/h* (elapsed time 6.175 sec) by Donald Glenn "Big Daddy" Garlits

Hannu Mikkola and Gunnar Palm celebrating their win after the World Cup Rally in 1970

307

(b. 1932) of Seffner, Florida driving his rear-engined *Swamp Rat 1-R* AA/F dragster, powered by a 7 751 c.c. supercharged Dodge V8 engine, during the National Hot Rod Association's 3rd Annual Gatornationals at Gainesville Dragway, Florida, U.S.A., on 19 March 1972. The lowest elapsed time recorded is 5.91 sec (terminal velocity 231.95 m.p.h. [*373,28 km/h*]) by Don Moody (U.S.A.) driving his rear-engined AA/F dragster, powered by a 7 931 c.c. supercharged Chrysler V8 engine, during the National Hot Rod Association's 1st All Pro Supernationals at Ontario Motor Speedway, Ontario, California, U.S.A., on 19 Nov. 1972.

Rocket or jet-engined The highest terminal velocity and lowest elapsed time recorded by any dragster is 311.41 m.p.h. *501,16 km/h* and 5.10 sec by Victor Wilson (b. 1944) of Sydney, Australia in the 22 ft *6,7 m* long 3-wheeled *Courage of Australia*, powered by a 6,000 lb. *2 700 kg* s.t. hydrogen peroxide rocket engine, at Orange County International Raceway, E. Irvine, California, U.S.A., in November 1971.

Terminal velocity is the speed attained at the end of a 440 yd 402 m run made from a standing start and elapsed time is the time taken for the run.

LAND SPEED RECORDS

The highest speed ever recorded by a wheeled vehicle was achieved by Gary Gabelich (b. San Pedro, California, U.S.A., 29 Aug. 1940) at Bonneville Salt Flats, Utah, U.S.A., on 23 Oct. 1970. He drove the Reaction Dynamics *The Blue Flame*, weighing 4,950 lb. *2 245 kg* and measuring 37 ft *11 m* long, powered by a liquid natural gas–hydrogen peroxide rocket engine developing a maximum static thrust of 22,000 lb. *9 979 kg*. On his first run, at 11.23 a.m. (local time), he covered the measured km *0.6 miles* in 3.543 sec (average speed 631.367 m.p.h. [*1 016,086 km/h*]) and the mile *1,6 km* in 5.829 sec (617.602 m.p.h. [*993,934 km/h*]). On the second run, at 12.11 a.m., his times were 3.554 sec for the km *0.6 miles* (629.413 m.p.h. [*1 012,942 km/h*]) and 5.739 sec for the mile *1,6 km* (627.287 m.p.h. [*1 009,520 km/h*]). The average times for the two runs were 3.5485 sec for the km *0.6 miles* (630.388 m.p.h. [*1 014,511 km/h*]) and 5.784 sec for the mile *1,6 km* (622.407 m.p.h. [*1 001,666 km/h*]). During the attempt only 13,000 lb. *5 900 kg* s.t. was used and a peak speed of 650 m.p.h. *1 046 km/h* was momentarily attained.

The most successful land speed record breaker was Major Sir Malcolm Campbell (1885–1948) of the United Kingdom. He broke the official record nine times between 25 Sept. 1924, with 146.157 m.p.h. *235,216 km/h* in a Sunbeam, and 3 Sept. 1935, when he achieved 301.129 m.p.h. *480,620 km/h* in the Rolls-Royce engined *Bluebird*.

The world speed record for compression ignition engined cars is 190.344 m.p.h. *306,328 km/h* (average of two runs over measured mile [*1,6 km*]) by Robert Havemann of Eureka, California, U.S.A. driving his *Corsair* streamliner, powered by a turbocharged 6 981 c.c. 6-cylinder GMC 6-71 diesel engine developing

Garry Gabelich, holder of the world land speed record for a wheeled vehicle after his record-breaking run

746 b.h.p., at Bonneville Salt Flats, Utah, U.S.A., in August 1971. The faster run was made at 210 m.p.h. *337 km/h*.

MISCELLANEOUS

Fastest pit stop Jackie Oliver took 9 sec to load 100 litres *22.0 Imperial gal* of fuel during the Francorchamps 1 000 km sports car race on 9 May 1971. This time was equalled by A. J. Foyt, Jr., during his first fuel stop (lap 14) in the Indianapolis 500 on 29 May 1971.

Duration record The greatest distance ever covered in one year is 400 000 km *248,548.5 miles* by François Lecot (1879–1949) an innkeeper from Rochetaillée, near Lyon, France, in an 11 c.v. Citroën (1 900 c.c., 66 b.h.p.), mainly between Paris and Monte Carlo, from 22 July 1935 to 26 July 1936. He drove on 363 of the 370 days allowed.

The world's duration record is 185,353 miles 1,741 yd *298 298 km* in 133 days 17 hours 37 min 38.64 sec (average speed 58.07 m.p.h. [*93,45 km/h*]) by Marchand, Presalé and six others in a Citroën on the Montlhéry track near Paris, France, during March-July 1933.

Go-kart circum-navigation The only recorded instance of a go-kart being driven round the world was a circumnavigation by Stan Mott, of New York, U.S.A., who drove a Lambretta engined 175 c.c. Italkart, with a ground clearance of 2 in *5 cm*, 23,300 land miles *37 500 km* through 28 countries from 15 Feb. 1961 to 5 June 1964, starting and finishing in New York, U.S.A.

MOUNTAINEERING

Origins Although bronze-age artifacts have been found on the summit of the Riffelhorn, Switzerland (9,605 ft [*2 927 m*]) mountaineering, as a sport, has a continuous history dating back only to 1854. Isolated instances of climbing for its own sake exist back to the 14th century. The Atacamenans built sacrificial platforms near the summit of Llullaillaco (22,058 ft [*6 723 m*]) in late pre-Columbian times c. 1490. The earliest recorded rock climb in the British Isles was of Stacna Biorrach, St. Kilda by Sir Robert Moray in 1698.

Mount Everest Mount Everest (29,028 ft [*8 847 m*]) was first climbed at 11.30 a.m. on 29 May 1953, when the summit was reached by Edmund Percival Hillary (born 20 July 1919), created K.B.E., of New Zealand, and the Sherpa, Tenzing Norkhay (born, as Namgyal Wangdi, in Nepal in 1914, formerly called Tenzing Khumjung Bhutia), who was awarded the G.M. The successful expedition was led by Col. (later Hon. Brigadier) Henry Cecil John Hunt, C.B.E., D.S.O. (born 22 June 1910), who was created a Knight Bachelor in 1953 and a life Baron on 11 June 1966.

SUBSEQUENT ASCENTS OF MOUNT EVEREST BY 29 CLIMBERS

Climbers	Date	Climbers	Date
Ernst Schmidt, Jürg Marmet (Swiss)	23 May 1956	Sonam Gyaltso, Sonam Wangyal	22 May 1965
Hans Rudolf von Gunten, Adolf Reist (Swiss)	24 May 1956	C. P. Vohra (India), Sherpa Ang Kami	24 May 1965
*Wang Fu-chou, Chu Yin-hua (China), Konbu	25 May 1960	Capt. H. P. S. Ahluwalia, H. C. S. Rawat (India), Phu Dorji	29 May 1965
James Warren Whittaker, Sherpa Nawang Gombu	1 May 1963	Nomi Uemura, Tero Matsuura (Japan)	11 May 1970
Barry C. Bishop (U.S.), Luther G. Jerstad (U.S.)	22 May 1963	Katsutoshi Hirabayoshi (Japan), Sherpa Chotari	12 May 1970
Dr. William F. Unsoeld (U.S.), Dr. Thomas F. Hornbein (U.S.)	22 May 1963	Sgt. Mirko Minuzzo, Sgt. Rinaldo Carrel (Italy) with	5 May 1973
Capt. A. S. Cheema (India), Sherpa Nawang Gombu	20 May 1965	Lapka Tenzing and Sambu Tamang	
		Capt. Fabrizio Innamorati, W. O. Virginio Epis and Sgt. Maj.	7 May 1973
		Claudio Benedetti (Italy) with Sonam Gallien (Nepal)	

Not internationally accepted as authentic.

Greatest wall The highest final stage in any wall climb is that on the south face of Annapurna I (26,504 ft [8 078 m]). It was climbed by the British expedition led by Christian Bonnington when on 27 May 1970 Donald Whillans, 36 and Dougal Haston, 27 scaled to the summit. The longest wall climb is on the Rupal-Flanke from the base camp at 3 560 m 11,680 ft to the South Point 8 042 m 26,384 ft of Nanga Parbat—a vertical ascent of 4 482 m 14,704 ft. This was scaled by the Austro-Germano-Italian Expedition led by Dr. Herrligkoffer in April 1970.

Greatest Alpine Wall Europe's greatest wall is the 6,600 ft 2 000 m North face of the Eigerwand (Ogre wall) first climbed on 20 Aug. 1932 by Hans Lauper, Alfred Zurcher, Alexander Graven and Josef Knubel. The first direct ascent was by Heinrich Harrar and Fritz Kasparek of Austria and Andreas Heckmair and Ludvig Vörg of Germany on 21–24 July 1938. The greatest alpine solo climb was that of Walter Bonatti (Italy) of the South West Pillar of the Dru, Montenvers now called the Bonatti Pillar in 126 hr 7 min on 17–22 Aug. 1955.

Rock climbing The world's most demanding XS (extremely severe) rock climb is regarded as the sheer almost totally holdless 3,000 ft 914 m Muir Wall of El Capitan 7,564 ft [2 305 m]) Yosemite, California, U.S.A., first climbed in November 1958. In 1968 Royal Robbins (U.S.A.) climbed this solo with *pitons*.

MOUNTAIN RACING

Descent Rates It is recorded that John Ekema descended Mount Cameroun from the summit 13,350 ft 4 069 m to Buea at 3,000 ft 914 m in 99 min on 10 March 1973 achieving a rate of 104 ft 31,8 m vertical per sec.

In the much shorter Skiddaw Fell Race (3,053 to 250 ft [930 to 107 m]) a descent rate of 128 ft 39 m vertical per sec was achieved by Jeff Norman (Altrincham A.C.) in the 1972 race.

Ben Nevis The record time for the race from Fort William to the summit of Ben Nevis and return is 1 hr 33 min

Sir Edmund Hillary, the first man to reach the summit of Mount Everest, twenty years ago, in May 1953

5 sec by Dave Cannon on 4 Sept. 1971. The feminine record is 1 hr 51 min for the ascent only, by Elizabeth Wilson-Smith on 14 Sept. 1909, and 3 hrs 2 min for the ascent and return by Kathleen Connachie, aged 16, on 3 Sept. 1965. The full course by the bridle path is about 14 miles 22 km but distance can be saved by crossing the open hillside. The mountain was first climbed in about 1720 and the earliest race was in 1895.

The Lakeland 24-hour record is 63 peaks achieved by Joss Naylor (b. 10 Feb. 1936) of Wasdale on 24–25 June 1972. He covered 92 miles 148 km with 35,000 ft 10 668 m of ascents and descents in 23 hrs 33 min. Naylor has won every Ennerdale mountain race over 23 miles 37 km since it was instituted in 1968 setting a record time of 3 hr 30 min 40 sec in 1972. The Yorkshire three peak record is 2 hr 36 min 26 sec by Jeff Norman on 25 April 1971.

The "Three Thousander" record over the 14 Welsh peaks of over 3,000 ft 914 m is 4 hr 46 min with pacemakers by Naylor on 17 June 1973 despite misty conditions.

Three peaks record The Three Peaks run from sea level at Fort William, Inverness-shire, to sea level at Caernarvon, *via* the summits of Ben Nevis, Scafell Pike and Snowdon, was uniquely achieved by the late Eric Beard, 37 of Leeds Athletic Club, in 10 days in June 1969.

Ten Peaks Record The Ten Peaks race is from Barnthwaite Farm, Wasdale Head, Cumberland to the top of Skiddaw *via* England's nine other highest mountains and tops: Great Gable, Sca Fell, Scafell Pike, Broad Crag,

Joss Naylor on the summit of Tryfan during his record-breaking run over the Welsh 14 peaks in June 1973

PROGRESSIVE MOUNTAINEERING ALTITUDE RECORDS

ft	m	Mountain	Climbers	Date
9,605	2 927	Riffelhorn, Zermatt, Switzerland	—	Bronze Age
14,300	4 360	Kaoshan Pass, Hindu Kush	Alexander the Great's army	327 B.C.
12,388	3 775	Fuji, Japan	—	prior A.D. 806
17,887	5 452	Popocatépetl, Mexico	Francisco Montano	1521
18,400	5 608	Mana Pass, Zaskar Range	A. de Andrade, M. Morques	1818
18,096	5 515	On Chimborazo, Ecuador	Dr. A. Humboldt, Goujand (France) and C. Montufar	July 1624
19,411	5 916	On Leo Pargyal Range, Himalaya	Gerrard and Lloyd	23 June 1802
22,260	6 784	On E. Ibi Gamin, Garhwal Himalaya	A. & R. Schlagintweit	Aug. 1855
22,606	6 890	Pioneer Peak on Baltoro Kangri	W. M. Conway, M. Zurbriggen	23 Aug. 1892
22,834	6 959	Aconcagua, Andes	M. Zurbriggen	14 Jan. 1897
23,394	7 130	On Pyramid Peak, Karakoram	W. H. Workman, J. Petigax Snr. & Jnr., C. Savoie	12 Aug. 1903
23,787	7 250	On Gurla Mandhata, Tibet	T. G. Longstaff, A. & H. Brocherel	23 July 1905
c.23,900	c.7 285	On Kabru, Sikkim-Nepal	C. W. Rubenson and M. Aas	20 Oct. 1907
24,607	7 500	On Chogolisa, Karakoram	Duke of the Abruzzi, J. Petigax, H. & E. Brocherel	18 July 1909
c.24,900	c.7 590	Camp V, Everest Tibet-Nepal	G. L Mallory, E. F. Norton, T. H. Somervell, H. T. Morshead	20 May 1922
26,986	8 225	On Everest (North Face), Tibet	G. L. Mallory, E. F. Norton, T. H. Somervell	21 May 1922
c.27,300	c.8 320	On Everest (North Face), Tibet	G. I. Finch, J. G. Bruce	27 May 1922
28,125*	8 570*	On Everest (North Face), Tibet	E. F. Norton	4 June 1924
28,125*	8 570*	On Everest (North Face), Tibet	P. Wyn Harris, L. R. Wager	30 May 1933
28,125*	8 570*	On Everest (North Face), Tibet	F. S. Smythe	1 June 1933
28,215*	8 599*	South Shoulder on Everest, Nepal	R. Lambert, Tenzing Norkhay	28 May 1952
28,721	8 754	South Shoulder on Everest, Nepal	T. D. Bourdillon, R. C. Evans	26 May 1953
29,028	8 847	Everest, Nepal-Tibet	E. P. Hillary, Sherpa Tenzing Norkhay	29 May 1953

* *Highest altitude attained without oxygen.*

PROGRESSIVE LIST OF HIGHEST SUMMITS CLIMBED

The progressive list of highest summits climbed after Aconcagua in 1897 is as follows:

ft	m		Climbers	Date
23,360	7 120	Trusil, Garhwal Himalaya	T. G. Longstaff, A. & H. Brocherel, Karbir	12 June 1907
23,385†	7 127	Pauhunri, Sikkim Himalaya	A. M. Kellas, Sonam and another porter	16 June 1911
23,383	7 127	Pik Lenin, Trans-Alai Pamir	E. Allwein, K. Wien, E. Schneider	25 Sept. 1928
23,442	7 145	Nepal Peak, Sikkim-Nepal	E. Schneider	24 May 1930
24,344	7 417	Jongsong Peak, Nepal-Sikkim-Tibet	E. Schneider, H. Hoerlin	3 June 1930
25,447	7 756	Kamet, Garhwal Himalaya	F. S. Smythe, R. L. Holdsworth, E. E. Shipton, Lewa	21 June 1931
25,645	7 816	Nanda Devi, Garhwal Himalaya	N. E. Odell, H. W. Tilman	29 Aug. 1936
26,492	8 047	Annapurna I, Nepal	M. Herzog, L. Lachenal	3 June 1950
29,028	8 847	Mount Everest, Nepal-Tibet	E. P. Hillary, Tenzing Norkhay	29 May 1953

(For subsequent ascents of Mount Everest, see above)

† *Survey of India height now listed as 23,180 ft 7 065 m.*

Ill Crags, Great End, Bow Fell, Helvellyn and Little Man. The record time is 15 hr 34 min by John Wadlow (b. 3 Jan. 1952) and Tony Zirkel (b. 8 Jan. 1955) in a race organised by the Cumbrian Community Trust on 16 Sept. 1972.

Pennine Way The record for traversing the 270 mile *434 km* long Pennine Way is 4 days 5 hr 10 min by Alan Heaton, 43 and Michael Meath, 25 of Clayton-le-Moor Harriers on 30 June to 4 July 1972.

African Two Peaks Record The climbing of Africa's two highest mountains, Kilimanjaro (19,340 ft [*5 890 m*]) and Mount Kenya (17,058 ft [*5 199 m*]) from summit to summit in 24 hours, was achieved on 9–10 Feb. 1964 by Rusty Baillie (Rhodesia) and Barry Cliff (G.B.). The descent of 15,300 ft *4 660 m* the 250 mile *400 km* drive and the 8,500 ft *2 600 m* ascent of Mount Kenya were achieved in 21 hr 50 min.

Fell running Bill Teasdale won the Guide's Race at the Grasmere Sports, Westmorland, for the eleventh time in 1966. It involves running to a turning point on Butter Crag (966 ft [*294 m*] above sea level) and back, a distance of about 1½ miles *2,4 km*. His time of 13 min 5.0 sec in 1965 constitutes the record time.

Greatest fall The greatest recorded fall survived by a mountaineer was when Christopher Timms (Christchurch University) slid 7,500 ft *2 300 m* down an ice face into a crevasse on Mt. Elie de Beaumont (10,200 ft [*3 100 m*]), New Zealand on 7 Dec. 1966. His companion was killed but he survived with concussion, bruises and a hand injury.

NETBALL

Origins The game was invented in the U.S.A. in 1891 and introduced into England in 1895 by Dr. Toles. The All England Women's Netball Association was formed in 1926. The oldest club in continuous existence, apart from business clubs such as the B.B.C. Netball club, is Tiffin Old Girls' Netball Club, Kingston-upon-Thames, Surrey re-instituted in October 1930.

World title World championships were inaugurated in August 1963 at Eastbourne, Sussex and were won by Australia. The 1971 world championships at Kingston, Jamaica were also won by Australia. The record number of goals in the World Tournament is 402 by Mrs. Judith Heath (b. 1942) in 1971.

Highest scores England has never been beaten in a home international. England's record score is 94 goals to 12 *v.* Wales in 1970 and 94 goals to 13 *v.* Northern Ireland in Jamaica in January 1971. The highest international score recorded was when New Zealand beat Northern Ireland 112–4 at Eastbourne, Sussex on 2 Aug. 1963.

Most internationals The record number of internationals is 43 by Anne Miles (b. 9 April 1942) of England to 1973.

Marathon An outdoor marathon netball match lasting 48 hr by 6 teams of 7 girls was played by Bungay 'Shell' Youth Club, Suffolk on 2–4 June 1972. An indoor marathon of 57 hr 2 min was sustained by players from Appleton Hall County Grammar School, Appleton, Lancs. ending on 15 July 1973.

OLYMPIC GAMES

Note: These records now include the un-numbered Games held at Athens in 1906, which some authorities ignore. Although inserted between the regular IIIrd Games in 1904 and the IVth Games in 1908, the 1906 Games were both official and were of a higher standard than all three of those that preceded them.

Origins The earliest celebration of the ancient Olympic Games of which there is a certain record is that of July 776 B.C., when Koroibos, a cook from Elis, won a foot race, though their origin dates from *c.* 1370 B.C. The ancient Games were terminated by an order issued in Milan in A.D. 393 by Theodosius I, "the Great" (*c.* 346–395), Emperor of Rome. At the instigation of Pierre de Fredi, Baron de Coubertin (1863–1937), the Olympic Games of the modern era were inaugurated in Athens on 6 April 1896.

Largest crowd The largest crowd at any Olympic site was 150,000 at the 1952 ski-jumping at the Holmenkollen, outside Oslo, Norway. Estimates of the number of spectators of the marathon race through Tōkyō, Japan on 21 Oct. 1964 have ranged from 500,000 to 1,500,000.

MOST MEDALS

Individual gold In the ancient Olympic Games victors were given a chaplet of olive leaves. Milo (Milon of Krotōn) won 6 titles at *palaisma* (wrestling) 540–516 B.C. The most individual gold medals won by a male competitor in the modern Games is 10 by Ray C. Ewry (U.S.A.) (b. 14 Oct. 1873 d. 29 Sept. 1937) (see Track and Field Athletics). The female record is seven by Vera Caslavska-Odlozil (b. 3 May 1942) (see Gymnastics). The most won by a British competitor is four by Paul Radmilovic (1886–1968) in Water Polo in 1908, 1912 and 1920 and in the 800 m team swimming event in 1908. The sculler and oarsman Jack Beresford, C.B.E. won the three gold and two silver medals in the five Olympics from 1920 to 1936.

National The total figures for most medals and most gold medals for all Olympic events (including those now discontinued) for the summer (1896–1972) and Winter Games (1924–1972) and for the Art Competitions (1912–1948) are:

	Gold	Silver	Bronze	Total
1. U.S.A.	621	473½	408½	1,503
2. U.S.S.R. (formerly Russia)	249	208	201	658
3. G.B. (including Ireland to 1920)	161½	197½	173	532

Oldest and youngest competitors The oldest recorded competitor was Oscar G. Swahn (Sweden), who won a silver medal for shooting (running deer) in 1920, when aged 73. The youngest ever winner was a French boy (whose name is not recorded) who coxed the Netherlands coxed pair in 1900. He was not more than 10 and may have been as young as 7. He substituted for Dr. Hermanus Brockmann, who coxed in the heats but proved too heavy. The youngest-ever female gold medal winner is Miss Marjorie Gestring (U.S.A.) (b. 18 Nov. 1922, now Mrs. Bowman), aged 13 yr 9 months, in the 1936 women's springboard event.

Longest span The longest span of an Olympic competitor is 40 years by Dr. Ivan Osiier (Denmark), who competed as a fencer in 1908, 1912 (silver medal) 1920, 1924, 1928, 1932 and 1948, totalling seven celebrations. He refused to compete in the 1936 Games on the grounds that they were Nazi-dominated. The longest feminine span is 24 years (1932–1956) by the Austrian fencer Ellen Müller-Preiss. The longest span of any British competitor is 20 years by George Mackenzie who wrestled in the Games of 1908, 1912, 1920, 1924 and 1928, and by Mrs. Dorothy J. B. Tyler (*née* Odam), who high-jumped in 1936–48–52 and 56. The only Olympian to win 4 consecutive individual titles has been Alfred A. Oerter (b. 19 Sept. 1936, Astoria, N.Y.) of the U.S.A., who won the discus title in 1956–60–64–68.

Most Countries and participants The greatest number of competitors in any summer Olympic Games up to 1972 has been 7,147 (including 1,070 women) from a record 122 countries at Munich in 1972. The fewest was 285 competitors in 1896. In 1904 only 11 countries participated.

Pierre de Coubertin, founder of the modern Olympic Games, begun in 1896

Modern celebrations have been voted for by the International Olympic Committee as follows. Dates indicate the span of Olympic competitions (excluding elimination contests). The first date is not necessarily that of the opening ceremony.

I	1896	Athens	6–15 April
II	1900	Paris	20 May–28 Oct.
III	1904	St. Louis	1 July–23 Nov.
*	1906	Athens	22 April–2 May
IV	1908	London	27 April–31 Oct.
V	1912	Stockholm	5 May–22 July
VI	1916	Berlin	not celebrated owing to war
VII	1920	Antwerp	20 April–12 Sept.
VIII	1924	Paris	4 May–27 July
IX	1928	Amsterdam	17 May–12 Aug.
X	1932	Los Angeles	30 July–14 Aug.
XI	1936	Berlin	1–16 Aug.
XII	1940	Tokyo, then Helsinki	not celebrated owing to war
XIII	1944	London	not celebrated owing to war
XIV	1948	London	29 July–14 Aug.
XV	1952	Helsinki	19 July–3 Aug.
XVI	1956	Melbourne[1]	22 Nov.–8 Dec.
XVII	1960	Rome	25 Aug.–11 Sept.
XVIII	1964	Tokyo	10–24 Oct.
XIX	1968	Mexico	12–27 Oct.
XX	1972	Munich	26 Aug.–10 Sept.
XXI	1976	Montreal	18 July–1 Aug.

* This celebration (to mark the 10th anniversary of the modern Games) was officially intercalated but is not numbered.
[1] The equestrian events were held in Stockholm 10–17 June 1956.

Separate Winter Olympics (there had been ice skating events in 1908 and 1920 and ice hockey in 1920) were inaugurated in 1924 and have been voted for as follows:

I	1924	Chamonix, France	25 Jan.–4 Feb.
II	1928	St. Moritz, Switzerland	11–19 Feb.
III	1932	Lake Placid, U.S.A.	4–15 Feb.
IV	1936	Garmisch-Partenkirchen, Germany	6–16 Feb.
V	1948	St. Moritz, Switzerland	30 Jan.–8 Feb.
VI	1952	Oslo, Norway	14–25 Feb.
VII	1956	Cortina d'Ampezzo, Italy	26 Jan.–5 Feb.
VIII	1960	Squaw Valley, California	18–28 Feb.
IX	1964	Innsbruck, Austria	29 Jan.–9 Feb.
X	1968	Grenoble, France	6–18 Feb.
XI	1972	Sapporo, Japan	3–13 Feb.
XII	1976	Innsbruck, Austria	4–13 Feb.

311

The first Winter Games in 1924 attracted 293 competitors from 16 nations.

Ever present Five countries have never failed to be represented at the 21 Celebrations of the Games: Australia, Greece, Great Britain, Switzerland and the United States of America.

Largest team France entered 880 men and 4 women in the 1900 Games at Paris.

ORIENTEERING

Origins Orienteering was invented by Major Ernst Killander in Sweden in 1918. World championships were inaugurated in 1966 and are held biennially. Annual British championships were instituted in 1967.

Most titles **World** Sweden won the world men's relay titles in 1966 and 1968 and the women's relay in 1966 with Ulla Lindkvist (Sweden) winning the individual titles in both 1966 and 1968.

Britain The most successful British team has been Edinburgh Southern Orienteering Club which won the Senior Men's title in 1969 and 1970 and the Senior Ladies' title in 1970. Gordon Pirie won the men's individual title in 1967 and 1968 and Carol McNeill won the women's title in 1967, 1969 and 1972.

Carol McNeill, three times winner of the women's individual orienteering title

PELOTA VASCA (JAI ALAI)

Origins The game, which originated in Italy as *longue paume* and was introduced into France in the 13th century, is said to be the fastest of all ball games with speeds of up to 160 m.p.h. *257,5 km/h*. Gloves were introduced *c.* 1840 and the *chisterak* was invented *c.* 1860 by Gantchiki Dithurbide of Sainte Pée. The long *chistera* was invented by Melchior Curuchage of Buenos Aires, Argentina in 1888. The world's largest *frontón* (the playing court) is that built for $4,500,000 (now £1,875,000) at Miami, Florida, U.S.A.

Longest Domination The longest domination as the world's No. 1 player was enjoyed by Chiquito de Cambo (*né* Joseph Apesteguy) (France), born 10 May 1881–died 1955, from the beginning of the century until succeeded in 1938 by Jean Urruty (France) (b. 19 Oct. 1913).

Games played in a *fronton* are *Frontenis*, *pelote* and *paleta* with both leather and rubber balls. The sport is governed by the International Federation of Basque Pelote.

PIGEON RACING

Earliest references Pigeon Racing was the natural development of the use of homing pigeons for the carrying of messages—a quality utilized in the ancient Olympic Games (776 B.C.–A.D. 393). The sport originated in Belgium and came to Britain *c.* 1820. The earliest major long-distance race was from Crystal Palace, South London, in 1871. The earliest recorded occasion on which 500 miles *800 km* was flown in a day was by "Motor" (owned by G. P. Pointer of Alexander Park Racing Club) which was released from Thurso, Scotland, on 30 June 1896 and covered 501 miles *806 km* at an average speed of 1,454 yds *1 329 m* per min (49½ m.p.h. [*79,6 km/h*]).

Longest flights The greatest recorded homing flight by a pigeon was made by one owned by the 1st Duke of Wellington (1769–1852). Released from a sailing ship off the Ichabo Islands, West Africa, on 8 April, it dropped dead a mile from its loft at Nine Elms, London on 1 June 1845, 55 days later, having flown an airline route of 5,400 miles *8 700 km*, but an actual distance of possibly 7,000 miles *11 250 km* to avoid the Sahara Desert. It was reported on 27 Nov. 1971 that an exhausted pigeon bearing a Hannover label was found 10,000 miles *16 100 km* away at Cunnamulla, Queensland, Australia. The official British duration record (into Great Britain) is 1,141 miles *1 836 km* by A. Bruce's bird in the 1960 Barcelona Race which was liberated on 9 July and homed at Fraserburgh, Aberdeenshire, Scotland on 5 Aug.

Highest speeds In level flight in windless conditions it is very doubtful if any pigeon can exceed 60 m.p.h. *96 km/h*. The highest race speed recorded is one of 3,229 yds *2 952 m* per min (110.07 m.p.h. [*177,14 km/h*]) in the East Anglian Federation race from East Croydon on 8 May 1965 when the 1,428 birds were backed by a powerful south south-west wind. The winner was A. Vidgeon & Son.

The highest race speed recorded over a distance of more than 1 000 km *621.37 miles* is 2,432.70 yds *2 224,45 m* per min (82.93 m.p.h. [*133,46 km/h*]) by a hen pigeon in the Central Cumberland Combine race over 683 miles 147 yds *1 099,316 km* from Murray Bridge, South Australia to North Ryde, Sydney on 2 Oct. 1971. The world's longest reputed distance in 24 hrs is 803 miles *1 292 km* (velocity 1,525 yds [*1 394 m*] per min) by E. S. Peterson's winner of the 1941 San Antonio R.C. event Texas, U.S.A.

The best 24-hour performance into the United Kingdom is 686 miles *1 104 km* by A. R. Hill's winner of the 1952 race from Hannover, Germany to St. Just, Cornwall—average speed 1,300 yds *1 188 m* per min (44.31 m.p.h. [*71,31 km/h*]).

312

POLO

Earliest games Polo is usually regarded as being of Persian origin having been played as *Pula c.* 525 B.C. Other claims have come from Tibet and the Tang Dynasty of China A.D. 250 The earliest polo club of modern times was the Kachar Club (founded in 1859) in Assam, India. The game was introduced into England from India in 1869 by the 10th Hussars at Aldershot, Hampshire and the earliest match was one between the 9th Lancers and the 10th Hussars on Hounslow Heath, west of London, in July 1871. The first all-Ireland Cup match was at Phoenix Park, Dublin, in 1878. The earliest international match between England and the U.S.A. was in 1886.

The game is played on the largest pitch of any ball game in the world. A ground measures 300 yds *274 m* long by 160 yds *146 m* wide with side boards, or as in India, 200 yds *182 m* wide without boards.

Highest handicap The highest handicap based on eight 7½-min "chukkas" is 10 goals introduced in the U.S.A. in 1891 and in the United Kingdom and in Argentina in 1910. The most recent additions to the select ranks of the 33 players ever to receive 10-goal handicaps are H. Heguy, F. Dorignac, G. Dorignac and G. Tanoira all of Argentina. The last (of six) 10-goal handicap players from Great Britain was G. Balding in 1939.

The highest handicap of any of the United Kingdom's 350 players is 7, by Paul Withers and J. Hipwood.

Highest score The highest aggregate number of goals scored in an international match is 30, when Argentina beat the U.S.A. 21–9 at Meadow Brook, Long Island, New York, U.S.A., in September 1936.

Most Olympic Medals Polo has been part of the Olympic programme on five occasions: 1900, 1908, 1920, 1924 and 1936. Of the 21 gold medallists, a 1920 winner, the Rt. Hon. Sir John Wodehouse, Bt., C.B.E., M.C., the 3rd Earl of Kimberly (b. 1883–k. 1941) uniquely also won a silver medal (1908).

Most internationals The greatest number of times any player has represented England is four in the case of Frederick M. Freake in 1900, 1902, 1909 and 1913. Thomas Hitchcock, Jr. (1900–44) played five times for the

An ancient Persian illustration of polo as it was originally played

U.S.A. *v.* England (1921–24–27–30–39) and twice *v.* Argentina (1928–36).

Most expensive pony The highest price ever paid for a polo pony was $22,000 (*now* £7,857), paid by Stephen Sanford for Lewis Lacey's *Jupiter* after the U.S.A. *v.* Argentina international in 1928.

Largest trophy The world's largest trophy for a particular sport is the Bangalore Limited Handicap Polo Tournament Trophy. This massive cup standing on its plinth is 6 ft *1,83 m* tall and was presented in 1936 by the Raja of Kolanka.

Largest crowd World record crowds of more than 50,000 have watched floodlight matches at the Sydney Agricultural Show, Australia.

POWER BOAT RACING

Origins The earliest application of the petrol engine to a boat was Gottlieb Daimler's experimental power boat on the River Seine, Paris, France, in 1887. The sport was given impetus by the presentation of an international championship cup by Sir Alfred Harmsworth in 1903, which was also the year of the first off-shore race from Calais to Dover.

Harmsworth Cup Of the 25 contests from 1903 to 1961, the United States has won 16, the United Kingdom 5, Canada 3 and France 1.

The greatest number of wins has been achieved by Garfield A. Wood with eight (1920–21, 1926, 1928–29–30, 1932–33). The only boat to win three times is *Miss Supertest III*, owned by James G. Thompson (Canada), in 1959–60–61. This boat also achieved the record speed of 115.972 m.p.h. *186,638 km/h* at Picton, Ontario, Canada in 1960.

Gold Cup The Gold Cup (instituted 1903) has been won four times by Garfield A. Wood (1917, 1919–20–21) and by Bill Muncey (1956–57, 1961–62). The record speed is 120.356 m.p.h. *193,694 km/h* for a 3 mile *4,8 km* lap by Rolls-Royce-engined *Miss Exide*, owned by Milo Stoen, driven by Bill Brow at Seattle, Washington, U.S.A. on 4 Aug. 1965.

Highest off-shore speeds The highest speed attained is 83.2 m.p.h. *133,9 km/h* by Dr. Carlo Bonomi of Rome in his 36 ft *10,97 m* *Aeromarine IX* (a Cigarette type hull) powered by two 468 in³ *7,669 c.c.* 600 h.p. Kiekhaefer Aeromarine engines. This average speed was recorded over the 215 statute miles *346 km* of the Tropheo Baleares Race at Palma di Mallorca, Spain on 27 May 1973. In this event a fastest British speed was set by Colonel Ronald Hoare of England, who recorded 80.9 m.p.h. *130,2 km/h* in his Don Shead designed, Aeromarine engined, *Unohoo*. The highest average race speed off British shores has been 69.5 m.p.h. *111,8 km/h* by Vincenzo Balestrieri (Italy) and Don Pruett in *Red Tornado* over 184 miles *296 km* from Southsea Pier,

Tommy Sopwith in his power boat, *Miss Enfield*. He is the only 3 time winner of the Cowes-Torquay race

Hampshire to Weymouth, Dorset to Hillhead Buoy, south of the Isle of Wight in the Wills International Race on 14 June 1969. The Countess of Arran drove her off-shore powerboat *Highland Fling* for a world's record of 85.63 m.p.h. *137,80 km/h* despite fuel trouble on the back-up run on Windermere on 21 Oct. 1971.

Longest races The longest race has been the Port Richborough London to Monte Carlo Marathon Off-Shore International event. The race extended over 2,947 miles *4 742 km* in 14 stages on 10–25 June 1972. It was won by HTS (G.B.) driven by Mike Bellamy, Eddie Chater and Jim Brooks in 71 hrs 35 min 56 sec (average 41.15 m.p.h. [*66,24 km/h*]). The *Daily Telegraph and B.P.* Round Britain event was inaugurated on 26 July 1969 at Portsmouth with 1,403 miles *2 257 km* in 10 stages west—about England, Wales and across Northern Scotland *via* the Caledonian Canal. The 1969 race (26 July to 7 Aug.) was won by *Avenger Too* (Timo Makinen, Alan Pascoe Watson and Brian Hendicott) in 39 hrs 9 min 37.7 sec. Of the 42 starters, 24 finished.

Cowes-Torquay race The record average for the *Daily Express* International Off-Shore Race (instituted 1961) is 66.47 m.p.h. *106,97 km/h* by *The Cigarette* (Don Aronow) over the 236 mile *379 km* course from Cowes, Isle of Wight to Torquay, Devon and back in 3 hrs 33 min on 30 Aug. 1969. The only 3 time winner has been Tommy Sopwith in 1961, 1968 and 1970.

Dragsters The first drag boat to attain 200 m.p.h. *321 km/h* was Sam Kurtovich's *Crisis* which attained 200.44 m.p.h. *322,57 km/h* in California in Oct. 1969 in a one-way run.

Longest journey The Dane Hans Tholstrup, 25, circumnavigated Australia in a 17 ft Caribbean Cougar fibreglass runabout with a single 80 h.p. Mercury outboard motor from 11 May to 25 July 1971.

Longest Jump The longest jump achieved by a power boat has been 110 ft *32,5 m* by Jerry Comeaux, 29 in a Glastron GT-150 with a 135 h.p. Evinrude Starflite on an isolated waterway in Louisiana, U.S.A. in mid-Oct. 1972. The take off speed was 56 m.p.h. *90 km/h*. The jump was required for a sequence in the eighth Bond film *Live and Let Die*.

RACKETS

Origins There is record of the sale of a Racket Court at Southernhay, Exeter, Devon dated 12 Jan. 1798.

Earliest world champion The first world rackets champion was Robert Mackay, who claimed the title in London in 1820. The first closed court champion was Francis Erwood at Woolwich in 1860. The first new court built in Great Britain since 1914 was the Second Court opened at Harrow School in 1965.

Longest reign Of the 19 world champions since 1820 the longest reign is held by British-born U.S. resident Geoffrey W. T. Atkins, who has held the title since beating the professional James Dear in 1954 and retired after a fourth successful defence of it in April 1970.

Most Amateur titles Since the Amateur singles championship was instituted in 1888 the most titles won by an individual is nine by Edgar M. Baerlein (1879–1971) between 1903 and 1923. Since the institution of the Amateur doubles championship in 1890 the most shares in titles has been eleven by David Sumner Milford (b. 7 June 1905), between 1938 and 1959. He also has seven Amateur singles titles (1930–52), an open title (1936) and held the world title from 1937 to 1947.

David Milford (extreme left) who has had eleven shares in Amateur Rackets Doubles Championships

RODEO

Origins Rodeo came into being with the early days of the North American cattle industry. The earliest references to the sport are from Santa Fe, New Mexico, U.S.A., in 1847. Steer wrestling came in with Bill Pickett (Oklahoma) in 1903. The other events are calf roping, bull riding, saddle and bare-back bronco riding.

The largest rodeo in the world is the Calgary Exhibition and Stampede at Calgary, Alberta, Canada. The record attendance has been 993,777 on 5–14 July 1973. The record for one day is 133,506 on 14 July 1973.

Most world titles The record number of all-round titles is five by Jim Shoulders (U.S.A.) in 1949 and 1956–57–58–59 and by Larry Mahan (U.S.A.) (b. 21 Nov. 1943) in 1966–67–68–69–70. The record figure for prize money in a single season is $60,852 (£24,340) by Phil Lyne (U.S.A.) (b. 18 Jan. 1947) of George West, Texas.

Time records Records for timed events, such as calf-roping and steer-wrestling, are meaningless, because of the widely varying conditions due to the size of arenas and amount of start given the stock. The fastest time recorded for roping a calf is 7.5 sec by Junior Garrison of Marlow, Oklahoma, at Evergreen, Colorado, U.S.A. in 1967, and the fastest time for overcoming a steer was 2.4 sec by James Bynum of Waxahachie, Texas, at Marietta, Oklahoma, in 1955.

The standard required time to stay on in bareback, saddle bronc and bull riding events is 8 sec. In the now obsolete ride-to-a-finish events, rodeo riders have been recorded to have survived 90+ min, until the mount had not a buck left in it.

Champion bull The top bucking bull is No. 17, a 1,700 lb. *770 kg* cross-bred owned by Beutler Bros. and Cervi, of Sterling, Colorado. When cowboys do manage to ride this seldom ridden beast they win first place.

Champion bronc Currently the greatest bronc is *Descent*, a 16 year old Palomino gelding, owned by Beutler Bros. and Cervi, which has been voted "Bucking Horse of the Year" for a record sixth year. Traditionally a bronc called *Midnight* owned by Jim McNab of Alberta, Canada was never ridden in 12 appearances at the Calgary Stampede.

ROLLER SKATING

Origins The first roller skate was devised by Joseph Merlin of Huy, Belgium, in 1760. Several "improved" versions appeared during the next century, but a really satisfactory roller skate did not materialize before 1866, when James L. Plimpton of New York produced the present four-wheeled type, patented it, and opened the first public rink in the world at Newport, Rhode Island, that year. The great boom periods were 1870–75, 1908–12 and 1948–54, each originating in the United States.

Largest rink The greatest indoor rink ever to operate was located in the Grand Hall, Olympia, London. It had an actual skating area of 68,000 ft² *6 300 m²*. It first opened in 1890, for one season, then again from 1909 to 1912.

Roller hockey Roller hockey (previously known as Rink Hockey in Europe) was first introduced in this country as Rink Polo, at the old Lava rink, Denmark Hill, London in the late 1870s. The Amateur Rink Hockey Association was formed in 1905, and in 1913 became the National Rink Hockey (now Roller Hockey) Association. Britain won the inaugural World Championship in 1936 since when Portugal has won most titles with 11 between 1947 and 1972.

Most titles Most world speed titles have been won by Miss A. Vianello (Italy) with 16 between 1953 and 1965. Most world pair titles have been taken by Dieter Fingerle (W. Germany) with four in 1959–65–66–67. The records for figure titles are 5 by Karl Heinz Losch in 1958–59–61–62–66 and 4 by Astrid Bader, also of West Germany, in 1965 to 1968. Leslie E. Woodley of Birmingham won 12 British national individual titles over the three regulation distances (880 yds [*804 m*], one mile [*1,6 km*] and five miles [*8 km*]) between 1957 and 1964. Chloe Ronaldson of London won 18 ladies' titles over 440 yds *402 m*, 800 m *874 yds* and 880 yds *804 m* in 1958–73.

Records The fastest speed put up in an official world record is 25.78 m.p.h. *41,48 km/h* when Giuseppe Cantarella (Italy) recorded 34.9 sec for 440 yds *402 m* on a road at Catania, Sicily on 28 Sept. 1963. The world mile record on a rink is 2 min 25.1 sec by Gianni Ferretti (Italy). The greatest distance skated in one hour on a rink by a woman is 20 miles 1,355 yds *33,407 km* by C. Patricia Barnett (G.B.) at Brixton, London on 24 June 1962. The men's record on a closed road circuit is 35,831 km *22 miles 465 yds* by Alberto Civolani (Italy) at Bologna, Italy on 15 Oct. 1967.

Marathon record The longest recorded continuous roller skating marathon was one of 197 hours performed by Walter Miller at the White City rink, Boise, Idaho, U.S.A. in June 1935. The longest reported skate was by Clinton Shaw from Victoria, British Columbia to St. John's, Newfoundland (4,900 miles [*7 900 km*]) on the Trans-Canadian Highway *via* Montreal from 1 April to 11 Nov. 1967.

ROWING

Oldest race The earliest established sculling race is the Dogget's Coat and Badge, which was rowed on 1 Aug. 1716 over 5 miles *8 km* from London Bridge to Chelsea and is still being rowed every year over the same course, under the administration of the Fishmonger's Company. The first English regatta probably took place on the Thames by the Ranelagh Gardens, near Putney in 1775. Boating began at Eton in 1793, 72 years before the "song". The Leander Club was formed *c.* 1818.

OLYMPIC GAMES

Olympic Since 1900 there have been 105 Olympic finals of which **medals most** the U.S.A. have won 26, Germany (now West Germany) 15 and Great Britain 14.

Four oarsmen have won 3 gold medals: John B. Kelly (U.S.A.) (1889–1960), father of H.S.H. Princess Grace of Monaco, in the sculls (1920) and double sculls (1920 and 1924); his cousin Paul V. Costello (U.S.A.) (b. 27 Dec. 1899) in the double sculls (1920, 1924 and 1928); Jack Beresford, Jr., C.B.E. (G.B.) (b. 1 Jan. 1899) in the sculls (1924), coxless fours (1932) and double sculls (1936) and Vyacheslav Ivanov (U.S.S.R. (b. 30 July 1938) in the sculls (1956, 1960 and 1964).

315

A Thames Regatta at Putney in the Victorian age

BOAT RACE

The earliest University Boat Race, which Oxford won, was from Hambledon Lock to Henley Bridge on 10′ June 1829. In the 119 races to 1973, Cambridge won 67 times, Oxford 51 times and there was a dead heat on 24 March 1877.

Record times The race record time for the course of 4 miles 374 yds *6,779 km* (Putney to Mortlake) is 17 min 50 sec by Cambridge in 1948. Oxford returned 17 min 37 sec in practice on 19 March 1965. The smallest winning margin was Oxford's win by a canvas in 1952. The greatest margin (apart from sinking) was Cambridge's win by 20 lengths in 1900. The record for the distance (rowed on the ebb from Mortlake to Putney) is 17 min 24 sec by the Tideway Scullers School in the Head of the River Race on 21 March 1964.

Intermediate times The record to the Mile Post is 3 min 47 sec (Oxford 1960 and 25 March 1967); Hammersmith Bridge 6 min 42 sec (Oxford 25 March 1967); Chiswick Steps 10 min 45 sec (Oxford 1965, in practice) and Barnes Bridge 14 min 39 sec (Oxford 19 March 1965, in practice.)

Oarsman Heaviest The heaviest man ever to row in a University boat has been David L. Cruttenden (b. Hartlepool, 1947) the No. 6 in the 1970 Cambridge boat at 16 st. 0 lb. *101 kg 604*. The 1972 Cambridge crew averaged a record 13 st. 11⅛ lb. *87 kg 600*.

Lightest The lightest oarsman was the 1882 Oxford Stroke, A. H. Higgins, at 9 st. 6½ lb. *60 kg 100*. The lighest cox was F. H. Archer (Oxford) in 1862 at 5 st. 2 lb. *32 kg 658*.

HENLEY ROYAL REGATTA

The annual regatta at Henley-on-Thames, Oxford-shire, was inaugurated on 26 March 1839.

Since 1839 the course, except in 1923, has been about 1 mile 550 yds *2 112 m* varying slightly according to the length of boat. In 1967 the shorter craft were "drawn up" so all bows start level. Prior to 1922 there were two slight angles.

Sculling The record number of wins in the Wingfield Sculls (instituted on the Thames 1830) is seven by Jack Beresford, Jr. (see Olympic Games), from 1920 to 1926. The fastest time (Putney to Mortlake) has been 21 min 11 sec by Leslie Southworth in 1933. The record number of world professional sculling titles (instituted 1831) won is seven by W. Beach (Australia) between 1884 and 1887. Stuart A. Mackenzie (Great Britain and Australia) performed the unique feat of winning the Diamond Sculls at Henley for the sixth consecutive occasion on 7 July 1962. In 1960 and 1962 he was in Leander colours.

Highest speed Speeds in tidal or flowing water are of no comparative value. The highest recorded speed for 2,000 m *2,187 yds* by an eight is 5 min 32.54 sec (13.45 m.p.h.

HENLEY ROYAL REGATTA—Classic Records (year in brackets indicates date the event was instituted)

			min sec	
Grand Challenge Cup (1839)	8 oars	Ratzeburger Ruderclub (West Germany)	6:16	3 July 1965
Ladies' Challenge Plate (1845)	8 oars	University of Wisconsin, U.S.A.	6:32	6 July 1973
Thames Challenge Cup (1868)	8 oars	Princeton University, U.S.A.	6:33	5 July 1973
		University of Wisconsin, U.S.A.	6.33	6 July 1973
Princess Elizabeth Challenge Cup (1946)	8 oars	Ridley College, Canada	6:38	6 July 1973
Stewards' Challenge Cup (1841)	4 oars	Quintin B.C.	6:55	3 July 1965
Visitors' Challenge Cup (1847)	4 oars	University of London	7:09	5 July 1973
Wyfold Challenge Cup (1855)	4 oars	Thames Tradesmen's R.C.	7:02	7 July 1973
Prince Phillip Challenge Cup (1963)	4 oars	North-eastern University, Rowing Association U.S.A.	7:00	6 July 1973
Britannia Challenge Cup (1969)	4 oars	Isis B.C.	7:15	5 July 1973
Silver Goblets (called Silver Wherries until 1850) (1845) and Nickalls' Challenge Cup (1895)	Pair oar	Peter Gorny and Gunther Bergau (ASK Vorwaerts Rostock, East Germany)	7:35	1 July 1965
Double Skulls Challenge Cup (1939)	Sculls	Michael J. Hart and Christopher L. Baillieu (Leander Club and Cambridge University)	6:59	6 July 1973
Diamond Challenge Skulls (1844)	Sculls	Donald M. Spero (New York A.C., U.S.A.)	7:42	3 July 1965

[21,65 km/h]) by East Germany in the European Championships in Copenhagen, Denmark on 21 Aug. 1971 and in the Olympic Games 5 min 54.02 sec (12.64 m.p.h. [20,34 km/h]) by Germany at Toda, Japan, on 12 Oct. 1964.

Fastest Cross Channel Row The fastest row across the channel has been 4 hrs 15 min from Sandgate, Kent to Boulogne, France by a coxed four (Jack Hughes (Stroke) Maurice Drummond, Samuel Osborne, George Edwards (bow) and Jimmy Ladlow (cox)) on 27 July 1947.

Loch Ness Loch Ness, the longest stretch of inland water in Great Britain (22.7 miles [36,5 km]), was rowed by a coxed four jollyboat from Eastern Amateur Rowing Club of Portobello on 11 Oct. 1969 in 4 hrs 11 min.

Oxford–London The fastest time registered between Folly Bridge, Oxford through 33 locks and 112 miles 180 km to Westminster Bridge, London is 15 hrs 16 min by an eight (no substitutes) from the Wallingford R.C. on 18 Oct. 1970 so beating a military record set in 1824.

Circum-navigation of Ireland Ireland, the world's twentieth largest island, was first circumnavigated by an oarsman when Derek Paul King, 25, of Dartford, Kent, landed at Rosnowlagh, County Donegal on 3 Oct. 1971 having rowed *Louise* 1,500 miles 2 400 km in 108 days since 11 June.

Marathon An eight from the Aramoho Boating Club, New Zealand covered 78 miles 125 km in 12 hrs a 4 mile 6 km long shuttle course on the River Wanganui on 20 Nov. 1971.

Whaler Pulling The Isle of Wight was circumnavigated in a 60 nautical mile 111 km pull in a 27 ft 8,22 m naval

A contemporary painting of an Oxford racing eight at the time of the first Boat Race in 1829

whaler by two crews from the Southampton City Fire Brigade in 12 hrs 34 min on 9 June 1973.

Punting Punting was a sport with both amateur and professional championships instituted in the 1870's. Victorians argued about the two styles of pole planting and running *versus* pricking. W. Haines won the Professional Championship of the Thames 8 times in the period 1897–1908. The longest recorded punt is one of 101 miles 162,5 km on the Lancaster Canal, England, by 4 male and 1 female punters on 3–5 Sept. 1972. Only two John Siddle and David Whitaker fell in.

SHINTY

Shinty (from the Gaelic *sinteag*, a leap) was recorded in the West and Central Highlands *c.* 1790 when it was known as *lomain* (driving forward). Games were contested between whole clans or parishes without limit as to numbers or time until darkness stopped play among the walking wounded. The field of play was undelineated except by the occasional pail of *uisge-beatha* (whisky). In an inter-clan match a combatant who had failed to disable at least one opponent within a reasonable time had his curved stick (caman) confiscated as a punishment by the Chieftain so that he could only kick the ball (*cnaige*) or his opponents.

This ungovernable game was first given some rules in 1879 and the present governing body was set up by C. I. Macpherson of Balavil near Kingussie, Inverness-shire on 10 Oct. 1893.

Most titles The most successful club has been Newtonmore, Inverness-shire which has won the Camanachd Association Challenge Cup (instituted 1896) nineteen times (1907–1971).

Highest scores The highest Cup score was in 1909 when Newtonmore beat Furnace 11–3 at Glasgow. Dr. Johnnie Cattanach scored eight hails or goals.

A war artist's impression of an early game of Shinty

SHOOTING

Olympic Games The record number of gold medals won is five by seven marksmen:—Carl Osburn (U.S.A.) (1912–1924); Konrad Stäheli (Switz.) (1900 and 1906); Willis Lee (U.S.A.) (1920); Louis Richardet (Switz.) (1900 and 1906); Ole Andreas Lilloe-Olsen (Norway) (1920–1924); Alfred Lane (U.S.A.) (1912 and 1920) and Morris Fisher (U.S.A.) (1920 and 1924). Osburn also won 4 silver and 2 bronze medals to total 11. The only marksman to win 3 individual gold medals has been Gulbrandsen Skatteboe (Norway) (b. 18 July 1875) in 1906–08–1912.

Record heads The world's finest head is the 23-pointer stag head in the Maritzburg collection, Germany. The outside span is 75½ in 191 cm the length 47½ in 120 cm and the weight 41½ lb. 18 kg 824. The greatest number of points is probably 33 (plus 29) on the stag shot in 1696 by Frederick III (1657–1713), the Elector of Brandenburg, later King Frederick I of Prussia.

The record head for a British Red Deer is a 47-pointer (length 33½ in [85 cm]) from the Great Warnham Deer Park, Sussex in 1892. The record for a semi-feral stag is a 20-pointer with an antler length of 45¾ in 115 cm from Endsleigh Wood, Devon, found in December 1950 and owned by G. Kenneth Whitehead.

Largest shoulder guns The largest bore shoulder guns made were 2 bores. Less than a dozen of these were made by two English wildfowl gunmakers c. 1885. Normally the largest guns made are double-barrelled 4-bore weighing up to 26 lb. 11 kg which can be handled only by men of exceptional physique. Larger smooth-bore guns have been made, but these are for use as punt-guns.

Highest muzzle velocity The highest muzzle velocity of any rifle bullet is 7,100 ft 2 164 m per sec (4,840 m.p.h. [7 789 km/h]) by a 1937 0.30 calibre, M 1903 Standard U.S. Army Ordnance Department rifle.

Clay pigeon Most world titles have been won by S. De Lamniczer (Hungary) in 1929, 1933 and 1939. The only woman to win two world titles has been Gräfin von Soden (West Germany) in 1966–67. The record number of clay birds shot in an hour is 1,308 by Joseph Nother (formerly Wheater) (born 1918) of Kingston-upon-Hull, Yorkshire, at Bedford on 21 Sept. 1957. Using 5 guns and 7 loaders he shot 1,000 in 42 min 22.5 sec.

BISLEY

The National Rifle Association was instituted in 1859. The Queen's (King's) Prize has been shot since 1860 and has only once been won by a woman—Miss Marjorie Elaine Foster, M.B.E. (score 280) on 19 July 1930. Only Arthur G. Fulton, M.B.E. has won 3 times (1912, 1926, 1931).

The highest score (possible 300) is 293 by Richard P. Rosling (City R.C.) and A. Narcon (Canada) on 28–29 July 1972 and by Keith Martin Pilcher on 20–21 July 1973. The record for the Silver Medal, 150 (possible 150) by M. J. Brister (City Rifle Club) and the Lord Swansea on 24 July 1971. Brister won the tie shoot.

Bench rest shooting The smallest group on record at 1,000 yds 914 m is 7.68 in 195 mm by Mary Louise De Vito with a 7 mm-300 Wetherby in Pennsylvania on 11 Oct. 1970.

Block tossing Using a pair of auto-loading Remington Nylon 66.22 calibre guns, Tom Frye (U.S.A.) tossed 100,010 blocks (2½ in [6 cm] pine cubes) and hit 100,004—his longest run was 32,860—on 5–17 Oct. 1959.

Annie Oakley's portrait in the Amateur Trapshooting Association Hall of Fame. She was the most famous trick shot of all time

Biggest bag The largest animal ever shot by any big game hunter was a bull African elephant (Loxodonta africana) shot by J. J. Fényközi (Hungary) 48 miles 77 km north-northwest of Macusso, Angola, on 13 Nov. 1955. It required 16 heavy calibre bullets from an 0.416 Rigby and weighed an estimated 24,000 lb. (10.7 tons [10,87 tonnes]), standing 13 ft 2 in 4,013 m at the shoulders. In November 1965 Simon Fletcher, 28, a Kenyan farmer, claimed to have killed two elephants with one 0.458 bullet.

The greatest recorded lifetime bag is 556,000 birds, including 241,000 pheasants, by the 2nd Marquess of Ripon (1867–1923). He himself dropped dead on a grouse moor after shooting his 52nd bird on the morning of 22 Sept. 1923.

Revolver shooting The greatest rapid fire feat was that of Ed. McGivern (U.S.A.), who twice fired from 15 ft 4,5 m 5 shots which could be covered by a silver half-dollar piece (diameter 1.205 in [3,060 cm]) in 0.45 sec at the Lead

INDIVIDUAL WORLD RECORDS

(for Olympic Games programme events)
(as ratified by the International Shooting Union (U.I.T.) as at 1 Jan. 1973)

			Possible—Score			
Free Rifle	300 m	3 × 40 shots	1,200—1,157	Gary L. Anderson (U.S.A.)	Mexico City, Mexico	23 Oct. 1968
Small-bore Rifle	50 m	3 × 40 shots	1,200—1,166	John Writer (U.S.A.)	Munich, W. Germany	30 Aug. 1972
Small-bore Rifle	50 m	60 shots prone	600— 599	Ho Jun Li (North Korea)	Munich, W. Germany	28 Aug. 1972
Free Pistol	50 m	60 shots	600— 572	Grigori Kosych (U.S.S.R.)	Pilsen, Czechoslovakia	1969
Rapid Fire Pistol	25 m	60 shots	600— 572	Giovanni Liverzani (Italy)	Phoenix, Arizona, U.S.A.	1970
Running (Boar) Target	50 m	60 shots "normal runs"	600— 569	Lakov Zhelezniak (U.S.S.R.)	Munich, W. Germany	1 Sept. 1972
Trap	200 birds		200— 199	Angelo Scaizone (Italy)	Munich, W. Germany	29 Aug. 1972
Skeet	200 birds		200— 200	Yevgeniy Petrov (U.S.S.R.)	Phoenix, Arizona, U.S.A.	1970
			200— 200	Yuri Tzuranov (U.S.S.R.)	Bologna, Italy	1971

The U.I.T. also ratifies 7 other men's events (including Air Rifle and Air Pistol) and 6 positional records for men and 7 events and 1 positional record for women and team events for all 29 world record events except women's trap and skeet. The nearest to a "possible" by a woman is 598/600 by E. Rolinska (Poland) for the Standard Rifle 50 metres 60 shots prone at Suhl, East Germany in 1971.

LARGEST BRITISH BAGS

Woodpigeon	550	1 gun	Major A. J. Coates, near Winchester		10 Jan. 1962
Pigeons	561	1 gun	K. Ransford, Shropshire-Montgomery		22 July 1970
Snipe	1,108	2 guns	Tiree, Inner Hebrides	25 Oct.–3 Nov. 1906	
Hares	1,215	11 guns	Holkham, Norfolk		19 Dec. 1877
Woodcock	228	6 guns	Ashford, County Galway		28 Jan. 1910
Grouse	2,929	8 guns	Littledale and Abbeystead, Lancashire		12 Aug. 1915
Grouse	1,070	1 gun	Lord Walsingham in Yorkshire		30 Aug. 1888
Geese (Brent)	704*	32 punt-guns	Colonel Russell i/c, River Blackwater, Essex	c. 1860	
Rabbits	6,943	5 guns	Blenheim, Oxfordshire		17 Oct. 1898
Partridges	2,015†	6 guns	Rothwell, Lincolnshire		12 Oct. 1952
Pheasants	3,937†	7 guns	Hall Barn, Beaconsfield, Buckinghamshire		18 Dec. 1913

* Plus about 250 later picked up.
† Plus 104 later picked up.

Club Range, South Dakota, U.S.A., on 20 Aug. 1932. On 13 Sept. 1932 at Lewiston, Montana, McGivern fired 10 shots in 1.2 sec from two guns at the same time double action (no draw) all 10 shots hitting two $2\frac{1}{4} \times 3\frac{1}{2}$ in *5,7 × 8,9 cm* playing cards at 15 ft *4,57 m*.

Quickest draw The super-star of fast drawing and, described as the Fastest Gun who was ever alive, is Bob Munden (b. Kansas City, Missouri, 8 Feb. 1942). His single shot records include Walk and Draw Level Blanks in 15/100ths sec at Arcadia, California on 4 June 1972. Standing Reaction Blanks (4 in [*10 cm*] balloons at 8 ft [*2,43 m*]) in 16/100ths sec at Norwalk, California on 21 Jan. 1973 and Self Start Blanks in 2/100ths sec at Baldwin Park, California on 17 Aug. 1968. At Las Vegas he got off 10 shots in 2.12 sec. His fastest shot with live ammunition is 21/100ths sec at 21 ft *6,40 m* hitting a man-sized Silhouette in 1963. The fastest (woman) gun alive is Linda Guerra, who shot 21/100ths sec in the Standing Reaction event at Norwalk.

Small Bore On 27 Jan. 1956 in the National Inter-County Association League at 25 yds prone the Kent team of 20 scored a possible 2,000 *ex* 2,000. The record score for a round in the British School's Small Bore Rifle Association (B.S.S.R.A.) contest is a team possible of 500 *ex* 500 by Gresham's School, Holt, Norfolk in Lent Term, 1972. S. J. Carter scored 500 *ex* 500 in the 5 rounds in this .22 contest.

Trick shooting The most renowned trick shot of all-time was Annie Oakley (*née* Moses) (1860–1926). She demonstrated

Bob Munden, the fastest draw alive, in action

the ability to shoot 100 *ex* 100 in trap shooting for 35 years aged between 27 and 62. At 30 paces she could split a playing card end-on, hit a dime in mid-air or shoot a cigarette from the lips of her husband—one Frank Butler.

SKIING

Origins The earliest dated skis found in Fenno—Scandian bogs have been dated to *c.* 2500 B.C. A rock carving of a skier at Rødøy, Tjøtta, North Norway, dates from 2000 B.C. The earliest recorded military competition was an isolated one in Oslo, Norway, in 1767. Skiing did not develop into a sport until 1843 at Tromsø, Norway. Skiing was known in California by 1856, having been introduced by "Snowshoe" Thompson from Norway. The Trysil Shooting and Skiing Club (founded 1861), Australia, claims it is the world's oldest. Skiing was not introduced into the Alps until 1883, though there is some evidence of earlier use in the Carniola district. The first Slalom event was run at Mürren, Switzerland, on 6 Jan. 1921. The International Ski Federation (F.I.S.) was founded on 2 Feb. 1924. The Winter Olympics were inaugurated on 25 Jan 1924. The Ski Club of Great Britain was founded on 6 May 1903. The National Ski Federation of Great Britain was formed in 1964.

Most Olympic wins The most Olympic gold medals won by an individual for skiing is four (including one for a relay) by Sixten Jernberg (b. 6 Feb. 1929) of Sweden, in 1956–60–64. In addition, Jernberg has won three silver and two bronze medals. The only women to win three gold medals are Klavdiya Boyarskikh (b. 11 Nov. 1939) and Galina Koulakova, 30, both of the U.S.S.R., who each won the 5 km and 10 km and were members of the winning 3 × 5 km relay teams at Innsbruck, Austria and at Sapporo, Japan in 1964 and 1972 respectively. The most Olympic gold medals won in men's alpine skiing is three, by Anton ("Toni") Sailer (b. 17 Nov. 1935) in 1956 and Jean-Claude Killy (b. 30 Aug. 1943) in 1968.

Most world titles The world alpine championships were inaugurated at Mürren, Switzerland, in 1931. The greatest number of titles won is 12 by Christel Cranz (b. 1 July 1914) of Germany, with four Slalom (1934–37–38–39), three Downhill (1935–37–39) and five Combined (1934–35–37–38–39). She also won the gold medal for the Combined in the 1936 Olympics. The most titles

won by a man is seven by Anton ("Toni") Sailer (b. 17 Nov. 1935) of Austria, who won all four in 1956 (Giant Slalom, Slalom, Downhill and the non-Olympic Alpine Combination) and the Downhill, Giant Slalom and Combined in 1958.

In the Nordic events Sixten Jernberg (Sweden) won eight titles (four at 50 km, one at 30 km, and three in relays) in 1956–64. Johan Gröttumsbraaten (b. 24 Feb. 1899) of Norway won six individual titles (two at 18 km and four Combined) in 1926–32. The record for a jumper is five by Birger Ruud (b. 23 Aug. 1911) of Norway, in 1931–32 and 1935–36–37.

The World Cup, instituted in 1967, has been won three times by Gustav Thöni (Italy) (b. 28 Feb. 1921) in 1971–72–73. The women's cup has been won three times by the 1,67 m *5 ft 6 in* 68 kg *150 lb.* Annemarie Proell (b. 27 March 1953) of Austria in 1971–72–73. In 1973 she won a unique 8 out of 8 downhill races and a record 28 World Cup events.

Most British titles The greatest number of British Ski-running titles won is three by Leonard Dobbs (1921, 1923–24), William R. Bracken (1929–31) and Jeremy Palmer-Tomkinson (1965–66–68). The most ladies Titles is four by Miss Isobel M. Roe (1938–39, 1948–49) and Miss Gina Hathorn (b. 6 July 1946) (1966–68–69–70). The most wins in the British Ski-jumping Championship (discontinued 1936) is three, by Colin Wyatt (1931, 1934, 1936).

Heaviest Heavyweight Champion The greatest winner of the "World Heavyweight Ski Championship" at Sugarloaf Mountain, Maine, U.S.A. was John Truden (U.S.) who weighed in at 401 lb. (28 st. 9 lb. [*182 kg*]) in 1972. It has been said that, apart from avalanches, his best event is giant slalom.

Highest speed The highest speed claimed for any skier is 114.479 m.p.h. *184,237 km/h* by Alessandro Casse (Italy) on the Kilometro Lanciato, Cervinia, Italy in July 1973. The

319

Heinz Wosipiwo during his world record ski-jump of 169 m *554 ft 6 in* in 1973

average speed in the 1968 Olympic downhill race on the Chamrousse course, Grenoble, France by Jean-Claude Killy (b. 30 Aug. 1943) of France was 86,79 km/h *53.93 m.p.h.*.

Duration The longest non-stop skiing marathon was one lasting 48 hours by Onni Savi, aged 35, of Padasjoki, Finland, who covered 305.9 km *190.1 miles* between noon on 19 April and noon on 21 April 1966.

Largest entry The world's greatest Nordic ski race is the "Vasa Lopp", which commemorates an event of 1521 when Gustav Vasa (1496–1560), later King Gustavus Eriksson, skied 85 km *52.8 miles* from Mora to Sälen, Sweden. The re-enactment of this journey in reverse direction is now an annual event, with 9,397 starters on 4 March 1970. The record time is 4 hours 39 min 49 sec by Janne Stefansson on 3 March 1968.

Longest jump The longest ski-jump ever recorded is one of 169 m *554 ft 6 in* by Heinz Wosipiwo (East Germany) at **World** Oberstdorf, East Germany, on 9 March 1973. The record for a 70 m hill is 85,49 m *280 ft 6 in* by Tauno Käyhkö at Falun, Sweden on 19 Feb. 1973 when scoring 247.8 points for distance and style.

British The British record is 61 m *200.1 ft* by Guy John Nixon (b. 9 Jan. 1909) at Davos on 24 Feb. 1931. The record at Hampstead, London, on artificial snow is 28 m *90.8 ft* by Reidar Anderson (b. 20 April 1911) of Norway on 24 March 1950.

Ski- Parachuting The greatest recorded vertical descent in parachute ski-jumping is 2,300 ft *700 m* by Rick Sylvester, 29, (U.S.) who on 31 Jan. 1972 skied off the 3,200 ft *975 m* sheer face of El Capitan, Yosemite Valley, California. His parachute opened at 1,500 ft *460 m*.

Longest run The longest all-downhill ski run in the world is the Weissfluhjoch-Küblis Parsenn course, near Davos, Switzerland, which measures 12,23 km *7.6 miles*. The run from the Aiguille du Midi top of the Chamonix lift (vertical lift 2 492 m [*8,176 ft*]) across the Vallée Blanche is 20,9 km *13 miles*.

Longest lift The longest chair lift in the world is the Alpine Way to Kosciusko Châlet lift above Thredbo, near the Snowy Mountains, New South Wales, Australia. It takes from 45 to 75 min to ascend the 3.5 miles *5,6 km*, according to the weather. The highest is at Chactaltaya, Bolivia, rising to 5 029 m *16,500 ft*.

Greatest descent The greatest reported descent in a 7 hour day is 104,000 ft *31 700 m* by Jean Mayer at Taos Ski Valley, New Mexico in 1964. He made 61 runs using a Poma lift for ascents.

Highest altitude Yuichiro Miura (Japan) skied 2,5 km *1.6 miles* down Mt. Everest starting from 26,200 ft *7 985 m*. In a run from a height of 24,418 ft *7 442 m* he reached speeds of 93.6 m.p.h. *150 km/h* on 6 May 1970. Sylvian Squdan (Switzerland) became the first man to ski down Mount McKinlay (20,320 ft [*6 193 m*]) on 10 June 1972. He took 7 hours to reach the 7,000 ft *2 133 m* level and made 2,700 jump turns on the 50–55° top slopes.

SKIJORING

The record speed reached in aircraft skijoring (being towed by an aircraft) is 175,78 km/h *109.23 m.p.h.* by Reto Pitsch on the Silsersee, St. Moritz, Switzerland, in 1956.

SKI-BOB

The ski-bob was invented by Mr. Stevens of Hartford, Connecticut, U.S.A., and patented (No. 47334) on 19 April 1892 as a "bicycle with ski-runners". The Fédération Internationale de Skibob was founded on 14 Jan. 1961 in Innsbruck, Austria. The Ski-Bob Association of Great Britain was registered on 23 Aug. 1967. The highest speed attained is 166 km/h *103.4 m.p.h.* by Erick Brenter (Austria) at Cervinia, N. Italy, in 1964.

World Champion- ships The only ski-bobbers to retain a world championship are Gerhilde Schiffkorn (Austria) who won the women's title in 1967 and 1969 and Gertrude Geberth, who won in 1971 and 1973.

SNOWMOBILE
The world record speed for a snowmobile stood at 127.3 m.p.h. *204,8 km/h* by a Ski Doo XR-2 as at 10 Feb. 1973.

SNOOKER

Origins Research shows that snooker was originated by Field Marshal Sir Neville Chamberlain, G.C.B., G.C.S.I. (1820–1902) as a variation of "black pool", in the Ootacamund Club, Nilgiris, South India in the summer of 1875. It did not reach England until 1885, where the modern scoring system was adopted in 1891. Championships were not instituted until 1916. World Professional Championships were instituted in 1927.

Highest breaks It is possible if an opponent commits a foul with 15 reds on the table that his opponent can exercise an option of nominating a colour as a red and then pots this free ball and then goes on to pot the black with 15 reds still on the table, he can score 155. The official world record break of the maximum possible (excluding handicaps or penalties) of 147 was set by Joe Davis, O.B.E. (b. 15 April 1901) against Willie Smith at Leicester Square Hall, London on 22 Jan. 1955 and by Rex Williams (G.B.) against Manuel Francisco at Cape Town, South Africa, on 22 Dec. 1965. At least 22 other "perfect" frames have been achieved under less rigorous conditions. The highest break by an amateur is one of 145 by Max Williams, seven-times Australian Amateur Snooker Champion (1961–1973). The first man to complete a 147 break was E. J. O'Donaghue (Australia) in 1934.

Marathon The most protracted snooker endurance record is one of 174 hr by 3 players (each resting for 1 frame in three) Mark Hetherington, Geoffrey Lambert and Iain Ross of the Royal Holloway College Students' Union Society on 16–24 Feb. 1973. Hetherington dropped out 8½ hr from the end by which time 351 frames (31,463 points) were completed.

SPEEDWAY

Origins Motor cycle racing on large dirt track surfaces has been traced back to 1902 in the United States. The first organized "short track" races were at the West Maitland (New South Wales, Australia) Agricultural Show in November 1923. The sport was introduced to Great Britain at High Beech, Essex, on 19 Feb. 1928. After three seasons of competition in Southern and Northern leagues, the National League was instituted in 1932. The best record is that of the Wembley Lions who won in 1932, 1946–47, 1949–53, making a record total of eight victories. Since the National Trophy knock-out competition was instituted in 1931, Belle Vue (Manchester) have been most successful with nine victories in 1933–34–35–36–37, 1946–47, 1949 and 1958. In 1965 the League was replaced by the British League in which Belle Vue have won three times in succession (1970–72).

Most world titles The world speedway championship was inaugurated at Wembley, London in September 1936. The only five-time winner has been Ove Fundin (b. Tranås, 1933) (Sweden), who won in 1956, 1960, 1961, 1963 and 1967. In addition he was second in 1957–58–59 and third in 1962, 1964 and 1965. Ivan Mauger (N.Z.) (b. Christchurch 1939) is the only rider to win three successive championships (1968–70). He also won in 1972.

Lap speed The fastest recorded speed on a British speedway track is 54.62 m.p.h. *87,90 km/h* on the 470 yd *429 m* 2nd Division track at Crewe by Barry Meeks. This track was shortened by 40 yd *36 m* in 1970 and the current fastest track record on a British circuit is an average of 51.49 m.p.h. *82,86 km/h* at Exeter by Ivan Mauger on 2 July 1973.

SQUASH RACKETS

(Note: "1971", for example, refers to the 1971–72 season.)

Earliest champion Although rackets (U.S. spelling racquets) with a soft ball was evolved *c.* 1850 at Harrow School (England), there was no recognized champion of any country until J. A. Miskey of Philadelphia won the American Amateur Singles Championship in 1906.

World title The inaugural international (world) championships were staged in Australia in August 1967 when Australia won the team title in Sydney and Geoffrey B. Hunt (Victoria) took the individual title, both these titles being retained in 1969 and 1971.

MOST WINS

Open Championship The most wins in the Open Championship (amateurs or professionals), held annually in Britain, is seven by Hashim Khan (Pakistan) in 1950–51–52–53–54–55 and 1957.

Amateur Championship The most wins in the Amateur Championship is six by Abdel Fattah Amr Bey (Egypt) later appointed Ambassador in London, who won in 1931–32–33 and 1935–36–37. Norman F. Borrett of England won in 1946–47–48–49–50.

An artist's impression of some Harrovians playing the game they invented—squash rackets

Professional Championship The most wins in the Professional Championship is five, a record shared by J. St. G. Dear, M.B.E. (Great Britain) in 1935–36–37–38 and 1949, and Hashim Khan (Pakistan) in 1950–51–52–53–54.

Most international selections The record for international selection is held by D. M. Pratt with 50 for Ireland from 1956 to 1972. The record for England is 40 by J. G. A. Lyon from 1959 to 1968; O. L. Balfour (Scotland) with 45 between 1954 and 1968, and for Wales 44 by L. J. Verney between 1949 and 1965.

Longest span of internationals Mrs. Henry G. Macintosh (née Sheila Speight), the 1960 British Champion, played for England v. Wales in April 1949 and in Dec. 1971—a span of 22 years. Among men P. Harding-Edgar first played for Scotland in 1938 and last played 21 years later in 1959.

Longest championship match The longest recorded championship match was one of 2 hr 13 min in the final of the Open Championship of the British Isles at the Edgbaston-Priory Club, Birmingham in December 1969 when Jonah P. Barrington, M.B.E. (Ireland) beat Geoffrey B. Hunt (Australia) 9–7, 3–9, 3–9, 9–4, 9–4 with the last game lasting 37 min.

Most wins women The most wins in the Women's Squash Rackets Championship is 12 by Mrs. Heather McKay, M.B.E. (née Blundell) of Australia, 1961 to 1972.

Marathon record In squash marathons a rest interval of 1 min is allowed between games and 2 min between the 4th and 5th games with 5 min additional rest per hour. The rate of play must not exceed 11 games per hour. The longest recorded squash marathon (under these competition conditions) has been one of 60 hr 10 min by Dennis Glennon at Ndola Squash Club, Zambia on 1–4 Dec. 1972. He played 925 games of which he won 610, against various opponents. The

Geoffrey Hunt (Australia) (nearer the camera), three times World Champion, playing Jonah Barrington (Ireland), who, in 1969, took 2 hr 13 min to beat Hunt

longest single marathon by a pair is 54 hr 45 min by Nick Chapman and Derek Thorpe at the New University of Ulster, Coleraine on 28–31 Mar. 1973. The longest time achieved in Great Britain has been 50 hrs 3 min by Alec W. Jones and David L. Farbrother at the Worcester County S.R.C. on 18–20 Aug. 1972.

SURFING

Origins The traditional Polynesian sport of surfing in a canoe (ehorooe) was first recorded by Captain James Cook, R.N., F.R.S. (1728–79) on this third voyage at Tahiti in December 1771. Surfing on a board (Amo Amo iluna ka lau oka nalu) was first described ("most perilous and extraordinary . . . altogether astonishing and is scarcely to be credited") by Lt. (later Capt.) James King, R.N., F.R.S. in March 1779 at Kealakekua Bay, Hawaii Island. A surfer was first depicted by this voyage's official artist John Webber.

The sport was revived at Waikiki by 1900. Australia's first body surfing events were run by the Bondi Surf Bathers Lifesaving Club, which was formed in February 1906. Australia's most successful champion has been Bob Newbiggin, who won the senior title in 1939–40–45–46–47 and the senior Belt Race in 1940. Hollow boards came in in 1929 and the light plastic foam type in 1956.

Highest waves ridden Makaha Beach, Hawaii provides the reputedly highest consistently high waves often reaching the rideable limit of 30–35 ft 9–10 m. The highest wave ever ridden was the tsunami of "perhaps 50 ft 15 m", which struck

Minole, Hawaii on 3 April 1868, and was ridden to save his life by a Hawaiian named Holua.

Longest ride *Sea wave* About 4 to 6 times each year rideable surfing waves break in Matanchen Bay near San Blas, Nayarit, Mexico which makes rides of c. 5,700 ft 1 700 m possible.

World Champions World Championships were inaugurated in 1964 at Sydney, Australia. The first surfer to win two titles has been Joyce Hoffman (U.S.) in 1965 and 1966.

River bore The longest recorded rides on a river bore have been set on the Severn bore, England. In 1968 local residents reported a ride of 4 to 6 miles 6–9 km by Rodney Sumpter of Sussex. In September 1971 Mick Evans succeeded in making a run from Rea to Maisemore Weir a distance of 4 miles 6,4 km.

Skid Boarding The sport in which a 15 lb. 7 kg fibreglass coated plywood disc is substituted for a surfboard was introduced in 1967 on the coasts around Bournemouth, England. Speeds of 25 m.p.h. 40 km/h and distances of 85 yds 77 m have been achieved.

SWIMMING

Earliest references It is recorded that inter-school swimming contests in Japan were ordered by Imperial edict of Emperor Go-Yoozei as early as 1603. In Great Britain competitive swimming originated in London c. 1837, at which time there were five or more pools, the earliest, of which had been opened at St. George's Pier Head, Liverpool in 1828.

Largest pools The largest swimming pool in the world is the seawater Orthlieb Pool in Casablanca, Morocco. It is 480 m 1,547 ft long and 75 m 246 ft wide, and has an area of 3.6 ha 8.9 acres. The largest land-locked swimming pool with heated water was the Fleishhacker Pool on Sloat Boulevard, near Great Highway, San Francisco, California, U.S.A. It measures 1,000 × 150 ft *304,8 × 45,7 m* and up to 14 ft *4,26 m* deep and contains 7,500,000 U.S. gallons *28 390 hectolitres* of heated water. The world's largest competition pool is that at Osaka, Japan, which accommodates 25,000 spectators. The largest in the United Kingdom is the Empire Pool, Cardiff, completed in 1958 with a seating capacity of 1,722.

Fastest swimmer Excluding relay stages with their anticipatory starts, the highest speed reached by a swimmer is 4.89 m.p.h.

7,86 km/h by Stephen Edward Clark (U.S.A.), who recorded 20.9 sec for a heat of 50 yds *45,72 m* in a 25 yds *22,86 m* pool at Yale University, New Haven, Connecticut, U.S.A., on 26 March 1964. Spitz's 100 m record of 51.22 sec required an average of 4.367 m.p.h. *7,028 km/h*.

Most world records Men, 32, Arne Borg (Sweden) (b. 1901), 1921–1929. Women, 42, Ragnhild Hveger (Denmark) (b. 10 Dec. 1920), 1936–1942.

WORLD RECORDS
(at distances recognized by the *Fédération Internationale de Natation Amateur*)

MEN

Distance	Time	Name and Nationality	Place	Date
FREESTYLE	min sec			
100 metres	51.22	Mark Andrew Spitz (U.S.A.)	Munich, W. Germany	3 Sept. 1972
200 metres	1:52.78	Mark Andrew Spitz (U.S.A.)	Munich, W. Germany	29 Aug. 1972
400 metres	4:00.11	Kurt Krumpholz (U.S.A.)	Chicago, Illinois, U.S.A.	4 Aug. 1972
800 metres	8:17.6	Stephen Holland (Australia)	Brisbane, Queensland, Australia	5 Aug. 1973
1,500 metres	15:37.8	Stephen Holland (Australia)	Brisbane, Queensland, Australia	5 Aug. 1973
BREASTSTROKE				
100 metres	1:04.94	Nobutaka Taguchi (Japan)	Munich, W. Germany	30 Aug. 1972
200 metres	2:21.55	John Hencken (U.S.A.)	Munich, W. Germany	2 Sept. 1972
BUTTERFLY STROKE				
100 metres	54.27	Mark Andrew Spitz (U.S.A.)	Munich, W. Germany	31 Aug. 1972
200 metres	2:00.70	Mark Andrew Spitz (U.S.A.)	Munich, W. Germany	28 Aug. 1972
BACKSTROKE				
100 metres	56.3	Roland Matthes (E. Germany)	Leipzig, E. Germany	9 Apr. 1972
100 metres	56.30†	Roland Matthes (E. Germany)	Munich, W. Germany	4 Sept. 1972
200 metres	2:02.8	Roland Matthes (E. Germany)	Leipzig, E. Germany	10 July 1972
200 metres	2:02.82	Roland Matthes (E. Germany)	Munich, W. Germany	2 Sept. 1972
INDIVIDUAL MEDLEY				
200 metres	2:07.17	Gunnar Larsson (Sweden)	Munich, W. Germany	3 Sept. 1972
400 metres	4:30.81	Gary Hall (U.S.A.)	Chicago, Illinois, U.S.A.	3 Aug. 1972
FREE STYLE RELAYS				
4 × 100 metres	3:26.42	United States (David H. Edgar, John Murphy, Jerry Heidenreich, Mark Andrew Spitz)	Munich, W. Germany	28 Aug. 1972
4 × 200 metres	7:35.78	United States (John Kinsella, Frederick Tyler, Steven Genter, Mark Andrew Spitz)	Munich, W. Germany	31 Aug. 1972
MEDLEY RELAY				
4 × 100 metres	3:48.16	United States (Michael E. Stamm, Thomas E. Bruce, Mark Andrew Spitz, Jerry Heidenreich)	Munich, W. Germany	4 Sept. 1972

† *Achieved in a Medley Relay.*

WOMEN

Distance	Time	Name and Nationality	Place	Date
FREESTYLE	min sec			
100 metres	58.12	Kornellia Ender (E. Germany)	Utrecht, Netherlands	18 Aug. 1973
200 metres	2:03.56	Shane Elizabeth Gould (Australia)	Munich, W. Germany	1 Sept. 1972
400 metres	4:19.04	Shane Elizabeth Gould (Australia)	Munich, W. Germany	30 Aug. 1972
800 metres	8:53.68	Keena Rothhammer (U.S.A.)	Munich, W. Germany	3 Sept. 1972
1,500 metres	16:56.9*	Shane Elizabeth Gould (Australia)	Adelaide, Australia	11 Feb. 1973
BREASTSTROKE				
100 metres	1:13.58	Catherine Carr (U.S.A.)	Munich, W. Germany	2 Sept. 1972
200 metres	2:38.5	Catie Ball (U.S.A.)	Los Angeles, California	26 Aug. 1972
BUTTERFLY STROKE				
100 metres	1:03.05*	Kornellia Ender (E. Germany)	East Berlin, E. Germany	14 April 1973
200 metres	2:15.57	Karen Patricia Moe (U.S.A.)	Munich, W. Germany	4 Sept. 1972
BACKSTROKE				
100 metres	1:05.39	Ulriche Richter (E. Germany)	Utrecht, Netherlands	18 Aug. 1973
200 metres	2:19.19	Melissa Belote (U.S.A.)	Munich, W. Germany	4 Sept. 1972
INDIVIDUAL MEDLEY				
200 metres	2:23.01*	Kornellia Ender (E. Germany)	East Berlin, E. Germany	13 April 1973
400 metres	5:01.10	Angela Franke (E. Germany)	Utrecht, Netherlands	19 Aug. 1973
FREESTYLE RELAY				
4 × 100 metres	3:55.19	United States (Sandra Neilson, Jennifer Jo Kemp, Jane Louise Barkman, Shirley Babashoff)	Munich, W. Germany	30 Aug. 1972
MEDLEY RELAY				
4 × 100 metres	4:20.75	United States (Melissa Belote, Catherine Carr, Deena Diane Dearduff, Sandra Neilson)	Munich, W. Germany	3 Sept. 1972

Those marked with an asterisk are awaiting ratification.
Only performances set up in 50 m or 55 yds baths are recognized as World Records. F.N.A. no longer recognize any records made for distances over non-metric distances.

BRITISH NATIONAL RECORDS
as ratified by the Amateur Swimming Association
(short course and record equalling performances are *not* recognised)

MEN

Distance	Time	Name	Place	Date
FREESTYLE	min sec			
100 metres	53.4	Robert Bilsland McGregor, M.B.E.	Tokyo, Japan	29 Aug. 1967
200 metres	1:56.68	Brian Brinkley	Coventry, Warwickshire	3 Aug. 1973
400 metres	4:06.44	Brian Brinkley	Munich, West German	1 Sept. 1972
800 metres	8:42.6	Brian Brinkley	Leeds, Yorkshire	28 May 1972
1,500 metres	16:39.6	Brian Brinkley	Crystal Palace, London	15 July 1972
BREAST STROKE				
100 metres	1:06.25	David Andrew Wilkie	Munich, West Germany	29 Aug. 1972
200 metres	2:23.67	David Andrew Wilkie	Munich, West Germany	2 Sept. 1972

BUTTERFLY

100 metres	58.13	John Maurice Mills	Munich, West Germany	30 Aug. 1972
200 metres	2:05.21*	Brian Brinkley	Coventry, Warwickshire	3 Aug. 1973

BACK STROKE

100 metres	1:00.3*	Colin Cunningham	Crystal Palace, London	15 July 1972
200 metres	2:08.6*	Colin Cunningham	East Berlin	19 Aug. 1973

INDIVIDUAL MEDLEY

200 metres	2:10.0	David Andrew Wilkie	Crystal Palace, London	23 Apr. 1973
400 metres	4:36.29*	Brian Brinkley	Coventry, Warwickshire	4 Aug. 1973

WOMEN

FREESTYLE

100 metres	1:00.5	Alexandra Elizabeth Jackson	Mexico City, Mexico	18 Oct. 1968
200 metres	2:11.19*	Lesley Allardice	Coventry, Warwickshire	3 Aug. 1973
400 metres	4:35.18*	Susan Stuart Edmondson	Leeds, Yorkshire	2 June 1973
800 metres	9:24.8	June Margaret Green	Crystal Palace, London	23 Apr. 1973
1,500 metres	(19:40.0)	This standard time not yet achieved		

BREAST STROKE

100 metres	1:16.53	Dorothy Elizabeth Harrison	Munich, West Germany	1 Sept. 1972
200 metres	2:44.2	Mrs. Pat Catherine Beaven	Edinburgh, Scotland	28 July 1972

BUTTERFLY

100 metres	1:06.26*	Jo Atkinson	Coventry, Warwickshire	4 Aug. 1973
200 metres	2:23.6	Jean Anne Jeavons	Crystal Palace, London	14 July 1972

BACK STROKE

100 metres	1:08.61*	Margaret Mary Kelly	Leeds, Yorkshire	2 June 1973
200 metres	2:26.2	Wendy Burrell	Barcelona, Spain	9 Sept. 1970

INDIVIDUAL MEDLEY

200 metres	2:29.5	Shelagh Hudson Ratcliffe	Kecskemet, Hungary	4 Apr. 1970
400 metres	5:15.4	Shelagh Hudson Ratcliffe	Los Angeles, California, U.S.A.	18 Aug. 1971

* Awaiting ratification.

OLYMPIC SWIMMING RECORDS

Most Olympic titles The greatest number of Olympic gold medals won is nine by Mark Andrew Spitz (U.S.A.) (b. 10 Feb. 1950):—

100 metres freestyle	1972
200 metres freestyle	1972
100 metres butterfly	1972
200 metres butterfly	1972
4 × 100 metres freestyle relay	1968 and 1972
4 × 200 metres freestyle relay	1968 and 1972
4 × 100 metres medley relay	1972

All but one of these performances (the 4 × 200 m relay of 1968) were also world records.

Women The record number of gold medals won by a woman is four shared by Mrs. Patricia McCormick (née Keller) (U.S.A.) (b. 12 May 1930) with the High and Springboard Diving double in 1952 and 1956 (also the female record for individual golds) and by Dawn Fraser O.B.E. (now Mrs Gary Ware) (Australia) (b. 4 Sept. 1937) with the 100 metres freestyle (1956–60–64) and the 4 × 100 metres freestyle relay (1956).

British The record number of gold medals won by a British swimmer (excluding Water Polo *q.v.*) is four by Henry Taylor (b. 17 March 1885 d. 1951) with the 400 metres freestyle (1908), 1,500 metres freestyle (1906 and 1908) and 4 × 200 metres relay (1908). None of the seven British women who have won a gold medal, won a second title.

Most Olympic medals The most medals won is 11 by Spitz, who in addition to his nine golds (see above), won a silver (100 m butterfly) and a bronze (100 m freestyle) both in 1968.

Women The most medals won by a woman is eight by Dawn Fraser, who in addition to her four golds (see above) won four silvers (400 metres freestyle 1956, 4 × 100 metres freestyle relay 1960 and 1964, 4 × 100 metres medley relay 1960).

British The British record is eight by Taylor who in addition to his four golds (see above) won a silver (400 m freestyle 1906) and three bronzes (4 × 200 m freestyle relay 1906, 1912, 1920). The most medals by a British woman is four by Margaret Joyce Cooper (now Mrs John Badcock) (b. 18 Apr. 1909) with one silver (4 × 100 m freestyle relay 1928) and three bronze (100 m freestyle 1928, 100 m backstroke 1928, 4 × 100 m freestyle relay 1932).

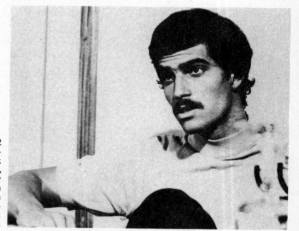

The 1972 multiple champion Mark Spitz (U.S.A.), who uniquely won seven gold medals in a single Olympic Games

Most individual gold medals The record number of individual gold medals won is four by Charles M. Daniels (U.S.A.) (b. 12 July 1884) (100 m freestyle 1906 and 1908, 220 yds freestyle 1904, 440 yds freestyle 1904); Roland Matthes (E. Germany) (b. 17 Nov. 1950) with 100 m and 200 m backstroke 1968 and 1972 and Spitz (see above). The most individual golds by a British swimmer is three by Taylor (see above).

Most difficult dives Those with the highest tariff (degree of difficulty 3.0) are the "3½ forward somersault in tuck position from the one metre board; the backward 2½ somersault piked; the reverse 2½ piked and the forward 3½ piked from the 10 m board". Joaquin Capilla of Mexico has performed a 4½ somersaults dive from a 10 m board, but this is not on the international tariff.

LONG DISTANCE SWIMMING

Longest Distance Ocean Swim The longest recorded ocean swim is one of 90¾ miles *146,0 km* by Walter Poenisch (U.S.A.) in the Florida Straits (in a shark cage) in 21 hrs 18 min on 27–28 June 1972.

A unique achievement in long distance swimming was established in 1966 by the cross-Channel swimmer Mihir Sen of Calcutta, India. These were the Palk Strait from India to Ceylon (in 25 hrs 36 min on 5–6 April); the Straits of Gibraltar (Europe to Africa in 8 hrs 1 min on 24 August); the Dardanelles (Gallipoli, Europe to Sedulbahir, Asia Minor in 13 hrs 55 min on 12 September) and the entire length of the Panama Canal in 34 hrs 15 min on 29–31 October. He had earlier swum the English Channel in 14 hrs 45 min on 27 Sept. 1958.

CHANNEL SWIMMING

Earliest Man The first man to swim across the English Channel (without a life jacket) was the Merchant Navy captain Matthew Webb (1848–83), who swam breaststroke from Dover, England, to Cap Gris-Nez, France, in 21 hrs 45 min from 12.56 p.m. to 10.41 a.m., 24–25 Aug. 1875. He swam an estimated 38 miles *61 km* to make the 21-mile *33 km* crossing. Paul Boyton (U.S.A.) had swum from Cap Gris-Nez to the South Foreland in his patent life-saving suit in 23 hrs 30 min on 28–29 May 1875. There is good evidence that Jean-Marie Saletti, a French soldier, escaped from a British prison hulk off Dover by swimming to Boulogne in July or August 1815. The first crossing from France to England was made by Enrique Tiraboschi, a wealthy Italian living in Argentina, who crossed in 16 hrs 33 min on 11 Aug. 1923, to win the *Daily Sketch* prize of £1,000.

Woman The first woman to succeed was Gertrude Ederle (U.S.A.) who swam from Cap Gris-Nez, France to Dover, England on 6 Aug. 1926, in the then overall record of 14 hrs 39 min. The first woman to swim from England to France was Florence Chadwick of California, U.S.A., in 16 hrs 19 min on 11 Sept. 1951. She repeated this on 4 Sept. 1953 and 12 Oct. 1955. The first Englishwoman to succeed was Ivy Gill on 14 Oct. 1927—the latest ever date in the year for any conquest.

Fastest The official Channel Swimming Association record is 9 hrs 36 min by Lynne Cox, 16 (U.S.A.) from England to France on 10 Aug. 1973. This beat by 8 min the fastest male time set by Richard David Hart, 26 (U.S.A.) on 21 Aug. 1972. The fastest crossing ever claimed is one of 9 hrs 35 min by Barry Watson, aged 25, of Bingley, Yorkshire, from Cap Gris-Nez, France, to St. Margaret's Bay, near Dover, on 15–16 Aug. 1964 but this is recognized at 9 hrs 47 min by the Association. The fastest crossing by a relay team is one of 9 hrs 29 min by Radcliffe Swimming Club of Lancashire, from Cap Gris-Nez to Walmer on 13 June 1966.

Slowest The slowest crossing was the third ever made, when Henry Sullivan (U.S.A.) swam from England to France in 26 hr 50 min on 5–6 Aug. 1923.

Earliest and latest The earliest date in the year on which the Channel has been swum is 6 June by Dorothy Perkins (England) aged 19, in 1961, and the latest is 14 October by Ivy Gill (England) in 1927. Both swims were from France to England.

Youngest The youngest conqueror is Leonore Modell of Sacramento, California, U.S.A., who swam from Cap Gris-Nez to near Dover in 15 hrs 33 min on 3 Sept. 1964, when aged 14 yrs 5 months. The youngest relay team to cross are from the Royal Tunbridge Wells Monson S.C. from England to France on 4 Sept. 1968. The team coached by John Wrapson, had an average age of 12 years 4 months and were David Young, Richard Field, Kim Taylor, Peter Chapman, Stephen Underdown and Peter Burns.

Oldest The oldest swimmer to swim the Channel has been William E. (Ned) Barnie, aged 55, when he swam from France to England in 15 hrs 1 min on 16 Aug. 1951.

Double crossing First Antonio Abertondo (b. Buenos Aires, Argentina), aged 42, swam from England to France in 18 hrs 50 min (8.35 a.m. on 20 Sept. to 3.25 a.m. on 21 Sept. 1961) and after about 4 min rest returned to England in 24 hrs 16 min, landing at St. Margaret's Bay at 3.45 a.m. on 22 Sept. 1961, to complete the first "double crossing" in 43 hrs 10 min. Kevin Murphy, 21, completed the first double crossing by a Briton in 35 hrs 10 min on 6 Aug. 1970. The first swimmer to achieve a crossing both ways was Edward H. Temme (b. 1904) on 5 Aug. 1927 and 19 Aug. 1934.

Miss Gertrude Ederle (U.S.A.), who in 1926 became the first woman to swim the English Channel. She swam from France to England in 14 hr 39 min

Fastest The fastest double crossing, and the second to be achieved, was one of 30 hrs 3 min by Edward (Ted) Erikson, aged 37, a physiochemist from Chicago, Illinois, U.S.A. He left St. Margaret's Bay, near Dover, at 8.20 p.m. on 19 Sept. 1965 and landed at a beach about a mile *1,6 km* west of Calais, after a swim of 14 hrs 15 min. After a rest of about 10 min he returned and landed at South Foreland Point, east of Dover, at 2.23 a.m. on 21 Sept. 1965.

Most conquests Brojan Das (Pakistan) swam the Channel six times in 1958–61. Greta Andersen-Sonnichsen (U.S.A.) also swam the Channel five times in the period 1957–1965.

Underwater The first underwater cross-Channel swim was achieved by Fred Baldasare (U.S.A.), aged 38, who completed the distance from France to England with Scuba in 18 hrs 1 min on 11 July 1962. Simon Paterson, aged 20, a frogman from Egham, Surrey, travelled underwater from France to England with an air hose attached to his pilot boat in 14 hrs 50 min on 28 July 1962.

Irish Channel The swimming of the 22 mile *35 km* wide Irish Channel from Donaghadee, Northern Ireland to Portpatrick, Scotland was first accomplished by Tom Blower of Nottingham in 15 hrs 26 min in 1947 and repeated by Kevin Murphy in 1970 and 1971.

Bristol Channel The first person to achieve a double crossing of the Bristol Channel is Jenny James of Pontypridd, South Wales, who swam from Sully, Glamorganshire to Weston-super-Mare, Somerset in 10 hrs 2 min on 18 Sept. 1949 and the return course in 8 hrs 21 min on 9 July 1950.

Solent The fastest time for swimming the Solent (Southsea to Ryde, Isle of Wight) has been 1 hr 13 min 3 sec by Keith Richards (Southsea) in 1970. The greatest number of crossings has been 19 single and 2 non-stop double crossings by Richard Glynn of Cheltenham.

Loch Ness The first person to swim the length of Great Britain's longest lake, the 22¾ mile *36,61 km* long Loch Ness, was Brenda Sherratt of West Bollington, Cheshire, aged 18, in 31 hrs 27 min on 26–27 July 1966.

Round the Isle of Wight Kevin Murphy of Harrow achieved the first circumnavigation of the Isle of Wight covering the 55 miles *88 km* in 26 hrs 51 min on 22–24 Sept. 1971.

Treading water The duration record for treading water (vertical posture without touching the lane markers in an 8 ft *2,43 m* square) is 24 hrs by David Bloch at Arlington, Nebraska, U.S.A., on 17–18 Aug. 1972.

Ice swimming Jenny Kammersgård, 53 swam 200 m *218 yds* in 7 min 13 sec in Denmark on 19 Feb. 1972 in water at a temperature of 1.5°C (34.7°F).

Most dangerous One of the most dangerous swims on record was the unique crossing of the Potoro River in Guiana just above the 741 ft *226 m* high Kaieteur Falls by Private Robert Howatt (the Black Watch) on 17 April 1955. The river is 464 ft *141 m* wide at the lip of the falls.

Relays The longest recorded mileage in a 24 hr swim relay (team of 5) is 63 miles 487 yds *101,833 km* by a relay team from the Paarl Amateur Swimming Club, South Africa, on 5–6 Jan. 1970. The fastest time recorded for 100 miles *160 km* by a team of 20 swimmers is 31 hrs 35 min 21.3 sec by Piedmont Swim Club, California, U.S.A., on 3–4 Sept. 1970.

Marathon relays In Buttermere, Westmorland, England on 18–28 July 1968 six boys, aged 13 to 15, covered 300 miles *482 km* in 230 hrs 39 min.

Underground swimming The longest recorded underground swim is one of 3,402 yds *3 110 m* in 87 min by David Stanley Gale through the Dudley Old Canal Tunnel, Worcestershire, in August 1967.

Sponsored swimming The greatest amount of money raised in a sponsored swim is £12,645.13 by the Lions Club of Jersey with 210 swimmers covering 352.6 miles *567,45 km* in 35 hrs at the Fort Regent Pool, St. Helier, Jersey on 23–26 Feb. 1973.

Underwater swimming Vladimir Kon covered 100 m *109 yds* underwater with flippers in 40.6 sec at Chelyabinsk, U.S.S.R. on 10 Mar. 1972. Nina Avdegeva (U.S.S.R.) recorded 48.2 sec at the same meeting. A team of eight from the Furness Sub-Aqua Club swam the 10½ mile *16,8 km* length of Lake Windermere from Lakeside Hotel Pier to Ambleside public beach in 10 hrs 0 min 58 sec on 18 July 1971. A Champagne bottle was used as the relay baton by the team which claimed a record for self-navigation.

TABLE TENNIS

Earliest reference The earliest evidence relating to a game resembling table tennis has been found in the catalogues of London sports goods manufacturers in the 1880s. The old Ping Pong Association was formed in 1902 but the game proved only a temporary craze until resuscitated in 1921. The English Table Tennis Association was formed on 24 April 1927.

The highest total of English men's titles (instituted 1921) is 20 by G. Viktor Barna (1912–72). The women's record is 18 by Diane Rowe (b. 14 April 1933), now Mrs. Eberhard Scholer. Her twin Rosalind (now Mrs. Cornett) has won 9 (two in singles).

Youngest international The youngest ever international (probably in any sport) was Joy Foster, aged 8, the 1958 Jamaican singles and mixed doubles champion.

Longest rally In the 1936 Swaythling Cup match in Prague between Alex Ehrlich (Poland) and Paneth Farcas (Romania)

Miss Diane Rowe (G.B.) (left) who won 18 English women's Table Tennis titles including six doubles wins with her twin sister Rosalind. Together they won two World Doubles titles

MOST WINS IN WORLD CHAMPIONSHIPS Instituted (1926–27)

Event	Name and Nationality	Times	Years
Men's Singles (St. Bride's Vase)	G. Viktor Barna (Hungary)	5	1930, 1932–33–34–35
Women's Singles (G. Geist Prize)	Angelica Rozeanu (Romania)	6	1950–51–52–53–54–55
Men's Doubles	G. Viktor Barna (Hungary) with two different partners	8	1929–35, 1939
Women's Doubles	Maria Mednyanszky (Hungary) with three different partners	7	1928, 1930–31–32–33–34–35
Mixed Doubles (Men)	Ferenc Sido (Hungary) with two different partners	4	1949–50, 1952–53
(Women)	Maria Mednyanszky (Hungary) with three different partners	6	1927–28, 1930–31, 1933–34

G. Viktor Barna gained a personal total of 15 world titles, while 18 have been won by Miss Maria Mednyanszky.
Note: With the staging of championships biennially the breaking of the above records would now be virtually impossible.

MOST TEAM TITLES

Event	Team	Times	Years
Men's Team (Swaythling Cup)	Hungary	11	1927–31, 1933–35, 1938, 1949, 1952
Women's Team (Marcel Corbillon Cup)	Japan	8	1952, 1954, 1957, 1959, 1961, 1963, 1967, 1971

MOST WINS IN ENGLISH OPEN CHAMPIONSHIPS (Instituted 1921)

Event	Name and Nationality	Times	Years
Men's Singles	Richard Bergmann (Austria, then G.B.)	6	1939–40, 1948, 1950, 1952, 1954
Women's Singles	Mrs. M. Alexandru (Romania)	5	1963–64, 1970–71–72
Men's Doubles	G. Viktor Barna (Hungary, then G.B.) with five different partners	7	1931, 1933–34–35, 1938–39, 1949
Women's Doubles	Miss Diane Rowe (G.B.) with four different partners	12	1950–56, 1960, 1962–65
Mixed Doubles (Men)	G. Viktor Barna (Hungary, then G.B.) with four different partners	8	1933–36, 1938, 1940, 1951, 1953
(Women)	Miss Diane Rowe (G.B.) (now Scholer) with three different partners	4	1952, 1954, 1956, 1960, 1969

the opening rally lasted 2 hrs 12 min. On 14 Apr. 1973 Nick Krajancie and Graham Lassen staged a 2 hrs 31 min rally in Auckland, New Zealand.

Marathon records In the Swaythling Cup final match between Austria and Romania in Prague, Czechoslovakia, in 1936, the play lasted for 25 or 26 hours, spread over three nights.

The longest recorded time for a marathon singles match by two players is 73 hrs 10 min by Peter Broad and Gary Stevenson of Maranui S.L.S.C. at Lyall Bay, New Zealand on 2–5 June 1973. On 20–23 Dec. 1971 Craig Harris, 16, played 77 hrs 7 min against a series of opponents in Davis, California, U.S.A.

The longest recorded marathon by 4 players maintaining continuous singles is 600 hours (25 days) by 4 players from the First Presbyterian Church, Belleville, Illinois on 31 July to 25 Aug. 1972. The longest doubles marathon by 4 players is 42 hrs 1 min by four members of the Chatham Technical High School for Boys, Kent on 27–29 June 1973.

Highest speed No conclusive measurements have been published, but Chuang Tse-tung (China) the world champion of 1961–63–65, has probably smashed the 2.5 g ball at a speed of more than 60 m.p.h.

TENNIS (REAL OR ROYAL)

Origins The game originated in French monasteries c. 1050.

Oldest court The oldest of the 17 surviving Tennis Courts in the British Isles is the Royal Tennis Court at Hampton Court Palace, which was built by order of King Henry VIII in 1529–30 and rebuilt by order of Charles II in 1660. The oldest court in the world is one built in Paris in 1496. There are estimated to be 3,000 players and 29 courts in the world.

World titles The first recorded World Tennis Champion was Clerge (France) c. 1740. Pierre Etchebaster (b. 1893) won the title at Prince's, Paris, in May 1928, last defended it in New York (winning 7–1) in December 1949 and retired undefeated in 1955, after 27 years. Etchebaster, a Basque, also holds the record for the greatest number of successful defences of his title with six.

British titles The Amateur Championship of the British Isles (instituted 1780) has been won 13 times by Edgar M. Baerlein (b. 1879) (1912 to 1930). The greatest number of international appearances has been 18 by Sir Clarance Napier Bruce, G.B.E., 3rd Baron Aberdare (1885–1957).

Pierre Etchebaster (France), whose 27 year reign as world champion at real tennis (1928–1955) did not end until he was over 60

TIDDLYWINKS

Origins This game was only espoused by adults in 1955 when Cambridge University issued a challenge to Oxford.

Guinness Trophy England has remained unbeaten against Scotland, Ireland and Wales since the Trophy's inception on 7 May 1960. The closest result has been their 59½–52½ win over Wales at Warwick on 7 April 1968.

Accuracy The lowest number of shots taken to pot 12 winks from 3 ft *91 cm* is 23, first achieved by M. Brogden (Hull University) on 18 Oct. 1962. This record has been many times equalled since including 3 occasions by

Alan Dean, Secretary of the English Tiddleywink Association and the unbeaten English Singles Champion since the championship was inaugurated in 1970.

Speed The record for potting 24 winks from 18 in *45 cm* is 21.8 sec by Stephen Williams (Altrincham Grammar School) in May 1966.

Marathon Allen R. Astles (University of Wales) potted 10,000 winks in 3 hours 51 min 46 sec at Aberystwyth, Cardiganshire in February 1966. The most protracted game on record is one of 170 hrs by six players of Quinton Kynaston School, St. John's Wood, London, on 1–8 Jan. 1973.

TRACK AND FIELD ATHLETICS

Earliest references Track and field athletics date from the ancient Olympic Games. The earliest accurately known Olympiad dates from 21 or 22 July 776 B.C., at which celebration Coroebus won the foot race. The oldest surviving measurements are a long jump of 7,05 m *23 ft 1½ in* by Chionis of Sparta in c. 656 B.C. and a discus throw of 100 cubits by Protesilaus.

Fastest runner Robert Lee Hayes (b. 20 Dec. 1942) of Jacksonville, Florida, U.S.A., was timed at the 60 (6.0 sec) and 75 yds (7.1 sec) marks in a 100 yard event at St. Louis,

Missouri, on 21 June 1963, which indicates a speed of 27.89 m.p.h. *44,88 km/h* Wyomia Tyus (b. Griffin, Georgia, U.S.A., 29 Aug. 1945) was timed at 23.78 m.p.h. *38,27 km/h* in Kiev, U.S.S.R. on 31 July 1965.

Highest jumper There are several reported instances of high jumpers exceeding the official world record height of 7 ft 6½ in *2,30 m*. The earliest of these came from unsubstantiated reports of Tutsi tribesmen in Central Africa (see page 18) clearing up to 8 ft 2½ in *2,50 m* definitely however, from inclined take-offs. The greatest height cleared above an athlete's own head is 17⅝ in *44,76 cm* achieved by Ni Chih-chin of China when clearing 2.29 m *7 ft 6⅛ in* in an exhibition at Changsha, Hunan on 8 Nov. 1970. He stands 6 ft 0½ in *1,84 m* tall and was born on 14 April 1942. The greatest height cleared by a woman above her own head is 19 cm *7.48 in* by Yordanka Blagoeva (Bulgaria) who stands 1,75 m *5 ft 8.9 in*, when she jumped 1,94 m *6 ft 4½ in* at Zagreb, Yugoslavia on 24 Sept. 1972.

Most Olympic titles The most Olympic gold medals won is ten (an absolute Olympic record) by Ray C. Ewry (U.S.A.) (b. 14 Oct. 1873 d. 29 Sept. 1937) with:

Standing High Jump	1900, 1904, 1906, 1908
Standing Long Jump	1900, 1904, 1906, 1908
Standing Triple Jump	1900, 1904

Women The most gold medals won by a woman is four shared by Francina E. Blankers-Koen (Netherlands) (b. 26 April 1918) with (100 m, 200 m, 80 m hurdles and 4 × 100 m relay, 1948) and Betty Cuthbert (Australia) (b. 20 April 1938) with 100 m, 200 m, 4 × 100 m relay, 1956 and 400 m, 1964.

British The most gold medals won by a British athlete (excluding Tug of War and Walking *qq.v.*) is two by: Charles Bennett (1,500 m and 5,000 m team, 1900); Alfred Tysoe (800 m and 5,000 m team, 1900); John Rimmer (4,000 m steeplechase and 5,000 m team, 1900) Albert G. Hill (b. 24 March 1889) 800 m and 1,500 m, 1920 and Douglas Gordon Arthur Lowe (b. 7 Aug. 1902) 800 m 1924 and 1928.

Most Olympic medals The most medals won is 12 (9 gold and 3 silver) by Paavo Johannes Nurmi (Finland) (b. 13 June 1897):

1920 Gold: 10,000 m; Cross Country, Individual and Team; silver: 5,000 m.

1924 Gold: 1,500 m; 5,000 m; 3,000 m Team; Cross Country, Individual and Team.

1928 Gold: 10,000 m; silver: 5,000 m; 3,000 m steeplechase.

Within eight years (1920–28) Paavo Nurmi (Finland) won nine Olympic gold medals—six individual and three team—including five at the Paris Games of 1924

WORLD RECORDS—MEN

The complete list of World Records for the 54 scheduled men's events (excluding the 6 walking records, see under WALKING) passed by the International Amateur Athletic Federation as at July 1973. *Denotes awaiting ratification.

RUNNING

Event	Min sec	Name and Nationality	Place	Date
100 yards	9.1	Robert Lee Hayes (U.S.A.)	St. Louis, Missouri, U.S.A.	21 June 1963
	9.1	Harry Winston Jerome (Canada)	Edmonton, Alberta, Canada	15 July 1966
	9.1	James Ray Hines (U.S.A.)	Houston, Texas, U.S.A.	13 May 1967
	9.1	Charles Edward Greene (U.S.A.)	Provo, Utah, U.S.A.	15 June 1967
	9.1	John Wesley Carlos (U.S.A.)	Fresno, California, U.S.A.	10 May 1969
	9.1*	Steve Williams (U.S.A.)	Fresno, California, U.S.A.	12 May 1972
220 yards (straight)	19.5	Tommie C. Smith (U.S.A.)	San Jose, California, U.S.A.	7 May 1966
220 yards (turn)	20.0	Tommie C. Smith (U.S.A.)	Sacramento, California, U.S.A.	11 June 1966
440 yards	44.5	John Smith (U.S.A.)	Eugene, Oregon, U.S.A.	26 June 1971
880 yards	1:44.6*	Richard Wohlhuter (U.S.A.)	Los Angeles, U.S.A.	27 May 1973
1 mile	3:51.1	James Ronald Ryun (U.S.A.)	Bakersfield, California, U.S.A.	23 June 1967
2 miles	8:14.0	Lasse Viren (Finland)	Stockholm, Sweden	14 Aug. 1972
3 miles	12:47.8	Emiel Puttemans (Belgium)	Brussels, Belgium	20 Sept. 1972
6 miles	26:47.0	Ronald William Clarke, M.B.E. (Australia)	Oslo, Norway	14 July 1965
10 miles	46:04.2	Willy Polleunis (Belgium)	Brussels, Belgium	20 Sept. 1972
15 miles	1 hr 12:48.2	Ronald Hill (United Kingdom)	Bolton, Lancashire, England	21 July 1965
100 metres	9.9	James Ray Hines (U.S.A.)	Sacramento, California, U.S.A.	20 June 1968
	9.9	Ronald Ray Smith (U.S.A.)	Sacramento, California, U.S.A.	20 June 1968
	9.9	Charles Edward Greene (U.S.A.)	Sacramento, California, U.S.A.	20 June 1968
	9.9	James Ray Hines (U.S.A.)	Mexico City, Mexico	14 Oct. 1968
	9.9	Eddie Hart (U.S.A.)	Eugene, Oregon, U.S.A.	1 July 1972
	9.9	Reynaud Robinson (U.S.A.)	Eugene, Oregon, U.S.A.	1 July 1972
200 metres (straight)	19.5	Tommie C. Smith (U.S.A.)	San Jose, California, U.S.A.	7 May 1966
200 metres (turn)	19.8	Tommie C. Smith (U.S.A.)	Mexico City, Mexico	16 Oct. 1968
	19.8	Donald O'Riley Quarrie (Jamaica)	Cali, Colombia	3 Aug. 1971
400 metres	43.8	Lee Edward Evans (U.S.A.)	Mexico City, Mexico	18 Oct. 1968
800 metres	1:43.7*	Marcello Fiasconaro (Italy)	Milan, Italy	27 June 1973
1,000 metres	2:16.0*	Daniel Malan (South Africa)	Munich, West Germany	24 June 1973
1,500 metres	3:33.1	James Ronald Ryun (U.S.A.)	Los Angeles, California, U.S.A.	8 July 1967
2,000 metres	4:56.2	Michel Jazy (France)	St. Maur des Fosses, France	12 Oct. 1966
3,000 metres	7:37.6	Emiel Puttemans (Belgium)	Aarhus, Denmark	14 Sept. 1972
5,000 metres	13:13.0	Emiel Puttemans (Belgium)	Brussels, Belgium	20 Sept. 1972
10,000 metres	27:31.0*	David Colin Bedford (G.B. & N.I.)	London, England	13 July 1973
20,000 metres	57:44.4	Gaston Roelants (Belgium)	Brussels, Belgium	20 Sept. 1972
25,000 metres	1 hr 15:22.6	Ronald Hill (United Kingdom)	Bolton, Lancashire, England	21 July 1965
30,000 metres	1 hr 31:30.4	James Noel Carroll Alder (G.B. & N.I.)	London (Crystal Palace)	5 Sept. 1970
1 hour	12 miles 1,609 yd 20 784 m	Gaston Roelants (Belgium)	Brussels, Belgium	20 Sept. 1972

HURDLING

Event	Min sec	Name and Nationality	Place	Date
120 yards (3′ 6″ [*106.4 cm*])	13.0	Rodney Milburn (U.S.A.)	Eugene, Oregon, U.S.A.	25 June 1971
	13.0*	Rodney Milburn (U.S.A.)	Eugene, Oregon, U.S.A.	20 June 1973
220 yards (2′ 6″ [*75.9 cm*]) (straight)	21.9	Donald Augustus Styron (U.S.A.)	Baton Rouge, Louisiana, U.S.A.	2 April 1960
440 yards (3′ 0″ [*91.1 cm*])	48.8	Ralph Mann (U.S.A.)	Des Moines, Iowa, U.S.A.	20 June 1970
110 metres (3′ 6″)	13.1*	Rodney Milburn (U.S.A.)	Zurich, Switzerland	6 July 1973
	13.1*	Rodney Milburn (U.S.A.)	Sienna, Italy	21 July 1973
200 metres (2′ 6″) (straight)	21.9	Donald Augustus Styron (U.S.A.)	Baton Rouge, Louisiana, U.S.A.	2 April 1960
200 metres (2′ 6″) (turn)	22.5	Karl Martin Lauer (West Germany)	Zürich, Switzerland	7 July 1959
	22.5	Glen Ashby Davis (U.S.A.)	Bern, Switzerland	20 Aug. 1960
400 metres (3′ 0″)	47.8	John Akii-Bua (Uganda)	Munich, West Germany	2 Sept. 1972
3,000 metres Steeplechase	8:14.0*	Ben Wabura Jipcho (Kenya)	Helsinki, Finland	27 June 1973

THE MARATHON

There is no official marathon record because of the varying severity of courses. The best time over 26 miles 385 yards *42 km* (standardized in 1924) is 2 hr 08 min 33.6 sec (av. 12.24 m.p.h. [*19,69 km/h*]) by Derek Clayton (b. 1942, at Barrow-in Furness, England) of Australia, at Antwerp, Belgium, on 30 May 1969.
The best time by a British international is 2 hr 9 min 28.0 sec by Ronald Hill of Bolton United Harriers, at Edinburgh, Scotland on 22 July 1970.
The fastest time by a female is 2 hr 46 min 30 sec (av. 9.53 m.p.h. [*15,33 km/h*]) by Adrienne Beames (Australia), at Werribee, Victoria, Australia on 31 Aug. 1971 in a time trial. Cheryl Bridge *née* Pedlow (U.S.A.) ran 2 hrs 49 min 40.0 sec at Culver City, California on 5 Dec. 1971.

RELAYS

Event	Min sec	Team	Place	Date
4 × 110 yards (two turns)	38.6	University of Southern California, U.S.A. (Earl Ray McCullouch, Fred Kuller, Orenthal James Simpson, Lennox Miller [Jamaica])	Provo, Utah, U.S.A.	17 June 1967
4 × 220 yards	1:21.7†	Texas Agricultural & Mechanical College (Donald Rogers, Rocklie Woods, Marvin Mills, Curtis Mills)	Des Moines, Iowa, U.S.A.	24 April 1970
4 × 440 yards	3:02.8	Trinidad and Tobago Lennox Yearwood, Kent Bernard, Edwin Roberts, Wendell A. Mottley)	Kingston, Jamaica	13 Aug. 1966
4 × 880 yards	7:10.4*	University of Chicago Track Club (Tom Bach, Ken Sparks, Lowell Paul, Richard Wohlhuter)	Durham, North Carolina, U.S.A.	12 May 1973
4 × 1 mile	16:02.8	New Zealand Team (Kevin Ross, Anthony Polhill, Richard Tayler, Richard Quax)	Auckland, New Zealand	3 Feb. 1972
4 × 100 metres (two turns)	38.2	United States National Team (Charles Edward Greene, Melvin Pender, Ronald Ray Smith, James Ray Hines)	Mexico City, Mexico	20 Oct. 1968
	38.2	United States National Team (Larry Black, Robert Taylor, Gerald Tinker, Eddie Hart)	Munich, West Germany	10 Sept. 1972
4 × 200 metres	1:21.5	Italian Team (Franco Ossala, Pasqualino Abeti, Luigi Benedetti, Pietro Mennea)	Barletta, Italy	21 July 1972
4 × 400 metres	2:56.1	United States National Team (Vincent Matthews, Ronald Freeman, G. Lawrence James, Lee Edward Evans)	Mexico City, Mexico	20 Oct. 1968
4 × 800 metres	7:08.6	West Germany "A" Team (Manfred Kinder, Walter Adams, Dieter Bogatzki, Franz-Josef Kemper)	Wiesbaden, West Germany	13 Aug. 1966
4 × 1,500 metres	14:49.0	France "A" Team (Gerard Vervoort, Claude Nicolas, Michel Jazy, Jean Wadoux)	St. Maur des Fosses, France	25 June 1965

† *The time of 1;20.7 achieved by University of Southern California (*Edesel Garrison, Lee Brown, William Deckard and Donald O'Riley Quarrie*) at Fresno, California, U.S.A. 13 May 1972 is not eligible because Quarrie is a Jamaican national.*

FIELD EVENTS

Event	ft	in	m	Name and Nationality	Place	Date
High Jump	7	6½	*2,30**	Dwight Stones (U.S.A.)	Munich, West Germany	11 July 1973
Pole Vault	18	5¾	*5,63*	Robert Seagren (U.S.A.)	Eugene, Oregon, U.S.A.	2 July 1972
Long Jump	29	2½	*8,90*	Robert Beamon (U.S.A.)	Mexico City, Mexico	18 Oct. 1968
Triple Jump	57	2¾	*17,44*	Viktor Saneyev (U.S.S.R.)	Sukhumi, U.S.S.R.	17 Oct. 1972
Shot Putt	71	7	*21,82**	Allan Dean Feuerbach (U.S.A.)	San Jose, California, U.S.A.	5 May 1973
Discus Throw	224	5	*68,40*	L. Jay Silvester (U.S.A.)	Reno, Nevada, U.S.A.	18 Sept. 1968
	224	5	*68,40*	Rickard Bruch (Sweden)	Stockholm, Sweden	5 July 1972
Hammer Throw	250	8	*76,40*	Walter Schmidt (Germany)	Lahr, Germany	4 Sept. 1971
Javelin Throw	308	8	*94,08**	Klaus Wolfermann (West Germany)	Leverkusen, West Germany	5 May 1973

DECATHLON

8,454 points	Nikolay Avilov (U.S.S.R.) (1st day: 100 m 11.0 sec, Long Jump 7,68 *25′ 2½″*, Shot Putt 14,36 *47′ 1½″*, High Jump 2,12 *6′ 11½″* 400 m 48.5 sec	Munich, West Germany (2nd day: 110 m Hurdles 14.31 sec, Discus 46,98 *154′ 1½″*, Pole Vault 4,55 *14′ 11¼″*, Javelin 61,66 *202′ 3½″*, 1,500 m 4:22.8 sec)	7–8 Sept. 1972

Women The most medals won by a woman athlete is seven by Shirley de la Hunty (*née* Strickland) (Australia) (b. 18 July 1925) with 3 gold, 1 silver and 3 bronze in the 1948, 1952 and 1956 Games.

British The most medals won by a British athlete is four by Guy M. Butler (b. 25 Aug. 1899) with a gold medal for the 4 × 400 m relay and a silver in the 400 m in 1920 and a bronze medal for each of these events in 1924. Two British women athletes have won three medals: Dorothy Hyman, M.B.E. (b. 9 May 1941) with a silver (100 m, 1960) and bronze (200 m, 1960 and 4 × 100 m relay, 1964) and Mrs. Mary Denise Rand, M.B.E. (now Toomey, *née* Bignal), (b. 10 Feb. 1940) with a gold (Long Jump), a silver (Pentathlon) and a bronze 4 × 100 m relay) all in 1964.

Most wins at one Games The most gold medals at one celebration is five by Nurmi in 1924 (see above) and the most individual is four by Alvin C. Kraenzlein (U.S.A.) (1876–1928) in 1900, with 60 m, 110 m hurdles, 200 m hurdles and long jump.

Most national titles The greatest number of national A.A.A. titles (excluding those in tug of war events) won by one athlete is fourteen individual and two relay titles by Emmanuel McDonald Bailey (b. Williamsville, Trinidad 8 Dec. 1920), between 1946 and 1953.

The greatest number of consecutive title wins is seven by Denis Horgan (Ireland) in the shot putt (1893–99), Albert A. Cooper (2 miles walk, 1932–38), Donald Osborne Finlay, D.F.C., A.F.C. (1909–70) (120 yds hurdles, 1932–38), Harry Whittle (440 yds hurdles, 1947–1953) and Maurice Herriott (3,000 m steeplechase, 1961–67). The record for consecutive W.A.A.A. titles is eight by Mrs. Judy U. Farr (Trowbridge & District A.C.) (b. 24 Jan. 1942), who won the 1½ mile 2 500 m walk from 1962–69.

Earliest landmarks The first time 10 sec ("even time") was bettered for 100 yds under championship conditions was when John Owen recorded 9⅘ sec in the United States A.A.U. Championship at Analostan Island, Washington, D.C., U.S.A., on 11 Oct. 1890. The first recorded instance of 6 ft *1,83 m* being cleared in the high jump was when Marshall Jones Brooks jumped 6 ft 0⅛ in *1,832 m* at Marston, near Oxford, England, on 17 March 1876. The breaking of the "4-minute barrier" in the one mile *1 609,34 m* was first achieved by Dr. Roger Gilbert Bannister, C.B.E. (b. Harrow, England 23 March 1929), when he recorded 3 min 59.4 sec on the Iffley Road track, Oxford, at 6.10 p.m. on 6 May 1954.

World record breakers *Oldest* The greatest age at which anyone has broken a world athletics record in a standard Olympic event is 35 years 255 days in the case of Dana Zátopkova, *née* Ingrova (b. 19 Sept. 1922) of Czechoslovakia, who broke the women's javelin record with 182 ft 10 in *55,73 m* at Prague, Czechoslovakia, on 1 June 1958. On 20 June 1948 Mikko Hietanen (Finland) (b. 22

WORLD RECORDS—WOMEN

The complete list of World Records for the 27 scheduled women's events passed by the International Amateur Ahtletic Federation as at July 1973. Those marked with an asterisk are awaiting ratification.

RUNNING

Event	Min sec	Name and Nationality	Place	Date	
100 yards	10.0	Chi Cheng (Tawian, China)	Portland, Oregon, U.S.A.	13 June	1970
220 yards (turn)	22.6	Chi Cheng (Taiwan, China)	Westwood, Calif., U.S.A.	3 July	1970
440 yards	52.2	Katheleen Hammond (U.S.A.)	UrbanaIllinois, U.S.A.	12 Aug.	1972
880 yards	2:01.0	Judith Florence Pollock (née Amoore) (Australia)	Helsinki, Finland	28 June	1967
1 mile	4:29.5*	Paola Cacchi (née Pigni) (Italy)	Viareggio, Italy	8 Aug.	1973
60 metres	7.2	Betty Cuthbert (Australia)	Sydney, N.S.W., Australia	21 Feb.	1960
	7.2	Irina Robertovna Bochkaryova (née Turova) (U.S.S.R.)	Moscow, U.S.S.R.	28 Aug.	1960
100 metres	10.9*	Renate Stecher (née Meissner) (East Germany)	Astrova, Czechoslovakia	7 June	1973
	10.9*	Renate Stecher (née Meissner) (East Germany)	Leipzig, East Germany	30 June	1973
	10.8*	Renate Stecher (née Meissner) (East Germany)	Dresden, East Germany	21 July	1973
200 metres (turn)	22.4	Chi Cheng (Taiwan, China)	Munich, West Germany	12 July	1970
	22.4	Renate Stecher (née Meissner) (East Germany)	Munich, West Germany	7 Sept.	1972
	22.4*	Renate Stecher (née Meissner) (East Germany)	Leipzig, East Germany	1 July	1973
	22.1*	Renate Stecher (née Meissner) (East Germany)	Dresden, East Germany	22 July	1973
400 metres	51,0	Marilyn Fay Neufville (Jamaica)	Edinburgh, Scotland	23 July	1970
880 metres†	51.0	Monika Zerht (East Germany)	Paris, France	4 July	1972
1,500 metres	1:58.8	Hildegard Falck (née Janze) (West Germany)	Stuttgart, West Germany	11 July	1971
	4:01.4	Lyudmila Bragina (U.S.S.R)	Munich, West Germany	9 Sept.	1972

† Shin Geum Dan (North Korea) has achieved 1;58.0 at P'yongyang, North Korea on 5 Sept. 1964; but she was under suspension by the I.A.A.F. at the time of performance.

HURDLING

Event	sec	Name and Nationality	Place	Date	
100 metres (2′ 9″ [83,7 cm])	12.5	Annelie Ehrhardt (East Germany)	Potsdam, East Germany	15 June	1972
	12.5	Pamela Ryan (née Kilborn) (Australia)	Warsaw, Poland	28 June	1972
	12.5*	Annelie Ehrhardt (East Germany) (twice)	East Berlin	13 Aug.	1973
	12.3*	Annelie Ehrhardt (East Germany)	Dresden,East Germany	22 July	1973
200 metres (2′ 6″ [75,9 cm])	25.7	Pamela Ryan (née Kilborn) (Australia)	Melbourne, Australia	25 Nov.	1971

FIELD EVENTS

Event	ft	in	m	Name and Nationality	Place	Date	
High Jump	6	4½	1,94	Jordanka Blagoyeva (née Dimitrova) (Bulgaria)	Zagreb, Yugoslavia	24 Sept.	1972
Long Jump	22	5¼	6,84	Heidemarie Rosendahl (West Germany)	Turin, Italy	3 Sept.	1970
Shot Putt	69	0	21,03	Nadyezhda Chizhova (U.S.S.R.)	Munich, West Germany	7 Sept.	1972
Discus Throw	221	8	67,58*	Faina Melnik (U.S.S.R.)	Moscow	11 July	1973
Javelin Throw	213	5	65,06	Ruth Fuchs (née Gamm) (East Germany)	Potsdam, East Germany)	11 June	1972

PENTATHLON (1971 Scoring Tables)

		Place	Date
4,831 points*	Burglinde Polak (East Germany)	Sophia, Bulgaria	11–12 Aug. 1973

RELAYS

Event	Min sec	Team	Place	Date	
4 × 110 yards	44.7	Tennessee State University (Diane Hughes, Debbie Wedgeworth, Mattline Render, Iris Davis)	Bakersfield, California, U.S.A.	9 July	1971
4 × 220 yards	1:35.8*	Australia (Marian Hoffman, Jennifer Lamy, Raelene Ann Boyle, Pamela Kilborn)	Brisbane, Australia	9 Nov.	1969
4 × 440 yards	3:33.9	U.S.A. National Team (Katheleen Hammond, M. Ferguson, Madeline Jackson [née Manning], D. Edwards)	Urbana, Illinois, U.S.A.	12 Aug.	1973
4 × 100 metres	42.8	United States National Team (Barbara Ferrell, Margaret Bailes [née Johnson], Mildrette Netter, Wyomia Tyus)	Mexico City, Mexico	20 Oct.	1968
	42.8	West Germany (Christiane Krause, Ingrid Mickler [née Becker], Annegret Richter, Heidemarie Rosendahl)	Munich, West Germany	10 Sept.	1972
	42.8	West Germany National Team (Christiane Krause, Ingrid Mickler, Annegret Richter, Heidemarie Rosendahl)	Munich, West Germany	10 Sept.	1972
4 × 200 metres	1:33.8	United Kingdom National Team (Maureen Dorothy Tranter, Della P. James, Janet Mary Simpson, Valerie Peat [née Wild])	London (Crystal Palace)	24 Aug.	1968
4 × 400 metres	3:23.0	East German National Team (Dagmar Käsling, Rita Kühne, Helga Seidler, Monika Zehrt)	Munich, West Germany	10 Sept.	1972
4 × 800 metres	8:08.6*	Bulgarian National Team (Svetla Zlateva, Lilyana Tomova, Tonka Petrova, Stefka Kordanova)	Sophia, Bulgaria	12 Aug.	1973

Sept. 1911) bettered his own world 30,000 m record with 1 hr 40 min 46.4 sec at Jyväskylä, Finland, when aged 36 years 272 days.

Youngest Doreen Lumley (b. September 1921) of New Zealand equalled the world record for the women's 100 yds of 11.0 sec at Auckland, New Zealand on 11 March 1939, when aged 17 years 6 months.

Most in a day Jesse Owens (U.S.A.) set six world records in 45 min at Ann Arbor, Michigan on 25 May 1935 with a 9.4 sec 100 yds (3.15 p.m.), a 26 ft 8¼ in *8,13 m* long jump (3.25 p.m.), a 20.3 sec 220 yds (and 200 m) at 3.45 p.m. and a 22.6 sec 220 yds low hurdles (and 200 m) at 4.0 p.m.

INTERNATIONALS

Most The greatest number of full Great Britain internationals won by a British male athlete is 53 by Crawford William Fairbrother, M.B.E. (b. 1 Dec. 1936), the high jumper, from 1957. The feminine record is 40 full internationals by Mary Denise Rand (now Toomey, née Bignal).

Oldest and youngest Of full Great Britain (outdoor) internationals the oldest have been Harold Whitlock (b. 16 Dec. 1903) at the 1952 Olympic Games, aged 48 years 218 days, and Mrs. Dorothy Tyler (née Odam) (b. 19 March 1920) at the 1956 Olympic Games, aged 36 years 269 days. The youngest have been William Land (b. 29 Nov. 1914) versus Italy in 1931, aged 16 years 271 days, and Miss Sylvia Needham (b. 28 March 1935) versus France in 1950, aged 15 years 166 days. Sonia Lannaman (b. King's Heath, Birmingham of Jamaican parentage, 24 March 1956) represented Great Britain versus East Germany indoors in East Berlin on 20 Feb. 1971, when she was 32 days short of her 15th birthday.

UNITED KINGDOM (NATIONAL) RECORDS—MEN

Event	Min sec	Name	Place	Date
100 yards	9.4	Peter Frank Radford	Wolverhampton	28 May 1960
220 yards (turn)	20.5	Peter Frank Radford	Wolverhampton	28 May 1960
440 yards	45.9	Robbie Ian Brightwell, M.B.E.	London (White City)	14 July 1962
880 yards	1:47.2	Christopher Sydney Carter	London (White City)	3 June 1968
1 mile	3:55.3	Peter John Stewart	London (Crystal Palace)	10 June 1972
2 miles	8:22.0	Ian Stewart	Stockholm, Sweden	14 Aug. 1972
3 miles	12:58.2	David Colin Bedford	Stockholm, Sweden	15 June 1971
6 miles	26:51.6	David Colin Bedford	Portsmouth, Hampshire	10 July 1971
10 miles	46:44.0	Ronald Hill	Leicester	9 Nov. 1968
15 miles	1H12:48.2	Ronald Hill	Bolton, Lancashire	21 July 1965
100 metres	10.1	Brian William Green	Bratislava, Czechoslovakia	3 June 1972
200 metres (turn)	20.3	David Andrew Jenkins	Edinburgh, Scotland	19 Aug. 1972
400 metres	45.2*	David Andrew Jenkins	Oslo, Norway	3 Aug. 1973
800 metres	1:45.1*	Andrew William Carter	London (Crystal Palace)	14 July 1973
1,000 metres	2:18.2	John Peter Boulter	London (Crystal Palace)	6 Sept. 1969
1,500 metres	3:38.2	Peter John Stewart	London (Crystal Palace)	15 July 1972
	3:38.2	Brendan Foster	Munich, West Germany	9 Sept. 1972
2,000 metres	5:03.2	David Colin Bedford	London (Crystal Palace)	8 July 1972
3,000 metres	7:46.4	David Colin Bedford	Louvain, Belgium	21 June 1972
5,000 metres	13:17.2	David Colin Bedford	London (Crystal Palace)	14 July 1972
10,000 metres	27:30.8*	David Colin Bedford	London (Crystal Palace)	13 July 1973
20,000 metres	58:39.0	Ronald Hill	Leicester	9 Nov. 1968
25,000 metres	1H15:22.6	Ronald Hill	Bolton, Lancashire	1 July 1965
30,000 metres	1H31:30.4	James Noel Carroll Alder	London (Crystal Palace)	25 Sept. 1970
1 hour	12 miles 1,268 yds 20 472 m	Ronald Hill	Leicester	9 Nov. 1968

HURDLING

Event	sec	Name	Place	Date
120 yards/110 metres	13.5*	Berwyn Price	Leipzig, East Germany	1 July 1973
200 metres (turn)	23.0	Alan Peter Pascoe	Loughborough, Leicestershire	5 June 1969
200 metres/220 yards (straight)	23.3	Peter Burke Hildreth	Imber Court, Surrey	27 Aug. 1955
200 metres/220 yards (turn)	23.7	Paul Ashley Laurence Vine	London (White City)	15 July 1955
	23.7	John Michael Waller Hogan	London (White City)	9 May 1964
400 metres	48.1	David Peter Hemery	Mexico City, Mexico	15 Oct. 1968
440 yards	50.2	David Peter Hemery	London (White City)	13 July 1968
3,000 metres Steeplechase	8:26.4	Andrew John Holden	London (Crystal Palace)	15 Sept. 1972

FIELD EVENTS

Event	ft	in	m	Name	Place	Date
High Jump	6	10¾	2,10	Alan Leslie Lerwill	Athens, Greece	18 July 1973
Pole Vault	17	1	5,21	Michael Anthony Bull	London (Crystal Palace)	15 July 1972
Long Jump	27	0	8,23	Lynn Davies, M.B.E.	Bern, Switzerland	30 June 1968
Triple Jump	54	0	16,46	Frederick John Alsop	Tokyo, Japan	16 Oct. 1964
Shot Putt	67	2	20,47	Geoffrey Lewis Capes	East Berlin	30 July 1973
Discus Throw	206	5	62,92	William Raymond Tancred	London (Crystal Palace)	12 Aug. 1973
Hammer Throw	233	7	71,20*	Barry Williams	Blackburn, Lancashire	28 July 1973
Javelin Throw	273	9	83,44	David Howard Travis	Zürich, Switzerland	2 Aug. 1970

DECATHLON (1962 Scoring Table)

7,903 (points)	Peter John Gabbett (1st day: 100 m 10.5 sec, Long Jump 24′ 7¾″ *7,51 m*, Shot Putt 43′ 8″ *13,31 m*, High Jump 6′ 1¼″ *1,85 m*, 400 m 47.4 sec)	Kassel, West Germany (2nd day: 110 m Hurdles 15.2 sec, Discus 151′ 0″ *46,02 m*, Pole Vault 13′ 9½″ *4,20 m*, Javelin 181′ 10″ *55,42 m*, 1 500 m 4:39.8 sec)	5–6 June 1971

RELAYS

Event		Name	Place	Date
4 × 110 yards	40.0	United Kingdom National Team (Peter Frank Radford, Ronald Jones, David Henry Jones, Thomas Berwyn Jones)	London (White City)	3 Aug. 1963
4 × 220 yard	1:26.0	London Team (David Henry Jones, Brian Andrew Smouha, Peter Frank Radford, David Hugh Segal)	London (White City)	30 Sept. 1959
4 × 440 yards	3:06.5	England Team (Martin John Winbolt-Lewis, John Austin Adey, Peter Warden, Timothy Joseph Michael Graham)	Kingston, Jamaica	13 Aug. 1966
4 × 800 metres and 4 × 880 yds†	7:17.4	United Kingdom National Team (Martin Bilham, David Cropper, Michael John Maclean, Peter Miles Browne)	London (Crystal Palace)	5 Sept. 1970
4 × 1 mile	16:24.8	Northern Counties Team (Stanley George Taylor, John Paul Anderson, Alan Simpson, Brian Hall)	Dublin, Ireland	17 July 1961
4 × 100 metres	39.3	United Kingdom National Team (Joseph William Speake, Ronald Jones, Ralph Banthorpe, Barrie Harrison Kelly)	Mexico City, Mexico	19 Oct. 1968
4 × 200 metres	1:24.1	Great Britain (Brian William Green, Roger Walters, Ralph Banthorpe, Martin Edward Reynolds)	Paris, France	2 Oct. 1971
4 × 400 metres	3:00.5	United Kingdom National Team (Martin Edward Reynolds, Alan Peter Pascoe, David Peter Hemery, David Andrew Jenkins)	Munich, West Germany	10 Sept. 1972
4 × 1,500 metres	15:06.6	Great Britain (Roy C. Young, Walter Wilkinson, Ian Stewart, Adrian P. Weatherhead)	Paris, France	2 Oct. 1971

† *A U.K. National Team recorded 7:14.6 for 4 × 880 yards at the Crystal Palace, London, on 22 June 1966, but lap times were illegally communicated to the runners.*

UNITED KINGDOM (NATIONAL) RECORDS—WOMEN

Event	Min sec	Name	Place	Date
100 yards	10.6	Heather Joy Young (*née* Armitage)	Cardiff	22 July 1958
	10.6	Dorothy Hyman, M.B.E.	London (White City)	7 July 1962
	10.6	Dorothy Hyman, M.B.E.	London (White City)	4 July 1964
	10.6	Mary Denise Rand (now Toomey, *née* Bignal), M.B.E.	London (White City)	4 July 1964
	10.6	Daphne Arden (now Slater)	London (White City)	4 July 1964
220 yards (turn)	23.6	Daphne Arden (now Slater)	Kingston, Jamaica	8 Aug. 1966
440 yards	54.1	Deirdre Ann Watkinson	London (White City)	2 July 1966
880 yards	2:04.2	Anne Rosemary Smith	Chiswick, Greater London	3 June 1967
1 mile	4:37.0	Anne Rosemary Smith	Leipzig, East Germany	30 June 1973
100 metres	11.2*	Andrea Joan C. Lynch	Budapest, Hungary	3 Oct. 1963
200 metres	23.2	Dorothy Hyman, M.B.E.	East Berlin	2 Aug. 1970
	23.2	Margaret Ann Critchley	Mexico City, Mexico	16 Oct. 1968
400 metres	52.1	Lillian Barbara Board, M.B.E.	Innsbrück, Austria	31 May 1973
	52.1	Verona Marolin Bernard	Munich, West Germany	3 Sept. 1972
800 metres	2:00.2	Rosemary Olivia Sterling (now Mrs. T. Wright)	Munich, West Germany	9 Sept. 1972
1,500 metres	4:04.8	Shelia Janet Carey (*née* Taylor)		

HURDLING

Event	sec	Name	Place	Date
100 metres	13.2	Judith Ann Vernon (*née* Toneboehn)	Helsinki, Finland	26 July 1972
200 metres	26.7	Sharon Colyear	London (Crystal Palace)	16 July 1971

FIELD EVENTS

Event	ft	in	m	Name	Place	Date
High Jump	6	1½	1,86	Barbara Jean Inkpen (now Mrs. Carl Lawton)	London (Crystal Palace)	15 Sept. 1972
Long Jump	22	2¼	6,76	Mary Denise Rand (now Toomey, née Bignal) M.B.E.	Tokyo, Japan	14 Oct. 1964
Shot Putt	53	6¼	16,31	Mary Elizabeth Peters	Belfast, Northern Ireland	1 June 1966
Discus Throw	190	4	58,02	Christine Rosemary Payne (née Charters)	Birmingham	3 June 1972
Javelin Throw	182	5	55,60	Susan Mary Platt	London (Chiswick)	15 June 1968

PENTATHLON

	Name	Place	Date
4,801 points (1971 Tables)	Mary Elizabeth Peters	Munich, West Germany	2–3 Sept. 1972

RELAYS

Event	Min sec	Name	Place	Date
4 × 110 yards	45.0	United Kingdom National Team (Anita Doris Neil, Maureen Dorothy Tranter, Janet Mary Simpson, Lillian Barbara Board)	Portsmouth, Hampshire	14 Sept. 1968
4 × 220 yards	1:37.6	London Olympiades A.C. (Della Patricia James [now Pascoe], Barbara M. Jones, Lillian Barbara Board, Janet Mary Simpson [now Mme. Clerc])	Solihull, Warwickshire	10 June 1967
4 × 100 metres	43.7	United Kingdom National Team (Anita Doris Neil, Maureen Dorothy Tranter, Janet Mary Simpson [now Mme. Clerc], Lillian Barbara Board)	Mexico City, Mexico	19 Oct. 1968
	43.7	United Kingdom National Team (Andrea Joan C. Lynch, Della Patricia Pascoe [née James], Judith Ann Vernon [née Toeneboehm], Anita Doris Neil) (for details see World record)	Munich, West Germany	10 Sept. 1972
4 × 200 metres	1:33.8			
4 × 400 metres	3:28.7	United Kingdom National Team (Verona Marolin Bernard, Janet Mary Simpson [now Mme. Clerc], Jeannette Veronica Roscoe, Rosemary Olivia Stirling)	Munich, West Germany	10 Sept. 1972
4 × 800 metres	8:23.8	Great Britain (Joan Florence Allison, Sheila Janet Carey [née Taylor], Patricia Barbara Lowe [now Cropper], Rosemary Olivia Stirling)	Paris, France	2 Oct. 1971

Mass relay record The record for 100 miles *160,9 km* by 100 runners belonging to one club is 8 hrs 9 min 42 sec by Shore Athletic Club at Monmouth College, West Long Branch, New Jersey, U.S.A., on 25 March 1973.

Three-legged race The fastest recorded time for a 100 yds three-legged race is 11.0 sec by Harry L. Hillman (d. 9 Aug. 1945) and Lawson Robertson (b. 1883 Aberdeen d. 22 Jan. 1951) at Brooklyn, New York City, N.Y., U.S.A., on 24 April 1909.

Running Backwards The fastest time recorded for running the 100 yds backwards is 13.5 sec by Bill Robinson (1878–1949) in the U.S. early in the century.

End to End Barefoot On 5–9 Sept. 1971 a group of members of the International Budo Association ran from John O'Groats to Land's End, barefoot—891 miles *1 443 km*.

Greatest caber toss The 230 lb. *104 kg* Braemar Caber, originally 21 ft *6,4 m* in length, defied all comers until it was successfully tossed by George Clark at the Braemar Gathering Aberdeenshire, Scotland, in September 1951.

Blind 100 yards The fastest time recorded for a 100 yds by a blind man is 11.0 sec by George Bull, aged 19, of Chippenham, Wiltshire, in a race at the Worcester College for the Blind, on 26 Oct. 1954.

Pancake race record The annual Housewives Pancake Race at Olney, Buckinghamshire, was first mentioned in 1445. The record for the winding 415 yds *380 m* course is 63.0 sec, set by Miss Janet Bunker, aged 17, on 7 Feb. 1967. The record for the counterpart race at Liberal, Kansas, U.S.A. is 59.1 sec by Kathleen West, 19, on 10 Feb. 1970.

Standing High Jump The best standing high jump is 5 ft 9¼ in *1,76 m* by Johan Christian Evandt (Norway) at Oslo on 4 March 1962.

Standing Long Jump Joe Darby (1861–1937) the famous Victorian professional jumper from Dudley, Worcestershire, jumped a measured 12 ft 1½ in *3,69 m without* weights at Dudley Castle, on 28 May 1890. Evandt (see above) achieved 3,65 m *11 ft 11¾ in* as an amateur in Reykjavik, Iceland on 11 March 1962.

TRAMPOLINING

Origins Trampolines were used in show business at least as early as "The Walloons" of the period 1910–12. The sport of trampolining (from the Spanish word *trampolín*, a springboard) dates from 1936, when the prototype "T" model trampoline was developed by George Nissen (U.S.A.).

Most difficult manoeuvres The three most difficult manoeuvres yet achieved are the triple twisting double back somersault, known as a Miller after the first trampolinist to achieve it— Wayne Miller (b. 1947) of the U.S.A. and eight consecutive triple somersaults by Ricky Virgin, 15 (Australia) (24 somersaults with 8 contacts with the bed) on 26 Aug. 1972. The most difficult for women is the Wills (5½ twisting back somersault), named after the five-time world champion Judy Wills (b. 1948) of the U.S.A., of which no analysable film exists.

Most titles The only men to win a world title (instituted 1964) twice have been Dave Jacobs (U.S.) the 1967–68 champion and Wayne Miller (U.S.), who won in 1966 and 1970. Judy Wills won the first 5 women's titles (1964–65–66–67–68). Both European men's titles (1969 and 1971) were won by Paul Luxon (G.B.), the 1972 world champion. Three United Kingdom titles have been won by David Curtis (1966–67–68) and Paul Luxon (1969–70–71), while Miss Jackie Allen (1960–61), Mary Hunkin (née Chamberlaine) (1963–64) and Lynda Ball (1965–66) have each won two British titles.

Marathon record The longest recorded trampoline bouncing marathon is one of 505 hrs, set by a team of 8 members, of the Ottawa Street Community Y.M.C.A. at Pro's Golf Centre, Stoney Creek, Ontario, Canada on 22 June–13 July 1971. The record for a 6-man team is 254 hrs set in Townsville, Queensland, Australia on 30 April–11 May 1971. The solo record is 63½ hrs (with 5 min breaks per hour permissible) by A. D. (Tony) Richardson of Dunedin Y.M.C.A., New Zealand on 20–22 Oct. 1972.

TROTTING AND PACING

Origins The trotting gait (the simultaneous use of the diagonally opposite legs) was first recorded in England in c. 1750. The sulky first appeared in harness-racing in 1829. Pacers thrust out their fore and hind legs simultaneously on one side.

Highest price The highest price paid for a trotter is $3,000,000 for *Nevele Pride* by the Stoner Creek Stud of Lexington, Kentucky from Louis Resnick and Nevele Acres in the autumn of 1969. The highest price ever paid for a pacer is $2,500,000 for *Albatross* in 1972.

Greatest winnings The greatest amount won by a trotting horse is $1,764,802 by *Une de Mai* to 15 April 1973. The record for a pacing horse is $1,201,470 by *Albatross*

which was retired to stud in Nov. 1972.

Most Successful Driver The most successful sulky driver in harness racing history has been Herve Filion (b. 1 Feb. 1940) of Quebec, Canada who reached a record 4,065 wins at Roosevelt Raceway, New York after a record 605 wins in the 1972 season.

Records against time	Trotting			Pacing			
World (mile [*1 609,34 m* track])	1:54.8	Nevele Pride (U.S.A.), Indianapolis, Indianao	31 Aug. 1969	1:52.0	Steady Star(U.S.A.) Lexington, Kentucky	1 Oct. 1971
Australia	2:01.2	Gramel, Harold Park, Sydney	1964	1:57.3	Halwes, Harold Park, Sydney	1968
New Zealand	2:02.4	Control, Addington, Christchurch	1964	1:56.2	Cardigan Bay, Hutt Park, Wellington	1963
World Record	1:55.6	Noble Victory (U.S.A) at Du Quoin, Illinois	31 Aug. 1966	1:54.6	Albatross (U.S.A.) at Sportsman's Park, Cicero, Illinois	1 July 1972

TUG OF WAR

Tug of War is a competitive sport in 14 countries. The term was first recorded in 1876 in England. It became an Olympic event in 1900 in Paris and was dropped after 1920. In 1958 a separate governing body, the Tug-of-War Association, was formed to administer Britain's 800 clubs.

Most Olympic Medals The only three men to win two gold medals (1908 and 1920) (all also won a silver medal in 1912) were James Shepherd, Frederick H. Humphreys, and Edwin A. Mills (all G.B.).

Longest Pull The longest recorded pull is one of 2 hours 41 min between "H" Company and "E" Company of the 2nd Battalion of the Sherwood Foresters (Derbyshire

Regiment) at Jubbulpore, India, on 12 Aug. 1889. "E" Company won.

The longest recorded pull under A.A.A. Rules (in which lying on the ground or entrenching the feet is not permitted) is one of 8 min 18.2 sec for the first pull between the R.A.S.C. (Feltham) and the Royal Marines (Portsmouth Division) at the Royal Tournament of June 1938.

Most A.A.A. titles Greatest team The catchweight Wood Treatment team (formerly the Bosley Farmers) of Cheshire, have represented and won for England every international against five countries since 1964. They have won 15 consecutive A.A.A. Championships since 1959. Hilary Brown, Mike Eardley, George Hicton, Peter Hirst and Norman Hyde have been in every team.

VOLLEYBALL

Origins The game was invented as *Minnonette* in 1895 by William G. Morgan at the Y.M.C.A. gymnasium at Springfield, Massachusetts, U.S.A. The International Volleyball Association was formed in Paris in April 1947. The Amateur (now English) Volleyball Association of Great Britain was formed in May 1955. The ball travels at a speed of 70 m.p.h. *112,5 km/h* when smashed over the net, which measures 2.43 m (7 ft 11.6 in). In the women's game the net is 2.24 m *7 ft 4.1 in.*

World titles World Championships were instituted in 1949. The U.S.S.R. has won six men's titles (1949, 1952, 1960, 1962, 1964 and 1968) in the eight meetings held. The U.S.S.R. won the women's championship in 1952, 1956, 1960, 1968 and 1970. The record crowd is 60,000 for the 1952 world title matches in Moscow, U.S.S.R.

Olympic The sport was introduced to the Olympic Games for

both men and women in 1964.

The only volleyball players of either sex to win there medals are Ludmila Bouldakova (U.S.S.R.) (b. 25 May 1938) and Inna Ryskal (U.S.S.R.) (b. 15 June 1944), who both won a silver medal in 1964 and golds in 1968 and 1972.

The record for gold medals for men is shared by four members of the U.S.S.R.'s 1968 team who won a second gold medal in 1972: Eduard Sibiryakov, Yury Poyarkov, Yvan Bugayenkov and Georgy Mondzolevsky.

Marathon The longest recorded volleyball marathon is one of 168 hrs played by 4 teams of six from Kirkby College of Further Education, Liverpool on 22–29 April 1973.

One Man Team Bob L. Schaffer, 45 of Newark, New Jersey specialises in taking on 6 men teams lone-handed. His latest reported life-time score is 1,200 wins since 16 Aug. 1963. His only loss was to Fordham University basketball team.

WALKING

Olympic Medals Most There have been 24 Olympic walking races covering every celebration since 1906 except for 1928.

The only walker to win three gold medals has been Ugo Frigerio (Italy) (b. 16 Sept. 1901) with the 3,000 m and 10,000 m in 1920 and the 10,000 m in 1924. He also holds the record of most medals with four (having additionally won the bronze medal in the 50,000 m in 1932) which total is shared with Vladimir Golubnitschyi (U.S.S.R.) (b. 2 June 1936), who won gold medals for the 20,000 m in 1960 and 1968, the silver in 1972 and the bronze in 1964.

The best British performance has been two gold

medals by George E. Larner for the 3,500 m and the 10 miles in 1908, but Ernest J. Webb won three medals being twice runner up to Larner and finishing second in the 10,000 m in 1912.

Trans-Continental The record for walking across the United States from Los Angeles, California, to New York is 53 days 12¼ hrs by John Lees (for details see page 221). The feminine record for the route from San Francisco to New York is 86 days by Dr. Barbara Moore (b. Varvara Belayeva, in Kalouga, Russia, 22 Dec. 1903), ending on 6 July 1960.

Longest Desert Walk The longest desert walk (made in high summer day-time) ever recorded is one of 316 miles *508 km* by Bill Collins (b. 22 Oct. 1923) of Las Vegas through Death

Valley, California in 10 days 10 hrs on 28 July–6 Aug. 1972. The maximum daily shade temperatures varied between 122°F *50°C* and a low of 115°F *46,1°C* with ground temperatures at 4 p.m. of 195°F *90,6°C* to a low of 178°F *81,1°C*. The route took in Devil's Golf Course Badwater (282 ft *85 m* below sea level), 14 miles *22,5km* of Salt Flats hitherto untraversed, and Furnace Creek.

"End to end" The record for walking from John o'Groats to Land's End (route varies between 876 and 891 miles [*1 409 and 1 433 km*]) is 10 days 23 hrs 53 min achieved by Malcolm Taylor of Milnsbridge, Huddersfield, Yorkshire on 28 July–7 Aug. 1973. The feminine record is 17 days 7 hrs by Miss Wendy Lewis ending on 15 March 1960. End to end and back has twice been achieved. Frederick E. Westcott, aged 31, finished on 18 Dec. 1966 and David Tremayne (Australia), aged 27, finished on 28 May 1971. The Irish "End to End" record over the 376 miles *605 km* from Mizen Head, Cork to Malin Head, Donegal is 7 days 22 hrs 10 min, set by Tom Casey (b. 1930) on 1–9 July 1972.

London to Brighton The record time for the London to Brighton walk is 7 hrs 35 min 12 sec by Donald James Thompson, M.B.E. (b. 20 Jan. 1933) on 14 Sept. 1957. The record time for London to Brighton and back is 18 hrs 5 min 51 sec by William Frederick Baker (b. 5 April 1889) of Queen's Park Harriers, London, on 18–19 June 1926.

1,000 miles 1,000 hours The first man to achieve 1,000 miles *1 609,34 km* in 1,000 hours at one mile each hour was Capt. Robert Barclay-Allardice, (b. Ury, Kincardineshire, 1780) at Newmarket from 1 June to 12 July 1809. He lost 32 lb. *14,5 kg* in weight during the ordeal.

Walking on crutches David Ryder, 21, a polio victim from Chigwell, Essex, arrived at Land's End from John o'Groats on 18 Aug.

American Bill Collins during his walk through Death Valley where the ground temperature reached 195 °F *90,6 °C*

1969 having completed the entire course on crutches. From 30 March to 14 Aug. 1970 he succeeded in walking on crutches 2,960 miles *4 763 km* across North America.

Road walking The world's best performances for the two Road Walking events on the programme of the last Olympic Games are: 20,000 m 1 hr 24 min 50.0 sec by Vincent Paul Nihill (G.B.) on the Isle of Man, 30 July 1972 and 50,000 m 3 hrs 52 min 44.6 sec by Bernd Kannenberg (West Germany) 1972.

Most titles The greatest number of national titles won by a British walker is 26 by Nihill from 1963 to 1972. These are A.A.A. 2 miles/3 km 1965–70–71; 7 miles/10 km 1965–66–68–69 and R.W.A. 10 miles 1965–68–69–72; 20 km 1965–66–68–69–71–72; 20 miles 1963–64–65–68–69–71 and 50 km 1964–68–71.

OFFICIAL WORLD RECORDS (Track Walking)
(As recognized by the International Amateur Athletic Federation) (*Awaiting ratification)

Distance	Time hr min sec	Name and Nationality	Place	Date
20,000 metres	1 25 19.4	Hans-Georg Reimann (East Germany)	Erfurt, East Germany	24 June 1972
	1 25 19.4	Peter Frenkel (East Germany)	Erfurt, East Germany	24 June 1972
30,000 metres	2 14 45.6	Karl-Heinz Stadtmüller (East Germany)	Berlin	16 Apr. 1972
20 miles	2 31 33.0	Anatoliy S. Vedyakov (U.S.S.R.)	Moscow, U.S.S.R.	23 Aug. 1958
30 miles	3 51 48.6*	Gerhard Weidner (West Germany)	Hamburg, West Germany	8 Apr. 1973
50,000 metres	4 00 27.0*	Gerhard Weidner (West Germany)	Hamburg, West Germany	8 Apr. 1973
2 hours	26 911 m *16 miles 1,270 yds*	Karl-Heinz Stadtmüller (East Germany)	East Berlin	16 Apr. 1972

WATER POLO

Origins Water Polo was developed in England as "Water Soccer" in 1869 and was first included in the Olympic Games in Paris in 1900.

Olympic Games Most medals Hungary has won the Olympic tournament most often with five wins in 1932, 1936, 1952, 1956 and 1964 Great Britain won in 1900, 1908, 1912 and 1920.

Five players share the record of three gold medals: George Wilkinson (b. 1880) in 1900–08–12; Paulo (Paul) Radmilovic (1886–1968), and Charles Sidney Smith (b. 1879) all G.B. in 1908–12–20; and the Hungarians Deszö Gyarmati (b. 23 Oct. 1927) and György Kárpáti (b. 23 June 1935) in 1952–56–64.

Radmilovic (see above) also won a gold medal for the 4 × 200 m relay in 1908.

A.S.A. championships The club with the greatest number of Amateur Swimming Association titles is Plaistow United Swimming Club of Greater London, with eleven from 1928 to 1954.

Most goals The greatest number of goals scored by an individual in a home international is eleven by Terry C. Miller (Plaistow United), when England defeated Wales 13–3 at Newport, Monmouthshire, in 1951.

Most caps The greatest number of internationals is 168 by Aurel Zahan (Romania) to 1970. The British record is 96 in 15 seasons by Peter Pass, M.B.E. of Chesham Bois, Buckinghamshire from June 1955 to August 1969.

WATER SKIING

Origins The origins of water skiing lie in plank gliding or aquaplaning. A photograph exists of a "plank-riding" contest in a regatta won by a Mr. S. Storry at Scarborough, Yorkshire on 15 July 1914. Competitors were towed on a *single* plank by a motor launch. The present day sport of water skiing was pioneered by Ralph W. Samuelson on Lake Pepin, Minnesota,

U.S.A., on two curved pine boards in the summer of 1922, though claims have been made for the birth of the sport on Lake Annecy (Haute Savoie), France, in 1920. The first World Water Ski Organization was formed in Geneva on 27 July 1946. The British Water Ski Federation was founded in London in 1954.

Longest jumps The first recorded jump on water skis was made by Ralph Samuelson off a greased ramp, at Miami Beach,

Florida, U.S.A. in 1928. The longest jump ever recorded is one of 169 ft *51,5 m* by Wayne Grimditch, 17 (U.S.A.) at Callaway Gardens, Pine Mountain, Georgia, U.S.A. on 15 July 1972. The women's record is 111 ft *33,8 m* by Barbara Clack, 27 (U.S.A.) at Callaway Gardens on 11 July 1971.

The British record is 157 *ft* 3½ in *47,95 m* by James Carne (Ruislip W.S.C.) at Temple-sur-Lot, Bordeaux, France on 30 July 1972. The Irish record is 134 ft *40,8 m* by Alan Dagg (Golden Falls W.S.C.) at Dublin on 25 Sept. 1971. Dagg, the six time Irish National Champion (1967–73) also won two Irish Open titles in 1971–72. The women's record is 106 ft 3½ in *32,39 m* by Jeannette Stewart-Wood (b. 1946) at Ruislip, Greater London on 11 June 1967. This could not be ratified as a world record because a minimum improvement of 8 in *20 cm* is required.

Buoys and Figures The world record for slalom is 38 buoys (6 passes through the short course plus two buoys with the 75 ft *22 m* rope shortened by 36 ft *10 m* by Mike Suyderhoud (U.S.) at Ruislip, Middlesex on 6 June 1970 and Roby Zucchi (Italy) at Canzo, Italy on 6 Sept. 1970. The record for figures is 5,970 points by Ricky McCormick (U.S.) at Bedfont, near London, in August 1970. The British records are 33 buoys by Ian Walker (Ruislip) at Canzo, Italy in September 1970 (5 passes plus 3 buoys with the 75 ft *22 m* rope shortened by 32 ft [*9,75 m*)] and 4,350 points by Paul Seaton at Princes W.S.C. on 10 Sept. 1972.

Longest run The greatest distance travelled non-stop is 818.2 miles *1 316,7 km* by Marvin G. Shackleford round McKellar Lake, Memphis, Tennesse, U.S.A. in 35 hrs 15 min in September 1960. The British record is 470.67 miles *757,46 km* (in 15 hrs 1 min 53.2 sec) by Charles Phipps, 30, on Lake Windermere from 4.4 a.m. to 7.5 p.m. on 4 Oct. 1969.

Highest speed The water skiing speed record is 125.69 m.p.h. *202,27 km/h* by Danny Churchill at the Oakland Marine Stadium, California, U.S.A., in 1971. Sally Younger (b. 1953), set a feminine record of 105.14

m.p.h. *169,20 km/h* at Perris, California on 17 June 1970. The fastest recorded speed by a British skier has been 76.542 m.p.h. *123,18 km/h* (average) at Holme Pierrepont, Nottinghamshire on 15 Nov. 1972 by the 1972 European Ski-Racing Champion, John Harvey.

Water-ski racing The record for the 58 mile *93 km* Cross Channel race from Greatstone-on-Sea, near New Romney, England to Cap Gris-Nez, France and back is 1 hr 37 min 30 sec by Robin Manwaring of Kent on 13 Aug. 1972.

Most titles World overall championships (instituted 1949) have been won twice by Alfredo Mendoza (U.S.A.) in 1953–55 and Mike Suyderhoud (U.S.A.) in 1967–69 and three times by Mrs. Willa McGuire (*née* Worthington) of the U.S.A., in 1949–50 and 1955. Mendoza won five championship events and McGuire and Elizabeth Allen (U.S.A.) seven each. The most British overall titles (instituted 1953) ever won by a man is four by Lance Callingham in 1959–60 and 1962–63, and the most by a woman is three by Maureen Lynn-Taylor in 1959–60–61 and by Jeanette Stewart-Wood in 1963–66–67.

Barefoot The barefoot duration record is 67 min over about 36 miles *57 km* by Stephen Z. Northrup (U.S.A.) in 1969. The backwards barefoot record is 33 min 19 sec by Paul McManus (Australia) in 1969. A barefoot jump of 43 ft *13 m* was reported from Australia. The barefoot speed records are 87.46 m.p.h. *140,75 km/h* by John Taylor on Lake Ming, California on 28 March 1972 and 61 m.p.h. *98 km/h* by Miss Haidee Jones (Australia). Alan Hargreaves (G.B.) reached 37 m.p.h. *59,54 km/h*, at Holme Pierrepont, Nottinghamshire on 14 Nov. 1972.

Water-ski flying The altitude record for a towed water-skier is 4,750 ft *1 460 m* by Bill Moyes of Sydney, Australia over Lake Ellesmere, New Zealand on 14 March 1972 towed by a 435 h.p. Hamilton jet boat. The duration record is 15 hrs 3 min by Bill Flewellyn, 29 (N.Z.) over Lake Bonney, Barmera, South Australia 1971.

WEIGHTLIFTING

Origins Amateur weightlifting is of comparatively modern origin and the first world championship was staged at the Café Monico, Piccadilly, London, on 28 March 1891. Prior to that time, weightlifting consisted of professional exhibitions in which some of the advertised poundages were open to doubt. The first 400 lb. *181 kg* clean and jerk is, however, attributed to Charles Rigoulot (1903–62), a French professional, in Paris, with 402½ lb. *182 kg 570* on 1 Feb. 1929.

Greatest back lift The greatest weight ever raised by a human being is 6 270 lb. *2 844 kg* (2.80 tons [*2 84 tonnes*]) in a back lift (weight raised off trestles) by the 26 st. *165 kg* Paul Anderson (U.S.A.) (born 1933), the 1956 Olympic heavyweight champion at Toccoa, Georgia, U.S.A., on 12 June 1957. The heaviest Rolls-Royce, the Phantom VI, weighs 5,600 lb. *2 540 kg* (2½ tons [*2,54 tonnes*]). The greatest lift by a woman is 3,564 lb. *1 616 kg* with a hip and harness lift by Mrs. Josephine Blatt *née* Schauer (1869–1923) at the Bijou Theatre., Hoboken, New Jersey, U.S.A., on 15 April 1895.

Greatest overhead lift The greatest overhead lifts made from the ground are the clean and jerks achieved by super-heavyweights which now exceed 4½ cwt. *2,2 quintal* (504 lb. [*228 kg*]) (see table p. 336). The greatest overhead lift ever made by a woman is 286 lb. *129 kg* in a continental jerk by Katie Sandwina, *née* Brummbach (Germany) (b. 21 Jan. 1884, d. as Mrs. Max Heymann in New York City, U.S.A., on 21 Jan. 1952) in *c.* 1911. This is equivalent to seven 40 lb. *18 kg* office typewriters. She

stood 5 ft 11 in *1,80 m* tall, weighed 210 lb. *95 kg* (15 st. 10 lb.) and is reputed to have unofficially lifted 312½ lb. *141 kg 747* and to have shouldered a cannon taken from the tailboard of a Barnum and Bailey circus wagon which allegedly weighed 1,200 lb. *544 kg*.

Power lifts Paul Anderson, as a professional, has bench-pressed 627 lb. *284 kg* and has achieved 1,200 lb. *544 kg* in a squat so aggregating, with an 820 lb. *371 kg* dead lift, a career total of 2,647 lb. *1 200 kg*. The A.A.U. of America record for a single contest is an aggregate of 2,370 lb. *1 075 kg* by Jon Cole (U.S.A.) set in October 1972. Jim Williams (U.S.A.) has bench-pressed 675 lb. *306 kg* in 1972.

The highest recorded two-handed dead lift is 882 lb. *400 kg* by Jon Cole (U.S.A.). Hermann Gorner (Germany) performed a one-handed dead lift of 734½ lb. *333 kg 10* in Dresden on 20 July 1920. Peter B. Cortese (U.S.A.) achieved a one-armed dead lift of 370 lb. *167 kg i.e.* 22 lb. *9 kg 90* over triple his bodyweight at York, Pennsylvania on 4 Sept. 1954.

Gorner (see above) raised 24 men weighing 4,123 lb. *1 870 kg* on a plank on the soles of his feet in London on 12 Oct. 1927 and also carried on his back a 1,444 lb. *654 kg* piano for a distance of 52½ ft *4,8 m* on 3 June 1921.

The highest competitive two-handed dead lift by a woman is 392 lb. *177 kg* by Mlle. Jane de Vesley (France) in Paris on 14 Oct. 1926.

It was reported that an hysterical 8 st. 11 lb. *55 kg 791* woman, Mrs. Maxwell Rogers, lifted one end of a 3,600 lb. *1 632 kg* (1.60 ton [*1,62 tonnes*]) station wagon which, after the collapsing of a jack, had fallen on top of her son at Tampa, Florida, U.S.A., on 24 April 1960. She cracked some vertebrae.

Brick Lifting Gorner (see above) is reputed to have lifted 14 bricks weighing 56 kg *123½* lb. horizontally using only lateral pressure.

Cue levering The only man ever to have levered six 16 oz. *453 g* billiard cues simultaneously by their tips through 90 degrees to the horizontal, is W. J. (Bill) Hunt of Darwen, Lancashire at the Unity Club, Great Harwood, Lancashire on 25 June 1954.

Olympic Games Most Gold Medals Of the 81 Olympic titles at stake the U.S.S.R. have won 21, the U.S.A. 15 and France 9. Eight lifters have succeeded in winning an Olympic gold medal in successive Games. Of these three have also won a silver medal:

Louis Hostin (France)	Gold, light-heavyweight 1932 and 1936; Silver 1928.
John Davis (U.S.A.)	Gold, heavyweight 1948 and 1952.
Tommy Kono (Hawaii/U.S.A.)	Gold, lightweight 1952; Gold, light-heavyweight 1956; Silver, middle-weight 1960.
Charles Vinci (U.S.A.)	Gold, bantamweight 1956 and 1960.
Arkady Vorobyov (U.S.S.R.)	Gold, middle-heavyweight 1956 and 1960.
Yoshinobu Miyake (Japan)	Gold, featherweight 1964 and 1968; Silver, bantamweight 1960.
Waldemar Baszanowski (Poland)	Gold, lightweight 1964 and 1968.
Leonid Schabotinsky (U.S.S.R.)	Gold, heavyweight 1964 and 1968.

OFFICIAL WORLD WEIGHTLIFTING RECORDS (As at 1 July 1973)

Bodyweight Class	Lift	Lifted lb.	Lifted kg	Name and Nationality	Place	Date
Flyweight (114½ lb. [*52 kg*])	Snatch	231¼	*105*	Gyi Aung (Burma)	Munich, W. Germany	27 Aug. 1972
	Jerk	292	*132,5*	Charlie Depthios (Indonesia)	Munich, W. Germany	27 Aug. 1972
	Total	512¼	*232,5*	Vladimir Smetanin (U.S.S.R.)	Warsaw, Poland	20 Sept. 1969
Bantamweight (123¼ lb. [*56 kg*])	Snatch	255½	*116*	Koji Miki (Japan)	Tashkent, U.S.S.R.	16 Mar. 1973
	Jerk	330½	*150*	Mohamed Nassiri (Iran)	Mexico City, Mexico	13 Oct. 1968
	Total	561¾	*255*	Mohamed Nassiri (Iran)	Mexico City, Mexico	13 Oct. 1968
Featherweight (132¼ lb. [*60 kg*])	Snatch	276½	*125,5*	Yoshinobu Miyake (Japan)	Matsuura, Japan	28 Oct. 1969
	Jerk	349¼	*158,5*	Yuri Golubtsov (U.S.S.R.)	Tashkent, U.S.S.R.	17 Mar. 1973
	Total	611½	*277,5*	Yoshinobu Miyake (Japan)	Matsuura, Japan	28 Oct. 1969
Lightweight (148¾ lb. [*67,5 kg*])	Snatch	303	*137,5*	Waldemar Baszanowski (Poland)	Lublin, Poland	23 Apr. 1971
	Jerk	391¼	*177,5*	Murkharbi Kirzhinov (U.S.S.R.)	Munich, W. Germany	30 Aug. 1972
	Total	688¾	*312,5*	Murkharbi Kirzhinov (U.S.S.R.)	Munich, W. Germany	30 Aug. 1972
Middleweight (165¼ lb. [*75 kg*])	Snatch	331¾	*150,5*	Leif Jensen (Norway)	Copenhagen, Denmark	28 Apr. 1973
	Jerk	414¼	*188*	Nedelcho Kolev (Bulgaria)	Madrid, Spain	14 June 1973
	Total	727¼	*330*	Nedelcho Kolev (Bulgaria)	Madrid, Spain	14 June 1973
Light-heavyweight (181¾ lb. [*82,5 kg*])	Snatch	354¾	*161*	Vladimir Rizhenkov (U.S.S.R.)	Madrid, Spain	15 June 1973
	Jerk	444	*201,5*	Vladimir Rizhenkov (U.S.S.R.)	Madrid, Spain	15 June 1973
	Total	782¼	*355*	David Rigert (U.S.S.R.)	Sochi, U.S.S.R.	24 Dec. 1972
Middle-heavyweight (198¼ lb. [*90 kg*])	Snatch	374¾	*170*	David Rigert (U.S.S.R.)	Madrid, Spain	16 June 1973
	Jerk	470½	*213,5*	David Rigert (U.S.S.R.)	Madrid, Spain	16 June 1973
	Total	837¾	*380*	David Rigert (U.S.S.R.)	Shakhty, U.S.S.R.	5 Apr. 1973
Heavyweight (242½ lb. [*110 kg*])	Snatch	391¼	*177,5*	Pavel Pervushin (U.S.S.R.)	Madrid, Spain	17 June 1973
	Jerk	492½	*223,5*	Pavel Pervushin (U.S.S.R.)	Madrid, Spain	17 June 1973
	Total	881¾	*400*	Pavel Pervushin (U.S.S.R.)	Madrid, Spain	17 June 1973
Super-Heavyweight (Over 242½ lb. [*110 kg*])	Snatch	402¼	*182,5*	Serge Reding (Belgium)	Brussels, Belgium	2 June 1973
	Jerk	529	*240*	Vasili Alexeev (U.S.S.R.)	Madrid, Spain	18 June 1973
	Total	920¼	*417,5*	Vasili Alexeev (U.S.S.R.)	Madrid, Spain	18 June 1973

(As supplied by Mr. Oscar State, O.B.E., General Secretary of the International Weightlifting Federation).

Most Medals The winner of most Olympic medals is Norbert Schemansky (U.S.A.) with four: Gold, middle-heavyweight 1952; Silver, heavyweight 1948; Bronze, heavyweight 1960 and 1964.

British The only British lifter to win an Olympic title has been Launceston Elliott the open one-handed lift champion in 1896 at Athens.

Most Successful British Lifter Louis George Martin, M.B.E., born Jamaica 1936, won four World and European mid-heavyweight titles in 1959–62–63–65. He won an Olympic silver medal in 1964 and a bronze in 1960 and also 3 Commonwealth gold medals in 1962–66–70. His total of British titles was 12.

Tonnage Record The highest reported tonnage lifted in 100 hrs is 453.22 tons *460,49 tonnes* by Jim Foster at King Alfred's Boys' Club, Winchester, Hampshire on 20–24 Oct. 1970.

Strand Pulling The International Steel Strand Association was founded by Gaum Pearson (Scotland) in 1940. The greatest ratified poundage to date is a super heavy-weight left arm push of 809 lb. *366 kg 90*.

WRESTLING

Earliest references The earliest depicting of wrestling holds and falls, are from the walls of the tomb of Ptahhotap so proving that wrestling dates from *c.* 2350 B.C. or earlier. It was introduced into the ancient Olympic Games in the 18th Olympiad in *c.* 704 B.C. The Greco-Roman style is of French origin and arose about 1860. The International Amateur Wrestling Federation (F.I.L.A.) was founded in 1912.

Most World Champion-ships The greatest number of world championships won by a wrestler is seven by the freestyler Aleksandr Medved (U.S.S.R.), born 1937 with the Light-heavyweight titles in 1964 (Olympic) and 1966, the Heavyweight 1967 and 1968 (Olympic), and the Extra heavy weight title 1969, 1970 and 1971. The only other wrestler to win world titles in 6 successive years has been Abdullah Movahad (Iran) in the lightweight division in 1965–70. The record for Greco-Roman titles is five shared by Roman Rurua (U.S.S.R.) with the featherweight 1966, 1967, 1968 (Olympic), 1969 and 1970 and Victor Igumenov (U.S.S.R.) with the Welterweight 1966, 1967, 1969, 1970 and 1971.

Most Olympic titles Three wrestlers have won three Olympic titles:

Carl Westergren (Sweden) (b. 13 Oct. 1895)	
Greco-Roman Middleweight, 75 kg	1920
Greco-Roman Light Heavyweight, 82,5 kg	1924
Greco-Roman Heavyweight over 87 kg	1932
Ivar Johansson (Sweden) (b. 31 Jan. 1903)	
Freestyle Middleweight, 79 kg	1932
Greco-Roman Welterweight, 72 kg	1932
Greco-Roman Middleweight, 79 kg	1936
Aleksandr Medved (U.S.S.R.) (b. 16 Sept. 1937)	
Freestyle Light Heavyweight	1964
Freestyle Heavyweight	1968
Freestyle Super Heavyweight	1972

The only wrestler with more medals is Imre Polyák (Hungary) who won the silver medal for the Greco-Roman featherweight class in 1952–56–60 and the gold in 1964.

Best record Osamu Watanabe (Japan) won the freestyle feather-weight event in the 1964 Olympic Games. This was his 186th successive win and he had never been defeated.

Longest bout The longest recorded bout was one of 11 hrs 40 min between Martin Klein (Estonia representing Russia) and Armas Asikainen (Finland) in the Greco-Roman middleweight "A" event in the 1912 Olympic Games in Stockholm, Sweden.

Longest span The longest span for B.A.W.A. titles is 24 years by G. Mackenzie, who won his first title in 1909 and his last in 1933. Mackenzie, also jointly holds (see Fencing) the record of having represented Great Britain in five successive Olympiads from 1908 to 1928.

Heaviest heavyweight The heaviest heavyweight champion in British wrestling history was A. Dudgeon (Scotland), who won the 1936 and 1937 B.A.W.A. heavyweight titles, scaling 22 st. *139 kg.*

Cumberland wrestling The British Cumberland and Westmorland Championships were established in 1904. The only 6 time champions have been J. Badderley (Middleweight in 1905–06–08–09–10–12) and E. A. Bacon (Lightweight in 1919–21–22–23–28–29).

GREAT BRITAIN—MOST TITLES

Heavyweight	10	Ken Richmond, 1949–60
Middleweight	7	Thomas Albert Baldwin (b. 27 Sept. 1905), 1942, 1944–46, 1948, 1951–52 (also Welterweight in 1941)
Welterweight	9	Joe Feeney, 1957–60, 1962, 1964–66, 1968
Lightweight	8	Arthur Thompson, 1933–40
Featherweight	8	H. Hall, 1952–57, 1961, 1963 and Lightweight 1958–59
Bantamweight	6	Joe Reid, 1930–35

PROFESSIONAL WRESTLING

Professional wrestling dates from *c.* 1875 in the United States. Georges Karl Julius Hackenschmidt (1877–1968) made no submissions in the period 1898–1908. The highest paid professional wrestler ever is Antonio ("Tony") Rocca, with $180,000 (*£75,000*) in 1958. The heaviest ever wrestler has been William J. Cobb of Macon, Georgia, U.S.A. (b. 1926), who was billed in 1962 as the 802 lb. *363 kg 781* (57 st. 4 lb.) "Happy" Humphrey. What he lacked in mobility he possessed in suffocating powers. By July 1965 he had reduced to a more modest 232 lb. *105 kg 233* (16 st. 8 lb.).

Most Successful Ed "Strangler" Lewis (1890–1966) *née* Robert H. Friedrich, fought 6,200 bouts in 44 years losing only 33 matches. He won world titles in 1920, 1922 and 1928.

Britain's greatest professional wrestler has been Bert Assirati (b. 1912) who in 21 years was never once pinned on the mat. At 5 ft 6 in *167 cm* and 266 lb. *120 kg* he could do a crucifix on the rings, 3 one arm pull-ups and dead lift 800 lb. *332,9 kg.*

Sumo wrestling The sport's origins in Japan certainly date from *c.* 200 A.D. The heaviest ever performer was probably Dewagatake, a wrestler of the 1920's who was 6 ft 5 in *195 cm* tall and weighed up to 30 st. *190 kg.* Weight is amassed by over alimentation with a high protein sea food stew called *chanko-rigori*. The tallest was probably Ozora, an early 19th century performer, who stood 7 ft 3 in *220 cm* tall. The most successful wrestler has been Koki Naya (b. 1940), *alias* Taiho ("Great Bird"), who won his 26th Emperor's Cup on 10–24 Sept. 1967. He was the youngest ever *Yokozuna* (Grand Champion) at the age of 21 in 1967. The highest *dan* is Makuuchi attained by Taiho in 1965.

YACHTING

Origins Yachting in England dates from the £100 stake race between Charles II and his brother James, Duke of York, on the Thames on 1 Sept. 1661 over 23 miles *37 km* from Greenwich to Gravesend. The earliest club is the Royal Cork Yacht Club (formerly the Cork Harbour Water Club), established in Ireland in 1720. The word yacht is from the Dutch to hunt or chase.

Highest speed The highest speed achieved in trials run by a national yachting governing body has been 26.3 knots 30.28 m.p.h. *48,73 km/h* by the 60 ft *18,28 m* proa *Crossbow* (sail area 932 ft² [*86,58 m²*]) designed by Rod McAlpine-Downie, with T. Coleman as helmsman, off Portland, Dorset on 6 Oct. 1972. The U.S. Navy experimental hydrofoil craft *Monitor* is reported to have attained speeds close to 40 knots (46 m.p.h. [*74 km/h*]).

Most successful The most successful racing yacht in history was the Royal Yacht *Britannia* (1893–1935), owned by King Edward VII, when Prince of Wales and subsequently by King George V, which won 231 races in 625 starts.

America's Cup The America's Cup was originally won as an outright prize by the schooner *America* on 22 Aug. 1851 at Cowes and was later offered by the New York Yacht Club as a challenge trophy. On 8 Aug. 1870 J. Ashbury's *Cambria* (G.B.) failed to capture the trophy from the *Magic*, owned by F. Osgood (U.S.A.). Since then the Cup has been challenged by Great Britain in 15 contests, by Canada in two contests, and by Australia thrice, but the United States holders have never been defeated. The closest race ever was the fourth race of the 1962 series, when the 12 m *13 yds* sloop *Weatherly* beat her Australian challenger *Gretel* by about 3½ lengths (75 yds [*68 m*]) a margin of only 26 sec on 22 Sept. 1962. The fastest time ever recorded by a 12 m *13 yd* boat for the triangular course of 24 miles *38 km* is 2 hrs 46 min 58 sec by *Gretel* in 1962.

Little America's Cup The catamaran counterpart to the America's Cup was instituted in 1961 for International C-Class catamarans. The British club entry has won on each annual occasion to 1968 *v.* the U.S.A. (1961–66 and 1968) and *v.* Australia in 1967. In 1969 Denmark beat G.B. and in 1970 Australia beat Denmark and has held the Cup since.

Largest yacht The largest private yacht ever built was Mrs. Emily Roebling Cadwalader's *Savarona* of 4,600 gross tons, completed in Hamburg, Germany in Oct. 1931, at a cost of $4,000,000 (*now £1.66 million*). She (the yacht), with a 53 ft *16,15 m* beam and measuring 407 ft 10 in *124,30 m* overall, was sold to the Turkish government in March 1938. Operating expenses for a full crew of 107 men approached $500,000 (*now £200,000*) per annum.

The largest private sailing yacht ever built was the full-rigged 350 ft *106 m* auxiliary barque *Sea Cloud* (formerly *Hussar*), owned by the oft-married Mrs. Marjorie Merriweather Post-Close-Hutton-Davies-May (born 1888), one-time wife of the U.S. Ambassador in the U.S.S.R. Her four masts carried 30 sails with the total canvas area of 36,000 ft² *3 344 m²*.

Largest sail The largest sail ever made was a parachute spinnaker with an area of 18,000 ft² *1 672 m²* (more than two-fifths of an acre [*0,1 ha*]) for Vanderbilt's *Ranger* in 1937.

Olympic Games The first sportsman ever to win individual gold medals in four successive Olympic Games was Paul B. Elvström (b. 25 Feb. 1928) (Denmark) in the Firefly class in 1948 and the Finn class in 1952, 1956 and 1960. He has also won 8 other world titles in a total of 6 classes. The lowest number of penalty points by the winner of any class in an Olympic regatta is 3 points (6 wins [1 disqualified] and 1 second in 7 starts) by *Superdocius* of the Flying Dutchman class (Lt. Rodney Stuart Pattisson, M.B.E., R.N. (b. 5 Aug. 1943) and Iain Somerled Macdonald-Smith, M.B.E. (b. 3 July 1945)) at Acapulco Bay, Mexico in October 1968.

Great Britain The only British yacht to win two titles was *Scotia* in the Open class and Half-One Ton class at the 1900

337

SPORTS, GAMES AND PASTIMES

Regatta with Lorne C. Currie, helmsman and crewed by J. H. Gretton and Linton Hope. The only British yachtsman to win in two Olympic regattas is Rodney Pattisson in 1968 (see above) and again with *Superdoso* crewed by Christopher Davies (b. 29 June 1946) at Kiel, West Germany in 1972.

Admiral's Cup The ocean racing series to have attracted the largest number of participating nations (three boats allowed to each nation) is Admiral's Cup held by the Royal Ocean Racing Club in the English Channel in alternate years. Up to 1973, Britain had won 5 times, U.S.A. twice and Australia and West Germany once.

Biggest Class The most numerous class of boat originating in Britain and the world's greatest two-man dinghy class is the Mirror Dinghy with 41,429 boats world wide on 1 June 1973.

24 Hour Dinghy Race The greatest distance covered in 24 hrs in the annual West Lancashire Yacht Club event at Southport is 112 miles *180 km* by a G.P. 14 from West Kirby Sailing Club on 11–12 Sept. 1968. On 19–20 July 1972 a National Squib (17 ft 3 in [*5,25 m*]), sailed by Charles Iliff and James Wilson, achieved 125 nautical miles, off the Flanders coast, in 24 hours to average 5.02 knots *9,64 km/h*.

Highest Altitude The greatest altitude at which sailing has been conducted is 14,212 ft *4 331 m* on Lake Pomacocha, Peru by *Nusta* a 19 ft *5,79 m* Lightning dinghy owned by Jan Jacobi, reported in 1959.

Crossbow setting a yachting speed record off Portland in the English Channel with 26.3 Knots

---

Acknowledgements

J. W. Arblaster, Esq., A.I.M.
James Bond
British Airways
British Museum (Natural History)
British Rail
British Travel
British Waterworks Association
A. W. Bulley, Esq.
Henry G. Button, Esq.
Kenneth H. Chandler, Esq.
Central Electricity Generating Board
Central Office of Information
Dr. A. J. C. Charig
Sq. Ldr. D. H. Clarke, D.F.C., A.F.C.
Clerk of Dail Eireann
Fédération Aéronautique Internationale
Fédération Internationale de l'Automobile
Fédération Internationale des Hôpitaux
George Fisher, Esq.
Frank L. Forster
Fortune
Dr. Francis C. Fraser
General Post Office
A. Herbert, Esq. (New Zealand)

Michael E. R. R. Herridge, Esq.
Dr. Arthur H. Hughes (Chairman Guinness Superlatives Ltd., 1954–1966)
Imperial War Museum
Institute of Strategic Studies
Kline Iron and Steel Company
The Library of Congress, Washington, D.C.
Lloyd's Register of Shipping
London Transport Board
Prof. K. G. McWhirter, M.A., M.Sc.
Meteorological Office
Metropolitan Police
Alan Mitchell, Esq.
Miss Carole Mortimer
Music Research Bureau
National Aeronautics and Space Administration
National Geographic Society
National Maritime Museum
National Physical Laboratory
Mrs. Susann Palmer
A. J. R. Purssell Esq. (Chairman since 1971)
Jean Reville, Esq.
Royal Astronomical Society
Royal Botanic Gardens

Royal Geographic Society
Royal National Life-boat Institution
Dr. Albert Schwartz
John W. R. Taylor, Esq.
Trinity House
U.N. Statistical Office
Water and Water Engineering
Gerry L. Wood, Esq., F.Z.S.
World Meteorological Organization
Zoological Society of London

Also to A. T. Albin, Esq., Mrs. Barbara Anderson, Mrs. Sally Bennett, Mrs. Christine Bethlehem, Mrs. Rosemary Bevan, Miss Suzi Biggar, D. Richard Bowen, Esq., Signa. Wendy Cirillo, Mrs. Pamela Croome, Miss Trudy Doyle, Mlle. Béatrice Frei, Miss Amanda Griffin, Harold C. Harlow, Esq., Miss Tessa Hegley, E. C. Henniker, Esq., David N. Hewlett, Esq., Mrs. Angela Hoaen, David F. Hoy, Esq., Mrs. Eileen Jackson, Mrs. Hilary Leavey, Mrs. Jane Mayo, G. M. Nutbrown, Esq., Mrs. Margaret Orr-Deas, Peter B. Page, Esq., John Rivers, Esq., Mrs. Judith Sleath, Mrs. Anne Symonds, Andrew Thomas, Esq. (Associate Editor 1964–68), Mrs. Winnie Ulrich, Miss Diana Wilford.

Photographic Credits

Aerofilms Ltd, 306 (col 2). Aero Pictorial, 212 (col 1). Associated Newspapers, 192 (3), 203. Associated Press, 18, 20, 43, 239 (col 2) 240 (col 1), 240 (col 2 top), 240 (col 2 bottom), 249 (bottom), 253 (col 1), 269, 272 (top), 282, 288, 296, 297, 308, 322. Barratts Photo Press, 271 (bottom). Belfast Telegraph, 250. Alfred Bennett, 157 (col 2). Birmingham Post, 208. The British Archer, 246. British Broadcasting Corporation, 118, 119. British Tourist Authority, 70 (col 2), 76, 98, 123, 130, 136, 210 (col 2). British Trans Americas Expedition, 206. Camera Press, 102, 144. Central Press, 261 (col 2), 262 (col 2), 264, 276, 294. China Morning Post, 232. Christies, 174. Cinema International Corp (UK), 117. John Cleare, 309 (col 1). J. P. Coates, 47. Croydon Advertiser, 22. Crown Copyright, 183. Cryer & Marchant Ltd, 146. Daily Press, 249 (top). Dept of the Environment, 96, 134 (col 1). Dryden of St Ives, 126. John Eagle, 286 (col 1). Esso Photo, 143 (col 1). Euclid Inc, 147 (col 2). The Evening Standard, 225 (col 2). HMS Excellent, 227. John Fairfax & Sons Ltd, 36. Julio Falabella, 38. Features International, 23. Ford, 121. J. Gateand, 59. General Aeronautique, 154 (col 2). Goodyear Aerospace Corpn, 122, 157 (col 1). Gravely, 150. Greyhound, 147 (col 1). Greyhound Magazine, 289. The

Guardian, 298. Hannon Engineering Inc. 93. Johnny Harms, 243. Gilbert Hawker, 177. Harland & Wolff, 163 (top). Hong Kong Government, 181. Hopkins Photo Agency, 278. Bobby Hopkins, 295 (bottom). J. B. Horne, 152. Imperial War Museum, 189. Irish University Press, 104. IBM Ltd, 95. Italian State Tourist Office, 134 (col 2). Marian Kaplan, 283. Keystone, 196, 254, 263 (col 1), 26 (col 2). J. W. Kitchenham Ltd, 169. Kobel Collection, 19. E. D. Lacey, 271 (top), 274, 286, 287, 290. La Moto (De Noel), 304 (col 2). Hank Lefebvre, 178. Michael Lewin, 225 (col 1). Eric Lindgren, 52. Lloyd's of London, 108. Loffland Bros Co, 138. London Express, 125, 314 (top). Mansell Collection, 218. Marks & Spencer, 166. C. V. Middleton, 62. Milwaukee Zoological Park, 38. Montana Highway Commission, 131. Motorcycle, 304 (col 1). Mount Everest Foundation, 309 (col 2). NASA, 238 (bottom). National Galley, 97. National Geographical Society, 57. National Park Service, 69. H. W. Neale, 284. Nelson, 170. R. Newberry, 210 (col 1). Novosti Press Agency, 158. Opal Skymine Ltd, 90. Oshkosh, 175 (col 2). Gene Pahnke, 204 (col 1). Walter Parker, 211 (col 1). Peterborough Citizen & Advertiser, 186. Photo Reportage, 198. Players, 172. Popperfoto, 324. Portuguese

Tourist Office, 135. Press Association, 260, 261 (col 1), 262 (col 1), 263 (col 2), 273. Psychic Press Ltd, 32. Radio City, 113. Radio Times Hulton Picture Library, 26, 27 (2), 29, 31, 68, 79, 81, 115 (col 1 top), 115 (col 2), 237 (col 2), 252, 293, 300, 313, 316, 317 (top), 325, 328. Royal Danish Ministry for Foreign Affairs, 162. Roy J. Sabine, 49. Salford City Reporter, 279. Scottish Electricity Board, 161 (col 2). Erika Seldel, 320. South African Tourist Corporation, 63, 127. Sikorsky Aircraft, 156. Miss E. D. Smith, 230. Sotheby & Co, 175 (col 1). Sport and General, 255, 306 (col 1), 314 (bottom). Abe Saperstein, 248. Steward Observatory 83. Syndication International, 221, 226, 257, 266, 275, 307 (col 2). L. Taylor, 177. Richard Thornd, 202. John Timbers, 233 (top). United Press International, 242, 247, 302. United Press Photos, 195. US Air Force, 154 (col 1). US Dept of the Interior, 64. US Navy Photograph, 142, 70. United Towing Ltd, 143 (col 2). Universal Pictorial Press, 105, 223, 238 (top), 239 (col 1). University of Massachusetts, 107. University of Michigan News Service, 110. Vestry House Museum, 145. Johnnie Walker, 167 (col 1). Western Morning News, 133. Wilson & Co, 159. G. L. Wood, 37, 41. James Young, 114. K. Ziolkowski, 99. Zoological Society of London, 45.

STOP PRESS

CHAPTER 1—THE HUMAN BEING

Page 18
Shortest dwarfs A rachitic dwarf named Nruturam (b. 28 May 1929) living in Naydwar, India is reported to be 28 in *71 cm* in height.
Joyce Carpenter d. 7 Aug 1973.

Page 19
Heaviest Heavy-weights *World* The Veteran's Administration Hospital, Houston, Texas, reported on 5 Jan. 1972 that they had discharged John Lang, 37, of Clinton, Iowa, who according to his manager weighed between 900 and 1,000 lb. *408 and 453 kg*. His symptoms, age, caravan, and many other details are identical to those attaching to Mike Walker (*q.v.*).

Page 22
Centenarian *Great Britain* Alice Stevenson died on 18 Aug. 1973 aged 112 years 39 days. Mrs. Elizabeth Watkins (b. 10 Mar. 1863) in Belfast City Hospital) succeeded as title-holder.

Page 24
Multiple great grand-parents Mrs Finch, aged 98, of East Ham, Greater London, was reported in May 1972 to be a great-great-great grandmother.

Page 30
Heart Transplant Harry Lewis (real name Lewis B. Russell) now of Indianopolis reaches the fifth anniversary of his operation on 27 Aug. 1973.

Page 31
Hunger strike It was reported on 15 July 1973 that Dennis Goodwin, serving 14 years in Wakefield Prison for rape and housebreaking, had completed his 382nd day on a hunger strike during which he has accepted only liquids.

CHAPTER 2—ANIMALS AND PLANTS

Page 34
G Force Record The highest g force encountered in nature is the 380 g of the acceleration of a 10 mm long click beetle when jumping 30 cm *11.7 in.* as measured by M. E. G. Evans of Manchester University.

Page 35
Rarest Mammals The World Wild-Life Fund reported in May 1973 that there were at least 44 Japan rhinoceros alive.

Page 45
Longest feathers In 1970 an Onagadori with tail feathers 34 ft 9½ in. *10,60 m* long was reported.

Page 58
Oldest Trees Reports from the Dendrochronological Department at the University of Arizona indicate that ring counts from fallen bristlecones now extend back another 850 years to 8,000 years or to nearly 6000 B.C.

Page 59
Longest Daisy chain Seven 11 to 14 year old girls from Brookfield School, Calver, Sheffield—Lindsey Crabb, Christine Douglass, Jennifer Geary, Adele Hickling, Judith and Karen Longmore, and Deborah Siney—completed a daisy chain 1,715 ft *522,72 m* in length from 18,000 daisies on 30–31 May 1973.

Page 61
Tallest Hedge Runs for 170 yds *155 m* and is 15 ft *4,57 m* thick at the base.

Page 62
Ten leafed clover The finder was Mrs Mildred Henry of Athens, Ohio whose 10 leafed specimen was collected on 3 Oct. 1967. For Phillipa Smith *read* Philippa Smith.

CHAPTER 3—NATURAL WORLD

Page 69
Mountains The highest insular *mountain* is Mt. Sukarno.

Page 72
Rivers For 20 *million million ft²* read *ft³*.

Page 74
Stalactites For Poll on Ionian *read* Ionain.

Deepest Caves By Countries—Latest Revisions for table on page 74

ft	m	Cave	Country
3,850	1,174	Resea de la Pierre Saint Martin	France
3,743	1,141	Gouffre Berger, Vercors	France
3,018	920	Abisso Michele Gortani	Italy
2,798	853	Sumidero de Cellagua, Cantabria	Spain
2,526	770	Jaskinia Sniezna, Tatras	Poland
2,463	751	Ghar Parau, Zagros Mts	Iran
2,460	750	Holloch, Muotathal Lucerne	Switzerland
2,329	710	Gruberhorn holhe, Dachstein	Austria
1,250	381	Yorkshire Pot, Crow's Nest Pass, Alberta	Canada
1,020	310	Khazad-Dum, Tasmania	Australia
1,010	307	Ogof Fynnon Ddu	Wales

Longest *Revised figures for the length of Mammoth Cave/Flint Ridge System are now 122 miles 196,3 km or 131.7 miles 212 km and for the Ogof Fynnon Ddu, Breconshire 25 miles 40 Km. The longest vertical pitch is El Sotano, Mexico at 410 m 1,345 ft.*

CHAPTER 4—UNIVERSE AND SPACE

Page 78
Sun Dimensions The latest revised mean diameter for the sun is 864,940 miles *1 391 986 km*, a decrease of 430 miles *692 km*.

Page 79
Longest Eclipses The eclipse of A.D. 717 which occurred in the Pacific lasted 7 min 15 sec. That in the South Atlantic on 16 July 2186 will last 7 min 28 sec.

Brightest Comet The Comet Kohoutek or 1973F was first identified by Luboš Kohoutek of Hamburg University on two plates exposed on 7 March 1973 as a diffuse 16th mag. object 440 million miles *708 million km* distant in the constellation Hydra. It will reach its perihelion of 13 million miles *21 million km* on 28 Dec. 1973 and a magnitude −5 to −10 and will thus be visible to the naked eye in broad daylight and at its most spectacular around 10–20 Jan. 1974. It will travel round the sun at 93,600 m.p.h. *150 500 km/h* and will not reappear for at least 10,000 years.

Page 80
Mars Nix Olympica rises some 79,000 ft *24,000 m* above its surrounding "terrain".
The distance of *Phobos* from Mars has now been revised to 5,828 ± 2 miles *9 380 ± 3 km*, an increase of 10 miles *16 km*.
The irregularly shaped *Deimos* is now quoted as having an average diameter of 7.1 miles *11,4 km*.

Page 81
Most Distant Quasars Estimates vary according to the adopted value of Hubble's constant and whether or not the Euclidean model is abandoned. According to the Sandage model of the Universe, the observable horizon, *i.e.* the distance at which receding quasars attain the speed of light and hence their luminosity disappears, is 11,400 million light years. Thus the distance of the faint blue QSO OQ 172 in Boötes would be, on *this* model, perhaps less than 11,000 million light years distant.

Page 85
Largest Satellite The 442 lb. *200 kg* U.S. RAE (Radio Astronomy Explorer) launched into lunar orbit in June 1973 has antennae 1500 ft *415 m* from tip to tip.

CHAPTER 5—THE SCIENTIFIC WORLD

Page 86
Particles *Number of* There are 35 known elementary particles and anti-particles whilst early in 1973 the existence of only 68 resonance *types* was accepted.
In late May 1973 cosmic-ray researchers at Leeds University announced the existence of a new heavy particle named the mandela, detected at Haverah Park near Harrogate, Yorkshire which has been variously described as the long awaited quark or a vector boson.

Highest melting points The non-metallic element with the highest solidification point is the graphite form of carbon which sublimes directly from solid to vapour at 4073 K or 3800° C.

Page 88
Most powerful Drugs The most powerful synthetically manufactured drug is d-Lysergic Acid Diethylamide tartrate (LSD-25, $C_{20}H_{25}N_{30}O$) first produced in 1938 in research for cure against the common cold and first intentionally manufactured by Dr. Albert Hoffmann (Switzerland) as a hallucinogen on 16–19 April 1943.

Page 89
Most expensive Wine The highest price for a *single* bottle (as opposed to a magnum or larger receptacle) has been 30,000 French Francs (*then* £2,470) for a Château Ausone 1900, Saint Emilion les Grand Cru Classé claret auctioned for charity by Mes. Ader, Picard et Tajan of Paris jointly with Sotheby's in Paris on 21 Nov. 1972.

Page 91
Largest Steerable Dish A High Court action to injunct the Meifod project was withdrawn on 17 July 1973.

Page 94
Wind Tunnels United Kingdom The intermittent compressed air type tunnel at the B.A.C. plant at Warton, Lancashire can be run at Mach. 4 and during discharge of stored compressed air can, by release, generate a power far higher than can be maintained by any continuous type of wind tunnel.

CHAPTER 6—ARTS AND ENTERTAINMENTS

Page 97
Longest Painting Thirty-three members of Class Six of the Sacred Heart School, Teddington, Middlesex expended nearly 1,000 man hours in Jan.–March 1973 in completing a painting *Scenes of England* which measured 150 yd *137 m* in length.

Page 102
Longest English Place Name The Northumbrian River Authority inquiry in June 1973 into the effects of building a projected dam at Saffronside revealed that a 19 letter place named Cottonshopeburnfoot would be drowned.

Page 106
Best Sellers The total number of Bibles and parts of the Bible produced in 1972 by Bible Societies worldwide was 218,429,595 in 255 languages. The *Book of A Thousand Tongues* republished in 1972 by the American Bible Society contains translations in 1,399 languages.

Longest Letter Physically the longest letter reported is one of 5,379 ft *1 639 m* mailed on 12 March 1973 by Steve Riley of Sacramento, California to his cousin Tim Knock of Kansas City, Missouri at a cost of $11.07 in postage. It contained 137,000 words.

Page 109
Organ Marathon Louis Fourie of Welkom, South Africa played for 73 hours ending on 13 Apr. 1973.

Largest Organ For 64 ft Gravissima *read* 64 ft *tone* Gravissima.

Page 116
Live Audience For 560,800 *read* 56,800. There were in addition 6,000 gate-crashers.

Loudest Pop Group The amplification of *Deep Purple* at 10,000 watts attains 117 decibels—sufficient to render 3 of the audience in the Rainbow Theatre, London unconscious.

Page 117
Cinema box Office The British record for a weeks takings was set at £52,000 by the Odeon, Leicester Square for *Live and Let Die* the eighth epic of James Bond featuring Roger Moore in the week starting 23 July 1973.

Page 119
Most Prolific Scriptwriter The most prolific television writer in the world is the Rt. Hon. Lord Willis (b. 13 Jan. 1918), who in the period 1949–73 has created 21 series, including the first seven years and 2,250,000 words of *Dixon of Dock Green*, which has been running since 1955, 20 plays and 21 feature films. In addition he has written 21 stage plays from farce to tragedy and one

musical of which 18 have been produced and is now working on a first novel. His total output since 1945 can be estimated at 75,000,000 words.

Highest T.V. Advertising The highest T.V. advertising rates in Great Britain are the I.T.V. peak time network 30 sec spots rate fixed in Sept. 1972 at £7,057 or or £235.23 per second.

CHAPTER 7—THE WORLD'S STRUCTURES

Page 122
Tallest Totem Pole A totem pole 173 ft *52,73 m* tall was raised on 6 June 1973 at Alert Bay, British Columbia, Canada. It tells the story of the Kwakiutl and took 36 man-weeks to carve.

Page 124
Most Expensive House The Georgian town house of 14,000 ft² *1 300 m²* at 30 Curzon Street, Mayfair, London, built in 1771 by Robert Adam for the 1st Marquess of Bath was sold at auction by Jones, Lang, Wootton for the Royal Worcester Co. to Daejan Holdings on 26 June 1973 for £2,720,000 freehold.

Page 126
Pub Visiting Mr. House reached his 2,500th pub on 31 July. 1973. Using public and private transport J. G. Lawton of the *Leeds Evening Post* has evidence of more than 13,000 visitations.

Page 128
Tallest structure For Emley Moore read Emley *Moor*. Tallest Tower: the balcony on the Ostankino tower is at 337 m *1,106 ft*.

Page 132
Tube Tunnel For East Fincley read East Finc*h*ley.

Page 135
Largest Oil Platform The tallest sea oil platform is that for Shell-Esso under construction by Redpath Dorman Long for the Brent Field, North Sea which will be 750 ft. *228,60 m* high is due for completion in May 1975.

Page 136
Scaffolding The greatest scaffolding structure ever erected was one comprising 750,000 ft (142 miles [*228,5 km*] of tubing) up to 486 ft *148 m* in height used in the reconstruction of Guy's Hospital, London in 1971.

Page 138
Deepest Ocean Drilling The deepest bore into the sea bed is 4,265 ft *1 300 m* by *Glomar Challenger* (US) as part of the Deep Sea Drilling Project. The deepest sea drill below sea level was 20,483 ft *6 243 m* as part of the same research project.

CHAPTER 8—MECHANICAL WORLD

Page 147
Dumper Truck A prototype Peerless V-Con End truck built in Dallas, Texas 28 ft *8,53 m* wide was operating in 1972.

Page 151
Railway Speeds for Crompton No 604 *read* Crampton No 604.

Page 153
Supersonic Flight for "Chick" E. Yeager *read* "Chuck" E. Yeager.

Page 154
Air Cargo for *11 040 m³* read *1104,0 m³*.

Page 155
Altitude Record A U.S.S.R. E-266 jet aircraft piloted by Aleksandr Fedotov climbed under its own power to a record 36 240 m *118,897 ft* or *22.51 miles* over the U.S.S.R., on 25 July 1973.

Page 157
Largest Balloon for *11,326 m³* read *1132,6 m³*.

CHAPTER 9—BUSINESS WORLD

Page 174
English Silver A pair of Queen Anne chandeliers of 1,970 oz. by John Bodington (1703-4) were bought by How of Edinburgh for a record £115,000 on 27 June 1973.

CHAPTER 10—HUMAN WORLD

Page 180
World Population The UN estimate for mid-1975 is now 4,021,758,000.

Page 184
Regnal Numbers Further research now confirms that HSH Prince Henry LXXIV Reuss had a cousin who died in infancy —Count Heinrich (or Henry) LXXV Reuss (1800–1801).

Page 190
Big Bertha The sobriquet Big Bertha was first applied to 17 in *431 mm* Krupp howitzers used against the Belgian forts early in World War I. The gun which shelled Paris, though referred to as a "Big Bertha" was as stated of only 210 mm 8.6 in calibre.

Page 197
Longest Prison Term Corona's 20th century US murder record was surpassed with the discovery on 13 Aug. 1973 of the body of the 27th victim of the pervert Dean Corll, 33 of Houston, Texas.

Page 198
Largest Ransom John R. Thompson, 50 of Firestone Tyre and Rubber Co was released in Buenos Aires, Argentina on 5 July 1973 by political kidnappers for a reputed $3,000,000 (£1.2 million).

Page 207
Most Unorthodox Driver Britain's most unorthodox driver was Mrs Viola Ireland, 78 who, on 11 June 1973 in Court at Basingstoke, Hampshire was banned from driving for a year and fined £40. In driving to Winchester she U-turned onto the M3 Motorway and drove south on the lanes normally reserved for north bound London traffic. Five hours later, having had "a nice tea" she was sighted by the self-same disbelieving police patrol man, who had earlier escorted her off, proceeding homeward at 15 m.p.h. *24 km/h* in what would have been the correct carriageway for her outward journey. An additional charge was one of parking at right angles across the road contrary to motorway rules.

Page 214
Worst Fire in U.K. The disaster of 1883 in the Victoria Hall, Sunderland was at a children's 1d entertainment in which 116 boys and 65 girls (and 2 others) aged between 3 and 14 expired not from fire but from suffocation after a stampede. Sixty nine children died in the major panic ensuing from the minor cinema fire at Paisley, Renfrewshire, Scotland on 31 Dec. 1929.

CHAPTER 11—HUMAN ACHIEVEMENTS

Page 216
Propeller Driven Speed Record Larry Hill drove the supercharged propeller driven hydroplane *Mr. Ed* at 202.42 m.p.h. *325,76 km/h* at Long Beach, California in August 1971. *Climax* recorded 205.19 m.p.h. *330,22 km/h* in a one-way run.

Page 220
Running The 24 hour running record was raised to 162.1 miles *269,3 km* by P. Skjoedt (Denmark) at Copenhagen, Denmark, 4–5 Aug. July 1973.

Page 223
Bath Tub Marathon The longest recorded propulsion of an unmodified bath tub was one of 24 hours by members of the Malvern Hills Round Table in July 1973.

Page 224
Most successful complainer Ralph Charell (b. 3 Dec. 1929), author of *How I Turn Ordinary Complaints into Thousands of Dollars*, between January 1963 and July 1973 amassed a total of $75,591.22 (£30,235) ranging between $6.95 and $25,000 in refunds and compensations.

Page 225–226
Limbo Dancing Marlene Raymond, 15, negotiated a flaming bar 6⅛ in *15,5 cm* off the floor at the Port of Spain Pavilion, Toronto on 24 June 1973.

Page 226
Escapology Léossen's escape from the cell was in Keflavik Airport prison on 23 Sept. 1972.

Page 227
High Diving The 491st suicide was committed from the Golden Gate Bridge in mid August 1973. There are seven know survivors of the 240 ft *73 m* plunge.

Page 228
Paper Chain Some 700 children of Writtle, Essex built a paper chain by the modern method of computer paper and staples 2 miles *3,2 km* in length on 16 June 1973.

Page 229
Pogo Stick Jumping Danny Koster of Clinton, Michigan, U.S.A. achieved 17,323 jumps on 5 July 1973.

Pole Squatting Kim Moren, 20 completed 253 days in a camper atop a 50 ft pole in Yakima, Washington, U.S.A. from 14 Oct. 1972 to 24 June 1973.

Page 230
Singing The marathon record was extended to 75 hr by Jerry Cammarata, 26 of Staten Island, New York with a repetoire of 917 songs sung in the bath tub during 24–27 July 1973.

Page 231
Teeth Pulling John Massis moved 4 railroad cars weighing 43 090 kg *42.4 tons* with his teeth harness on 15 Nov. 1972.

Page 232
Tunnel of Fire John Bridgeman passed through a tunnel of fire 114 ft *34,75 m* long at Bishop's Stortford, Hertfordshire on 28 May 1973. Note the fatal run of Stephen Ladd (p. 232) was on the return run of a 82 ft *25 m* tunnel. Reo Ruiters (South Africa) rode through a 62 m *200 ft* tunnel in Johannesburg in March 1973 but this was 12 ft by 12 ft against the now standard 6 ft 8 in square.

Page 233
Wealthiest U.K. Citizen The assets to which John Moores (b. Eccles, Lancashire 1896), founder of Littlewoods Football Pools (see page 282) has title were estimated at £400 million in mid 1973.

Page 235
Beer Upsidedown Moalwyn Howell, 26 of Beckenham, Kent consumed 2 pints *113,5 centilitres* upsidedown in a reported 13.8 sec on 11 July 1973.

CHAPTER 12—SPORTS, GAMES AND PASTIMES

Page 275
Football Association Heading: Tony Marshall, 17 of St. Austell, Cornwall completed 6,375 headers in 44 min in November 1972.

Transfer Fee Johann Cruyff was transferred from Ajax Amsterdam to F.C. Barcelona for £922,300 announced on 20 Aug. 1973.

Page 287
Golf, Most Major titles Jack Nicklaus surpassed R. T. Jones's record with a 14th major title by winning his third U.S. P.G.A. championship at Cleveland, Ohio on 12 Aug. 1973.

Page 312
Parachuting (new entry) Origins Parachuting graduated from pure life saving, through stunt exhibitions to a regulated sport with the Institution of world championships at Lesce-Bled, Yugoslavia in 1951. A team title was introduced at the second Championships at Saint Yan, France in 1954 and women's events were included at the third Championships near Moscow, U.S.S.R. in 1956.

World Titles The U.S.S.R. won the men's team titles in 1954–56 60–66–72 and the women's team title in 1956–58–68–68–72. No individual has ever won a second world overall title.

Accuracy Records Kumbar (Czechoslovakia) scored nine consecutive dead centre strikes (10 cm disc) in the 11th World Championships at Tahlequah, U.S.A. in 1972.

British Mr. John Meacock (Peterborough) has thrice won the British title (1969–71–72).

Page 332
One legged High Jump One legged Anthony Willis, 18 (City of Plymouth A.C.) cleared 6 ft *1 m 83* at Plymouth, Devon, England on July 1973.

Page 334
Walking End to End Johnnie Savile, 54 (one lung) and John Ryder covered the 886 miles *1 425 km* distance in 10 days 18 hr 20 min on 8–18 Aug. 1973.

INDEX

SUBJECT INDEX

An asterisk against a page reference indicates that there is a further reference in the Stop Press section.

343

LIQUEUR, *most expensive 89*
LIQUOR, *most alcoholic, smallest bottle 88–89*
LITIGATION, *most protracted 192*
LITTER, *largest 36, puppies 41, kittens 42*
LIVESTOCK RECORDS, *176–177*
LIVING STANDARD, *greatest cost increase 182–3*
LIZARD, *largest 45, oldest 46, largest extinct 54*
LOAD, *heaviest draught 41, heaviest and largest, tallest (overland) 148, heaviest (railway) 152, greatest air 154, heaviest pushed in a barrow 223, parachute 229*
LOAF, *longest 204*
LOBSTER, *largest 50*
LOCH, *longest sea, largest inland U.K., longest, deepest, highest 73*
LOCK, *largest, deepest, highest lock elevator, longest flight 130*
LOCOMOTIVE, *see Engine, Railway*
LOCUSTS, *largest swarm 51*
LOG ROLLING, *longest contest 228*
LONGEVITY, *21–22**
LORRY, *largest 147*
LOSS, *biggest paper 234*
LOUDEST POP GROUP, *340*
LUGEING, *250*
LUNAR CONQUEST, *215*
LUPIN, *tallest 61*
LYNCHING, *worst, last in U.K. 197*

MACHINERY, *oldest 159*
MACHINE TOOL, *largest 159*
MACH NUMBER, *highest attained with air 94, scale for aircraft speeds 152*
MAGAZINE, *largest circulation 108–109, highest advertising rates 109*
MAGNET, *strongest and heaviest 94*
MAGNETIC FIELD, *strongest 94*
MAGNITUDE, *Stellar 77, 80*
MAIL, *greatest robbery 198*
MAJORITY: *Electoral see Elections; Parliamentary see Parliament*
MAMMALS, *35–43, largest, tallest, smallest, rarest 35*, fastest 35–36, slowest, longest lived, highest living, largest herd, gestation periods, largest litter, fastest breeders 36, largest toothed 37, highest and lowest blood temperatures 40, largest prehistoric 56, earliest 57, largest marine 63*
MAMMOTH, *heaviest tusks, tallest 56*
MAN, *tallest 15–17, shortest 17–18, most variable stature, heaviest world 18–19, heaviest U.K., thinnest, lightest 19, greatest slimming feat, greatest weight gain 20, earliest 20–21, oldest 21–22, largest chest 26, most fingers, longest finger nails, longest hair, beard, moustache, richest natural resources, most alcoholic, highest, lowest temperature 28, first space flight 84, greatest altitude 216, fastest 215–216, most travelled 216, most married 221, richest in world, U.K. 233, highest salary in world, U.K., highest, lowest income 234, most bemedalled 236, most statues 238*
MANUFACTURING COMPANY, *largest 167*
MANUSCRIPT, *highest price; Bible, at auction 104*
MAP, *oldest 107*
MARATHON, *fastest 329 (see also separate activities)*
MARBLE, *largest slab 90*
MARBLES, *302*
MARCH (Military), *longest 190, fastest 191*
MARINE DISASTER, *worst world, U.K. 214*
MARQUEE, *largest 136*
MARRIAGE, *most 221–222, oldest bride and groom, longest, most married, largest mass ceremony 222, lowest, highest average ages 182*
MARSUPIALS, *largest, smallest, rarest, longest jump 40*
MASER, *first illumination of moon 95*
MASSACRES, *greatest 194*
MASS ARREST, *greatest 197*
MASS KILLINGS, *greatest 194*
MASTS, *Radio and T.V. 127, 128*
MATADOR, *greatest 257*
MATCHBOX LABELS, *oldest, longest and dullest set 174*
MATERNITY HOSPITAL, *largest world, U.K. 183*
MATTER, *rarest form 87*
MAYPOLE, *tallest 133*
MEASUREMENT, *smallest particle 93*
MEASURE OF WEIGHT, *earliest 92*
MEAT, *eating record 235, biggest consumers 203*
MEAT PIES, *eating record 235, largest 203*
MEDALS, *oldest, rarest, commonest, most expensive 235, V.C.—most bars, oldest, youngest, longest lived, most awards; record number of bars; most mentions in despatches, highest decorations U.S.S.R., U.S.A., most bemedalled man 236*
MEDICAL CENTRE, *largest 183*
MELTING POINT, *lowest and highest for gases 86, metals 87**
MEMBER OF PARLIAMENT, *largest, narrowest personal majority, fewest votes, most rapid change of fortune, greatest swing, highest poll, youngest, oldest 186, longest span of service, earliest women M.P.s, longset speech 187*
MEMORIAL, *tallest (progressive records) 127, tallest 133*
MEMORY (human), *most retentive 31*
MENTAL ARITHMETIC, *greatest feat 31*
MENTAL HOSPITAL, *largest 183, longest sentence in Broadmoor, longest escape 197*
MERCHANDISING FIRM, *largest 167*
MERCHANT SHIPPING, *world total largest fleet 205*
MERGER, *largest 165*
METAL, *lightest, densest, lowest and highest melting and boiling points, highest and lowest expansion, highest ductility, highest tensile strength, rarest, commonest, most non-magnetic, newest 87, purest 88*
METEOR, *greatest shower 77*
METEORITE, *largest world, U.K., Ireland 77, largest craters 77–78*
METEOROIDS, *77*
METROPOLITAN CENSUS AREA, *largest world 181*
MICROBE, Bacteria: *largest, highest, longest lived, toughest.* **Viruses:** *largest, smallest, most primitive 56*
MICROSCOPE, *most powerful, electron 93*
MIDGET, *shortest 17, lightest 19*
MILESTONE, *oldest 207*
MILITARY ENGINE, *largest 190*
MILK, *drinking record 235*
MILKING, *hand milking record 177*
MILK YIELD, *cows, lifetime, one lactation, day; goats 177*
MILLIONAIRESSES, *world, U.K. 233 youngest, earliest 234*
MILLION AND ONE (Darts), *270*
MILLIPEDE, *most legs 52*
MINARET, *tallest 212*
MINCE PIE, *largest 204*
MINE, *progressive records 138, earliest 138–139, deepest world, U.K., largest gold, richest gold, largest iron, copper, silver, lead and zinc, spoil heap, largest open pit, deepest open pit 139, winding cage speed 161, greatest depth, shaft sinking record 220*
MINERALS, *see Gems*
MINERAL WATER, *largest firm 167*
MINING, *winding cage speed 161, greatest depth, shaft sinking record 220, disaster world, U.K. 214*
MINT, *largest 202*
MIRROR, *largest (solar furnace) 159*
MISER, *greatest 234*
MOATS, *world's largest 123*
MOBILE, *largest, heaviest 98*
MODEL AIRCRAFT, *altitude, speed, duration record 157–158*
MODEL RAILWAY, *record run 152*
MODERN PENTATHLON, *302–303*
MOLLUSC, *largest squid, octopus, most ancient, largest, smallest, rarest, longest lived, shells; snail; largest, speed 53, earliest 57*
MONARCH, *longest descent, longest, shortest reign; British; longest, shortest reign 183, longest lived, youngest, most children, most married 184*
MONETARY VOTE, *largest Parliamentary 240*
MONEY, *200–202*
MONKEY, *largest, smallest, rarest, longest lived 38*
MONOCYCLE, *tallest, distance record 149, duration record 221*
MONOPOLY, *most protracted game 166*
MONORAIL, *highest speed 152*
MONUMENT, *tallest 133, largest prehistoric 133–134, youngest ancient, largest 134, most 183*
MOON, *distance extremes, diameter, earliest radar echo, speed, first direct hit, first photographs hidden side, first soft landing, blue moon, largest and deepest craters, brightest spot, highest mountains, temperature extremes, oldest samples 78, eclipses; earliest, longest, most, least frequent 79, longest lunar mission, duration record on 84, first man on 215*
MOON ORBITS, *records 85*
MORBIDITY, *highest 27*
MORSE, *highest speed 228*
MORTALITY, *infant, lowest, highest 182*
MORTAR, *largest 190*
MOSAIC, *largest 98*
MOSQUE, *largest 212*
MOSS, *smallest, longest 61*
MOTH, *largest 51–52, smallest, rarest, most acute sense of smell 52*
MOTHER, *most prolific in world, U.K., oldest in world, U.K., Ireland 23*
MOTIONLESSNESS, *longest 31*
MOTOR CAR, *see Car*
MOTORCYCLE, *earliest, earliest factory, fastest road machine, track machines, largest, most expensive 149, greatest body jump 223*
MOTOR CYCLING, *303–305*
MOTOR RACING, *305–308*
MOTOR RALLY, *round Britain record 148, earliest, longest, 307*
MOTOR VEHICLE, *see Car*
MOTORWAY, *most complex interchange, highest 206*
MOUND, *largest artificial 134*
MOUNTAIN, *highest submarine 66, highest world, highest from Earth's centre, highest insular*, highest U.K. and Ireland 69, highest unclimbed, largest, greatest ranges 71, highest points U.K. and Ireland by counties 70, highest lunar 78, racing 309 (see also 339)*
MOUNTAINEERING, *conquest of Everest, highest summit by woman 220, worst disaster world, U.K. 214, sport 308–310*
MOUSE, *smallest 39*
MOUSTACHE, *longest 28*
MULTIPLE BIRTHS, *24–25*
MULTIPLE GREAT GRAND-PARENTS, *24*
MURAL, *earliest, largest 97*
MURDER, *trial, longest, shortest, best attended 192, highest rate 194–195, lowest rate, most prolific murderer, world U.K., most gang murders 195*
MURDERESS, *most prolific 195*
MUSCLE, *largest, smallest 26, fastest movements 28, 51*
MUSEUMS, *oldest, largest 98*
MUSHROOM, *largest farm 176*
MUSIC, *109–113, longest silence 111*
MUSICAL FILM, *best-selling record 116, most expensive, highest price rights, highest box office gross 117*
MUSICAL INSTRUMENTS, *109–110 oldest, largest and loudest 109, greatest manpower required, highest and lowest notes 110*
MUSICAL NOTATION, *oldest 109*
MUSICAL NOTE, *generated by "laser" beam 93, highest and lowest orchestral 101–111*
MUSICAL SHOW, *longest runs, most costly, shortest run 114*
MUSICIANS, *most for one instrument 110, highest paid 111*
MUZZLE VELOCITY, *highest 241*

NAILS (finger), *longest 28*
NAME, *longest chemical 101; place; longest 101–102, shortest, earliest, commonest 102; personal; earliest, longest, shortest, commonest 102–103, most contrived 103, longest Biblical 105*
NARCOTICS, *greatest haul 198*
NATION, *largest 179, richest, poorest 200*
NATIONAL ANTHEM, *oldest, longest shortest, longest rendition 111*
NATIONAL DEBT, *largest 200*
NATIONAL INCOMES, *highest 182*
NATIONAL PRODUCT, *largest 200*
NATIONAL SAVINGS, *highest total 200*
NATIONAL WEALTH, *total 200*
NATURAL BRIDGE, *longest 74*
NATURAL INCREASE (population), *highest, lowest rates 182*
NATURE RESERVE, *smallest world 62*
NATURISTS, *first and largest camps 136*
NAVAL BATTLE, *greatest 189*
NAVE, *longest world, U.K. 210*
NAVY, *largest, greatest battle 189*
NEBULAE, *farthest visible 82*
NECK, *longest 27*
NEEDLE THREADING, *record strands 228*
NERVE GAS, *most powerful 88*
NETBALL, *310*
NEWSPAPER, *most durable comic strip 106, most in world 107, most readers 107–108, oldest world, U.K., most expensive, largest, largest page, smallest, highest circulation, "earliest", most read 108*
NEWSREELS, *most durable commentator 118*
NEWT, *largest, smallest world, U.K. 47*
NEW TOWN, *largest 124*
NIGHT CLUB, *oldest, largest, highest, lowest 125*
NOBEL PRIZE, *highest cash value, most awards by country 237, individual 237–238, oldest prize-man, youngest 238*
NOISE, *loudest 93*
NONUPLETS, *24*
NORTHERN LIGHTS, *78*
NORTH POLE, *conquest 218*
NOTE, *highest and lowest attained by human voice 30, highest generated by "laser" beam 93, highest and lowest orchestral 110–111*
NOUNS, *most cases 99*
NOVEL, *longest 104, highest sales 106*
NOVELIST, *most prolific, fastest, top-selling, youngest 105*
NUCLEAR EXPLOSION, *greatest 191*
NUDIST CAMP, *first, largest 136*
NUGGET, *largest gold, silver 90*
NUMBER, *highest named, lowest and highest prime, lowest and highest perfect, most primitive, most decimal places 92*
NUMBER PLATE (Car), *earliest, most expensive 145*
NUMEROLOGY, *expression of large numbers 92*
NUT (Engineering), *largest 160*
NYLON, *sheerest 174*

OAK, *largest U.K., tallest 58*
OARS, *earliest 140*
OBELISK, *oldest, largest 134*
OBITUARY, *longest 184*
OBJECT, *smallest visible to human eye 30, farthest visible 82, remotest (universe) 82–83*
OBSERVATORY, *highest, oldest 91*
OCEAN, *(see also Sea), largest (area, depth, weight, volume), most southerly deepest, world, British, temperature, remotest spot from land 66, greatest descent 220, progressive descent records 220*
OCEANARIUM, *earliest, largest 63*
OCTOPUS, *largest 53*
OCTUPLETS, *24*
ODDS (Gambling), *longest, shortest 282–283*
OFFICE BUILDING, *administrative, commercial world's largest, tallest in U.K. 120*
OIL COMPANY, *largest 168*
OIL FIELD, *largest world, greatest gusher, greatest fire 138*
OIL FIRE, *greatest 138*
OIL GUSHER, *most prolific 138*
OIL PIPELINE, *longest world, U.K. 160*
OIL PLATFORM, *largest 144*
OIL POLLUTION, *greatest 144*
OIL REFINERY, *largest 168*
OIL TANK, *largest 160*
OIL WELL, *deepest world, U.K. 138*
OLD SCHOOL TIE, *oldest 209*
OLD SOLDIERS, *oldest 189*
OLYMPIC GAMES, *310–311*
OMELETTE, *greatest number 228, largest 204*
ONAGER, *largest 190*
ONIONS, *picked, eating record 235*
OPAL, *largest 90*
OPERA, *longest, longest aria, cadenza 111*
OPERA HOUSE, *largest 111–12, most tiers 112,*
OPERATION, *longest, oldest, youngest subjects, heart transplants, earliest appendicectomy, anaesthesia 30, fastest amputation 31*
ORCHESTRA, *most, largest, largest attendance, highest and lowest notes 110*
ORCHID, *rarest U.K. 57, largest, tallest, smallest, highest priced 60, smallest seed 62*
ORDER OF MERIT, *longest lived holder, oldest recipient, youngest recipient 240*
ORDERS AND MEDALS, *235–236*
ORGAN, *largest, largest church, loudest stop, marathon 109*, highest and lowest notes 110*
ORGANISM, *smallest, largest, most basic 56, earliest 56–57*
ORIENTEERING, *312*
OSCARS, *most 117*
OSTRICH, *largest, running speed 43, largest egg 44*
OWL, *rarest, most acute vision 44*
OX, *heaviest England 176, eating record 235*
OYSTERS, *eating record 235*

PACIFIC CROSSING, *fastest 141, marine records 219*
PACING *332–333*
PAGODA, *tallest 212*
PAINTER, *most prolific 97*
PAINTING, *earliest, largest world U.K. 96, most valuable 96–97, highest price Old Master, auction records, world, by British artist, highest price modern, living artist, pop art 97, highest priced (progressive records) 98, oldest and youngest R.A., 97, shortest apprenticeship, earliest, largest mural 97**
PALACE, *largest world, U.K., largest ever 123*
PALINDROME, *longest 100*
PANCAKE RACE, *fastest 332*
PANCAKE TOSSING, *228*
PANDEMIC, *worst world, U.K. 214*
PANIC, *worst world, U.K. 214*
PAPER, *most expensive writing 175*
PAPER MILL, *largest 168*
PAPER MONEY, *200–201*
PAPERWEIGHT, *highest auction price 174*
PARACHUTING, *longest fall without parachute, parachuting records 229, 341*
PARISH, *longest incumbency 213*
PARISH REGISTER, *oldest 213*
PARK, *largest 62*
PARKING METERS, *earliest 207*
PARLIAMENT, *world; oldest, largest, smallest quorum, highest paid legislators 184, longest membership 184–185, filibusters, largest elections, closest, most one-sided elections, highest personal majority; U.K.; earliest, longest, shortest, longest sittings, most time-consuming legislation, most divisions 185, party majorities 185–186, largest personal, narrowest, most recounts, fewest votes, most rapid change of fortune, greatest swing, highest poll; M.P.s; youngest, oldest 186, longest span, earliest women M.P.s, House of Lords; oldest, youngest member, longest speech, greatest petition; Premiership; longest term, shortest term, most times, longest lived, youngest; Chancellorship; longest and shortest tenures, most appointments; Speakership; longest 187*
PARTICLE, *number, lightest and heaviest sub-nuclear, fastest 86**
PARTICLE ACCELERATOR, *most powerful 94*
PARTIES, *largest communist, country with most 185*
PARTY GIVING, *most expensive 222*
PASS, *highest 206*

Indexing by
Gordon Robinson

349

1. ORKNEY ISLANDS World's Shortest Scheduled Flight: Westray to Papa Westray—120 sec

2. OUTER HEBRIDES World's Tallest True Giant: The 7 ft 9 in *236 cm* Angus Macaskill born Island of Berneray in 1825

   Highest Ever Recorded Wind Speed 408 m.p.h. *656 km/h* 154,200 ft *47 000 m* above South Uist 13 Dec. 1967

3. ROCKALL The World's most isolated small rock 191 miles *307 km* from St. Kilda. Also the Most Westerly point in the E.E.C.

4. ABERDEENSHIRE World's Earliest Spider and Earliest Insect: *Palaeostenzia crassipes* and *Rhyniella proecursor* dating from 370,000,000 B.C.

5. PERTHSHIRE World's Tallest Hedge: The beech hedge at Meikleour, planted 1746 now stands 85 ft *25,90 m* tall

6. DUNBARTONSHIRE World's Largest Ever Liner: *R.M.S. Queen Elizabeth* (83,673 gross tons) launched 27 Sept. 1938

7. WEST LOTHIAN-FIFE World's Longest Bridge Span (in period 1890 to 1917): Forth Railway Bridge—1,710 ft *521 m*

8. BERWICKSHIRE World's Longest Bridge Span (in period 1820 to 1826): Union Bridge—449 ft *136,85 m*

9. LANCASHIRE World's Highest Speed on Water: Donald Campbell was measured at 328 m.p.h. *527 km/h* on Coniston Water in "Bluebird" K-7 on 4 Jan. 1967

10. YORKSHIRE Earliest "Water Skiing": Plank-riding behind a motor-boat was an event at the Scarborough Regatta on 15 July 1914

    Earliest Man-Carrying Glider: Sir George Cayley's glider carried his coachman (possibly John Appleby) 500 yds *460 m* in 1853

11. World's Top Selling Recording Group. The four Beatles, b. Liverpool 1940–43, sold more than 545,000,000 singles equivalents (1963–1972)

12. YORKS-LINCS World's Longest Bridge Span: The Main span of The Humber Bridge, due for completion in 1977, will be 4,626 ft *1 410 m*—365 ft *111,25 m* longer than the Verrazano Bridge, New York

13. LINCOLNSHIRE World's Tallest Structure: The 525 ft *160 m* tall central spire of Lincoln Cathedral completed in 1307 was the world's tallest structure and was unsurpassed for 5½ centuries till 1884

14. NORTH WALES World's Oldest Life Form: The microscopic organism *Kakabekia barghoorniana* collected near Harlech, Merioneth in 1964 dated from 2,000 million years ago

15. MIDLANDS Absolute Human Altitude Record: On 17 July 1862 James Glaisher ascended in a balloon from Wolverhampton to 25,400 ft *7 700 m* and again on 5 Sept. to a record height not certainly surpassed till 1927

    Tallest Giantess in Medical History: Jane Bunford (1895–1922) the Northfield giantess, probably measured 7 ft 11 in *241 cm*

16. WARWICKSHIRE The world's largest tapestry *Christ in Glory* in Coventry Cathedral measures 315 yds² *263 m²*

17. OXFORD World's First Sub-Four Minute Mile Run: Roger Bannister's 3 min 59.4 sec on 6 May 1954

18. LONDON World's Largest Diamond: The Royal Sceptre kept in the Jewel House, Tower of London, contains the Star of Africa of 530.2 carats

    World's Longest Vehicular Tunnel: The London Underground tunnel from Morden to East Finchley completed in 1939 measures 17 miles 528 yds *27,841 km*

    The world's most expensive land is prime freehold land in the City of London where one large site was valued in 1973 at £1,950 per ground ft² or £21,230 per m²

    The world's oldest proven female centenarian: Miss Alice Stevenson (b. 10 July 1861, d. 18 Aug. 1973) celebrated her 112th birthday at Sutton, Surrey

19. THAMES ESTUARY Sound Barrier First Encountered?: Geoffrey de Havilland's D.H. 108 Swallow disintegrated over Egypt Bay on 27 Sept. 1946

20. SOUTH WALES World's Earliest Locomotive to run on Rails. Richard Trevithick (b. 1771) demonstrated his first steam locomotive on a 9 mile *14,48 km* track at Penydarran, Glamorgan in 1804

21. CORNWALL Earliest Transatlantic Signal: Marconi's first transatlantic signal (letter S in morse) sent from Poldhu and received in Newfoundland on 12 Dec. 1901

22. SOLENT First Man to Exceed 400 m.p.h. *643,737 km/h*: Flt. Lt. Stainforth flew the Supermarine S.6B at 415.2 m.p.h. *668,19 km/h* on 29 Sept. 1931

23. R. SHANNON AT PORTUMNA, CO. GALWAY Ireland's greatest fishing story is the landing of a pike in excess of 92 lb. *41 kg 730* in about 1796 (double the official world record)

24. DUN LAOGHAIRE, CO. DUBLIN The world's longest strike was over a dismissed barman from a pub, ending on 5 Dec. 1953—14½ years after it was called

25. KINSALE, CO. CORK The highest succession number borne by any peer is that of the 35th Baron Kingsale (b. 1941). The barony dates from 1223

26. CORK The world's longest hunger strike was one of 94 days by 9 Irishmen from 11 Aug. to 12 Nov. 1920

27. POLL ON IONAIN, CO. CLARE The world's largest free-hanging stalactite at 38 ft *11,60 m*

28. CLIFDEN, GALWAY Capt. J. W. Alcock and Lt. A. Whitten-Brown completed the first non-stop Trans-Atlantic flight on 14-15 June 1919

29. ALL IRELAND Ireland holds the world's natural record for high average ages for marrying—31.4 years for males and 26.5 years for females

    The world's most earthquake-free area. No epicentre has ever been instrumentally recorded on this the 20th largest island in the world